# The SAGE Handbook of
# Web History

# The SAGE Handbook of Web History

Edited by
Niels Brügger and
Ian Milligan

SAGE reference
Los Angeles | London | New Delhi | Singapore | Washington DC | Melbourne

SAGE

Los Angeles | London | New Delhi
Singapore | Washington DC | Melbourne

SAGE Publications Ltd
1 Oliver's Yard
55 City Road
London EC1Y 1SP

SAGE Publications Inc.
2455 Teller Road
Thousand Oaks, California 91320

SAGE Publications India Pvt Ltd
B 1/I 1 Mohan Cooperative Industrial Area
Mathura Road
New Delhi 110 044

SAGE Publications Asia-Pacific Pte Ltd
3 Church Street
#10-04 Samsung Hub
Singapore 049483

Editor: Michael Ainsley
Editorial Assistant: Umeeka Raichura
Production Editor: Anwesha Roy
Copyeditor: Sunrise Setting
Proofreader: Sunrise Setting
Indexer: Elske Janssen
Marketing Manager: Lucia Sweet
Cover Design: Wendy Scott
Typeset by: Cenveo Publisher Services
Printed in the UK



**Library of Congress Control Number: 2018960265**

**British Library Cataloguing in Publication data**

A catalogue record for this book is available from the British Library

ISBN 978-1-4739-8005-1

# Contents

# List of Figures and Box

## FIGURES

## BOX

# List of Tables

# Notes on the Editors and Contributors

## THE EDITORS

**Niels Brügger** is Professor at Aarhus University, the School of Communication and Culture. In 2000 he co-founded the Centre for Internet Studies, Aarhus University, and has headed the centre since 2010. Since 2014 he has been Head of NetLab, a research infrastructure for the study of the archived web. His research interests are web historiography, web archiving, and media theory. Within these fields he has authored a number of publications, including *Web 25: Histories from the first 25 years of the World Wide Web* (Ed., Peter Lang, 2017), *The Web as History: Using Web Archives to Understand the Past and the Present* (Ed. with Ralph Schroeder, UCL Press, 2017), and *The Archived Web: Doing History in the Digital Age* (MIT Press, 2018). He is co-founder (2017) and managing editor of the international journal *Internet Histories: Digital Technology, Culture and Society* (Taylor & Francis/Routledge).

**Ian Milligan** is an Associate Professor of History at the University of Waterloo, where he teaches Canadian and digital history. Ian's work explores how historians can use web archives, the large repositories of cultural information that the Internet Archive and many other libraries have been collecting since 1996. He has published two books: the co-authored *Exploring Big Historical Data: The Historian's Macroscope* (2015) and *Rebel Youth: 1960s Labour Unrest, Young Workers, and New Leftists in English Canada* (2014). In 2016, Ian was named the Canadian Society for Digital Humanities/Sociétè canadienne des humanités numériques (CSDH/SCHN)'s recipient of the Outstanding Early Career Award.

## THE CONTRIBUTORS

**Adam Amram** is a scientific programmer. He holds an MSc from the Department of Information and Knowledge Management at Haifa University. His research focuses on developing computational tools for web research.

**Belinda Barnet** is Senior Lecturer in Media at Swinburne with research interests in digital cultures, social media, the app economy, data analytics, AI, and the history of digital media. Her current projects include examining the role of automation in speech rehabilitation in order to improve the use of cochlear implants in deaf children. Alongside her research work, she has worked as Service Delivery Manager (Wireless Content Services) for Ericsson Australia. She is the author of *Memory Machines: The Evolution of Hypertext* (Anthem Press UK, 2013). You can find her on Twitter at @manjusrii.

**Valérie Beaudouin** is a Professor of Social Sciences at Telecom ParisTech. She studies the changes in social practices related to the digital era. She has been directing and conducting research on online communities, self-publication, author's networks, online amateur critiques, and currently the construction of heritage and digital memories about WWI with the French National Library. Information technology as a tool for humanities is one of her special interests: she specialized in text mining and social network tools and more generally on digital methods for social sciences. She graduated from ENSAE ParisTech as a Statistician Economist in 1991 and obtained a PhD in Linguistics in 2000 at EHESS (Higher School of Social Sciences). Her most recent publication, with Dominique Pasquier, is 'Forms of contribution and contributors' profiles: An automated textual analysis of amateur on line film critics' in *New Media & Society*.

**Anat Ben-David** is a Senior Lecturer in the Department of Sociology, Political Science and Communication, and Head of the Open Media and Information Lab at the Open University of Israel. Her research focuses on national web studies and digital sovereignty, web history and web archive research, and the politics of online platforms. Methodologically, her work specializes in developing and applying digital and computational methods for web research.

**Finn Brunton** (finnb.net) is an Assistant Professor in the Department of Media, Culture, and Communication at New York University. He is the author of *Spam: A Shadow History of the Internet* (MIT Press, 2013), *Obfuscation: A User's Guide for Privacy and Protest* with Helen Nissenbaum (MIT Press, 2015), *Communicate* with Mercedes Bunz (University of Minnesota Press, 2018), and *Digital Cash: The Unknown History of the Anarchists, Immortalists, and Utopians Who Created Cryptocurrency* (Princeton University Press, 2019), as well as numerous articles and papers.

**Anthony Cocciolo** is the Dean at Pratt Institute School of Information in New York City. His research and teaching are in the area of archives and digital preservation. He recently published *Moving Image and Sound Collections for Archivists* (Chicago: Society of American Archivists). Cocciolo completed his doctorate from the Communication, Media and Learning Technologies Design program at Teachers College, Columbia University, and his B.S. in Computer Science from the University of California, Riverside.

**Matthew Crain** is an Assistant Professor in the Department of Media, Journalism, and Film at Miami University. His research interests include the commercial development of the Internet, the political economy of the media, communications policy, and critical studies of advertising. His work has been published in academic journals including *New Media & Society* and the *International Journal of Communication*. He previously taught at Queens College, City University of New York.

**Andy Famiglietti** is a Professor of Digital Rhetoric at West Chester University in Pennsylvania. He has previously published on the rhetoric of Wikipedia editors in *First Monday*. His ongoing research projects adapt digital humanities distant reading methods to better understand rhetorical strategies utilized in Wikipedia and other online spaces. He is also a software developer, working to build open source educational tools for writing classrooms.

**Gerard Goggin** is Professor of Media and Communications and ARC Future Fellow, University of Sydney. He is a leading figure in mobile media and communication research, with key books including *Cell Phone Culture* (2006), *Global Mobile Media* (2011), the *Routledge Companion to Mobile Media* (2014), the four-volume *Major Works: Mobile Technologies* (2016), and *Location Technologies in International Context* (2018). Goggin is also a founding editor of the journal *Internet Histories*, and editor of the *Routledge Companion to Global Internet Histories* (2017).

**Dene Grigar** is Professor and Director of The Creative Media and Digital Culture Program at Washington State University Vancouver, whose research focuses on the creation, curation, preservation, and criticism of electronic literature. She is President of the Electronic Literature Organization. Grigar has authored 14 media works, including *Curlew* (2014), *A Villager's Tale* (2011), and *When Ghosts Will Die* (2008). She curates exhibits of electronic literature and media art, and has mounted shows at the British Computer Society, the Library of Congress, the Symposium on Electronic Art, and the Modern Language Association (MLA), among other venues. With Stuart Moulthrop she developed the methodology for documenting born-digital media, a project that culminated in an open source, multimedia book, entitled *Pathfinders* (2015), and a book of media art criticism, entitled *Traversals* (2017), for The MIT Press. In 2017, she was awarded the Lewis E. and Stella G. Buchanan Distinguished Professorship by her university.

**Alexander Halavais** is an Associate Professor of Social Technologies in the School of Social and Behavioral Sciences at Arizona State University, where he researches ways in which social media change the nature of scholarship and learning and allow for new forms of collaboration and self-government. He directs the Masters in Social Technologies program. The second edition of his *Search Engine Society* was published by Polity in 2017, and he is working on a book tentatively entitled *All Seeing*.

**Anne Helmond** is Assistant Professor of New Media and Digital Culture at the Department of Media Studies at the University of Amsterdam. She is a member of the Digital Methods Initiative and App Studies Initiative research collectives where she focuses her research on the infrastructure of social media platforms and mobile apps. Her research interests include digital methods, software studies, platform studies, app studies, infrastructure studies, and web history. She currently holds a Veni grant from the Netherlands Organisation for Scientific Research (NWO) for the project 'App ecosystems: A critical history of apps' (2017–20). More info: annehelmond.nl.

**Tanja Jadin** is a Professor for E-Learning at the Study Programme Communication and Knowledge Media at the University of Applied Sciences Upper Austria. She holds a doctoral degree in Psychology from the University of Salzburg. Her main research interests are computer-supported collaborative learning, self-regulated learning, informal learning, teaching and learning with new media, and media literacy.

**Steve Jones** is a UIC-Distinguished Professor of Communication, Research Associate in the UIC Electronic Visualization Laboratory, Adjunct Professor of Computer Science, and Adjunct Research Professor in the Institute of Communications Research at the University of Illinois at Urbana-Champaign. His research interests include the social history of communication technology, health and new media, human augmentics, virtual environments and virtual reality, popular music studies, Internet studies, and media history. He was the founder and first President of the Association of Internet Researchers and served as Senior Research Fellow at the Pew Internet and American Life Project. He is editor of *New Media & Society*, co-editor of *Mobile Media & Communication*, and edits the Digital Formations book series for Peter Lang Publishing. His research has been funded by the National Science Foundation, National Institutes of Health, National Cancer Institute, Centers for Disease Control, and the Tides Foundation. Jones was named a Fellow of the International Communication Association in 2012.

**Justin Joque** is a scholar of philosophy, technology and media and the visualization librarian at the University of Michigan. He completed his PhD in Communications and Media Studies at the European Graduate School and holds a Masters in Science of Information from the University of Michigan. He is most recently the author of *Deconstruction Machines: Writing in the Age of Cyberwar* (University of Minnesota Press, 2018).

**Allie Kosterich** is an Assistant Professor in the Department of Media, Communications, and Visual Arts at Pace University. Allie's research examines transformation in the media industry, particularly at the intersection of organizations, institutions, and digital technologies. Her recent work focuses on institutional change in news media in reaction to new forms of media production. This includes a large-scale study examining career histories and skill sets of professional journalists in the United States. Allie uses mixed methods in her work, including archival research, interviews, and social network analysis. Allie received her PhD in 2017 from Rutgers University School of Communication and Information.

**Ditte Laursen** is Head of Department for Digital Cultural Heritage at The Royal Danish Library. She is experienced in collection management, IT governance, and research and development. Her special interests include digital cultural heritage, digital humanities, and digital research infrastructures. She is the author or co-author of numerous publications on digital archives, social interaction in, around, and across digital media, and users' engagement with museums and libraries, all published in international peer-reviewed journals and anthologies.

**Stine Lomborg** is Associate Professor in Communication and IT at the University of Copenhagen. She holds a PhD in Media Studies from Aarhus University. Her research centers on new models of communication in the context of digital media and empirical studies of the uses of social and mobile media in the context of self-tracking and online communication. She is the author of *Social Media – Social Genres: Making Sense of the Ordinary* (Routledge), which uses web archival research on social media use in Denmark to understand the development of new forms of everyday communication and sociality, and has also authored several articles reflecting on the methodological, ethical and regulatory implications of digital media.

**Madhavi Mallapragada** is Associate Professor in the Department of Radio-Television-Film at the University of Texas at Austin. Her research interests are in the areas of new media, cultural studies, media and diaspora, race and ethnicity, media industries, Asian American media, and immigrant culture. She is the author of *Virtual Homelands: Indian Immigrants and Online Cultures in the United States* (University of Illinois Press, 2014). She is currently working on a book-length project on the politics of race and ethnicity in US media industries. Her research has been published in the journals *Television and New Media*, *Communication, Culture & Critique*, *New Media and Society*, *South Asian Popular Culture*, and in the edited anthologies *Global Asian American Popular Cultures* (2016), *Re-Orienting Global Communication: Indian* *and Chinese Media Beyond Borders* (2010), *Critical Cyberculture Studies: Current Terrains, Future Directions* (2006), and *Web.studies: Rewiring New Media for the Digital Age* (2000).

**Jim McGrath** is a Postdoctoral Fellow in Digital Public Humanities at the John Nicholas Brown Center for Public Humanities and Cultural Heritage (Brown University). His research interests include digital humanities, public humanities, community archives, electronic literature, and Internet subcultures. He received his PhD in English from Northeastern University, where he was also Project Co-Director of *Our Marathon: The Boston Bombing Digital Archive*. He is on Twitter @JimMc_Grath.

**Mark McLelland** is a Professor in the Sociology program at the University of Wollongong. He is author or editor of over ten books focusing on Japanese popular culture and cultural and media history.

**Gareth Millward** is a Wellcome Trust Research Fellow at the Centre for the History of Medicine, University of Warwick. He held a bursary from the British Library and Institute of Historical Research to help develop new search tools for historians accessing the Library's web archive data in 2014–15. Since then, he has been keen to integrate web archives into his research, particularly for contemporary events. He specializes in British health policy since World War II. His PhD focused on disability policy since the 1960s, and he has recently completed a monograph on the history of British childhood vaccination policy. Since 2017 he has been researching the policy and rhetoric around British sickness certification from 1945 to the present.

**Jeremy Wade Morris** is an Associate Professor of Media and Cultural Studies in the Department of Communication Arts at the University of Wisconsin-Madison. His research interests include the digitization of cultural goods and commodities, software and app culture, the history of sound technologies, and the current state of the popular music industries. He is the author of *Selling Digital Music, Formatting Culture* (University of California Press) and co-editor of a collection on apps and software called Appified: Culture in the Age of Apps (with Sarah Murray, University of Michigan Press 2018). His work has also appeared in journals such as *New Media & Society*, *Critical Studies in Media Communication*, and *Popular Communication*. He is the founder of PodcastRE.org, a database to preserve podcasts and make them more researchable for scholars of media and audio history.

**Francesca Musiani** is Associate Research Professor at the French National Centre for Scientific Research (CNRS), Institute for Communication Sciences (ISCC – CNRS/Sorbonne University). Her current research focuses on science and technology studies approaches to the study of Internet governance and privacy. She is one of the Principal Investigators of the NEXTLEAP project (2016–18, *Next-Generation Techno-Social and Legal Encryption Access and Privacy*), funded by the European Commission. Francesca is the author of *Internet et vie privée [Internet and Privacy]* (Uppr Editions, 2016) and *Nains sans géants. Architecture décentralisée et services Internet [Dwarfs Without Giants. Decentralized Architecture and Internet Services]* (Presses des Mines, 2013 [2015], was awarded the *Prix Informatique et Libertés* by the French Privacy and Data Protection Commission).

**Federico Nanni** is a Postdoctoral Researcher at the Data and Web Science Group and the Political Science Department of the University of Mannheim. His research focuses on the issues that arise when using born-digital documents as primary sources to study the present times and on adopting (and adapting) Natural Language Processing methods for supporting works in the digital humanities and computational social sciences. His previous studies have been published in relevant digital humanities journals, such as *Digital Scholarships in the Humanities* and *Digital Humanities Quarterly*, as well as at important computer science venues, such as EMNLP, JCDL, and EACL.

**Michael L. Nelson** is a Professor of Computer Science at Old Dominion University. Prior to joining ODU, he worked at NASA Langley Research Center from 1991–2002, where he developed the NASA Technical Report Server (NTRS). He is a co-editor of the OAI-PMH, OAI-ORE, Memento, ResourceSync, and Robust Links specifications. His research interests include repository-object interaction and web preservation. More information about Michael can be found at http://www.cs.odu.edu/~mln.

**Michael Nycyk** is an independent technology and social researcher affiliated with the Department of Internet Studies at Curtin University, Perth, Australia and a graduate of the University of Queensland, Brisbane, Australia, in Information Management and Communication and Language Studies. His primary interest is in understanding the behaviors of Internet users, policies to manage these, and the shaping of online identity. His areas of research include understanding adult cyberbullying, Internet trolling, members' flaming strategies on YouTube, computer hackers' behaviors, and analyzing people's online behaviors, and their management, on social media. He has published in these areas, including self-published books, and other publications. Additional areas he has researched and published in include: the use of technologies by older adults and effective learning strategies, minimizing the digital divide, online learning methods, knowledge management and electronic records management, and child fostering practices.

**Christina Ortner** is Professor for Online Communication at the Study Programme Communication and Knowledge Media at the University of Applied Sciences Upper Austria. She also teaches communications and qualitative social science at the University of Salzburg and the University of Applied Science Salzburg. Her research interests include online communication, social media, audience and reception studies, children, youth and the media, and citizen communication.

**James O'Sullivan** is Lecturer in Digital Arts and Humanities at University College Cork (National University of Ireland). He has previously held faculty positions at the University of Sheffield and Pennsylvania State University. His work has been published in a variety of interdisciplinary journals, including *Digital Scholarship in the Humanities*, *Digital Humanities Quarterly*, and *Hyperrhiz: New Media Cultures*. He and Shawna Ross are the editors of *Reading Modernism with Machines* (Palgrave Macmillan, 2016). He is the author of several collections of poetry, including *Courting Katie* (Salmon Poetry, 2017), and is the founding editor of New Binary Press. Further information on James and his work can be found at josullivan.org.

**Susanna Paasonen** is Professor of Media Studies at University of Turku, Finland. With an interest in studies of popular culture, sexuality, affect, and media theory, she is the author of *Carnal Resonance: Affect and Online Pornography* (MITP, 2011) and *Many Splendored Things: Thinking Sex and Play* (Goldsmiths Press, 2018), co-author of *Not Safe for Work: Sex, Humor and Risk in Social Media* with Kylie Jarrett and Ben Light (MITP, forthcoming), and co-editor of *Working with Affect in Feminist Readings: Disturbing Differences* (Routledge 2010, with Marianne Liljeström) and *Networked Affect* (MITP, 2015, with Ken Hillis and Michael Petit). She serves on the editorial boards of the journals *Sexualities*, *Porn Studies*, *New Media & Society*, *Social Media + Society*, and *International Journal of Cultural Studies*.

**Zeynep Pehlivan** is a Research Engineer in the legal deposit team of Ina (French National Audiovisual Institute). She holds a PhD in Computer Science from the University of Pierre and Marie Curie (thesis title: 'Access to web archives: querying, navigating and optimizing'). Her research focuses on web archiving and access methods to web archives and their optimization. Before joining Ina, she participated in national and international R&D projects such as SCAPE (Scalable Preservation Environments, EU FP7) and the LabEx-founded 'Pasts in the Present: History, heritage, memory'. She is currently working on social media archiving and mining (e.g. with Twitter).

**Lindsay Poirier** is a cultural anthropologist and recently completed her Ph.D. in Science and Technology Studies at Rensselaer Polytechnic Institute. As of January 2019, she will be Assistant Professor of Data Studies in the Science and Technology Studies Department at University of California Davis. Her research focuses on digital expertise, data cultures, and the theorization of digital infrastructure. She has conducted historical research on approaches to digital knowledge representation in the artificial intelligence community and has conducted fieldwork within both the Semantic Web community and a community of practitioners building data standards for the human services. She is also the lead platform architect for the Platform for Experimental Collaborative Ethnography (PECE) – an open source digital humanities platform, which now supports several international research projects.

**Richard Rogers** is Professor of New Media and Digital Culture, Media Studies, University of Amsterdam. He is also Director of the Digital Methods Initiative as well as the Netherlands Research School for Media Studies (RMeS).

**Valérie Schafer** has been Professor of Contemporary European History at $C^2DH$ (Centre for Contemporary and Digital History) at the University of Luxembourg since February 2018. She was previously a researcher at the French National Centre for Scientific Research (CNRS). Her current research deals with the Internet and Web history. She led the Web90 project funded by the French National Research Agency (ANR) and dedicated to the French Heritage, Memories and History of the Web in the 1990s. She is the author of *La France en réseaux (années 1960–1980)* [France in Networks (1960–1980)] (2012) and she co-authored with Benjamin Thierry *Le Minitel, l'enfance numérique de la France* [The Minitel, the French Digital Childhood] (2012) and with Bernard Tuy *Dans les coulisses de l'Internet. RENATER, 20 ans de technologie, d'enseignement et de recherche* [On the Internet's Sidelines: RENATER, 20 Years of Technology, Teaching and Research] (2013).

**Ralph Schroeder** is Professor at the Oxford Internet Institute. Before coming to Oxford University, he was Professor in the School of Technology Management and Economics at Chalmers University in Gothenburg (Sweden). His recent books include *Rethinking Science, Technology and Social Change* (Stanford University Press, 2007), *An Age of Limits: Social Theory for the 21st Century* (Palgrave Macmillan), *Knowledge Machines: Digital Transformations of the Sciences and Humanities* (MIT Press, 2015, co-authored with Eric T. Meyer), and *Social Theory after the Internet: Media, Technology and Globalization* (UCL Press). He is currently doing research on the social implications of big data and on the uses of digital media by right-wing populists.

**Gabriele de Seta** holds a PhD in Sociology from the Hong Kong Polytechnic University and recently completed a postdoctoral fellowship at the Institute of Ethnology, Academia Sinica in Taipei, Taiwan. His research work, grounded in ethnographic engagement across multiple sites, focuses on digital media practices and vernacular creativity in Chinese-speaking areas. He is also interested in experimental music, Internet art, and the collaborative intersections of anthropology and art practice. Gabriele has published in a wide range of journals, including *Fibreculture*, *The Information Society*, *Anthropology Now*, and *Medien&Zeit*, and authored numerous chapters for handbooks and edited volumes. More information is available on his website http://paranom.asia

**Ignacio Siles** is a Professor in the School of Communication at Universidad de Costa Rica. He is the author of *Networked Selves: Trajectories of Blogging in the United States and France* (Peter Lang, 2017), *Por un Sueño En.red.ado* (EUCR, 2008), and several articles about technology and society. He obtained his PhD in the Media, Technology, and Society program at Northwestern University. His current book project examines the transnational history of computer networks in Central America in the 1990s as a political project of integration and development.

**Philip Sinner** is a Research Associate and Lecturer at the Department of Communications, University of Salzburg. His research interests concern aspects of audio visual and online communication with a special focus on social media, younger people, sports, and soccer as well as on processes of media socialization. Since 2011 he has been a member of the European Research Network EU Kids Online and the saferinternet.at advisory board, and a committee member since 2016 of the Austrian No Hate Speech Movement (http://www.nohatespeech.at). Since 2018 he has been the Early Career Scholars Representative of the newly created 'Division Media Sport and Sport Communication' in the German Communication Association.

**Michael Stevenson** is a web historian, and Associate Professor of New Media and Digital Culture in the Media Studies department at the University of Amsterdam. His work is broadly about the roots and foundations of media practices, genres, and forms that are considered 'web-native' or otherwise specific to the new media landscape. He is currently working on 'The Web that Was', a project funded by the Dutch National Science Foundation (NWO), about the Perl programing language and the early web. He is still figuring things out.

**Peter Stirling** is a digital curator in the digital legal deposit team at the Bibliothèque nationale de France (BnF). He works on the definition of services and tools for users of the web archives and on digital preservation of the collections. He also participates in day-to-day web archiving activity and the international activity of the team in the context of the International Internet Preservation Consortium. He holds an MA in English Literature and an MSc in Information and Library Studies, and previously worked for an online information portal for health professionals in the UK and in online information monitoring for the French National Cancer Institute, before joining the BnF in 2009.

**Benjamin G. Thierry** is Associate Professor at Sorbonne Université and a researcher at the French National Center for Scientific Research (Institute for Communication Sciences, CNRS – Sorbonne Université). He specializes in history of computing and telecommunications. His long-term research interests involve the socialization of IT (man–machine communication, digital culture, and links to the general public). He is the co-author with Valérie Schafer of *Le*

*Minitel, l'enfance numérique de la France* [The Minitel, the French Digital Childhood] (2012). He is currently the Vice-President for Digital Projects at Sorbonne Université.

**Herbert Van de Sompel** is an information scientist at the Los Alamos National Laboratory and leads the Prototyping Team in the Research Library. The team does research regarding various aspects of scholarly communication in the digital age. Herbert has played a role in various interoperability efforts (OAI-PMH, OpenURL, OAI-ORE, info URI, Open Annotation, ResourceSync, SharedCanvas, Memento, Robust Links) and in the design of scholarly discovery tools (SFX linking server, bX recommender engine). More information about Herbert can be found at http://public.lanl.gov/herbertv.

**Marc Weber** is Curatorial Director of the Internet History Program (computerhistory.org/nethistory) at the Computer History Museum in Silicon Valley. He established Web history as a topic starting in 1995 with help from Sir Tim Berners-Lee and other online pioneers, and co-founded two of the first organizations in the field. The Internet History Program has further expanded the Museum's leading collection of networking history materials and developed its galleries and exhibits on connected topics, including the permanent Web, Mobile, and Networking galleries. Weber has conducted oral histories with several hundred online pioneers. He speaks and publishes widely and consults to companies, filmmakers and museums on the history of the online world and has been interviewed on related topics by major media from the BBC to *Wired*. He serves on the editorial board of *Internet Histories* and co-chairs the W3C Web History Community Group. He is author of an upcoming book from Thomas Dunne Books/St. Martin's Press on the evolution of the online world.

**Matthew Weber** is an Associate Professor in the Hubbard School of Journalism and Mass Communication at the University of Minnesota. Matthew is an expert on organizational change and the use of large-scale Web data. His recent work includes a large-scale longitudinal study examining strategies employed by media organizations for disseminating news and information through online hyperlink networks. Subsequent research includes an examination of the effectiveness of adopting social media within organizations in order to share knowledge and collaborate with teammates. Matthew is also leading an initiative to provide researchers with access to the Internet Archive (archive.org) in order to study digital traces of news networks. Matthew received his PhD in 2010 from the Annenberg School of Journalism and Communication at the University of Southern California.

**Peter Webster** is an independent scholar and consultant based in the UK. He has published widely on various aspects of contemporary British religious history from the 1920s to the 1990s, including church and state, the religious arts, evangelicalism, and the relationship of faith and technology. He has also written extensively on the implications of the digital turn for historical research, and on web archives in particular. His most recent book, on Walter Hussey, Anglican patron of the arts, was published in 2017 by Palgrave Macmillan. After working with digital archives for the University of London, the British Library, and the International Internet Preservation Consortium, he founded Webster Research and Consulting in 2014. WR&C works with libraries and archives to understand what users need from digital resources for research, and works with technologists to meet those needs.

**Jane Winters** is Chair of Digital Humanities at the School of Advanced Study, University of London. She has led or co-directed a range of digital projects, including Big UK Domain Data for the Arts and Humanities; Digging into Linked Parliamentary Metadata; Traces through Time: Prosopography in Practice across Big Data; and Born Digital Big Data and Approaches for History and the Humanities. Recent publications include 'Tackling complexity in humanities big data: From parliamentary proceedings to the archived web', in *Big and Rich Data in English Corpus Linguistics: Methods and Variations*, ed. T. Hiltunen, J. McVeigh and T. Säily (Helsinki: Varieng, 2017); 'Breaking in to the mainstream: Demonstrating the value of internet (and web) histories', *Internet Histories* (March 2017); and 'Web archives for humanities research: Some reflections', in *The Web as History: Using Web Archives to Understand the Past and Present*, ed. N. Brügger and R. Schroeder (London: UCL Press, 2017).

# Foreword

# The Web as Counterpart

Steve Jones

In late 2017 the US-based Starz cable television network launched a science fiction espionage drama titled *Counterpart* based on the premise that in 1987, during a science experiment, East German scientists accidentally created a parallel Earth. While a crossing point existed in Berlin that allowed people to physically move between the worlds, from that point in 1987 onward the two worlds diverged. Part of the drama involved moments when a person would meet their counterpart, or a friend, acquaintance or co-worker, from the other world. What would be the consequences of such encounters? Could one recognize or reconcile with the other?

One way, of the admittedly many, to read *Counterpart* is as an allegory for the Web. Invented in 1989, one could imagine its existence as a kind of parallel universe, with crossing points at screens, perhaps. The interesting element of such a reading, as with most all allegories, is not in the match or mismatch of the allegorical details so much as it is in the lesson of the parable. The lesson in this case is not an end result, a single consequence resulting from some prior actions or motives. It is in the consequences that arise from the moment of divergence. What becomes of one's identity, indeed, what becomes of the notion of identity, in a strangely split, parallel, universe? Therein lies the importance of understanding the history of the Web. It is not merely a technology, a product of scientific invention. Nor is it merely a new way to do things we had already been doing (writing, communicating, reading, etc.) or even to do new things altogether. And it is also not merely a platform on which we share thoughts, ideas, images and sounds. It is all those things, but greater than their sum.

The Web is, like the parallel Earth of *Counterpart*, us, and not us, a recognizable, yet strange, place. How did it come about, what was its development? We can find points of origination but from those moments onward multiple trajectories emerge. How do we hold the Web still enough to achieve a degree of satisfactory scrutiny? Numerous scholars are now, thankfully, asking, and answering, questions such as these. The research and discussion presented in *The SAGE Handbook of Web History* provide the context for pressing on with discovery of the Web as an indivisible part of contemporary human experience, and provide the foundation for future successful archiving and preservation of the Web's history.

The significance of *The SAGE Handbook of Web History* is, among other things, in its recognition of the need for a multifaceted approach to the preservation and study of the history of the Web. Although the Web seems to be a relatively new phenomenon, it is as if time passes on it in 'dog years', at a rate that feels like seven years for each time the Earth travels around the sun. To many people it likely feels as if it has been around forever, or as long as they can remember, at least. As I write this foreword Facebook is in the early stages of the Cambridge Analytica controversy; by the time it is published other controversies will likely have come and gone, too.

The question, then, is how do we capture the essence of the Web, the experience, and the consequences, of it? Even if we can entirely preserve it, from the bits to the screens, the links to the machines, what might we do to capture the myriad uses to which it is put as well as the affective dimension of its use?

I am reminded of the early days of the Pew Internet & American Life Project in late 1999 and early 2000 when survey instruments were being developed for use in telephone interviews. Would it be better to ask respondents if they went online, or if they used the Internet, or if they accessed the Web? What would be the consequences for the answers we would get with each question? Even a simple question, such as 'Did you check your e-mail today?' elides numerous questions, not the least of which is whether the Web was used for e-mail and how such use matters, whether it renders e-mail different from other forms of access. Similarly, Web access via mobile devices and the increasing use of apps, some of which do little more than offer Web pages while others seem completely apart from it, alters the perception of the Web. The phenomenological turn expressed in some of the pages in this *Handbook* is therefore particularly welcome, necessary and important. While I do not wish to argue that there is a distinctive 'essence' to the experience of the Web nor to set historical fact apart from experience, it does seem to me useful to acknowledge that if there is ever to be an interpretive dimension to the Web's history then we need to think through the elements of what that dimension might be and find ways to preserve it, too. Doing so would provide the means for reconstituting the Web as greater than the sum of its parts and aid in understanding the Web as a multifaceted technology, at once a medium, built on another medium, that facilitates other media.

It is important to remember therefore that the Web is not merely a technological web but also an affective one. Consider, for instance, if during the present Cambridge Analytica controversy Facebook were to find millions of its users deleting their accounts. What would happen to conversation threads on Facebook if the company permitted users to delete all of their posts along with their accounts? Furthermore, those accounts are implicated in how people log in to other sites and to apps, illustrating that the reach of the Web is at once both outside the scope of what we consider the Web proper and connected to apps, and also impenetrable as Web content is increasingly proprietarily held. Users have experience, loyalties, relationships with other users as well as with sites and with the private and public entities that operate sites.

Furthermore, the Web, by means of its interconnection with other aspects of online (and sometimes offline, as might be the case with, say, credit card use, travel arrangements, etc.) activity that is facilitated by the tracking of Web use through cookies and other means, is implicated in a panoply of engagements that people have, often determined by algorithm, whether with other people, private companies, public institutions or machines and digital assistants. The rapid shift from plain HTML to Java, Javascript, APIs, JSON and other software tools that have made Web browsers a form of operating system have altered not only the experience of the Web but also its nature. In all likelihood, the majority of the interactions that we have on the Web are not only irreproducible but also unable to be preserved insofar as capturing them involves more than the storage of information but also a replication of the processes involved between the moment of a click and rendering of pixels on the screen. The Web is now greater than the sum of its parts in no small part because of the processing involved in rendering information on it, in putting data through the mill that delivers it to our screens.

I realize it may seem as if I am lamenting the development of the Web since the late 1990s, and while I will admit to not being completely without nostalgia I am not by any means calling for a return to a simpler Web. I am merely wanting to emphasize that it is important to understand just how complicated the Web has become and with that added complexity how difficult yet how very necessary it is to preserve it and to mine its history for insight. Indeed, when I reflect on the complexity and importance of the Web (and the Internet generally) I am reminded of John Steinbeck's plaintive edict about journalism, written in a letter to John P. McKnight, then at the United States Information Service in Rome, in 1956. 'What can I say about journalism?', Steinbeck wrote,

> It has the greatest virtue and the greatest evil. It is the first thing a dictator controls. It is the mother of literature and the perpetrator of crap. In many cases it is the only history we have and yet it is the tool of the worst men. But over a long period of time and because it is the product of so many men, it is perhaps the purest thing we have. Honesty has a way of creeping into it even when it was not intended (Steinbeck and Wallsten, 1976: 526).

It takes little imagination to substitute the words 'Web' or 'Internet' for 'journalism' in Steinbeck's first sentence, and no more imagination to wonder whether it may be true about new media. Whether it could truly be said about the Web, perhaps history will tell. That it might be true is nevertheless a compelling reason to expeditiously and rigorously preserve all that we can of the Web.

## REFERENCE

Elaine Steinbeck and Robert Wallsten, *Steinbeck: A Life in Letters*. Penguin Books, 1976, p. 526.

# Introduction

Niels Brügger and Ian Milligan

The Web has now been with us for over 25 years: new media is simply not all that new anymore. It has developed to become an inherent part of our social, cultural, economic, political, and social lives, and accordingly is now an object of historical study. With web archiving having begun in 1996, we are also now living in a time when over two decades of the Web have been collected, preserved, and made accessible – a detailed documentary record of society and events. Two key points thus lie at the heart of this *Handbook*: that the history of the Web itself needs to be studied, but also that its value as an incomparable historical record needs to be inquired as well.

If researchers today want to fully understand the present, as well as our past from the mid 1990s onwards, the Web will play a critical role. While there is no common rule for when a topic becomes 'history', the timeframe seems to be shortening as the speed of information dissemination accelerates. For example, as Ian Milligan argues in this book's first chapter, it took less than 30 years after the events of 1968 for a varied, developed, and contentious historiography to emerge; in 2021, we will be marking the 30th anniversary of the creation of the first website.

Within the last decade, considerable scholarly interest in the Web's history has emerged. However, there has yet been no comprehensive review of the field. Digital historians and their colleagues in the digital humanities have approached changing historical methods more generally, but without specific focus on the Web (see for example Cohen and Rosenzweig, 2005; Gold and Klein, 2016; Graham et al., 2015; Terras et al., 2013). Internet histories provide specific (and invaluable) accounts of particular technologies – the Web, or the Internet, or pre-Web technologies like the Minitel for example (Abbate, 2000; Brunton, 2013; Mailland and Driscoll, 2017) – but this *Handbook* aims to pull its gaze back from the particular stories, and present a multifaceted understanding of a developing field. The history of the Web itself remains relatively understudied, with only a few exceptions (Banks, 2008; Brügger, 2017, 2010; Brügger and Schroeder, 2017; Foot and Schneider, 2006; Gillies and Cailliau, 2000). In any case, these books only offer specific perspectives on web history, as opposed to the multifaceted *Handbook* you are now reading. The *SAGE Handbook of Web History* also shares ground with the growing literature within the fields of 'digital methods', such as Richard Rogers' award-winning *Digital Methods*, but delves deeper into the specific questions around the Web (Rogers, 2013). Finally, there is a body of work exploring the archived Web from the perspective of those who collect, curate, and preserve it; these are useful complementary works, but do not approach web archives from the perspective of a scholarly user (Brown, 2006; Masanès, 2006).

Time is ripe for this *Handbook*. In this introduction, we introduce the twin dimensions of 'web history' and discuss the structure and content of this *Handbook* a bit more. We then provide an overview of the six sections, with some thoughts on how the pieces fit together to suggest the emergence of a new field of study.

## THE TWO DIMENSIONS OF 'WEB HISTORY'

The title of this *Handbook* speaks to the book's emphasis on two different, yet related, forms of web history. On the one hand, 'web history' may refer to the use of the Web of the past as a historical source in any kind of historical study. Imagine a scholar of higher education who uses the webpages of universities and government agencies to tell her story; not a history of webpages, per se, but a history that happens to use archived websites to craft her narrative. On the other hand, 'web history' can also refer to any study of the history of the Web itself (and where the Web, of course, can also be a source). The *SAGE Handbook of Web History* focuses on both of these two meanings: histories written *with* the Web as well as histories written *of* the Web. The Web is both a historical source and an object of study in its own right.

As a historical source, web archives are unique. Unlike traditional institutional archives, the snapshots that comprised the archived Web are artifacts created by the archival process itself (Brügger, 2018). They are in many cases assembled by digital robots, 'spiders' which crawl publicly accessible webpages by starting on a given page, downloading it, following all the links, downloading that content, following links, and beyond – a potentially infinite process, as even if the crawler found enough content and ended up back where it started, the Web is always changing and the process must begin anew (Milligan, 2016). These reconstructions of the live Web are never exact replicas, even though they may at first glance look complete. This makes an understanding of web archives especially important. For these reasons, scholars, researchers, and students who wish to use archived web content as historical documents need to be familiar with both the technical and material aspects of web archives, as well as the related theoretical and epistemological concerns that arise when dealing with these digital artifacts. Thus, this book offers historians and other researchers a comprehensive resource for navigating web archives when undertaking historical research.

At the same time, this collection is also a text that aims to organize and present distinct approaches to studying histories of the Web. Although 'the World Wide Web' is commonly addressed in the singular, the following chapters include diverse examples of web histories that consider various national contexts, popular and subcultural practices, material and technological considerations, and beyond. By bringing this collection of historical case studies together, the *Handbook* is a valuable resource for new media scholars looking to ground contemporary digital cultures and practices historically.

## STRUCTURE AND CONTENT

The *Handbook* you are now reading speaks to many different scholarly communities across a diverse set of fields. Represented within the *Handbook* are communications scholars, historians, digital humanists, media and cultural studies practitioners, and researchers from the world of library and information sciences. An international book, bringing together scholars from multiple continents, the *SAGE Handbook of Web History* highlights the varied interdisciplinary perspectives that scholars take towards an understanding of web history.

This book is intended for academics, graduate students, and upper-level undergraduates within the humanities and the social sciences, in particular those with an interest in how the past of the Web and of our more recent history can be and has been studied. This is a wide audience, ranging from scholars of media studies and communication history, to digital humanists, and historians in general. With growing interest in this field – as several contributors argue, it would be difficult to imagine doing a history of the 1990s or beyond without using these kinds of sources – some insight and overall approaches to the field of web history are necessary.

The book is divided into six sections, discussed in more depth below. Each chapter can be read as a standalone contribution, of course, but also has fruitful interactions with its fellow chapters in the section: a perspective from a historian, for example, subsequently complemented by that of a computer scientist.

## *Part One: The Web and Historiography*

In the 'Web and Historiography', we provide the basic fundamentals that underpin the field. In short: what does it mean to do web history? What is a web archive? Do archived websites represent a new kind of primary source, or do they fundamentally represent continuity? These chapters in some ways serve as an extended introduction to the field: from learning about the existing web archives, to how they have been framed and understood by historians and other new media scholars, to how they can be used ethically.

The first chapter, 'Historiography and the Web', by **Ian Milligan**, fleshes out some of the discussions around what it means to think of the Web as a primary source, crucially highlighting dimensions of both scale and scope. With web archives, historians have more information, created by people who never before would have been part of the historical record. But how can this information be accessed? Drawing on concepts from the digital humanities, notably that of distant reading, this chapter argues that the growing centrality of web archives to the historical profession will require a rethinking of historical methodology – and an understanding of the place of technology within the historical profession since the Second World War.

We continue these themes in the *Handbook*'s second chapter, 'Understanding the Archived Web as a Historical Source', by **Niels Brügger**. In this chapter, the fundamental elements of web archives are articulated: how they rapidly change (even during the process of collection!) and how they are fundamentally different from many other kinds of digitized primary sources. The chapter then articulates a theoretical and methodological framework to carry out web history. To use web archives requires fundamental knowledge of how they work, which this chapter provides.

With the basic contours of web archives presented, we then pivot towards talking about 'Existing Web Archives', a chapter by **Peter Webster**. Not all web archives are created the same, and when using them researchers need to be aware of how their scope and structure can dramatically differ. This chapter presents a historical overview of web archives, looks at how they are created today, and examines how that affects our current historical arguments and interpretations.

The 'Web and Historiography' section then comes to an end, appropriately, with a chapter by **Richard Rogers** which explores 'Periodizing Web Archiving: Biographical, Event-Based, National and Autobiographical Traditions'. Rogers looks at the different approaches taken to web archiving since the advent of the Internet Archive: from trying to save single sites, to understanding events, to national web domains or self-expression on social media. After this periodization, Rogers then proposes new methodological approaches to access web archives, from screencast documentaries to digging into the underlying code that makes a website display.

Taken together, these four chapters serve in many ways as a crash course into the world of web archives and web archiving: who does it, what it means, how to use it, and the unique aspects that underlie this type of primary source. From these four unique perspectives, we hope that readers can come away with an interest in conceiving their own research questions – but can do so fully informed of the opportunities and pitfalls that may arise.

## *Part Two: Theoretical and Methodological Reflections*

The section of the book involves theoretical and methodological reflections on how to do web history: from understanding it from various intellectual perspectives (such as science and technology studies or taking a quantitative approach) to more technical approaches such as using network analysis or large-scale text mining to understand the past. With a solid understanding of how web archives are created as established in the last section, we now seek to put them to work.

The section begins with **Valérie Schafer** and **Benjamin G. Thierry's** 'Web History in Context', an exploration of how 'the' Web needs to be put into context. How has the Web spread and diffused around society? How can we write a history of the mid 1990s, for example, and take the Web into proper account? In short, if we are to use the Web as a historical source, we need to use it properly – and realize that there is no singular 'the' Web.

With the Web put into context, what sorts of approaches can one take to its study? One such perspective is offered in the following chapter, 'Science and Technology Studies Approaches to Web History', by **Francesca Musiani** and **Valérie Schafer**. The two authors introduce critical STS concepts and notions, illuminating them with case studies from web history. The chapter then fleshes out an in-depth example of web governance as a case study, showing how the Web can thus be understood as a complex and changing socio-technical system.

If STS offers one theoretical framework, what other approaches could be taken as well? In 'Theorizing the Uses of the Web', **Ralph Schroeder** discusses various approaches to how the Web is used and aims to point the way forward by developing a new theoretical framework – and thinking about the implications for policy, ethics, and future scholarship.

Now that we know how to theorize and contextualize collections, the next question is how we should do so. Ethics are a critical issue when using such diverse digital archives, as **Stine Lomborg**'s chapter on 'Ethical Considerations for Web Archives and Web History Research' explains. Her article introduces the several dimensions that researchers should consider, from contexts, subjects of study, methods of data collection, analytical types, and beyond; it is not about firm answers, but a way of thinking.

With the theoretical underpinnings of the last four chapters under the reader's belt, we then transition to discussions of method. How best to explore these archives? **Federico Nanni**'s 'Collecting Primary Sources from Web Archives: A Tale of Scarcity and Abundance' explores two case studies where web archives have been put to use to advance historical scholarship: from reconstructing a university webpage to the study of contemporary events. As a scholar bridging computer science and history, Nanni notes how combining traditional historical methods with the methods of Internet studies and natural language processing could form an intriguing route forward.

The final four chapters in this section form a series of methodological pieces, outlining various approaches a scholar can adopt when exploring web history. **Michael Stevenson** and **Anat Ben-David** introduce critical concepts in their 'Network Analysis for Web History', providing a conceptual background for how these key strategies can be applied: both an introduction to network analysis as well as hands-on cases on how network analysis has assisted research, search, social media, and the state of the art with web archives.

Networks are one way to uncover the structure of a site – but so are other methods for taking lots of web archival data, translating them to numbers, and drawing conclusions from analysis. **Anthony Cocciolo**'s 'Quantitative Web History Methods' chapter explains how to do this, introducing the field of quantitative research methods and explaining the field through an in-depth analysis of how we can study the archived Web to see the decrease in text and the rise in image-based layouts and communication.

What much of the last three chapters have in common is their use of computers – computers to collect, count, and analyze information. Accordingly, **Anat Ben-David** and **Adam Amram**'s chapter on 'Computational Methods for Web History' explores how computational methods can help us explore web archives, but provides cautionary notes around how methods, tools, and techniques need to be adapted to the specific nature of the source. They do so through four computational techniques, drawn from their research projects, showing both the benefits of this form of research and the limitations.

Finally, working with web archives, given their scale, brings challenges in representing research. Continuing on from earlier discussions of network analysis, quantitative methods, and computational approaches more generally, **Justin Joque**'s 'Visualizing Historical Web Data' works us through how we can represent and explore web archives through data visualization. Some of this builds on networks specifically, and other parts of the chapter address how we can visualize both text and change over time as well.

## *Part Three: Technical and Structural Dimensions of Web History*

Web history, indelibly associated with a particular platform – the World Wide Web – requires that students, scholars, and practitioners have a basic technical understanding of underlying protocols, infrastructure, and access materials. We need to understand the structure of the Web as well, such as the hyperlinks that users explore to move from page to page, or the Web browsers such as NCSA Mosaic or Internet Explorer that they used to access it from the early 1990s onwards.

What better place to start with an exploration of the technical underpinnings of web history than with the Hypertext Transfer Protocol (or HTTP) itself and how it has been extended through the Memento Protocol to allow the integration of past and present Web. **Michael Nelson** and **Herbert Van de Sompel** accordingly discuss the history of Unix, HTTP, and introduce the Memento Protocol in their 'Adding the Dimension of Time to HTTP' chapter. Through these explorations, we can see how the original vision of the Web was stymied in part due to issues with the filesystem. The work discussed in this chapter has made large amounts of web history scholarship possible, by allowing versioning and the integration of web archives all around the world.

We often take the HT in HTTP for granted – the hypertext that underpins the Web today. Yet, as **Belinda Barnet** notes in her 'Hypertext Before the Web – or, What the Web Could Have Been' chapter, hypertext stretches back much earlier. Looking at three early systems – Douglas Engelbart's NLS, Ted Nelson's Xanadu,[1] and Nelson and Andies van Dam's HES – this chapter both introduces the early conceptual underpinnings of the ever-present hyperlink today, and also allows us to imagine alternative visions of what it could have been.

Focusing more specifically on the hyperlink itself, but continuing to question existing narratives and putting aside a more simplistic Web 1.0 to Web 2.0 paradigm, **Anne Helmond**'s 'A Historiography of the Hyperlink' explores how the link itself has evolved. Using six key moments, from proto hypertext to the role of the link before search to how the link is disappearing today, the chapter illuminates the history of the Web itself as well as the link.

Taking a similar historical approach, **Alexander Halavais** looks at 'How Search Shaped and Was Shaped by the Web'. Taking aim at traditional narratives that saw search engines as having been 'bolted on' to the Web, this chapter notes how the Web and search have co-evolved together – a process that continues to shape and evolve with our modern Web today. Users used to 'surf' the Web, using links, a process which has been profoundly reoriented by search.

Roads taken – or not – lie at the heart of **Lindsay Poirier**'s chapter on 'Making the Web Meaningful: A History of Web Semantics'. In the original vision of Tim Berners-Lee's Web, nodes that linked to each other would represent not documents but individuals or objects; while the Web that emerged was not like this, since 1994 Berners-Lee and others have been calling for the realization of a 'semantic Web'. This chapter explores the semantic Web community, looking back to the 1970s and forward to help us understand how the semantic Web shapes our understanding of knowledge today.

The final two chapters in this section then address two stories in how we use the Web. The first, 'Browsers and Browser Wars', by **Marc Weber**, explores the history of how the Web is accessed: through a web browser. It argues that in the Web's early days browsers became the main battleground for overall control of the Web. The first struggle, between the original browser-editor vision and the simpler "read-only" model that prevailed, was followed by two commercial "browser wars." While these mostly ended by 1999, a mobile war continues today.

This last current is picked up in the section's final chapter, with **Gerard Goggin**'s 'Emergence of the Mobile Web'. Users increasingly browse the Web on mobile devices, and it is increasingly mediated through different social media platforms, apps, and other software. This chapter explores how the mobile Web can be defined and studied.

## *Part Four: Platforms on the Web*

On top of the Web's structure exist platforms: from collaboratively written encyclopedias like Wikipedia, to blogging software, to nearly ubiquitous advertisements and social media networks like Twitter, Facebook, and, in the past, web publishing platforms like GeoCities. This section gathers five chapters which take explicitly historical approaches to explore their very different 'platforms'. Useful for an understanding both of those particular sites, and how the Web evolved from the mid 1990s to the present, they help to contextualize the more targeted case studies that follow.

The first platform we explore is Wikipedia, in **Andy Famiglietti**'s 'Wikipedia'. The story travels from 2001, when Larry Sanger sent his first note about 'Nupedia' to a small number of people on their mailing list, to today, when Wikipedia's millions of articles constitute the fifth most visited website in the world. Yet, while it is occasionally understood as an exemplar new media project, Famiglietti instead shows how it is a historically contingent project, growing out of the free and open source software movement. Many of these themes come together in an extensive case study on the 2008 Gaza War article.

With the Web today seemingly dominated by advertising, a historical perspective can help us understand its growth: how did an information retrieval tool become so saturated by commercial messaging? In 'A Critical Political Economy of Web Advertising History', **Matthew Crain** looks at the development of technologies, standards, and practices that brought advertising onto the mainstream of the Web. By using a critical political economy approach, Crain is able to weave in the interplay between the Web and larger political and economic questions.

While the Web was developed as a read–write medium, it was difficult for many early web users without technical knowledge to find a place to contribute – GeoCities provided one such important platform. In his chapter 'Exploring Web Archives in the Age of Abundance', **Ian Milligan** argues that these sorts of platforms allow more democratic, accessible historians – Big Data as an avenue into social history on a large scale – but that the steps to explore such sources will require a profound rethinking of how historians understand the past.

If GeoCities was an early platform, by the turn of the twenty-first century many web users were turning to blogs as an outlet for self-expression. In his aptly named chapter 'Blogs', **Ignacio Siles** explores the story of blogs in the United States: why they arose and how they continue to develop today. It is also a fascinating example of mixed-method research: drawing on over 100 interviews, archival research in traditional archives as well as on the Web, and ethnographic studies.

Finally, in our last chapter in this section, **Christina Ortner**, **Philip Sinner**, and **Tanja Jadin** explore 'The History of Online Social Media'. Their chapter provides an overview of the social media phenomenon as it emerged in the late 1990s before expanding dramatically throughout the 2000s. They do so through a four-phase periodization that explores online interaction before social media, web-based services, the emergence of diverse social media services, and the ecosystem of mobile apps today. This big picture exploration of modern social media platforms is a perfect way to round out this section.

## *Part Five: Web History and Users, some Case Studies*

With the foundational pieces complete – including historiography, theory, technical, structural, and platform dimensions – the *SAGE Handbook of Web History* then turns itself to the largest section of the book: understanding web history and users through a series of 14 case studies. Each of these chapters are exemplars, ranging from an understanding of online news through web history, to streaming media file formats, to the Chinese Web, to trolling and memes. A diverse assemblage of authors and topics, these chapters shed light not only on their particular topic but also on various methods for undertaking web history.

Like many of our voyages on a web browser, we begin appropriately at 'home' – in this case, with **Madhavi Mallapragada**'s 'Cultural Historiography of the "Homepage". Her piece interrogates the concept of the homepage, exploring it as both a technical and cultural concept. Taking a historical approach, Mallapragada explores the emergence and shifting significance of the homepage in the 1990s and 2000s, as well as its continued relevance today.

Change is also key to any understanding of news media in the context of web history. **Allie Kosterich** and **Matthew S. Weber** explore the dramatic shifts that have transformed how consumers engage with news in light of the Web in their chapter 'Consumers, News and a History of Change'. Their historical lens allows them to convincingly demonstrate that many contemporary shifts in how we consume media today can be traced back, through web history, to shifts on the Web.

Many of our case studies throughout the book, like the last two and several others, are grounded in particular national contexts. This should not be surprising, **Niels Brügger** and **Ditte Laursen** argue in the next chapter, 'Historical Studies of National Web Domains'. Despite the global nature of the Web – we can access content made half the world away as easily as something written next door – users tend to situate themselves in nations. Accordingly, the two authors introduce the national Web as an object of analytical inquiry.

The next 11 chapters then move into specific case studies, each of which illuminates the field of web history as well. **James O'Sullivan** and **Dene Grigar** explore 'The Origins of Electronic Literature as Net/Web Art', a chapter which explores the story of e-lit, from its diskette-based origins to its Web-based homes today. This shift onto the Web had profound consequences for this medium – similarly, the authors note, to many other cultural objects migrated to the Web.

Historians who study memory have similarly seen their scholarship transformed by the Web – our collective memory of events over a century ago is shaped by the Web as well.

**Valérie Beaudouin**, **Zeynep Pehlivan**, and **Peter Stirling** approach this question in their chapter 'Exploring the Memory of the First World War Using Web Archives: Web Graphs Seen from Different Angles'. By creating a map of links between First World War websites, they are able to see how online communities socially organize the memory of the war.

Just as the Web can be studied to see the spread of memory, so too can web archives help explore the historical roots of contemporary issues such as vaccine refusal. **Gareth Millward** addresses this in his 'A History with Web Archives, Not a History of Web Archives: A History of the British Measles–Mumps–Rubella Vaccine Crisis, 1998–2004'. His chapter both explores the MMR vaccine controversy through several archived webpages and demonstrates his substantive findings as well as the methodological issues he encounters when trying to work with this material – necessitating engagement with both web archives as well as traditional resources.

This theme of considering web archives as just one among many primary documents is also foundational to **Peter Webster**'s chapter on 'Religion and Web History'. To study religion over the last 20 years is to also, in many cases, consider the Web: both how religions are shaped by the Web, and how web history has interacted with major themes in the field, from secularization to the place of religion in society. Webster also explores future directions in this field.

We then shift gears away from specific case studies to explorations of particular aspects of the Web. **Jeremy Wade Morris** explores the sonic element in his 'Hearing the Past: The Sonic Web from MIDI to Music Streaming'. While we tend to focus on visual and text, Morris explores what we can learn from web history by listening – accordingly, he covers the history of sound on the Web (from technological developments to commercialization) – and also explores the barriers that we face due to obsolete and proprietary file formats.

Considering a broad range of media types, the next chapter, 'Memes', by **Jim McGrath,** explores how text, images, animated GIFs, sound, and short movies can spread around the Internet. After an introduction to the concept in general, McGrath explores where memes emerged on the Web, beginning in early-1990s Usenet groups, through the recent rise of the 'meme' term itself on the Internet, using it as an avenue to look at just how quickly the Web has transformed.

Transformation underpins the next chapter as well, by **Gabriele de Seta**. 'Years of the Internet: Vernacular Creativity before, on, and after the Chinese Web' explores the evolution of the Internet in China, focusing on six years – from the first email, to BBSs, and messaging and chat services. Showing continuities in the vernacular creativity of Chinese Internet users, the unique evolution of the Web in China can be seen in this important story.

Pulling the gaze back from China alone to considering East Asia as a region, **Mark McLelland**'s 'Cultural, Political and Technical Factors Influencing Early Web Uptake in North America and East Asia' explores Taiwan, mainland China, Japan, and Korea. Given the Euro-American assumptions that underpinned much of the early Web – from QWERTY keyboards to non-Roman script encoding – the adoption of the Web took a different route there. His chapter begins with East Asian pre-Web systems before exploring how these early encounters led to unique web cultures by the mid-to-late 1990s.

Our final three chapters in this section cover three aspects that the Web's designers may not have had in mind. The first, 'Online Pornography', by **Susanna Paasonen**, explores the world of online pornography. The pornography industry, Paasonen argues, has underpinned much of the Web's technical development over the last two decades – from credit card processing to streaming video and advertisements – and the Web has had considerable impact on pornography as well.

Spam, the mild irritant that we all face in our inboxes, is another critical element that we need to understand to grasp how the Web has evolved – just as pornography shaped the Web, so too did spam, influencing search engines, how we use the Web, legal frameworks, and beyond. **Finn Brunton** explores this in his 'Spam' chapter, using spam as an avenue into a counter history of the Web.

The section then concludes with **Michael Nycyk**'s 'Trolls and Trolling History: From Subculture to Mainstream Practices'. This story of a small Internet-based subculture that ended up shaping the mainstream social media and web platforms helps us take an alternate vision of the Web's history. From Usenet to Web 2.0, trolls have evolved alongside the Web.

### *Part Six: The Roads Ahead*

After this array of case studies and web history approaches, it becomes clear that there are many roads forward in the field of web archives. We give the closing words of the book to **Jane Winters**, a professor of digital history, whose chapter 'Web Archives and (Digital) History: A Troubled Past and a Promising Future?' investigates the failure of historians to meaningfully engage with web archives as of 2018 – despite pressing reasons to do so. She then proposes a new future, one which sees historians mixing both qualitative and quantitative approaches, to reclaim the stories of everyday people.

## THE NEW FIELD OF WEB HISTORY

If we are going to be able to write histories of the 1990s and beyond, not only of the Web but of any social, cultural, political, economic, or beyond phenomenon that was itself reflected in the Web, we need to understand the context in which these sources were created. In this lies the importance of web history as a field. A spam message in 1994, or a troll in 2008, or a homepage in 1999 were all created in particular contexts – which all need to be understood for their responsible use. Similarly, while those who study web history need not be coders, they do need some understanding of the underlying technological platforms and interfaces, from the origins of the hyperlink to an understanding of how the web browsers that users used to access the Web changed over time.

The Web has now been with us for over a quarter of a century. Historians are not soothsayers, able to magically use the past to understand the future, but they can begin to get a sense of the broad contours of an evolving historical force with an eye to what it might mean for particular outcomes. With such a rich historical record and legacy to draw on, any contemporary understanding of the Web can only be enriched by an understanding of its historical context; and any breathless exploration of what the future might hold can benefit from an understanding of the legacies at play.

## ACKNOWLEDGMENTS

Our sincerest thanks, in the first place, to our contributors. We couldn't have asked for a better group of scholars to work with as we put this collection together. Many of the contributors picked up the gauntlet and drafted expansive chapters, informed both by their existing research agendas but in many cases by moving into new areas and avenues. It goes without saying that this book would not be possible without their phenomenal work.

Our gracious thanks as well to Chris Rojek, the Sociology publisher at SAGE who provided so much initial support on the project before passing on the baton to editors Mila Steele and Michael Ainsley. Thanks also to Colette Wilson, Anwesha Roy, Serena Ugolini, and Matthew Oldfield at SAGE for all of their support with making this *Handbook* a reality!

We would also both like to thank Megan Sapnar Ankerson from the University of Michigan for her assistance and guidance in the first stages of bringing our ideas together. Ian Milligan would also like to thank his colleagues in the Web Archives for Historical Research Group: Nick Ruest, Jimmy Lin, Ryan Deschamps, and Samantha Fritz, for providing continual encouragement and insights into the world of web archiving research.

## Note

1 Xanadu is a registered trade and service mark of Project Xanadu, Sausalito CA 94965, US.

## REFERENCES

Abbate, J. (2000) *Inventing the Internet*. Cambridge: MIT Press.

Banks, M. (2008) *On the Way to the Web: The Secret History of the Internet and Its Founders*. Berkeley: Apress.

Brown, A. (2006) *Archiving Websites: A Practical Guide for Information Management Professionals*. London: Facet Publishing.

Brügger, N. (2010) *Web History*. New York: Peter Lang.

Brügger, N. (Ed.) (2017) *Web 25: Histories from the First 25 Years of the World Wide Web*. New York: Peter Lang.

Brügger, N. (2018) *The Archived Web: Doing History in the Digital Age*. Cambridge: MIT Press.

Brügger, N., and Schroeder, R. (Eds) (2017) *The Web as History*. London: UCL Press.

Brunton, F. (2013) *Spam: A Shadow History of the Internet*. Cambridge: MIT Press.

Cohen, D., and Rosenzweig, R. (2005) *Digital History: A Guide to Gathering, Preserving, and Presenting the Past on the Web*. Philadelphia: University of Pennsylvania Press.

Foot, K.A., and Schneider, S.M. (2006) *Web Campaigning*. Cambridge: MIT Press.

Gillies, J., and Cailliau, R. (2000) *How the Web was Born: The Story of the World Wide Web*. Oxford: Oxford University Press.

Gold, M.K., and Klein, L.F. (Eds) (2016) *Debates in the Digital Humanities 2016*. Minneapolis: University of Minnesota Press.

Graham, S., Milligan, I., and Weingart, S. (2015) *Exploring Big Historical Data: The Historian's Macroscope*. London: Imperial College Press.

Mailland, J., and Driscoll, K. (2017) *Minitel: Welcome to the Internet*. Cambridge: MIT Press.

Masanès, J. (2006) *Web Archiving*. Berlin: Springer.

Milligan, I. (2016) 'Lost in the Infinite Archive: The Promise and Pitfalls of Web Archives', *International Journal of Humanities and Arts Computing*, 10(1): 78–94.

Rogers, R. (2013) *Digital Methods*. Cambridge: MIT Press.

Terras, M., Nyhan, J., and Vanhoutte, E. (Eds) (2013) *Defining Digital Humanities: A Reader*. London: Routledge.

PART I

# The Web and Historiography

1

# Historiography and the Web

Ian Milligan

## INTRODUCTION

The advent of the Web as a primary source will dramatically affect the practice of researching, writing, and thinking about history. Historians are entering into an era where we will have more information than ever before, left behind by people who rarely before entered the historical record. Web archives will fundamentally transform much of what a historian does, requiring a move towards computational methodologies and the digital humanities.

Web archives matter. One cannot write most histories of the 1990s or later without reference to web archives, or at the very least to do so would be to neglect a major medium of the period. Web archivists and other institutions are today engaged in the collaborative effort to ensure that people in the future know what happened in 1996, or 2001, or 2006, or today. This ensures that we as a society will have the information that we need to make arguments for justice, for equality, for policy, for a better understanding of ourselves, and beyond. Web archives will be a foundation for history.

Crucially, historians need to be ready for this shift. They will soon be writing histories of the 1990s that require web archives to do justice to their topics – and they need to be ready. While there is no exact metric for when past events become fodder for historical interpretations, it is worth noting that the first historical narratives of the 1960s in the United States and Canada for example began to appear in the 1980s; by the 1990s, established monographs and doctoral studies could be undertaken (Gitlin, 1987; Isserman, 1987; Kostash, 1980; Levitt, 1984; Owram, 1997). As the Web is now well over 25 years old, we are roughly at the time when the first serious historical studies will begin to be undertaken, and it is likely that many trailblazing doctoral students in the field are now beginning to contemplate their first degrees. To not use web archives would run the very real possibility of fundamentally misrepresenting any of the above topics. This will happen sooner than we think, too. Not only are the 1990s history, the Web is now over 25 years old, with widespread web archiving beginning over two decades ago with the Internet Archive in 1996.

This chapter explores what the changing nature of historical scale will mean for historians. It begins by discussing how web archives will become increasingly central to the historical profession. Following this, drawing upon Franco Moretti's concepts of close reading versus distant reading, it advances a typology of research projects carried out to date. The chapter then discusses the next directions for the field, especially the growing importance of metadata analysis rather than exploring content itself. It concludes by situating our contemporary trend into a 'third wave of computational history', suggesting how historians could profit by understanding themselves in their own historical context.

## THE GROWING CENTRALITY OF WEB ARCHIVES TO THE HISTORICAL PROFESSION

To reinforce the importance of web archives, consider all of the things that one could not write a history of without using web archives. Without web archives, one could not write histories of the late 1990s Tamagotchi trend, figuring out what that meant about our relationship to animals, each other, and technology; or political histories of the late 1990s on early Internet censorship, from the V-Chip to the *Communications Decency Act* in the United States, critical moments in our early Web history that might have fundamentally changed how we interacted with the medium; or economic and business histories of the 1990s dot.com bubble; or even events of pivotal significance like the attacks of September 11$^{th}$, 2001. Each of the above would be innumerably enhanced by the use of web archives, and considerably diminished by not considering these sources. This is not a niche area. Crucially, they underscore that Web histories will not just be histories of the World Wide Web (although those are important and well represented in this *Handbook*), but histories that happen to use the Web as a primary source because of its significant role in knowledge production and communication.

The novelty of these web archives can be seen in two respects: that of scale, in that we have more data than ever before, and that of scope, where different kinds of sources that were rarely preserved before are now being so. In this section, I will explore scale and scope in turn.

We are now working with sources that are being preserved on a different scale than historians are previously used to working with. In this we are seeing the insights of the late American historian Roy Rosenzweig borne out, as he foresaw in a 2003 *American Historical Review* article that historians were shifting from an environment of scarcity to one of abundance (Rosenzweig, 2003). In other words, historians have traditionally wished we had more information about the past – now, when working with web archives, historians are threatened by having too many sources to parse and explore.

Some examples can bear out the sheer scale of born-digital content being generated every day. A constantly updated page, 'My Data is Bigger than Your Data', published by University of Waterloo computer scientist Jimmy Lin, gives a tally of the ever-changing boasts of just how big datasets are. A few examples help to bring this into contrast. In January 2017, Twitter announced that it was storing over 500 petabytes of information (one petabyte is 1,000 terabytes). The Internet Archive has over 30 petabytes of archives, with approximately 13 to 15 terabytes per day being added to its collections. Spotify, a music streaming service, collects over a terabyte of user data every day from its over 75 million users and one and a half *billion* playlists. YouTube sees a petabyte of data uploaded every single day (Lin, n.d.). Not all of this will be kept. Content on Snapchat, for example, is filled with largely intended transient content; similarly, Facebook and many corporate databases will likely not be archived for historical consumption. Given ethical concerns and rights to privacy, this is not necessarily a bad thing! But even if a fraction of the above is kept, historians will be challenged to no end. In particular, the Internet Archive's activities are of interest, as they are collecting with an eye to future research access. In short, the amount of information generated on the Web means that our historical record is dramatically changing.

The expansive scope of web archives, too, has the prospect of bringing more people into the historical record. Much of what can be found in the Internet Archive are primary sources authored by people who never before would have been part of the historical record. It is not simply that instead of learning about Tamagotchis from *The New York Times* or *The Guardian* we can learn about them from Web-based sources, but that we can begin to work with the pages of people who actually used Tamagotchis. Young kids and their parents created sites in the GeoCities child-focused section, for example, allowing us to work with this innovative primary source (see my chapter on GeoCities in this *Handbook*). It is emblematic of a broader shift in the categories of people who we can learn about (Milligan, 2016). Think of the long list of sources that we will now have thanks to the widespread advent of web archiving. Pages by children, blogs by everyday teenagers, students, and adults, or even individuals who can give a unique perspective on unfolding world events (such as the Russian soldier who posted the MH17 missile launch on Facebook) (Taylor, 2014).

Web archives do not provide a perfect representation of the past – they offer facsimiles of the original pages, and much is missing or of reduced functionality (Brügger, 2013a) – but neither do traditional archives, which have had to be very selective with what they select, appraise, and preserve. We need to mind gaps in coverage and inclusion. This can be done by looking at who uses the Web and how, often drawing on studies of contemporary or historical studies (Blank and Dutton, 2014; Duggan, 2015). Additionally, we need to understand gaps in how web archives find content on the Web and what gets preserved and what does not (Thelwall and Vaughan, 2004). But while we need to understand the context in which web archives are created, we also need to understand how these collections will in many cases be broader than what has been left behind in the past. Historical practice has been dominated by archival study since the nineteenth century, often government and institutionally dominated repositories of information about what has come before. While web archives certainly have an institutional perspective, such as collections from governments or of university calendars, for example, the new forms of citizen histories present a more democratic record of the past.

To reinforce this shift, I often think to my own first book on Canada's 1960s, where I studied how young workers, students, and activists engaged with each other (Milligan, 2014). These were difficult questions to explore, even though the events had only taken place 40 years before. Student activists do not keep minutes of meetings that took place late in pubs, coffee houses, or communal homes; nor do young workers who are engaged in illegal wildcat strikes. Union newsletters tended to stress official lines, leaving little room for alternative visions. My sources then were crumbs of the past: memories from a few, garnered through around 70 oral interviews, though it was hard to find names or contemporary contact information: police reports, including of graffiti on the side of an industrial building; informants; bewildered newspaper articles in the mainstream media; occasional write-ups in a student newspaper or a manifesto saved in a university archive. Tackling a similar question today would be different. Think of the resources collected around Occupy Wall

Street, or the Canadian First Nations #idlenomore movement, or just the regular activities of youth culture.

Indeed, this animated my own first foray into studying web archives, when I worked with an old collection of websites that were created by Canadian youth in the 1990s under the auspices of a Canadian federal training project. When I found these archived websites over a decade later, I began to realize that these sources were different from what I had seen before (Milligan, 2012). In digging into youth footprints, I realized that I could even find my own first trace of a digital past, from when I was an 11-year-old boy in 1995 asking for help about a board game online. Eleven-year-old boys did not, as a rule, leave sources – yet now they do. This does not make things easier, of course – one still needs to find these sources, identify who is who if they want to, and begin to think about what is being crawled and what is not. It is an incomplete record, affected by profound issues of access, but is certainly bigger and more expansive than what we had before.

## *The Infinite Archive*

Historians work with a necessarily incomplete record of the past. Indeed, the two terms – history and the past – are not synonyms. The past happened, whereas history is created from the traces of the past that persist (from memories, to physical fragments, to archival documents, to tweets). The vast majority of things that happen are never recorded, something which philosophically remains the same. But right now a web crawler is following links, downloading pages, following links, working in that potentially infinite process that creates the archives of our lives. In this section, I would like to provide some reasons for how these traces of the past that now exist that would never have existed before matter and have the potential to reshape our historiography.

The advent of web archives has the potential to expand scholarship in several respects. Think of the blogs and social media that document what people are eating – indeed, one of the canards against social media is often 'I don't care what you had for dinner'. But a sense of what everyday people eat, consume, and idealize when it comes to food is going to be valuable; historians have long struggled with really understanding what we eat in our private homes, relying largely on memory, raw material information, government reports, how people responded to rationing, and the like (Mosby, 2014). Alternatively, we can have new understandings of social movements like Occupy Wall Street. If you relied on *The New York Times* or the *Washington Post* to understand what happened in Zuccotti Park in New York City, you would have more of a skewed vision than if you were able to use the Occupy websites themselves (used for coordination, publicity, and making the organization come together).

Occupy is also a good way to underline the importance of preserving Web materials. It can help underline the importance of preserving and documenting this material, and how this is the sort of work that needs to be done without delay. Of all the Occupy sites, created in the heat of an ever-evolving movement, two years later only 41% of the sites were active (LaCalle and Reed, 2014). Unlike physical media, which can – especially if printed on acid-free paper – be surprisingly durable (imagine a book, placed on a shelf, and coming back to it 20 years later; you can probably access the content, even if there have been some moisture problems and the like), these sources require active preservation. Server fees need to be paid, and with only brief interruption, they can disappear. And apart from high-profile projects that had considerable funding and expertise, such as the reconstruction of the first web page hosted at CERN or the first North American site at Stanford, once it is gone it is gone (Karampelas, 2014; Tsukayama, 2013).

## *Web Archiving Scholarship Today: A Quick Glimpse*

All of this is to say that the research landscape for historians seeking to study the 1990s is changing, and that it matters that historians are ready to engage with this material now. So what are historians doing with it? We are only now just beginning to see what users can do with web archives, beyond nostalgic explorations and the such. These largely fall into two rough categories: traditional close reading, and the computational digital humanities approach of distant reading (Moretti, 2007).

Some of these histories are close readings, or the inquiry of one website or a few different sites – dozens, or hundreds even, but still of a scale where the historian can click, scroll, read, and explore the individual sites to a very high degree. This builds on a great textual tradition within the historical field, where we dive deeply into one story, flesh out the stories, and in so doing learn something far more about the broader context of the events that we are studying as well. Several of these approaches appear in the *Handbook* chapters that follow in part. Federico Nanni, for example, has explored the University of Bologna's website in depth and has tried to reconstruct the story of that one page, drawing on the Internet Archive, university IT departments, and eventually using oral histories and personal contacts to tell this deeply textured story. In so doing, it becomes a good entryway into the robots.txt exclusion protocol and how websites can be removed, even retroactively, from the Internet Archive; and how a recent history of the website can be done through a close reading of one domain (Nanni, 2016). Similarly, Stanford University Libraries carried out an in-depth process to reconstruct the first web server's page outside of Europe, that of the Stanford Linear Accelerator Center's website, using the SLAC backup system (AlSum, 2015; Deken, 2017). It is an in-depth story of digital preservation, drawing on source code, newsgroups, generating web archive files from a non-standard web archive, and beyond. In so doing, this essential work helps us understand the broader challenges of digital preservation, and how much work goes into individual stories.

Yet we also have operations on a completely different scale, requiring 'distant reading'. This leverages the power of what modern data mining and text analysis tools can do on large amounts of data. This approach of distant reading is inspired by the literary work of Franco Moretti, or the wide gulfs of time and space that earlier Annales historians like Fernand Braudel explored (Braudel, 1972; Moretti, 2007). These are stories on a massive, unprecedented scale, aided by computational analysis. Peter Webster, a pioneering UK historian, has used the link graphs of the UK Web Archive to explore who linked to creationist websites. Did governments, academics, bloggers, Christian media, or the mainstream media, for example, link to these sorts of sites? This was large-scale analysis that would not have been possible if it were to be carried out manually. In this study, Webster noted that creationists mostly talk to themselves, and are ignored by academia, media, and the churches; underscoring that even among evangelicals this was a particularly minority view (Webster, 2014). This use of link graphs was also employed in a recent piece by Webster, looking at how linking patterns changed in the wake of the Sharia Law controversy in the United Kingdom; and, for example, how these links might reflect real-world interest in various dioceses (Webster, 2017). Or, at times, this has even involved looking at entire national country-code top-level domains (ccTLDs), such as the Danish .dk. Recent work by Niels Brügger has explored the general challenges and opportunities presented by exploring a nation's web domain (Brügger, 2017). There is even promising work that looks at now-defunct top-level domains, such as the deleted Yugoslavian .yu. Anat Ben-David of the Open University of Israel conducted pioneering research into the shape of this deleted domain, looking at how the networked structure of millions of pages dramatically changed between 1996 and 2010. She found that the internal links emerged after the fall of autocrat Slobodan Milosevic, and then began to fall apart as new domains for the independent countries emerged; as she puts it, 'the intra-domain linking patterns of the .yu domain are closely tied with stability and sovereignty' (Ben-David, 2015, 2016).

We can see from this very brief overview that there is great power and potential in being able to use these web archives. Yet the number of scholars working with web archives today is still relatively small, due in no small part to the problem of access.

## *Going Wayback: Closely Reading Web Archives*

One of the major limitations of a web history, however, is the sheer difficulty of doing this sort of work. There is a necessity to democratize access to this material, so that historians and everyday people have better access to this important digital cultural resource.

Currently, most historians and other researchers access web archives via some flavor of a 'Wayback' instance. You can see a version of the Internet Archive's instance in Figure 1.1. The Wayback Machine, which is what the Internet Archive calls its version of the Wayback, was launched in 2001 to provide access to its collections. It is now also available as an open-source project known as 'Open Wayback'.

The Wayback Machine allows a user to temporally browse 'back in time', by rendering collected pages and making links find the closest snapshot to the page that they are launching their search from. In short, one can load up the American White House's home page from December 27th, 1996 and when clicking on links within the Wayback Machine, one is brought to snapshots of that page as close to that day as possible.

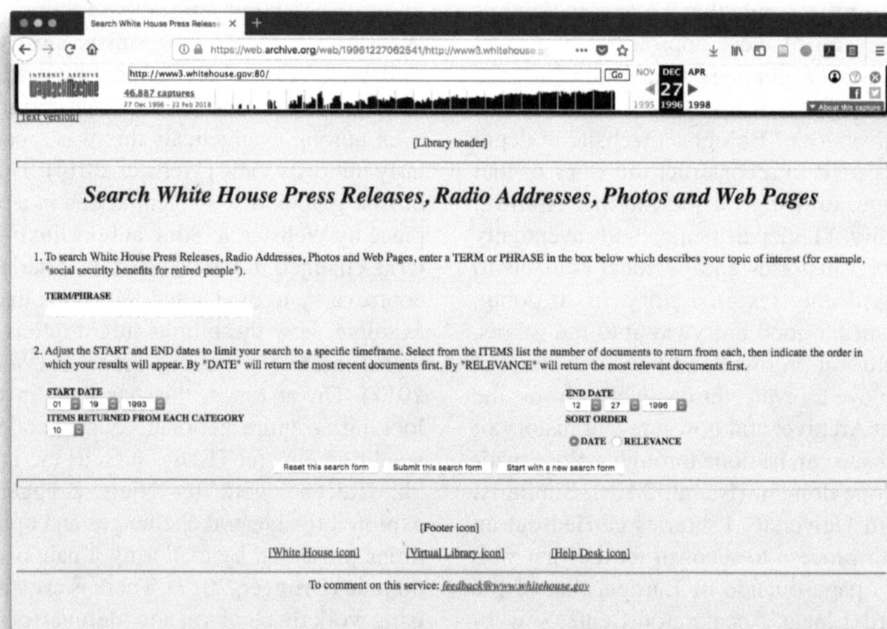


**Figure 1.1 The White House viewed in the Wayback Machine.**

Users can find content in the Wayback Machine by two means. First, they can type in the URL of the address that they know they want to find (nytimes.com, for example). Second, they can do a limited full-text search on the home pages of websites (type 'New York Times' and you find the URL of the page, which can be very useful when pages have changed their URL several times over their life).

Researching with the Wayback Machine lends itself to close reading. A user browses one page at a time, and is limited by the speed of the Wayback Machine and the underlying server. It is not a speedy experience, but it does in many ways replicate the experience of working with traditional documents. Even when working with the Web in other ways, finding URLs through various discovery methods discussed below, the end point is usually a Wayback Machine. It is how we view the documents themselves. Yet for most research projects, the Wayback Machine will not be enough. When working at scale, such as the millions of pages of GeoCities, one cannot click through each page manually; and the basic search functionality that the Internet Archive provides is limited only to home pages.

But imagine trying to use the Wayback Machine at scale: you would have to click through pages manually, limited to home page searches, and beyond – it would take decades, if not more, just to look at all the pages. Accordingly, new systems of access are being developed to explore this. Some of these are simply various full-text search interfaces, designed not to handle the massive amount of data within the Wayback Machine, but to be implemented on relatively smaller collections. Enter the world of distant reading.

## *Computational Access to Web Archives: We Want to Read It All but Cannot*

Historians like to work with content – but the scale of web archives makes that difficult to achieve. What should historians then do? Traditionally, the historian's approach can be likened to that of a microscope: closely exploring small numbers of documents; in an era of ever-growing datasets, the macroscope may be the better metaphor (Graham et al., 2015). Niels Brügger has identified five different layers when it comes to studying the Web: the Web as a whole, web spheres, web pages, and web elements (Brügger, 2009, 2018). The concept of web spheres comes from Schneider and Foot, who define this as 'not simply a collection of websites, but as a hyperlinked set of dynamically defined digital resources that span multiple websites and are deemed relevant, or related, to a central theme or "object"' (Schneider and Foot, 2004: 118).

The debate between a wider focus – thinking of the Web as a whole à la Schneider, Foot, and Brügger – and a narrower one speaks to the importance of both close and distant reading. In related work, I have argued that larger perspectives benefit our understanding of the Web, given the importance of context for understanding single documents (Milligan, 2012, 2016). Other scholars have noted the importance of a 'Big Data' perspective to derive meaning from large amounts of cultural data (Aiden and Michel, 2013; Mayer-Schönberger and Cukier, 2013; Schroeder, 2014). Some historians, however, based on their experience with web archives have questioned the idea that bigger is necessarily better. Gareth Millward, who worked with web archives as part of the BUDDAH project, argued as much in a *Washington Post* opinion piece:

> We're going to have to realize that we can't read everything. We already do this with printed documents, but we need to be more explicit about it and more willing to admit it. Smaller samples of websites, specifically chosen for their historical importance, can give us a much better understanding. We can begin to ask questions about how sites are constructed and what information people and organizations chose to reveal. Similarly, much more focussed searches on smaller time periods, more marginal topics, or specific cultural groups can produce a more manageable 'corpus'

> for reading and manipulating in the same way we would on our trips to traditional archives. (Millward, 2015)

Millward also argues that metadata, the links between websites, might be the most useful way forward – finding common ground with other scholars (Brügger, 2013b).

Metadata is an important concept that thus lies at the heart of web archival research. While a difficult-to-define term, it can perhaps be best understood – as the American National Security Agency (NSA) does – as 'information about content (but not the content itself)' (Greenwald, 2014: 132). Indeed, the NSA's definition is a useful beginning point, as the NSA itself underscores the power of metadata. The 2013 Edward Snowden revelations that the agency had been engaged in widespread harvesting of American metadata, such as the records of phone calls (who you call, who calls you, and how long you spoke for), shocked many Americans. Despite agency denials that this was not surveillance as it did not engage with content, authors such as journalist Glenn Greenwald convincingly hold that metadata can actually be *more* revealing than the content itself. A single call, even if it were to be transcribed and published, would not tell you much about your life. However, a recurring pattern over months or years, would begin to (Greenwald, 2014). The MIT Immersion Lab's tool at https://immersion.media.mit.edu/ also helps to illustrate this, as it takes a user's Gmail account, extracts the to, from, cc, and timestamp fields, and begins to reconstruct your life based on social ties.

A similar approach works well with web archives, as later chapters in this *Handbook* discuss. Stevenson and Ben-David explore this at depth, but here is an example. Recall the Toronto Political Parties and Political Interest Groups collection, collected by the University of Toronto between 2005 and today. There are some 14 million documents in total, too many to read. Indeed, some domains consist of thousands of different pages. Using Warcbase, a software program that works with the underlying WARC files in the collection, we extracted all the hyperlinks between sites and aggregated them by domain.[1]

For example, any time a page within the left-wing New Democratic Party of Canada domain (ndp.ca) linked to another page, we counted the domain that it came from (ndp.ca) and the domain that it was going to (for example, NewYorkTimes.com). By doing so we could tell stories about the web archive that eluded single page readings. In these hyperlink graphs, for example, we can see the left-wing New Democratic Party of Canada (ndp.ca) linking heavily to the centrist Liberal Party of Canada (liberal.ca), and largely ignoring the right-wing Conservative Party of Canada (conservative.ca). This is due to several reasons, notably that the Liberals are in power at this time. Even though they are ideologically closer, it makes more sense to link to attack and critique the party in power than an opposition party.

This example helps underscore the importance of metadata for exploring archived web material. At first, the inability to explore web archival data in a manner we are used to in traditional archives may seem like a downside, but increasingly by leveraging the structured metadata within archives we are able to quickly find material of relevance.

Other projects have explored the potential of distant reading to explore web archives. In the United Kingdom, for example, the Big UK Domain Data for the Arts and Humanities (BUDDAH) project sought to develop technical and methodological approaches for the historical uses of web archives. Partnering with the British Library to 'co-produce tools', the team moved towards new access methods. The ensuing Shine viewer (Figure 1.2) allows a user to see trends in a large web archival collection obtained by the British Library from the Internet Archive, which covers the .uk domain between 1996 and 2013. Consider the example query in Figure 1.2, which compares the relative frequency of three prime ministers between these years. We can see the blue line (Tony Blair) diminish in

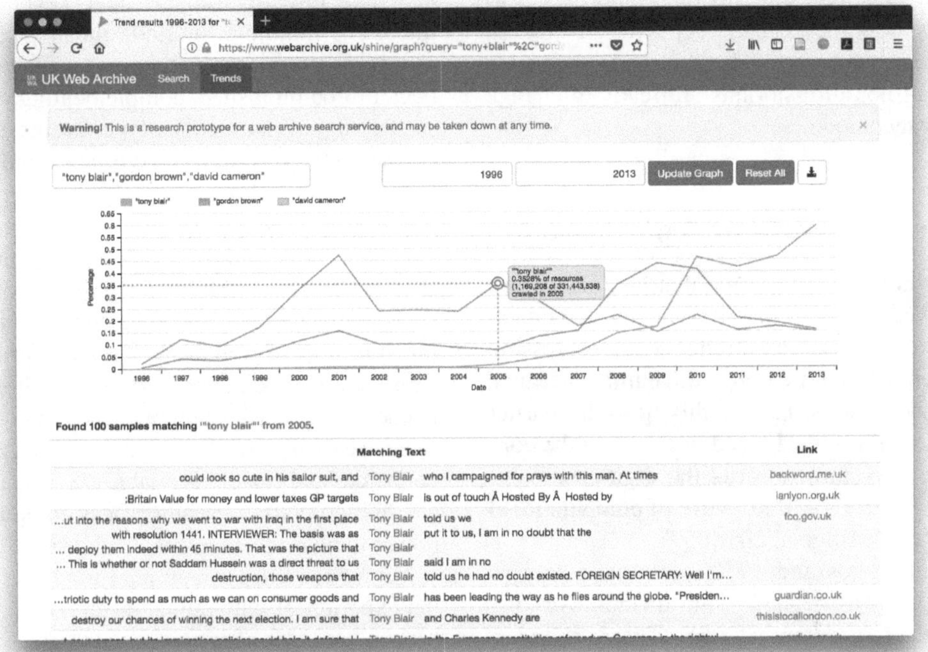


**Figure 1.2 Three Prime Ministers seen in the UK Web Archive's Shine interface. Image used with thanks to the British Library.**

frequency, replaced by the red line (Gordon Brown) when he is prime minister, and finally both are eclipsed by the yellow line (David Cameron). A user can click on the lines, and then be brought to a sample page containing that phrase (Jackson et al., 2016).

These interfaces are not perfect. In the above case, the samples are arranged in the order by which they were crawled – earliest to last. While a laudable reaction to the 'black box' of a search engine (like Google) that we may not understand, when working at scale we need to begin to engage with ranking algorithms. Eschewing relevance ranking is akin to doing research where archives are Twitter timelines – ordered only by date, meaning we understand the order they are in but at any scale it begins to overwhelm the human capacity to reason and engage. Yet it can still build considerable interest. In 2015, for example, our research team at the University of Waterloo and York University used the Shine platform to provide access to a ten-year-old collection of Canadian political party and political interest group websites (webarchives.ca). The University of Toronto had been collecting these sites since 2005, comprising some 50 domains of all of Canada's major political parties, minor political parties, and a somewhat nebulous assemblage of political interest groups covering topics as varied as campaigns to ban land mines, protect the Canadian environment, or fight for social justice for Canada's First Nations. Given the importance of this collection, once we provided access to it, we had thousands of visitors after the media picked up the story. This underscores the power of an easy-to-use interface.

Shine, and other similar interests, speak to the new methods that historians will need as they facilitate both distant and close reading. Later in this book, my *Handbook* chapter on

GeoCities uses some of these approaches to show how they can be deployed in modern historical research. The downside, however, is that not all historians are ready to change their technique.

### *The Third Wave of Digital History*

This is not the first time that historians have worked at scale, but it comes at a moment when the mainstream historical profession appears to be retreating from numbers, teams, and computers. Part of this lies with earlier historical follies. Indeed, we can see the contemporary turn towards the digital humanities as part of a 'third wave of computational history' (Milligan, 2012: 30).

The 1960s and 1970s saw computers as indelibly associated with quantitative histories (Anderson, 2008). These pioneering computational historians relied on large mainframe computers and stacks of punchcards, saw considerable advancements in the realms of demographic history and studies of large censuses, and generated arguments foundational to our understanding of social mobility and migration today (Anderson, 2008; Katz, 1975). Others, however, brought hubris to their work, claiming 'scientific' rigor (Fogel and Elton, 1984). Perhaps the height of this was the debate around Fogel and Engerman's *Time on the Cross: The Economics of American Negro Slavery*, seen by critics as reducing the terrible, human experience of slavery to numbers and tables (Fogel and Engerman, 1974); by the late 1970s, this first wave of computational history was in retreat. Some of these earlier debates tempered enthusiasm for computational histories, which reappeared in the early 1990s with the personal computing revolution. This second wave of computational history was marked by graphical user interfaces, word processing, and the rise of the World Wide Web and attendant scholarly networks such as H-Net. Instead of scholars needing to use punchcards to interact with mainframe computers, they could interact with computers and data directly through their keyboards, mice, and monitors. In 1998, the *Journal of the Association for History and Computing* began to be published, complementing other 1990s digital humanities-type events such as the 1994 conference Hypertext and the Future of the Humanities (Graham et al., 2015). Since the early 2010s, we are now in a third wave of computational history due to several factors, notably decreasing storage costs, the power of distributed cloud computing, the rise of digital preservation professionals, and open-source software. Storage is cheaper than ever before, we can put it to good use thanks to all of the data that is being collected and made available to researchers, and crucially we can harness computing power to begin to access it (Milligan, 2012).

Yet we can learn something from these earlier experiences with digital history. First, as I have argued elsewhere, we need to recognize the subjectivity of the tools that are designed and used (Graham et al., 2015; Milligan, 2012). Claims towards scientific rigor alienated other historians during the first wave of computational history. The results from a 'distant reading' algorithm over a web archive may appear to be objective, in that the data and the algorithm combined will produce the same answer. But the subjectivity of tools is embedded in the machines that we use: the decisions on how we structure datasets, tokenize sentences, calculate central nodes in a network diagram, and beyond, all rely on generations of scholars as well as human agency. Just as importantly, even if historians are basing their argument off the *exact same evidence*, they will not draw the same historical conclusions or arguments. Results always need interpretation. In short, Big Data is not better than earlier forms of exploration, simply different.

## CONCLUSIONS

Historians are in some ways at a crossroads, as we seek to grapple with the implications of scale in the digital age. This also holds true for non-Web-based research, drawing on databases and beyond (Milligan, 2013; Putnam, 2016). Imagine a historian trying to understand the rise of somebody like Donald Trump, elected US president in late 2016. Search interfaces can only get them so far, especially if they rely on keywords; imagine the number of hits they would get if they put his name into the equivalent of a Google search, or newspaper database search, or beyond. They would have no sense of what was important, or what was not important. As Ted Underwood has noted, 'in a database containing millions of sentences, full-text search can turn up twenty examples of anything' (Underwood, 2014). In this dystopian scenario, as the historian cannot read tens of thousands of hits on one keyword search in one small archive alone, as they begin to put pen to paper, while they imagine they've chosen the right sources – the ranking algorithm is really writing the work.

To do this work will require algorithmic and computational literacy. But imagine a more sophisticated approach. They decide to take part of a web archive, say a series of blogs around a particular incident during the Trump campaign; or a circumscribed corpus of media articles. Perhaps they use network analysis to filter away extreme, unrepresentative voices, focusing instead on pages that both mentioned Trump prominently and had many other pages (themselves trustworthy based on linking patterns) linking to them. They consult the information they have about the programs they are using to explore this material, recognize the biases in the archive and the algorithm, and begin to pare it down. After this filtering process, perhaps they are down to a manageable set of 500 web pages, which can be closely read. Spanning distant and close, hard work lies ahead but the historian at least has a rigorous pathway forward.

None of this will be easy or straightforward. Our society has been grappling with a profound medium shift with the advent of the World Wide Web. Historians will be no different. It has been over 25 years since the Web was launched, and over 20 years since the beginning of widespread web archiving with the Internet Archive. This will require a new toolkit, ethical sensitivity, and innovative approaches to access. In the *Handbook* chapters that follow, we will explore the various dimensions that this rethinking can play out.

## Note

1 WARC, or Web ARChive files, are the ISO-standardized file format that web archives use to store their content. In a nutshell, they aggregate all the products of a crawl together with metadata. The best way to understand a WARC file is a tangible example. Imagine we are preserving a university's website. Within it are potentially millions of files: HTML files, Word and PDF documents, JPG and PNG images, video, stylesheets, and beyond. A WARC file can aggregate these resources with description, allowing them to be preserved and crucially accessed.

## REFERENCES

Aiden, E., and Michel, J.B. (2013) *Uncharted: Big Data as a Lens on Human Culture*. New York: Riverhead.

AlSum, A. (2015) 'Reconstruction of the US First Website', *Proceedings of the 15th ACM/IEEE-CS Joint Conference on Digital Libraries*: 285–286.

Anderson, I. (2008) 'History and Computing' (http://www.history.ac.uk/makinghistory/resources/articles/history_and_computing.html). Accessed 22 June 2018.

Ben-David, A. (2015) 'What Does the Web Remember of Its Deleted Past?' (https://webarchivehistorians.org/2015/09/07/what-does-the-web-remember-of-its-deleted-past/). Accessed 4 October 2016.

Ben-David, A. (2016) 'What Does the Web Remember of Its Deleted Past? An Archival Reconstruction of the Former Yugoslav Top-Level Domain', *New Media and Society*, 18(7): 1103–1119.

Blank, G., and Dutton, W.H. (2014) 'Next Generation Internet Users: A New Digital Divide', in M. Graham and W.H. Dutton (Eds.), *Society and*

*the Internet: How Networks of Information and Communication Are Changing Our Lives*. New York: Oxford University Press. pp. 36–52.
Braudel, F. (1972) *The Mediterranean and the Mediterranean World in the Age of Philip II*. Berkeley: UC Press.
Brügger, N. (2009) 'Website History and the Website as an Object of Study', *New Media and Society*, 11(1–2): 115–132.
Brügger, N. (2013a) 'Web Historiography and Internet Studies: Challenges and Perspectives', *New Media and Society*, 15(5): 752–764.
Brügger, N. (2013b) 'Historical Network Analysis of the Web', *Social Science Computer Review*, 31: 306–321.
Brügger, N. (2017) 'Probing a Nation's Web Domain: A New Approach to Web History and a New Kind of Historical Source', in G. Goggin and M. McLelland (Eds.), *The Routledge Companion to Global Internet Histories*. New York: Routledge. pp. 61–73.
Brügger, N. (2018 forthcoming) *The Archived Web: Doing Web History in the Digital Age*. Cambridge: MIT Press.
Deken, J.M. (2017) 'The Web's First "Killer App": SLAC National Accelerator Laboratory's World Wide Web Site, 1991–1993', in N. Brügger (Ed.), *Web 25: Histories from the First 25 Years of the World Wide Web*. New York: Peter Lang Publishing. pp. 57–78.
Duggan, M. (2015) 'The Demographics of Social Media Users' (http://www.pewinternet.org/2015/08/19/the-demographics-of-social-media-users/). Accessed 10 December 2015.
Fogel, R.W., and Engerman, S.L. (1974) *Time on the Cross: The Economics of American Negro Slavery*. New York: W. W. Norton & Company.
Fogel, R., and Elton, G. (1984) *Which Road to the Past?: Two Views of History*. New Haven: Yale University Press.
Gitlin, T. (1987) *The Sixties: Years of Hope, Days of Rage*. New York: Bantam Books.
Graham, S., Milligan, I., and Weingart, S. (2015) *Exploring Big Historical Data: The Historian's Macroscope*. London: Imperial College Press.
Greenwald, G. (2014) *No Place to Hide: Edward Snowden, the NSA, and the U.S. Surveillance State*. New York: Metropolitan Books.
Isserman, M. (1987) *If I Had a Hammer: The Death of the Old Left and the Birth of the New Left*. New York: Basic Books.
Jackson, A., Lin, J., Milligan, I., and Ruest, N. (2016) 'Desiderata for Exploratory Search Interfaces to Web Archives in Support of Scholarly Activities', *Proceedings of the 16th ACM/IEEE-CS on Joint Conference on Digital Libraries*: 103–106.
Karampelas, G. (2014) 'Stanford Libraries Unearths the Earliest U.S. Website' (http://news.stanford.edu/news/2014/october/slac-libraries-waybback-102914.html). Acessed 4 April 2017.
Katz, M.B. (1975) *The People of Hamilton, Canada West: Family and Class in a Mid-Nineteenth-Century City*. Cambridge: Harvard University Press.
Kostash, M. (1980) *Long Way from Home: The Story of the Sixties Generation in Canada*. Toronto: Lorimer.
LaCalle, M., and Reed, S. (2014) 'Poster: The Occupy Web Archive: Is the Movement Still on the Live Web?', presented at Digital Preservation 2014, Washington, DC.
Levitt, C. (1984) *Children of Privilege: Student Revolt in the Sixties: A Study of Student Movements in Canada, the United States, and West Germany*. Toronto: University of Toronto Press.
Lin, J. n.d. 'My Data Is Bigger Than Your Data' (http://lintool.github.io/my-data-is-bigger-than-your-data/). Accessed 22 June 2018.
Mayer-Schönberger, V., and Cukier, K. (2013) *Big Data: A Revolution That Will Transform How We Live, Work, and Think*. Boston: Eamon Dolan/Houghton Mifflin Harcourt.
Milligan, I. (2012) 'Mining the "Internet Graveyard": Rethinking the Historians' Toolkit', *Journal of the Canadian Historical Association*, 23(2): 21–64.
Milligan, I. (2013) 'Illusionary Order: Online Databases, Optical Character Recognition, and Canadian History, 1997–2010', *Canadian Historical Review*, 94(4): 540–569.
Milligan, I. (2014) *Rebel Youth: 1960s Labour Unrest, Young Workers, and New Leftists in English Canada*. Vancouver: UBC Press.
Milligan, I. (2016) 'Lost in the Infinite Archive: The Promise and Pitfalls of Web Archives', *International Journal of Humanities and Arts Computing*, 10(1): 78–94.
Millward, G. (2015) 'I Tried to Use the Internet to Do Historical Research. It Was Nearly

Impossible', *Washington Post* (https://www.washingtonpost.com/posteverything/wp/2015/02/17/i-tried-to-use-the-internet-to-do-historical-research-it-was-nearly-impossible/?utm_term=.77cd9f605120). Accessed 19 February 2015.

Moretti, F. (2007) *Graphs, Maps, Trees: Abstract Models for Literary History*. New York: Verso.

Mosby, I. (2014) *Food Will Win the War: The Politics, Culture, and Science of Food on Canada's Home Front.* Vancouver: UBC Press.

Nanni, F. (2016) 'Reconstructing a Website's Lost Past: Methodological Issues Concerning the History of www.unibo.it', ArXiv160405923.

Owram, D. (1997) *Born at the Right Time: A History of the Baby Boom Generation*. Toronto: University of Toronto Press.

Putnam, L. (2016) 'The Transnational and the Text-Searchable: Digitized Sources and the Shadows They Cast', *American Historical Review*, 121(2): 377–402.

Rosenzweig, R. (2003) 'Scarcity or Abundance? Preserving the Past in a Digital Era', *American Historical Review*, 108(3): 735–762.

Schneider, S.M., and Foot, K.A. (2004) 'The Web as an Object of Study', *New Media and Society*, 6(1): 114–122.

Schroeder, R. (2014) 'Big Data: Towards a More Scientific Social Science and Humanities?', in M. Graham and W.H. Dutton (Eds.), *Society and the Internet: How Networks of Information and Communication Are Changing Our Lives*. New York: Oxford University Press. pp. 164–176.

Taylor, N. (2014) 'The MH17 Crash and Selective Web Archiving' (https://blogs.loc.gov/thesignal/2014/07/21503/). Accessed 12 April 2017.

Thelwall, M., and Vaughan, L. (2004) 'A Fair History of the Web? Examining Country Balance in the Internet Archive', *Library and Information Science Research*, 26(2): 162–176.

Tsukayama, H. (2013) 'CERN Reposts the World's First Web Page', *Washington Post* (https://www.washingtonpost.com/business/technology/cern-reposts-the-worlds-first-web-page/2013/04/30/d8a70128-b1ac-11e2-bbf2-a6f9e9d79e19_story.html). Accessed 10 June 2014.

Underwood, T. (2014) 'Theorizing Research Practices We Forgot to Theorize Twenty Years Ago', *Representations*, 127(1): 64–72.

Webster, P. (2014) 'Reading Creationism in the Web Archive' (https://peterwebster.me/2014/11/18/reading-creationism-in-the-web-archive/). Accessed 23 May 2017.

Webster, P. (2017) 'Religious Discourse in the Archived Web: Rowan Williams, Archbishop of Canterbury, and the Sharia Law Controversy of 2008', in N. Brügger and R. Schroeder (Eds.), *The Web as History*. London: UCL Press. pp. 190–203.

# 2

# Understanding the Archived Web as a Historical Source

Niels Brügger

Like any other historical study, web histories should be based on a variety of source types such as written documents, print and electronic media, oral histories, and the web itself. As is the case with all source types, the online web must have been collected by someone – an archiving institution, a researcher, or any other person – and it has to be preserved so that it can later be made available to historians.

However, the online web changes rapidly. The lifetime of web content has been debated since at least the late 1990s, and there seems to be agreement that large portions of the web are very ephemeral (cf. e.g. Cho and Garcia-Molina, 1999; Ntoulas et al., 2004; Agata et al., 2014; Jackson, 2015). Web content may have been changed, moved, or deleted for various reasons, and sometimes in the hope of not being found out. For instance, in 2013, news media reported that the UK Conservative Party had deleted more than a decade's political speeches from its website, some of which might not be in line with the party's present politics.[1] In other cases content is changed or deleted as part of institutional routines, such as is seen with online news media outlets, and sometimes things are just taken off-line without much reflection about why this is done.

This rapid changeability is an everyday experience for web users that they have probably learned to live with, but to those who have taken on the task of collecting and preserving the web for future studies the speed of change constitutes a great challenge. Therefore, much of the online web from the first formative years has been lost, which is a well-known phenomenon within media history where it often takes decades until the technical, organisational, and economic conditions are in place to launch preservation initiatives. Nevertheless, large portions of the online web have been collected since the mid 1990s and are now available in a great number of web archives all over the world, which enables web historians to document and study the changes that have taken place;

for instance, the UK Conservative Party's political speeches had been archived by the British Library.[2]

As will be shown in this chapter, the archived web is in many ways fundamentally different from other digital sources, such as digitised documents, print and audio-visual media, and even online media, and therefore web historians have to become familiar with this type of source, its characteristics, and how these characteristics impact its scholarly use. In short, a critical approach to the archived web is needed.

This chapter outlines some key elements in a theoretical and methodological framework for doing web history based on the archived web as a historical source. To provide a starting point for the identification of the specific nature of the archived web, a brief outline is drawn of the wider landscape of digital media and what is termed their 'digitality'. Before digging deeper into the characteristics of the archived web, the chapter investigates what characterised the online web that was archived as well as the process of web archiving where the online web became the archived web. The stage is then set to outline the nature of the archived web, compared with the online web and other types of archived documents and media.[3] Finally, some of the main impacts that the nature of the archived web has on how it can be used as a scholarly source by the web historian are discussed.[4]

## DIGITALITY AND THE ONLINE WEB

The point of departure of this chapter is that all digital media come with their own 'digitality', that is their own way of being digital (cf. Brügger, 2018). A digital medium's digitality sets up an array of possible ways of interacting with the medium and with the textual and semiotic systems that the medium enables (for a general discussion of the 'relatively fixed features' of a medium, see Meyrowitz, 1994: 50). Therefore, when setting out to investigate the possible use of the archived web it is pivotal to identify the archived web's digitality, that is its specific ways of being digital.

### *Forms of Digitality: Digitised, Born Digital, Reborn Digital*

Despite the fact that digital media are different because they each come with their own digitality, they also share some features. An important criterion for determining a digital medium's digitality is how it became digital, and therefore grouping digital media based on the provenance of their digital nature is reasonable. Based on this approach, three main types can be distinguished: digitised, born digital, and reborn digital material (Brügger, 2012: 104).

Digitised material is material that has previously existed in a non-digital form, but has been transformed to become digital. The non-digital original can, for instance, be handwritten documents, print media, or electronic audio-visual media, and they may have been digitised in a number of ways, from being keyboarded and transferred to punched cards to the scanning of document prints and photos to image files, or the digital recording of analogue sound and moving images.

Born-digital material has never existed in any other form than digital. This type of material was created for and only made available on digital media such as CD-ROMs, DVDs, or computer networks.[5] Therefore this type of material does not have any non-digital original to go back to.

Reborn-digital material is born-digital material that has been collected and preserved, and that has been changed in this process to such a degree that it is not identical to the born-digital of which it was made. This could be an emulated computer game, a screen film of an app, or material in a web archive.

Distinguishing between these three specific types of digital material is important because the digitality of each type has a decisive impact on how it can be interacted with in the processes of collecting and preserving it as well as making it available, for instance to researchers who want to use it as a historical source.

## Characteristics of the Online Web

When investigating the archived web, it is often overlooked that it was created on the basis of the online web. The archived web is reborn at the nexus of the online web and the chosen archiving forms and strategies (cf. below), and therefore a number of the main characteristics of the online web influence the nature of the archived web. Or, to use the vocabulary above: the digitality of the archived web is a function of the digitality of the online web as it is combined with specific web archiving forms and strategies. Any form of the online web shares the following three characteristics: it is born with two semiotic layers, it is fragmented, and it is hyperlinked.

### The web is born with two semiotic layers

The web consists of two distinct semiotic layers: on the one hand, the text that the web user sees in a browser window on the screen (or hears in the speakers), and, on the other hand, the text that enables the presentation of the semiotic elements on the screen, namely the text written in an HTML file (code and textual content) as well as the elements that are requested and retrieved from one or more web servers. When the web user enters a web address – a URL – in the location bar of a web browser (or clicks a hyperlink), a request is sent to the relevant web server, which then returns the requested HTML document as well as the files to which the HTML document may point (image files, audio or video files, feeds, etc.), and when all the requested material is received it is interpreted in the web browser and displayed in a browser window.[6] To highlight this point one can compare the online web to a digitised newspaper. They both come with a visible side – what can immediately be seen when displaying the document – but they differ significantly when it comes to the hidden text 'below' this visible surface. The digitised newspaper usually consists of an image file (bitmap or similar) that is then immediately interpreted as a newspaper page when displayed, whereas the online web page has an extra layer of HTML and attached files. Digitised image files may become enriched with character recognition (OCR), but in contrast to the online web this is not an indispensable and inherent part of the document since it is added after digitisation, and the information it conveys is not as rich and complex as is the case with the hidden web text.

### The web is born fragmented

The second characteristic of the web is its fragmented nature. What is presented to the web user in the web browser window appears to be a unified web page, but as mentioned above this apparent unity hides the fact that the page comprises patched-together fragments. The HTML file is in itself a structured patchwork of bits and pieces, including textual content and commands, and the various files that are retrieved also constitute individual entities that have to be combined with the rest to form a coherent web page.

Digitised collections can also come as partly fragmented – for instance if parts of the text have been marked with a mark-up language – but these fragments are not there from the outset as an inherent part of the material, as is the case with the online web.

### The web is born hyperlinked

Finally, the web is born hyperlinked, since it is possible to connect any fragment of text on one computer with any other semantic entity on the same or on another computer in the computer network.[7] One could argue that hyperlinks are not necessary for the web, which may in principle be correct, but in practice a web without hyperlinks would not work; for instance, one would then have to write exact web addresses in the location bar every time one wanted to go to another web page.

As was the case with the two semiotic layers and the fragmentation of the web, the use of the hyperlink also differs from what is the case in a digitised collection. Hyperlinks may be added to digitised newspapers, but they are not an inherent part of the material since they are added later, and they need not be added.

## *Web Archiving*

Knowledge about the inherent properties of the online web is only one element in the understanding of the archived web, since the archived web is constructed as a combination of the online web and the different forms and strategies used when collecting and preserving it. Therefore, it is important to have a closer look at web archiving. As shall be shown in the following, the process of collecting and preserving the web is in many cases more complex, complicated, and opaque than is the case with establishing a digitised collection.

### *Forms of collecting and preserving the web*

The online web may have been collected and preserved in various ways. The most widespread archiving form is web crawling, which is used by most major national and international web archiving initiatives, but it is also possible to use other forms. Since web historians may have to combine the archived web from different collection types, a broad understanding of web archiving is preferable. Thus, web archiving can be understood as any form of deliberate and purposive collecting and preserving of web material.

The simplest way of preserving a web page is by making an image, either in the form of a screenshot or by the use of dedicated software that contacts a web server and transforms the rendered web page to an image file.

An extended version of preserving the web as an image file is to make a screen movie, that is, filming what happens on the screen when a user moves around on a website, clicks hyperlinks, watches streamed video, etc. When making a screen movie there is no direct connection to a web server, and therefore what is archived is not a function of a hidden HTML file, but rather of the movements made by the individual who records the screen.

Another simple form of web archiving is the downloading of individual files from the web, be that audio or video files that have been part of a web page, or files with only parts of an HTML file such as hyperlinks.

The most complex form of web archiving is web crawling. Web crawling is a sophisticated, systematic, and scalable version of the collecting of individual files, basically because the process can be automated and it scales to large amounts of web material. A list of the web addresses one wants to collect is created (a so-called seed-list), and the archiving software goes through this list by contacting the listed web servers one by one, retrieves the web pages in question, strips all the hyperlink information on each web page, retrieves the material to which these hyperlinks point, strips the hyperlink information on these web pages, etc. And the software continues with this iterative process as far away from the starting points as the web archivist has asked for. The result of web crawling is a collection of HTML files and the files that make up a given web page, whether they are saved as they are retrieved or aggregated into dedicated file formats such as ARC or WARC. Thus, in contrast to the first three mentioned methods of web archiving, web crawling is inextricably linked with the online web's hidden HTML code, to its fragments, and to its hyperlinks, in brief to the three characteristics of the digitality of the online web. And for the very same reason it is based on a wide range of settings, for instance it has to be specified how many levels away from the original URL the software is allowed to follow hyperlinks, which specific file types should be included/excluded, if the web crawler is to remain within the limits of a particular web domain, when the archiving should stop, etc. Thus, because web crawling is based on following hyperlinks, and because of the large number of possible and required settings, it can be maintained that to a large extent the archiving actor does not know exactly what is archived.[8]

## Strategies of web archiving

One of the main challenges for the individual or institution who wants to collect and preserve the online web is that in most cases it is not possible to archive the entire web in all dimensions, exactly as it looked when online. Therefore, strategies have to be used to collect as much as possible of what is intended to be collected.[9]

When considering the different possible archiving strategies, the archiving actor had to decide how the strategy should relate to three variables – space, time, and possible use – by placing the archiving on a continuum in relation to each variable. As for space the strategies either aim at archiving as much as possible of the web, or they are designed to archive specific fractions of the web. With regard to time, the strategy must address the question of the archiving frequency: either the archiving is continuous, or it focuses on certain delimited points in time. Finally, regarding the possible use of what is archived, the archiving actor must reflect on whether the later use is either unknown or a well-known and precise use case. Thus, the strategies used for archiving the web can be placed at different cross-sections of a grid with all/fractions, continuous/once, and unknown/known use.

## Challenges of web archiving

When an archiving actor in the past set out to collect and preserve the web, the overall challenge was how the relations between the concrete form of the online web at the specific period, and the different archiving forms and strategies at hand should be negotiated. However, no matter how this was done the web archivist was facing at least five challenges that all influence the later use of the archived material.

The first challenge is that in most cases there exists no stable original on the web against which the quality of the archiving can be checked. Unlike a digitised newspaper or broadcast programme, the online web may – or may not – be the same when quality is checked as when it was archived, given the possible rapid speed of change of the web.

Second, compared with most other forms of collecting and preserving, including digitisation, the choices of 'what' and 'how' to preserve are embedded in a much more complex, unsystematic, and less transparent environment. When digitising a collection of newspapers or radio programmes, problems such as brightness or file compression have to be addressed, but although these choices influence the outcome, the number of options is limited and their possible scope is transparent, and if any other actor proceeded in the same way, the result would likely be identical. In contrast, the combination of the online web's complex digitality and the many forms and strategies for archiving, as well as their mutual calibration, multiplies the number of possible options. And in particular regarding web crawling, the 'what' tends to be obscured by the 'how', since one may have a clear idea about 'what' to archive at the outset, but as a consequence of the multiple choices of the 'how', either one does not get what was intended, or one gets more than what was expected.

A third challenge that the web archivist had to struggle with in the past is related to what can be termed the dynamics of updating (Schneider and Foot, 2004: 115; Brügger, 2005: 22–4). As stated above, the web changes rapidly, but updates are not necessarily predictable and regular. Compared with printed or electronic media, the temporality of the web is not that of an entity published on a regular basis, like daily newspapers or a scheduled radio and television programme.

This implies that what was archived at the beginning of one archiving process may have changed as the process progresses. As if, when page 10 was scanned, page 2 was suddenly changed, or halfway through the digitisation of a radio programme, the beginning was altered.

The fourth challenge to the web archive actor was that things are likely to have gone wrong during the web archiving process. Even with simple archiving forms like saving the web as images, the software may not have processed the web page correctly. And with more complex web archiving forms such as web crawling, the number of error sources grows significantly. In contrast, if errors occur during digitisation, they are generally systematic and recurring.

Finally, the fifth challenge revolves around the chosen archiving strategy and the relationship between time and space in the different strategies. Regarding space, the biggest challenge is that web archiving takes time, which means that the closer the strategy is to 'all', the longer the archiving will require since it is not possible to archive 'all' at the same time. But the closer the strategy approaches 'fractions', the less the problem becomes. Regarding time, the closer the archiving strategy is to 'continuous', the more space is a problem because the archive cannot archive large amounts of the online web continuously. Finally, with regard to the possible scenarios for the use of what is archived, the less that is known about the possible use, the harder it is to choose the right forms and strategies for archiving.

In addition to these five challenges that cut across forms and strategies, the archiving actor has had to face challenges that are specific to how each of the different archiving forms handle the archiving of the three fixed features of the online web's digitality.

On the one hand, archiving in the form of a picture or a screen movie has only preserved what was visible on the computer screen or in the browser window while the HTML is not archived. In this case what you see is what you get.

On the other hand, web crawling has only preserved the HTML and possibly integrated files or services (images, graphics, a feed, etc.). Therefore, what is collected with web crawling does not mirror what users of the past saw in their browser as such, but rather the HTML code found on the web server in an HTML file, as well as the files that were linked to and that were eventually interpreted in the user's browser to form the displayed web page.

Therefore, the web archivist was facing the challenge of either preserving a given web entity exactly as it appeared online (or close to), while at the same time excluding the HTML code for good, or preserving the HTML code and other elements that can later be patched to get as close as possible to what once was online.

## *The Archived Web as a Historical Source*

When a web historian finds the archived web and intends to use it as a historical source, it is important to critically reflect on how the online web of the past has been transformed to the archived web that the web historian is interacting with. In short, the web historian needs to start thinking about how the web archivist's approach to the challenge of combining the online web's digitality with specific archiving forms and strategies has affected the result, and how this may impact the next steps in the research process. This section shall present some of the main characteristics of the archived web as it can be found in a web collection, whereas the possible impact on the research process is debated in the next section.

### *Constitutive characteristics of the reborn web*

No matter the choice of archiving forms and strategies, the following four constitutive characteristics apply to the archived web. They are considered constitutive since they are a function of the archiving of the digitality of the online web as such.

### Lack of an original

The online web changes fast, and over time it is very likely that the original that was once online has disappeared or changed. Therefore, if things are missing or are not functioning correctly in an archived web entity, one cannot expect to return to the online web to verify the original. The absence of a stable original is one of the most important differences between the digitised collection and the archived web.

### Incompleteness

Incompleteness is inherent of any collection. But the incompleteness of the archived web comes in different forms and for various reasons compared with other collections, including digitised collections. By and large the degree of completeness of a digitised collection can be assessed systematically, as the causes of possible shortcomings are more transparent, but it is very difficult to assess the degree of (in)completeness of the archived web compared with what was online with the same level of systematic approach. Due to an opaque combination of the chosen archiving strategy, deliberate omissions, updating during the archiving, and archiving errors, the web historian using a collection of the archived web should expect that things are missing one way or another.

### A unique version and not a copy

Compared with what was once online, the archived web is best understood as a unique version and not a copy on a 1:1 scale. The archiving forms and strategies combined with the fact that things may be missing implies that the same online entity that was collected by two different archiving actors may very well be different versions instead of identical copies of what was online. In addition, each version is only one version among other versions, and it is difficult to maintain that one of them constitutes an original. This uniqueness of each archived web entity is different from what usually happens with a digitised collection, where the result of the digitisation process to a larger extent can be considered a copy that is much closer to being an identical copy of an original.

### Temporal and spatial inconsistency between the archived fragments

In their online form the many bits and pieces of the web are always present at the same time and in the same space. The source and target of a hyperlink are there at the same time, and a given website has the extension it has at any given moment. The online web is consistent with regard to time and space, but this is not the case with the archived web.

The possible temporal inconsistency affects all instances of the archived web where hyperlinks are involved since the source of the hyperlink and its target may not have been archived at the same time. Considering that the hyperlink is an inherent element in the digitality of the online web, the temporal inconsistency is very likely to be a widespread phenomenon in a collection of archived web, in particular where strategies close to archiving 'all' 'continuously' have been used. This possible lack of temporal consistency between link source and target is not seen in a digitised collection, simply because hyperlinks are an optional and controlled complement.

The possible spatial inconsistency is caused by the fact that all web entities were not necessarily archived with the same spatial extension, which can happen because of deliberate choices to discard specific parts of the web during the archiving, because of unexpected problems, or because parts of the web have been deleted or moved during the archiving process. As if, in a digitised newspaper collection, the size of the newspapers was random, some of the copies had only the cover, others only pages 2 and 4, and yet others had all pages.

## *Specific Characteristics of the Reborn Web*

All archived web instances share the constitutive phenomena described above to some extent, but also each of the different types of collection may have specific properties that are a function of how the content of the collection was created. As mentioned above, a fundamental distinction can be made between what is actually collected and preserved, and as a consequence a given web collection may display what was photographed or recorded at the time of archiving, much like 'What you see is what you get', or the collection has to re-assemble the archived fragments in a meaningful way to enable the display or otherwise provide access to the collection's holdings.

### *'What you see is what you get'*

Screenshots do not come with any other immediate form of interaction than to look at the image, and moving web elements are not included, nor do hyperlinks work. Individual web pages archived with dedicated software are also still images and therefore do not show moving elements, but hyperlinks may work, although they point to the online web and not to another archived entity; and it is possible to scroll up and down to view the entire web page.

Since screen movies are movies, they allow for moving backwards or forwards. But insofar as they mirror the movements of the individual who initially created the movie, it is only possible to move around in the archived web as filmed. Video may be part of the film, and hyperlinks may have been clicked, but in both cases these features can only be interacted with as part of the movie and not as autonomous entities.

### *'What you get is what can be assembled'*

A collection of crawled web can best be understood as a giant bucket with billions and billions of individual, but potentially interlinked, files. This implies that the web archive can decide to take files (or parts of them, such as specific code lines in an HTML file) out of the bucket again and combine them in a great variety of ways, some of which may even be different from when the bits and pieces were collected, including ways that by no means make the material appear like what it looked like when it was browsed in the past. A crawled web collection is therefore malleable and there is no predetermined way to make the fragments available.

The web collection owner may decide to re-assemble the fragments in a way as close as possible to what the web looked like in a browser when it was online, which is what is done in the Wayback software, the replay software that was developed by the Internet Archive and is used by many major web archives. The web archive may also give access to hyperlink information whereby the web collection would not look like anything seen in a web browser, but would rather have the form of a file with information about link source and target. Or image files could be singled out to support image analysis, and the collection would then have the form of a collection of this specific file type. In any case it is difficult to say which way best reflects the web that was once online. And the possibilities are almost endless.

In contrast to a digitised collection where textual fragments such as mark-up or OCR are only added at a later stage, if at all, the crawled web collection is reborn as fragmented and marked-up and therefore it can be made available in more – and more differentiated – ways than is possible to do with a digitised collection. However, this high level of flexibility comes at a price, since the collection's volatile nature also makes it a more unstable source, compared with a digitised collection where one file very often equals one copy of what was initially digitised. In a crawled web collection, what is stable is each of the fragments, but not their re-assembling.

When it comes to completeness, a collection of crawled web is different from a digitised collection as well as the online web, because it is incomplete and too complete at the same time. On the one hand, there is often too little in the collection, basically because all the fragments that were initially online may not have come into the archive, among others because of the choice of archiving form and strategy, the dynamics of updating, and technical deficiencies. On the other hand, there may be too much in the collection, because there may exist more versions of 'the same' that may be close to identical, without being exactly identical; one reason for this is that more crawled hyperlinks may have pointed to the same web entity that has then been archived several times, but often not at the exact same time.

The fact that fragments are being placed in the same bucket in a crawled web collection also affects temporal inconsistency, but in different ways, depending on how the fragments are made available. One example is the Wayback Machine, where the temporal inconsistency comes in an almost imperceptible form, but nevertheless it is there. As previously mentioned on the online web, a web page is patched together of bits and pieces retrieved from a web server at the time they were requested, and something similar happens in the Wayback Machine, except that the bits and pieces are not retrieved from an online web server, but from the web archive's own collection. But if all the needed bits are not there from the same date and time as the web page itself, the Wayback Machine's software retrieves the missing elements from a time as close as possible to the time of the web page. Since this can be a question of days, weeks, or even months, the web page that the user is looking at may be patched together of fragments from different points in time: a two-day-old banner ad, an image from the following week, etc. (cf. Hockx-Yu, 2015). What appears to be a temporally 'flat' and consistent web page with only one temporality ('now') may hold several invisible temporalities, thus including a temporal drift that stretches back and forth in time, whereby it becomes temporally inconsistent as a whole.

## THE ARCHIVED WEB'S POSSIBLE IMPACT ON THE SCHOLARLY USE

The characteristics outlined above constitute some of the main elements in the digitality of the archived web, and they should be acknowledged as such by any web historian who intends to use the archived web as a historical source. Furthermore, they should serve as the point of departure for a critical assessment of how they unfold in the specific collection(s) that the web historian intends to use, and thereby of how they can possibly impact the research process, from searching and selecting material to creating a corpus to study.

### *No Original to Go Back to, Incompleteness, and Unique Versions*

The major challenge for any web historical project based on the archived web is the fundamental uncertainty as to the character of the archived web. As we have seen, this is an effect of the combination of the lack of an original, that things are very likely to be missing, and that what are found in a web collection are unique versions. And each of these uncertainties is aggravated because of the opacity of what is actually the case, often due to lack of documentation.

Incompleteness in the source material is as such familiar to any historian, and it is always relative to the concrete research aim, since it is only a problem if what is missing was to be included in the study at all. Nevertheless, the specific challenges related to web archives are different from those related to other collection types, since the main problem is not only a possible lack of (parts of) sources, but rather that it can be very difficult to evaluate to what extent the available versions are identical or not to what was online in the past.

Although the digitality of the online web is one of the reasons that one can sow doubt about the status of the archived web, it also opens up new possibilities that may even help to remedy the above challenges, at least to some extent. What is missing may have left digital traces; for instance, HTML files may provide valuable information about what should have been displayed – for instance, a file type extension such as .img tells us that an image should have been displayed, and files may even have names that reveal their content.

When it comes to corpus creation – that is, the process of identifying and extracting selections of a web collection – the presence of 'too much' of the same may constitute a challenge. When constructing a corpus from a web collection this has to be done in two steps: first, an initial corpus is delimited in time and space, and then the versions that should be included have to be identified and selected.

### *Possible Temporal and Spatial Inconsistency Between the Archived Fragments*

The temporal and spatial inconsistencies between the archived fragments that are potentially inherent to any collection of the archived web constitute a challenge to studies that intend to focus on relations between fragments, which de facto usually means including hyperlinks in the study.

If a project aims to study the hyperlink network between images on a number of websites, based on a collection of websites that spans several weeks, it is very likely that link sources and link targets are not archived at the same time, or that some link targets are not archived at all. In the analysis this will have two implications: first, that linked-to pages or images may have changed or disappeared, and, second, that if the hyperlinks on the linked-to page are also to be included in the analysis as link sources pointing to yet other link targets, the latter targets may have been archived even later, and so on.[10]

A similar phenomenon may happen in terms of spatial extension, if the study is based on a collection where some websites were archived in depth, including all levels below the front page, whereas on other websites only the front page or maybe a couple of levels of the website were archived.

In both cases there are no good solutions to overcome these challenges, but only ways of handling and minimising the problems in ways where one has to balance the need for consistency against the need for having something to study. When creating a corpus, the following general rule applies regarding temporal inconsistency: one can select either a short period of time, which will reduce the possible temporal inconsistency, while probably also reducing the amount of material to be studied. Or a longer interval can be chosen, which will raise the possibility of temporal inconsistency, while probably also raising the amount of material to be included. How this trade-off shall be negotiated depends on the concrete research project and on a critical assessment of what is available in a given collection. As to the spatial inconsistency, it is not possible to proceed as with the temporal inconsistency, in the main because of the lack of something similar to a timestamp that could help determine the spatial extent of the individual web entities.

### *Two Collection Types and their Impact on Web History*

In addition to the above-mentioned constitutive characteristics' impact on the web historian's use of web collections, it is also important to reflect on how the two types of collections previously identified affect the research process.

#### *Studying a 'what you see is what you get' collection*

First, source material such as screen images or movies is not easy to search in any systematic and detailed way. Files with individual web pages may be searched individually, but as for the rest, the only way of finding relevant material is to go through all the sources manually. In addition, screen movies can be challenging to navigate since they follow the movements of the individual who did the filming. Second, combining images of web pages to form an entire website is challenging to do in a consistent way, and just getting an overview of the pages' interrelations may be difficult, in the main because clickable hyperlinks are missing. Third, in cases where hyperlinks are to be studied, it is a great disadvantage that the code level is not available. Fourth, in terms of possible forms of analysis, the most obvious way of analysing this type of material is a traditional manual document/image analysis. Finally, because of the manual approach in both search and analysis, research projects based on images and movies do not scale well.

Despite these challenges, screen dumps, files with individual web pages, and screen movies also come with some important advantages. First, and most importantly, the images and movies are (by and large) showing exactly what the web entities looked like, thus providing the 'look and feel' of the past web, without any possible temporal inconsistencies in the replay. Second, creating a corpus and preserving it is relatively straightforward and can simply be done by creating the needed folders on a computer desktop. Third, although the form of the material tends to enhance reading the text as one would do in a non-digital medium, automated textual analyses cannot be ruled out, since screen shots are bitmaps and they can therefore be enriched with OCR (cf. Cocciolo, 2015).

### *Studying a 'what you get is what can be assembled' collection*

If the web historian intends to use a collection of crawled web, this raises new challenges and opens up other possibilities.

For the web historian who wants to analyse the visible side of the web, the fundamental challenge with a crawled web collection is that the visible web has not been archived as such. The researcher does not have immediate access to what the web of the past actually looked like. On the contrary, what is accessible is the previously mentioned giant bucket of possibly interlinked bits and pieces that have to be assembled. One way of doing this is the Wayback Machine. The use of the Wayback Machine affects the steps of the research process in various ways. The first thing is search, and here the main challenge is that as such the Wayback software does not allow for other entry points than the web address (URL), and if the researcher does not know the URL it is impossible to find the relevant material to study. However, some web archives have created indexes that allow for full text search. Once the relevant web pages are found, replayed by the Wayback software they are shown one by one, each with the possible temporal inconsistency previously described. Obviously, the doubt as to whether the web page embeds a temporal inconsistency or not is a challenge to any researcher wanting to make claims about what a given web page exactly looked like in the past. But the possible remedy may be nearby, because with crawled web the HTML code is available and it is therefore possible to check the timestamps of each individual web element to find out the extent of temporal drift. However, despite the possible inconsistencies, the many possibilities offered by the Wayback Machine's presentation should also not be forgotten, most notably that researchers have access to a browsable web page with working hyperlinks, although the challenges are just below the surface, since hyperlinks may very well make the user jump in time by each click. If a corpus of web pages has been identified in the Wayback Machine then the next research step would be to analyse the material, and if focus is only on the visible side, historiographical approaches and methods that are usually used for this type of source can be used. However, since the sources come in the form of individual web pages, as seen in the Wayback Machine, the scale of the analysis probably has to be limited.

But the researcher may not want to analyse the visible side at all. The source of such a study would then be the hidden text only, without any interest in what the web actually looked like when online in the past. This could, for instance, be a study of the hyperlink network, the number of specific file types, streamed video, or the use of blog software (see Brügger and Schroeder (2017) for examples of this type of study). The phases of research look different when studying the hidden side of the web only. Searching in the non-visible texts is often not possible, but if the possibility exists it is usually in the form of access to a file with the index that the Wayback software uses when looking up which bits and pieces to combine in the web page view (a CDX file), which can support users with information about URLs, timestamp, and file type. Creating a corpus based on such access forms to the web collection may also be challenging. Although an index of the collection's holdings enables the material to be searched, it is not straightforward to come from the identification of the websites one wants to study to the material itself as preserved in the collection. For instance, if the aim is to study the written text on all web pages, access to the body text is needed, and in most web archives this is not possible to get in its HTML form, but only as displayed in its visible form with the Wayback software (cf. Lin et al., 2017). If a researcher has succeeded in creating the corpus she needs, she then has to do the analysis, and this is where the possibilities outcompete the challenges, simply because a corpus based on the above formats is machine-readable, and therefore the analysis can be automated, and analyses of large amounts of data are made possible, just as the analysis can focus on each type of archived fragment that is expressed in the code, thereby making the analysis very fine grained, despite the large scale.

## CONCLUDING REMARKS

The web historians who set out to base their study on the archived web should start by acknowledging that although at first sight an archived web collection may look like a digitised collection or the online web, it is fundamentally different from both, and shall thus be approached differently.

Therefore, it is important to become familiar with the specific digitality of the collection one uses by providing as much information about provenance as possible, and by digging more into how the general characteristics of the archived web play out in each collection. Then it is possible to make as informed choices as possible as to how it makes sense to make selections, create a corpus to study, and perform the analysis in each case. And – most importantly – it is essential to continuously explain and document these methodological reflections about the nature and provenance of the archived web. In many ways these steps resonate traditional historiographical skills, but the concrete critical work with the sources come in new forms because of the digitality of the archived web, and therefore traditional approaches have to be reinterpreted and translated to fit this new source environment.

## *Notes*

1 For an overview of other examples see Winters (2017).
2 Histories of web archiving and web archives can be found in Brügger (2011: 29–32; 2018); Webster (2017); Koerbin (2017); and Laursen and Møldrup-Dalum (2017). The latter two mainly focus on web crawling and national web archives. See also Rogers (2018) and Webster (2018).
3 There exist a great variety of international, national, and local web archives, cf. the overviews in IIPC Members, and in List of Web archiving initiatives.
4 The following sections reiterate some of the insights presented in Brügger (2018).
5 The term born digital is also used in Berry (2012: 4); Kirschenbaum (2013); Rogers (2013); and Jones (2014: 6).
6 This is obviously a very simple scenario, but even with more complicated and dynamic web pages, this is basically what happens. In the following the term HTML is used as an umbrella term to cover the different versions of HTML, including XHTML and XML.

7 See Brügger (2017) for a pre-history of the hyperlink, and Helmond (2018) and Barnet (2018) for different approaches to the history of the hyperlink.
8 It is also possible to collect web material from a database, made available through an Application Programming Interface (API), or to collect web material that has been taken off-line and preserved unchanged (backups and the like); for space reasons these archiving forms are not presented here, but they are discussed in Brügger (2018).
9 In addition to the technical challenges outlined in the following paragraphs, a number of legal, curatorial, and organisational issues are also at stake in relation to web archiving strategies.
10 For an overview of historical network analysis of hyperlinks, see Brügger (2013) and Stevenson and Ben-David (2018).

## REFERENCES


Agata, T., Miyata, Y., Ishita, E., Ikeuchi, A., and Ueda, S. (2014) Life span of web pages: A survey of 10 million pages collected in 2001, in Proceedings of the 14th ACM/IEEE-CS Joint Conference on Digital Libraries. IEEE Press. pp. 463–464.

Barnet, B. (2018) 'Hypertext before the web – or, what the web could have been', in N. Brügger & I. Milligan (Eds.), The SAGE Handbook of Web History. pp. 215–226. London: Sage.

Berry, D.M. (2012) 'Introduction: Understanding the digital humanities', in D.M. Berry (Ed.), Understanding Digital Humanities. New York, NY: Palgrave Macmillan. pp. 1–20.

Brügger, N. (2005) Archiving websites: General considerations and strategies. Aarhus: Centre for Internet Studies.

Brügger, N. (2011) 'Web archiving – between past, present, and future', in M. Consalvo & C. Ess (Eds.), The Handbook of Internet Studies. Oxford: Wiley-Blackwell. pp. 24–42.

Brügger, N. (2012) 'When the Present Web is Later the Past: Web Historiography, Digital History, and Internet Studies', Historical Social Research, 37(4), 102–117.

Brügger, N. (2013) 'Historical Network Analysis of the Web', Social Science Computer Review, 31(3), 306–321. DOI: 10.1177/0894439312454267

Brügger, N. (2017) 'Connecting textual segments: A brief history of the web hyperlink', in N. Brügger (Ed.), Web 25: Histories from the First 25 Years of the World Wide Web. New York: Peter Lang Publishing. pp. 3–28.

Brügger, N. (2018) The archived web: Doing history in the digital age. Cambridge, MA: MIT Press.

Brügger, N., and Schroeder, R. (Eds.) (2017) The web as history: Using web archives to understand the past and the present. London: UCL Press.

Cho, J., and Garcia-Molina, H. (1999) 'The evolution of the web and implications for an incremental crawler', in Proceedings of the 26th International Conference on Very Large Databases.

Cocciolo, A. (2015) 'The rise and fall of text on the Web: A quantitative study of Web archives', Information Research, 20(3), http://www.informationr.net/ir/20-3/paper682.html#.W6Kcpy863OQ [Accessed 19 Sep 2018].

Helmond, A. (2018) 'A historiography of the hyperlink: Periodizing the web through the changing role of the hyperlink', in N. Brügger & I. Milligan (Eds.), The SAGE Handbook of Web History. London: Sage. pp. 227–241.

Hockx-Yu, H. (2015) 'The Unknown Aspects of Web Archives', paper presented at the conference 'Web archives as scholarly sources: Issues, practices and perspectives', 8–10 June, Aarhus.

IIPC Members (n.d.) http://netpreserve.org/about-us/members.

Jackson, A. (2015) 'Ten years of the UK web archive: What have we saved?', paper presented at the 2015 IIPC GA, Palo Alto.

Jones, S.E. (2014) The emergence of the digital humanities. New York: Routledge.

Kirschenbaum, M. (2013) 'The .txtual condition: Digital humanities, born-digital archives, and the future literary', Digital Humanities Quarterly, 7(1), n.p.

Koerbin, P. (2017) 'Revisiting the World Wide Web as artefact: Case studies in archiving small data for the National Library of Australia's PANDORA Archive', in N. Brügger (Ed.), Web 25: Histories from the First 25 Years of the World Wide Web. New York: Peter Lang Publishing. pp. 191–206.

Laursen, D., and Møldrup-Dalum, P. (2017) 'Looking back, looking forward: 10 years of development to collect, preserve, and access the Danish web', in N. Brügger (Ed.), Web 25: Histories from the First 25 Years of the World Wide Web. New York: Peter Lang Publishing. pp. 207–227.

Lin, J., Milligan, I., Wiebe, J., and Zhou, A. (2017) 'Warcbase: Scalable analytics infrastructure for exploring web archives', Journal on Computing and Cultural Heritage, 10(4), link: https://dl.acm.org/citation.cfm?id=3097570 [Accessed 19 Sep 2018].

List of Web archiving initiatives (n.d.) https://en.wikipedia.org/wiki/List_of_Web_archiving_initiatives.

Meyrowitz, J. (1994) 'Medium theory', in D. Crowley & D. Mitchell (Eds.), Communication Theory Today. Cambridge: Polity. pp. 50–77.

Ntoulas, A., Cho, J., and Olston, C. (2004) 'What's new on the web? The evolution of the web from a search engine perspective', in www2004, May 17–22, 2004. New York.

Rogers, R. (2013) Digital methods. Cambridge, MA: MIT Press.

Rogers, R. (2018) 'Periodizing web archiving: Biographical, event-based, national and autobiographical traditions', in N. Brügger & I. Milligan (Eds.), The SAGE Handbook of Web History. London: Sage. pp. 42–56.

Schneider, S.M., and Foot, K.A. (2004) 'The web as an object of study', New Media & Society, 6(1), 114–122.

Stevenson, M., and Ben-David, A. (2018) 'Network analysis for web history', in N. Brügger & I. Milligan (Eds.), The SAGE Handbook of Web History. pp. 125–137. London: Sage.

Webster, P. (2017) 'Users, technologies, organisations: Towards a cultural history of world web archiving', in N. Brügger (Ed.), Web 25: Histories from the First 25 Years of the World Wide Web. New York: Peter Lang Publishing. pp. 175–190.

Webster, P. (2018) 'Existing web archives', in N. Brügger & I. Milligan (Eds.), The SAGE Handbook of Web History. London: Sage. pp. 30–41.

Winters, J. (2017) 'Breaking in to the mainstream: Demonstrating the value of internet (and web) histories', Internet Histories, 1(1–2), 173–179.

# Existing Web Archives

Peter Webster

Web archives are fast becoming the fundamental source with which the history of the Web is written. Scholars coming to them for the first time are in need of some orientation, however, since those archives are brought into being by many different organisations for varying purposes and by different means. Their scope and structure also vary widely, as do the means of first locating and then using them. This chapter begins with a brief historical sketch of the development of Web archiving over the last 20 years. It then moves on to outline the different means by which archives are created, and what implications those differences have for how they must be interpreted. It outlines the varied kinds of collections in existence, and the different questions of method that this variety raises for scholars. Finally, it details the means by which scholars may first locate archived Web content, and (once located) how it may be used. It is based throughout on the literature available but (as is the nature of very contemporary activity such as this) much of the business of Web archiving has yet to come under systematic scholarly scrutiny. As such, some of the perspectives here are those of a scholar who has also been a participant-observer in some of the developments described; it is in part the articulation of a kind of institutional memory.

## A BRIEF HISTORY OF WEB ARCHIVING

Users of traditional paper archives have always known that to understand how the archive came into being is a prerequisite to using it well. (For an extended meditation on this theme, see Thomas et al., 2017). By which criteria was material selected for inclusion (if it was selected at all)? Who was it that devised those criteria, and whose particular interests might they have served, and which others have they occluded? These may seem obvious questions to ask, but users of digital resources have approached them in different ways to traditional print and manuscript resources, with a critical engagement which, whether greater or less, is surely different in kind. And in order to answer those questions successfully, some acquaintance with the 'cultural history' of an archive is necessary. Who (or, which organisations) have created these Web archives, over which time period(s), and in response to which internal and external drivers: legal, economic, organisational? A full history of Web archiving as it has unfolded over 20 years remains to be written, but a brief historical sketch of what content has been collected, by whom and why, is in order here. What follows is in large part derived from my own sketch of the history (Webster, 2017b).

The most well-known of all Web archives was also one of the very first: the Internet Archive, which celebrated 20 years of operation in 2016. Uniquely, it began without any link – personal or institutional – to the library and archive sector. Brewster Kahle, the Archive's co-founder and still its director, set up the Archive as a non-profit counterpart to his Alexa Internet, an early Web browser toolbar which both helped users navigate the Web and archived it based on those users' actions. Although Alexa was subsequently acquired by Amazon, the Archive continued its work, motivated by a vision of a comprehensive library of the world's content (Kimpton and Ubois, 2006; an ethnography of the Archive's current work is Ogden et al., 2017). Given this maximally comprehensive policy of selection, the Archive's holdings dwarf those of any other Web archive. By October 2016 it held archived copies of 273 billion webpages from 361 million sites, comprising 510 billion individual time-stamped digital objects (Goel, 2016b). At the same time, it operates without any broader institutional remit or legal or regulatory framework (except for US law in general) and is, in the final instance, answerable only to itself and (indirectly) to its users. The Archive has become a landmark in the information landscape, is very heavily used and has been foundational to the rest of the wider Web archiving community. However, it is under no formal obligation to continue either to collect or to provide access to its content. This is no criticism, but is merely to note the different conditions under which different archives are created.

The other Web archiving organisation with a globally comprehensive selection policy is the Common Crawl Foundation. Like the Internet Archive, its genesis was in the technology hub of California's Silicon Valley, and (also like the Archive) it operates as a non-profit foundation. Founded in 2007 by former senior Google executive Gil Elbaz, it began comprehensive crawls of the Web in 2008, based on a mission to provide access to Web data at a scale previously only available to large corporations, in order to facilitate research, innovation in business, and use by the general public (Green, 2011).

At about the same time that the Internet Archive was founded, national libraries on three continents were also taking their first steps towards systematic archiving of the Web. In Canada, what was then the National Library of Canada (now part of Library and Archives Canada) instigated the Electronic Publications Pilot Project, which reported in 1995. In common with the majority of national libraries, the NLC had a remit to collect and make available 'Canada's published heritage', now understood to include publications delivered on physical storage media such as disks, or via the Internet (National Library of Canada, 1996). The National Library of Australia was similarly charged with maintaining a comprehensive collection of materials relating to Australia and the Australian people. The PANDORA project was established in 1996, again as a natural extension of that older remit to take in material made available via the Internet. Faced with the need to obtain permission from the owners of websites to harvest their material, and a simple lack of resources, the NLA took a pragmatic decision to take a selective approach from the beginning (Koerbin, 2004: 1–2).

In Sweden, the Royal Library had been responsible for collecting, preserving and providing access to Swedish printed publications since 1661. Once again, the archiving of the Web as analogous to published works was viewed as a natural extension of that remit. In contrast to the Australian case, the Swedish approach was comprehensive, on the grounds that it was in fact more cost-effective than a selective approach, and also due to agnosticism about the relative potential value of different kinds of content: '[o]ne doesn't know what information future generations will consider important' (Arvidson et al., 2000).

Several countries have long-established systems of legal deposit that entitle national libraries or their analogues to receive copies of everything published within that country. In nations where print legal deposit was in force there have been moves to extend that legal framework to cover non-print content. This movement has of course been wider in scope than the Web, since it tends also to include digital objects that are more obviously 'published', in particular scholarly journals and electronic books. One of the first nations to implement such a new law was Denmark in 1997. The relevant act for New Zealand was the National Library Act of 2003, the same year as the Legal Deposit Libraries Act in the UK (Elliott, 2011; Field, 2004; Larsen, 2005). The relevant French legislation dates from 2006, and several others have since followed (Aubry, 2010).

World Web archiving has been shaped to a large extent by the key role taken by the national libraries, who were in close contact and collaborated extensively. In relation to legal deposit in particular, there was international collaboration from the first. A working group on non-print legal deposit was set up by the Conference of Directors of National Libraries, and worked between 1994 and 1996 (Field, 2004: 90). The International Internet Preservation Consortium was formed in 2003 by the Internet Archive and a group of national libraries and has been of vital importance in the growth of the movement (Illien, 2011). The IIPC has acted as a key clearing-house of ideas – technical, curatorial and organisational – as well as being a direct funder of education, research and technical development projects.

Alongside these large-scale and (sometimes) comprehensive approaches, there have been a number of organisations, large and small, that have taken on the task of archiving the Web for more specific purposes. Chief amongst these are university-based archives, acquiring content as part of their wider content development, to support students and staff. One early example, beginning in 2008, is the Columbia University Human Rights Web Archive, a project of the Center for Human Rights Documentation and Research, located within the Columbia University Libraries in New York (CHRDR, 2016). A rather different type of organisation that archives the content of other organisations is the Archive Team, a 'loose collective of rogue archivists, programmers, writers and loudmouths dedicated to saving our digital heritage' (Archive Team, 2016). The Archive Team began work in 2008 in response to a growing sense of the vulnerability of user-generated content to arbitrary closure by the platforms that hosted it (Scott, 2008, 2011). One such archive is that of the early online community Geocities, abruptly closed by Yahoo in 2009, which is now becoming an object of study for historians (Milligan, 2017: 140). On other occasions, interested citizens have acted to create Web archives in response to rapidly unfolding events of importance, such as the informal grouping of activist librarians that produced the Dale Askey Archive, relating to a lawsuit in Canada that involved issues of freedom of speech (Milligan et al., 2016).

Alongside these several ventures that preserve the content of others, the more recent past has seen an increase in the number of organisations taking steps to preserve their own content. Quite apart from the longer-term interest to scholars, organisations have tended to see the issue in terms of orderly management of closure (in the cases where a site is to be shut down), but also as a logical extension of older practices of corporate record-keeping: as an aid to future decision-making, and (particularly in industries subject to statutory regulation) as a means of managing risk and as a resource in the case of litigation. Some such archives are publicly available, such as that of the Smithsonian Institution in the United States, or of the UK Parliament.[1] However, at present, many of these archives are not open to public use, and as such are hard to document, but they would appear to be a feature of the scene that is growing in importance.

Public organisations operate under a different set of imperatives than private companies, and the final significant strand in the history of Web archiving is the archiving of government records. In some countries there is a clear division between a national library (dealing with the published record) and a national archive (dealing with the unpublished record of government). However, the archiving of government Web estate has not always been easy to place: of which organisation should it be the responsibility? The division has become particularly unclear since the move in several countries towards the delivery of government services on a 'digital by default' basis, particularly since 2011 (Lips, 2014). One of the earliest national archives to take on the task was the National Archives of the UK. The government had in 1999 decided that all newly created public records were to be stored and retrieved digitally by 2004, and subsequently also decided that all services to business and to the citizen should be delivered online by 2005. Websites used to deliver those services were to be considered as public records, and so the UK Government Web Archive was formally founded in 2003 (Brown, 2006: 178–9).

## HOW IS A WEB ARCHIVE MADE?

Even as the Internet Archive and the national libraries were beginning their work in 1996, there was already a small but growing group of scholars who were studying the early Web and its predecessor technologies (Wellman, 2011). For these, there was no alternative but to act as their own archivist, and this strand of small-scale individual archiving has persisted alongside the larger-scale efforts of libraries, archives and other organisations. In some cases, this has taken the form of image-based records of the visual appearance of a page: either screenshot images or (more recently) using facilities within Web browsers to save a page as a PDF file. This approach involved the loss of much if not all of the functionality of a site. This problem could be avoided by the archiving instead of HTML files and associated objects. This approach, whilst it retained the functionality in the short term, was always vulnerable to potential loss both of the appearance of a resource and its functionality, as the ways in which Web browsers rendered content changed over time. All this having been said, there most likely exists a considerable body of highly significant early Web content in the possession of individual scholars, largely inaccessible to others.

For some researchers, interested in larger bodies of materials than single pages, there were developed various desktop applications that would allow larger-scale and finer-grained crawling of websites. One such was Wget, which allows the harvesting of whole sites and also recursive crawling: the following of a certain number of links from a seed URL. Crucially, in later versions Wget also allowed the output of archived files in the ISO standard WARC file format used by most libraries and archives. Storage in WARC is currently the standard means of avoiding the loss of functionality and appearance inherent in other approaches. Another commonly used tool was HTTrack, which additionally came with a graphical user interface where Wget must be operated from the command line. Most recently the Webrecorder service has allowed users to capture content as they browse it in their own browser, a different approach again.

The most commonly used crawler for crawling at the scale of whole national domains is Heritrix, first developed by the International Internet Preservation Consortium and made available to the wider archiving community on an open source basis (Kimpton and Ubois, 2006: 211). Each of these scaleable alternatives allows efficient collection of material at scale, but presents the end user with additional questions of interpretation. Each particular crawl must begin with an initial list of seeds, the composition of which has some influence on the content which is collected and in which order. The harvested content is also influenced by other decisions taken when programming the crawl: were the captures from a particular domain capped at a certain file size? Were certain areas on a particular site excluded from the crawl? Did the crawl observe the robots.txt protocol, by which website administrators request (but cannot enforce) that their sites are not crawled? These matters are at present not widely documented in such a way to aid user understanding of the composition of the final archive.[2]

Although the precise configuration of people and technologies varies, the several Web archiving organisations that conduct large-scale archiving with their own staff and infrastructure all must cover certain activities. (A useful early summary of the issues was Masanès, 2006.) Policies must be devised to specify which content should be archived, how frequently, at what depth and with which levels of quality assurance (how good a copy is good enough?). Both staff and information systems are required to record the implementation of those policies at an operational level. More staff (and often different individuals) are then required to operate the crawling process itself. Hardware is required to store the data once harvested; further applications to index it for searching, if required (the most commonly used are Apache Solr and ElasticSearch); and specialist expertise is required for long-term preservation of that data. In most cases, some means of making that content discoverable is also then required (of which more below). This often requires the integration of a new kind of data into existing library and archival catalogue systems, and the support of reference librarians who support users directly. New and different kinds of Web application are also often required to render archived content to users both locally and remotely. The most commonly used basic application is known as Wayback (or its open source sibling Open Wayback), but several institutions are now developing tools that go beyond its capabilities (for which, see the 'Finding and using Web archives' section, below). As such, operating an end-to-end operation requires a partnership of managers, librarians and/or archivists, and technology professionals specialising in Web crawling, indexing, network and hardware management, digital preservation and application development.

Operating a full end-to-end Web archiving operation at large scale, then, imposes a very particular set of costs on an archiving organisation. Although the costs for hardware and storage capacity are significant, those things are not in short supply; the major limitation is often that on the availability of technical staff. As the technologies used to deliver Web content evolve very quickly, so must the skills of those charged with obtaining successful captures of that content. In contrast, libraries and archives are often already well endowed with expertise in the selection of content for archiving, its description and the necessary quality assurance work. As such, there has developed a small but significant group of providers of outsourcing services for Web archiving. Typically, the lead organisation continues to select and describe content, whilst contracting with one of these providers to conduct the crawling, carry out indexing and provide access.

The various providers in this market may by and large be divided between non-profit organisations and private-sector providers, and between those providing open access to the final archives and those providing access restricted to certain groups (typically the client and their staff). In fact, it has been the private-sector providers which have tended most often to provide restricted-access archives. These have most often met the needs of individual organisations, most particularly in regulated areas of the private sector, as a means of meeting regulatory requirements for record-keeping and for use in possible litigation. The non-profit providers are dominated by two players, both of whom generally provide openly accessible archives. The Archive-It service was launched by the Internet Archive in 2006, with a particular concentration on serving libraries, archives, universities and other public and third-sector clients, predominantly although not exclusively in North America. In Europe, similar services have been offered since 2004 by the Internet Memory Foundation, via its Internet Memory Research subsidiary. First established as the European Web Archive in Amsterdam in 2004, Internet Memory Research at the time of writing served several European clients from the library and archive sector (Brown 2006: 18).

## HOW ARE WEB ARCHIVES STRUCTURED?

This chapter has dwelt at length on the various means by which a Web archive comes into existence, and the cultural and institutional setting in which that creation occurs. No less important for interpreting the archive correctly is an understanding of its scope: which kinds of content were selected for inclusion. In some cases, notably those of the Internet Archive and Common Crawl, the question is at one level easy to answer: everything. Neither the Archive nor Common Crawl limit their collecting geographically to particular national or local domains, or on grounds of subject matter, or by the technological format in which content is delivered.

This intention of comprehensiveness presents both an unprecedented opportunity and a potential trap for the unwary. The frequency at which individual pieces of content are archived varies significantly, and so the scholar must always reckon with the fact that content on the live Web may appear, be altered and indeed disappear without ever being visited by a crawler. Given this, great care must be taken not to equate *comprehensiveness* as a selection policy with *completeness* in the archive itself. To add to this indeterminate incompleteness – the ineluctable product of the nature of the medium itself – studies have shown that the unintended effect of the very nature of the crawl process has introduced systematic bias into the composition of the archive. Thelwall and Vaughan (2004) showed significant weighting in the Internet Archive towards certain countries, due to the nature both of the Web itself and of the crawl process. Web archivists in many institutions work hard to eliminate such biases as far as possible, but one of the key challenges in the next few years ahead is for scholars and archivists to work together to understand the ways in which archives are created and the information which scholars need in order to be able to allow for the inevitable gaps and biases they contain.

Amongst those Web archive collections that are bounded by a particular selection policy, by far the largest are those relating to whole national domains, held for the most part by national libraries, and collected under legal deposit provisions. Such archives now exist for Denmark, France, Iceland and the UK, amongst others, and more are being added gradually to the list. Once again, however, some caution is required in understanding precisely how the national domain is defined, as the definition varies considerably between nations. For those nations with one or more country code top-level domain (such as .uk for the UK and .fr for France), registration within that ccTLD defines a particular domain as within scope for legal deposit. The matter is much less clear for nations whose political boundaries do not map precisely onto any one ccTLD: the United States, without any such ccTLD of any size, is a case in point. In any case, studies show that a large proportion of domains published from within a particular nation are not registered in the local ccTLD, although neither the extent of nor the reasons for this are well understood (Milligan and Smyth, 2018; Webster, 2018). Recognising this, other means are also often used to determine whether a domain may be considered in scope, such as the geographic location of the servers on which content is hosted, or of the residence of the organisation or individual which registered the domain. In addition, some nations with a national language that is wholly or largely unique to that country, such as Denmark, have cast their legal deposit legislation to include content written in that language, even if published elsewhere. There remain broader questions about the nature of the nation that each individual disposition posits. However, a knowledge of the basic assumptions made is essential for scholars wishing to use national legal deposit archives.

To date it has been the national and supranational Web archiving initiatives that have attracted the most attention and attained the highest profile. Although established more recently, there are also many other collections that are also demarcated by geopolitical divisions but focussed on smaller units. This has been a relatively weak tradition in Europe, although there are notable examples, such as in the Belgian city of Antwerp (Boudrez and Van den Eynde, 2002). In the United States, there is a somewhat stronger tradition of independent action by individual state archives, such as North Carolina (Martin and Eubank, 2007). Some of these initiatives have a broad remit to capture content relating to the affairs of a city or state more generally; in the case of North Carolina, the content is restricted to state government sites and related content.

Some Web archives are created and made available along different lines than the geographic. Partly due to the very particular technical issues involved in their capture, some archives are focussed solely on audio-visual content. Two prominent examples of this are the Netherlands Institute for Sound and Vision (Nederlands Instituut voor Beeld en Geluid), and (in France) L'Institut nationale de l'audiovisuel. Both have a national remit, and work closely with the respective national libraries. As a result, it is important that users understand the demarcation of the collections between the pair of institutions in each country.

Other means of demarcation include the sectoral: materials relating to a particular sphere of political, economic or cultural life. This chapter has already described the history of the archiving of national government Web estate, such as the UK Government Web Archive (part of the National Archives) or the Australian Government Web Archive (an initiative of the National Library of Australia). In some cases, an institution is of such particular and singular significance that its corporate archive is at the same time an archive of a whole sphere of activity: a case in point is the Parliamentary Web Archive in the UK. (The UK has only one parliament, after all.) One particular gap in current provision is of business archives: Web archives of the estate of private companies to match the extensive network of paper archives for the same corporations. This is not to say that such content is not being archived, but more that it is (so far) rarely made available for public and scholarly use, apart from within the mass of larger legal deposit collections.

Rather more various, and thus more difficult to interpret, are the many collections that are based on particular subjects. Alongside archiving under legal deposit, the national libraries also have a strong tradition of subject-based collecting. This has often been associated with significant political and cultural events, such as elections or major sporting events. These events, of a wide general interest, and of which the significance is not often in dispute, have served in many cases as a means of demonstrating the importance of Web archiving and of establishing a programme. One of the earliest collections in the UK Web Archive relates to the 2005 general election; in 1996 the Internet Archive collected the sites of candidates for the presidency of the United States, in partnership with the Smithsonian Institution, and again in 2000 on behalf of the Library of Congress (Kimpton and Ubois, 2006: 202–3). The first collaborative collections created by the members of the IIPC related to successive Olympic Games. These large general collections have tended to be projects undertaken by the national libraries. However, both the national libraries and university initiatives have focussed collecting on themes that are wider and longer-lasting than particular events. Examples within the UK Web Archive include collections relating to diasporic communities, health, video games and the practice of oral history. From within the universities, one of the earliest examples was the Digital Archive of Chinese Studies (DACHS), a German–Dutch venture (Lecher, 2006). Amongst the collections hosted by Archive-IT are the Digital Art Web Archive (Cornell University), Resources in Religion and Theology (Princeton Theological Seminary) and the Innsbruck Newspaper Archive (University of Innsbruck).

These subject-based collections, selective in nature, present the user with a different set of methodological challenges to the comprehensive collections. Since the collections are selective, users must first understand the selection criteria used: criteria which are not always fully documented at the point at which users access the collection. It is also essential to understand the cases where a resource was selected for archiving, but could not be archived, either for technical reasons (that a successful capture could not be obtained) or for legal reasons (that, where the permission of the site owner was required, it could not be obtained). Without this information, robust analytical use of a whole collection is made more difficult.

## FINDING AND USING WEB ARCHIVES

One of the consequences of the advent of digital resources has been a fundamental change in the relationship between the providers of objects for study (libraries and archives, by and large) and those who use those objects. Whatever intellectual use a reader might make of a manuscript or printed book, the means by which that object is brought to the reader's desk does not affect how it is used. With digital resources, design decisions made during the creation of the applications that deliver digital objects to users affect what may or may not be done with those objects. As such, users need not only to engage critically with the object itself and how it came into being, but also with the systems by which they are able to gain access to it. Access to Web archives has been enabled in several different ways, each of which is in a state of constant development as technologies change.

The earliest and most pervasive means of accessing an archived object is by means of a search for its original URI, the unique string of characters that identified it online (also often commonly referred to as the URL, although the two are not strictly synonymous). Most crawler softwares produce the data necessary to enable this as a matter of course as part of the crawl process, often in the CDX format, a kind of finding list for locating an individual URI in a larger WARC file. URI search is the primary way of locating objects in Wayback. Indeed, the Wayback Machine (the main means of accessing the holdings of the Internet Archive) had URI search as its only means of access until 2016. URI search on its own, however, presents some challenges to use of the archived Web as an historical source as it presupposes that the URI of a resource, perhaps long since disappeared from the live Web, is either known by the user or can be discovered by some other means. This point is writ large in the work of Anat Ben-David on reconstructing the defunct domain of the former Yugoslavia; a case in which *all* the resources from an entire national top-level domain have gone from the live Web (Ben-David, 2016).

In digital scholarly resources for research at large, a standard means of access and one which users now expect as standard is searching of the full text. This is widely available in Web archives, particularly those which are freely available online. However, at the time of writing, by no means all of the larger Web archives provide full-text search as standard, partly due to the not insignificant technical difficulties in creating the necessary indexes at the scale required. For its first 20 years the Internet Archive – the largest of them all – did not offer full-text search, and the functionality implemented in 2016 offers a search of only part of the full archive, based on the homepages of each domain (Goel, 2016a).[3]

Both of these modes of access presuppose that the key object of study in a Web archive is an individual archived object, page or site, replayed in a Web browser using Wayback or a similar graphical user interface. Attention amongst Web archives has relatively recently turned to means of representing the contents of Web archives at a more abstract level, and visually, in line with a more general trend towards visualisation of data both for research and in other spheres, not least journalism. The SHINE interface, developed by the British Library and now being used elsewhere, incorporated a visualisation of trends, a means of showing the frequency with which particular search terms appeared within each archived year. Experimentation is also at an early stage with ways to visualise the link graph, the patterns of hyperlinks between different parts of the Web.

Recent years have seen scholars widen their interest to include Web archives as data: either as ARC/WARC files (the standardised file format for Web archives), or metadata derived from them. Relatively few individual researchers have access to the size of local infrastructure necessary to handle data at scale. One response to this is that of Common Crawl, where access to (extremely large) collections of WARC files is via a third-party cloud storage service, on which researchers with the necessary programming skills can run their own scripts for a fee. As well as WARC files, there is now also a proliferation of derived data made available for download and local use. The CDX format, as well as being critical for the provision of a URL search service, also provides a data source with which to begin to analyse the contents of a Web archive at a more abstract level. The British Library has also begun to make available other kinds of derived data about its collections, not least the JISC UK Web Domain Archive Dataset. As well as the associated CDX files from this data, there is available derived data relating to postal codes, file format and host-to-host links, some of which is already being used by scholars (Webster, 2017a; Webster, 2018). Both Common Crawl and the Internet Archive have begun to allow users to exploit other file formats derived from Web archives, notably WAT files (Web Archive Transformation) and WET files (which contain extracted plain text); these too have attracted the attention of Web historians (Milligan, 2016).

Niels Brügger has noted the confusion that surrounds the use of the term 'archive' in the context of Web materials; the term 'webrary', whilst perhaps less elegant, captures better the rather stronger analogy that exists between websites and traditional publication (Brügger, 2016). However, the ways in which such 'publication-like' things may be integrated into traditional library catalogue systems are yet to solidify into conventions and standards that apply across different services, and much Web archive discovery is through dedicated user interfaces which stand alone. Within a Web archive, the particular object of study could be a particular individual website, or a related group of them (a 'web sphere'); it could equally well be a single PDF document or image file. As such, the appropriate level at which Web archives should be described is more difficult to fix than for printed works. In addition, the traditional library catalogue assumes (for the most part) a relationship in which each individual object is catalogued. In the context of legal deposit archives, containing many millions of domains, and billions of individual resources, such a relationship is inconceivable in the traditional sense. The vast bulk of archived Web resources will almost certainly never be manually described by a human being, although automated means may well be developed that infer certain descriptive characteristics of a resource from an analysis of its content. As a result, a user's awareness of a Web archive needs to include an understanding of how and to what extent it has been described, and how that affects the ways in which individual resources may be discovered.

It is also the case that the means by which archives may be accessed varies between and within individual institutions. In many cases, archived content may be accessed freely online and between nations, such as is the case with the Internet Archive, or the Portuguese Web Archive (arquivo.pt). However, the situation is more complex in relation to legal deposit archives, such that in the British case, the Open UK Web Archive is freely available online whereas the UK Legal Deposit Web Archive is not. Most legal deposit dispensations are marked by a compromise between the opposing interests of the owners of content who wish to exercise their rights in that content and generate revenue from it, and scholars and the general public who have an interest in there being a public record of that content. As a result, the routine archiving of copyright material has entailed certain restrictions on access and reuse of that content. (For an example of these negotiations in the UK, see Green, 2012.) In other contexts, access is restricted not so much for these commercial reasons but in order to protect individuals to whom the content may refer. Whatever the underlying reason, access to legal deposit content is often restricted to the premises of the national library, as is the case in France and the UK. In other cases, such as Denmark, access may be gained away from library premises but only to academic users after a process in which their credentials are verified. Access arrangements to Web archives depend on the circumstances in which those archives were created.

## CONCLUSION

This chapter has sought to outline some of the key patterns into which Web archiving has fallen over its first 20 years, in terms of organisations, techniques, collections and access. Along the way, it has raised several axes of necessary critical engagement for Web historians regarding the archived Web as a new class of primary source. Some of these issues have their analogues in print, manuscript or other sources; a scholar needs to understand who produced an object, whether it be a manuscript, a painting or an archived PDF. But some of the issues presented here are peculiar to the archived Web, and must be thought through afresh. As this chapter outlined, the technologies that are used to create archived Web resources fundamentally shape those resources, and so understanding those technologies is a prerequisite to understanding the archive. Crucial also is an understanding of how the archive is structured: along national lines, by the institution or sector that created the content, by file format or by a more general subject. Finally, users must also understand something of the means by which they discover, search within, view and analyse archived objects, since those means are both relatively new and in a state of flux and development. That thinking will be greatly enabled by close collaboration between scholars and archivists: a partnership of mutual benefit which shows welcome early signs of growth.

### *Notes*

1 Smithsonian Institution: https://archive-it.org/organizations/660; the UK Parliament Web Archive is at http://webarchive.parliament.uk

2 An example of a well-documented crawl is that of the Internet Archive from 2011: https://archive.org/details/wide00002&tab=about

3 The limitations of this approach are evident in the case of homepages of organisations or individuals that do not have their own domains, such as blogs hosted by platforms such as Blogger or Wordpress.

## REFERENCES


Archive Team (2016) 'Homepage', retrieved 3 May 2016 from http://www.archiveteam.org.

Arvidson, A., Persson, K., and Mannerheim, J. (2000) 'The Kulturarw3 Project: the Royal Swedish web archive – an example of "complete" collection of web pages'. Paper given at 66th IFLA Council and General Conference, retrieved 15 April 2016 from http://archive.ifla.org/IV/ifla66/papers/154-157e.htm

Aubry, S. (2010) 'Introducing Web archives as a new library service: the experience of the National Library of France', *LIBER Quarterly*, 20(2): 179–99.

Ben-David, A. (2016) 'What does the Web remember of its deleted past? An archival reconstruction of the former Yugoslav top-level domain', *New Media and Society*, 18(7): 1103–19.

Boudrez, F., and Van den Eynde, S. (2002) 'Archiving websites' [DAVID project report], accessed 10 January 2017 from http://www.expertisecentrumdavid.be/davidproject/teksten/Rapporten/Report5.pdf

Brown, A. (2006) *Archiving websites. A practical guide for information management professionals*. London: Facet.

Brügger, N. (2016) 'Webraries and Web archives: the Web between public and private', in W. Evans and D. Baker (Eds), *The End of Wisdom? The Future of Libraries in a Digital Age*. Oxford: Chandos. pp.185–90.

CHRDR [Centre for Human Rights Documentation and Research] (2016) 'Human rights Web archive', retrieved 5 May 2016 from http://library.columbia.edu/locations/chrdr/hrwa.html

Elliott, A. (2011) 'Electronic legal deposit: the New Zealand experience'. Paper given at IFLA conference, retrieved 1 April 2016 from http://www.ifla.org/past-wlic/2011/193-elliott-en.pdf

Field, C.D. (2004) 'Securing digital legal deposit in the UK: the Legal Deposit Libraries Act 2003', *Alexandria*, 16(2): 87–111.

Goel, V. (2016a) 'Beta Wayback Machine – now with site search!', Internet Archive Blogs, retrieved 12 January 2017 from http://blog.archive.org/2016/10/24 beta-wayback-machine-now-with-site-search/

Goel, V. (2016b) 'Defining Web pages, Web pages and Web captures', Internet Archive Blogs, retrieved 3 January 2017 from https://blog.archive.org/2016/10/23/defining-web-pages-web-sites-and-web-captures/

Green, A. (2012) 'Introducing electronic legal deposit in the UK: a Homeric tale', *Alexandria*, 23(3): 103–9.

Green, L. (2011) 'Common Crawl enters a new phase', retrieved 1 January 2017 from http://commoncrawl.org/2011/11/common-crawl-enters-a-new-phase/

Illien, G. (2011) 'Une histoire politique de l'archivage du web', Bulletin des bibliothèques de France, 2, retrieved 1 December 2013 from http://bbf.enssib.fr/consulter/bbf-2011-02-0060-012

Kimpton, M., and Ubois, J. (2006) 'Year-by-year: from an archive of the internet to an archive on the internet', in J. Masanès (Ed.), *Web Archiving*. Berlin: Springer. pp.201–12.

Koerbin, P. (2004) 'Managing Web archiving in Australia. A case study'. Paper given at IWAW, 2004, retrieved 1 May 2016 from http://iwaw.net/04/

Larsen, S. (2005) 'Preserving the digital heritage: new legal deposit Act in Denmark', *Alexandria*, 17(2): 81–7.

Lecher, H. (2006) 'Small scale academic Web archiving: DACHS', in J. Masanès (Ed.), *Web Archiving*. Berlin: Springer. pp.213–26.

Lips, M. (2014) 'Transforming government – by default?', in M. Graham and W.H. Dutton (Eds), *Society and the Internet. How Networks of Information and Communication are Changing our Lives*. Oxford: Oxford University Press. pp.179–94.

Martin, K.E., and Eubank, K. (2007) 'The North Carolina state government Web archives: a case study of an American government web archiving project', *New Review of Hypermedia and Multimedia*, 13(1): 7–26.

Masanès, J. (2006) 'Web archiving: issues and methods', in J. Masanès (Ed.), *Web Archiving*. Berlin: Springer. pp.1–53.

Milligan, I. (2016) 'Lost in the infinite archive: the promise and pitfalls of Web archives', *International Journal of Humanities and Arts Computing*, 10(1): 78–94.

Milligan, I., Ruest, N., and St Onge, A. (2016) 'The great WARC adventure: using SIPS, AIPS and DIPS to document SLAPPS', Digital Studies / Le Champ Numerique, retrieved from https://www.digitalstudies.org/articles/10.16995/dscn.18/

Milligan, I. (2017) 'Welcome to the Web: the online community of GeoCities during the early years of the World Wide Web', in N. Brügger and R. Schroeder (Eds), *The Web as History*. London: UCL Press. pp.137–58.

Milligan, I., and Smyth, T. (2018) 'Studying the Web in the shadow of Uncle Sam: the difficult case of the Canadian web sphere', in N. Brügger and D. Laursen (Eds), *The Historical Web and Digital Humanities: the Case of National Web domains*. London: Routledge.

National Library of Canada (1996) 'Electronic Publications Pilot Project (EPPP). Summary of the final report', retrieved 22 April 2016 from http://epe.lac-bac.gc.ca/100/200/301/nlc-bnc/eppp_summary-e/ereport.htm

Ogden, J., Halford, S., and Carr, L. (2017) 'Observing Web archives. A case for an ethnographic study of Web archiving'. Proceedings of WebSci '17, Troy, NY, USA, 25–28 June 2017, https://doi.org/10.1145/3091478.3091506

Scott, J. (2008) 'Eviction, or the coming datapocalypse', retrieved 1 May 2016 from http://ascii.textfiles.com/archives/1617

Scott, J. (2011) 'Presentation at personal digital archiving conference, Internet Archive', retrieved 1 April 2016 from https://archive.org/details/PDA2011-jasonscott

Thelwall, M., and Vaughan, L. (2004) 'A fair history of the Web? Examining country balance in the Internet Archive', *Library and Information Science Research*, 26(2): 162–76.

Thomas, D., Fowler, S., and Johnson, V. (2017) *The silence of the archive*. London: Facet.

Webster, P. (2017a) 'Religious discourse in the archived Web: Rowan Williams, archbishop of Canterbury, and the sharia law controversy of 2008', in N. Brügger and R. Schroeder (Eds), *The Web as History*. London: UCL Press. pp.190–203.

Webster, P. (2017b) 'Users, technologies, organisations: towards a cultural history of world web archiving', in N. Brügger (Ed.), *Web 25: Histories from the First 25 Years of the World Wide Web*. New York: Peter Lang. pp.175–90.

Webster, P. (2018) 'Lessons from cross-border religion in the Northern Irish web sphere: understanding the limitations of the ccTLD as a proxy for the national web', in N. Brügger and D. Laursen (Eds), *The Historical Web and Digital Humanities: the Case of National Web domains*. London: Routledge.

Wellman, B. (2011) 'Studying the Internet through the ages', in M. Consalvo and C. Ess (Eds), *The Handbook of Internet Studies*. Chichester: Wiley-Blackwell. pp.17–23.

# Periodizing Web Archiving: Biographical, Event-Based, National and Autobiographical Traditions

Richard Rogers

## INTRODUCTION: HISTORIOGRAPHIES BUILT INTO WEB ARCHIVES

The purpose of this chapter is to periodize web archiving, in order to discuss four ongoing traditions that form an overlapping and layered history of both the implementation but more so the study and use of archived websites. The most contemporary period of web archiving, as with most recent periods generally, is perilous to characterize, but the self-archiving and selfie culture undertaken most visibly on social media platforms such as Facebook and Instagram appears to sit at the end of a spectrum that commenced with the Internet Archive and preserving single websites, and has witnessed a chronology of efforts that include both event-based as well as national web making. I argue that each of these periods corresponds to a particular historiographical tradition, inviting certain kinds of content-based history-writing with the web archives. The piece discusses not only the research that each tradition of web archiving affords but also approaches to studying web archives that (perhaps counter-intuitively) are not based on a study of website content. Code-based analysis of archived websites allows for avenues of research both about web archiving – such as the historical reconstruction of the websites missing in archives (through an historical hyperlink network analysis) – as well as histories of the web that are broader social observations, such as the rise of tracking that gathers data on web users (through an overtime analysis of trackers and cookies embedded in archived websites). Ultimately the chapter concludes with a discussion of the so-called 'crisis in web archive use' and ways to address it, such as repurposing and building atop existing web archives.

To trace the history of web archiving, I argue, is to appreciate the distinctive historiographical points of view built into web archives since the mid 1990s: from the biographical (or single site) and the event-based to the national and autobiographical traditions. A discussion of each would concern the implications for (web) history-writing as well as web archiving practices, including a call for the consideration of other scholarly uses of web archives. In order to address the 'crisis in web archive use', which primarily concerns their under utilization, one may look to such creative uses as making screencast documentaries of website histories, curating thematic or issue-based collections from existing archives, undertaking historical hyperlink analysis to conjure a past state of the web as well as examining the underlying code of archived websites (for cookies, for example, in order to study tracking or surveillance). It also may be of interest to expand upon archival regimes that privilege only the national and 'official' definitions of the public interest that drive selection (national methodologies), in order to enable historical projects that are currently unintended, such as a reconstruction of the Yugoslav web (Ben-David, 2016).[1]

Before developing the argument, I would like to mention four caveats about the periodization. The first is that I offer a contemporary rather than a sweeping periodization of *longue durée* such as the medieval, early modern, modern or postmodern. The time span is but two decades. The second is that periodization does not shutter one tradition as it calls another into ascendancy. Whilst epistemologically distinctive and related to specific touchstones in the history of web archiving, the biographical, event-based, national and autobiographical historiographies overlap in time. Each may endure, but one may lack the vibrancy of its early period, having experienced pioneer's regress; it may have matured. The third caveat is that the periodization does not rest upon a single cause of change, whereupon one would follow back-end technology, front-end interface, institutional involvement or academic paradigm formation (to name a few), and be able to identify the triggering event from one area that prompted the next period. Moreover, the effort here is not to develop a framework that explains (social) change in web archiving outlooks, however much the four areas I just alluded to may be of assistance. Finally, the periodization itself is from a point in time, and as such could be rewritten anew in future, or itself be conceptualized as a period in theory, e.g., the early days of web archiving theory when initial thoughts were formed on how to periodize web archiving history.

The periodization rests on touchstones that in retrospect brought into being archival regimes or repertoires that inform the web historiographies on offer. Here the notion of archival regime refers to the work of Wolfgang Ernst, defining it as 'not an idiosyncratic choice, but a rule-governed, administratively-programmed operation of inclusions and exclusions' (2006: 114). These regimes inform the kinds of histories that are in some sense given by the archives, or afforded to be written, if you will. The archives are also historicizable, and may be studied for their periodicity, or reflecting a particular web time when they were created.

## SINGLE-SITE HISTORIES, OR THE BIOGRAPHICAL TRADITION

The Internet Archive was founded by Brewster Kahle in 1996 to archive 'everything': 'I usually work on projects from the "you've-got-to-be-crazy stage"' (Reiss, 1996; Livingston, 2008; Kahle and Parejo Vadillo, 2015). The Sisyphean improbability of the 'everything archive' project (or its 'craziness') lies in at least two elements: one may never capture all of the web (at any one time), and as it grows one is presumably increasingly capturing less of it. At its very outset the Internet Archive presented itself less in the service of future generations, web and other history scholars, the court of law (and copyright infringement) or other use cases to which it subsequently lent itself.

Rather, it offered a solution to a major issue of its time, the '404 File Not Found' problem (Kahle, 1997). Beginning at least in February 1998, Alexa Internet, shortened from Alexandria, made available a browser toolbar with a small button that would pulsate if the website visited on the live web was not found (Alexa, 1998). 'Wayback', as the button was named, remarkably supplied the missing page from the Internet Archive.

In exchange for receiving these offline webpages from the archive, one would agree to allow one's surfing history to be logged so that the archive's crawlers could visit the sites to archive them. That was the data exchange, in one of the earlier 'free' business models (Anderson, 2009). Through the Alexa toolbar, one also could retrieve information about the website one was visiting, such as how fresh (or stale) it was. One also can view related websites, the speed with which the website loads and even its inlink count as a sign of its popularity or authority. The Wayback Machine (and the toolbar) are thus period pieces, and as such of interest to web historians in how they capture the mid 1990s, where loading speeds, broken links and related destinations were all considered of the moment for the 'surfer'.

Indeed, even without the toolbar the Wayback Machine, launched in 2001, later maintained the web as a surfer's medium rather than the searcher's medium that came after it. The surfing continued within the archive itself. Rather than allowing broken pathways, the archive directed hyperlinks on archived webpages to take the user to the page closest in time to the original, or to the live webpage, if it had not been saved. This multi-temporal archival experience arguably made surfing into one of the Wayback Machine's uses, together with various forms of historical reconstruction.

From a historiographical point of view, the Internet Archive, with its Wayback Machine, organized the history of the web in a specific manner. Whilst since 2016 one may search for keywords (that appear in URLs or in metatext), the Wayback Machine from the beginning invited one to type in a single URL, such as http://www.google.com, and navigate its history through a listing or calendar of archived instances as well as a timeline.[2] The interface thus sees the web as a history of single websites (or more specifically URLs) that evolve through time; one may view their stories through the interface.[3]

The default setting on the timeline is a monthly impression, with a chunky arrow that invites the user to click through the changes to the website at that historical pace, though through the calendar there is also the opportunity to choose specific dates as well as times of the day of those frequently archived sites. The ones archived most frequently are likely from 'focused crawls' rather than the 'broad crawls' that capture the vast majority of distinct sites in the archive (Kimpton et al., 2003; Sigurðsson, 2005).

## EVENT-BASED SPECIAL COLLECTIONS, OR EVENT-BASED HISTORIOGRAPHY

The second period's touchstone is the Webarchivist project, and its readiness when 9/11 transpired (Webarchivist, 2001). There were collection concepts ('web sphere'), server capacity and researchers in place when the airplanes struck the World Trade Center and the Pentagon, out of which came not only the pioneering 9/11 web collection but solidified event-based web archiving, an *idée fixe* in the selection repertoire of web archives. The historiographical tradition it spawned is thus based on collecting websites around events, predominantly elections, disasters and (papal and presidential) transitions. It actually began with the Internet Archive's first project (with the Smithsonian), archiving the 1996 US presidential elections, and the Webarchivist project followed in those footsteps with its plans to capture the 2002 US congressional and other elections, when disaster struck on September 11, 2001. With this agile, just-in-time archiving, they were able to amass some 25,000 websites (over some four months), now part of the US Library of Congress's 'digital collections'. Subsequently, the Webarchivist project continued to collect websites around elections and further expanded its disaster collection work with the special collection surrounding the Asian Tsunami of 2004 (1,500 websites).

Event-based archiving of 'elections and disasters' owes greatly not only to the Webarchivist project but also to a particular pioneering collection technique. 'Web sphere analysis' is a demarcation technique that defines a collection space substantively, temporally as well as web-topologically. Foot and Schneider describe a web sphere as 'a set of dynamically defined digital resources, often connected by hyperlinks, spanning multiple websites relevant to a central event, concept or theme and bounded temporally' (Foot and Schneider, 2002: 225; Schneider and Foot, 2005). Akin to Kahle's 'everything' collection which necessarily evolves as it discovers new websites, the web sphere definition is also innovative for its webbiness, allowing for its dynamic collection through discovering new websites through hyperlink analysis. It is also historicizable, having borrowed from the emergence at the time of hyperlink mapping techniques to map networks of websites around the same issue (Rogers, 2012). The project also was contiguous with contemporaneous assumptions of the metaphysics of the web, portions of which are organized (and readily archivable) as spheres, like (in its day) the up-and-coming blogosphere.

## NATIONAL WEB ARCHIVES, OR NATIONAL HISTORIOGRAPHY

The third derives from not so much a moment but rather a long march of the national institutions onto the web, and the growing acceptance of the very idea of the 'Danish part of the internet', or the Swedish part or the Czech part, to be archived separately, either by law or custom (Schostag and Fønss-Jørgensen, 2012). Rather than a cyberspace (where everything can be collected) or a sphere (where a thematic event is to be located), from the national point of view the web is carved into relatively tidy, geographical (content) portions for national institutions keeping public records as well as national heritage. In such an archival regime it would be remarkable for national institutions to collect subaltern materials that archive more than national content, be it (in order of importance) from the top-level country domain, lists of nationally significant websites and social media pages, events as well as language detection.

The third corresponding historiographical tradition is thus the national, which began (as with the event-based tradition) as an Internet Archive service to Swedish and Icelandic national libraries, before they and other national libraries settled into their own collecting in the mid 2000s. The Internet Archive would crawl a top-level country domain and make it available to the national library for preservation and access, whereas nowadays, in a turn of the tables, national libraries crawl their 'own' domains, without subsequently uploading them as collections to the Internet Archive (often out of concern for copyright infringement, which also keeps them offline and accessible only on site), with the exception of Portugal, which both uploads and makes accessible its archive online (Internet Archive, 2017). Indeed, one of the stated aims of the national web archiving projects is to reduce dependence on foreign services (Gomes et al., 2008). Most other national web archiving initiatives have gradually developed their own archiving capacity, with particular definitions of what constitutes the national.

National libraries and archives are tasked with archiving public records as well as other content of national interest, so the question asked with regards to web archiving by national libraries has to do with what constitutes public interest. What should count, methodologically, as valuable 'national content'? Archiving traditions are often adjoined to the technical infrastructure of the web, so the national becomes the websites using the top-level country domain as well as the language, together with public interest and heritage definitions. Along these lines the national libraries have existing appraisal and selection traditions as well as vehicles to undertake this kind of work, such as national deposit laws, which obligate archiving. Some countries, such as the Netherlands, do not have such deposit laws, but have similar principles concerning collecting and preserving the public record as well as cultural heritage. Whether with or without deposit laws, one could argue the collection approach preserves some combination of public record for official history and heritage for national history.

Amongst the influential definitions of the constitution of heritage is the Danish, which collects and stores 'Danica' or national cultural heritage, but also incorporates the history of web archiving into its regime, collecting a couple of events per year. For the Danes, as well as for other national libraries, websites that use the top-level country domain are to be archived as well as those intended for a Danish audience, and written in Danish. Websites about the Danish people, significant Danish personalities or well-known figures, or simply about Denmark (no matter the language) also would be candidates for archiving. Therefore, if there is a website in English about the nineteenth-century Danish writer Hans Christian Andersen, that website could be included. In the crawling regimes, apart from regularly archiving significant websites and periodically archiving lesser ones, there are also 2–3 'events' (such as Danish elections) that Netarkivet, the archiving authority, is prepared to save. The Dutch (without the legal deposit) make use of a similar definition of 'the national', as do the Portuguese and French, whilst the latter is somewhat broader in its special collections – apart from the French elections, examples of special collections are more expansive than events, such as 'blogs, sustainable development, Web activism' (BnF, 2017). In all the descriptions of collection-making by national libraries, the national interest takes precedence.

Such an archiving routine editorializes the web as a national story, and moves web archivalism far away from the Internet Archive's initial approach of crowdsourcing URLs through people installing a toolbar in a 'grab them all' tradition, or the hyperlink analysis for event-based, 'web sphere' collections. It often turns 'events' largely into national ones. These days an Asian tsunami likely would not be archived by a European national library. As a case in point the last international event collected by the UK web archive is from 2004; the Danish archive appears increasingly to concentrate on national events, with the exception of international collaborations with, for example, the Czech archive and its Vaclav Havel collection.[4]

## AUTOBIOGRAPHICAL ARCHIVING

Finally, with the rise of social media (especially Facebook) and mobile platforms challenging the web as the dominant online content and activity space, has come the lessened capacity to archive it, or as archival studies scholars have put it: 'the responsibility of archiving Facebook data [lies with] individual users' (Sinn and Syn, 2014); hence the notion of the autobiographical. In practice, each of the three traditions mentioned above have the means to retain some social media (and occasionally do archive Facebook 'pages' such as We are all Khaled Said, crucial in the Egyptian Revolution of 2011). That archiving, however, does not pertain to individual profiles after login.

This fourth tradition (loosely defined) is the development of the capacity of archiving oneself, especially one's social media use, which is outside the purview of the other web archiving traditions. One could refer to such activities as life blogging and quantifying oneself as precursors to self-archiving online, since these, often health-related, authoring practices are often in the style of public diaries, worthy of saving, like eighteenth-century chapbooks and other 'popular' sources of everyday life (Darnton, 2009). 'Mommy' as well as 'DIY fatherhood' blogging are examples from the web, as are the 'wounded healers of Instagram' from social media (Ammari et al., 2017; Sanchez-Querubin, 2017). Posting entries on Facebook (and even Snapchat) could be construed similarly; however it is the request for the data dump that could be understood at least initially as self-archiving. That is to say, awareness of the capacity to create collections of one's own history first relied on knowing one's digital rights (so to speak) and asking companies to comply with them. There have arguably been larger developments in terms of opportunities for self-archiving, and I would like to discuss four recent ones.

The first development concerns health apps, and the data retained from fitness bands and watches such as Apple's iWatch. Here there are opportunities for 'personal data requests' that relate less to one's writings than to one's physical state. The second development concerns the movement of activity from the web to smartphones, and the question as to what to archive. Apart from making software app collections (practiced by the Internet Archive, for example), there is a shift in collection from 'content' to data. One may access mobile-related activity data through an API, or application programming interface (Littman et al., 2017). Such is a more general strategy for social media archiving, be it originating from the web or from a mobile device (Thomson, 2016). The third development, recording a period of one's life in social media, is exemplified by the social media artistic 'performance' by Amalia Ulman called 'Excellences & Perfections' (2014). In a period of six months Ulman documents on Instagram her aspiration to become a Los Angeles 'It girl', gaining followers as she moves through aspirational stages of becoming from 'trying to be discovered' to 'bad girl' and finally to 'healthy lifestyle' before (surprisingly) posting 'the end'. Rhizome, the digital arts group, in producing this work of art, introduced its Web Enact software to capture such coming of age or other personal developments on social media. Later called webrecorder.io, it allows one to 'record' a social media page. This approach stands in contrast to requesting a data dump, downloading or taking screenshots of the website, or tapping into the API for data. Finally, I would like to briefly mention 'selfie archiving', however much it has been undertaken by neither self-archivers nor web archivists. Researchers have created collections of Instagram photos hashtagged #selfie. In one project by TIME magazine, the goal was to crown the 'Selfiest Cities in the World' (Wilson, 2014). The researchers created a database of 400,000 Instagram photos that were tagged #selfie, determined each selfie's geolocation and created a ranked list of cities, where in the event Makati City and Pasig in the Philippines had the most selfies per 100,000 people, followed by Manhattan, Miami and so forth; the list is dominated by Asian and North American cities that were subsequently plotted onto a map showing selfie density. Conducted by a team of researchers led by Lev Manovich, the second selfie archiving project – Selfiecity – created selfie collections from New York, São Paulo, Berlin, Bangkok and Moscow (using #selfie and city geolocations in the queries). The researchers subsequently measured the formal properties of the faces (tilt of the head, smile, etc.). Amongst other findings, the project found that selfies are largely an undertaking for 23- to 26-year-olds, though in Moscow they tend to trend older and in São Paulo younger. Furthermore, in Moscow people are slightly gloomier, whereas in São Paulo happier. Thus, the project outputs city mood gradations. It should be noted that Instagram (and the moody selfies) are accessible on the web, though most users are mobile-based (on smartphones), pointing up a number of issues such as the movement of users and their content production from the web to the app space and also how web archiving may assist with mobile content archiving.

What are the prospects for archiving social media institutionally? With respect to the single-site or biographical tradition (and the contents available via the Wayback Machine), attempts to crawl and archive social media as websites are fraught with issues. Whilst hardly clear-cut, one could put forward a distinction between social media that are principally social networking sites or user-generated content platforms, and expect the content platforms to be more open to crawling and archiving than the social networking ones (Thomson, 2016) (see Table 4.1). In the event, Facebook and LinkedIn (seeing themselves as principally social networking sites) do not allow archive crawlers, having opted out through placing a robots.txt file respected (and archived) by the Internet Archive; most other platforms allow the archiving of their 'about' pages, terms of service, FAQs and other non-password-protected webpages.[5] With respect to archiving the user-generated content, platforms (Flickr, Pinterest, Reddit, YouTube) allow archiving of their materials, though in certain cases the materials are personalized (and ranked), so there is skewing.

The overall exception is Twitter, which donates its historical tweets (and archive) to the Library of Congress, where they are stored. The girth of such big data, however, has proven too great to make it available to researchers (Zimmer, 2015). Tweet collections also may be made (but not shared with others) with software tools, such as the Digital Method Initiative's TCAT (Twitter Capture and Analysis Tool), which queries Twitter's streaming and REST APIs for hashtags, keywords and user accounts (as well as @ mentions). US President Donald Trump's tweet collection (i.e., just his user account's tweets) is significant as are collections made from the US presidential elections of Hillary Clinton and Trump supporters, respectively. There are also hashtag collections, such as the infamous #iranelection (around which a great deal of debate ensued concerning the very idea of a 'Twitter revolution'). Given rate limits, questions of collection completeness arise; there is a Twitter-owned service (GNIP) that provides historical tweet sets at often exorbitant prices.

Each of the other traditions sketched above would tackle archiving social media somewhat differently. From the event-based tradition, archiving of Facebook pages (rather than individual profiles) has been practiced, especially in the case of the Egyptian Revolution of 2011 (Runyon and Houlihan, 2012; Urgola and Runyon, 2016). In the national tradition,

**Table 4.1. Select social media platforms with principle function in order of importance (adapted from Thomson, 2016)**

| *Platform* | *Year launched* | *URL* | *Principal functions in order of importance* |
|---|---|---|---|
| Facebook | 2005 | facebook.com* | social networking, user-generated content |
| Flickr | 2004 | flickr.com% | user-generated content, social networking |
| Instagram | 2010 | instagram.com% | user-generated content, social networking |
| LinkedIn | 2003 | linkedin.com* | social networking, user-generated content |
| Pinterest | 2010 | pinterest.com% | user-generated content, social networking |
| Reddit | 2005 | reddit.com#% | user-generated content, social networking |
| Twitter | 2006 | twitter.com#% | user-generated content, social networking |
| YouTube | 2005 | youtube.com# | user-generated content, social networking |

*robots.txt exclusion file in place

# ranked content archived

% terms of service archived

one may wish to archive national public figures and official institutions (Facebook pages as well as Twitter feeds), as is practiced by the UK National Archive, for example. As mentioned there is also a movement afoot to shift attention from the html to the data, and tap into and archive the API streams offered by the social media companies. One could imagine, methodologically, that there would be 'everything', 'event-based' as well as 'national' strategies for API polling. At least with Facebook, which closed down the availability of extracting personal information, including one's own as well as that of friends with its 1.2 API version (mid 2015), the full autobiographical (all data about oneself across Facebook) still would rely on the data dump, though Archive-It's software would allow one to grab one's own profile page, and webrecorder.io affords the means to capture its dynamic history (Rieder, 2015).

## ADDRESSING THE CRISIS IN WEB ARCHIVE USE

In 2010 web archiving theorists referred to a crisis in the scholarly use of web archives, for there were so few users (Dougherty et al., 2010). The crisis has been illustrated through regular queries in Google Scholar and Google Web Search for the use of the citation preferred by the Library of Congress; for some years now, typing 'Archived in the Library of Congress Web' into Google Scholar has returned very few results (Rogers, 2013). The search engine returns are mainly self-citations. The Library of Congress Web has largely special collections in the event-based tradition, which could account for the low usage. In the single-site tradition, the employment of the Wayback Machine of the Internet Archive in scholarly work is greater; however, most articles are about Wayback URLs as references in legal cases and academic papers (and how Wayback combats live link rot), rather than as sources for web or digital history, with some notable exceptions (Musso and Merletti, 2016; Chakraborty and Nanni, 2017). In the national tradition, most national libraries have very few visitors to their web archives, given access policies. The computers allocated to web archive use by the National Library of France often lie idle. Annual users of the web archives in Denmark and the Netherlands number perhaps in the double digits.[6]

How might one address the crisis? Are there signs that it may be abating? Scholars have introduced ways and means to increase the use of web archives, such as making available full text search, building tools to visualize the contents of web archives, treating web archives as big data, concatenating archives with a common interface or promulgating the creation of one's own archives (Hockx-Yu, 2011; Padia et al., 2012; Huurdeman et al., 2013; Memento, 2015; Archive-It, 2017; Cowls, 2017; Meyer et al., 2017). For (contemporary) historians working with (web) archivists, one may wish to make one's own archive with the Archive-It service, and study it, as in the case of the Egyptian Revolution of 2011 (the uprising of the 25th of January), a project of the American University of Cairo. The historical account of the rise and fall of an Islamic punk scene is also illustrative of the approach of making a collection to study it (Dougherty, 2017).

Another general approach, described below, is making creative use of existing archives with digital methods (Rogers, 2009). By a digital methods approach is meant the repurposing of dominant devices and platforms for social and medium research (or, in this case, digital and web history). How to repurpose the Wayback Machine's output of single websites? One captures a website's history and plays it back in the style of time-lapse photography as a screencast documentary with voiceover (Rogers, 2017).[7] One example is the history of google.com, called 'Google and the Politics of Tabs' (Rogers and Govcom.org, 2008). Using the Wayback Machine, all unique historical instances of google.com are captured, i.e., those pages that contained changes as signified by an asterisk on the Wayback Machine's (classic) user interface. These are loaded into a moviemaker (QuickTime), and then played back to choose themes for a voiceover. The story is told by noting the gradual changes made over time to the front page of google.com, especially to the tabs above the search box, where different services came and went, such as the Google directory, or the human-edited listing. After appearing with great fanfare in 2000 it was gradually relegated to the 'more' button, and then placed behind 'even more', until the directory was finally removed altogether in 2004. Other services made it all the way to the front-page interface before disappearing, or have staying power, such as images (Google Image Search). The story told is a web history: in the screencast documentary of google.com, there is an evident, gradual decline of the directory over time (and with it the human librarian), and the simultaneous rise of the algorithm or the back end of search. Other examples of screencast documentaries have been made for media history (e.g., the evolution of a newspaper on the web) as well as digital history (the evolution of the US White House, whitehouse.gov).

The second contribution to web archive usage is to create one's own thematic collection of websites from one or more existing archives, first demonstrated by the Dutch newspaper, the *NRC Handelsblad* (Dohmen, 2007). By largely using the Wayback Machine, the researchers made a collection of Dutch right-wing and right-wing extremist websites, and devised a keyword query strategy to answer the question: is Dutch culture hardening and becoming more extreme? To answer this question, they examined how the language on the websites changed over time, demonstrating that on the right-wing websites in particular, the language used was becoming increasingly extreme, approximately that on the right-wing extremist sites. The researchers cautiously concluded that Dutch culture is hardening, thereby making a contribution, however modest, to social history. Here it should be noted that such a project could not be realized with a national archival regime that saves 'significant' websites in the public interest for heritage or, for that matter, an event-based approach. Being able to make a collection of extremist sites would demand an 'everything' approach, augmented perhaps by combing multiple national web archives that sometimes stray from the national (heritage) methodology.

The third example is a project that again creates a thematic collection of websites within existing web archives, and conjures a past state of the web, so as to study the missing web and its significance through historical hyperlink analysis. The past state in question is the early blogosphere. There is an archived website called Eaton Web, which for many years had an authoritative list of blogs, and it was considered the portal (or leading directory) for the blogosphere (albeit largely American and English-language ones). In the summer of 2001, the website owner, Eaton, gave up listing new blogs because of abundance. To the researchers this was the sign that the period of the 'early blogosphere' was over. Eaton's last list was batch queried in the Wayback Machine, and it was found that only 20% or so of blogs were missing (see Figure 4.1). Consequently, historical hyperlink analysis was performed, which enabled the researchers to determine the significance of each of the websites in the blogosphere, including the missing ones, according to network measures. Thus, all the sites were given historical context, and the past 'blogosphere' was depicted (or conjured) as a network. Using a similar technique of historical hyperlink analysis, the evolution of the Dutch blogosphere has also been mapped (Weltevrede and Helmond, 2012).

Finally, the fourth approach is to study not the content of a single website, a thematic set over time, or a past state of the web through hyperlink analysis (including the unarchived sites), but rather the underlying code of one or more websites. This is a technique colleagues and I discovered coincidentally by

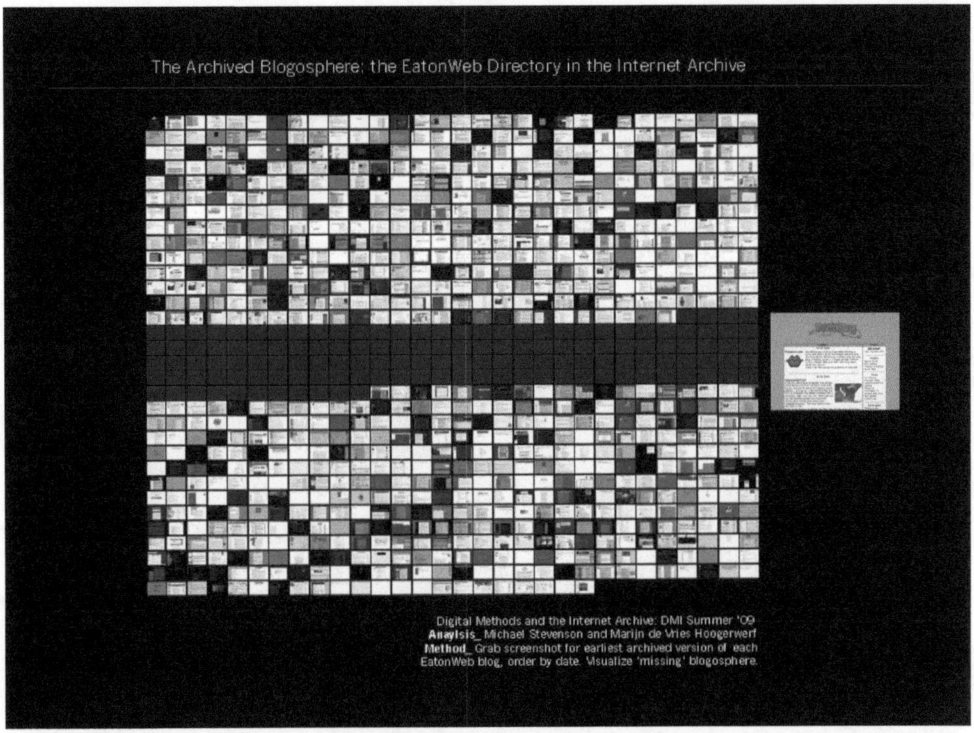


**Figure 4.1 Early blogosphere, with missing archived websites. Collection based on Eatonweb. Digital Methods Initiative, Amsterdam, 2009.**

using the browser add-on Ghostery whilst visiting historical websites in the Wayback Machine. Ghostery shows third-party elements embedded in webpages when visited, including trackers, third-party cookies and so forth. With Ghostery enabled whilst visiting an archived webpage, one can view historical trackers (van der Velden, 2014; Deville and van der Velden, 2015). These trackers may be captured over time for specific websites, showing for example the history of tracking behavior by *The New York Times* (Helmond, 2015) (see Figure 4.2).

## CONCLUSIONS: FROM SINGLE SITE HISTORIES TO HISTORICAL NETWORK ANALYSIS

The effort here is to periodize web archiving, in order to describe how archival regimes and periodicity produce distinctive historiographical traditions. Historicized and described is the single-site (or website biography) approach built into the interface of the Internet Archive (mid 1990s), the event-based tradition from the Webarchivist project (and particularly the 9/11 archive), the long march of the national institutions and heritage methodologies making their own national webs (mid 2000s), and a variety of efforts to save social media, and particularly individual accounts through recording (as well as data dumps) in the autobiographical tradition (early 2010s). There is a distinctive chronology of web archiving with particular key moments per tradition, such as the Alexa toolbar, the 'web sphere', the 'Danish part of the web', and webrecorder.io, but each archiving regime and associated historiographical tradition continues.

The dominant approaches to web archiving and their in-built historiographies do not

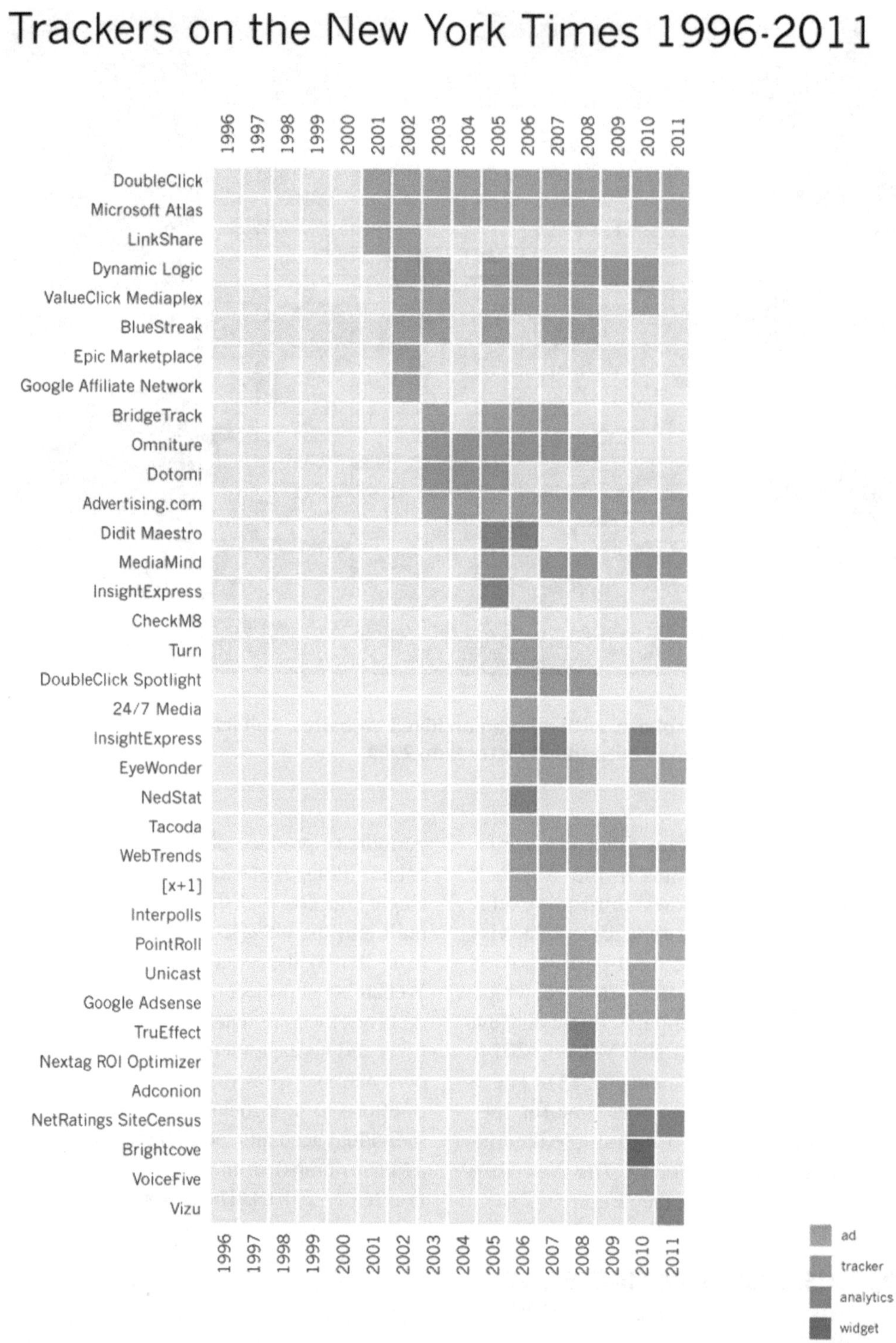


**Figure 4.2 Trackers embedded in *The New York Times*. Output from Tracker Tracker tool showing trackers embedded in archived newspaper webpages over time. Digital Methods Initiative, Amsterdam, 2012.**

preclude others, however much (with the exception of the Internet Archive and some smaller projects) the emphasis is increasingly on the public interest remit of a heritage institution.[8] As a result, one is able to write national (web) histories from the contents stored by the national institutions. Such an emphasis, however, would preclude projects such as the reconstruction and transformation of the Iraqi web before, during and after the Iraq War, 2003–11. Given the refrain concerning the urgency of archiving the web and born-digital content, a rejoinder would add: when does it become urgent to archive other cultures than one's own (Beunen & Schiphof, 2006)?

Web archives are also underutilized. Many can only be accessed from a library reading room; for the German national web archive, for example, one would sit behind a national library computer in Frankfurt or Leipzig. Few do, creating an air of crisis in web archive use. Brightening the archive is the task of scholars researching archive use, and building tools atop. Other engagement comes from making one's own (with Archive-It) or curating collections from existing archives. Indeed, amongst the creative use of archives for scholarly purposes is building a thematic collection (e.g., right-wing and right-wing extremist websites in the Netherlands) and posing research questions about (the hardening of) culture. Other uses of web archives put forward in the digital methods approach above include the technique of creating a screencast documentary of the history of a website, conjuring a past state of the web through historical hyperlink analysis and examining the underlying code of archived websites and fishing out trackers and third-party cookies with the aid of a tracker database, in order to put forward a history of (online) surveillance or behavioral targeting. Each approach rests on the capacity to build software on top of an online web archive, query it, extract data and make derivative works, which is a research practice different from visiting a library's reading room and browsing its web archive.

## Notes

1 National web archival regimes have taken root in at least the following countries, whose national libraries or archives are members of the International Internet Preservation Consortium (IIPC): Canada, Chile, China, Croatia, Czech Republic, Denmark, Estonia, Germany, Finland, France, Iceland, Ireland, Israel, Japan, Latvia, Luxembourg, the Netherlands, New Zealand, Norway, Poland, Portugal, Scotland, Serbia, Singapore, Slovenia, South Korea, Spain, Sweden, Switzerland, the UK and the United States. Numbering some 50, there are additional representatives from provinces (Catalonia and Quebec) as well as ones from universities and other (governmental) institutions. See Niu (2012).

2 The Memento project (mementoweb.org), the initiative that strives to source and output archived websites from multiple web archives, also invites the single URL as input.

3 The Internet Archive originally was provided to users of the Alexa Toolbar as a solution to the '404 file not found' error, providing single webpages. The Wayback Machine, as its interface, also provides single webpages. Since one is prompted to type a URL into the interface, users presumably would type front pages, or website domains, into the interface, and proceed from there. I thus refer to the Wayback Machine as organizing single-site histories. There are other use cases, too, such as pasting a longer URL, in order to look up copyright infringement. One may paste a specific historical URL that is now offline, thereby employing it in the manner of the Alexa Toolbar of old.

4 When collaborating with other international institutions (such as with the Czech web archive), the Danish web archive occasionally makes collections that are not primarily or partially Danish in focus. Since the early days, however, there appears to be an increasing tendency to follow the Danish heritage preservation policy, and archive events where Denmark is involved (Olympics, EU elections), as well as particularly national events such as the teacher lock-out, a Copenhagen science festival and a national scandal involving credit card transaction monitoring.

5 Web archiving software, such as Archive-It, has the option to ignore robots.txt, thereby enabling the archiving of social media pages, groups and profiles, if one is logged in, and has given user credentials. Otherwise one archives default prompt pages, such as Facebook's 'log in or sign up'. (Archive-It does have a default user, Charlie Archivist, who has no friends.) Archive-It's instructions are explicit in their call to exclude personal profiles (Lohndorf, 2017). It should be added

that social media companies such as Facebook and LinkedIn explicitly prohibit crawling without permission, and list on the robots.txt exclusion page which types of content archive crawlers may access, i.e., Facebook pages of public figures rather than personal profiles.
6 In the Netherlands it often has been a handful of users. In Denmark special workshops at Netarkivet organized by the NetLab at Aarhus University have bolstered the numbers.
7 One employs the Wayback Machine link ripper to harvest the URLs of all historical instances of a webpage, from which one chooses the ones to screenshot. Loading a select list of URLs into 'Grab them all' or another batch screenshot generator creates files to be imported into a moviemaker.
8 The Common Crawl project (commoncrawl.org) is another exception.

## REFERENCES

Alexa (1998) 'Support', Alexa.com, https://web.archive.org/web/19980209020820/http://www.alexa.com:80/support/details/index.html

Ammari, T., Schoenebeck, S., and Lindtner, S. (2017) 'The Crafting of DIY Fatherhood', Proceedings of CSCW '17, New York: ACM, 1109–1122.

Anderson, C. (2009) Free: The Future of a Radical Price. New York: Hyperion.

Archive-It (2017) 'Archive-It. Web archiving services for archives and libraries', San Francisco: Internet Archive.

Ben-David, A. (2016) 'What does the Web remember of its deleted past? An archival reconstruction of the former Yugoslav top-level domain', New Media & Society, 18(7): 1103–1119.

Beunen, A., and Schiphof, T. (2006) 'Legal aspects of web archiving from a Dutch perspective', Centre for Law in the Information Society. Leiden: University of Leiden.

BnF (2017) Digital legal deposit: four questions about Web Archiving at the BnF, Paris: Bibilotheque national de France, http://www.bnf.fr/en/professionals/digital_legal_deposit/a.digital_legal_deposit_web_archiving.html

Chakraborty, A., and Nanni, F. (2017) 'The changing faces of science museums: A diachronic analysis of museum websites', in Niels Bruegger (Ed.), Web 25: Histories of the First 25 Years of the World Wide Web. New York: Peter Lang. pp.157–172

Cowls, J. (2017) 'Cultures of the UK Web', in Niels Brügger and Ralph Schroeder (Eds.), The Web as History. London: UCL Press. pp.220–237.

Darnton, R. (2009) The Case for Books: Past, Present and Future. New York: Public Affairs.

Deville, J., and van der Velden, L. (2015) 'Seeing the invisible algorithm', in Louise Amoore and Volha Piotukh (Eds.), Algorithmic Life: Calculative Devices in the Age of Big Data. London: Routledge. pp.87–105.

Dohmen, J. (2007) 'Opkomst en ondergang van extreemrechtse sites', NRC Handelsblad, 25 August.

Dougherty, M. (2017) '"Taqwacore is Dead. Long Live Taqwacore" or punk's not dead?: Studying the online evolution of the Islamic punk scene', in Niels Brügger and Ralph Schroeder (Eds.), The Web as History. London: UCL Press. pp. 204–219.

Dougherty, M., Meyer, E.T., Madsen, C., van den Heuvel, C., Thomas, A., and Wyatt, S. (2010) 'Researcher Engagement with Web Archives: State of the Art', London: JISC.

Ernst, W. (2006) 'Dis/continuities: Does the archive become metaphorical in multi-media space?', in Wendy Chun and Thomas Keenan (Eds.), New Media, Old Media. A History and Theory Reader. New York: Routledge. pp.105–123.

Foot, K.A., and Schneider, S.M. (2002) 'Online Action in Campaign 2000: An Exploratory Analysis of the U.S. Political Web Sphere', Journal of Broadcasting & Electronic Media, 46(2): 222–244.

Gomes, D., Nogueira, A., Miranda, J., and Costa, M. (2008) 'Introducing the Portuguese web archive initiative', Proceedings of IWAW '08, Heidelberg: Springer.

Helmond, A. (2015) 'The Platformization of the Web'. PhD dissertation, Amsterdam: University of Amsterdam.

Hockx-Yu, H. (2011) 'The Past Issue of the Web', Proceedings of WebSci '11, New York: ACM.

Huurdeman, H.C., Ben-David, A., and Samar, T. (2013) 'Sprint methods for web archive research', Proceedings of WebSci '13, New York: ACM.

Internet Archive (2017) Arquivo.pt: the Portuguese web-archive, San Francisco: Internet

Archive, https://archive.org/details/portuguese-web-archive
Kahle, B. (1997) 'Archiving the Internet', Scientific American, March: 157–172.
Kahle, B., and Parejo Vadillo, A. (2015) 'The Internet Archive: An Interview with Brewster Kahle', 19: Interdisciplinary Studies in the Long Nineteenth Century, issue 21.
Kimpton, M., Stata, R., and Mohr, G. (2003) 'Internet Archive Crawler Requirements Analysis', Heritix Internet Archive Webteam Confluence. San Francisco: Internet Archive.
Littman, J., Chudnov, D., Kerchner, D., Peterson, C., Tan, Y., Trent, R., Vij, R., and Wrubel, L. (2016) 'API-based social media collecting as a form of web archiving', International Journal on Digital Libraries, 28: 1–18.
Livingston, J. (2008) Founders at Work: Stories of Startups' Early Days. New York: Apress.
Lohndorf, J. (2017) 'Archiving Facebook', Archive-It Help Center, September, https://support.archive-it.org/hc/en-us/articles/208333113-Archiving-Facebook
Memento (2015) Memento Guide – Introduction to Memento. Mementoweb.org
Meyer, E., Yasseri, T., Hale, S., Cowls, J., Schroeder, R., and Margetts, H. (2017). 'Analysing the UK web domain and exploring 15 years of UK universities on the web, in Niels Brügger and Ralph Schroeder (Eds.), The Web' as History. London: UCL Press. pp.23–44.
Musso, M., and Merletti, F. (2016) 'This is the future: A reconstruction of the UK business web space (1996–2001)', New Media & Society, 18(7): 1120–1142.
Niu, J. (2012) 'An overview of web archiving', D-Lib Magazine, 18(3/4).
Padia, K., AlNoamany, Y., and Weigle, M.C. (2012) 'Visualizing Digital Collections at Archive-It', Proceedings of JCDL '12, New York: ACM.
Reiss, S. (1996) 'Internet in a Box', Wired, 1 October, http://www.wired.com/wired/4.10/scans.html
Rieder, B. (2015) 'The end of Netvizz (?)', blog post, The Politics of Systems blog, http://thepoliticsofsystems.net/2015/01/the-end-of-netvizz/
Rogers, R. (2009) The End of the Virtual: Digital Methods. Amsterdam: Amsterdam University Press.
Rogers, R. (2012) 'Mapping and the politics of the web', Theory, Culture & Society, 29(4/5): 193–219.
Rogers, R. (2013) Digital Methods. Cambridge, MA: MIT Press.
Rogers, R. (2017) 'Doing web history with the Internet Archive: Screencast documentaries', Internet Histories, 1(1–2): 160–172.
Rogers, R., and Govcom.org (2008) 'Google and the Politics of Tabs', video, Amsterdam: Govcom.org.
Runyon, C., and Houlihan, M. (2012) 'Revolutionary libraries: Building collections and promoting research about the January 25th uprising in Egypt', Alexandria, 23(2): 73–77.
Sanchez-Querubin, N. (2017) 'The Wounded Healers of Instagram', Paper presented at Trauma Studies in the Digital Age workshop, Netherlands Institute for Advanced Study in the Humanities and Social Sciences, Amsterdam, 10–12 May.
Schneider, S.M., and Foot, K.A. (2005) 'Web sphere analysis: An approach to studying online action', in Christine Hine (Ed.), Virtual Methods: Issues in Social Research on the Internet. Oxford: Berg. pp.157–170.
Schostag, S., and Fønss-Jørgensen, E. (2012) 'Webarchiving: Legal deposit of internet in Denmark. A curatorial perspective', Microform & Digitization Review, 41(3/4): 110–120.
Sigurðsson, K. (2005) 'Incremental crawling with Heritrix', Proceedings of IWAW '05, Vienna.
Sinn, D., and Syn, S.Y. (2014) 'Personal documentation on a social network site: Facebook, a collection of moments from your life?', Archival Science, 14(2): 95–124.
Thomson, S.D. (2016) 'Preserving Social Media: DPC Technology Watch Report 16-01', Glasgow: Digital Preservation Coalition.
Ulman, A. (2014) 'Excellences and Perfections', New York: Rhizome, http://webenact.rhizome.org/excellences-and-perfections
Urgola, S., and Runyon, C. (2016) 'Participatory archives: Building on traditions of collaboration, openness, and accessibility at the American University in Cairo', in Raymond Pun, Scott Collard and Justin Parrott (Eds.), Bridging Worlds: Emerging Models and Practices of U.S. Academic Libraries Around the

Globe. Chicago: Association of College and Research Libraries. pp.91–103.
van der Velden, L. (2014) 'The third party diary: Tracking the trackers on Dutch governmental websites', NECSUS. European Journal of Media Studies, 25 June.
Webarchivist (2001) 'Please help us build a Web Archive of the Sept 11 Attack', webpage, Webarchivist.org, 1 October, https://web.archive.org/web/20011001200536/http://webarchivist.org:80/
Weltevrede, E., and Helmond, A. (2012) 'Where do bloggers blog? Platform transitions within the historical Dutch blogosphere', First Monday, 17(2).
Wilson, C. (2014) 'The Selfiest Cities in the World: TIME's Definitive Ranking', TIME Magazine, 10 March.
Zimmer, M. (2015) 'The Twitter archive at the Library of Congress: Challenges for information practice and information policy', First Monday, 20(7).

# PART II

# Theoretical and Methodological Reflections

# Web History in Context

Valérie Schafer and Benjamin G. Thierry

## INTRODUCTION

Insisting on a contextualised history of the Web may at first appear tautologous, given the central role of contextualisation in the practice of history. Nonetheless, the number of factors involved in the deployment, diffusion and usage of the Web raises important questions about the hierarchies to be operated, the periodisation to be adopted and the active strategies to be emphasised.

Emerging from a context to be apprehended on many different levels (global, national and also individual) and within many different areas (technical, economic, political and cultural), the Web also gives rise to new dynamics. They have implications for temporality, for conceptions of space and even of events. Constructing a historical narrative of the Web from the early 1990s until the present should take full account of a phenomenon both global and present in an ever-growing number of human activities. It means that we need to pay equal attention to everything encompassing or encompassed by the history of the Web as an object affecting numerous areas of the economic, political, technical and personal lives of the actors involved (an object determining its own context), no less than as an object set within numerous already identifiable contexts (of time, space and material reality).

This perspective entirely meets the tendencies and issues raised in the history of information technology. Within less than 15 years, this history has developed in a number of directions, as highlighted by Tom Misa (2007) in *Understanding How Computing Has Changed the World*. An initial focus on technology has given way to work on the wider roots of the information age. Tom Misa anticipated the development of a field that would seek to understand the meeting of information technology and society, increasingly important with the development of networks and of the Web. The dissemination of information technology not only in the professional world, but also, thanks to micro-computing, in the home, along with the increasing presence of networks in daily life, has led to new approaches taking greater account of social factors. The willingness to take on board the complexity of innovation from multiple perspectives, to rethink the articulation of top-down and bottom-up approaches, along with, for example, Nathan Ensmenger's advocacy (2012) of a reassessment of the social history of computing, have influenced historians' views of information technology as well as of networks and the Web.

The presence now of the Web in every area of life demands studies which constitute it simultaneously both as itself a contextualising object and as anchored in a context. Contextualising because today it directly influences an infinite number of objects, which can no longer be studied without taking account of their echoes online. In transmedia dynamics in particular, we can see how the Web is increasingly becoming an ever-present backdrop to controversies, to the configuration of information and even to interpersonal relationships.

Equally, the Web must find its own contextualisation, first of all – since we are historians – from a diachronic perspective. The first challenge is not to remain within the limits set by the technology itself.

This twofold approach (the Web *in* context and the Web *as* context) suggests how focused we need to be on the construction of an ever-changing socio-technical reality – a return to a totalising, process-focused history which takes account of ongoing developments. We should resist the effects of any discourse tending to fix realities or establish, in hieratic or metonymic fashion, an image of 'THE' Web.

The present analysis falls into three main sections, which interrogate, in turn, the diachronic or temporal contextualisation, the boundaries or spatial contextualisation and finally collective and individual experiences of the Web.

## THE WEB FROM A DIACHRONIC AND CHRONOLOGICAL PERSPECTIVE

> Can you describe for the reader the D-day, or the H-hour or the M-minute, the precise moment when you invented the World Wide Web?
>
> (His expression suggests he is lost in memories) Well, I was coming down a footpath in the Swiss Alps... (silence) Then the clouds started getting thicker... and darker... (silence) There was a flash of lightening, a peel of thunder, a storm was beginning to blow, when suddenly the clouds parted and...
>
> And?
>
> And nothing! I'm making this up... Ideas never arrive like that, you're not suddenly struck by an illumination or a revelation, everything you read about Newton's apple or Archimedes shouting 'Eureka!' in his bath-tub, these are fantasies! [...].
>
> Tim Berners-Lee (2014)

With this touch of humour Tim Berners-Lee questions the vision – sometimes still present in part of the general public – of a seminal revelation that would give rise to the emergence of an invention. The Web did not come out of the blue in the late 1980s. The notion of hyperlink already existed, and Mosaic was not the first browser; therefore it is the uses, creativity, circulation and appropriation of the World Wide Web and Mosaic, as much as the innovation itself, which ensure success. Thus, it is the genealogies, but also the turning points, and the breaks as well as the continuities, that the history of the Web has to question, interweaving the temporalities of innovation, uses, communication and media.

### *Genealogies and Transitions: A Process-Focused History*

The origins of the Web are the subject of a rich literature featuring two essential aspects. The first of these consists of (infinitely varied) definitions of a finished Web, in a state allowing it to be defined as such, something existing from that point onwards and not before. The fetishisation of dates has led to the over-determination of particular characteristics, which vary from one writer to another: the appearance of a graphic interface and the marketing of the first search engine are the best-known examples.

The second aspect is the genealogy established in order to explain 'how the Web happened'. This draws on notions of a longer-term genealogy. The work of Paul Otlet at the turn of the twentieth century or Ted Nelson's Xanadu project are thus posited as early versions of hypertext, even though the latter is also viewed as an example of *vaporware* (Wolf, 1995). Meanwhile, other developments, like that of the French Minitel (a videotex online service), are often ignored because they took place in geographical locations discounted by the historiography of modern technologies. Niels Brügger (2016: 1059–60) has already pointed to the many omissions in existing historical works:

> Should we celebrate the moment when the idea for an innovation was formulated? Should the thoughts and technologies paving the way for the idea be included? Should the prototype or the finished product be celebrated? Or was the technology not invented until it was made publicly or commercially accessible, or maybe not even until its number of users reached a critical mass? How these questions are to be answered is in part a function of each individual scholar's specific research question, focus and interest.

He argues that the choice of founding event, the timespan considered and the types of factor taken into account are determined by a researcher's own background and objectives, as well as by the stated aims of a study.

There is considerable justification for this view. From a more polemical perspective, we should also look to the vested interests that are bound to influence writing and writers on the Web. In particular, these influence genealogical choices concerning the technologies to be studied, sometimes to anachronistic effect. An example of this is Paul Otlet's Mundaneum. This bibliographic tool (Mazower, 2012; Van den Heuvel and Rayward, 2011) originated in Belgium at the end of the nineteenth century and is now presented as a founding element in genealogies of the Web. Some have even sought to define it as an – at least conceptual – prototype. However, it is unclear whether those working on the technologies essential to the development of the Internet, and then of Web interfaces, had even heard of such tools. Some journalists and writers, for example, have described Mundaneum as a 'paper Google'. This is not to deny the influence of Otlet's arguments, despite the presentism inherent in such an anachronistic approach. It does, however, serve to underline the fact that a genealogical history involving elements just as complex as the Web itself requires the most rigorous analysis of any point of contact before actual effects can be deduced or given any weight.

Bearing this in mind, the 'actual creation' of an artefact, rather than its abstract conception, is these days taken as the crucial element in a historical narrative. Thus, Paolo Bory, Eleanora Benecchi and Gabriele Balbi (2016), in *How the Web was Told: Continuity and Change in the Founding Fathers' Narratives on the Origins of the World Wide Web*, have clearly established the dual narrative of how Ted Nelson invented the term *hypertext* and Berners-Lee made the system a reality:

> Paola Castellucci (1999) argues that, in *Weaving the Web*, Nelson was portrayed as the artistic and eclectic inventor of the *term* hypertext, whereas Berners-Lee depicted himself as the inventor of the *thing* hypertext (pp. 12–18). This thesis has been strengthened by Mike Sendall: 'Ted Nelson had thought about this forty years ago but it was Tim who went and did it!' (Gillies and Cailliau, 2000: 201). In other words, depicting Nelson's hypertext as a potential idea that 'Berners-Lee transformed into reality [...] made Berners-Lee himself the innovator who "activated" and systematised the hypertext technology' (Bory et al., 2016).

The notion of solitary inventors is now increasingly giving way to the study of the background movements that shaped the Web. It allows us to appreciate the collective and international elements of co-construction. The different ways in which the Web has been used are increasingly recognised as defining actual milestones in the history of networks too.

## *The Periodisation of Web History*

Every historical phenomenon has its own periodisation (Prost, 2010: 118), which the historian must unravel in order to construct the chronology of his/her object. The periodisation of Web history is a challenge facing the historian on several levels.

First to be considered is an overall chronology of the Web, which must not only take account of technological turning points, but also consider developments in media, mediatised and information culture. We can think, for example, of how gifs, memes (Eppink, 2014), spam (Brunton, 2013) and audio formats have been used. We can consider how video usage has grown, with wider and wider transmedia circulation, as well as of the ways in which different applications and communication empires, as they develop, offer platforms and services, like Google, YouTube and Twitter, which have tended to establish their own rhythms. Also important is a grasp both of network hybridisation in the creative field (Shifman, 2013) and of network influence on other media systems (content shared with television, cinema, etc.).

Historians need also to consider a communication era that is both heterogeneous in terms of Internet and Web users and global in terms of countries and continents (we return to this in the next section). Temporalities to be distinguished should not simply include the Web 1.0 period, followed by the Web 2.0 (O'Reilly, 2005) and CMS period.

Alongside – and not always corresponding precisely to – the chronological division between the 'early adopter' and 'newbie' periods, and finally that of adoption by a general public, the division between personal websites, followed by blogs and wikis, and then digital social networks, etc., should be refined too.

Thinking of digital culture should also lead us to question the significant and commonly duplicated historical breaks within the history of the Web, in particular that of Web 2.0, or the 'participatory turn'.

Like many important concepts, Web 2.0 doesn't have a hard boundary, but rather a gravitational core. Tim O'Reilly (2005) explains that you can visualise Web 2.0 as a set of principles and practices that tie together a veritable solar system of sites that demonstrate some or all of those principles, at a varying distance from that core. Discourses of actors like Tim O'Reilly demonstrate how much they can be performative. Convinced of the importance of the participatory shift, O'Reilly reverses the burden of proof by explaining that an 'important concept' has no solid boundaries but works much like our solar system, with its ellipses and its gravitational influences. For the historian, it is the reverse: a solid concept not only has borders, but it allows complementary boundaries to be drawn at its margins to identify and articulate other objects.

We should thus be taking some distance from the discourses, so widely relayed by the media, of certain digital actors such as Tim O'Reilly or Chris Anderson. Their formulaic skills ('An attitude, not a technology', 'Data as the Intel Side', etc.; see O'Reilly (2005)) should not lead us to neglect other earlier practices and antecedents, as highlighted by Michael Stevenson (2016):

> From celebrations of the electronic frontier and cyberspace to pronouncements of Web 2.0 and, more recently, 'the sharing economy', each new paradigm shift on the Web may be conceptualised not just as technological innovation but also as a rhetorical move that revitalises familiar oppositions between the old and the new, thus 'consecrating' a new genre or technology as a true departure from old media. How might the persistence of such discourses be explained?

In 'Rethinking the Participatory Web', Stevenson (2014) turns to the history of *HotWired* to illustrate how debates about the value of amateur participation have long been fundamental to the imagination of the Web.

The values attached to interaction or participation have also been subject to developments not confined to the Web. Forms of expression on the Web are inextricable from the social representations behind the formats concerned. They relate in turn to imaginaries demanding analysis in terms of both the short-term history of the Web and the longer-term history of written work (Herrenschmidt, 2007).

While the famous rise of the amateur, the place of user-generated content and, more widely, the question of user participation are heuristic structures vital to historians, they do well to take equal account of the rhythms of a particular object. Commercial usage, for example, has not developed at the same rhythm as the activist Web, does not form part of the same structures and does not have the same relationship to the media.

Furthermore, it is important that historians situate the objects of their studies within a broader historical process: an archived web page dedicated, for example, to the abdication of Pope Benedict XVI may be accessed by historians of the papacy and historians of the religious press or of online communication, may be examined and analysed in different ways and also may be inserted into a periodisation particular to the researcher's own field of study (Schafer and Thierry, 2015). As noted by Antoine Prost (2010: 116), 'The historian does not reconstruct an entire temporality in every research project, but encounters a time already worked on, already periodised, by other historians'. Any analysis of websites also involves a further temporal dimension, in addition to those already highlighted. On the one hand, as noted by Claude Mussou (2012: 264, our translation): [...] whereas an archive is traditionally composed of documents whose usage value is no longer recognised, selected or organised in accordance with already identified and fixed criteria, the Web archive is constructed 'in real time' by the automatic collection of content that, to some extent at least, has not lost its usage value.

On the other hand, as Niels Brügger (2012: 161–3) puts it, 'in general it is impossible to archive online web content on a scale of 1:1. [...] On the contrary: the web archiving process creates unique versions, each with their own individual "aura"'. Web archives create reconstructions and offer content from the past set within contemporary interfaces where we find temporal leaps created by the reconstruction of links, constituting hybrid and unpublished content that overturns the notion of authenticity (Schafer and Thierry, 2015). As Louise Merzeau (2014) has noted, these are also inextricable from the rhythms of the organisations that have archived the content. She highlights how in less than 20 years the archiving of the Web has passed through different paradigms: from the documentary model, aimed at comprehensive archiving on earlier models like that of the library, it became a dynamic, temporal archive in the image of the Web itself, recognising instability as an indispensable dynamic, not forgetting the notion of the archive as memory, with the model of the intelligent copy or exemplar. As Niels Ole Finneman emphasises (2015), the archiving of the Web also involves taking account of a temporal dimension with three aspects: the dimension of original content, the 'cumulative and transformative' dimension of archiving and finally the dimension of the researcher's reading, which again becomes a kind of hypertextuality. We can also add a fourth dimension, that of a reading inextricable from its own time and not always immune to presentism or nostalgia.

We see this nostalgia particularly in relation to the 1990s. Historians seeking to reconstruct the Web of that time encounter not only a nostalgic discourse on the Web itself, but also the nostalgia of those for whom that period was a golden age. To them it represents the time of proselytising 'early adopters' sharing their knowledge and skills and developing what came to be known as Netiquette (a portmanteau composed of net and etiquette qualifying courtesy on online discussions groups). This was the time, too, of the 'handmade Web', of endless inventiveness, creativity, new kinds of publication that gradually became standardised, especially in the wake of the Internet bubble. Such representations give only a partial picture of the Web of the 1990s, of course, but their prominence highlights the DIY aesthetic and practices and the active involvement of Internet users in creating web pages, which decreased with the introduction of simple publication tools[1].

And as Megan Sapnar Ankerson (2009) has shown by studying the splendour and decadence of the Flash technology, the Web then assumed a new simplicity, a kind of contrition for past excesses. In the salvage work of the Geocities Archive Team and in the Geocities-izer site[2], which enables the user to give his/her site a '90s look', we see some renewal of interest in a 'vernacular' digital heritage (Milligan, 2017) and in the folklore and the coding of those early days.

We can state, therefore, that constructing a chronology of the Web depends on our capacity to establish a multiple genealogy for an object at a crossroads – in technical terms, of course, but also in terms of the *offline* usages, representations and variations accompanying the diffusion of the Web.

## THE BOUNDARIES AND SPATIAL CONTEXTUALISATION OF THE WEB

> In 1993 we were not in a position to say where the future home for the Web would be.
>
> In 1995, I am happy to say that two renowned institutions, INRIA and MIT, have allowed us to build one. The idea of having a single location, in the United States, always seemed out of the question to me.
>
> Tim Berners-Lee, Launch of the European Branch of the W3C, 2 November 1995

As noted above by Berners-Lee, the Web did not appear on a specific D-day, H-hour or M-minute, but its British founder reminds us that the Web and the W3C – the consortium that sustains its development and its governance, have several locations too. A general history of the Web has therefore to take into account geopolitical, institutional and legal contexts. It thereby claims a historical geography of the Web, both a 'classic' one, based on the centres of power and on national and international issues, and a 'new' one of flows (of diffusion, acculturation and adaptation) within particular spaces (local, regional or national).

### *A Multinational, International and Transnational History*

Central to the history and development of the Web is Tim Berners-Lee's decision to ask CERN to place his invention in the public domain and his preference for open innovation with equally open structures of governance (Berners-Lee, 2000). A focus on the governance of the Web allows us to situate it historically, once again both technically and politically, as well as within a global arena where stakeholder and geographical interests are nonetheless important.

Meanwhile, in 1993, the University of Minnesota decided that companies should pay to use Gopher[3], though, at the request of Tim Berners-Lee, CERN agreed to allow free use of Web protocols. The next year, the MIT Laboratory for Computer Science (LCS) became the first host of the World Wide Web Consortium (WC3). In his introduction to *Weaving the Web*, the head of MIT-LCS, Michael L. Dertouzos, notes that 'As technologists and entrepreneurs were launching or merging companies to exploit the Web, they seemed fixated on one question: "How can I make the Web mine?". Meanwhile, Tim Berners-Lee was asking "How can I make the Web yours?"' (Berners-Lee, 2000: viii). Berners-Lee (2000) also recalls that he wanted the consortium to run on an open process like the IETF's, but 'one that was quicker and more efficient, because we would have to move fast'.

Recalling the establishment of WC3, and the decision to base it in three locations, in the United States, in Europe and finally at Keio in Japan in the mid 1990s, suggests a number of reflections concerning issues of normalisation, regulation, internationalisation and globalisation involved in the development of the Web, and the importance of viewing these in context. Below we highlight two such issues.

First and foremost is Tim Berners-Lee's decisive preference for openness and multi-stakeholder governance, which Internet actors have continued to develop ever since the 1960s. As Andrew Russell notes in a paper (2003) highlighting the influence of consensus-based, non-hierarchical values throughout the history of the Web and of W3C, 'consensus is a predominant cultural value of Internet governance, most notably in the Internet Engineering Task Force (IETF). The IETF's motto and operating philosophy: "We reject: kings, presidents, and voting; we believe in rough consensus and running code" is widely cited as a model for deliberative governance'. The history of Web governance thus suggests a chronology going back to the 1960s, the formation of the Network Working Group[4], the creation of 'Requests for Comments' in the Arpanet project[5] and even further back. W3C represents a stance on patents and openness inherent in the development of information and network technologies. Nonetheless, Tim Berners-Lee did not place the Web within existing governance structures, particularly those of the Internet, although he was in contact with the IETF:

> Berners-Lee understood that 'running the consortium would always be a balancing act, between taking the time to stay as open as possible and advancing at the speed demanded by the onrush of technology'. He admired the openness of the IETF process, but felt that, given the fast pace of the commercial world that was increasingly adopting the Web, the Web would benefit from a quicker and more efficient process (Russell, 2003).

The decisive factors in his choice thus arose both from a particular historical context – that of openness and the influence of the structures within which software and even the Internet were being developed – and from an immediate context of wishing to propel the development of the technology, the transition of Gopher to a payment model and his own departure from CERN, among other things.

Second, we should note that while the Web was established within a global dynamic, as evidenced not least in its name, it was inextricable from the start from continental and regional geopolitical and institutional interests. Tim Berners-Lee, having left CERN and joined MIT, was keen to retain a European base for the Web – a desire that would lead in particular to the competition to host W3C…

> […] a 'divine surprise' for Europe and for INRIA.
>
> After CERN's withdrawal, the Web could have left for the other side of the Atlantic with Berners-Lee, its founding father, had he not promoted a prominent European role. Despite CERN's innovations, Europe did not have its own critical mass of activity and development.
>
> It had immediately to collaborate with transnational communities, helping to integrate European building of infrastructure into the larger context of globalization in recent decades. (Griset and Schafer, 2011: 368)

## *National Adaptations*

Beyond these international, transnational and multinational spaces, there is clearly a rich history of adaptations of the Web to specific contexts with different technical cultures and industrial and commercial antecedents, as well as those subject to varying national legislation. Examples are provided by several studies in *The Routledge Companion to Global Internet Histories* (Goggin and McLelland, 2017), such as Nicholas John's chapter on the emergence and structuring of ISPs in Israel, or Ignacio Siles's chapter on the slow passage from X25 to TCP/IP in Costa Rica (and the occurring rivalries and debates within the country). Other examples include the studies dedicated to Mexico or Brazil, situating them in specific political and economic contexts, or those focusing on Korea and Taiwan, addressing more specific uses such as BBS and e-mails. All of these are enlightening national paths, which involve the political, economic, technological, cultural and social history of these countries, their inclusion in regional groups and environments and their relationship to the United States.

As regards the case of France specifically, which is very familiar to the authors, the delay in French adoption of the Web at the end of the 1990s was often emphasised by advocates of a faster transition from Minitel to the Internet. The Internet access figure of 100,000 in 1995 increased by 1997 to 381,000 for domestic access and 621,000 for workplace access. Despite this rapid take-off, Reuters in 1997 estimated the number of French websites at 21,367, as compared with 825,385 in the United States. Thus, while early adapters in the United States had to deal with the huge number of novice arrivals on the Net from 1993 – an 'eternal September' provoked by AOL's opening of Usenet forums to general access, it was only in the second half of the 1990s that France would experience the still very cautious appearance of newbies on the Web:

> In 1988, the regulation of domestic traffic was only a matter of taming a herd of elephants. In 1995, all our online relationships were ambushed by millions of little mice, which were much more difficult to control. And of course releasing the mice only in clusters, as Netscape did, solved nothing. (Huitema, 1995, authors' translation)

This highlights the need for national, as much as transnational, histories. We should also note, despite these clearly different timescales, a convergence of reactions on the part of early adopters on both sides of the Atlantic (Auray, 2002; Paloque-Bergès, 2011), raising questions about the spread of digital culture in different production contexts.

The question of whether there is really just one Web or a plurality of Webs is thus a crucial one. A useful image for how national communities have participated in the creation of discrete information spaces, defined by language usage and specific reference points and sometimes governed by the will of national institutions, may be that of the archipelago. This is also currently becoming an even more appropriate image for the various services, applications and spaces on the Web, with the effects of GAFAT (Google, Amazon, Facebook, Apple, Twitter) and of digital social networks and digital environments thus requiring the most sophisticated analysis.

## FROM WEB TO WEBS? COLLECTIVE AND INDIVIDUAL EXPERIENCES

> Virtual reality came before reality, not the other way around; the reality was in our heads
>
> when we imagined the exploits of *Captain Fracasse*[6], and we didn't have to pay for a connection or a modem.
>
> Bruno Latour on the *France Culture* radio programme *Place de la Toile*[7], 20 November 2009.

Bruno Latour's somewhat provocative formula that challenges the idea of a virtuality specific to the digital world by insisting on its material dimensions, which are also put forward by approaches related to Internet Studies or Infrastructure Studies, invites us to grasp the context that gives birth to these infrastructures, whether informational or material. We must therefore rethink the place of the hardware and software computer industry, as well as the economic, regulatory and political characteristics that frame, or sway under, the development of uses of networks. Speeches concerning the information highways, from those of Al Gore (Vice President of the

United States during the Clinton administration) in 1993 and their rework in Europe (e.g. the Théry report in France, or the European Bangemann report on 'Europe and the Global Information Society' in 1994, for instance) reflect the growing importance of political and economic stakes at work since the 1990s. Individual, private and domestic aspects also come into play in the history of the Web; together, these factors contribute to experiences that are both singular and plural, individual and collective.

## *Beyond Technology: Economics and Politics*

Technical approaches are beginning to give way to analyses that take account of the relationship of the Web to both politics and economics.

This sometimes focuses on the changing environment of the Web itself and the impact it has on its historical development, challenging its roots and values, as highlighted by Andrew Russell (2003) with the historical study of some debates within the W3C. He enriches the socio-technical approach of protocols and governance that Sandra Braman (2014) had raised for Internet development by also studying the Request for Comments. With particular reference to the debates that took place between 1999 and 2003 around the use of patents in W3C recommendations, Andrew Russell throws light on the impact of a changing context, for example the widespread diffusion of the Web and the growth of commercial interests in the period preceding the Internet bubble. Thus:

> [the] history of PPWG[8] provides an excellent case study for testing the ability for the W3C to garner consensus around an issue that pitted the 'open code' values of grassroots Web developers against the commercial interests that concerned Dertouzos and Berners-Lee in the early 1990s. (Russell, 2003)

However, the influence of the Web and of networks more generally on our political ideas (Loveluck, 2015) and democratic practices (Badouard et al., 2016; Mabi, 2016) is increasingly a focus. While the role of the State in the development of information technology before the network era has been the subject of several pioneering studies from the 1990s onwards (Griset, 1998), the role of political contexts in the adoption of the Web has yet to be sufficiently appreciated. Nonetheless, national political configurations have played a crucial role. To return to the example of Minitel, the catch-up period seen in France from the second half of the 1990s highlights a public initiative well behind that seen in the United States. Following a dozen years when France led the way in public access technology, Minitel assumed all the hallmarks of a 'technical-industrial mis-step' (Thierry, 2013).

To this must be added the way in which a current and widespread political discourse depicts digital communication, including the Web, as a solution to everything, a tendency denounced by some analysts as solutionism (Morozov, 2014). Here, too, only a long-term perspective on both 'network politics' and the 'politics of networks' will allow us to see the actions of Snowden, Julian Assange or Bradley Manning in the context both of governments' digital activity (Rey, 2016) and of a secrecy whose development is only in part attributable to power relations mediated through the Web. Such a perspective allows us to see that not everything happening online is completely new.

## *Towards a Phenomenology of Web Experience*

The position assumed by the Web during the 1990s in the workplace as well as in the private sphere is also a powerful argument for approaching our relationship with all things digital from an experiential perspective as much as through economic and political analysis. Far from reviving the now-dated metaphor of early analysts who depicted Web users as traversing a virtual world removed from reality, on science-fictional, 'cyberpunk' lines (Dery, 1994), the time has come to develop a phenomenology of our real relationship with the Net.

The first stage, unarguably, is to validate the real foundations of our experience and compile a history of the real culture of the virtual, no longer arbitrarily separating real and virtual. Studies, for example, of the economic conditions of consultancy, undertaken from the perspective of a history of pricing and supply (Rebillard, 2012), of the elements of environmental interaction defined by a long-term history of our relationship with digital tools (Bardini, 2000), or indeed of early practitioner communities (Thierry, 2012), can become the basis for appreciating recent innovations and their impact on our everyday experience of the Net (adoption of smartphones, new pricing structures, etc).

As the most common elements of our practice continue to change, we also need to establish a periodisation of such change, along the lines of Anne Helmond's work on the hypertext link and how its meaning has changed over time. She has shown, for example, how much the meaning of the term 'hyperlink' has changed over time, studying:

> the history of the hyperlink from a medium-specific perspective by analyzing the technical reconfiguration of the hyperlink by engines and platforms over time. Hyperlinks may be seen as having different roles belonging to specific periods, including the role of the hyperlink as a unit of navigation, a relationship marker, a reputation indicator and a currency of the web. (Helmond, 2013)

The tools available to historians for carrying out this type of study are developing. For example, Oldweb.today, a service that allows for the navigation of Web archives with browsers from their own time, reminds us that the study of Web archives demands their contextualisation. Beyond the importance of considering the visual and material specificities which framed the context of production and accessibility of these pages – terminal, network and bandwidth – the reading of a Web archive implies an understanding of what the web page, the website and its hyperlinks meant in their time (Schafer et al., 2016).

Finally, analysis of how the Web has changed our understanding of the world is still in its infancy, but is already indicating new and fertile topics for research (such as the massive adoption of smartphones or the online availability of digital photographs (Gunthert, 2015) or, again, the growth of online communities of medical patients, political activists or users of technology).

The pioneers and research centre archives which are clearly identified are now being joined by new knowledge banks and new tools that the historian must take advantage of. Web archives revealing the websites (lost or not), the presentation tools (the technologies invoked, the real dissemination and usage of these technologies and the degree to which they have been mastered by the actors involved) and the digital landscapes composed by the various interfaces (especially the structures for presenting information) can lead to the formation of a corpus that will give us access to the various ways in which the Web has been used. This allows us to go beyond the boundaries of how technicians use technology.

The involvement of digital tools in almost every area of society should thus encourage studies both on their diffusion and on their usage.

- Diffusion especially in terms of how this is anchored in reality. For example, the place of cybercafés as spaces of discovery, learning and relaxation is a striking example from the first period of the 'mobile Web' before the advent of the smartphone.
- Usage approached through Web archives and other archives that historians are used to consulting. Looking no further than the social adaptations of the Web since the time of laboratories

and universities, we have the manuals that flourished in the 1990s (Laquey, 1995), the press and the other 'traditional' media that allow us to re-anchor the Web within a society in the adoption phase.

## CONCLUSION

Building the history of the Web consists above all of confronting multiple problems of categorisation of the objects that make up this complex reality. The Web must be viewed in relation to all the fields that act upon it, not all of which are technical in nature: the experience of users, the political and economic consequences of its development, and so on. To grasp the Web as a whole requires a seemingly paradoxical division in order to emphasise its dimension of *global social fact*. This paper stressed three essential dimensions, which can contribute to it: temporalities, spaces and materialities.

By introducing the reader to the temporalities, spatialities and materialities that should frame the history of the Web, our narrative takes its roots in Fernand Braudel's reflections (1969) on history but also revisits recent works such as Geoffrey Bowker's analysis in *Memory Practices in the Sciences*, which advocated:

> We need to open a discourse – where there is no effective discourse now – about the varying temporalities, spatialities and materialities that we might represent in our databases, with a view to designing for maximum flexibility and allowing as possible for an emergent polyphony and polychrony. Raw data is both an oxymoron and a bad idea; to the contrary, data should be cooked with care. (Bowker, 2006: 183–4)

In context, the Web is polychronous. Here, as already emphasised, we must find the means to articulate complex genealogies and go beyond a history of successes that can only serve to rubber-stamp a dominant model of development. Its profound roots, sometimes unforeseen by its actors themselves, have many long-term genealogies: the search for an effective system of technology-based documentation has haunted minds since at least Vannevar Bush and his famous Memex (Nyce and Kahn, 1991), and even long before a global network of computers was considered. This calls for a reassessment of the importance given to older innovations, but with the risk of an anachronism, as shown by the discourses that try to make the Mundaneum a Google 'before its time', which is an obvious sign of the contamination of the past with an obsessive present.

In context, the Web then comes about and develops in spaces that are interwoven with each other and that must be articulated. In its early years of development and after its birth at CERN in Europe, the Web becomes rooted in the North American context and expands rapidly, coming in contact with national spaces that adopt it according to specific constraints and contexts. As a context, the Web pushes us today to think of globalisation in terms of technology and media. However, as a deeply deterritorialised space too, it questions the notion of border and sovereignty, but also the possibility of plurilingualism and the position of States in the governance of the world communications.

In context, the Web can finally be grasped as the emerging place of many individual and collective experiences. These experiences are distributed across time and lead to the succession of definitions of the Web in the minds and discourses of actors that is dependent on the instant at which they experience the Web. The myriad of mediums (screens, devices, interfaces, etc.), speeds and contents draw up as many possibilities for the historian to explore the phenomenologies of the Web. From a 56 kilobits connection, at home or in a cybercafé and with a 13- or 14-inch CRT screen, to the ubiquitous 4G smartphone's connection, is it always the same Web or is it different experiences of the same artefact?

Finally, as context, what the historian experiences of the Web constitutes the ultimate frontier to be taken into account.

Following what sociologists have been assiduously practising for a while, the historian must make a reflexive analysis of his own history with the Web, in order to avoid taking the current Web for the state of culmination of what is in fact an ever-evolving story. Such consideration of internal and external contexts then further allows us to give due weight to the development of a Web that is constantly being redefined and to analyse recent developments (for example the way that HTML and the page format as the basic unit of information now face competition from the creation of data silos, data encapsulation and the appearance of major new capturers of attention like Facebook), in sum to consider the Web in all its dynamic process of becoming, rather than through a rigid and inevitably outdated definition of what it is presumed to be.

## ACKNOWLEDGEMENTS

This study has been carried out within the framework of the Web90 project supported by the French National Research Agency (ANR-14-CE29-0012-01).

### *Notes*

1 See Kyle Chayka (28 October 2014), The Great Web 1.0 Revival, gizmodo.com, http:/gizmodo.com/the-great-web-1-0-revival-1651487835 'Nostalgic for intimacy
When it first got popular, Facebook was like the back room at a club: A cozy space filled with just your friends, everyone clearly connected to everyone else. Now, it's more like a stadium [...]
Nostalgic for free-form self-expression
Niche communities that aren't overseen by giant companies also have the freedom to evolve on their own and embrace identities and designs that wouldn't be possible on Facebook [...]'.
See also Anil Dash (13 December 2012), The Web We Lost, http://dashes.com/anil/2012/12/the-web-we-lost.html

2 http://www.wonder-tonic.com/geocitiesizer/

3 Gopher is a protocol that was designed for distributing, searching and retrieving documents over the Internet. It would remain free for educational and non-profit institutions.
'This was an act of treason in the academic community and the Internet community. Even if the university never charged anyone a dime, the fact that the school had announced it was reserving the right to charge people for the use of the gopher protocols meant it had crossed the line. To use the technology was too risky. Industry dropped gopher like a hot potato' (Berners-Lee, 2000: 73).

4 A group led by Steve Crocker, to develop the host-to-host software in Arpanet.

5 An early packet switching network launched by the Advanced Research Projects Agency (ARPA) of the United States Department of Defense in 1969.

6 A nineteenth-century French adventure novel.

7 Web Square.

8 Patent Policy Working Group.

## REFERENCES

Ankerson, M.S. (2009) 'Historicizing Web Design: Software, Style and the Look of the Web', in Janet Staiger and Sabine Hake (eds), *Convergence Media History*. New York, London: Routledge. pp. 192–203.

Auray, N. (2002) 'L'Olympe de l'internet français et sa conception de la loi civile', *Les Cahiers du Numérique,* 3(2): 79–90. https://www.cairn.info/revue-les-cahiers-du-numerique-2002-2-page-79.htm

Badouard, R., Mabi, C. and Sire, G. (2016) 'Beyond "Points of Control": Logics of digital governmentality in Internet Policy Review' [online] https://policyreview.info/articles/analysis/beyond-points-control-logics-digital-governmentality

Bardini, T. (2000) 'Les promesses de la révolution virtuelle. Genèse de l'informatique personnelle, 1968–1973', *Sociologie et Sociétés*, 32(2): 57–72.

Berners-Lee, T. (2014) 'Oui, le Web est né en France', Challenges, 17 June. https://www.challenges.fr/high-tech/tim-berners-lee-oui-le-web-est-ne-en-france_151444

Berners-Lee, T. (2000) *Weaving the Web*. New York: Harper Business.

Bory, P., Benecchi, E. and Balbi, G. (2016) 'How the Web was told: Continuity and change in the founding fathers' narratives on the origins of the World Wide Web', *New Media & Society*, 18(7): 1066–87.

Bowker, G. (2006) *Memory Practices in the Sciences*. Cambridge, MA: The MIT Press.

Braman, S. (2014) 'The geopolitical and the network political: Internet designers and governance', *International Journal of Media and Cultural Politics*, 9(2): 277–96.

Braudel, F. (1969) *Écrits sur l'Histoire*. Paris: Flammarion.

Brügger, N. (2016) 'Introduction: The Web's first 25 years', *New Media & Society*, 18(7): 1059–65.

Brügger, N. (2012) 'Web history and the Web as a historical source', *Zeithistorische Forschungen/Studies in Contemporary History*, 9: 316–25, http://www.zeithistorische-forschungen.de/2-2012/id%3D4426

Brunton, F. (2013) *SPAM: A Shadow History of the Internet*. Cambridge, MA: The MIT Press.

Castellucci, P. (1999) *Dall'ipertesto al web*. Bari: Laterza.

Dery, M. (1994) *Flame Wars: The Discourse of Cyberculture*. Durham: Duke University Press Books.

Ensmenger, N. (2012) 'The digital construction of technology: Rethinking the history of computers in society', *Technology and Culture*, 53(4): 753–76.

Eppink, J. (2014) 'A brief history of the GIF', *Journal of Visual Culture*, 13(3): 298–306, http://journals.sagepub.com/doi/pdf/10.1177/1470412914553365

Gillies, J. and Cailliau, R. (2000) *How the Web Was Born: The Story of the World Wide Web*. Oxford: Oxford University Press.

Goggin, G. and McLelland, M. (eds) (2017) *The Routledge Companion to Global Internet Histories*. New York/Abingdon: Routledge.

Griset, P. and Schafer, V. (2011) 'Hosting the World Wide Web Consortium for Europe: From CERN to INRIA', *History and Technology*, 27(3): 353–70.

Griset, P. (1998) *Informatique, Politique Industrielle, Europe, entre Plan Calcul et Unidata*, Institut d'Histoire de l'Industrie. Paris: Éditions Rive Droite.

Gunthert, A. (2015) *L'Image Partagée. La Photographie Numérique*. Paris: Textuel.

Helmond, A. (2013) 'The algorithmization of the hyperlink', *Computational Culture*. http://computationalculture.net/article/the-algorithmization-of-the-hyperlink

Herrenschmidt, C. (2007) *Les Trois Écritures: Langue, Nombre, Code*. Paris: Gallimard.

Huitema, C. (1995) 'Les touristes, les éléphants et les souris', *Planète Internet,* November–December: 78.

Laquey, T. (1995) *Sésame pour Internet: Initiation au Réseau Planétaire*. Paris: Addison Wesley France.

Loveluck, B. (2015) *Réseaux, Libertés et Contrôle. Une Généalogie Politique d'Internet*. Paris: Armand Colin.

Mabi, C. (2016) 'Analyser les dispositifs participatifs par leur design', in Christine Barats (ed.), *Manuel d'Analyse du Web*. Paris: Armand Colin. pp. 33–7.

Mazower, M. (2012) *Governing the World, The History of an Idea, 1815 to the Present*. London: Allen Lane.

Merzeau, L. (2014) 'Vers un Web temporel', Talk at the IIPC General Assembly. http://merzeau.net/vers-un-web-temporel/

Milligan, I. (2017) 'Welcome to the Web: The Online Community of GeoCities and the Early Years of the World Wide Web', in Ralph Schroeder and Niels Brügger (eds), *The Web as History*. London: UCL Press. pp. 137–58.

Misa, T.J. (2007) 'Understanding how computing has changed the world', *IEEE Annals of the History of Computing*, 29(4): 52–63.

Morozov, E. (2014) *To Save Everything, Click Here: The Folly of Technological Solutionism*. New York: PublicAffairs.

Mussou, C. (2012) 'Et le Web devint archive: Enjeux et défis', *Le Temps des Médias,* 2(19): 259–66.

Nyce, J.M. and Kahn, P. (1991) *From Memex to Hypertext: Vannevar Bush and the Mind's Machine*. Boston: Academic Press.

Ole Finneman, N. (2015) 'Hypertextual relations in digital born Materials', RESAW conference, 'Web Archives as Scholarly Sources: Issues, Practices and Perspectives', 8 – 10 June, Aarhus University, Denmark.

O'Reilly, T. (2005) 'What Is Web 2.0, Design Patterns and Business Models for the Next Generation of Software', oreilly.com. Retrieved from: http://www.oreilly.com/pub/a/web2/archive/what-is-web-20.html

Paloque-Bergès, C. (2011) *Entre trivialité et culture: Une histoire de l'Internet vernaculaire. Émergence et médiation d'un folklore de réseau*, Thèse de Doctorat en Sciences de l'Information et de la Communication, Université Paris VIII.

Prost, A., 2010 [1996] *Douze Leçons sur l'Histoire*. Paris: Éditions du Seuil.

Rebillard, F. (2012) 'La genèse de l'offre commerciale grand public en France (1995–1996): Entre fourniture d'accès à l'Internet et services en ligne "propriétaires"', *Le Temps des Médias*, 18: 65–75.

Rey, O. (2016) *Quand le Monde s'est Fait Nombre*. Paris: Stock.

Russell, A. (2003) 'The W3C and its Patent Policy Controversy: A Case Study of Authority and Legitimacy in Internet Governance', http://arussell.org/papers/alr-tprc2003.pdf

Schafer, V. and Thierry, B. (2015) 'L'ogre et la toile. Le rendez-vous de l'histoire et des archives du Web', *Socio*, 4: 75–96.

Schafer, V., Musiani, F. and Borelli, M. (2016) 'Negotiating the Web of the past', *French Journal for Media Research*, 6, http://frenchjournalformediaresearch.com/lodel/index.php?id=952

Shifman, L. (2013) *Memes: In Digital Culture*. Boston: The MITPress.

Stevenson, M. (2016) 'The cybercultural moment and the new media field', *New Media & Society*, 18(7): 1088–102.

Stevenson, M. (2014) 'Rethinking the participatory Web: A history of HotWired's "new publishing paradigm", 1994–1997', *New Media & Society*, 18(7): 1331–46.

Thierry, B. (2013) 'De Tic-Tac au Minitel: la télématique grand public, une réussite française', *Actes du colloque Les ingénieurs des Télécommunications dans la France contemporaine. Réseaux, innovation et territoires (XIXe–XXe siècles)*. Paris: IGPDE editor.

Thierry, B. (2012) '"Révolution 0.1". Utilisateurs et communautés d'utilisateurs au premier âge de l'informatique personnelle et des réseaux grand public (1978–1990)', *Le Temps des Médias*, 1(18): 54–64.

Van den Heuvel, C. and Rayward, B. (2011) 'Facing interfaces: Paul Otlet's visualizations of data integration', *Journal of the American Society for Information Science and Technology*, 62(12): 2313–26.

Wolf, G. (1995) 'The curse of Xanadu', *Wired* 3, https://www.wired.com/1995/06/xanadu/

# Science and Technology Studies Approaches to Web History

Francesca Musiani and Valérie Schafer

## INTRODUCTION

A decade ago, Barry Wellman affirmed that the mid nineties had corresponded to the 'prehistoric' era in the emerging field of study seeking to explore, analyze and understand the complexity of the social, legal, political and economic relations subtending the development of the Internet (Wellman, 2004: 127). This approach goes hand in hand with Web development, and this interest in renewed approaches to Internet studies is most likely related to the widespread diffusion of the Internet allowed by the Web in the late nineties. Leveraging approaches issued from science and technology studies (STS), researchers have progressively emphasized a critical approach to the complex nexus of Internet and society. More recently, Janet Abbate notes that:

> STS can be useful to address the complex links between Internet technology and culture, which have blurred the frontiers of traditional categories. One of STS' tenets is to 'open the black box' of technology to understand its functioning, and understand how social relations and aims translate into artifacts. STS similarly offer models to describe how human and non-human actors exert joint agency in mediated environments. (Abbate, 2012:170)

This chapter introduces STS approaches, applying them to Web history, with the intent to show how they can shed further light on it and enrich it. In its first part, the chapter introduces key STS concepts and notions such as agency, co-construction, *dispositif*, actor–network, boundary object (Star and Griesemer, 1989), controversy and trial, and links them to case studies and examples drawn from the history of the Web such as the creation of W3C, the rise of spam, GIFs and memes, the development of Wikipedia and the role of APIs. The second part of the chapter delves into the governance of the Web as a particularly interesting case study of how STS notions and concepts can be leveraged to advance the analysis of objects and dynamics central to the Web and its history. Important Web governance-related concepts, such as multi-stakeholderism (Malcolm, 2008) and algorithmic governmentality (Rouvroy and Berns, 2013), are 'put to the test' through a STS lens.

This chapter seeks to show the value of a relational, practice-oriented approach – what in STS vocabulary is called 'unpacking black boxes', or doing a sociology 'of assemblages'. The chapter examines how this approach can shed light on the hybrid mobilizations of innovators, consumers, users and entrepreneurs – alongside their creations and cultures – that have made the Web the complex socio-technical system it is today.

## WHEN STS AND WEB HISTORY MEET

The encounter between the field of science and technology studies (STS) and the Internet as a subject of study has already proven interesting and fertile in recent times. Notably, an emerging field of study is born in the bridging of STS and Internet governance research. Thus, it is interesting to revisit the history of the Web, and more generally of the Internet, through the lens of key concepts in STS. The first part of this chapter aims to demonstrate the effectiveness of a few core STS concepts in the field of Web history. The meeting of STS and the Web first happened with studies of information and communication technologies (ICTs), the Internet in particular. Thus, as a background to this endeavor, the chapter first retraces this meeting, and proceeds to show that more recently, STS have crossed paths with media studies, thus reinforcing the nexus between approaches to the communication field in its past and present dimensions.

### *When STS Meet ICTs*

The '*STS turn*' is founded in the sociology of innovation's interest in technical objects and social practices of appropriation of emerging technologies, in media sociology's increasing interest in ICTs, and the development of information and communication sciences: ICTs become 'interactional artifacts' (de Fornel, 1994: 126). With the advent of the Internet, then of the Web, an 'object-centered', interdisciplinary field of study follows at the end of the nineties, with the creation of Internet studies. The 'STS turn' within this field calls for a particular attention paid to context and situated practices, the unveiling of the 'invisible work' of Internet and Web innovation. STS approaches put emphasis on the practices that shape the management and the governance of the Internet and its uses as a living reality, and determine the ways in which it operates, works, resists and functions. Furthermore, STS approaches invite us not to consider values and rationalities of Internet and Web practitioners as *indicators* of how they perceive the world, but to problematize them as *resources and categories* that they deploy in specific circumstances in order to create and uphold specific configurations – in short, to actively organize their world.

### *When STS Meet Media Studies*

Several disciplines have attempted to 'think themselves anew' through the STS lens, or proposed conceptual hybrids. Noortje Marres and Carolin Gerlitz (2015) argue, for example, that digital social research should adopt 'interface methods' – a 'critical and creative engagement with methods development at the intersection of sociology, STS and digital research' (Marres and Gerlitz, 2015: 21), despite the strong bias in favor of purely quantitative methods that currently informs research on digital media.

Even more recently, Gabriele Balbi, Alessandro Delfanti and Paolo Magaudda (Balbi et al., 2016) have facilitated a conversation on the cross-fertilization of STS and media studies approaches (Badouard et al., 2016). The convergence between the two fields is revealed to be far from linear, with numerous points of friction appearing and notions such as *dispositif* (which we will come back to later in more detail) revealing their multiple meanings. However, several objects and sensibilities are shared by media studies and STS, especially in terms of common ancestors – e.g. domestication theory as discussed by Oudshoorn and Pinch (2003) – or a shared interest in infrastructures. All these contribute to the dialogue of the sociology (and the history) of the Web, and STS. Their encounter is, in particular, driven by the concept of materiality.

As Balbi et al. (2016) note, the 'material' and 'physical' aspects of social life have been a crucial object of investigation for STS since the inception of the field. A 'material turn' in the study of the Internet and ICTs is fostered by hybrid work between STS and media and communication studies (Hondros, 2015). This work has not always been linear, as Lievrouw (2014) notes, due to STS' and media studies' respective tendencies to give prominence to different processes – the co-determinism of the social and the material for STS, versus media studies' understanding of technology's materiality as a product of discourses and visions. However, it is increasingly producing notable work, such as Parikka's media archaeology (2012) and Gitelman's work (2013) on the infrastructures subtending data.

Badouard et al. (2016), drawing from Latour and Callon's 'classic' STS literature, observe that STS have helped recognize technical artifacts' status of 'mediators', inasmuch as they can modify the performativity of social actions. In this conception, it makes less sense to consider discourses and objects as separate spheres, and more sense to understand discourses as circulating within objects, both spheres co-constructing each other (Boczkowski and Lievrouw, 2007; Gillespie et al., 2014).

The notion of *dispositif* (in the Foucauldian sense, often translated as 'device' in English) and boundary object are among the notable concepts at the intersection of media studies and STS. In classic actor–network theory vocabulary, a socio-technical *dispositif* (device) is defined as an assemblage of human and non-human actants, where competencies and performances are distributed, and whose existence is enabled by the workings of innovation. Moreover, the notion allows agency (Proulx, 2009) to be integrated in the analysis, for a more fine-grained appreciation of its collective dimension. As Muniesa et al. (2007: 2) point out, 'devices do things. They articulate actions, they act or make others act', they make phenomena of translation materially possible. Several authors have underlined the suitability of the 'device' notion to be expanded beyond the strictly Foucauldian focus on power relations, social control, disciplinary and normative connotations. Indeed, the more recent uses of the notion by social science researchers call for a reflection on the different forms of tension and mediation that articulate and interact in a number of constantly evolving media, digital and communication devices, including the Web (Appel et al., 2010).

## *When Web History Meets STS Concepts: The Example of 'Boundary Objects'*

Concepts such as *dispositif* and mediation prove useful for articulating STS and media studies in a pragmatic approach to the 'power relations' inscribed in information and communication tools, as Badouard et al. (2016) conclude. Indeed, the notions of mediation and re-mediation can usefully be applied to the Web and to its archives – which increasingly act as sources for historians. In recent work, we have shown the extent to which mediations and agencies need to be taken into account in order to think of the Web of the past and the archived Web:

> Technical and human negotiations at both levels of collection and consultation of the Web archive

> include many operations: the choices of particular crawl frequencies, depths, domains to be collected, programming of robots, data deduplication processes; the recreation of links and filling of URLs by the access software; the exclusion of specific elements such as advertisements; the creation of platforms and consultation environments offering different designs and functionalities. All these operations bear witness to the ongoing choices that reflect the scope and ambitions established by and for the actors of Web archiving (Schafer et al., 2016).

We can attempt to go further, by showing how several features of born-digital heritage allow us to qualify it as a boundary object, i.e. the concept coined by Susan Leigh Star and James Griesemer (1989) to analytically describe those processes where actors coming from different social worlds, and called upon to cooperate, manage to coordinate despite their diverging points of view: 'how do they create mutual understandings without losing the diversity of social worlds?' (Trompette and Vinck, 2009: 6–7). This concept was meant to reduce the inherent asymmetry enshrined in Michel Callon's original 'translation' notion (1986): from a top-down initiative by the innovator or the science entrepreneur, enrolling other actors by exerting control via mandatory passage points, to a more organic view taking into account the co-existence of several translation processes.

This notion is, indeed, to be handled with care – as Susan Leigh Star herself suggests in a subsequent article (2010): since its creation, the concept has mostly been used for its 'interpretive flexibility', i.e. the property that allows it to operate as a support of heterogeneous translations, a device of integration for different types of knowledge, of mediation in the processes of coordination of experts and amateurs. However, as Trompette and Vinck (2009) emphasize, other dimensions have been unjustly overlooked or downright forgotten; for example, boundary objects incorporate sets of conventions, standards and norms, typical of specific communities of practice, and allow us to account for the processes of delegation of work or other activities, or for the performative action of artifacts in the production of knowledge. By fully re-instating these dimensions, one is able to account more broadly for the work of coordination, alignment, alliance and translation between the different actors and the worlds they mobilize.

The notion of boundary object, seen in this light, can be applied to the study of born-digital heritage on the Web and beyond the Web, e.g. the discussion lists, newsgroups and websites of the early nineties. For instance, with a view to reconstructing the trajectories of innovation within pioneering user groups, Camille Paloque-Berges (2017) highlights the uses of these technologies in the mid 1990s, and observes that they served a logic of confrontation to social, political and economic norms – such as, respectively, rules of sociability in online public speaking, equipment and techno-scientific development, governance and regulation of networks, and the transition from non-commercial networks to a full-fledged digital economy. Interestingly, the author notes that not only the discussions, but the processes of their archiving facilitated negotiations and cooperation between programmers and pioneer users and within the programing community. Indeed, those processes helped to clarify and make explicit the reconfigurations and re-appropriations of innovation, and contributed to the emergence of the spatial and temporal practical dimensions of innovation (Latzko-Toth, 2010).

As noted previously (Schafer et al., 2016: 13), sufficiently 'malleable to adapt itself to the local needs and constraints of its different user-types', capable of existing in different social worlds, all the while satisfying the 'informational needs' of each, and being sufficiently robust to maintain a common identity throughout these adaptations (Star and Griesemer, 1989), born-digital heritage carries within itself the challenges of its maintenance, memory, but also of its governance, as we explore in the second part of this chapter.

The prism of boundary objects can be used to investigate several 'objects' in Web history – such as the protocols and formats that have contributed to make the Web what it is today, or the animated images GIFs. Indeed, taking the issue of formats and particularly of blogs, Ignacio Siles proposes an STS entry into Web history via the notion of closure (Siles, 2011). He observes that practitioners largely consider that weblogs merged other types of sites (diaries, journals) only after 1999 as a result of the emergence of automated blogging software, considered as a defining moment in the early history of blogs. However, Siles remarks, this particular account of the history of blogs neglects other factors that STS perspectives can help to unveil. Examples of this are the conditions under which this Web 'format' emerged and how it has merged with other practices and technologies, as well as the 'shaping' role of relevant social groups of Web users (diarists, personal publishers), and more broadly the agency of users at large in appropriating both the technical and content dimensions of these sites, which paralleled the development of the software itself. Thus, the author argues:

> [b]ecause it involved interactions between several groups of users around a technology and the partial stabilization of its meaning, this case can be conceptualized as an instance of early 'closure' (Pinch and Bijker, 1987) [, referring to] the process through which 'artifacts appear to have fewer problems and become increasingly the dominant form of the technology' (Kline and Pinch, 1996: 766). Stabilization thus designates the process through which technologies acquire material form and meaning. (Siles, 2011: 738–739)

As for blog formats, the history of the Web provides myriad examples of processes and practices that contribute to attach meaning to artifacts, of different actors' engagement in the material appropriation of such artifacts, and of their social and technical 'stabilization' via ongoing processes of shaping and reshaping. Web history is about the mutual shaping of content and artifacts, developers and users; STS concepts contribute to shed light on the mundane and taken-for-granted practices and discourses that constitute the design, regulation and maintenance of the Web, a system whose crucial importance in our lives today was shaped by its early days in the nineties. Ultimately, these approaches speak to, and unpack, more 'macro' issues of politics, power and governance, which will be the subject of the next section.

## WEB GOVERNANCE HISTORY THROUGH 'A STS LENS'

This mutual shaping between artifacts and contents calls for a long-term understanding of the history of the Web and of the shaping of knowledge infrastructures. It also invites us, following Philip Agre, to explore the relation between technical architectures and institutions, particularly the difference between 'architecture as politics' and 'architecture as a substitute for politics' (Agre, 2003), an argument that is, of course, closely linked to Lawrence Lessig's famous motto 'code is law' and its offspring. Agre argues that technology often comes to us 'wrapped in histories about politics', which raises the issue of Web governance.

The notion of Internet governance – since its first widely consensual definition elaborated at the World Summit on the Information Society in Geneva, 2003, and Tunis, 2005 – has led to a number of recent studies seeking to merge it with STS perspectives (e.g. DeNardis, 2014; Epstein et al., 2016). In 2005, the Working Group on Internet Governance defined Internet governance as 'the development and application by Governments, the private sector and civil society, in their respective roles, of shared principles, norms, rules, decision-making procedures, and programmes that shape the evolution and use of the Internet', adding that 'it also includes other significant public policy issues, such as critical Internet resources, the security and safety of the Internet, and developmental aspects and issues pertaining to the use of the Internet'.

This definition is centered on the Internet, not specifically on the Web; furthermore, Web governance has led to a far more limited number of studies that explicitly place this notion at their heart. However, we argue that said definition is relevant for Web governance as well, and can be usefully explored via STS tools, as we will show in the remainder of this section via three cases that speak to three levels of the Web and of its history: the 'institutional' governance of the Web as expressed in a wide standardization body such as the W3C; the governance of a Web 'system' – as speaking of a mere 'website' may now be too reductive – i.e. the foremost online encyclopedia, Wikipedia; and, finally, that of Web archiving, which has in several respects reproduced and prolonged a number of critical issues in Internet governance.

### *From CERN to the W3C*

As previously showed, STS approaches are strongly linked to the sociology of translation, and influenced by the actor–network theory (ANT) (Callon, 1986; Latour, 1987; Law, 1992). By proposing an analysis of the very 'practical' ways in which humans and non-humans connect and stabilize, ANT allows an articulate understanding of the interactions leading to the hybrid and unstable associations of 'the technical', 'the political', 'society' and 'organizations', and their temporary stabilizations due to 'translations'. Giving center stage to technical objects in the making, to processes, to the unstable and the transient, ANT considers that the keys to understanding innovation and its politics are the process, the movement and the negotiation, rather than the object or the artifact themselves at any given moment. This framework proves useful to analyze arenas of Internet governance that are, indeed, places of constant and articulate negotiation – such as the World Wide Web Consortium (W3C) – but it also allows us to re-instate the actors of Web history in its socio-technical complexity, showing how the unfolding of this history is most often about alliances and consultations with an increasing number of stakeholders.

The historian can produce an ex post socio-technical analysis of the ways in which choices were made. However, actors have at times taken upon themselves, often in very empirical ways, to undertake a situated socio-technical analysis. As John Law noted, actors become 'heterogeneous engineers', able to understand and support the organization of actors and objects – humans and non-humans (Law, 1987). The success of innovation, in this vision, partly relies on innovators' capacity to interest and enroll other actors around their vision of innovation and their way of articulating it (Callon, 1986).

This approach helps redefine the emergence of the Web, since the work of Tim Berners-Lee and Robert Cailliau, in a specific manner. The emergence of the W3C, further detailed by the 'Web History in Context' chapter in this *Handbook*, can indeed be read according to this particular angle. Let us recall, for example, Tim Berners-Lee's decision to ask CERN to place his invention in the public domain and his preference for open innovation with equally open structures of governance (Berners-Lee, 2000). At the request of Tim Berners-Lee, CERN agreed to allow free use of Web protocols. The next year, the first international World Wide Web Conference was held at CERN, and the MIT Laboratory for Computer Science (LCS, now CSAIL) became the first host of the World Wide Web Consortium (W3C). In his introduction to *Weaving the Web*, the head of MIT-LCS, Michael L. Dertouzos, notes that 'As technologists and entrepreneurs were launching or merging companies to exploit the Web, they seemed fixated on one question: "How can I make the Web mine?". Meanwhile, Tim Berners-Lee was asking "How can I make the Web yours?"' (Berners-Lee, 2000: viii); indeed, this citation seems to emphasize Berners-Lee's capacity to 'enroll' around open protocols. Similarly, the establishment of the W3C, and the decision to base it in three locations, in the United States, in Europe (Griset and Schafer, 2011) and finally at Keio in Japan, further sustains this argument – this capacity of enrollment and translation that originated with Berners-Lee's newsgroups announcement of the WWW in 1991.

Other examples in Web history provide us with the needed opportunity to study the negotiations that took place within the W3C, but also among actors of a governance that was soon made broader, including, in particular, organized civil society. Janet Abbate (2012: 174–5) demonstrates this with clarity when she describes the controversy that took place at the end of the nineties between the W3C and American activists for civil liberties, on the content filtering system called Platform for Internet Content Selection (PICS). Tim Berners-Lee argued that PICS was a mere tool that allowed users to choose their preferred content, and that Web developers were inspired by 'a vision of the way in which society needed to be improved [as] nowadays the social can evolve thanks to technology, while earlier on, the only way was to produce laws' (Harmon, 1998, quoted in Abbate, 2012: 174, our translation). However, civil liberties activists were worried about the power of technologists, summarized under Lessig's formula 'Code is Law' in 1999, a year after *The New York Times* had dedicated time and space to PICS. As Abbate shows, the PICS system was never widely spread to the general public, and it was replaced ten years or so later by a new filtering system, this time at the service of advertisers seeking to target consumers. Yet it serves as an illustration of Web governance as a complex socio-technical system of systems and it invites an analysis of the plurality and 'networkedness' of hybrid devices and arrangements that populate, shape and define the Web (Musiani, 2015).

Other work is reminiscent of this approach, whether it touches upon the general history of the Web and its governance or more precise aspects, for example on the relation we establish to information via search engines. In this regard, Badouard et al. (2014) note that a large majority of links is the prerogative of a small number of websites, and the majority of sites are targeted by only a very small number of links. The authors conclude that this phenomenon implies a specific relation between users and information, which translates, in particular, into a daily imbalance in the agendas of online media, between a minority of over-exposed current news and a majority of confidential subjects. This approach invites historical studies of hyperlinks, such as those of Ian Milligan (2014) and Anne Helmond (2013) – and shows the interest in making these studies STS-informed and revealing of these imbalances and their evolutions.

Similarly, current research on Web tracking appears to fuel both media studies and STS, looking at Web history as an ongoing, technical and human negotiation and hybridization. Lerner et al. (2016) used the tool TrackingExcavator to conduct the most extensive longitudinal study of the third-party web tracking ecosystem to date, retrospectively from 1996 to the present; they argue that:

> understanding the trends in the web tracking ecosystem over time – provided for the first time at this scale by our work – is important to future discussions surrounding web tracking, both technical and political. Beyond web tracking, there are many questions about the history and evolution of the web (Lerner et al., 2016).

This study, as those previously mentioned, will certainly contribute toward shedding further light onto the performative function of Web arrangements and the invisibility, pervasiveness and agency of infrastructure that shape the Web. The next section examines how these phenomena can be analyzed at the scale of a single website, such as Wikipedia.

## From Wikipedia Governance to Algorithmic Governmentality

Pierre-Carl Langlais' work (2015) on the emergence of a Wikipedian normativity during the 2000s suggests governance issues can be understood and analyzed via STS tools. Langlais builds his work on Dominique Cardon and Julien Levrel's (2009) framework analyzing 'participatory vigilance' – a notion developed through their interest in the mechanisms of norm integration in the francophone Wikipedia. He remarks that, until the end of 2003, the issue of references was not present in the foremost online encyclopedia. Indeed, the processes of modification and discussion were prevalent before the situation evolved in the mid 2000s. The 2004 recommendation 'cite your sources' is arguably born out of the important augmentation in readership, increasing tensions, and multiple 'editing wars'. Analyzing the process through which a norm is imposed – which entails heavy discussions on the initial obligation it signifies – Langlais explains:

> In early 2007, the normative exigence of reference citation has reached its maturity [...] Actually, all is left to do. Non-referenced contributions keep on coming [...] Created in January 2007, the References Project initially gathers fifteen or so contributors. The emphasis is placed on the evangelization of the community [...] Several practical tools are created to facilitate this evangelization process, including a number of banners signaling the lack or the necessity of a reference. Parallel to this external diffusion work, the References Project promoters develop an important clarification work. The first discussions center on suggestions of tools, and on proposals of rules to adopt. This strong coalescence of the technical sublayer and human organization appears as consubstantial of the wiki system. (2015: 85–6, our translation)

Prominent Internet historian Janet Abbate (2012: 171) argues that since its early stages, the network of networks has been about the merging of infrastructure and culture, which has constituted hybrid agencies, complex interactions between machine- and human-originated agencies in the creation of content and the elaboration of communication practices (*ibid.*: 176). In this light, we can conceive of Wikipedia as a nexus between technical and human infrastructures, and examine the ways in which contributions and collective, individual behaviors and tools intersect, the different layers of human and technical agency at work. Indeed, increasingly often, robots are undertaking correction and signaling tasks, and the Recent Change patrol, looking for vandalism episodes, benefits from a number of automatic tools to supervise new modifications. As Dominique Cardon emphasizes: 'The epistemic rationale guiding a large majority of behaviors on Wikipedia must not be looked for in people, nor in the interface, but in the mutual adjustments allowing people to interact on the wiki' (2015: 19, our translation).

The example of Wikipedia shows how digital environments raise multiple questions on how much autonomy users have, when faced with automatized decision-making. More broadly, architectures, programs, computer codes, algorithms, interfaces and recommendation systems influence and co-shape the possible choices and decision-making capacities of users. In which ways do digital environments introduce visible or invisible elements that are susceptible to influencing participation and decision? Indeed, Web history would greatly benefit from a diachronic study of environments, platforms and Web architectures exploring the evolutions that took place via a strong integration of hardware and software, of material and informational infrastructures, from the DIY of the nineties to the development of Content Management Systems (see, in this volume, the 'Web History in Context' chapter).

Code, software, bots or hardware are no longer conceived as 'mere' technical devices but as actors themselves, and the result of human decisions at once – in short, as socio-technical constructions. In this view, an analytical examination of the place of robots, of interfaces, of algorithms or infrastructures (Musiani and Schafer, 2011; Star, 1999) is no longer an 'internalist' approach consisting in the exploration of 'black boxes' and an 'already-made' assessment of technology's capacity to constrain human decision. Instead, it becomes the analysis of a social, political, technical and economic co-construction, to be conducted all along the digital 'chain', from developers to users, exploring technical architectures, upper and lower layers, design, applications, aggregation techniques and algorithms (Barocas et al., 2013; Rieder, 2012), and platforms (Gillespie, 2010).

In this regard, the notion of governmentality seems appropriate as the cornerstone of a theoretical framework that enables us to think of the ways in which technical devices tend to co-structure the range of possible actions (Foucault, 2004). Within the more specific field of digital technologies, the notion of 'algorithmic governmentality' (Rouvroy and Berns, 2013) invites us to think how the digital 'makes' Internet users do things, and simultaneously, highlights its empowering dimension. In digital environments, different possibilities and multiple constraints merge and simultaneously express themselves in the development of action (Badouard et al., 2016). This fusion of what is possible and what constrains can also be found in the constant negotiations taking place in the field of Web archiving and, in the historian's eyes, introduce further arenas of 'mediation' within the Web of the past.

## *Web Archiving as a Microcosm of Internet Governance*

In 1980, Langdon Winner's seminal paper asked: 'Do artefacts have politics?' By 'politics', Winner meant the 'arrangements of power and authority in human associations as well as the activities that take place within those arrangements' (Winner, 1980: 123). Applying this hypothesis to the study of Web archiving means to study how its distributed, diffused and technology-embedded nature (DeNardis, 2014: 8) 'can embody specific forms of power and authority'. Observing infrastructures, Web archives' design and their stakeholders' 'coming together' entails looking into the scripts (Akrich, 1992) that perform role-sharing, the distribution of competencies and some delegation of rule enforcement to algorithms and automated devices. As noted by Star (1999: 337–9): '[...] Study an information system and neglect its standards, wires, and settings, and you miss equally essential aspects of aesthetics, justice, and change'.

This 'relational' approach entails important changes in methods, as STS-informed fieldwork can go as far as including the arenas where the shaping of infrastructures and architectures are observed, deconstructed and reconstructed. Arenas where political decisions – explicitly so, or *de facto* – are taken concerning the code, the technical norms, the 'tinkering' and reconfigurations of technical objects (Star and Bowker, 2006: 151–2). In recent work (Schafer et al., 2016) we have set out to apply this perspective to the study of Web archiving, thus seeking to respond to Tim Hitchcock's interrogation:

> Where I end up is seriously jealous of the possibilities; and seriously wondering what the 'object of study' might be. In the nature of an archive, the UK Web Archive imagines itself as an 'object of study'; created in the service of an imaginary scholar. The question it raises is how do we turn something we really can't understand, cannot really capture as an object of study, to serious purpose? How do we think at one and the same time of the web as alive and dead, as code, text, and image – all in dynamic conversation one with the other. And even if we can hold all that at once, what is it we are asking? (Hitchcock, 2015)

By opening the black boxes of Web archiving (Musiani and Schafer, 2015) and by observing the processes through which the Web of the past is 'negotiated' in several arenas of formal and informal governance today (Schafer et al., 2016), we have been able to demonstrate how Web archiving, as several other arenas in the past and the current Internet, relies upon a multi-stakeholder model of governance.

Indeed, the dialectic between different practices and sources of normativity – concurring or complementary – that can be found in Internet governance may as well be found in Web archiving. The initial 'anarchistic' and flamboyant elements of the early Internet, for example, meet their match in the Archive Team's ironic motto ('We are going to rescue your shit!'), which has indeed opened up the way to some iconic rescues, such as Geocities from the shutdown by Yahoo!. Twitter and Facebook's collection and capture of private data for archiving purposes is a testament to the component of Web archiving governance that is dependent upon the role of the private sector. National and international institutions occupy a central role, as illustrated by projects such as the French legal deposit and by entities such as the UNESCO chart on Digital heritage in 2003, the Internet Archive and the International Internet Preservation Consortium (IIPC) – with nuances ranging from the 'international' as the sum of national initiatives, to the 'transnational' approaches. Finally, the role of standardization bodies and technical discussions that occupy such a prominent place in Internet governance, like the W3C and the IETF, can also be found in Web archiving with the IIPC meetings.

We have also shown how the notion of co-construction has found its way into Web archiving, where the main categories of Internet governance actors may be found – as well as their tensions. It is the case, for example, of controversies between the common good and proprietary formats, and between different imaginaries of the Internet and the Web. In this regard, the missions established by, or delegated to, Web archiving organizations are interesting to observe, as are the geopolitical and political tensions that contribute to shaping and reshaping them. Brewster Kahle's September 2014 and November 2016 appeals, respectively (Kahle, 2014, 2016), show how a reflection on the perimeter and mission of his project took place when he raised public attention to China's blocking of the Internet Archive:

> China started blocking the Internet Archive again a couple of months ago, we believe, because they do not like our open access policies. In this way, we have started to understand the power in the hands of the Internet service providers. Let's keep our access to Internet sites 'Neutral' and not at the discretion of companies and governments. (Kahle, 2014)

And when he appealed for funding to create a complete copy of the Archive's digital collections in Canada after the November 2016 elections in the United States:

> We are building the Internet Archive of Canada because, to quote our friends at LOCKSS, 'lots of copies keep stuff safe.' [...] On November 9th in America, we woke up to a new administration promising radical change. [...] It means preparing for a Web that may face greater restrictions. (Kahle, 2016)

As shown in Schafer et al. (2016), Web archiving reactivates the same polarizations, negotiations and dynamics between actors which had emerged at the time of Internet governance's birth – and it mirrors the fact that the present-day digital world is still developing unevenly.

## CONCLUSION

This chapter has made an argument for – and illustrated by means of several examples – the suitability and usefulness of an STS-informed perspective on the history of the Web and Web archives. We have looked back to the first 'encounters' between STS and ICTs, and then, with the Internet in particular, and with other disciplines that have sought to investigate the 'media' potential of such tools, the chapter has come to examine how STS concepts, in particular that of boundary object in its multiple facets, may be of use in shedding light on Web history and, in particular, on its governance.

Indeed, as the second part of this chapter has shown, 'tackling the macro questions of politics and power related to IG requires unpacking the micro practices of governance as mechanisms of distributed, semi-formal or reflexive coordination, private ordering, and use of internet resources' (Epstein et al., 2016). STS can shed light on how, in the wide and vast march of history producing seemingly stable arrangements, small 'histories' of taken-for-granted, mundane activities of design and use contribute to *doing and making* the Web and its governance.

Incorporating into the analysis of Web history(ies) the intertwining of technical and political governance, the ever-changing games of alliances and power balances between very different actors, the visions, imaginaries and social worlds they each bring to the table, the agency of non-human actors and infrastructures as loci of mediation… these STS sensibilities enable us to connect the micro actions of individuals and the affordance of particular technical artifacts with emergent attributes of large, complex systems (*ibid.*, 2016). As such, they add another layer of understanding and appreciation of how the Web of our (recent) past was negotiated – and still is.

## *Acknowledgments*

This study has been carried out within the framework of the Web90 project supported by the French National Research Agency (ANR-14-CE29-0012-01).

## REFERENCES

Abbate, J. (2012) 'L'histoire de l'Internet au prisme des STS', *Le Temps des Médias*, 18: 170–80.

Agre, P. (2003) 'Peer-to-peer and the promise of Internet equality', *Communications of the ACM*, 46(2): 39–42.

Akrich, M. (1992) 'The de-scription of technical objects', in Bijker, Wiebe & Law, John (eds.), *Shaping Technology/Building Society. Studies in Sociotechnical Change*. Cambridge, MA: The MIT Press, pp. 205–24.

Appel, V., Boulanger, H. and Massou, L. (eds., 2010) *Les Dispositifs d'Information et de Communication. Concepts, Usages et Objets*. Bruxelles: De Boeck.

Badouard, R., Mabi, C. and Sire, G. (2014) 'Numérique et gouvernementalité. Les technologies entre possibles et contraintes', *SFSIC Annual Conference 2014*, https://sfsic2014.sciencesconf.org/30651/document

Badouard, R., Mabi, C., Mattozzi, A., Schubert, C., Sire, G. and Sørensen, E. (2016) 'STS and media studies: Alternative paths in different countries', *Tecnoscienza*, 7(1): 109–28.

Balbi, G., Delfanti, A. and Magaudda, P. (2016) 'Digital circulation: Media, materiality, infrastructures. An introduction', *Tecnoscienza*, 7(1): 7–16.

Barocas, S., Hood, S. and Ziewitz, M. (2013) 'Governing Algorithms: A Provocation Piece', *Discussion Paper for the Governing Algorithms conference*, NYU, May 16–7, 2013, http://ssrn.com/abstract=2245322

Berners-Lee, T. (2000) *Weaving the Web*. New York: Harper-Business.

Boczkowski, P. and Lievrouw, L. (2007) 'Bridging STS and communication studies: Scholarship on media and information technologies', in Hackett, Edward, Amsterdamska, Olga, Lynch, Michael and Wajcman, Judy (eds.), *The Handbook of Science and Technology Studies, third edition*. Cambridge, MA: The MIT Press, pp. 949–77.

Callon, M. (1986) 'Some elements of a sociology of translation: Domestication of the scallops and the fishermen of St Brieuc Bay', in Law, John (ed.), *Power, Action and Belief: A New Sociology of Knowledge?* London: Routledge, pp. 196–223.

Cardon, D. (2015) 'Surveiller sans punir', in Barbe, Lionel, Merzeau, Louise and Schafer, Valérie (eds.), *Wikipedia, Objet Scientifique non Identifié*. Nanterre: Presses Universitaires de Paris Ouest, pp. 15–39.

Cardon, D. and Levrel, J. (2009) 'La vigilance participative. Une interprétation de la gouvernance de Wikipédia', *Réseaux*, 2(154): 51–89.

de Fornel, M. (1994) 'Le cadre interactionnel de l'échange visiophonique', *Réseaux*, 64: 107–32.

DeNardis, L. (2014) *The Global War for Internet Governance*. New Haven: Yale University Press.

Epstein, D., Katzenbach, C. and Musiani, F. (2016) 'Doing internet governance: Practices, controversies, infrastructures, and institutions', *Internet Policy Review*, 5(3): DOI: 10.14763/2016.3.435

Foucault, M. (2004) *Sécurité, Territoire, Population, Cours au Collège de France 1977–1978*. Paris: Seuil.

Gillespie, T. (2010) 'The politics of "platforms"', *New Media & Society*, 12(3): 347–64.

Gillespie, T., Boczkowski, P. and Foot, K. (eds., 2014) *Media Technologies: Essays on Communication, Materiality and Society*. Cambridge, MA: The MIT Press.

Gitelman, L. (ed., 2013) *Raw Data is an Oxymoron*. Cambridge, MA: The MIT Press.

Griset, P. and Schafer, V. (2011) 'Hosting the World Wide Web Consortium for Europe: From CERN to INRIA', *History and Technology*, 27(3): 353–70.

Harmon, A. (19 January 1998) 'Technology to Let Engineers Filter the Web and Judge Content', *The New York Times*.

Helmond, A. (2013) 'The algorithmization of the hyperlink', *Computational Culture*. http://computationalculture.net/article/the-algorithmization-of-the-hyperlink

Hitchcock, T. (2015) 'The UK Web archive, born-digital sources, and rethinking the future of research', *Web Archives for Historians* blog, http://webarchivehistorians.org/tag/tim-hitchcock/

Hondros, J. (ed., 2015) 'The Internet and the material turn. Special issue', *Westminster Papers in Communication and Culture*, 10(1): http://www.westminsterpapers.org/27/volume/10/issue/1/

Kahle, B. (2014) 'Please Help Protect Net Neutrality', *Internet Archive Blog*, https://blog.archive.org/2014/09/10/please-help-protect-net-neutrality/

Kahle, B. (2016) 'Help Us Keep the Archive Free, Accessible, and Reader Private', *Internet Archive Blog*, https://blog.archive.org/2016/11/29/help-us-keep-the-archive-free-accessible-and-private/

Kline, R. and Pinch, T. (1996) 'Users as agents of technological change: The social construction of the automobile in the rural United States', *Technology and Culture*, 37(4): 763–95.

Langlais, P.-C. (2015) '{{Référence nécessaire}} L'émergence d'une norme wikipédienne (2003–2009)', in Barbe, Lionel, Merzeau, Louise and Schafer, Valérie (eds.), *Wikipedia, Objet Scientifique non Identifié*. Nanterre: Presses Universitaires de Paris Ouest, pp. 77–90, http://books.openedition.org/pupo/4106

Latour, B. (1987) *Science in Action: How to Follow Scientists and Engineers Through Society*. Cambridge, MA: Harvard University Press.

Latzko-Toth, G. (2010) *La co-construction d'un dispositif socio-technique de communication: Le cas de l'Internet Relay Chat*. PhD dissertation, Université du Québec à Montréal.

Law, J. (1987) 'Technology and heterogeneous engineering: The case of Portuguese expansion', in Bijker, Wiebe E., Hughes, Thomas P. and Pinch, Trevor (eds.), *The Social Construction of Technological Systems. New Directions in the Sociology and History of Technology*. Cambridge, MA: The MIT Press, pp. 111–34.

Law, J. (1992) 'Notes on the theory of actor-network: Ordering, strategy and heterogeneity', *Systems Practice*, 5(4): 379–93.

Lerner, A., Kornfeld Simpson, A., Kohno, T. and Roesner, F. (2016) 'Internet Jones and the Raiders of the Lost Trackers: An Archaeological Study of Web Tracking from 1996 to 2016', *Proceedings of the 25th USENIX Security Symposium (USENIX Security 16)*, August 2016, https://trackingexcavator.cs.washington.edu/InternetJonesAndTheRaidersOfTheLostTrackers.pdf

Lievrouw, L.A. (2014) 'Materiality and media in communication and technology studies: An unfinished project', in Gillespie, Tarleton, Boczkowski, Pablo and Foot, Kirsten (eds.), *Media Technologies: Essays on Communication, Materiality and Society*. Cambridge: The MIT Press, pp. 21–52.

Malcolm, J. (2008) *Multi-Stakeholder Governance and the Internet Governance Forum*. Wembley, WA: Terminus Press.

Marres, N. and Gerlitz, C. (2015) 'Interface methods: Renegotiating relations between digital social research, STS and sociology', *The Sociological Review*, 64(1): 21–46.

Milligan, I. (2014) 'Extracting links from Geocities and throwing them at the wall', Blog *Digital History, Web Archives, and Contemporary History*, https://ianmilligan.ca/2014/07/23/extracting-links-from-geocities-and-throwing-them-at-the-wall/

Muniesa, F., Millo, Y. and Callon, M. (2007) 'An introduction to market devices', *Sociological Review*, 55(2): 1–12.

Musiani, F. (2015) 'Practice, plurality, performativity and plumbing: Internet governance research meets science and technology studies', *Science, Technology and Human Values*, 40(2): 272–86.

Musiani, F. and Schafer, V. (2011) 'Le modèle Internet en question (années 1970–2010)', *Flux*, 85–86(3–4): 62–71.

Musiani, F. and Schafer, V. (2015) 'Opening the Black Box of Web Archiving: STS Approaches and the Governance of Born-Digital Heritage', First RESAW Symposium, *Web Archives as Scholarly Sources: Issues, Practices, Perspectives*, June 8–10, 2015.

Oudshoorn, N. and Pinch, T. (eds., 2003) *How Users Matter. The Co-Construction of Users and Technologies.* Cambridge, MA: The MIT Press.

Paloque-Berges, C. (2017) 'Vers des lieux de mémoire réticulaires? Construire un patrimoine de la communication des sciences et des techniques du numérique', *RESET*, 6, http://reset.revues.org/839

Parikka, J. (2012) *What is Media Archaeology?* Cambridge: Polity Press.

Pinch, T.J. and Bijker, W.E. (1987) 'The social construction of facts and artifacts', in Bijker, Wiebe E., Hughes, Thomas P. and Pinch, Trevor (eds.), *The Social Construction of Technological Systems. New Directions in the Sociology and History of Technology.* Cambridge, MA: The MIT Press, pp. 17–50.

Proulx, S. (2009) 'L'intelligence du grand nombre: La puissance d'agir des contributeurs sur Internet – limites et possibilités', *7ème colloque du chapitre français de l'ISKO, Intelligence collective et organisation des connaissances*, Lyon, 24–26 juin 2009. http://pro.ovh.net/~iskofran/pdf/isko2009/PROULX.pdf

Rieder, B. (2012) 'What is in PageRank? A historical and conceptual investigation of a recursive status index', *Computational Culture*, (2).

Rouvroy, A. and Berns, T. (2013) 'Gouvernementalité algorithmique et perspectives d'émancipation', *Réseaux*, 177(1): 163–96.

Schafer, V., Musiani, F. and Borelli, M. (2016) 'Negotiating the Web of the past. Web archiving, STS and governance', *French Journal for Media Research*, 6, http://frenchjournalformediaresearch.com/lodel/index.php?id=952

Siles, I. (2011) 'From online filter to web format: Articulating materiality and meaning in the early history of blogs', *Social Studies of Science*, 41(5): 737–58.

Star, S.L. (1999) 'The ethnography of infrastructure', *American Behavioral Scientist*, 43(3): 377–91.

Star, S. L. (2010) 'This is not a boundary object: Reflections on the origin of a concept', *Science, Technology & Human Values*, 35(5): 601–17.

Star, S.L. and Bowker, G. (2006) 'How to Infrastructure', in Lievrouw, Leah A. (ed.), *Handbook of New Media*. London: Sage, pp. 151–62.

Star, S.L. and Griesemer, J. (1989) 'Institutional ecology, "translations" and boundary objects: Amateurs and professionals in Berkeley's Museum of Vertebrate Zoology, 1907–39', *Social Studies of Science*, 19(3): 387–420.

Trompette, P. and Vinck, D. (eds., 2009) 'Retour sur la notion d'objet-frontière', *Revue d'Anthropologie des Connaissances*, 3(1): 5–27.

Wellman, B. (2004) 'The three ages of Internet studies: Ten, five and zero years ago', *New Media & Society*, 6(1): 123–9.

Winner, L. (1980) 'Do artifacts have politics?', *Daedalus*, 109(1): 121–36.

# Theorizing the Uses of the Web

Ralph Schroeder

## INTRODUCTION

The web has been with us for more than a quarter century. It has clearly become a major medium, but it is equally clear that how the web is used does not fit existing theories of mass or interpersonal media. Apart from media and communication studies, the main discipline that might be expected to provide insights into the web is information science. But information science has a rather limited perspective on the web, and hardly deals with how people seek information in everyday life. This chapter will discuss various approaches to how the web is used and point the way forward by developing a theoretical framework. It may seem futile to try to fit the uses of the web into an overarching framework since they are rapidly changing, but a case can also be made for the opposite view: that we can only understand the social implications of the web if we start to pin down how the web fits into people's overall information and communication uses. And, in the context of this *Handbook*, unless we know how the web is used, it is difficult to understand other questions about the web, such as how the web should be archived, or how we should think about its history, or tackle various policy questions.

This chapter will give an overview of various perspectives on web uses which can be seen as elements that need to come together for an overall framework for understanding their implications. It will begin by discussing various disciplinary approaches to the web. Next, it will review what is known about everyday information practices related to the web. In the following section, we can take the concrete example of Wikipedia, one of the most well-known and important sources of online information. At that point, we can turn the shape of the web, its scale, scope, and interconnectedness. Finally, against this background, it will be possible to examine the web as a new information infrastructure. The conclusion can then point to the implications of the framework that has been developed, for policy, ethics, and future web scholarship.

## DISCIPLINARITY

The reason why people's information-seeking behaviours are poorly understood is partly due to the legacies of disciplinary specialization. Media and communication scholars have studied email and more recently social media, but they are only beginning to study the web as such. Information scientists have been mainly interested in how researchers and students seek information, but not the population-at-large. And political communication researchers have been concerned with whether digital media democratize or enable greater control – but less so with how people seek political information. The web also has features which set it apart from other media: for example, user-generated content is a major portion of web content, but where does it fit into theories of traditional mass or interpersonal media?

Information seeking has so far been poorly theorized in the social sciences (Sonnenwald, 2016) and there has been scant research on the role of information seeking in everyday life (Rieh, 2004; Savolainen, 2008; Aspray and Hayes, 2011). Information can be defined as codified accounts that can answer questions such as 'who', 'what', 'where', and 'why'; or, as a cognitive input that makes a difference to the person's relation to the physical and social environment (a 'cybernetic' definition; see Gleick, 2011). This sets information apart from the more complex 'knowledge', which can be seen as the more analytical processing or organization of information on one side (Stehr, 1994; Meyer and Schroeder, 2015 for scientific knowledge) and the simpler or raw 'data' (Schroeder, 2016) on the other. Information can also be distinguished from communication: information is one way, communication two way – whether one-to-one (interpersonal) or one-to-many (mass). This also makes it possible to distinguish the web from other sources; the web is primarily a one-way online source of information. One complication is that the web allows sharing, via sending links, for example (for sharing news, see Kümpel et al., 2015). Still, these are first sought – and then shared or communicated. There are other complications and clarifications to be discussed below, but the idea of 'seeking' information – one way – will do for now.

The problem that information seeking falls between disciplines will only become more acute over time since, increasingly, most forms of accessing any content, including the consumption of news and entertainment, will take place online. However, it may become necessary to distinguish between when people go online to actively seek information as opposed to when they passively consume the pre-packaged sources of news and entertainment with which they are provided in mass media. Another distinction that can be made is between serious and non-serious information, a distinction that can be found (though it is not developed) in Savolainen (2008). Serious information relates to needs, or the practical means to develop one's capabilities (Sen, 2009), as opposed to wants, which are not required for capabilities but rather for leisure or consumption.

There is a further requirement, related to individuals' access to and ability to use serious information, which needs to be part of a theory of information, which is that information (like other media) must be reliable, open, and diverse. If it is not, information could be misleading, asymmetric in terms of access (because of paywalls and the like), and skewed towards being dominated by certain groups. Yet as long as there is such a rich and inclusive environment, the need for serious information can be met, which will also enable social scientists to identify the types of information that are central to social change and which types are less so (and in the latter case, more a matter of documentation or academic specialisms rather than part of the role of the web and other media as integral to social transformation). Clearly, identifying information use that is integral to social change in this way is a contentious issue. Yet making such distinctions is part of any social science of media, just as it is a (somewhat different) task for historians, including historians of the web or those who use the web as a resource for analysing history.

To analyse information seeking on the web, a number of disciplines – media and communications, sociology, information science, and some areas within computer science – can be drawn upon, but there is no single discipline which has done so in a unified way to date. Search engine companies and marketing companies, of course, have lots of knowledge about 'user behaviour' in information seeking, though this knowledge hardly finds its way into academia. Yet the main purpose of their knowledge of user behaviour is to tailor information more precisely to certain users or groups and to target them, which can be seen as a more powerful or refined form of mass communication. Still, there are some emerging areas of research, Web Studies (Brügger, 2012) and Web Science (a computer science, ACM, conference, see http://www.websci16.org/) that will be helpful. However, these will need to be connected to established social science disciplines and to long-standing social science debates since social scientists are interested in what information people actually routinely search for.

On this topic, there is as yet little research, though Hektor (2001) undertook a pioneering study even before the web was widely used, examining mostly offline sources. Yet Hektor's study also points to how little is known about information uses from another perspective, because what he examined, via an in-depth study of Swedes' daily information uses, is how they sought information from various sources, such as libraries, bus timetables, printed encyclopaedias, recipe books, noticeboards, other people (in person), and the media. What this highlights is that the sources of information before the web were not studied as such (but see Aspray and Hayes, 2011); instead 'the media' were studied and other (offline) sources of information fell into various other disciplinary niches without being theorized as part of the information infrastructure of society as seen from an everyday user perspective.

One potential objection to treating the web separately must be confronted: why treat the online separately from offline, and why separate the web when it encompasses so much online material yet overlaps with many internet uses such as sharing links in emails, using apps, and much more? One reason is that the boundaries of content are themselves changing: news, for example, could formerly be restricted to traditional print and television and (often) primarily national news sources, but blogs and YouTube videos and many other sources can now also be regarded as news, and they often transcend borders. And even where audiences for content are still mainly defined by nationality and language, perhaps the most interesting new forms of accessing information are cross-border (for example, diasporas) or across language (as when people use tools like Google Translate). The same applies to other categories of content such as advertising, educational videos, and blogs. It makes little sense to examine only a narrow slice of online content when people often browse and stumble upon unexpected sources across boundaries. And while web uses are comparable to offline and other online sources, it is clearly also a separable entity, and information seeking on the web a separable activity.

There is a final point about disciplinarity that must be mentioned here: there is the emerging specialist discipline of studying the history of the internet and the web. That is the backdrop to – but not the focus of – this chapter. Instead, the focus here is: what do the uses of the web, in everyday life and for seeking information (though 'seeking', as we shall see, is a subset of 'uses'), tell us about how our media habits (again, media = communication + information) are changing? In other words, what place do web uses and information have in the social science of media? The major part of this change is that the web has added information uses to communication uses, making information seeking a much greater part of everyday life. If this argument is correct, then this analysis of web uses must inform web history: on the analogy with the history of newspapers, why study the history of newspapers – though that is also a separate enterprise – without also looking at the role of those who read them, and what role they played in society in general? Similarly, with the web: what role does it play as part of our uses and sources of information – in all media, or generally? How do the web's uses among other media vary? Which groups use this source among other sources? Without this context, any web history will be incomplete.

All this can be put differently: what kind of social science of media, with the web as one medium, does web history need? Web history may be concerned with lots of individual topics – the history of companies on the web, the history of fandom on the web, the history of literatures on the web, and many more. But a social science of media provides the most encompassing frame for all these (the uses of the web and other media), while also singling out or separating out the most important ones (serious uses), while more detailed uses are allocated their place for more specialist disciplinary treatments (by, say, business historians, cultural historians, literary historians, and the like). As will be readily apparent, this is partly a matter of the division between social science of the media and the various fields of history, which could be drawn differently. But there must be, for social science, a general impact of the web or way in which the web can be seen as resulting in social change, and understanding this impact or change, I would argue, is a precondition for doing web history, even if it does not determine or limit it.

## INFORMATION SEEKING IN EVERYDAY LIFE

Seeking online information is still changing, but it has also become so commonplace as to be invisible: we can think here of how often we, or anyone with internet access, 'googles' something every day. We can also think of the variety of questions that are 'googled': persons, places, schedules, brands, services, scientific and technological novelties, diseases, popular culture references, and much more. Or again, think of how often we say: 'what did we do before Google?' Social science has simply not caught up with how to make sense of the changes brought about by the web as a central and new part of our lives. It is in any event a departure from traditional media, which were, in terms of seeking information, constrained by their physical availability. Note that the perspective taken here is that the important aspect for understanding web uses is what people seek and do with the information – not with how it is produced. The structure of what is available and how this material is used is central to everyday life, and can be seen as an extension of society's media infrastructure (which will be discussed below). The question of how information is produced, even if the possibility of producing user-generated content has also become more widespread, is a separate one.

One approach in respect of what is new here might be to argue, as Castells does (2009), that the main change is 'self-selection', whereby people choose the online material that best fits their needs. Yet this approach overlooks that there are new gatekeepers even when information is chosen, as with search engines or social media feeds or other constraints on the visibility or accessibility of web pages. And people do not select information from a limitless set of possibilities; there are constraints to what they seek and find, dictated, among other things, by their digital literacy and their routines or habits, and also how these carry over from traditional media. However, it is true that, apart from these gatekeepers, some online resources both extend existing sources and are openly accessible, and so increase what can be 'selected'.

In any event, the web as an information source is distinct from the information sources of traditional mass and interpersonal media, but it also competes with other digital media for attention: for example, even if Wikipedia is often among the top results when using a search engine, there are many other online and offline sources that could be used (with and without the use of search engines). Further, online information sources are examples of content being pushed towards users in a targeted way, as when search results prioritize finding Wikipedia articles (or other information) for particular users because the search algorithm has been tailored towards specific users (Pariser, 2011). Finally, these new online sources add to and complement others, but media systems also shape them: in China, the Chinese-language version of Wikipedia has been blocked for certain periods, and a different online encyclopaedia, Baidu Baike, with content controlled by the company Baidu (one of the biggest in China), which is in turn influenced by the government, is dominant on the mainland (Liao, 2009).

A number of methods have been used to understand information behaviours, including interviews (Rieh, 2004; Savolainen, 2008) and focus groups (Hargittai et al., 2012). Focus groups are useful because they can elicit responses people may not be aware of in their own behaviours (information seeking is often of this nature, since people do not consider it a separate activity, even though researchers do). What Hargittai et al. (2012) found in their study of information seeking is that Americans did not think of themselves as overburdened by the flood of diverse types of information; in other words, there was no self-report of 'information overload'. What people found objectionable was the low quality and repetitive nature of this information – scandals, endless crime reports, and tabloid-type news. Tellingly, however, they nevertheless consumed this information in abundance.

A different approach is quantitative, and here the study of search engine use in Australia (Waller, 2011a) can be highlighted. This study was based on access to commercial data about users, both their search query keywords and demographic information about who searches for what. The study found that the vast bulk of content sought relates to consumer activity and popular culture. Less than 2% of search queries related to 'serious information' (recall the distinction made earlier between serious and non-serious information), such as civic, health, and political information. Yet this small percentage still amounts to millions of searches per day in a country with a relatively small population. Another surprising finding was that search queries hardly varied between socio-economic groups. In any event, the fact that such a small proportion of information is 'serious' also raises the question whether information 'seeking' is appropriate: most uses of the web are for leisure, 'surfing' the web, rather than looking for material. This difference is sometimes labelled 'directed' as against 'undirected' seeking, but speaking of 'seeking' as a subset of 'uses' may be more appropriate in the context of everyday life.

Another study, also by Waller (2013), provides a 'bottom-up' perspective, since a top-down or quantitative perspective misses how information is actually used. To be sure, online information may be reliable and available, but can people actually use it? Waller (2013) gives the example of an immigrant woman in urban Australia seeking information that she needed to obtain from the Red Cross. Because of her situation, she was unable to access any of the information she needed online. Instead, she had to make several arduous trips to find the relevant Red Cross office in person, and then wait in queues to be seen. This took her several days, information that a young person with the requisite educational and linguistic and digital skills would have found online in minutes! This is admittedly an extreme example, but it behoves researchers who have access to devices, online resources and skills, and with the ability to ask others in their networks – the most extreme 'information haves' – to think about people who have access neither to the devices or skills, nor to others who could help them, the 'information-have-less' or 'information-have-nots' (see Qiu, 2009).

It is also worth bringing to mind how access to appropriate – or again, serious – information is increasingly becoming a vital resource in all walks of life; not just access to, but the ability to find and use information, again, can be seen as a question of justice, essential to developing one's 'capabilities' (Sen, 2009).

The advantage of a bottom-up user perspective is that it can challenge conventional wisdom. One further example can suffice: it is often said that China's censorship is highly effective and that it is particularly aimed at preventing 'harm' by strictly and effectively censoring (among other things) pornographic materials. This may be true for some materials, but as Hockx (2015) has shown in his study of 'internet literature', it is also highly misleading. First, by way of context, he notes that around 40% of Chinese access online literature (a specific literary genre rather than simply reading books on Kindle-type devices, and nowadays often on mobile apps) – a uniquely high proportion worldwide. This surprising result is itself worth pursuing from a comparative perspective: is seeking out a web-specific form of literature uniquely popular to China, or can similar phenomena be found around the globe? Second, Hockx documents the popularity of erotic fiction, bordering on pornographic, and particularly among women. While the government partly censors this material, and online publishers are working to contain this phenomenon within limits, it is clear that censorship here, as in politics, is widely circumvented, and that online literature represents a source of online material that transgresses or pushes the boundaries of what is acceptable. These widespread ways of seeking material online are not much discussed in top-down analyses of government internet policies, or indeed in the study of literary and cultural tastes. Yet understanding commonplace ways of accessing online materials such as these is highly revealing about Chinese cultural tastes.

From a bottom-up perspective, it is also important to consider the device that people use to access information. For many in high-income countries, and certainly for the majority in lower-income countries like China and India, smartphones are already the main means of engaging with the internet and the web (Donner, 2015). This is a momentous shift, opening up new 'digital divides' (Napoli and Obar, 2015): it may not be vastly important whether people contact each other via apps on smartphones, since they also have other means to do so. But for information, and since their smartphones are becoming constant companions and means for mastering ever greater parts of most people's lives, and as non-digital sources of information disappear – how people access information via smartphones, and what they access, will become an ever more central question in the social sciences. But the experience of the web on smartphones can be quite different from the experience of the web on a PC.

Another example of these differences or divides is the use of the voice interface for search on smartphones (Siri, the assistant on the Apple iPhone, is the most well-known example): how is what people find via voice different from text searches? Only one technical paper (Guy, 2016) on this question exists to date, which finds that search queries are indeed quite different: longer (unexpectedly so) and more like spoken language (expected). But there is much more research to do on this topic. In the United States, more than 50% of younger people already use voice search on a daily basis (Guy, 2016). This way of searching for information will be important for those who mainly or exclusively use smartphones, or more widely among those who simply find it more convenient in certain situations to search via voice. If the results for search via voice differ in important ways from those obtained via text-based search, then it can be anticipated that significant new information divides will open up.

Not just search engine results, but also how information is passed to 'audiences' or 'consumers' has changed profoundly. That is because the expertise and commercial competition for 'attracting eyeballs' in the 'marketplace of attention' (Webster, 2014) are changing quickly for the web (and for traditional media). One reason that has already been mentioned in passing is that information is increasingly shared via social media. Hence the analytics for measuring attention and visibility will have to measure web links that are shared. This is an exciting new area which has already yielded some interesting and non-obvious findings (for example, Bright, 2016), for example that what is most shared from the BBC news website does not correspond to what is most read in terms of the stories on the main page.

Finally, it might be possible to develop a taxonomy of the main types of information sought (from studies such as Waller (2011a), discussed earlier). That would also make it possible to examine how people search for particular topics. Anderegg and Goldsmith (2014) show, for example, how interest in climate change waxed and waned, and the search terms used in seeking information on a particular issue ('global warming' or 'global warming hoax') can be instructive. The popularity of topics could be combined with national and global website rankings and most frequently searched keywords. On the qualitative side, this taxonomy could be further refined with individual web browsing histories to provide rich ('thick') descriptions of the types of information people look for – and how this information fits into their everyday lives, meets their needs, and is part of their overall information environment of old and new sources and media.

## WIKIPEDIA

Against this background, we can turn to some specific examples. Wikipedia is the only non-commercial website in the top ten around the world (http://www.alexa.com/topsites/countries). Much has been written about the content of Wikipedia and how it is edited (Schroeder and Taylor, 2015), but almost nothing is known about what content is read, even though there are computational tools and data sources for finding out (https://en.wikipedia.org/wiki/Wikipedia:Web_statistics_tool). Global differences in accessing Wikipedia content by language and in different countries are bound to be highly revealing. Equally revealing would be to compare Wikipedia with its rival in China, Baidu Baike, which, as mentioned, is more popular than the Chinese-language version of Wikipedia in China because the government has championed it and curbed Wikipedia (Liao, 2009).

Wikipedia, like other openly available online information sources, extends the range of sources of information available: it is more accessible and more comprehensive than other, similar sources, such as offline encyclopaedias. It has also become a widely used resource for a range of topics for many internet users. Yet there are also new gatekeepers: Waller finds that in Australia, 93% of clicks on Wikipedia come via Google, and Google is the dominant search engine in Australia, with more than a 90% share (Waller, 2011b) of search engine uses (Australia is the country for which the most detailed analysis of Wikipedia uses and online information seeking is available). This new information source also creates new divides: some Australians do not have access to the internet or the digital skills to use it even if they do have access.

An interesting exception to how little we know about Wikipedia web audiences are articles about medicine. According to Heilman and West (2015), there are more than 155,000 of these, more than 29,000 of them in English. How often are they read? In 2013, this English content received 2.28 billion (non-mobile) page views, just under half of medical content in all languages on Wikipedia. 'Medical content accounted for 0.64% (0.029/4.5 million) of all articles on English Wikipedia, yet these received 2.49% (2277/91,252 million) of all English Wikipedia page views' (Heilman and West, 2015: 7). This makes medical content on

Wikipedia the single largest source of online health information in English, followed by the websites of the National Institutes of Health (NIH), WebMD, and the Mayo Clinic. It can be mentioned that over half the editors of medical content pages were health care professionals. And mobile views of English Wikipedia were over 30% in 2014. This kind of audience or readership information tells us a lot about where people find medical information, subject only to knowing more about how this fits into and complements the other online and offline sources they use.

But while Wikipedia provides a source that is widely regarded as reliable for serious matters (though this will continue to be a matter of debate), most of the content that is sought on Wikipedia via the dominant search engine Google concerns popular culture and the like, which arguably falls into the category of leisure rather than 'serious' information (Waller, 2011a). But this is also true of search engine uses generally, which are mainly used for leisure and consumer-related information seeking around the world (Segev and Ahituv, 2010). Thus, even if online information seeking, in this case using Wikipedia as a resource, is mainly for topics that are not crucial, it is nevertheless easy to see that some categories of information (such as for health, science, and civic topics) can play an important role in people's lives, even if they are far less common. Finally, it can be mentioned that Wikipedia, too, can be seen as part of a new infrastructure: Wikipedia is the only non-commercial site in the top ten, but the top websites worldwide (as we shall see) make up a vast proportion of the uses of the web as a whole.

## SCALE, SCOPE, AND INTERCONNECTEDNESS OF THE GLOBAL WEB

How global is this new information environment? To start with, we can say with certainty that there are fundamental divides or boundaries. The best example is China, which is often said to be cut off from the global web. Yet this is misleading in some senses. One reason is that, even in this restrictive environment, savvy internet users who wish to get access to information from within and outside the country can for the most part do so, except where online information has been removed altogether. A different way to gauge the global web is to ask: how many companies dominate online attention? (Schroeder, 2014; Pan, 2017) It turns out that, despite the global dominance of Google and Facebook in online advertising (and of Tencent and Baidu in China), media concentration among old and new media is in fact surprisingly varied across the globe (see Noam, 2016). Finally, Google, Facebook, and Amazon are among the top ten in most countries. Yet, even in China, there are dominant websites that closely emulate these three: Baidu the search engine, Alibaba a major retailer, and Tencent with its social network site WeChat.

Web visibility can be measured by several methods: examining top websites globally and nationally, use of keywords in search queries (Google Trends) and, as discussed, trending keywords for particular topics (Anderegg and Goldsmith, 2014). In addition, more specialized tools can be used, for example for Wikipedia article readership (https://en.wikipedia.org/wiki/Wikipedia:Web_statistics_tool. Hyperlink analysis, which has been a common method to gauge web visibility in the past, has been found to be a poor indicator of online visibility and web audiences (Barnett and Park, 2014; Wu and Ackland, 2014; Taneja, 2016). This is because hyperlinks are often an indication of the aims of webmasters, but they can also serve a number of other functions. Other methods include shared website use for the most frequently visited websites, globally or nationally, using Alexa.com (http://www.alexa.com/) rankings (Barnett and Park, 2014).

Among the most advanced methods to measure global (and national) visibility is to measure online attention. This method (using data from comScore) was used by Taneja and Webster (2016) and is based on two million panellists from more than 170 countries, measured once per month, and includes the top 1,000 web domains and subdomains, which together account for 99% of web user visits. This method is also able to capture different formats and genres (Taneja and Wu 2014; Wu and Taneja 2016). Among the findings is that 'similarity of languages and a common geographical focus of any two websites offer the best explanations of audience overlap between sites' and 'the number of hyperlinks between websites explains very little audience overlap' (Taneja and Webster, 2016: 175). This finding is based on the idea of 'audience duplication', whereby the likelihood of a user visiting one site if he or she visits another is higher than chance. These data are then aggregated to establish patterns of audience attention, which can then be correlated with other factors.

The authors (Wu and Taneja 2016) found that the clusters of visibility and the most popular websites have changed quickly within the space of the last six years: whereas in 2009, a global/US cluster was most central on the web and at the same time the largest, in 2011 it was overtaken by a Chinese cluster, and there was no longer a global/US cluster, but rather in second place was an US/English cluster followed by a global cluster. The same two clusters occupied the top two spots by size in 2013, but the global cluster (of websites that are not language specific, such as Mozilla and Facebook) had slipped to eighth place (India was ninth and Germany tenth), followed by a number of other clusters including sites in Japan and Russia, but also Spanish-language sites and those in Brazil and France.

What we see here is the evolution of the web as it becomes more oriented towards the global South (Spanish-language sites and sites in Brazil and also India). We also see, with time, that websites of 'global' status have become fewer in number among the world's top 1,000 sites, and we see language playing an increasing role. State policies promoting information and communication technologies are one factor here, and shared language another. Whatever the most important factors may turn out to be, the web is not becoming a single whole, but rather a series of clusters: linguistic, and those that develop due to the policies of states and sites promoting shared interests, such as commerce or personal relations.

More work is necessary to situate these findings within theories of patterns of online attention and visibility and information-seeking behaviours. And 'online attention' and 'online visibility' are of course different. Yet in a sense what people seek and what is most visible to people should amount to the same thing: 'attention' and 'visibility' should be two sides of the same coin, much as 'supply' should meet 'demand' in markets. And ultimately different approaches to measuring what information is sought should converge; as with measuring the most visible and most frequently accessed websites and the surveys which ask people how often they seek information about what. These include the national surveys undertaken by the World Internet Project (http://www.worldinternetproject.net/#about), the International Telecommunications Union (http://www.itu.int/en/ITU-D/Statistics/Pages/default.aspx), or the China Internet Network Information Center (http://www.cnnic.net.cn/). Other measures and approaches, as discussed, include focus groups and browsing histories.

## INFORMATION INFRASTRUCTURE

Another way to think about the web is as an infrastructure of information. In this respect, the web is part of a larger 'infrastructure' or 'large technological system' (Hughes, 1987): the internet. The internet encompasses a wider set of functions, including two-way communication, and seeking information is only one part of what people do online. And online information and communication are only part of a larger infrastructure of information and communication (that includes print, broadcast, and landline telephony). In this respect there is a deepening and broadening of this infrastructure – rather than an information or communication revolution; people's uses of information have not changed radically since the internet and the web. To make it even more complicated, only part of the internet and web are (public) infrastructures; much of the internet and web are private (think here of 'intranets'), and so there are large technological systems rather than infrastructures in the strict sense. But it is important not to exaggerate the influence of this new extension of the information infrastructure: the problem with those who talk of an information flood (Gleick, 2011), or measure the radical increase in the amount of information available (which is true: Hilbert and Lopez, 2011), or talk of an information overload, is that even though the supply of information has increased dramatically, there are limits to the amount of online information that is routinely used (Hargittai et al., 2012; Neuman et al., 2012).

Furthermore, only a small proportion of online information use is interesting for social science – search engine optimization and online advertising and shopping may be interesting for marketing and business scholars, but they are of limited significance to media and communication scholars and those concerned with social transformations. Nevertheless, there has clearly been a change, perhaps not on the scale of the print revolution (Eisenstein, 2005), but a change that can be appreciated when we think of the extent to which people use the web on an everyday basis, now also on mobile devices. People have become tethered to information, just as, with email and social media, they have become more tethered to each other (Schroeder, 2010; 2018).

At the same time, both information-seeking behaviours and the infrastructure are still changing. On the seeking side, for example, there are 'apps', which need to be downloaded and in this sense are not part of the open web but are still increasingly used in seeking and using information. There are other 'walled gardens' within the web or internet infrastructure, reminiscent of an early era of the web when companies and others sought to be 'portals' to the web. At the same time, it can be anticipated that information at our fingertips will come to be 'taken for granted' (Ling, 2012) as smartphones and other devices become commonplace, and as the online information infrastructure becomes more enveloping. Put differently, people are becoming dependent on the web infrastructure in a similar way to how they rely on electricity and roads today. This makes it imperative to understand how the web extends the information and communication infrastructure – without exaggerating its effects.

## CONCLUSION

Over the course of the coming decades, the web will continue to be only one source of information for people among many, but it is arguably becoming the single most important one. This means that there are policy implications, above all about the diversity, accuracy, and openness of information online. More concretely, is the information diverse enough, or do pages that are manipulated to achieve a high page rank, for example, but that are of low quality, dominate the results? Are the sources reliable when it comes, for example, to political or health-related information? Are results in different languages and the results obtained by people with different levels of digital skills and education (Hargittai and Hsieh, 2013) of equal quality? It may be that skills and coverage of different topics in different languages become more important than, say, questions of access to or censorship of online information – though all these questions will continue to shape the role of the web.

This chapter has discussed a variety of perspectives on uses of the web. It has suggested that an overall framework of understanding web uses must consist of the infrastructure of the web (and how it is part of broader infrastructures of information), of the content of the web – its scale, scope, and how it is interlinked, and how these relate to how the web is actually used in terms of content that is accessed in everyday life – all in the context of how this fits with or extends other media. Such a framework must be based on what web content is most visible and what receives attention, also compared with other offline, online, and traditional information and communication technology sources (Schroeder, 2016). While this is an ambitious undertaking, it is also possible to examine particular areas, such as the uses of Wikipedia, or access to political information, within this framework. And while this chapter has provided the elements of an overall framework, pulling these elements into a full theoretical account of the web still eludes us; that would require a more comprehensive analysis that includes more empirical material about web uses combined with a close theoretical integration of these elements. Still, it is only against this background that it will be possible to answer other larger questions about the web, such as those addressed in this *Handbook*, but also the ethical or policy questions raised in the previous paragraph.

In any event, for future media historians and sociologists of new media technologies, the web will provide a treasure trove of data. Questions such as 'what did people want to know in the early 21st century?' or 'what kinds of information did the web provide?' will open up new ways of understanding the past and the present. The availability of web data means that there will be plenty of data about content that people actively seek out and these data are also more granular than data for traditional media: how do people make choices when faced with alternative search engine results? When do they prefer text or visual types of information when both are available? When are they satisfied with what can be displayed on a small smartphone screen as opposed to needing a full screen and better input controls via a full-size keyboard and mouse? And: when do they use the web, as opposed to asking a friend online or offline or consulting printed sources? As information becomes more ubiquitous, complex, and variegated, scholarship has unique opportunities to produce anatomies of these multifaceted types of social behaviour, which, even though they are still evolving, are also becoming more embedded in all aspects of our lives.

Note: earlier versions of portions of this chapter were published previously in chapter 5 of Schroeder (2018).

## REFERENCES

Anderegg, W.R., & Goldsmith, G.R. (2014) 'Public interest in climate change over the past decade and the effects of the "climategate" media event'. *Environmental Research Letters*, 9(5): 054005.

Aspray, W., & Hayes, B. (eds.) (2011) *Everyday Information: The Evolution of Information Seeking in America*. Cambridge, MA: MIT Press.

Barnett, G., & Park, H.-W. (2014) 'Examining the international internet using multiple measures: New methods for measuring the communication base of globalised cyberspace'. *Quality and Quantity*, 48: 563–75.

Bright, J. (2016) 'The social news gap: How news reading and news sharing diverge'. *Journal of Communication*, 66(3): 343–65.

Brügger, N. (2012) 'Web historiography and internet studies: Challenges and perspectives'. *New Media & Society*, doi: 1461444812462852.

Castells, M. (2009) *Communication Power*. Oxford, UK: Oxford University Press.

Donner, J. (2015) *After Access: Inclusion, Development, and a More Mobile Internet*. Cambridge, MA: MIT Press.

Eisenstein, E.L. (2005) *The Printing Revolution in Early Modern Europe*. Cambridge: Cambridge University Press.

Gleick, J. (2011) *The Information*. London: Harper Collins.

Guy, I. (2016) 'Searching by talking: Analysis of voice queries on mobile web search'. In *Proceedings of the 39th International ACM SIGIR conference on Research and Development in Information Retrieval,* ACM, pp. 35–44.

Hargittai, E., & Hsieh, Y.P. (2013) 'Digital inequality'. In W. Dutton (Ed.), *Oxford Handbook of Internet studies*. Oxford, UK: Oxford University Press, pp. 129–50.

Hargittai, E., Neuman, W.R., & Curry, O. (2012) 'Taming the information tide: Perceptions of information overload in the American home'. *The Information Society*, 28(3): 161–73.

Heilman, J., & West, A. (2015) 'Wikipedia and medicine: Quantifying readership, editors, and the significance of natural language'. *Journal of Medical Internet Research*, 17(3): e62.

Hektor, A. (2001) *What's the use?: Internet and information behavior in everyday life*. PhD Thesis, Linkoeping University.

Hilbert, M., & López, P. (2011) 'The world's technological capacity to store, communicate, and compute information'. *Science*, 332(6025): 60–5.

Hockx, M. (2015) *Internet Literature in China*. New York, NY: Columbia University Press.

Hughes, T. (1987) 'The evolution of large technological systems'. In W. Bijker, T. Hughes, and T. Pinch (Eds.), *The Social Construction of Technological Systems*. Cambridge, MA: MIT Press, pp. 51–82.

Kümpel, A.S., Karnowski, V., & Keyling, T. (2015) 'News sharing in social media: A review of current research on news sharing users, content, and networks'. *Social Media + Society*, 1(2): doi: 2056305115610141.

Liao, H.-T. (2009) 'Conflict and consensus in the Chinese version of Wikipedia'. *IEEE Technology and Society Magazine*, 28(2): 49–56.

Ling, R. (2012) *Taken for Grantedness: The Embedding of Mobile Communication into Society*. Cambridge, MA: MIT Press.

Meyer, E.T., & Schroeder, R. (2015) *Knowledge Machines: Digital Transformations of the Sciences and Humanities*. Cambridge, MA: MIT Press.

Napoli, P., & Obar, J. (2015) 'The emerging mobile internet underclass: A critique of mobile internet access'. *The Information Society: An International Journal*, 30(5): 323–4.

Neuman, W.R., Park, Y.J., & Panek, E. (2012) 'Info capacity: Tracking the flow of information into the home: An empirical assessment of the digital revolution in the US from 1960–2005'. *International Journal of Communication*, 6: 20.

Noam, E. (2016) *Who Owns the World's Media?: Media Concentration and Ownership around the World*. New York: Oxford University Press.

Qiu, J. (2009) *Working-Class Network Society: Communication Technology and Information Have-Less in Urban China*. Cambridge, MA: MIT Press.

Pan, J. 2017. 'How Market Dynamics of Domestic and Foreign Social Media Firms Shape Strategies of Internet Censorship'. *Problems of Post-Communism,* 64(3-4): 167–88.

Pariser, E. (2011) *The Filter Bubble: What the Internet is Hiding from You*. Harmondsworth: Penguin.

Rieh, S.Y. (2004) 'On the Web at home: Information seeking and Web searching in the home environment'. *Journal of the American Society for Information Science and Technology*, 55(8): 743–53.

Savolainen, R. (2008) *Everyday Information Practices: A Social Phenomenological Perspective*. Lanham MD: Scarecrow Press.

Schroeder, R. (2010) 'Mobile phones and the inexorable advance of multimodal connectedness'. *New Media and Society*, 12(1): 75–90.

Schroeder, R. (2014) 'Does Google shape what we know?', *Prometheus: Critical Studies in Innovation*, 32(2): 145–60.

Schroeder, R. (2016) 'Big Data and Communication Research', *Oxford Research Encyclopedia of Communication*, http://communication.oxfordre.com/

Schroeder, R. (2018) *Social Theory after the Internet: Media, Technology, and Globalization*. London: UCL Press.

Schroeder, R., & Taylor, L. (2015) 'Big data and Wikipedia research: Social science knowledge across disciplinary divides'. *Information, Communication and Society*, 18(9): 1039–56.

Segev, E., & Ahituv, N. (2010) 'Popular searches in Google and Yahoo!: A "Digital Divide" in information uses?'. *The Information Society*, 26(1): 17–37.

Sen, A. (2009) *The Idea of Justice*. London: Allen Lane.

Sonnenwald, D. (ed.) (2016) *Theory Development in the Information Sciences*. Austin: University of Texas Press.

Stehr, N. (1994) *Knowledge Societies*. London: Sage.

Taneja, H. (2016) 'Mapping an audience-centric World Wide Web: A departure from hyperlink analysis'. *New Media and Society*, http://doi.org/10.1177/1461444816642172

Taneja, H., & Webster, J.G. (2016) 'How do global audiences take shape? The role of institutions and culture in shaping patterns of web use'. *Journal of Communication*, 66(2): 161–82.

Taneja, H., & Wu, A.X. (2014) 'Does the Great Firewall really isolate the Chinese? Integrating access blockage with cultural factors to explain web user behavior'. *The Information Society*, 30(5): 297–309.

Waller, V. (2011a) 'Not just information: Who searches for what on the search engine Google?'. *Journal of the American Society for Information Science and Technology*, 62(4): 761–75.

Waller, V. (2011b) 'The search queries that took Australian internet users to Wikipedia'. *Information Research*, 16(2), online at http://search.ebscohost.com/login.aspx?direct=true&db=lxh&AN=62852994&site=ehost-live

Waller, V. (2013) 'Diverse everyday information practices in Australian households'. *Library and Information Research*, 37(115): 58–79.

Webster, J.G. (2014) *The Marketplace of Attention: How Audiences Take Shape in a Digital Age*. Cambridge, MA: MIT Press.

Wu, A.X., & Taneja, H. (2016) 'Reimagining Internet geographies: A user-centric ethnological mapping of the World Wide Web'. *Journal of Computer-Mediated Communication*, 21(3): 230–46.

Wu, L., & Ackland, R. (2014) 'How Web 1.0 fails: The mismatch between hyperlinks and clickstreams'. *Social Network Analysis and Mining*, 4(1): 1–7.

# Ethical Considerations for Web Archives and Web History Research

Stine Lomborg

## INTRODUCTION: ARCHIVES, EVERYWHERE

Digital archives are everywhere. They are repositories of digital communications generated through human activity, different in size and scope, and created by a diverse range of actors – public institutions, commercial actors such as digital media insights companies, researchers and private citizens, to name just a few (Beer and Burrows, 2013). Digital archives serve to fixate and order data that might otherwise quickly vanish or change. Digitalization has enabled a dramatic upsurge in the sheer number and kinds of archives available, owing to the relative ease of archiving, storing and maintaining digital records. Hence, a wealth of information which was not previously saved and organized in databases for later retrieval is now being archived, from entire company intranets and websites to posts on debate forums or social media, to personal profile data and metadata such as time stamps, location, click-through patterns etc. At the same time, the analogue materials of pre-digital archives are digitized and included in cultural heritage archives such as the Europeana collections of European art and mass media content (Europeana.eu).

Web archives constitute a specific type of digital archive, comprising segments of the worldwide web – snapshots of specific sites, collections of communication about a specific event or the entire WWW in the moment and across time. Web archives are typically created using software to 'crawl' a portion of the publicly accessible web (e.g. company websites, but not intranets; open Facebook pages, but not private profiles). The process of collecting the archive is automated and unobtrusive (Lomborg, 2012b; Webb et al., 2000), yet the perimeters are predefined by the archiving actor (Brügger, 2011, 2017) (see also Brügger, this volume). The archived data may include different communication modalities (text, images, video, audio), links, metadata etc. While web archives do not comprise a 1:1 copy of what was actually on the live web at a given point in time, they constitute web corpora in a form that makes for a useful source for researching the history of the web itself as well as for studying aspects of late modern cultural history since the 1990s and up until today. Web archives may be constructed by the researcher for a specific project, for instance by harvesting data through APIs of specific sites and services (e.g. archives of digital memorial websites as data on practices of online grieving, or the development of specific social networks or political debates on social media across time). Researchers may also use data from existing archives (e.g. the Internet Archive's Wayback Machine or national web archives), typically larger in scope and maintained by public and private institutions with broader purposes, such as supporting research infrastructures or preserving cultural heritage.

The abundance of archives cannot be separated from the enabling technologies and infrastructures that support them. Digital media not only allow for easy access to a wide range and unprecedented amount of (personal) data, they also provide tools that enable a wide range of actors to collect and mine such data, often requiring little technical knowledge (Kennedy, 2016). Perhaps for this reason, research ethics questions have surfaced quite forcefully in digital media research. At the same time, there is very little research ethics literature to consult for specific guidance when it comes to web historiography and web history research, a specialized, interdisciplinary field of study that has developed at the intersection of history research and internet research proper. Although ethics mix into ongoing epistemological debates in the discipline of history (e.g. on how to use and treat diverse sources of evidence), the vocabulary of research ethics is largely absent (Gallois, 2011). This is perhaps also a result of historians traditionally working with comparably old sources, the appropriate use of which is formally stipulated by archival legislation and local regulations. Old sources may present detailed accounts of specific individuals who lived hundreds of years ago. But questions of future harm and beneficence for these individuals seem irrelevant when weighed against the greater societal good of writing the history of mankind. Yet web history and web archives put the question of harm to persons back into the research frame. As will be evident, ethics are of crucial importance when writing the histories of the users of the web, their online communications and communities. Therefore, the purpose of this chapter will be to address web history research ethics through the general perspective of internet research ethics, and to sensitize web history to areas of ethical concern, such as expectations of privacy, based on established ethics principles and discussions. This will, hopefully, serve as a starting point for future conversations around ethics in web history research.

Ethics questions regard not just what kinds of data can be collected and archived, but also what can be used in research. There is some convergence in digital research ethics discussions towards the idea that there is no fixed recipe for ethically sound research on digital media – it has proven unfruitful, even impossible, to establish firm rules that can apply across contexts, cultures, research fields etc. What instead seems to crystallize as the mainstream stand in humanistic and social science research ethics regarding digital media is the need for a case-by-case approach, considering a range of issues throughout the research process: from the kinds of data solicited in order to answer a research question and the procedures and tools used for data collection, storage, processing and documentation, to the publication of research findings. Following from this general trend, this chapter does not offer a fixed recipe for ethical decision-making in web history research. It offers guidance by way of reflecting on the kinds of issues and dilemmas that researchers are likely to face in digital media research, and web archival research specifically. It also offers concepts to 'think with' in order to reach ethically sound decisions for specific research endeavours and contexts.

## FROM INTERNET RESEARCH ETHICS TO WEB HISTORY ETHICS: DEBATES, PRINCIPLES AND SENSITIZING CONCEPTS

In digital media, ethics questions encompass the responsible and careful collection, processing, storage, reuse and reporting of digital data across contexts – commercial, governmental, personal etc. Internet research ethics deals with these same practices in a specific context, namely that of research, understood as the generation and dissemination of knowledge for the public good and benefit of society. At the core of ethics discussions is the balancing of respect for human subjects with the prospect of societal and human benefits, such as information technology and data-driven innovations. As will be evident below, I base the ethics discussions largely on the human subjects model. Since the purpose of my chapter is to bring web history in dialogue with digital media research, the basis of such dialogue must be to benchmark the new research area against the existing, interdisciplinary best practice.

The core questions of internet research ethics have developed in parallel with the development of digital media – questions about anonymity and authenticity in computer-mediated communication were central in the early days of internet research ethics, whereas today's ethics debates largely revolve around algorithms, artificial intelligence and big data. Internet research ethics discussions are mainly anchored at the intersection of information and computer ethics and social scientific, empirical inquiry into the uses of digital media. It is roughly modelled after human subjects' rights and protection principles rooted in medical science, and consolidated in the UN Declaration of Human Rights (1948), the Nuremberg Code (1949) and the Belmont Report (1979) (Buchanan, 2011). It is also influenced by standards and best practices in the various research disciplines that are involved in digital media research. As a result, internet research ethics is pluralistic in nature. Ethics guidelines and recommendations, such as the broadly endorsed guidelines from the Association of Internet Researchers (Ess and Committee, 2002; Markham and Buchanan, 2012), reflect this pluralism. There is no general agreement on specific standards for how to conduct ethically responsible research (e.g. when to seek informed consent), beyond the ground rule that the user's right to privacy must be balanced against researchers' rights to pursue knowledge for the benefit of society.

In this section I review key debates in the internet research ethics literature to reveal grey areas and concepts with which to think about ethics and making ethically responsible decisions in research etc. I consider these debates against the context of web history to make a case for when and how it is relevant to apply internet research ethics to this field.

### *Text Versus Person: What is the Ontological Status of the Data we are Dealing with?*

At the heart of internet research ethics discussions lies a distinction between seeing digital data as texts and as human subjects (Markham and Buchanan, 2012; McKee and Porter, 2009), echoing the models of broadcast and interpersonal communication. On the web, ordinary users are productive in new ways, including in the creation of the texts that make up the WWW. This fact provides crucial fuel for the 'text versus human' debate. Is a status update on Facebook or a comment uploaded to a news website to be considered a finished product, a textual artefact authored and published by someone? Or should it be seen as a communicative trace or extension of the person? In some cases, the determination of whether to consider digital data as texts or persons may be more or less clear-cut. A piece of digital art or a news article would typically classify as cultural products attributable to an author, who may or may not hold copyright over this material. But in other cases, say a personal blog post, a tweet, a homepage or chat functions on an organization's intranet, it may be argued that the communication resembles an ongoing interpersonal exchange or a personal confession rather than a textual product, which, in turn, implies seeing the produced data as traces of a person's practices, or expressions of the person's self. Both framings of digital data – as text or person – may be valid depending on the study object and research questions of a specific scientific inquiry.

The distinction between data as textual representations or as a form of personhood has disciplinary origins in humanistic and social scientific thinking about the internet as an object of study (Bassett and O'Riordan, 2002; White, 2002). Historiography and web history seems largely aligned with the former, considering archival material as historical artefacts – products of human activity. In some cases, this seems unproblematic, e.g. in studies of the development of the internet and WWW or analyses of the evolution of the design of professional websites over time. In other cases, e.g. the study of the development of specific sub-cultures on the web (e.g. sexual minority groups, political extremist debate fora or camgirls' websites), using archival data on the participants and their online communications may be more problematic, if only because of the risk of exposing and causing harm to specific private individuals, based on their prior affiliation to a sub-culture. The case-by-case ethical judgement starts with reflections about the textuality or humanness of the data in question.

The human subjects model dominates in ethics discussions, most likely because ethics dilemmas, guidelines and discussions tend to surface in research on the uses and users of the internet. Web traffic patterns, social media network graphs, likes and recommendations, user comments on news sites, personal blogs and so on are all data directly or indirectly traceable to the individuals that have browsed, connected, endorsed, commented and created 'stuff' online. Therefore, they are in a sense data on human subjects. To the extent that web archives include such data, which would be the case for archives of social media, for instance, but also other forms of web material traceable to individuals, broadly accepted research ethics standards such as the respect for human subjects, protection from harm and by extension the need to seek informed consent etc. become relevant to historical research that uses such web archival data. The personal data may be of a more or less sensitive nature. For instance, according to the EU Data Protection Directive, information regarding, for example, religion, political leaning, sexuality and personal health are *by law* defined as more sensitive than other types of personal information. It is important to note that sensitive information may often be gleaned from the context of communication, or by cross-referencing archives, even if the content itself does not explicitly reveal it.

A case-based approach to research ethics as dealt with during, not just before, the research process, is typically called for in the study of 'live' or 'recent' events, e.g. a debate of a specific political issue on the agenda in the comment section of an online news outlet, fandom practices in relation to a contemporary artist as displayed on social media etc. But to what extent does it apply to research on the historical web? What difference does temporality, and the temporal distance between researcher and researched implied in historical research, make in terms of research ethics? In principle, why should it make an ethical difference if personal data is found in an archive of the web or on the live web? Ontologically speaking, the data does not change in 'kind' over time. Given that the data still refers back to identifiable individuals, ethics dilemmas and questions regarding beneficence, harm, vulnerability and so on must still apply, prompting the same kind of ethical treatment as research into the live web, if possible. Furthermore, in a historical perspective the temporal distance between personal data put on the web ten or 20 years ago and the present is very small: digital media are comparatively young. Even though this challenge will gradually become smaller as time passes, it seems futile to suggest that some web data is so old that questions of harm – to the involved individuals or their descendants – are no longer relevant to consider. However, sometimes temporality does make a difference for research ethics, at least in practical terms. Seeking informed consent from research subjects encountered in historical archives may be impossible, because the source of data cannot be identified and traced, or because the person is no longer alive, in which cases the researcher may consider asking relatives (who might be harmed due to their affiliation with the deceased in question) to give their consent or otherwise protect the research subject. Informed consent, while certainly not a new problem for historians, thus presents a specific challenge for web history research, one that I will return to at the end of the chapter.

## *Risk Assessment and Protection from Harm: Who are the Researched?*

The question of harm and the ethical responsibility to protect research subjects from harm is crucial. Yet it may be difficult to anticipate the possibly harmful outcomes of being a subject in a digital media research project. How can we ensure that the voluntary sharing of personal data at one point in time does not come to negatively impact the research subject at a later point in time? As Enyon et al. (2017) have argued, it may be particularly difficult to access harm to and offence of research subjects in the data collection process on digital media, simply because it may be more difficult to establish a rapport with and between them. This challenge is emphasized when dealing with archival data, as will be unpacked at length later in the chapter. Furthermore, it may cause harm if personal data is not stored, encrypted and secured properly, or if a promise or expectation of confidentiality is breached through a third party's de-anonymizing or hacking of the data set.

One additional point has to be made about the pertinence of web history research reflecting on the issue of harm. When compared with physical, historical archives, digital archives, including web archives, hold three main characteristics, albeit with some variation among archives: increased and easy accessibility across space and time, increased and more thorough search and indexing facilities and easier cross-referencing of archives (Crossen-White, 2015). Some modification must be added: the ease of search, indexing and cross-referencing is conditioned by the degree to which the Archiving Body has managed to organize the vast and complex data, and this is certainly not always the case. But in principle, as a consequence, for the individual whose data is included in the archives, there is increased chance or risk of their data being discovered and re-identified (e.g. through cross-referencing between archives), and by extension, a greater risk of causing harm and distress for the individual, or descendants of the individual.

One way to begin addressing the question of harm is by considering the types of actors involved in our research. Some require more careful ethical treatment than others: researching children, socially or politically marginalized groups and physically or mentally vulnerable individuals entails a great ethical responsibility to protect participants from being bullied or put on undesirable public display, regardless of whether the online activities we study revolve around their vulnerability (e.g. a patient community for a specific chronic disease; political dissident communication in authoritative regimes etc.) or are seemingly trivial. Public figures such as politicians, celebrities or commercial actors may not expect the same degree of cautious treatment. This is because their public communication online is typically tied to their professional capacity and role – a role that carries with it an awareness of the possibility of being put to public scrutiny. Hence, ethical decision-making should start by considering the types of actors from which we gather data in terms of whether they are public figures communicating in their professional role or private individuals, and the perceived vulnerability of these private individuals.

For web history, reflecting on the kinds of subjects involved is particularly crucial, and arguably complements existing practices in historical research around the fair handling of sources. Traditional, physical archives of the past largely comprise material of sufficient public interest or value for cultural heritage, since it was not possible to archive everything. Therefore, to the extent that traditional archives revolve around human subjects, these tend to be public figures (politicians, artists, prominent business men and women etc.). To be sure, archives may include both professional and personal artefacts and records of these persons (e.g. excerpts from public appearances, but also private letters, to which special archival regulations may apply). In comparison, ordinary individuals – their public activities as well as their personal lives – may be less well-represented in historical records. In web archives lay people's social activities arguably figure more substantially. Many of these activities – interactions and communications – were previously oral and face-to-face only (and therefore not archived), but are now taking place increasingly in writing and images on the web, and therefore they are archived. As a consequence, web archives may involve a shift in the kinds of history that can be written: if everything and anything can be archived at the push of a button and stored on servers or in the cloud, it becomes increasingly possible to write history 'from below', giving voice to lay people sources and mundane artefacts, and to the margins of society, e.g. specialized communities or radical sub-cultures. With the democratizing potential comes an increasing ethical responsibility, and an obligation to reflect upon whose stories we are telling, to what extent we are equipped to tell their story, and what kinds of vulnerability and harm we might encounter and nurture when doing it. Finally, while the temporal distance implied in web history research does not weaken the distance between the data and the subject who produced it, time may in some instances change the risk of research, causing them harm.

## *Private and Public Contexts*

One additional key distinction concerns whether data is public or private, a principle mainly inherited from the ethics of participant observation in public and private spaces. Yet the distinction also comes in a more textually oriented guise, for instance, differentiating between intent of publication and publicity (Treadwell, 2014). A similar distinction is found in web history and web archival research where the concept of 'publication' refers to the kinds of material that have been made available to the public (e.g. Brügger, 2017). The distinction between public and private has been and continues to be promoted by scholarship, claiming that if the data is publicly accessible, then it can be collected without further ethical considerations and procedures such as seeking informed consent. Yet this distinction is contested in digital media research, because many digital media sites and services blur the lines between what is public and private. This blurring of lines in part has to do with the affordances of digital media, including the support for many-to-many communication alongside broadcasting one-to-many and interpersonal communication one-to-one; and the networked infrastructure allowing for easy distribution and interoperation of data between services and platforms etc. Although many social media services are publicly accessible by default (e.g. Twitter), or semi-public such as Facebook (some parts are open, and it simply requires a profile to access other user profiles, pages and open groups), one of the primary uses of social media is for personal communication – one-to-one and many-to-many. Furthermore, even though users seemingly care about their privacy and ideally *should* be aware of the possibility of unintended audiences (including researchers, social media insights companies and governmental institutions) gleaning their personal information and communicative exchanges on social media, they are often not. The media are rife with stories about (in particular young) people who share personal and possibly sensitive information on social media, potentially causing harm for those involved. In a historical perspective, similarly personally compromising content may be found in historical archives of specialized forums for discussing contentious issues such as politics, religion or hacktivism, or chatrooms for exploring one's sexuality. Hence, what was – in the moment of posting – a relatively unnoticeable, safe context at the outskirts of the web (which was, in the early days, a niche medium), may over time become part of public records of the web to which the user cannot regulate access. Several studies have suggested that users may not understand the possible ramifications of sharing personal data, that the impetus of sharing and relating to others is stronger than the concern for privacy, that they perceive social media as relatively private contexts, or simply that they find it difficult to understand and manage their privacy settings and control their information once posted (e.g. Acquisti and Gross, 2006; Boyd and Hargittai, 2010; Hargittai and Marwick, 2016; Taddicken, 2014). The possible unease that follows from not knowing what one's data may be used for, not having the means to control access to one's personal information etc., prompts ethical reasoning about how to handle users' data in digital media in a responsible manner. That is to say, the user's perceptions of *privacy*, understood here roughly in terms of personal information, calls for attention in discussions of ethics, even if it is legal to collect and use data in a specific digital context, because it is already in the public realm. This suggests that the distinction between what is a public and private setting is not that helpful for making ethical decisions in digital media research. Instead, as argued by Markham and Buchanan (2015) and Tiidenberg (2017), among others, we must take people's expectations of privacy seriously in ethical decision-making. In the following I put forward two concepts that do this, and that therefore seem particularly useful when doing web history research and developing web history ethics.

The concept of 'contextual integrity' (Nissenbaum, 2010) is an expectations-based framework for ethical reasoning about privacy and the protection of human subjects from harm in digital contexts. Nissenbaum's point of departure is a rebuttal of historically robust approaches to determining and justifying individuals' right to privacy in the United States: the individual's right to protection from the interference of the state (or other specific actors) in private matters, and the right to restricting access if so-called sensitive personal information is at stake, or if there is a reasonable expectation of privacy in context (e.g. the home as a setting in which it is reasonable to expect privacy). These three approaches fall short in a digital context. It may be difficult to determine and control who gets access to an individual's data (think, for instance, of the case of reselling user data to third parties). It may also be difficult to determine what counts as sensitive information and thus identify possible risks associated with personal data. Personal data that seemed non-sensitive in one context may turn sensitive at a later point in time or a different context. For instance, users of the OkCupid dating site may have felt that sharing information about their sexuality etc. was fairly non-sensitive in this particular context, or at least a reasonable part of the trade of getting access to potential partners on the site, but then in May 2016 students leaked OKCupid data from 70,000 users in a database in an alleged attempt to benefit the scholarly community. They had scraped the data from the site and made it public without the knowledge and consent of the users. Finally, it may be debatable what counts as a reasonable expectation of privacy in the context of digital media. Thus, instead of thinking of privacy as a matter of universal principles about who should have access to what information in which contexts, Nissenbaum suggests the lens of privacy as 'contextual integrity' as a means to consider whether something must be treated as private or not by looking at the specific context, data and actors involved. Every communicative context is guided by two types of norms of information flow: norms regarding what kind of information is appropriate to share in the specific context, and norms regarding who can control the information flow and by extension share, publish or use this information. These norms must be upheld in order to protect individual privacy. From a research ethics perspective, contextual integrity highlights how privacy expectations may be breached if we as researchers collect and use data on users' digital profiles, communications and actions without their knowledge and consent. The principle of contextual integrity invites web historians to dwell on the possible ethical consequences of repurposing historical web data – from the original context, to the archive and on to the context of web history.

Another useful ethics concept to reflect on the relationship between actors, content and contexts, and specifically the norms of appropriate information flows, is 'the distance principle', which refers to the distance between the object of study and the person who produced it (Lomborg, 2012a; Markham and Buchanan, 2015). The distance principle urges the researcher to consider the private/public continuum in terms of the experiential distance between a specific data point and the person who produced it in the first place (Lomborg, 2012a; Markham and Buchanan, 2015). A personal status update is likely to be considered more 'private' than a shared news article on Facebook, although this is not always the case. Although both are instances of an individual communicating, the status update originates from the user herself and emphasizes the user as the producer. The personal stakes of the individual are higher in research that reports discursive analyses of web-based communication than in research analysing and visualizing aggregate data, such as communication networks around a specific hashtag on Twitter. In the former example, the research participant is represented through specific instances of communication that are directly linked to the individual, whereas in the latter example, the individual is simply represented as a node in a network. The distance principle stipulates that it may be difficult for the researcher to determine beforehand whether a specific set of data is perceived as private or not for specific research participants. Rather, it must rely on a continuous assessment throughout the research process and possibly involve asking the participants themselves.

The distance principle helps unpack the ethics of working with archived web data to document histories of web cultures and identities. In essence, the archive inserts a distance between researcher and research subjects, which is not possible in online ethnographic research, which would typically partly rely on the same kinds of material to study the lived experience and practices of users. Given that the same material is used, one should expect similar ethical dilemmas and procedures. But the nature of the method and the temporal expansion of the data collection process in online ethnography is, in ethical terms, an advantage: research subjects can be approached slowly to build trust, and ethical measures can be built into the process ad hoc through negotiation with the participants throughout the process.

For instance, it is possible to differentiate between different types of participants if necessary. If a research subject discloses information that makes him vulnerable in the sense discussed above, additional measures may be taken to protect their privacy. In contrast, archiving techniques standardize data collection from the outset, because the tools for archiving require the researcher to specify what should be included and left out of the data set. Furthermore, owing to the initial distance between the researcher using the archive and the persons represented in it, it may be more difficult to approach the research subjects for informed consent etc. That is to say, the creation of trustful and respectful relationships with those under study is not built into the method; in fact, contacting participants to establish a rapport would diminish the advantage of the unobtrusiveness of archiving. That it to say, it is the web historian's job to then think about the possible ethical implications of using the archived data for specific projects with/without measures of privacy protection, consent and so on. As Crossen-White (2015) observes, the distance implied in archival research is likely to lower the researcher's sense of obligation and responsibility for the research subject, even if – according to the distance principle – the experiential distance between person and data, and researcher and object of the research is fairly small. Arguably, this sense of distance is further enhanced in historical web research, due to the temporal distance between the researcher and the historical data. At the same time, especially when engaging personal stories over time, as documented on a homepage or blog over time, historical research may bring us a sense of closeness to research subjects even if we don't directly connect with them.

### *Data 'found' in existing archives or archives 'made' by the researcher*

Web archives consist of 'found' data, insofar as the data was already on the web before becoming included in the archive. Yet they are also 'made', because the very process of archiving entails a number of methodological choices about what to include and leave out, how to represent the material in a database and so forth (Jensen, 2012; Lomborg, 2012b). Adding to this basic distinction, the data used for research may be found in preexisting archives of the web (e.g. the Internet Archive, or the Danish Netarkivet) or made, if the researcher creates the data archive herself. If data is found in an existing archive, the legal issues have been 'outsourced' from the research process and already dealt with by the archiving institution, namely those which have to do with the collection of data and data storage. In Denmark, for instance, researchers have to apply for access to Netarkivet by explaining the purpose of research and consent to not use personal information that may be derived from the archive. In the case of the Internet Archive, anyone can access the archives if they subscribe to the general Terms of Service, which include general agreements not to violate anyone's privacy, for instance by collecting and storing personal data from the Wayback Machine. It also grants special access to specific collections by application (internetarchive.org). Furthermore, the archival institution or gatekeeper may stipulate ethical rules for the researcher to consent to if using personal data from the archive (McKee and Porter, 2009). The archival gatekeeper's code of ethical research conduct may vary a great deal according to context and content, and many archives do not explicitly address ethics – only legal matters. Therefore, the researcher should at least maintain ethical reflection regarding data processing, documentation and display of research results based on the archived data. In ethical terms, it may be useful to distinguish between collection and use of the data in question. Arguably, ethical caution is particularly important in the researcher's selection of material from the archive for documentation in publications and other presentations of research, which put the archived data of human subjects on public display beyond the archive.

If the archive is produced and maintained by the researcher, their responsibility is to ensure adherence to the legal requirements for protecting personal data as well as all the ethics decisions regarding whether or not to obtain informed consent from those included in the archive, and if so how to anonymize the data, ensure secure data storage and deletion and so on. This responsibility may be an ethical advantage, because it puts the researcher in control of ethical decision-making. Yet it may be complicated further with the pressure of funding bodies to make digital data banks available for future research projects. For instance, the researcher may initially have obtained informed consent from those whose data is included in the archive for the specific research project, but this informed consent does not necessarily apply to later research projects using this data. Even if the data is re used in a new research project by the researcher, informed consent may need re-confirmation. Tiidenberg (2017), for instance, describes how she continually asks her informants in studies of sexy selfies on social media for consent when her research moves into a new phase.

### Informed consent and anonymization: procedures and obstacles

Seeking the consent from research participants is a standard procedure when collecting personal data on research participants. The idea of informed consent enforces individual autonomy and beneficence as key principles in human subjects research (Marzano, 2012) and can be modelled as an opt-in ethical procedure, in contrast to the opt-out policies often employed in web archiving, where users typically are included by default and have to request to be removed or 'muted' from the archive. Informed consent involves ensuring that research participants receive information about the purpose, methods, perceived risks and benefits of a given study before deciding whether to agree to be part of a given research project. It also allows them to withdraw at any point during the project. Hence, informed consent is an ongoing negotiation between the researcher and the researched. It may be formally ensured through a written and signed consent form, or given orally, for instance before a research interview. One recent study, the emotional contagion study conducted by Facebook (Kramer et al., 2014), caused scholarly and public furore for, among other things, failing to get informed consent from participants (Flick, 2016). The study deployed a large-scale experimental setup and manipulated user newsfeeds to assess the possibly contagious effect of emotions in the network. Contagion was documented, but the result suggested possible harm arising directly from the research setup.

Informed consent is tied to a number of obstacles, some of which are general, some of which are more likely to surface in digital media research, and web history in particular. One general issue involves how the researcher can verify that people are actually properly informed (Enyon et al., 2017). Do they understand the possible ramifications of being part of the study? One specific issue for digital media regards the question of informed consent from *whom*? For instance, should a researcher studying the uses of a specific hashtag on Twitter, or personal profiles on Facebook, seek informed consent from every user whose data may be present in the data set (e.g. friends tagged in a status update on the Facebook profile)? In reality, such an approach is hardly feasible. Ní Bhroin (2015) has proposed a distinction between core and ancillary research participants as a response to this problem, suggesting that informed consent need only be obtained from core participants. Finally, considering informed consent in connection with specific types of actors involved in research, it seems to pose a dilemma in the context of studying vulnerable subjects and sensitive topics. Such contexts can be tricky to study openly, and as Enyon et al. (2017) observe, asking for informed consent may cause subjects to withdraw and close the gates for this kind of research before it begins. At the same time, seeking informed consent from perceivably vulnerable subjects is a crucial ethical demand.

While there is no principal distinction between personal data of the (in the case of the web) not-so-distant past and present, in terms of the ethical treatment of such data, doing web history in an ethically sound manner may be particularly tricky and cumbersome, owing to the possible disappearance of the subjects 'behind' the data. In such cases, seeking informed consent from the person is futile. Consent to use the data must be negotiated with multiple other stakeholders, including relatives of the person in question and the archival institution that included the person's data in the archive in the first place (McKee and Porter, 2009).

Another gold research ethics standard regards confidentiality, typically handled by ensuring data access only to those authorized by the research participant and by anonymizing research participants in data sets and publications. This would imply removing personally identifying information such as name or user IDs, profile information and personal photos. Often in digital media research this is impracticable. Zimmer (2010), for instance, has forcefully demonstrated that even with large, anonymized data sets, it may be possible to re-identify anonymized participants. By way of combining data points in a publicly released data set on an entire cohort of Facebook users from a US college in 2006, Zimmer shows how easy it may be to de-anonymize participants in a data set, with possibly harmful implications. Interestingly, the researchers who had published the study had allegedly been in good faith, that is, tried to ensure respect for the involved participants, and the anonymized data set had been publicly released owing to a demand from the funding body for the project. Zimmer uses the case to argue that personally identifiable information not only includes personal characteristics such as name, age, gender, ethnicity etc., but also 'social' characteristics such as one's unique social graph (e.g. the personal network of friends on Facebook) or the combination of cultural tastes (see also Beaulieu and Estalella, 2012). In studies of online discourse, anonymization of participants is similarly difficult insofar as examples of discourse are published as part of the validation and documentation of analysis. In such cases, a simple string search may identify the participant (Lomborg, 2012a). Possibilities of cross-referencing archives could contribute further to making anonymization tricky (Crossen-White, 2015).

If anonymization is not possible, this may imply that some research is off-limits: how can vulnerable subjects and sensitive topics be researched in the context of digital media if we cannot protect their privacy? At the same time, such research is arguably extremely important in order to advance public understanding of, say, mental and physical illness, online racism and bullying etc. with the prospect of general beneficence. The difficulty of ensuring proper anonymization as well as informed consent, as described above, has led scholars to argue for a need to develop other procedures of ethical oversight and handling of subjects (Boyd, 2016), e.g. allowing for fabrication by remixing material from several participants into composite narratives or altering words in quotes to disable string search de-anonymization (Markham, 2012), or a greater emphasis on the 'ethics of care' (Held, 2006) to hold researchers accountable for their research subjects (Tiidenberg, 2017). One step in that direction is acknowledging that research ethics and ensuring respect for human subjects is a process that must be built into our research inquiries, not a check-box. Shifting towards opt-in principles and practices might be one crucial step for web archiving institutions and web historians in that direction.

### *Conclusion: when do human subjects transform into historical artefacts?*

Most historical web data of interest may be considered human subjects data, because it stems from the online activities of private individuals, e.g. personal homepages, comments to online newspaper articles and social media use. It enables researchers to tell tales of the development of (specific sites, practices and discourses on) the WWW over the past 25 years. Even though archived web data becomes historical web data from a researcher's perspective, in the lives of the persons who produced the data, such data is (sometimes a defining) part of their personal history, and may still hold significant value to them. There is no easy and clear line to suggest when human subjects on the live web become text, or historical artefacts of the web over time. Therefore, web history research deals with similar kinds of ethical dilemmas to those experienced by the broader field of digital media ethics outlined in this chapter. These to some extent challenge existing disciplinary norms and consensus in historical research and archival practices, as outlined through this chapter. On a general level, new digital territories for historical research call for renewed attention to ethical issues and perhaps more explicit responses from historians to general research ethics debates across disciplines.

There are no firm answers to ethics questions; they depend… on the context of inquiry, the types of actors involved, the activities they perform, the methods used for data collection and analysis, the kinds of data sought and so on. Based on exactly these premises, the Association of Internet Researchers, for instance, has developed internationally endorsed guidelines for case-based ethical reflections, which may be useful to consult before and during any digital media research project (Markham and Buchanan, 2012). The case-based approach is advocated in other official national and international guidelines (e.g. the Norwegian National Committees for Research Ethics), as well as in handbooks (Buchanan, 2011; Tiidenberg, 2017) and other research ethics publications (McKee and Porter, 2009). Guidelines, rather than fixed recipes, have the main advantage that they are adaptable to the dynamic nature of digital media, and the methods we use to study them. As technology evolves, new issues may emerge. These developments may twist and turn the directions and recommendations of internet and web history research ethics discussions in the future.

## REFERENCES

Acquisti, A. & Gross, R. 2006. Imagined communities: Awareness, information sharing, and privacy on the Facebook. *Lecture Notes in Computer Science,* 4258, 36–58.

Bassett, E. H. & O'Riordan, K. 2002. Ethics of Internet research: Contesting the human subjects research model. *Ethics and Information Technology,* 4, 233–247.

Beaulieu, A. & Estalella, E. 2012. Rethinking research ethics for mediated settings. *Information, Communication & Society,* 15, 23–42.

Beer, D. & Burrows, R. 2013. Popular culture, digital archives and the new social life of data. *Theory, Culture & Society,* 30, 47–71.

Boyd, D. 2016. Untangling research and practice: What Facebook's 'emotional contagion' study teaches us. *Research Ethics,* 12, 4–13.

Boyd, D. & Hargittai, E. 2010. Facebook privacy settings: Who cares? *First Monday,* 15, np.

Brügger, N. 2011. Web archiving – between past, present, and future. *In:* Consalvo, M. & Ess, C. M. (eds.) *The Blackwell Handbook of Internet Studies,* pp. 24-42. Oxford: Wiley-Blackwell.

Brügger, N. 2017. Webraries and Web archives: The Web between public and private. *In:* Baker, D. & Ewans, W. (eds.) *The End of Wisdom?: The Future of Libraries in a Digital Age,* pp. 185–190. Oxford: Chandos Publishing.

Buchanan, E. A. 2011. Internet research ethics: Past, present, future. *In:* Consalvo, M. & Ess, C. M. (eds.) *The Blackwell Handbook of Internet Studies,* pp 83–108. Oxford: Oxford University Press.

Crossen-White, H. L. 2015. Using digital archives in historical research: What are the ethical concerns for a 'forgotten' individual? *Research Ethics,* 11, 108–119.

Enyon, R., Fry, J. & Schroeder, R. 2017. The ethics of online research. *In:* Fielding, N. G., Lee, R., M. & Blank, G. (eds.) *The Sage Handbook of Online Research Methods,* pp. 19–37. *2nd edition.* London: Sage.

Ess, C. M. & Committee, A. E. W. 2002. Ethical decision-making and internet research: Recommendations from the AoIR Ethics Working Committee. Retrieved January 21, 2007, from http://www.aoir.org/reports/ethics.pdf.

Flick, C. 2016. Informed consent and the Facebook emotional manipulation study. *Research Ethics,* 12, 14–28.

Gallois, W. 2011. Ethics and historical research. *In:* Gunn, S. & Faire, L. (eds.) *Research Methods for History,* pp. 201–219. Edinburgh: Edinburgh University Press.

Hargittai, E. & Marwick, A. 2016. 'What can I really do?' Explaining the privacy paradox with online apathy. *International Journal of Communication,* 10, 3737–3757.

Held, V. 2006. The Ethics of Care: Personal, Political, Global, Oxford, Oxford University Press.

Jensen, K. B. 2012. Lost, found, and made: Qualitative data in the study of three-step flows of communication. *In:* Volkmer, I. (ed.) *Handbook of Global Media Research,* pp. 435–450. Malden, MA: Wiley-Blackwell.

Kennedy, H. 2016. Post, Mine, Repeat: Social Media Data Mining Becomes Ordinary, London, Palgrave Macmillan.

Kramer, A. D. I., Guillory, J. E. & Hancock, J. T. 2014. Experimental evidence of massive-scale emotional contagion through social networks. *Proceedings of the National Academy of Sciences,* 111, 8788–8790.

Lomborg, S. 2012a. Personal internet archives and ethics. *Research Ethics,* 9, 20–31.

Lomborg, S. 2012b. Researching communicative practice: Web archiving in qualitative social media research. *Journal of Technology in Human Services,* 30, 219–231.

Markham, A. N. 2012. Fabrication as ethical practice: Qualitative inquiry in ambiguous internet contexts. *Information, Communication & Society,* 15, 334–353.

Markham, A. N. & Buchanan, E. 2012. Ethical Decision-Making and Internet Research: 2012. Recommendations from the AoIR Ethics Working Committee.

Markham, A. N. & Buchanan, E. 2015. Ethical considerations in digital research contexts. *In:* Wright, J. (ed.) *Encyclopedia for Social & Behavioral Sciences,* pp. 606–613. Elsevier Press.

Marzano, M. 2012. Informed consent. *In:* Gubrium, J. F., Holstein, J. A., Marvasti, A. B. & Mckinney, K. D. (eds.) *The Sage Handbook of Interview Research: The Complexity of the Craft,* pp. 443–456. London: Sage.

Mckee, H. A. & Porter, J. E. 2009. The Ethics of Internet Research: A Rhetorical, Case-Based Process, New York, Peter Lang.

Ní Bhroin, N. 2015. Lost in Space? Social Media-Innovation and Minority Language Use. PhD, Oslo University.

Nissenbaum, H. 2010. Privacy in Context: Technology, Policy, and the Integrity of Social Life, Stanford, Stanford University Press.

Taddicken, M. 2014. The 'privacy paradox' in the social Web: The impact of privacy concerns, individual characteristics, and the perceived social relevance on different forms of self-disclosure. *Journal of Computer-Mediated Communication,* 19, 248–273.

Tiidenberg, K. 2018. Ethics in digital research. *In:* Flick, U. (ed.) *The Sage Handbook of Qualitative Data Collection,* pp. 466–481. London: Sage.

Treadwell, D. F. 2014. Introducing Communication Research: Paths of Inquiry. 2. ed., London, Sage.

Webb, E. J., Campbell, D. T., Schwartz, R. D. & Sechrest, L. 2000. Unobtrusive Measures (Revised edition), Thousand Oaks, CA, Sage.

White, M. 2002. Representations or people? *Ethics and Information Technology,* 4, 249–266.

Zimmer, M. 2010. 'But the data is already public': On the ethics of research in Facebook. *Ethics & Information Technology,* 12, 313–325.

# Collecting Primary Sources from Web Archives: A Tale of Scarcity and Abundance

Federico Nanni

La diversité des témoignages historiques

est presque infinie.

(Bloch, 1949)

The World Wide Web is the largest collection of human testimonies that we have ever had at our fingertips. Spanning from institutional websites to digital libraries, from personal blogs to Twitter accounts of prominent politicians, from online newspapers to large-scale knowledge bases, an immense number of born-digital testimonies are waiting to be retrieved, selected and studied by future historians. In addition to this, while these new resources are piling up steadily in front of our eyes, they are also rapidly replacing their analog counterparts, from printed news articles to personal diaries, from letter correspondences to scientific publications.

By acknowledging this sudden transition in production from printed to digital documents, the goal of this chapter is to present and discuss some of the new methodological issues that arise when these materials are to be employed as primary sources for studying the recent past. First, an overview of the debate on the historian's craft is offered. Then, two different case studies that have dealt with the difficulties of adopting born-digital materials in historical work will be described: the first is focused on reconstructing the past of university websites as a new way for studying the recent past of academic institutions; the second retrieves materials from large-scale archives of the web in order to study contemporary socio-political events. Through these descriptions, it will be highlighted how a fruitful combination of the historical methods with approaches from other research areas, such as internet studies and natural language processing, could support future historians in successfully addressing them.

## THE HISTORICAL METHOD: TODAY AND TOMORROW

In order to understand how the transition from analog to digital sources is about to change the historian's craft, it is first of all essential to examine how the 'historical method' (Shafer, 1974) is generally defined and which are its major steps.

**Defining a Subject**: In the first part of any historical research, the scholar broadly defines the subject of investigation and – together with it – an initial question. The research question, first presented at a coarse-grained level, will be sharpened through the recursive process of collecting sources, interpreting them and by doing so discovering the underlying narrative.

**Collecting the Evidence**: In order to address the research question, the historian identifies the testimonies upon which she/he builds a narrative through a complex process of collection, analysis and selection of the remains of the past. These testimonies could be physical remains (e.g. buildings, statues), oral memories or printed documents (e.g. chronicles, diaries, articles, census data) and will soon become born-digital documents, such as websites, online forums, email threads, large-scale databases, etc. The process of collecting primary sources has been shaped and sharpened by decades of discussions in historiography both on how to establish the reliability of these materials, for example through source criticism, and on how much 'true knowledge' can be derived from them (there are as many interpretations of the same text as many readers, as Barthes (1967) has taught us).

**Interpreting the Evidence**: The interpretation of the collected textual sources represents the core of any historical research. Due to this reason, it has been the central focus of debate across twentieth-century historiography and has experienced drastic transitions in methodology. As a matter of fact, the analysis and interpretation of sources can be conducted in many different ways: traditional historiography scholarships have strongly relied on hermeneutics and on the careful qualitative examination of documents, while other approaches – which emerged during the second part of the twentieth century, inspired by social science methodologies (see the advent of Cliometrics; Greif, 1997) – have employed census data or economic reports in order to conduct large-scale quantitative analyses.

Through the 1970s and 1980s, postmodern and deconstructionist theories (starting from the works of Barthes, 1967; Derrida, 1997 and Lyotard, 1984, among others) have posed major critiques to the underlying assumption of both traditional and social science historical scholarships that it is possible to discover a 'unique truth' about the past through careful analysis of the remains. The enormous impact of these critiques has been remarked by many historians (Burke, 2008; Munslow, 2006) and has led to the so-called cultural turn in the profession, which is still reflected strongly today in the community[1].

**Presenting a Narrative**: The final step of any historical research is to define a narrative and write a history. The creation of a narrative, which is highly connected with the initial definition of the research question, gives the historian the possibility of placing the work she/he is writing as part of a larger contribution to the field. This is achieved in two interconnected ways: first of all, by offering a new/different perspective on the topic under study; in addition to this, by participating in the larger debate in historiography regarding the ways the past can be rediscovered, examined, described and – for certain authors[2] – even modeled.

## *A Computational Turn of the Craft?*

History has been part of the so-called digital humanities (Schreibman et al., 2004) since their very beginning.[3] In particular, during the second part of the twentieth century the potential of computational methods and their impact over the historian's craft have been recurrent topics in historiography. As Thomas III (2004) remarked, already in 1945 Vannevar Bush, in his famous essay 'As We May Think', pointed out that technology could be the solution that would enable us to manage the abundance of scientific and humanistic data (Bush, 1945); in his vision, the Memex could become an extremely useful instrument for historians.

The use of the computer in historical research, which grew significantly between the 1960s and 1970s thanks both to the efforts of the Annales school (see for example Daumard and Furet, 1959) and to its application to the analysis of economic and census data (Greif, 1997), has been strongly related to the adoption of social science practices in historical studies (Evans, 2001). A pioneering work on the use of database technologies for historical research was conducted by Manfred Thaller during the 1980s (Thaller, 1991).

However, as Milligan (2012) and Robertson (2016) have already remarked, a large majority of the historian community has remained skeptical towards the adoption of computational methods in the craft. This attitude has consolidated in opposition to other humanities disciplines: for example, in the last 30 years the field of literary study has largely experimented with the potential of what they have defined as 'distant reading' techniques, in order to extract quantifiable information from large amount of texts (Moretti, 2013). Instead, during the same time, the so-called digital history community (Cohen et al., 2008) has decided to focus primarily on the potentialities of the web as a platform for the collection, presentation and dissemination of material (Cohen and Rosenzweig, 2005) and on the more 'communicative aspects' of doing research in the humanities (Robertson, 2016). This can be noticed by observing the importance given to digital public history topics (Noiret, 2015), the relevance of teaching in digital history (Cohen et al., 2008) and the tradition of digital history mapping (Knowles and Hillier, 2008).

In the second decade of the 2000s, thanks in particular to the prompt availability of digitized historical primary sources and the potentialities of web technologies, this skeptical attitude towards computational methods has slowly changed and a few interdisciplinary teams have developed tools in order to help other traditionally trained historians to employ these methods in their work. As Nelson (2016) remarked, the first fruitful applications of these methods for supporting historical narratives can be found in the works of Wilkens (2013) and Blevins (2014), which are robust examples of the beginning of a mature season of digital history.

While these early scholarships based on the use of computational approaches are essential for refreshing the historiographic debate, it is argued in this chapter that the adoption of computational methods could not be considered *per se* as a revolutionary turning point for the profession. In fact, use of these approaches is similar to other methodological turning points that historians have already experienced before. Milligan (2012), for example, identifies 'three waves' of computational history; moreover, during the last ten years the use of computational methods in humanities research has been strongly sustained and encouraged by public and private institutions (from the NEH Digital Humanities Advancement Grants to the Volkswagen Stiftung on 'Mixed Methods' in the Humanities) as well as private companies (e.g. Google's 'commitment' to the Digital Humanities) and often mainstream media sources (Rothman, 2014).

Nevertheless, it is argued in this chapter that historiography is about to experience a new and far more conspicuous turning point and that this will have a very strong impact on a specific step of the historian's craft, namely the way sources are collected from now on. Born-digital documents shared online, their ephemerality, preservation, availability and access are about to pose a large set of new challenges for future historians. In the next decades, the methodological debate in historiography will not only be centered around qualitative over quantitative, distant versus close, hermeneutics against statistical significance, but will also address the needs of the community in finding ways of acquiring knowledge on our recent (digital) past.

## The Born-Digital Turn

The transition from analog to born-digital materials is influencing the way historians study the past: materials such as websites, forums, blogs, tweets and emails are in fact very different from traditional analog and digitized primary sources. Born-digital materials have an extremely short life compared with printed documents as they are significantly more difficult to archive and preserve (LaFrance, 2015). This is due to a vast number of reasons (Brügger, 2005) and the consequence of it has been summarized by Rosenzweig (2003) with the concept of 'scarcity' of digital primary sources.

Web pages disappear constantly from the live web (because they are removed by the author or by the owner of the platform, for instance due to copyright issues), leaving a familiar trace of 404 status code messages. Several scholars (Brügger, 2012; Rosenzweig, 2003, among others) have already remarked on the great impact that the ephemerality of web materials will have on the sharing and accessibility of the knowledge produced in the digital age for the next generations of historians – as has been already said, in opposition to the fact that 'paper survives benign neglect for a long time' (Davis, 2014):

> The life cycle of most web pages runs its course in a matter of months. In 1997, the average lifespan of a web page was 44 days; in 2003, it was 100 days. Links go bad even faster. A 2008 analysis of links in 2,700 digital resources – the majority of which had no print counterpart – found that about 8 percent of links stopped working after one year. By 2011, when three years had passed, 30 percent of links in the collection were dead. (LaFrance, 2015)

Moreover, while some types of pages disappear more frequently than others (e.g. social media messages as opposed to official statements on administrative websites), those that do survive tend to change very frequently (Dougherty et al., 2010). For example, articles in newspapers (Nanni, 2013) as well as official administrative pages have often been modified without a specific mention (Owen and Davis, 2008). While initiatives such as the Internet Archive have a long tradition of preserving born-digital materials for future research, several issues still exist and new issues continue to emerge – not in the least due to constant innovations in web technologies. Therefore, researchers have to deal with the collected materials in a highly critical way, as Brügger (2012) described when he introduced his definition of web archive documents as reborn-digital materials:

> One of the main characteristics of web archiving is that the process of archiving itself may change what is archived, thus creating something that is not necessarily identical to what was once online. [...] And, second, that a website may be updated during the process of archiving, just as technical problems may occur whereby web elements which were initially online are not archived. Thus, it can be argued that the process of archiving creates the archived web on the basis of what was once online: the born-digital web material is reborn in the archive. (Brügger, 2012: 108)

The difficulties in the preservation of digital sources present a new set of issues for historians who plan to employ them in their work; however, they remain only part of the overall problem. In fact, already in 2003, Rosenzweig envisioned that future historians will not only deal with a consistent scarcity of primary sources, but they will also be challenged by a never before experienced abundance of records of our past. The indispensable need of computational methods for processing and retrieving materials from these huge collections of primary sources has been a central topic of Milligan's publications (2012, 2016). From his works it emerges that now that the community is dealing with the abundance of born-digital sources, the use of computational approaches cannot be a choice for the digital humanities researcher anymore. Therefore, it becomes essential that the researchers adopt these solutions critically, always knowing their potential and limitations, and learn how to combine them fruitfully with the traditional historical method.

While the consequences of the advent of born-digital sources will be revolutionary for our profession, so far 'very little attention has been paid to the new digital media as historical sources' (Brügger, 2012), highlighting the fact that, while 'new media is not that new anymore' (Milligan, 2016: 80) for our society, they remain a novelty for historians.

The next sections will remark further on this topic by describing two very different case studies that have dealt with the use of born-digital documents as primary sources for historical research. The first that will be introduced focuses on examining the online presence of the University of Bologna since the early nineties, and remarks on the importance of combining the traditional historian's craft with approaches from the field of internet studies.

## STUDYING THE RECENT PAST OF ACADEMIC INSTITUTIONS: A TALE OF SCARCITY

Multiple historians have considered academic institutions as political, economic and social actors; they have also argued how their power, role and influence changed over time, especially in relation to other actors, such as the city, the church and the national government (Brockliss, 1978). In particular, the comprehensive four-volume book series '*A History of the Universities in Europe*', commissioned by the European University Association, edited by Hilde de Ridder-Symoens and Walter Rüegg and published between 1992 and 2011 (Rüegg and de Ridder-Symoens, 1992), offers an unprecedented overview on how universities have transformed over centuries: what they have taught and researched, how they have been institutionalized and how they have interacted with the society.

Historians of higher education, who presented their research in the volume, have adopted a large variety of primary and secondary sources in their works, from university-archive materials such as matriculation and graduation statistics to academic dissertations, from public reports to large-scale statistical analyses. Based on these data, researchers have described and drawn conclusions on the history of universities on a large variety of topics, such as the way universities have managed resources, the way the admission process changed before and after 1970 and how sciences and humanities have been taught and studied.

The current prompt availability of a large variety of born-digital materials such as syllabi (Cohen, 2005), bachelor, master and doctoral theses (Ramage, 2011), academic websites (Holzmann et al., 2016b) and their hyperlinked structure (Hale et al., 2014) is about to become a new relevant component of this field of research (Nanni, 2017b). An emblematic example of the new challenges that born-digital documents will pose to historians of higher education is a study on reconstructing the recent past of the University of Bologna, through its digital sources (Nanni, 2017a).

The University of Bologna's website (Unibo.it), initially created in 1993, represents a new category of relevant resource for historians of higher education. The website collects and offers to the reader a large variety of documents, from descriptions of educational projects to overviews of research groups, from reports of collaboration with international institutions to information on opportunities of interactions with the private sector. In addition, it also shows how different departments, professors and research teams have been adopting the web – especially in its early days. Among the many relevant examples, one that deserves special mention is that the Astronomy Department of the university was already sharing preprints of their publications online in 1994 as html pages, in an early attempt to benefit from the potential of the World Wide Web.

Nevertheless, while Unibo.it represents a useful collection of primary sources, the website was modified several times during its first 20 years and the majority of pages that were published in the past are no longer available on the live web. In particular, the transition to the so-called 'Portale D'Ateneo', which started in the early 2000s, required that all department pages change their structure and adopt a common layout and organization of their content. This has often forced the creation of brand-new department subdomains and the removal of previous versions of the same from the live web. As an additional issue, the team that has managed the website during this entire transition has not consistently archived the previous versions of the website and documented their work.

Given the fact that, as of 2017, the National Libraries of Florence and Rome are still not part of the International Internet Preservation Consortium (IIPC) and no coordinated project with the specific purpose of preserving the national web-sphere currently exists in Italy, the Internet Archive remains the only resource available for recollecting all the materials that are no longer available on the University of Bologna website. However, in 2002 a removal request[4] from the administrative team of Unibo.it was sent to the Internet Archive, and for this reason Unibo.it was inaccessible through the Wayback Machine for more than 13 years. This highly complex situation reflects a new level of difficulties that future historians will encounter while attempting to collect born-digital sources. In the next section, an overview of the variety of sources and methods that have been used to deal with this issue and to reconstruct the past of Unibo.it will be presented.

**Library and Archive Materials**: As an initial step in the research, materials available in the university library and archives were consulted. Among many other documents, a very useful source has been the university yearbook. In the early 1990s only a few pieces of information regarding the website were mentioned in the yearbook; nevertheless, this source offered an initial diachronic overview of the official teams that were managing Unibo.it and was useful for drawing up a list of people to interview.

**Interviews**: In order to capture the rationale and the changing architecture of the website, the different teams who managed the website were interviewed, together with technicians and researchers who worked on the development of the pages of various departments, especially during the 1990s. Yet another interesting finding, presumably highly relevant for future historians, was that frequently during the interviews the subjects used public and private backups of emails in order to recollect the memories of their experience at working on Unibo.it and to confirm passages of the historical reconstruction.

**Newspapers**: As already done in previous work (Brügger, 2011), where printed media were used to retrieve information about the web of the past, information related to Unibo.it and the role of the website for the University of Bologna was identified in local and national newspaper archives. During the 1990s, newspapers such as *La Repubblica* and *Il Resto del Carlino* published a few short articles covering the new functionalities on the website (e.g. free email account for all students, online fee payments, etc.). These publications, together with materials collected from the university digital magazines (*Alma2000*, *AlmaNews*, *Unibo Magazine*), offered an additional overview on how the university decided to promote the website to its audience.

**Online Forums**: To get a closer look at the everyday use of the website by students and researchers, other materials have been collected and analyzed, starting with student forums (e.g. *UniversiBo*) and Usenet discussions preserved by Google. These documents, especially those from the 1990s, present the perspective and enthusiasm of a rather small but specific subset of the university community, namely students, researchers and professors in STEM fields, whose departments were among the first ones to offer access to the web.

**Live Web Materials**: While the website has been restructured multiple times during its first 20 years online, many resources are still available on the live web and can reveal the current role of the website in the university's organization and management (e.g. attracting national and international students and researchers, promoting collaborations with the private sector, etc.). Additionally, the social media pages of the institution (such as Facebook, Youtube and Twitter profiles) are becoming key components of its presence online, showing alternative and more informal ways of interaction with the users.

**Presence of Italian Websites in Other National Web Archives:** Aside from the Internet Archive, since 1996 national libraries from all around the world have also begun to preserve their national web past. PANDORA, started in 1996 by the National Library of Australia, the UK Web Archive (2004), the Netarkivet in Denmark (2005) and the Portuguese Web Archive (2011) are just a few examples of this international endeavor. Given the complexity of defining and preserving what is called a 'national web-sphere' (Brügger, 2009), this research also explored the use of foreign web archives as a proxy for studying Unibo.it. The practice of retrieving primary sources related to an Italian university website in foreign web archives could seem rather odd as the goal of a national web archive is precisely to preserve the web of its country; however, from time to time part of the non-national web also ends up being preserved, unintentionally, by these digital archives.

For example, to archive national web-spheres in an automatic way, archivists could set up crawlers with a maximum number of hyperlinks they can follow, with a specific set of starting points. A crawler that is set to go at most ten links away from one of these URLs could also end up crawling non-national content, as it will systematically follow all the hyperlinks. For this reason, if the University of Bologna were to organize a Summer School and Aarhus University had linked it from its website, the University of Bologna website (or at least part of it) would be unintentionally preserved in the Danish Web Archive.

As a part of this work, it has been found that both the Portuguese (Arquivo) and Danish (Netarkivet) web archives have preserved parts of Unibo.it several times since 2006.

**Cloned Versions of the Website**: Among the variety of sources available, one deserves a specific mention. In May 2007, a group of activists decided to create a copy of the Unibo.it web interface, as part of a protest against the European Credit Transfer and Accumulation System (ECTS) for the evaluation of the number of hours of study. In the URL *http://www.unibologna.eu* an identical version of the website was available, with a description of the reasons for the protest.

This source has not only been important in this study as it documented an innovative way of conducting a protest against an academic institution (by targeting its website), but also because the cloned website was preserved by the Internet Archive.

**A Critical Combination of Sources and Methods**: The combination of traditional archival practices with approaches from the field of internet studies is essential in the attempt to tackle this emblematic example of scarcity of born-digital primary sources and reconstructing the past of the University of Bologna website. This new methodology for collecting born-digital evidence has been especially useful in identifying the narrative behind the early years of Unibo.it, which involves the arrival of a Turkish professor from the United States at the university in 1988, the establishment of the second Italian node to the internet and the creation of arguably one of the most relevant university websites in the country[5].

While the difficulties in reconstructing the recent past of a university website could surprise the reader, as fewer than 30 years have passed since its creation, they only represent a few of the new issues that born-digital sources will pose to future historians.

As has been previously remarked and will be expanded on in the next section, future historians will in fact also be challenged by a never before experienced abundance of records of our past. The second case study presented in this chapter focuses on obtaining small topic-specific collections from large-scale archives of the web; by presenting the encountered challenges and describing the adopted solutions, the importance of fruitfully combining the traditional historical method with approaches from the field of natural language processing will be remarked on.

## CREATING POLITICAL EVENT COLLECTIONS: A TALE OF ABUNDANCE

The World Wide Web provides the research community with an unprecedented abundance of primary sources for diachronically tracing, examining and understanding major events and transformations in our society. For two decades, public and private institutions have preserved these born-digital materials for future analysis (Gomes et al., 2011). However, these collections are now so large that – in the rare cases that they are fully available for research (Hockx-Yu, 2014) – it is not feasible for scholars to study political and social phenomena by examining them in their entirety. If, for instance, we consider the Internet Archive, during its first 20 years it has preserved almost 500 billion web pages, and as of 2017 it has a collection of around 25 petabytes of data. Since 2001, this collection has become available for research through a URL search tool on the Wayback Machine. In the most recent years, information retrieval systems supporting keyword search over the diachronic layers of web archives have been developed by the research community and employed by institutions such as the UK Web Archive and – since 2017 – also partially by the Internet Archive. In addition to this, out-of-the-box tools such as ArchiveSpark (Holzmann et al., 2016a) and Warcbase (Lin et al., 2017) have been developed by the research community with the specific goal of supporting scholars in gathering information from large-scale web archive collections.

One of the main endeavors of web archive institutions for fostering the use of these new resources is to offer manually curated sub-collections regarding recent socio-political events. On Archive-It – a subscription web archiving service provided by the Internet Archive – a few collections regarding large-scale events such as the Boston marathon shooting, the Black Lives Matter movement and the Charlie Hebdo terrorist attack are available. The collections are curated by the Archive-It team in conjunction with curators and subject matter experts from institutions around the world.

In addition to manual selection, another solution employed by digital archivists for creating and sharing these event collections is to adopt a filtering approach that presents to the user only those documents that mention the name of the event. This type of approach is common in event-harvesting from Twitter, where researchers collect all tweets that – for example – mention the hashtag of the event.

While both collecting documents from web archives through manual selection and retrieving materials through name-filtering have already proved their usefulness in supporting researchers in the humanities and social sciences (e.g. Small, 2011), they have a few crucial limitations. On the one hand, manual selection is obviously a painstakingly long process – given the previously mentioned difficulties of retrieving information from web archives. On the other hand, collecting documents using the event-name heuristics presents the crucial limitation of often missing information on background stories as well as the premises of the examined events. To give a specific example, let us imagine that the goal is to collect primary sources regarding the 2004 Ukraine Orange Revolution. If the adopted method only retrieves documents that mention the name of the event, it will not collect materials that connect the premises of the revolution to the previous controversial presidential election in the country. And the same issue will emerge when studying the first free Algerian elections since their independence (1990), which is a premise of the Algerian civil war, or even when investigating the economic crisis behind Fujimori's auto-golpe in Peru (1992). In this last case, the documents that discuss the adoption of austerity measures will not be part of the collection. Moreover, the name used for referring to an event might change over time or vary between countries and languages: for example, one of the early hashtags used for the 2011 Egyptian Revolution was #jan25, referring to the day it started.

The second case study presented in this chapter is an interdisciplinary project between computer science and political history focused on building more comprehensive sub-collections regarding events such as elections, protests and political crises from large-scale web archives. As part of this research, a system that employs natural language processing methods and information retrieval approaches has been developed, which is able to gather and organize a highly comprehensive collection of sources describing a specific event (Nanni et al., 2017).

The developed approach is inspired by the fact that, when historians are conducting the same task manually (i.e. identifying relevant materials across an entire archive), they do not necessarily search only for documents that mention the name of the event. What historians will try to collect are also those documents that talk about related aspects that provide the context, involving for example some of the participants to the event, but not others. If we consider the previous example regarding the Orange Revolution, historians will also be interested in materials from the same period of time discussing the political career of Yulia Tymoshenko or addressing the state of the political relations between Ukraine, Russia and the European Union.

**Identifying Related Concepts and Entities**: In order to achieve this goal in an automated fashion, the first step is to be able to identify a set of concepts and entities that are relevant to an event. To do so, DBpedia (Auer et al., 2007) was employed. This is a large-scale knowledge base extracted from Wikipedia, where events (such as the Orange Revolution) are represented by nodes and connected through edges (i.e. hyperlinks in Wikipedia) to other related entities.

**Retrieving Contextual Passages**: For each collected entity and concept, a textual passage presenting it in the context of the event was also extracted from Wikipedia (for example: 'Yulia Tymoshenko co-led the Orange Revolution and was the first woman appointed Prime Minister of Ukraine'). This is an optimal solution for identifying other terms that could be useful to identify relevant documents.

**Ranking Concepts and Entities**: Having obtained an initial set of potentially relevant concepts and entities, the goal is to score each of them on how relevant they are to the event. For example, while Yulia Tymoshenko is highly relevant for the Orange Revolution, the European Union played only a marginal role in the event. Different approaches for ranking entities and concepts for relevance were tested and the best performing solution was to compute distances between entities and the event employing out-of-the-box RDF vector representations (Ristoski and Paulheim, 2016).

**Finding Mentions in Text**: Having our ranked set of entities and concepts, other documents mentioning them in relevant contexts were retrieved from the web archive. In order to go beyond simple string-matching of concepts that were considered relevant (e.g. 'protests', 'revolution', 'crisis', 'election'), word-embedding representations (Mikolov et al., 2013) have been adopted. Embedding techniques represent each word, entity or concept (e.g. 'protest') as a numeric vector of *n* dimensions. This allows us to measure similarity across different words and to collect relevant materials even if they talk about 'demonstration' or 'crisis', instead of, for example, mentioning 'protest' or 'revolution'.

**Final Collection Building**: It could happen that documents mention relevant entities and concepts out of context, for example as part of a comparison: 'The popular opposition to Ethiopia's current corrupt regime is comparable to the Orange Revolution in Ukraine'. In order to filter them out and select only the documents that should be included in the event collection, a machine learning system called Learning to Rank (Liu, 2009) was employed, which, given an initial set of relevant and not relevant documents, learns how to abstract this property and to automate the ranking process.

**A Critical Combination of Sources and Methods**: The combination of traditional practices of historical research with methodologies and approaches from the fields of natural language processing and information retrieval is essential for dealing with the large abundance of born-digital primary sources. Some of the approaches presented in this chapter have already been adopted in political science research. One of these first studies focused on retrieving documents that referred to political events (e.g. elections) from institutional web collections of the US government in order to define a new measure of 'attention' of the US Congress and the president to democratization and electoral practices in other countries, from Zimbabwe to Haiti and Egypt (Elshehawy et al., 2017). By doing so, this initial work highlights both the potential and challenges of using born-digital documents and computational methods for obtaining new insights into the recent political past.

The two case studies presented in this chapter reveal the importance of adopting a highly interdisciplinary approach when dealing with born-digital sources; methodologies from the field of internet studies could support historians in reconstructing lost web pages, while natural language processing methods could guide them in retrieving documents from large-scale web archives. The final part of this chapter will remark further on this, by discussing the importance of offering this interdisciplinary preparation to future historians in their educational programs.

## CONCLUSION: A NEW GENERATION OF HISTORIANS

In recent years, researchers have argued that history, like other humanities disciplines, is reaching a turning point in its methodology (Graham et al., 2015; Nelson, 2016; Scheinfeldt, 2012): sustained by the efforts of many digitization projects, the community has been employing computational methods in order to examine these vast resources and obtain new insights. This change in methodology has reopened a long-term debate regarding the ways textual evidence of the past can and should be properly interpreted.

While for the historical profession it is of course beneficial to constantly debate and criticize the validity of established practices of acquiring knowledge from sources, it is argued in this chapter that the adoption of digitized datasets and computational methods cannot be considered, by itself, the triggering factor of a fundamental turning point in our profession. In fact, adopting (or not) large-scale datasets of digitized sources, together with computational methods, will always remain a choice for the history scholar: Charles Darwin can still be studied without conducting text mining over the collections presented on Darwin Online, just as the London of the eighteenth century can be examined without reading the Proceedings of the Old Bailey Online.

However, it is also argued that history is in fact about to face a paradigm-shifting transition in its methods, but the triggering cause of this transition relies on the born-digital nature of the large majority of sources produced by contemporary societies. This change affects any type of document we create and consume in our everyday life, from bureaucratic forms collected by the public sector to newspaper articles to political mail correspondence to university websites, and it is about to present its multifarious consequences on historical research.

Born-digital sources are significantly more complex to archive, collect, analyze and select compared with traditional materials. Websites (such as Unibo.it) are large and variegated collections of documents, which are often not preserved in their entirety by web archive initiatives and can be reconstructed only through the meticulous combination of various pieces of information from different sources. When a resource, such as the institutional website of an administration, is finally re-created, it is often so vast that computational technologies (i.e. natural language processing methods and information retrieval approaches) are necessary for identifying and retrieving specific documents.

The methodological steps overviewed in this chapter for collecting, analyzing and selecting born-digital documents require strong interdisciplinary competences and a highly critical attitude towards sources and methods. In this complex scenario, this chapter concludes by raising a very pressing question: how can the new generations of historians be prepared to face these new challenges?

In recent years, the digital history community has already offered many educational activities on computational methods to its students. From workshops to panels, from courses to summer schools, from tutorials to hackathons, these initiatives have almost always been focused on presenting the potential of new resources, tools and platforms to the history students, following an attitude that has been branded 'more hack, less yack' (Nowviskie, 2014). While offering hands-on experiences with computational tools is important in order to introduce history students to the digital humanities, a critical approach is strongly needed in order to properly deal with born-digital sources and computational methods.

For this reason, it is essential that students will first of all be guided in shaping their research topics and receive early on in their studies the preparation necessary to support a critical analysis of the born-digital documents and computational methods at their disposal. This will be imperative for a generation of historians who will be able to go beyond an unquestioned adoption of the new sources and tools at their disposal and will instead critically employ them, in search of new historical perspectives.

## Notes

1 It is also important to acknowledge that reactions to postmodern approaches are present as well in the historiographic debate (see for example Evans, 2001).
2 See for example the adoption of social science methodologies in historical research in Fogel and Engerman (1974).
3 However, the relationship between history and computing on the one side and literary and linguistic computing on the other side has always been complicated (see for example Robertson, 2016).
4 As described in the FAQ section of the Internet Archive, a website owner can request crawling or archiving of a site to stop and the Internet Archive will endeavor to comply. This will be signaled by a 'blocked site error' message such as 'This URL has been excluded from the Wayback Machine'.
5 In 2001 the University of Bologna website won the 'WWW' prize from the Italian economic newspaper *Il Sole 24 Ore* for the best website in the category 'School, university and research'. Then, for three consecutive years (2005–7) Unibo.it received the 'Osc@r del web' prize for the best Italian public administration website. In 2007 Luigi Nicolais, the Italian Minister of Public Administration, was also present to confer the prize.

## REFERENCES


Auer, S., Bizer, C., Kobilarov, G., Lehmann, J., Cyganiak, R., and Ives, Z. (2007) 'DBpedia: A Nucleus for a Web of Open Data', *Proceedings of the 6th International and 2nd Asian Conference on Semantic Web:* 722–735.

Barthes, R. (1967) 'Discourse on History', *Social Science Information*, 6(4): 65–75.

Blevins, C. (2014) 'Space, Nation, and the Triumph of Region: A View of the World from Houston', *The Journal of American History*, 101(1): 122–147.

Bloch, M. (1949) *Apologie pour l'Histoire, ou, Métier d'Historien*. Armand Colin: Paris.

Brockliss, L.W. (1978) 'Patterns of Attendance at the University of Paris, 1400–1800', *The Historical Journal*, 21(3): 503–544.

Brügger, N. (2005) *Archiving Websites: General Considerations and Strategies*. The Centre for Internet Research: Aarhus.

Brügger, N. (2009) 'Website History and the Website as an Object of Study', *New Media & Society*, 11(1–2): 115–132.

Brügger, N. (2011) 'Web Archiving – between Past, Present, and Future', in M. Consalvo and C. Ess (Eds), *The Handbook of Internet Studies*, Wiley-Blackwell: Oxford.

Brügger, N. (2012) 'When the Present Web is Later the Past: Web Historiography, Digital History, and Internet Studies', *Historical Social Research/Historische Sozialforschung*, 37(4): 102–117.

Burke, P. (2008) *What is Cultural History?* Polity: Cambridge (UK).

Bush, V. (1945) 'As We May Think', *The Atlantic Monthly*, 176(1): 101–108.

Cohen, D.J. (2005) 'By the Book: Assessing the Place of Textbooks in US Survey Courses', *The Journal of American History*, 91(4): 1405–1415.

Cohen, D.J., and Rosenzweig, R. (2005) *Digital History: A Guide to Gathering, Preserving, and Presenting the Past on the Web*. University of Pennsylvania Press: Philadelphia, PA.

Cohen, D.J., Frisch, M., Gallagher, P., Mintz, S., Sword, K., Taylor, A.M., and Turkel, W.J. (2008) 'Interchange: The Promise of Digital History', *The Journal of American History*, 95(2): 452–491.

Daumard, A., and Furet, F. (1959) 'Méthodes de l'Histoire Sociale: Les Archives Notariales et la Mécanographie', *Annales: Histoire, Sciences Sociales*, 14(4): 676–693.

Davis, C. (2014) 'Archiving the Web: A Case Study from the University of Victoria'. *code {4} lib Journal*, 26 (http://journal.code4lib.org/articles/10015)

Derrida, J. (1997) *Of Grammatology*. John Hopkins University Press: Baltimore, MD.

Dougherty, M., Meyer, E.T., Madsen, C.M., Van den Heuvel, C., Thomas, A., and Wyatt, S. (2010) 'Researcher Engagement with Web Archives: State of the Art', *Preprint on SSRN* (https://ssrn.com/abstract=1714997)

Elshehawy, A., Marinov, N., and Nanni, F. (2017) 'Quantifying Attention to Foreign Elections with Text Analysis of US Congress and the Presidency', *Preprint on SSRN* (https://ssrn.com/abstract=2981486)

Evans, R.J. (2001) *In Defence of History*. Granta Books: London.

Fogel, R.W., and Engerman, S.L. (1974) *Time on the Cross*. University Press of America: Lanham, MD.

Gomes, D., Miranda, J., and Costa, M. (2011) 'A Survey on Web Archiving Initiatives', *Proceedings of the 15th International Conference on Theory and Practice of Digital Libraries*: 408–420.

Graham, S., Milligan, I., and Weingart, S. (2015) *Exploring Big Historical Data: The Historian's Macroscope*. Imperial College Press: London.

Greif, A. (1997) 'Cliometrics After 40 Years', *The American Economic Review*, 87(2): 400–403.

Hale, S.A., Yasseri, T., Cowls, J., Meyer, E.T., Schroeder, R., and Margetts, H. (2014) 'Mapping the UK Webspace: Fifteen Years of British Universities on the Web', *Proceedings of the 2014 ACM Conference on Web Science*: 62–70.

Hockx-Yu, H. (2014) 'Access and Scholarly Use of Web Archives', *Alexandria: The Journal of National and International Library and Information Issues*, 25(1–2): 113–127.

Holzmann, H., Goel, V., and Anand, A. (2016a) 'Archivespark: Efficient Web Archive Access, Extraction and Derivation', *Proceedings of the 2016 IEEE/ACM Joint Conference on Digital Libraries (JCDL)*: 83–92.

Holzmann, H., Nejdl, W., and Anand, A. (2016b) 'The Dawn of Today's Popular Domains: A Study of the Archived German Web Over 18 Years', *Proceedings of the 2016 IEEE/ACM Joint Conference on Digital Libraries (JCDL)*: 73–82.

Knowles, A.K., and Hillier, A. (Eds) (2008) *Placing History: How Maps, Spatial Data, and GIS are Changing Historical Scholarship*. ESRI: New York.

LaFrance, A. (2015) 'Raiders of the Lost Web', *The Atlantic*, 14 (https://www.theatlantic.com/technology/archive/2015/10/raiders-of-the-lost-web/409210/)

Lin, J., Milligan, I., Wiebe, J., and Zhou, A. (2017) 'Warcbase: Scalable Analytics Infrastructure for Exploring Web Archives', *Journal on Computing and Cultural Heritage (JOCCH)*, 10(4): 22.

Liu, T.Y. (2009) 'Learning to Rank for Information Retrieval', *Foundations and Trends in Information Retrieval*, 3(3): 225–331.

Lyotard, J.F. (1984) *The Postmodern Condition: A Report on Knowledge*. University of Minnesota Press: Minneapolis, MN.

Mikolov, T., Sutskever, I., Chen, K., Corrado, G.S., and Dean, J. (2013) 'Distributed Representations of Words and Phrases and their Compositionality', *Proceedings of the 26th International Conference on Neural Information Processing Systems*: 3111–3119.

Milligan, I. (2012) 'Mining the "Internet Graveyard": Rethinking the Historians' Toolkit', *Journal of the Canadian Historical Association/Revue de la Société Historique du Canada*, 23(2): 21–64.

Milligan, I. (2016) 'Lost in the Infinite Archive: The Promise and Pitfalls of Web Archives', *International Journal of Humanities and Arts Computing*, 10(1): 78–94.

Moretti, F. (2013) *Distant Reading*. Verso Books: London.

Munslow, A. (2006) *Deconstructing History*. Routledge: New York.

Nanni, F. (2013) 'L'Archiviazione delle Pagine dei Quotidiani Online', *Diacronie. Studi di Storia Contemporanea*, 15(3) (http://www.studistorici.com/wp-content/uploads/2013/10/02_NANNI.pdf)

Nanni, F. (2017a) 'Reconstructing a Website's Lost Past: Methodological Issues Concerning the History of www.unibo.it', *Digital Humanities Quarterly*, 11(2) (http://www.digitalhumanities.org/dhq/vol/11/2/000292/000292.html)

Nanni, F. (2017b) 'The Web as a Historical Corpus: Collecting, Analysing and Selecting Sources on the Recent Past of Academic Institutions', PhD Dissertation, University of Bologna.

Nanni, F., Ponzetto, S.P., and Dietz, L. (2017) 'Building Entity-Centric Event Collections',

*Proceedings of 2017 IEEE/ACM Joint Conference on Digital Libraries (JCDL)*: 199–209.

Nelson, R.K. (2016) 'Digital Humanities as Appendix', *American Quarterly*, 68(1): 131–136.

Noiret, S. (2015) 'Digital Public History: Bringing the Public Back In', *Public History Weekly*, 3(13) (http://hdl.handle.net/1814/38393).

Nowviskie, B. (2014) 'On the Origin of "Hack" and "Yack"', in M.K. Gold and L.F. Klein (Eds), *Debates in Digital Humanities (2nd ed.)*, University of Minnesota Press (http://dhdebates.gc.cuny.edu/debates/text/58)

Owen, D., and Davis, R. (2008) 'Presidential Communication in the Internet Era', *Presidential Studies Quarterly*, 38(4): 658–673.

Ramage, D.R. (2011) 'Studying People, Organizations, and the Web with Statistical Text Models', PhD Dissertation, Stanford University.

Ristoski, P., and Paulheim, H. (2016) 'RDF2vec: RDF Graph Embeddings for Data Mining', *Proceedings of the 2016 International Semantic Web Conference*: 498–514.

Robertson, S. (2016) 'The Differences Between Digital History and Digital Humanities', in M.K. Gold and L.F. Klein (Eds), *Debates in Digital Humanities (2nd ed.)*, University of Minnesota Press (http://dhdebates.gc.cuny.edu/debates/text/76).

Rosenzweig, R. (2003) 'Scarcity or Abundance? Preserving the Past in a Digital Era', *The American Historical Review*, 108(3): 735–762.

Rothman, J. (2014) 'An Attempt to Discover the Laws of Literature', *The New Yorker*.

Rüegg, W., and de Ridder-Symoens, H. (Eds) (1992) *A History of the University in Europe*. Cambridge University Press: Cambridge.

Scheinfeldt, T. (2012) 'Sunset for Ideology, Sunrise for Methodology', in M.K. Gold and L.F. Klein (Eds), *Debates in Digital Humanities (1st ed.)*, University of Minnesota Press. pp. 124–127.

Schreibman, S., Siemens, R., and Unsworth, J. (Eds) (2004) *A Companion to Digital Humanities*. Blackwell Publishing: Oxford.

Shafer, R.J. (1974) *A Guide to Historical Method*. Dorsey Press: Belmont, CA.

Small, T.A. (2011) 'What the Hashtag? A Content Analysis of Canadian Politics on Twitter', *Information, Communication & Society*, 14(6): 872–895.

Thaller, M. (1991) 'The Historical Workstation Project', *Computers and the Humanities*, 25(2): 149–162.

Thomas III, W.G. (2004) 'Computing and the Historical Imagination', in Schreibman, S., Siemens, R., and Unsworth, J. (Eds), *A Companion to Digital Humanities*. Blackwell Publishing: Oxford. pp. 56–68.

Wilkens, M. (2013) 'The Geographic Imagination of Civil War-Era American Fiction', *American Literary History*, 25(4): 803–840.

# Network Analysis for Web History

Michael Stevenson and
Anat Ben-David

This chapter provides a conceptual background for applying network analysis in web history research. Rather than a detailed discussion of the methods of network analysis (e.g. Wasserman and Faust, 1994) or a hands-on guide to using network analysis software for web and social media research (e.g. Hansen et al., 2010), this chapter serves as both a brief introduction to network analysis and a critical reflection on its potential for web historical research. It is divided into three main sections discussing: (1) the history and key concepts of network analysis, including the paradigm's aims and assumptions, (2) the influence of network analysis on the important web genres of search and social media, as well as how network analysis has been applied in research on the 'live web' and (3) the main challenges as well as the state of the art for network analysis using web archives. Finally, we conclude with a discussion of future directions for network analysis in web history research.

## INTRODUCTION TO NETWORK ANALYSIS

To understand how network analysis may be applied to web history and what is at stake in adopting the network approach, it is necessary to understand the historical and conceptual foundations of social network analysis. This section discusses how this 'paradigm' emerged as an approach to studying and explaining social phenomena and highlights how this intellectual history relates to the key assumptions, concepts and methods associated with network analysis.

### *Roots and Basic Concepts*

The roots of network analysis can be found in sociology in the 1930s, in particular in the work of famed psychoanalyst Jacob Moreno (1934), who developed an approach to mapping the interrelationships of groups called 'sociometry'. For Moreno, as for later proponents of network analysis, the key to understanding social structure was to see it as a 'network' of relations rather than relatively homogenous 'groups' of individuals. Moreno devised methods to capture and analyze networks of affinity within communities, and in one case famously argued that an 'epidemic' of runaways from a young women's reformatory school in New York could be explained in large part by looking at the ties of friendship and dislike between them, or their 'sociometric organization' (ibid.: 407). Moreno's key insight was that this spontaneous event was not indicative of 'mass' hysteria, but rather reflected how emotions and behaviors could quickly spread within an existing structure of relations 'In a way that even the girls themselves may not have been conscious of, it was their location in the social network that determined whether and when they ran away' (Borgatti et al., 2009: 892).

In subsequent decades, sociologists and anthropologists similarly developed a 'network' view of social ties, and in the 1970s social network analysis emerged as a well-defined discipline and 'formal methodology' in sociology (Carrington and Scott, 2011: 2). As a formal methodology, social network analysis draws on a branch of mathematics called 'graph theory', which provides vocabulary and techniques related to the study of relationships between objects. Graph data may be structured in different ways but is typically formatted as a matrix (Table 10.1) or a set of columns and rows (Table 10.2) representing objects and their connections. In social network analysis a typical matrix will list actors (individuals, institutions, etc.) along each axis and labels inside the matrix will represent information about their relationships (e.g. 'admires' or 'is friends with …'). Relationships are either *directed* (e.g. one person admires another) or *undirected* (e.g. kinship).

**Table 10.1 Example of a matrix with undirected social network data (x signifies a tie)**

| | *Person A* | *Person B* | *Person C* |
|---|---|---|---|
| Person A | - | | x |
| Person B | | - | x |
| Person C | x | x | - |

**Table 10.2 Social ties represented in two columns (using the same data as in Table 10.1)**

| *Person* | *Shares tie with* |
|---|---|
| A | C |
| C | B |

Graph data may be visualized in a network diagram, which consists of *nodes* (or *vertices*) representing the graph's objects and *lines* (or *edges*) representing their relationships. This process requires a set of decisions about how the data should be analyzed and depicted. For example, one might only want to visualize certain connections (e.g. only mutual expressions of friendship), while most network diagrams are composed using an algorithm (essentially, a set of rules or instructions) that positions nodes spatially according to the connections between them.

Key aspects of networks that can be represented and explored visually include *center* and *periphery*. Although different methods for calculating centrality exist, a central node typically has a high number of connections relative to other nodes, and such measurements may indicate a node's level of involvement and/or prestige within a network (Wasserman and Faust, 1994: 169–75). Other key characteristics include network *density*, a ratio between the actual and potential total number of connections in the network, and *distance*, a measurement of the path between two nodes. Nodes are said to have *structural equivalence* when they have identical ties, and other (less strict yet more complex) notions of equivalence may be used to identify classes of similar actors (Wasserman and Faust, 1994: 461–502). Along these lines, White et al. (1976) developed the notion of *blockmodels* to denote sets of nodes with similar patterns of connections within a larger network. Each block is essentially a subgrouping of nodes with a shared *position* within the network as well as a shared *role*, where the latter is also defined in terms of a pattern of links to other blocks (as opposed to inherent characteristics of actors within the group). For example, data from a network of researchers may reveal blocks related to status: a block of leading researchers is defined as those known by the vast majority of the network and connected to each other through interactions and collaborations, while at the same time generally unaware of and not connected to lower-tier researchers (ibid: 747–9).

## *Social Network Analysis as a Sociological 'Perspective'*

Although it is tempting to think of network analysis simply as a toolbox for capturing, visualizing and analyzing network data, it is important to see how this methodology is embedded in a larger sociological paradigm or 'perspective' that prioritizes social 'relations' over social 'categories' (Emirbayer and Goodwin, 1994: 1414). For example, the typical sociological survey will seek to find correlations between a particular behavior (e.g. websites visited) and commonly held attributes or demographics (e.g. income level, gender, etc.). By contrast, a network analysis approach would assume that behaviors are more accurately predicted by close examination of one's network of social ties.

As social network analysis has become widely adopted, one can see this basic assumption about the importance of 'relations' at work in a wide range of studies, from questions about the link between power and physical attraction (Martin, 2005) to the study of patent networks in exploring geographical regions of innovation (Fleming et al., 2007). Within this diverse literature, however, general 'moves' and concepts can be distilled (Borgatti et al., 2009) that have developed alongside methods for analyzing social networks (Wasserman and Faust, 1994).

In addition to a wealth of tools, concepts and existing theory, previous work on social network analysis provides a good deal of critical self-reflection that will benefit applications within web history. Criticism of network analysis centers on three related issues. First, the concepts, methods and tools offered by social network analysis are all geared towards answering questions of *structural context* rather than *content*. Network analysis may provide insight into how, say, a video or meme spreads on the web, or help to identify clusters and cliques among bloggers or social media users, but says very little about the meaning of such content or the character of such communities. Moreover, given the commitment to a relational understanding of social action, a 'pure' form of network analysis would seek to transform any questions of content into network terms: the meaning of a meme or video is to be found in the networks it traverses and connects, the character of a community is understood in terms of the connections between its members and its position in relation to other communities. Second, because most network analysis assumes the primacy of networks over their content, it does not address how networks are constituted, maintained and dissolved by cultural practices (Emirbayer and Goodwin, 1994). Third, focusing only on structure leads to narrow explanations (if any) of historical change:

> [Network analysis] provides a useful set of tools for investigating the patterned relationships among historical actors. These tools, however, by themselves fail ultimately to make sense of the mechanisms through which these relationships are reproduced or reconfigured over time. (ibid: 1447)

There is thus an inherent tension between network analysis and the central aim of historical inquiry, namely to provide explanations of events and processes that occur over time. Of course, this does not preclude its use in web history, but any studies that build on the language and methods of network analysis should consider this central tension.

### *Citation Analysis*

One form of network analysis that deserves a special mention in relation to the web is citation analysis, as this has influenced both web technology (such as search engines and social media) as well as tools for web research.

Citation analysis is the study of connections between scientific texts by way of bibliographic references. The technique was pioneered in the 1950s by Eugene Garfield to help researchers find the journals and articles that would most interest them, as well as providing libraries with an evaluation tool for managing their journal collections (Garfield, 1955). In addition to information retrieval purposes, Garfield and others were quick to see the potential for employing citation analysis in the history and sociology of science (e.g. de Solla Price and Beaver, 1966).

Citation networks can be compiled and studied in different ways for different purposes. The basic form is the study of *direct citations*, producing a graph that is particularly suited to overall measures of popularity and centrality. *Bibliographic coupling* compares references from scientific papers, and serves to indicate topical similarity. A third technique that is particularly prevalent in the sociology of science is *co-citation analysis*, where a tie between two papers is registered when they are cited together by a third paper. The more often two papers are cited together, the stronger their connection. According to Small (1973), the significance of these ties is 'subject similarity' and 'the association or co-occurrence of ideas', and co-citation analysis thus offers a potential view not only of structures of influence, but of relationships between particular concepts, ideas or arguments.

Together, social network analysis and citation analysis provide long histories of research and a rich foundation of problems, concepts, vocabularies, methods, tools and critical reflections that may be mined in order to give depth to network analyses of web data and web history. However, the importance of this existing knowledge is not limited to *applying* network analysis. As we argue in the next section, there is a triadic relationship between network analysis, the web as a medium and web research that is crucial to understanding the web (including its history) as well as the dominant questions and modes of explanation that characterize the body of research that has grown around it.

## THE WEB AND NETWORK ANALYSIS

In this section we discuss two important ways the web and social network analysis are related. On the one hand, network analysis is part of the fabric of our experience of the web, as network analysis has influenced key technologies such as search engines and social media. On the other hand, web data and social media data have strong affordances for network analysis, and the growth of the web has been accompanied by a great deal of interest in network analysis as well as the proliferation of network analytical tools.

As a hypertext document system, the World Wide Web is rooted in the science and practice of information retrieval. Given this common lineage with citation analysis, it is no surprise that the web's basic design has two major affordances for network analysis.

First, hyperlinks serve as an analogy to ties or citations in the sense that social network analysis uses these concepts. Even in his original 1989 proposal, Berners-Lee speculated that the web would allow for (automatic) analysis of connections between researchers, for example to guide the creation of project groups. Second, IP and HTTP data logged by web servers (and data gathered through browser cookies and other tracking technology) align with the kinds of data used for network analysis, including spatial and temporal data (through IP addresses and timestamps), interaction data and data about information flows (c.f. Borgatti et al., 2009).

One key application of network analysis is in search technology, most famously in Google's PageRank algorithm. Google co-founders Larry Page and Sergey Brin (together with colleagues) specifically drew on citation analysis and described their algorithm as 'a method for rating web pages objectively and mechanically' (Page et al., 1999: 1; cf. Rieder, 2014). Google's engine marked a major shift in search because of how little the rankings depended on the *content* of sites, instead relying almost entirely on the larger structure of connections on the web to make determinations about the quality and relevance of a website. Although counting links was one of the many methods used by previous search engines, Google's algorithm stood out for how it used network structure to make further inferences about the *quality* of links: a link from a website prominent in the network (such as Yahoo! or the BBC) is valued more highly by PageRank than a link from a website on the periphery (i.e. one with fewer links from the network). In accordance with the central tenet of network analysis, then, the algorithm does not take into account internal attributes of web pages, but instead defines authority in relational terms. As is clear in their descriptions of PageRank and discussion of the search engine elsewhere, Page and Brin see this emphasis on network structure as the key to achieving objective, or 'organic', search results, thus echoing Garfield's (1955) argument that citation analysis provides a more objective measure of scientific quality.

A similar connection is seen between network analysis and social media, particularly in methods for 'socially' recommended content. Starting in 2007, Facebook began to see its product less as a specialized 'social network' and more as a generalized utility (Farber, 2007). This turn towards seeing itself as a platform – not just for users but for developers, content providers and advertisers – went hand in hand with the company's promotion of its core feature as a 'social graph', or 'the network of connection and relations between people on the service' (ibid, n.p.). Around the same time, the company was developing algorithms for selecting and recommending content for users' news feeds that would come to be known collectively as EdgeRank (Kincaid, 2010). EdgeRank, like Google's PageRank, is a ranking algorithm that employs a relational approach: it uses data about relationships and user activities to calculate a relevance score, and thus explicitly does not seek to define this importance by looking at the substance of shared content. Where PageRank sorts websites based on hyperlink analysis, EdgeRank sorts newsfeed posts and other timely information based on explicit and implicit ties between people, pages, groups and other entities on Facebook's social graph.

The blind spots of PageRank and EdgeRank are in some sense also those of network analysis in general. Their relational approaches must be considered when discussing past and present controversies about how they order and recommend content, from issues related to controversial search results to the (discontinued) use of human editors on Facebook. What the examples of PageRank and EdgeRank suggest, then, is that network analysis is not simply a method to be applied to the web's past, but also a set of ideas and techniques that informed important events and innovations in the medium's history. They also raise the question of how network analyses in web research in some sense 'extend' the methods already embedded in the medium (Rogers, 2013). This is the question we turn to now.

## Network Analysis and Web Research

In this section we examine how network analysis has been used to study the live web. Although uses of network analysis are more widespread, we highlight three genres in particular: webometrics, issue networks and controversy mapping, and studying social media data.

Examples of network analysis in web research prior to the late 2000s were focused nearly exclusively on hyperlinks, considered the ultimate 'thread' that seamlessly weaves the web. Park and Thelwall (2003) distinguish between webometrics – an approach rooted in information science – and hyperlink network analysis as an approach rooted in social network analysis. The two approaches, albeit sharing the same object of study and a similar method of quantitatively extracting and mapping hyperlink networks, differ in their focus and research questions. The webometrics approach is primarily focused on the hyperlink's role in the context of information retrieval and search engine algorithms (Thelwall et al., 2005), with practical aims such as website discovery and ranking. The hyperlink network analysis paradigm, meanwhile, hosts a variety of research questions and interests, ranging from studying social structures and computer-mediated communication to the study of social movements or specific issues (De Maeyer, 2013). Interestingly, the distinction between information science and social sciences as parallel approaches to the study of online networks is also characteristic of the literature on web archive research and historical network analysis in particular, as we will see later.

Among other forms of research, hyperlink network analysis is used in Science and Technology Studies approaches to mapping issues and controversies online (Marres and Rogers, 2008; Marres, 2015). The Issue Crawler (http://www.issuecrawler.net/) is a web-based application that uses concepts and techniques from co-citation analysis to map 'issue networks', or heterogeneous sets of actors organized around an issue of public concern. Beginning with a set of websites that act as starting points, the Issue Crawler mines a network of hyperlinks and outputs a network diagram based on 'co-links'. Examples of issue network analysis include research on how local political issues may be 'subsumed' or redefined by the structures of transnational issue networks (Marres and Rogers, 2008), and comparative research on how structures of issue networks relate to the degree to which issue 'narratives' are shared (Bennett et al., 2011).

Since the late 2000s, network analysis on the web has increased dramatically, moving beyond the hyperlink-based approaches such as webometrics and issue network analysis to incorporate many more types of (social) network data – a development made possible by the rise of social media. Where a number of studies use social media data for traditional network analysis questions such as identifying 'influencers' within social groups (Aral and Walker, 2012; Stieglitz and Dang-Xuan, 2013), others employ network analysis of social media data in other domains such as news discussion (Bruns and Burgess, 2012). Meanwhile, network analysis tools designed with web and social media data in mind include NodeXL (Smith et al., 2009; Hansen et al., 2010) and Gephi (Bastian et al., 2009).[1]

The popularity of network analysis for social media is unsurprising, given the many affordances social media data has for this approach. In addition to formalized relationship and activity data, the commercial incentive of turning social networks into 'platforms' for developers has ensured structured access in the form of APIs. However, this commercial value means companies exert control over this access, often making it more difficult for researchers to study social media. In addition to issues of access, researchers must engage with the question of what exactly social media data represents, and what assumptions and consequences are attached to different approaches to gathering and analyzing that data. For example, how we study and interpret Twitter data depends on what relations are represented by 'follows'. Kwak et al. (2011) demonstrate that the structure of relations on Twitter deviates considerably from that of existing social networks, and combine this finding with others to suggest that the medium should be understood as a news medium rather than a social utility. Meanwhile, an analysis of Facebook's 'social graph' suggests commonalities with other social networks, and provides evidence of its 'small-world' nature, meaning relatively few 'steps' are necessary for content to be shared across a large portion of the network (Ugander et al., 2011). Where computer scientists have examined the nature of social media data through large-scale topological mappings, media studies researchers have done so through specific case studies. In a study of a political and cultural 'refraction chamber' on Twitter, Rieder (2012) analyzes the assumptions embedded in different approaches to collecting the platform's network data. As Rieder argues, approaches that focus too narrowly on the traditional network analysis topic of 'diffusion' will miss out on important ways in which communities appropriate news and information in culturally distinct ways (ibid.).

As we have seen in this section, network analysis and the web are closely linked, from the influence of network analysis on key web genres to a large body of network analytical research and a range of network analysis tools for web research. Now we turn to how network analysis has been applied in web history research, focusing on the key challenges this brings.

## APPLYING NETWORK ANALYSIS IN WEB HISTORY RESEARCH

Before discussing the applicability of network analysis in web history research, let us introduce web archives as the primary source used for historical network analysis. Earlier in this chapter, we outlined the historical ties between hyperlink, search engines and scientometrics. As with Google's PageRank algorithm, the history of web archives is also rooted in scientometrics and in the history of search engines. Brewster Kahle, the founder of the Internet Archive, was the CEO and founder of Alexa Internet. After Alexa Internet was sold to Amazon in 1996, the Internet Archive was founded as a non-profit organization, taking its harvesting technology and data donation from Alexa Internet. In an early piece about web archiving, Kahle identifies the Internet Archive's mission with scientometric analysis, noting that the web's hyperlinked structure functions as an informal citation system and that 'the study of the evolution of the web's hyperlink topology may provide insights into what any given community thought was important' (1997, n.p.). Thus, the Internet Archive, and subsequently many national web archives that were founded in the early 2000s, follow the logic of search engines. However, unlike search engine crawlers, which add newly found pages to the search engine's index, web archiving crawlers preserve a snapshot of any found page (Masanes, 2006).

Unlike the popular application of network analysis as a paradigm and method for conducting web research, historical network analysis of the web has thus far been limited in scope, primarily due to numerous methodological challenges that relate to the difficulty in adding a temporal dimension to the network diagram, as well as to ontological problems in using archived websites as the primary source from which historical networks are generated.

### *Temporal Challenges*

The network diagram is a spatial representation of relational ties between entities at a given point in time. As long as the temporal dimension is held static, there is no principle difference between network analyses of contemporary ties – for example, a network of interlinked websites of university students (Adamic and Adar, 2003) – and network analyses of historical ties – for example, a network of the social structure of Roman society (Alexander and Danowski, 1990). Since the web is a dynamic medium in which content and ties change constantly and rapidly, the static network diagram fails to capture the dynamic changes that a network undergoes over time.[2] It should be noted that this constraint poses challenges to any network analysis of web data, whether of the present or of the past, as the content and structure of the network may have changed minutes after the data was captured.

Therefore, one of the first problems in applying historical network analysis to web data is the lack of temporal or longitudinal data. To solve this problem, several researchers proposed to proactively collect web data in order to analyze changes in its hyperlinked structure over time. Foot et al. (2003), for example, proposed a method that involves proactive data collection involving machine network mapping and human ethnographic coding to retrospectively study the evolution of linking practices of Congressional candidates during the 2002 campaign season. Baeza-Yates and Poblete (2003) also used proactive crawling of Chilean websites in order to study the evolution of the structure of the Chilean web.

A second challenge in applying historical network analyses of the web relates to the difficulty in determining websites' specific timestamps. The live web hosts various websites that were published or recently updated at different points in time, and the exact time of publication or update can be estimated through various methods, such as the timestamps embedded in a website's code, or a response to a HTTP server request. However, as SalahEldeen and Nelson (2013) argue, such timestamps may vary in format or time zone. While SalahEldeen and Nelson propose a method for 'carbon-dating' websites through a web application that estimates the creation date for a URI by polling various sources of evidence (such as Bitly for the first time a URI was shortened, a Memento aggregator for the first time it appeared in a public web archive or Google's time of last crawl), other researchers use web resources with known timestamps to study the evolution of networks over time.[3] Buriol et al. (2006), for example, used the explicit timestamps associated with Wikipedia's entries to study the evolution of Wikipedia's linked structure over time. Like Wikipedia, web archives also attach specific timestamps to each page or element from the archived website. In this way, Toyoda and Kitsuregawa (2005) used six Japanese web archives to develop a system for visualizing and analyzing the evolution of the web's structure with a series of website captures from 1996 to 2003.

Despite the advantage of web archives as repositories of longitudinal web data with exact timestamps that may lend themselves to historical network analysis, there are several additional challenges to their use as historical sources for this purpose, as outlined in the following section.

## *Challenges Related to Web Archives as Specific Historical Sources*

On its face, web archives should lend themselves to historical network analysis not only because of the exact timestamps attached to each archived snapshot, but also because of an assumed fit between the network paradigm and methods for web archiving. Many web archives are created using a harvesting method that relies on the web's networked structure to crawl websites and discover more pages. At the same time, the archived websites are preserved as discrete files that are stripped of their original networked structure and contextual environments (Rogers, 2013). Therefore, unlike hyperlink networks of the live web, network analyses of the archived web involve reconstruction, rather than mapping.

One of the challenges in reconstructing historical hyperlink networks from the archived web involves the normalization and selection of the relevant timestamps of the archived snapshots. Since the frequency of archiving is irregular, one cannot ensure that all of the network's actors have been archived at the same time. Instead, the reconstructed network might represent an artifact of mixed temporalities, rather than a coherent representation of spatial ties at a specific moment in time. As a hypothetical example, consider a researcher who is interested in following up on the study of Foot et al. (2003) mentioned above, to study the hyperlink network of Congressional candidates' websites before and after the 2008 US presidential election. The researcher would collect a list of candidates' websites, and fetch their archived snapshots from the Internet Archive from 2007 and 2009. Subsequently, she would compare differences in the hyperlink network that each list generates. However, a closer inspection of the websites in each list would reveal that some of the websites were archived at the beginning of the year, while others were archived towards its end. The question arises whether the ties that the networks display indeed exist on the live web, even though the websites from which the ties were extracted are dated almost a year apart.

To address this problem, researchers from the Digital Methods Initiative created a tool that renders hyperlink networks based on a selection of archived versions that are closest to 1 July in each year (Weltevrede and Helmond, 2012). A similar initiative that facilitates the reconstruction of hyperlink networks from the archived web is the Web Archives for Longitudinal Knowledge (WALK) project, which offers ready-made graph files for visualizing hyperlink networks of the Canadian national web archiving portal (Milligan et al., 2016). While various approaches will address the issue of inconsistency differently, it should be noted that the problem of temporal difference is an artifact of the archiving process and is not 'solved' through any particular mode of analysis, especially since network diagrams – given their emphasis on spatial organization – serve to deemphasize or smooth over such temporal inconsistencies.

Other challenges that are specific to the archived web as a historical source relate to the scope and depth of the archive. Web archives such as the Internet Archive crawl the live web using a 'breadth-first' method, focusing on discovering links to other websites from a given homepage of a website. While the majority of national libraries use Heritrix, the breadth-first crawler developed by the Internet Archive (Mohr et al., 2004), some national web archives employ a 'depth-first' crawling method that aims to completely archive all the pages of a given website, or choose for a 'selective method' of archiving a given set of curated websites (Masanes, 2006). As a result, historical hyperlink analyses of web archives may be incomplete, due to differences between the crawling methods employed (Milligan et al., 2016; Samar et al., 2016).

The problem of completeness of web archives as a historical source for network analysis is addressed by Niels Brügger (2013), who argues that while all web archives are incomplete – both due to partial archiving but also due to missing elements in the archiving process, such as video and images, which analytical network analysis software cannot address – web archives are also too complete, since there are many archived versions of the same website, from which the researchers have to select.

Finally, it should be noted that most hyperlink network analyses of web archives are in fact reconstructions of ties between outbound links from the archived snapshots, rather than a reconstruction of possible inbound links from other websites outside of the researchers' corpus. Put differently, as Brügger (2013) notes, while there is only one live web, the reconstructed network is always one instance of many possible networks. To solve this problem, he suggests performing historical network analysis across different web archives.

## Examples

Despite the abovementioned challenges, there is a growing literature on web history that employs historical network analysis using web archives, especially from the perspective of the study of national webs. The application of network analysis in web historical research can be broadly described in three areas of historical questions: (1) the study of the evolution of networks over time – emphasizing the shifting roles of content, issues and actors. (2) The evolution of the web as a medium – emphasizing changes in technologies, features and structure. (3) A critical study of web archives as a primary source for historical research. While each of these questions can be performed separately, they are often combined. A combination of historical questions on the evolution of networks of actors and of the web as a medium is evident in a study by Weltevrede and Helmond (2012), who reconstructed the hyperlinked structure of the Dutch blogosphere, to study the history of the web's blogging platform transitions. Hale et al. (2014) traced the changing hyperlink structure of networks of British universities and found an inverse relationship between the density of links and the geographical distance between universities. Ben-David (2016) reconstructed from the Internet Archive the now vanished domain of the former Yugoslavia, .yu, and performed historical network analysis of the historical domain to demonstrate ties between sovereignty and the cohesive structure of a national web, thereby combining questions on the evolution of historical national webs with a critique of web archives as a primary source for web historiography. Historical network analysis of the archived web has also been used as a method to discover evidence of historical materials that have not been archived. Huurdeman et al. (2015) proposed a method for recovering evidence of the past existence of pages that were crawled but not preserved during the archiving process, using a combination of hyperlink analysis, anchor text and crawl logs.[4]

As we have seen in this section, researchers interested in applying historical network analysis either proactively archive their own corpora, or rely on archived web data. The plethora of ontological and methodological challenges related to the use of historical network analysis with archived web materials might deter researchers from applying this method. However, when carefully planned, historical network analysis of the archived web may be particularly useful in gaining broad insights about the structural evolution of historical networks over time, as well as for answering different sets of questions on the web's history. The following section concludes this chapter by putting forward a reflexive approach to the application of network analysis in web history.

## BACK IS THE WAY FORWARD

This chapter has sought to provide the necessary concepts, history and theory needed to apply network analysis in web history research. In conclusion, we would like to propose two ways in which 'back is the way forward' for both network analysis and those who wish to apply it to web history. First, if methodological innovation follows from novel research problems, web history provides fruitful grounds for new insights relating to network analysis. Whereas social media increasingly offer highly formalized data suitable for network analyses (even if access to this data remains highly controlled), the archived web remains notoriously incomplete. In addition to considering how to approach the material constraints and uneven temporality of web archives, researchers must consider what other, perhaps offline, sources can be mined for historical network data that can be used to triangulate findings from archived web pages. The challenge is perhaps to realize that web history is more 'networked' than conventionally understood: beyond hyperlinks, there are implicit links between a range of people, institutions, technologies and so on that can be mapped in order to produce better descriptions of structural relations in the web's history.

Second, web historians making use of network analysis may find inspiration from further engagement with existing work in network sociology. For example, further work on the histories of networked groups like the early blogging community (Ammann, 2009; Siles, 2012) may find useful concepts and theory on how structures of relations are co-constituted with shared identities (White, 1992). More generally, web historians will likely seek approaches that transcend the divide between studies of 'big' and 'small' data, as well as the divide between structural dynamics and situated meaning. Another existing body of work that should prove useful is qualitative approaches to gathering and analyzing network data (Hollstein, 2011). Overall, the challenge is to go beyond understanding network analysis as a methodological toolbox and instead engage with it as a paradigm, one that is suited to particular kinds of research problems and questions.

## ACKNOWLEDGMENTS

Research for this chapter was supported by the Dutch National Science Foundation (NWO) in connection with the Veni research project 'The web that was' (275-45-006).

### *Notes*

1 Note that some tools such as the Issue Crawler are designed specifically to crawl and analyze the live web. Users provide data for other tools such as NodeXL and Gephi, making these tools more suitable when using historical web data.

2 It should be noted that although the literature on social network analysis proposes statistical methods for studying the coevolution of networks using longitudinal data, these models have not been widely adopted in historical network analyses of the web. Snijders (2005), for example, puts forward several statistical models that conceive of network dynamics as a continuous process rather than being bound to the observation moments, because at each moment the current network structure is an important determinant of the likelihood of the changes that might occur next.

3 Memento (Van de Sompel et al., 2009) is a framework for locating past versions of a given web resource through an aggregator of resources from multiple web archives.

4 More examples of network analysis in web history can be found in Brügger and Schroeder (2017).

## REFERENCES

Adamic, L.A., and Adar, E. (2003) 'Friends and Neighbors on the Web', *Social Networks*, 25(3): 211–230.

Alexander, M.C., and Danowski, J.A. (1990) 'Analysis of an Ancient Network: Personal Communication and the Study of Social Structure in a Past Society', *Social Networks*, 12(4): 313–335.

Ammann, R. (2009) 'Jorn Barger, the Newspage Network and the Emergence of the Weblog Community', *Proceedings of the 20th ACM Conference on Hypertext and Hypermedia*. Torino, Italy: ACM: 279–288.

Aral, S., and Walker, D. (2012) 'Identifying Influential and Susceptible Members of Social Networks', *Science*, 337(6092): 337–341.

Baeza-Yates, R.A., and Poblete, B. (2003) 'Evolution of the Chilean Web Structure Composition', *Proceedings of the IEEE/LEOS 3rd International Conference on Numerical Simulation of Semiconductor Optoelectronic Devices*, 11–13.

Bastian, M., Heymann, S., and Jacomy, M. (2009) 'Gephi: An Open Source Software for Exploring and Manipulating Networks', *Proceedings of the Third International ICWSM Conference*, 8: 361–362.

Ben-David, A. (2016) 'What Does the Web Remember of Its Deleted Past? An Archival Reconstruction of the Former Yugoslav Top-Level Domain', *New Media & Society*, 18(7): 1103–1119.

Bennett, W.L., Foot, K., and Xenos, M. (2011) 'Narratives and Network Organization: A Comparison of Fair Trade Systems in Two Nations', *Journal of Communication*, 61(2): 219–245.

Borgatti, S.P., Mehra, A., Brass, D.J., and Labianca, G. (2009) 'Network Analysis in the Social Sciences', *Science*, 323(5916): 892–895.

Brügger, N. (2013) 'Historical Network Analysis of the Web', *Social Science Computer Review*, 31(3): 306–321.

Brügger, N., and Schroeder, R. (Eds.) (2017) *The Web as History: Using Web Archives to Understand the Past and the Present*. London: UCL Press.

Bruns, A., and Burgess, J. (2012) 'Researching News Discussion on Twitter', *Journalism Studies*, 13(5–6): 801–814.

Buriol, L., Castillo, C., Donato, D., and Leonardi, S., Millozzi. (2006) 'Temporal analysis of the Wikigraph', *2006 IEEE/WIC/ACM International Conference on Web Intelligence (WI 2006 Main Conference Proceedings)(WI'06)*: 45–51.

Carrington, P.J., and Scott, J. (2011) 'Introduction', in J. Scott and P.J. Carrington (Eds.), *The SAGE Handbook of Social Network Analysis*. London: Sage. pp. 1–8.

De Maeyer, J. (2013) 'Towards a Hyperlinked Society: A Critical Review of Link Studies', *New Media & Society*, 15(5): 737–751.

de Solla Price, D.J., and Beaver, D. (1966) 'Collaboration in an invisible college,' *American Psychologist* 21: 1011–1018.

Emirbayer, M., and Goodwin, J. (1994) 'Network Analysis, Culture, and the Problem of Agency', *American Journal of Sociology*, 99(6): 1411–1454.

Farber, D. (2007) 'Facebook: The Social Web Utility Company', ZDnet, 25 Jan. (http://www.zdnet.com/article/facebook-the-social-web-utility-company/)

Fleming, L., King, C., and Juda, A.I. (2007). 'Small Worlds and Regional Innovation', *Organization Science*, 18(6): 938–954.

Foot, K., Schneider, S.M., Dougherty M., et al. (2003) 'Analyzing Linking Practices: Candidate Sites in the 2002 US Electoral Web Sphere', *Journal of Computer-Mediated Communication*, 8(4) (https://doi.org/10.1111/j.1083-6101.2003.tb00220.x)

Garfield, E. (1955) 'Citation Indexes for Science. A New Dimension in Documentation through Association of Ideas', *International Journal of Epidemiology*, 35(5): 1123–1127.

Hale, S.A., Yasseri, T., Cowls, J., Meyer, E.T., Schroeder, R., and Margetts, H. (2014) 'Mapping the UK Webspace: Fifteen Years of British Universities on the Web', *Proceedings of the 2014 ACM Conference on Web Science*: 62–70.

Hansen, D., Shneiderman, B., and Smith, M.A. (2010) *Analyzing Social Media Networks with NodeXL: Insights from a Connected World*. Burlington, MA: Morgan Kaufmann.

Hollstein, B. (2011) 'Qualitative Approaches', in J. Scott and P.J. Carrington (Eds.), *The SAGE Handbook of Social Network Analysis*. London: Sage. pp. 404–416.

Huurdeman, H., Kamps, J., Samar, T., et al. (2015) 'Lost but Not Forgotten: Finding Pages on the Unarchived Web', *International Journal on Digital Libraries*, 6(3–4): 247–265.

Kahle, B. (1997) 'Preserving the Internet', *Scientific American*, 276(3): 82–83.

Kincaid, J. (2010) 'EdgeRank: The Secret Sauce That Makes Facebook's News Feed Tick', *Techcrunch*. 22 April (http://social.techcrunch.com/2010/04/22/facebook-edgerank/).

Kwak, H., Chun, H., and Moon, S. (2011) 'Fragile Online Relationship: A First Look at Unfollow Dynamics in Twitter', *Proceedings of the SIGCHI Conference on Human Factors in Computing Systems*. ACM, 16 July.

Marres, N. (2015) 'Why Map Issues? On Controversy Analysis as a Digital Method', *Science, Technology, & Human Values*, 40(5): 655–686.

Marres, N., and Rogers, R. (2008) 'Subsuming the Ground: How Local Realities of the Fergana Valley, the Narmada Dams and the BTC Pipeline Are Put to Use on the Web', *Economy and Society*, 37(2): 251–281.

Martin, J.L. (2005) 'Is Power Sexy?', *American Journal of Sociology*, 111(2): 408–446.

Masanes, J. (2006) 'Web Archiving Methods and Approaches: A Comparative Study', *Library Trends*, 54(1): 72–90.

Milligan, I., Ruest, N., and Lin, J. (2016) 'Content Selection and Curation for Web Archiving: The Gatekeepers vs. the Masses', *IEEE/ACM Joint Conference on Digital Libraries (JCDL)*: 107–110.

Mohr, G., Stack, M., Ranitovic, I., et al. (2004) 'Introduction to Heritrix', *4th International Web Archiving Workshop*: 1–15.

Moreno, J. (1934) *Nervous and mental disease monograph series: Who Shall Survive? A New Approach to the Problem of Human Interrelation*. Vol. 58. Washington, D.C.: Nervous and Mental Disease Publishing.

Page, L., Brin, S., Motwani, R., and Winograd, T. (1999) 'The PageRank Citation Ranking: Bringing Order to the Web', *Stanford InfoLab* (http://ilpubs.stanford.edu:8090/422/).

Park, H.W., and Thelwall, M. (2003) 'Hyperlink Analyses of the World Wide Web: A Review', *Journal of Computer-Mediated Communication*, 8(4) (https://doi.org/10.1111/j.1083-6101.2003.tb00223.x)

Rieder, B. (2012) 'The Refraction Chamber: Twitter as Sphere and Network', *First Monday*, 17(11) (http://firstmonday.org/ojs/index.php/fm/article/view/4199).

Rieder, B. (2014) 'What Is in PageRank? A Historical and Conceptual Investigation of a Recursive Status Index', *Computational Culture*, 2 (http://computationalculture.net/article/what_is_in_pagerank).

Rogers, R. (2013) *Digital Methods*. Cambridge, MA: MIT Press.

SalahEldeen, H.M., and Nelson, M.L. (2013) 'Carbon Dating the Web: Estimating the Age of Web Resources', *arXiv*:1304(5213) (https://arxiv.org/abs/1304.5213).

Samar, T., Traub, M.C., and van Ossenbruggen, J., and de Vries, A.P. (2016) 'Comparing Topic Coverage in Breadth-First and Depth-First Crawls Using Anchor Texts', *TPDL 2016: Research and Advanced Technology for Digital Libraries*, 10 August.

Siles, I. (2012) 'The Rise of Blogging: Articulation as a Dynamic of Technological Stabilization', *New Media & Society*, 14(5): 781–797.

Small, H. (1973) 'Co-Citation in the Scientific Literature: A New Measure of the Relationship between Two Documents', *Journal of the Association for Information Science and Technology*, 24(4): 265–269.

Smith, M.A., Schneiderman, B., Milic-Frayling, N., et al. (2009) 'Analyzing (Social Media) Networks with NodeXL', *Proceedings of the Fourth International Conference on Communities and Technologies*. ACM: 255–264.

Snijders, T. (2005) 'Models for Longitudinal Network Data', in P.J. Carrington, J. Scott, and S. Wasserman (Eds.), *Models and Methods in Social Network Analysis*. Cambridge: Cambridge University Press. pp. 215–247.

Stieglitz, S., and Dang-Xuan, L. (2013) 'Social Media and Political Communication: A Social Media Analytics Framework', *Social Network Analysis and Mining*, 3(4): 1277–1291.

Thelwall, M., Vaughan, L., and Björneborn, L. (2005) 'Webometrics', *ARIST* 39(1): 81–135.

Toyoda, M., and Kitsuregawa, M. (2005) 'A System for Visualizing and Analyzing the Evolution of the Web with a Time Series of Graphs', *Proceedings of the Sixteenth ACM Conference on Hypertext and Hypermedia*. ACM: 151–160.

Ugander, J., Karrer, B., Backstrom, L., and Marlow, C. (2011) 'The Anatomy of the Facebook Social Graph', *arXiv*:1111(4503).

Van de Sompel, H., Nelson, M., Sanderson, R., Balakireva, L., Ainsworth, S., and Shankar, H. (2009) 'Memento: Time Travel for the Web', *arXiv*:0911(1112) (https://arxiv.org/abs/0911.1112).

Wasserman, S., and Faust, K. (1994) *Social Network Analysis: Methods and Applications*. Cambridge: Cambridge University Press.

Weltevrede, E., and Helmond, A. (2012) 'Where Do Bloggers Blog? Platform Transitions within the Historical Dutch Blogosphere', *First Monday*, 17(2–6). (http://firstmonday.org/ojs/index.php/fm/article/view/3775/3142)

White, H.C. (1992) *Identity and Control: A Structural Theory of Social Action*. Princeton, NJ: Princeton University Press.

White, H.C., Boorman, S.A., and Breiger, R.L. (1976) 'Social Structure from Multiple Networks. I. Blockmodels of Roles and Positions', *American Journal of Sociology*, 81(4): 730–780.

# Quantitative Web History Methods

Anthony Cocciolo

## INTRODUCTION

This chapter explores how historical research questions, including research questions about the history of the web, can be addressed through quantitative research methods applied to web archives. At a basic level, quantitative methods involve applying a variety of mathematical or statistical analyses on numerical data. These mathematical techniques can be as simple as adding up the occurrence of some word, to more sophisticated techniques such as analysis of variance (ANOVA), which will be described in more depth in this chapter. Through the use of web archives, quantitative methods can be used to show patterns and changes over time, thus having utility in addressing historical research questions.

In this chapter, a personal use of quantitative research methods with web archives will be discussed as a way of illustrating how they can be used more broadly (Cocciolo, 2015). In 2014, I was interested in what I perceived as a decreased use of text on the web in favor of image-based content, such as video and photographs. I was particularly interested in what seemed like an erosion of written content online in favor of a form of communication that seemed to share commonalities with children's books, where photographs were accompanied with small amounts of text. In seeing what looked like a movement away from the written word, I was reminded of the work of Walter Ong who noted the tenacity of orality, or a tendency to attempt to return to an oral culture despite the success and obvious benefits of literacy (Ong, 2002). An oral culture is one without knowledge of literacy, where information, knowledge, and culture is communicated and passed down through means other than the written word, such as through oral storytelling, music, and other non-written means. Was the internet, with its newfound ability to easily stream video and high-resolution imagery, allowing for Ong's return to orality?

Although I realized that I could not make such sweeping arguments in an academic study – reviewers would be none too pleased – I was still interested in developing a sound method for determining changes in the amount of text delivered to users over time. To study this, web archives are essential because they contain copies of webpages from the past. Although some countries have extensive web archives of their national domain or other collecting areas, in the United States – which was my main study site – the most extensive web archive is the one kept by the Internet Archive that it displays through its WayBack Machine. Thus, I knew that if I was to study changes in the presentation of text over websites used by people in the United States, the web archives kept by the Internet Archive would be an essential resource.

Before I discuss how I applied web archives in my research, I will outline the general steps for engaging in quantitative research using web archives. Each of these steps will be described in more detail in the following sections and will draw on this personal example. These steps are:

1 *Developing a research question* – First, a research question should be developed that can be addressed in full or in part through web archives. Types of questions that can be explored through such methods will be explored, as well as those that are better suited for other methods.
2 *Securing a corpus* – Second, the corpus of web archived content that provides coverage of the areas appropriate to the research question ought to be secured, and ways to gain access to such corpora will be discussed.
3 *Numerical translation* – Third, the corpus of text needs to be translated into numerical data based on the research question.
4 *Analysis* – Fourth, using the numerical datasets created in the earlier step, mathematical or statistical analysis techniques can be employed. This can be as simple as mathematical functions such as summation, average, or standard deviation, to more complex analysis, including statistical techniques such as analysis of variance (ANOVA).
5 *Drawing conclusions* – Fifth, like all research, conclusions should be drawn based on the analysis.

The aim of this chapter is to offer a starting point for historians interested in applying quantitative research methods to web archives to answer historical research questions, using personal experience as an illustration. However, before the stages are discussed, relevant literature on using quantitative research methods with web archives will be introduced.

## RELEVANT LITERATURE

Using quantitative research methods with web archives may be somewhat new to historians. In a traditional sense, historical research involves the close examination of textual records to address historical research questions. The question of whether to use quantitative or qualitative research methods is not generally directed at the historian but rather at the social scientist, such as the psychologist, sociologist, and education researcher. Quantitative and qualitative research – when referred to by social scientists – typically involves studying living people, which may or may not be the case for historians. In social science, qualitative research methods such as interviews and focus groups are often used to get at people's understanding of something that is not well understood, such as motivations or opinions on some topic. Quantitative research can be used to study an issue or topic that may be better understood. However, there is greater interest in seeing how wide or generalizable a given view is. Whereas qualitative research may involve analysis of data such as interview transcripts, quantitative research may involve analysis of numerical data such as that generated from a survey. In this paper, 'quantitative research' is used to refer to performing analysis using numerical and statistical techniques on data, specifically web archives. While this method may not be commonly used by historians, it can be used to help address historical research questions in conjunction with other sources of evidence.

Studying webpages and web-based phenomena using quantitative methods is not new as it is captured in the research subfield of information science known as webometrics. According to Thelwall and Vaughan, 'Webometrics encompasses all quantitative studies of web-related phenomenon' (2004: 1213). Thelwall (2009) notes that webometrics can be used for studying a variety of web-based phenomena, such as issues relating to election websites, online academic communication, bloggers as amateur journalists, and social networking. The methods can be used for understanding aspects like web impact assessment, citation impact, trend detection, and search engine optimization, among other possible uses. Webometrics grows out of the subfield of information science known as bibliometrics, which uses quantitative analysis to make measurements related to published books and articles, such as citation analysis to determine impact. Related subfields include infometrics, which is the quantitative study of information and can combine analysis of information in whatever form it may occur.

Björneborn and Ingwersen (2004) highlight four main areas of webometric research: 1) webpage content analysis; 2) web link structure analysis; 3) web usage analysis; and 4) web technology analysis. Notably missing from this list is a longitudinal or time-based dimension. However, webometrics researchers highlight the possibilities opened up by web archives. Björneborn and Ingwersen highlight that 'Web archaeology… could in this webometric context be important for recovering historical Web developments, for example, by means of the Internet Archive (www.archive.org)' (2004: 1217). When webometrics was in its early development in the 2000s, web archives such as the Internet Archive only contained a few years of content, making them less appealing for long-term, longitudinal analysis. However, as web archives have persisted, and notable web archives such as the Internet Archive have surpassed 20 years of crawling websites, new opportunities for historical and longitudinal analysis are increasingly possible.

In the field of communication and media studies, researchers have begun to use web archives to create web histories, which Brügger defines as 'a necessary condition for the understanding of the Internet of the present as well as of new, emerging Internet forms' (2011: 24). Web histories can include studies of multiple facets of the web, such as national domains, which may look at factors such as volume, space, structure, and content, among others (Brügger, 2014).

## STAGE 1 – DEVELOPING A RESEARCH QUESTION OR QUESTIONS

Before progressing further, I must make a quick note on the language used in this article as it varies to some degree by country. By 'homepage', I am referring to the start page or initial page of a website. I also use the term website, which refers to an entire collection of webpages under a given domain. For example, the website 'pepsi.com' is composed of a homepage and other webpages that are hyperlinked together to form the website.

When engaging in quantitative research using web archives, it is necessary to have a research question that lends itself to such methods. For my project mentioned in the introduction, my research questions are the following:

> Is the use of text on the World Wide Web declining? If so, when did it start declining, and by how much has it declined?

The above research questions are well-suited for quantitative methods using web archives. The first reason why is that the question is essentially quantitative in nature: a 'decline' and by 'how much' is something that can be readily measured numerically by comparing data from some specific year in the past and measuring it against a more recent year. The second reason is that web archives are the essential resource for seeking answers to the above questions. As the Internet Archive has been archiving the web since 1996 (Goel, 2016), it is possible to use it to analyze homepages for nearly the entire lifespan of the World Wide Web. Although web archives are generally not available for the first few years of the World Wide Web, by the end of the 1990s good web archives – specifically through the WayBack Machine – exist. Thus, web archives work well for studying content from the late 1990s to the present day.

The major limitation when making comparisons between the past and present is that not all present-day webpages existed in the past, and not all past websites continue into the future. Further, some webpages blocked web crawlers because they feared losing control of their content, thus leaving sites like Time Magazine (time.com) poorly represented in 1990s web archives. A further limitation is that most web archives do not copy every webpage within a given domain, but only go a few levels deep off of the homepage. While the Internet Archive has very extensive copies of homepages of top-level domain names for many months and years, webpages several levels below the homepage are less well-represented. Thus, using web archives to make comparisons between homepages is much more feasible than making comparisons against some webpage many levels below the homepage. Understanding the strengths and limitations of a particular web archive necessarily impacts the types of research questions and analysis that it can be used to address.

Although there are an infinite number of possible research questions that may make use of quantitative research methods with web archives, some particular components are more appropriate than others. Research questions that are looking into the occurrence of some 'thing' are particularly noteworthy, which can include the occurrence of a word, image, phrase, visual element, hyperlink, person, or place. Basically, if it can be readily identified by a computer or human, it can be used in the research question. Another component can be the co-occurrence of one 'thing' with another. Co-occurrence analysis can factor in the distance between each 'thing', such as word distance, pixel distance, or number of links away. More sophisticated relationships between one or more 'things' can also be studied, such as the nature of sentiments relating one element to another (Liu, 2012). The more complicated the phenomenon – such as sentiment – the more complex the algorithms for identifying them must be. With the increased complexity, there is greater chance that the algorithm could perform poorly and not correctly identify the sentiment. Thus, simpler phenomena, such as occurrence or co-occurrence, are more straightforward to determine than more sophisticated relationships. Emerging practices that use machine learning and artificial intelligence in algorithms have the potential for identifying complex phenomena and relationships (Kelleher et al., 2015). Although well beyond the scope of this article, machine learning techniques that leverage artificial intelligence have potential application to research questions that are inherently historical in nature.

Questions well-suited for web archives research could be the timeframe of the late 1990s to the present, which are the years that are well-represented in some web archives. If earlier years are being included, web archives may need to be augmented with more traditional sources, such as newspapers, magazines, and books. Analysis of such sources can be expedited to some extent by using digitized copies of such works, but print holdings may be needed as not everything has been digitized or, if it has, is it necessarily available to researchers?

In a perfectly linear world, researchers move from creating research questions, to devising methods for addressing those questions, to implementing the methodology, analyzing the data, generating results, and drawing conclusions. However, as many researchers know, the questions are developed in dialectic with the available research methods and data sources available; thus each aspect influences the other. Hence, it would not be unusual to refine research questions based on the data that can be secured, or the analysis options available. In the next section, securing the web archive corpus will be discussed.

## STAGE 2 – SECURING A WEB ARCHIVE CORPUS

The next step in the research process is securing or identifying a corpus of web archived webpages that can be used or analyzed to address the research questions. Before obtaining a corpus, it is important to understand the ways in which web archives come into existence. Some of the methods used to archive web content are client-side archiving, server-side archiving, and non-web archiving (Masanès, 2006). Client-side archiving is the most popular form of web archiving and is used by the Internet Archive (2018) to collect webpages for display on the WayBack Machine. In this approach, web crawlers act like normal web users and 'start from seed pages, parse them, extract links, and fetch the linked document', then re-iterate (Masanès, 2006: 23). This method works well for simpler webpages, but could encounter difficulty when encountering webpages that exchange content in between webpage loads, which is popularly known as the Asynchronous JavaScript and XML (AJAX) approach to creating web interfaces. Many social media sites make extensive use of this approach, and without special provisions for web archiving, could make retrieving this content challenging. This could be overcome, but may require manual intervention by a skilled web archivist. This approach is also challenging when attempting to download large collections of webpages, which could take a long time to completely download. For example, Masanès notes 'it will take more than three days to archive a site with 100,000 pages' (2006: 24).

Some of the limitations of client-side web archiving are overcome by server-side web archiving, in which files are copied directly from the server in conjunction with the site owner's cooperation. This method was used by the Library of Congress to create an archive of Twitter (Osterberg, 2013). The limitation of this approach is re-creating the webpages so that they are authentic to what the user would have experienced, and the extensive effort required negotiating the transfer of data.

Perhaps the simplest form of web archiving is to create non-web archives, where web content is printed out or converted to a format like Adobe Acrobat PDF or PNG files and stored using something other than the web (e.g., file folders, directories on a computer) (Masanès, 2006). Although this method has some appeal because of its simplicity, it loses the context in which users experienced the content and the way it was navigated using hyperlinks. It also could lose some of the graphical look and feel of the webpage, which is readily evident when most webpages are saved as PDFs or printed out.

In the case of my research project on the decline of text on the web, I was interested in making comparisons between webpages from today with those in the past. Thus, I needed to use webpages that I know existed in the past and persist until today. I developed a list of 100 popular and prominent websites in the United States that existed from 1999 to 2014 which were available through the WayBack Machine, using indexes like Alexa's Top 500 English-language Website index (Alexa, 2003). Popular and prominent websites were selected – rather than websites that may be obscure and unused – because they may better reflect the interests and desires of the general user population. The list is repeated below in Table 11.1.

**Table 11.1 Website categories with respective websites**

| *Category* | *Total websites* | *Websites* |
|---|---|---|
| Consumer products and retail | 10 | Amazon.com, Pepsi.com, Lego.com, Bestbuy.com, Mcdonalds.com, Barbie.com, Coca-cola.com, Intel.com, Cisco.com, Starbucks.com |
| Government | 11 | Whitehouse.gov, SSA.gov, CA.gov, USPS.com, NASA.gov, NOAA.gov, Navy.mil, CDC.gov, NIH.gov, USPS.com, NYC.gov |
| Higher education | 10 | Berkeley.edu, Harvard.edu, NYU.edu, MIT.edu, UMich.edu, Princeton.edu, Stanford.edu, Columbia.edu, Fordham.edu, Pratt.edu |
| Libraries | 8 | NYPL.org, LOC.gov, Archive.org, BPL.org, Colapubliclib.org, Lapl.org, Detroit.lib.mi.us, Queenslibrary.org |
| Magazines | 12 | USNews.com, TheAtlatnic.com, NewYorker.com, Newsweek.com, Economist.com, Nature.com, Forbes.com, BHG.com, FamilyCircle.com, Rollingstone.com, NYMag.com, Nature.com |
| Museums | 10 | SI.edu, MetMuseum.org, Guggenheim.org, Whitney.org, Getty.edu, Moma.org, Artic.edu, Frick.org, BrooklynMuseum.org, AMNH.org |
| Newspapers | 9 | NYTimes.com, ChicagoTribune.com, LATimes.com, NYDailyNews.com, Chron.com, NYPost.com, Suntimes.com, DenverPost.com, NYPost.com |
| Online service | 8 | IMDB.com, MarketWatch.com, NationalGeographic.com, WebMD.com, Yahoo.com, Match.com |
| Technology site | 11 | CNet.com, MSN.com, Microsoft.com, AOL.com, Apple.com, HP.com, Dell.com, Slashdot.org, Wired.com, PCWorld.com, IBM.com |
| Television | 11 | CBS.com, ABC.com, NBC.com, Weather.com, PBS.org, BBC.co.uk, CNN.com, Nick.com, MSNBC.com, CartonNetwork.com, ESPN.go.com |
| **Total** | **100** | |

Although the Internet Archive has archived webpages from 1996 onward, the range of webpages archived improved as years advanced, and by 1999 many more websites were being archived than in 1996. Thus, I would begin my comparisons at the year 1999. To show changes over time, I would analyze those websites every three years (1999, 2002, 2005, 2008, 2011, and 2014). In sum, all websites needed to continuously exist between 1999 and 2014, and all those in Table 11.1 met that criteria.

The way that I chose to secure the archived webpages was to use Memento (2018). Memento is a technical framework aimed at a better integration of the current and the past web, and provides a way to issue requests and receive responses from web archives (Van de Sompel et al., 2009). For example, you can submit to the web service a URL and date, and it will bring back the URL for the web archived content. The URL returned can be from a variety of web archives, but for all my sites submitted the Internet Archive was the web archive that was brought back by Memento. I developed a PHP script that issued requests to the Memento web service for the 100 websites for six years, and in each case it returned a URL of the content from the Internet Archive, thus producing 600 web archived pages. Note that websites originally included in the 100 websites that were not archived for any given year were removed and replaced with a website that had all years archived from the respective category. Thus, each homepage was inspected manually to ensure that it was there and was not some type of error page that would throw off the analysis.

Web archived webpages (the HTML and binary files) can be downloaded in a web browser window (using the File -> Save As option), or a script can be used to download the HTML file and related files needed to render the page. For example, the command-line based tool 'wget' makes downloading webpages and related binary files relatively straightforward. For example, issuing the following command via the Windows command line or Macintosh terminal using 'wget' will download the Internet Archive's July 1997 homepage of the Pratt Institute's website:

**Box 11.1 Example use of command line tool wget**

```
wget -p -e robots=off https://web.archive.org/web/19970713123416/
   http://www.pratt.edu/
```

Note that in the above example, an option is passed to wget to ignore the robots.txt file on the Internet Archive's WayBack Machine, which explicitly blocks all crawlers. It is a strange irony that the site that was built on crawling websites does not allowing crawling! However, this is likely not so problematic as long as large amounts of content are not downloaded all at once, which can place strain on a webserver. In fact, the above request will only download a small amount of data. If too many requests are being issued too quickly, it is likely that you could be temporarily blocked. The 'p' option included with the wget command ensures that the crawler downloads all the page pre-requisites, such as GIF and JPG files referenced in the HTML page.

In my case, I was not interested in getting the HTML and related binary files (e.g., JPGs, GIFs), but wanted large visual presentations of the webpage. This was because the method I intended to use to determine which parts of the webpage were graphics and which were text was to use a computer vision algorithm, which will be discussed more in the next section. To download the full print-screens, I used a simple Firefox extension called 'Grab Them All', which creates full webpage screenshots of pages as PNG files using a seed list of URLs (Grab Them All, 2018). I was able to give it a seed list of 600 URLs, and in half an hour I had large PNG visual representations of those archived webpages.

Brügger writes that a web archived website is typically faulty and deficient compared with the original (Brügger, 2008). Web archived websites can have problems with the link or with the content displayed, among other possible issues. One advantage of creating a graphic version of a web archived webpage is that it stabilizes it: since a PNG file can be only opened and rendered one way, there is no chance that it will be displayed differently on different computers or browsers. However, it has the disadvantage of eliminating the special functions of webpages (e.g., hyperlinks, interactive content, moving image content, etc.). Thus, while it eliminates some problems (e.g., browser obsolescence that may render some functions inoperable), it introduces new limitations (e.g., transforming an inherently interactive medium into a static image).

For projects where only the text is important and not the HTML or related binary files, scripts can be developed which remove the HTML. For example, a regular expression script, implemented in PHP or Python, can remove all HTML markup from a file, leaving only the readable text. Further, the PHP function strip_tags() can remove HTML information from a webpage, leaving only the visible text. Lastly, specialized libraries, such as the Beautiful Soup library for Python, can be used for extracting information from HTML and XML files (Beautiful Soup, 2018; PHP.net, 2018).

When engaging in such tasks as stripping the HTML from a file, it is always a good idea to maintain copies of your data in stages. This is because if you realize further in the process that you made an error (e.g., stripped out more content than was expected), you can refer to copies of the data from the earlier stages.

Note that this is only one method to get access to web archived content. This method diverges from the 'big-data' approaches to working with web archives, such as using gigabytes, terabytes, or even petabytes of web archived content in analyses. To gain access to big datasets of web archived content, it is necessary to work more directly with providers, rather than downloading small bits from the web. For example, the non-profit organization Common Crawl provides researchers access to web archived data (Common Crawl, 2018). Since these datasets are so large, it can be inefficient to make copies of the data, and thus sites like Common Crawl allow users to run their analysis against the cloud-based data using computing services provided by Amazon.

Before discussing big-data approaches in more detail, it is important to make a distinction between data and metadata. Metadata can be defined as 'data about data'. A familiar example is that a telephone conversation could be considered the data, but the phone number dialed to enable the connection and the duration of the call might be considered metadata. In the case of web archives, the data could be the HTML of a webpage where the metadata may be the URL and the date the copy of the HTML was made.

Common Crawl provides users with access to the web archive data and metadata in three formats: WARC file, metadata-only format (WAT) and text-only format (WET). WARC files are a standard-based, text-based format for representing web-crawled webpages. WARC files include the HTML for crawled webpages, metadata on the crawl (e.g., what day and time the site was crawled), and the binary files encoded in the text-based format. WARC files can be large and difficult to deal with, especially if you are not using all the data provided in them. For example, all the JPGs, GIFs, or other binary data that are part of a webpage get encoded in WARC files, easily making the majority of WARC files comprise nonsensical content because the binary data is not human-readable but machine-readable. If the binary data, such as images, are not necessary for a particular research project, the other formats Common Crawl offers may be better options. These include the metadata-only format (WAT), which provides information like the page title and outgoing links on the page, making it useful for creating networks of webpage linkages. The last format provided is the text-only format (WET), which removes the HTML, Javascript, and other parts of a webpage that are not shown to users via a web browser. This format can be especially useful if you are interested in the textual content on a webpage.

One limitation of Common Crawl's data is that its earliest is from 2008 and 2009, stored in ARC format, which was an earlier web archiving format that preceded WARC. ARC is very similar to WARC, and many tools support both formats, so this should not be a major impediment. However, because this data only begins in 2008, it would not be useful for studying the earliest years of the web. To study webpages from the 1990s, the Internet Archive is likely the best source.

## STAGE 3 – NUMERICAL TRANSLATION

Once the corpus has been secured, whether this comprises WARC files, metadata of web crawls, text from crawls, screenshots of webpages, or other manifestations of data from web archives, it is necessary to begin to prepare the data for numerical analysis. Web archives have many facets, and thus the ways in which the data gets translated into numerical data is going to depend very much on the research questions. In the case of my research project described earlier, I was interested in using the 600 full-length screenshots, representing 15 years of homepages from 100 popular and prominent websites, to see if the amount of text presented to users was declining. Thus, I needed a method to decipher the textual content from other content, such as images, videos, or whitespace.

I ended up modifying an open-sourced web browser extension called Project Naptha (2018), which could be used for detecting blocks of text within an image. This extension implemented an innovative computer vision algorithm called the Stroke Width Transform (SWT). SWT was created by a Microsoft research team who observed that the 'one feature that separates text from other elements of a scene is its nearly constant stroke width' (Epshtein et al., 2010: 2963). During their initial evaluation the algorithm was able to identify text regions within natural images with 90% accuracy.

For example, Figure 11.1 shows this process used on the Library of Congress webpage from Internet Archive's 2002 collection, with the black boxes identifying the text regions from the images. The algorithm is not without minor inaccuracies. It has identified part of the dome incorrectly as a text area, as well as some other very small areas. Nevertheless, it has an accuracy that is consistent with the findings of the Microsoft researchers. A second example provided is that of the White House website from 2002 using this same process (shown in Figure 11.2).

Using the bounding boxes produced by Project Naptha, a percentage of webpage text to non-text was computed, and recorded into a MySQL database. For example, the

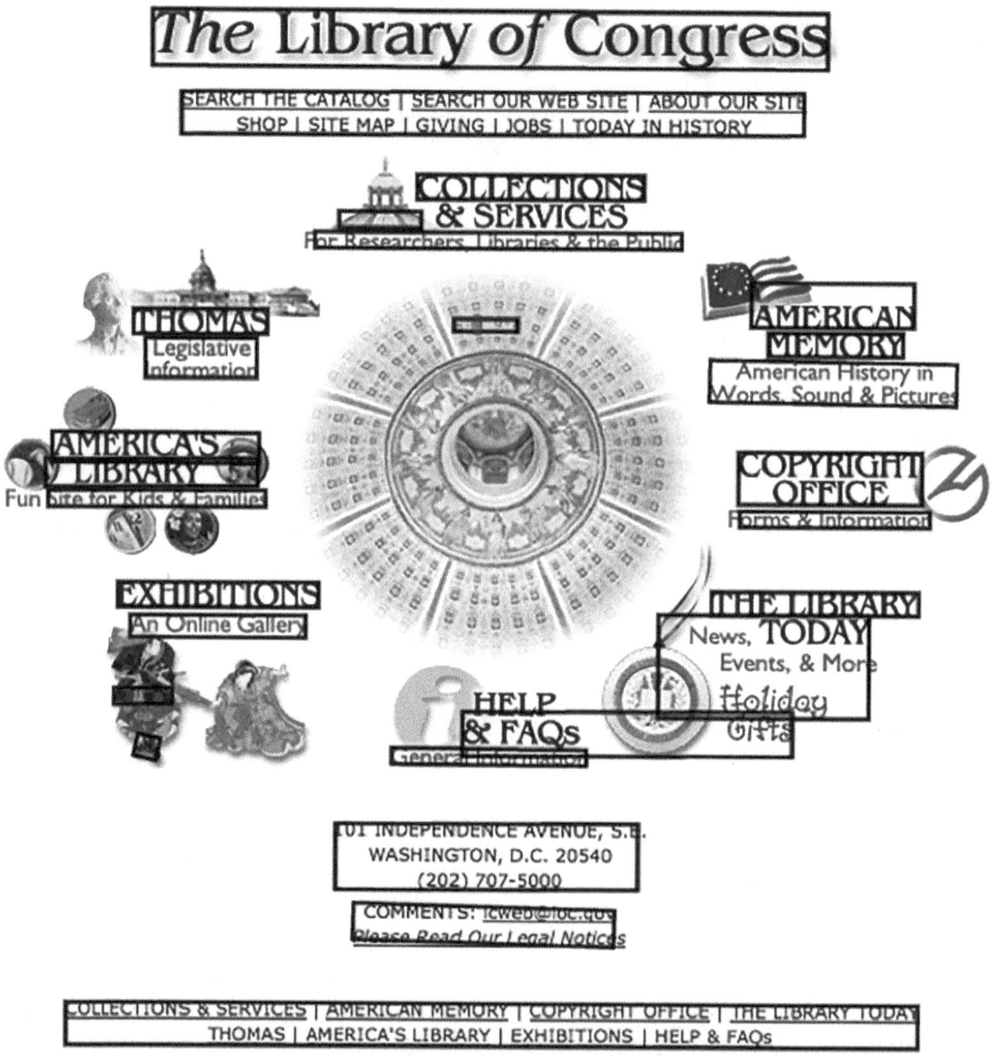


**Figure 11.1 Library of Congress website from year 2002, with text areas highlighted with black bounding boxes. Webpage is 23.33% text using this method.**

webpage shown in Figure 11.1 is 23.33% text, whereas the webpage shown in Figure 11.2 is 46.10% text, which indicates what is readily visible: that Figure 11.2 is more text-heavy than Figure 11.1.

Thus, at this point in my research project, I had created numerical data from 600 screenshots of webpages. The data included URL, percentage of text to non-text, and year. This is only one narrow slice of data that can be generated, and other numerical data can be derived. For example, this could include recording information like word counts, properties of images or videos,

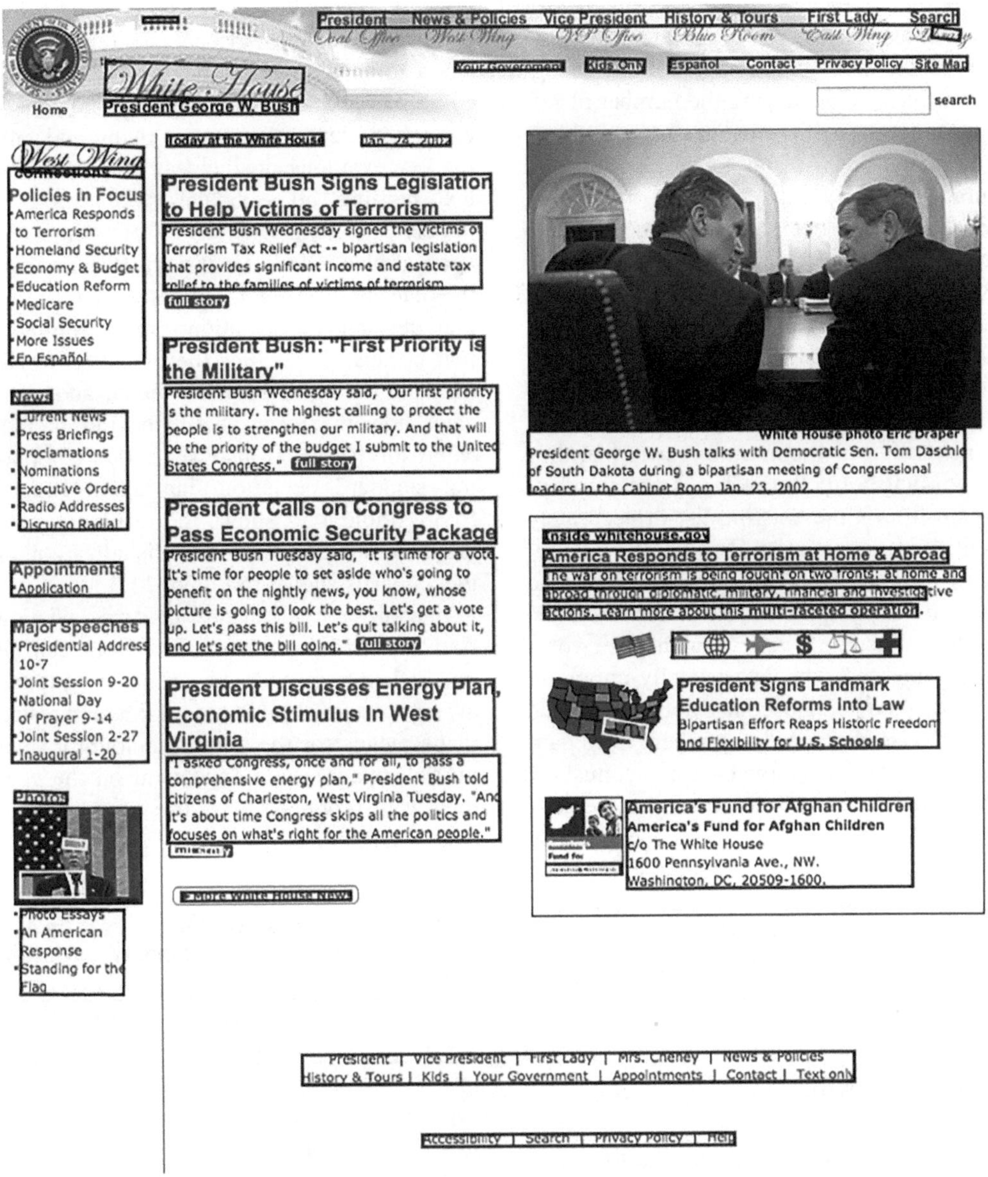


**Figure 11.2 WhiteHouse.gov from 2002 with text areas highlighted with black bounding boxes. Webpage is 46.10% text using this method.**

relative amount of executable code to HTML on webpages, and file sizes, among many other possible numerical properties.

Other methods for translating web archives into numerical data include the use of topic modeling, text mining, and natural language processing (NLP) tools (Graham et al., 2016). NLP is a research field within the discipline of computer science, and has a number of applications that can readily produce numeric data. These can include named entity recognition, such as identifying the number of references to a specific person, place, or thing; sentiment analysis; and topic identification (Jurafsky and Martin, 2008). A number of free tools and open-toolkits are available for engaging in natural language processing (Bird et al., 2018; Natural Language Toolkit, 2018; Open NLP, 2018; Stanford CoreNLP, 2018). All of these tools require some experimentation, as well as verification that they are producing the desired result. If such tools are being used, it is important to verify that they are working correctly, such as correctly identifying from a pre-existing list or accurately identifiying a sentiment. Evaluating the utility of these NLP tools can be accomplished through sampling the source material and the resulting outcome to verify that they are working as expected. This is especially important if the method being used has not been proven to work elsewhere. Although there is no hard and fast rule of how large the sample must be, I suggest at least 10% for unproven methodologies. The evaluation can be enhanced by using two independent evaluators to measure how well the tools are working on the sample data. Ensuring this consistency is often referred to as interrater reliability.

## STAGE 4 – ANALYSIS

Once web archives have been used to generate numerical data, this data can be used in analysis. In the research project described here, I was interested in knowing if the amount of text online was declining. I had 600 data points which included URL, year, and percentage of text from non-text that was generated using the computer vision algorithm described in the earlier step. An analysis step that I was interested in engaging in was the average percentages for each year available: 1999, 2002, 2005, 2008, 2011, and 2014. Although this analysis could be readily achieved in any spreadsheet program such as Microsoft Excel, I used the statistics package SPSS. However, average values alone are not enough evidence that text is rising and falling. For example, say the year 2014 was 30% text because all webpages were approximately 30% text, whereas in 1999 the average was also 30% but half were 15% text and the other half 45% text. In cases such as this one, the standard deviation statistic is important because it clarifies the extent to which the data diverges from the mean, and indicates how the mean should be interpreted. Microsoft Excel can also be used for computing standard deviation, but again I used SPSS. Table 11.2 shows the results of both these computations, and a visualization of the values is shown in Figure 11.3.

In addition to mean and standard deviation statistics, additional statistical work can be undertaken to provide greater meaning to the average values. In this case, I was interested if the means (or the average amount of text on a webpage) were dependent on the year they were produced, or if these means were simply random. Although standard deviation

**Table 11.2 Mean percentage of text on a webpage pear year, with standard deviation values**

| *Year* | *Mean percentage of text on a webpage* | *Standard deviation* |
|---|---|---|
| 1999 | 22.36 | 15.45 |
| 2002 | 30.89 | 14.93 |
| 2005 | 32.43 | 14.60 |
| 2008 | 31.31 | 15.88 |
| 2011 | 28.51 | 15.47 |
| 2014 | 26.88 | 13.23 |

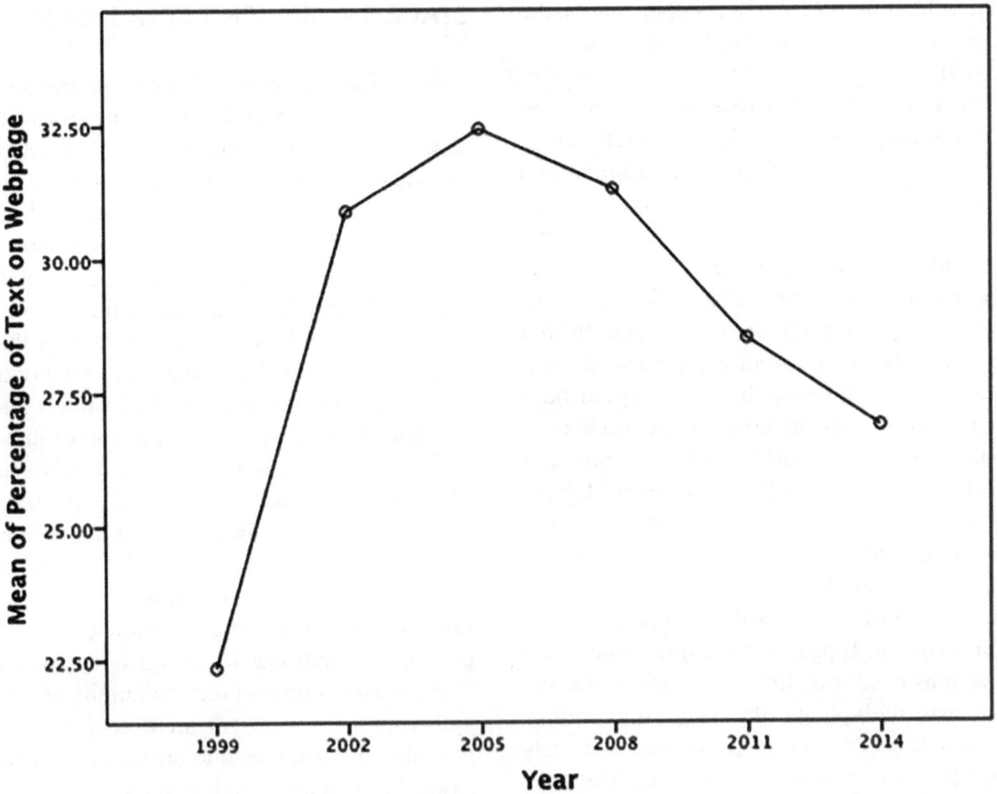


**Figure 11.3 Percentage of text on webpages.**

can measure variation, statistical significance tests can ensure that this variation is not merely chance but is dependent on some other variable or variables. In this case, that variable is the year the webpage was produced, which is referred to as the independent variable because it is a fact that does not depend on other variables. The percentage of text on a webpage could then be considered a dependent variable, whose value is hypothesized to be dependent on the year the webpage was produced.

When engaging in statistical tests, a finding of 'statistical significance' indicates that the dependent variable's values are not pure chance but are influenced one way or another by the independent variable. In this project, the specific test I used was the one-way analysis of variance, which is often referred to as one-way ANOVA. The SPSS software facilitates the computation work for this test, and provides results that can be interpreted to conclude whether there is indeed a statistically significant relationship between these variables. When using statistical tests like ANOVA, the existence of a statistically significant relationship is determined by the 'p-value' or probability value. Although explaining how p-values work is beyond the scope of this article, this particular research ANOVA produced a p-value of less than .0005, which led to the conclusion that there was a statistically significant relationship between the percentage of text on a webpage and the year it was produced. In the case of the research project discussed here, a 'one-way ANOVA revealed that the percentage of text on a webpage are not chance occurrences but rather this percentage is dependent on the year the website was produced' (Cocciolo, 2015).

It should be acknowledged that many historians may not be particularly well-versed in statistics. I received doctoral training at a school of education, where statistics coursework is generally required. However, historians interested in using big data can become more experienced in statistics through their own independent study or through formal coursework. As I do not always use statistical tests in my research, I find myself having to brush up on how to use such tests and how to implement them in computer software, such as SPSS. However, I have found some resources useful, most notably the Laerd Statistics (2018) tutorials on the web. Although they provide some free information, most of it is available via a monthly subscription. It provides comprehensive discussions of all the different types of statistical tests, with plenty of examples, as well as information on how to implement the tests in SPSS and interpret the results. The subscription costs are low and well worth the small investment. Consulting resources such as this, as well as other resources such as statistics textbooks (e.g., Mendenhall et al., 2012), can be useful in understanding how statistical tests work and how the results should be interpreted, including knowing whether there is a statistically significant relationship between the variables. A further option is to explore online courses, such as courses available through Khan Academy and Coursera.

Note that there are some limitations to using statistics. If the dataset is small, such as under 30 data points, statistics may not be the best tool and results can be augmented with qualitative information. The study described here could be significantly enhanced by making use of a dataset larger than 600 data points. When using statistics, in general, large datasets are better than small, so 6,000, or even six million, data points could enhance the overall significance of the study.

## STAGE 5 – DRAWING CONCLUSIONS

Before drawing conclusions from research using quantitative methods, it is necessary to describe the limitations. As mentioned earlier, quantitative methods are well-suited for large datasets, such as ones with at least 30 data points. Beyond concerns of dataset size, other limitations can be articulated in the conclusion. For example, in the research study described here, one limitation was that that it only included websites that were popular and prominent in the United States, and thus the changes to the composition of those webpages over time may not be a universal phenomenon but rather US-specific. Although webpages in the United States have significant use from individuals outside of the United States, being able to highlight how aspects like website selection impact the conclusions that can be drawn is necessary. Further, issues around the limitations of web archiving – or what got archived and what got missed – could lead to erroneous conclusions. For example, in this study I noted that some popular and prominent websites – such as Time Magazine – are poorly web archived in the WayBack Machine because of limitations defined by Time in its robots.txt file.

The conclusion reached in the study was that 'the percentage of text on the Web climbed during the turn of the twentieth century, peaked in 2005, and has been on the decline ever since' – with the caveat that this finding is based on popular and prominent websites in the United States (Cocciolo, 2015). Other issues arising from limitations of the web archive corpus can also be discussed when drawing conclusions from the research.

## CONCLUSION

In conclusion, this paper offered a starting point for historians interested in using quantitative research methods using web archives.

Although the use of such methods requires some study of statistical research methods, as well as implementing scripts using tools like PHP and Python, these can all be readily learned using resources described in this chapter, including online resources. Such methods allow for making sense of large amounts of data and addressing historical research questions with precision. In some cases, the best option may be engaging with others who have the necessary expertise to study the phenomena. These can include computer programmers, statisticians, and those with access to facilities with web archives. Through such collaborations, historians can open up exciting new research avenues using web archives.

## REFERENCES

Alexa (2003) 'Alexa's Top 500 English-language Website index (2003 web archive)'. Available at: https://web-beta.archive.org/web/20031209132250/http://www.alexa.com/site/ds/top_sites?ts_mode=lang&lang=en [18 February 2018].

Beautiful Soup Python Library (2018) Available at: https://www.crummy.com/software/BeautifulSoup/bs4/doc/ [18 February 2018].

Bird, S., Klein, E., and Loper, E. (2018) 'Natural Language Processing with Python – Analyzing Text with the Natural Language Toolkit'. Available at: http://www.nltk.org/book/ [19 February 2018].

Björneborn, L., and Ingwersen, P (2004) 'Toward a basic framework for webometrics', *Journal of the American Society for Information Science and Technology* 55(14): 1216–1227.

Brügger, N. (2008) 'The archived website and website philology: A new type of historical document', *Nordicom Review* 29(2): 155–175.

Brügger, N. (2011) 'Web Archiving – Between Past, Present and Future', in M. Consalvo and C. Ess (Eds.), *The Handbook of Internet Studies.* Malden, MA: Wiley-Blackwell. pp. 24–42.

Brügger, N. (2014) 'Probing a Nation's Web Domain: A New Approach to Web History and a New Kind of Historical Source', in G. Goggin and M. McLelland (Eds.), *The Routledge Companion to Global Internet Histories.* New York: Routledge. pp. 61–73.

Cocciolo, A. (2015) 'The rise and fall of text on the Web: A quantitative study of Web archives', *Information Research* 20(3). Available at: http://www.informationr.net/ir/20-3/paper682.html [19 February 2018].

Common Crawl (2018) Available at: http://commoncrawl.org/ [18 February 2018]

Epshtein, B., Ofek, E., and Wexler, Y. (2010) 'Detecting text in natural scenes with stroke width transform', in Proceedings of 2010 IEEE Conference on Computer Vision and Pattern Recognition in San Francisco, CA. New York, NY: IEEE. pp. 2963–2970.

Goel, V. (2016) 'Defining Web pages, Web sites and Web captures', *Internet Archive Blogs.* Available at: https://blog.archive.org/2016/10/23/defining-web-pages-web-sites-and-web-captures/ [19 February 2018].

Grab Them All (2018). Available at: https://addons.mozilla.org/en-US/firefox/addon/grab-them-all/ [19 February 2018].

Graham, G., Milligan, I., and Weingart, S. (2016) *Exploring Big Historical Data: The Historian's Macroscope*. London: Imperial College Press.

Internet Archive (2018) 'The Way Back Machine'. Available at: http://archive.org

Jurafsky, D., and Martin, J.H. (2008) *Speech and Language Processing*, 2nd edition. New York: Pearson Prentice Hall.

Kelleher, J.D., Mac Namee, B., and D'Arcy, A. (2015) *Fundamentals of Machine Learning for Predictive Data Analytics: Algorithms, Worked Examples and Case Studies*. Cambridge, MA: MIT Press.

Laerd Statistics (2018). Available at: https://statistics.laerd.com/ [19 February 2018].

Liu, B. (2012) *Sentiment Analysis and Opinion Mining.* San Rafael, CA: Morgan & Claypool.

Masanès, J. (2006) 'Web Archiving: Issues and Methods', in J. Masanès (Ed.), *Web Archiving.* Berlin: Springer. pp. 1–53.

Memento (2018) 'time travel'. Available at: http://timetravel.mementoweb.org/ [19 February 2018].

Mendenhall, W., Beaver, R.J., and Beaver, B.M. (2012) *Introduction to Probability and Statistics*. Stamford, CT: Duxbury Press.

Natural Language Toolkit (2018). Available at: http://www.nltk.org/ [19 February 2018].

Ong, W.J. (2002) *Orality and Literacy: The Technologizing of the Word*. London: Routledge.

Open NLP (2018) Available at: http://opennlp.sourceforge.net/projects.html [19 February 2018].

Osterberg, G. (2013) 'Update on the Twitter Archive at the Library of Congress', *Library of Congress Blog*. Available at: http://blogs.loc.gov/loc/2013/01/update-on-the-twitter-archive-at-the-library-of-congress/ [19 February 2018].

PHP.net (2018) 'strip_tags'. Available at: http://php.net/manual/en/function.strip-tags.php [18 February 2018].

Project Naptha (2018) Available at: https://projectnaptha.com/ [18 February 2018].

Stanford CoreNLP (2018) Available at: http://stanfordnlp.github.io/CoreNLP/ [19 February 2018].

Thelwall, M. (2009) *Introduction to Webometrics: Quantitative Web Research for the Social Sciences*. San Rafael, CA: Morgan & Claypool.

Thelwall, M., and Vaughan, L. (2004) 'Webometrics: An introduction to the special issue', *Journal of the Association for Information Science and Technology* 55(14): 1213–1215.

Van de Sompel, H., Nelson, M.L., Sanderson, R., Balakireva, L.L., Ainsworth, S., and Shankar, H. (2009) 'Memento: Time travel for the Web'. Available at: http://arxiv.org/abs/0911.1112 [18 February 2018].

12

# Computational Methods for Web History

Anat Ben-David and Adam Amram

## INTRODUCTION

In light of the exponential growth in digital data characterizing the twenty-first century, future historians of our time will have to rely on born-digital materials as primary sources for establishing historical facts. Yet born-digital materials challenge historians' well-established source criticism techniques used for establishing facts based on the authenticity, authorship and authority of documents, for they are ephemeral, immaterial, fragile and easy to manipulate. For example, the content of websites can be easily modified, tweets are frequently deleted, the number of social media comments and likes can be artificially boosted through click farms and dubious sources spreading misinformation can be disguised as reliable news organizations. With the commercialization of the web, more than ever before, web data is primarily proprietary, and therefore subjected to platforms' policies and constraints.

Compared with the fragility and contestation of born-digital data, web archives are one of the last non-commercial knowledge devices that can be used to establish historical facts from web data. Web archives capture snapshots of websites at a specific point in time and preserve them for eternity. However, despite the fact that archived websites are stable, reliable, public and non-commercial digital primary sources, they are difficult to study with digital and computational methods.

In recent years, a 'computational turn' is advocated as a paradigmatic shift in the digital humanities. Arguably, such justification seems unnecessary for the web, for there is no need for a 'turn' if the web is a computational medium to begin with. On its face, many of the computational techniques already in use by digital humanists and web researchers (such as methods for text and image analysis, geo-mapping or network analyses) can be easily used with archived web materials.

The question remains, if web archives are conceived, curated and distributed in digital form, why are they so difficult to study computationally?

One of the reasons accounting for the difficulty in using computational methods on the archived web is the distinctive ontological status of archived websites, compared with other digital materials. According to Niels Brügger, web archives differ from other digital material, whether they are analogue documents that have been digitized (for example, scans of historical newspapers, letters or books), or born-digital documents (such as copies of contemporary newspapers, letters, books and other documents that were originally produced in digital form). Termed by Brügger (2016) as 're-born digital materials', the archived web is a static representation of an ephemeral medium, which would not have existed prior to its archiving. Brügger outlines further challenges regarding the unique characteristics of the archived web, including, among others, the fact that differences in the technical settings and collection policies of web archiving institutions may result in different archived versions of the same websites. In addition, there are difficulties in representing the temporal aspects of the archived snapshots, and in deciding which archived version of a given website should be used, where there is either scarcity of versions or a multiplicity of nearly identical versions from similar time stamps. Put differently, web archives are not just another repository of digital documents, but call for particular methods that would take into account their unique characteristics.

In this chapter, we argue that the use of computational methods for web archive research is possible – and even desired – provided that the methods, tools and techniques are adapted to the specific characteristics of web archives, and the challenges involved in studying them. To support this argument, we begin with an overview of the theoretical justifications for the use of computational methods in computational social sciences and digital humanities. Thereafter, we discuss specific methodological challenges put forward by web archives, and how computational methods may be helpful in overcoming some of them. We further outline four computational techniques – drawn from our previous research projects – that illustrate ways in which computational tools have enabled us to use the Internet Archive as a primary source, and to answer web historical questions. Finally, we discuss the limits of the computational methods approach.

## THEORETICAL BACKGROUND

Broadly defined, the term 'computational methods' relates to the application of analytical methods and techniques – originally developed by computer scientists – to answer research questions in other disciplines such as the humanities and the social sciences. It is fair to say that these mathematical techniques, involving data processing, numerical analysis, simulation and modeling, algorithms, visualization, artificial intelligence and other forms of computation, are agnostic to disciplinary boundaries, as long as the data is digital. For example, a computer program designed to identify topics in a large corpus of texts can be applied to analyze a corpus of poems, of historical manuscripts or of corporate emails.

However, the introduction of computational methods in the humanities and social sciences has been far from trivial. David Berry (2011) describes a 'computational turn' in digital humanities as a result of three paradigmatic waves: in the first, computational techniques were primarily a means to digitizing texts and to building infrastructures for digital archives, which, in turn, were analyzed by humanists as they would analyze any other non-digitized text; the second wave looked at the digital historian's toolkit as one that can be applied not only to digitized texts, but also to any other 'born-digital' data.

Finally, the third wave turned its gaze to computation itself – the mediation of computer code and the digitality of the objects it works with – as producing new ontologies and effecting epistemic changes.

Indeed, in the past decade, advances in computational technologies opened new possibilities for storing and processing data at a scale which was unimaginable only a few years ago. The analytical possibilities that accompany new computational analyses promise new kinds of knowledge that were impossible before. Big data analysis and computational methods are termed the new historians' 'macroscope' (Graham et al., 2015), alluding to the revolutionary impact the invention of optical instruments such as the microscope and telescope had on the natural sciences in the seventeenth century. This promise is epitomized in two papers published in the journal *Science*. In the first, Michel et al. (2011) put forward the notion of 'culturomics', involving computational analyses of large volumes of literary texts to quantitatively investigate cultural trends. Resonating Moretti's distinction between close and distant readings (2007), the researchers computationally analyzed a corpus of digitized texts containing about 4% of all books ever printed from 1800 to 2000, and demonstrated that this approach can provide insights about fields as diverse as lexicography, the evolution of grammar, collective memory, the adoption of technology, the pursuit of fame, censorship and historical epidemiology. The second paper discusses the application of a computational approach in the social sciences (Lazer et al., 2009). Here too, the researchers argue that the increasing datafication of almost every realm of human activity paves the road to new research opportunities that can identify patterns, trends and proximities in huge and diverse datasets, and draw new insights in many fields in the social sciences.

Going back to Berry's definitions of three waves of digital humanities, it can be argued that the study of the web and its history can be situated between the second and the third – by bringing together the humanist's and the social scientist's research questions and toolkits, and by studying born-digital texts, as well as data about almost any aspect of human activity. On the face of it, arguments for adopting a computational approach for web history do not require further justification, as they draw from both the digital humanities and the computational social sciences. As Graham et al. note:

> While big data is often explicitly framed as a problem of the future, it has already presented fruitful opportunities for the past. The most obvious place where this is true is archived copies of the publicly accessible Internet. The advent of the World Wide Web in 1991 has had revolutionary effects on human communication and organization, and its archiving presents a tremendous body of non-commercialized public speech. There is a lot of it, however, and large methodologies will be needed to explore it. It is this problem that we believe makes the adoption of digital methodologies for history especially important. (2015: 27)

The ability to perform new computational analyses at scale seems to be a unified justification for the adoption of computational and digital methods for history, social sciences and web research. Nevertheless, web historical research – with the archived Internet as its primary source – still posits somewhat different justifications for the use of computational methods, since the web is a computational medium to begin with. If the 'computational turn' in the digital humanities and the social sciences began with the digitization of printed texts on one hand, and with the 'datafication' of social phenomena on the other, for the web – there has never been a need for such a computational turn.

The question then remains: if there is such a structural fit between the web as a computational medium and computational methods for studying its history, why are computational methods not widely used in web historical research?

The answer to these questions may be found in Brügger's alternative periodization of digital humanities, which focuses on the evolution of digital material, rather than on research practices (2016). Compared with digitized and born-digital materials, Brügger argues that web archives should be considered re-born digital materials, which grants it a distinct ontological status and calls for a methodological treatment that takes its unique characteristics into account. Therefore, the apparent structural fit between the 'digitality' of the archived web and digital methods designed for studying born-digital material, such as the live web, is misleading.

In the next section, we follow Brügger's argument about the distinctiveness of the archived web as re-born digital material, by tracing the historical roots of the use of computational methods in web history, and by outlining specific challenges that hinder the adoption of computational methods in web archival research. We then offer possible computational solutions to some of these challenges.

### *Roots of Computational Methods in Web History*

The establishment of the Internet Archive in 1996 marked the emergence of web archiving practices, now shared by many institutions, organizations and researchers around the world. Five years later, snapshots of archived websites became available for browsing and viewing through an interface developed by the Internet Archive and aptly labeled the 'Wayback Machine'. In many ways, the introduction of the Wayback Machine has paved the road for both qualitative and quantitative analyses of the archived web.

Historically, however, computational and quantitative methods for studying web archives were the realm of information scientists, and not historians, media scholars or social researchers. The early information science literature on web archives offered computational tools for improving retrieval of archived web content, for example by using metadata (Rauber and Bina, 1999; Rauber and Merkl, 1999). Researchers have also started publishing results from longitudinal studies analyzing the structure and persistence of web pages, based on archived web data (Koehler, 2002). After the turn of the millennium, studies in information retrieval created large temporal web collections for the development and evaluation of retrieval techniques for the temporal web (Baeza-Yates et al., 2004; Bordino et al., 2008; Chen and Roy, 2009; Chung et al., 2009). Historical analysis of the dynamic evolution of websites' markup style was picked up by information scientists much later, less as a means for historical research and more as a method for evaluating the retrieval effectiveness of the modern web (Gyllstrom et al., 2012).

Meanwhile, social science researchers – mainly political scientists, and later on web historians and other media scholars – started using web archives for studying social and political phenomena on the web. The early methods used for the social studies of archived web materials were either manual, or only semi-automated. Researchers in the Netherlands, for example, started archiving websites of Dutch political parties and electoral campaigns (Voerman, 1998). In a series of publications, Schneider and Foot put forward the method of web sphere analysis, as 'a framework for web studies that enables analysis of communicative actions and relations between web producers and users developmentally over time' (Schneider and Foot, 2005: 2). The method involves dynamically selecting and archiving a set of web pages around a theme or an event, web pages which are subsequently analyzed by triangulating hyperlink, content and qualitative analyses (Foot and Schneider, 2010; Foot et al., 2003; Schneider and Foot, 2004).

Gradually, along with the widespread establishment of web archiving initiatives at national libraries, as well as with developments in the ways the web was structured and organized (i.e. through search engines) and with methodological developments in the fields of Internet research (such as automated hyperlink analysis and web scraping), digital and computational methods for the study of web archives began to emerge (Rogers, 2015).

For social scientists and historians who engage with Internet histories, web archives enabled very specific types of research based on a single archived web page as unit of analysis. Rogers describes one such research scenario as website histories – performed through screencast documentaries. Rogers claims that such a research scenario is native to the medium, as it 'makes explicit what the Wayback Machine implies, with its invitation to tell the history of a website and through it the history of the web' (Rogers, 2017: 90).

Following the idea of repurposing the web's natively digital objects and organizing devices to conduct 'natively digital' web research, Rogers and researchers from the Digital Methods Initiative also developed tools that output a list of direct links to all archived snapshots of a given URL[1], and which extract a historical hyperlink network from archived snapshots of a set of URLs[2]. These tools have been used by Weltevrede and Helmond (2012) to study the evolution of the Dutch blogosphere.

It is only around the time of the emergence of the 'computational turn' in digital humanities and computational social sciences that large-scale historical analyses of web archives became more widespread. This has been primarily facilitated by emerging collaborations between academic researchers, digital libraries and web archives, such as the Big UK Domain Data for the Arts and Humanities (BUDDAH) project (Winters, 2017), the Netherlands Web Archive Retrieval Tools (WebART) project (Huurdeman et al., 2013) and the Danish probing of a national web project (Brügger, 2017). These projects – all initiated around 2013 – aim to highlight the value of web archives as a source for arts and humanities researchers, develop access tools and methods for research and provide research scenarios – as well as research findings – of historical studies of a national web archive as a (huge) single unit of analysis of several terabytes, which is highly dependent on computational analyses as well as on infrastructures suitable for big data analysis. In line with these developments are recent calls to think of computational methods as the new toolkit of the web historian (Milligan, 2012, 2016). Despite this, it should be noted that, to date, the ability to access and process an entire national web archive as a unit of analysis is reserved to a handful of researchers who collaborate with national libraries or with the Internet Archive, while other members of the research community need to resort to available resources such as the Wayback Machine, which, as previously noted, is designed for viewing the history of a single website, rather than for performing large-scale data analyses. The following section further elaborates on the challenges that hinder the widespread application of computational methods to archived web materials.

## CHALLENGES IN APPLYING COMPUTATIONAL METHODS FOR WEB HISTORY

Though the application of computational methods to study web history has become more widespread in recent years, most of the published literature on the use of web archives for historical research focuses on technical and theoretical challenges limiting the application of computational and digital methods for web history (Brügger, 2013; Dougherty et al., 2010; Milligan, 2016). These challenges can be organized analytically around four topics: issues of access, the limits of current interfaces to web archives, and problems of contextualization and completeness of archived web materials. All four challenges affect the historian's ability to make sense of the primary materials. Below we briefly discuss these challenges that hinder the application of computational approaches, or 'distant reading', to web archives (Lin et al., 2014).

## Access

User statistics of web archives hosted by national libraries show relatively low access rates. To name two examples, both the French and Danish web archives keep full domain harvests of the .fr and .dk domains, respectively, under legal deposit law, and access is restricted to researchers. In 2012, the National Library of France reported 30–50 monthly consultations of the web archive, whereas in Denmark only 20 researchers received access between 2007 and 2012 (Schostag & Fønss-Jørgensen, 2012; Stirling et al., 2012).

There is a growing divergence between the technological ability to preserve and archive the web, and the legal barriers related to copyright and privacy that hinder online access to archived web materials. With the exception of the Internet Archive and the national web archives of Japan and Portugal, most web archiving initiatives held by national libraries can only allow offline access, and only to those physically located in the libraries' reading rooms. As a consequence, only a handful of researchers who actively collaborate with national web archives or with the Internet Archive are able to conduct large-scale computational analyses of the archived web[3].

## Interfaces

The problem of legal access to archived web materials is coupled with a problem of existing access tools and interfaces to web archives. The design of the Internet Archive's Wayback Machine – currently the dominant access interface to most institutional web archives around the world – reflects the perception that the unit of analysis is a single website, and that archives are best consulted, or browsed, one website at a time (Brügger, 2012a; Rogers, 2013, 2017). The single-site approach hinders researchers from increasing their analytical scope from one page to a collection of websites, or even the entire archive (Ben-David and Huurdeman, 2014; Milligan, 2016).

User studies indicate that most users (whether they are journalists, litigators, lay people or academic researchers) expect to consult web archives in the same fashion they consult the live web: through search (Ball, 2010; Costa and Silva, 2009, 2011; Jatowt et al., 2008; Meyer et al., 2011; Ras and van Bussel, 2007). Although several web archives are already developing full text search interfaces, some of which were designed specifically for data analysis purposes (Holzmann et al., 2017), these have still not been widely implemented.

Indeed, current web archiving infrastructures are not well-suited for computational research. The technical infrastructure of most web archives – the Internet Archive among them – was built before the 'computational turn'. Arguably, web archiving infrastructures are also mirrors through which the history of the web can be studied. The Wayback Machine's slogan, 'surf the web as it was', denotes that it was conceived at a period in the web's history when 'browsing' and 'surfing' were the common mode of engaging with the web, before the takeover of the search paradigm (Ben-David and Huurdeman, 2014). From an infrastructural point of view, modern technologies designed to process petabytes of data, such as Hadoop Distributed File System (HDFS) and Hadoop MapReduce, are underutilized. The lack of those contemporary big data technologies as infrastructure for web archive preservation and access makes it difficult for researchers to perform 'distant reading' and macro analytics on web archives (Lin et al., 2014).

## Contextualization

Another critique often made about the archived web as a primary source for historical research is a problem of contextualization. As Featherstone (2006) argued, digital storage allows for expanding the boundaries of the archive, as well as the boundaries of what is considered worthy of archiving. Yet this poses tremendous difficulties for the traditional practices of source appraisal and provenance, which are central principles in archival sciences. Web archives may include millions of web pages, yet the archived snapshots lack significant contextual information about the wider media ecology in which the website operated when it was archived, and lack significant provenance information (Ben-David and Amram, 2018; Dougherty et al., 2010; Milligan, 2016; Rogers, 2013). While web archives keep the seed lists and crawl logs of the archiving process, this important metadata is usually not made available to researchers. As a result, little is known about the circumstances of archiving a specific website at a particular point in time, about the specific archiving method, or whether or not a specific website has been archived deliberately (as part of a seed list), or serendipitously (as a linked website to a seed list) (Huurdeman et al., 2015)[4]. Even though the lack of sufficient contextual information and metadata limits the ability to draw significant findings from large-scale analyses of archived websites, as we soon demonstrate, a 'distant reading' of web archives may be fruitful in re-introducing some of the missing context to archived web materials.

## Completeness

Completeness is another issue web historians need to address when working with web archives as primary sources, and where computational methods may be of crucial relevance. Niels Brügger (2012b) poignantly reminds us that web archives are both incomplete – since many pages are not archived – and too complete – since there may be many duplicates and archived versions of the same page. Making sense of archived web materials is therefore aided by assessments of the degree of their completeness, or incompleteness. Here, completeness can be measured as an evaluation of the archiving process itself (what has been preserved and what has been lost), or of the outcome of the archiving process (which sources are missing from a given corpus of archived websites, and whether or not the archiving of websites is complete). For example, a study by Thelwall and Vaughn (2004) shows significant differences in the archival coverage of national webs on the Internet Archive. Research by Ainsworth et al. (2011) shows that an estimated 35%–90% of websites have at least one archived copy; however, these figures are challenged by Hale et al. (2017), who found that the archival coverage of the popular website TripAdvisor is only 24%; Alkwai et al. (2015) estimated the completeness of archived snapshots of Arabic websites on the Internet Archive by comparing them with a list of URLs that were found in web directories. Interestingly, Huurdeman et al. (2015) put forward the notion of the 'aura' of a web archive – representations of unarchived content that are represented by hyperlinks and anchor text data from archived URLs of a national web archive.

While such assessments of archival coverage and completeness are crucial for contextualizing web archive materials for historical research, they can only be performed computationally, since it is necessary to assess the whole volume of a given archive (and, as is the case with the studies referenced above, estimate the size of the entire web) in order to indicate or infer what parts of it may be incomplete or missing.

To summarize this section, the relatively low usage rate of web archives for historical research, and the adoption of computational methods for this type of study, can be explained as a chicken and egg problem. On the one hand, there is growing scholarly interest in accessing and using archived web data for various types of analysis. While there are emerging initiatives to develop frameworks for allowing access, data extraction and analysis of web archives[5], limited access to most existing web archives, along with the limits of interfaces and processing infrastructures, and lack of sufficient contextualization information about appraisal, provenance and completeness, drive many historians away from using web archives for web history, and especially from applying various data analysis methods that would be native to the medium. In the following section of this chapter, we attempt to evoke the web historians' interest in applying simple computational methods when using web archives for historical research. This is not proposed as a solution to the existing challenges described above; rather, such simple computational methods can be seen as a means to allow for distant readings of archived web materials, by stretching the limits of existing access channels, interfaces and infrastructures of web archives.

The techniques described in the following section are based on simple scripts specifically designed for researchers who may not be well versed in computational methods, and who do not have institutional access to web archives as big data corpora. This is provided so as to assist more researchers in attaining as many analytical benefits as possible, when using the Internet Archive's Wayback Machine as their entry point for conducting research on the web's pasts.

## COMPUTATIONAL SOLUTIONS TO THE CHALLENGES OF ACCESS, INTERFACE, CONTEXTUALIZATION, APPRAISAL AND COMPLETENESS

In the previous sections of the chapter, we reviewed some of the literature that applied a computational approach to studying web archives from diverse disciplines and perspectives, ranging from assessments of the archives' coverage, to the characterization of national webs. In this section, we report on findings from our own work, by outlining specific and simple computational techniques that we developed and applied to web historical research. These techniques are designed to overcome specific challenges related to archived web materials and their current interfaces, as outlined above. Furthermore, they significantly increase the scope of analysis enabled by the Wayback Machine. While these methods are tailored to specific questions, they serve here as a proof of concept, which can then be adapted and used for other research purposes. Above all, they are listed here as a means to lower the threshold preventing web historians from engaging in critical, born-digital, web historical research, such that can critique the historical, technical and infrastructural history of archived websites, and that can further contextualize them as primary sources for historiography.

Our previous work has primarily focused on the Internet Archive and the Wayback Machine as a primary source. The research questions – related to the history of national webs – were not computational in nature; rather, we used computational methods where a methodological challenge hindered us from increasing the scope of the analysis or from gaining wider contextual knowledge about our corpus. Below, we outline four research scenarios where the use of relatively simple python scripts has helped us enhance the utility and scope of historical research with the Wayback Machine.

### *1. Increasing the Scope: Finding more URLs*

As previously mentioned, the Wayback Machine allows for viewing and browsing archived snapshots, but does not lend itself easily to analyses that wish to extend their scope beyond the single page as the unit of analysis. Furthermore, in order to use the Wayback Machine, users are expected to know the URL they are looking for[6]. But what if one does not know which URL to look for? And what if it is impossible to know the URL address of historical websites that can no longer be found on the live web?

This is the case of the .yu domain, the historical country code top-level domain of the former Yugoslavia, which was entirely removed from the Internet's Domain Name System (DNS) in 2010. DNS is the hierarchical universal system responsible for the resolution of web addresses from IP numbers. As such, if the IP addresses associated with a given domain are removed from the DNS, they cannot be resolved, even if the websites are still hosted on a server connected to the Internet.

Our research question was relatively broad: what does the web 'remember' of its deleted past? Is it possible to reconstruct from the Wayback Machine a deleted national web, if the live web cannot disclose any .yu URL as a starting point to the archive? (Ben-David, 2016). To answer this question, we used the hyperlinked structure of archived websites to our advantage. Using lists of seed URLs which were obtained from an expert, we used a python script that fetched all the seeds from the Wayback Machine, and snowballed their outlinks, searching for more .yu URLs[7]. We iterated the method several times until no new .yu URLs were found. This outlink extraction method enabled the scope of the analysis to be increased from a seed list of about 4,000 hosts, to 17,460 unique websites in the .yu domain, estimated to comprise 53% of the registered addresses in the .yu domain at its peak. The partial reconstruction does not necessarily indicate that the undiscovered portions of the domain represent a limitation of the method; instead, it may indicate that almost half of the domain was not archived by the Internet Archive, as we will soon explain.

With the extracted dataset, we performed historical network analysis (a method outlined in Chapter 10 of this *Handbook*; see also Weltevrede and Helmond (2012) and Hale et al. (2014)) to examine the strength of ties within the .yu domain, as well as among national domains of former-Yugoslavia republics. Furthermore, the data we extracted from the Internet Archive allowed us to ask further questions about the history of the .yu domain, as well as about the appraisal of the Internet Archive as a primary source for web history, as outlined below.

## 2. Source Critique: Comparing Web Cultures of Seed Lists

As noted by Rogers (2017), archived websites face scrutiny as a primary source for historiography, and for legal evidentiary purposes. Such scrutiny is realized through traditional appraisal of sources in historiography, such as determining the originality of a document, the authenticity of authorship and the source's reputation. While web archives complicate all of the above (Brügger, 2012a; Rogers, 2017), the question is which techniques can be used to appraise archived websites as sources? While the screencast documentary of a single website is one possible venue for source criticism, we put forward a technique for appraising lists of URLs, as starting points or seeds for archival web research.

Historical analysis of archived web materials that extends beyond the single website as its unit of analysis greatly depends on a seed list of initial URLs from which the corpus is created. Different URL lists may lead to very different corpora, even though they may be seen as covering the same topic. For example, a study by Mataly (2013) compared corpora created about the former UK Prime Minister Margaret Thatcher using three born-digital source lists: curated website collections from the UK Web Archive, temporal search on Google (with query results set to past years) and a domain harvest of the .uk domain. The differences between the generated lists were rather striking: the corpus created by searching the UK Web Archive's collections was primarily governmental; the sources referring to Thatcher that appeared on Google with time stamps from the exact same period were primarily commercial (large newspaper and e-commerce platforms) and the corpus of the domain harvest was more diverse, containing a variety of types of sources.

This example shows that seed lists are embedded in specific web cultures, which may have internal preferences or biases. To understand these cultures and potential biases, in our case study of the reconstruction of the .yu domain from the Internet Archive, we used a fairly simple technique for comparing the seed lists that generated the reconstruction. This simple technique, initially coined by the Digital Methods Initiative as a triangulation tool[8], compared the source lists from which our reconstruction began (Google search results, Wikipedia, a computer magazine, and an ISP). First, we removed duplicates from each list, and then we identified the URLs shared among source types, and the URLs unique to each source type. The ties between the shared and unique sources can be read as a table, or visualized as a network graph. In the case of the .yu domain, we found that, relative to the other source lists, Wikipedia was the most diverse source to be used as a seed list for reconstructing topical corpora from the Internet Archive.

### 3. Assessing Incompleteness

Earlier in this chapter, we argued that an assessment of the (in)completeness of web archives is necessary for contextualizing historical research done with archived web materials. It should be noted that assessments of incompleteness greatly depend on metadata that is often unavailable or inaccessible for researchers, such as information about the collection policy, or access to the archiving crawler's logs.

Despite these limits, computational methods may give researchers the ability to assess the whole by comparing the archived dataset against different datasets and data sources, as was previously done by Thelwall and Vaughn (2004), Ainsworth et al. (2011), Alkawi et al. (2015) and Hale et al. (2017). In the case of the .yu domain, we assessed the number of *accessible* archived snapshots of .yu websites on the Internet Archive, compared with the number of .yu URLs recovered by our outlink extraction method. Here, we queried the Internet Archive's Wayback Machine CDX server API[9] and documented the response code for each URL – indicating whether it can or cannot be accessed on the Wayback Machine. Using a python script and the urllib2 module, we sent GET queries to the REST API of the Internet Archive CDX server to lookup captures of our known Yugoslav URLs. With the help of filtering and collapsing features of the CDX server, we requested only successful snapshots and selected only one for each year. Using this method, we found that the level of archival coverage of the historical domain is a function of temporal proximity to the live web: the shorter the temporal gap between a live website and its archived snapshot, the better its archival coverage on the Internet Archive.

### 4. Culturomics: Histories of Non-Textual Elements

At the outset of this chapter we argued that some computational methods for textual analysis can be applied to any type of text, independently of their affiliation to various academic disciplines. This also applies to the archived web, where, for example, methods such as Topic Modeling have already been used to analyze the evolution of the textual content of historical websites over time (Milligan, 2016). At the same time, we also argued that the history of websites not only comprises text, but also other elements documenting the history of the medium, and the socio-technical 'ecology' in which a given website operated at the time it was archived (Berry, 2012; Fuller, 2005). We also mentioned the 'culturomic' approach (Michel et al., 2011), which calls for analyzing cultural patterns in large volumes of data. Although the archiving process does not and cannot capture the full ecosystem in which the live website operated, it still captures a wealth of data that can be of significant importance to web historians – especially those interested in technological and cultural histories. Apart from text, web archives contain images, video, various document formats such as MS Word, PDF or PowerPoint presentations; each HTML page also contains code, within which one can find historical 'treasures' such as embedded advertisements and cookies. Is it possible to conduct large-scale culturomics analysis of non-textual elements found in the Wayback Machine?

Inspired by Lev Manovich's work on cultural analytics (2009, 2012), we also argue that large-scale analyses of the non-textual elements of web archives may open up a variety of new historical analyses. To this end, we developed a computational tool for analyzing the evolution of color in non-photographic images of the reconstructed .yu domain, focusing on archived snapshots dated between 1997 and 2000 (Ben-David et al., 2018). We used a technique based on Machine Learning, to summarize the three dominant colors of each of the non-photographic images in the reconstructed domain, in order to study the history of the ties between web design, cultural digital practices and preferences, and nationalism. Specifically, we compared the three-color histograms summarizing the images of the .yu domain with the colors of the Yugoslav flag, and calculated the overall 'distance' of the entire domain from the colors of the flag during the Kosovo war[10].

To summarize this section, it is evident that none of the computational techniques that we used for studying the history of the .yu domain are new. Rather, we adapted existing methods for web research and data analysis, and tailored them to meet the challenges of performing large-scale analysis of data with the Internet Archive's Wayback Machine. The following section concludes this chapter by discussing the limits of the computational approach to web historical research.

## CONCLUSIONS

Although a computational approach brings with it a revolutionary promise of new paradigms of knowledge, and of writing and reading history, most of the advocates of this approach argue that it should be adopted judiciously – not necessarily as a replacement to existing humanist and social scientific methods, but rather as an important aid, a necessary instrument for gaining knowledge in a datafied world (Berry, 2012; Graham et al., 2015). In this chapter, we charted some of the new computational methods-based analysis strategies and approaches to studying archived websites accessed from the Wayback Machine. We have shown that despite the limits of the access interface – which is designed for viewing single archived pages rather than a distant reading of millions of them – python scripts can increase the analytical scope of historical web research, as well as answer important questions that improve the contextualization of archived web data (such as evaluation of sources and of archival coverage). We also demonstrated that computational methods can turn archived websites into a fascinating playground for identifying cultural trends by using the wealth of multimodal information they harbor.

Despite the benefits of the computational approach outlined above in stretching the analytical possibilities of historical research using the Wayback Machine, there are also several limits to consider. Chief of them is the production of analytical artifacts and their misinterpretation as historical facts. As previously mentioned, awareness of the cultures of sources and devices from which web archive research begins is crucial to the interpretation of the archival corpora and of the historical networks that each may produce. A possible way of overcoming the problem of analytical artifacts is triangulation of sources. In addition, analyses aided by computational methods, tools and techniques are able to answer specific quantifiable questions. They are good at 'probing web archives' (Brügger, 2017) when dealing with huge corpora of archived websites, and when there is no alternative way of 'knowing' the archive as a whole. Nevertheless, this knowing is limited to quantifiable information, and macro analyses of millions of documents, or of petabytes of data, do not always suffice for answering deeper questions about historical processes (Winters, 2017). Further critical thinking and reflexive analysis are required to place the outputs of computational tools in context (Schafer et al., 2016).

## Notes

1 Digital Methods Initiative, Wayback Machine Link Ripper, https://wiki.digitalmethods.net/Dmi/ToolInternetArchiveWaybackMachineLinkRipper (visited 01.02.18).
2 Digital Methods Initiative, Internet Archive Wayback Machine Network per Year, https://wiki.digitalmethods.net/Dmi/ToolInternetArchiveWaybackMachineToNetwork (visited 01.02.18).
3 There are several exceptions to this claim. The UK web archive is freely accessible online for the collections made before 2014, whereas the ccTLD archivings of the .uk domain (from 2014 onwards) can only be accessed onsite at one of five national libraries. As for the Danish web archive, researchers who receive permission can browse the web archive remotely, while MA students are allowed access to the web archive only in the reading rooms of the national library.
4 Since 2016, this problem is slightly mitigated in the new interface of the Wayback Machine, which now provides information about the collection of web captures associated with the specific web crawl the capture came from. See https://blog.archive.org/2016/10/24/faqs-for-some-new-features-available-in-the-beta-wayback-machine/ (visited 01.02.18).
5 See, for example, the Archives Unleashed Toolkit (Lin et al., 2017) and the ArchiveSpark project (Holzmann et al., 2016).
6 Since 2016, the new version of the Wayback Machine allows for basic keyword search on phrases from the URL, yet full site search is not yet available. See https://blog.archive.org/2016/10/24/faqs-for-some-new-features-available-in-the-beta-wayback-machine/ (visited 01.02.18).
7 Open Media and Information Lab, The Open University of Israel (2017). Internet Archive Link Extractor. https://github.com/omilab/internet-archive-link-extractor (visited 01.02.18).
8 Digital Methods Initiative (2008). Triangulation. https://wiki.digitalmethods.net/Dmi/ToolTriangulation (visited 01.02.18).
9 The Wayback CDX server API is a standalone HTTP servelet that serves the index that the Wayback Machine uses to lookup captures. https://github.com/internetarchive/wayback/blob/master/wayback-cdx-server/README.md. (visited 01.02.18). For further research scenarios using the CDX file, see Milligan (2016).
10 Open Media and Information Lab, the Open University of Israel (2016). Image Color Analysis. https://github.com/omilab/image-color-analysis (visited 22 September 2017).

## REFERENCES

Ainsworth, S.G., AlSum A., SalahEldeen H., Weigel, M.C., and Nelson, M. (2011) 'How much of the web is archived?' In: *Proceedings of the 11th Annual International ACM/IEEE Joint Conference on Digital Libraries*, pp. 133–136.

Alkwai, L.M., Nelson, M.L., and Weigle, M.C. (2015) 'How well are Arabic websites archived?' In: *Proceedings of the 15th ACM/IEEE-CE Joint Conference on Digital Libraries*, 2015, pp. 223–232.

Baeza-Yates, R., Lalanne, F., Castillo, C., and Dupret, G. (2004) '*Comparing the Characteristics of the Korean and the Chilean Web' Korea-Chile IT Cooperation Center ITCC*. Technical Report. Available at: http://chato.cl/papers/baeza_04_comparing_chilean_web_korean_web.pdf

Ball, A. (2010) *DCC state of the art report: Web archiving*. Available at:http://www.dcc.ac.uk/sites/default/files/documents/reports/sarwa-v1.1.pdf

Ben-David, A. (2016) 'What does the web remember of its deleted past? An archival reconstruction of the former Yugoslav top-level domain', *New Media & Society*, 18(7): 1103–1119.

Ben-David, A. and Amram, A. (2018) 'The Internet Archive and the socio-technical construction of historical facts', *Internet Histories*, 2(1–2): 179–201.

Ben-David, A., Amram, A., and Bekkerman, R. (2018) 'The colors of the national web: Visual data analysis of the historical yugoslav web domain', *International Journal on Digital Libraries*, 19(1): 95–106.

Ben-David, A. and Huurdeman, H.C. (2014) 'Web archive search as research: Methodological and theoretical implications', *Alexandria*, 25(1–2): 93–111.

Berry, D. (2011) 'The computational turn: Thinking about the digital humanities', *Culture Machine*, 12: n.p. Available at: http://www.culturemachine.net/index.php/cm/article/viewarticle/440

Berry, D. (2012) Life in Code and Software: Mediated Life in a Complex Computational Ecology. Open Humanities Press.

Bordino, I., Boldi, P., Donato, D. Santini, M., and Vigna, S. (2008) 'Temporal evolution of the UK Web', In: *Proceedings of the IEEE International Conference on Data Mining Workshops, ICDM Workshops*, 2008, pp. 909–918.

Brügger, N. (2012a) 'Web history and the Web as a historical source', *Zeithistorische Forschungen*, 9(2): 316–325.

Brügger, N. (2012b) 'When the present Web is later than the past: Web historiography, digital history, and Internet Studies', *Historical Social Research/Historische Sozialforschung*: 102–117. Available at: https://www.ssoar.info/soar/bitstream/handle/document/38378/ssoar-hsr-2012-4-brugger-When_the_present_web_is.pdf?sequence=1 (accessed 20 October 2015).

Brügger, N. (2013) 'Web historiography and Internet Studies: Challenges and perspectives', *New Media & Society*, 15(5): 752–764.

Brügger, N. (2016) 'Digital humanities in the 21st century: Digital material as a driving force', *DHQ: Digital Humanities Quarterly*: 10(3). Available at: http://www.digitalhumanities.org/dhq/vol/10/3/000256/000256.html

Brügger, N. (2017) 'Probing a nation's web domain: A new approach to web history and a new kind of historical source', In: Gerard Goggin and Mark McLelland (eds), *The Routledge Companion to Global Internet Histories*. New York: Routledge. pp. 61–73.

Chen, L. and Roy, A. (2009) 'Event detection from flickr data through wavelet-based spatial analysis', In: *Proceedings of the 18th ACM Conference on Information and Knowledge Management*, 2009, pp. 523–532.

Chung, Y.-J, Toyoda, M. and Kitsuregawa, M. (2009) 'A study of link farm distribution and evolution using a time series of web snapshots', In: *Proceedings of the 5th International Workshop on Adversarial Information Retrieval on the Web*, 2009, pp. 9–16.

Costa, M. and Silva, M.J. (2009) 'Towards information retrieval evaluation over web archives', In: *Proceedings of the SIGIR 2009 Workshop on the Future of IR Evaluation*, 2009, pp. 37–38.

Costa, M. and Silva, M.J. (2011) 'Characterizing search behavior in Web archives', In: *TWAW*, pp. 33–40.

Dougherty, M., Meyer, E.T., McCarthy Madsen, C., van den Heuvel, C., Thomas, A., and Wyatt, S. (2010) 'Researcher engagement with web archives: State of the art'. Joint Information Systems Committee Report.

Featherstone, M. (2006) 'Archive', *Theory, Culture & Society*, 23(2–3): 591–596. DOI: 10.1177/0263276406023002106.

Foot, K. and Schneider, S. (2010) 'Object-oriented web historiography', In: Niels Brügger (ed.), *Web History*. New York: Peter Lang. pp. 61–80. Available at: http://faculty.washington.edu/kfoot/Publications/Foot_Schneider.pdf (accessed 22 September 2017).

Foot, K., Schneider, S.M., Dougherty, M., Xenos, M., and Larsen, E. (2003) 'Analyzing linking practices: Candidate sites in the 2002 US electoral web sphere', *Journal of Computer-Mediated Communication* 8(4). Available at: https://doi.org/10.1111/j.1083-6101.2003.tb00220.x.

Fuller, M. (2005) *Media Ecologies: Materialist Energies in Art and Technoculture*. London: MIT Press.

Graham, S., Milligan, I., and Weingart, S. (2015) *Exploring Big Historical Data: The Historian's Macroscope*. London: Imperial College Press.

Gyllstrom, K., Eickoff, C., de Vries, A.P., and Moens, M.F. (2012) 'The downside of markup: Examining the harmful effects of css and javascript on indexing today's web', In: *Proceedings of the 21st ACM International Conference on Information and Knowledge Management*, 2012, pp. 1990–1994.

Hale, S.A., Blank, G., and Alexander, V.D. (2017) 'Live versus archive: Comparing a web archive to a population of web pages', In: Niels Brügger and Ralph Schroeder (eds), *Web as History: Using Web Archives to Understand the Past and the Present*. London: UCL Press. pp. 45–61. Available at: http://www.jstor.org/stable/j.ctt1mtz55k.8.

Hale, S.A, Yasseri, T., Cowls, J., Meyer, E.T., Schroeder, R., and Margetts, H.. (2014) 'Mapping the UK webspace: Fifteen years of British universities on the web', In: *Proceedings of the 2014 ACM Conference on Web Science*, 2014, pp. 62–70.

Holzmann, H., Goel, V., and Anand, A. (2016) 'Archivespark: Efficient web archive access, extraction and derivation', In: *Digital Libraries (JCDL), IEEE/ACM Joint Conference on*, 2016, pp. 83–92.

Holzmann, H., Nejdl, W., and Anand, A. (2017) 'Exploring Web archives through temporal anchor texts', In: *Proceedings of the 2017 ACM on Web Science Conference*, 2017, pp. 289–298.

Huurdeman, H.C., Ben-David, A., and Sammar, T. (2013) 'Sprint methods for web archive research', In: *Proceedings of the 5th Annual ACM Web Science Conference*, 2013, pp. 182–190.

Huurdeman H.C., Kamps, J., Samar, T., de Vries, A.P., Ben-David, A., and Rogers, R. (2015) 'Lost but not forgotten: Finding pages on the unarchived web', *International Journal on Digital Libraries* 16(3–4): 247–265. DOI: 10.1007/s00799-015-0153-3.

Jatowt, A., Kawai, Y., Ohshima, H., and Katsumi, T. (2008) 'What can history tell us?: Towards different models of interaction with document histories', In: *Proceedings of the 19th ACM Conference on Hypertext and Hypermedia*, 2008, pp. 5–14.

Koehler, W. (2002) 'Web page change and persistence – A four-year longitudinal study', *Journal of the Association for Information Science and Technology,* 53(2): 162–171.

Lazer, D., Pentland, A. (Sandy), Adamic, L., Aral, S., Barabasi, A. L., Brewer, D., Christakis, M., Contractor, N., Fowler, J., Gutmann, M., Jebara, T., King, G., Macy, M., Roy, D., and Van Alstyne, M. (2009) Life in the network: the coming age of computational social science. Science (New York, N.Y.), 323(5915), 721–723. http://doi.org/10.1126/science.1167742. (2009) 'Life in the network: The coming age of computational social science', *Science* 323(5915): 721–723. Available at: https://www.ncbi.nlm.nih.gov/pmc/articles/pmc2745217/ (accessed 22 September 2017).

Lin, J., Kraus, K., and Punzalan, R. (2014) 'Supporting "distant reading" for web archives', *Proceedings of Digital Humanities*: 239–241.

Lin, J., Milligan, I., Wiebe, J., and Zhou, A. (2017) 'Warcbase: Scalable analytics infrastructure for exploring Web archives', *Journal on Computing and Cultural Heritage,* 10(4): 1–30.

Mataly, J. (2013) 'The Three Truths of Margaret Thatcher: Creating and Analyzing Archival Artefacts'. M.A dissertation, University of Amsterdam.

Manovich, L. (2009) The practice of everyday (media) life: From mass consumption to mass cultural production? *Critical Inquiry,* 35(2): 319–331.

Manovich, L. (2012) How to compare one million images? In: David M. Berry (ed.), *Understanding Digital Humanities*. London: Palgrave Macmillan. pp. 249–278.

Meyer, E.T., Thomas, A., and Schroeder, R. (2011) 'Web archives: The future (s)'. Available at SSRN: https://ssrn.com/abstract=1830025 or http://dx.doi.org/10.2139/ssrn.1830025.

Michel, JB., SHEN, Y.K., Presser Aiden, A., Veres, A. Gray, M.K., The Google Books Team, Picket, J.P., Hoiberg, D., Clancy, D., Norvig, P., Orwant, J., Pinker, S., Nowak, M.A., and Liberman Aiden, E. (2011) 'Quantitative analysis of culture using millions of digitized books', *Science* 331(6014): 176–182. Available at: http://science.sciencemag.org/content/331/6014/176.short (accessed 22 September 2017).

Milligan, I. (2012) 'Mining the "Internet graveyard": Rethinking the historians' toolkit',

*Journal of the Canadian Historical Association*, 23(2): 21–64.

Milligan, I. (2016) 'Lost in the infinite archive: The promise and pitfalls of web archives', *International Journal of Humanities and Arts Computing* 10(1): 78–94.

Moretti, F. (2007) *Graphs, Maps, Trees: Abstract Models for Literary History*. New York: Verso.

Ras, M. and van Bussel, S. (2007) 'Web archiving user survey'. National Library of the Netherlands (Koninklijke Bibliotheek). Available at: https://www.kb.nl/sites/default/files/docs/kb_usersurvey_webarchive_en.pdf (accessed 22 September 2017).

Rauber, A. and Bina, H. (1999) 'A metaphor graphics based representation of digital libraries on the world wide web: Using the libviewer to make metadata visible', In: *Proceedings. Tenth International Workshop on Database and Expert Systems Applications*. IEEE, pp. 286–290.

Rauber, A. and Merkl, D. (1999) 'Mining text archives: Creating readable maps to structure and describe document collections', In: Jan M. Żytkow and Jan Rauch (eds), *Principles of Data Mining and Knowledge Discovery: Third European Conference, PKDD'99 Prague, Czech Republic*. Berlin: Springer. pp. 524–529.

Rogers, R. (2013) *Digital Methods*. Cambridge, MA: MIT Press.

Rogers, R. (2015) 'Digital methods for Web research', In: Robert A. Scott and Marlis C. Buchmann (eds), *Emerging Trends in the Social and Behavioral Sciences*. DOI: 10.1002/9781118900772.

Rogers, R. (2017) 'Doing Web history with the Internet Archive: Screencast documentaries', *Internet Histories*, 1: 160–172.

Schafer, V, Musiani, F., and Borelli, M. (2016) 'Web archiving, governance and STS'. *French Journal of Media Research*, 6: 1–23.

Schneider, S.M. and Foot, K.A. (2004) 'Web campaigning by US presidential primary candidates in 2000 and 2004', In: John C. Tedesco and Andrew Paul Williams (eds), *The Internet Election: Perspectives on the Web in Campaign*. Lanham: Rowman & Littlefield Publishers. pp. 21–36.

Schneider, S.M. and Foot, K.A. (2005) 'Web sphere analysis: An approach to studying online action', In: Christine Hine (ed.), *Virtual Methods: Issues in Social Research on the Internet*. New York: Berg. pp. 157–170.

Schostag, S. and Fønss-Jørgensen, E. (2012) 'Webarchiving: Legal deposit of internet in Denmark. A curatorial perspective', *Microform & Digitization Review*, 41(3–4): 110–120.

Stirling, P., Chevallier, P., and Illien, G. (2012) 'Web archives for researchers: Representations, expectations and potential uses', *D-Lib* 18(3/4), Available at: http://www.dlib.org/dlib/march12/stirling/03stirling.html

Thelwall, M. and Vaughan, L. (2004) 'A fair history of the Web? Examining country balance in the Internet Archive', *Library & Information Science Research*, 26(2): 162–176.

Voerman, G. (1998) 'Dutch political parties on the Internet', *ECPR News*, 10(1): 8–9.

Weltevrede, E. and Helmond, A. (2012) 'Where do bloggers blog? Platform transitions within the historical Dutch blogosphere', *First Monday* 17(2). Available at: http://first monday.org/ojs/index.php/fm/article/view/3775/3142 (accessed 23 December 2015).

Winters, J. (2017) 'Breaking in to the mainstream: Demonstrating the value of internet (and web) histories', *Internet Histories* 1(1–2): 173–179. DOI: 10.1080/24701475.2017.1305713.

# Visualizing Historical Web Data

Justin Joque

The emerging field of web history offers unique opportunities to understand media at scales and levels of complexity never before possible. The expansion of various web archives provides massive and complex datasets that can reveal important insights into culture and our practices of computation. As Milligan (2012) argues, the availability of these massive and rich data sources opens up the space for a third wave of digital history, working directly on these already digitized, hyperlinked and temporally differentiated texts. To navigate, analyze and comment upon these documents requires a set of tools and methods that are quickly being developed in history and other humanities fields. While many of these methods and techniques draw heavily from other fields, such as computer science, information retrieval, data mining, etc., their use and translation into the humanities requires additional considerations. One of the key methods in this third wave of digital history is the use of data visualization techniques, especially for representing and exploring large datasets.

While visualization techniques offer a powerful set of methods for dealing with the diverse types of data that can be extracted from historical web data, it is not always clear how to best display this data. The amount of data, skewed distributions, complex interactions and the difficulty of displaying change over time all confound to make visualization a difficult task. In light of these challenges, this chapter attempts to outline some critical issues and suggestions for visualizing historical web data, drawing heavily on methodologies developed in data visualization and related fields, such as network analysis, text mining, etc. The chapter explores general data visualization techniques, network visualization, text analysis visualization and concludes with a discussion of visualizing change over time.

It should be noted that data visualization is as much an artistic process concerned with questions of design and legibility as it is a scientific practice for representing data. There is no simple formula or single process that can represent web data or any other type of data immediately and 'correctly'. Effective data visualization requires experimentation and knowledge of one's data. Furthermore, the audience and purpose of data visualization have immense impacts on best practices. Data visualization generally serves three different purposes: monitoring data to track ongoing processes, exploring data to understand it and communicating data to explain what we have discovered to others. Working with historical data it is most likely researchers will have the latter two goals in mind. In differentiating these purposes, it is important to remember who the audience of a given visualization will be. While one may use complex visualizations with little explanation as part of one's own research, if the intention of a visualization is to communicate some result it is of the utmost importance that what is being displayed is comprehensible to the audience and for the media through which it will be displayed (e.g. it would be imprudent to create a complex high-resolution graph for a slideshow that the audience will only see for a few seconds). With these considerations in mind, it is possible to outline a number of issues and possible solutions that arise in working with historical web data.

## VISUALIZATION IN GENERAL

Websites offer diverse types of metadata and data that lend themselves to well-known types of graphs. Exploring and presenting data in such straightforward ways can often be more compelling than complex visualizations whose ultimate aim is not entirely clear. For example, we may be interested in the relationship between the number of links on a page and the amount of text; in this case a standard scatterplot, which simply places a dot where data lies along two axes, would serve us well. Histograms do well for showing distributions of single variables, by creating 'bins' for the data (e.g. 0–5, 5–10) and representing the count of data points by vertical bars; bar charts excel at showing the composition of a dataset broken into categories, etc. It would be imprudent to attempt to provide an exhaustive list of such graphs here, but a few general principles will be helpful as one explores datasets, graphs and software for visualization.

Any single static two-dimensional data visualization can show at most approximately eight variables. This definitely does not mean one should always strive to show eight variables at a time, as even that limited number can quickly make seeing relationships, patterns or structure difficult. In his 1964 book *Semiology of Graphics*, Bertin divides these eight variables into two positional variables (e.g. x and y or $\phi$ and r in polar coordinates) and six 'retinal' variables: color, size, shape, value (i.e. light to dark), orientation and texture. He further suggests that some of these variables are better at showing different types of data (e.g. shapes are well suited for categorical data). I will refrain from recounting Bertin's entire semiology here, but one should consider which visual variables can best represent the type of data that is being visualized. Furthermore, spending some time with Bertin's book should be high on any list of ways to become skilled in data visualization.

Tufte (1983: 93) also provides a number of important insights that are helpful in constructing any visualization. He sums up one of his major contributions to the field of data visualization by stating, 'A large share of ink on a graphic should present data-information, the ink changing as the data change. Data-ink is the non-erasable core of a graphic, the non-redundant ink arranged in response to variation in the numbers represented'. Building on this he further defines the data-ink ratio as the ratio of ink used to display data to the total amount of ink used in a visualization. We could of course update this from ink to non-background colored pixels; but the principle remains the same. Good visualizations should tend to maximize this ratio as much as possible, eliminating superfluous marks on charts.

Wainer (1984: 139) summarizes the conclusion from Tufte's metric by stating, 'Although arguments can be made that high data density does not imply that a graphic will be good, nor one with low density bad, it does reflect on the efficiency of the transmission of information. Obviously, if we hold clarity and accuracy constant, more information is better than less'. In short, visualization is most effective when the viewer is presented with as much information as possible, and as little ink as possible, provided that neither of these stand in the way of clarity.[1] Thinking in terms of Bertin's list of visual variables, this does not mean that one should always attempt to use all eight visual variables, as that is often an easy way to destroy the clarity of any graph. Rather, one should be judicious in their use, providing only the information that is relevant but presenting it as directly as possible.

This raises a related consideration, especially for comparing aggregate information: when representing small amounts of data, tables often outperform charts. Tables, or even sentences describing data, can maximize the data-ink ratio for small amounts of data and have the added benefit of presenting the reader with the raw information from which they can easily see relationships. With these general considerations in mind, let us move onto specific types of graphs (and their challenges) that often arise in working with historical web data.

## NETWORKS

Some of the most interesting and readily computable data available from websites and web archives are the link structures. Arguably, for the first time ever, historians, literary scholars and others can easily explore massive networks of citation, reference and intertextuality. It is common practice to represent these structures as network diagrams. While the exponential growth of networks as a means of visual representation and as a metaphor for understanding everything from capitalism (Castells, 2011) to science and society (Latour, 1993, 2005) to computers and beyond (Barabási, 2014) may make network diagrams seem instantly obvious, there is a risk that this ubiquity actually serves to obfuscate their nuance and function. Thus, taking a moment to reiterate exactly what network diagrams represent can be fruitful in preparation for deciding the most efficacious way to represent data.

Networks consist of two distinct elements: nodes and edges. Nodes generally represent things and edges represent some sort of relationship between things. For example, we could construct a network out of webpages and relationships could represent links between pages. Such a network would likely be represented as *directed*, since a link goes from one page to another. Other networks, such as a co-author network, may be *undirected* since writing a paper with someone implies that they wrote a paper with you. Additionally, a network can either be made up of one type of thing (e.g. authors) or multiple types of things (e.g. authors and articles) and often it is possible to convert the latter into the former (e.g. by directly linking co-authors rather than linking them to their articles). This immediately suggests one of the first important decisions that can drastically alter network visualizations: what the nodes and edges will be. As both Foot (2006) and Brügger (2009) argue, we should think carefully about exactly what the object of study is when we are researching 'the web' and its history. Creating a network out of domains or subdomains rather than individual pages can create networks that provide different information and look substantially different. In addition, it should be noted that multiple connections between two nodes (e.g. multiple links from a single page to another page) can either be represented by multiple individual lines or a single line that is given a *weight*, which can then be mapped to a visual property of the line if desired (e.g. line thickness, color, etc.).

When executed well, network visualizations can provide a striking representation of the complex structure of data. They excel at showing local clusters (e.g. communities of websites that are in conversation with each other), disconnected components and the general density of networked relationships. They can also be extremely powerful for showing the difference between two related networks, for example two different blogs, or for showing how a single network has changed by visualizing two different moments in time.

While networks can be powerful visual representations, one of the most challenging aspects of representing them is that large tightly interwoven networks tend to produce uninterpretable masses of nodes and connections that look more like hairballs than a meaningful representation of data (See Figures 13.1 and 13.2). Various automatic layout algorithms can have a considerable impact on the readability of a network, especially if nodes can be clustered in such a way that interesting patterns emerge in the density of connections between clusters (e.g. separating subcommunities, subdomain or types of pages can often be fruitful) (see Figure 13.3). Furthermore, in general, networks that have clear clusters tend to be easier to visualize than networks with a single tightly connected component. Luke (2015) discusses a number of automatic layout algorithms and some of the ways they can be modified, variations of which can be found in most network visualization software.

Furthermore, since many of the most often used automatic layouts (e.g. variations of force-directed layouts) simulate physical systems in order to distribute nodes in space to most clearly present network structures, adjusting the parameters of these simulations can have significant impact on the readability of the resultant graph. For example, one of the earliest but still often used algorithms – Fruchterman and Reingold (1991) – makes each node repel every other node and treats each edge as a spring (that has a default length and a given strength that pulls nodes towards that default length). It then updates positions based on the various forces until it settles into a low-energy state that keeps related nodes close together and at the same time spreads nodes out as much as possible, making the resultant visualization readable. Adjusting the spring length, the spring strength and the repellent force between nodes can significantly change the output of the simulation. Most network visualization software will allow these parameters to be adjusted and taking a little time to do so can often be of great benefit.

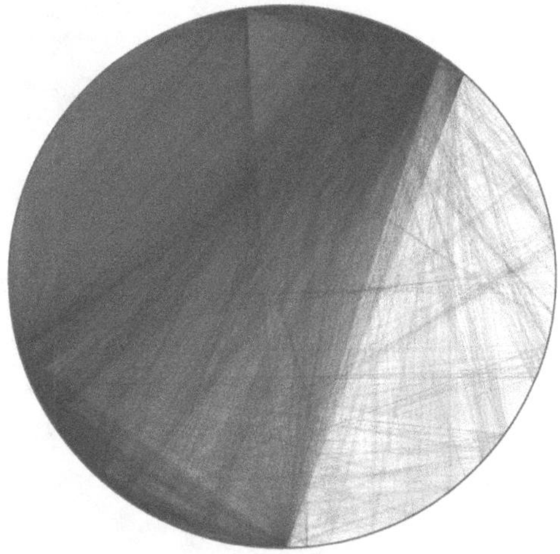

**Figure 13.1 The network of all pages from http://ai.umich.edu a newer unit at the University of Michigan focused on academic innovation in the digital age. Each circle (node) around the outside represents a single page and each line (edge) between them represents a link from one page to another. The nodes are sorted around the circle based on the next directory in the url. It is already evident that the left is the highly connected component while the right is very sparsely connected. This and all of the other network diagrams made by the author (Figures 13.1 through 13.6) were made using Cytoscape (Shannon et al., 2003).**

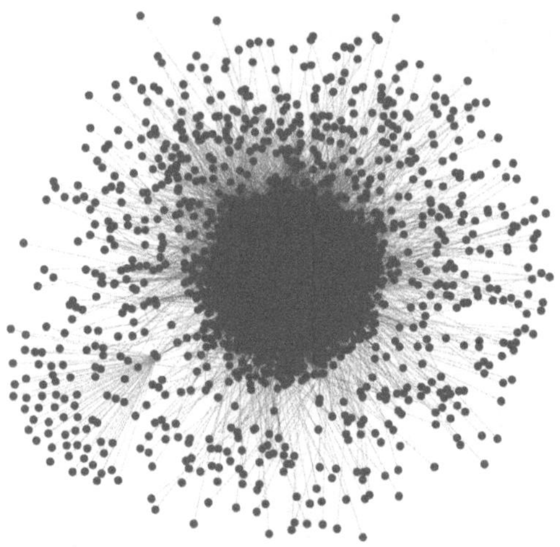

**Figure 13.2 The force-directed visualization of the same network from Figure 13.1 is difficult to read due to its density. Perhaps the only structural element that is noticeable is the relatively large group of nodes in the lower left that appear to be exclusively linked from a single node.**

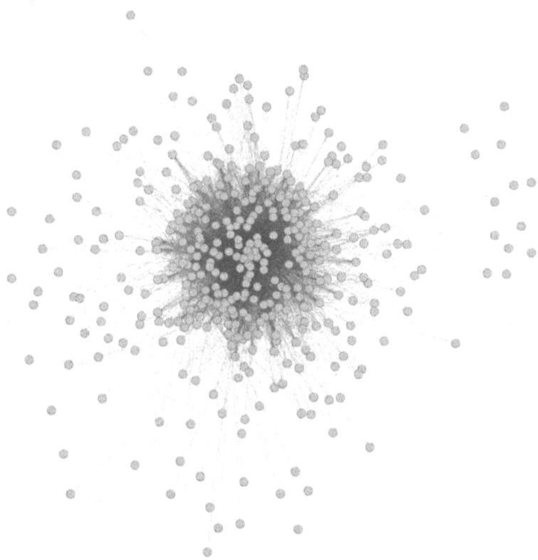

**Figure 13.3 Looking just at links between the top-level directories (e.g. http://ai.umich.edu/blog and http://ai.umich.edu/about-ai) gives a smaller network that is slightly more manageable but still difficult to learn very much from.**

While layout of networks can greatly increase the aesthetic quality and readability of a network, many networks (especially link networks extracted from websites) have such a high density of edges and number of nodes that no level of finesse with layout alone is able to extract a meaningful visual representation, unless of course one merely desires to communicate the sheer density of a network. Luckily, as the use of network visualization has grown in many fields alongside the ease of creating large network datasets, a number of techniques have recently been developed for making such networks more visually understandable.

## *Edge Pruning and Edge Bundling*

Rarely do an excessive number of nodes cause a network to be too crowded, since nodes can take up a very small amount of visual space. Rather, it is usually the number of edges connecting these nodes that tend to overwhelm attempts at a network visualization, hiding any existing structure behind an impenetrable mass of lines. One possible solution to this problem is *edge pruning*, wherein edges are removed based either on some value in the data itself or in the network structure. The former is the most straightforward: for example, if one is looking at links between blogs, any connection with fewer than, say, 25 links can be removed, leaving only connections where there is a continual habit of linking rather than one or two incidental links. Edge pruning is doubly helpful for force-directed layouts as it both removes a mass of lines and also decreases the number of springs that hold the network tightly together, thus allowing it to spread out more (see Figure 13.5). The visualizations and analysis in Adamic and Glance (2005) offer a number of examples of the effect of removing data in order to make visuals more understandable. For example, in one visualization they first remove edges that represent fewer than five links and then remove those links that represent fewer than 25 links – each step makes the underlying structure of connection clearer.

Another option for edge pruning, especially when there are no clear variables that could help discern the importance of connections (e.g. unweighted friendship networks, blogrolls, co-authorship, etc.), is to use the structure of the network itself to prune edges. By generating various metrics that describe the importance of edges to the network, it is possible to maintain and even clarify the general structure while simultaneously minimizing the overall number of visualized edges. Zhou et al. (2010) and Dianati (2016) offer procedures for removing edges while maintaining the connectivity of a network. Hennessey et al. (2008) even provide an algorithm for network simplification by node removal. Such a process more aggressively changes the visualization of the network into an abstraction of its structure, but for especially dense networks such measures may be called for.

*Edge bundling* provides a slightly different approach for minimizing excessive amounts of ink spent displaying edges. Edges that trace similar paths can be bent so that they run together. Like edge pruning, bundling can either be done based on information in the data (e.g. hierarchical relationships can be bundled together, such as if one were visualizing links both between sites and between individual pages) or using the structure of the layout itself; Holten (2006; Holten and Van Wijk, 2009) offers algorithms for both, the latter using a force-directed algorithm (similar in concept to one discussed previously for graph layout) to bend nearby edges together (see Figures 13.5 and 13.6). A number of network visualization software packages now have built-in options for edge bundling.

Meyer et al. (2017) include a slightly different example of bundling that effectively includes edge and node bundling. Their graph shows the size of the node based on the length of the bar in the outside circle and the size of connections as the width of the edges. The graph presents a compelling display of the size of connections between domains (see Figure 13.7).

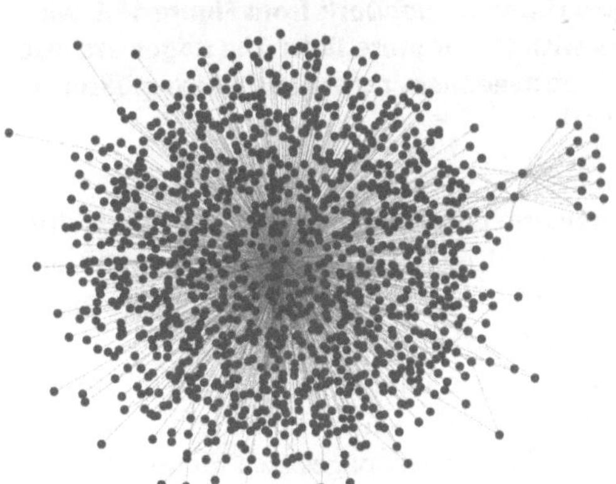

**Figure 13.4 The same set of pages from Figure 13.1, but only showing edges where a page links to another page five or more times. This most likely shows structural links such as those that appear in headers and footers along with a few places on a page rather than single mentions in the body of the text. The main page in the middle is the About page.**

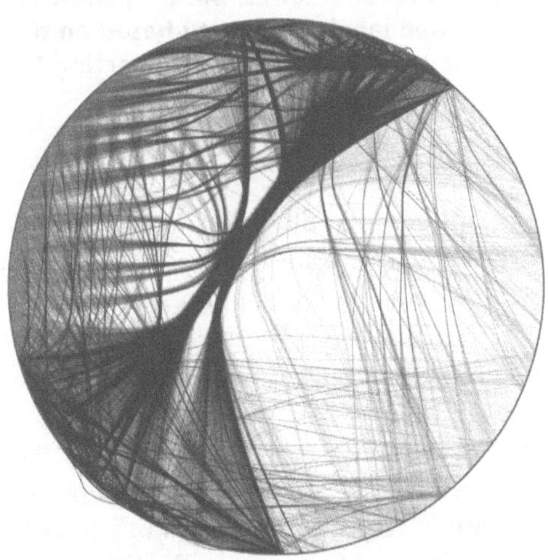

**Figure 13.5 Bundling the edges from Figure 13.1 provides a clearer visualization. Edge bundling can be powerful for circle layouts as one can see the general direction of movement.**

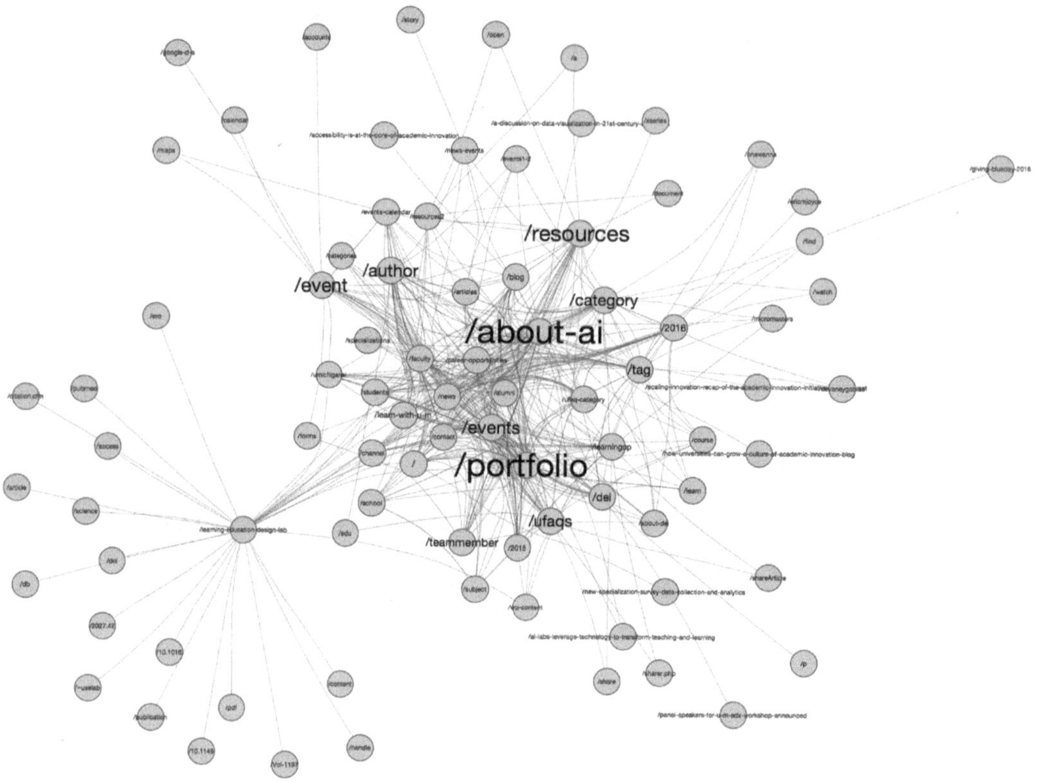


**Figure 13.6 This final network visualization shows the same network from Figure 13.3 with the first-level directories, but only showing edges with ten or more links. The edges are also bundled and labels are scaled based on the node's betweenness centrality, which measures how important a node is for connecting the network.**

## *Hive Plots*

A modification on the basic layout of a network, known as a hive plot, offers another possibly elucidating option (Krzywinski et al., 2012). A hive plot most often involves three radially arranged axes that contain all nodes in a network and edges are drawn between the three axes.[2] Such a layout then provides a number of options for emphasizing various aspects of the data. The three axes can be used to categorically differentiate nodes; for instance, if one were visualizing connections between different groups of online communities they could be divided between the axes more clearly showing links that connect across communities. Likewise, numeric data, either from the network structure or elsewhere, can be mapped to distance along the axis. For example, nodes can be placed further out depending on the number of incoming links or the amount of text on a given page, clearly delineating the most linked or longest pages (see Figures 13.8 and 13.9).

Hive plots allow one to choose what are the most interesting aspects of a network dataset and stress those in the visualization. As such they can be very effective in representing extremely complex networks. While the edge segments all end up being of nearly similar length, they all move in the same direction – rather than crossing each other as in a force-directed network – and so improve the display

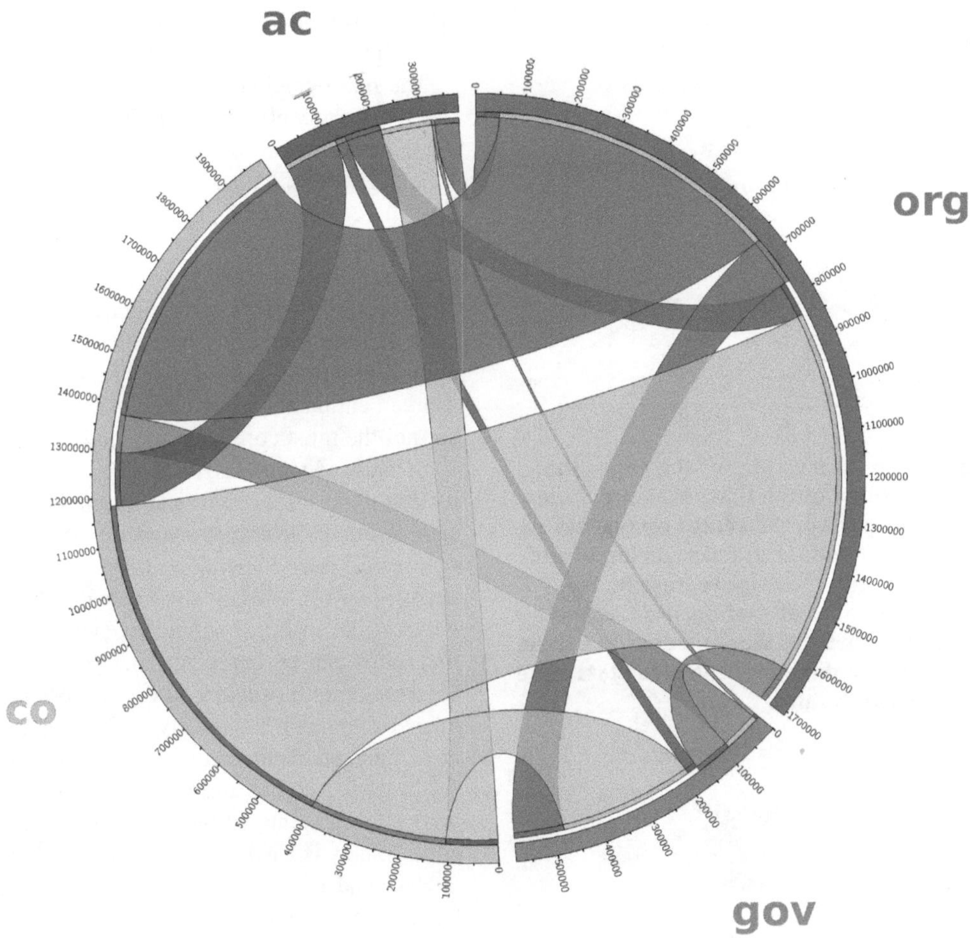


**Figure 13.7 An example of edge and node bundling showing connections between high-level domains (Meyer et al., 2017).**

of the density of connections between parts of the network. Furthermore, hive plots can be subjected to the same modifications as other networks, e.g. edge or node pruning, bundling, etc., to further clarify the network structure.

Another benefit to a hive plot is that, unlike a force-directed layout whose final layout is dependent on initial starting locations, the layout is deterministic and hence always reproducible given the same data and decisions about what values to map to the axes. Furthermore, hive plots have the added advantage of being robust in the face of minor changes. Various other layouts can be drastically affected by minor modifications, whereas most hive plots will merely delete or add data as it is changed, leaving other nodes and edges exactly where they are.

### *Heatmaps*

While standard node and edge diagrams tend to instantly evoke our sense of 'network-ness', aesthetically appearing as what many of us think of when we think of networks, other representations can also reveal important properties of a given network

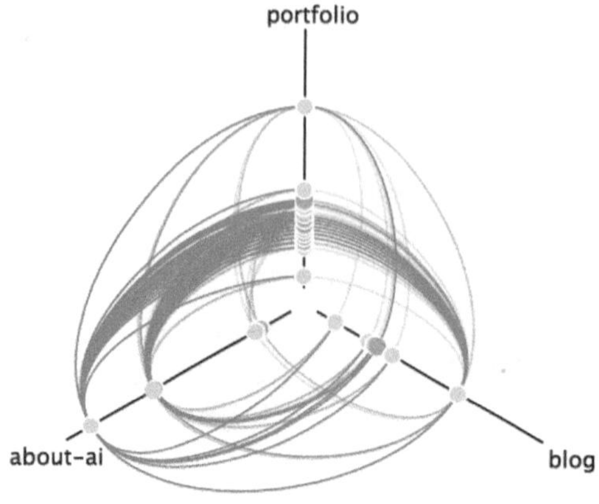


**Figure 13.8 A hive plot of the pages that make up three of the first-level directories. The distance from the center represents the degree (number of links coming in and going out) and the color represents the number of nodes at that position on the axes. Note that this diagram does not show links within a directory. The hive plots were produced with Jhive.**

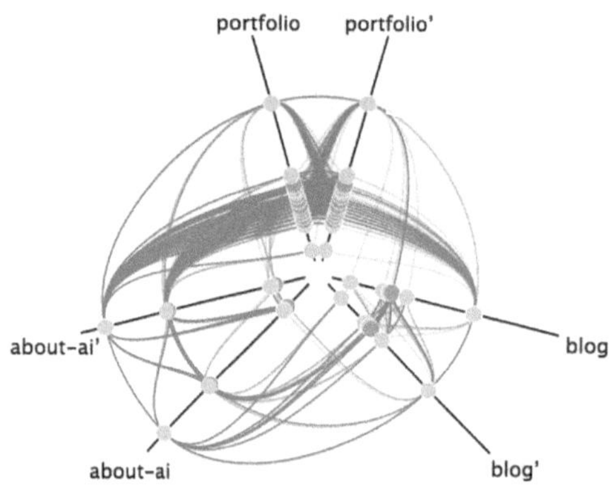


**Figure 13.9 The same plot as Figure 13.7, but with the axes expanded to show inter-directory links. Each page is thus shown twice, once on the main axis and once on the repeated axis.**

(and sometimes more cleanly and clearly than network diagrams). One common option is a heatmap, which displays connections as a colored node–node matrix. Each node is listed once along both the x and y axes and where they meet is then colored based on whether (or how much) they are connected (see Figures 13.10 and 13.11).

The main challenge that arises with using heatmaps for web visualization is that while these networks are dense they are often significantly sparser than many other networks (i.e. there are lots of pages that do not link to each other). Especially if a heatmap is automatically clustered, one can end up with large swaths of white space since sinks (websites that are linked to but do not link out to anything) will all cluster together. Incredibly sparse heatmaps can be difficult to read and are not the most compelling visualization.

Because edges add no more visual complexity, but extra nodes significantly increase the size of a map, heatmaps are especially strong options for datasets with high edge density in networks with a relatively small number of nodes. Like in other network visualizations, the nodes can be organized and grouped by attribute or data structure (e.g. clusters can be placed together). Especially when heatmaps are organized by attribute, they can be powerful tools for comparing either different networks or the same network over time, since edge density is easily perceptible.

Heer and Kandel (2012) provide an excellent example of the power of heatmaps for displaying network structure, especially as a tool for diagnosing data problems. They extract a network dataset from friendship relations on Facebook and plot them first as a standard force-directed layout; a large central cluster is visible along with a few smaller clusters, as we would expect from a social network such as this. They then plot the same data as a heatmap, reordering the data in order to group tightly connected nodes close to each other. Finally, they plot the dataset in id order and a large blank space becomes apparent, suggesting there is a gap in the dataset. Indeed, it turns out that the Facebook API is rate limited and so failed to return the entire dataset, offering no warning that the data was truncated. While one hopes to avoid such situations, the example speaks to the clarity that heatmaps can provide in understanding networks.

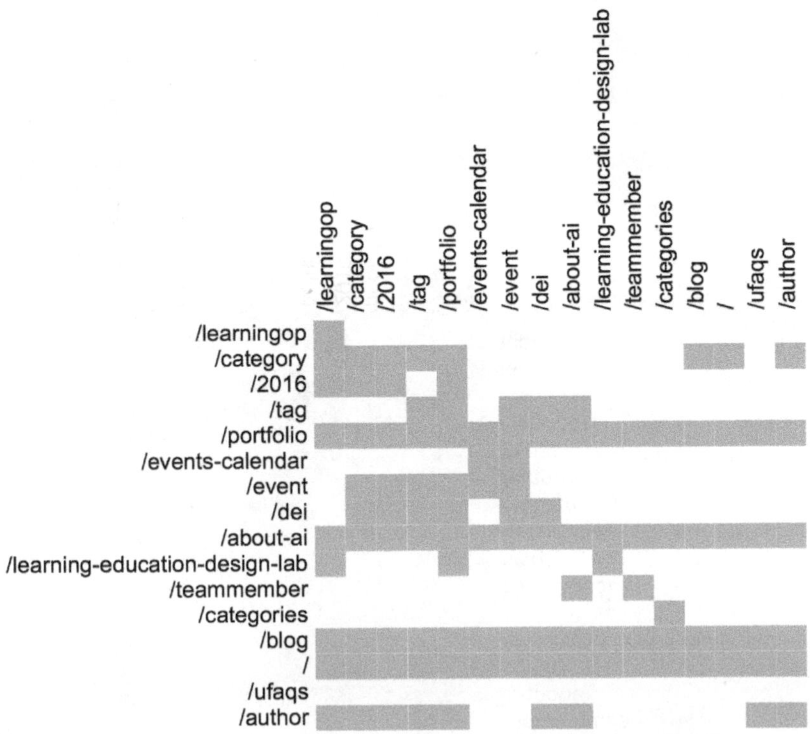


**Figure 13.10 A heatmap showing a subset of first-level directories from http://ai.umich.edu. A gray square represents a link between pages in those directories. The directory on the left is the directory the link originates from and the directory at the time is the destination directory. It should be noted that directed graphs do not produce symmetrical heatmaps. These heatmaps were made using the statistical software R (R Core Team, 2013).**

## *Metrics*

Finally, we should remember that various metrics can describe the abstract structures of networks and these metrics can be visually compared. For instance, if one were researching subcommunities in an online community, understanding how tightly clustered link networks are within these various subcommunities may be more important than the visual display of the networks themselves. In such a case, we could calculate the global clustering coefficient (Luce and Perry, 1949), which measures the ratio of connected triplets that are closed to all connected triplets (i.e. if a website links to two other websites, how often do those two websites link to each other). Graphing the clustering coefficients of the various subcommunities – possibly against another metric such as the size of the network – can in many circumstances be more informative than the network graphs themselves.

It can also be compelling to graph network metrics against other data that describes the pages one is working with. Cowls and Bright (2017) include a nice example, graphing the number of hyperlinks to each high-level country domain (e.g. .it websites for Italy) against the number of mentions of that country during the study period. The resultant graph is quite compelling and straightforward (see Figure 13.12).

Any number of network metrics can be elucidating, and the vast majority of structural characteristics can be quantified. There is not space here to list and detail all of the possible

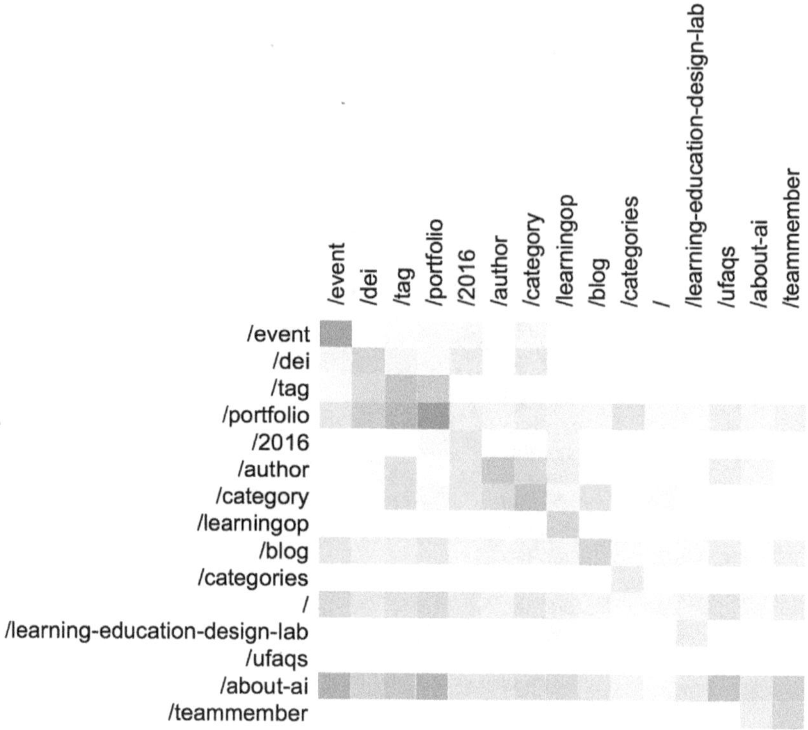


**Figure 13.11 The same heatmap from Figure 13.9, but colored based on the number of links.**

metrics one could use, but most network visualization software will automatically calculate a fair number of these. Any introductory text to social network analysis should detail the vast majority of these and explain how to utilize them. Furthermore, spending time with such a text and learning more about network analysis can offer great insights into the process of visualization as well.

## TEXT

Another obviously important aspect of web data is the actual text of websites. Such large-scale corpora of text offer themselves well to a variety of text analysis methodologies, from simply counting the occurrences of a few key words to complex algorithms for topic modeling. One of the main challenges of visually representing the result of text mining is that many of these algorithms function in very high-dimensional spaces (e.g. they treat each unique word as a dimension and run computations in this space) so that any visualization of the results requires some form of dimensionality reduction, such as projecting the data onto an algorithmically selected two-dimensional plane. While projections of the three-dimensional earth onto two-dimensional maps are generally understandable, one merely has to look at the complicated mathematical and political discussions involved in this process to get a sense of how complex projections from this three-dimensional space to a two-dimensional space can be (let alone a 10,000-dimensional space).

### *Simple Text Visualizations*

Relatively simple text analyses, such as counting words, can often be incredibly

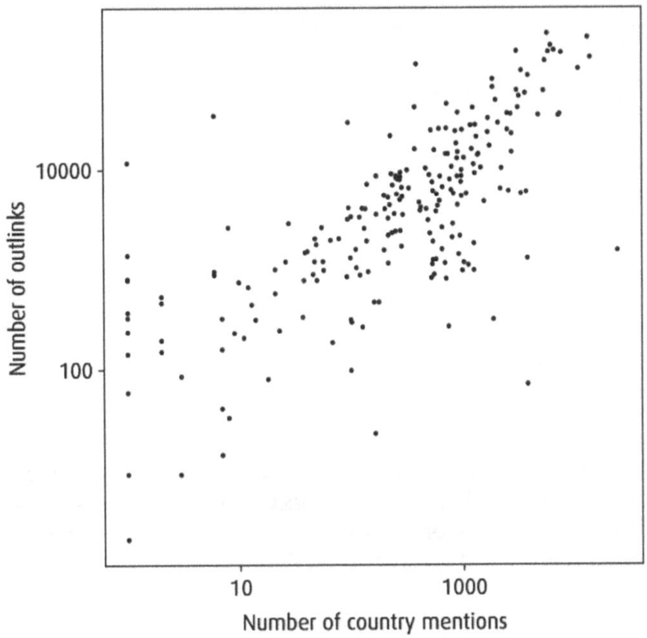


**Figure 13.12 A scatterplot showing the relationship between links to country high-level domains and mentions on the BBC website (Cowls and Bright, 2017).**

insightful and such analyses lend themselves well to compelling data visualizations (e.g. the continued use of Google N-grams despite methodological concerns that have been raised (Pechenick et al., 2015)). Even lists of sentences including a given word in a corpus can be elucidating (this is known as a concordance). For relatively small datasets with longer texts, dispersion plots can quickly show the distribution of words throughout a corpus. A dispersion plot shows where terms occur by word position in a document, or in a series of documents that have been ordered in some way (see Figure 13.13).[3]

Similarly, cumulative frequency plots, which show the combined number of occurrences of the most frequent words (e.g. the number of times the first most common words occur; then the number of times the first two most common words occur, etc.), are informative. By showing these plots together for subsections of a corpus, one can display both the most common terms and information about the lexical diversity of a set of documents. In this case, it may be desirable to remove stop words (i.e. common words that tell us little about the documents in question, such as 'the', 'a', etc.); or depending on exactly what is interesting about a set of websites, one may decide to leave stop words in the count.

In general, it should be remembered that visualization need not show everything about a corpus. It is likely that the only way to know every element of a corpus is to read every document in it; the purpose of data mining and visualization is to find interesting occurrences or structures. It is not to recreate the corpus, like the imagery empire in Borges' short story that created a map the exact size of the territory.[4] In short, if there are interesting aspects of a dataset one should seek to show only those elements. This is especially true when working with text mining. While complex algorithms and analyses can be elucidating, the most striking visualizations tend to be those that are easily understood and

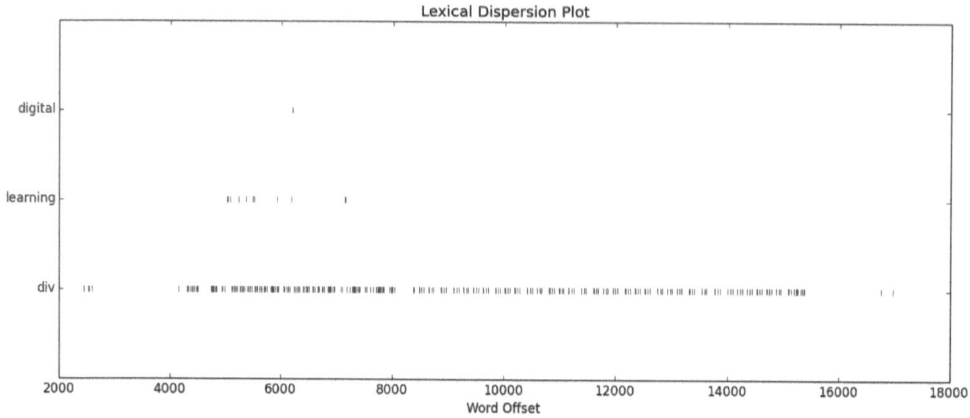


**Figure 13.13 A dispersion plot showing the frequency of the terms 'digital', 'learning' and 'div' from http://ai.umich.edu/about-ai. The text includes all of the html and it is readily apparent how much greater the proportion of code is to the human-readable text. This graph was made using the Natural Language Toolkit (NLTK), a package for Python (Bird et al., 2009b).**

represent elements of the text or metadata that could be counted directly if one had the time.

## *Algorithmic Approaches*

Beyond such direct ways of extracting data from text and visualizing it, many data-mining algorithms, especially those that reduce the final dimensionality of the output data to two or three dimensions, lend themselves to various visualizations. Principle component analysis allows one to visualize two or three derived components as axes with each website as a point on a scatterplot. Latent Dirichlet Allocation (LDA, one of the more popular algorithms for topic modeling in the humanities) is often presented simply as lists of words that determine topics, but since LDA assigns a percentage of each document to each topic, multiple visualization opportunities arise. One could again use a heatmap, to show each document along one axis and each topic along the other, coloring each square based on the percentage of the topic that corresponds to the document.[5]

One possible, though relatively infrequently used, option with great potential is the use of self-organizing maps (SOMs) as a means to display related and divergent topics in a large corpus. SOMs use artificial neural networks to map high-dimensional spaces to a two-dimensional plane, trying to maintain the proximity of related items. A third dimension can then be used to display how similar or dissimilar nearby items are. Skupin (2002; Skupin et al., 2013) has used SOMs to great effect to visualize concepts in large text corpora, placing central terms throughout the map and making 'valleys' of related terms (see Figure 13.14). One of the major advantages of SOMs over other visualizations of algorithmic text analysis is that they replicate a type of visualization, a contour map, that viewers are often familiar with. Related concepts are proximate, and the addition of topography supplements this with an additional sense of how related nearby terms are.

Of course, if a specific algorithm is necessary for an analysis, it will be worth the time and space to describe the functioning of that algorithm and any visual output it may produce. But if one is agnostic about the specific algorithm to be used or an algorithmic treatment of the text is merely being used to provide a sense of the data, it can be beneficial to select an algorithm whose output is sensible without significant additional explanation of the algorithm. Furthermore, some algorithms, such as LDA, or even simple analysis, such as calculating terms that most clearly differentiate between two corpora or two times, lend themselves well to simply listing words with scores or counts. Again, the communicative power of tables and lists should not be underestimated.

## CHANGE OVER TIME

While the discussion up to this point has focused largely on displaying various aspects of web data, one of the most important elements of history has been left to the side, namely displaying change over time. It has been left to the end because it is simultaneously one of the most difficult and most simple things to deal with in terms of visualization. There is a growing interest and number of tools for animating visualizations or creating interactive visualizations that allow a user to move through time. While such animations are a sensible way to deal with time and are easy for the viewer as they map time to time (though usually scaled so one can see a number of years in a few minutes), they have some drawbacks. First, animations or interactive visualizations are not as easily distributable as static visualizations; they often require certain software to run or host online. Furthermore, some of the technology that is used for these visualizations is not easily archived.

Second, and more fundamentally, one of the strengths of data visualization is the ability to take large amounts of information

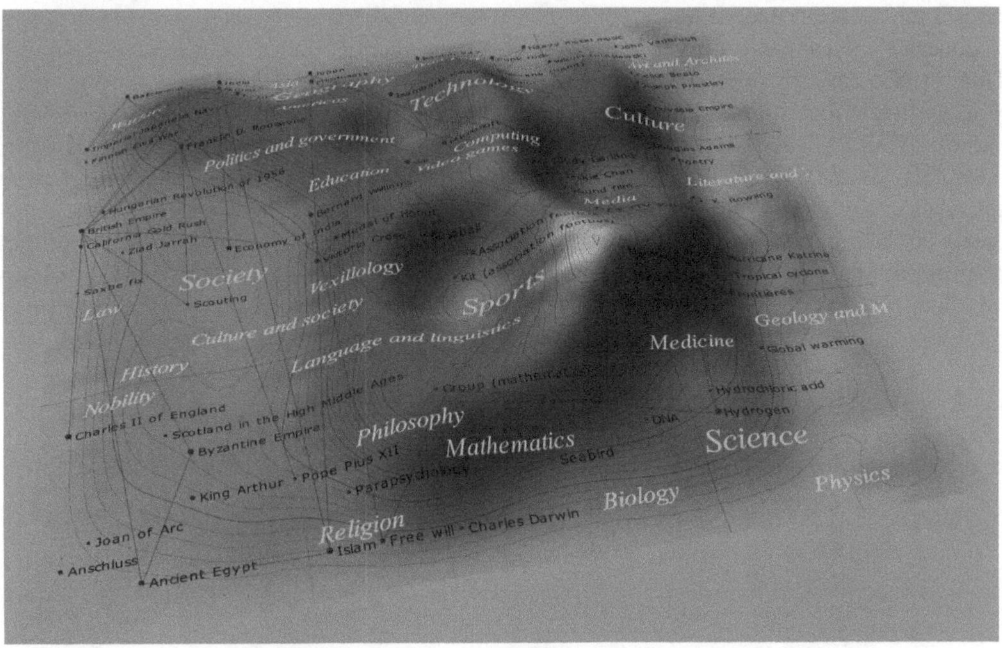


**Figure 13.14 Self-organizing map based on Wikipedia featured article data. Closer items are more similar. The 'mountains' are edges between clusters and the straight lines are links between articles. (Denoir, 2013 - Creative Commons Attribution-ShareAlike 3.0 License, available: https://en.wikipedia.org/wiki/File:Self_oraganizing_map_cartography.jpg).**

and distribute it spatially, allowing the eye to quickly discern similarities, differences, patterns, etc. Animations and interactions require the viewer to compare not what is seen but what is remembered. Thus, in a sense, animation works against the greatest strengths of data visualization. In his book, Bertin (2011) explicitly excises animation from the discussion of data visualization, suggesting that its understanding lies more with a discussion of cinematic time. While animation and interaction are much more easily achieved now than they were at the time of Bertin's writing, his statement on this matter should be understood philosophically rather than merely technologically.

In this light, one efficacious technique for displaying change over time is the use of small multiples. Small multiples consist of multiple graphs showing how the graph changes over time (or another variable). Using them to display time requires periodizing one's data (i.e. each graph represents a month, year, decade, etc.), but if this is done well it can be used to great effect. Tufte (1983: 169) says of small multiples (a term and technique that he helped to popularize): 'Well-designed small multiples are inevitably comparative, deftly multivariate, shrunken, high-density graphics, usually based on a large data matrix drawn almost entirely with data-ink, efficient in interpretation, and often narrative in content'. Meyer et al. (2017) include an exceptional example of the use of small multiples for web data, depicting the strength of hyperlinked connections between universities in the UK over time (see Figure 13.15).

Boyandin et al. (2012:1005) even offer a user study comparing animated geographical visualizations with small multiples. They conclude, 'We observed that with animation the subjects tended to make more findings concerning geographically local events and changes between subsequent years. With small-multiples more findings concerning longer time periods were made'. While animations may allow one to follow specific areas in a graph, understanding large-scale structural changes is likely significantly aided by displaying data over space rather than time.

In addition to small multiples, time can be treated as a variable in any graph. For example, one could graph any network metric, such as clustering coefficient or average degree, over time. Furthermore, the change in a distribution, such as betweenness centrality, which is a node-level metric, can be represented as a series of small multiples, with a histogram for each time point. This is not to say that animations should not be used: these can be very effective for showing the exponential growth in size or complexity of data over time and interaction excels at allowing users to explore subsets that may be of

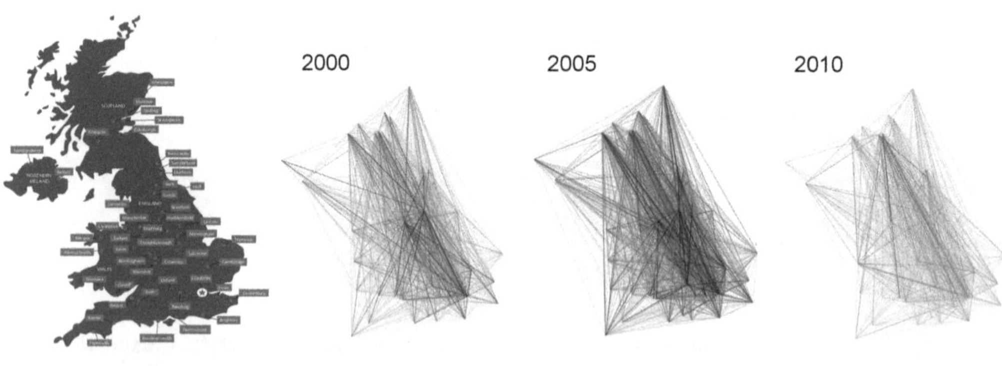


**Figure 13.15 Small multiples showing the strength of hyperlinked connections between UK universities under study for 2000, 2005, 2010 (Meyer et al., 2017).**

particular interest to them. Still, the use and necessity of either should be carefully considered and chosen for what it can explicitly add.

## CONCLUSION

Wainer (1984: 145–6) concludes his article, which attempts to teach visualization by offering advice on displaying data badly, with a final suggestion: if something has been done well in the past figure out a new and different way to do it. Of course, our goal is to display data well, and so the opposite suggestion should be taken; many of the visualization problems that one runs into have already been addressed by others either using similar data or even unrelated data (many of the advances in network visualization have been made dealing with social networks, gene expression networks, etc.). While this chapter has attempted to address some of the most common issues that arise in visualizing historical web data, it is impossible that all of the potential issues could have been dealt with. There are many challenges that are beyond the scope of this chapter, but it is still highly likely that someone else has confronted a related set of issues and written about them. Even a bad example can be instructive in suggesting against possible approaches.

Finally, it is good practice to look at examples with an agnosticism towards specific software and technologies. Much of the software available today prematurely limits a user's options for making charts and graphs; exploring visualization outside of the limits of a particular piece of software will allow one to make the best decisions about how to represent data. You can then choose the best software for transforming your data into a visualization.

Websites, and especially web archives, offer a multitude of rich data types that have much to tell us about information, communication, writing and culture. Researchers working with such data do not lack information that can be quantified, analyzed and visualized. The challenge in working with this type of data, and especially in visualizing it, is to exclude the information that distracts from the most interesting structures and stories contained with the data. Spending time exploring your data and seeing what is most visually compelling (and distracting) can pay dividends in the quality and communicative power of data visualization.

### Notes

1 It should also be noted that axes and scales can have a considerable impact on clarity. Especially when dealing with heavily skewed data (such as the number of links pointing to a page and other web data that often presents a Zipfian distribution), logarithmic scales can be of great use.
2 It is also possible to double the axes, such that axis 1 and axis 1′ show connections within the group.
3 For both concordances as dispersion plots see NLTK chapter 1 part 3 (Bird et al., 2009a).
4 Borges' one paragraph short story (1975), "On Exactitude in Science", recounts, "The Cartographers Guilds struck a Map of the Empire whose size was that of the Empire, and which coincided point for point with it. The following Generations, who were not so fond of the Study of Cartography as their Forebears had been, saw that that vast map was Useless".
5 For more examples of visualizing LDA see (Riddell, 2015).

## REFERENCES


Adamic, L.A., and Glance, N. (2005) 'The political blogosphere and the 2004 US election: Divided they blog', in *Proceedings of the 3rd international workshop on Link discovery*: 36–43.

Barabási, A.-L., and Frangos, J. (2014) *Linked: The new Science of Networks*. New York: Basic Books.

Bertin, J. [1964(2011)] *Semiology of Graphics: Diagrams, Networks, Maps*, trans. W Berg. Redlands: ESRI Press.

Bird, S., Klein, E., and Loper, E. (2009a) *NLTK Book*. Available: http://www.nltk.org/book/ (accessed: November 20, 2016)

Bird, S., Loper, E., and Klein, E. (2009b) *Natural Language Processing with Python*. Sebastopol, CA: O'Reilly Media Inc.

Borges, J.L. (1975) 'On Exactitude in Science', in *A Universal History of Infamy*, trans. Norman Thomas de Giovanni. London: Penguin Books: 131.

Boyandin, I., Bertini, E., and Lalanne, D. (2012) 'A qualitative study on the exploration of temporal changes in flow maps with animation and small-multiples', *Computer Graphics Forum*, 31(3) pt 2: 1005–1014.

Brügger, N. (2009) 'Website history and the website as an object of study', *New Media & Society*, 11(1–2): 115–132.

Castells, M. (2011) *The Rise of the Network Society: The Information Age: Economy, Society, and Culture* (Vol. 1). New York: John Wiley & Sons.

Cowls, J., and Bright, J. (2017) 'International hyperlinks in online news media', in Brügger, N. and Schroeder, R. (Eds), *The Web as History*. London: University College London Press: 101–116.

Dianati, N. (2016) 'Unwinding the hairball graph: Pruning algorithms for weighted complex networks', *Physical Review E*, 93(1): 012304.

Foot, K. (2006) 'Web sphere analysis and cyberculture studies', in Silver, D. and Massanari, A., (Eds), *Critical Cyberculture Studies*. New York: NYU Press: 88–96.

Fruchterman, T.M., and Reingold, E.M. (1991) 'Graph drawing by force-directed placement', *Software: Practice and Experience*, 21(11): 1129–1164.

Heer, J., and Kandel, S. (2012) 'Interactive analysis of big data', *XRDS: Crossroads, The ACM Magazine for Students'*, 19(1): 50–54.

Hennessey, D., Brooks, D., Fridman, A., and Breen, D. (2008) 'A simplification algorithm for visualizing the structure of complex graphs', in *2008 12th International Conference Information Visualisation*. July, 2008: 616–625.

Holten, D. (2006) 'Hierarchical edge bundles: Visualization of adjacency relations in hierarchical data', *IEEE Transactions on Visualization and Computer Graphics*, 12(5): 741–748.

Holten, D., and Van Wijk, J.J. (2009) 'Force-directed edge bundling for graph visualization', *Computer Graphics Forum*, 28(3): 983–990.

Krzywinski, M., Birol, I., Jones, S.J., and Marra, M.A. (2012) 'Hive plots – rational approach to visualizing networks', *Briefings in Bioinformatics*, 13(5): 627–644.

Latour, B. (1993) *The Pasteurization of France*. Cambridge: Harvard University Press.

Latour, B. (2005) *Reassembling the Social: An Introduction to Actor-Network-Theory*. Oxford: Oxford University Press.

Luce, R.D., and Perry, A.D. (1949) 'A method of matrix analysis of group structure', *Psychometrika*, 14(2): 95–116.

Luke, D. (2015) *A User's Guide to Network Analysis in R*. Berlin: Springer.

Meyer, E., Yasseri, T., Hale, S., Cowls, J., Schroeder, R., and Margetts, H. (2017) 'Analysing the UK web domain and exploring 15 years of UK universities on the web', in Brügger, N. and Schroeder, R. (Eds), *The Web as History*. London: University College London Press: 23–44.

Milligan, I. (2012) 'Mining the "Internet graveyard": Rethinking the historians' toolkit', *Journal of the Canadian Historical Association*, 23(2): 21–64.

Pechenick, E.A., Danforth, C.M., and Dodds, P.S. (2015) 'Characterizing the Google Books corpus: Strong limits to inferences of socio-cultural and linguistic evolution', *PloS One*, 10(10): e0137041.

R Core Team (2013) *R: A language and environment for statistical computing*. R Foundation for Statistical Computing: Vienna, Austria.

Riddell, A. (2015) *Text Analysis with Topic Models for the Humanities and Social Sciences*. Available: https://de.dariah.eu/tatom/ (accessed November 15, 2016)

Shannon, P., Markiel, A., Ozier, O., Baliga, N.S., Wang, J.T., Ramage, D., Amin, N., Schwikowski, B., and Ideker, T. (2003) 'Cytoscape: A software environment for integrated models of biomolecular interaction networks', *Genome Research*, 13(11): 2498–2504.

Skupin, A. (2002) 'A cartographic approach to visualizing conference abstracts', *IEEE Computer Graphics and Applications*, 22(1): 50–58.

Skupin, A., Biberstine, J.R., and Börner, K. (2013) 'Visualizing the topical structure of the medical sciences: A self-organizing map approach', *PloS One*, 8(3): e58779.

Tufte, E. (1983) *The Visual Display of Quantitative Information*. Cheshire, CT: Graphics Press.

Wainer, H. (1984) 'How to display data badly', *The American Statistician*, 38(2): 137–147.

Zhou, F., Malher, S., and Toivonen, H. (2010) 'Network simplification with minimal loss of connectivity', in *2010 IEEE International Conference on Data Mining*: 659–668.

# PART III

# Technical and Structural Dimensions of Web History

14

# Adding the Dimension of Time to HTTP

Michael L. Nelson and Herbert Van de Sompel

## INTRODUCTION

While the web is distributed, most web archives are centralized silos that do not cooperate with each other. This is partially because the technology that is necessary to replay the archived content and keep it from being influenced by material on the live web also makes it difficult for web archives to cooperate. The Memento Protocol (which we played a central role in defining) addresses this problem by defining an extension to the Hypertext Transfer Protocol (HTTP) that allows for standardized, machine-readable integration of both the past web and the present web. The Memento Protocol extends the concept of HTTP content negotiation to include not only well-known dimensions such as Multipurpose Internet Mail Extensions (MIME) types (e.g., JPEG vs. PNG) and file encodings (e.g., gzip vs. compress), but also the dimension of Coordinated Universal Time (UTC) as a universal versioning system. The protocol can be supported by all systems that hold temporal resource versions, including conventional web archives, as well as resource versioning systems such as wikis.

The Memento Protocol introduces some standard terminology with which to discuss web archiving, the most fundamental of which are: original resource (the resource on the live web), Memento (an archived version of an Original Resource, frozen in time), TimeGate (a resource capable of datetime content negotiation to discover a temporally appropriate Memento), and TimeMap (a machine-readable list of all Mementos for an Original Resource). Furthermore, the Memento Protocol is the first web archiving API, enabling aggregation of access to disparate web archives. Web archiving has been dominated by the Internet Archive's Wayback Machine, but via the Memento Protocol it is possible to leverage the more than a dozen publicly accessible web archives throughout the world for increased completeness, consistency, verifiability, resilience, and availability.

This chapter begins by introducing the history of Unix and HTTP and how they continue to influence the design of web archives today, then reviews the Memento terminology and concepts that allow for standardized discussion of the basic mechanics of web archiving. Next, we review how different web archives can be aggregated and how user agents (i.e., web browsers) can interact with Memento-enabled archives, and then conclude with a brief review of our activities in areas of open research that result when there is an integrated, distributed network of web archives.

## HISTORY OF HTTP AND UNIX

HTTP is the protocol (Fielding et al., 1999) that underpins what we know colloquially as 'the web'. A simple version, HTTP version 0.9, was documented in 1991 (Berners-Lee, 1991), and in 1996 a version similar to the version still in use today was defined (Berners-Lee et al., 1996). Unix, in various vendor-specific formats, was the predominant operating system during this timeframe for workstations and mainframes, so the development of HTTP, while technically independent of Unix, is ultimately deeply intertwined with the operating system that made it possible. As such, the history of HTTP is one of incrementally implementing the original vision of a fully featured, distributed filesystem. Initially conceived with read-write and versioning capabilities, early implementations fell short of the original vision due in part to the tight integration with the Unix filesystem. Advances in encryption and authentication have made the read-write capability more widespread, but it was not until the development of the Memento Protocol that the versioning capability was added for HTTP.

Despite versioning (described in terms of generic vs. specific resources) being part of an early design document for the Web (Berners-Lee, 1996), the historical coupling of HTTP and Unix filesystems stood in the way of embracing a time dimension for the web. Since most of the early HTTP servers were implemented on Unix workstations, the Unix filesystem and HTTP were co-deployed in almost all cases. Metadata about files in the Unix filesystem is stored in 'inodes' (a contraction of 'index node'), and the original description of the Unix filesystem defined three notions of time to be stored in an inode: file creation, last use, and last modification (Ritchie and Thompson, 1974). However, at some early point the storage of the file creation time in the inode was replaced with the last modification time of the inode itself. The result was that the last modification and access times of a file are defined, but the creation time, a crucial part of establishing provenance, cannot be stored in a standard Unix filesystem. Thus, files stored on a Unix filesystem, which are subsequently served through HTTP, inherit the semantic limitations of the filesystem, and as a result HTTP has only two notions of time in server responses: the 'Date' header, which provides the date of the response, and the 'Last-Modified' header, which is inherited from the inode.

To better understand how the Memento Protocol integrates with HTTP, many of the figures listed below provide raw, actual HTTP requests and responses. The web browsers we use everyday (e.g., Firefox, Chrome) hide these detailed and verbose HTTP requests and responses from us, but in this chapter we choose to surface these details because they are integral to understanding the web archiving infrastructure that the Memento Protocol enables. We recognize the HTTP responses can be intimidating to those not used to reading them, but with a short primer they quickly become invaluable. We will walk through how to read the HTTP session in Figure 14.1.

First, for every HTTP response, we include the curl request, with all the appropriate arguments, that generated the response. 'Curl' is a command line web browser that does not render web pages (like Firefox, Chrome, etc.), but rather shows the raw HTTP response from the web server. The '$' symbol in the figures is the command line prompt, and what follows is what the user types. If you are in a terminal program, you should be able to copy and paste everything after the '$' and get a similar response (keep in mind that responses will change over time). Not all curl options and other command line arguments are fully explained in this chapter, but in the interest of reproducibility they are provided as executed. For example, the following line uses curl to return just the metadata (via the '-I' argument) for an image at lanl.gov:

```
$ curl -I http://www.lanl.gov/_assets/
   images/lanl-logo-footer.png
```

The next line is the response from the server and has three components: 'HTTP/1.1' is an acknowledgment from the server that it is supporting the 1.1 version of HTTP (new and older versions exist, but 1.1 is still currently the most commonly deployed). Next, '200' is the numerical code that provides the semantics of the response; in this case '200' means the request was understood, processed, and there were no errors. The next portion is a human-readable phrase, in this case 'OK', which is explanatory for the '200' response code. The phrase is for human readability and web browsers only process the numeric code. In Figure 14.1, the full response is:

```
HTTP/1.1 200 OK
```

There are many other HTTP response codes defined, but in this chapter we will focus on '200' and '302'. The following 302 responses are equivalent, since the text phrase is for humans and only the code '302' is processed by browsers:

```
HTTP/1.1 302 Found
```

Or:

```
HTTP/1.1 302 Moved Temporarily
```

The 302 response is a redirection from the requested URI to another URI. The response provides metadata, but also instructs the browser to issue a new request for a different URI (which in turn may also issue a redirection, until the process stops with a '200' response). Redirections frequently occur, but regular web browsers hide them and users are typically unaware of this fundamental HTTP event. The argument '-L' will cause curl to automatically follow the redirection.

The final part of an HTTP response is a series of lines of metadata (which can appear in any order), arranged in a 'key: value' format, followed by a carriage return. For example, these four lines indicate the date of the response (2017-02-07), when the resource was last modified (2014-10-28), that the returned representation is an image in 'PNG' format, and that the image is 8,719 bytes long:

```
Date: Tue, 07 Feb 2017 00:08:10 GMT
Last-Modified: Tue, 28 Oct 2014
   22:12:02 GMT
Content-Length: 8719
Content-Type: image/png
```

Now we can examine the HTTP response in Figure 14.1 and see that the Los Alamos National Laboratory (LANL) logo PNG file was last modified in 2014, over two years ago from the request in 2017. Thus, if the file were stored in a cache after the Last-Modified date, it does not need to be downloaded again.

On the other hand, pages that are dynamically generated typically do not set the 'Last-Modified' header, in part because it is not stored by default in the filesystem and thus is extra work to track and compute. The result is that the web is losing expressiveness about time, not gaining it. For example:

```
$ curl -I http://www.lanl.gov/_assets/
   images/lanl-logo-footer.png
HTTP/1.1 200 OK
Date: Tue, 07 Feb 2017 00:08:10 GMT
Last-Modified: Tue, 28 Oct 2014
   22:12:02 GMT
Content-Length: 8719
Content-Type: image/png
```

**Figure 14.1 The Last-Modified response header often exists for images, pdfs, and other typically static files.**

Figure 14.2 is for the HTML home page that embeds (among other resources) the PNG from Figure 14.1. The HTML home page has surely changed from 2014, but it might not have changed from yesterday or even last week. Unfortunately, without the Last-Modified header we cannot be sure and we are likely to have unnecessary downloads if we visit the page often.

A careful inspection of Figure 14.2 shows the 'Vary' response header, indicating that the server can perform content negotiation on this resource; in this case the server is capable of transmitting a compressed version of this HTML page for quicker download times, and the users' browser will uncompress it on their behalf. Note that while the 'Vary' header indicates that content negotiation is possible, it is the presence of the 'Content-Encoding' response header that indicates that compression has actually occurred (Figure 14.3).

Tim Berners-Lee's original design document about 'generic' and 'specific' resources that formed the basis for content negotiation did not anticipate character sets or encodings (Berners-Lee, 1996), but it did describe 'target

```
$ curl -I http://www.lanl.gov/
HTTP/1.1 200 OK
Date: Tue, 07 Feb 2017 00:08:46 GMT
Vary: Accept-Encoding
Content-Type: text/html; charset=UTF-8
```

**Figure 14.2 The Last-Modified response header is typically absent from resources with dynamically constructed representations (i.e., almost all HTML files).**

```
$ curl -I -H "Accept-Encoding: gzip"
   http://www.lanl.gov/
HTTP/1.1 200 OK
Date: Tue, 07 Feb 2017 05:05:31 GMT
Vary: Accept-Encoding
Content-Encoding: gzip
Content-Length: 20
Content-Type: text/html; charset=UTF-8
```

**Figure 14.3 Based on the 'Accept-Encoding' request header, the server responds with a gzipped HTML page, as declared in the 'Content-Encoding' response header.**

mediums' (or 'features'), which have now been replaced with cascading style sheets (CSS) functionality, and time, which the Memento Protocol made possible nearly 20 years later.

## MEMENTO TERMINOLOGY AND CONCEPTS

To better understand the Memento Protocol (Van de Sompel et al., 2009, 2010, 2013), we must clarify some terminology that is often used imprecisely even in technical writing. Figure 14.4 is from the seminal Web Architecture document (Jacobs and Walsh, 2004), and shows: 1) Uniform Resource Identifiers (URI), 2) Resources, and 3) Representations.

*URIs*, which are a superset of the more commonly known Uniform Resource Locators (URLs), identify *resources*. At any given moment, resources exist in a certain state, and that state can be serialized into a *representation* of the resource. It is this representation that is transmitted via HTTP, rendered by the browser, etc. – the resource itself is not transferred, and indeed can be a real-world object (i.e., non-digital). When a URI is dereferenced (most commonly with HTTP, though many other URI schemes (i.e., protocols) are defined), the representation of that resource is returned. As shown in Figures 14.2 and 14.3, the representation can vary based on input from the client (e.g., compressed or not), which means there can simultaneously be different representations that capture the current state of the resource.

The Memento Protocol specifies how to retrieve a representation of a prior, not current, state of a resource by allowing a client to express the datetime of the prior state it is interested in. Building on the Web Architecture, the Memento Protocol introduces standard terminology with which to discuss the mechanics of versioning on the web (Van de Sompel et al., 2013):

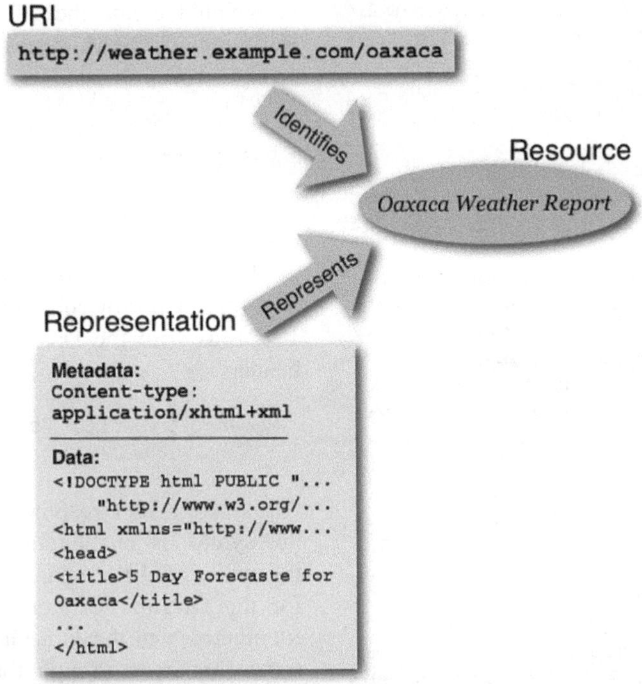


**Figure 14.4 URIs, resources, and representations (Jacobs and Walsh, 2004).**

- Original Resource: an Original Resource (identified by URI-R) is a resource that exists or used to exist, and for which access to one of its prior states may be required.
- Memento: a Memento (identified by URI-M) for an Original Resource is a resource that encapsulates a prior state of the Original Resource. A Memento for an Original Resource as it existed at time T is a resource that encapsulates the state the Original Resource had at time T.
- TimeGate: a TimeGate (identified by URI-G) for an Original Resource is a resource that is capable of datetime negotiation to support access to prior states of the Original Resource.
- TimeMap: a TimeMap (identified by URI-T) for an Original Resource is a resource from which a list of URIs of Mementos of the Original Resource is available.

When an archive crawls an Original Resource, it saves the state of the resource at the time it was crawled. This state now becomes its own frozen resource, a Memento, and the time at which it was crawled is stored in the resource's Memento-Datetime response header. Note that the value for Memento-Datetime can be different from the Last-Modified header sent from the archive, since the archives can continually update banners, archive logos, and other extra information injected into the Memento when it is replayed (Nelson, 2011). For example, the banner at the top of Figure 14.18 is supplied by the web archive itself and the contents of the banner are updated over time, necessitating updated values for Last-Modified even though the Memento-Datetime value does not change.

For the Original Resource http://www.lanl.gov/, the first known Memento is in the Internet Archive's Wayback Machine (the first (operational in 1996) and by far the largest public web archive (Negulescu, 2010)) with a URI-M of http://web.archive.org/web/19961221031231/http://lanl.gov/. We can examine its HTTP response in Figure 14.5.

```
$ curl -I http://web.archive.org/web/
   19961221031231/http://lanl.gov/
HTTP/1.1 200 OK
Server: Tengine/2.1.0
Date: Wed, 08 Feb 2017 02:26:53 GMT
Content-Type: text/
html;charset=utf-8
Content-Length: 9237
Memento-Datetime: Sat, 21 Dec 1996
   03:12:31 GMT
Link: <http://lanl.gov/>;
   rel="original", <http://web.
   archive.org/web/timemap/link/
   http://lanl.gov/>; rel="timemap";
   type="application/link-
   format", <http://web.archive.
   org/web/http://lanl.gov/>;
   rel="timegate", <http://web.
   archive.org/web/19961221031231/
   http://lanl.gov/>; rel="first
   memento"; datetime="Sat, 21 Dec
   1996 03:12:31 GMT", <http://web.
   archive.org/web/19981212015212/
   http://lanl.gov/>; rel="next
   memento"; datetime="Sat, 12 Dec
   1998 01:52:12 GMT", <http://web.
   archive.org/web/20170201114455/
   http://lanl.gov/>; rel="last
   memento"; datetime="Wed, 01 Feb
   2017 11:44:55 GMT"
```

**Figure 14.5 HTTP response for a Memento from the Internet Archive.**

In this case, the Original Resource and Memento-Datetime are extractable from the URI-M as www.lanl.gov and 19961221031231, respectively. However, not all archives follow this convention and extracting strings from URIs violates the practice of URI opacity as recommended by the Web Architecture (Jacobs and Walsh, 2004). In short, URI opacity means that one should not rely on extracting semantics from substrings in a URI. For example, the string '19961221031231' might not always indicate the Memento-Datetime that it appears to indicate. Furthermore, not all archives use URIs with apparent semantics. For example, the WebCite web archive has archived www.lanl.gov on 2011-06-28, and that page is available at both of these URIs, neither of which indicate the URI of the Original Resource nor the Memento-Datetime:

```
http://webcitation.org/query?
   id=1309246026894208
http://webcitation.org/5zm0eNcVU
```

The standardized, machine-readable method is to return the Memento-Datetime in the response header, with the datetime in a format borrowed from Email (Crocker, 1982), as with the Date and Last-Modified headers:

```
Memento-Datetime: Sat, 21 Dec 1996
   03:12:31 GMT
```

Inside the Link response header, although the syntax is challenging, a careful reading will reveal the unambiguous statements for the Original URI, first, last, and next Mementos, and the TimeGate and TimeMap (note that even though the line wraps, it is a single logical 'key: value' line, where the value has multiple, comma-separated sub-values):

```
Link: <http://lanl.gov/>; rel=
   "original", <http://web.archive.
   org/web/timemap/link/http://
   lanl.gov/>; rel="timemap";
   type="application/link-
   format", <http://web.archive.
   org/web/http://lanl.gov/>;
   rel="timegate", <http://web.
   archive.org/web/19961221031231/
   http://lanl.gov/>; rel="first
   memento"; datetime="Sat, 21 Dec
   1996 03:12:31 GMT", <http://web.
   archive.org/web/19981212015212/
   http://lanl.gov/>; rel="next
   memento"; datetime="Sat, 12 Dec
   1998 01:52:12 GMT", <http://web.
   archive.org/web/20170201114455/
   http://lanl.gov/>; rel="last
   memento"; datetime="Wed, 01 Feb
   2017 11:44:55 GMT"
```

In Figure 14.6 we see the HTTP response for the URI-M http://archive.is/OYfTd, and from just this URI-M we cannot extract the URI-R and Memento-Datetime (similar to the WebCite example above); thus the Link

```
$ curl -I http://archive.is/OYfTd
HTTP/1.1 200 OK
Date: Wed, 08 Feb 2017 02:52:25 GMT
Content-Type: text/
   html;charset=utf-8
Memento-Datetime: Wed, 17 Dec 2014
   21:16:53 GMT
Link: <http://www.lanl.gov/>;
   rel="original", <http://archive.
   is/timegate/http://www.lanl.
   gov/>; rel="timegate", <http://
   archive.is/timemap/http://www.
   lanl.gov/>; rel="timemap";
   type="application/link-format";
   from="Sat, 15 Oct 2011 08:20:59
   GMT"; until="Wed, 17 Dec 2014
   21:16:53 GMT", <http://archive.
   is/20141106023554/http://www.
   lanl.gov/>; rel="prev memento";
   datetime="Thu, 06 Nov 2014
   02:35:54 GMT", <http://archive.
   is/20111015082059/http://www.
   lanl.gov/>; rel="first memento";
   datetime="Sat, 15 Oct 2011
   08:20:59 GMT", <http://archive.
   is/20141217211653/http://www.
   lanl.gov/>; rel="last memento";
   datetime="Wed, 17 Dec 2014
   21:16:53 GMT"
```

**Figure 14.6 HTTP response for a Memento from archive.is.**

and Memento-Datetime response headers are crucial.

We established that the Memento in Figure 14.5 is the first Memento available for http://www.lanl.gov/. There are two ways to verify this with the Internet Archive. The first is to download the TimeMap for http://www.lanl.gov/ and check the first value. Figure 14.7 only shows the first few entries since the TimeMap is quite large, with over 1,800 Mementos.

Some TimeMaps are already larger than 100,000 Mementos, so even though they are sorted by datetime, it can still be a lot to download and parse. To address this need, TimeGates perform datetime content negotiation and will issue an HTTP redirect to the most appropriate Memento. For conventional web archives that are unaware of the change rate of the Original Resource, the TimeGate simply chooses the closest Memento to the requested datetime (as expressed in the Accept-Datetime request header). This algorithm is known as 'mindist' for 'Minimum Distance'. Figure 14.8 shows the client asking the Internet Archive for a Memento closest to October 16, 2013.

```
$ curl --silent http://web.archive.org/web/timemap/link/http://lanl.gov/ |
   head -10
<http://lanl.gov/>; rel="original",
<http://web.archive.org/web/timemap/link/http://lanl.gov/>; rel="self";
   type="application/link-format"; from="Sat, 21 Dec 1996 03:12:31 GMT";
   until="Wed, 01 Feb 2017 11:44:55 GMT",
<http://web.archive.org/web/http://lanl.gov/>; rel="timegate",
<http://web.archive.org/web/19961221031231/http://lanl.gov/>; rel="first
   memento"; datetime="Sat, 21 Dec 1996 03:12:31 GMT",
<http://web.archive.org/web/19981206235030/http://lanl.gov/>; rel="memento";
   datetime="Sun, 06 Dec 1998 23:50:30 GMT",
<http://web.archive.org/web/19981212015212/http://lanl.gov/>; rel="memento";
   datetime="Sat, 12 Dec 1998 01:52:12 GMT",
<http://web.archive.org/web/19981212030449/http://www.lanl.gov/>;
   rel="memento"; datetime="Sat, 12 Dec 1998 03:04:49 GMT",
<http://web.archive.org/web/19990117014439/http://lanl.gov/>; rel="memento";
   datetime="Sun, 17 Jan 1999 01:44:39 GMT",
<http://web.archive.org/web/19990117083819/http://lanl.gov/>; rel="memento";
   datetime="Sun, 17 Jan 1999 08:38:19 GMT",
<http://web.archive.org/web/19990125090547/http://lanl.gov/>; rel="memento";
   datetime="Mon, 25 Jan 1999 09:05:47 GMT",
```

**Figure 14.7 The first ten lines of the TimeMap for http://www.lanl.gov/.**

```
$ curl -I -H "Accept-Datetime: Wed,
   16 Oct 2013 22:59:48 GMT" http://
   web.archive.org/web/http://lanl.
   gov/
HTTP/1.1 302 Found
Server: Tengine/2.1.0
Date: Wed, 08 Feb 2017 03:38:20 GMT
Content-Type: text/html
Content-Length: 0
Location:     /web/20131019030442/
   http://www.lanl.gov/
Vary: accept-datetime
Link:        <http://lanl.gov/>;
   rel="original",    <http://web.
   archive.org/web/timemap/link/
   http://lanl.gov/>; rel="timemap";
   type="application/link-format",
   <http://web.archive.org/
   web/19961221031231/http://lanl.
   gov/>;   rel="first   memento";
   datetime="Sat,   21   Dec   1996
   03:12:31   GMT",   <http://web.
   archive.org/web/20131014072106/
   http://lanl.gov/>;    rel="prev
   memento"; datetime="Mon, 14 Oct
   2013 07:21:06 GMT", <http://web.
   archive.org/web/20131019030442/
   http://lanl.gov/>; rel="memento";
   datetime="Sat,   19   Oct   2013
   03:04:42   GMT",   <http://web.
   archive.org/web/20131020082626/
   http://lanl.gov/>;    rel="next
   memento"; datetime="Sun, 20 Oct
   2013 08:26:26 GMT", <http://web.
   archive.org/web/20170201114455/
   http://lanl.gov/>;    rel="last
   memento"; datetime="Wed, 01 Feb
   2017 11:44:55 GMT"
```

**Figure 14.8 Negotiating with a TimeGate for a Memento of http://www.lanl.gov/ close to October 16, 2013.**

In Figure 14.8, the TimeGate issues a redirection to URI-M http://web.archive.org/web/20131019030442/http://lanl.gov/, which although off by three days (October 19, 2013) is the closest available Memento to October 16, 2013 that the Internet Archive has.

The Memento Protocol also applies to transactional archives, such as LANL's SiteStory (Brunelle et al., 2013), and content management systems that act as their own archives, such as wikis. Figure 14.9 shows the HTTP response from the World Wide Web Consortium (W3C, a standards body for the web) wiki which implements our Memento for MediaWiki extension (Jones et al., 2014), and the server is specifying its own TimeGate for the URI-R https://www.w3.org/wiki/SpecProd/Restyle. One could consult the Internet Archive to discover Mementos for this URI-R, but since this is a MediaWiki, the wiki is its own archive and is authoritative on which versions existed at different points in time (see Jones et al., 2016a for an analysis of missed updates and redundant Mementos when web archives interact with wikis). Figure 14.10 shows datetime negotiation requesting a Memento one second before the Memento-Datetime for the last Memento in the wiki. If this were a conventional web archive that did not know the complete version history, it would use mindist and choose the Memento that was one second into the future. But since this is a content management system with a complete version history, it selects the closest Memento with a Memento-Datetime value less than or equal to the Accept-Datetime value because that is the version that was the current one at the requested datetime. This algorithm is known as 'minpast' for 'Minimum Past' and in Figure 14.10 it results in the redirection to a Memento two years in the past instead of one second in the future, which the mindist algorithm would have chosen.

The entire Memento framework comes together as shown in Figure 14.11, where ideally the Original Resource links to the TimeGate (URI-G); if this link is not provided the user's browser can be configured to know the location of a suitable TimeGate. It is the TimeGate's job to handle the datetime negotiation and redirect the user to the closest available Memento. The Mementos in the web archive provide machine-readable links to each other, as well as back to the Original Resource, allowing for seamless navigation between the current and past webs. Because the Memento Protocol is an

```
$ curl -I https://www.w3.org/wiki/
   SpecProd/Restyle
HTTP/1.1 200 OK
Link: <https://www.w3.org/wiki/
   SpecProd/Restyle>; rel="original
   latest-version",<https://www.
   w3.org/wiki/Special:TimeGate/
   SpecProd/Restyle>;
   rel="timegate",<https://www.
   w3.org/wiki/Special:TimeMap/
   SpecProd/Restyle>; rel="timemap";
   type="application/link-format";
   from="Thu, 08 Dec 2011 20:09:41
   GMT"; until="Fri, 11 Mar 2016
   16:02:35GMT",<https://www.w3.org/
   wiki/index.php?title=SpecProd/
   Restyle&oldid=55833>; rel="first
   memento"; datetime="Thu,
   08 Dec 2011 20:09:41
   GMT",<https://www.w3.org/
   wiki/index.php?title=SpecProd/
   Restyle&oldid=97718>; rel="last
   memento"; datetime="Fri, 11 Mar
   2016 16:02:35 GMT"
Content-language: en
Last-Modified: Mon, 13 Feb 2017
   09:44:38 GMT
Content-Type: text/html;
   charset=UTF-8
Content-Length: 22688
Date: Mon, 13 Feb 2017 17:08:03 GMT
```

**Figure 14.9 HTTP response with Memento headers from the W3C MediaWiki.**

extension of HTTP and content negotiation, it retains HTTP's compliance with the architectural principles of Representational State Transfer (REST) and Hypermedia as the Engine of Application State (HATEOAS) (Fielding, 2000). In its simplest form, this means that clients interact with the state of resources using only the methods defined in HTTP (i.e., REST) and 'follow their nose' and interact with self-describing resources to discover navigable links to related, typed resources, such as other Mementos, TimeGates, and TimeMaps (i.e., HATEOAS). In summary, the Memento Protocol is not a service separate and apart from a web archive, it is embedded within the normal HTTP operations of a web archive.

## MEMENTO AND AGGREGATING MULTIPLE ARCHIVES

In Figure 14.8, the Internet Archive did not have a Memento for the exact date of October 16, 2013 and redirected to one of October 19 instead. For many applications, this three-day difference is inconsequential, but what if it was essential to view the state of that URI-R on October 16, 2013? Users could query different web archives separately, but keeping track of the publicly accessible web archives that natively support the Memento Protocol would require more knowledge than most users possess. For example, the earliest Memento for the Smithsonian Institute's home page (http://www.si.edu/) is in the Portuguese Web Archive and not the Internet Archive (October, 1996 vs. May, 1997) (Fuhrig, 2014). Too much time has passed to definitely say why the Portuguese Web Archive has the earliest page, but the Memento Protocol facilitated the discovery of the Memento in an archive that many people in the United States may not have known.

Fortunately, the Memento Protocol makes it easy to combine various web archives into *aggregators*, which provide a single TimeGate and a single TimeMap for all the web archives that it aggregates (Sanderson, 2012). For example, Los Alamos National Laboratory runs an aggregator available at: http://timetravel.mementoweb.org. To revisit the query in Figure 14.8, finding a Memento of http://www.lanl.gov/ close to October 16, 2013, Figure 14.12 shows the response from the TimeTravel aggregator.

Since the aggregator at timetravel.mementoweb.org currently knows of approximately 30 publicly accessible web archives, it can redirect the client to exactly the desired Memento for http://www.lanl.gov/ on October 16, 2013. These examples are from the publicly accessible aggregator at timetravel.mementoweb.org, but there is no requirement to use this aggregator. Old Dominion University (ODU) runs a

```
$ curl -I -L -H "Accept-Datetime: Fri, 11 Mar 2016 16:02:34 GMT" https://www.
   w3.org/wiki/Special:TimeGate/SpecProd/Restyle
HTTP/1.1 302 Found
Vary: Accept-Encoding,Accept-Datetime
Location: https://www.w3.org/wiki/index.php?title=SpecProd/
   Restyle&oldid=77827
Link: <https://www.w3.org/wiki/Special:TimeMap/SpecProd/Restyle>;
   rel="timemap"; type="application/link-format"; from="Thu, 08 Dec 2011
   20:09:41 GMT"; until="Fri, 11 Mar 2016 16:02:35 GMT",<https://www.w3.org/
   wiki/index.php?title=SpecProd/Restyle&oldid=55833>; rel="first memento";
   datetime="Thu, 08 Dec 2011 20:09:41 GMT",<https://www.w3.org/wiki/index.
   php?title=SpecProd/Restyle&oldid=97718>; rel="last memento"; datetime="Fri,
   11 Mar 2016 16:02:35 GMT",<https://www.w3.org/wiki/SpecProd/Restyle>;
   rel="original latest-version"
Content-Type: text/html; charset=UTF-8
Content-Length: 0
Date: Mon, 13 Feb 2017 17:17:07 GMT

HTTP/1.1 200 OK
Memento-Datetime: Fri, 10 Oct 2014 04:07:37 GMT
Link: <https://www.w3.org/wiki/SpecProd/Restyle>; rel="original latest-
   version",<https://www.w3.org/wiki/Special:TimeGate/SpecProd/Restyle>;
   rel="timegate",<https://www.w3.org/wiki/Special:TimeMap/SpecProd/Restyle>;
   rel="timemap"; type="application/link-format"; from="Thu, 08 Dec 2011
   20:09:41 GMT"; until="Fri, 11 Mar 2016 16:02:35 GMT",<https://www.w3.org/
   wiki/index.php?title=SpecProd/Restyle&oldid=55833>; rel="first memento";
   datetime="Thu, 08 Dec 2011 20:09:41 GMT",<https://www.w3.org/wiki/index.
   php?title=SpecProd/Restyle&oldid=97718>; rel="last memento"; datetime="Fri,
   11 Mar 2016 16:02:35 GMT"
Content-language: en
Vary: Accept-Encoding,Cookie
Content-Type: text/html; charset=UTF-8
Content-Length: 21235
Date: Mon, 13 Feb 2017 17:17:07 GMT
```

**Figure 14.10 Datetime negotiation with a MediaWiki TimeGate for one second before the latest Memento; MediaWiki uses the minpast algorithm instead of mindist.**

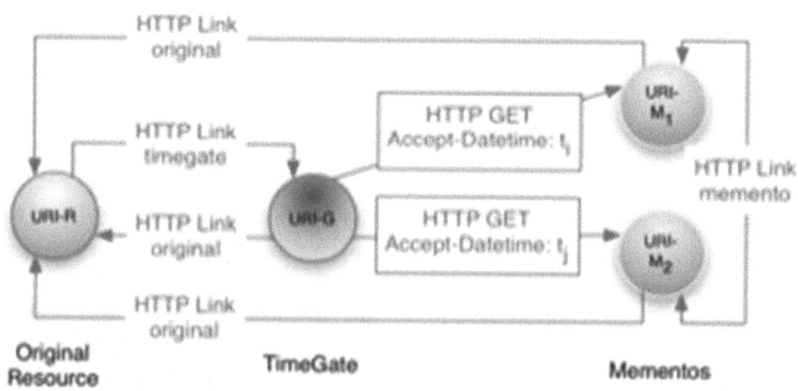


**Figure 14.11 Architectural overview of how the Memento framework allows a representation of a prior state of a resource to be accessed.**

```
$ curl -I -H "Accept-Datetime:
   Wed, 16 Oct 2013 22:59:48 GMT"
   http://timetravel.mementoweb.org/
   timegate/http://www.lanl.gov/
HTTP/1.1 302 Moved Temporarily
Server: nginx/1.10.1
Date: Thu, 09 Feb 2017 17:50:37 GMT
Content-Type: text/plain;
   charset=iso-8859-1
Content-Length: 0
Location: http://archive.
   is/20131016225948/http://www.
   lanl.gov/
Vary: Accept-Datetime
Last-Modified: Wed, 08 Feb 2017
   04:27:12 GMT
Link: <http://www.lanl.
   gov/>;rel="original", <http://
   timetravel.mementoweb.org/
   timemap/link/http://www.
   lanl.gov/>;rel="timemap";
   type="application/link-
   format",<http://archive.
   is/20131016225948/http://www.
   lanl.gov/>;rel="memento";
   datetime="Wed, 16 Oct 2013 22:59:48
   GMT",<http://web.archive.bibalex.
   org:80/web/19961221031231/
   http://lanl.gov/>;rel="memento
   first"; datetime="Sat, 21 Dec
   1996 03:12:31 GMT",<http://web.
   archive.org/web/20170201114455/
   http://lanl.gov/>;rel="memento
   last"; datetime="Wed, 01 Feb 2017
   11:44:55 GMT"
```

**Figure 14.12 A response from an aggregated TimeGate, redirecting to http://archive.is/20131016225948/http://www.lanl.gov/.**

separate aggregator at memgator.cs.odu.edu, and a query to this aggregator shows that Mementos for http://www.lanl.gov/ can be found in at least eight publicly accessible web archives with native Memento Protocol support (Figure 14.13). While the Internet Archive (archive.org) clearly has the most with 1,810 Mementos and Archive-It (a separate subscription service of the Internet Archive) is second with 311, there are still more than 250 Mementos in other web archives.

```
$ curl --silent http://memgator.
   cs.odu.edu/timemap/link/http://
   www.lanl.gov/ | grep datetime |
   awk '{print $1}' | awk -v FS=/
   '{print $3}' | sort | uniq -c
   36 archive.is
3 arquivo.pt
6 swap.stanford.edu
311 wayback.archive-it.org
1 wayback.vefsafn.is
1810 web.archive.org
228 webarchive.loc.gov
1 webarchive.parliament.uk
```

**Figure 14.13 The processed TimeMap showing the hostnames of the eight public web archives with Mementos for http://www.lanl.gov/ and their respective Memento counts.**

The MemGator software is available for download and local installation (Alam and Nelson, 2016), making it possible to set up a Memento aggregator with custom sets of web archives, suitable for local or private deployments.

## RIGHT-CLICK TO THE PAST

To this point, we have discussed the Memento Protocol in terms of HTTP interactions, using the curl command line user-agent and examining raw HTTP responses. While this is necessary to understand the mechanics of the Memento Protocol, there are a range of more user-friendly clients and services using the Memento Protocol that provide a more seamless integration of the current and past web.

The easiest way to get started is to visit http://timetravel.mementoweb.org/ and input the desired URI-R and datetime. In Figure 14.14, we use http://www.lanl.gov/ and 2013-10-16, respectively; this is effectively the user-friendly version of the curl request shown in Figure 14.12. In Figure 14.15, we see the results, sorted by web archives with a Memento closest to the desired datetime,

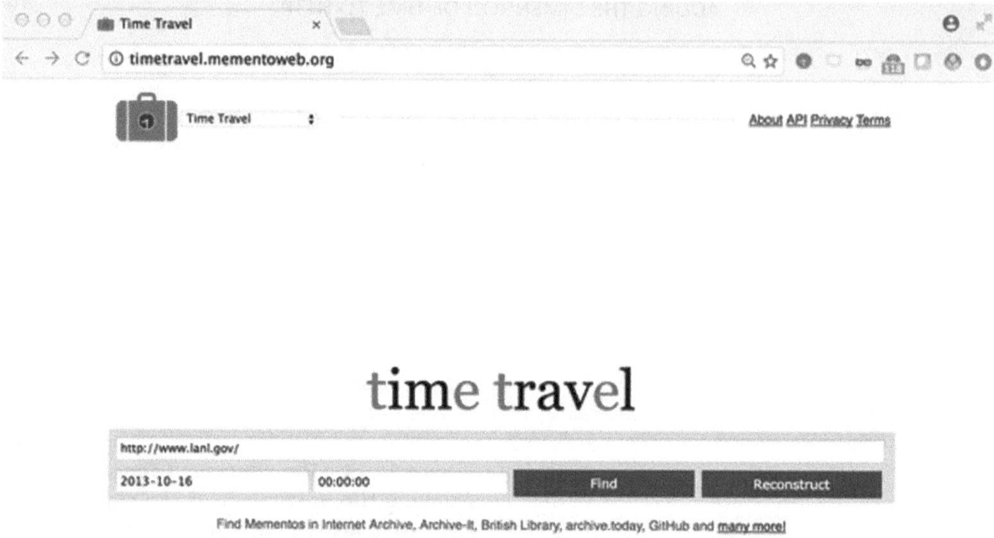


**Figure 14.14 A request to the TimeTravel service with URI-R = http://www.lanl.gov/ and datetime=2013-10-16.**

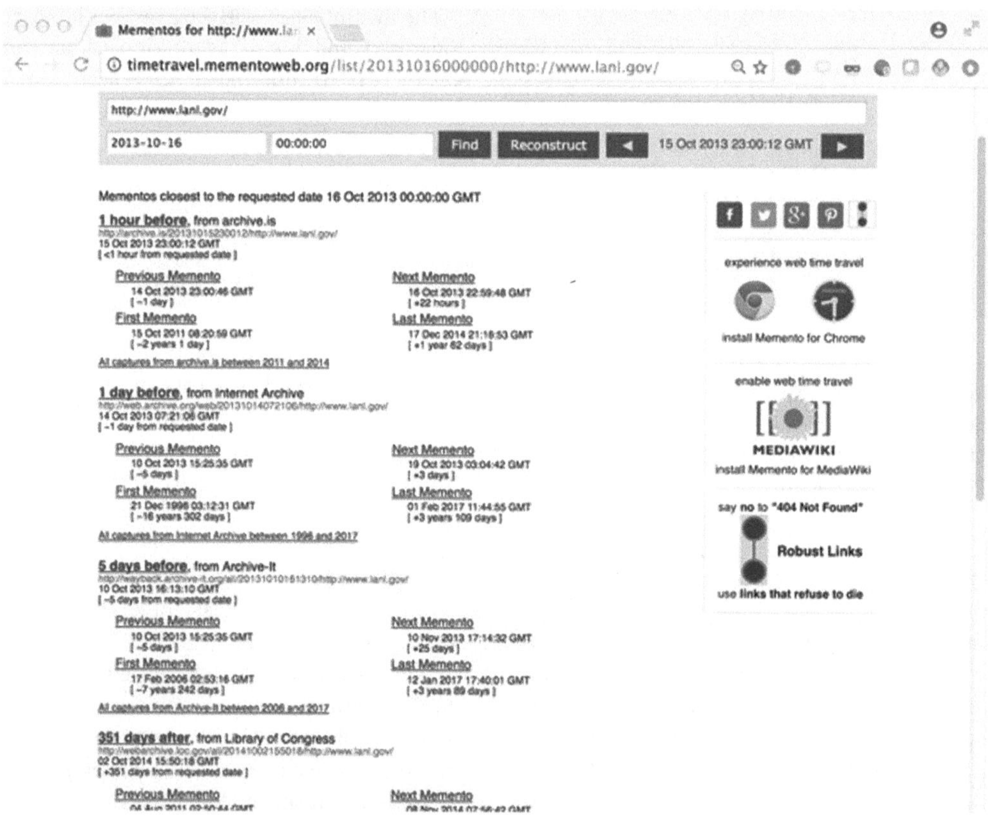


**Figure 14.15 The response to the request shown in Figure 14.12, with seven archives holding Mementos for this URI-R (available at: http://timetravel.mementoweb.org/list/20131016000000/http://www.lanl.gov/).**

with the archive.is Memento at the top of the list, followed by the Internet Archive, and a total of seven different archives (when the page scrolled to the bottom). The archives differ slightly from the ODU aggregator result shown in Figure 14.13, in part because of a prediction interface employed by the LANL Time Travel service, which is discussed below.

While the Time Travel service is an attractive and easy to use interface, it is still a destination separate from the live web, meaning that users need to know of its location and choose to navigate there to explore the past web. While this is suitable for extended sessions of interacting with the past web, such sessions do not reflect how most humans use web archives. In a study of accesses to the Internet Archive, AlNoamany found that 82% of human sessions begin with referrals from live web pages (the majority of which come from Wikipedia), and 86% of those links no longer exist on the live web (AlNoamany, 2014). In short, web archives are primarily used as a versioning system to supplement failures in the live web, so we should have user agents that support this modality.

There are several clients for providing Memento-based access, including the original MementoFox (now deprecated) (Sanderson et al., 2011), Mink (which also facilitates archiving of live web pages) (Kelly et al., 2014b), and Memento for iOS (Tweedy et al., 2013). We will focus on the 'Memento for Chrome' extension, which provides Chrome users the capability to 'right-click to the past' (Nelson, 2013). Regular clicks provide the expected navigation (i.e., staying on the live web), but users can choose to right-click on a link or just in the middle of the page for the current URI to seamlessly provide access to the same functionality shown in Figures 14.12, 14.14, and 14.15. Figure 14.16 shows the user setting the desired datetime (October 16, 2013) with a calendar widget (the extension will use this value in the Accept-Datetime request header). Figure 14.17 shows the user right-clicking in the middle of the page, indicating the desired URI-R is 'this' page, i.e., http://www.lanl.gov/. There are several datetime options, but here the user is selecting the datetime as set in Figure 14.16. After selecting the link in Figure 14.17, the client then communicates with the Time Travel aggregator (effectively issuing the request shown in Figure 14.12), and the result is the client is directed to the URI-M http://archive.is/20131016225948/http://www.lanl.gov/ (Figure 14.18). To navigate back to the live web, the user right-clicks in the middle of the page again and selects 'get at current date' (Figure 14.19). The described interactions are also possible for links in pages and embedded resources such as images.

## ONGOING RESEARCH

The Memento Protocol has opened up entirely new areas of research regarding inter-archive access and collaboration. Though not an exhaustive list, we provide an overview of some of our recent research activities which the Memento Protocol has made possible and, in some cases, necessary.

### *Routing URI Requests to the Proper Web Archives*

When there was only one archive (i.e., the Internet Archive), access was simple: the archive either had the desired Memento or it did not. The addition of multiple web archives, which began in earnest in the mid to late 2000s (Bailey et al., 2013; Gomes et al., 2011), increases the complexity significantly. Either the user has to navigate to different web archives and check for existence, which is limited by the user's time and knowledge of the archives, or a service has to aggregate access to these archives (cf. the Time Travel service in Figures 14.14 and 14.15). When the number of web archives an aggregator has to select is small, it is easy to broadcast the URI lookup to all

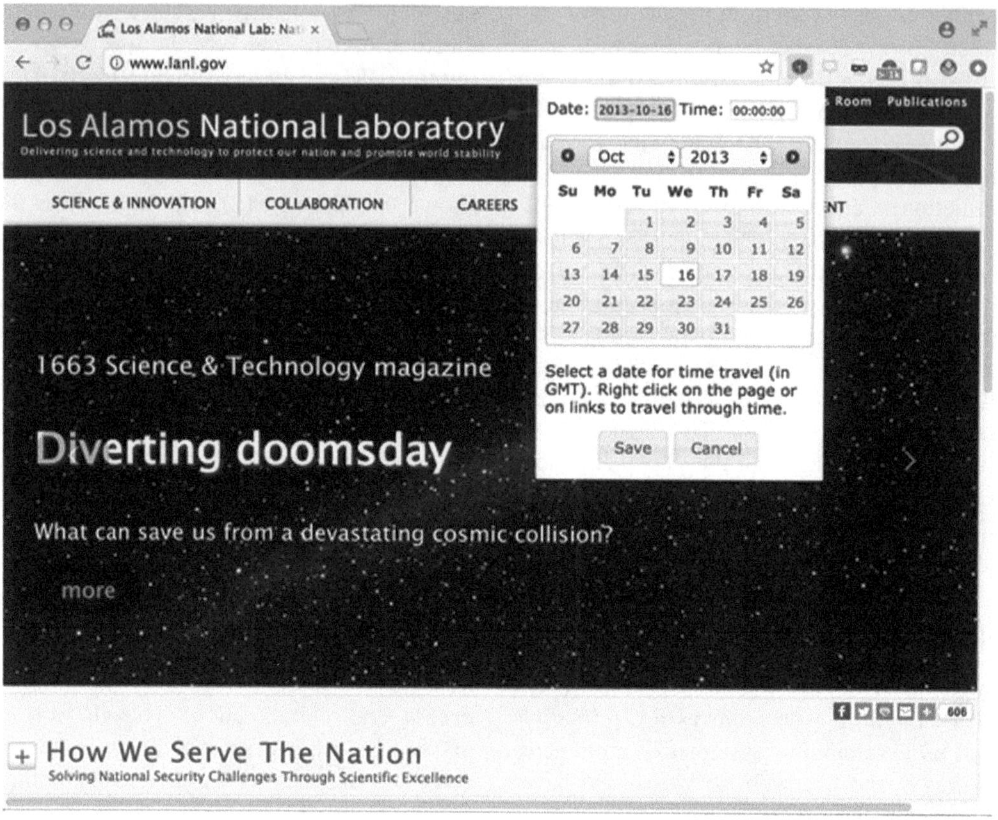


**Figure 14.16 Setting the datetime to October 16, 2013 for http://www.lanl.gov/.**

known web archives and then synthesize the results. As the number of web archives grows this become untenable, with responses waiting for the slowest archive to respond, while all along most of the web archives do not hold the desired Memento (i.e., a 404 HTTP response). This problem is well-known in the distributed search community as the query routing problem (Callan, 2002), even though URI lookups are not exactly like full-text queries in that the archives either have the Memento or they do not, and there is no ranked list of potentially relevant hits. For web archives, we want to predict where to send URI lookup requests such that we only query archives which are likely to have Mementos for the requested Original URI. This is not as obvious as it first seems – crawling scope is notoriously difficult and imprecise and archives often capture more than they intended.

In our earliest research in URI routing (AlSum et al., 2013, 2014), we proved that 52% of the time we can still produce a complete TimeMap querying only the top three (of a possible 12 available at that time) web archives even if we exclude the Internet Archive. Querying the top six web archives (excluding the Internet Archive) produces a complete TimeMap 77% of the time. In summary, despite a growing number of web archives, we need only query a few of them to get the complete list of all available Mementos, and even if the Internet Archive were to disappear, over one-half of the Original URIs would be unaffected.

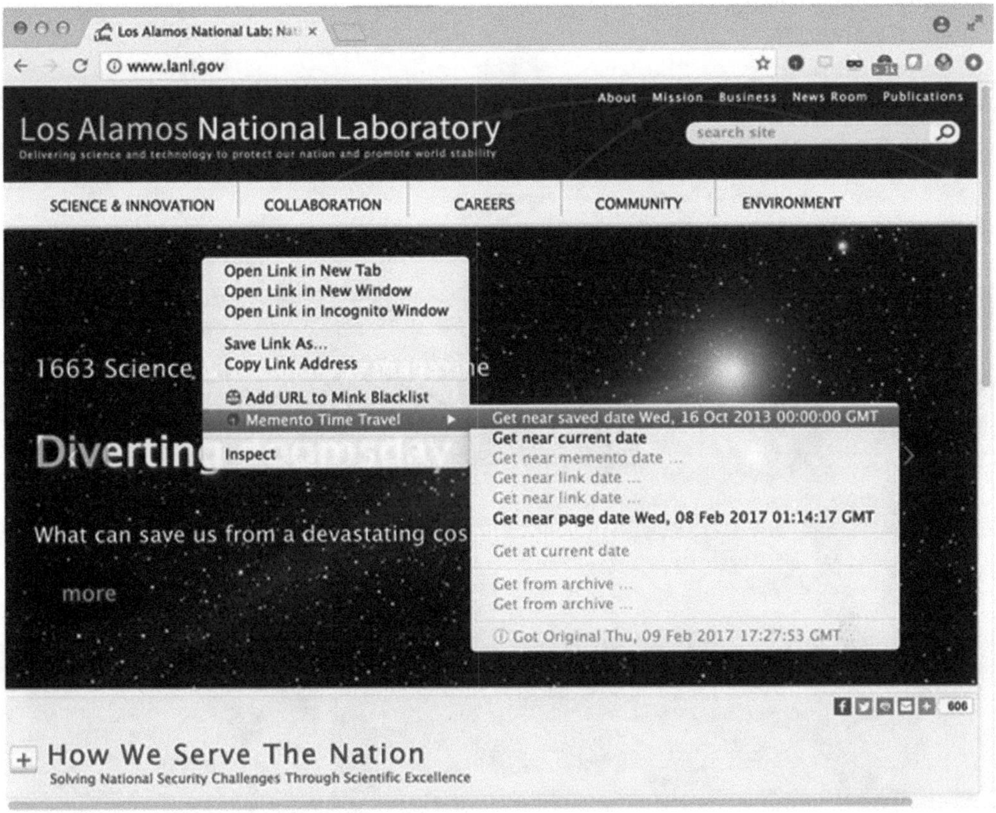


**Figure 14.17 Right-clicking in the middle of the page to expose datetime negotiation options for http://www.lanl.gov/.**

Of course, the question is: how do we know where to send the URI lookups? We have explored a variety of methods, including building web archive profiles using their CDX files (produced for playback in the Wayback Machine archival playback software) and HTTP access logs of web archives (Alam et al., 2015; Alam et al., 2016b), machine learning techniques based training data from responses of web archives for a fixed set of URI lookups (Bornand et al., 2016) (this method is in production in the Time Travel service shown in Figures 14.14 and 14.15), and – for web archives that have a full-text index – extracting terms from archived documents and using those as queries back into the archive (Alam et al., 2016a).

All of these methods have trade-offs. Using CDX files and HTTP access logs requires cooperation from the participating archives to make those files available for processing into a profile. Profiles built from learning from responses to lookups are sensitive to the URIs used in the training phase and thus will not reveal Original URIs that you do not know to ask for. Using keywords extracted from documents assumes a full-text search interface is available (which is often available only in smaller archives) and requires a large number of full-text queries to extract enough documents to profile its holdings. Our current research in this area involves developing approaches that are hybrids of the methods described above, as well as addressing

**Figure 14.18 The user is now at the Memento http://archive.is/20131016225948/ http://www.lanl.gov/.**

optimum approaches for updates and reevaluating baseline profiles.

## *How to Use Multiple Archives*

Figures 14.12, 14.14, and 14.15 show an aggregator consulting multiple web archives and then redirecting the requesting client to the web archive that contains the closest available Memento. But once the client follows that redirection, all the requests for embedded resources are relative to the archive holding the root HTML page (in the case of Figures 14.12, 14.14, and 14.15, all requests are relative to http://archive.is/). This means if there are links, images, or other embedded resources missing, the client is unable to take advantage of the other web archives that might hold those resources.

Some embedded resources, links, or even entire sites might not be present in the Internet Archive. One reason an entire site might not be present is because the site, for any number of reasons, is using a 'robots.txt' file on the live web to limit access by the Internet Archive, for both future crawls and any content they currently hold (Rossi, 2016). Figure 14.20 shows the Internet Archive's response for the URI-R https://www.quora.com/, and Figure 14.21 shows that there are several hundreds of Mementos in other web archives that do not implement the Internet Archive's robots.txt policy.

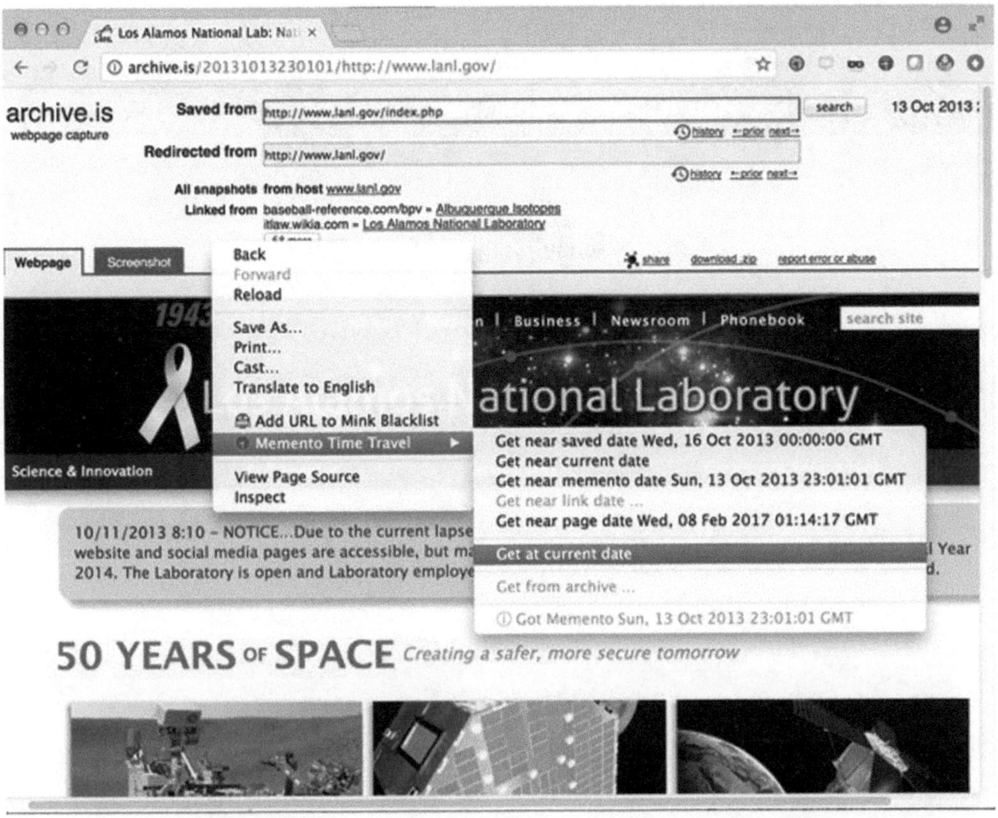


**Figure 14.19 Right-clicking in the middle of the Memento to go back to the live web (i.e., from http://archive.is/20131016225948/http://www.lanl.gov/ back to http://www.lanl.gov/).**

## *Memento Quality and Temporal Coherence*

Although the gold standard for assessing web archiving quality is still human interaction with a Memento to ensure all embedded resources, links, and functionality are preserved, this level of assessment is clearly not scalable. We have been involved with a range of automated evaluations of the web archiving process, including the Archival Acid Test (Kelly et al., 2014a), which evaluates the capabilities of crawling and playback technology stacks (e.g., the Heritrix crawler (Mohr et al., 2004) and the Wayback Machine playback engine), and assessing Memento damage (Brunelle et al., 2014, 2015) which provides weights to missing embedded resources based on heuristics for determining if the missing resource was 'important'.

Of particular note is our work on 'Temporal Violations', which are combinations of root HTML pages and embedded resources (e.g., images, CSS, JavaScript) that are combined during archival replay to produce a combination that never existed on the live web (Ainsworth et al., 2014; 2015). This can happen when the root HTML page is crawled and the embedded images (for example) are modified in between the time the root HTML page was crawled and the images themselves were crawled.

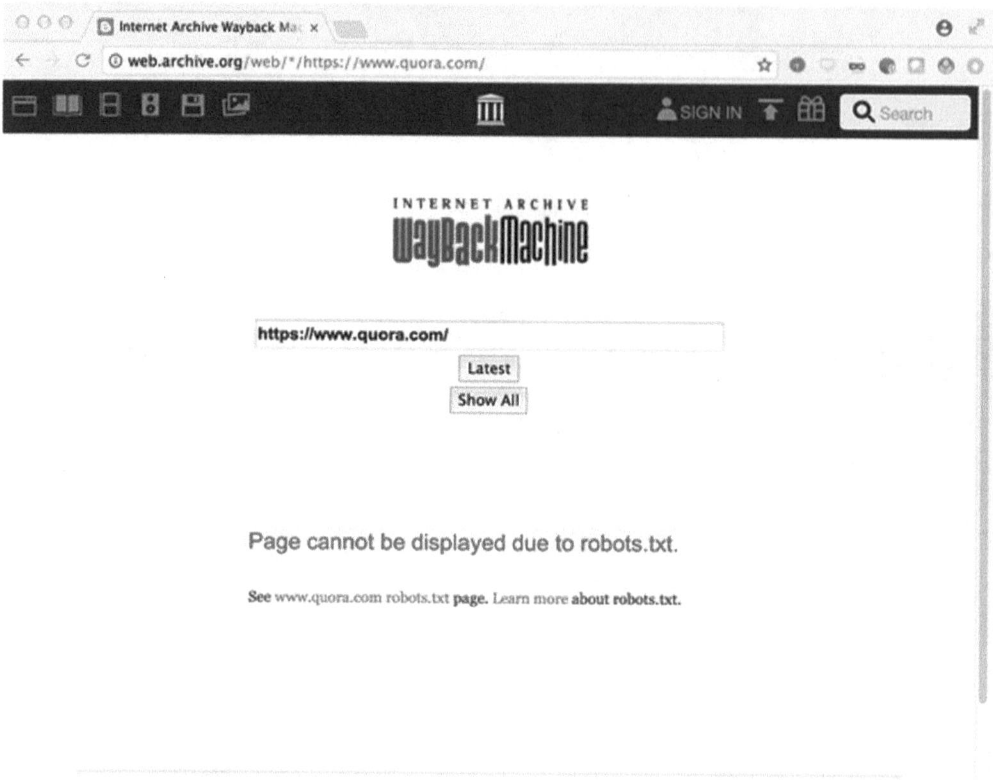


**Figure 14.20 The Internet Archive may hold Mementos for https://www.quora.com/ but is blocking them due to the directives found in https://www.quora.com/robots.txt.**

```
$ curl --silent -i http://memgator.
   cs.odu.edu/timemap/link/https://
   www.quora.com/ | grep datetime |
   awk '{print $1}' | awk -v FS=/
   '{print $3}' | sort | uniq -c
44 archive.is
3 arquivo.pt
219 wayback.archive-it.org
77 wayback.vefsafn.is
182 webarchive.loc.gov
4 webarchive.nationalarchives.gov.uk
6 webarchive.parliament.uk
```

**Figure 14.21 https://www.quora.com/ is not in the Internet Archive but is archived 500+ times in seven other archives.**

We defined four categories for discussing the temporal coherence of composite Mementos (root HTML plus embedded resources):

1 Prima Facie Coherent – the combination of embedded resources and a root HTML page can be shown to have existed as presented at the time of crawling (i.e., Memento-Datetime).
2 Prima Facie Violative – the embedded resources can be shown to have been modified since the Memento-Datetime of the root HTML page.
3 Possibly Coherent – the embedded resources have Memento-Datetimes earlier than their root HTML page, and although they cannot be shown to be coherent since embedded resources are typically static, they are possibly coherent.
4 Probably Violative – the embedded resources have Memento-Datetimes later than their root HTML page, and although they cannot be shown to be violative, as root HTML pages are often dynamically generated and modified at a faster rate than embedded resources, they are probably violative.

```
$ curl -I http://web.archive.org/web/20141113140512im_/http://www.lanl.gov/
   _assets/images/lanl-logo-footer.png
HTTP/1.1 200 OK
Server: Tengine/2.1.0
Date: Mon, 13 Feb 2017 05:46:48 GMT
Content-Type: image/png
Content-Length: 8719
Connection: keep-alive
Memento-Datetime: Thu, 13 Nov 2014 14:05:12 GMT
Link: <http://www.lanl.gov/_assets/images/lanl-logo-footer.png>; rel="original",
   <http://web.archive.org/web/timemap/link/http://www.lanl.gov/_assets/images/
   lanl-logo-footer.png>; rel="timemap"; type="application/link-format",
   <http://web.archive.org/web/http://www.lanl.gov/_assets/images/lanl-logo-
   footer.png>; rel="timegate", <http://web.archive.org/web/20120912040310/
   http://www.lanl.gov/_assets/images/lanl-logo-footer.png>; rel="first
   memento"; datetime="Wed, 12 Sep 2012 04:03:10 GMT", <http://web.archive.
   org/web/20141009211301/http://www.lanl.gov/_assets/images/lanl-logo-footer.
   png>; rel="prev memento"; datetime="Thu, 09 Oct 2014 21:13:01 GMT", <http://
   web.archive.org/web/20141113140512/http://www.lanl.gov/_assets/images/lanl-
   logo-footer.png>; rel="memento"; datetime="Thu, 13 Nov 2014 14:05:12 GMT",
   <http://web.archive.org/web/20141122060334/http://www.lanl.gov/_assets/
   images/lanl-logo-footer.png>; rel="next memento"; datetime="Sat, 22 Nov 2014
   06:03:34 GMT", <http://web.archive.org/web/20170204070650/http://www.lanl.
   gov/_assets/images/lanl-logo-footer.png>; rel="last memento"; datetime="Sat,
   04 Feb 2017 07:06:50 GMT"
X-Archive-Orig-last-modified: Tue, 28 Oct 2014 22:12:02 GMT
X-Archive-Orig-content-type: image/png
X-Archive-Orig-date: Thu, 13 Nov 2014 14:03:55 GMT
X-Archive-Orig-content-length: 8719
```

**Figure 14.22 The Memento-Datetime and X-Archive-Orig-last-modified headers establish a range of temporal validity.**

The combination of Last-Modified and Memento-Datetime headers are critical for determining a range of temporal validity for an embedded resource with respect to a root HTML page in which it appears. Embedded resources, such as images, CSS, and JavaScript, tend to be static files with Last-Modified response headers available (cf. Figure 14.1), and most HTML files are dynamically generated and thus rarely have the Last-Modified response header (cf. Figure 14.2). For example, in the Memento http://web.archive.org/web/20141031175656/https://www.lanl.gov/, with a Memento-Datetime of 'Fri, 31 Oct 2014 17:56:56 GMT', the logo at the bottom of the page (http://web.archive.org/web/20141113140512im_/http://www.lanl.gov/_assets/images/lanl-logo-footer.png) has a Memento-Datetime of 'Thu, 13 Nov 2014 14:05:12 GMT', which means it was crawled after the root HTML page in which it appears. However, as shown in Figure 14.22, the Last-Modified date of the logo as it was when the logo was crawled is echoed in the 'X-Archive-Orig-last-modified' response header (indeed, many of the original HTTP response headers are echoed by the web archive with the prefix 'X-Archive-Orig-').

In Figure 14.23, we see a NOAA page with a Memento-Datetime of January 29, 1999 with an embedded image as the primary content. However, when we dereference the URI-M for the image, we see that the Last-Modified and Memento-Datetime headers (Figure 14.24) have values of April 10, 2003. This combination of HTML page and embedded JPEG never existed on the live web.

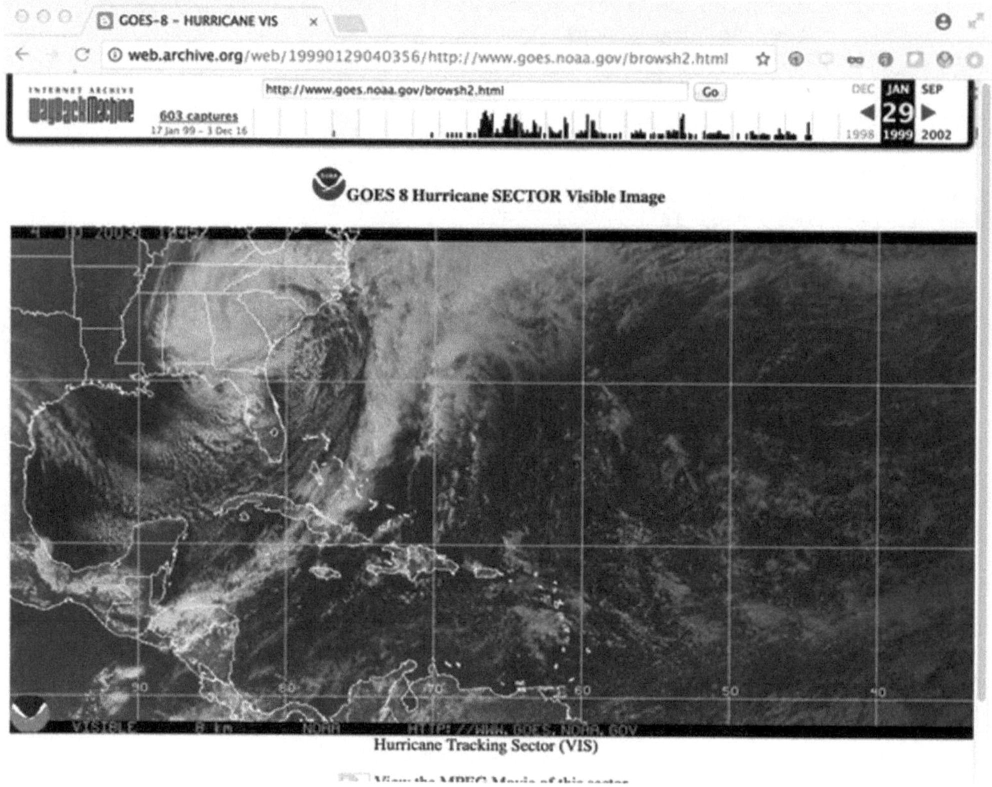


**Figure 14.23 Memento http://web.archive.org/web/19990129040356/http://www.goes.noaa.gov/browsh2.html.**

In our study of temporal violations (Ainsworth et al., 2015), we found that approximately 76% of composite Mementos were complete (i.e., missing no embedded Mementos), and utilizing additional Memento-enabled web archives could raise that number to 80% complete. More concerning is that 6% of composite Mementos are Prima Facie Violative and 2.5% are Probably Violative. When multiple archives are used, the Probably Violative composite Mementos actually goes up to 5%, in part because not all web archives provide the X-Archive-Orig-last-modified response header (Ainsworth, 2015). So, while multiple archives increase the completeness, they can potentially decrease the temporal coherence. When taken altogether, only 18% of composite Mementos are both complete and Prima Facie Coherent. In summary, web archives probably provide a faithful rendering of the past web approximately only one in five times.

## *Linking to Archives or the Live Web?*

The existence of multiple web archives introduces the question, similar to the 'appropriate copy' problem of reference linking (Caplan and Arms, 1999), of which version to link to when writing HTML: the live web version, or an archived version, and, if an archived version, in which archive? Increased

```
$ curl -IL http://web.archive.org/web/19990129040356/http://www.goes.noaa.
  gov/GIFS/HUVS.JPG
HTTP/1.1 302 Found
Server: Tengine/2.1.0
Date: Tue, 14 Feb 2017 04:02:10 GMT
Content-Type: image/jpeg
Content-Length: 0
Location: /web/20030410203138/http://www.goes.noaa.gov/GIFS/HUVS.JPG
Link: <http://www.goes.noaa.gov:80/GIFS/HUVS.JPG>; rel="original"

HTTP/1.1 200 OK
Server: Tengine/2.1.0
Date: Tue, 14 Feb 2017 04:02:11 GMT
Content-Type: image/jpeg
Content-Length: 141380
Memento-Datetime: Thu, 10 Apr 2003 20:31:38 GMT
Link: <http://www.goes.noaa.gov/GIFS/HUVS.JPG>; rel="original", <http://
  web.archive.org/web/timemap/link/http://www.goes.noaa.gov/GIFS/HUVS.JPG>;
  rel="timemap"; type="application/link-format", <http://web.archive.org/
  web/http://www.goes.noaa.gov/GIFS/HUVS.JPG>; rel="timegate", <http://web.
  archive.org/web/20030410203138/http://www.goes.noaa.gov/GIFS/HUVS.JPG>;
  rel="first memento"; datetime="Thu, 10 Apr 2003 20:31:38 GMT", <http://web.
  archive.org/web/20030602014329/http://www.goes.noaa.gov/GIFS/HUVS.JPG>;
  rel="next memento"; datetime="Mon, 02 Jun 2003 01:43:29 GMT", <http://web.
  archive.org/web/20170201134641/http://www.goes.noaa.gov/GIFS/HUVS.JPG>;
  rel="last memento"; datetime="Wed, 01 Feb 2017 13:46:41 GMT"
X-Archive-Orig-last-modified: Thu, 10 Apr 2003 20:05:23 GMT
X-Archive-Orig-content-type: image/jpeg
X-Archive-Orig-date: Thu, 10 Apr 2003 20:31:33 GMT
X-Archive-Orig-content-length: 141380
X-Archive-Orig-server: Apache/2.0.45 (Unix)
```

**Figure 14.24 Prima Facie Violative: the embedded JPEG from Figure 14.23 was actually modified and archived in 2003, not 1999.**

interest in link rot ('soft 404s' (Bar-Yossef et al., 2004) or actual 404 HTTP responses) and content drift (the page persists, but the content is no longer relevant to the author's original intent when creating the link) in our scholarly, legal, and other corpora has raised interest in linking directly to Mementos instead of Original URIs (Jones et al., 2016b; Klein et al., 2014; Zittrain et al., 2014). The current practice in sites like Wikipedia is to replace broken links to the live web to point directly to a URI-M in the Internet Archive (AlNoamany, 2014). However, this fails to take advantage of the other public web archives that might also have copies. One could link to an aggregator, but there is a better way that allows providing both URI-R and URI-M values, along with a prefered datetime for use in archives the author of the HTML might not have knowledge of. This approach increases the chances to be able to revisit originally linked content by including information that can be used to look up Mementos in any archive (URI-R and archival datetime) in addition to the key that can only be used in a single archive (URI-M). This fallback mechanism is relevant because the brief history of web archives provides plenty of illustrations that their accessibility can be hindered by a wide range of challenges including technical failures, financial woes, take-down requests, and geo-politically induced censorship.

The Robust Links specification takes advantage of the HTML5 'data-' attribute for extensible metadata fields not otherwise

```
<a href="http://www.lanl.gov/"
data-versionurl="http://archive.
   is/3IEj0"
data-versiondate="2013-10-16">my
   robust link to the LANL home
   page</a>
```

**Figure 14.25 Primary link is to URI-R, alternate link to URI-M, and a preferred datetime.**

defined in HTML5 (Van de Sompel et al., 2015). For example, if we wanted to link to the URI-R with an alternate link to a URI-M, we could write the HTML shown in Figure 14.25. The URI-R and value in the 'data-versiondate' attribute can be combined for URI lookups in any web archive, for example, using the Memento Protocol.

Similarly, it is possible to reverse the primary and alternate link. Figure 14.26 shows the primary link to an aggregator service that will dynamically determine and redirect the client to the closest available Memento; the URI-R is the alternate link, and the datetime is also provided. If that aggregator is no longer online, the URI-R and datetime values can be combined for discovery in other web archives or aggregators.

Variations of the examples in Figures 14.25 and 14.26 are possible, but all require the desired datetime to be expressed either in the 'data-versiondate' link attribute or in the datePublished or dateModified attributes for the HTML meta tag if the datetime is applicable to the entire page. A demonstration of Robust Links in action can be found in the links of one of our recent papers (Van de Sompel and Nelson, 2015).

```
<a href="http://timetravel.mementoweb.
   org/memento/20131016000000/
   http://www.lanl.gov/" data-
   originalurl="http://www.lanl.gov/"
   data-versiondate="2013-10-16">my
   robust link to the LANL home
   page</a>
```

**Figure 14.26 Primary link is to an aggregator, alternate link to URI-R, and a preferred datetime.**

## CONCLUSIONS

The Memento Protocol is the de facto standard for integrating the now dozens of publicly accessible web archives, and it works equally well in intranets and private archives. For example, the browsers and tools we at LANL and ODU use to access the Internet Archive and other public web archives are the same tools we use to access our research group's private wiki. The Memento Protocol is an implementation of datetime negotiation in HTTP, fulfilling one of the original design goals of Tim Berners-Lee that was deferred in part because of the lack of temporal semantics in the Unix filesystem. The Memento Protocol provides a standardized, machine-readable mechanism for bi-directional linkage between the current and past webs, where before there had just been an ad hoc set of conventions and archive-specific heuristics for naming and accessing the past web. TimeMaps provide lists of Mementos for an Original Resource, and TimeGates provide the datetime negotiation to the closest available Memento.

In 2006, Julien Masanes expressed a vision of an interconnected, global grid of web archives:

> Such a grid should link Web archives so that they together form one global navigation space like the live Web itself. This is only possible if they are structured in a way close enough to the original Web and if they are openly accessible. (Masanes, 2006, p. 21)

The Memento Protocol achieves this goal by changing web archives from strictly destinations into infrastructure that supports the live web by providing a standardized and integrated versioning for the web indexed by global datetime. In the future when the web transitions from dozens to 100s or even 1,000s of web archives, public and private, the faithful and complete rendering of past web pages will depend on the ability to identify, query, and access the appropriate subset of web archives.

The history of the early twenty-first century cannot be told without significant evidence from web archives. The websites and their contents are fleeting, and are too culturally important to be left to the care of a single web archive. The web is distributed and largely uncoordinated, with interoperability emerging from simple protocols such as HTTP. So too must be our web archives: distributed and largely uncoordinated, with interoperability made possible via time semantics that are part of HTTP and finally transcend the limitations of the Unix operating system.

## ACKNOWLEDGMENTS

The Memento Protocol was originally supported by grants from the Library of Congress. Additional research was supported in part by NSF IIS 1009392, NSF IIS 1526700, and the Andrew Mellon Foundation. Numerous people supported the Memento Protocol through software development and installation, many of whom appear below as our co-authors. Figures 14.16 through 14.19 are courtesy of the Los Alamos National Laboratory.

## REFERENCES

Ainsworth, S.G. (2015) *Original header replay considered coherent*. [blog] Web Science and Digital Library Research Group. Available at: http://ws-dl.blogspot.com/2015/08/2015-08-28-original-header- replay.html [Accessed 1 Mar. 2018].

Ainsworth, S.G., Nelson, M.L., and Van de Sompel, H. (2015) 'Only one out of five archived web pages existed as presented', in: *HT '15, Proceedings of the 26th ACM Conference on Hypertext and Hypermedia*, [online] Guzelyurt: ACM, pp. 257–266. Available at: https://doi.org/10.1145/2700171.2791044 [Accessed 1 Mar. 2018].

Ainsworth, S.G., Nelson, M.L., and Van de Sompel, H. (2014) *A framework for evaluation of composite memento temporal coherence*. [online] Available at: http://arxiv.org/abs/1402.0928 [Accessed 1 Mar. 2018].

Alam, S., and Nelson, M.L. (2016) 'Memgator – a portable concurrent memento aggregator: Cross-platform CLI and server binaries in Go', in: *JCDL '16. Proceedings of the 16th ACM/IEEE-CS Joint Conference on Digital Libraries*, [online] Newark: ACM, pp. 243–244. Available at: https://doi.org/10.1145/2910896.2925452 [Accessed 1 Mar. 2018].

Alam, S., Nelson, M.L., Van de Sompel, H., Balakireva, L., Shankar, H., and Rosenthal, D.S.H. (2015) 'Web archive profiling through CDX summarization', in: *TPDL '15, Proceedings of Theory and Practice of Digital Libraries*, [online] Poznań: Springer, pp. 3–14. Available at: https://doi.org/10.1007/978-3-319-24592-8_1 [Accessed 1 Mar. 2018].

Alam, S., Nelson, M.L., Van de Sompel, H., and Rosenthal, D.S.H. (2016a) 'Web archive profiling through fulltext search', in: *TPDL '16, Proceedings of Theory and Practice of Digital Libraries*, [online] Hannover: Springer, pp. 121–132. Available at: https://doi.org/10.1007/978-3-319-43997-6_10 [Accessed 1 Mar. 2018].

Alam, S., Nelson, M.L., Van de Sompel, H., Balakireva, L.L., Shankar, H., and Rosenthal, D.S.H. (2016b) 'Web archive profiling through CDX summarization', *International Journal on Digital Libraries*, [online] 17(3):223–228. Available at: https://doi.org/10.1007/s0079 [Accessed 1 Mar. 2018].

AlNoamany, Y. (2014) '*Using Web Archives to Enrich the Live Web Experience Through Storytelling*'. PhD. Old Dominion University, Department of Computer Science.

AlSum, A., Weigle, M.C., Nelson, M.L., and Van de Sompel, H. (2013) 'Profiling web archive coverage for top-level domain and content language', in: *TPDL '13, Proceedings of Theory and Practice of Digital Libraries*, [online] Valetta: Springer, pp. 60–71. Available at: https://doi.org/10.1007/978-3-642-40501-3_7 [Accessed 1 Mar. 2018].

AlSum, A., Weigle, M.C., Nelson, M.L., and Van de Sompel, H. (2014) 'Profiling web archive coverage for top-level domain and content language', *International Journal on Digital Libraries*, [online] 14(3):149–166.

Available at: https://doi.org/10.1007/s00799-014-0118-y [Accessed 1 Mar. 2018].

Bailey, J., Grotke, A., Hanna, K., Hartman, C., McCain, E., Moffatt, C., and Taylor, N. (2013) *Web archiving in the United States: A 2013 survey*. [online] Available at: https://blogs.loc.gov/thesignal/2014/10/results-from-the-2013-ndsa-u-s-web-archiving-survey/ [Accessed 1 Mar. 2018].

Bar-Yossef, Z., Broder, A.Z., Kumar, R., and Tomkins, A. (2004) 'Sic transit gloria telae: Towards an understanding of the web's decay', in: *WWW '04, Proceedings of the 13th International Conference on World Wide Web*, [online] New York: ACM, pp. 328–337. Available at: https://doi.org/10.1145/988672.988716 [Accessed 1 Mar. 2018].

Berners-Lee, T. (1991) *The original http as defined in 1991*. [online] Available at: https://www.w3.org/Protocols/HTTP/AsImplemented.html [Accessed 1 Mar. 2018].

Berners-Lee, T. (1996) *Web architecture: Generic resources*. [online] Available at: http://www.w3.org/DesignIssues/Generic.html [Accessed 1 Mar. 2018].

Berners-Lee, T., Fielding, R., and Frystyk, H. (1996) *Hypertext Transfer Protocol – HTTP/1.0, Internet RFC 1945*. [online] Available at: https://tools.ietf.org/html/rfc1945 [Accessed 1 Mar. 2018].

Bornand, N.J., Balakireva, L., and Van de Sompel, H. (2016) 'Routing memento requests using binary classifiers', in: *JCDL '16, Proceedings of the 16th ACM/IEEE-CS Joint Conference on Digital Libraries*, [online] Newark: ACM, pp. 63–72. Available at: https://doi.org/10.1145/2910896.2910899 [Accessed 1 Mar. 2018].

Brunelle, J.F., Kelly, M., SalahEldeen, H., Weigle, M.C., and Nelson, M.L. (2014) 'Not all mementos are created equal: Measuring the impact of missing resources', in: *JCDL '14, Proceedings of the 14th ACM/IEEE-CS Joint Conference on Digital Libraries*, [online] London: ACM, pp. 321–330. Available at: https://doi.org/10.1109/JCDL.2014.6970187 [Accessed 1 Mar. 2018].

Brunelle, J.F., Kelly, M., SalahEldeen, H., Weigle, M.C., and Nelson, M.L. (2015) 'Not all mementos are created equal: Measuring the impact of missing resources', *International Journal on Digital Libraries*, [online] 16(3–4):283–301. Available at: https://doi.org/10.1007/s00799-015-0150-6 [Accessed 1 Mar. 2018].

Brunelle, J.F., Nelson, M.L., Balakireva, L., Sanderson, R., and Van de Sompel, H. (2013) 'Evaluating sitestory with the ApacheBench tool', in: *TPDL '13, International Conference on Theory and Practice of Digital Libraries*, [online] Valetta: Springer, pp. 204–215. Available at: https://doi.org/10.1007/978-3-642-40501-3_20 [Accessed 1 Mar. 2018].

Callan, J. (2002) 'Distributed Information Retrieval' in: Croft W.B. (ed) Advances in Information Retrieval. The Information Retrieval Series, vol 7. Springer, Boston, MA, [online]. Available at: https://doi.org/10.1007/0-306-47019-5_5 [Accessed 1 Mar. 2018].

Caplan, P., and Arms, W.Y. (1999) 'Reference linking for journal articles', *D-Lib Magazine*, [online] 5(7/8). Available at: https://doi.org/10.1045/july99-caplan [Accessed 1 Mar. 2018].

Crocker, D.H. (1982) *Standard for the Format of ARPA Internet Text Messages, Internet RFC-822*. [online] Available at: https://tools.ietf.org/html/rfc822 [Accessed 1 Mar. 2018].

Fielding, R., Gettys, J., Mogul, J., Frystyk, H., Masinter, L., Leach, P., and Berners-Lee, T. (1999) *Hypertext Transfer Protocol – HTTP/1.1, Internet RFC-2616*. [online] Available at: https://tools.ietf.org/html/rfc2616 [Accessed 1 Mar. 2018].

Fielding, R.T. (2000) *'Architectural Styles and the Design of Network-based Software Architectures'*. PhD. University of California, Irvine, Department of Computer Science.

Fuhrig, L.S. (2014) *Tracking down the elusive 'treasure house for learning'*. [blog] Smithsonian Institution Archives blog. Available at: https://siarchives.si.edu/blog/tracking-down-elusive-'treasure-house-learning' [Accessed 1 Mar. 2018].

Gomes, D., Miranda, J., and Costa, M. (2011) 'A survey on web archiving initiatives', in: *TPDL '11, Proceedings of Theory and Practice of Digital Libraries*, [online] Berlin: Springer, pp. 408–420. Available at: https://doi.org/10.1007/978-3-642-24469-8_41 [Accessed 1 Mar. 2018].

Jacobs, I., and Walsh, N. (2004) *Architecture of the world wide web, volume one. Technical Report W3C Recommendation 15 December*

*2004, W3C*. [online] Available at: https://www.w3.org/TR/webarch/ [Accessed 1 Mar. 2018].

Jones, S.M., Nelson, M.L., Shankar, H., and Van de Sompel, H. (2014) *Bringing web time travel to mediawiki: An assessment of the memento mediawiki extension*. [online] Available at: http://arxiv.org/abs/1405.2330 [Accessed 1 Mar. 2018].

Jones, S.M., Van de Sompel, H., and Nelson, M.L. (2016a) 'Avoiding spoilers: Wiki time travel with Sheldon Cooper', *International Journal on Digital Libraries*, [online] 19(1):77–93. Available at: https://doi.org/10.1007/s00799-016-0200-8 [Accessed 1 Mar. 2018].

Jones, S.M., Van de Sompel, H., Shankar, H., Klein, M., Tobin, R., and Grover, C. (2016b) 'Scholarly context adrift: Three out of four uri references lead to changed content', *PloS One*, [online] 11(12):e0167475. Available at: https://doi.org/10.1371/journal.pone.0171057 [Accessed 1 Mar. 2018].

Kelly, M., Nelson, M.L., and Weigle, M.C. (2014a) 'The archival acid test: Evaluating archive performance on advanced HTML and JavaScript', in: *JCDL '14, Proceedings of the 14th ACM/IEEE-CS Joint Conference on Digital Libraries*, [online] London: ACM, pp. 25–28. Available at: https://doi.org/10.1109/JCDL.2014.6970146 [Accessed 1 Mar. 2018].

Kelly, M., Nelson, M.L., and Weigle, M.C. (2014b) 'Mink: Integrating the live and archived web viewing experience using web browsers and Memento', in: *JCDL '14, Proceedings of the 14th ACM/IEEE-CS Joint Conference on Digital Libraries*, [online] London: ACM, pp. 267–276. Available at: https://doi.org/10.1109/JCDL.2014.6970229 [Accessed 1 Mar. 2018].

Klein, M., Van de Sompel, H., Sanderson, R., Shankar, H., Balakireva, L., Zhou, K., and Tobin, R. (2014) 'Scholarly context not found: One in five articles suffers from reference rot', *PloS One*, [online] 9(12):e115253. Available at: https://doi.org/10.1371/journal.pone.0115253 [Accessed 1 Mar. 2018].

Masanes, J. (2006) *Web Archiving*. Springer, Berlin, Heidelberg.

Mohr, G., Kimpton, M., Stack, M., and Ranitovic, I. (2004) 'Introduction to heritrix, an archival quality web crawler', in: *IWAW '04, 4th International Web Archiving Workshop*, [online] Bath. Available at: https://web.archive.org/web/20170809135759/http://iwaw.europarchive.org/04/Mohr.pdf [Accessed 1 Mar. 2018].

Negulescu, K.C. (2010) *Web archiving @ the internet Archive; presentation at the 2010 Digital Preservation Partners Meeting*. [online] Available at: http://www.digitalpreservation.gov/meetings/documents/ndiipp10/NDIIPP-072110FinalIA.ppt [Accessed 1 Mar. 2018].

Nelson, M.L. (2011) *Memento-Datetime is not Last-Modified*. [blog] Web Science and Digital Library Research Group. Available at: http://ws-dl.blogspot.com/2010/11/2010-11-05-memento-datetime-is-not-last.html [Accessed 1 Mar. 2018].

Nelson, M.L. (2013) *Right-click to the past – Memento for Chrome*. [blog] Web Science and Digital Library Research Group. Available at: http://ws-dl.blogspot.com/2013/10/2013-10-14-right-click-to-past-memento.html [Accessed 1 Mar. 2018].

Ritchie, D., and Thompson, K. (1974) 'The UNIX time-sharing system', *Communications of the ACM*, [online] 17(7):365–375. Available at: https://doi.org/10.1145/361011.361061 [Accessed 1 Mar. 2018].

Rossi, A. (2016) *Robots.txt Files and Archiving .gov and .mil Websites*. [blog] Internet Archive Blogs. Available at: https://blog.archive.org/2016/12/17/robots-txt-gov-mil-websites/ [Accessed 1 Mar. 2018].

Sanderson, R. (2012) 'Global web archive integration with Memento', in: *JCDL '06, Proceedings of the 12th ACM/IEEE Joint Conference on Digital Libraries*, [online] Washington: ACM, pp. 379–380. Available at: https://doi.org/10.1145/2232817.2232900 [Accessed 1 Mar. 2018].

Sanderson, R., Shankar, H., Ainsworth, S., McCown, F., and Adams, S. (2011) 'Implementing time travel for the web', *Code4Lib Journal*, [online] 13. Available at: http://journal.code4lib.org/articles/4979 [Accessed 1 Mar. 2018].

Tweedy, H., McCown, F., and Nelson, M.L. (2013) 'A Memento web browser for iOS', in: *JCDL '013, Proceedings of the 13th ACM/IEEE-CS Joint Conference on Digital Libraries*, [online] Indianapolis: ACM, pp. 371–372. Available at: https://doi.org/10.1145/2467696.2467764 [Accessed 1 Mar. 2018].

Van de Sompel, H., and Nelson, M.L. (2015) 'Reminiscing about 15 years of interoperability efforts', *D-Lib Magazine*, [online] 21(11/22). Available at: https://doi.org/10.1045/november2015-vandesompel [Accessed 1 Mar. 2018].

Van de Sompel, H., Nelson, M.L., and Sanderson, R. (2013) *HTTP framework for time-based access to resource states – Memento, Internet RFC 7089*. [online] Available at: http://tools.ietf.org/html/rfc7089 [Accessed 1 Mar. 2018].

Van de Sompel, H., Nelson, M.L., Sanderson, R., Balakireva, L.L., Ainsworth, S., and Shankar, H. (2009). *Memento: Time Travel for the Web*. [online] Available at: http://arxiv.org/abs/0911.1112 [Accessed 1 Mar. 2018].

Van de Sompel, H., Sanderson, R., Nelson, M.L., Balakireva, L.L., Shankar, H., and Ainsworth, S. (2010) 'An HTTP-based versioning mechanism for linked data', in: *LDOW '010, Proceedings of the Linked Data on the Web Workshop,* [online] Raleigh: CEUR 628. Available at: http://ceur-ws.org/Vol-628/ldow2010_paper13.pdf [Accessed 1 Mar. 2018].

Van de Sompel, H., Shankar, H., Wincewicz, R., and Nelson, M.L. (2015) *Robust links – link decoration*. [online] Available at: http://robustlinks.mementoweb.org/spec/ [Accessed 1 Mar. 2018].

Zittrain, J., Albert, K., and Lessig, L. (2014) 'Perma: Scoping and addressing the problem of link and reference rot in legal citations', *Legal Information Management*, [online] 14(02):88–99. Available at: https://doi.org/10.1017/S1472669614000255 [Accessed 1 Mar. 2018].

# Hypertext before the Web – or, What the Web Could Have Been

Belinda Barnet

Historiography is always guided by specific tropes; it is 'infected by what it touches as the past' Demeulenaere (2003). Much has been written about the history of hypertext over the last 20 years, and I've contributed to that literature; in the process I've been infected by the vision behind the early systems from the 60s and 70s. This might be because I've got to know some of the inventors – I conducted 22 interviews with inventors for my book on pre-web systems *Memory Machines* (Barnet, 2013) – and drank the same Kool-Aid. The first system was built in counterculture-soaked 1960s California, though, so a bit of dreaming is appropriate, along with the occasional Yoga Workstation. This was an era when people had grand visions for their pre-web hypertext systems, when they believed that the solution to the world's problems might lie in finding a way to organize the mess of human knowledge: to represent its true interconnections.

Now for the important bit: this story stops before the Web. More accurately, it stops before hypertext became synonymous with the Web; as Ted Nelson[1], who coined the term 'hypertext' among other things, put it to me in 1999, 'People saw the Web and they thought, "Oh, that's hypertext, that's how it's meant to look"'. But hypertext is not the Web; the Web is one particular implementation of hypertext. In this chapter we will use Ted Nelson's definition of hypertext: branching and responding text read at a computer screen (Nelson, 1992). The Web is without a doubt the most successful and prevalent version of hypertext, but it is also an arguably limited one. Hypertext existed well before the Web – the systems here were imagined (and in some cases built and obsolete) well before Google and Facebook. Insofar as the Web is a hypertext system, it continues an already established line of evolution, and it is important to understand this pre-history to fully understand the Web.

The first hypertext systems were deep and richly connected, and in some respects more powerful than the Web. These early systems were not, however, connected to hundreds of millions of other users. You could not reach out through FRESS and read a page hosted in Thailand or Libya. The early systems worked on their own set of documents in their own unique environments. Although Nelson certainly envisioned that Xanadu would have the domestic penetration of the Web, and NLS had nifty collaborative tools and chalk-passing protocols, none of the early 'built' systems we look at either briefly or in depth in this chapter – NLS, HES and FRESS – was designed to accommodate literally billions of users. That's something only the Web can do.

As Jay Bolter put it in our interview,

> What the World Wide Web did was two things. One is that it compromised as it were on the 'vision' of hypertext. It said, 'This is the kind of linkage it's always going to be, it's always going to work in this way', [but] more importantly it said that the really interesting things happen when your links can cross from one computer to another… So global hypertext – which is what the Web is – turned out to be the way that you could really engage, well, ultimately hundreds of millions of users. (Bolter, 2011)

The goal of this chapter is to explore the visions of the early hypertext pioneers, starting over 60 years ago, and in the process, to broaden our conception of what hypertext could be. The chapter begins by exploring NLS, then Xanadu and on to HES.

## DOUG ENGELBART'S ON-LINE SYSTEM (NLS)

Dr Douglas Carl Engelbart, who died in 2013, was a softly spoken man. His voice was low yet persuasive, as though 'his words have been attenuated by layers of meditation', his friend Nilo Lindgren wrote in 1971 (Rheingold, 2000: 178). I struggled to hear him in our interview, being deaf myself, but that didn't matter; he had been describing the same vision in great detail to journalists, historians and engineers for over 60 years. Engelbart wanted to improve the model of the human, to 'boost our capacity to deal with complexity' as a species (Engelbart, 1999).

> Here's a human… He's got all these capabilities within his skin we can make use of, a lot of mental capabilities we know of, and some of it he's even conscious of. Those are marvellous machines there – motor machinery to actuate the outside world, and sensor and perceptual machinery to get the idea of what's going on… (Engelbart, 1998: 213)

For Engelbart, the most important element of the 'human system' was language; language is a powerful machine. Engelbart would seek to harness its nonlinear relationships with a computer system and externalize its 'networked' structure.

Engelbart still remembers reading about Vannevar Bush's Memex (hypothetical proto-hypertext system that Bush described in his 1945 *The Atlantic Monthly* article 'As We May Think'), and the moment when he became 'infected' with the idea of building a means to extend and navigate this great pool of human knowledge. He was a military radar technician out in the Philippines when he first picked up a reprint of Bush's article, in the summer of 1945, and wandered into a Red Cross library that was built up on stilts to read it. News of Hiroshima was devastatingly fresh; Engelbart was 20 years old and deep in thought (Barnet, 2013). He was wondering how he could 'maximize [his] contribution to humankind' as an engineer (Engelbart, 1999).

In this article Bush looked towards the postwar world as an engineer and predicted an exponential increase in human knowledge, especially scientific and technological knowledge. How are we to keep track of it all? How are we to prevent great ideas from being lost? Some ideas are like seeds. 'Or viruses. If they are in the air at the right time, they will infect exactly those people who are most susceptible to putting their lives in the idea's service' (Rheingold, 2000: 176). Although he didn't think about the article again for many years, the ideas in it infected Engelbart.

But five years after he had read 'As We May Think' in the Philippines, Engelbart claims, 'I formulated [my] goal on…human intellectual effectiveness' (Engelbart, 1962a: 236). These three 'flashes' were to become the framework he worked from for the rest of his career:

1 FLASH-1: The difficulty of mankind's problems was increasing at a greater rate than our ability to cope.
2 FLASH-2: Boosting mankind's ability to cope with complex, urgent problems would be an attractive candidate as an arena in which a young person might 'make the most difference'.
3 FLASH-3: Ahah – graphic vision surges forth of me sitting at a large CRT console, working in ways that are rapidly evolving in front of my eyes (beginning from memories of the radar-screen consoles I used to service). (Engelbart, 1988: 189)

This vision of a radar-screen console attached to a computer is important. Engelbart transferred this technology from the radars he was servicing in the Philippines to computers as he had learnt about them in engineering school (CRT phosphors came into common use around WWII). This image of a human sitting at a screen is the image from which all future work would depart. By the time Engelbart started work on NLS ten years later, progress had been made on 'presenting computer-stored information to the human… by which a cathode-ray-tube (of which the television picture tube is a familiar example) can be made to present symbols on their screens of quite good brightness, clarity, and with considerable freedom as to the form of the symbol' (Engelbart, 1962b). In 1951, however, Engelbart had to mentally extrapolate from radar screens. As he told me in 1999,

> I put together what I knew about computers and what I knew about radar circuitry etc. to picture working interactively, and it just grew from there' (Engelbart, 1999).

This was a radical idea in the 1950s. At that time, computers were large electronic devices stored in air-conditioned rooms, at many degrees of separation from the 'user'. They were attended to by technicians and fed their information out to these technicians on punch cards and printouts. The idea that a screen might be attached to a computer, and that humans might interact directly via this surface, was far left field.

The computer, screen and mouse would become Engelbart's parallel to Memex's microfilm storage desk, tablet display and stylus. With these technologies, Engelbart would 'update' an image of potentiality from a different era and bring it to digital computing. But his ideas did not garner the peer support Engelbart was seeking.

> After I'd given a talk at Stanford, [three angry guys] got me later outside at a table. They said, 'All you're talking about is information retrieval.' I said no. They said, 'YES, it is, we're professionals and we know, so we're telling you, you don't know enough so stay out of it, 'cause goddamit, you're bolloxing it all up. You're in engineering, not information retrieval.' (Engelbart, 1999)

Computers, in large part, were still seen as number crunchers, and computer engineers had no business talking about the human beings who used these machines. Fortunately, one of the few people who had the disciplinary background to be able to understand the new conceptual framework was moving through the ranks at the Advanced Research Projects Agency (ARPA). This man was J.C.R. Licklider, a psychologist from MIT. 'The hope is that, in not too many years, human brains and computing machines will be coupled together very tightly, and the resulting partnership will think as no human brain has ever thought', wrote Licklider in a 1960 paper called 'Man-Computer Symbiosis' (Licklider, 1960: 131).

Licklider began financing projects that developed thought-amplifying technologies. ARPA support began in 1963, 'at varying levels – during 1965, about eighty thousand dollars' (Bardini, 2000: 23). But as Bardini points out (in his book and in a personal communication), it was Bob Taylor, initially working as a psychologist at NASA, who mustered the strongest support for the project. Initially he put in 85,000 dollars from NASA mid 1964 to mid 1965 (Bardini, 2000: 23). Then when he moved from NASA to ARPA in 1964 he told Engelbart that IPTO 'was prepared to contribute a million dollars initially to provide one of the new time-sharing systems, and about half a million dollars a year to support the augmentation research' (Rheingold, 2000: 86). That is the equivalent of around 14 million in today's dollars.

Around this time Engelbart asked a bright young SRI engineer named Bill English if he'd present a paper for him. English said yes, and joined Engelbart's project shortly thereafter. As English told me in 2011, 'I saw what he was doing and I was interested in it. So I joined him and that's how it all began' (English, 2011). He became Engelbart's chief engineer in 1964, and began work on some of the basic ideas we'll explore in the next section.

Bill Duvall joined SRI in 1966, but didn't start work on the NLS project until 1968. He asked to be moved onto Engelbart's team, but first he had to meet with the head of engineering at SRI.

> [He] was a very traditional engineer. I was a 24-year-old kid, or 23 years old, and he had this big corner office that had bookshelves to the ceiling and the little ladder that goes around, and a big desk. He sat on the other side of his desk, and I sat in a chair and he looked at me, and he said, 'You don't really think what they're doing up there is science, do you?' I think that reflected a lot of the official attitude towards what Doug was doing. (Duvall, 2011)

The freshly outfitted laboratory, the Augmentation Research Center (ARC), began its work in 1965. It started with a series of experiments focused on the way people select objects on a computer screen. In the context of screen-based interactivity, Engelbart and English's 'mouse' consistently beat other devices for fast, accurate selection in a series of controlled tests. Yet it took over 20 years to enter the commercial market, a time period that Engelbart considers strikingly long (Engelbart, 1988: 196).

At the heart of NLS was a basic philosophy that you should be able to link to anything, anywhere ('unless there was a specific reason not to do so' (Duvall, 2011)). This approach to information was entirely new – an approach that assumed from the outset that connectivity is important, that the relationship between and among ideas was just as important as the unit of information (or 'statement') itself. As Duvall remembers,

> The thing that I would say distinguished NLS from a lot of other development projects was that it was sort of the first – I'm not sure what the right word is – 'holistic' is almost a word that comes to mind – project that tried to use computers to deal with documents in a two-dimensional fashion rather than in a one-dimensional fashion. (Duvall, 2011)

Content insertion and navigation involved four basic commands: Insert, Delete, Move and Copy. The mouse served as a pointer to indicate where content was to be inserted or deleted in existing text. Most important, however, the Link function allowed cross-referencing to another statement – and the user could define cross-references at any level in the hierarchy. Links were character strings within a statement 'indicating a relationship' (Engelbart, 1999) to another statement, and they could be made in the same file or between different files.

The NLS design changed as it was created, evolving around the technical activities of the project team itself as they documented their efforts. In the process of designing the software, the team generated a number of technical reports, source code versions, communications, release notes, problems and associated solutions. These were linked together and tracked by date and version.

Consequently, between 1969 and 1971 (Bardini, 2000) NLS was changed to include an electronic filing arrangement that served as a linked archive of the development team's efforts. This eventually cross-referenced over 100,000 items (Engelbart, 1988). It was called the software Journal, the most explicit model of a hypertextual environment with embedded associative links to surface in the digital environment in the 1960s.

As mentioned previously, the entire NLS system was set up for perfect storage and recall. Everything was tracked and identifiable. Every object in the document was intrinsically addressable, and most important, these addresses never disappeared (Engelbart, 1999). They were permanent, attached to the object itself, which meant that they followed the object wherever it was stored, so links could be made at any stage to any object in the system. As Duvall remembers,

> [In NLS] we had it that every object in the document was intrinsically addressable, right from the word 'go'. It didn't matter what date a document's development was, you could give somebody a link right into anything, so you could actually have things that point right to a character or a word or something. (Duvall, 2011)

The NLS team called this a 'frozen state' addressing scheme (Engelbart, 1997), which is in contrast to the World Wide Web, where the finest level of intrinsic addressability is the URL (Universal Resource Locator, a character string that identifies an Internet resource, invented by Tim Berners-Lee in 1994[2]). Unlike the NLS object-specific address, the URL is simply a location on a server; it is not attached to the object itself. That said, NLS was working in its own little environment, on its own documents – not with billions of users.

By 1968 NLS had matured into a massive database and set of paths through this database, the first digital hypertext system. It was time to take NLS out of the Petri dish and set it to work in front of the engineering community. Engelbart took an immense risk and applied for a special session at the ACM/IEEE-CS Fall Joint Computer Conference in San Francisco in December 1968. 'The nice people at ARPA and NASA, who were funding us, effectively had to say "Don't tell me!", because if this had flopped, we would have gotten in trouble' (Engelbart, 1988: 203).

The conference was set up using a video projector pointing at a huge, 20-foot screen that was linked to a host computer and piped back to the group at SRI via a temporary microwave antenna. The setup was very expensive, and although no special system capabilities were employed (NLS was run just as it was used back at the lab), the organizational and presentational machinery used almost all the remaining research funds for the year.

Engelbart sat up on the stage beneath the projection screen, a mouse in one hand and his other hand playing a special one-handed keyset. He manipulated the audience's attention by controlling their view of the information being explored; he drilled down through the data structure and presented it in multiple different views, each piece connected to the last by a link. The screen was divided into neat windows containing explanatory text or graphics about NLS, and also about the presentation itself in the hypertext Journal. It was dubbed 'The Mother of all Demos' by Andries van Dam. A video of this demo is now available on the Web.

This was the first public appearance of the mouse and the first public appearance of hypertext, screen splitting, computer-supported associative linking, computer conferencing and a mixed text/graphics interface. It proceeded without a hitch and received a standing ovation (Rheingold, 2000).

As a result of the NLS demo, many of the user interface technologies from NLS also migrated into computing over the next few years, the mouse in particular. Ted Nelson eventually incorporated the mouse into his Xanadu design (Barnet, 2013). NLS also allowed consideration of the modern windows-icon-menu-pointing-device (WIMP) interface.

Engelbart was working from a vision he had as a young engineer. This vision changed the world. Technical visions have no essence; there is no transcendent design, no Platonic form we are striving towards. There is, however, a recurrent dream – an elusive 'blessed break' – and this dream is an ancient one. It comes from long-standing cultural desires and anxieties about the ephemerality of human memory and knowledge.

The dream is to create a perfect archive for human knowledge, a machine that might 'extend, through replication, human mental experience' (Nyce and Kahn, 1991: 124) and capture the interconnected structure of knowledge itself. Most important, this would be a machine that we can control, whose workings are transparent to us and whose trails do not fade. Which brings us to the next system – my favorite system and recurring vision: the Magical Place of Literary Memory: Xanadu®.

## THE MAGICAL PLACE OF LITERARY MEMORY: XANADU

> What I thought would be called Xanadu® is called the World Wide Web and works differently, but has the same penetration. (Nelson, 1999)

It was a vision in a dream. A computer filing system that would store and deliver the great body of human literature, in all its historical versions and with all its messy interconnections, acknowledging authorship, ownership, quotation and linkage. Like the Web, but much better: no links would ever be broken, no documents would ever be lost, and copyright and ownership would be scrupulously preserved. The Magical Place of Literary Memory: Xanadu. In this place, users would be able to mark and annotate any document, see and intercompare versions of documents side by side, follow visible hyperlinks from both ends ('two-way links') and reuse content pieces that stay connected to their original source document. There would be multiple ways to view all this on a computer screen, but the canonical view would be side-by-side parallel strips with visible connections. Just imagine. This vision – which is older than the Web, and aspects of it are older than *personal computing* – belongs to hypertext pioneer Theodor Holm Nelson, who dubbed the project Xanadu in October 1966.[3]

The name comes from the famous poem by Samuel Taylor Coleridge, 'Kubla Khan'. In his tale of the poem's origin, Coleridge claimed to have woken from a laudanum-laced reverie with 'two or three hundred' lines of poetry in his head. He had noted down but a few lines when he was interrupted by a visitor, and when he returned to his work later he found that the memories had blurred irretrievably. His mythical landscape, this vision of Xanadu, had passed away 'like the images on the surface of a stream into which a stone had been cast' (Coleridge, cited in Nelson, 1987: 142).

One of Nelson's most cherished memories is based on a vision of gently moving water. When he was about four or five he trailed his hand in the water as his grandfather rowed a boat. He studied the different 'places' in the water as they passed through his fingers, the 'places that at one instant were next to each other, then separated as my finger passed. They rejoined, but no longer in the same way' (Nelson, 2010: 35). These connections were infinite in number and in complexity, and they changed as the water moved. It was a religious experience, a vision that has stayed with him for 70 years. At that moment he started thinking about what he calls 'profuse connection', the interconnections that permeate life and thought: How can one manage all the changing relationships? How can one represent profuse connection? Xanadu was proposed as a vast digital network to house this corpus of ideas and evidential materials, facilitated by a special linking system.

The story of Xanadu is the greatest image of potentiality in the evolution of hypertext. Nelson invented a new vocabulary to describe his vision, much of which has become integrated into contemporary hypermedia theory and practice – for instance, the words 'hypertext' and 'hypermedia'. As he told me in 1999, 'I think I've put more words in the dictionary than Lewis Carroll. Every significant change in an idea means a new term'. Nelson came up with many significant changes, and consequently many new terms, some of which I discuss below. He also recruited or inspired some of the most visionary programmers and developers in the history of computing, many of whom went on to develop the first hypertext products (although this doesn't impress him: 'the problem with inspiring people is that they then try to credit you with things you don't like' (Nelson, 2010).

Much has been written about Project Xanadu over the years (the ones I cite throughout this chapter are Landow, 1992; Rheingold, 2000). Nelson himself doesn't have the time to keep up with it all – and even when he does, as he put it to me in 2010, 'anything people write about me will be insufficiently praising, and so it's very hard to read it' (his comments on my own work were prolific). The remarkable thing about Xanadu is that, despite countless setbacks, it refuses to die. Its logo is, appropriately enough, the Eternal Flaming X. Paisley and Butler (cited in Smith, 1991: 262) have noted that 'scientists and technologists are guided by "images of potentiality" – the untested theories, unanswered questions and unbuilt devices that they view as their agenda for five years, ten years, and longer'. Often accused of hand waving and lucid dreaming, Nelson's Xanadu has nonetheless become the most important vision in the history of computing.

Nelson wears a lanyard across his neck and shoulder with three pens attached to it (when I first met him in 1999 it had sticky notes, at another point a stapler – the 'system is evolving' as he put it in a personal communication, 2012). He has been wearing it since 1997. The belt is filled with tools to connect things with, tools to deal with a world of paper. Like Bush, Nelson is painfully aware that ideas are easily lost in conventional indexing systems, that they are disconnected from each other, and that 'serious writing or research' demands connecting ideas together. Frustrated by the lack of a global, real-world system that might do this for him, and 'outraged' by the confines of paper (Nelson, 1998: 1–2), he feels the need to do this manually.

Nelson's struggle against the paradigm of paper led him to design an alternative. In 1960, at Harvard University, he took a computer course for the humanities, 'and my world exploded' (Nelson, 2010: 99). He understood immediately that computers were all-purpose machines that could be put in the service of information handling. Like Engelbart, he did not believe that computers were mathematical tools for engineers. He saw a solution to his problem of information handling, and he also saw a future where paper might be eliminated. 'The prison of paper, enforcing sequence and rectangularity, had been the enemy of authors and editors for thousands of years; now at last we could break free' (Nelson, 2010: 120).

One of the first ideas was based on his own 'terrible problem' keeping notes on file cards. The problem was that his cards really needed to be in several different places at once; new projects were built on earlier ideas, new documents were built on earlier ideas, so these items should be reusable by reference. Perhaps the computer might solve that problem; it could link them together. This idea would later prove important in the design of Xanadu.

> Many of my file cards belonged in several places at once – several different sequences or projects. Each card – call it now an entry or an item – should be stored only once. Then each project or sequence would be a list of those items. (Nelson, 2010: 103)

Imagine if the same item could appear in multiple places. You could connect each item to its original by an addressing method and retrieve them on a computer screen. Because this would be reuse by reference rather than by copying, you could trace each item back to its original source. This idea – that you should be able to see all the contexts of reuse, and that you should be able to trace items back to their original source – would 'drive my work to the edge of madness' (Nelson, 2010: 104). It would later become the kernel of Nelson's most innovative idea: transclusion. Transclusion, and also the ability to visually compare prior or alternative versions of the same document on-screen ('intercomparison') were integral to the design of Xanadu. Over the next 40 years, Nelson would hone these ideas and experiment with them in various incarnations.

In 1960 Nelson announced his term project: a writing system for the IBM 7090, the only computer at Harvard at the time, stored in a big, air-conditioned room at the Smithsonian Observatory. In the 1960s computers were 'possessed only by huge organizations to be used for corporate tasks or intricate scientific calculations' (Nelson, 1965: 135). The idea that expensive processing time might be wasted on writing, of all things, was deemed crazy by the engineering community. Nelson ignored this. He proposed a machine-language program to store documents in the computer, change them on-screen with various editorial operations and print them out. But this was no mere word processor (which in any case didn't exist at the time); Nelson envisioned the user would be able to compare alternative and prior versions of the same document on-screen.

The second part of Nelson's idea took shape in the early 1960s, when there was 'a lot of talk around Cambridge [Massachusetts, where Harvard is located] about Computer-Assisted Instruction, for which there was a lot of money' (Nelson, 1992: 1/26). It was not so much a design at this point, Nelson stressed in response to my request for paper, 'it was an idea that may have been on only one file card' (Nelson, 2010). At this time he conceived of what he called 'the thousand theories program', an explorable computer-assisted instruction program that would allow the user to study different theories and subjects by taking different trajectories through a network of information.

This led to another idea, which Nelson drafted as an academic paper while teaching sociology at Vassar College in 1965. He wants to stress at this point that there was no single eureka moment as 'the ever-changing designs had been swirling in my head for five years' (Nelson, 2012). The concept was clear enough, however, to put it down on paper. This revised design combined two key ideas: side-by-side intercomparison and the reuse of elements (transclusion). He thought about the architecture of the system and decided to have sequences of information that could be linked sideways. As with his first design, this would all occur on a computer screen, visually, in real time. He called this system 'Zippered Lists'.

Zippered Lists permitted linking between documents: like the teeth in a zipper, items in one sequence could become part of another ('EXCEPT', Nelson wrote in response to this chapter, 'the two sides of the zipper don't have to be in the same order'). Versions of a document could be intercompared; an item could be an important heading in one sequence and a trivial point in another, and all items could be written or retrieved in a nonsequential fashion. Links could be made between large sections, small sections or single paragraphs. Writers could trace the evolution of an idea.

Crucially, the design also got him published. Nelson's first paper explaining the term 'hypertext' was presented at the ACM 20th National Conference in August 1965. It was not the first time that the word 'hypertext' had appeared in print, though. That was in an invitation to a talk Nelson gave at Vassar College, 'Computers, Creativity and the Nature of the Written Word', on 5 January 1965. (Actually, it's the word 'hypertexts'. A copy of this invitation appears in *Possiplex*.)

One of the first people who thought they might try to build *part* of Nelson's design was Andries van Dam (I stress 'part' here because van Dam had ideas of his own that he wanted to explore at the same time, such as print text editing). We explore this in the next section.

Van Dam would be the first person to attempt to build part of Nelson's vision.

## SEEING AND MAKING CONNECTIONS: HES AND FRESS

We will now trace the development of two important hypertext systems built at Brown: the Hypertext Editing System (HES), co-designed by Ted Nelson and van Dam and developed by van Dam's students, and the File Retrieval and Editing System (FRESS), designed by van Dam and his students. Brown University has played a major role in the development of hypertext systems and humanities computing since 1967, due in no small part to van Dam's work in this area, and the Institute for Research in Information and Scholarship (IRIS) he helped establish there with William Shipp and Norman Meyrowitz in 1983.

Ted Nelson was co-designer of HES, and his ideas about hypertext inspired the HES project in the first place; van Dam credited Nelson for this contribution both in our interviews (1999; 2011) and in his public talks and published work. Nelson still feels, however, that he has been 'given no more credit than his [van Dam's] undergraduate students' (Nelson, 2012). Unfortunately, Nelson fell out with the HES team during its design and implementation in 1967, and he has stated in several interviews with the author that he was unhappy with the result. He is bitter about the experience, largely because he feels his vision was sidelined in favor of print text editing (Nelson, 1999; 2011). We explore this in more detail shortly.

Along with Engelbart's landmark NLS system, HES and FRESS constitute the first generation of hypertext systems. These are not dusty old antiques from the dawn of computing science, however; in many respects, FRESS by 1968 was more interactive than present-day HTML. As working prototype systems, HES and FRESS had technical chutzpah.

## The Design of HES

Van Dam bumped into Nelson at the 1967 Spring Joint Computer Conference in Atlantic City. Passionate and eloquent, Nelson told van Dam about what he'd been doing since he left Swarthmore: hypertext. 'He had nothing to show for this idea, no prototypes or work in the sense that computer scientists talk about work – i.e. software, algorithms, things that are concrete', recalled van Dam (1999). What Nelson did have was a vision of what hypertext should look like, and an infectious enthusiasm for the idea. Nelson had in mind an entirely new genre for literature, and he had a new word to describe this vision: hypertext.

> Nelson's vision seduced me. I really loved his way of thinking about writing, editing and annotating as a scholarly activity, and putting tools together to support that... He talked me into working on the world's first hypertext system and that sounded cool. (van Dam, 1999)

Van Dam gathered a team together at Brown and began work later that year, with the objective of trying out this hypertext concept. He stressed in his communications to me that the idea was never to 'realize' Xanadu in its entirety. The intention was much smaller and more circumspect: to 'implement a *part* of his vision. We were not able to implement or even understand the breadth and scope of that [larger] vision' (van Dam, 2011). Nelson, however, was under the impression that his designs would be honored.

Nelson was initially very excited. He went up there 'at his own expense' (van Dam, 1988: 87) to consult in the development of HES, but found the experience frustrating. As observed previously, van Dam and his team wanted to explore the hypertext concept, but they also had their own plans for print text editing (which Nelson strenuously opposed). The team set out to design a dual-purpose system for authoring, editing and printing documents such as papers, proposals and course notes, which could also be used to browse and query written materials nonsequentially. From Nelson's perspective, this was a compromise on his design: it was simulating paper, and hypertext was a mere footnote to the system.

This sentiment is understandable; the reader knows by now that Nelson feels his vision was sidelined. But the HES team were trying to convince the world that the whole concept of handling text on computers was not a waste of time and processing power. The world knew text handling as a paper-based thing. 'Not only were we selling hypertext, but at the same time document processing, interaction. Many people were still computing with cards', recalls van Dam (1999).

HES was set up on an IBM 360/50 with a 2250 display, and ran in a 128k partition of the operating system that controlled the 512k of main memory available (there was a complete times-haring system operating in another partition). The user sat facing a 12-inch-by-12-inch screen, browsing through portions of arbitrarily sized texts. Original text was entered directly via a keyboard, and the system itself was controlled by pressing function keys and by pointing at the text with a light pen or with the keyboard (Carmody et al., 1969: 4). The activities of the user corresponded directly to the operations normally performed upon text by writers and editors. The user was able to manipulate pieces of text as though they were physical items: correcting, cutting, pasting, copying, moving and filing drafts.

The HES team did not wish to store text in numerical pages or divisions known to users, except as they might deliberately divide text, create links or number headings. Rather than filing by page number or formal code name, HES stored text as arbitrary-length fragments or 'strings' and allowed for edits with arbitrary-length scope (for example, insert, delete, move, copy). This approach differed from NLS, which imposed a hierarchical tree structure of fixed-length lines or statements upon all content; Engelbart used 4,000-character limits on his statements to create a tighter, more controlled environment. HES was deliberately made to embody a freewheeling character, as non-structured as possible.

The system itself comprised text 'areas' that were of any length, expanding and contracting automatically to accommodate material. These areas were connected in two ways: by links and by branches. A link went from a point of departure in one area (signified by an asterisk) to an entrance point in another, or the same, area.

The HES team used Ted Nelson's concept of a hypertext link (though from Nelson's perspective they 'flattened' this by making the jumps one-way), as Doug Engelbart was incorporating the same idea into NLS independently, unbeknownst to van Dam, who wishes he was aware of this work. 'I hadn't heard of Engelbart. I hadn't heard of Bush and Memex. That came quite a bit later', van Dam recalls (1999). Links were intended to be optional paths within a body of text – from one place to another. They represented a relationship between two ideas or points: an intuitive concept. Branches were inserted at decision points to allow users to choose 'next places' to go.

In early 1968 HES did the rounds of a number of large customers for IBM equipment, for example, *Time/Life* and *The New York Times*. All these customers based their business on the printed word, but HES was too far out for them. Writing was not something you did at a computer screen. They had seen programs that set type, and maybe some programs for managing advertisements, but the concept of sitting in front of a computer and writing or navigating text was foreign to them.

> The best I ever got was from people like Time-Life and the New York Times who said this is terrific technology, but we're not going to get journalists typing on computer keyboards for the foreseeable future. (van Dam, 1999)

As we now know, however, in less than a decade journalists (and executives) would be typing on computer keyboards.

In late 1968 van Dam finally met Doug Engelbart and attended a demonstration of NLS at the Fall Joint Computer Conference. As we explored, this presentation was a landmark in the history of computing, and the audience, comprising several thousand engineers and scientists, witnessed innovations such as the use of hypertext, the computer 'mouse' and screen and telecollaboration on shared files via videoconferencing for the first time.

For van Dam this system set another, and entirely different, technical precedent.

The line or context editor was old technology. NLS was the prototype for creating, navigating and storing information behind a tube and for having a multiuser, multiterminal, cost-effective system. He went on to design the File Retrieval and Editing System (FRESS) at Brown with his team.

Nelson is adamant that the legacy of HES is modern word processing, and that it also led to today's web browser.

> The design of HES became the design of FRESS... then Intermedia, then imitated by Notecards and then by the World Wide Web. (Nelson, 2012)

Van Dam, for his part, thinks this is overreaching. 'I think Nelson, when he feels that the "bad example" that HES set had reverberations in the bad design of the Web or browsers, is giving our humble little effort an order of magnitude more credit than it deserves' (van Dam, 2011).

We do not have space here to go into van Dam's next system (FRESS): interested readers can find it in my book. I shall stop here, 40 years before the Web, and conclude.

## CONCLUSIONS

I hope that this chapter has presented you with some earlier models of the hypertext concept, and in the process, demonstrated that every model has its benefits and its shortcomings. Hypertext is not the Web; the Web is but one particular implementation of hypertext. It's the best we've come up with insofar as it actually works, most of the time – and it has stayed the course for 22 years. It is not, however, the only way hypertext can be done – as the systems described in this chapter show.

We have also inherited a vision from these projects: a device that 'enables associative connections that attempt to partially reflect the 'intricate web of trails carried by the cells of the brain"' (Wardrip-Fruin, 2003: 35). More precisely, a tool for thought – a tool that might both organize and 'permanize' (to use Nelson's term again) the mass of deeply tangled data that surrounds us. For the world grows more and more complex every day, and the information we are expected to keep track of proliferates at every click. How are we to keep track of it all?

The problem Nelson, Engelbart and van Dam identified is just as urgent today. The Web has *not* solved this problem for us – arguably it has highlighted it, in razor-sharp text and 16.7 million colors. The Web is without doubt a world-changing and world-opening technology; as van Dam put it to me in 1999, 'the fact that I can reach out and touch stuff in Ethiopia, as it were, is still a surprise to me' (van Dam, 1999). Unlike any of the hypertext systems we have looked at here, the Web stretches between countries and engages literally billions of people. But there are things we could improve on.

Imagine a system whose trails did not fade. Imagine if documents and objects could be stored permanently, with their own unique address that never vanished, and retrieved at will. Imagine if any version of these documents could be visually intercompared side by side, like the teeth in a zipper – and the quotes or ideas in those documents could be traced back to their original source with a click. Imagine if we could separate the linking structure from the content, and that content could consequently be reused in a million different formats. Imagine if we could capture the deeply tangled structure of knowledge itself, but make it better, make it permanent.

### *Notes*

1 Note that his full name is Theodor Holm Nelson.
2 An anchor tag is not an intrinsic address.
3 While working at Harcourt.

## REFERENCES

Bardini, T. (2000) *Bootstrapping: Douglas Engelbart, Coevolution, and the Origins of Personal Computing*. Stanford, CA: Stanford University Press.

Barnet, B. (2013) *Memory Machines: The Evolution of Hypertext*. London & New York, NY: Anthem Press.

Carmody, S., Gross, W., Nelson, T.H., Rice, D. and van Dam, A. (1969) 'A Hypertext Editing System for the /360'. In M. Faiman and J. Nievergelt (eds), *Pertinent Concepts in Computer Graphics*, 291–330. Urbana: University of Illinois Press.

Demeulenaere, A. (2003) 'An Uncanny Thinker: Michel de Certeau' in *Image & Narrative*, 5.

Engelbart, D. (1962a) 'Letter to Vannevar Bush and Program on Human Effectiveness'. In J. Nyce and P. Kahn (eds), *From Memex to Hypertext: Vannevar Bush and the Mind's Machine*, 1991, 235–44. London: Academic Press.

Engelbart, D. (1962b) 'Augmenting Human Intellect: A Conceptual Framework'. *Report to the Director of Information Sciences,* Air Force Office of Scientific Research, Menlo Park, CA, Stanford Research Institute.

Engelbart, D. (1997) Interview with David Bennehum. Online: http://memex.org/meme3-01.html

Engelbart, D. (1998) 'The Augmented Knowledge Workshop'. In A. Goldberg (ed.), *A History of Personal Workstations*, 185–249. New York: ACM Press.

Landow, G. (1992) *Hypertext*. London: Johns Hopkins University Press.

Licklider, J.C.R. (1960) 'Man-Computer Symbioses'. In A. Goldberg (ed.), *A History of Personal Workstations*, 1988, 131–40. New York: ACM Press.

Nelson, T. (1965) 'A File Structure for the Complex, the Changing and the Indeterminate'. In *Proceedings of the ACM 20th National Conference*. New York: ACM Press.

Nelson, T. (1987) *Computer Lib/Dream Machines*. Redmond, WA: Microsoft Press.

Nelson, T. (1992) *Literary Machines*. Sausalito, CA: Mindful Press.

Nelson, T. (1998) *What's on My Mind*. Online: http://www.xanadu.net/xybrap.html

Nelson, T. (2010) Possiplex: Movies, Intellect, Creative Control, My Computer Life and the Fight for Civilization. Available at Lulu.com http://www.lulu.com/spotlight/tandm [March 2012].

Nyce, J. and Kahn, P. (eds) (1991) *From Memex to Hypertext: Vannevar Bush and the Mind's Machine*. London: Academic Press.

Rheingold, H. (2000) *Tools for Thought: The History and Future of Mind-Expanding Technology* (2nd Edition). Cambridge, MA: MIT Press.

Smith, L.C. (1991) 'Memex as an Image of Potentiality Revisited'. In J. Nyce and P. Kahn (eds), *From Memex to Hypertext: Vannevar Bush and the Mind's Machine*, 261–86. London: Academic Press.

Tofts, D. (1998) *Memory Trade: A Prehistory of Cyberculture*. North Ryde, NSW: Interface Press.

Van Dam, A. (1988) 'Hypertext '87 Keynote Address' in *Communications of the ACM* Volume 31 Issue 7, July, 887–95.

Wardrip-Fruin, Noah (2003) 'Introduction: As We May Think'. In Noah Wardrip-Fruin and Nick Montfort (eds), 2003, 35.

Wardrip-Fruin, Noah and Montford, Nick (eds) (2003) *The New Media Reader*. Cambridge, MA: MIT Press

## PERSONAL COMMUNICATIONS

Bolter, Jay (2011) Interview with the author.

Duvall, Bill (2011) Interview with the author (recorded via phone, Melbourne).

Engelbart, Doug (1999) Interview with the author, Baltimore.

English, Bill (2011) Interview with the author (recorded via phone, Melbourne).

Nelson, Ted (1999) Interview with the author at Kyoto University Japan.

Nelson, Ted (2010) Interview with the author at Swinburne University.

Nelson, Ted (2012) Comments on the manuscript for *Memory Machines*.

Van Dam, Andries (1999) Interview with the author at Brown University.

Van Dam, Andries (2011) Interview with the author via phone.

# A Historiography of the Hyperlink: Periodizing the Web through the Changing Role of the Hyperlink

Anne Helmond

## INTRODUCTION: PERIODIZING THE WEB THROUGH THE HYPERLINK

In this chapter I provide a historiography of one of the core elements of the web, the hypertext link. I do so with the specific purpose of tracing the various roles of this central web object as a way to understand social, technical, and commercial transformations of the web. That is, the hyperlink is positioned as a way to historicize larger web developments and as an alternative way to periodize the web.

The dominant way of web periodization is through what Allen calls a 'discourse of versions' (2013), established by Tim O'Reilly who labeled the period after the dot-com crash 'Web 2.0' (2005), a marketing term he used to claim this period as new and upgraded, whilst at the same time promising a sense of continuity (Allen, 2013: 5). In doing so, O'Reilly invented the idea of Web 1.0 in retrospect and created a perception of the web before, Web 1.0, and after, Web 2.0, the dot-com crash (Allen, 2013). Whilst O'Reilly stresses the continuities between the two periods and is careful to not position the shift as a technological upgrade, he nonetheless creates a juxtaposition by characterizing Web 1.0 as a web for 'publishing' and Web 2.0 as a web for 'participation' (2005). This supposed shift from Web 1.0 as the 'read-only' static publishing web to Web 2.0 as the 'read-write' participatory social web has since become the web's dominant historical narrative (Song, 2010; Allen, 2013; Ankerson, 2015; Helmond, 2015; Stevenson, 2016).

Following Allen's interpretation and critique of this narrative, Megan Ankerson proposes to 'put aside the discourse of versions and approach the web and web historiography as a site of ongoing configuration' by employing Lucy Suchman's notion of 'configuration' as 'a device for studying how material artifacts and cultural imaginaries are joined together' and how these are connected to specific production practices (Ankerson, 2015: 3). Like Ankerson's consideration of web historiography through forms of alignment and configuration, I approach my periodization of the web through one of the core infrastructural elements of the web, the hyperlink, by tracing its production and use practices within a view of the web as a complex social, techno-commercial configuration. Such focus does not aim to merely describe the technological progress of the hyperlink as a material artifact, but rather, to situate its development within the diverse practices of end-users, webmasters, bloggers, and developers within the context of the software, platforms, search engines, and apps that are involved in the creation, distribution, and consumption of hyperlinks. At the same time, I consider the hyperlink's imagined capabilities by the actors involved in its production and distribution. Which social, political, or economic purpose does the hyperlink serve for them? I argue that there is an ongoing – and sometimes conflicting – interpretation of what the hyperlink is or should be, and that there is a constant negotiation between specific production and use practices as well as an unfolding alignment with social and economic incentives.

In what follows, I argue that the hyperlink is not a timeless object and that it may be employed to analyze changes in the social, technical, and commercial configuration of the web. I do so by providing a periodization of the hyperlink based on its historically diverse roles at six key moments (or episodes) that are characterized by distinct devices. I provide a history that discusses these six episodes individually whilst demonstrating their interconnections, thus highlighting how these episodes may run parallel. First, the proto-hyperlink as envisioned in early hypertext systems; second, the hypertext link as fabric of the web and navigational object in the early pre-search web; third, the hyperlink as the currency of the web in the heydays of the search engine era; fourth; the role of hyperlinks in building the blogosphere and the introduction of new link types; fifth, the effects of platformization on the hyperlink by social media platforms turning the link into an analytical device for data-harvesting; and sixth, the disappearance of the 'traditional' hypertext link as the prime connection mechanism with the rise of mobile apps.

## TRACING THE HYPERLINK

The history of the hyperlink as a reference and navigational object is often traced back to the footnote (De Maeyer, 2013), which functions as a way to explicitly link to additional information and source material within a text (Grafton, 1997), and to even older forms of inter textual connections (Halavais, 2008; Brügger, 2017). In his genealogy of the hyperlink, Niels Brügger positions the hyperlink within the longer and broader history of links as mechanisms for interconnecting pieces of text (2017). He identifies three phases in his history of intertextual linking and observes how each period is characterized by a specific type of media: first, links in non-digital media such as clay tablets, printed books, and mechanical systems; second, links in stand-alone digital computers; and third, links in networked digital computers (2017). The history of the link presented here mainly focuses on the third period, which is characterized by the advent of interconnected computer systems, digital hypertext systems, and the rise of the World Wide Web. In particular I focus on the role of search engines, blog software, social media platforms, and apps in the evolution of the role of the hyperlink on the web and the mobile space.

On the web hyperlinks have evolved beyond citations to serve a wide range of social and technical functions (Halavais, 2008). Thus, instead of thinking about hypertext and hyperlinks as 'remediations' of older media types and linkages (cf. Bolter, 1990), I follow Elmer's call that if we wish to understand links and linking on the web 'we must also come to grips with the specific architectural logic of the web' and consider the hyperlink within its web-native environment (2001). That is, I consider the medium-specificity of the hyperlink as a web-native object (Helmond, 2013; Rogers, 2013) by focusing on the infrastructure of the web and the actors involved in the production and distribution of hyperlinks. In what follows next, I discuss the changing purpose, use, and function of the hyperlink over time in six episodes, each characterized by a number of human and non-human protagonists that have played a major role in the history of the hyperlink.

## EPISODE 1. THE PROTO-HYPERLINK IN EARLY HYPERTEXT SYSTEMS

Most commonly, the lineage of the hypertext link is traced back to pre-web hypertext systems (Barnet, in this volume; Elmer, 2001), as a way to interconnect and make accessible our ephemeral human knowledge (Barnet, 2014). In her history of hypertext, Barnet (in this volume; 2014) describes different visions, models, and implementations of hypertext systems before the web in order to emphasize that the web is just but one famous realization of a hypertext system. It is beyond the scope of this chapter to describe the development of these systems at length. The history of hypertext has been extensively discussed elsewhere by scholars from literature studies, game studies, information science, and new media studies (see Bolter, 1990; Landow, 1991; Aarseth, 1997; Elmer, 2001; Kirschenbaum, 2001; Wardrip-Fruin, 2004; Krapp, 2006; Halavais, 2008; Barnet, in this volume; Barnet, 2014; Wright, 2014a; Brügger, 2017).

However, it is important to briefly consider a number of proto-hypertext systems and the types of interconnections they conceived to understand links as part of technical infrastructures for organizing and distributing information. One of the earliest proto-hypertext systems was Paul Otlet's Mondothèque, a device for researchers, providing one of the many visions on how to organize the world's information (Rayward, 1994; Wright, 2014a; Wright, 2014b). Otlet aimed 'to promote universal access to human knowledge through a global information network that he dubbed the "Mundaneum"' (Wright, 2014a: 5). Knowledge was stored in and connected to the universal library of the Mundaneum via a personalized multimedia workstation called the 'Mondothèque' (van den Heuvel & Rayward, 2011; Wright, 2014a). The Mondothèque, which remained an unrealized prototype, should be understood as 'more than just a platform for consuming information; it was an active tool for knowledge production' (Wright, 2014a: 235) enabling users to create links between various types of media documents and pieces of knowledge. Wright sees Otlet's Mondothèque as the forgotten European precursor to Vannevar Bush's Memex, a proto-hypertext system in which (hyper)links were conceptualized as associational markers to establish 'trails' between documents (Bush, 1945). The Memex aimed to organize, sort, and structure the world's knowledge via associative indexing. However, what distinguishes Otlet's from Bush's visions is that 'Otlet saw the network as essential to his vision of a worldwide platform for knowledge sharing; Bush envisioned the Memex as a stand-alone machine' (Wright, 2014b). Otlet and Bush's devices were analog machines that relied on microfilm for the storage of data, but both remained unbuilt prototypes. The advent of the (networked) computer introduced new ideas about organizing and connecting the world's information. Ted Nelson and Doug Engelbart were two pioneers working on early hypertext systems before the advent of the web.

The word 'hyperlink' has been attributed to Ted Nelson, who worked on the first hypertext system, Project Xanadu, in the 1960s. The system was never entirely built but a number of partially functioning Xanadu prototypes have been released since the late 1990s (Nelson, 2016). Nelson coined the word 'hypertext' (Nelson, 1965) in a paper outlining an evolutionary file structure for an automatic personal filing system, in which he quotes Bush's ideas about the Memex at length. Nelson used the word hypertext to describe how text within the system could be accessed and retrieved in a nonlinear fashion whereby readers could follow hypertext links to read additional information. A noteworthy core element of Nelson's Xanadu was the idea of unbreakable two-way links as a way to implement 'transclusion', a type of interlinking of 'the same thing knowably and visibly in more than one place' (Nelson, 1999: 1).

Around the same time as Nelson was working on Xanadu, Doug Engelbart was creating the oN-Line System (NLS), inspired by Bush's Memex. NLS was a system for cross-referencing, based on the basic premise that you could link to anything and to anywhere through the Link function (Barnet, in this volume). The NLS system had fine-grained linking capabilities and links within the system represented a relationship (Barnet, in this volume).[1] Both Xanadu and NLS were never adopted on a wide scale and it wasn't until the late 1980s, when Apple started selling computers with a pre-installed version of HyperCard, a piece of hypermedia software, that hypertext became available to the larger public and became '*de facto* the archetype of what hypertext – and hyperlinking – was' (Barnet, 2014: xxii; Brügger, 2017). With the advent of the World Wide Web (the web), the ideas of hypertext and hyperlinking would be further exposed to a larger public.

## EPISODE 2. THE HYPERLINK AS FABRIC OF THE WEB

In his book *Weaving the Web* on the history of the web, Tim Berners-Lee acknowledges the ideas of Bush, Nelson, and Engelbart in developing a hypertext system (2000: 5–6). He describes how his creation was also inspired by the organizing structures of the mind in terms of making and storing connections through (random) associations (2000: 10). Berners-Lee describes his task as to 'marry' the development of the internet with early ideas of hypertext and hypertext links (2000: 6) to form 'a web of information' (2000: 4). His vision of the web was inspired by the following idea: 'Suppose all the information stored on computers everywhere were linked [...]. Suppose I could program my computer to create a space in which anything could be linked to anything. [...]' (2000: 4). To create such an interlinked information space, Berners-Lee created the Universal Resource Identifier (URI) to identify any object on the web, the Hypertext Transfer Protocol (HTTP) for transferring hypertext, and the Hypertext Markup Language (HTML) as a common language or 'basic lingua franca' for writing and representing hypertext pages (2000: 36–40). Berners-Lee considered the URI the 'most fundamental innovation of the web' because the hypertext link contains the destination URI telling the browser where to find the document (2000: 37). HTML in its turn functions as 'the fabric' (Berners-Lee et al., 1994) or 'connective tissue' (Berners-Lee, 1998) of the web. One of the central elements of HTML is the hypertext link as 'the basic hypertext construct' enabling connections between different resources on the web (W3C, n.d.). Hypertext links, commonly referred to as hyperlinks, web links, or just simply links, allow the creation of interconnections between websites, web pages, and other web objects. As such, they bear the capacity to weave disparate entities of the web together into 'a single, global information space', which Berners-Lee called the World Wide Web (2000: 4). Universality was key to the design of the web as '[a] hypertext link must be able to link to anything' (107) and anyone should be able to create links. Berners-Lee considered 'the right to link' as 'the very basic building unit for the whole Web' (139). Similar to, but distinct from, Nelson's implementation of the two-way link, Berners-Lee contemplated designing the web with bidirectional links (Berners-Lee, n.d.) but these were never implemented as part of an architectural decision because mono-directional links enabled the web to scale quickly (Berners-Lee, 1998). Another important aspect in the design of the link was that whilst Berners-Lee saw that it could be used as 'a way of transmitting judgements of quality', he made clear that 'the intention in the design of the web was that normal links should simply be references, with no implied meaning' (Berners-Lee, 1997) and that the hyperlink does not imply any type of endorsement (2000: 139).

Key to the initial popularization of hyperlinks was the introduction of graphical browsers such as Mosaic by indicating clickable hyperlinks in blue-colored underlined text, which became the de facto standard for displaying links on the web (Weinreich et al., 2001). Whilst anyone could potentially create hyperlinks by learning HTML, in these early days of the web this act was reserved to webmasters who could make and run their own websites. With the advent of HTML editors, content management systems, blog software, and free website services such as Tripod and Geocities, it became easier to create websites and to link to other sites. This period of mass amateur website building, which Olia Lialina refers to as the 'vernacular web', was driven by a do-it-yourself ethos with very few design rules – except for a valid HTML – and led to an explosion of websites with an amateur aesthetic (Lialina, 2009: 27). According to Lialina this web was 'fascinated by the power of links' and 'people felt it was their responsibility to configure the environment and build the infrastructure' by linking to other pages and by listing external link lists on their websites (27). In addition to building the web's infrastructure, people also built communities through links by engaging in 'web rings', a way of interlinking websites with similar topics (Elmer, 1999; Lialina, 2009: 27). These web rings also contributed to the discoverability of new websites and offered a subject-based index of a set of websites (Elmer, 1999).

With the growth of the web it became more and more difficult to find interesting and relevant websites. This led to the creation of new services that aimed to index the web (Halavais, in this volume), with search engines like Aliweb, Excite, and AltaVista, expert directories of links[2] like DMOZ and the Yahoo! Directory, and portals like MyNetscape and My Yahoo!, which positioned themselves as entry points to the web by providing professionally curated links. These mostly new commercial actors made money off hyperlinks through the strategic placement of links or 'featured links' on their websites (Hargittai, 2000; Rogers, 2002). Thus, hyperlinks have given rise to an industry of new commercial actors on the web such as content aggregators, web portals, and search engines (cf. Dellarocas et al., 2013: 2360). A new company, Google, would turn hyperlinks and the interlinked infrastructure of the web into a very successful business model.

## EPISODE 3. THE HYPERLINK AS CURRENCY OF THE WEB

An important moment in the history of both the web and the hyperlink has been the introduction and rise of search engines. Here, I focus on the role of Google as the search engine that 'built its empire from an appreciation of the Net's underlying architecture', as it conceived of a 'web/info-centric business model that was built upon the harvesting and crawling of hyperlinks' (Elmer, 2006: 9). What distinguished Google from previous search engines is that it employed hyperlinks as a way to calculate the relevance and reputation of a site, by considering – amongst other factors – who links to whom and how often a site is linked to (Brin and Page, 1998). Google's PageRank algorithm calculates the relevance of a website based on the quality or importance of other websites linking to it (Brin and Page, 1998) and as a result not all hyperlinks have equal value for Google. Whilst Google currently takes over 200 signals into account, PageRank is still an important factor in determining a site's relevance (Search Console Help, n.d.).

Google's 'industrialization' of the hyperlink (Turow, 2008: 3) has created the so-called 'link economy' (Rogers, 2002; Walker, 2002) in which search engines determine the value of links and where links are exchanged, bought, or sold by webmasters and spammers. Google turned the link from a navigational object into 'the currency of the web' by interpreting links as 'objective, democratic and machine-readable signs of value' (Walker, 2002: 72). Google's business model is built on the 'open web', a web built on open standards and where links can be followed from one page to another and indexed by search engines. The foregrounding of the link as a sign of value and medium of exchange raises questions about the actors involved in the production, indexation, and distribution of links. In this sense, the hyperlink provides a way to understand the early commercialization of the web, which has traditionally focused on businesses 'rushing' to the web to build websites as a form of presence (cf. Rogers, 2002), but instead focuses on the political economy of the link. Such a perspective considers its role as a currency (Walker, 2002) and draws attention to the rise of new web-specific services that monetize the hyperlink as the core feature of the web, and the rise of new linking practices and strategies. With the new role of the link as the currency of the web, actors involved in creating hyperlinks became aware of their strategic value, leading to a whole new industry of manipulation around search engines to achieve higher rankings (Halavais, 2008: 49–50). Next, I elaborate on the political economy of linking and the constant negotiation between those creating links and those indexing and distributing links by focusing on the role of links and the practices of linking in the blogosphere and the creation of new types of links.

## EPISODE 4. BUILDING THE BLOGOSPHERE AND THE INTRODUCTION OF NEW LINK TYPES

Besides directories, web portals, web rings, and search engines trying to organize the web in the late 1990s, there were also very important individual actors such as webmasters and bloggers who would point other users to interesting websites and pages through link lists on their websites and blogs. Blogs are often seen as a specific genre of websites (Siles, in this volume),[3] defined by their form as 'frequently updated, reverse-chronological entries on a single Web page' (Blood, 2004: 53). These entries, called 'posts', constitute the main units or building blocks of the blog, in contrast to the 'page' unit of the website. In order to be able to link to a single post, instead of a whole page, blogger Jason Kottke started implementing permanent URLs for each entry on his blog (Kottke, 2000). This idea was quickly taken up by developers from the blog software company Blogger, who implemented 'permalinks' into their software to give 'each blog entry a permanent location – a distinct URL – at which it could be referenced' (Blood, 2004: 54). This new link type was quickly adopted by other bloggers and blog software developers and the permalink became 'a canonical component of the standard Weblog entry' (Blood, 2004: 54). Early blogger Rebecca Blood argues that the 'original weblogs were link-driven sites' (2000) and that the prototypical blog focuses on linking to other blogs to provide commentary on interesting blog posts (Blood, 2000; Herring et al., 2005). But links did not only play an important role within a blog entry; bloggers also often created 'blogrolls' to link to other interesting blogs in the sidebar of their blogs. All these links between blogs create an interconnected network of blogs called 'the blogosphere', although the degree of its interconnectedness might be overestimated (Herring et al., 2005). The ritual practices of linking stabilized the blog as a web format and created a sense of community as bloggers would start referring to themselves as the 'weblog community' (Ammann, 2009; Siles, 2011: 745).

Before the advent of blog software, which originated and gained popularity between 1997–9, bloggers would manually create hyperlinks to link to other blogs (Blood, 2000; Helmond, 2008). The practice of blogging and linking was made easier with the implementation of linking features into blog software and What You See Is What You Get (WYSIWYG) editors (Blood, 2004: 54). Hereafter, bloggers would only have to insert a URL and the blog software would automatically generate the corresponding HTML code for the hyperlink. Blog software also enabled automated interlinking between blogs with the creation of two new link types that were built on top of the permalink: the trackback and pingback. Blog software can 'ping' or notify other blog software of an incoming link by automatically 'placing a reciprocal link – a trackback – in the entry they have just referenced' (Blood, 2004: 55). Trackbacks are a semi-manual type of notification and interlinking system since bloggers have to manually send the trackback notification from within the software's interface. Receiving trackbacks could be automated since blog software can be configured to automatically receive and place trackbacks underneath a post. Unfortunately, trackbacks turned out to be very prone to spam since the receiving software did not verify the incoming link and incoming links could therefore very easily be faked. Spammers used trackbacks to artificially boost the ranking of their sites in search engines and pingbacks were developed to partially solve the problems of trackbacks. Pingbacks automatically send notifications to other blogs and the receiving blog software verifies the incoming link. Both trackbacks and pingbacks (semi-)automatically interlink blogs and render the links between blogs visible on both ends, resembling the idea of a two-way link. Trackbacks and pingbacks draw attention to the changing configuration of actors involved in the production and distribution of links. Blog software introduced and standardized new types of links such as the permalink, the trackback, and pingback, and became an active agent in creating links between blogs and the interlinking of blogs into a blogosphere (Helmond, 2008; Weltevrede and Helmond, 2012; Helmond, 2013).

Another important blog feature that highlights the constant negotiations taking place between various actors involved in creating, distributing, and exploiting links is the blog comment. Whilst previously the act of linking was mainly reserved to webmasters and bloggers,[4] blog comments underneath blog posts opened up the blog to links from blog visitors. This form of user-generated linking expanded the participatory ideals of blogging as a way 'to democratize publishing' (Blood, 2004: 55) by also giving blog readers a voice. However, opening up the comment space made blogs even more prone to spam. Spammers would not only target the trackback mechanism but also the comment space with links to boost their own rankings. This time an attempt to create a solution to combat link spam was developed by Google, the key actor in the link economy, who suffered from spam in its search engine results as a result of the new linking capabilities. On January 18, 2005, Google announced its measure to prevent comment spam, a new hyperlink attribute called 'nofollow'. In HTML, elements can have parameters called attributes where the <a> element defines the hypertext link, the 'href' attribute defines the destination of a link, and the 'rel' attribute specifies 'the relationship between the document containing the hyperlink and the destination resource' (W3C, 2014). Google introduced the 'nofollow' value as part of the hyperlink's 'rel' attribute to indicate a particular type of relationship between the source and destination link: 'From now on, when Google sees the attribute (rel="nofollow") on hyperlinks, those links won't get any credit when we rank websites in our search results'

(Cutts and Shellen, 2005). No credit meant no value for a website's PageRank, severely diminishing the intended goal of the spammers. The nofollow attribute was introduced in collaboration with a number of partners, including major blog software developers such as Blogger and WordPress, who implemented it into their software so that every link in a blog comment would automatically receive the nofollow attribute. The effect of nofollow is that, in Google's world, not all links have equal value, since links in comments with the nofollow attribute do not pass on value for a site's PageRank. The role of 'nofollow' in preventing spam is still a pressing issue today, as Google regularly warns webmasters to follow their linking guidelines and to use 'nofollow' where appropriate or else they may see their sites' rankings penalized (Google Webspam Team, 2017).

## EPISODE 5. THE EFFECTS OF PLATFORMIZATION ON THE HYPERLINK

Whilst the hyperlink has technically not changed since its inception, in the previous episodes I have demonstrated how search engines and blog software have appropriated or added features to the hyperlink for their own purposes. This next episode discusses the implications of the 'platformization' of the web (Helmond, 2015), a term used to refer to the rise of social media platforms and the consequences of their extension into the web, for the hyperlink. It provides a way to conceptualize how social media platforms have imposed their own infrastructural and economic model onto the web by repurposing web-native objects, such as the hyperlink, for their own gain. I discuss the consequences of the rise of social media for the hyperlink by addressing three issues: first, the further automation of linking through social buttons; second, the reconfiguration of the hyperlink through social buttons to fit the underlying business models of the associated social media platforms; and third, the increasing invisibility of the hyperlink in social media.

With the introduction of social bookmarking icons, now commonly known as social buttons, social media platforms have developed ways to facilitate easy link sharing across platforms (Helmond, 2013).[5] Sharing a website article using a social button such as Facebook's Share button automatically creates a status update displaying a preview of the link's content: the article's title, subtitle, image, domain name, and author.[6] The status update with the link preview does not show the linked URL but instead is reduced to the URL's domain name, which then links to the individual article. Sharing an article directly on Facebook is handled slightly differently since posting a link both shows the full URL in the status update and creates a link preview underneath the post. The automation of link sharing via social buttons creates a two-way link:

> Facebook also employs linking mechanisms that closely resemble the bidirectional links proposed by Bush, Nelson, and so on. Whereas a typical Web hyperlink usually goes in one direction – from source document to target hyperlink – links on Facebook typically work both ways; a comment or 'like' interaction will show up in multiple threads; and a user may follow a link back to see the original commenter's page. (Wright, 2014a: 290)

However, Facebook does not support traditional linking practices of being able to create a hyperlink by linking a word in a Facebook post to a specific URL destination on the web. The only 'links' you can create are to internal Facebook items such as users and pages (Berners-Lee, 2010). Software developer Dave Winer is a strong advocate of implementing hyperlinking into Facebook. The current implementation, he argues, is not a form of linking and is 'really hurting the rest of the web' by not allowing users to freely link to other places on the web (Winer, 2016). Tim Berners-Lee has also expressed his concerns in regard to websites and web services that develop their own linking mechanisms that do not interoperate with the web's open standards and formats (Berners-Lee, 2010). He argues that they are undermining the web's principle of universality meaning that you can link to anything, where 'the URI is the key to universality' (2010). He explains how social media platforms are becoming silos by walling off their information: 'The isolation occurs because each piece of information does not have a URI. Connections among data exist only within a site'. Berners-Lee warns that '[t]he more this kind of architecture gains widespread use, the more the Web becomes fragmented, and the less we enjoy a single, universal information space' (2010: 82). Links are essential in weaving the web into a single place and social media platforms are prohibiting a specific type of linking practice, the traditional hyperlink, using instead their own forms of interlinking. In addition, many social media platforms also reconfigure links posted to their platforms so that they fit the underlying platform architectures and business models. They do so by turning links shared to their platforms into shortened URLs, a new type of link which gained popularity on Twitter.

On Twitter, users can only use up to 140 characters for their tweets, which means that posting a link will take up a significant number of valuable characters. Users turned to URL shorteners such as TinyURL to shorten their long links into shortened links, e.g. http://tinyurl.com/newlink. In June 2011 Twitter built its own URL shortener t.co into its platform architecture and from that moment onwards every link posted to Twitter is automatically shortened into a t.co URL.[7] Twitter hides this transformation of the hyperlink from its users, by displaying an abbreviated version of the original long link in the front-end, the platform's user interface as visible in the browser, whilst using the actual shortened link for a variety of different purposes in the back-end, the platform's data infrastructure.[8] By routing all links through its platform, Twitter can not only detect and filter out spam links but it can also collect valuable link data. Twitter can now easily track how many times a link has been shared, clicked on, by whom, and when, on its platform. But it can also gather many of these statistics when the link is distributed outside of its platform boundaries. As I have argued elsewhere, platforms have turned the link into an analytical device by repurposing it into a data-rich shortened URL:

> By automatically wrapping links in tweets with a t.co URL, Twitter makes this shared data on its platform 'algorithm ready' by reconfiguring the hyperlink to fit the platform. The automatic processing of the hyperlink and its reconfiguration into an analytical device in order to become part of an algorithmic system is what I refer to as the algorithmization of the hyperlink. (Helmond 2013)

On social media platforms, the link no longer just functions as a navigational device where a link in a tweet points to another location on the web, but also provides valuable data such as link statistics. This data serves as input for the platform's various algorithms that determine relevant and trending content but is also used by Twitter's marketing partners for their own commercial purposes such as advertising (Helmond, 2013). Platforms have appropriated the link as an object to measure web activities, attention, and other forms of engagement to fit their own economic agendas.

Next, I briefly turn to the current state of web development to reflect on the decline of the hyperlink and the introduction of new link types such as mobile deep links and app links with the rise of mobile apps.

## EPISODE 6. BEYOND THE WEB: MOBILE APPS AND DEEP LINKING

The previous sections have argued that in order to understand the evolution of the hyperlink and associated linking practices we should consider the actors involved in the production and reconfiguration of the hyperlink. In the changing political economy of linking a variety of actors has been involved over time: from webmasters, bloggers, and social media users to search engines, blog software, and social media platforms, to only name a few. I have argued that in order to understand what the hyperlink is, can do, or is made to do, we should consider its role within the transforming socio-techno-commercial environment of the web. When considering the present role of the hyperlink, its evolution and implementation should also be considered beyond the web. That is, with the introduction of mobile phones and the increasing ubiquity of mobile network data, in recent years we have seen the development of the mobile web (Goggin, in this volume) with pages specifically built for or adjusted to smaller screens and lower bandwidth. However, instead of building mobile web pages or services many companies have built dedicated mobile apps. For many, apps have become the main entry point to the web and internet-based platforms (comScore, 2016). Whilst the mobile web is based on the same standards as the web, and links between pages are created using hyperlinks, apps employ proprietary linking mechanisms. They use so-called mobile or app 'deep links' to enable app interlinking but these deep links are not based on open standards. In his defense of the open web, Berners-Lee describes how deep linking in apps works and the consequences of this type of linking: 'Apple's iTunes system, for example, identifies songs and videos using URIs that are open. But instead of "http:" the addresses begin with "itunes:", which is proprietary. You can access an "itunes:" link only using Apple's proprietary iTunes program' (2010: 83). Apps do not employ open link standards, which, similar to the practices of social media platforms, turns them into stand-alone objects or little unlinkable islands that often function separate from the web, thereby turning them into 'closed worlds' or centralized 'walled gardens' (Berners-Lee, 2010: 83).

To create interconnections between apps and the web, companies such as Apple, Google, and Facebook have introduced new link types for linking between apps and for linking to specific content within apps. Facebook launched App Links at its F8 Developer Conference in 2014 as 'an open cross platform solution for deep linking to content in your mobile app' (Facebook for Developers, n.d.). For Facebook, these App Links also provide a way to gather app analytics such as 'traffic and usage information' on who is using your app (Facebook for Developers, n.d.), thereby positioning App Links as both navigational and analytical devices. In May 2015 Google announced its own 'App links, along with App Indexing for Google search' (Eason, 2015). A month later, during the WWDC, Apple also announced its own version, entitled 'Universal Links' (Apple Developer, n.d.-a), seemingly referring to the universality principle of hyperlinks on the web. Similar to websites and web pages, which are linked or 'woven' together by hyperlinks to create the World Wide Web, Apple explicates how 'an app exists as part of an ecosystem' of other apps (Apple Developer, n.d.-b). Universal Links are Apple's way of linking apps into an ecosystem similar to but separate from the web. Whilst these current developments may aim to address the current barriers of app-interlinking, they are not providing a universal solution.[9] With the introduction of deep links, Facebook's App Links, Google's app links, and Apple's Universal Links these companies have contributed their own – mostly proprietary – solutions for app linking (and indexing) and have created a proliferation of new app link standards outside of the scope of W3C, which oversees open web standards such as HTML and the hypertext link. In addition, deep links provide not only an app-native way of linking, but also an app-native way to track users, and to collect valuable information for advertisers. At the same time this new link type points to the diminishing role of the hyperlink in the app space as a universal interconnector.

## CONCLUSION

The hyperlink as one of the core infrastructural elements of the web has a long and rich history – not only if we consider its potential precursors of intertextual links and its early employment in proto-hypertext systems, but also, and especially, its implementation on the web. In this chapter I have provided a historiography of the hyperlink by narrating its role in six episodes in the history of the web. These episodes demonstrate how the hyperlink has evolved from a feature to interlink information within technical knowledge infrastructures such as the Mondothèque, the Memex, Xanadu, and the World Wide Web, to a feature that may be used to collect valuable information about the interlinked structure of the web as well as about the people clicking and viewing those links. That is, the hyperlink's long-established role as a navigational tool has been supplemented with its new function as an analytical device for data-harvesting. As such, the evolution of the hyperlink provides an important entry point into understanding the increasing commercialization of the web. The way in which the hyperlink has been employed *socially* by users and *economically* by search engines, social media platforms, and apps has changed significantly. By tracing how these actors have handled and appropriated the hyperlink over time we gain insights into its novel additional functions on the web and in the app space.

The six episodes focused on the relation between the main actors involved in the production, distribution, and valorization of hyperlinks. These protagonists included human actors, such as webmasters, bloggers, blog software developers, and technology entrepreneurs, as well as non-human actors such as blog software, search engines, social media platforms, apps, and the companies behind them such as Google, Facebook, Twitter, and Apple. Each of these actors comes with its own very specific ideas, agendas, or economic incentives of what the hyperlink is, could, or should be. That is, there is a constant interplay between the material object of the hyperlink and the various actors involved in its production, distribution, and valorization. Instead of providing a lineage or teleological account of the hyperlink, the six episodes focused on the changing constellations of actors and how they employ the hyperlink for their own social, technical, and economic incentives. The episodes demonstrate a number of continuities and discontinuities in the role of the hyperlink. First, the hyperlink is still a core element of the web and a central mechanism for creating and navigating connections between web pages and sites. On the one hand links are created manually by webmasters, bloggers, and other types of web users, and, on the other hand, their production has become increasingly (semi-)automated with the introduction of blog software and social buttons. As a consequence, the way in which the web becomes interconnected has changed. Second, social media platforms and companies involved in app development have created their own interconnection and interlinking mechanisms, their own types of links, which function similarly to, but are different from, the traditional hyperlink. As a result, social media platforms and in particular apps are seen as walled gardens which operate on their own logic of connection, largely disconnected from the World Wide Web at large. Custom linking mechanisms are not only developed for creating connections, but especially for tracing and tracking the movement of users and their data through social media platforms and apps.

By focusing on the political economy of linking over time, I have drawn attention to the increasing commercialization of the hyperlink. The hyperlink has seemingly lost its innocence since it is no longer just a way of navigating the web but has also become an object that can be monetized and that can be employed to track users. Linking is no longer just 'weaving the web' but contributing to an infrastructure of valuation.

## Notes

1 See Barnet in this volume for more detail on the role of links and types of linking in Doug Engelbart's oN-Line System (NLS) and Ted Nelson's Xanadu.
2 Berners-Lee's first website at CERN also contained two directories of websites, one organized by subject and the other by type of service, see: http://info.cern.ch/hypertext/DataSources/Top.html (Accessed: 8 March 2017).
3 See danah boyd's (2006) critique of defining blogging as a form or genre – she argues that, instead, it should be seen as both a medium and a practice.
4 As well as users from web fora, message boards, and other early forms of web-based communication groups.
5 See Helmond (2013) on the history of social buttons and the technical details of link automation.
6 Which elements are visible in the preview depends on whether or not the website with the Share button has optimized itself for Facebook's crawler by employing Open Graph tags, Facebook's markup language.
7 See Helmond (2013) on the history of link shorteners, the technical details behind link shortening, and the role of shortened URLs in social media.
8 Technically this means that the browser displays the long URL, whilst the short URL is coded into the underlying HTML.
9 For example, Apple's Universal Links only works with iOS 9 or higher and not with Android apps, thereby only interlinking Apple apps into an ecosystem.

## ACKNOWLEDGMENTS

The author wishes to thank Fernando van der Vlist, the reviewer, and the editors for their valuable comments on this chapter. This work is part of the research program Innovational Research Incentives Scheme Veni with project number 275-45-009, which is (partly) financed by the Netherlands Organisation for Scientific Research (NWO).

## REFERENCES

Aarseth, E.J. (1997) *Cybertext: Perspectives on Ergodic Literature*. Baltimore: Johns Hopkins University Press.

Allen, M. (2013) 'What was Web 2.0? Versions as the dominant mode of internet history', *New Media & Society*, 15(2): 260–275. doi: 10.1177/1461444812451567.

Ammann, R. (2009) 'Blogosphere 1998: Analysis', *Tawawa*, 5 November. Available at: http://tawawa.org/ark/2009/11/5/blogosphere-1998-analysis.html (Accessed: 13 January 2013).

Ankerson, M.S. (2015) 'Social media and the "read-only" Web: Reconfiguring social logics and historical boundaries', *Social Media + Society*, 1(2): 1–12. doi: 10.1177/2056305115621935.

Apple Developer (n.d.-a) *Seamless Linking to Your App, WWDC 2015 – Videos*. Available at: https://developer.apple.com/videos/play/wwdc2015/509/ (Accessed: 4 March 2017).

Apple Developer (n.d.-b) *Universal Links for Developers, Apple Developer*. Available at: https://developer.apple.com/ios/universal-links/ (Accessed: 4 March 2017).

Barnet, B. (2014) *Memory Machines: The Evolution of Hypertext*. London: Anthem Press.

Berners-Lee, T., Cailliau, R., Luotonen, A., Nielsen, H.F., and Secret, A. (1994) 'The World-Wide Web', *Communications of the ACM*, 37(8): 76–82. doi: 10.1145/179606.179671.

Berners-Lee, T. (1997) 'Links and law', *Commentary on Web Architecture*, April. Available at: http://www.w3.org/DesignIssues/LinkLaw.html (Accessed: 29 October 2012).

Berners-Lee, T. (1998) *Web Architecture from 50,000 feet, W3C*. Available at: https://www.w3.org/DesignIssues/Architecture.html (Accessed: 17 February 2017).

Berners-Lee, T. (2000) *Weaving the Web: The Original Design and Ultimate Destiny of the World Wide Web*. New York: Harper Business.

Berners-Lee, T. (2010) 'Long live the Web: A call for continued open standards and neutrality', *Scientific American*, December. Available at: http://www.scientificamerican.com/article/long-live-the-web/ (Accessed: 24 March 2014).

Berners-Lee, T. (n.d.) *Topology, W3 Archive 1990*. Available at: https://www.w3.org/DesignIssues/Topology.html (Accessed: 17 February 2017).

Blood, R. (2000) 'Weblogs: A history and perspective', *Rebecca's Pocket*, 7 September. Available at: http://www.rebeccablood.net/essays/weblog_history.html (Accessed: 14 March 2014).

Blood, R. (2004) 'How blogging software reshapes the online community', *Communications of the ACM*, 47(12): 53–55.

Bolter, J.D. (1990) *Writing Space: The Computer, Hypertext, and the History of Writing*. Hillsdale: Routledge.

boyd, danah (2006) 'A blogger's blog: Exploring the definition of a medium', *Reconstruction*, 6(4). Available at: http://www.danah.org/papers/ABloggersBlog.pdf (Accessed: 27 September 2012).

Brin, S. and Page, L. (1998) 'The anatomy of a large-scale hypertextual Web search engine', *Computer Networks and ISDN Systems*, 30(1): 107–117.

Brügger, N. (2017) 'Connecting textual segments: A brief history of the web hyperlink', in Brügger, N. (ed.) *Web 25: Histories from the first 25 Years of the World Wide Web*. New York: Peter Lang Publishing, pp. 3–28.

Bush, V. (1945) 'As we may think', *The Atlantic*, July. Available at: http://www.theatlantic.com/magazine/archive/1945/07/as-we-may-think/303881/ (Accessed: 29 October 2012).

comScore (2016). The 2016 U.S. Mobile App Report. Available at: http://www.comscore.com/Insights/Presentations-and-Whitepapers/2016/The-2016-US-Mobile-App-Report (Accessed: 5 March 2017).

Cutts, M. and Shellen, J. (2005) *Preventing comment spam, Official Google Blog*. Available at: http://googleblog.blogspot.nl/2005/01/preventing-comment-spam.html (Accessed: 29 October 2012).

Dellarocas, C., Katona, Z., and Rand, W. (2013) 'Media, aggregators, and the link economy: Strategic hyperlink formation in content networks', *Management Science*, 59(10): 2360–2379.

De Maeyer, J. (2013) 'Towards a hyperlinked society: A critical review of link studies', *New Media & Society*, 15(5): 737–751. doi: 10.1177/1461444812462851.

Eason, J. (2015) 'Android M Developer Preview & Tools', *Android Developers Blog*, 28 May. Available at: https://android-developers.googleblog.com/2015/05/android-m-developer-preview-tools.html (Accessed: 4 March 2017).

Elmer, G. (1999) 'Web rings as computer-mediated communication', *CMC Magazine*, January. Available at: http://www.december.com/cmc/mag/1999/jan/elmer.html (Accessed: 27 February 2017).

Elmer, G. (2001) 'Hypertext on the Web: The beginnings and ends of Web Path-ology', *Space and Culture*, 10: 1–14.

Elmer, G. (2006) 'Re-tooling the network: Parsing the links and codes of the Web world', *Convergence: The International Journal of Research into New Media Technologies*, 12(1): 9–19. doi: 10.1177/1354856506061549.

Facebook for Developers (n.d.) *App Links – Documentation, Facebook for Developers*. Available at: https://developers.facebook.com/docs/applinks/analytics (Accessed: 14 February 2017).

Google Webspam Team (2017) 'A reminder about links in large-scale article campaigns', *Official Google Webmaster Central Blog*, 25 May. Available at: https://webmasters.googleblog.com/2017/05/a-reminder-about-links-in-large-scale.html (Accessed: 26 May 2017).

Grafton, A. (1997) *The Footnote: A Curious History*. Cambridge: Harvard University Press.

Halavais, A. (2008) 'The hyperlink as organizing principle', in Turow, J. and Tsui, L. (eds) *The hyperlinked Society*. Ann Arbor: The University of Michigan Press, pp. 39–55.

Hargittai, E. (2000) 'Open portals or closed gates? Channeling content on the World Wide Web', *Poetics*, 27(4): 233–253.

Helmond, A. (2008) *Blogging for engines. Blogs under the influence of software-engine relations*. University of Amsterdam. Available at: http://www.annehelmond.nl/2008/09/23/blogging-for-engines-blogs-under-the-influence-of-software-engine-relations/ (Accessed: 2 March 2017).

Helmond, A. (2013) 'The algorithmization of the hyperlink', *Computational Culture*, (3). Available at: http://computationalculture.net/article/the-algorithmization-of-the-hyperlink (Accessed: 4 February 2017).

Helmond, A. (2015) 'The platformization of the Web: Making Web data platform ready', *Social Media + Society*, 1(2): 1–11. doi: 10.1177/2056305115603080.

Herring, S.C. *et al.* (2005) 'Conversations in the blogosphere: An analysis "from the bottom up"', in *System Sciences, 2005. HICSS'05. Proceedings of the 38th Annual Hawaii International Conference on*. IEEE, pp. 1–11. Available at: http://ieeexplore.ieee.org/xpls/

abs_all.jsp?arnumber=1385453 (Accessed: 24 May 2015).
van den Heuvel, C. and Rayward, W.B. (2011) 'Mondothèque. A multimedia desk in a global internet', Poster for the 7th Iteration on 'Science Maps as Visual Interfaces to Digital Libraries' of the Places & Spaces Mapping Science Exhibition. Available at: http://www.narcis.nl/publication/RecordID/oai:pure.knaw.nl:publications%2F2c037a94-f0c7-4829-8d86-a7e2341991eb (Accessed: 25 February 2017).
Kirschenbaum, M. (2001) 'Materiality and matter and stuff: What electronic texts are made of', *Electronic Book Review*, 3. Available at: http://www.altx.com/ebr/riposte/rip12/rip12kir.htm (Accessed: 15 December 2014).
Kottke, J. (2000) *Finally. Did you notice the, kottke.org*. Available at: http://kottke.org/00/03/finally-did-you-notice-the (Accessed: 3 March 2017).
Krapp, P. (2006) 'Hypertext avant la lettre', in Chun, W. and Keenan, T. (eds) *New Media, Old Media: A History and Theory Reader*. New York: Routledge, pp. 359–374.
Landow, P.G.P. (ed.) (1991) *Hypertext: The Convergence of Contemporary Critical Theory and Technology*. Baltimore: The Johns Hopkins University Press.
Lialina, O. (2009) 'A vernacular Web', in Lialina, O. and Espenschied, D. (eds) *Digital Folklore*. Stuttgart: Merz Akademie, pp. 19–35.
Nelson, T.H. (1965) 'Complex Information Processing: A File Structure for the Complex, the Changing and the Indeterminate', in *Proceedings of the 1965 20th National Conference*. New York, NY, USA: ACM (ACM '65), pp. 84–100. doi: 10.1145/800197.806036.
Nelson, T.H. (1999) 'Xanalogical structure, needed now more than ever: Parallel documents, deep links to content, deep versioning, and deep re-use', *ACM Computing Surveys*, 31(4es). doi: 10.1145/345966.346033.
Nelson, T.H. (2016) *THE XANADU® PARALLEL UNIVERSE*. Available at: xanadu.com/xUniverse-D6 (Accessed: 2 March 2017).
O'Reilly, T. (2005) *What is Web 2.0: Design patterns and business models for the next generation of software, O'Reilly*. Available at: http://oreilly.com/web2/archive/what-is-web-20.html (Accessed: 4 November 2012).
Rayward, W.B. (1994) 'Visions of Xanadu: Paul Otlet (1868–1944) and hypertext', *Journal of the American Society for Information Science (1986–1998)*, 45(4): 235.
Rogers, R. (2002) 'Operating issue networks on the Web', *Science as Culture*, 11(2): 191–213.
Rogers, R. (2013) *Digital Methods*. Cambridge: The MIT Press.
Search Console Help (n.d.) *How Google Search Works, Google*. Available at: https://support.google.com/webmasters/answer/70897?hl=en (Accessed: 26 May 2017).
Siles, I. (2011) 'From online filter to web format: Articulating materiality and meaning in the early history of blogs', *Social Studies of Science*, 41(5): 737–758.
Song, F.W. (2010) 'Theorizing web 2.0: A cultural perspective', *Information, Communication & Society*, 13(2): 249–275.
Stevenson, M. (2016) 'Rethinking the participatory web: A history of HotWired's "new publishing paradigm," 1994–1997', *New Media & Society*, 18(7): 1331–1346. doi: 10.1177/1461444814555950.
Turow, J. (2008) 'Introduction: On not taking the hyperlink for granted', in Turow, J. and Tsui, L. (eds) *The Hyperlinked Society: Questioning Connections in the Digital Age*. Ann Arbor: University of Michigan Press, pp. 1–18.
Twitter (2011) 'Link sharing made simple', *Twitter Blog*, 7 June. Available at: https://blog.twitter.com/2011/link-sharing-made-simple (Accessed: 11 July 2013).
W3C (2014) *4.2.4 The link element, W3C Recommendation*. Available at: https://www.w3.org/TR/html5/document-metadata.html (Accessed: 2 March 2017).
W3C (n.d.) *Links, W3C Recommendation*. Available at: https://www.w3.org/TR/html401/struct/links.html (Accessed: 2 March 2017).
Walker, J. (2002) 'Links and power: The political economy of linking on the Web', in *Proceedings of the Thirteenth ACM Conference on Hypertext and Hypermedia*. ACM, pp. 72–73. Available at: http://dl.acm.org/citation.cfm?id=513358.
Wardrip-Fruin, N. (2004) 'What hypertext is', in *Proceedings of the Fifteenth ACM Conference on Hypertext and Hypermedia*. ACM, pp. 126–127.
Weinreich, H., Obendorf, H., and Lamersdorf, W. (2001) 'The look of the link – concepts for

the user interface of extended hyperlinks', in *Proceedings of the 12th ACM Conference on Hypertext and Hypermedia*. New York, NY, USA: ACM (HYPERTEXT '01), pp. 19–28. doi: 10.1145/504216.504225.

Weltevrede, E. and Helmond, A. (2012) 'Where do bloggers blog? Platform transitions within the historical Dutch blogosphere', *First Monday*, 17(2). doi: 10.5210/fm.v17i2.3775.

Winer, D. (2016) 'Facebook and linking is a big deal', *Scripting News*, 3 January. Available at: http://scripting.com/liveblog/users/davewiner/2016/01/03/0783.html (Accessed 4 March 2017).

Wright, A. (2014a) *Cataloging the World: Paul Otlet and the Birth of the Information Age*. Oxford: Oxford University Press.

Wright, A. (2014b) 'The secret history of hypertext', *The Atlantic*, 22 May. Available at: https://www.theatlantic.com/technology/archive/2014/05/in-search-of-the-proto-memex/371385/ (Accessed 18 February 2017).

17

# How Search Shaped and Was Shaped by the Web

Alexander Halavais

Search engines have long been seen as a set of services somehow 'bolted on' to the larger web experience. In this view, search engine technology allowed for an ever-more complete indexing of a rapidly growing new World Wide Web, and as the card catalog provided an index to the library stacks, the search engine was seen as somehow separate from the rest of the web. This is more than a metaphor: the technologies that make up web search trace their lineage directly to library cataloging, among other sources. But for many reasons, the relationship of search engines to the larger web is far messier. The architecture of the web has co-evolved with the development of search engine technologies, and the biases of those technologies have shaped – and continue to shape – the modern web.

This chapter traces the large-scale shift from web surfing to web searching, and what this has meant for the organization of the web over time. The massive reorganization from intentionally chaotic distributed hypertext to a largely indexed and searchable web marks one part of that shift. This has been driven not only by the technology of search, but by the commodification of attention online. As the search engine came to be the main gatekeeper of online attention, search became the economic engine and came to be closely tied to online advertising and marketing.

But this is far from unidirectional. While it is true that the technologies of search have had wide-ranging effects on the organization of information, those search engines did not emerge from a vacuum. In many cases, search evolved to meet specific needs brought about by new uses of the growing web. The development of search engines and the web were deeply intertwined and co-evolutionary. This chapter begins by tracing the changes in search over time, from the period before the emergence of the web to the present. It then examines the question of how new markets of attention and online socialization have both affected and been affected by the structures and biases of search engines.

By understanding search, we are better able to understand how the web as a whole works, and how it has changed over time.

## THE LONG HISTORY OF THE SEARCH ENGINE

The World Wide Web changed the face of the internet, in many ways subsuming it. We still use a number of applications outside of the web, from email to chat to gaming, and video content takes up roughly three-quarters of total internet traffic (Cisco, 2016), but the World Wide Web was the application that took the internet to the masses. Within several years of the first web browser being introduced, there were at least a couple dozen search engines that sought to make sense of the rapidly expanding web (Chu and Rosenthal, 1996). Many of these engines owed their existence to pre-web search technologies. In each of these cases, search answered a need. The information structure was not efficiently browsable; a technology was needed that would make it more effective for the user.

It is difficult to identify a clear starting point for search engines. The process of indexing large collections of digital text generally comes under the aegis of 'information retrieval'. While that field has received far more attention and engagement since the early 1990s, it certainly did not begin with the internet – it grew up with digital computing. Some draw a connection to Vannevar Bush's prophetic 'As We May Think' (1945), which described an imagined device (the 'Memex') that allowed the researcher to easily query a large collection of text and retrieve the appropriate document. He and his team built prototypes that did this with microfilm in the 1930s, and others similarly indexed systems for punch cards (Sanderson and Croft, 2012). The first examples of purely electronic machines that could do something similar soon followed. By the 1960s the digital computer's ability to not just crunch numbers but store data was becoming apparent, and it was during this period that many of the models for representing documents and algorithms for searching were developed, especially as part of Gerard Salton's research groups at Harvard and then Cornell. His measure of document similarity (as the coefficient of the cosine between vectors described by the totality of the terms found in each document) and other ideas developed during the period became the core of early search engine functionality (Salton, 1975).

Early mechanical and digital computing is not the only starting point. The systems eventually used to index digital data had been used to catalog printed and written information for as long as those have existed. For very modest collections, such an index could be held in the head of the owner or librarian. Especially as the collection increased in size, creating an externalized index became an essential task, and the power initially vested in the librarian moved to the technical embodiment of that person: the index (Kaser, 1962). That index, and the metadata that accompanies it, has been a part of what we traditionally think of as libraries for thousands of years.

By the 1980s, traditional printed card catalogs were largely being replicated digitally and displaced by online indexes (Borgman, 1986). And with the growth of the internet during the same decade, a new and rapidly growing source of digital data emerged. With it came the need to search. Applications intended to search through the files of a single computer were expanded to include indexes of other computers on the network. New forms of searching also emerged. The Unix command 'finger', for example, provided information about a particular user, including when that user last logged on, and often some personal contact information. Its creator, Les Earnest, designed 'finger' in 1971 to aid in social networking at the Stanford Artificial Intelligence Lab (quoted in Shah, 2000):

> People generally worked long hours there, often with unpredictable schedules. When you wanted to meet with some group, it was important to know who was there and when the others would likely reappear. It also was important to be able to locate potential volleyball players when you wanted to play, Chinese food freaks when you wanted to eat, and antisocial computer users when it appeared that something strange was happening on the system.

When computers were networked via the internet, it became possible to 'finger' individuals from across the country or the world, to find out more about them, and in the days before the web was among the more widely used protocols for searching for information about individuals online.

The development of the File Transfer Protocol (FTP) led to even more disconnected collections of files. Often public FTP servers allowed individuals to upload or download files anonymously. Since a file name was rarely descriptive enough to be of particular use, these servers often had an index file, updated by hand, that listed the available files and briefly described their contents. This quickly became unsustainable, and as a result, arguably the first search engine appeared in 1990 (Deutsch, 2000). Archie provided a way of searching across FTP servers to find a particular file. After it launched, it grew quickly: 'From 30 hits a day, we soon went to 30 an hour, then 30 a minute'. Archie's approach to gathering information from distributed servers and then providing it as a search service became the model for the search engines that followed. This included Veronica, a search engine for Gopher, an intermediate step toward the World Wide Web that made it possible to browse files available on the internet via a menu structure. Like Archie, it searched through the titles of files and indexed them by crawling through the menus of 'gopherspace' (Parker, 1994).

In 1989, when Tim Berners-Lee prototyped the 'WorldWideWeb', a project that provided distributed access to hypertexts, he already could draw on several years of development around hypermedia. The ACM Hypertext conferences had started two years earlier, and had already examined the question of searching hypertext when the amount of information grew too large to be made sense of through browsing (Frisse, 1987). Indeed, Berners-Lee himself saw the project as a melding of information retrieval and browsable hypertexts. In one of the early announcements of the project (1991) he notes:

> The WWW world consists of documents, and links. Indexes are special documents which, rather than being read, may be searched. The result of such a search is another ('virtual') document containing links to the documents found. A simple protocol ('HTTP') is used to allow a browser program to request a keyword search by a remote information server.

Much of the growth of the web can be attributed to how open ended it was. Adding to the growing web was as simple as making a link. Exploring this new web of information was as exciting as it was intimidating. But as the web grew exponentially, and particularly as it came to be used commercially, the need to be able to rapidly find what you were looking for became acute. The web needed to be searchable as well as surfable.

## WEB SEARCH BEFORE GOOGLE

For many people, Google represents the way one accesses the content of the internet. It can be easy to forget that there were a number of popular web search engines during early popularization of the web, and even after Google came to dominate. The earliest search engines had a single challenge: effectively accessing and indexing the rapidly growing web. But as search engines did a better job keeping up with the web, they faced a new challenge: there was a growing effort across the web to become more easily noticed by the search engines.

One of the earliest web search engines was Wandex, developed by Matthew Gray at the Massachusetts Institute of Technology. Gray initially created a crawler, the World

Wide Web Wanderer, in an effort to measure the size of the growing web, but by the end of 1993 the resulting index made the web searchable. Even after initial search engines were made available, the discovery of useful websites was often human-curated through the distribution of 'what's new' emails, shared collections of bookmarks, collaborative 'webrings' that linked together like sites (Elmer, 1999), or web catalogs like Yahoo! or DMOZ (Callery, 1996). Carefully organized 'bookmark files' with the URLs of interesting or oft-revisited sites (Abrams et al., 1998) could easily be published as pages with web-ready versions generated by some of the early web browsers. As a result, many personal home pages included a list of favored sites, a practice that eventually dovetailed with 'blogrolls' once blogging became popular. Reports of new and interesting sites could be found in a number of places, from magazines like *Wired* to emailed bulletins.

While bookmark files certainly helped users to 'refind' sites – something search engines are now frequently relied on to provide – they were of less use in finding specific information. Especially early in the evolution of the web, this is hardly surprising. Today, there is the general expectation that if something (an idea, a company, a person) exists, there is some indicator of it somewhere on the web; it is simply a matter of finding it. In the case of the early web, it was far more likely to be a surprise when something you were interested in had some sort of presence on the web. As a result, the early web was ripe for exploration and discovery. *Searching* the web only made sense as its size increased.

That size increased quickly. The web consisted of just over 600 sites by the end of 1993. That number was over 10,000 by the end of 1994 and crossed the million mark in the first half of 1997 (Zakon, 2017). While surfing through several hundred sites, even at the slow speeds of the early 1993 internet, was entirely possible, visiting a million – and eventually a billion – certainly was not. And with commercialization, the ways in which people used the web were changing as well. Brian Pinkerton (1994) indicates this issue as central to the development of one of the first web search engines, WebCrawler:

> Imagine trying to find a book in a library without a card catalog. It is not an easy task! Finding specific documents in a distributed hypertext system like the World-Wide Web can be just as difficult. To get from one document to another users follow links that identify the documents. A user who wants to find a specific document in such a system must choose among the links, each time following links that may take her further from her desired goal. In a small, unchanging environment, it might be possible to design documents that did not have these problems. But the World-Wide Web is decentralized, dynamic, and diverse; navigation is difficult, and finding information can be a challenge. This problem is called the resource discovery problem.

Wandex largely replicated the functionality of Veronica, with a crawler that was able to find and follow links. But like that predecessor, it also indexed only the titles of pages, not the content. Brian Pinkerton's WebCrawler and the Repository-Based Software Engineering (RBSE) spider and indexer each extended this to indexing the textual content of the page. By the end of 1994, the WebCrawler had received its millionth query, and had been joined by more than a half-dozen other early search engines.

In terms of overall design, these shared very similar architectures, each crawling the web with robots, constructing an index, and providing a front end to handle queries and generate a list of search engine results. Competition was fierce, but largely revolved around coverage: how broadly their robots crawled and how often. As Bharat and Broder noted in 1998, a cottage industry had emerged around comparing the most popular search engines, with scores of articles and a dedicated website. They estimated the coverage and overlapped four of the most popular search engines of the time: HotBot, AltaVista, Excite, and Infoseek. The search engines had different sizes of coverage, but the authors note that their most startling discovery was how very little overlap the search engines had: 'less than 1.4% of the total coverage, or about 2.2 million pages appeared to be indexed by all four engines'. Dogpile and other meta-search engines could help a bit here, by aggregating the results across search engines, but there was concern that much of the web was undiscoverable.

Moreover, a clear financial model to provide these resources had yet to emerge. Serving an advertisement for AT&T in 1994, *HotWired* was a pioneer in selling web banner ads, which helped to make their HotBot search engine a profitable venture. They claim (Singel, 2010) that this was the spark that led to the 'portal war' and eventually the dot-com bubble. While there is no doubt that search engines played an important part in the commercial development of the web, that may apportion too much of the credit – and blame – to the role of advertising online. Nonetheless, the ad-supported model would make search one of the few profitable industries on the early web, and drive out other financial models for search, including paid submission, paid inclusion, and paid placement. Directly paying to manipulate search results undermines the value of an engine, at least in a competitive market (see Henshaw, 2001), and eventually it drew the scrutiny of regulators as well. Many search engines, especially a young Google, also provided customized search and enterprise solutions that helped to fund their efforts. Others shifted in this direction as well, including Inktomi, which provided search results for several engines, and Northern Light, which launched a search engine in 1997 that included links results in proprietary databases, and eventually closed down their public search engine to focus on enterprise search.

Because search engines always yielded more potential results than an individual could make use of, all of them provided some form of prioritization; as Schwartz (1998) wryly notes: 'Although experience with search engines sometimes makes this hard to believe, search results are usually ranked by relevance…'. The disbelief was natural, since it was often difficult to discern the reasoning behind the ranking. First, the specific algorithm that determined where in the list a site fell was almost always a closely held secret. Second, without any semantic data, there were limited ways of determining the most 'important' pages. These included measuring the frequency and proximity of the query terms on the page, as well as whether pages had been clicked through on earlier searches, or whether it was part of a human-reviewed list of sites (sometimes taken from category-based sites like DMOZ). Third was an influence that gradually changed the dynamic between search engines and the searchable web: site owners sought any advantage they could in rising in the ranks of relevance.

The formal restrictions on commercial activity on the internet were lifted just as the web was taking off. By the late 1990s the 'search engine wars' largely focused on ways of ranking search results, while those who had things to sell online were particularly interested in influencing those rankings. The basic problem of assembling and keeping current an index had been superseded by the question of 'relevance' (Introna and Nissenbaum, 2000). For some – including Tim Berners-Lee (1996), one of the architects of the web – for it to be useful, the web would need to be coded with semantic data, allowing computers to make sense of it in a more comprehensive fashion:

> To date, the principle [sic] machine analysis of material on the web has been its textual indexing by search engines. Search engines have proven remarkably useful, in that large indexes can be searched very rapidly, and obscure documents found. They have proved to be remarkably useless, in that their searches generally take only vocabulary of documents into account, and have little or no concept of document quality, and so produce a lot of junk. (Berners-Lee, 1996)

While a number of efforts were made toward the inclusion of semantic data for search, the web at large remained – and remains today – wildly unstructured. Moreover, the cat-and-mouse game between search engines and marketers continued unabated. Into this fray came a new weapon that would significantly disrupt that ongoing conflict: PageRank.

## THE GOOGLE REVOLUTION

In early 1996, Stanford University doctoral students Larry Page and Sergey Brin started working on BackRub, which would eventually come to be called Google. The initial advantage of Google over the existing search engines was embodied in the PageRank algorithm, which took a page from academic citation analysis and used the information from hyperlinks as a kind of peer review. Those pages that received the most links from popular pages floated to the top of the 'relevant' results. Page and Brin described it not in terms of citation, but, from an intuitive sense, from the perspective of a 'random surfer' (Page et al., 1999). A user who randomly surfs links on the web would be more likely to wind up on a page with a high PageRank.

PageRank is far from the only reason for Google's long-term rise to search engine dominance, but there can be little doubt that the algorithm changed the balance of power between search engines and the marketers hoping to gain an advantage through them – at least temporarily. For the first time, web authors had to think not only about how to make the site appealing to the search engine robots that visited it, but how to make its hyperlinked 'location' in the web ecosystem more appealing. Much like retailers in the physical world have to think about neighborhoods, foot traffic, and visibility, suddenly it was more important than ever before that others linked to your site.

Naturally, having a large number of inbound hyperlinks (or 'backlinks') was always important to website owners. After all, it was not just the theoretical surfer envisioned by PageRank who followed hyperlinks: that is how many people found their way to your website, especially before the turn of the millennium. If you wanted to be found, you had to be linked. And if you were linked by a particularly influential site – especially some of the group blogs and news filters like Slashdot and its descendants – you could see your web traffic spike to an extreme degree. These flash crowds were at one point called the 'Slashdot Effect', but could be seen as a result of sites that followed the group news approach Slashdot pioneered: Kuro5hin, Fark, Digg, Reddit, and – although it is not an exact analog – now Facebook and Twitter. So, even if backlinks were not important to the process of search, they would be of interest to the web author. Naturally, these two functions went hand-in-hand, though. Once a site had received traffic from a flash mob, it was likely to receive more links, and higher search rankings – a cumulative process that is common among a number of networked environments (Price, 1976).

While the initial work on what would become Google web search began in 1996, and the search engine was launched by 1998, Google really came into its own at the turn of the millennium, and Search Engine Land (Sullivan, 2010) called what followed 'The Google Decade'. Much of this had to do with Google's seemingly incessant march into everything from ecommerce to social networking. In particular, the basis for Google's most significant source of income – the AdWords advertising network – was launched in 2000, providing the basis for its steady rise to one of the most profitable businesses on the planet.

Starting with the acquisition of an archive of Usenet messages called Dejanews in 2001, much of Google's expansion occurred via acquisitions that became products for advertising, blogging, mapping, cloud-based services, artificial intelligence, online sales and coupons, video sharing, ebooks, robotics, social networking, facial recognition, health, telephony, mapping, natural language systems, customer relationship management, and mobile software, among many more. These helped Google to produce a popular email service, a mobile phone operating system, and a range of other services that seemingly have little to do with search. Just as PageRank shifted the focus to the web ecosystem, Google used the data collected from these services to create a more effective search engine and a more effective advertising network.

If the period before Google represented a war of attrition and attention among search engines seeking to discover a new market, the period since Google's inception has been marked by consolidation. Certainly, Google continues to have significant challenges from rivals. In particular, the Chinese search engine Baidu is often the first choice for those seeking materials from China or in Chinese, though it may not have the broader global coverage of Google (Jiang, 2014). And Microsoft's Bing search engine continues to attract a segment of searchers. And a handful of search engines with names familiar to long-time denizens of the web continue to operate, including Yahoo!, AOL, Excite, and Ask.com (though in several cases these sites deliver search results provided by Google or Bing). Nonetheless, by most measures, of every five people searching the web, roughly four are likely to be googling (NetMarketShare, 2017). Though the basic technologies that make up the web as a whole had not changed, the architecture had, moving from a browsable to a searchable space.

## MONETIZING ATTENTION

By 2006, the Oxford English Dictionary had added 'to google', as a synonym for searching the internet. The web come to be a mainstay in the media diet for a good portion of the world, and as audiences left traditional mass media, advertisers needed to make sense of a new and challenging medium. They naturally focused on the search engine as a technology that acted as a gatekeeper and provided a clear space for influencing users.

Google was in a prime position for addressing these new interests. As Siva Vaidhyanathan (2011) persuasively writes, Google is more than merely an application for searching the web, or an extraordinarily successful internet company. The process of 'googlization' reaches into nearly every corner of our information ecosystem, coloring our social interactions, our political processes, and the ways in which we come to know the world. Of course, media have always shaped our experience of the world, setting the agenda of our political debates, or influencing what we see as risks and threats. In some ways, the internet should have reversed the ways in which global media attenuated our sources of information. After all, with broad access to the web, everyone now had their own 'printing press'.

While the early web might have looked like a distributed conversation, where information could only be found by 'surfing' from page to page, search engines changed that, making pages increasingly more findable, but less discoverable. Search engines became a point of control, focusing attention on some parts of the web while ignoring others. On the early web, it was perfectly reasonable to publish something and hope to be 'discovered' by people who happened by and were willing to recommend your site to others. When the recommendations came from a search engine instead, influencing those engines became more important. And as Google gradually became synonymous with search, it also became the central switch for information and knowledge on the internet.

It initially wrested some control over attention that online marketing and search engine optimization (SEO) had begun to accrue, evening out the playing field somewhat. By 1995, the 'Multi-Media Marketing Group' had been founded, which produced a popular newsletter with tips for influencing search engines (Knowles, 2017). The SEO industry grew continuously until 2016, when salaries and demand for SEO expertise abated slightly. Especially in the early days, the term 'spamdexing' was far more popular (Torok, 1996). Initially, the focus of

SEO practitioners was on 'keyword stuffing': determining which keywords were worth targeting in searches and then including as many of them as high on the page as possible. Early on, these might have appeared in the metadata tags for the page, including those that specifically indicated keywords chosen by the author, but once search engines began ignoring such metadata for the purposes of ranking, authors turned to new approaches. These included repeating targeted keywords throughout the text of the page, sometimes with text with the same color as the page background, or otherwise hidden from all but the search engine. This could result in visitors using a search engine and arriving at a page that had absolutely nothing to do with their search terms.

This was particularly true for pornography. During the 1990s, there was significant concern over the availability of pornography online, especially to children. Part of this was because, as Susanna Paasonen describes elsewhere in this volume, pornography was one of the earliest commercially successful ventures on the web. Users often searched for pornographic content, and providers sought buyers who could make an instant purchase. In many ways search engines served as a natural intermediary between those seeking out pornography – often with little interest in paying – and those seeking to provide it at a price. Online pornography providers innovated in a range of areas, from advertising networks to pop-ups to the use of online video and safe online payments. One of those areas of innovation was affiliate networks: developing automated systems that provided rewards for bringing paying customers to a site. Those who created these affiliate sites were single-mindedly interested in drawing searchers' attention, and one of the most effective ways of doing this was to attract not just their legitimate searches for adult content, but searches on just about any topic.

Naturally, this reduced the effectiveness of the search engine for the user, who was seeking 'relevant' results. Those searching AltaVista or HotBot would often have to wade through a number of pornographic results – including, at times, those illegal in their jurisdiction – regardless of the information sought. During a period in which search engines were in direct competition, those that could avoid misdirecting users had an advantage. Obviously, as the number of pages on the web ballooned, and as the web became even more commercial, the question of not just returning results, but returning the most 'important' results became a priority. Search engines responded to spamdexing as quickly as they could, but it rapidly became a game of cat-and-mouse.

It took a bit longer for spamdexers to figure their way around PageRank, and many celebrated Google for bringing some measure of balance back to the web. While spamdexers had developed a repertoire of techniques for manipulating their own websites to achieve high rankings in search engine results pages, they had not needed to think about the broader web ecosystem, and the effect of linkages, before Google came along. As Page et al. (1999) noted, the low ranks of these pages were likely 'because people do not want to link to pornographic sites from their own webpages'. Google rapidly gained in popularity against the other search engines thanks to its reputation of presenting a view of the web that had been manipulated far less and provided what were sometimes considered more useful results.

But Google was certainly not a one-trick pony. Soon after it gained significant popularity, website owners targeted PageRank. Rather than making changes to their own site, they would create rings of sites that linked to one another, or seek to have links made from other sites. And it was not just the link that mattered: the context of the link could affect how Google interpreted a site. This effect was noted and exploited by some, before it became common knowledge. In early 2001, Farhad Manjoo noted a strange effect: searching for 'dumb motherfucker' on Google presented you with a link for merchandise relating to the US president at the time.

He hypothesized some potential reasons for this, but in the coming years it became clear that including keywords in links to a page could affect how Google's search engine indexed it. The technique, called a 'Google bomb', was used for several years to collectively shape what Google indexed.

While Google bombing represented, largely, an amusing diversion, it also provided a small peek into the ways in which Google continuously changed its technology to prevent manipulation by SEO practitioners and spamdexers. The rise of the Google bomb occurred around the time of the rise of the blogosphere. Thanks to heavy linking and frequently updated pages, blogs came to exert a significant influence on Google. When a collection of bloggers decided to, they could collect this power to create a Google bomb (Kahn and Kellner, 2004). But more broadly, blogs had natural advantages when it came to achieving high search rankings, and some complained that the blogosphere was taking over Google's results pages. Others used this to their advantage, either creating their own blog networks or spamming comments on blogs from around the web to provide links to the page they were promoting. (Eventually, the latter was dampened through the 'nofollow' tag, which excluded links in comments from providing the 'googlejuice' that adds to a site's prominence in results.)

Today, Google uses dozens of 'signals' beyond PageRank in order to provide results and counter attempted manipulation. Nonetheless, it relies heavily on reading the environment around a site, and attempts to manipulate those links in order to gain ranking continue to be used, and are one of the few reasons for Google to execute a 'manual action', which is sometimes referred to as a 'Google death sentence' (Malaga, 2010). There have been a number of examples of Google's removal of a site from the web resulting in substantial financial repercussions for the violating site. Even larger companies that have been penalized by Google, including American retailer JC Penney (Segal, 2011), and BMW's site in Germany (Blakely and McCormack, 2006), have felt the sting of being shunned. A US court recently decided that Google has the absolute right to delist companies if it so chooses (*e-ventures* v. *Google*, 2017). Google's ability to effectively silence voices on the web – not by removing them, but by making them unfindable – is remarkable.

Google advises the creators of websites to simply make their sites usable for human visitors, and they will do the rest. Nonetheless, producers of websites have continuously tried to gain an advantage and Google has continuously adjusted their algorithms to counter this. This process has been called by some the 'Google Dance', as pages climb and fall according to new criteria for relevance. There have also been large-scale changes that significantly reorganize the results pages and determine who new winners and losers are. Sometimes these are explained by the search engine (though rarely in detail), and other times they are noted by keen observers in the SEO community. Sometimes these changes can be quite substantial, with major elements of the ranking or interface systems changed. For example, in late August of 2013, Google deployed 'Hummingbird', which provided for more conversational queries. These changes are often tested with a subset of searches made by unsuspecting visitors before they are used more broadly.

The idea that search is a neutral conduit, a switchboard that allows you to reach your desired page, is part of the mythology of the search engine. It occupies an important space both in terms of the distribution of knowledge, and the flow of commerce. As such, it is difficult to imagine that it would not be subject to substantial efforts to influence its functionality. The primary way this has been achieved is by changing the way web pages appear, and how the web itself is linked together. Despite a design that was intended to be 'bottom up', the web has evolved in an effort to reflect the biases of search engines, and particularly the biases of Google.

## THE BIASING ENGINE

Critics of search often seek to determine whether Google is 'biased'. This is the wrong question to ask: search is inherently a biasing process, favoring some results over others. This does not mean that Google wishes to present a particular position or idea, necessarily, but rather that any system that acts as a filter must also introduce some form of bias.

As one early newspaper article (Pegoraro, 1999) had it, Google 'sees the Web as a popularity contest'. In that respect, Google has become more biased over time, as it aims to provide better results. But just as the word 'biased' is problematic, so is the word 'better'. The natural question is: better for whom? Given that Google's product is its users' attention, which it sells to advertisers in order to produce a profit, Google's aim is to create a bias that attracts users back to Google. Because of this, 'better' is often better for the user.

But a number of criticisms have suggested that what the user gets from Google is biased in ways that are not necessarily better for society, and some of these critiques find parallels with those of journalism and mass media more broadly. There has long been a concern that Google presents a bias toward, broadly, its advertisers. Others suggests that it commodifies knowledge, presenting it in brief, easily digestible chunks that draw us away from more considered forms of learning and make us collectively more stupid (Carr, 2008). Another concern – especially with search results that since 2009 are influenced by our past searches, our activity on the web, or what our friends look for – is that we may find information that satiates us by playing to our preconceptions (Pariser, 2011). A search engine created in 2008 as an alternative to this kind of 'filter bubble', called DuckDuckGo, has enjoyed some modest success by not tracking its users' searches, and therefore allowing them to escape from self-reinforcing echo chambers (Wauters, 2011).

One of the more longstanding challenges to the issue of what Google considers 'important' comes from a particular US-centric (or, alternatively, a globalized) view that might miss important national or cultural nuance. Baidu played directly to that difference in advertising its search engine. An article in *Computerworld* (Lemon, 2007: 26) described an early ad for the search engine:

> 'I get it', the Western man says, speaking heavily accented Chinese. Surrounded by beautiful Chinese women in the video advertisement, he grins with self-satisfaction. Nearby, a suave Chinese man dressed in scholar's robes laughs. 'You don't necessarily get it', he says. As the ad unfolds, the Chinese scholar proceeds to humiliate the Westerner, mocking his poor Chinese-language skills. In the end, the women flock to the scholar's side, and the Westerner is left confused, alone and humiliated.

In order to protect its cultural capital – as well as some degree of political control – China has supported the development of alternative search engines like Baidu, through both direct funding and policy that has been at times antagonistic toward Google.

And China is not alone in this regard. In his 2007 book, Jean-Noël Jeanneney suggested, for example, that a Google search is likely to lead to an Anglo-centric view of the French revolution; not necessarily ignoring French sources, but favoring those from the perspective of English observers. The title of his book – *Quand Google défie l'Europe* – also hints at issues of national control. Driven in part by the concern regarding such control (Abelson et al., 2008: 159), France and Germany partnered in an attempt to create an alternative to Google with the Quaero project (2007–13). While other national search engines, including the Swiss Search.ch, continue to attract visitors, none of these have reached anything approaching the traffic of Baidu, let alone Google.

At least for the time being, Google remains a central gateway for ideas and money on the web. While nations can attempt to influence that filter through policy or the courts, the most frequent attempt to change what Google delivers is by reshaping the web. Search engines began as an attempt to inflict order on the chaotic and dynamic web of interconnected pages that made up the growing World Wide Web. Today, web authors are just as likely to use their own pages in an attempt to inflict a new order on the global search engine. But that centrality is facing a new set of challenges.

## EVOLVING WITH THE SOCIAL WEB

The term 'social search' is a bit of a misnomer; how could search be anything but social? However, over the last decade a significant amount of online interaction has moved to platforms that support social participation. Naturally, there has been a question about how search engines might shift as internet users' attention and focus has shifted.

One version of the question relates to how search engines might be used to index social media platforms and provide search for and with them. These systems represent a significant challenge in terms of the volume and velocity of change: making Twitter and Facebook searchable is no small problem, and requires a more direct connection than is available via the web interface. So it makes sense, for example, that Google might partner directly with Twitter to more easily index their 9,000 tweets per second (Patel, 2015). Likewise, Facebook, Google, Microsoft, and Amazon, among others, have partnered to research how artificial intelligence might make their systems for filtering and finding more effective.

At the same time, these platforms have direct access to their own data and are creating their own, internal search engines to help make sense of it. In 2012, Facebook saw more than a billion queries a day to its search engine, and by 2016 that number was up to two billion and still growing (Constantine, 2016). If Facebook considered itself a search engine, that would make it the second most popular search engine in the world, and the fastest growing. And like Google, Facebook sees effective search as the gateway to selling advertisements.

Even before the rise of the social media platforms, search engines focused on their forerunners: blogs. Though the blogosphere had its own search engines, the largest of which was Technorati, Google focused on blogs not just because of the currency and interest of their topics, but because their link structure was so essential to finding the 'important' sites on the web. It was a bit surprising then that Google initially showed little interest in using signals from social media platforms to aid their search process. Microsoft's Bing experimented with ways of directly indicating which results your friends found interesting, and Google did the same for a short time. There is a great deal of speculation as to how important social signals are to prioritizing results on these two search engines today, and while Google continues to indicate that it does not use social signals (Schwartz, 2015), there is some consensus that results rankings correlate to social media attention.

The real impact of 'social search' has yet to be felt. Over the last few years news organizations have noticed a trend in the way people end up on their sites. Many still go directly to the websites of trusted news sources, but a significant number arrive not thanks to a search engine results page, but rather via a shared message on Facebook, Twitter, or another social media platform. Google, which for a time was so ubiquitous it was coming to be seen as the internet itself, is gradually being supplanted by Facebook, and especially by Facebook on mobile devices, a shift that has accelerated rapidly during the 2010s.

This shift away from the search engine interface is something that Google predicted in the earliest days of the company, but it remains unclear what search without visible search engines will become. Certainly, the collaborative filtering function of Facebook holds part of the key, as do increasingly sophisticated systems for analyzing both the content of the web and the meaning of online messages. The future will continue to require search, but we may no longer see the search process as clearly, or find the need to identify things called 'search engines'.

## CO-EVOLVING SEARCH

Understanding the history of the web requires not just an archive of the pages that were created, but a broad understanding of the context in which audiences encountered those materials. The web, as a broad environment, is far more than its pages, their content, and a collection of hyperlinks. Much of how individuals experience the web has to do with how they find and encounter the information on it. That alone would make it important to understand how search engines have developed over time.

But perhaps more importantly, it is impossible to cleanly divide search engines from the larger web; the web makes little sense outside of the context of the search engine. It is not just an essential 'feature' of the web, it represents a technology for organizing our social experiences and our collective knowledge. And just as the content and experience of the web is not entirely in the hands of the authors of websites, the nature of search engines is only partially determined by their engineers. The search engine has evolved to meet the needs of users and web authors, and these groups have each contributed significantly to the evolution of web search. That back and forth is likely to continue, and so understanding the search engine requires an understanding of how the web has changed, and any hope of understanding the nature of the web relies on a thorough understanding of the search engine.

## REFERENCES

Abelson, H., Ledeen, K., and Lewis, H.R. (2008) *Blown to Bits: Your Life, Liberty, and Happiness After the Digital Explosion*. Upper Saddle River, New Jersey: Addison-Wesley.

Abrams, D., Baecker, R., and Chignell, M. (1998) 'Information Archiving with Bookmarks: Personal Web Space Construction and Organization', *CHI '98 Proceedings of the SIGCHI Conference on Human Factors in Computing Systems*, Los Angeles, California, April 18–23, New York: ACM, pp. 41–8.

Berners-Lee, T. (1991) WorldWideWeb: Summary, Usenet: alt.hypertext, 9 August 1991. Available at: https://groups.google.com/forum/#!msg/comp.archives/CfsHISNYPUI/DTs60INnuzcJ [Accessed 15 June 2018].

Berners-Lee, T. (1996) The World Wide Web: Past, Present and Future. Available at: https://www.w3.org/People/Berners-Lee/1996/ppf.html [Accessed 15 June 2018].

Bharat, K., and Broder, A. (1998) 'A Technique for Measuring the Relative Size and Overlap of Public Web Search Engines', *Computer Networks and ISDN Systems*, 30(1): 379–88.

Blakely, R., and McCormack, H. (2006) 'Google's "Death Penalty" for BMW', *The Times*, February 6. Available at: https://www.thetimes.co.uk/article/googles-death-penalty-for-bmw-wpbtz992h8v [Accessed 15 June 2018].

Borgman, C.L. (1986) 'The User's Mental Model of an Information Retrieval System: An Experiment on a Prototype Online Catalog', *International Journal of Man-Machine Studies*, 24(1): 47–64.

Bush, V. (1945) 'As We May Think', *Atlantic Monthly*, 176: 101–8.

Callery, A. (1996) 'Yahoo! Cataloging the Web', *Untangling the Web: Proceedings of the Conference Sponsored by the Librarians Association of the University of California, Santa Barbara, and Friends of the UCSB Library*. Available at: http://files.eric.ed.gov/fulltext/ED403886.pdf [Accessed 15 June 2018].

Carr, N. (2008) 'Is Google Making Us Stupid? What the Internet Is Doing to Our Brains', *The Atlantic*, July/August. Available at: https://www.theatlantic.com/magazine/archive/2008/07/is-google-making-us-stupid/306868/ [Accessed 15 June 2018].

Chu, H., and Rosenthal, M. (1996) 'Search Engines for the World Wide Web: A Comparative Study and Evaluation Methodology', *Proceedings of the Annual Meeting – American Society for Information Science*, 33: 127–35.

Cisco (2016) White Paper: Cisco VNI Forecast and Methodology, 2015–2020. Available at: http://www.cisco.com/c/en/us/solutions/collateral/service-provider/visual-networking-index-vni/complete-white-paper-c11-481360.html.

Constantine, J. (2016) 'Facebook Sees 2 Billion Searches per Day, But It's Attacking Twitter, Not Google', *TechCrunch*, July 27. Available at: https://techcrunch.com/2016/07/27/facebook-will-make-you-talk/

Deutsch, P. (2000) 'Archie: A Darwinian Development Process', *IEEE Internet Computing*, 4(1): 69–71.

Elmer, G. (1999) 'Web Rings as Computer-Mediated Communication', *CMC Magazine*, January. Available at: http://www.december.com/cmc/mag/1999/jan/elmer.html

e-ventures v. Google (2017) Memorandum and Order, US District Court, Middle District of Florida, Fort Meyers Division. Available at: http://digitalcommons.law.scu.edu/cgi/viewcontent.cgi?article=2410&context=historical.

Frisse, M.E. (1987) 'Searching for Information in a Hypertext Medical Handbook', in Stephen Weiss and Mayer Schwartz (eds.), *Proceedings of ACM Hypertext 87 Conference*, November 13–15, 1987, Chapel Hill, North Carolina, pp. 57–66.

Henshaw, R. (2001) 'What Next for Internet Journals? Implications of the Trend towards Paid Placement in Search Engines', *First Monday*, 6(9). Available at: http://firstmonday.org/ojs/index.php/fm/article/view/884/793 [Accessed 15 June 2018].

Introna, L.D., and Nissenbaum, H. (2000) 'Shaping the Web: Why the Politics of Search Engines Matter', *The Information Society*, 16: 169–85.

Jeanneney, J.-N. (2007) *Google and the Myth of Universal Knowledge*, Teresa Lavender Fagen (trans.). Chicago: University of Chicago Press.

Jiang, M. (2014) 'The Business and Politics of Search Engines: A Comparative Study of Baidu and Google's Search Results of Internet Events in China', *New Media & Society*, 16(2): 212–33.

Kahn, R., and Kellner, D. (2004) 'New Media and Internet Activism: From the "Battle of Seattle" to Blogging', *New Media & Society*, 6(1): 87–95.

Kaser, D. (1962) 'In principium Erat Verbum', *Peabody Journal of Education*, 39(5): 258–63.

Knowles, M. (2017) The History of SEO. Available at: http://www.thehistoryofseo.com [Accessed 15 June 2018].

Lemon, S. (2007) 'Out-Googling Google: Chinese Search Giant Baidu is Beating Google at Its Own Game in China, But It's Playing by Different Rules', *Computerworld*, April 30, p. 26.

Malaga, R.A. (2010) 'Search Engine Optimization: Black and White Hat Approaches', in Marvin V. Zelkowitz (ed.), *Advances in Computers: Improving the Web*, London: Academic Press, pp. 1–41.

Manjoo, F. (2001) 'Google Link is Bush League', *Wired News*, January 25. Available at: http://archive.wired.com/science/discoveries/news/2001/01/41401 [Accessed 15 June 2018].

NetMarketShare (2017) 'Desktop Search Engine Market Share, January 2017'. Available at: http://www.netmarketshare.com/search-engine-market-share.aspx [Accessed 15 June 2018].

Page, L., Brin, S., Motwani, R., and Winograd, T. (1999) 'The PageRank Citation Ranking: Bringing Order to the Web', Stanford Infolab, 422. Available at: http://ilpubs.stanford.edu:8090/422/ [Accessed 15 June 2018].

Pariser, E. (2011) *The Filter Bubble: What the Internet Is Hiding from You*. New York: Penguin.

Parker, G. (1994) Internet Guide: Veronica. Available at: http://web.archive.org/web/20040808093422/http://www.lib.umich.edu/govdocs/godort/archive/elec/intveron.txt.old [Accessed 15 June 2018].

Patel, N. (2015) 'Everything You Need to Know about the Google-Twitter Partnership', Search Engine Land, March 20 Available at: http://searchengineland.com/everything-need-know-google-twitter-partnership-216892 [Accessed 15 June 2018].

Pegoraro, R. (1999) 'Googly Eyes', *The Washington Post*, January 22, p. N62.

Pinkerton, B. (1994) 'Finding What People Want: Experiences with WebCrawler', presented at the Second World Wide Web Conference, Chicago, October 17–19.

Price, D. De S. (1976) 'A General Theory of Bibliometric and Other Cumulative Advantage Processes', *Journal of the American Society for Information Science*, 27(5): 292–306.

Salton, G. (1975) *A Theory of Indexing*. Philadelphia: Society for Industrial and Applied Mathematics.

Sanderson, M., and Croft, W.B. (2012) 'The History of Information Retrieval Research', *Proceedings of the IEEE, 100* (Special Centennial Issue): 1444–51.

Schwartz, B. (2015) 'Google: Again, Social Signals Do Not Influence Your Ranking', Search Engine Roundtable. Available at: https://www.seroundtable.com/google-social-signals-ranking-20803.html [Accessed 15 June 2018].

Schwartz, C. (1998) 'Web Search Engines', *Jounal of the American Society for Information Science*, 49(11): 973–82.

Segal, D. (2011) 'The Dirty Little Secrets of Search', *The New York Times*, February 12. Available at: http://www.nytimes.com/2011/02/13/business/13search.html [Accessed 15 June 2018].

Shah, R. (2000) History of the Finger Protocol. Available at: http://www.rajivshah.com/Case_Studies/Finger/Finger.htm [Accessed 15 June 2018].

Singel, R. (2010) 'Oct. 27, 1994: Web Gives Birth to Banner Ads', Wired.com Available at: https://www.wired.com/2010/10/1027hotwired-banner-ads/ [Accessed 15 June 2018].

Sullivan, D. (2010) 'The Google Decade: Search in Review, 2000 to 2009', Search Engine Land, February 1. Available at: http://searchengineland.com/the-google-decade-search-in-review-2000-to-2009-34830 [Accessed 15 June 2018].

Torok, A.G. (1996) 'Internet Search Engines: Are Users Ready?' in Ahmed H. Helal and Joachim W. Weiss (eds.), *Towards a Worldwide Library: A Ten Year Forecast*, 19th International Essen Symposium, September 23–26, 1996, Essen: Publications of Essen University Library, 21: 241–53.

Vaidhyanathan, S. (2011) *The Googlization of Everything (And Why We Should Worry)*. Berkeley: University of California Press.

Wauters, R. (2011). 'DuckDuckGo to Google, Bing Users: Escape Them Filter Bubbles!' *Tech Crunch*, June 20. Available at: https://techcrunch.com/2011/06/20/duckduckgo-to-google-bing-users-escape-them-filter-bubbles/ [Accessed 15 June 2018].

Zakon, R.H. (2017) Hobbes' Internet Timeline 24. Available at: https://www.zakon.org/robert/internet/timeline/ [Accessed 15 June 2018].

# Making the Web Meaningful: A History of Web Semantics

Lindsay Poirier

## INTRODUCTION

While working at CERN as a contract programmer in 1989, Tim Berners-Lee submitted a proposal to his boss Mike Sendall for an information system that would help organize information distributed across the multinational laboratory without requiring researchers to agree on a standard technology or information model (Berners-Lee, 1999). This system evolved into what we today call the World Wide Web (WWW).

Today, the WWW is understood as an information space where documents, or Web pages, can be referenced and linked to from other documents using hypertext links. However, the system Berners-Lee described in his proposal aimed to do more than link documents; it aimed to link data, or specific nodes on Web pages. To illustrate the system in the proposal, Berners-Lee described a complex information system diagramed with a series of nodes and arrows. Nodes represent people, software models, groups of people, concepts, documents, etc., and arrows describe the relationships between nodes – for instance, that node A depends on node B or that node A is a part of node B. In designing a system that could link nodes and describe their relationships, it would not only be possible to organize information in more intuitive ways, it would also be possible to perform data analysis on the system, determining, for instance, when groups of people had few ties or when certain software had several dependencies. Importantly, Berners-Lee notes, 'Ideally, [each node] represents or describes one particular person or object' (Berners-Lee, 1989).

However, the Web did not evolve this way. After releasing the WWW to the public in 1991, it began to proliferate rapidly and evolved towards a document-based Web. Rather than hypertext linking data points, the document-based Web linked Web documents that each described many objects and people. This made it difficult to perform data analysis on Web data; computers could not distinguish between data points within Web documents and how they related to documents from which they were linked. Thus, in his keynote speech at the first international WWW conference in 1994, Berners-Lee lamented that Web documents were 'flat' and 'devoid of meaning' when in fact they 'describe real objects and imaginary concepts'. He called for adding 'semantics to the web' so that information within documents could become machine-readable, and relationships could be described between information. This was the first public reference to what today is called the *Semantic Web*.

As the WWW has developed into one of the world's largest information repositories, there have been notable efforts to structure Web data with semantics – to design the technologies and standards to enable a Semantic Web. In the Semantic Web, data points on Web pages have unique identifiers and metadata and can be linked with other data points on other Web pages. Using terms defined in openly available schemas to describe the links between data points helps the computer interpret meaning from Web data. Early efforts to enable a Semantic Web aimed to improve Web search capacities and support automated agents in making sense of data. More recent efforts have aimed to build out knowledge graphs that link together relevant data from all over the Web.

Notably, standardizing the protocols needed to enable a Semantic Web involved bringing together stakeholders with different understandings of where meaning comes from and how best to represent it to a computer. Thus, many arguments emerged in the undertaking. I begin by showing how these arguments are, to a certain extent, rooted in conflicts in the history of artificial intelligence (AI), and more specifically, knowledge representation. I then begin drawing on oral history interviews that I conducted with members of the Semantic Web community, along with archival research that I conducted on the World Wide Web Consortium (W3C)'s public forums (data collected as part of a research project documenting the histories of information infrastructures) to show how different styles of thought that guided knowledge representation work in the 1970s and 1980s have become interwoven in the design of the Semantic Web. Finally, I argue that the lessons learned in attempting to structure Web data for machine consumption have pushed researchers to reevaluate how they think about data structures, semantics, and logic.

Strategies in knowledge representation shape how information is organized, contextualized, presented, and accessed. Understanding how knowledge representation on the Web has progressed gives us insight into how the Web organizes cultural, social, and political life. Sociological literature examining the Semantic Web has shown how its affordances have gone on to shape how knowledge is produced and understood (Halford et al., 2013; Waller, 2016; McCarthy, 2017). Philosophical literature has examined how digital objects and the way they are related through code have come to define meaning (Veltman, 2006; Hui, 2016). In focusing on the history of Semantic Web design in this chapter, I aim to demonstrate how history, politics, and diverse epistemologies are reflected in the design and use of information architectures.

## KNOWLEDGE REPRESENTATION AND ONTOLOGIES

For decades, knowledge representation has been a central concept in AI research. Research in knowledge representation questions: how can we model the mind? How do we get machines to mimic the mind's recognition and understanding of everyday objects? How do we get machines to understand information about a complex world?

In the 1970s, debates about how to address these questions and challenges began to divide the knowledge representation community. Over the past 50 years, there have been calls to merge elements of research across the divisions (Minsky, 1991), and yet, within the Semantic Web community, and particularly in conversations that emerged in the development of the Web Ontology Language (OWL) in the early 2000s, classic debates continued to divide the way that researchers approached knowledge representation on the Web. In what follows, I describe early work in knowledge representation, tracing how divisions came to structure the way that Semantic Web researchers approached their work.

## Minsky's Frames

In 'A Framework for Representing Knowledge', Marvin Minsky (1974), often considered alongside John McCarthy to be a father of AI, introduced the frame concept. For Minsky, a frame is 'a data structure for representing stereotyped information':

> Here is the essence of the theory: When one encounters a new situation...one selects from memory a structure called a Frame. This is a remembered framework to be adapted to fit reality by changing details as necessary. (1974: 1)

The 'terminals' or slots of a frame have certain requirements that the values assigned to them must meet. In order to recognize and understand a situation, one must match the values of the situation to the terminals in various frames.

Applying this to AI involved creating 'frame languages' based on descriptions of objects (rather than algorithms for how data should be manipulated). As a machine is exposed to a new object, it compares and tries to match the object to the description for a frame it holds in memory. If the object's values can't be assigned to the terminals of a frame, the machine has to select other frames from memory or 'de-bug' existing frames to create new ones. Frame languages provided an alternative to reasoning with first-order predicate calculus by offering structures that could approach new and mundane situations and make sense of them based on a prior understanding of the world.

These ideas challenged earlier approaches to knowledge modeling in AI and came at a time when many AI researchers were confronting how 'smart' systems with intricate algorithms (such as chess-playing computers) were unable to perform more common-sense tasks. Prior to proposing frames as a framework for representing knowledge, Minsky himself, along with Seymour Papert, an AI researcher who worked closely with Minsky at MIT, had attempted to tackle the challenges of teaching computers common-sense knowledge through the construction of 'micro-worlds' – or bounded environments with little complexity where computers could learn. Upon mastering knowledge in a micro-world, computers could slowly be introduced to more complex thinking.

Yet Minsky critiqued the micro-world approach to knowledge representation as he introduced the frame concept. Minsky (1974: 74) argued that, while modeling logic in a micro-world often produced favorable results, '...as we approach reality the obstacles become overwhelming'. Minsky also lamented that 'logicist' approaches to AI focused intently on producing 'consistency and completeness'[1]:

> I cannot state strongly enough my conviction that the preoccupation with Consistency, so valuable for Mathematical Logic, has been incredibly destructive to those working on models of mind. At the popular level it has produced a weird conception of the potential capabilities of machines in general. At the 'logical' level it has blocked efforts to represent ordinary knowledge, by presenting an unreachable image of a corpus of context-free 'truths' that can stand separately by themselves. This obsession has kept us from seeing that thinking *begins with defective networks that are slowly (if ever) refined and updated.* (1974: 78, italics in original)

Frames, on the other hand, focused not on the internal structure of knowledge, but on how the mind came to recognize and structure external situations. While using first-order logic to model knowledge assumed that concepts completely, consistently, and rationally followed the same set of rules, the architecture of the frame assumed that we can't possibly model this way since every situation is marked with a new set of components or conditions. Minsky argued that our assessments and expectations of any given situation can never be more than imperfect approximations; we can only adapt a concept or situation from frames we already possess – to what we have already been exposed to. They will thus never be complete or consistent.

## *Divides*

Minsky's approach to modeling knowledge, along with others that were emerging in the early 1970s, such as Roger Schank and Robert Abelson's (1975) scripts, represented a more 'procedural' approach to knowledge representation than 'logicist' or 'declarativist' approaches, which had been championed by prominent AI researchers like John McCarthy and Patrick Hayes (who would go on to make important contributions to the Semantic Web). This binary marked a schism in the knowledge representation community that emerged in the early 1970s. Logicists/declarativists tended to apply first-order logic to knowledge representation problems, whereas proceduralists tended to model knowledge representation problems by defining structures and then manipulating them with programing procedures. Further debates over the value of consistency and the aesthetic of knowledge representation solutions marked another schism in the community – one that Roger Schank, an AI theorist and computer science professor at Yale University, coined as the 'neats vs. the scruffies' in the early 1970s (Crevier, 1994). Neats sought clean and consistent solutions to knowledge representation problems, whereas scruffies tended to employ hacks, testing out different solutions to see what would work versus what wouldn't.

These divisions were made more precarious as researchers on either side of the debate addressed the shortcomings of the approaches. John McCarthy and Patrick Hayes (1969), who may be characterized as the quintessential neat and logicists, described one such shortcoming to logic-based knowledge representation in the late 1960s. In what is now a classic AI paper, they suggested the difficulty of using logic to model dynamic facts – or, in other words, facts that change over time. This problem led some logicists, like Drew McDermott, a computer science professor at Yale University, to question the enduring value of logical approaches:

> At some point one has to ask, Why bother? When all the other boys and girls are out playing with their computers, why must the logicists stay indoors and practice finger exercises? Can we really believe that the insights gained will eventually allow logic to leapfrog other approaches to inference? It seems far more likely that logic will trail behind, struggling to stuff all sorts of inference patterns into its own view of the world, whether they fit or not. (McDermott, 2014: 116)

Terry Winograd (1980), a computer scientist at MIT who later moved to Stanford University, also inclined towards a proceduralist and scruffy approach to knowledge representation in the mid to late 1970s after coming to terms with the inability of his 'micro-worlds' system SHRDLU to scale to real-world contexts. Describing the 'controversy' between procedural and declarative epistemologies, Winograd (1975) argued that approaches to knowledge representation based solely in formal logic tended to separate 'facts' from 'processes' and ultimately went on to model facts as discrete units. Proceduralist approaches, on the other hand, were based more on 'interactions' between data and subroutines that manipulated them. Terry Winograd and Daniel Bobrow's Knowledge Representation Language called KRL – 'organized around conceptual entities with associated descriptions and procedures' — is considered one of the first knowledge representation languages to be based on Minsky's frames (Bobrow and Winograd, 1977: 2). Distinguishing this language from logic-based approaches, Winograd described, 'There is a fundamental philosophical and mathematical difference between truth-based systems of logic, and process-based systems like KRL' (1980: 220).

Yet Hayes (1977) went on to critique the distinctions researchers like Winograd had drawn between proceduralist and declarativist approaches, arguing that the controversy was based in a false dichotomy. Logic, he argued, was not a programing language or even a style of programing. It was simply a set of ideas for justifying inferences (conclusions drawn in formal reasoning). Proceduralists had been advocating for particular *data structures* and styles of programing, whereas the role of logic was to enrich these data structures and processes with interpretations of their meaning in the world. Thus, he went on to assert that representation languages that purported to adhere to a proceduralist model, such as KRL, incorporated elements of logic in their design (Hayes, 1980).

In a similar vein to Hayes's critique, in the late 1970s and early 1980s more researchers began to position frames and other structures for modeling knowledge (such as semantic networks (see Quillian, 1968)) as providing a *syntax*, or structure, for knowledge representation but lacking a *semantics* that would enable machines to interpret its meaning. This led to calls for systems that would blur the lines between declarativist and proceduralist trends in AI. For instance, Eugene Charniak, a computer science professor at Brown University, introduced Frame-based Artificial Intelligence Language (FRAIL) that 'use[d] both predicate calculus and frames' (1981: 1083). Drawing on the neat/scruffy distinction, Charniak (1986) went on to propose a 'neat' theory for language interpretation.

It was in this spirit of merging descriptive features of object-oriented representation languages and inferential features of logic-based knowledge representation that description logics (DL) – one of the most influential frameworks for modeling knowledge on the Semantic Web – emerged.

## Genealogies of Description Logics

Interested in building systems that could automate intelligent behavior, Ronald Brachman, a PhD candidate at Harvard University who would go on to be considered the 'Father of description logics', began conceptualizing a new system for knowledge representation in his 1978 dissertation. Brachman outlined the shortcomings of semantic networks – frameworks for representing the relationships between concepts. He argued that semantic networks lacked consistency and precision in semantics, or, in other words, an explicit 'epistemology' – defined by Brachman as 'a set of primitive structures for encoding knowledge… and rules for combining those structures into well-formed representations of individuals and classes of individuals' (Brachman, 1978: 44). He argued that existing frame languages, such as KRL, while offering notable models for *describing* concepts, could not explain how sub-units composed wholes: how concepts were built up from representational units that related to each other. From this, Brachman introduced the structural inheritance network – a model for knowledge representation that would not only characterize the properties of objects, but would also establish what could be called a 'neat' semantics for formalizing relationships between objects. Perhaps, most notably, Brachman introduced the concept of 'subsumption', or the ability to categorize nodes so that a reasoner can eventually infer (or draw conclusions about) the relationships between concepts.

Other research emerging in the early 1980s was concerned with making object-oriented representation languages, such as frames, more 'functional' (Levesque, 1984). In other words, this research aimed to design systems that could do more than simply 'describe' knowledge through neat semantic structures; it also aimed to design systems that could make 'assertions', or statements arrived at through coding procedures, based on these structures. In 1982, Brachman and Levesque suggested that 'competence' in knowledge representation required both 'terminological adequacy' – where the structures of relations between terms could be characterized to a machine – and 'assertional adequacy' –

where the machine could interpret these structures in order to make assertions about what is known and what is not known in a knowledge base. However, frames did not make a distinction between these two forms of adequacy; according to Brachman et al. (1983), in many frame-based representation systems, it wasn't clear whether the frame was describing a concept or asserting the existence of a concept. They thus began to conceptualize systems that would differentiate between descriptive and assertional components of the language; the descriptive components were based on frames, while the assertional components were based on elements of first-order logic. Both subsumption and the distinction between descriptive and assertional components oriented the design of KL-ONE, a frame-based knowledge representation system that would become the primary model for description logics (DL) in the early 1990s (Brachman and Schmolze, 1985).

Systems like KL-ONE posed tricky tradeoffs. Brachman and colleagues aimed to build systems that could at once provide rich, or 'expressive', descriptions of concepts, but also make inferences about the relationships between concepts within a finite number of computational steps. However, the more expressive knowledge representation languages are, or the more complexity they attempt to model, the more challenging it is to guarantee the system will be sound, complete, and 'decidable' (capable of producing a conclusion) (Patel-Schneider, 1985; Levesque and Brachman, 1987). Because of this, KL-ONE-like systems often restricted the number of constructors, or 'primitives', of the language to a small set. It offered a substantially limited logic. Thus, throughout the 1980s, a great deal of attention was devoted to 'cleaning' semantics in object-oriented systems, advancing the inferential capabilities of these systems, and theorizing the computational limits of the work. In the late 1980s, this research merged into the DL[2] framework.

Throughout the 1990s, researchers went on to experiment how far they could push the tradeoffs between expressivity and decidability in DL-based systems. At one end of the spectrum, systems like CLASSIC (Borgida et al., 1989) considerably limited the expressivity of the language in order to ensure the system could produce inferences in a reasonable amount of time, while offering advice on how to work with and extend the limited language for practical representation and reasoning (Brachman et al., 1991). On the other hand, systems like LOOM 'conced[ed] that it might be acceptable to deliberately build an incomplete system' (MacGregor, 1991b: 90). Robert MacGregor, who served as a Senior Project Leader of the University of Southern California's Information Sciences Institute, argued that knowledge representation systems may need to sacrifice completeness and offer users more expressivity in order to prevent systems from becoming too 'scruffy':

> A small, elegant KRS embedded in a larger, incomplete (i.e. scruffy) application yields a scruffy application. ... Our experience with NIKL and LOOM suggests that when application programmers need to represent something, and the [knowledge representation system] can't help them, they invent their own representation, and the result is nearly always inferior to what a skilled knowledge representation developer could produce. (MacGregor, 1991a: 396)

Later work by Ian Horrocks (1998) and Peter Patel-Schneider (1998), who would both come to be important figures in the development of the Web Ontology Language (OWL), sidestepped the expressivity/decidability tradeoff by implementing powerful reasoners that could draw inferences from expressive knowledge bases in reasonable timeframes. Deborah McGuinness (2001) suggests that it was working through these tensions in the 1990s that prepared DLs to 'emerge from ivory towers' into WWW usage.

## KNOWLEDGE REPRESENTATION ON THE WEB

When Ora Lassila, a computer scientist and research fellow at Nokia Labs, came to MIT as a visiting scholar in 1996, Tim Berners-Lee asked him what he believed was wrong with the Web. Lassila replied that he would like the Web to be able to do more things without human intervention; Berners-Lee agreed.

The origins of the Semantic Web are often traced back to the publication of the *Scientific American* article 'The Semantic Web' in 2001 (Berners-Lee et al., 2001), but the work to formalize standards and protocols for applying knowledge representation on the Web had begun in the mid 1990s, with the development of the Resource Description Framework (RDF). RDF offers syntax for enabling computers to interpret Web content. Based on RDF, Web data gets organized into 'triples', consisting of a subject, a predicate, and an object. The subject is a piece of data on the Web that has a universal identifier; the object can either be another piece of data on the Web that has a universal identifier or a reference to something that exists outside of the Web[3]. The predicate describes the relationship between the subject and the object. For instance, one triple may be John Doe (http://johndoe) is a Person. Here John Doe would be a piece of data on the Web; 'person' would refer to an entity that exists outside of the Web; and 'is a' would describe the relationship between the two. Another triple may be John Doe (http://johndoe) is married to Jane Doe (http://janedoe).

RDF emerged from a lineage of work that aimed to develop standard formats for making metadata, or descriptions of data, machine-readable. An early predecessor to RDF was the Platform for Internet Content Selection (PICS) – a system that allowed users to associate metadata with Web content designed initially to help parents control what children could access. Perhaps the most notable pre-cursor to RDF was the Meta-Content Framework (MCF). Ramanathan Guha began developing MCF at Apple in the mid 1990s. Guha had long been involved in knowledge representation work, playing a key role in the Cyc project – an ambitious (and often described 'scruffy' (Matuszek et al., 2006)) effort to build a machine-readable corpus of common-sense knowledge. MCF aimed to structure metadata so that information could flow between software products with different information models and data structures.

When Guha left Apple for Netscape in 1997, he met Tim Bray, who had developed the first version of the W3C's XML specification – a standard for storing and transporting data on the Web. Together, they adapted MCF using XML, and this project became the basis for the Resource Description Framework (RDF)[4].

Work to formalize RDF into a Web standard through the W3C began in 1997, and the standard was formalized into a recommendation in 1998. The group of practitioners that participated in the formalization of the W3C RDF standard had diverse backgrounds and agendas. Some represented major search engines, aiming to build tools that could enable machines to better interpret the content of a Web page to improve search. Some came from industry, seeing an economic benefit to enabling smarter browsing. Another group of practitioners came from the knowledge representation community, excited by the idea of building a worldwide knowledge representation system.

On the working group many argued that RDF had to be simple – like a basic programing language with which more complicated programs could be written. Others did not believe RDF should be treated like a programing language – that knowledge representation was not necessarily reducible to simpler forms. The recommendation emerged as a compromise between these viewpoints.

However, many individuals in the knowledge representation community still considered RDF too messy and inconsistent to enable knowledge representation. In fact, without provocation or prior introduction, Pat Hayes, who was still revered in the knowledge representation community, emailed the working group chairs to complain about the recommendation's sloppiness. He was later asked to join the working group. Reflecting earlier concerns surrounding the limitations of frame-based systems based solely in procedural methodologies, RDF provided syntax for knowledge representation, but lacked a neat semantics (Lassila and McGuinness, 2001). This played an important role in the development of OWL.

## *Web Ontology Language*

In the late 1990s, the US Defense Advanced Research Projects Agency (DARPA) was becoming interested in designing systems that could control and coordinate autonomous software agents. One vein of this research involved designing languages that could identify, understand, and integrate information sources across distributed agents through 'semantics'. The DARPA Agent Markup Language (DAML) Program was introduced in 2000, and James Hendler, then a computer science professor at the University of Maryland, was appointed as the program manager.

At the time of his appointment, Hendler, along with colleagues Jeff Heflin and Sean Luke, had been working to develop a system that could 'mark up' Web pages with semantics. SHOE (Simple HTML Ontology Extensions) enabled website designers to reference an ontology where a series of terms were defined and then annotate data on their HTML documents with these terms. The system would enable search engines to 'look up' the meaning of annotated content on a Web page by referencing the ontology.

Placing this project in the context of research being conducted in the field of knowledge representation (citing systems like KL-ONE, CLASSIC, and LOOM), Heflin, Hendler, and Luke argued that applying a knowledge representation language on the Web would require considerably rethinking what knowledge bases could enable:

> Web systems simply cannot assume that all of the information has been entered solely under a knowledge engineer's watchful eye, and is therefore correct and consistent. As authority on the Internet is distributed, it cannot and does not make any such promise. This lack of central control leads to a number of serious problems. Since there is often no editorial review or quality control of Web information, each page's *reliability* must be questioned. Since a web page that was useful one day can disappear the next, there is no guarantee on the *availability* of information. Since there are no integrity constraints on the Web, information from different sources can be in disagreement, leading to *inconsistency*. Some inconsistencies may be due to error, others due to philosophical differences. In addition, there are quite a number of well-known "web hoaxes" where information was published on the Web with the intent to amuse or mislead – the computational agent typically cannot tell the difference! (Heflin et al., 1999: 2–3, italics in original)

Thus, rather than aiming to build a complete, consistent, or neat knowledge base, the guiding design principle for SHOE became 'a little semantics goes a long way'.

When Hendler got to DARPA, he was given funding to distribute to three laboratories that would build out proofs of concept for DAML. One funded group was the Knowledge Systems Laboratory at Stanford University – where McGuinness had moved after being quite active in the description logic community throughout the 1990s, both designing DL languages and co-building large DL applications, including a family of industrial-strength configurator applications (McGuinness and Wright, 1998). Another funded group was the Massachusetts Institute of Technology Laboratory for Computer Science and W3C, where Berners-Lee and others were advancing research towards what they were calling the 'Semantic Web'. Several folks that had long been involved in the knowledge representation community also became involved in the project, including Drew McDermott, Pat Hayes, and Peter Patel-Schneider. Together, these groups and other collaborators formalized DAML into a language in October 2000. Soon after, they joined efforts with other researchers who had been designing the Ontology Interface Layer (OIL) in the European Union. DAML+OIL was released in January 2001.

The W3C working group for the Web Ontology Language (OWL) began in 2001, tasked with shaping DAML into a Web standard. With over 40 participants, the committee was very large in comparison to other W3C committees. Consisting primarily of academic researchers, there were not so much different stakeholder positions on the working group, but instead schisms in what members believed the ontology should do and how it should be structured. In an interview I conducted with Pat Hayes, he described:

> The RDF working group ... had sort of a collegiate atmosphere and eventually ... after some initial fights, we got each other calibrated, and were able to sort of work together. Occasionally people would get exasperated with one another, but that sort of thing happens. The OWL working group was much more of a real genuine schism. It had an on-going fight, which was still ongoing, between two very different points of view about what OWL should be.

Some of the early controversies in formalizing the mark-up language into a Web standard were identified in a 'Trends and Controversies' section of the March/April 2002 issue of the *IEEE Intelligent Systems* journal (van Harmelen et al., 2002). In the section, eight participants on the working group – each from different backgrounds – were asked to comment on the process of defining a standard ontology language for the Web. Frank van Harmelen, a knowledge representation and reasoning professor at Vrije Universiteit Amsterdam, suggested that the styles of frame-based modeling that he had seen used in both academia and industry 'directly conflict with the DL [description logic] style of DAML+OIL' (van Harmelen et al., 2002: 2–3). He called on the working group to reduce the complexity of the ontology's formal semantics. Guus Schreiber, also a computer science professor at Vrije Universiteit Amsterdam and co-chair of the OWL working group, wrote:

> The debate about what a Web ontology language should look like is reminiscent of past neat-scruffy struggles. Knowledge modelers want expressiveness, logicians stress decidability. The main difference is that the Semantic Web actually forces us to make some choices: there is a strong need for real-world knowledge representation. (van Harmelen et al., 2002: 78)

Indeed, many of the arguments that arose in the working group reflected earlier neat–scruffy struggles. As James Hendler, chair of the working group of OWL, noted in one email to the group:

> In fact, if one goes back to a famous talk given by Roger Schank...he referred to the neats and the scruffies and at that time, this particular debate we're still having today was one of the examples used as a differentiator! ...the issue being discussed here gets so much to the heart of things and the differences in how frame and DL folks see the world that it's hard to even know where to begin.

The issues that arose in the conversations to formalize the ontology had to do with the syntax, the semantics, and the usability of the language. Syntactically, there was considerable concern held by some from the DL community that designing first-order logic on top of RDF syntax would prevent the ontology from producing decidable results.[5] Pat Hayes, who described in his interview with me that (despite his historical positioning) he played the role of a scruffy in the OWL working group, went on to propose a proof that this was not a paradox as long as the logic gave up decidability.

Another issue that arose in the working group concerned the type of logic on which the ontology should be based. Should the ontology be based on DLs – first-order logics with considerably limited expressivity that could ensure the system could produce results in a reasonable amount of time – or should the ontology be based on full logic where any RDF statements could be combined in any way without guarantees that there would be soundness and completeness?[6] Finally, there was concern about whether the system would be usable by everyday webmasters.

While early efforts attempted to sort out these controversies, eventually the working group decided to propose three versions of OWL – one emphasizing simplicity and usability (OWL-Lite), one emphasizing decidability (OWL-DL), and one emphasizing expressivity (OWL-Full) (Horrocks et al., 2003). Ora Lassila told me in an interview, 'I think the distinction between these two [OWL-DL and OWL-Full] represents the rift that exists between the knowledge representation community, or it did at the time anyway'. In an email thread with many working group members throwing around ideas for naming each version, Frank van Harmelen offered one possibility:

OWL Light: ?

wimpy

OWL fast: OWL/FOL-style

Neat

OWL large: OWL/RDF-style

Scruffy [7]

Recommending three versions of OWL signified that overcoming the epistemological and technological binds of knowledge representation with a one-size-fits-all solution was likely impossible – particularly in a space as messy as the WWW.

## *Web 3.0 Meets Web 2.0*

As the Semantic Web progressed, there was growing concern that its vocabularies and ontologies were being developed to tackle specific tasks and could not scale out for structuring large-scale, heterogeneous, and dynamic Web data (Shadbolt et al., 2006). Particularly as the emergence of social Web applications (such as blogging and social networking sites) made it easier for users to produce their own Web data, some Semantic Web practitioners began considering the role that individual tagging of Web data could play in building out a Semantic Web. Around this time many in the community began emphasizing building capacity for 'linked data' over reasoning with Web data (Bizer et al., 2009). Aiming specifically to make structured data publicly available on the Web, the 'linked data movement' was less concerned with getting ontologies sound and complete and more concerned with enabling diverse users to publish data on the Web with linking protocols (Berners-Lee, 2009). For Wendy Hall, a computer scientist at the University of Southampton whose work on hypertext and hypermedia had influenced the design of the Semantic Web, this was exactly what was needed to get the Semantic Web out of an 'AI rat-hole'. As she described to me in an interview: 'We needed to get data out there that could be linked so that people could see what the power of [the Semantic web] was. The argument being that if you did the theory first, you'd never achieve it'.

At around the same time, several of the researchers who had contributed to the OWL working group honed their attention on fixing inconsistencies in OWL 1. OWL 2 was largely designed as an attempt to extend and revise the original, with an explicit aim to improve the ontology's soundness and expressivity (Grau et al., 2008). Yet, several researchers that I have interviewed argued that creating yet another version of OWL only served to further confuse Web users. Further, with more everyday webmasters producing their own Web data, there were far more instances of OWL being used in ways that did not adhere to the strict specifications outlined in the ontology (Halpin et al., 2010). This trend posed the threat of breaking many of the inferential features championed by the DL community.

Thus, in the early 2010s, 'microformats', such as schema.org and hCard, began popping up as simplified alternatives to RDF and OWL. Much like RDF's predecessors, these tools involved marking up data within HTML documents with vetted schemas. Popular discourse seems to suggest that these tools, while incredibly scruffy, inconsistent, and unlikely ever to be able to serve as a base for sound inferences, are 'winning out' in the Semantic Web domain (Norvig, 2016). Figure 18.1 demonstrates how these technologies are part of a lineage of knowledge representation systems.

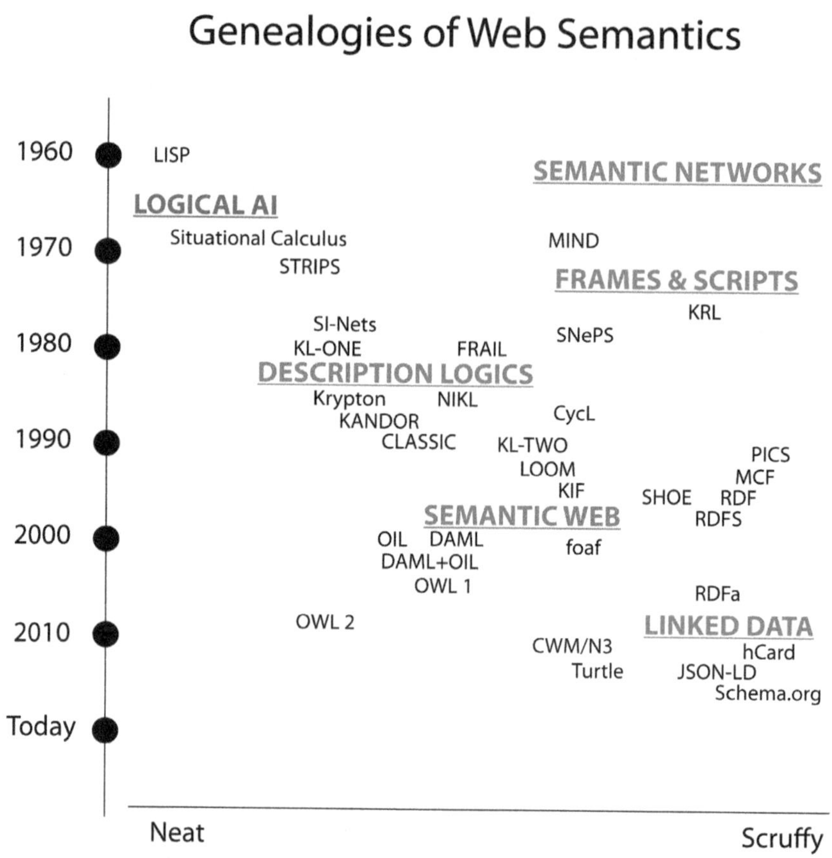


**Figure 18.1 This figure depicts a timeline of systems, languages, and frameworks that have been advanced in the field of knowledge representation since the 1960s. It shows how the field has toggled between neat and scruffy approaches to knowledge representation. Many of the Semantic Web technologies introduced in the 2000s and 2010s can be said to derive from earlier systems – sharing common creators, design directives, and worldviews.**

## CONCLUSION

In his commentary 'The Myth of One True Logic', DL pioneer Ronald Brachman (1987: 169) acknowledged the 'turn for the 'neat' that was emerging in the knowledge representation community in the mid to late 1980s. He lamented the emergence of what he called 'TOTL[(the one true logic)]-imperialism', noting how an emphasis on capital-L logicism had rendered other, less neat, forms of logic illegitimate in the community. He concluded that what was needed in the community was more 'give-and-take' between logicist and procedural approaches.

In the mid 2010s, after years of firmly staking grounds over how data structures, semantics, and logic should formalize and organize Web data, members of the Semantic Web community are turning again to call for a 'give-and-take' approach to knowledge representation on the Web. Responding to a long email thread considering how greater consistency could be brought to schema.org, Mike Bergman, a specialist in knowledge representation and active contributor to schema.org community discussions, replied, 'Let's not revisit the tiresome RDF v. OWL wars in this forum'. He went on to suggest, 'The trick is to be consistent in the face of pragmatic realities'.[8]

The history of knowledge representation on the Web can be read as an effort to navigate, argue over, and eventually creatively endure these binds. In one sense, there is considerable consensus that the Web could benefit from 'smarter data' – that adding meaning to Web data can add context to data, make data easier to discover, and enable us to draw disparate data together in novel ways. On the other hand, the Web itself is quite scruffy, full of inconsistencies and paradoxes (see Barnet, this volume, for how HTTP embodies this). Making this space meaningful is a very hard enterprise. Yet, as schema.org and other linked data technologies that tolerate inconsistencies and paradoxes 'win out' on the Web, the field of Web semantics seems to be taking a 'turn for the scruffy' (Poirier, 2017) – a turn perpetuated by persistent reminders that the worldviews and concepts diverse people use to describe their world often don't fit so 'neatly' into tighter systems of representation.

## Notes

1 In mathematical theory, 'completeness' suggests a mathematical system where 'all true statements can be proven', and 'consistency' suggests a mathematical system where 'no false statements can be proven'.

2 Unlike when referencing Web documents, when URIs are used to reference real-world objects, the real-world object cannot be retrieved through the computer. Agreeing on a solution to this problem generated a great deal of debate in the Semantic Web community (see Hayes and Halpin, 2008). The current W3C guidelines around this problem are summarized at: https://www.w3.org/TR/2008/NOTE-cooluris-20081203/.

3 Both MCF and RDF went on to influence the design of RSS – another Web arena where the 'neat/scruffy' divides played out (see Robbins, 2006: 108–9).

4 https://lists.w3.org/Archives/Public/www-webont-wg/2002Jan/0170.html

5 Peter Patel-Schneider, a particularly strong proponent for moving away from RDF syntax, acknowledged that scruffier approaches could overcome this issue, but 'it would be a gigantic mess, at best'. https://lists.w3.org/Archives/Public/www-webont-wg/2001Dec/0081.html

6 Jim Hendler described to me that this is an issue about whether infinity is permitted in the logic. 'Logic', he argued, 'loves infinity'. However, infinity is not decidable and will break a DL reasoner.

7 https://lists.w3.org/Archives/Public/www-webont-wg/2002Oct/0130.html

8 https://lists.w3.org/Archives/Public/public-vocabs/2014Jan/0047.html

## REFERENCES


Berners-Lee, T. (1989) Information Management: A Proposal (https://www.w3.org/History/1989/proposal.html) Accessed February 16, 2016.

Berners-Lee, T. (1999) *Weaving the Web: The Original Design and Ultimate Destiny of the World Wide Web by Its Inventor*. San Francisco: Harper Business.

Berners-Lee, T. (2009) The next Web. TED2009 (https://www.ted.com/talks/tim_berners_lee_on_the_next_web?language=en.) Accessed June 8, 2016.

Berners-Lee, T., Hendler, J., and Lassila, O. (2001) 'The Semantic Web', *Scientific American*, 284(5): 29–37.

Bizer, C., Heath, T., and Berners-Lee, T. (2009) 'Linked Data: The Story So Far', in Sheth Amit (ed.), *International Journal on Semantic Web and Information Systems*, 5(3): 1–22. (doi:10.4018/jswis.2009081901)

Bobrow, D.G., and Winograd, T. (1977) 'An Overview of KRL, a Knowledge Representation Language', *Cognitive Science*, 1(1): 3–46. (doi:10.1207/s15516709cog0101_2)

Borgida, A., Brachman, R.J., McGuinness, D.L., and Resnick, L.A. (1989) 'CLASSIC: A Structural Data Model for Objects', in *Proceedings of SIGMOD International Conference on Management of Data*. New York: ACM, 58–67. (doi:10.1145/67544.66932)

Brachman, R.J. (1978) 'A Structural Paradigm for Representing Knowledge'. PhD dissertation, Harvard University.

Brachman, R.J. (1987) 'The Myth of the One True Logic', *Computational Intelligence*, 3(1): 168–72. (doi:10.1111/j.1467-8640.1987.tb00187.x)

Brachman, R.J., Fikes, R.E., and Levesque, H.J. (1983) 'Krypton: A Functional Approach to Knowledge Representation', *Computer*, 16(10): 67–73. (doi:10.1109/MC.1983.1654200)

Brachman, R.J., and Levesque, H.J. (1982) 'Competence in Knowledge Representation', in *Proceedings of Second National Conference on Artificial Intelligence*. Philadelphia: Morgan Kaufmann Publishers Inc., 189–92. (http://www.aaai.org/Papers/AAAI/1982/AAAI82-045.pdf) Accessed February 13, 2017.

Brachman, R., McGuinness, D., Patel-Schneider, P., Resnick, L.A., and Borgida, A. (1991) 'Living with CLASSIC: When and How to Use a KL-ONE-like Language', in John Sowa (ed.), *Principles of Semantic Networks: Explorations in the Representation of Knowledge*. San Mateo, CA: Morgan Kaufmann, 401–56.

Brachman, R.J., and Schmolze, J.G. (1985) 'An Overview of the KL-ONE Knowledge Representation System', *Cognitive Science*, 9(2): 171–216. (doi:10.1207/s15516709cog0902_1)

Charniak, E. (1981) 'A Common Representation for Problem-Solving and Language-Comprehension Information', *Artificial Intelligence*, 16(3): 225–55. (doi:10.1016/0004-3702(81)90001-1)

Charniak, E. (1986) 'A Neat Theory of Marker Passing', in *Proceedings of the Fifth AAAI National Conference on Artificial Intelligence*. Philadelphia, Pennsylvania: AAAI Press, 584–88. (http://dl.acm.org/citation.cfm?id=2887770.2887869) Accessed February 21, 2017.

Crevier, D. (1994) *AI: The Tumultuous History of the Search for Artificial Intelligence*. New York: BasicBooks.

Grau, B.C., Horrocks, I., Motik, B., Parsia, B., Patel-Schneider, P., and Sattler, U. (2008) 'OWL 2: The next Step for OWL', *Web Semantics: Science, Services and Agents on the World Wide Web, Semantic Web Challenge 2006/2007*, 6(4): 309–22. (doi:10.1016/j.websem.2008.05.001)

Halford, S., Pope, C., and Weal, M. (2013) 'Digital Futures? Sociological Challenges and Opportunities in the Emergent Semantic Web', *Sociology*, 47(1): 173–89. (doi:10.1177/0038038512453798)

Halpin, H., Hayes, P.J., McCusker, J.P., McGuinness, D.L., and Thompson, H.S. (2010) 'When owl:sameAs Isn't the Same: An Analysis of Identity in Linked Data', in Peter F. Patel-Schneider, Yue Pan, Pascal Hitzler, Peter Mika, Lei Zhang, Jeff Z. Pan, Ian Horrocks, and Birte Glimm (eds.), *The Semantic Web – ISWC 2010*. Lecture Notes in Computer Science 6496. Berlin Heidelberg: Springer, 305–20. (doi:10.1007/978-3-642-17746-0_20)

Harmelen, F. van, Horrocks, I., Clark, P., Patel-Schneider, P.F., Uschold, M., Rousset, M.-C., Hendler, J., and Schreiber, G. (2002), 'Ontologies' KISSES in Standardization', *IEEE Intelligent Systems*, 17(2): 70–9. (doi:10.1109/MIS.2002.999223)

Hayes, P.J. (1977) 'In Defense of Logic', in *5th International Joint Conference on Artificial Intelligence – Volume 1*. San Francisco: Morgan Kaufmann Publishers Inc, 559–65. (http://dl.acm.org/citation.cfm?id=1624435.1624559) Accessed February 14, 2017.

Hayes, P.J. (1980) 'The Logic of Frames', in Dieter Metzing (ed.), *Frame Conceptions and Text Understanding*. New York: Walter de Gruyter, 46–61.

Hayes, P.J., and Halpin, H. (2008) 'In Defense of Ambiguity', *International Journal on Semantic Web and Information Systems*, 4(2): 1–18. (doi:10.4018/jswis.2008040101)

Heflin, J., Hendler, J., and Luke, S. (1999) SHOE: A Knowledge Representation Language for Internet Applications (http://drum.lib.umd.edu/handle/1903/1044) Accessed February 17, 2017.

Horrocks, I. (1998) 'Using an Expressive Description Logic: FaCT or Fiction?', in *Proceedings of Knowledge Representation*. San Mateo, CA: Morgan Kaufmann Publishers Inc., 636–47.

Horrocks, I., Patel-Schneider, P.F., and Harmelen, F. van. (2003) 'From SHIQ and RDF to OWL: The Making of a Web Ontology Language', *Web Semantics: Science, Services and Agents on the World Wide Web*, 1(1): 7–26. (doi: 10.1016/j.websem.2003.07.001)

Hui, Y. (2016) *On the Existence of Digital Objects*. Minneapolis: University of Minnesota Press.

Lassila, O., and McGuinness, D. (2001) 'The Role of Frame-Based Representation on the Semantic Web', Knowledge Systems Laboratory Report KSL-01-02. Stanford University.

Levesque, H.J. (1984) 'Foundations of a Functional Approach to Knowledge Representation', *Artificial Intelligence*, 23(2): 155–212. (doi:10.1016/0004-3702(84)90009-2)

Levesque, H.J., and Brachman, R.J. (1987) 'Expressiveness and Tractability in Knowledge Representation and Reasoning', *Computational Intelligence*, 3(1): 78–93. (doi:10.1111/j.1467-8640.1987.tb00176.x)

MacGregor, R. (1991a) 'The Evolving Technology of Classification-Based Knowledge Representation Systems', in John Sowa (ed.), *Principles of Semantic Networks: Explorations in the Representation of Knowledge*. San Mateo, CA: Morgan Kaufmann Publishers, Inc, 385–400.

MacGregor, R. (1991b) 'Inside the LOOM Description Classifier', *SIGART Bulletin*, 2(3): 88–92. (doi:10.1145/122296.122309)

Matuszek, C., Cabral, J., Witbrock, M., and Deoliveira, J. (2006) 'An Introduction to the Syntax and Content of Cyc', in *Proceedings of the 2006 AAAI Spring Symposium on Formalizing and Compiling Background Knowledge and Its Applications to Knowledge Representation and Question Answering*. Menlo Park, CA: AAAI Press, 44–9.

McCarthy, J., and Hayes, P.J. (1969) 'Some Philosophical Problems from the Standpoint of Artificial Intelligence', in B. Meltzer and D. Michie (eds.), *Machine Intelligence 4*. Edinburgh: Edinburgh University Press, 463–502.

McCarthy, M. (2017) 'The Semantic Web and Its Entanglements', *Science Technology, and Society*, 22(1): 21–37. (doi:10.1177/0971721816682796)

McDermott, D. (2014) 'AI, Logic, and the Frame Problem', in Frank M. Brown (ed.), *The Frame Problem in Artificial Intelligence: Proceedings of the 1987 Workshop*. San Francisco: Morgan Kaufmann, 105–18.

McGuinness, D.L. (2001) 'Description Logics Emerge from Ivory Towers', in *Proceedings of the International Workshop on Description Logics*. Stanford, CA, 201–3.

McGuinness, D.L., and Wright, J.R. (1998) 'An Industrial-Strength Description Logic-Based Configurator Platform', *IEEE Intelligent Systems and Their Applications*, 13(4): 69–77. (doi:10.1109/5254.708435)

Minsky, M. (1974) 'A Framework for Representing Knowledge', Massachusetts Institute of Technology A.I. Laboratory, Memo No. 306. (http://hdl.handle.net/1721.1/6089) Accessed October 15, 2015.

Minsky, M. (1991) 'Logical Versus Analogical or Symbolic Versus Connectionist or Neat Versus Scruffy', *AI Magazine*, 12(2): 34–51. (doi:10.1609/aimag.v12i2.894)

Norvig, P. (2016) 'The Semantic Web and the Semantics of the Web: Where Does Meaning Come From?', Keynote presented at the *www2016*, Montreal, Quebec.

Patel-Schneider, P.F. (1985) 'A Decidable First-Order Logic for Knowledge Representation', in *Proceedings of the 9th International Joint Conference on Artificial Intelligence – Volume 1*. San Francisco, CA, USA: Morgan Kaufmann Publishers Inc, 455–58. (http://dl.acm.org/citation.cfm?id=1625135.1625224) Accessed February 17, 2017.

Patel-Schneider, P.F. (1998) 'DLP System Description', in *Collected Papers from the International Description Logics Workshop*, 87–9.

Poirier, L. (2017) 'A Turn for the Scruffy: An Ethnographic Study of Semantic Web Architecture', in *Proceedings of WebSci'17*. Troy, NY: ACM, 359–67. (doi:https://doi.org/10.1145/3091478.3091505)

Quillian, M.R. (1968) 'Semantic Memory', in Marvin Minsky (ed.), *Semantic Information Processing*. Cambridge, MA: MIT Press, 27–70.

Robbins, J.N. (2006) *Web Design in a Nutshell: A Desktop Quick Reference*. Sebastopol, CA: O'Reilly Media, Inc.

Schank, R.C., and Abelson, R.P. (1975) 'Scripts, Plans, and Knowledge', in *Proceedings of the 4th International Joint Conference on Artificial Intelligence – Volume 1*. San Francisco, CA, USA: Morgan Kaufmann Publishers Inc, 151–7. (http://dl.acm.org/citation.cfm?id=1624626.1624649)

Shadbolt, N., Berners-Lee, T., and Hall, W. (2006) 'The Semantic Web Revisited', *IEEE Intelligent Systems*, 21(3): 96–101. (doi:10.1109/MIS.2006.62)

Veltman, K. (2006) 'Towards a Semantic Web for Culture', *Journal of Digital Information*, 4(4). (https://journals.tdl.org/jodi/index.php/jodi/article/view/113 Accessed February 16, 2016.)

Waller, V. (2016) 'Making Knowledge Machine-Processable: Some Implications of General Semantic Search', *Behaviour & Information Technology*, 35(10): 784–95. (doi:10.1080/0144929X.2016.1183710)

Winograd, T. (1975) 'Frame Representations and the Declarative/Procedural Controversy', in Daniel Bobrow and Allan Collins (eds.), *Representation and Understanding: Studies in Cognitive Science*. New York: Academic Press, Inc, 185–210.

Winograd, T. (1980) 'What Does It Mean to Understand Language?', *Cognitive Science*, 4(3): 209–41. (doi:10.1207/s15516709cog0403_1)

# Browsers and Browser Wars

Marc Weber

Browsers are the part of the Web that users actually see and touch with a mouse or finger. As such, they've long gotten more attention than their counterparts: the equally important Web server software off somewhere at the end of a wire or radio link. But in the Web's first years, browsers (Figure 19.1) also served as the main battleground for control of its future. The features they emphasized, or left out, would shape the new medium at the most fundamental levels – how you would find information, pay online, use multimedia, even whether you could easily contribute knowledge or simply absorb it. While the Web is an open standard, the creators of the dominant browser could hope to become its de facto masters.

This chapter traces that history, starting with the Web's background and invention, and the loss of control by its creators, whose vision for the Web's features was radically different from what it became. It moves on to the two great 'browser wars', and how those were intertwined with the existential question of the early Web – how to make it pay for itself. Where older online systems charged by the minute or hour (Bourne and Hahn, 2003; Gillies and Cailliau, 2000; Hafner, 2001; Mailland and Driscoll, 2017), the Web was an open standard running over an (initially) academic network. The ad-driven and 'freemium' models that finally succeeded have fundamentally shaped not only the economy of the online world, but its character and its content[1].

The chapter finishes by showing how the battleground has gradually shifted from browser vs. browser to mobile vs. personal computers, and to apps vs. the Web itself. The competition has also moved steadily server side. Not to Web server software itself, but to the massively profitable content it serves up from giant banks of hard disks: social media, keyword search, shopping, and more.

## DAVID VS. GOLIATH

At the start of the 1980s it was hard to imagine that the Advanced Research Projects Agency (ARPA)'s Internet protocols would

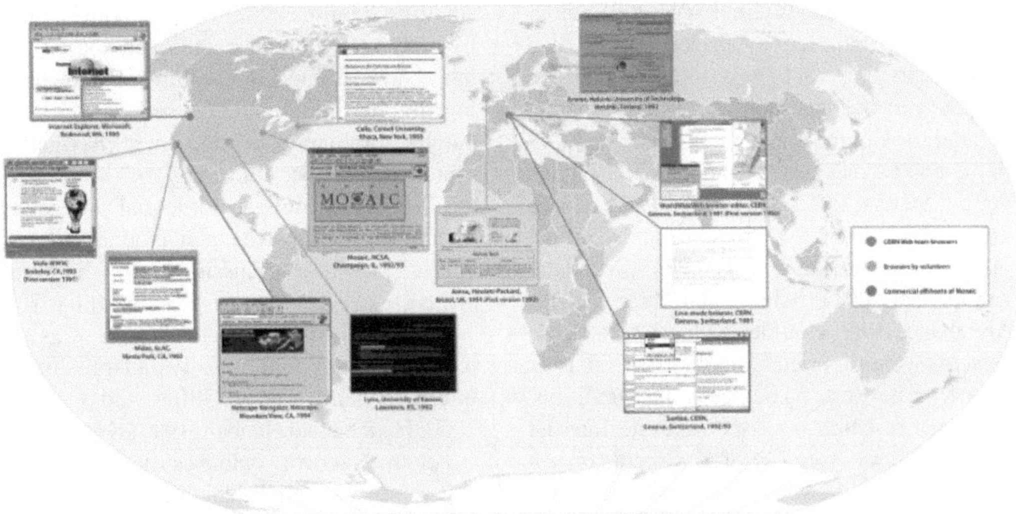

**Figure 19.1 Early Web browsers, family tree.**

*Source*: Computer History Museum

become the 'one ring to rule them all', with dominion over the earth's wires and switches from national payment systems to smart refrigerators. They were just one of several experimental standards for how to tie different networks together at the lower plumbing levels, a process known as *internetting*.

In fact, as that decade's bitter standards wars unfolded around which internetting standard should prevail, the Internet we use today was a scrappy but research-oriented David facing several Goliaths: Open Systems Interconnect (OSI), the lumbering official favorite of industry and standards bodies, and two proprietary systems from computing giants DEC and IBM.

But then David began taking steroids – in the form of US government cash. With infusions from the military, the National Science Foundation, and other agencies, while building on its loyal base of open-source hackers, the Internet started bulking up (Pelkey, 2009–2018).

It didn't hurt that the Internet had working hardware and software when its most serious rival, the Europe-based OSI, was still mostly vaporware tied down in endless meetings. As an official international standard, OSI had to painstakingly heed input from all major stakeholders (Russell, 2014).

The Internet community, by contrast, was a seeming contradiction: a captive democracy of brilliant hackers presided over by philosopher-geeks with absolute power. Those leaders – the directors of the computing research program at ARPA – generally let the iconoclastic volunteers self-organize in a kind of online meritocracy, deciding standards through a mutual respect for '…rough consensus and running code'[2]. But the leaders could also step in to settle a standards debate by fiat, or use their funding muscle to force a grant recipient – UC Berkeley – to build Internet protocols into UNIX[3].

It also didn't hurt that the Internet was backed by technology-obsessed young senator Al Gore, whose eponymous bill put nearly a billion dollars into Internet protocols for education[4]. Those protocols began to spread like wildfire, even though OSI remained the official future of networking for the US government, among others. Looking back, it's clear that by the end of the 1980s the Internet had already won, even if many insiders didn't realize it at the time (Pelkey, 2009–2018; Segal, 1995).

But because the Internet was still a noncommercial net used by geeks, nobody had bothered to write slick, easy-to-use online systems to run over it, such as the mass-market Minitel, or CompuServe, or PLATO, or AOL, or even LexisNexis (Campbell-Kelly and Garcia-Swartz, 2013; Carey and Elton, 2009; CHM, 2011; Dear, 2017; Gillies and Cailliau, 2000; Jones and Latzko-Toth, 2017; Mailland and Driscoll, 2017; Schafer and Thierry, 2012; Marchand, 1987; Mounier-Kuhn, 2002). Those systems were proprietary, and mostly ran over their own networks. The geeks who traditionally used research networks like the Internet got by with an assembly of fussy tools only a power user could love (Hafner and Lyon, 1996; Salus, 1995). To grow beyond those core users, something had to change.

Who would put an online system on the Internet?

Back in the 1960s ARPA itself had kick-started some of the world's very first such systems, from timesharing to Doug Engelbart's eponymous NLS (oNLine System). But the ARPA community's champions of these upper 'user' layers – including J.C.R. Licklider, Engelbart, and Bob Taylor – had long since moved on (Bardini, 2000; Barnet, 2014, and this volume; Markoff, 2005; Nielsen, 1995; Waldrop, 2001).

So the vacuum above the Internet began to get slowly filled by a rag-tag collection of small-time online systems. They were written by lone wolf volunteers and open-source collaborations, some from within the freewheeling Internet community itself. There was Gopher, a barebones document navigation system from the University of Minnesota, and WAIS, a mildly commercial navigation system similar to a search engine. Usenet, whose sprawling discussion boards had long hosted lively discussions on everything from sadomasochism to particle physics, was the biggest existing system to get adapted to the Internet (CHM, 2011; Gillies and Cailliau, 2000; Hauben and Hauben, 1997; Krol, 1993).

Another set of online systems featured hypertext, the clickable links so familiar today. These included Viola (Figure 19.2), built around Java-like applets by brilliant and bored Berkeley student Pei Wei; Hyper-G, a slickly packaged and very complete system by Austrian researcher Hermann Maurer (Nielsen, 1995); Lynx by Michael Grobe and Lou Montulli at the University of Kansas, and several others (Berners-Lee and Fischetti, 1999; CHM, 2011; Gillies and Cailliau, 2000)[5].

## WorldWideWeb

One of the more obscure of the late 1980s attempts to create an online system for the

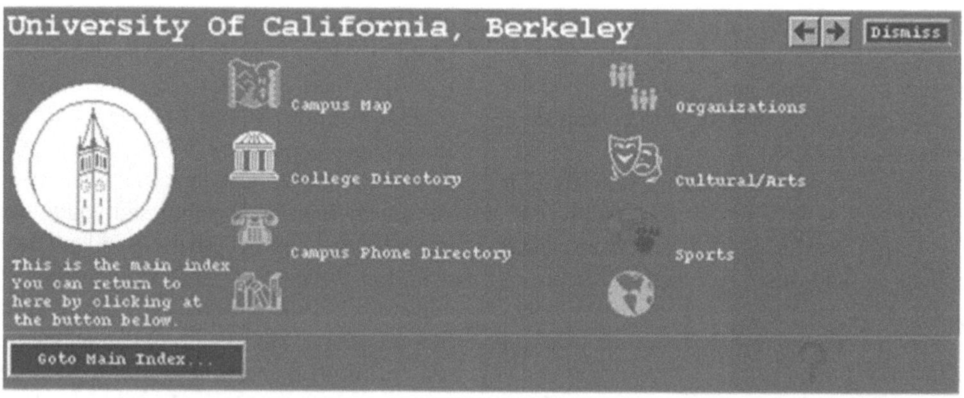


**Figure 19.2 Viola hypertext system, 1989. Viola was a powerful hypertext system by student Pei Wei, based around Java-like applets. He later turned it into an early Web browser. Courtesy of Pei Wei.**

Internet came out of CERN, the huge physics laboratory in Geneva, Switzerland. The tiny project had a comically ambitious name: 'WorldWideWeb'. Its inventor, English physicist turned programmer Tim Berners-Lee, created the Web as a partly underground effort – with help from colleague Robert Cailliau and their students and assistants, and with limited official support from CERN.

I've noticed that many of the people strongly attracted to hypertext share personality traits that could be labeled Attention Deficit Disorder: distractible, absent-minded, and creative[6]. To these folks, traditional hierarchical categories can seem numbingly predictable, the cyber equivalent of chloroform. But a clickable hyperlink might lead anywhere. It offers an intoxicating glimpse of what it's like to make tangible your own fleeting thoughts and associations; to pin the butterfly of insight. In fact, the man who originally coined the word 'hypertext', Ted Nelson, may have co-invented the medium as a crutch to compensate for his own troubles focusing[7].

With his habit of talking in a rapid stream of half-finished insights and wry asides, Tim Berners-Lee has been described as '...a hand grenade with ears'[8]. The son of early computer professionals, he had come up with his own hypertext system (ENQUIRE) nearly a decade before the Web. The idea stayed with him through a series of contracts and a startup venture, and by the late 1980s had turned into an obsession. He mercilessly pestered his managers to send him to an emerging series of hypertext conferences in the late 1980s.

Most creators of online systems had started with a blank slate, without worrying too much about compatibility. From Engelbart's NLS in the 1960s to Hyper-G in the late 1980s, they had assumed their adopters would put in some effort just to get the system going; converting existing information to the new format, perhaps even buying custom equipment.

Berners-Lee could assume no such thing. The 1980s were a Babel of conflicting standards for both online systems and the networks that underpin them. But if there was one place that lived that chaos fully, it was CERN. Because it is funded by over a dozen countries, the institution not only had all the many competing standards of the era, but also obscure national ones thrown into the mix, plus a bevy of home-grown contenders developed just for physics (Berners-Lee and Fischetti, 1999; Gillies and Cailliau, 2000; Segal, 1995).

That meant Berners-Lee's hypertext-based WorldWideWeb had to work *within* the mix of existing systems – instantly. It needed to be something a network administrator could install without licenses, or purchase orders, or days of training. It would be best if it could connect to current databases and documents.

In terms of features, his system was rudimentary compared with the elegant visions of earlier pioneers like Nelson and Engelbart– something those pioneers would not be shy about later pointing out (Gillies and Cailliau, 2000; Nelson, 2008; Weber and Hughes, 1997). But his goal was less to create a self-contained online realm than bridges between existing ones.

Some of that compatibility was based on a new role for hypertext. Berners-Lee had realized that hypertext links were not just a useful way to navigate knowledge in general, or to get around *within* a particular information system like HyperCard or NLS. They might also be the practical breakthrough he needed to unify information across a rat's nest of those different information systems:

> To follow a link, a reader clicks with a mouse (or types in a number if he or she has no mouse). To search an index, a reader gives keywords (or other search criteria). These are the only operations necessary to access the entire world of data.
>
> — Tim Berners-Lee, The W3 Book, early 1990s

You would search, and click. Behind the scenes those actions could be translated into tortured queries for a database, or arcane passwords and credentials, or the trigger for intricate commands – perhaps even for a whole virtual page to be created on the fly.

But as a user you need neither know nor care about such details. You would be surfing.

Berners-Lee submitted a funding proposal for what would become the Web in early 1989. He re-submitted it in mid 1990 with Robert Cailliau, who had been planning a networked hypertext system of his own. The response from upper management was silence.

Berners-Lee's boss Mike Sendall had pushed him to go ahead and create prototypes for the main elements of the Web we know today. He set to work over two months in the fall of 1990. He tried hard to farm out the browser-editor, though – he and Cailliau begged hypertext vendors including Microcosm and OWL to adapt their existing client software to work with the Web. There were no takers.

By Christmas Berners-Lee had URLs for addresses, HTML for pages, HTTP for links, and his own Web browser. Unlike those we use today, the prototype browser was also an editor – you could author Web pages as easily as in a word processor.

Editing was common to other hypertext systems. But it was an especially pivotal part of his vision for the Web; not only to be able to read information anywhere in the world, but to be able to contribute to it, and make references to anything, anywhere, in your own personal notes and to-do lists as well as shared documents. His hope was that a Web of knowledge – you might even call it a 'world brain' – would gradually assemble itself from the millions of links made by users in the course of their everyday lives.

How could they make all those links? Very simply – clicking on the top-level Links menu in the browser-editor would let a user instantly link to either existing places or a new, blank page. Making links would become

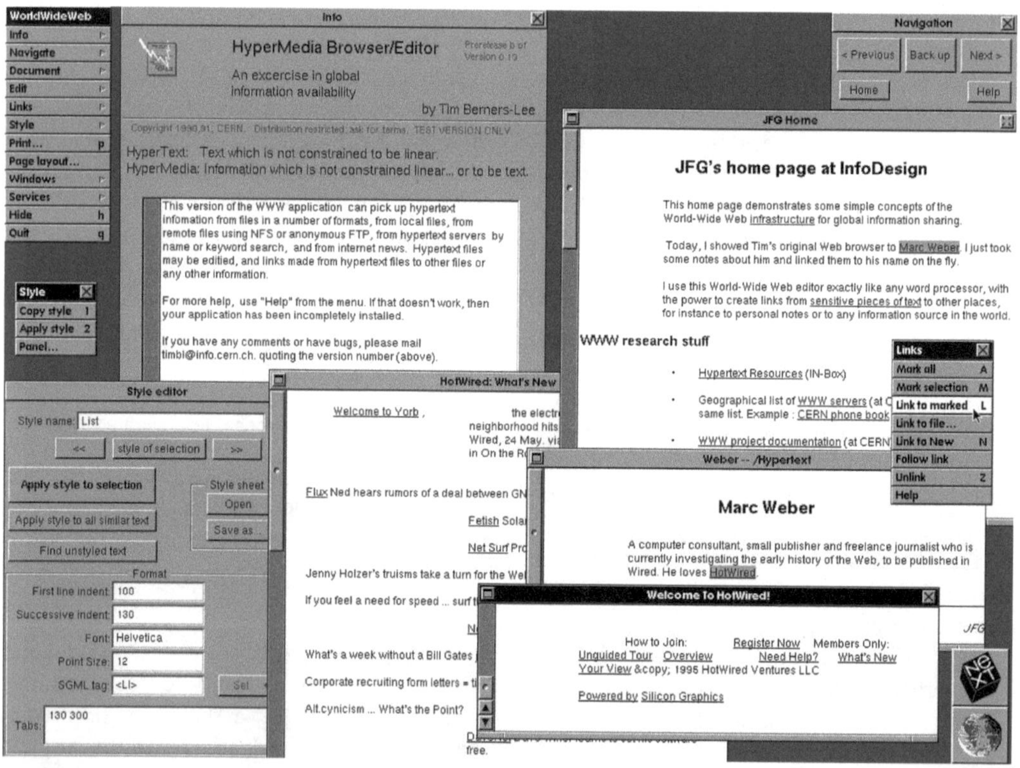


**Figure 19.3 WorldWideWeb browser-editor on the NeXT computer. Courtesy of Jean-François Groff.**

as ordinary as typing text. Users wouldn't have to deal with any complex codes unless they wanted to. With the built-in editing, there was no reason to edit HTML by hand. URLs were also hidden by default; the idea was to navigate with simple links and keyword searches.

The Web was born.

The next year was perhaps the richest creative period in the Web's early development as Berners-Lee, student Nicola Pellow, Robert Cailliau, programmer Jean-François Groff, mentor Ben Segal, and a growing circle of students and colleagues fleshed out a vision, which included a number of features not implemented in the Web today[9]: typed links, Web-to-print scripts that would translate links into paper cross-references[10], Next and Previous buttons to follow a "trail" through content, and so on.

The Web's design was also fumbling its way toward another goal. From his ENQUIRE system a decade before, Berners-Lee had been interested in hypertext links as not only a convenient navigation aid, but a way to map the real-world relationships between people, projects, ideas, and things. A few years later, he would flesh out these loose ideas into his vision for a 'Semantic Web', covered in other chapters in this *Handbook*.

But back in 1991 there was an elephant in the room. He had written his browser-editor on a powerful but rare computer built by Steve Jobs' NeXT Inc. and known for its rapid prototyping features. The same work on a more conventional machine might have taken over a year. To demo the Web on other platforms he'd had student Nicola Pellow create a simple text-only browser that could run on anything from a mainframe terminal to a Psion handheld computer. (Many early users would mistakenly believe this was the only browser the Web team had created[11].)

But for the Web to grow, Graphical User Interface (GUI) browsers were now needed for other platforms, like PCs, Macs, and the UNIX workstations common in computer science. CERN's upper management declined to fund that development. For an organization whose real job is smashing the building blocks of the

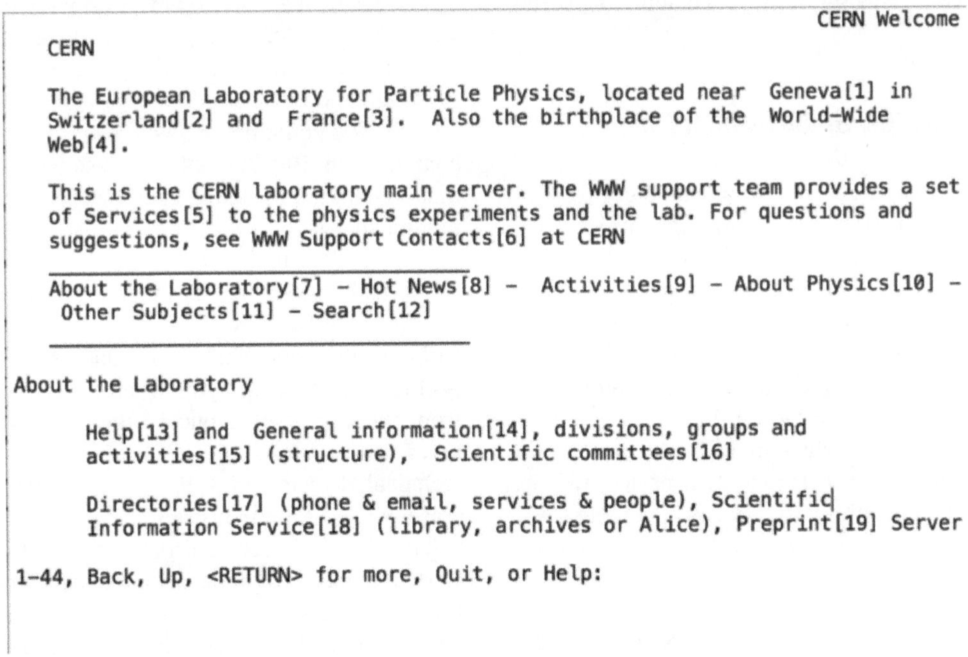


**Figure 19.4 Screenshot, CERN line-mode browser. © CERN.**

universe to see what makes them tick, the Web seemed like a stretch. The project was stuck.

So Berners-Lee and Cailliau took a leap of faith that was both desperate and hopeful. They had programmer Jean-François Groff create a library of ready-to-use Web code, like a roll-your-own browser kit, along with a standardized server. They put out an appeal: could volunteers from the budding Web development community use that library to write the needed browsers?

Looking back, this is where the Web's history split off in a very different direction from other online systems. From Minitel to LexisNexis to PLATO and CompuServe, most such systems provided the equivalent of a 'browser' in the form of their own client or physical terminal. But this was simply a tightly coupled – often proprietary – tool for viewing content on the system's servers. The same model would apply to the Web's direct competitors like Gopher and Hyper-G. Had CERN funded versions of the NeXT browser-editor for popular platforms, the Web, too, would have had its own client tightly coupled to the system as a whole. Because they didn't, a whole new set of players entered the scene.

## A FISTFUL OF BROWSERS

The response to the Web team's cry for help was fast, and heartening. Pei Wei of UC Berkeley converted his Viola hypertext system (Figure 19.2) into the first Web browser beyond CERN (Figure 19.5). Viola and the Midas browser (Figure 19.6) by Tony Johnson of SLAC laid out the familiar features of a browser we still use today. A computer science class in Helsinki created the Erwise browser as a student project (Figure 19.1). Law professor Tom Bruce wrote Cello (a riff on Viola), the first browser for the PC (Gillies and Cailliau, 2000)[12]. And so on (Figure 19.1).

For the Web team at CERN, it felt like a barn-raising; brilliant volunteers from all around the globe pitching in and meeting and chatting on the www-talk discussion group. But however beautifully conceived, these were one-man or student efforts; unpolished side projects that frequently crashed and could take even an experienced programmer part of a day to successfully install.

The next volunteer browser changed all that. It was called Mosaic (Figure 19.7), and it was written in early 1993 by brilliant student Marc Andreessen and UNIX guru Eric Bina at the National Center for Supercomputing Applications (NCSA). At first it seemed little more than a me-too browser on the model of Viola and Midas. But NCSA, a major site in the 1980s expansion of the Internet, had created and distributed the most popular program to run over the Internet so far, NCSA Telnet.

Recognizing the Web's potential, NCSA software manager Joseph Hardin quickly assembled formal teams for UNIX, Mac, and PC browsers as well as a server, and he and NCSA director Larry Smarr turned the ignition key on the institution's formidable support and PR machines.

The result was the first Web browser that was properly tested, supported, and easy for non-geeks to install. Like the Viola and Midas browsers it was modeled on, Mosaic left out editing; you could browse Web pages but not change them. But Berners-Lee was confident that could soon be added back (Weber, 1995 unpublished)[13].

Few readers today can imagine just how small and incestuous the Web community was in 1993, or how deeply the results of early events shape what we see and use now. As in those creation myths where, say, a hair from the eyebrow of one of the gods who gives birth to all trees, a seemingly minor technical decision in 1993 could spawn or erase whole future industries[14].

The first real technical battle of the Web started off as a footnote in an e-mail from Marc Andreessen. It ended with Andreessen politely, but clearly, defying Tim Berners-Lee. What was the struggle about? On its

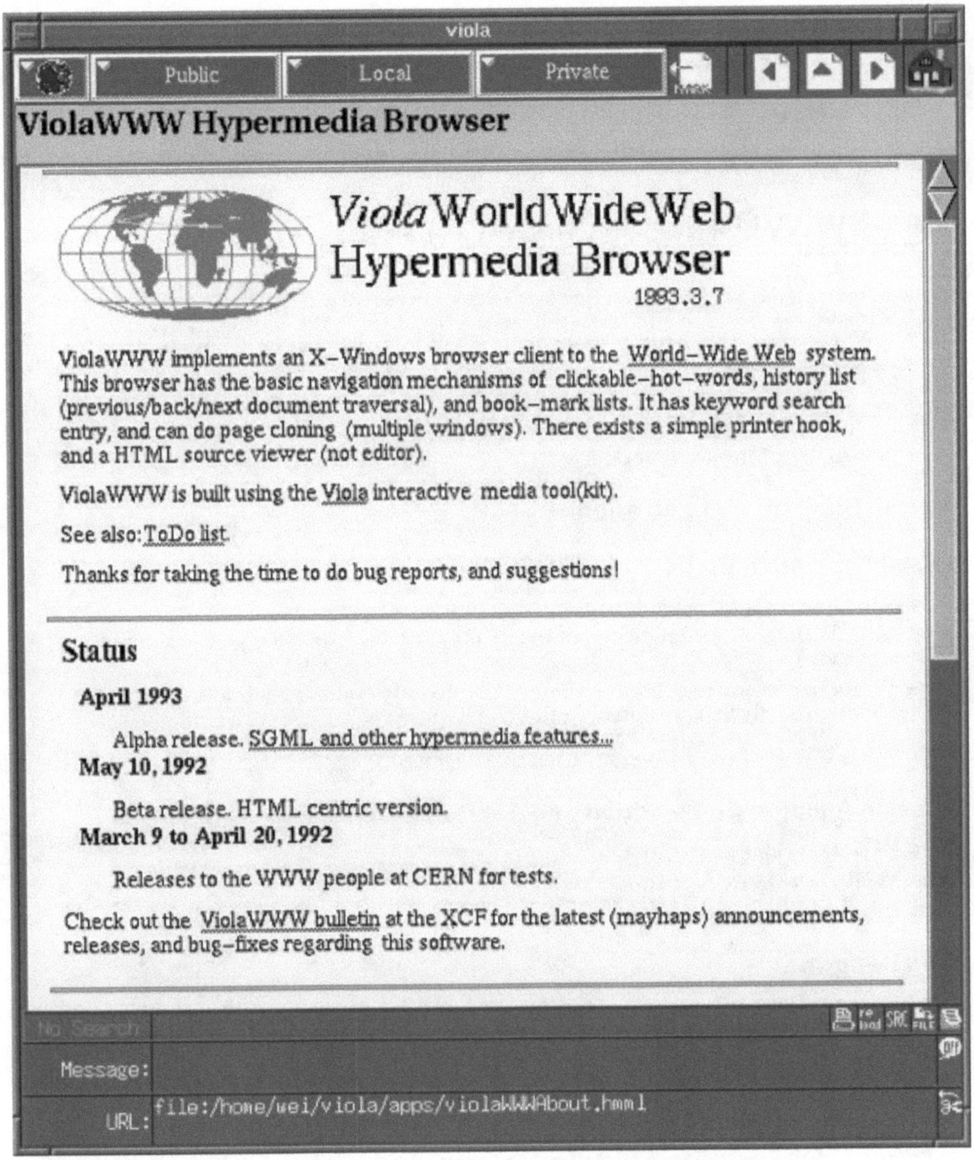


**Figure 19.5 Viola browser, screenshot from later version 1993. Courtesy of Pei Wei.**

face, how to best integrate images, sounds, and other media into a still text-heavy Web. But the real issue, of course, was who would shape its future.

Since Berners-Lee's first Web proposal in 1989, support for integrating a rich variety of multimedia had been a major goal. But nobody on the Web team felt much sense of urgency when it came to actually implementing that support. It was one of many features that could be worried about when the Web was better established. The NeXT browser-editor, Midas, Cello, and others were full GUI (Graphical User Interface) browsers in the sense that they could display text in different sizes and fonts (Figure 19.1). Yet images

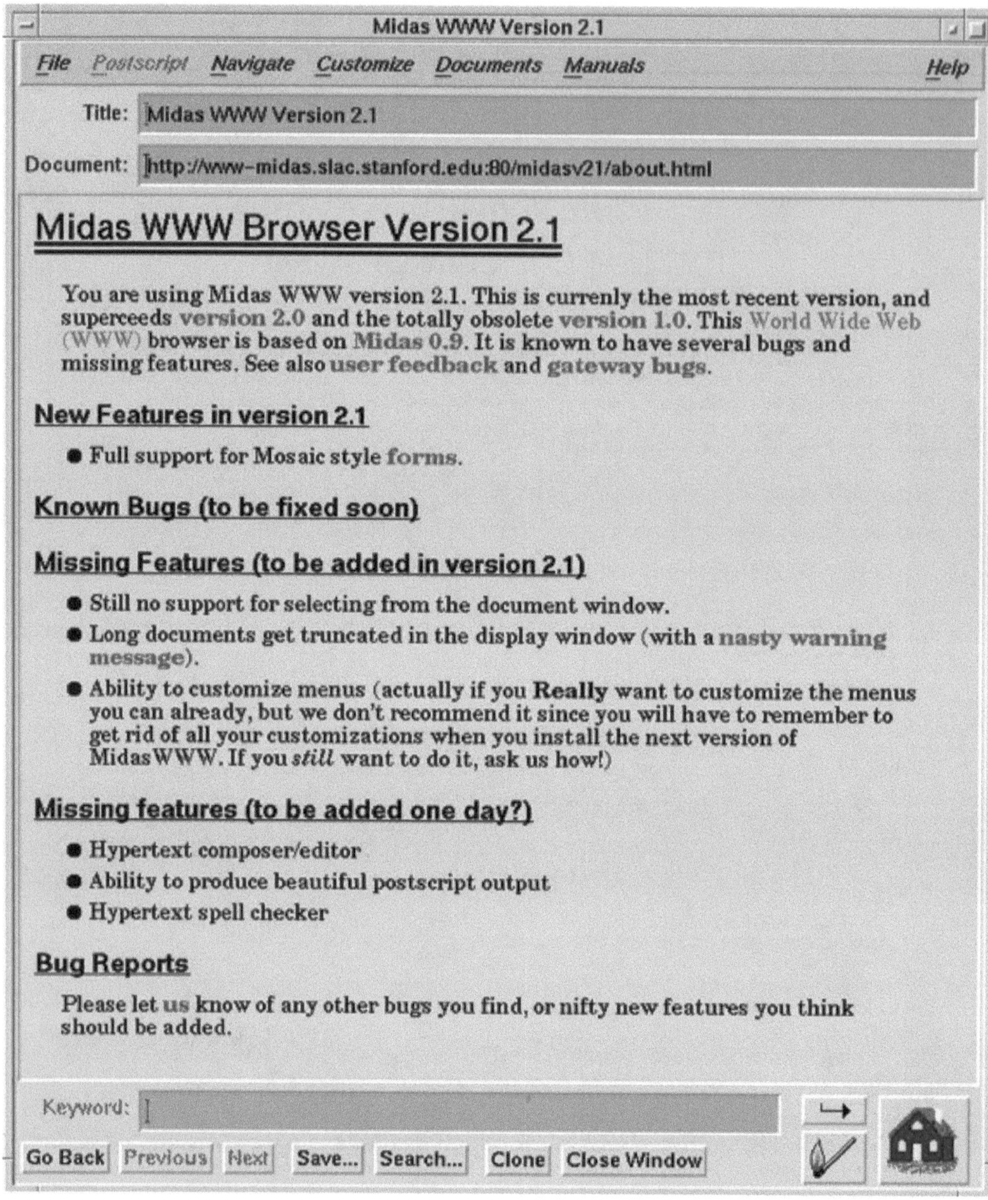


**Figure 19.6 Midas browser, screenshot from later version 2.1. Courtesy of Tony Johnson.**

and other media could only be displayed in a separate window, not mixed with the text.

Multimedia over networks was a complicated and fast-evolving technical issue at the time, with a major standard (MIME) just being defined. Berners-Lee had spent part of the summer of 1992 at Xerox's famed Palo Alto Research Center (PARC), partly to study different options. He wanted to create a single HTML tag that could not just handle different media, but display them in different ways – combined with text on a page, in a separate browser window, collapsible as in an outline view, or in a helper app[15].

But Andreessen had a crucial insight: images, at least, weren't something that could wait until after the Web was established. Without them, the Web might never get there at all.

In late February of 1993 Andreessen wrote to the www-talk mailing list announcing that Mosaic would incorporate a new HTML tag specifically to display bit-mapped images, called IMG. Berners-Lee responded with his recommendation for a future, more general INCLUDE tag that would be the single gateway for integrating all media, not just images. INCLUDE was meant to be incorporated into standard links, and offer flexibility about how media were shown (embedded in the page, in a separate window, in an 'outline' view the user could toggle on or off).

The debate became a heated topic on www-talk, with nearly all the main folks weighing in. Many agreed with Berners-Lee that IMG could set a bad precedent. Would there need to be special-case tags for every new class of media? IMG could also make it harder to implement the kind of scalability and format negotiation they felt were important. Tony Johnson was considering adding media to the Midas browser, with a simple tag like IMG coupled to a general one like INCLUDE. Though he didn't mention it on the list, Pei Wei was already experimenting with multimedia in Viola.

In the end, Berners-Lee decided to put an end to the back and forth with a simple ruling: 'Let the IMG tag be INCLUDE...'[16]. After a silence, Andreessen announced that he and Eric Bina would go ahead with IMG despite the objections[17], saying that the complexities of a more general tag like INCLUDE could be worked out later.

It was the first time somebody had seriously challenged Berners-Lee's authority over the Web. It was also the first real rift in a friendly, idealistic Web development community which so far had just been thrilled to find others with like interests.

But users loved the pictures! It's probably no coincidence that the version of Mosaic that seized the imagination of the tech press was the one that let you mix text and graphics.

The year before, the number of computers connected to the Internet had passed a million. The time was ripe for something like the Web to go world-wide.

## FAME

Mosaic took the technology press by storm in the spring of 1993, aided by a strong PR campaign from NCSA as well as years of pent-up dreams of an 'information superhighway'.

For the still-clubby little Web community it was mostly a period of thrill after thrill, as everyone rode a delicious wave of success together. The tensions of the IMG debate receded into the past. All the late-night dreams of lonely years suddenly seemed not just possible, but likely, whether your personal vision of cyber-utopia was an infinitely linked library, or a world brain, or a global marketplace.

It was perhaps like the excitement at the dawn of the auto or radio industries, but now on a time scale compressed from years to months. Serious new Web sites were appearing, from the Louvre to Kevin Hughes' pioneering multimedia Hawaii site. For the Web team, there was an especially warm feeling whenever former rivals jumped on the bandwagon – the Lynx hypertext system joined Viola in transforming itself into a Web browser, and Austrian hypertext pioneer Hermann Maurer added Web support to his sophisticated Hyper-G.

Then, in a stroke of luck that would seem contrived in fiction, the system which had become the Web's mortal rival began to almost magically melt away. Gopher ran over the Internet like the Web, but was larger and was growing faster (Figure 19.8). Suddenly, Gopher's home institution – the University of Minnesota – announced in early 1993 that it would begin to charge licensing fees for Gopher servers. That same spring Tim Berners-Lee finally convinced CERN to

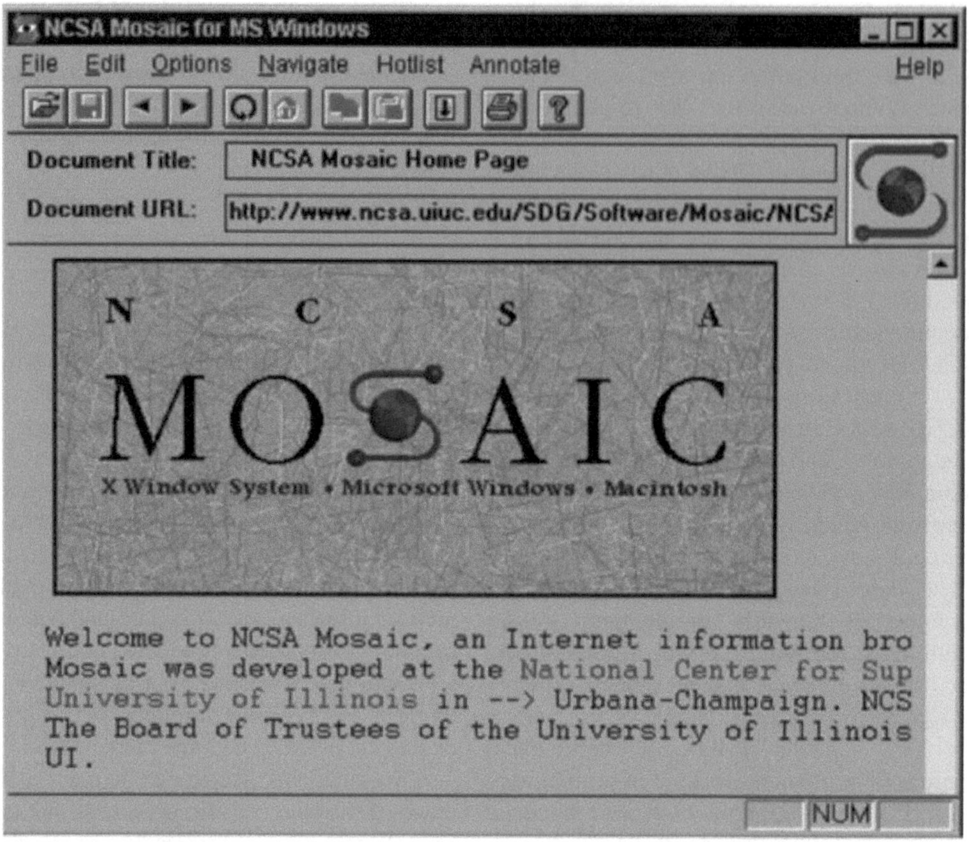


**Figure 19.7 NCSA Mosaic browser, 1993. Mosaic brought the Web to ordinary users. NCSA's 'What's New' page effectively became a home page for the entire early Web. Credit: © Board of Trustees of the University of Illinoi.**

release the Web into the public domain. The Web would be free – forever. Gopher servers withered like snowmen in a spring rain. As we'll see, Vice President Al Gore would help deliver the coup de grâce.

In the summer, technical publisher O'Reilly teamed up with Viola author Pei Wei to launch Global Network Navigator, or GNN. This was the first portal on the Web, with travel, news, shopping, and – perhaps an even more important first – advertising (Figure 19.9).

With the Web's first success came things to fight over.

To the world, NCSA was having the ride of its life, with journalists virtually camping outside the software development lab that housed the Mosaic teams, and data center staff scrambling to add machines and bandwidth fast enough to meet the exploding demand. Company after company licensed their code (some not realizing they could build their own browser and server from the Web team's public code library).

The 'What's New' page updated by Marc Andreessen and Eric Bina had become both the front door and the front page to the infant Web. It was the launching pad for several services still familiar today.

But behind the scenes there was growing bitterness between the Mosaic programing team and their managers, Joseph Hardin and Larry Smarr. Each side felt the other was expendable, while their own efforts were the crux of Mosaic's success.

**Figure 19.8 Gopher t-shirt in the style of hot-rod artist Big Daddy Roth, ca. 1994. Gopher was the Web's most serious competitor. It was developed by Mark McCahill, Paul Lindner, and Farhad Anklesaria at the University of Minnesota. © Mark Richards.**

Mosaic's success also created tensions over credit and control between NCSA and the CERN Web team. In fact, much of the world came to know the Web not as itself, but under an alias, as Mosaic. NCSA called its generic Web server a Mosaic server, and its marketing materials rarely mentioned the W-word (Figure 19.10).

The CERN Web team chafed at the slight. Much of the code in Mosaic came out of the WWW code library they had provided. Mosaic's features were modeled on the Viola and Midas Web browsers. But they chafed privately. While NCSA was chatting up top journalists from around the world, Berners-Lee's and Cailliau's passive silence was only matched by the spectacular inaction on the part of the CERN press office. Mosaic – and the United States – won the day.

But Mosaic's rise did accelerate Berners-Lee and Cailliau's activities in another direction: trying to form non-profit Web bodies

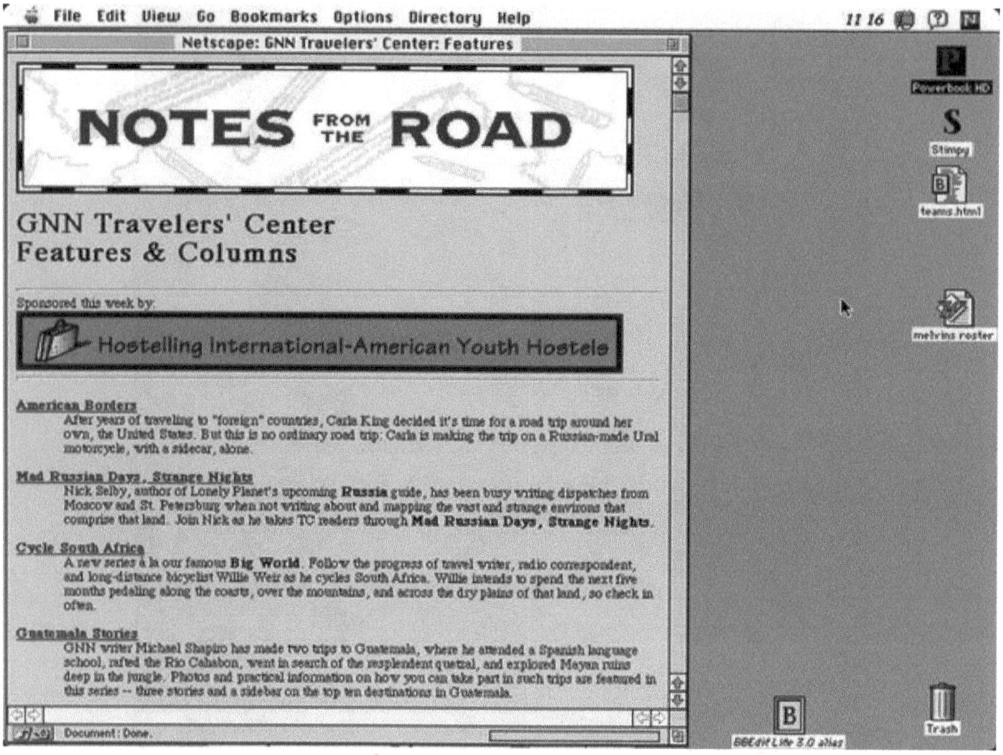


**Figure 19.9 Web portal site GNN pioneered Web advertising in 1993, with embedded ads similar to this example from 1995. GNN evolved from a bookstore kiosk version of 'The Whole Internet User's Guide' based on the early Viola browser. Courtesy of O'Reilly Media.**

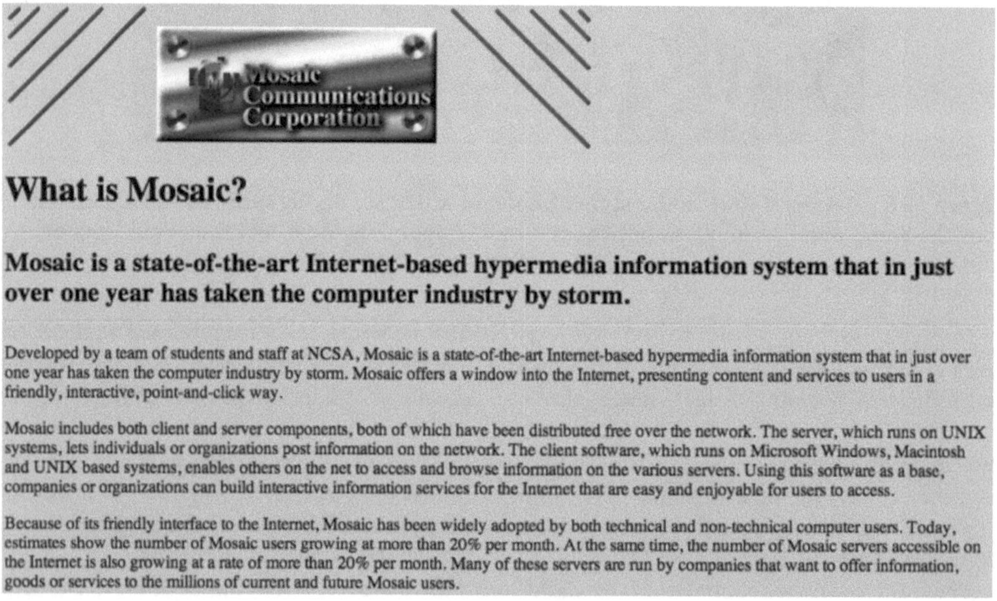


**Figure 19.10 Mosaic marketing materials. Credit: © Board of Trustees of the University of Illinois.**

that could help assure its future. Cailliau made contacts at the European Union, and Berners-Lee began to seriously consider overtures from MIT to host the US part of an organization there.

## THE GREAT MIGRATION WESTWARD

By 1994 companies, institutions, advertisers, and news media were jumping on the Web bandwagon in geometrically increasing numbers. There was also the first serious interest from three harder-to-get players: the highest levels of government, the publishing industry, and perhaps most important of all, Silicon Valley.

Progress happened fastest in the United States. The combination of CERN (and Geneva's) indifference to the Web with Silicon Valley's growing interest pushed along a general move westward: from Europe to the United States, and from everywhere else to Silicon Valley (Figure 19.1).

At the end of 1993 the tensions within the NCSA Mosaic team had reached toxic levels. Marc Andreessen quit NCSA and took a job at pioneering Internet company Enterprise Integration Technologies (EIT) in Silicon Valley, which would later launch the CommerceNet consortium.

But Andreessen was soon recruited by the larger-than-life founder of Silicon Graphics, Jim Clark, to help start a new Web company. Andreessen suggested creating a new browser and server, codenamed 'Mozilla' – a mashup of the idea of Godzilla and what they hoped would be a Mosaic-killing browser[18]. They threw down the gauntlet by poaching around half the Mosaic team from NCSA, including Mosaic coauthor Eric Bina, and the whole group founded Mosaic Communications in early 1994.

NCSA took them to court over their reuse of the Mosaic name and, potentially, code. The terms of the settlement that followed were secret. But one result was that the new company changed its name to that of its

**Figure 19.11 White House site, 1994. Available at public domain.**

new browser, Netscape, which then became Netscape Navigator (Figure 19.12).

NCSA had assigned commercial rights for Mosaic to its corporate partner, Spyglass, and Browser War I was on. Spyglass made some good sales, including to one pivotal player – Microsoft. But to little avail. Netscape's Navigator seemed to support its programmer's claims that they had rewritten the new browser from the ground up: it was slick, reliable, and faster than Mosaic. It also offered full support to large paying customers, a prerequisite for many corporations to adopt it. NCSA Mosaic was dead within a year. It would be Navigator that first showed the Web – and the online world – to the rest of us.

The Web's westward movement got help from an unexpected quarter – the US White House. Vice President Al Gore personally demoed the Web to cabinet heads, and encouraged them to put up Web sites for their departments. The White House's own site (whitehouse.gov, (Figure 19.11)) led the way (CHM, 2011)[19], a final knock for one-time Web rival Gopher, which had early use by Congress.

As a major center for both computing and the 1960s counterculture, the San Francisco Bay Area as a whole had long been a mixing ground for technology with vivid, sometimes utopian, dreams for its future.

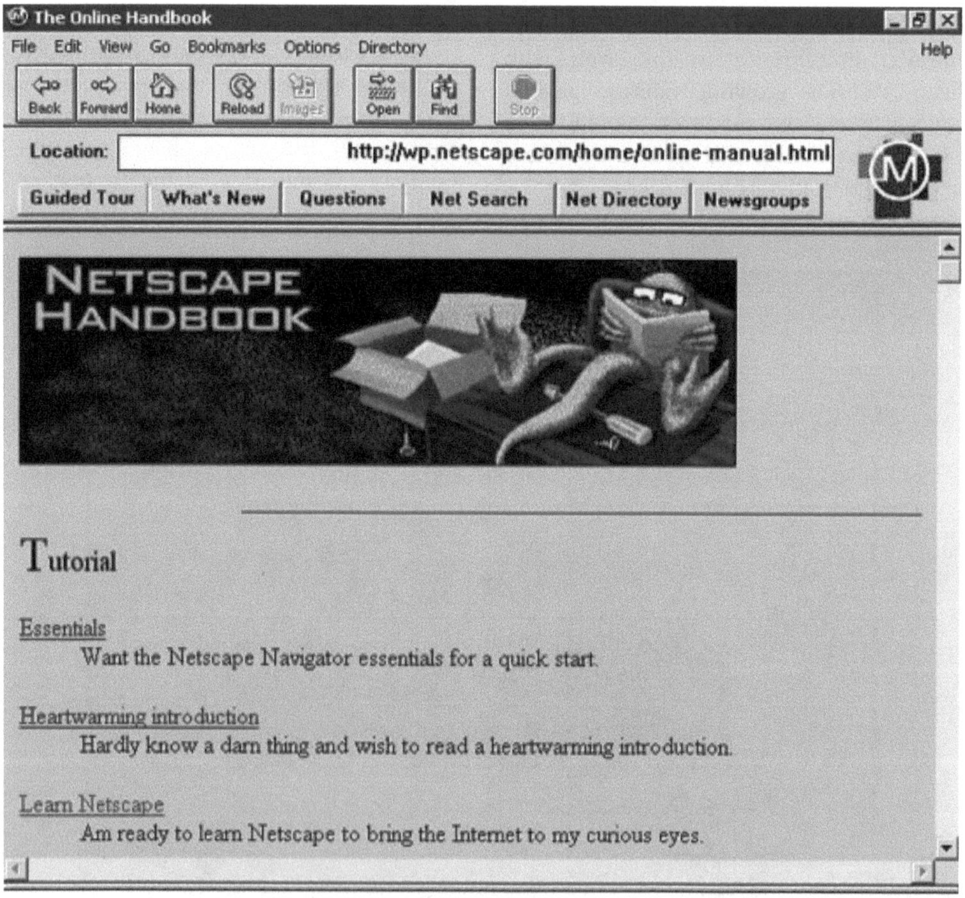


**Figure 19.12 Screenshot from Netscape Navigator. Credit: ©AOL.**

The ideas for VRML, or Virtual Reality Markup Language, were hammered out against a background of technical inspiration, LSD and hot tub parties, and espresso. Mark Pesce and Tony Parisi's vision was of a world where most browsers supported virtual reality, and the most basic operations on the Web took place in a virtual world[20].

That meant not just games or virtual online communities like the later Second Life, but navigating your way from site to site, and browsing information once you got there. A site's designer might choose to have you arrive in a virtual room where you could talk with someone else's avatar or choose a book or a video from a shelf, as well as more 'conventional' uses of VR like a virtual walk-through of a building, collaborative engineering projects[21], or visualization of molecules.

VRML was a surprise hit at the vastly oversubscribed first international Web conference at CERN, an event Web programmer Jean-François Groff called 'the Woodstock of the Web'. Held in the summer of 1994, it was a follow-up to the Wizard's Workshop hosted by publisher O'Reilly and Associates the summer before. The participants at both events shared a palpable sense that they were going to change the world in wonderful ways, that they were on the cusp of something Big.

But the westward pull continued. Only months later, Tim Berners-Lee announced that he would run the new World Wide Web Consortium (W3C) from MIT, in an attempt to combat his eroding control over the Web and its potential fragmentation as a standard. This left Robert Cailliau and others at CERN in a diminished role. CERN would host merely the European office, not the headquarters.

Mosaic's eclipse by Netscape was no great surprise, given the sheer power and momentum of Silicon Valley. Nor was Tim Berners-Lee's shift to the United States. But the complete end of Web development at CERN was sudden. In December of 1994, CERN management decided to hand the Web project off to the French national computing research institute. Part of the impetus was that the lab had just gotten funding approval from its member states to build a major new accelerator, the Large Hadron Collider (LHC), to hunt for the elusive Higgs-Boson particle. CERN had always been ambivalent about supporting the Web, given its physics mission. But the shift would effectively scatter what little center of gravity was left to Web development in Europe and in the Geneva region[22]. When Europe fully woke up to the Web, it would be as an American import.

Yet despite its rocketing popularity, the Web still didn't have a way to pay for itself. The next section explores how that changed.

## MAKING THE WEB SAFE FOR BUSINESS

> If it wasn't for Netscape, you'd be calling the Web Microsoft Network or AOL by now.
>
> — Lou Montulli, Netscape founding programmer, coauthor of the Lynx browser

To a savvy business person in the mid 1990s, the Web looked like a waste of time. There were two big reasons. First, it was an open standard, with open access. That meant no obvious way to charge by the minute, which had been the bread and butter of commercial online systems from 1960s timesharing to Minitel to CompuServe – and of telephone companies since before living memory. How would you make money?

Second, the Web ran over the Internet. Not only was that government-funded network based on another open standard, but until mid 1995 it had actually *forbidden* commercial use. It didn't help that many of the better-known spokespeople for both the Web and Internet were hippie hackers, academics, civil liberties advocates, or otherwise seen as less than enthusiastic about conventional business. For many of these folks the Internet felt like the antidote to commercial online services like CompuServe and AOL, a shared

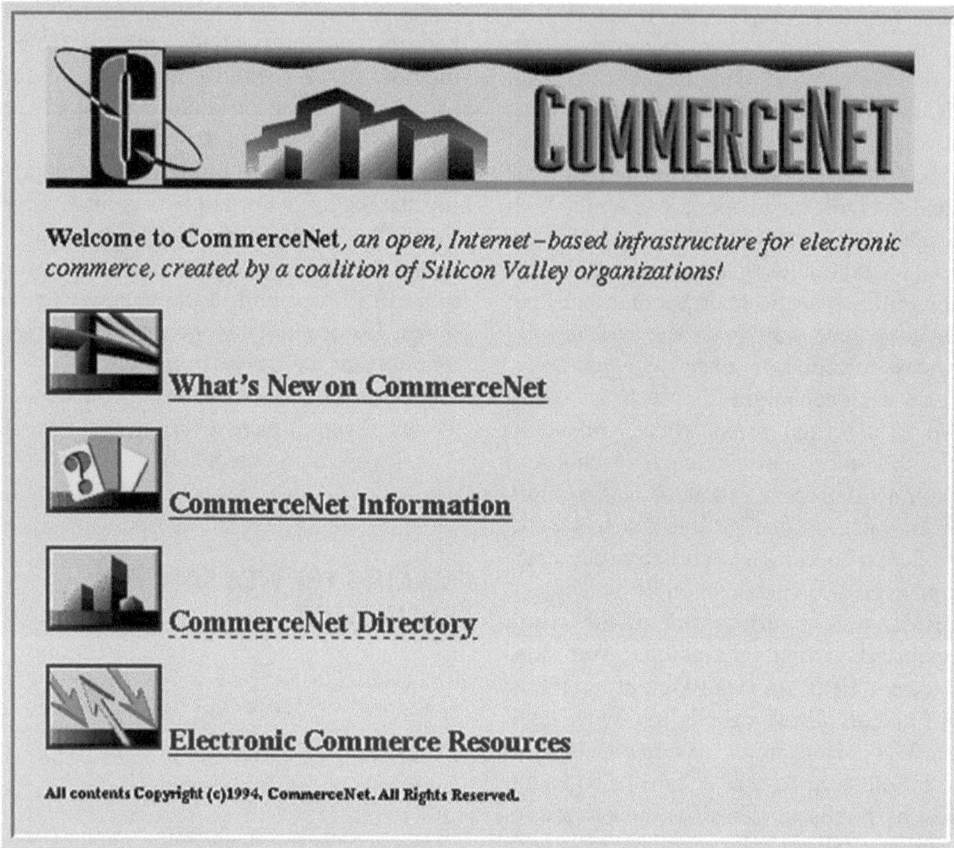


**Figure 19.13 CommerceNet Consortium page, 1994 Courtesy of Kevin Hughes.**

commons on which crass commercialization would be as appetizing as blaring TV ads in a public library.

Of course, we all know the Web and Internet went commercial in the end. But it took a number of kick-starts to get them there. Their open, non-commercial roots were a big contrast with much of the history of automated information systems. The long history of electrically enhanced business leads from nineteenth-century telegraphy and Western Union money transfers through 1930s Telex, and then the flowering of computerized transaction systems – ERMA, SWIFT, ATMs, etc. – from the 1950s onward. In fact, the first dedicated e-commerce device may have been the telegraph-era ticker tape machine for stock quotes (Figure 19.14).

Many pre-Web online systems had been very friendly to business indeed. For instance, France Telecom generated billions in annual sales on Minitel (Mailland and Driscoll, 2017). Even iconoclastic, alternative online community The Well had a rock-solid business model with its hourly connection charges.

As the Web took off, a few pioneers tried to prove that the once anti-commercial Internet could indeed support business. By 1993, publisher O'Reilly's pioneering commercial portal GNN (Global Network Navigator) was running online ads, soon joined by *Wired* Magazine's online venture *HotWired*. The mid 1990s was also the first flowering of would-be digital currencies, from anonymous, cypherpunk-inspired DigiCash to the more conventional CyberCash. In 1994, Enterprise

**Figure 19.14 Universal 3-A stock ticker, ca. 1870–80. Among the first dedicated e-commerce devices, ticker tape machines printed stock prices in real time. They were named for their ticking sound © Mark Richards.**

Integration Technologies (EIT) – the same firm which had hired Marc Andreessen after he left NCSA – founded the influential CommerceNet consortium to develop Web commerce (Figure 19.13), with members including Wells Fargo, Netscape, and Visa.

While mainstream businesses were still trying to figure out how to monetize clicks, pornography and gambling sites were quietly starting to earn serious profits and pioneering the nuts and bolts of Web transactions along the way. The first online lottery started in Liechtenstein in 1995, and soon there was a wildly growing new industry loosely centered around London; a freewheeling world of online casinos, offshore shell companies, and wild Caribbean parties, all threaded through legal loopholes with the skill of a master tailor[23]. At the same time, sex and pornography were evolving from earlier models on bulletin board systems (BBSs), Minitel, and Usenet to a new and highly profitable kind of Web industry.

But it was Netscape's spectacular 1995 IPO that kicked off the dot-com boom, and the success of online firms like Amazon, Yahoo!, and eBay that finally convinced mainstream business to follow the pioneers into Web commerce. Netscape's innovative business model – free to individuals, commercial licenses to companies – began to answer the skeptic's question of how an open standard could pay.

In terms of tech cred, it didn't hurt that Sun Microsystems had picked up the radical dream that net-based applications could make operating systems irrelevant (Gillies and Cailliau, 2000)[24]. Java applets would give your browser all the functions you needed, and eventually eliminate the need for Microsoft or Apple. Sun's slogan was: 'The Network is the Computer', and Netscape among others was happy to come along for the ride.

## CLOSING THE FRONTIER

By the mid 1990s there were working models for some of the main pillars of Web commerce: 'freemium' software and services with Netscape, ad-supported information portals like GNN and Yahoo!, and direct sales of goods as with 1-800-FLOWERS, Amazon's virtual mega-bookstore, and eBay's unique auction model.

The frontier was closing fast. The next story would be one of settlement: not how to make the Web, but who would control it.

The Web fully joined the mainstream in the late summer of 1995. The giddy expansion of the last couple of years had finally produced a critical mass of users, developers, journalists, companies, and government support. Equally important, Microsoft got involved.

Netscape had been riding high, particularly when its August IPO made it the first famous 'dot-com'. Then the sleeping giant in Seattle finally woke up, and the result was the long, cold Browser War II. As in the real Cold War, many other, smaller conflicts slowed down, and what followed were three years of locked combat in which the World Wide Web reached the rest of us.

But the software giant's entry into Web development was a reluctant one, since it meant scrapping plans for its own competing Microsoft Network (MSN), a standalone environment with its own networking protocols (Figure 19.15). The surviving 'walled gardens' of the era – CompuServe, AOL, Minitel in France – were already beginning to fade out or become Web access points. But the tens of millions of copies of Windows 95 that Microsoft expected to sell in the first year came ready to plug right in to MSN. Even if just a small percentage subscribed, MSN would have instantly become a walled garden bigger than CompuServe and AOL.

In a single document, Bill Gates' 'Internet Tidal Wave' memo dictated a complete change of direction for the huge firm, akin to turning a battleship around a buoy. Microsoft became a Web company. It was a recognition that the Web – and the business models that Netscape and others had pioneered for making an open standard pay – had gotten too big to simply crush.

But Microsoft could still crush Netscape. Gates decided to use his firm's near-monopoly over the desktop to take on the browser market. Microsoft bundled its own licensed version of Mosaic, which it named Internet Explorer, with every later copy of Windows 95 and its successors. MSN became a Web portal as Microsoft challenged Netscape's Navigator browser head on. At its peak, the Explorer team reportedly grew to a thousand strong (Sink, 2003).

Browser War II was fought on largely the same grounds as Browser War I: Mosaic clone vs. Mosaic clone. Neither company seriously revisited the early Web or other hypertext systems to expand the basic footprint of what a browser could do for the user. Netscape Gold was the only major try at a browser-editor: painfully slow, it made editing and browsing two separate modes as in very early word processors. Microsoft did try to integrate the Web and connectivity into a variety of products, from Word to Windows, with varying degrees of success. But Internet Explorer kept mostly to the tried and true. This meant it was easy for users to switch browsers, since they all did roughly the same things.

By the late 1990s the design of Web pages was professionalizing fast. While HTML had originally been aimed at ordinary users with word-processor-level graphics needs (and skills), the lack of easy editing pushed content production to professionals. The kinds of crude pages done by techie webmasters were giving way to serious graphic design, aided by various changes to HTML[25].

The world at large was just in the first throes of Web mania. But to those most involved in the Web's launch, the wild ride of the last few years seemed to be palpably slowing down. By the end of 1995, the results of the struggles you've been reading about would produce the first durable balance of power for the major players in the Web's technical development.

For nearly four years – an eternity in those early days when a 'Web year' was jokingly defined as around three months[26] – Microsoft and Netscape were locked in a slow war of attrition, with the World Wide Web Consortium (W3C) in the middle. Started by Tim Berners-Lee, W3C was the Web's standards body, with over 100 corporate members. It also served as a field of combat, as Microsoft and Netscape proposed their own additions to HTML, HTTP, and so on. Netscape tended to be the challenger, adding new tags that infuriated HTML architects like Dave Raggett, while Microsoft often found it a useful competitive strategy to assiduously follow W3C rules.

Browser War II was over by 1999. Netscape Navigator's share of the browser market had faded to an echo of Internet Explorer's, and Netscape was bought by AOL. But in 1998, some of Netscape's core programmers had started the open-source Mozilla foundation. The Firefox browser was one of the main fruits of that effort, and in a sense continued the battle against Internet Explorer for another 14 years until Explorer was retired by Microsoft.

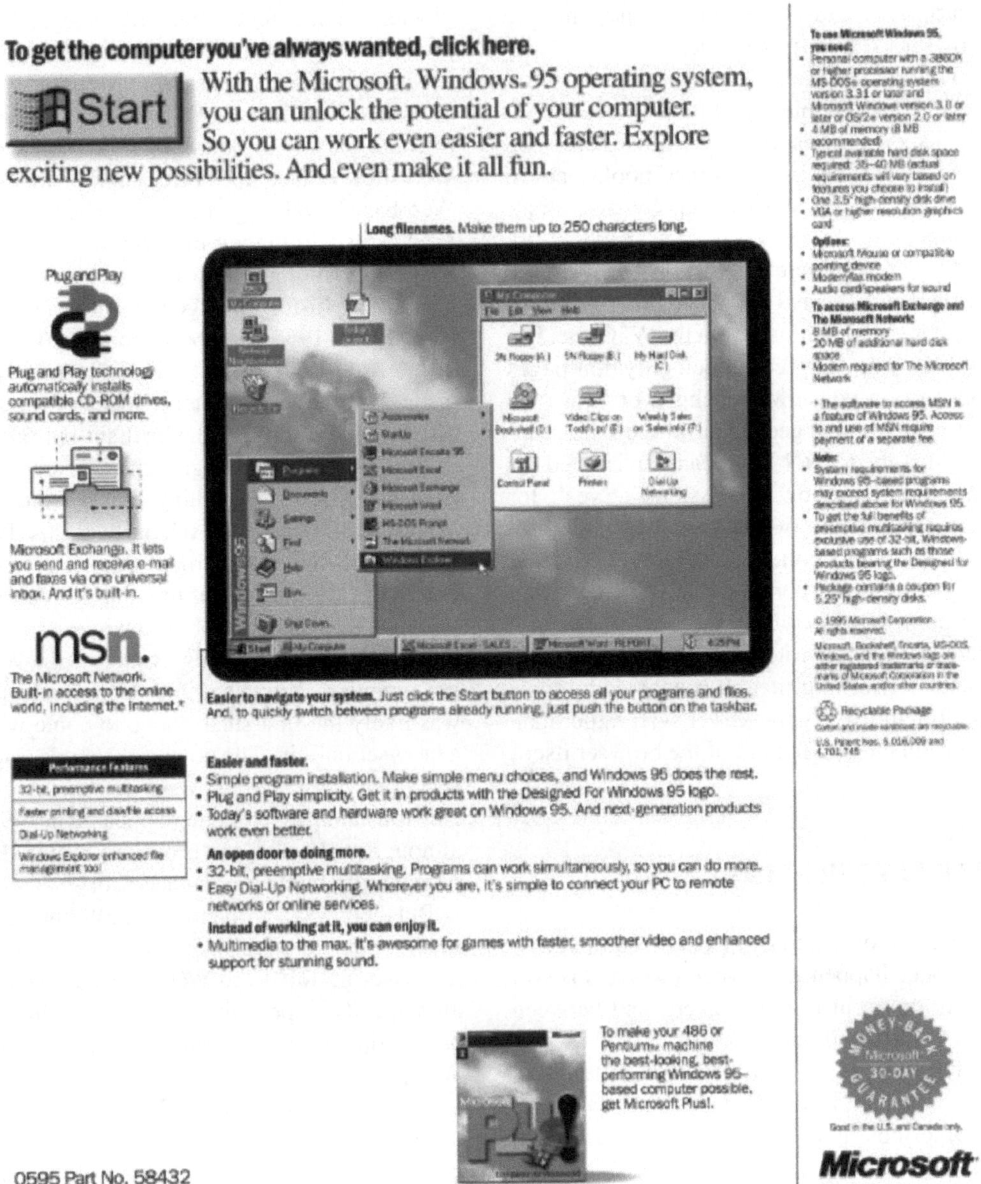


**Figure 19.15 Windows 95 box with Microsoft Network (MSN) logo. Windows 95 came ready to connect to this initially proprietary network and online service, the last major challenger to the Web and Internet. MSN soon switched to providing internet access. *Source*: Computer History Museum.**

There has been no Browser War III. Why? The main battleground for 'mindshare' on the Web has shifted away from browsers to mostly server-based (aka 'cloud') services – search, shopping, and user-generated content from Wikipedia to social media. It has also shifted form factor. As we'll see shortly, the battle lines have increasingly become smartphone vs. computer, and mobile browser vs. smartphone app.

Tim Berners-Lee's NeXT browser-editor, with its idea of integrated browsing and editing as extensions of word processing and our daily to-do lists, address books, notes, etc., was never followed up by any major product[27].

The most concrete example today might be the aging Amaya reference browser-editor you can still download from the W3C site. But in 2018 you can pretty much only edit pages that live on your own machine, or your own server if you're a geek. The whole infrastructure that the CERN Web team envisioned for handling authoring permissions – 'yes', for instance, for your own pages at work but 'no' for editing your colleague's – was never built.

Instead, what comparatively little editing we do in 2018 is within the confines of particular 'Web 2.0' sites, like blogs, wikis, and social networking sites. It is enabled by tools that run mostly on the server side, rather than being an integral feature of the browser itself.

## WEB IN YOUR POCKET

The kind of take-no-prisoners competition that once happened between browsers is still going on – but in our pockets, and between our pockets and our desks (or laps)!

There are more functional differences between Safari on an iPhone and Safari on a MacBook than between nearly any two desktop Web browsers ever written. Ditto for Chrome on Android vs. Chrome on a Google Chromebook. Those differences aren't just about user interface issues, like where the bookmark's menu is or how to enter URLs. They're about how you use the browser – where, for what, and for what kind of sites.

Then there is the rivalry between mobile Web browsers and Internet apps. At a technical level, a mobile Web browser itself is just an especially well-established Internet 'app'. But in societal terms the Web embodies a global, open-source standard designed to promote interoperability and cross-linking.

Most apps, by contrast, are proprietary and often fleeting. They aren't generally designed to share data with other apps, or with most Web sites. In fact, apps offer another way for Web-based 'walled gardens' like Facebook to keep users within their manicured confines.

Pre-Web mobile 'browsing' has a long and fascinating history that goes back at least to Alan Kay's 1968 Dynabook concept (CHM, 2011; Kay, 1972), if not Nikola Tesla's fantastic 1905 'World System' ideas (Carlson, 2013), and up through the brilliant but failed efforts of General Magic, the startup that tried to bring us something like the mobile Web – and beyond – in the early 1990s. But that lies beyond the scope of this chapter, as does a detailed history of the mobile Web[28].

In broad outline, mobile devices tried to incorporate Web browsing as soon as the Web got popular. Nokia's 1996 Communicator was likely the first smartphone to come with a browser built in. The powerful Newt's Cape (play on Netscape) browser for the Apple Newton handheld computer appeared in 1995, although truly wireless browsing required a pricey radio modem as an accessory[29].

But there was a problem. The still-emerging mobile data networks of the time weren't up to delivering full-sized Web pages at reasonable speeds, especially without the kind of bandwidth-sensitive format negotiation the Web team had originally favored.

Mobile makers tried a series of clever but ultimately unsatisfying workarounds. For instance, the Palm IV organizer optimized caching of data on servers to permit browsing of a sort over low-speed pager networks[30]. On many 'dumb' phones, Wireless Access Protocol (WAP) let users access selected Web content. But the text-only 'browser' could only connect to sites which had paid to be included on a central WAP server.

Others tried to make the basic language of Web pages, HTML, more compact. In 1996 HTML senior architect Dave Raggett roughed out a version of HTML optimized

**Figure 19.16 Kinokuniya bookstore, i-mode site. Credit: © Kinokuniya.**

**Figure 19.17 Cybird's mobile map, i-mode site. Credit: ©Cybird.**

for speed[31]. But the first such effort to reach consumers was in Japan.

So in 1999, while American dot-com CEOs were famously dancing on tables in pleather pants (Helmore, 2001; Paternot, 2001)[32] at the peak of the dot-com boom, Tomihisu Kamada of ACCESS and other Japanese pioneers hired by telephone operator NTT DoCoMo were deploying the mass mobile Web – eight long years before the iPhone and Android brought it to the rest of us.

i-mode sites (Figures 19.16, 19.17) used a compact version of the HTML language, called – appropriately enough – Compact HTML (Matsunaga, 2001; Wallace et al., 2002)[33]. By 2002, over 34 million Japanese subscribers were using i-mode phones for Web access, e-mail, banking, live maps, streaming video, news, and pretty much everything else we do with smartphones today (Wallace et al., 2002)[34].

Early devices looked like conventional 'dumb' phones, but pushing the 'i' (information) mode button opened the i-mode browser, and a whole new set of options. The phones even served as mobile electronic wallets, for buying anything from a soda to a train ticket. NTT DoCoMo handled billing and shared the revenues with official i-mode sites (Mallon, 2013; Matsunaga, 2001; Wallace et al., 2002)[35]. Domestic competitors to i-mode soon followed, though attempts to spread beyond Japan fizzled.

Smartphones finally started to get global traction around 2001: Symbian phones from Europe, Blackberrys from Canada, Palm/Handspring Treos from Silicon Valley. All had browsers, as did some handheld computers for use with a landline modem. Opera and ACCESS were two of the major mobile browser makers. But small screens, limited support for plugins, and still-poky speeds on full-sized Web pages limited user interest.

iPhone didn't start as a phone. Galvanized by the success of its iPod, Apple began developing a minimalist tablet – all screen, no keyboard. But when the skunkworks tablet team stumbled across a multi-touch pointing device, management got excited. Could using your fingers to pinch, scroll, and zoom be the basis for a new kind of user interface – one that might let a phone-sized screen easily browse documents or a full Web page?

The rest is history. In combination with networks that were finally fast enough to deliver full-sized Web pages wirelessly, the iPhone – and its Android imitators – took the mass Web mobile. At least the passive browsing part. The finger interface was heavily optimized for displaying content, not creating it.

The original iPhone had no third-party apps. With the exception of included apps like iTunes, the only connection to the net was through the built-in Safari browser. But in 2008, Apple opened up the iPhone to third-party developers, who quickly produced thousands of them[36]. Apps could, of course, only run on iPhones. But more remarkably, they could only be accessed through Apple's highly profitable (and 'curated', including censorship) App Store[37], an update on the wild success of the iTunes Store for the iPod.

Android apps followed suit, though with less of a proprietary lock.

An ironic result was to partly freeze Web browsers. Rather than push the limits of what could be done within a browser, or in the shared environment of the Web, developers began to put their most innovative features into native iOS or Android apps. You may be walking down the street as you pinch and scroll with your fingers rather than clicking on a mouse, but the main features of mobile browsers in 2018 have changed little from Viola, and Midas, and Mosaic a quarter century before.

Looking back, another reason browsers have become less of a focus is that the server side has finally caught up. The centers of gravity for the Web today are the masters of great server banks[38] – and even greater user bases – like Facebook, Weibo, Wikipedia, Amazon, Alibaba, Google, and Yandex. As we've seen, the gradual oozing of power to the server side was accelerated by the fact that browsers lost two key battles.

Modern browsers have neither become de facto operating systems as in the Java dreams of the later 1990s[39], *nor* our personal word processors, to-do lists, hypertext authoring tools, etc. as Tim Berners-Lee originally envisioned (Berners-Lee and Fischetti, 1999). Either of these roles could have kept particular browsers 'sticky' for users, less interchangeable than they are today. What authoring and PIM (Personal Information Management) functions we do now are mostly on the server side, through social media, online calendars and notes, Google docs, blogs, or wikis. This keeps our loyalties with the owners of the servers, not the browsers we use to access them.

Whether the Web's drift toward the server-side dominance of older commercial online systems like Minitel, CompuServe, etc. is permanent remains to be seen. In the last decade there have been attempts to put more functionality in the browser, including Google's ChromeBook with its browser-as-operating system, and the Mozilla Foundation's similar Firefox OS for smartphones (Mims, 2013). Neither have exactly taken the world by storm. But unlike older online systems, with their tightly coupled clients and servers, the client (browser) side of the Web is a fulcrum from which powerful players once shaped our online future. It remains a wild card.

## ACKNOWLEDGMENTS

The author thanks Niels Brügger and Ian Milligan for their help and advice in the preparation of this chapter, Hansen Hsu for exploring the history of Apple browsers together, and his agent Laurie Fox for helping him think through some of the material that led to its contents. He thanks Kirsten Tashev, Len Shustek, Dag Spicer, Chris Garcia, Paula Jabloner, Karen Kroslowitz, Al Kossow, Jon Plutte, and many, many others at CHM for educating him about interpretation and preservation in a museum context. He thanks Ben Segal, Jean-François Groff,

Tim Berners-Lee, Stevan Keane, Dave and Jenny Raggett, and Kevin Hughes for getting him hooked on the topic in the first place.

## Notes

1 'Fake news' is one highly discussed consequence of the ad-driven model, and the decline of traditional subscription models for media may be related to the rise of 'freemium'.

2 Attributed to Internet pioneer Dave Clark, IETF plenary presentation 1992; also quoted in Resnick (1992).

3 Personal confirmation, 2017, Marshall Kirk McKusick, member of Berkeley UNIX team at the time. According to McKusick, ARPA made the inclusion of support for TCP/IP into Berkeley UNIX a prerequisite for further ARPA funding.

4 Then-Senator Al Gore's High-Performance Computing and Communication Act of 1991 created the National Information Infrastructure, which promoted and funded over $600 million of various networking initiatives. Gore called this the 'information superhighway' (Gore, 1991).

5 Also based on my own interviews with creators of Viola in 1996, Hyper-G in 1996, Lynx in 1996, and Montulli of Lynx for a second time in 2006.

6 This observation is also supported for Berners-Lee by his statements about himself in my interviews with him in 1995–7, by Nelson about himself in my interview with him in 2013, and in the case of Engelbart by Markoff, 2005, among other biographical accounts.

7 Weber, interview with Ted Nelson, 2013.

8 Weber, Interviews with Tom Bruce, 1996.

9 Weber, interviews with Jean-François Groff, 1995, 1996, 2010; interviews with Tim Berners-Lee, 1995–6; interviews with Robert Cailliau, 1995–6.

10 Weber, interviews with Jean-François Groff, 1995, 1996, 2010.

11 Weber, interviews with Jean-François Groff, 1995, 1996, 2010; interviews with Tim Berners-Lee, 1995–6; interviews with Robert Cailliau, 1995–6.

12 Cello was the only very early browser not based on the CERN code library; Bruce rewrote all the needed code himself. Interviews with Tim Berners-Lee, 1995–7; Tom Bruce, 1996.

13 Weber, interviews with Tim Berners-Lee, 1995 and 1996.

14 For instance, the decision by most browser creators to leave out authoring flipped the Web as a whole to a read-only medium, and much later gave rise to server-side editing (social media, blogs, Google Docs, etc.). The de facto standard created by NCSA's IMG tag accelerated the adoption of simple images (and possibly of the Web as a whole!) while likely delaying common standards for other media, and taking multiple link display modes as proposed in Berners-Lee's INCLUDE tag off of the table.

15 The following is based on Weber, interviews with Tim Berners-Lee, 1995 and 1996, Weber, 1995 unpublished, and interviews with Jean-François Groff, 1995–6 and 2010, and Dave Raggett, 1996–7. Berners-Lee's eventual goal was to have multimedia automatically adjust to the capabilities of the browser and connection being used. This was part of a larger goal for the Web to be scalable to different browsers and devices. For instance, text tagged as 'Heading 2' in HTML might show up as bolded, with extra space above and below, and in a larger font size on a full GUI browser like Viola or the original NeXT browser-editor. On a text-only browser it might be bolded, if the browser handled that, or separated by an extra line and marked by asterisks at either end. On a special browser for the deaf, the narrating voice might simply pronounce those words with more volume and emphasis. Similarly, lines of text would automatically 'wrap' to fit the width of a browser window, rather than having a fixed width that could dangle beyond the right margin.

How would that principle apply to multiple media? As an example, a video clip could appear in its original, full resolution on a fast graphical browser connected with broadband. But with a slow connection, that might get knocked down to a lower resolution video, or even an image. On a text-only browser, a caption might simply describe what the video was about and note that it couldn't be shown. All this would happen through format negotiation – the browser would automatically send the server a list of the formats it could handle, and the server would then send back appropriate choices.

16 www-talk mailing list for 1993, preserved at webhistory.org (http://1997.webhistory.org/lists/lists.html), among other sites.

17 Eric Bina initially had opposed adding graphics at all because he was concerned they would waste bandwidth. From Weber and Hughes, interview with Eric Bina and Marianne Winslett, 1996.

18 Jamie Zawinski 1994–6, 'The Netscape Dorm', https://www.jwz.org/gruntle/nscpdorm.html (accessed February 2018).

19 Also from Weber, interviews with Jock Gill, Phillip Hallam-Baker, John Mallery, 1996–7.

20 Weber, interviews with Tony Parisi, 1996, Mark Pesce, 1996.

21 VENUS project at CERN led by Silvano de Gennaro, for prototyping the Large Hadron Collider in virtual reality; http://venus.web.cern.ch/VENUS/ (accessed February 2018).

22 In early 1995 CERN held a both sad and funny last-minute Web event for the previously overlooked European tech press; a combined coming-out party and wake. Many attending journalists were turned on to the Web for the first time just as it was being kicked out of the nest – including myself. The unanswered questions of that event helped pique my own interest in researching the history of the Web.

23 Interview with Adriaan Brink, 2009. Interview with anonymous source, 2009.

24 Pei Wei's 1989 Viola hypertext system was based around downloadable Java-like applets and was intended to be part of a more general environment. Even the browser (later adapted into the ViolaWWW Web browser) was written from them. The idea was that functionality could be downloaded as needed over the net. Gillies and Cailliau (2000); Weber, interview with Pei Wei, 1996, various personal communications. A precursor to this vision was the MUPID hypertext videotex system by Hermann Maurer, who later developed Web competitor Hyper-G. MUPID had downloadable applets and the intelligent terminal could also function as a standalone PC. Also Weber, interview with Hermann Maurer, 1996, personal communications, 2007.

25 Weber, interviews with Kevin Hughes, 1996–7, 2010.

26 Quotes from 1996 Tim Berners-Lee interview in *World Wide Web* journal: http://whatis.techtarget.com/definition/Web-year (accessed February 2018).

27 Netscape Gold was an attempt to combine browsing and editing features in the same product. But instead of being able to edit text 'live' as in a modern word processor or Berners-Lee's original Web browser-editor, the user had to switch into a separate editing mode, then back to browse mode to see how their changes looked. The Mac version of Netscape Gold was also slow and memory intensive. See Wodaski (1996), and a tutorial page on a late version of Netscape Gold: http://www.zisman.ca/netgold/ (accessed February 2018).

28 I plan to briefly summarize this history in an upcoming book with Thomas Dunne Books/St. Martin's Press.

29 Weber and Hansen Hsu, interview with Greg Christie, 2017. Newt's Cape (http://www.howdesign.com/web-design-resources-technology/graceful-degradation-on-a-newton-pda/, accessed February 2018) was the most capable browser for the Apple Newton. It was also a multimedia e-book creation tool using NewtonScript, http://newtonglossary.com/terms/newts-cape (accessed February 2018).

30 Weber, interview with Jeff Hawkins, 2010.

31 The working name was EZWeb. Tom Greene of W3C and I came up with a set of proposals for a mobile device with a browser-editor based on EZWeb or a similarly compact version of HTML, called WebGirl as a joke on GameBoy. There were doubtless others thinking along similar lines.

32 TheGlobe.com co-founder Stephan Paternot. See Paternot (2001).

33 'Compact HTML for Small Information Appliances', W3C NOTE 09-Feb-1998. Boston: World Wide Web Consortium. https://www.w3.org/TR/1998/NOTE-compactHTML-19980209/ (accessed February 2018).

34 In contrast with WAP's rigid centralization or the iOS App Store's lock on native apps, i-mode was a semi-open ecosystem – a bit like Minitel, or the later Android Play Store with its 'curated' contents. Since CHTML was an official W3C standard as a variant of HTML, anybody could set up a CHTML server. The result was a mix of official i-mode sites listed and registered by NTT DoCoMo, and renegade 'black' or 'grey' sites. i-mode browsers could also connect to normal Web sites, albeit slowly (Batista, 2000; Weber, interview with Tomihisu Kamada, 2008).

35 A later example of this kind of revenue sharing is the later Apple App Store; an earlier one the Minitel Kiosk system (Mailland and Driscoll, 2017).

36 Weber and Hansen Hsu, interview with Richard Williamson and Ken Kocienda, 2017.

37 With its apps and App Store, Apple had not only taken complete control – and a 30% cut – of the software it would allow to be used on its new handheld computing platform. It had in effect created a proprietary hardware terminal for an open standard, the Internet.

38 Note that this is different from the evolution of Web server software itself. Following the first Web servers from CERN and then NCSA in the early to mid 1990s, much server software was supplied by Apache and other open-source packages for decades, with Sun and later Microsoft servers in a more minor role. The graph on this page from Netcraft.com shows the changes over time: http://news.netcraft.com/archives/2016/07/19/july-2016-web-server-survey.html (accessed February 2018).

39 Recent attempts to put more operating systems on the client side include Google Chrome, and Mozilla's short-lived Firefox OS.

## REFERENCES


Bardini, T. (2000) Bootstrapping: Douglas Engelbart, Coevolution, and the Origins of Personal Computing. Stanford, CA: Stanford University Press.

Barnet, B. (2014) Memory Machines: The Evolution of Hypertext. London: Anthem Press.

Barnet, B. (2018) 'Hypertext Before the Web – or, What the Web Could Have Been', in. N. Brügger and I. Milligan (Eds), The SAGE Handbook of Web History (n.p.). London: Sage.

Batista, E. (2000) 'WAP or I-Mode: Which Is Better?' Wired Magazine, 8/30/00.

Berners-Lee, T., and Fischetti, M. (1999) Weaving the Web: The Original Design and Ultimate Destiny of the World Wide Web by its Inventor. San Francisco: Harper.

Bourne, C.P., and Bellardo Hahn, T. (2003) A History of Online Information Services, 1963–1976. Cambridge, MA: The MIT Press.

Campbell-Kelly, M., and Garcia-Swartz, D.D. (2013) 'The history of the internet: The missing narratives', Journal of Information Technology, 28(1): 18–33.

Carey, J., and Elton, T.J. (2009) 'The other path to the web: The forgotten role of videotex and other early online services', New Media and Society, 11(1–2): 241–260.

Carlson, W.B. (2013) Tesla: Inventor of the Electrical Age. Princeton, NJ: Princeton University Press.

Computer History Museum (CHM) (2011) 'Revolution: The First 2000 Years of Computing', Web version. Mountain View, California, http://www.computerhistory.org/revolution.

Dear, B. (2017) The Friendly Orange Glow: The Untold Story of the PLATO System and the Dawn of Cyberculture. New York: Pantheon.

Gillies, J., and Cailliau, R. (2000) How the Web Was Born: The Story of the World Wide Web. New York: Oxford University Press.

Gore, A. (1991) 'High-Performance Computing Act of 1991', 102d Congress, Public Law, Government Printing Office, https://www.gpo.gov/fdsys/pkg/STATUTE-105/pdf/STATUTE-105-Pg1594.pdf (accessed February 2018).

Hafner, H., and Lyon, M. (1996) Where Wizards Stay Up Late: The Origins of the Internet. New York: Simon and Schuster.

Hafner, K. (2001) The Well: A Story of Love, Death, and Real Life in the Seminal Online Community. New York: Carroll & Graf.

Hauben, M., and Hauben, R. (1997) Netizens: On the History and Impact of Usenet and the Internet. Los Alamitos, CA: IEEE Computer Society Press.

Helmore, E. (2001) 'So who's crying over spilt milk?', The Guardian, May 10, 2001, https://www.theguardian.com/technology/2001/may/10/internet.onlinesupplement (accessed February 18).

Jones, S., and Latzko-Toth, G. (2017) 'Out from the PLATO cave: Uncovering the pre-Internet history of social computing', Internet Histories, 1(1–2): 60–69.

Kay, A. (1972) 'A personal computer for children of all ages', Boston, MA: Proceedings of the ACM National Conference.

Krol, E. (1993) The Whole Internet: User's Guide and Catalog. Cambridge, MA: O'Reilly and Associates.

Mailland, J., and Driscoll, K. (2017) Minitel: Welcome to the Internet. Cambridge, MA: The MIT Press.

Mallon, D. (2013) 'Where Are They Now? i-mode' Ubertech, ZDnet.com, http://www.zdnet.com/article/where-are-they-now-i-mode/ (accessed February 2018).

Marchand, M. (1987) Minitel (La grande aventure). Paris: Larousse.

Markoff, J. (2005) What the Dormouse Said: How the Sixties Counter Culture Shaped the Personal Computer Industry. New York: Penguin USA.

Matsunaga, M. (2001) The Birth of i-mode: An Analogue Account of the Mobile Internet. Singapore: Chuang Yi Publishing Pte Ltd.

Mims, C. (2013) 'With a new web-based mobile phone, Mozilla is out-Googling Google', Quartz, July 1, 2013, https://qz.com/99505/with-a-new-web-based-mobile-phone-mozilla-is-out-googling-google/ (accessed February 2018).

Mounier-Kuhn, P.-E. (2002) 'Les premiers réseaux informatiques en France', Entreprises et Histoire, 29: 10–20.

Nelson, T. (2008) Geeks Bearing Gifts: How the Computer World Got This Way. Sausalito, CA: Mindful Press.

Nielsen, J. (1995) Multimedia and Hypertext: The Internet and Beyond. Chestnut Hill, MA: Academic Press.

Paternot, S. (2001) A Very Public Offering: A Rebel's Story of Business Excess, Success, and Reckoning. New York: Wiley.
Pelkey, J. (2009–2018) A History of Computer Communications: 1968–1988, http://www.historyofcomputercommunications.info/ (accessed February 2018).
Resnick, P. (1992) 'On Consensus and Humming in the IETF', IETF (Internet Engineering Task Force) RFC (Request for Comments) 7282, also in IETF plenary presentation 1992.
Russell, A. (2014) Open Standards and the Digital Age: History, Ideology, and Networks. Cambridge, UK: Cambridge University Press.
Salus, P.H. (1995) Casting the Net: From Arpanet to Internet and Beyond. Reading, MA: Addison-Wesley Professional.
Schafer, V., and Thierry, B.-G. (2012) Le Minitel, l'Enfance Numérique de la France. Paris: Nuvis.
Segal, B. (1995) 'A Short History of Internet Protocols at CERN', Internet Society, History pages: https://www.internetsociety.org/internet/history-internet/, then http://ben.home.cern.ch/ben/TCPHIST.html (accessed February 2018).
Sink, E. (2003) 'Memoirs from the Browser Wars', https://ericsink.com/Browser_Wars.html (accessed February 2018).
Waldrop, M.M. (2001) The Dream Machine: J.C.R. Licklider and the Revolution That Made Computing Personal. New York: Viking.
Wallace, P., Hoffman, P., Blut, Z., Barrow, K., Scuka, D. (2002) i-Mode Developer's Guide. Boston: Addison-Wesley Professional.
Weber, M. (1995, unpublished) 'The Untold History of the World Wide Web (and Why We're Only using Half its Power)', feature article for Wired Magazine UK, fact-checked by Tim Berners-Lee, Robert Cailliau, Jean-François Groff, Ben Segal, and Mike Sendall. Unpublished due to demise of first version of Wired UK as joint venture with The Guardian.
Weber, M., and Hughes, K. (1997) Web History Events and Exhibit program, 1997 International World Wide Web Conference, http://1997.webhistory.org/historyday/ (accessed February 2018).
Wodaski, J. (1996) Creating Cool Navigator Gold Web Pages. New York: John Wiley & Sons Inc.

20

# Emergence of the Mobile Web

Gerard Goggin

## INTRODUCTION

When the World Wide Web consortium celebrated the 25th anniversary of the Web in 2014, inventor Sir Tim Berners-Lee issued a call for a crowd-sourced Magna Carta. Noting that 40 per cent of the world's population were Web users, Berners-Lee opened up discussion on 'what could we do to get the other 60 per cent on board [to the Web] as quickly as possible'. 'Obviously', Berners-Lee noted, 'it's going to be around mobile' (Berners-Lee, 2014).

As we approach the 2020s, there is a very different role for the Web, compared with the early 2000s. Circa 2000 the Web was often seen *as* the Internet. Now, many of the world's users access the Internet, including the Web, via *mobile* technologies (Donner, 2015; Herman et al., 2015). The mobile Web is still integral to the public Internet, but the mobile Web is also – and often rather challengingly – woven into much of the fabric of the private, enclosed, 'walled gardens' of the commercial and institutionally controlled Internet.

Here lies the challenge for how we, as researchers, historians, users, and non-users, understand the mobile Web. True, browsing the Web (old school!) on a mobile device is common. Yet what now represents the common or definitive Internet and Web experience comprises diverse encounters with a range of other mobile technologies. Many of the new and emergent Internet technologies have evolved or been 'born-mobile' – in terms of their socio-technical characteristics, diffusion, take-up, and meanings (Goggin, 2014; Ito et al., 2005). It is often difficult to strictly declare what kinds of mobile Internet, media, and data technologies and cultures are authentically 'mobile Web', and which don't really engage the Web at all.

So, in this chapter, I offer a perspective on how one might define and approach mobile Web, as a distinctive area of the general Web and its histories. There are various ways of framing and telling the story of the development of mobile Web. Much of the literature, especially concerning the early history of mobile Web, has focussed on convergence, standardization, global and local development, commercialization, and so on. Here Indrek Ibrus's work has been outstanding, in its sophisticated examination of the tensions between the forces for autonomy of the mobile Web versus convergence with the general Web; and, more recently, the continued push of infrastructure companies for 'maximum convergence of all versions of web access platforms', contrasted with the 'measured divergence', cross-platform strategies of content and service providers (Ibrus, 2016). The story I wish to tell in the chapter revolves around the interplay between the shifting interests of various factions of industry (mobile Web platform companies, telecommunications companies, handset vendors, software providers, content and service providers) with users and the contexts of use, especially internationally. The chapter comprises four key aspects of the mobile Web:

1 The emergence of the mobile Web, especially focussing on the Wireless Access Protocol (WAP) as the first dedicated standards initiative;
2 The invention of the 'classic' mobile Web browser, Opera;
3 Internet standards-focussed mobile Web development and the brief flowering of mobile Web 2.0;
4 Smartphones and the dramatic change of the mobile Web, in the face of apps, social media, and the internationalization of mobile media.

As I proceed, I hope to highlight the key issues grasping and theorizing the changing nature of mobile Webs, and especially to draw attention to the importance in recent times of attending to how different actors and groups have imagined, shaped, and adapted these technologies. As much as anything, as I shall outline, mobile Web histories represent a set of limit-cases for thinking about what the Web and Internet have been, are, and will be.

## BECOMING MOBILE WEB: MOBILE BROWSING AND THE STRUGGLES OF WAP

Defining the mobile Web can be tricky. On a narrow view, the definition appears obvious: it is the Web or Web content as these exist, or are adapted, for mobile devices. For the World Wide Web Consortium (W3C) on its 'Mobile Web Initiative' home page, the tagline is simple: 'Combining the power of the Web with the strengths of mobile devices' (W3C, 2014). As we shall see, however, the dividing line between 'mobile Web' (= Web + mobile) versus non-mobile Web can be quite blurry.

As I have already noted, for a brief moment the Web, and indeed Web studies, promised to be nearly co-extensive with the Internet itself, a moment captured by David Gauntlett's collection *Web.Studies* (Gauntlett, 2000). This was roughly the same time also we see the emergence of the mobile Web. From the early 1990s onwards, an increasing number of mobile phones and wireless devices were designed to support Web browsing. The Nokia Communicator 900 in 1996 (Nokia, 1996) is often seen as the first successful case of a dedicated mobile Web device (Ibrus, 2010: 35). The Communicator was a cellular mobile phone with a hinged keyboard, initially marketed as a top-end product for business executives keen for email and Internet access. It was advertised as a glamour accessory, for instance in the 1997 movie *The Saint* (Nokia, 1997). As the Communicator developed through more advanced models, the device was increasingly used for mobile Web access (cf. Figure 20.1).

It is fair to say that the ways the mobile Web was imagined in its first decade were fairly limited (Hansmann et al., 2003), when viewed from a historical vantage point some two decades onwards. An important advance occurred in December 1997, when Nokia, Ericsson, Motorola, and Phone.com formed the WAP Forum, creating the Wireless Access Protocol (WAP) to unify the already diverse kinds of mobile and wireless technologies and networks that were available. WAP was invented before the smartphone, to run on the mobile phones available from the late 1990s to mid 2005s, in particular. WAP is a protocol that allowed mobile phones to display webpages. To make this possible, webpages needed to be written in a particular

**Figure 20.1 Nokia Communicator 9300 Model displaying Wikipedia home page.**
*Source*: Wikimedia, https://upload.wikimedia.org/wikipedia/commons/5/5e/Nokia9300.png).

Web 'language': Wireless Markup Language (WML). WML was different from the default language used for websites at the time – Hypertext Markup Language (or HTML) – and the requirement to learn WML was an additional barrier to website providers customizing websites for WAP. On the positive side, WAP had quite minimum processing and software requirements, including a very small or micro browser. Over the next decade, a slowly growing number of website and Web content providers fleshed out WAP mobile Web offerings. Mostly early WAP services involved transactions conceived in a narrow sense, such as finding basic information on services or direction, making simple purchases, booking tickets or checking schedules, sport scores, news and weather, stock quotes, and so on:

> The vast majority of WAP content is text-based, so any kind of graphical content is rare to find. Don't expect to find a WAP-ready YouTube, Google Video, or anything of that sort. (NTE, 2002)

For the first few years of its life WAP was not widely used, and often widely derided as a 'failure' (Teo and Pok, 2003). Commentators suggested that its promoters had failed to appreciate the capabilities and design issues of mobiles, dazzled instead by the Internet and tech boom of the late 1990s (Jenson, 2005: 307). An obstacle to the take-up of WAP was that it required mastery of the new and specialized WML, rather than using HTML. Surmounting such criticisms, the WAP Forum developed WAP 2.0 based on directions in mainstream Internet and thereafter WAP websites grew steadily.

As the same time as WAP was developing, so did an alternative technology: Japan's i-mode. I-mode was not just another competitor, it represented another way of imagining the mobile and the mobile Web. In 1998, Digital Phone Tokyo Group launched a simple text browsing service called *SkyWeb*, which did not include graphic functions (Haas, 2006: 123). With fast-developing competition, this quickly evolved into *J-Sky*, offered under the brand J-Phone. The prime competitor was i-mode, introduced in February 1999 by dominant Japanese telecommunications carrier NTT DoCoMo. I-mode was an ecosystem of mobile Internet, mobile Web, content, and services, and, crucially, an integrated billing system that included 'the monthly subscription fee, the packet transmission fee, and the i-mode information fee [paid to information or content service providers]' (Ishii, 2004: 46). In technical terms, i-mode was underpinned by a version of the HTML Web standard, called c-HTML. The i-mode was tightly controlled by DoCoMo, allowing subscribers to access a wide range of mobile data services (forerunners to mobile premium services, as well as mobile apps), offered by approved third-party providers. As well as the most popular services such as search, transportation information and maps, news, and weather (2001 survey of accessed websites via PC and mobile telephone quoted in Ishii, 2004: 50), popular i-Mode services included music, ringtones, and games. As one contemporaneous study notes: 'Web pages that can be accessed via I-mode phones are either official sites registered on the Imenu, or unofficial sites' (Jonason and Eliasson, 2001: 343). I-mode rapidly attracted users, numbering an estimated 14 million subscribers by October 2001 (Natsuno, 2003: 22), then 33 million just three years after launch (Ishii, 2004: 44).

Due to i-mode, in particular, Japan became the celebrated and widely debated case internationally for mobile Web and mobile Internet use. In particular, in the WAP vs. i-mode contest, we see the cross-currents of ongoing tensions in the mobile Web, parsed in the distinctions drawn between 'closed' and 'open' visions of the Internet. In no small part, the achievement of i-mode is due to strong operator control (Tee and Gawer, 2009). Further still, the consumer ease of use of i-mode and its quick take-up relied upon a carefully constructed and tightly controlled ecosystem, something that was quite a contrast with WAP, as various researchers noted (e.g. Wallace et al., 2002: 150). Various efforts were made to export i-mode to other markets, but it never attracted a following. One issue was timing: the marketing of i-mode in foreign markets in 2002 onwards, including the Netherlands, Taiwan, and Australia (Goggin, 2006: 168; Tee and Gawer, 2009), coincided with the rise of mobile premium services, and eventually the advent of the smartphone and mobile apps (Goggin and Spurgeon, 2007).

Woven into these dynamics of competing mobile Web systems are cultural factors. An insight that resonates across the history of the mobile Web is offered by Japanese scholar Kenichi Ishii, who notes that the mobile Internet in that country 'evolved from mobile phones and pagers … rather than from PCs', and that the 'Japanese experience after 1995 demonstrates that user needs have brought about the high penetration rate and unique usage patterns' (Ishii, 2004: 56, 57). Accordingly, the lesson to be drawn from i-mode, Ishii argues, is 'the mobile Internet may develop in a diverse manner throughout the world, depending on local culture and customs' (Ishii, 2004: 57). The deep cultural, social, political, economic, and infrastructural underpinning of i-mode and the mobile Internet in Japan is something that is richly established in the pioneering 2005 volume on mobiles in Japanese life, *Personal, Portable, Pedestrian* (Ito et al., 2005). Internet historians have offered revisionary accounts of the development of the Japanese Internet, noting, among other factors, the challenges of language scripts on Japanese computer keyboards, compared with innovative solutions offered by mobile devices (McLelland et al., 2018). Such an emphasis on cultural, social, and linguistic dynamics in relation to the mobile Web and Internet applies even more so in the decade and a half after these debates – when WAP has played a crucial role in extending mobile Internet access globally, especially in countries of the 'global south' (Ling and Horst, 2011).

Early adoption of the mobile Web in emerging economies is documented in a range of research. Among others, the key work of Jonathon Donner on the evolving mobile nature of the Internet has shown users seeking to access a wide range of particular mobile messaging, chat, music, file-sharing, information, and other technologies and apps, but then often having resource to WAP as a way to 'venture out onto the broader Internet' (Donner et al., 2011: 577). Much mobile Web usage happens over Wi-Fi networks rather than mobile cellular networks (Donner, 2015: 34, 129). A 2009 study of digital media usage among low-income urban school students in rural South Africa found that 'different kinds of media downloaded from WAP mobile phone portals are often used side by side with locally produced digital media, (Kreutzer, 2009: 53). It also noted 'the absence of walled garden portals among students' [mobile] web usage' (Kreutzer, 2009: 62).

Yet another picture of the complex emergence of WAP is offered by the Chinese case. In comparison to Japan (Harwit, 2012), in China the PC remained the only interface until 2000 when China Mobile started its WAP business. WAP was initially slow to take up in China (Yan, 2003), with only 50,000–60,000 users by end 2000, or some 2 per cent of the total market at that time (Wang & Cheng, 2012: 5). However, the 2003 launch of QQ mobile (a version of the highly popular QQ messaging software) played an important role in popularizing WAP phones, such as the Nokia 7110 (McLelland et al., 2018). For some users, such as migrant women, the advent of this mobile Web represented 'necessary convergence', as 'many migrants' only means of going online (outside of Internet cafés) is with Internet-enabled mobile phones' (Wallis, 2013: 107). Reflecting on this study, Cara Wallis argues that for these users, such mobile Web is 'important in alleviating digital inequality', but that many would prefer the more unconstrained ways to access QQ and other programs via a computer (Wallis, 2013: 107). This is an argument that various others develop in other directions, in relation to other jurisdictions, such as Philip Napoli and Jonathon Obar's critique of mobile Internet access as raising the spectre of an emerging underclass (Napoli and Obar, 2014). Such trends across a range of settings are taken up and systematically considered in Donner's 2015 book *After Access*, notable for its argument that the 'shift to a more mobile Internet may be accelerating this departure away from the Web ideal – and in so doing, altering the relationship between mobile-only users and the Internet itself' (Donner, 2015: 156). For its part, WAP still exists and thrives today across many international settings – but it still very much flies under the radar of dominant industry and research trends alike.

## OPERA: THE CLASSIC MOBILE WEB BROWSER

An instructive case study of the emergence of the mobile Web can be found in the browser synonymous with it: Opera. Like WAP, Opera was invented years before the smartphone redefined what most consumers thought of the mobile phone.

Opera was developed by two computer programmers, Jon Stephenson von Tetzchner and Geir Ivarsøy. They worked in Televerkets Forskninginstitutt (TF), the celebrated research group in the Norwegian telecommunications incumbent Telenor that also included Finn Trosby, a central figure in the invention of SMS, and mobile communication scholar Rich Ling (Ling, 2015: 443), among others. Von Tetzchner and Ivarsøy began coding their own Web browser in December 1994 (Opera, 2009), and at the end of 1995 left Telenor to found Opera Software ASA (Manes, 1998; Opera, 2017). In 1996, the Opera browser was offered for sale to the public, competing with the free Microsoft Internet Explorer and Netscape Navigator (Manes, 1998). Opera soon attracted praise from users and technology writers (Manes, 1998). Fitting on one floppy disk, Opera also included a magnification tool that allowed zooming in or out, leading a reviewer in *The Guardian* to note that it 'can be used by those with impaired vision' (Jennings, 1998). Opera had some limitations, as it could not yet handle certain kinds of content, such as Java and ActiveX; did not come with its own plug-ins (though it could accept Real Audio, and some other multimedia plug-ins); had limitations with handling email addresses (Manes, 1998); and had a barrier to use with its 'try-before-you-buy retail model' (as the premium version cost £25). As *The New York Times* journalist Stephen Manes memorably put it: 'Opera's story is a Norse saga of smaller size, clever features, reasonable speed and occasional annoyances' (Manes, 1998).

Opera's reputation for innovation was the reason that a third former Telenor colleague, Håkon Wium Lie, joined the company in 1999 as Chief Technology Officer (Lie and Bos, 2005: 351), a position he held until 2016.[1] Lie was impressed that Opera was only the third browser to implement Cascading Style Sheets (CSS), a feature of the Web he had created while working at CERN in 1994, when he proposed the concept to Berners-Lee and Robert Cailliau (Lindberg, 2016).[2] Lie joined Opera after a four-year stint at W3C, so it is no surprise that he was a flag bearer for the pivotal role of standards in mobile Web technology development and the future of the market.

By the early 2000s, Opera had gained an enthusiastic, although still minority, following, with its price seen as a continuing issue as well as its difficulties in keeping up with the developments in Web technology and design (Taylor, 2002). Making a virtue of its lightness and speed, Opera chose to stake its reputation on being the best browser for mobile devices (*The Guardian*, 2002). In 2005, Opera launched the Opera Mini, a cut-down version of its mobile browser, designed for fast-loading content (see Figure 20.2 and Figure 20.3).

Opera also featured as a fully fledged combatant in the 'browser wars' among the different companies vying to rule the Web. In 2007, it lodged a complaint with the European Commission against Microsoft tying Internet Explorer to the Windows Operating System, and 'hindering interoperability by not following accepted Web standards' (Opera, 2007). In 2009, the EC rendered legally binding Microsoft's commitments to offer its OS users a choice of browsers, and eventually fined the company €561 million for a 2011–12 breach of this commitment (EC, 2013). Otherwise, in this heyday period, Opera was regularly announcing partnerships with a wide range of mobile phone vendors and carriers. It also sought to capitalize on its pole position as a mobile Web pioneer, by trailblazing the emerging mobile markets internationally, including various countries in Asia and Africa. Opera is an excellent example of the way in which the market became 'attuned to the needs of bandwidth-constrained mobile users', resulting in important innovations in mobile Web browsing technology (Donner, 2015: 131).

Opera continued development, and managed to forge on with modest success in the smartphone era, reaching 71 million active users for its mobile browser in 2010 (Sengupta, 2010), rising to 281 million mobile users in 2016 (Dredge, 2016), due to 'pockets of strength' as a leading browser in Africa, India, Indonesia, and China (Tsang

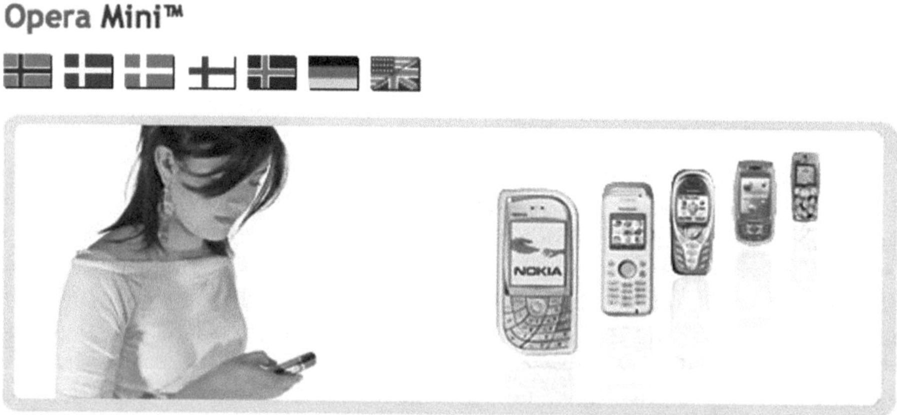


**Figure 20.2 Opera Mini advertising, Opera.com website, 31 December 2005.**
*Source*: Internet Archive, https://web.archive.org/web/20051231034658/http://www.opera.com:80/products/mobile/operamini).

**Figure 20.3 Mobile website browsing on Opera Mini, Opera.com website, 31 December 2005.**

and Mozur, 2016). However, tensions were revealed when von Tetzchner departed the company in 2010, criticizing Opera's new directions in a blaze of acrimonious interviews (Orlowski, 2014). Von Tetzchner set up a new company, Vivaldi (vivaldi.com), revolving around a new, fully customizable, premium browser, 'redefining what a browser is' (Schofield, 2016; Toulas, 2016).

In 2016 Opera's consumer businesses (Mobile Advertising, Consumer, and Tech Licencing) were the subject of a US$1.2 billion takeover bid by Chinese investors. The offer was accepted by Opera SA but foundered on the shoals of US regulatory approvals, allegedly due to concerns about privacy and security of user data. In November 2016, a consortium of Chinese firms quietly acquired the Opera consumer businesses for US$575 million (Opera, 2016). In new hands, the Opera browser limped on; however, its fate underscored the profound changes unfolding in the mobile Web.

## WEB CUSTODIANS AND MOBILE WEB 2.0 VISIONARIES

The trend of mobile manufacturers designing devices that were optimized for the Web deepened with the parallel developments in Internet Web technologies themselves (W3C, 2015). As WAP emerged, there were parallel developments in the mainstream world of Internet standards and protocols responding to the urgent need for the Internet to cope with mobility of connections (something evident in the creation of the IPv6 protocol). The two efforts from the mobile industry and Internet sector formally came together in 1998 when the World Wide Web Consortium (W3C) and the WAP Forum released a White paper which identified areas of future cooperation, expressing a desire to achieve 'the seamless integration of mobile devices into the Web' (W3C, 1998).

Of course, the reality was that the future turned out to be dauntingly seamful. As W3C explained in a 2015 overview document: 'Mobile devices not only differ widely from traditional computers, but they also have a lot of variations among themselves, in term of screen size, resolution, type of keyboard, and media recording capabilities' (W3C, 2015). Indeed, the mobile Web presents many challenges for Web design and implementation:

> Mobile devices have a lot of power compared with the desktop computer of 10 years ago, but they

> also have severe limitations that don't have to be dealt with when developing Web sites solely for the desktop … Mobile devices force Web developers to think about things they have never had to think about before. (Zakas, 2013)

The development of mobile phones as computer devices, as data processing and networking devices, for use with different kinds of software applications – and, into the mix, with different kinds of Internet and Web technologies, is a process that takes some years to unfold. As convergence gathered pace, W3C, as the official custodians of the Web, picked up the pace on their standards development activities. In May 2005, the W3C launched its mobile Web initiative, to make 'browsing the web from mobile devices a reality' (W3C, 2005). 'Mobile access to the Web has been a second-class experience for far too long', according to Berners-Lee, who enjoined developers to make 'the mobile device as a first-class participant, and … produce materials to help developers make the mobile Web experience worthwhile' (W3C, 2005).

Vaulting over this worthy initiative was a dramatic, even faintly millenarian, movement to reimagine the future of media by conjuring up 'Mobile Web 2.0', as it was dubbed by developers Ajit Jaokar and Tony Fish (Jaokar and Fish, 2006). This vision of a multimedia, collaborative, participatory digital media had a dramatically expanded mobile Web at its heart, keen to untap the innovation possibilities in mobile data technology (Jaokar and Fish, 2004). Even scholars saw mobile Web 2.0 as significantly altering the possibilities of technology, for instance, in urban life (viz. Bilandzic and Foth, 2009: 62). The discourse of mobile Web 2.0 was relatively shortlived, compared with its much more widely taken-up counterpart, Web 2.0. What happened next was a major detour in the career of the mobile Web – the arrival of smartphones. The furious development of smartphones, and their associated operating systems and software (especially apps), ushered in a new phase for the mobile Web.

## REIMAGINING THE MOBILE WEB IN THE SMARTPHONE AND SOCIAL MEDIA MOMENT

The incubation of the mobile Web that we have tracked in the 1997–2006 period entered a fateful and largely unforeseen situation with the arrival of smartphones and tablet computers, which quickly became regarded as the dominant mobile phone technology (Frith, 2015; Goggin, 2011; Helmond, 2015; Vincent and Haddon, 2018).

While there is some complexity to the 'smartphone moment', what is evident is that many kinds of services previously consumed via the mobile Web are now accessed via apps (Morris and Murray, 2018). Apps are a kind of mobile software designed and optimized to work with particular mobile devices, operating systems, and mobile networks (see, for instance, FTC, 2017). Mobile apps also have the advantage of operating within an apps ecosystem that allows the kind of billing, access to third-party providers, and ease of customer experience (often fraught, however) previously associated with i-mode. Apps are tightly integrated with the user's mobile device, allowing unprecedented tracking of user behaviour and information. Smartphones also include a range of sensor, gestural, haptic, and location technology (Frith, 2015), which adds new dimensions to the affordances of technology coupled with the apps. Since 2007, and increasingly, much consumer experience of online communication has occurred inside and via apps, especially apps for social media and mobile chat platforms. However, there are distinct differences between apps and the mobile Web that have been widely noticed and debated (Brügger, 2018).

First and foremost, the mobile Web can be accessed from any browser on a smartphone, without the user needing to install or pay for an app. Second, in a context of rising concerns concerning data privacy and surveillance, while the user is surfing the mobile Web from their browser, their behaviour and data cannot be tracked as effectively and comprehensively as it can with an app. Third, with the mobile Web any provider can potentially offer a website, without having to get permission from, and abide by the terms and conditions of, the particular app store or marketplace. Fourth, the mobile Web browser also supports the possibility to jump from one website to another, whereas a user cannot jump easily from one app to another, as 'an app cannot link out of itself directly to other apps' (Brügger, 2016: 1064). Against these advantages, it can be contended that, even vastly improved with the advent of the HTML standard, the mobile Web user experience is much more variable than is the case with apps. A key issue here is the lack of integration between website, device, carrier, website service or content provider, and so on – a typically tight coherence in apps.

In brief, over the 2006–18 period, we see a world of difference between apps and the mobile Web. In response to such issues, we can also observe many efforts to join up apps and the mobile Web – and, partly as a result of such bridging efforts, important interdependencies between the two technologies. These close relationships have led various commentators, such as *Computerworld*'s Ira Brodsky, to predict that 'in the end, you won't be able to tell them apart' (Brodsky, 2015):

> The mobile Web and mobile apps are not mutually exclusive. In fact, the two solutions often work together ... Neither the mobile Web nor mobile apps are going to die. They are going to converge. (Brodsky, 2015)

To understand this better, consider the common experience of consuming news from a mobile device. A user might get her news from *Buzzfeed*, the online news outlet, via an app. However, reading a story on the app might lead to a link, which takes the user to a story on the *Buzzfeed* website, or another website. This would then be viewed via a mobile browser, which would launch on the device. So-called 'native apps' (that is, running on the device, inside the operating system) can offer better support for sharing content, viewing videos, and downloading content for later, off-line consumption, as well as offering advantages for advertising. Complicating the picture are Web apps. These are software applications that run inside a Web browser. Web apps have an important advantage, because they are in the control of the website provider, rather than the entity controlling the app store.[3] A good example of the respective merits of 'native' apps versus Web apps can be found in the case of the *Financial Times*. A global brand thriving in the age of digital disruption of news, the *Financial Times* switched from having an iOS app in 2011. The apparent reason was to avoid paying Apple a 30 per cent cut of subscription revenue, as well as to avoid allowing Apple to collect payment information and other data directly from customers when they purchase the app and thus subscribe (Marshall, 2017; Owen, 2017). Instead, *Financial Times* subscribers viewed content via a Web app. In August 2017, the *Financial Times* reverted to an iOS app, hoping to 'boost subscriber engagement with its content and in turn increase the revenue it is able to extract from its customers over the long term' (Marshall, 2017). Like other media brands, such as Spotify, Apple softened the blow by only allowing existing subscribers to be able to download the iOS app (Marshall, 2017). As a result, consumers have to subscribe via the *Financial Times* website, and cannot purchase a subscription within the app itself – thus denying Apple access to the subscriber data (Marshall, 2017).

As this example indicates, with the majority of their traffic coming from mobile consumption, news and entertainment companies have a strong investment in such intricate strategies for navigating the mobile Web. From a mobile Web designer's perspective, mobile (i.e. 'native') apps are crucial, depending on the business. However, there still exists the general imperative of grasping the nettle of 'the subtler issues of mobile web', as one textbook author puts it, arguing in 'favour of providing a mobile-friendly website' (Esposito, 2016: 381). These kinds of discourses and contests over the mobile Web, apps, and mobile technology can be better understood by the case of HTML5 standardization.

As Andrew Schrock notes, since the 'demise of Flash on mobile, HTML5 is an increasingly essential infrastructure of the mobile web' (Schrock, 2014: 827). He explains that the mobile Web 'connects web pages developed in HTML5 with various web browsers', and the 'distinctions between apps and the mobile web are starting to blur due to HTML5 increasingly being used for cross-platform app development' (Schrock, 2014: 829). While HTML5 is an example of an 'open' standard, Schrock shows the various ways that companies 'work open-source standards to their advantage by introducing features into the W3C, while ignoring or downplaying features introduced by others' (Schrock, 2014: 830), which he aptly characterizes as 'a milder version of the infamous "browser wars" in the mid-1990s' (Schrock, 2014: 830). A key challenge is that W3C is hamstrung by its lack of enforcement powers, so is left to find other ways to marshal support and collective agreement. For instance, in late 2015, the two-year EU-funded HTML5 Apps project concluded, which hoped to accelerate 'the development of standard Web technologies required to make HTML5 apps competitive with native apps, specifically in the areas of Web payments and rich mobile Web APIs' (ERCIM, 2015). It aimed to close the gap between native and HTML5 apps, through the 'standardization of missing HTML5 functionalities' (ERCIM, 2015). Such initiatives deserve closer scrutiny by historians and scholars, especially as buried in such detail lie key coordinates of how the Internet is being shaped for the future (Ibrus, 2016; Schrock, 2014: 830).

## CONCLUSION

Apart from a few studies cited here, notably the work of Idrus as well as others such as Donner and Schrock, there is little systematic scholarly research on the emergence of the mobile Web, and its implications for how we understand the Web, the Internet, and contemporary media. Invaluable in their own right, such mobile Web histories – another kind of 'missing net histories' (Driscoll and Paloque-Berges, 2017) – can also contribute to more accurate, comprehensive, and nuanced understandings of Internet histories. Added to which, mobile Web histories can shed important light on how the development of technology, standards, uses, cultural and media forms, social meanings, and imaginaries play out now and into the future. In concluding, I wish to outline key items for the research agenda.

First, while there is growing recognition of the archival and methodological challenges of Web histories, most rigorously put in the work of Niels Brügger (e.g. Brügger, 2011), and registered in a range of emergent work pertaining to Internet histories, as yet there is little specific discussion of these issues when it comes to mobile Web histories. There is a threshold ontological issue as the mobile Web is a different entity or object from the Web itself (cf. Brügger, 2009). Much of the content may be similar, and there is a broad similarity among mobile Web, the Web, and other markup languages. However, it is unclear to what extent we might be able to reconstruct a particular mobile Web artefact or have sufficient documentation to analyse mobile Web practices and experiences. How and where are mobile Web artefacts and texts archived? And how might they be retrieved, for what kinds of purposes? (Davis, 2014; McCown et al., 2015; Schneider and McCown, 2013).

A key issue for the mobile Web arises with stand-alone, proprietary social media systems. How does one gain access, for instance, to Facebook or Twitter or Weibo or Instagram (as perhaps four of the most harvested and researched platforms at present)? Typically, it involves either: purchasing access from the company; purchasing access via a third-party provider (e.g. via a 'fire hose'); or gathering and scraping what particular data from the platform is available via the publicly accessible Web and Internet. Because of their nature, as we have seen from reviewing their histories, mobile Webs involve a significant component of technology, software, and data that is owned by mobile companies.

The issues for the mobile Web unfolding with the advent of mobile apps are an important case in point here. Apps are key to the Internet, when accessed via tablets and mobile phones, yet writing a history of apps is a considerable challenge – because it is difficult to gain reliable information on what apps are available and how they are developed and used, especially due to the reluctance of app store owners to allow access to information. There exist potential 'workarounds' – creative techniques to gain a picture and details of apps, for instance, via Web and Internet archives (which will include websites with details of apps), a strategy adopted by Anne Helmond in her critical history of apps (Helmond, 2017). However, in apps and elsewhere, the basic foundational work in scrutinizing the archives, historical remnants, traces, and infrastructures of the mobile Web remains to be done.

Moving from the foundational questions of archives, materials, and methods, there are various areas of mobile Web histories that deserve attention. Much existing scholarly research on the mobile Web focusses on key periods of the early mobile Web, WAP, i-mode, or mobile Web work by W3C. Future historical research needs to much more systematically cover and revise this terrain, from different perspectives that better incorporate the different industries, players, and institutions they entail.

Consider, for instance, that we know very little empirically of actual mobile websites themselves. There is little recuperative or analytical work, or wider scholarly discussion on websites, Web culture, or Web design (for example, in retrospective scholarly conferences) when it comes to the mobile Web. Mobile browsers have received little or no attention.

Finally, a key area for future research is to grapple with the implications for Web historians of mobile Internet being developed and appropriated differently depending on local cultures, economics, infrastructures, and so on. Here researchers face the imperative of acknowledging, documenting, and exploring the very different mobile Webs, mobile Web cultures of use, social practices and functions, providers, and industries to be found across the whole international range of settings, cultures, and languages. Such research trajectories are now on the agenda in relation to global Internet histories (Goggin and McLelland, 2017), and promise to be especially rich in relation to the babel of international mobile Webs – the journey through which will surely help us assemble a much richer and adequate set of Web, Internet, and other histories.

## Notes

1 Håkon Wium Lie had an illustrious career in technology and activism, and was a founding member of the Norwegian Pirate Party (see his website at http://www.wiumlie.no/en). Interestingly, he also edited a 1993 special issue of Telenor's in-house journal *Telektronik* on 'Cyberspace' (https://www.w3.org/People/howcome/p/telektronikk-4-93/).

2 While at Opera, Håkon Wium Lie wrote his PhD thesis on Cascading Style Sheets, which included a chapter on CSS for small screens (Lie, 2005: chapter 8).

3 As well as 'native' mobile OS apps and Web apps, there are also hybrid apps: 'Hybrid apps are built with web technologies and mobile web implementations and run inside a native container on a mobile device' (Vakintis and Panagiotakis, 2016: 233).

## REFERENCES

Berners-Lee, T. (2014) 'A Magna Carta for the Web'. TED Talks. Vancouver, 19 March. Retrieved from https://www.ted.com/talks/tim_berners_lee_a_magna_carta_for_the_web. [Accessed 14 July 2018]

Bilandzic, M., and Foth, M. (2009) 'Social navigation and local folksonomies: Technical and design considerations for a mobile information system', in S. Hatzipanagos and S. Warburton (Eds), Handbook of Research on Social Software and Developing Community Ontologies. Hershey, PA: IGI Global. pp. 52–66.

Brodsky, I. (2015) 'Deathmatch: The mobile web vs. mobile apps', Computerworld, 21 December. Retrieved from https://www.computerworld.com/article/3016736/mobile-wireless/the-mobile-web-vs-mobile-app-death-match.html. [Accessed 14 July 2018]

Brügger, N. (2018) 'Web history and social media', in J. Burgess, A. E. Marwick, and T. Poell (Eds), The SAGE Handbook of Social Media. London: Sage. pp. 196–212.

Brügger, N. (2016) 'Introduction: The Web's first 25 years', New Media & Society, 18(7): 1059–1065.

Brügger, N. (2011) 'Web archiving – between past, present, and future', in M. Consalvo and C. Ess (Eds), The Handbook of Internet Studies. Oxford: Blackwell. pp. 24–42.

Brügger, N. (2009) 'Website history and the website as an object of study', New Media & Society, 11(1–2): 115–132.

Davis, C. (2014) 'Archiving the Web: A case study from the University of Victoria', Code{4}Lib, 26. Retrieved from http://journal.code4lib.org/articles/10015. [Accessed 14 July 2018]

Donner, J. (2015) After Access: Inclusion, Development, and a More Mobile Internet. Cambridge, MA: MIT Press.

Donner, J., Gitau, S., and Marsden, G. (2011) 'Exploring mobile-only Internet use: Results of a training study in urban South Africa', International Journal of Communication, 5: 574–597.

Dredge, S. (2016) 'Browser maker Opera in line for $1.2bn acquisition by Chinese consortium', The Guardian, 11 February. Retrieved from https://www.theguardian.com/technology/2016/feb/11/browser-maker-opera-acquisition-chinese. [Accessed 14 July 2018]

Driscoll, K., and Paloque-Berges, C. (2017) 'Searching for "missing" net histories', Internet Histories, 1(1): 47–59.

Esposito, D. (2016) Modern Web Development: Understanding Domains, Technologies, and User Experience. Redmond, WA: Microsoft Press.

European Commission (EC). (2013) 'Antitrust: Commission fines Microsoft for non-compliance with browser choice commitments', media release, 6 March. Retrieved from http://europa.eu/rapid/press-release_IP-13-196_en.htm. [Accessed 14 July 2018]

European Research Consortium for Informatics and Mathematics (ERCIM). (2015) 'HTML5Apps paves the way to future W3C payment standards and advances mobile Web standardization roadmap', media release, 29 September. Retrieved from https://www.ercim.eu/news/396-html5apps-paves-the-way-to-future-w3c-payment-standards-and-advances-mobile-web-standardization-roadmap. [Accessed 14 July 2018]

Federal Trade Commission (FTC). (2017) 'Understanding mobile apps'. Retrieved from https://www.consumer.ftc.gov/articles/0018-understanding-mobile-apps. [Accessed 14 July 2018]

Frith, J. (2015) Smartphones as Locative Media. Hoboken, NJ: Wiley.

Gauntlett, D. (Ed.) (2000) Web.Studies: Rewiring Media Studies for the Digital Age. London: Arnold/Hodder and Oxford University Press.

Goggin, G. (2014) 'Facebook's mobile career', New Media & Society, 16(7): 1068–1086.

Goggin, G. (2011) Global Mobile Media. London and New York: Routledge.

Goggin, G. (2006) Cell Phone Culture: Mobile Technology in Everyday Life. London and New York: Routledge.

Goggin, G., and McLelland, M. (Eds) (2017) Routledge Companion to Global Internet Histories. New York: Routledge.

Goggin, G., and Spurgeon, C. (2007) 'Premium rate culture: The new business of mobile interactivity', New Media & Society, 9(4): 753–770.

The Guardian. (2002) 'Opera is staging a coup', The Guardian, 24 October, p. 7.

Haas, M. (2006) Management of Innovation in Network Industries: The Mobile Internet in Japan and Europe. Wiesbaden: Deutscher Universitäts-Verlag.

Hadlaw, A. Herman, A., and Swiss, T. (Eds) (2015) Theories of the Mobile Internet: Materialities and Imaginaries. New York: Routledge.

Hansmann, U., Merk, L., Nicklous, M.S., and Stober, T. (2003) Pervasive Computing: The Mobile World. 2nd ed. Berlin: Springer.

Harwit, E. (2012) 'Comparative development of the mobile Internet in China and Japan', in R. W.-C. Chu, L. Fortunati, P.L. Law, and S. Yang (Eds), Mobile Communication and Greater China. New York: Routledge. pp. 80–95.

Helmond, A. (2017) 'NWO Veni grant for App ecosystems: A critical history of apps', Blog post, 28 July. Retrieved from http://www.annehelmond.nl/2017/07/28/nwo-veni-grant-for-app-ecosystems-a-critical-history-of-apps/ [Accessed 14 July 2018]

Helmond, A. (2015) 'The platformization of the Web: Making Web data platform ready', Social Media + Society, 1(2). Retrieved from https://doi.org/10.1177/2056305115603080. [Accessed 14 July 2018]

Ibrus, I. (2016) 'Web and mobile convergence: Continuities created by re-enactment of selected histories', Convergence, 22(2): 147–161.

Ibrus, I. (2010). Evolutionary Dynamics of New Media Forms: The case of the Open Mobile Web. PhD thesis, London School of Economics.

Ishii, K. (2004) 'Internet use via mobile phone in Japan', Telecommunications Policy, 28(1): 43–58.

Ito, M., Okabe, D., and Matsuda, M. (Eds) (2005) Personal, Portable, Pedestrian: Mobile Phones in Japanese Life. Cambridge, MA: MIT Press.

Jaokar, A., and Fish, T. (2006) Mobile Web 2.0. London: Futuretext.

Jaokar, A., and Fish, T. (2004) Opengardens: The Innovator's Guide to the Mobile Data Industry. London: Futuretext.

Jennings, C. (1998) 'To buy or not to buy – Say boo to bloatware', The Guardian, 17 September, p. 14.

Jenson, S. (2005) 'Default thinking: Why consumer products fail', in R. Harper, L. Palen, and A. Taylor (Eds), The Inside Text: Social, Cultural and Design Perspectives on SMS. Dordrecht: Springer, pp. 305–324.

Jonason, A., and Eliasson, G. (2001) 'Mobile Internet revenues: An empirical study of the I-mode portal', Internet Research, 11(4): 341–348.

Kreutzer, T. (2009) Generation Mobile: Online and Digital Media Usage on Mobile Phones among Low-Income Urban Youth in South Africa. Report. Centre for Film and Media Studies. Retrieved from University of Cape Town. Retrieved from tinokreutzer.org/mobile [Accessed 14 July 2018]

Lie, H.W. (2005) Cascading Style Sheets. PhD thesis, University of Oslo. Retrieved from http://www.wiumlie.no/2006/phd/ [Accessed 14 July 2018]

Lie, H.W., and Bos, B. (2005) Cascading Style Sheets: Designing for the Web. 3rd edition. Upper Saddle River, NJ: Addison-Wesley.

Lindberg, O. (2016) 'Interview with Håkon Wium Lie', Net Magazine, 625. 11 April. Retrieved from https://medium.com/net-magazine/interview-with-h%C3%A5kon-wium-lie-f3328aeca8ed [Accessed 14 July 2018]

Ling, R. (2015) 'Rich Ling: An intellectual autobiography', in Z. Yan (Ed.), Encyclopedia of Mobile Phone Behaviour. Vol. 1. Hershey, PA: IGI Global. pp. 442–452.

Ling, R., and Horst, H. (2011) 'Mobile communication in the global south', New Media & Society, 13(3): 363–374.

Manes, S. (1998) 'For specialty users, browser price may be right', The New York Times, 28 April, p. 3.

Marshall, J. (2017) 'Financial Times returns to Apple's app store after a six-year hiatus', Wall Street Journal, 7 August. Retrieved from https://www.wsj.com/articles/financial-times-returns-to-apples-app-store-after-six-year-hiatus-1502092855 [Accessed 14 July 2018]

McCown, F., Yarbrough, M., and Enlow, K. (2015) 'Tools for discovering and archiving the mobile Web', D-Lib Magazine, 21: 3–4.

McLelland, M., Yu, H., and Goggin, G. (2018) 'Alternative histories of social media in Japan and China', in J. Burgess, A.E. Marwick, and T. Poell (Eds), SAGE Handbook of Social Media. Los Angeles, CA: Sage. pp. 53–68.

Morris, J.W., and Murray, S. (Eds) (2018) Appified. Ann Arbor, MI: University of Michigan Press.

Napoli, P.M., and Obar, J.A. (2014) 'The emerging mobile Internet underclass: Critique of mobile Internet access', The Information Society, 30(5): 323–334.

Natsuno, T. (2003) i-Mode Strategy. Chichester, England: John Wiley.
Nokia. (1997) 'Nokia 9000 Communicator makes a visible appearance in The Saint', media release, 9 April. Retrieved from http://www.nokia.com/en_int/news/releases/1997/04/09/nokia-9000-communicator-makes-a-visible-appearance-in-the-saint [Accessed 14 July 2018]
Nokia. (1996) 'First GSM-based communicator product hits the market', media release, 15 August. Retrieved from http://www.nokia.com/en_int/news/releases/1996/08/15/first-gsm-based-communicator-product-hits-the-market-nokia-starts-sales-of-the-nokia-9000-communicator [Accessed 14 July 2018]
NTE. (2002) 'What is WAP Mobile Web', LovetoKnow. Retrieved from http://cellphones.lovetoknow.com/What_is_WAP_Mobile_Web [Accessed 14 July 2018]
Opera. (2017) 'FAQS: When was Opera founded?'. Retrieved from http://www.operasoftware.com/press/faq [Accessed 14 July 2018]
Opera. (2016) Annual Report. Retrieved from http://www.operasoftware.com/company/investors [Accessed 14 July 2018]
Opera. (2009) 'Celebrating the 15th anniversary of the Opera browser's origin', media release, 28 April. Retrieved from http://www.operasoftware.com/press/releases/general/1994-the-year-that-started-it-all [Accessed 14 July 2018]
Opera. (2007) 'Opera files antitrust complaint with the EU', media release, 13 December, http://www.operasoftware.com/press/releases/general/opera-files-antitrust-complaint-with-the-eu.
Orlowski, A. (2014) 'Opera founder von Tetzchner: It's all gone to crap since I quit', The Register, 7 February. Retrieved from https://www.theregister.co.uk/2014/02/07/opera_founder_its_all_gone_to_crap/ [Accessed 14 July 2018]
Owen, L.H. (2017) 'Six years later, the Financial Times is back in the App Store', Nieman Lab, 7 August. Retrieved from http://www.niemanlab.org/2017/08/six-years-later-the-financial-times-is-back-in-the-app-store-apple-still-wont-get-a-cut-of-subscriptions/ [Accessed 14 July 2018]
Schneider, R., and McCown, F. (2013) 'First steps in archiving the mobile web: Automated discovery of mobile websites', JCDL '13: Proceedings of the 13th ACM/IEEE-CS Joint Conference on Digital Libraries. Indianapolis, IN: ACM. pp. 53–56.
Schofield, P. (2016) 'Vivaldi – the new web browser for power users', The Guardian, 6 April. Retrieved from https://www.theguardian.com/technology/2016/apr/06/vivaldi-the-new-web-browser-for-power-users [Accessed 14 July 2018]
Schrock, A.R. (2014) 'HTML5 and openness in mobile platforms', Continuum, 28(6): 820–834.
Sengupta, D. (2010) 'Opera is the oldest browser, and it is still surviving: Jon Tetzchner, founder, Opera software', Economic Times, 9 December. Retrieved from http://economictimes.indiatimes.com/opinion/qna/opera-is-the-oldest-browser-and-it-is-still-surviving-jon-tetzchner-founder-opera-software/articleshow/7068303.cms [Accessed 14 July 2018]
Taylor, P. (2002) 'Faster and smarter', Financial Times, 13 October.
Tee, R., and Gawer, A. (2009) 'Industry architecture as a determinant of the successful platform strategies: A case study of the i-mode mobile Internet service', European Management Review, 6(1): 217–232.
Teo, T.S.H., and Pok, S.H. (2003) 'Adoption of the Internet and WAP-enabled phones in Singapore', Behaviour & Information Technology, 22(4): 281–289.
Toulas, B. (2016) 'Vivaldi browser: Interview with Jon Stephenson von Tetzchner', Utappia blog, 21 September. Retrieved from https://utappia.org/2016/09/21/vivaldi-browser-interview-with-jon-stephenson-von-tetzchner/ [Accessed 14 July 2018]
Tsang, A., and Mozur, P. (2016) 'Chinese group bids $1.2 billion for company behind Opera Web browser', The New York Times, 10 February. Retrieved from https://www.nytimes.com/2016/02/11/business/dealbook/china-opera-kunlun-qihoo-golden-brick.html [Accessed 14 July 2018]
Vakintis, I., and Panagiotakis, S. (2016) 'Middleware platform for mobile crowd-sensing applications using HTML5 APIs and web technologies', in C.X. Mavromoustakis, G.

Mastorakis, and J.M. Batalla (Eds), Internet of Things (IoT) in 5G mobile technologies. Chaim: Springer. pp. 231–274.

Vincent, J., and Haddon, L. (Eds) (2018) Smartphone Cultures. London and New York: Routledge.

Wallace, P., with Hoffman, A., Scuka, D., Blut, Z., and Barrow, K. (2002) i-Mode developer's guide. Indianapolis, IN: Addison-Wesley.

Wallis, C. (2013) Technomobility in China: Young Migrant Women and Mobile Phones. New York and London: NYU Press.

Wang, J., and Cheng, C.-T. (2012) 'History of the mobile phone in China', in R.W.-C. Chu, L. Fortunati, P.L. Law, and S. Yang (Eds), Mobile Communication and Greater China. New York: Routledge. pp. 64–79.

WAP Forum. (2000) 'Wireless Application Protocol: White paper'. Retrieved from https://www.wapforum.org/what/WAP_white_pages.pdf [Accessed 14 July 2018]

W3C. (2014) 'The Web and mobile devices'. Retrieved from https://www.w3.org/Mobile/ [Accessed 14 July 2018]

W3C (2005) W3C launches 'Mobile web initiative'. Retrieved from https://www.w3.org/2005/05/mwi-pressrelease [Accessed 14 July 2018]

W3C (1998) WAP Forum – W3C Cooperation White Paper. Retrieved from https://www.w3.org/TR/NOTE-WAP [Accessed 14 July 2018]

Yan, X. (2003) 'Mobile data communications in China', Communications of the ACM, 46(12): 80–85.

Zakas, N.C. (2013) 'The evolution of web development for mobile devices', Commnications of the ACM, 55(4):42–48.

PART IV

# Platforms on the Web

21

# Wikipedia

Andy Famiglietti

## INTRODUCTION

Today Wikipedia is arguably one of the most important information sources on the planet. Wikipedia is the fifth most visited website worldwide (Alexa Top 500 Global Sites, n.d.). Wikipedia information has been cited in a wide variety of high-stakes real-world implications, including peer-reviewed medical literature (Bould et al., 2014) and judicial opinions (Peoples, 2009). During the 2008 presidential race, the McCain campaign was suspected of attempting to 'clean-up' the Wikipedia article of their vice-presidential nominee, prior to the announcement of Sarah Palin's nomination (*All Things Considered*, 2008). The struggle over the student use of Wikipedia in classroom assignments has been so extensive that when Middlebury College's history department banned the use of Wikipedia as a source for student essays it made national news (Cohen, 2007).

However, for a significant cohort of early twenty-first-century new media scholars, Wikipedia's significance extends far beyond its visibility as an information source. For these scholars, who focused on the economics of digital information production, Wikipedia quickly became the defining example of the vast creative power they believed was being unleashed by the internet. Yochai Benkler, in his influential account of the new media economy, *Wealth of Networks*, refers to Wikipedia, along with several other examples, as evidence that 'the networked environment makes possible a new modality of organizing production: radically decentralized, collaborative, and nonproprietary; based on sharing resources and outputs among widely distributed, loosely connected individuals who cooperate with each other without relying on either market signals or managerial commands' (Benkler, 2006: 60). Internet scholar and public intellectual Clay Shirky was even more emphatic in his use of Wikipedia as an exemplar of new media potential. In his short piece 'Gin, Television, and Social Surplus', Shirky argues that the internet will unleash a 'cognitive surplus' by allowing individuals to make productive use of time they previously wasted watching television. He measures the productive potential of this surplus in terms of Wikipedia, claiming that if 'the internet-connected population' devoted even 1% of their TV-watching time to productive volunteer online activity, that would amount to 'one hundred Wikipedia projects per year worth of participation' (Shirky, 2012: 240).

For Shirky, then, Wikipedia was not merely an example of the potential of new media, it was a general-purpose unit for measuring this potential. The application of Wikipedia as a template for what could be expected of a 'free' and 'open' internet went far beyond Shirky's literal use of Wikipedia as a unit of measure. Many scholars (Ghosh, 2006; Lessig, 2004; Tapscott and Williams, 2010; Zittrain, 2008) argued that Wikipedia's example could be generalized, and could provide a model for understanding the economics of internet-based information production more broadly. These authors, whose work was widely cited in debates surrounding copyright, net neutrality, and other policy issues, argued that the Wikipedia model showed that free, open internet-based collaboration could create a fairer, freer, more democratic information economy.

From the vantage point of 2018, however, this belief that Wikipedia would provide a model for a new, better, more democratic information environment seems misplaced. Instead of 'hundreds' of Wikipedia-like, Wikipedia-scale projects, our contemporary internet is dominated by a handful of massive social media platforms. Wikipedia, and other collaborative internet projects, are understood not to be idealized spaces for democratic participation, but spaces in which historical forms of power and privilege operate, sometimes in new and even more virulent forms. This chapter seeks to correct our understanding of Wikipedia, by moving away from understanding the project as a general-purpose template for new media and towards embracing Wikipedia's existence as a historically contingent and specific project. To that end, I examine the early Wikipedia and show how the project grew out of a specific historical heritage: that of the free and open source software movement. This movement, which developed in response to historically contingent dotcom era concerns over top-down control of information, shaped Wikipedia in important ways during its first years of existence. Wikipedia inherited both important resources from this movement, and significant anxieties about information control. These resources and anxieties have, in turn, shaped Wikipedia's own record of historical events. I explore this influence using the Wikipedia article documenting the 2008 Gaza War as a case study.

## WIKIPEDIA AND THE FREE/OPEN SOURCE SOFTWARE MOVEMENT

Free and open source software (or F/OSS) encompasses a diverse set of software projects. The source code of these projects is released so that anyone with the requisite knowledge can modify or redistribute the program. It is easy to forget that F/OSS is a relatively recent phenomenon. The Google n-gram chart in Figure 21.1 below is one way to visualize the sudden emergence of the larger F/OSS movement. Note how 'open source' grows rapidly, while once common terms for earlier experiments with software that users could obtain at no cost decline.

The story of this emergence has been told many times. It has been told by practitioners within the F/OSS movement (Raymond, 2000; Stallman, 2002; Torvalds, 2001), by anthropologists embedded within the movement (Coleman, 2012; Kelty, 2008), and by legal scholars, economists, and others interested in the implications of F/OSS for their fields (Benkler, 2006; Ekstrand et al., 2013; Lessig, c.1999; Weber, 2004). In this section, I draw from these sources to construct a summary of the history of F/OSS that

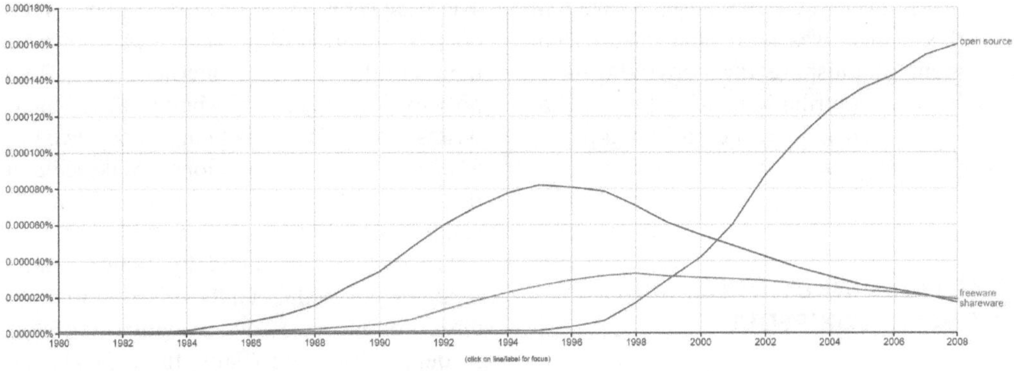


**Figure 21.1: The rise of 'open source'.**

makes salient the conceptual and organizational resources F/OSS provided the early Wikipedia project. I want to show how these resources come out of a very particular history. Namely, the resources inherited by Wikipedia from F/OSS are shaped by historically specific concerns about centralized *information control* stemming from the rise and fall of the 'dotcom bubble' at the close of the twentieth century.

Many within F/OSS stress its continuity with earlier practices. For example, Richard Stallman, founder of the Free Software Foundation (FSF) and the GNU[1] project, describes his project's origin as reaching back to practices established in mid-twentieth-century computer science departments. When he was at the MIT AI lab in the 1970s, he writes, 'we did not call our software, "free software", because that term did not yet exist; but that is what it was. Whenever people from another university or a company wanted to port and use a program, we gladly let them' (Stallman, 2002: 15). While the acceptance of software as something to be 'shared' in the 1970s was not as universal as Stallman's quote here suggests, larger patterns of source-sharing in early academic computing have been documented, especially in academic contexts (Kelty, 2008; Levy, 1984; Turner, 2006; Weber, 2004).

While the FSF and GNU project would go on to make important technical and legal innovations (including the first free software license, the GNU GPL), the larger F/OSS movement's push against information being controlled as property would not happen for nearly another 15 years. Chris Kelty's account of the F/OSS movement in *Two Bits* helps us to understand why. Kelty establishes how F/OSS's emergence into the public eye was propelled by the mid-1990s' move away from 'free software' and towards 'open source'. This move, which, Kelty argues, serves to shear the practices of non-property-based software production from Stallman's ethics of 'freedom', was driven in no small part by the peculiar economics of the dotcom era. As Kelty puts it, 'the Internet giveaway was a conflict of propriety: hackers and geeks who had built the software that made it all work, under the sign of making it free for all, were seeing that software generate untold wealth for people who had not built it' (Kelty, 2008: 110). Thus, even as the shift from 'free' to 'open source' served to make F/OSS more 'business friendly', this shift also represented a strategic move designed to ensure those producing information were not alienated from the fruits of their labor.

This commitment to using free licenses to prevent information producers from being expropriated by information owners was part of Wikipedia's F/OSS inheritance. Wikipedia was initially released under the GFDL, a documentation license developed by the Free Software Foundation. As we will see, this license was more than just a legal document establishing the copyright status of Wikipedia contributions; it was also a rhetorical tool that helped the early Wikipedia organize and grow.

## HOW F/OSS INHERITANCE SHAPES THE EARLY WIKIPEDIA

In this section, I examine the F/OSS resources inherited by the early Wikipedia. In particular, I am interested in the state of Wikipedia during the project's first two years of development, an era when the success of Wikipedia was hardly assured, and the project built important policies and practices. In this analysis of the early Wikipedia, I draw off of several archival resources: the archives of the Wikipedia-L and Intlwiki-L mailing lists, and an internet archive Wayback Machine snapshot of the state of Wikipedia.com in April of 2001 (because Wikipedia switched the wiki software it used to maintain the site early in its existence, the archives of site activity maintained on the current Wikipedia via 'history' pages are unreliable during the very early period of the site's existence). The archives of the first two years of Wikipedia's existence contain ample evidence of how the site inherited both a motivated user base, and anxieties over information control from F/OSS. Furthermore, they allow us to see how this inheritance would shape how the project would work in a lasting way.

It is no secret Wikipedia drew on the idea of 'openness' as articulated in F/OSS. However, the concept of 'openness' wasn't all that Wikipedia borrowed; it also borrowed something much more tangible: a population of developers already exposed to F/OSS-style organization. Some of these developers entered the project after Wikipedia was written up favorably on blogs like Slashdot and Kuro5hin, early in 2001 (Nupedia and Project Gutenberg Directors Answer – Slashdot, n.d.). There are signs that Wales and Sanger actively courted attention from these sites, known for their ability to direct internet traffic. In a post to Wikipedia-L in March 2001, Sanger writes, 'JimboWales is being interviewed by Slashdot [...]. He mentioned Wikipedia in the interview, and we may experience a substantial surge in traffic' (Sanger, 2001d).

Others were recruited by Wales from a rival encyclopedia, GNUpedia[2], started by GNU volunteers. I have recounted this story in detail elsewhere (Famiglietti, 2011), but significant to my account of Wikipedia's history here is the way in which Wikipedia's license serves Wales as a rhetorical tool, allowing him to persuade GNUpedia volunteers to join Wikipedia. In one series of GNUpedia mailing list posts, Wales characterizes GNUpedia as a 'fork' (duplicate) of Nupedia (Wikipedia is barely a week old at this time) and writes, 'But since the license is compatible (the same) there is probably no reason to have two projects...' (Wales, 2001a). The fact that the projects use the same license becomes a way for Wales to convince GNUpedia volunteers that their effort is a wasteful duplication.

The successful recruitment of F/OSS hackers was an important resource for the early Wikipedia, since these volunteer workers were accustomed to the F/OSS philosophy and coordination style. However, it also helped sow the seeds of what would later be understood as an important problem: the gender skew of Wikipedia's editor community. As late as 2007, the Wikipedia editor community was overwhelmingly (over 90%) male. This gender imbalance stems in part from the gender imbalance in the F/OSS community that Wikipedia relied on to build its initial editor base. F/OSS project contributors are only 2% female (Ghosh et al., 2002). As early as January 2002, Wikipedia editors had started to notice the community's gender imbalance. One female editor, posting to the list about an unrelated issue, asked, 'Are there no other women taking part in this? I feel a bit like I've snuck into the boys room'

(T., 2002). List members acknowledged the project was heavily male, but also pointed to a number of high-profile women at work on Wikipedia. This focus on a few high-profile women may have blinded them to the ongoing gender disparity. While early editors may have not been particularly conscious of Wikipedia's gender skew, it has since been widely recognized (Reagle, 2012) that unequal gender participation in Wikipedia is a significant complication of the site's claim to be a democratic community where 'anyone can edit'.

In addition to developers, Wikipedia inherited the F/OSS movement's anxieties over information control. For many early Wikipedia users, the dotcom bust (which early in 2001 was still in the process of happening) showed that information control was a failed, but still dangerous, method of doing business online. While early Wikipedians were mostly confident that the GFDL limited their vulnerability to outside corporate actors capturing and controlling their content, they had some concerns about the possibility of untoward actions by Wales's company Bomis, which hosted Wikipedia. These concerns would ultimately help to propel Wikipedia's shift to a non-profit business model. Just as important, they would help to shape some key Wikipedia content policies.

Copyright was one of the issues tightly tied to anxieties over information control. Like F/OSS coders before them, early Wikipedia editors were keenly aware of copyright law and perceived it as a possible stumbling block. During 2001 and 2002, Wikipedia-L would frequently discuss copyright issues, ranging from whether an editor could retain some copyright protections for his work while simultaneously releasing 'excerpts' under the GFDL (Rybo, 2001), to concerns about Wikipedia users' ability to re-use content under another content license (Sanger, 2001b), to questions about the copyright protections afforded to 'a list of all the winners of major sporting events' (Owen, 2001).

While Wikipedia editors were united in the process of trying to negotiate building a resource using an open content license in a world governed by copyright, they had a range of interpretations of copyright law's purpose and legitimacy. This can perhaps most clearly be seen in a March 2001 mailing list conversation between Sanger and Wikipedia editor Lee Crocker. Crocker criticizes the current warning against including copyrighted material in Wikipedia, which chastised editors, 'DO NOT STEAL'. Crocker writes that this language is 'personally offensive to me and other dedicated, moral, hard-working, law-abiding, intelligent people working to abolish copyright law as it is today' (Crocker, 2001). Sanger responds, defending his language, and the broader notion of intellectual property, saying, 'There are excellent reasons why intellectual property rights exist and have existed in one form or another in so many places and for so long; probably the most important is that, without them, artists and inventors lose an extremely important incentive' (Sanger, 2001c). Wales, for his part, responds by attempting to limit the debate on the mailing list, writing 'O.k., well, I'm thinking we shouldn't argue too much about this here on the Wikipedia list', and saying he has made a change to the notice that he hopes will address Crocker's concerns (Wales, 2001d). Clearly, ideological positions on copyright varied within the early Wikipedia.

Perhaps the most interesting opinion on copyright expressed in the debate above is Wales's pragmatic centrist approach. Perhaps the reason Wales was not terribly interested in engaging in a debate over the ideology of copyright in spring 2001 is that the collapse of the dotcom economy had convinced him traditional copyright protections were, regardless of their philosophical foundations, a practical liability for doing business on the internet. Hints of such a position can be found in another March 2001 mailing list post by Wales, in which he shares a Yahoo news article reporting the problems the traditional encyclopedia Britannica was having building online content. Wales writes, 'Britannica's woes will only deepen. It's hard to compete against free volunteer projects' (Wales, 2001b). For Wales, long debates over copyright's legitimacy are simply irrelevant in an economy where 'free' projects will naturally outcompete 'non-free' competitors.

While Wales was confident the economics of the internet favored free projects like Wikipedia over traditional content like Britannica, he elsewhere deploys concern over unpopular corporate actors capturing Wikipedia content for their own use as a rhetorical tool when debating Wikipedia policy. One example of this use occurred in an October 2001 Wikipedia-L thread where Wales debated Wikipedia's interpretation of the GFDL, the GNU-derived 'free documentation license' that the project then used. At the time Wikipedia was making somewhat creative use of a clause in the GFDL that allowed authors to specify an 'invariant section' re-users had to copy verbatim when redistributing the work. While this clause had originally been intended to allow authors of software documentation to include a stable page of author acknowledgments and other information, Wikipedia in mid-2001 was using the 'invariant section' clause to ask anyone re-using Wikipedia content to include an HTML table of links back to the original page on Wikipedia itself. For some Wikipedia editors, this use of the GFDL represented an over-reach. One objected that 'the requirement is most likely in violation of the terms of the [GFDL]', and speculated, 'requiring them to be in HTML seems to be violative of the FDL as well. What if I wanted to do my website in some other markup language' (Kissane, 2001).

Wales responds, pushing back on the interpretation of the exact permissions granted by the GFDL (Wales, 2001c), and then posts a broader defense of requiring attribution, in which he uses the threat of Microsoft capturing Wikipedia content and altering it as a reason to maintain the invariant section (Wales, 2001e). However, editors are not entirely convinced. Instead, many users argue that Wikipedia would be better off making its method of attribution more adaptable to the needs of re-users. Another prominent Wikipedia user at that time writes, 'if we really want large websites to adopt Wikipedia [...], there is absolutely no way that we can hope to dictate layout decisions to them. Their site designers will laugh us out the door' (Boldt, 2001). Many Wikipedia editors are keen to give re-users more freedom and are unconcerned with corporate re-use. Instead, they suggest that attribution is less important than the wide spread of Wikipedia's content to many different users and hosts.

This desire for Wikipedia content to spread to a variety of places is perhaps a reflection of the fact that the chief source of anxiety over information control for early Wikipedians was the Bomis company itself. This anxiety frequently surfaced over the issue of 'forking', a F/OSS term for splitting a project. Forking emerges as a concern within the F/OSS community precisely because of the way source code is treated as a shared resource. Since no one entity 'owns' F/OSS code, any project member is potentially free to take that code and use it to create their own version of the project. Forking is seen by F/OSS community members both as a source of freedom, since anyone unhappy with the direction of a project is free to leave and create something to their own liking, and of danger, since splitting projects can split the pool of labor available to accomplish tasks and lead to duplicate work and incompatible results (Weber, 2004).

Posts to the Wikipedia-L list show early Wikipedia editors also see forking as a source of both freedom and danger. These ideas surface frequently in conversations about the potential for a future fork of Wikipedia. For example, in August 2001 one Wikipedia editor posts concerns about Bomis either failing or attempting to force users to pay for access in the future, writing, 'I feel that while wikipedia is doing so great I'm anxious what will it be in the future. How can we be sure that they won't shut down the server or make it payable [sic]. This is a commercial company after all, not the FSF' (Jasiutowicz, 2001). Another editor replies, reassuring, 'the GFDL allows you to download everything and start your own server' (Hidders, 2001). In another reply, an editor writes he believes that, in order to fully comply with the GFDL, Wikipedia needs to be easier for a user to copy. He argues Wikipedia is not in compliance with the GFDL requirement for a 'transparent copy to be easily available' simply because 'spidering' Wikipedia (using a script to follow each link on the site and automatically download the linked page) is a possibility (Bihlmeyer, 2001).

This exchange touches off a conversation that would go on via the mailing list for weeks and involve multiple Wikipedia editors, along with Sanger and Wales. Wales is generally supportive of the idea of making Wikipedia's content easier to replicate, but he hopes those providing copies of Wikipedia will 'do so in a "read only" way' (Wales, 2001f). Editor Bryce Harrington, one of the editors who was persuaded by Wales to leave the GNUpedia project and join Wikipedia, writes 'The reason many people got involved (at the very least, *me*) was the willingness to hold the content under the GFDL. As I see it, what folks are asking is simply to deliver on the promises made at the outset' (Harrington, 2001a). In a later post, he demonstrates concern that a business failure for Bomis could result in a loss of the Wikipedia project if forking isn't technically easy:

> while none of us have any wish to see Bromis [sic] go out of business, we must admit that these days this is not unheard of. If Bromis were to go under, and we did not have a backup of the site that the community could resurrect quickly and easily, then there is a question whether wikipedia would exist if Bromis did not (Harrington, 2001b).

Here, Harrington's offhand remark that the failure of Internet companies like Bomis is something that 'these days [...] is not unheard of' ties his anxieties over information control to the historical moment of the dotcom crash. In an era where companies were frequently failing, some believed it dangerous to give even a trusted company unilateral control over important information.

Anxiety over Bomis's control over Wikipedia did ultimately lead to a project fork. The 2002 'Spanish Fork' of Wikipedia occurred after Larry Sanger announced Bomis might start running ads on Wikipedia to help restore his salary (which had been cut due to declining revenue at Bomis). This fork, which is still well remembered in the Wikipedia community, has been documented in detail elsewhere (Tkacz, 2011). However, a brief exploration of the Spanish Fork helps demonstrate the particular anxieties over information control that led to an actual fork of Wikipedia. Furthermore, while the Spanish Fork was not permanent, it did influence Wikipedia's policies in the longer term.

The unhappiness of Spanish Fork participants was based on a sense that Bomis was taking control of information they had provided, against their wishes. Their concerns were informed by ideas of national identity and autonomy. An interview with Enyedy conducted in 2011 demonstrates how national identity informed his decision. In a discussion with Nathanial Tkacz, Enyedy discusses how tension had existed between the Spanish- and English-language Wikipedia (which Enyedy refers to as the 'American Wikipedia') from the beginning. He says that the fact that the initial software and policy pages were all in English cast an 'American shadow' over the international Wikipedia projects. He further elaborates on this tension between the 'American' and Spanish projects when asked about the relationship between the Spanish Wikipedia and Larry Sanger, saying, 'The American Wikipedia might have seen [Sanger] as a "facilitator", but we regarded Sanger more like an obstacle. [...] I have to admit that he brought some good ideas to us, but the American Wikipedia was too caught up in the interests of Bomis Inc' (Tkacz and Enyedy, 2011).

Here, Enyedy explicitly equates Sanger, 'Bomis Inc', and the American Wikipedia, suggesting that allowing the 'American' dotcom company to control the Spanish Wikipedia project was unacceptable. For Enyedy, then, Wikipedia is not a general, universal example of information production, but a specific, American project.

How Wikipedia was shaped by the specific history of the American dotcom crash is further demonstrated by the larger impact of the Spanish Fork. Ultimately, the Spanish Fork would help to ensure Sanger's exit from the Wikipedia project, as the ad revenue that would have restored his salary never materialized. This happened after a larger discussion about ads on Wikipedia. This discussion demonstrates how at least some early Wikipedians thought about online business models in the wake of the dotcom crash. One site of discussion was a page at meta.wikipedia.com entitled 'Making Wikipedia Profitable', where a variety of editors expressed their concerns about the ad-based plan to raise revenue for Wikipedia. One writes, 'I just wrote a page on the dotcom death. The only sort of financing that I believe in for a site like this is a fat, one-time donation from someone who has too much money. Don't tax the users with subscription fees or advertisements. These plans are doomed'. Bryce Harrington, who Wales had recruited from GNUpedia, writes an extensive plea for a non-profit model for the site, in which he argues, 'First, I think we could generally say that if Wikipedia were to start making a profit, some authors would feel cheated, or that the site had "sold out" and was no longer sufficiently community-controlled'. Another editor prefaced his opposition to ads by writing:

> I am a recent slashdot inductee, and I have to say first of all that this site seems to me to be a fulfillment of the real promise of the internet, which is not to make megabucks for corporations, but to facilitate communication and sharing of ideas, and to make the world a better place in the process ('Making Wikipedia profitable', 2002).

All of these editors voiced the notion that adding advertisements would be unable to generate revenue to pay for content creation and would alienate critical unpaid content creators, a lesson they seem to have learned from watching the failed business grabs of the dotcom era.

## QUALITY ANXIETY AND WIKIPEDIA POLICY

Without ad revenue to pay his salary, Sanger departed the Wikipedia project. This solves one problem for Wikipedia by resolving volunteer editors' anxieties over misuse of the information they were producing. However, it exacerbates another of the project's anxieties, namely concern over the ability of a 'free' project to create high-quality information. Retracing how this anxiety shaped Wikipedia policy helps us to understand how the specific history that led to Sanger's departure had a profound effect on the larger Wikipedia environment.

Even very early on, Wikipedians were aware of quality concerns surrounding their project. For example, as of April 2001 the 'Welcome Newcomers!' page, intended to introduce new users to the project, included the following language:

> Maybe you think that Wikipedia would end up being a rather low-quality product, since it's open to everyone. But perhaps it's the fact that it is open to everyone that makes a lot of these articles pretty good, and ever-improving. To alter a now-famous catchphrase: 'Given enough eyeballs, all errors are shallow.' We tend to cater to the highest common denominator – 'lower denominators' tend politely not to touch articles they know nothing about! There are a lot of Ph.D.'s and graduate students and other very smart and knowledgeable people at work here – but everyone is welcome. (Wikipedia: Welcome, newcomers, 2001)

The 'Welcome Newcomers' page displays a curious tension, attempting to at once reassure users Wikipedia is a quality product, one that 'cater[s] to the highest common denominator', while at the same time reassuring them 'everyone is welcome' to contribute.

One of the biggest tools allowing Wikipedia to navigate this tension is its 'Verifiability' policy. This policy, which grows out of language contained in the Neutral Point of View policy, is summarized in its current version: 'in Wikipedia, verifiability means that other people using the encyclopedia can check that the information comes from a reliable source. Wikipedia does not publish original research. Its content is determined by previously published information rather than the beliefs or experiences of its editors' (Wikipedia, 2017). This policy allows Wikipedia to accept contributions from a wide range of participants, as its F/OSS-informed model demands, without allowing those participants total authority to decide on truth for the encyclopedia. As we will see in the next section, while the policy allows Wikipedia to function in the face of its quality anxiety, it also influences what sorts of truth claims have validity within the project.

## THE GAZA WAR ARTICLE AS A CASE STUDY IN THE INFLUENCE OF 'VERIFIABILITY'

Wikipedia's Verifiability policy (Wikipedia shorthand WP:V) continues to play an important role in the process of producing information as practiced on Wikipedia. Since WP:V flows from Wikipedia's attempt to resolve the problem of creating a reliable resource without centralized control, the way WP:V shapes Wikipedia's process can be seen as a part of the continuing influence of its particular F/OSS-inflected history.

To better understand how WP:V shapes Wikipedia, we can examine how it was deployed in the case of the article documenting the 2008 Gaza War. This article provides a useful case study for investigating the policy environment of the mature Wikipedia project. In particular, the fraught environment for the Gaza War article demonstrates the compromises and negotiations made by Wikipedia editors dealing with contested subject matter. The section below will demonstrate how use of WP:V allows editors to defer questions of truth onto relatively simpler and more resolvable questions about existing accounts in secondary sources, while also reinforcing existing power inequalities within Wikipedia. In particular, the case study demonstrates how Wikipedia finds compromises when dealing with real-world conflicts, but also how 'Western' sources of information are privileged by WP:V.

One example demonstrating how WP:V allows editors to reach compromises was the incredibly fraught debate over the listing of 'civilian' casualties. In the case of this article, the problem of defining who was and was not a 'civilian' casualty of the conflict was a seemingly irreconcilable issue, and one where Wikipedia was vulnerable to accusations of inaccuracy. Questions over defining civilian casualties first surface in a post to the article's talk page dated December 29, 2008. In this post one editor challenges the way civilian casualties of the conflict are then being counted:

> It seems to me like somebody is trying to put a spin on things by stating that there are '29+ civilians' dead among the 287 on the basis of an ABC article stating that among those dead, at least 20 were children and 9 were women. That is quite biased, and should be changed ASAP. (Talk:Gaza War/Archive 1 – Wikipedia, the free encyclopedia, 2009).

We can see in this quote two related questions editors of the Gaza War article would return to frequently. First there is a methodological question: how should civilians be counted? Can civilian casualty counts be inferred by counting some other demographic category, such as women or children, or is some other method needed? Second, and perhaps more difficult, is what could be called a question of ontology. Given the complicated political status of Gaza, the question of where the line between civilian and combatant should be drawn in this conflict is one

Wikipedia editors find themselves unable to resolve. Two arguments made by editors early in the article demonstrate just how difficult it would be for Wikipedia editors to attempt to reconcile definitions of 'civilian' based on 'real-world' ethical and legal considerations. One editor, Wikifan12345, argues that Hamas's decentralized nature blurs the line between civilian and military casualties. He writes, 'Hamas runs like a terrorist organization, in the sense that support comes from many locales, homes, libraries, things that we consider ordinary is often used there to conceal weapons/soldiers/etc.' (Talk:Gaza War/Archive 4 – Wikipedia, the free encyclopedia, 2009), and thus he feels the counts of 'civilians' being made by NGOs and Palestinian sources have been unfairly inflated. In contrast, another editor, NonZionist, argues, 'Almost ALL Palestinians are civilians. If my home is invaded and I attempt to defend my family, do I lose my civilian status? International law recognizes the right of people under occupation to RESIST' (Talk:Gaza War/Archive 4 – Wikipedia, the free encyclopedia, 2009).

Other editors quickly point out that these arguments are irrelevant in the face of WP:V, yet heated debate over them grows to involve several other editors and many more threads of conversation. Despite repeated pleas, neither Wikifan12345 nor NonZionist has very much luck in swaying their fellow editors to define 'civilians' in the way that they see best. In one particularly telling moment, editor Nableezy tells NonZionist:

> NonZionist, I completely agree with you, but for the purposes of this article, unless we can find a reliable source, and probably people would want multiple sources, that make this point, there is not really any way of doing this. But as a philosophical discussion, I do agree that in an occupying force killing somebody, regardless of the situation, would best be described as killing a victim of occupation. (Talk:Gaza War/Archive 15 – Wikipedia, the free encyclopedia, 2009)

Here we can see how Nableezy articulates a separate moral space for the Wikipedia community, distinct from one's moral sense of real-world conflict. His or her own moral values say, 'an occupying force killing somebody, regardless of the situation, would best be described as killing a victim of occupation', but Nableezy stresses the need for information included on Wikipedia to meet the shared values of the community, especially the value placed on reliable sources.

Unlike Nableezy's articulation of shared values, NonZionist and Wikifan12345 continue to advocate on behalf of their own values, to little avail. Both eventually stop trying to influence the course of this article. The cases of both of these editors speak to the apparent difficulty of being an advocate for a particular set of moral values on Wikipedia, without taking into consideration the shared values of the Wikipedia community itself, in particular the shared values embedded in WP:V. This policy also serves to project matters of values onto sources. These sources, however, become a source of values and a contested terrain for editors in and of themselves.

## RELIABLE SOURCES AS CONTESTED TERRAIN

This deferral of the difficult questions of truth onto sources, while clearly a useful way for Wikipedia editors to build effective compromises on controversial matters, also raises difficult questions of its own. Namely, the question of what does, and does not, constitute a 'reliable' source. Editors challenged the reliability of sources cited by others on a regular basis. In addition to the debate over the PCHR (Palestinian Center for Human Rights) and IDF (Israeli Defense Force) sources used for casualty count numbers discussed in the previous section, heated discussion took place over the use of such sources as a statement by the official spokesperson of the Palestinian Popular Resistance Committees (Talk:Gaza War/Archive 1 – Wikipedia, the free encyclopedia, 2009), the American Center for Law and Justice (Talk:Gaza War/Archive 6 – Wikipedia, the free encyclopedia, 2009), the Pakistani newspaper website Dawn.com (Talk:Gaza War/Archive 6 – Wikipedia, the free encyclopedia, 2009), and the activist website antiwar.com (Talk:Gaza War/Archive 16 – Wikipedia, the free encyclopedia, 2009).

Over the course of these exchanges a pattern emerges. Both Palestinian and Israeli advocates argue against sources from the opposite side that they feel are too extreme to be reliable. For example, Wikifan12345 objects to complaints that the article cites too many Western sources by arguing, 'Arab and Palestinian media is a sham at best, and I'm being generous here' (Talk:Gaza War/Archive 4 – Wikipedia, the free encyclopedia, 2009). In another instance, an editor objects to the fact that, as he or she sees it, a section on 'Palestinian Militant Activity' is slanted, since 'almost every piece of information here can be traced back to IDF sources', and argues that 'we need to use more neutral sources' (Talk:Gaza War/Archive 29 – Wikipedia, the free encyclopedia, 2009). A third group of editors positions itself as being between the two sides, and advocates for pluralism and inclusiveness in Wikipedia sourcing. One such editor articulates his understanding of reliable sources as:

> A reliable source can be partisan and non-neutral [...] The more controversy around a topic, the more need for verifiability. Hence, there needs to be more sources and more variety of POV in sources. (Talk:Gaza War/Archive 1 – Wikipedia, the free encyclopedia, 2009)

Given these three positions, what is the actual outcome of the contest over 'reliable sources' for the Gaza War article? Because the lines of conflict here are closely tied to national identity, as well as to the larger conflicts involving the supra-national formation of 'the Western world', investigating what countries are represented by sources cited in the Gaza War article might help to establish the relative success of the pro-Israel, pro-Palestine, and pro-plurality factions in shaping the article. Figure 21.2 displays the countries of origin of these sources in graphic form. As the graph shows quite clearly, the overwhelming majority of the sources for this article were attributable to Israel, the US, and the UK. Sources from occupied Palestine itself were very rare.

There are several factors that may account for this disparity between 'Western' and

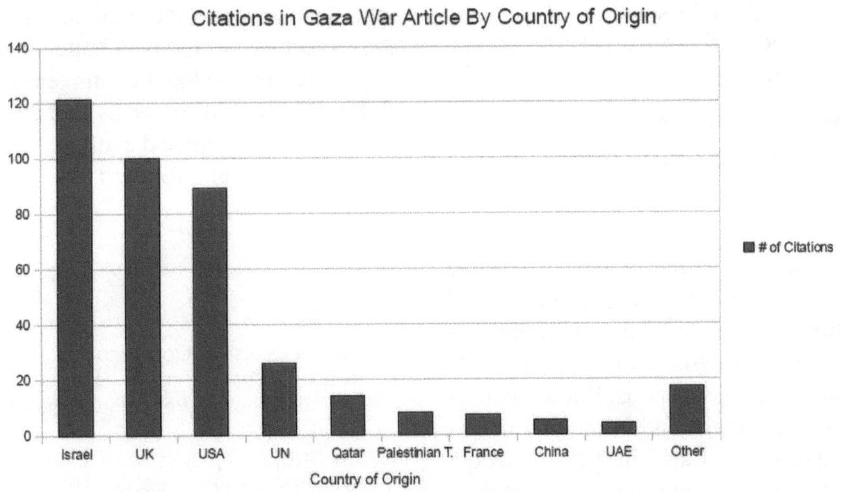


**Figure 21.2 Citations in Gaza War article by country of origin.**

*Source*: Wikipedia, the free encyclopedia (2010)

'non-Western' sources in the composition of this article. The first is that the English Wikipedia's Verifiability policy favors sources in English, as this renders them easier for the majority of English Wikipedia editors to check up on. The second is the advantage Western sources enjoy in material conditions, internet access, and distribution, which was noted by Wikipedia editors themselves during their discussion of sources on several occasions. Finally, in the face of consistent and often very hostile opposition to non-Western sources as demonstrated by the actions of Wikifan12345 and others, described above, editors may have chosen to cite Western sources for facts they wished to include, rather than go through the trouble of making the case for inclusion of non-Western media.

In any event, this lopsided inclusion of Western sources undermines the expansive, pluralist position advocated by some editors for Wikipedia sources. It suggests strongly that, in this way at least, Wikipedia's content policies[3], policies shaped by Wikipedia's need to manage anxieties over the quality of 'free' information, make the site somewhat inherently conservative, bound to reflect historical inequalities of access and media power as it defers difficult questions of 'truth' to its sources.

## CONCLUSION: A HISTORICALLY SPECIFIC AND CONTINGENT WIKIPEDIA

While the above is hardly an exhaustive survey of the historical conditions that shaped the creation of Wikipedia, the evidence presented establishes Wikipedia's historically specific and contingent status. Rather than an example of a general trend in the production of information in our internet-connected society, Wikipedia is the outcome of a specific confluence of ideas and labor coming from the F/OSS community in the era following the dotcom crash.

In particular, I have shown how the anxiety over centralized information control in the post-dotcom moment gave Wikipedia's early volunteer editors tremendous leverage in shaping the early Wikipedia. The early editor community was able to use this leverage, via the Spanish Fork, to resist the imposition of advertising on their work. While this editor autonomy allowed Wikipedia to become a non-profit information source, it also meant that the initial, heavily male, editor population was able to 'self-govern' in ways that may have continued the 'locker room' atmosphere reported by some early female Wikipedians, and that may still be encountered on the site today.

Furthermore, the resistance to adding advertisements to Wikipedia also meant removing Larry Sanger from his paid role as chief editor of the project. This removal exacerbated already existing anxieties about the quality of information Wikipedia could produce. As we saw in the case of the 2008 Gaza War article, while Wikipedia is able to successfully handle these anxieties via policies like Verifiability, these same policies tend to privilege 'Western' information sources within the project

Thus, we can see how Wikipedia's F/OSS inheritance creates the particular encyclopedia project we see today. A better understanding of the complex and contingent history of Wikipedia should allow us to better understand the still living and evolving community of Wikipedia going forward.

### Notes

1 GNU, a recursive acronym that stands for 'Gnu's Not Unix', is the name given to Stallman's attempt to build a free clone of the Unix operating system.

2 The GNUpedia project was a short-lived attempt to build a free encyclopedia. While it's impossible to know what form this project would have ultimately taken, had it survived, it was understood by its volunteers as fundamentally an encyclopedia project.

3 These content policies include WP:V, which we have been discussing, but also the Neutral Point of View (NPOV) and No Original Research (NOR) policies, along with other policies and guidelines designed to shape Wikipedia's content.

## REFERENCES

Alexa Top 500 Global Sites (n.d.) Available at: http://www.alexa.com/topsites (accessed 13 August 2017).

*All Things Considered* (2008) Palin's Wikipedia Entry Gets Overhaul. NPR. Available at: http://www.npr.org/templates/story/story.php?storyId=94118849.

Benkler Y. (2006) *The Wealth of Networks: How Social Production Transforms Markets and Freedom*. New Haven, CT: Yale University Press.

Bihlmeyer R. (2001) [Wikipedia-l] Wikipedia teamwork. Available at: https://lists.wikimedia.org/pipermail/wikipedia-l/2001-August/000316.html (accessed 13 August 2017).

Boldt A. (2001) [Wikipedia-l] GFDL and Wikipedia, II. Available at: https://lists.wikimedia.org/pipermail/wikipedia-l/2001-October/000644.html (accessed 13 August 2017).

Bould M.D., Hladkowicz E.S., Pigford A.-A.E., et al. (2014) References that anyone can edit: Review of Wikipedia citations in peer reviewed health science literature. *BMJ* 348: g1585. DOI: 10.1136/bmj.g1585.

Cohen N. (2007) A History Department Bans Citing Wikipedia as a Research Source. *The New York Times*, 21 February. Available at: https://www.nytimes.com/2007/02/21/education/21wikipedia.html (accessed 13 August 2017).

Coleman E.G. (2012) *Coding Freedom: The Ethics and Aesthetics of Hacking*. Princeton. NJ: Princeton University Press.

Crocker L. (2001) [Wikipedia-l] 'DO NOT STEAL'. Available at: https://lists.wikimedia.org/pipermail/wikipedia-l/2001-March/000038.html (accessed 13 August 2017).

Ekstrand V.S., Famiglietti A., and Nicole C. (2013) The Intensification of Copyright: Critical Legal Activism in the Age of Digital Copyright. *IDEA* 53: 291.

Enyedy E. (n.d.) [Intlwiki-l] Good luck with your wikiPAIDia. In: *Intlwiki-l*. Available at: http://git.net/ml/science.linguistics.wikipedia.international/2002-02/msg00038.html (accessed 24 August 2017).

Famiglietti, A. (2011) The right to fork: A historical survey of de/centralization in Wikipedia. In: Lovnik, G. and Tkacz, N. eds. *Critical Point of View: A Wikipedia Reader*. Amsterdam: Institute of Network Cultures, pp. 296–308.

Ghosh R. (ed.) (2006) *CODE: Collaborative Ownership and the Digital Economy*. Cambridge, MA: The MIT Press.

Ghosh R.A., Glott R., Krieger B., et al. (2002) *Free/libre and open source software: Survey and study*. Part iv: 'Survey of developers'. Available at: http://www. infonomics. nl/FLOSS/report/FLOSS_Final4.pdf. Available at: http://www.math.unipd.it/~bellio/FLOSS%20Final%20Report%20-%20Part%204%20-%20Survey%20of%20Developers.pdf.

Harrington B. (2001a) [Wikipedia-l] Wikipedia teamwork. Available at: https://lists.wikimedia.org/pipermail/wikipedia-l/2001-August/000325.html (accessed 13 August 2017).

Harrington B. (2001b) [Wikipedia-l] Wikipedia teamwork. Available at: https://lists.wikimedia.org/pipermail/wikipedia-l/2001-August/000326.html (accessed 13 August 2017).

Hidders J. (2001) [Wikipedia-l] Wikipedia teamwork. Available at: https://lists.wikimedia.org/pipermail/wikipedia-l/2001-August/000312.html (accessed 13 August 2017).

Jasiutowicz K.P. (2001) [Wikipedia-l] Wikipedia teamwork. Available at: https://lists.wikimedia.org/pipermail/wikipedia-l/2001-August/000306.html (accessed 13 August 2017).

Kelty C. (2008) *Two Bits: The Cultural Significance of Free Software*. Durham, NC: Duke University Press.

Kissane S. (2001) [Wikipedia-l] GNU FDL & HTML Table Requirement. Available at: https://lists.wikimedia.org/pipermail/wikipedia-l2001-October/ 000627.html (accessed 13 August 2017).

Lessig L. (c.1999) *Code: and other laws of cyberspace*. New York, NY: Basic Books.

Lessig L. (2004) *Free Culture: How Big Media Uses Technology and the Law to Lock down Culture and Control Creativity*. New York: Penguin Press.

Levy S. (1984) *Hackers: Heroes of the computer revolution*. 1st ed. Garden City, NY: Anchor Press/Doubleday.

Making Wikipedia profitable: encyclopedia article from Wikipedia. (2002, March 2). Available at: http://web.archive.org/web/20020302113625/meta.wikipedia.com/wiki.phtml?title=Making+Wikipedia+profitable (accessed 13 August 2017)

Nupedia and Project Gutenberg Directors Answer – Slashdot (n.d.) Available at: https://news.slashdot.org/story/01/03/02/1422244/nupedia-and-project-gutenberg-directors-answer (accessed 18 August 2017).

Owen G. (2001) [Wikipedia-l] Copyright question. In: *Wikipedia-L*. Available at: https://lists.wikimedia.org/pipermail/wikipedia-l/2001-June/000227.html (accessed 13 August 2017).

Peoples L.F. (2009) The citation of Wikipedia in judicial opinions. *Yale JL & Tech* 12: 1.

Raymond E.S. (2000) The Cathedral and the Bazaar. Available at: http://catb.org/~esr/writings/cathedral-bazaar/cathedral-bazaar/ (accessed 25 June 2010).

Reagle J. (2012) 'Free as in sexist?' Free culture and the gender gap. *First Monday* 18(1). DOI: 10.5210/fm.v18i1.4291.

Rybo S. (2001) [Wikipedia-l] Copyright forking. In: *Wikipedia-L*. Available at: https://lists.wikimedia.org/pipermail/wikipedia-l/2001-June/000171.html (accessed 13 August 2017).

Sanger L. (2001a) [Nupedia-l] Let's make a wiki. In: *Nupedia-l*. Available at: http://web.archive.org/web/20030414014355/http://www.nupedia.com:80/pipermail/nupedia-l/2001-January/000676.html (accessed 13 August 2017).

Sanger L. (2001b) [Wikipedia-l] License question. Available at: https://lists.wikimedia.org/pipermail/wikipedia-l/2001-June/000207.html (accessed 13 August 2017).

Sanger L. (2001c) [Wikipedia-l] Response. Available at: https://lists.wikimedia.org/pipermail/wikipedia-l/2001-March/000043.html (accessed 13 August 2017).

Sanger L. (2001d) [Wikipedia-l] Slashdotted? Available at: https://lists.wikimedia.org/pipermail/wikipedia-l/2001-March/000025.html (accessed 13 August 2017).

Shirky C. (2012) Gin, Television and Social Surplus. In: Mandiberg M. ed. *The Social Media Reader*. New York: New York University Press.

Stallman R.M. (2002) *Free Software, Free Society: Selected Essays of Richard M. Stallman*. First Printing, First Edition. Gay J (ed.). Free Software Foundation.

T. L. (2002) [Wikipedia-l] Another copyright issue. Available at: https://lists.wikimedia.org/pipermail/wikipedia-l/2002-January/001087.html (accessed 13 August 2017).

Talk:Gaza War/Archive 1 – Wikipedia, the free encyclopedia (2009) Available at: http://en.wikipedia.org/wiki/Talk:Gaza_War/Archive_1 (accessed 15 July 2010).

Talk:Gaza War/Archive 4 – Wikipedia, the free encyclopedia (2009) Available at: http://en.wikipedia.org/wiki/Talk:Gaza_War/Archive_4 (accessed 15 July 2010).

Talk:Gaza War/Archive 6 – Wikipedia, the free encyclopedia (2009) Available at: http://en.wikipedia.org/wiki/Talk:Gaza_War/Archive_6 (accessed 15 July 2010).

Talk:Gaza War/Archive 15 – Wikipedia, the free encyclopedia (2009) Available at: http://en.wikipedia.org/wiki/Talk:Gaza_War/Archive_15 (accessed 15 July 2010).

Talk:Gaza War/Archive 16 – Wikipedia, the free encyclopedia (2009) Available at: http://en.wikipedia.org/wiki/Talk:Gaza_War/Archive_16 (accessed 15 July 2010).

Talk:Gaza War/Archive 29 – Wikipedia, the free encyclopedia (2009) Available at: http://en.wikipedia.org/wiki/Talk:Gaza_War/Archive_29 (accessed 15 July 2010).

Tapscott D. and Williams A.D. (2010) *Wikinomics: How Mass Collaboration Changes Everything*. Expanded edition. New York, NY: Portfolio.

Tkacz N. (2011) The Politics of Forking Paths. In: Lovink G. and Tkacz N. eds. *Critical Point of View: A Wikipedia Reader.* Amsterdam: Institute for Network Cultures, pp. 94–109.

Tkacz N. and Enyedy E. (2011) 'Good Luck with your wikiPAIDia': Reflections on the 2002 Fork of the Spanish Wikipedia. An interview with Edgar Enyedy. In: Lovink G. and Tkacz N. eds. *Critical Point of View: A Wikipedia Reader.* Amsterdam: Institute for Network Cultures, pp. 94–109.

Torvalds L. (2001) *Just for Fun: The Story of an Accidental Revolutionary*. 1st ed. Diamond D. ed. New York, NY: HarperBusiness.

Turner F. (2006) *From Counterculture to Cyberculture: Stewart Brand, the Whole Earth*

*Network, and the Rise of Digital Utopianism*. Chicago, IL: University of Chicago Press.

Wales J. (2001a) Re: [Bug-gnupedia] Nupedia. In: *Bug-Gnupedia*. Available at: http://lists.gnu.org/archive/html/bug-gne/2001-01/msg00108.html (accessed 7 June 2010).

Wales J. (2001b) [Wikipedia-l] Britannica news. Available at: https://lists.wikimedia.org/pipermail/wikipedia-l/2001-March/000044.html (accessed 13 August 2017).

Wales J. (2001c) [Wikipedia-l] GNU FDL & HTML Table Requirement. Available at: https://lists.wikimedia.org/pipermail/wikipedia-l/2001-October/000629.html (accessed 13 August 2017).

Wales J. (2001d) [Wikipedia-l] Response. Available at: https://lists.wikimedia.org/pipermail/wikipedia-l/2001-March/000041.html (accessed 13 August 2017).

Wales J. (2001e) [Wikipedia-l] Why an attribution requirement? Available at: https://lists.wikimedia.org/pipermail/wikipedia-l/2001-October/000630.html (accessed 13 August 2017).

Wales J. (2001f) [Wikipedia-l] Wikipedia teamwork. Available at: https://lists.wikimedia.org/pipermail/wikipedia-l/2001-August/000357.html (accessed 13 August 2017).

Weber S. (2004) *The Success of Open Source*. Cambridge, MA: Harvard University Press.

Wikipedia (2017) Wikipedia:Verifiability. Available at: https://en.wikipedia.org/w/index.php?title=Wikipedia:Verifiability&oldid=795820786 (accessed 13 August 2017).

Wikipedia, the free encyclopedia (2010) Gaza War (2008-2009) Available at: https://en.wikipedia.org/w/index.php?title=Gaza_War_(2008%E2%80%9309)&oldid=376497374 (accessed 15 July 2010).

Wikipedia: Welcome, newcomers (2001) Available at: https://web.archive.org/web/20010406105416/http://www.wikipedia.com:80/wiki/Welcome,_newcomers (accessed 13 August 2017).

Zittrain J. (2008) *The Future of the Internet – And How to Stop It*. New Haven, CT: Yale University Press.

22

# A Critical Political Economy of Web Advertising History

Matthew Crain

The rise of web advertising over the past two and a half decades has been meteoric. Global online ad spending has risen steadily since the World Wide Web's creation, proving resilient in the face of two financial crises and generally tepid economic growth. Consulting firm McKinsey & Company (2015) predicts that 'digital media', which includes the web and mobile platforms, will account for more than 50% of worldwide advertising spending by 2019. The web has been the primary carrier of digital advertising and its expansion has been accompanied by a great build-up of consumer data collection capacity. For a majority of users, pervasive advertising and monitoring are now default components of web engagement.

As internet access continues its uneven proliferation, web advertising seems to grow apace. But why is this so? The web was created as an information retrieval tool and released into the public domain in the hope that it might become a 'universal medium for sharing information' (Berners-Lee and Fischetti, 1999: 84). It was designed to be open-ended, but was hardly optimized to serve the marketing needs of business. Support for advertising was not a standard feature of web technology, nor was it particularly welcome within early web cultures. Yet today the web is saturated in commercial messaging and significant efforts are ongoing to enhance and extend digital advertising capabilities. Is it simply the natural state of affairs that the web's diffusion entails integration within advertising systems? A look at the origins of web advertising in the United States suggests otherwise. The capacities for advertising and consumer monitoring had to be constructed along technical, but also political economic, lines.

Using the United States as a case study, this chapter outlines the history of web advertising from a critical political economy of media (CPE) approach. While web advertising does not have a sole country of origin, US companies, in partnership with the federal government, were among the first to bring advertising to 'cyberspace'. As part of the broader privatization of the internet, policy-makers sought to position American businesses at the forefront of the web's global commercial expansion. The US government embraced a hands-off regulatory approach to web advertising, hoping to bolster the industry's early growth. Throughout the 1990s, US companies developed leading technologies, standards, and practices that brought fringe web advertising markets into the mainstream. At the time of this writing, US-based transnational corporations dominate the global digital advertising sector. At the forefront are Google and Facebook, both of which have come to stand among the world's most valuable companies by pushing the technical and political boundaries of web advertising and consumer surveillance. In so doing, they have helped to solidify advertising's place at the center of the digital media economy. CPE provides valuable insights into the historical roots of this state of affairs.

## A CRITICAL POLITICAL ECONOMY APPROACH

One of the primary aims of CPE is to clarify how media and communications systems work in relation to larger structures of political and economic power (Hardy, 2014; Mosco, 2009; Wasko et al., 2011; Winseck and Jin, 2011). Historical analysis is foundational to this effort because it denaturalizes prevailing institutional arrangements and social relations, showing the structural forces and human agency at work in the construction of media systems. In her classic study of social construction of technology, Carolyn Marvin (1988) unpacks the history of electronic communication by taking readers back to the moments *When Old Technologies Were New*. In a complementary fashion, CPE posits that it is also necessary to consider what is 'old' about new technologies. Foremost among what is old about web advertising is that it grew out of the century-in-the-making interdependency of media and marketing within capitalism. Adapting a term from John Sinclair (2016), a 'marketing/media complex' emerged in the late nineteenth century as manufacturers, retailers, advertising agencies, and commercial media outlets found common interest in building national consumer markets. These entities grew symbiotic as markets matured and advertising became a cornerstone of corporate strategy. In increasingly prevalent oligopoly scenarios, advertising functioned as a barrier to would-be competitors and a means of brand maintenance. Advertising expenditures grew rather quickly to account for around 2% of US GDP and have remained relatively stable ever since. Large swaths of the media sector became reliant on advertising revenues and, on the whole, business was good. Media empires were forged as advertising became a 'leading edge of global consumerism' (Schiller, 1969: 13), serving the ideological and market-building needs of an astonishingly productive corporate industrial economy.

In a word, advertising became integral to industrial capitalism and evolved in relation to its overarching political economic currents. A rich CPE literature chronicles these developments, unearthing the contested processes whereby marketing imperatives came to govern the structure and content of successive media systems and highlighting attendant social problems including constraints on journalism, class bias of media fare, and deepening commercialism (Baldasty, 1992; McChesney, 1993; Ohmann, 1996). From this perspective, the history of mass media is intertwined with the history of creating large markets for consumer goods and services. Advertising took a variety of forms, but mass marketing became the prevailing strategy in alignment with the affordances of industrial printing and broadcasting technologies, i.e. mass communication. As new information communication technologies developed, particularly computers and advanced telecommunications networks, the marketing/media complex responded with renewed dynamism, seeking to exploit emerging business opportunities and evade destructive competition. This lineage is the starting point for a CPE analysis of web advertising history.

Public policy is a focal point for CPE, which emphasizes the central role of politics in media development. Successive media and advertising systems have been heavily shaped by the formative policy decisions that Paul Starr (2004) calls 'constitutive choices'. For example, legislation, regulation, and government subsidy were foundational to the establishment of commercial broadcasting in the United States, particularly in the form of the Radio Act of 1927 and Communications Act of 1934. It was the Federal Radio Commission/Federal Communications Commission, at the behest of Congress and with executive branch backing, that 'cleared the dial' of many public and non-profit broadcasters to give exclusive licenses (for free) to a commercial broadcast oligopoly owned by some of the nation's most powerful technology companies. Early policies often have structuring 'path dependence' effects on subsequent system development. Television's brisk subsumption by commercial radio broadcasters is one example, though CPE scholars point out that early commercial broadcasting was highly controversial, as evidenced not only by organized citizen opposition, but also by the decisions of peer nations like Great Britain to reject advertising and establish alternative public broadcasting models (McChesney, 1993). CPE attends to such complexities by looking for moments of contestation and putting policy-making to questions of 'for whom and for what' (Schiller, 1978).

There are numerous examples of the US government's historical stewardship of the marketing/media complex, from subsidizing basic communication technology research to chameleon-like public interest regulations to a tax code that allows companies to write off advertising as a business expense. The takeaway here is that public policy has always been fundamental to media system development and that, despite strong structural pressures towards commercialization, there are real political choices to be made, especially during a platform's formative years (McChesney, 2007; Starr, 2004). The World Wide Web is no exception. Web advertising's history is in many ways the story of the internet's assimilation into the capitalist political economy. At the same time, important elements of web advertising's construction can be attributed to variously contested policy choices, rather than inevitable technological advance or market predestination. The balance of this chapter demonstrates the CPE approach by highlighting how public policy-making, financial investment, and the structural imperatives of capitalism shaped the web's formative moments, drove the rapid build-up of online advertising, and propelled consumer monitoring.

## FOUR 'STAGES' OF WEB ADVERTISING

The history of web advertising in the United States can be mapped into several cascading stages of development: electronic billboards, ad networks, search advertising, and surveillance advertising. Of course, reality has a habit of being too complex to fit neatly into distinct categories. There was and remains a great deal of experimentation, investment, and conflict within the institutions, technologies, and practices of web advertising. A new historical 'stage' does not come along and simply replace its predecessor. Instead, it is useful to think of these categories as trajectories, progressing in varying degrees of overlap, sometimes in opposition, but generally in an additive fashion. Tim Berners-Lee (1999) noted that the web's technical protocols were established by means of 'accretion'. The same is true of web advertising in that contemporary practices reflect an amalgamation of prior developments.

The first three stages come from the United States' pre-broadband era, roughly the mid 1990s to the mid 2000s, during which the economy was overtaken by a massive boom and bust of speculative investment that centered on information and communication technologies: the dotcom bubble. The web advertising trends of this period have since converged around the collection and exchange of consumer information for application to a wide range of digital marketing activities. Terms like 'one-to-one marketing' and 'big data' have been used to describe such practices, which signify the fourth and current stage of development. I use the term surveillance advertising to emphasize that targeted messaging and consumer profiling are now at the core of digital advertising. Surveillance also suggests a power imbalance among the watched and watchers that reflects a troubling disparity of control over contemporary advertising data practices.

## ELECTRONIC BILLBOARDS AND CORPORATE HOME PAGES

By the time the web came on the scene in the early 1990s, the multi-faceted privatization of the larger internet was well underway (Abbate, 1999; Greenstein, 2017). In the midst of a recession, policy-makers at the highest levels of government sought to catalyze economic growth through privatizing and deregulating finance and telecommunications. There was bi-partisan support among policy-makers for the commercial development of what was often called the 'information superhighway'. President Bill Clinton's administration, taking power in 1993, made private-sector investment and control the cornerstone of federal internet policy, which enabled web advertising to flourish. Major technology and media companies were afforded high-level access to policy-making processes and were ultimately given broad leeway to develop the web as they saw fit. This extended to the advertising industry, members of which quite literally wrote a laissez-faire approach to web advertising into the administration's 1997 internet policy manifesto, *A Global Framework for Electronic Commerce*. Notwithstanding exceptions concerning encryption and regulation of 'indecent' content, the government made good on its promise to 'let the private sector lead'. This established a baseline of so-called 'self-regulation' for the web advertising industry, a regulatory approach Des Freedman (2014) describes as 'negative policy', a form of non-intervention where the private sector charts its own course relatively free from public oversight. These measures fell under the presiding logic of what scholars have variously described as 'marketization' (Hesmondhalgh, 2013), 'corporate libertarianism' (Pickard, 2015), and, more broadly, 'neoliberalism' (Harvey, 2005).

Despite a favorable policy environment, online advertising did not advance smoothly. The first web advertisement is usually attributed to the online tech magazine HotWired.com in the fall of 1994; however, marketers had been experimenting with older 'interactive services' for at least a decade (Mosco, 1982). Though limited in scope, commercial messaging appeared on early data transmission systems like teletext and videotex, bulletin board services like Usenet, and to a greater extent on commercial online services such as CompuServe, Prodigy, and America Online (AOL). For our purposes, all of these efforts fall under the electronic billboard stage, whereby primarily static ad messages were placed in front of audiences as they navigated through content. The most prevalent format was the banner ad, known in the industry as 'display advertising' because it mixed text and graphical elements in a manner similar to print and outdoor advertising. But web banners went beyond existing forms by adding layers of interactivity, the most notable of which was the click-through function. HotWired.com's famous first banner was a partnership with AT&T that read: 'Have you ever clicked your mouse right HERE? You will'. Users who clicked were transported to AT&T's website, which, along with sparse information about long-distance telephone services, featured hyperlinks to a handful of websites created by fine art museums.

The unpolished and scattershot nature of early banners and corporate sites reflected the medium's unfamiliarity, but also exposed the ambivalence among marketers regarding the web's utility as an ad channel. The broader 'information superhighway' was still shaking out and it was by no means certain that the web would prevail over competing systems such as AOL's 'walled garden' online service or the cable industry's pilot programs for 'interactive television'. As a result, very few marketers spent any money on the web in the mid 1990s and those that did only carved out a fraction of their ad budgets to test the waters (Turow, 2006). A handful of 'digital ad agencies' cropped up to help marketers experiment on the web, but many traditional agencies remained cautious about the new interactive landscape. In 1995 web ad spending barely registered on the scale compared with more established media, but rapid growth was just around the corner.

## AD NETWORKS AND THE DOTCOM BUBBLE

By 1996 it was clear that the web would emerge as the winning interactive platform for popular use, due in no small part to Netscape's 'killer app', the graphical web browser and competitive internet service provision markets. Commercial online services were compelled to open their walled gardens, giving millions of users new access to the open web. The dotcom financial bubble funded a host of web start-ups seeking to draw users to their sites, which generated the first big wave of demand for web advertising (Crain, 2014). But the young industry was plagued by logistical problems. There was an absence of standard business practices to grease the wheels of ad sales. Web publishers lacked sales staff and technical expertise to implement banner campaigns. For marketers, it was difficult to reach users at scale and to measure the impact of advertising outlays. Despite attempts from television ratings companies like Nielson to establish audience metrics systems on the new medium, it proved difficult to build a consensus about how ads should be bought, sold, and evaluated.

Finding opportunity in this disorder, a new breed of advertising company emerged: the ad network. Blending well-established practices of ad sales outsourcing with the web's capacity for multi-directional communication, ad networks positioned themselves as intermediaries between web publishers looking to sell ad inventory and marketers seeking sizable audiences. The 'third-party' ad network strategy relied on centralized ad serving systems to manage banner delivery across bundles of disparate websites, an innovation enabled by the distributed nature of the web's communication protocols. Web publishers could use their own servers to host content, while ad networks hosted and delivered the ads from afar. By building their own distribution infrastructure, ad networks offered publishers fully outsourced advertising services, easing the burdens of labor and technical expertise and effectively lowering barriers to participation in the web advertising market. Various iterations of outsourced ad services proliferated and were utilized by most major publishers, from start-ups like Yahoo to established media companies like NBC and the *Wall Street Journal*. Leading ad networks such as DoubleClick and MatchLogic were able to aggregate far more users than any single publisher and thereby brought the first iteration of large-scale advertising to the web.

These logistical improvements were significant, but the industry had still other equally vexing problems. As banners spread their novelty quickly wore thin. It was something of an open secret among publishers and ad networks that the vast majority of users never clicked on ads. This was especially troublesome because much of the hype surrounding the web's commercialization hinged upon its interactivity, which was supposed to enable marketers to engage consumers directly rather than simply shout in their general direction. Without interactivity the low-bandwidth web seemed a poor substitute for existing branding platforms like television. As marketers began to complain about dismal click-through rates, a flurry of activity centered on ways to move 'beyond the banner'. There were attempts to jazz up ads with 'rich media' experiences and pop-up formats that were harder to ignore, but the idea that gained the most traction was that ads simply needed to be more 'relevant' to consumers. Through much trial and error, greater personalization of messaging was positioned as a solution for making advertising work on the web. Of course, these efforts required increased knowledge about web users, which dovetailed with emerging needs for data collection and user identification in the nascent online retailing and banking sectors.

The web's broader commercialization impelled its transformation from an anonymous to an identifying platform. Without delving too deeply into the technical details, the web's data protocols had originally been designed to facilitate series of discrete communications, rather than persistent connections. This made web browsing anonymous, but limited the scope of applications, especially those of a commercial nature. For example, in order for online shopping to function, websites had to recognize that a given series of actions (like putting items into a virtual shopping cart) were connected to a single user. The commercial web needed the ability to collect and store user data. It needed a memory. Netscape developed an elegant solution in the HTTP cookie, which gave web browsers a unique identifier and enabled a new frontier of data collection practices. Released as an open technical standard, cookies were rapidly adopted by major browser makers and websites.

The web advertising industry seized upon cookies as a means to gather information about consumers to inform ad targeting. Though disquiet persisted regarding whether clicks or impressions were the most appropriate metrics, it quickly became standard practice to pair tracking cookies with banner ad delivery. Ad networks led this charge as they sought to leverage the scale of their distribution networks to offer new forms of targeted banner advertising across their partner sites. To achieve these goals ad networks developed proprietary ad serving technologies that used databases and algorithms to store, combine, and deploy consumer data for targeted advertising. As early as 1997, DoubleClick's DART (Dynamic Advertising, Reporting, and Targeting) system could serve targeted ads in near real-time by cross-referencing its profile databases with information collected on the fly. The company's tagline during this period spoke of delivering the 'right message to the right person at the right time'. It is important to note that the data collection and ad targeting practices implemented in the 1990s were rudimentary by today's standards. Information gathering was largely limited to standard browser meta-data like IP addresses and time stamps, which could be strung together to create records of browsing history, but were bounded by a range of technical and organizational factors.

Nonetheless, the ad network stage represented web advertising's first generational leap. Early ad networks solved basic logistical problems and pioneered not only targeted advertising, but targeted advertising at scale in which every ad served was also an opportunity to gather consumer information. Moreover, since third-party tracking was implemented behind-the-scenes, most web users remained oblivious. These components would become important building blocks of the contemporary surveillance advertising model, which integrates targeting and profiling across the gamut of advertising practices. As consumer data increasingly occupied the center of the web advertising economy, the brunt of the industry's technical, organizational, and, as we shall see, political efforts went towards deepening and expanding web surveillance. By 2000, a cadre of top-tier ad networks were serving billions of ads per day across thousands of popular websites and building large profile databases to improve their targeting capacities. Though much of this activity was based in the United States, DoubleClick in particular worked to globalize its reach, creating sales offices and operating partnerships in some 30 countries.

The US government's stewarding of the dotcom investment bubble was a key policy program that impacted this stage of web advertising's development, funneling large amounts of capital to both the supply and demand sides of the nascent industry. Most concretely, ad networks like DoubleClick used venture capital and sky-high stock valuations to pursue aggressive growth strategies, roll out new services, acquire competitors, and invest in infrastructure, all while operating at losses. On the demand side, start-ups were among the web's biggest ad spenders. Venture capitalists, eager to maximize returns on dotcom investments, used their managerial power to direct resources to ad campaigns in order to build market share and 'get big fast', increasing valuations before public stock offerings and buyouts. These activities accelerated the construction of web advertising markets and legitimized the medium at a time when many traditional marketers were still ambivalent about the web's prospects as a sales channel.

## SEARCH ADVERTISING

Search advertising developed in parallel to the ad network model. As the number of web users and websites increased, portals and search engines emerged to organize and curate the online experience. Companies like Yahoo, AltaVista, and Lycos experimented with banner advertising to monetize their growing user bases, often partnering with ad networks to get their start. As portals gave way to the more user-directed and comprehensive search engine model, search engines like Infoseek, GoTo (later called Overture), and Google developed paid search advertising as an alternative to the ad network banner model.

Search ads, like web advertising more broadly, exhibited many variations but coalesced in the early 2000s around the approach advanced by Google, far and away the sector's most successful company. Like the ad network approach, search advertising utilized sophisticated software and hardware and hinged upon the promise of making ads relevant to consumers. But instead of targeting ads based on inferences made from stores of consumer data, search advertising used the search terms keyed in by users. For example, a person using Google's search engine to research a trip to Yellowstone National Park might see ads for nearby hotels or campsites alongside their search results. While the ad network model was growing increasingly complex and multivariate, search advertising emphasized simplicity and speed. Google heavily monitored the format and quality of its ads, limiting them to text only and weeding out misleading and poorly executed appeals. Google also demarcated paid advertising from so-called 'organic' results, helping to build user trust. Importantly, search advertising also introduced major changes in the ways that web ads were bought and sold. Banners were generally peddled on a cost-per-impression basis at a negotiated rate, so marketers paid for every ad delivered regardless of whether users clicked or not. Search ads came to be sold via auctions on a cost-per-click basis, meaning marketers bid on the rights to display ads in conjunction with search terms of their choosing and only paid when an ad was clicked.

Many marketers were enticed by search advertising's contextual approach to targeting and the cost-per-click pricing scheme in particular. A group of national marketers led by Procter & Gamble had already been pushing for cost-per-click pricing since web advertising's early days. Responding to these demands, contextual search ads moved away from impression-based pricing and placed greater emphasis on measurable results. Finding early success with paid search ads on its own sites, in 2003 Google took a page from the ad network playbook and created a program called AdSense that enabled any web publisher to host Google contextual ads, broadening its reach considerably. Search advertising exploded in the early 2000s, quickly growing to account for 40% of all web advertising expenditures, while banner advertising began to level off (Pricewaterhouse Coopers, 2005). Google rapidly became web advertising's most dominant company, capturing not only the lion's share of the search advertising market but a significant chunk of the entire online advertising sector. Google's incredible success in the early 2000s seemed to suggest that web advertising could work without relying on consumer surveillance.

## SURVEILLANCE ADVERTISING: PROFILES, PLATFORMS, AND DATA FUSION

After a brief but dramatic stall in the wake of the dotcom stock market crash, web advertising resumed strong growth, outpacing all other US media sectors. By the mid 2000s the two major thrusts in web advertising were paid search, grounded in contextual placement, and targeted display, which relied upon consumer monitoring. Together these formats accounted for three-quarters of industry revenues (Pricewaterhouse Coopers, 2005). The archetypes were Google and the ad network DoubleClick, which emerged from the dotcom stock crash considerably leaner, but newly profitable. Each company relied on scale to achieve 'relevance' in ad targeting, but took different approaches to consumer data collection. While Google analyzed user data to improve its search engine and other services, it did not monitor and profile users for advertising purposes like DoubleClick.

In the second half of the 2000s the distinctions between targeted display and search advertising fell away, most literally when Google acquired DoubleClick in 2007. After a bidding war with Microsoft (which was rapidly advancing into web advertising), Google bought DoubleClick at a $1 billion premium over its estimated valuation. No doubt the search giant wanted to move into the display advertising market, but also up for grabs were DoubleClick's massive trove of consumer data and surveillance infrastructure. Soon after the acquisition, Google reversed its policy on collecting consumer information for advertising purposes and in the years since has integrated surveillance into the core of its operations, including its flagship search advertising products. Google's buyout of DoubleClick was a high-profile marker for web advertising's industry-wide embrace of consumer surveillance.

Surveillance advertising gathered momentum along various fronts in the second half of the 2000s. Google's acquisition of DoubleClick paralleled a number of similar mergers, with Microsoft, AOL, Yahoo, and the advertising holding giant WPP all buying major ad networks with core competencies in consumer monitoring. Again, policy impacted these institutional changes. The largest of these mergers raised anti-trust concerns, triggering reviews and subsequent approvals by the Federal Trade Commission. The continued diffusion of broadband internet service, which reached over 50% of US households in 2007, enabled bandwidth-intensive applications like video streaming to flourish (Organization for Economic Co-operation and Development, 2011). User-generated video sites like YouTube achieved popularity, as did hubs for commercial content like Hulu, a joint partnership between major television networks. Video presented opportunities for marketers to bring familiar TV ad formats online, which were then augmented by the surveillance-based targeting methods of banner and search advertising. For example, after purchasing YouTube in 2006, Google began to integrate targeted advertising services into the video platform, building out new capabilities over time. Today marketers can target YouTube ads based on Google's profiles of individual users, which include information like web search histories, demographics, and interest categories.

Social networking services characterized by sites like MySpace, Facebook, and Twitter also factored heavily into the development and normalization of surveillance advertising. Immensely popular with web users, social networks amassed vast stores of personal information that could be deployed to inform advertising campaigns, including data on demographics, attitudes, and social connections – what Facebook CEO Mark Zuckerberg called the 'social graph'. The core 'value-added' from social networks stemmed from their arguably superior capacities to collect and deploy consumer data, and the explosive growth of Facebook in particular, which amassed over one billion worldwide users in its first decade, put strong competitive pressure on the entire web advertising industry to ramp up data collection efforts.

As digital media moved from the fringes to the center of the 'marketing mix', the industry pursued several threads that had been percolating since the 1990s, but had not achieved widespread implementation. Many of the biggest players adopted a 'platform approach', brokering a broadening array of advertising transactions among publishers, marketers, and ad agencies, all grounded in the collection and exchange of increasingly detailed consumer information. Google, Facebook, and their competitors prioritized ease of use, emphasizing simple set-ups, low-budget options, automation, and customization. The recent trend of 'programmatic' advertising aims to automate much of the ad buying process while giving campaign managers the tools to make highly specific adjustments as needed. These efforts have lowered barriers to participation in surveillance advertising, effectively turning the collection and monetization of consumer data into an 'app' accessible to anyone on the web.

The trajectory of surveillance not only broadens, but also deepens as companies collect new forms and greater quantities of data. Moving beyond HTTP cookies, the industry has developed myriad new types of 'digital fingerprinting' methods to monitor web users, embedding surveillance into technical architectures of web communication such as the flash video format. Another major trend is what might be called data fusion, whereby various entities collaborate to merge disparate consumer information for marketing purposes. The biggest development along these lines has been the combination of online and offline data, including personally identifiable information such as names and addresses, to 'close the loop' between advertising campaigns and consumer behaviors like retail transactions and movement through physical space. For example, Facebook partners with third-party data brokers to help marketers link their ad campaigns to product purchases. One way this is accomplished is by tracking the movements of users who have downloaded a Facebook-owned application to their mobile device and cross-referencing this data with ad campaign metrics. Here web advertising becomes increasingly indistinguishable from activities like credit reporting and consumer information reselling, business sectors that took hold decades before the web's creation, but have accelerated in recent years.

'Negative policy' (Freedman, 2014) has been instrumental in enabling surveillance practices to flourish. As data collection became more prevalent, civil liberties groups and journalists began to put public pressure on web advertising companies to address mounting privacy concerns. Privacy policy has been at the forefront of web advertising's political agenda ever since. An early backlash against the combination of offline and online data in the late 1990s produced a potential crisis for the industry as an emergent advocacy community, led by groups like the Electronic Frontier Foundation and Center for Media Education, pressured Congress to consider 'opt-in' legislation mandating that companies obtain prior consent from users before collecting their data. Seeing affirmative consent as a threat to the developing surveillance business model, a coalition of marketing trade associations and newly formed online ad industry groups successfully lobbied to install a regime of advertising 'self-regulation'. Privacy concerns have remained and periodically resurface when particularly egregious abuses come to light, but industry lobbies have been largely successful in maintaining self-regulation, cementing a policy framework based on principles of 'notice and choice'. The implementations of this 'consumer empowerment' approach are deeply flawed, primarily relying on unintelligible privacy policies and tepid opt-out mechanisms (Crain, 2018). With little access to the levers of political power, web users have become resigned to commercial surveillance, believing it 'futile to [attempt to] manage what companies can learn about them' (Turow et al., 2015: 3).

The point is not to overstate the cohesion and sophistication of surveillance advertising practices, but rather highlight the major trends of the web advertising industry that are discernable from the strategies of market leaders. By the end of the 2000s, the five most powerful US internet advertising companies – Google, Facebook, Microsoft, AOL, and Yahoo (the latter two now owned by Verizon) – all served profile-based targeted advertising and collected consumer data across expansive networks that included their own web properties and millions of other sites and applications. Numerous studies have shown that the web's most popular sites and services not only overwhelmingly monitor their users, but share user data with third parties, often by giving them direct access to collect user information via their platforms (Nordrum, 2016). On a global scale, from banners to search to video, surveillance has been embedded into advertising on the web to a greater extent than any other marketing channel in history.

## WHY SURVEILLANCE?

Technology looms large in scholarly and popular understandings of the web for self-evident reasons. Few would deny that the character and speed of technology change during the web's formative decades have been remarkable. The stages of web advertising presented above might be read as functions of various technological innovations: the centralized ad server, HTTP cookie, search term auction, profile database, targeting algorithm, and so on. Without a doubt these technologies have played a central role in shaping the particulars of web advertising. An important thrust of media history scholarship has been to interrogate and unpack technological forms and practices, as evidenced by a flowering of research approaches including science and technology studies, infrastructure studies, and media archaeology. At the risk of oversimplification, what is collectively useful about these various approaches is their attempt to weave together technology's determinative effects and social construction, to bring specificity to complex questions about the composition and consequences of the social-material assemblages we call 'technology'.

Critical political economy of media brings an important 'decentering' dimension to this research program, situating media and communications technologies within a historical context that foregrounds the structural dynamics and differential power relations that characterize capitalism. This is not to deny that technologies can exhibit significant biases or affordances, but to emphasize how and why specific technologies and elements thereof have been elevated or suppressed as media systems congeal around capitalist imperatives. Specifically, CPE draws attention to how web advertising has been constructed by human beings making decisions within organizational and political economic bounds that exert what Raymond Williams [2008 (1971)] referred to as 'pressures and limits'. In other words, research in CPE puts front and center the notion that, as Jonathan Hardy (2014: 112) succinctly put it, 'capitalism influenced the internet more than vice versa'.

Situating web advertising within the broad currents of capitalism helps to answer the question: why surveillance? Media business relations began to shift around 1970 as US capitalism in particular faced a crisis of profitability (Brenner, 2002) that spurred a host of political economic activity around information and communication technology (ICT) development. It is no coincidence that this is the period when packet-switched networks and computerization began to kick off major changes in the composition of global capitalism. Nor that the ideology of neoliberalism and its policies of privatization, deregulation, and 'free trade' would soon achieve mainstream political orthodoxy. Dan Schiller (1999, 2007) has shown that while commodification of information has always been involved in capital accumulation, the last 50 years have seen ICTs become a foundational pole of growth for an emergent 'digital capitalism'. Web advertising is part and parcel of this broader political economic project.

Capitalist investment, innovation, and appropriation of ICTs induced significant changes not only in production, but also consumption, and, most importantly for our purposes, the production of consumption otherwise known as advertising. Audience fragmentation, shifting demographics, and profit squeezes put national marketing under growing strain. In 1965, a marketer could reach 80% of 18- to 49-year-old women by purchasing just three television commercials; three decades later it required nearly 100 prime-time spots to achieve the same reach (Narisetti, 1998). These dynamics manifested in the marketing/media complex in significant ways, catalyzing and expanding advertising practices and technologies related to what Philip Napoli (2011) calls the 'rationalization of audience understanding'. Such rationalization boils down to efforts to enhance the comprehension, predictability, and control of consumer behavior (Pridmore and Zwick, 2011). Advertising began to recompose around an increasingly segmented system. Just as inventory was tracked across transnational commodity chains, pressure mounted to track audiences as they moved from activity to activity, both nationally and internationally (Schiller, 2014). A succession of new media technologies were incorporated into these functions, with the web and surveillance advertising forming a center of gravity in the 1990s and beyond.

The web presented a range of prospects for 'one-to-one' marketing, a chance to improve return-on-investment by separating 'targets' from 'waste' (Turow, 2011), to perhaps solve once and for all the legendary problem posed by department store magnate John Wanamaker: 'Half the money I spend on advertising is wasted; the problem is I don't know what half'. Evaluative methods such as A/B testing proliferated, offering improved ad campaign optimization and increasingly granular measurements of outcomes. As Joseph Turow (2006) put it, the web became a 'test bed', a prototype for a mode of advertising that found its purchase in distributing data gathering capacities, connecting heretofore disparate data silos, building out what Julia Angwin (2014) calls a surveillance 'dragnet', and creating a dispersed but integrated digital enclosure movement (Andrejevic, 2007) to power increasingly intensive information commodification.

This does not mean that web advertising developed smoothly or without episodes of contestation, dysfunction, or resistance. Competition and the struggle to overcome it are definitional to capitalism and drive its dynamism. Disparate entities within the marketing/media complex worked in conjunction *and at odds* to construct a social-material infrastructure for online advertising. The web emerged in the 1990s, simultaneously a threat and opportunity, at once conceivable as a platform for individual empowerment, commercial media's mortal wound, and potential horn of plenty for consumer data gathering. It was an unknown quantity, threatening to further splinter audiences and provide individual consumers with new degrees of autonomy, perhaps even the power to excise media advertising altogether. Marketers risked the loss of control over a media system that had long been dictated by their interests. As the CEO of marketing giant Procter & Gamble famously put it: the ad industry needed to 'grab technology change in its teeth' or chance obsolescence in the digital future (Artzt, 1994). Workaday rivalries aside, a broad range of companies maintained a common interest in bringing advertising to as many areas of social life as possible and sought to redefine the web accordingly. As the stages presented above highlight, policy-making was a preferred venue for action, as has been the case throughout US history.

This sketch of a critical political economy approach contributes to a web advertising historiography that denaturalizes technology, accounts for continuity and change, foregrounds policy-making, and situates marketing and media within the dynamics of the global capitalist political economy. As Robert McChesney (2008: 12) notes, 'assessing policies, structures, and institutions cannot answer all of the important questions surrounding media, but [political economists] believe their contributions are indispensible to the comprehensive study of media'. Calling out the undemocratic history of US media policy-making and web advertising in particular, CPE continues to articulate politics as a necessary site of intervention into the structural composition of media. Historical work in this tradition provides valuable lessons about future prospects (see Dolber, 2017; Dunbar-Hester, 2014; Gillespie, 2007; McChesney, 1993; Niesen, 2012; Pickard, 2015; Stole, 2006). Comparative and international studies represent a particularly important area for further research. The European Union, for example, has proven much more willing to constrain online commercial surveillance, prompting major regulatory conflicts and legal challenges from the transnational web advertising sector.

Another area in need of further study is the continuing role of finance capital, which has remained a potent driver of web advertising and consolidator of market power. Google and Facebook have relied on finance capital to expand, building up powerful barriers to competition. In the United States, three-quarters of digital ad revenues are divided among just ten companies, while European and Asian markets also exhibit high degrees of concentration (Pricewaterhouse Coopers, 2016). Google alone claims its ads can reach over 90% of global internet users. One estimate put the number of ads Google serves on a daily basis close to 30 billion, roughly ten times the number of people on the planet with internet access (Koetsier, 2012). This kind of market dominance raises important concerns about the bottlenecking of surveillance and influence capacities, especially when digital advertising intermingles freely between the ostensibly separate domains of commerce and politics. At the time of this writing, Facebook and other purveyors of surveillance advertising face mounting scrutiny over their roles in political manipulation and what, if any, civic responsibilities fall on their shoulders. One thing is certain. If the surveillance status quo is to be confronted, political activism and public policy must play fundamental roles.

## REFERENCES

Abbate, J. (1999) *Inventing the Internet*. Cambridge, MA: MIT Press.

Andrejevic, M. (2007) *iSpy: Surveillance and Power in the Interactive Era*. Lawrence, KS: University Press of Kansas.

Angwin, J. (2014) *Dragnet Nation: A Quest for Privacy, Security, and Freedom in a World of Relentless Surveillance*. New York: Times Books.

Artzt, E. (1994, May 12) P&G's Artzt: TV Advertising In Danger Remedy Is To Embrace Technology And Return To Program Ownership. *Advertising Age*. Available at: http://adage.com/article/news/p-g-s-artzt-tv-advertising-danger-remedy-embrace- technology-return-program-ownership/87052/ (accessed 5 March 2017).

Baldasty, G. (1992) *Commercialization of News in the Nineteenth Century*. Madison, WI: University of Wisconsin Press.

Berners-Lee, T. and Fischetti, M. (1999) *Weaving the Web: The Original Design and Ultimate Destiny of the World Wide Web by its Inventor.* New York: HarperCollins.

Brenner, R. (2002) *The Boom and the Bubble*. New York: Verso.

Crain, M. (2014) 'Financial markets and online advertising demand: Reevaluating the dotcom investment bubble', *Information, Communication & Society,* 17(3): 371–394.

Crain, M. (2018) 'The limits of transparency: Data brokers and commodification', *New Media & Society,* 20(1): 88–104.

Dolber, B. (2017) *Media and Culture in the U.S. Jewish Labor Movement: Sweating for Democracy in the Interwar Era*. New York: Palgrave.

Dunbar-Hester, C. (2014) *Low Power to the People*. Cambridge, MA: MIT Press.

Freedman, D. (2014) *The Contradictions of Media Power*. London: Bloomsbury.

Gillespie, T. (2007) *Wired Shut: Copyright and the Shape of Digital Culture*. Cambridge, MA: MIT Press.

Greenstein, S. (2017) *How the Internet Became Commercial*. Princeton, NJ: Princeton University Press.

Hardy, J. (2014) *Critical Political Economy of the Media: An Introduction*. New York: Routledge.

Harvey, D. (2005) *A Brief History of Neoliberalism*. New York: Oxford University Press.

Hesmondhalgh, D. (2013) *The Cultural Industries*. 3rd edn. London: Sage.

Koetsier, J. (2012, October 25) 30 Billion Times a Day, Google Runs an Ad. *Venture Beat*. Available at: https://venturebeat.com/2012/10/25/30-billion-times-a-day-google-runs-an-ad-13-million-times-it-works/ (accessed 15 February 2018).

Marvin, C. (1988) *When Old Technologies Were New: Thinking About Electric Communication in the Late Nineteenth Century*. New York: Oxford University Press.

McChesney, R. (1993) *Telecommunications, Mass Media, and Democracy: The Battle for the Control of U.S. Broadcasting, 1928–1935*. New York: Oxford University Press.

McChesney, R. (2007) *Communication Revolution: Critical Junctures and the Future of Media*. New York: New Press.

McChesney, R. (2008) *The Political Economy of Media: Enduring Issues, Emerging Dilemmas*. New York: Monthly Review Press.

McKinsey & Company (2015, September) Global Media Report: Global Industry Overview.

Mosco, V. (1982) *Pushbutton Fantasies*. Norwood, NJ: Ablex.

Mosco, V. (2009) *The Political Economy of Communication*. 2nd edn. Thousand Oaks, CA: Sage.

Napoli, P. (2011) *Audience Evolution: New Technologies and the Transformation of Media Audiences*. New York: Columbia University Press.

Narisetti, R. (1998, November 16) New and Improved: Ad experts talk about how their business will be transformed by technology. *Wall Street Journal*, 33.

Niesen, M. (2012) 'The little old lady has teeth: The U.S. Federal trade commission and the advertising industry, 1970–1973', *Advertising & Society Review,* 12(4). Available at: https://muse.jhu.edu/article/468049 (accessed 4 Sept 2018).

Nordrum, A. (2016, August 23) You're being tracked (and tracked and tracked) on the web. *IEEE Spectrum*. Available at: https://spectrum.ieee.org/tech-talk/telecom/internet/youre-being-tracked-and-tracked-and-tracked (accessed 15 February 2018).

Ohmann, R. (1996) *Selling Culture: Magazines, Markets, and Class at the Turn of the Century*. New York: Verso.

Organization for Economic Co-operation and Development (2011) Households with Broadband Access. OECD Broadband Portal (https://www.oecd.org/sti/broadband/oecdbroadband-portal.htm).

Pickard, V. (2015) *America's Battle for Media Democracy*. New York: Cambridge University Press.

Pricewaterhouse Coopers (2005) IAB Internet Advertising Revenue Report.

Pricewaterhouse Coopers (2016) IAB Internet Advertising Revenue Report.

Pridmore, J. and Zwick, D. (2011) 'Marketing and the rise of commercial consumer surveillance', *Surveillance & Society,* 8(3): 269–277.

Schiller, D. (1999) *Digital Capitalism*. Cambridge, MA: MIT Press.

Schiller, D. (2007) *How to Think about Information*. Urbana, IL: University of Illinois Press.

Schiller, D. (2014) *Digital Depression*. Urbana, IL: University of Illinois Press.

Schiller, H. I. (1969) *Mass Communications and American Empire*. Boulder, CO: Westview Press.

Schiller, H. I. (1978) 'Computer systems: Power for whom and for what?', *Journal of Communication,* 28(4): 184–193.

Sinclair, J. (2016) 'Advertising and media in the age of the algorithm', *International Journal of Communication,* 10: 3522–3535.

Starr, P. (2004) *The Creation of the Media: Political Origins of Modern Communications*. New York: Basic Books.

Stole, I. (2006) *Advertising on Trial: Consumer Activism and Corporate Public Relations*. Urbana, IL: University of Illinois Press.

Turow, J. (2006) *Niche Envy: Marketing Discrimination in the Digital Age*. Cambridge, MA: MIT Press.

Turow, J. (2011) *The Daily You: How the New Advertising Industry is Defining Your Identity and Your Worth*. New Haven, CT: Yale University Press.

Turow, J., Hennessy, M., and Draper, N. (2015) The Tradeoff Fallacy: How Marketers Are Misrepresenting American Consumers and Opening Them Up To Exploitation. Annenberg School for Communication, University of Pennsylvania, Pennsylvania PA.

Wasko, J., Murdock, G. and Sousa, H. (eds) (2011) *The Handbook of Political Economy of Communications*. New York: Wiley.

Williams, R. (2008) *Television: Technology and Cultural Form*. New York: Routledge (1st edn, 1971).

Winseck, D. and Jin, D. Y. (2011) *The Political Economies of Media: The Transformation of The Global Media Industries.* New York: Bloomsbury.

23

# Exploring Web Archives in the Age of Abundance: A Social History Case Study of GeoCities

Ian Milligan

## INTRODUCTION

When I think of the challenges – technical, ethical, historiographical – facing historians seeking to explore the social history of web archives, a particular archive comes to mind: GeoCities. GeoCities.com, founded in 1994 and closed in 2009 by Yahoo! corporation, was a place where many people had their first home on the World Wide Web. One simply needed to open their web browser, enter GeoCities.com into the browser bar, provide their e-mail address, and they would receive their free megabyte to create a website. These could be on any topic: their love of Buffy the Vampire Slayer, their family tree, a lamentation or celebration of a favorite sports team, an online diary, or even a child's tribute to their love of Winnie the Pooh. People took to GeoCities.com with a passion, and today the GeoCities.com web archive contains the sites of seven million people, about 186 million URLs in total. While there were many other ways to create web pages, services like GeoCities helped to democratize the Web: no need to know the inner workings of FTP, or servers, or beyond; web design could be as easy as Word processing.

While the actual definition of 'Big Data' is debatable – computer scientists might dismiss the 4TB that comprise a GeoCities web archive as small compared with the petabytes of data generated by the Large Hadron Collider – for historians something like GeoCities represents the new scope of historical abundance as they enter the web age of historiography (Graham et al., 2015). In this chapter, I begin by exploring the state of historical abundance in this field. I then use GeoCities as an example to show what researchers can do with web archives at scale using tools that historians and computer scientists have developed. In particular, I explore how historians can fruitfully analyze links, text, and images to begin to reconstruct traces of the past for analysis. Ultimately, I argue that in archives like GeoCities scholars have the potential to create more democratic, accessible histories but that doing so will require substantial rethinking of the historian's craft.

## FROM SCARCITY TO ABUNDANCE

In 2003, the late great American historian Roy Rosenzweig wrote 'Scarcity or Abundance? Preserving the Past in a Digital Era' in the *American Historical Review*. This prescient piece foresaw the shift from 'a culture of scarcity to a culture of abundance', which has now occurred on a scale that may have defied even what Rosenzweig could have imagined a decade and a half ago (Rosenzweig, 2003). An example that I like to use to underscore this is to compare the sorts of sources that historians have traditionally had with the resources that they might face in this web age of abundance.

Ordinary people did not generally leave behind historical records. When a historian tried to reconstruct an earlier time period, they were often forced to dig for the scarce records that individuals left behind: a birth or death notice, for example, or a record of a marriage or an inclusion in a national census. For insight into the rich lives of everyday people, historians have often had to read against the grain in sources such as criminal transcripts or fire insurance records. One of the best examples of information about the lives of modern England was the Old Bailey, the central London criminal court which produced court transcripts in part to sate a salacious public appetite. Between 1674 and 1913, the Old Bailey produced and preserved 197,745 trial transcripts. Today's Old Bailey website correctly describes its holdings as the 'largest body of records documenting the lives of non-elite people ever published' (Old Bailey Proceedings Online, 2013). For 239 years, the 197,745 trials are indeed the golden standard of historical documentation. Compare that, however, with GeoCities today – in the 15 years between 1994 and 2009, seven million users created some 186 million documents. Even creating a list of Uniform Resource Locators (URLs) within the collection leads to a 7GB text file and can take several hours even on a powerful server. This is what abundance looks like.

The Web was originally framed along the lines of a 'memory machine', as the title of Belinda Barnet's book puts it (Barnet, 2013). Vannevar Bush's Memex, or Ted Nelson's Project Xanadu both aimed to improve the memory of the individual user – transcending the problem of the 'absent-minded professor'. In so doing, hypertext and the Web ended up improving the collective memory of our society. Researchers today now have far more information about everyday people than ever before. Traditionally, elites shaped our historical record; increasingly, all of us act in ways and leave behind traces that shape the historical record for the next generation. James Gleick explains this well in his masterful *The Information: A History, A Theory, A Flood*: 'the information produced and consumed by humankind used to vanish – that was the norm, the default. The sights, the sounds, the songs, the spoken word just melted away. Marks on stone, parchment, and paper were the special case' (Gleick, 2012).

For GeoCities is just part of the broader constellation of web archived material being retained. In their *Uncharted: Big Data as a Lens on Human Culture*, Erez Aiden and Jean-Baptiste Michel note that a literary scholar studying Edgar Allen Poe has 422 letters to explore. Think of your own digital record – chances are somebody studying you could find more than 422 letters! As they note, 'this material comprises an astonishingly detailed record of the lives of billions of people – a record that did not exist at all mere decades ago. It has no precedent in human history' (Aiden and Michel, 2013). Billions of new documents are created every day, with millions being saved for future access.

GeoCities helps us remember, however, that it is not just scale – preserving millions of documents where we used to only save thousands, for example – but scope. People who never before would have been part of the historical record are now suddenly part of it. Teenagers who write about their love of video games, a retired Canadian vacationing in Florida who posts their pictures on a personal website, a young girl who posts poetry on her page under the watchful eyes of a parent. In the past historians might have only had fortunate glimpses: in the extremely rare event that a diary was made available to a historian, or if they appeared in the 'letters to the editor' section of a magazine or were interviewed in a community newspaper or fan magazine, or if they had been caught fleetingly in a radio or television interview. These insights into the thoughts and activities of everyday people have been invaluable to social historians, in part because they are so rare within the collections of formal libraries and archives. With GeoCities, what was rare is now common, if a researcher knows how to find it. This is both a challenge and an opportunity.

## A BRIEF HISTORY OF GEOCITIES: FROM RISING STAR TO DEAD WEBSITE

GeoCities.com, like many startups today, had humble beginnings. In November 1994, in Beverly Hills, California, a new service – Beverly Hills Internet – launched. Founded by David Bohnett, a software industry veteran who had just lost his companion, the aim was to create a new service to bring Internet users together. As Bohnett later recalled, 'We all have something to share with each other, which enriches both their lives and ours as well' (Ocamb, 2012). While Beverley Hills Internet was part of a broader trend of site providers including Tripod (1994) and Angelfire (1996), it had a unique focus on community (which I have argued in a separate piece). The name Beverly Hills Internet itself spoke to the geographic metaphors which became integral to the site, a trend which was solidified in its 1995 renaming as GeoCities.

That GeoCities would come to emphasize and stress spatial metaphors was part of a broader trend on the Web of the 1990s, that of the 'frontier', as Fred Turner has argued in his 2008 *From Counterculture to Cyberculture.* While 1960s counterculture adherents had been suspicious of or even hostile to technology – burning punch cards at Berkeley, for example – by the 1980s and 1990s their intellectual successors saw the power of utopian social transformation in technology (Turner, 2008). Notably, this current expressed the belief that the Web, unlike broadcast mediums like the television, could 'put you [the user] in command again' (Turner, 2008). Geographic metaphors additionally helped anchor the web – think of the Electronic Frontier Federation, for example, an early and still significant digital rights group – and GeoCities quickly became promoted as an ever-expanding geographic space.

GeoCities had several unique features, many of which were anchored to its conception of geographic space. Spatial metaphors reigned in the site's very being. The most apparent was the 'neighborhood' structure which was the site's main organizing feature. Rather than a 'vanity address' containing the user's name or preferred word (think of a URL such as http://geocities.com/~historycave), users selected a neighborhood for their site to belong in. These took many shapes and sizes. Some were broad in scope, such as the 'Heartland' neighborhood focusing on 'families, pets, hometown values'. Golf aficionados would go to Augusta; political wonks to the CapitolHill; philosophers, teachers, and book lovers to Athens; LGBT topics were found in WestHollywood; and discussions of technology in ResearchTriangle or SiliconValley. URLs would take the form of http://geocities.com/Heartland/1005, where the site number was a value between 1,000 and 9,999. As GeoCities grew, those site numbers would be exhausted, forcing the creation of suburbs. Heartland, as the largest and most expansive neighborhood, would eventually have 41 suburbs (Heartland/Hills, or Heartland/Plains).

These neighborhoods played a critical role in the life of the community, as I have argued elsewhere (Milligan, 2017). Each area had its own community leaders, volunteers who enforced community standards and taught people the ropes of HTML and site creation, or who ran community newspapers. Webrings (a series of websites that join together in a 'ring' of links so that readers can move between them – i.e. websites on Cairn Terriers that join together so that a visitor can surf between many like-minded pages), awards, and other connecting tendrils also connected these areas as discussed below. In short, the neighborhoods were what held GeoCities together and kept it from just being a collection of parked websites. They were an attempt to cluster users based on pre-existing interests, and to facilitate greater traffic within and throughout the community.

It quickly became successful. A press release in 1995 noted that it had received over 600,000 hits within its first five weeks, and by summer 1995 there were 1,400 websites on board. A succession of press releases underscored the dramatic growth: the first 100,000 by August 1996, and the first million by October 1997. By mid 1998, GeoCities was one of the top ten sites in terms of traffic and was growing by over 18,000 users a day (Motavalli, 2004). In its popularity lay the seeds of its eventual acquisition and downfall. The media promoted GeoCities as a place for people who wanted to join the Web. 'What if you want to do more than just look at live images from Hollywood? What if you want to live there? Now you can', noted *The Independent* newspaper in 1996 (Ridey, 1996). It articulated a vision of the Web that would not just be consumed by most web users, but a place where people could actively contribute.

With users came money. In August 1998, GeoCities went public with an initial offer of $17 a share, which soon rose to $40 a share. Yahoo! purchased GeoCities in January 1999 for $4.6 billion, or a valuation of $117 a share. It was then the third most visited site on the Web, with 55 million page views a day, behind only Yahoo! and AOL (Motavalli, 2004). Yahoo! GeoCities, as the new site was branded, quickly saw rapid change. The neighborhood structure was scrapped for new users, and for this and other reasons the site began to rapidly decline.

We can see how quickly the zeitgeist moved on by looking at media discussions of GeoCities. In 1998 and 1999, the Lexis|Nexis database had 208 and 247 articles respectively on GeoCities; by 2000 there were 20, and by 2003 only seven articles contained that keyword. The Web was quickly moving on from the garish, custom-designed websites of GeoCities. In 2009, Yahoo! decided to shutter GeoCities and delete all user content (save for GeoCities Japan, which continues today). While notice was given, e-mails went to accounts set up in the 1990s. More glaringly, they provided no export tool and users who wanted to save their content had to go page-by-page and preserve them by using their browser's 'save file as' function. Fortunately, the Internet Archive had been preserving this material since 1996 as part of its general archiving of the Web, and it carried out an end-of-life comprehensive crawl of GeoCities. Simultaneously, a team of guerrilla web archivists known as Archive Team carried out a collective effort to download this material. If it had not been for their efforts, there would be no record of GeoCities today.

## ACCESSING A WEB ARCHIVE TODAY

For a scholar interested in studying a collection of sites like GeoCities, they have a number of different ways to approach the problem: from the Wayback Machine, to the end-of-life collection from Archive Team, to more boutique arrangements with the Internet Archive itself. In this, we can see the particularities of GeoCities but also the issues of doing web history more generally.

As Rogers notes in this volume, for most scholars the starting point to working with GeoCities will be the Internet Archive's Wayback Machine (http://archive.org/web/). It provides two ways of working with web archived material. First, if a user knows the exact URL of a resource, they can 'go back in time' to that date. For GeoCities, then, a user would enter 'GeoCities.com', find a date that they are interested in, and select it. Figure 23.1 shows the earliest collected crawl of the GeoCities.com homepage on 22 October 1996. They would then subsequently click on links on the page to temporally browse around the page in October 1996 – as they select a link, the browser will go to the nearest available timestamp for the page requested. Slowly, the user can find the content they are looking for. The website is not fully functional – search functions, for example, will not work nor will any dynamic content. But one can begin to find websites. In the above example, the user could select 'neighborhoods', find the neighborhood of interest, and then begin to look at the pages within one-by-one.

The second option is to use the full-text search option, which explores home pages. Unfortunately, geocities.com is treated as one home page – so searching can only find the splash page. As I will note below, indexing the entirety of GeoCities.com would be challenging so this is an understandable decision taken by the Internet Archive.

The Wayback Machine is invaluable – the catch is actually locating the URLs of pages of interest. These can come from a variety of places: from browsing page-by-page through the Wayback Machine, to finding websites listed in old books or newspapers, or finding sites by other possible means.

Some of these other means of finding websites can come from working with the archive itself, outside of the confines of the Wayback Machine. As a high-profile digital deletion, multiple groups saved GeoCities when Yahoo! announced its 2009 erasure. Archive Team was ready to help save GeoCities, as it had been formed in the wake of the 2008 deletion of AOL Hometown, another early collection of personal websites. Jason Scott, a digital archivist, had called for teamwork to grab files. His December 2008 battle cry is worth quoting at length:

> Fuck the EULAs and the clickthroughs. This is history, you bastards. We're coming in, a team of multiples, and we will utilize Tor [a way to anonymously surf the Web by concealing the origin and destination of web traffic] and scripting and all manner of chicanery and we will dupe the hell out of your dying, destroyed, losing-the-big-battle website and save it for the people who were dumb enough to think you'd last. (Scott, 2009)

In April 2009, when news spread about GeoCities' deletion, Scott and Archive Team sprang into action. Yahoo! limited each downloading computer to 15 megabytes an hour: a limit that a regular user might not encounter, but if you were trying to preserve this material, it meant that many people would have to act in concert to save GeoCities. To make sure that the workload was distributed evenly across hundreds of people, Archive Team had volunteers download and run virtual machines on their own computers – these pre-configured machines could run pre-configured programs, acting in concert with the hundreds of other virtual machines. Archive Team found themselves in a crash course in GeoCities history: figuring out the 'neighborhood' system.

They succeeded in grabbing much of GeoCities before it went down (it is impossible to know just how much). Archive Team, in the end, was not alone in saving this material: a testament to the growing interest in digital preservation and in GeoCities itself. GeoCities was also mirrored by ReoCities, the Internet Archive carried out one last big download, and another website, Internet Archeology, also collected a subset. A year

**Figure 23.1 GeoCities.com from 22 October 1996, via Wayback Machine.**

later, the end-of-life GeoCities crawl was released as a Torrent; at the time, the largest Torrent on the Web, some 643GB of user-generated content. As Scott noted on his blog, this was 'a collection for historians, for researchers, for developers. For those who want to do study on the heritage on something so soon gone and yet so much of a part of how we got here' (Scott, 2011). Today, you can download the 634GB of GeoCities either through the Torrent or via the Internet Archive at https://archive.org/details/2009-archiveteam-geocities-part1. Working with the Torrent is somewhat challenging, as the files are the result of a wget download (wget is a command line tool that can be used to download or mirror websites and other files). It requires boutique sets of scripts or expertise with the command line to wrangle into a useful format.

For many web historians, files in the WARC format are ideal. The Internet Archive also preserved GeoCities at the end of it, and through a research agreement with them our project team at the University of Waterloo was able to get the WARC files. The WARC file format, which is certified by the International Standards Organization, preserves web archived information in a concatenated form. This is useful because if you consider all the material that goes into making a large website possible – the thousands of images, PDFs, Word documents, HTML files, CSS stylesheets, etc. – you would rather have them all in one container, with metadata to help find the information that you need.

The rise of an ISO standard has fortunately enabled the development of an ecosystem of tools to study web archives through WARC files. One such tool that our research team at the University of Waterloo and York University has developed is the Archives Unleashed Toolkit (archivesunleashed.org), or AUT. AUT provides in part for scalable analytics of web archives, and has the goal of being a usable tool for humanists and social scientists without formal computer science training. It allows researchers to do the following four steps: filtering, analyzing, aggregating, and visualizing, or what we term the FAAV cycle. Filtering allows a user to find a particular portion of the web archive – pages within the 'Enchanted Forest', for example, or political party pages that link to a certain domain and contain a particular keyword. Analyzing allows a scholar to extract information, say the hyperlinks from the pages that they have filtered, or find commonly recurring person names. Aggregating allows one to summarize or aggregate the output of the analysis from the previous step. And, finally, visualizing allows them to see results in a table, network graph, or some other form of custom visualization (Lin et al., 2017). This approach can allow the fruitful exploitation of a web archive.

## USING PAGERANK TO FIND SITES OF INTEREST

With so many files, the difficulty is finding which actual pages to explore. There are several different ways to find sites of relevance: using network analysis, specifically by leveraging the power of hyperlinks throughout GeoCities (which I assume to be a deliberate practice), extracting text to explore the various 'topics' that one can find in the collection, and finally by establishing a search engine to find topics of considerable interest. As a starting point for historical inquiry, however, network analysis is the most fruitful (Brügger, 2013).

A useful starting point when doing web history at scale is to find the pages that users tended to link to and visit. Many users wanted others to come to their site, as seen in their guestbooks, hit counters, and beyond. While today web content creators often rely on search engines to drive traffic to pages, links were critical in the 1990s.

Given the frequency of links around GeoCities, I used AUT to extract links from the entire site. The ensuing results were too large, so the first step was to filter (the first step of the FAAV cycle) the results by 'neighborhood'. In this case, I decided to focus on the child-focused Enchanted Forest. I then subsequently analyzed the links, aggregated how often pages linked to each other, and visualized them in Table 23.1 below.

**Table 23.1 Origin and destination links in GeoCities**

| *Origin* | *Destination* | *Number of links* |
|---|---|---|
| http://geocities.com/EnchantedForest/Meadow/1134 | http://www.geocities.com/EnchantedForest/1004 | 83 |
| http://geocities.com/Area51/Stargate/1357 | http://www.geocities.com/Area51/EnchantedForest/4213 | 33 |
| http://geocities.com/Eureka/1309 | http://www.geocities.com/EnchantedForest/Tower/7555 | 27 |

What does the above show? It means that on all of the pages in EnchantedForest/Meadow/1134 – the Enchanted Forest Meadow Community Center (including numerous subpages such as the Meadow newsletter, the webring, the community leader register, etc.), there were 83 links to the EnchantedForest/1004 site – the main community center. Eighty-three links between two community centers is not surprising, given the constant references and affinities.

If this is scaled across the entirety of GeoCities, as a researcher I can begin to see what particular websites had more incoming links and outgoing links, and by using an algorithm called PageRank, we can begin to see which sites would most likely be found during random user adventures around GeoCities. This latter is particularly important because if we begin to rank websites based on these metrics, just relying on the sheer numbers of incoming links as a metric of popularity can be skewed. Link farms, or pages that had lots of outgoing links and little content, existed to 'game' search engines and raise certain sites up in the rankings. PageRank, the core of which powers the Google search engine today, can help us find useful sites. In brief, PageRank is based upon links to other sites, each of which can be considered a 'vote of confidence' in that site. However, these votes are weighted according to the PageRank of the site that is issuing the link, helping us get around shenanigans (Brin and Page, 1998; Kamvar et al., 2003; Rogers, n.d.). For example, a link from *The New York Times* should be worth more than a link from Bob's Random website, and PageRank values the former more than the latter – not due to intrinsically knowing the trustworthiness of *The New York Times*, but because lots of other sites that in turn are linked from highly valued sites link to it.

Let's use one particular example now to outline how I can use link analysis to see these patterns. Consider Figure 23.2 below, which shows the link structure of one neighborhood: the Enchanted Forest.

In this figure, the bigger the dot – or node – the higher the PageRank value. By tracing the bigger nodes in the above visualization (or the spreadsheet that powers it), users can begin to see the sites that had the highest votes of confidence throughout the site. They would be the most likely to be stumbled upon by users.

By exploring them, we see great variety in the highly ranked pages. Some were simply pages by children which managed to achieve a particular impact; more of them, however, were aimed at building community and had themselves baked into the GeoCities infrastructure. Indeed, the commonality across the highly ranked pages was that they had thrown themselves into GeoCities: they received 'awards' from other users, they shared images with other people, they had become 'featured' by the GeoCities administration, and in general they were part of a vibrant ecosystem of pages. The highest-ranked site can be seen in Figure 23.3.

This page was the Enchanted Forest Awards Page (http://web.archive.org/web/20010721183753/http://www.geocities.com/EnchantedForest/Glade/3891/), which gave out the main awards, such as the Enchanted Forest Award of Excellence. A user would go there and apply for an award, and then

**Figure 23.2 The link structure of one GeoCities neighborhood, the Enchanted Forest.**

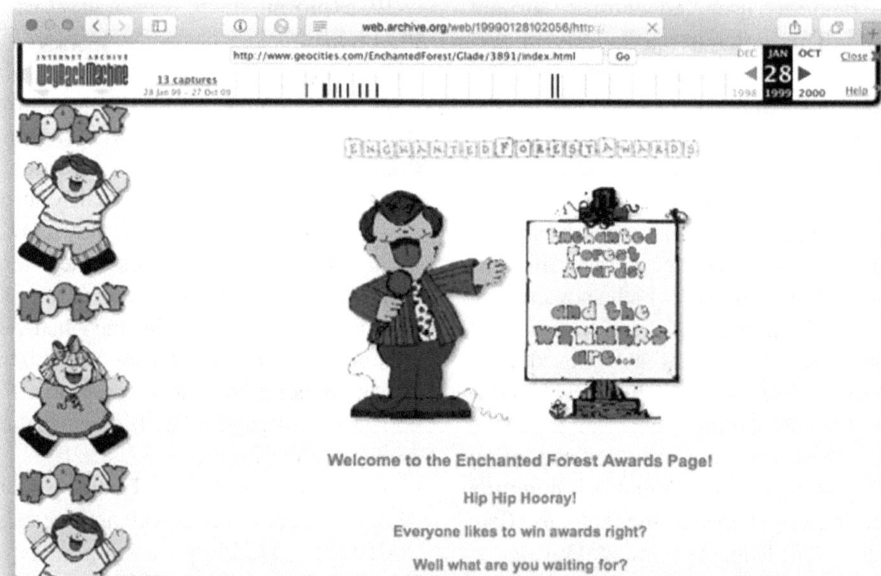


**Figure 23.3 EnchantedForest/Glade/3891 — the highest-ranked site.**

community leaders would visit and review the user's page, and if it met a long list of characteristics the user would receive the award. Other pages that I can find using PageRank include news websites, community centers, and 'cyberpet' images that people would put on their site.

The best use of this PageRank method, however, is to find the individual web pages of children and avid users themselves. The following pages I explore were found by finding highly ranked pages, which had many links to them from other highly linked-to pages. These pages were all written by children who threw themselves into the community fabric of GeoCities, joining webrings, accumulating awards, and having especially active guestbooks. Webrings were one of the most consistent features throughout the Enchanted Forest; our survey of 430 sites found that fully one-quarter of websites were a member of at least one (107 hits, or 24.8%). Other interesting pages from my PageRank exploration run the gamut from those aimed at children, those that built community either through services or award provision, to – of course – those written by children themselves. Let's take one well-connected example. Brandon's page, at Dell/4543, is worth exploring in detail. Like many other websites, it was active until some point in 2001, when it ceased to be updated any further (Brandon was ten years old in April 2001, and his age remained unchanged on the home page until the closure in 2009). His home page was an introduction to himself:

> Hi! My name is Brandon. I am 10 years old. As you can tell from the music, I am a big fan of Star Wars. My hobbies include baseball (I hate that my season is over), football, watching nascar races (my favorite driver is Ernie Ervin), riding my bike, and playing my games. My favorite game on Virtual Boy is Mario Tennis, Sonic and Knuckles on Sega Genesis, Willy Beamish on Sega CD, Teenage Mutant turtles on Super Ninetendo [sic], and Star wars on 32x. When I grow up, I want to be a baseball player. We live in S.C. I would like to hear from you! (https://web.archive.org/web/20010404081732/http://www.geocities.com/EnchantedForest/Dell/4543)

Elsewhere on his page, he had an aquarium page – 'my mom won't let me and my sister have an aquarium … so this is what we came up with' – which was a watery-background page with dozens of animated fish GIFs. He also had other pages, such as one focusing on Batman and another on Spiderman, mostly consisting of pictures and frames from the movies. An extensive Star Wars site makes for interesting viewing as well, connected to many other sites through two webrings that Brandon maintained. More crucially, Brandon also received 36 awards from other users, stretching back to his first award on 31 July 1997: most of these were from other kids on the Web, although some were from adults or others ('Clara's Special Children's Award', which offered 'a prayer for you [and] blessings all year through'). Brandon was part of this ecosystem too, offering his own 'Batman' award that other people could have: they would need to fill out a form to apply for the award, consisting of their name, e-mail address, home page, what it was about, and whether or not they had signed the guestbook. Some 25 people received his award: other kids, 'fellow treasure hunters', Power Rangers or Will Smith fan sites, Peter Pan, and so forth.

Brandon's site was just one of tens of thousands. For many, the sites reflect childhood interests and pastimes, or, in some cases, both. Kim's Pooh place, for example, combined an interest in Winnie the Pooh with online games, prizes, and connectivity. Others just had lots of content. Fans of the Backstreet Boys, expressing excitement at finishing elementary school and beginning high school, guidelines on how to do magic tricks, stories about their favorite country or historical figures (South Africa and Nelson Mandela in one case, Anne Frank in another), and beyond.

This is what we can learn from exploring networks. But we can also use the text contained within GeoCities to garner substantial insights from the historical material that we are exploring.

## TOPIC MODELING: FINDING CLUSTERS OF WORDS IN GEOCITIES

In a recent chapter for the UCL Press anthology *The Web as History*, I explored how we could use various methods to find community within GeoCities. One approach that I used there was topic modeling. This is an approach that finds clusters of words that appear frequently together, or topics (Blei et al., 2003). For example, when we write about our families we use words such as *husband*, *wife*, *kids*, *pets*, and *home*. Or when we write about work we use words such as *productivity*, *office*, *commute*, *pain*, and *boss* (Jockers, 2011). Latent Dirichlet allocation, or topic modeling, uses a sophisticated mathematical algorithm to go through documents and put the words back into the baskets from which they came. A researcher reading e-mails in the future might then see two bags of words: husband, wife, kids, and office, commute, pain and call them home and work, respectively. Without reading individual e-mails, researchers can gain a sense of what the user wrote about.

We can do something similar for GeoCities neighborhoods. In Table 23.2, I explore the top two topics for a specific subset of neighborhoods.

In general, we are seeing that topics appeared in the neighborhoods that they should have. The data demonstrates that such correlation was not universal, however. The Enchanted Forest remained child focused, due in part to the efforts of engaged community leaders in a context of fears around online child exploitation. The Pentagon expanded beyond its initial aim of connecting widely deployed and constantly moving military members: it became a forum for military history and for activism and political discussion (as seen in the two topics highlighted in the table below). Heartland, a significant GeoCities hub, advanced a particular vision of 'family': focused on the Christian faith, domestic issues, and – significantly – genealogy. Topic modeling can only tell us so much, however. Many users want a search engine.

## SEARCHING THE HAYSTACKS: A SEARCH ENGINE ON GEOCITIES

One additional experiment that we did was playing around with search engines. On a

**Table 23.2 Topics in GeoCities**

| *Neighborhood* | *Top two topics in each neighborhood* |
|---|---|
| Athens<br>*'... based on education, teaching, reading, writing, and philosophy'.* | people things time person sense life man work world human good mind soul make nature body case made point<br>part parts goddess witch healing incense witchcraft love energy pagan shaman witches sun spirit protection light circle earth religion |
| EnchantedForest<br>*'A place for and about kids. Games, stories, educational sites, and homepages created by kids themselves'.* | blue page school home day kids clues fun<br>time year room birthday family mom jordan play great party friends<br>jq battalion show st jonny horse battery<br>armored lt artillery camp sailor army field col pingu war area quest |
| Heartland<br>*'A family-oriented neighborhood that represents Main Street in cyberspace. This is the place to find parenting, pets, and home town values'.* | people time children book years child information year work make life school person system state world books government good<br>family county church home years information st city born state war school mrs history birth records great cemetery death |
| Pentagon<br>*Military men and women.* | war people president government american world states power state united general military public soviet political clinton america make army<br>fort war civil island iran world adams army british history badge rhode german french american forts walther cap newport |

corpus of this size, keyword searching is hit and miss. We decided that a search engine based on TF-IDF would help users find pages of particular interest. TF-IDF, or term frequency–inverse document frequency, finds what words make a given document (or in this case, page) special. As a quick example, consider a collection of trial transcripts: the word 'trial' or even 'murder' might not make a document special, but the names of the victim, offender, or location would be things that were unique to it. Accordingly, TF-IDF controls for the fact that some words naturally appear more than others. Our TF-IDF search engine can be seen in Figure 23.4.

Developed by researchers at the University of Waterloo, this search engine allowed us to type in keywords and find the pages that seemed most relevant. Figure 23.4 shows results for a search for 'Canada'. Each page leads to a thumbnail that can be clicked on to bring you right to the page itself. Searches for 'high school' lead to high schools; 'high school Canada' leads to Canadian educational sites, and beyond.

I found that this search engine was a useful complement to the above. By finding

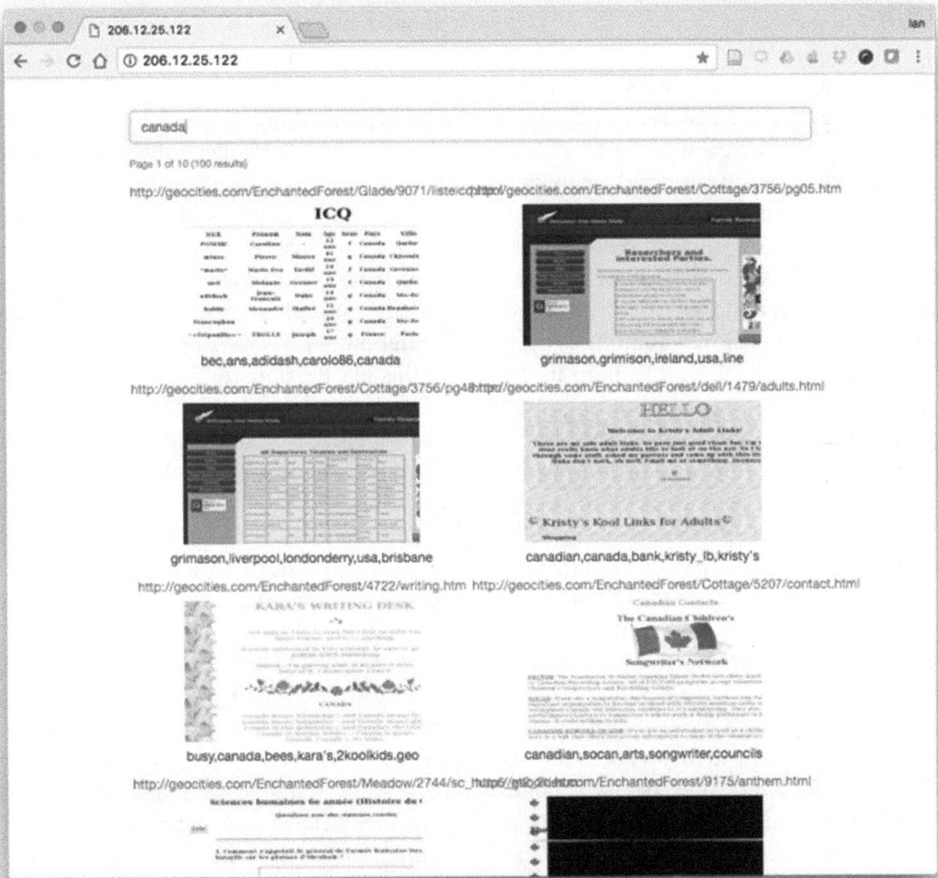


**Figure 23.4 The TF-IDF search engine.**

topics and hubs of interest in the network analysis as well as topic modeling, this led to search topics: 'awards' led to a list of awards pages, 'community leaders' helped find the community hubs, or 'Star Wars' could find those fan pages. But just by starting with the search page, we would not know if it would be worth searching for awards or community hubs. The recommendation I would give would be to begin with network analysis, get a sense of what was in a community, and then to begin to search down by using the search engine itself.

## FROM DISTANT TO CLOSE READING

In some respects, what we have seen above is simply steps to get the historian to the right place for them to do their work. The scale of GeoCities can elude meaningful analysis – you cannot read every page, and even if you could, by the time you finished reading them all it would be difficult to make sense of it all – unless it is filtered down to a subset of information for traditional reading. All of the above examples ultimately help us get a sense of the context surrounding individual pages, which are read closely to tell the actual narratives that a historian wants. Learning the topics and overall link contours helps reveal a 'distant reading' of a web archive, in the sense articulated by literary scholar Franco Moretti. This form of distant reading involves pulling one's gaze back to consider the 'collective system, that should be grasped as such, as a whole', as a result making the individual pages intelligible for the historian (Moretti, 2007: 3–4). Reading one or two pages could be misleading; reading thousands to see the overall shape of the archive can give us insights into the entire system as well as the individual documents themselves.

At the end of the process, one needs to ensure that they are able to reach the sites themselves: that a historian can read the actual web page (close reading) but that they understand how they would find it. The methods described above all facilitate reproducible and understandable research methods: using hyperlink analysis to find pages of interest with open-source platforms and well-documented algorithms; exploring the text of pages using well-traveled text-analysis algorithms like TF-IDF; or finding particular facets of the pages such as images in the case of GifCities.

With the 186 million pages within GeoCities, one could find anything to prove any narrative that they wanted to: pages about cats, dogs, particular fashion trends, or developments in web archives. Traditional archives had a selection process, and by virtue of something being kept in a national library or special collections there was a significance test passed; the same is not true with web archives, as pages like GeoCities contain millions of documents that never would have been preserved under traditional appraisal criteria. Indeed, archival theory is an uneasy bedfellow with web archives (Bailey, 2013). In this lies the opportunity to explore the lives of everyday people and their records, but also the challenge of abundance. It also makes it all the more important to understand the *context* of the documents that a historian is looking at.

Just because it is in the GeoCities web archive does not mean that it is important, as it must be contextualized. Is a website one of a kind? Is it representative? Is it influential? Is it marginal? All of the above questions matter when reading the document. They matter when working with traditional archival documents too, of course, but at the scale of a web archive – and the fact that more information was kept without formal selection criteria – they are even more important. Yet just because it is in GeoCities does not mean, as this chapter has sought to show, that it is not important.

## CONCLUSIONS

Everyday people, in general, did not leave behind information about their everyday lives. While epistemologically true in the age of web archives, the changing scale of preservation of information about interactions on the Web has changed this in absolute numbers. We are now confronted with millions of sources produced by everyday people in the course of their days: pages about their hobbies, their childhoods, their schools, their favorite sports teams, even the minutiae of daily life. Yet what seems so liberating about this shift – historical abundance – also presents challenges as we begin to experience the problems of abundance.

GeoCities.com bears this out. This chapter has demonstrated that, through sites like GeoCities, we have the ability to find more democratic histories of the past: histories that include the voices of everyday people who just happened to have a website in the late 1990s, and what that means for the historian's craft. Using GeoCities as a case study, it has also demonstrated one computational approach to studying the past: from leveraging hyperlinks, to exploring topics in text, to text-ranking algorithms like TF-IDF to find the information that a historian might want. By moving between the levels of close and distant reading, this helps us understand the tools and approaches that a historian might need to take. There are many other questions that a historian might ask of GeoCities, and this has just scratched the surface. But it hopefully suggests one path forward.

## REFERENCES


Aiden, E., and Michel, J.B. (2013) *Uncharted: Big Data as a Lens on Human Culture*. New York: Riverhead.

Bailey, J. (2013) 'Disrespect des Fonds: Rethinking Arrangement and Description in Born-Digital Archives', *Archive Journal* (http://www.archivejournal.net/essays/disrespect-des-fonds-rethinking-arrangement-and-description-in-born-digital-archives/).

Barnet, B. (2013) *Memory Machines: The Evolution of Hypertext*. London: Anthem Press.

Blei, D.M., Ng, A.Y., and Jordan, M.I. (2003) 'Latent Dirichlet Allocation', *Journal of Machine Learning Research*, 3: 993–1022.

Brin, S., and Page, L. (1998) 'The Anatomy of a Large-Scale Hypertextual Web Search Engine', paper presented at the Seventh International World-Wide Web Conference, Brisbane, Australia.

Brügger, N. (2013) 'Historical Network Analysis of the Web', *Social Science Computer Review*, 31(3): 306–321.

Gleick, J. (2012) *The Information: A History, A Theory, A Flood*. New York: Vintage.

Graham, S., Milligan, I., and Weingart, S. (2015) *Exploring Big Historical Data: The Historian's Macroscope*. London: Imperial College Press.

Jockers, M.L. (2011) The LDA Buffet is Now Open; or, Latent Dirichlet Allocation for English Majors (http://www.matthewjockers.net/2011/09/29/the-lda-buffet-is-now-open-or-latent-dirichlet-allocation-for-english-majors/). Accessed 18 July 2013.

Kamvar, S., Haveliwala, T., Manning, C., and Golub, G. (2003) 'Exploiting the Block Structure of the Web for Computing PageRank' (http://ilpubs.stanford.edu:8090/579/). Accessed 22 June 2018.

Lin, J., Milligan, I., Wiebe, J., and Zhou, A. (2017) 'Warcbase: Scalable Analytics Infrastructure for Exploring Web Archives', *ACM Journal of Computing and Cultural Heritage*, 10(4): 22:2–22:29.

Milligan, I. (2017) 'Welcome to the Web: The Online Community of GeoCities and the Early Years of the World Wide Web', in N. Brügger and R. Schroeder (Eds.), *The Web as History*. London: UCL Press. pp. 137–158.

Moretti, F. (2007) *Graphs, Maps, Trees: Abstract Models for Literary History*. New York: Verso.

Motavalli, J. (2004) *Bamboozled at the Revolution: How Big Media Lost Billions in the Battle for the Internet*. New York: Penguin.

Ocamb, K. (2012) 'David Bohnett: Social Change Through Community Commitment', *Frontiers*, 18.

Old Bailey Proceedings Online. (2013) Old Bailey Online – The Proceedings of the Old Bailey, 1674–1913 (http://www.oldbaileyonline.org/). Accessed 22 June 2018.

Ridey, R. (1996) 'Roger Widey travels under the volcano, and also discovers a Web full of creepy-crawlies', *The Independent*, 15.

Rogers, I. (n.d.) 'Pagerank Explained Correctly with Examples' (http://www.cs.princeton.edu/~chazelle/courses/BIB/pagerank.htm). Accessed 20 April 2016.

Rosenzweig, R. (2003) 'Scarcity or Abundance? Preserving the Past in a Digital Era', *American Historical Review*, 108(3): 735–762.

Scott, J. (2011) 'The Geocities Torrent: Patched and Posted' (http://ascii.textfiles.com/archives/3046). Accessed 22 June 2018.

Scott, J. (2009) 'Datapocalypso' (http://ascii.textfiles.com/archives/1649). Accessed 13 June 2014.

Turner, F. (2008) *From Counterculture to Cyberculture: Stewart Brand, the Whole Earth Network, and the Rise of Digital Utopianism*. Chicago: University of Chicago Press.

# 24

# Blogs

Ignacio Siles

The emergence of the blog (originally known as 'weblog') constitutes one of the most important developments in the history of the Web. Perhaps more than any other practice, blogging embodied widespread ideas about the potential of the Web for self-expression at the turn of the twenty-first century. By the mid 2000s, blogs were the icon of the 'Web 2.0' discourse, the key example that revealed the dynamic nature of the Web, the new kind of business models it entailed, and the challenge the Web posed to social institutions such as the mainstream media (O'Reilly, 2005). More recently, blogs have played a crucial role in helping to conceptualize the emergence and development of other Web technologies. The term 'microblogging', typically employed to label technologies such as Tumblr and Twitter, suggests that the relationship between blogs and other Web artifacts is of continuity and refinement. In this sense, the history of the blog encapsulates the history of the Web as a technology for self-performance.

Scholars have historicized blogging in several ways. Some studies have situated blogs within the wide history of practices and technologies that predate them. The main insight from this strand of research is that the blog's most defining features and use practices can be traced back to multiple sources (Herring et al., 2005; Miller and Shepherd, 2004). Another line of work has investigated how blogs acquired a recognizable set of characteristics at the end of the 1990s (Blood, 2002; Lovink, 2011; Siles, 2012a). Ammann (2009) thus studied the role played by Jorn Barger in the rise of an early group of users. Other scholars have investigated how, after its origins in a close community of practitioners, blogging was widely adopted in a variety of fields. For example, Rosenberg (2009) discussed how blogging developed into political and commercial phenomena. Finally, there has been a growing interest in documenting the specific configurations that the development of blogging has acquired in national settings (Locatelli, 2014; Moe, 2011;

Russell and Echchaibi, 2009; Weltevrede and Helmond, 2012).

This chapter contributes to this body of work by tracing how blogs emerged, stabilized, and developed in the United States from the mid 1990s to the present day. I focus on the United States not only because blogging emerged there but also because of the significance that the country has played in shaping an imaginary around blogging that has been influential in other contexts.[1] Although negotiated in important ways, the evolution of blogging in the United States provided Web users and developers in other parts of the world with a framework for making sense of the cultural meaning of this practice (Siles, 2017). This is not to suggest that the international uptake of blogging has been uniform. As Russell and Echchaibi (2009) remind us, blogging 'is being conceptualized differently in distinct cultural contexts. A blog can be more things that we are presently imagining, a vehicle of democratic expression, yes, but also a means to revive tradition, to explore identity, [or] to conduct public relations' (2009: 8). The role of blogging in non-liberal democracies or during major political events attests to the importance of this remark.

To account for this historical process, I draw on the theory of 'articulation', or the notion that meanings are partially established through the connection between elements with no necessary relation, such as 'values, feelings, beliefs, practices, structures, organizations, [and] ideologies' (Slack, 2006: 225). I argue that the identities of blogs in the United States developed as Web users and software developers established links between certain kinds of websites, metaphors, and practices of content creation. This approach allows me to depart from a 'heroic innovators approach', that is, the idea that 'behind every successful innovation in human endeavor is likely a champion, an articulate visionary, an inventor perhaps at the margins of the social institutions of the day' (Neuman, 2010: 8). Thus, rather than focusing on events and figures, I make my focus the historical *processes* that these important cases illustrate.

I begin by examining how blogs emerged in the second half of the 1990s. I look at how blogs absorbed the identities of other existing websites and content-creation practices on the Web. The result was the stabilization of blogs as a malleable 'format' for sharing an expansive variety of content types.[2] Second, I analyze the evolution of blogs in the early years of the new millennium. It was during this period that practitioners in the United States and abroad adopted blogs in a variety of ways and began speaking of sub-types of blogs, as opposed to the generic format that characterized the early days. I also illustrate how users adopted blogs internationally through the example of France. Third, I discuss how technologies created in the second half of the 2000s that sought to replace or extend blogging came to be associated with the notion of 'microblogging'. The final remarks bring this chapter to a close by discussing recent evolutions in the history of blogs. I argue that blogs are 'paradigmatic' in the sense that they shaped the terms for understanding the history of the Web as a technology for self-performance.

My historical analysis draws on a mixed-methods research design conducted in two countries: the United States and France.[3] The study on which this chapter is based integrated findings from 105 interviews with Web users, software developers, investors, entrepreneurs, commentators, and analysts, among others (conducted between 2009 and 2014); traditional archival research and Web archival techniques; both content and material analyses of a sample of websites; ethnographic participation in meetings of Web users and developers; and visits to numerous software companies and organizations that have appropriated blogs.

## CREATING A FORMAT FOR SELF-PERFORMANCE ON THE WEB

In December 1997, Jorn Barger started *Robot Wisdom*, a website devoted to sharing annotated hyperlinks to other sites on the Web. This computer programmer referred to his new project as a 'weblog' or 'a daily running log of the best webpages I visit', as he described it in an online forum one week after its launch (Barger, 1997b). In his first post, Barger reflected on information about gangs in Chicago and linked to another site where his readers could discover 'a ton of details – names, symbols, alliances – you never see anywhere else' (Barger, 1997a). Barger was not shy about making predictions about the impact his new online venture would have and invited other Web users to join the inescapable expansion of weblogs. In his words, 'I suspect that in a year there'll be hundreds of people maintaining pages like this, and that this will allow good URLs to spread much more quickly' (Barger, 1997b).

In the following months, several users fulfilled Barger's prophecy. Throughout 1998, many Web users created their own weblogs, sharing comments and hyperlinks to other online sources. By 1999, blogs caught the attention of the mainstream media. Journalist Scott Rosenberg (1999) maintained that '[the] phenomenon known as the weblog is one of the fastest-growing and most fertile creative areas on the Web today'. Press articles like this one illustrate the growth of this online activity in a short period of time. By 1999, users and journalists recognized the blog as a specific type of website with a defining set of features.

How did the blog gain a relatively stable identity as a specific kind of website? To make this happen, users began by creating patterns of similarity between certain existing websites. Throughout 1997 and 1998, several Web users identified sites that seemed to share various characteristics. Male individuals related to the technology development field, such as software producers, computer programmers, and Web designers, created most of these websites. These sites were characterized by features such as relatively short comments on recent news about technology, the Internet, and Web design. They were also full of hyperlinks that pointed to other sources of information online. Bill Humphries, a programmer and early user, recalls, 'The early mindset of [users] was to find interesting things and link to them. It was description or comment and link' (interview with author, 2009).

Users posted the most recent information in reverse chronological order to make content easier to read for others. According to Wesley Felter, a software developer and early weblog user, 'The idea was that someone was coming to read the weblog every day, and they wanted to see what's new since yesterday, so [we would] put the more interesting or more important links at the top' (interview with author, 2009). These sites also included a menu that linked the most recent entries to other sections of the website, options for allowing readers to configure the site's color scheme, automated search functions of keywords, archives of older posts, and mechanisms for sharing a link with the creator of the site.

To conceptualize what they considered to be similar kinds of websites, users employed a variety of metaphors. For example, Jorn Barger highlighted their role in the distillation of the Web's content: 'We vacuum the Net for stories that the major outlets haven't noticed yet, and pass along our sources so we can all get more and more efficient at this vacuuming' (Barger, 1998). Other users also employed the notion of 'pre-surfing' the Web for readers (Graham, 1998).

Another dynamic of articulation that shaped the emergence of blogs was the adoption of a name to identify websites that shared this common set of traits. Throughout 1998, a set of competing names circulated among users. A small group of users adopted Barger's weblog concept. But this term was only one among other possibilities. Some users, for the most part associated with a community of developers that coalesced around a software named Frontier, had been naming these sites 'news pages' since at least 1997. This term described websites created with Frontier, organized in reverse chronological order, and devoted to sharing news, comments, and hyperlinks to other Web sources mostly about technology issues. Another common name at the time was 'microportals', defined by one of its advocates as 'indy [sic] sites that change all the time [usually] run by one person, or a small group. Most of them belong to presurfers, or people who find links and share the best with others. Other sites are newsfeeds' (Wallace, cited in Siles, 2017). Finally, other names included 'filters' – inspired by an influential website created by a Web developer named Michael Sippey that included a section called *The Filter* (later named *Filtered for Purity*) – or simply 'personal websites' or 'homepages'.

The weblog became the standard name mostly because influential users (such as Barger and others) employed it as an articulatory concept to link existing approaches to Web publishing. By the end of 1998 and beginning of 1999, many users began referring to their websites as weblogs. In February 1999, Pete Prodoehl (1999), an early Frontier user, wrote: 'I didn't even know this site was a "weblog," but now I do ....' Similarly, in May 1999, John SJ Anderson (1999), a molecular biologist who created a site in 1998, announced: 'I've decided: GeneHack is now a web log, as opposed to the mess o' links that I previously thought of it as'. In addition to a common set of traits, this group of websites were now also linked by a common name. This name got shortened after one user, Peter Merholz, announced early in 1999 his decision to pronounce it as 'wee-blog' or 'blog'.

Throughout 1999, users implemented different means to communicate with other practitioners. Early references to a small set of 'sites like mine' evolved into recurrent allusions to a 'weblog community'. Certain users played a crucial role in the formation of this sense of community. According to Ammann (2009), Jorn Barger 'shaped the concept of the weblog community [...] by setting a prolific and inspiring example in his *Robot Wisdom Weblog* and by meticulously crediting his fellow practitioners in its pages' (2009: 284). Online forums were also a key dynamic of community building. In July 1999, Web developer Matt Haughey launched *MetaFilter*, a 'community weblog', that is, a blog updated by multiple users. According to Haughey, *MetaFilter* sought to crystallize the sense of community arising from interactions between early weblog users (interview with author, 2011). By early 2000, this site had become a central site of discussion for many users. In August 1999, Barger also created a mailing list for weblog users that was established as an important mechanism to build a sense of community between them.

The constitution of this community involved a parallel process of identity formation by which members of this group conceived of themselves as representative figures of a particular type of Internet user, expressed by concepts such as the Web's 'pre-surfer' or the 'weblogger' (Siles, 2012b). Establishing a distinction between 'webloggers' and 'online diarists' allowed the former to further define themselves as a community. As participants of the technology and Internet development fields, early bloggers knew a variety of programing languages and technical skills. Users envisioned these skills as a marker of identity and a source of differentiation with respect to other users who coded their sites in HTML (most notably online diarists). This sense of community led to various efforts to meet in person. A memorable gathering of early bloggers took place in March 2000, at the South by Southwest conference. During this event, many users met each other in person for the first time and discussed in roundtables and informal conversations the possibilities and limitations of blogs.

In the final years of the 1990s, more users began appropriating blogs for a variety of purposes (Siles, 2011). A key factor in making this possible was the emergence of automated software. Unlike Frontier, which was 'an integrated development environment for building and managing [...] websites [devised for] a webmaster or web developer with experience in system-level scripting'

(Winer, 1996), these new tools were specifically designed for a wide audience interested in automating the process of publishing a website. Andrew Smales released software for blogging called Pitas in July 1999 and, four months later, Diaryland for online diarists. Paul Kedrosky, a business school professor, launched Groksoup in August 1999. In San Francisco, a company named Pyra launched an automated Web application called Blogger in August 1999.

As users kept creating more and different content and software programs standardized these sites' features, a notion gained traction that defined blogs as a 'format' suited 'for publishing all kinds of information on the Web', as Evan Williams, one of the developers behind Blogger, described it (from an interview in Turnbull, 2002: 83). Users and software developers utilized the notion of 'format' to suggest that blogs were a content-agnostic medium (Siles, 2011). Meg Hourihan (2002), a co-creator of Blogger, suggested, 'What we write about does not define us as bloggers; it's how we write about it (frequently, ad nauseam, peppered with links)'. In this way, users shifted the focus of blogging from a singular end to the necessary means for creating, storing, and sharing various content online. 'Format' also tied the blog to the notion of *genre*, a particular arrangement of technological features crystallized in standardized software templates. Finally, 'format' designated the *size* of the blog as a publication outlet, which users and software developers described as being in opposition to the 'page paradigm'. Blogs, they argued, revolved around the 'post', a unique, smaller unit for producing meaning. In this way, by the end of the 1990s, blogs had gained a new identity as a malleable means for publishing on the Web.

## THE PROLIFERATION OF BLOGGING

In the early years of the new millennium, the identities of blogs proliferated, that is, they multiplied quantitatively and transformed qualitatively. The generic concept of the blog format that characterized the early days was gradually replaced by the notion that blogging had a multiplicity of sub-types: the 'news blog', the 'political blog', the 'video blog', the 'gadget blog', the 'fashion blog'… The identity of blogging was thus re-articulated: practitioners established a set of different connections between the blog format and other practices, metaphors, and meanings. Several factors worked as conditions of possibility for these re-articulations: the availability of software programs that afforded new, specific content-creation practices; transformations in the daily life of actors; and larger economic, political, and cultural processes. In particular, neoliberalization infused these re-articulations as it provided a framework for making sense of the purpose and nature of blogging. Users and software developers thus re-articulated blogs as a response to these factors.[4]

By making visible these factors, it becomes easier to understand how and why some of the most popular kinds of blogging developed. Thus, although in this chapter I focus particularly on the examples of 'news blogging' and 'political blogging', the goal is to provide an account of the *process* through which multiple blogging identities emerged. I concentrate on these cases because of how they captured public imagination in the early years of the 2000s in the United States. I also discuss briefly the case of France as an example of how the evolution of blogging acquired an international flavor.

The proliferation of blogging in the first years of the new millennium built on the availability of automated software that envisioned blogs as a 'blank canvas', as software developer Meg Hourihan described them (interview with author, 2009). In contrast to early popular applications, such as Blogger, these new programs required an installation on the user's server. Noah Grey thus described the creation of a software program named Greymatter in late 2000: 'I simply wanted to give myself more control and organization. [...] I couldn't find another tool to do what I wanted to do, so I wrote my own' (interview with author, 2012). In a similar manner, developer Mena Trott (n.d.) narrated the design of a popular software program named Movable Type as a tale of experimentation.

For users, the availability of novel software programs created fertile grounds for new content-creation practices that shaped significantly the identities of blogs. For example, these tools naturalized the post with several paragraphs as an important part of blogging. According to Tom Coates, a key figure in the development of blogging in the UK:

> When it started, [Blogger] was a box you could type stuff into and press the button. And then Moveable Type came on. And the first implication [...] was that people felt much more compelled to write a lot of things. It's like, 'I've got to write; I've got a whole page just sitting there!' I certainly felt the pressure to write more and more intelligently. (interview with author, 2011)

In addition to the transformation of software, the context of blogging changed at the turn of the century. The early days of blogging had been a fruitful period for self-exploration (Siles, 2011). But the political moment changed in the early years of the new millennium in ways that made it necessary for users to share their voice online. A key example of this was the appropriation of blogs as a mechanism to intervene in public life and make the voices of citizens heard in society (a practice originally known as 'warblogging' and then 'political blogging') (Welch, 2002). The context of this phenomenon was the aftermath of 9/11 and the US invasion of Afghanistan. To give an opinion about these events became pressing for people who felt they had no place to go other than the Web. According to Jerome Armstrong, an activist who created a website named *MyDD* (*My Due Diligence*) in 2001, and Markos ('Kos') Moulitsas Zúniga, a journalist and political scientist who built his own site (*Daily Kos*) in 2002, 'Both of us started our blogs because we wanted a voice in our nation's politics' (2006: vi–vii). Seen in this way, blogging was a response to significant events in the life of actors and larger cultural, political, and social processes.

According to these users, the political and economic climate of the early 2000s made it imperative to transform the public sphere outside of established power centers, notably the mainstream media. This required a capacity to translate the analysis of current events into an opinion and perspective that could contribute to democratic life (Walton, 2004). The privileged notion to conceptualize the product of these practices was the 'blogosphere'. It is possible to trace this notion back to 1999, when Brad Graham, an avid early user, deployed it half-jokingly to characterize the sense of community that was forming among blogging practitioners. In the early years of the 2000s, it was used in all seriousness to suggest that blogging embodied a possibility to reach the Habermasian ideal of the public sphere, that is, a symbolic space where citizens could meet to deliberate rationally about public affairs (Habermas, 1989). In the case of blogs, this was interpreted as the formation of a network of websites exchanging opinions and news to monitor the state and change politics from the bottom up.

Against the background of a crisis of legitimacy experienced by traditional institutions and organizations such as the state, the mainstream media, political parties, and large enterprises, actors from these organizations began exploring the world of blogging with the hope to reconnect with citizens. Already in 1999, James Romenesko, a journalist who covered technology news at the *St. Paul Pioneer Press*, had created a website to aggregate news called *Media Gossip*. 'My goal', he recalls, 'was to try to find things, journalism items, that most readers would not find on their own, and that meant going to some more obscure publications and media criticisms' (interview with author, 2009). In a similar manner, technology journalist Dan Gillmor started a column in October 1999 as a weblog at the *San Jose Mercury News*. He appropriated blogs to expand the content of his newspaper columns. Based on the experiences of these precursors, early in the new century newspapers began blogging as they sought to bring transparency to their inner workings and thus provide a solution to the crisis of legitimacy (Nielsen, 2012). These efforts came to be known as 'news blogs', By the mid 2000s, news organizations had gradually institutionalized these practices and expectations.

The invention of 'news blogs' and 'political blogs' posed a singular challenge: to generate a steady income to turn blogging into a full-time activity. During the early years of the new millennium, users began experimenting with ways to generate this income, notably by inviting readers to donate to their sites and implementing various advertising regimes. Underlying these efforts was a transformation of the identity of blogging. Rather than being hailed as the 'soapbox' of the 'John and Jane Does of the Net' (Yahoo! Internet Life, 2002: 57–8), as an outlet described them at the turn of the century, blogs were re-articulated as a commodity. This, in turn, required re-imagining the blogger as the digital avatar of the neoliberal entrepreneur.

Henry Copeland, a journalist and consultant, emphasized the need for a new economic model to highlight the entrepreneurial dimension of blogging. He defined it as 'blogonomics': 'a model of economic and informational collaboration through cross linking that creates ad hoc networks and communities' (interview with author, 2012). Thus, according to Copeland (2002), bloggers were better described as 'idea entrepreneurs, living in a clickocracy, risking their time and passion on writing'. Such a conception would 'enable hundreds of thousands of new idea entrepreneurs to carve out local, ideological or conceptual niches and make a living'. Projects to turn blogs into profitable ventures and enterprises, such as *Gawker* (2003), *The Huffington Post* (2005), and Weblogs, Inc. (2003), were outcomes of this larger process of commodification. In this way, blogs became 'enterprise solutions [...] [and] empires of nano-publishing', as UK blogger Tom Coates (2003) put it.

To be sure, the proliferation of blogging was not exclusive to the United States (Russell and Echchaibi, 2009). The case of France illustrates how certain notions about blogging coalesced into an imaginary that acquired particular flavors worldwide (Siles, 2017). Like in the United States, the blog absorbed the identities of early websites in France, most notably the *page perso* (short for personal page), the quintessential embodiment of self-performance on the 1990s French Web. This was a generic term used to describe websites where users discussed their passions and interests. By mid 2001, some users were debating intensively about the success of blogs in the United States and how it could be replicated in France. A computer scientist named Stéphane Gigandet thus reflected: 'Weblogs may be a triumph in the United States, but in the French-speaking world, they are in their infancy' (Gigandet, 2001a). The following day, Gigandet (2001b) published an essay to argue for the need to Frenchify blogs: in his view, they represented an opportunity to revive self-performance practices that had given life to sites like *pages persos*.[5]

It is difficult to overstate the excitement that the discovery of blogs caused among Web users in France over the following years. This was not lost on the international press. *The New York Times* noted in 2006, 'Already famed for angry labor strikes and philosophical debates in smoke-filled cafés, the French have now brought these passions online to become some of the world's most intensive bloggers. The French distinguish themselves, both statistically and anecdotally, ahead of Germans, Britons and even Americans in their obsession with blogs' (Crampton, 2006).

By the mid 2000s, ideas about the political potential of blogging, largely advanced in the United States, gained wide notoriety in France. These ideas emphasized the possibilities afforded by blogging to shape the public sphere outside of traditional power centers. Early users appropriated the American imaginary around blogging as a solution to a very French problem: the proximity between journalists in the mainstream media and the political elite. 'Just like the 2004 campaign in the United States', wrote Pô and Vanbremeersch (2007), 'the 2007 campaign in France signal[ed] the rise and structuration of [a] new political space' (2007: 155). This new political space, users argued, could now be occupied by 'ordinary' citizens. Like in the United States, although at a slower pace, the appropriation of blogs in France was also characterized by commodification and neoliberalization dynamics. As the decade progressed, actors in France argued more explicitly for defining the blogger as an entrepreneur and defining the blogosphere as a marketplace of attention (Le Meur and Beauvais, 2005).

Rosenberg (2009) argues that, since the early 2000s, 'blogging has fragmented [...]: there are not just craft bloggers, but whole cadres of knitting bloggers and weaving bloggers; not just foodie bloggers, but beer bloggers and sushi bloggers. [...] Each subculture has its own norms of behavior' (2009: 263–4). It is these blogging 'subcultures' that have captured public attention since the mid 2000s. For example, referring to one specific 'fashion blog', a writer in *The New York Times* stated in 2017: 'It paved the way for the fast fashion news cycle, creating an appetite for trade sites [...] [and] catwalk images [...]. For better or for worse, it was instrumental in the democratization of fashion as we know it' (Taylor, 2017).

Underlying this evolution of blogging into a matter of 'subcultures', 'niches', or 'communities' are the factors outlined above: the availability of software to enact specific blog sub-types; transformations in the daily life of actors; and larger economic, political, and cultural processes. The promises of combining the cultural force of blogging and an entrepreneurial spirit – borrowing the expression from Boltanski and Chiapello (1999) – is the drive behind most sub-types of blogging that have emerged since the mid 2000s: 'mommy blogs', 'video blogs', and 'fashion blogs', to name a few. These phenomena need to be situated within a context marked by the prevalence of a cultural discourse – or a subject position – that compels users to think of themselves as neoliberal entrepreneurs who forge market transactions with others online (Duffy and Hund, 2015).

## THE INVENTION OF 'MICROBLOGGING'

By the mid 2000s, developers built a set of technologies that came to be defined as 'social network sites' and 'microblogging' tools. Although instances of these kinds of applications can be found from the initial days of Web-based automated software, it wasn't until the mid to late 2000s that these services (and notions) stabilized.

These tools sought to both capture early blogging practices and enable new conceptions of what it meant to be in public online. In the months that followed the creation of tools such as Twitter and Tumblr, a specific concept emerged to refer to these applications and link (or articulate) them together: 'microblogging' (Waters and Nuttall, 2007). Before 2007, the term 'microblog' was occasionally used as a synonym of 'niche blog', a site devoted to discussing a specific topic (Rowan, 2003). Commentators also employed the notion of 'miniblog' to describe blogs about specific topics that were incorporated within larger websites (Faler, 2005). But as artifacts such as tumblelogs, Jaiku, and Twitter further stabilized by early 2007, the term 'microblogging' acquired a specific definition.

The notion of 'microblogging' played an articulatory role in several important ways. It enabled its proponents to bring together a group of technologies that had no necessary relation.[6] The possibility to publish short-form content functioned as the glue that tied these technologies together. As a concept, 'microblogging' also allowed advocates to link the blogging imaginary and this group of technologies. In this sense, the term 'micro-blogging' worked to suggest that blogging had been 'remediated' (Bolter and Grusin, 1999). David Karp, the creator of Tumblr, defined both Tumblr and Twitter as 'blogging that favors short-form data' (from an interview in Gwinn, 2007). Evan Williams, a co-developer of both Blogger and Twitter, argued that these tools were linked by an ontological property of the Web. He claimed: '[Twitter is] like we'll take blogging, we'll take out all these features and we'll limit the size of the post and that will be a whole thing. [...] [It] is like a molecule that is everywhere' (cited in Moggridge, 2010: 278). In this view, 'microblogging' technologies allowed blogging to be re-imagined in new ways.

Underlying these assertions was the belief that blogging required a major transformation to maintain its relevance in a shifting Web ecology. A post called *The Huffington Post is Not a Blog*, written by Jorn Barger – the programmer who coined the term 'weblog' in 1997 – aptly captures the dissatisfaction of some users about the commodification of blogs. Barger (2005) maintained: '[I] was distressed to discover that the original intent of the expression "web logging" (to log your websurfing with public annotations) has gone entirely by the boards'. Specifically, Barger criticized the notions of 'niche blog' and 'blog aggregators' illustrated by blog networks such as *The Huffington Post*.

For other users, blogs had standardized in unproductive ways and, at the center of this standardization, were unnecessarily long posts and certain technological features made to enable such form of writing. In the words of Tumblr's creator:

> The blogosphere [...] had matured to a place where it was really designed for editorial publishing. Everything after Movable Type had a title, several paragraphs of text, a footer, a permalink page with comments [...] but something that I really wanted out of my website, out of my blog, was much more freeform. (From an interview in Schonfeld, 2011)

In his view, the solution to this problem came in the form of the short post.

The invention 'microblogging' thus rested on the belief in the need for simplifying self-performance on the Web. This drive towards simplicity must be interpreted as an expression of a wider cultural concern with complexity (Maeda, 2006). By simplicity, software developers typically referred to the size of posts, the speed at which they could be made available to others, and minimalism in technological design. In short, simplicity meant reducing the number of technological features to the minimum required to enable social interaction (Siles, 2013). According to Evan Henshaw-Plath, one of the original developers of Twitter, during the creation of the tool 'there was a discussion about what you could strip away. [...] What [was] the simplest thing that [could] possibly work as opposed to what [was] featured complete?' (interview with author, 2011). These conceptions of simplicity found cultural resonance. In the media, 'microblogging' technologies were typically associated with notions of speed, simplicity, originality, purity, brevity, and minimalism (Glaser, 2007; Gwinn, 2007).

As the 2000s came to an end, the 'micro-blogging' notion reached the status of a keyword. For Williams (1983), keywords 'are significant, indicative words in certain forms of thought [that] bound together certain ways of seeing culture and society' (1983: 15). As such, the concept functioned to fill what seemed like a semantic void created by the availability of software programs that extended the history of blogs through the prism of simplicity. However, the 'microblogging' keyword was not accepted unanimously. Some blatantly rejected it and the assumptions on which the term relied. These critics contended that 'microblogging' was a vague and imprecise word with no major conceptual value that tended to freeze what were fluid and dynamic processes of technological design and appropriation (Selvitelle, 2008).

## A HISTORY OF NOW

The rise of 'microblogging' and 'social network sites' technologies has led to a reassessment of the place of blogging in the contemporary Web ecology. Far from a linear evolution, this can be conceptualized a site of struggle. From this perspective, reconsiderations of blogging can be situated within a spectrum of positions that range from those who construe the rise of 'microblogging' as a threat to those who envision it instead as a spring of new possibilities for blogging and the Web.

For some, the rise of 'microblogging' technologies has signaled the imminence of the blog's demise. In this view, the gradual commodification and standardization of blogging killed the merits of this practice. Nicholas Carr (2008), for example, argued that blogs had 'become mainstream' and thus 'lost much of their original personality'. Instead, these commentators emphasize the virtues of simplicity and the technologies that enable it. *Wired*'s Boutin (2008) thus asked: '[W] hy bother [blogging]? The time it takes to craft sharp, witty blog prose is better spent expressing yourself on Flickr, Facebook, or Twitter'.

An alternative position in the struggle for establishing the blog's contemporary meaning comes from users and developers, who argue for hybrids between both blogging and 'microblogging'. In their view, the materiality of software programs makes this combination come to fruition in productive ways. Thus, blogging is not about to perish because of 'microblogging' but can be reinvigorated instead by integrating 'microblogging' into its defining set of technologies and practices.

Finally, some actors justify the importance of blogging by emphasizing its renewed singularity in the Web ecology. This view posits fundamental differences between blogging and 'microblogging' – as both technologies and practices – but argues for reconciling them rather than keeping them apart. Blogging and 'microblogging' are defined neither in terms of competition nor hybridity, but rather as forming a symbiotic relationship: they supplement each other through their alternative strengths. According to WordPress's co-creator, Matt Mullenweg:

> Blogging [...] is the natural evolution of the lighter publishing methods – at some point you'll have more to say than fits in 140 characters, is too important to put in Facebook's generic chrome, or you've matured to the point you want more flexibility and control around your words and ideas. [...] You don't stop using the lighter method, you just complement it – different mediums afford different messages. (Mullenweg, 2011)

For Mullenweg, then, to write long posts remains fundamental for self-elaboration dynamics in that it allows the short post to be expanded in more substantial ways. Blogging, as it were, is back (or never went away).

The processes and trajectories discussed in this chapter reveal the centrality of the blog in defining the history of the Web as a technology for self-performance. Put differently, the history of the blog is the history of how and why we have used the Web repeatedly to make ourselves 'public' to others. From this perspective, blogs may be defined as a paradigmatic technology in Agamben's (2009) sense, that is, they are the case that makes intelligible singular aspects of a whole set of artifacts (such as sites and tools for self-elaboration online). According to Agamben, 'paradigms establish a broader problematic context that they both constitute and make intelligible' (2009: 17). As a paradigmatic technology, the history of the blog is also the history of how its most defining features have become standard affordances of the new media ecology. Rather than technological necessities, these features are the result of specific historical contexts that need to be carefully interrogated.

## Notes

1 In their analysis of the international uptake of blogging, Russell and Echchaibi (2009) also speak of an 'American blogging model'. Referring to the case of Italy, Locatelli (2014: 50–1) argues that 'the U.S. model remains a point of reference' and suggests that the 'imitation of the American experience' was a key factor driving the early appropriation of blogs. See also Siles (2017) for a comparison of the trajectories of blogging in the United States and France.

2 In the vocabulary of Science and Technology Studies (STS), stabilization refers to the process through which groups of interest actors negotiate the identity and meaning of an artifact (Bijker et al., 1987).

3 The project from which this chapter stems began as doctoral dissertation research.

4 Drawing on both genre and medium theories, Miller and Shepherd (2009) provide a similar explanation. As an alternative, and inspired mostly by STS literature, I conceptualize the history of blogging as a mutual shaping process in which the technology of blogging acquired certain configurations (depending on the specific sub-type of blogs that users enacted to respond to their changing contexts), and cultural expectations have found recurrently in blogging a material expression.

5 In a similar manner, Locatelli (2014) refers to the 'cultural adaptation' to which blogs were subjected in Italy. Siles (2007–2008) also shows that blogs absorbed the identities of previous sites in Costa Rica and that localizing them (through names that referred to typical Costa Rican expressions) was crucial in their early development.

6 In this sense, the 'microblogging' notion functioned as a crucial link between what Flichy (2007: 82) calls a frame of functioning – 'the body of knowledge and know-how mobilized or mobilizable' in the design of media technologies such as tumblelogs and Twitter – and a frame of use – the 'social activities proposed by the technology, the integrated routines of daily life, sets of social practices, kinds of people, places and situations connected to the technical artifact' (Flichy, 2007: 83), in this case, blogs. Flichy argues that it is precisely through the articulation of these two frames that technologies acquire social meaning.

## REFERENCES

Agamben, G. (2009) *The Signature of all Things: On Method*. New York: Zone Books.

Ammann, R. (2009) 'Jorn Barger, the NewsPage network, and the emergence of the weblog community', paper presented at the 20th Association for Computing Machinery Conference on Hypertext and Hypermedia, Italy.

Anderson, J.S. (1999) No title, *Genehack* (http://genehack.org/1999/05/). Accessed June 18, 2018.

Armstrong, J., and Moulitsas Zúniga, M. (2006) *Crashing the Gate: Netroots, Grassroots, and the Rise of People-Powered Politics*. White River Junction, VT: Chelsea Green Publishing.

Barger, J. (1997a) 'Robot Wisdom Weblog', *RobotWisdom* (http://web.archive.org/web/20000817183237/www.robotwisdom.com/log1997m12.html). Accessed June 18, 2018.

Barger, J. (1997b) '"Weblogs" are the best format for hotlists', *comp.infosystems.www.announce* (http://groups.google.com/group/comp.infosystems.www.announce/browse_frm/thread/7de977b747c34d3e/4af6ac27dad974fd?pli=1). Accessed June 18, 2018.

Barger, J. (1998) 'My weblog press release', *rec.arts.books* (http://groups.google.com/group/rec.arts.books/browse_thread/thread/a01e262d08703942). Accessed June 18, 2018.

Barger, J. (2005) 'The Huffington Post is not a blog', *Robot Wisdom Auxiliary* (http://robotwisdom2.blogspot.com/2005/12/huffington-post-is-not-blog.html). Accessed June 18, 2018.

Bijker, W.E., Hughes, T.P., and Pinch, T.J. (eds.) (1987) *The Social Construction of Technological Systems: New Directions in the Sociology and History of Technology*. Cambridge, MA: MIT Press.

Blood, R. (2002) 'Weblogs: A history and perspective', in J. Rodzvilla (ed.), *We've Got Blog: How Weblogs are Changing our Culture*. Cambridge, MA: Perseus. pp. 7–16.

Boltanski, L., and Chiapello, È. (1999) *Le Nouvel Esprit du Capitalisme*. Paris: Gallimard.

Bolter, J.D., and Grusin, R. (1999) *Remediation*. Cambridge, MA: MIT Press.

Boutin, P. (2008) 'Twitter, Flickr, Facebook make blogs look so 2004', *Wired* (http://www.wired.com/entertainment/theweb/magazine/16-11/st_essay). Accessed June 18, 2018.

Carr, N. (2008) 'Who killed the blogosphere?', *Roughtype.com* (http://www.roughtype.com/?s=who+killed). Accessed June 18, 2018.

Coates, T. (2003) '(Weblogs and) the mass amateurisation of (nearly) everything…', *PlasticBag* (http://www.plasticbag.org/archives/2003/09/weblogs_and_the_mass_amateurisation_of_nearly_everything/). Accessed June 18, 2018.

Copeland, H. (2002) 'Blogonomics: Making a living from blogging', *Pressflex.com* (http://web.archive.org/web/20020802074241/http://www.pressflex.com/news/fullstory.php/aid/54/Blogonomics:_making_a_living_from_blogging.html). Accessed June 18, 2018.

Crampton, T. (2006, July 27) 'France's mysterious embrace of blogs', *NYTimes.com* (http://www.nytimes.com/2006/07/27/technology/27iht-blogs.2314926.html). Accessed June 18, 2018.

Duffy, B.E., and Hund, E. (2015) '"Having it all" on social media: Entrepreneurial femininity and self-branding among fashion bloggers', *Social Media + Society*, July-December: 1–11.

Faler, B. (2005) 'A Capitol Hill presence in the blogosphere', *The Washington Post*. p. A15.

Flichy, P. (2007) *Understanding Technological Innovation: A Socio-Technical Approach*. Cheltenham, UK: Edward Elgar.

Gigandet, S. (2001a) 'Le triomphe des weblogs', *C-est-tout.com* (http://web.archive.org/web/20010716062349/http://c-est-tout.com/infos/info_883.shtml). Accessed June 18, 2018.

Gigandet, S. (2001b) 'Les balbutiements des jouebs', *C-est-tout.com* (http://web.archive.org/web/20010803181835/http://c-est-tout.com/infos/info_886.shtml). Accessed June 18, 2018.

Glaser, M. (2007) 'Twitter founders thrive on micro-blogging constraints', *PBS* (http://mediashift.org/2007/05/twitter-founders-thrive-on-micro-blogging-constraints137/). Accessed June 18, 2018.

Graham, B. (1998) No title, *BradLands* (https://web.archive.org/web/19991018212708/http://www.bradlands.com:80/archive/arc_120198.html). Accessed June 18, 2018.

Gwinn, E. (2007) 'World gets 21st century totem poles', *Chicago Tribune* (http://articles.chicagotribune.com/2007-03-20/features/0703200287_1_blog-twitter-messaging)

Habermas, J. (1989) *The Structural Transformation of the Public Sphere: An Inquiry into a Category of Bourgeois Society*. Cambridge: Polity Press.

Herring, S.C., Scheidt, L.A., Wright, E., and Bonus, S. (2005) 'Weblogs as a bridging genre', *Information, Technology & People*, 18(2): 142–71.

Hourihan, M. (2002) 'What we're doing when we blog', *O'Reilly Networks' Web DevCenter* (http://www.oreillynet.com/pub/a/javascript/2002/06/13/megnut.html). Accessed June 18, 2018.

Le Meur, L., and Beauvais, L. (2005) *Blogs pour les Pros*. Paris: Dunod.

Locatelli, E. (2014) *The Blog Up! Storia Sociale del Blog in Italia*. Milano: FrancoAngeli.

Lovink, G. (2011) *My First Recession: Critical Internet Culture in Transition*. Amsterdam: Institute of Network Cultures.

Maeda, J. (2006) *The Laws of Simplicity (Simplicity: Design, Technology, Business, Life)*. Cambridge, MA: MIT Press.

Miller, C.R., and Shepherd, D. (2004) 'Blogging as social action: A genre analysis of the weblog', in L. Gurak, S. Antonijevic, L.A. Johnson, C. Ratliff, and J. Reyman (eds.), *Into the Blogosphere: Rhetoric, Community, and Culture of Weblogs* (http://blog.lib.umn.edu/blogosphere/blogging_as_social_action_a_genre_analysis_of_the_weblog.html)

Miller, C.R., and Shepherd, D. (2009) 'Questions for genre theory from the blogosphere', in J. Giltrow and D. Stein (eds.), *Genres in the Internet: Issues in the Theory of Genre*. Amsterdam: John Benjamins. pp. 263–90.

Moe, H. (2011) 'Mapping the Norwegian blogosphere: Methodological challenges in internationalizing Internet research', *Social Science Computer Review*, 29(3): 313–26.

Moggridge, B. (2010) *Designing Media*. Cambridge, MA: MIT Press.

Mullenweg, M. (2011) 'Blogging drift', *Ma.tt* (http://ma.tt/2011/02/blogging-drift/). Accessed June 18, 2018.

Neuman, W.R. (2010) 'Theories of media evolution', in W. Russell Neuman (ed.), *Media, Technology, and Society: Theories of Media Evolution*. Ann Arbor: University of Michigan Press. pp. 1–21.

Nielsen, R.K. (2012) 'How newspapers began to blog', *Information, Communication & Society*, 15(6): 959–78.

O'Reilly, T. (2005) 'What is Web 2.0. Design patterns and business models for the next generation of software' (http://oreilly.com/web2/archive/what-is-web-20.html). Accessed June 18, 2018.

Pô, J.-D., and Vanbremeersch, N. (2007) 'La campagne électorale de 2007 et le débat politique en ligne', *Commentaire*, 30(117): 147–55.

Prodoehl, P. (1999) No title, *Rasterweb* (http://rasterweb.net/raster/199902.html)

Rosenberg, S. (1999) 'Fear of links', *Salon* (https://www.salon.com/1999/05/28/weblogs/). Accessed June 18, 2018.

Rosenberg, S. (2009) *Say Everything: How Blogging Began, What It's Becoming, and Why It Matters*. New York: Crown.

Rowan, D. (2003) 'Technobabble', *The Times*. p. 21.

Russell, A., and Echchaibi, N. (2009) *International Blogging: Identity, Politics, and Networked Publics*. New York: Peter Lang.

Schonfeld, E. (2011) 'Why David Karp started Tumblr: Blogs don't work for most people', *TechCrunch.com* (http://techcrunch.com/2011/02/21/founder-stories-why-david-karp-started-tumblr-blogs-dont-work-for-most-people/). Accessed June 18, 2018.

Selvitelle, B. (2008) 'Why I loathe the word "microblogging"', *life.i.think* (http://lukewarmtapioca.wordpress.com/2008/06/09/why-i-loathe-the-word-microblogging/). Accessed June 18, 2018.

Siles, I. (2007–2008) '"Blogueando" a la tica: Una mirada al uso de los blogs en Costa Rica', *Anuario de Estudios Centroamericanos*, 33–34: 325–57.

Siles, I. (2011) 'From online filter to Web format: Articulating materiality and meaning in the early history of blogs', *Social Studies of Science*, 41(5): 737–58.

Siles, I. (2012a) 'The rise of blogging: Articulation as a dynamic of technological stabilization', *New Media & Society*, 14(5): 781–97.

Siles, I. (2012b) 'Web technologies of the self: The arising of the "blogger" identity', *Journal of Computer-Mediated Communication*, 17(4): 408–21.

Siles, I. (2013) 'Inventing Twitter: An iterative approach to new media development', *International Journal of Communication*, 7: 2105–27.

Siles, I. (2017) *Networked Selves: Trajectories of Blogging in the United States and France*. New York: Peter Lang.

Slack, J.D. (2006) 'Communication as articulation', in G.J. Shepherd, J. St. John, and T. Striphas (eds.), *Communication as…: Perspectives on Theory*. London: Sage. pp. 223–31.

Taylor, T. (2017) 'Where fashion blogging began', *The New York Times* (https://www.nytimes.com/2017/02/01/fashion/fashin-where-fashion-blogging-began.html?_r=0)

Trott, M. (n.d.) 'The beginning', *Six Apart/About* (http://archive.li/7bw4C). Accessed June 18, 2018.

Turnbull, G. (2002) 'The state of the blog part 2: Blogger present', in J. Rodzvilla (ed.), *We've got blog: How weblogs are changing our culture*. Cambridge, MA: Perseus. pp. 81–5.

Walton, M. (2004) 'Bloggers get convention credentials', *CNN.com* (http://edition.cnn.com/2004/TECH/internet/07/23/convention-bloggers/). Accessed June 18, 2018.

Waters, R., and Nuttall, C. (2007) 'Mini-blog is the talk of Silicon Valley', *Financial Times* (http://www.ft.com/cms/s/2/d0ccbc46-daf7-11db-ba4d-000b5df10621.html-ixzz-1I04qzm6t). Accessed June 18, 2018.

Welch, M. (2002) 'Don't miss the Lileks response!', *MattWelch* (https://web.archive.org/web/20020405100057/http://mattwelch.com:80/warblog.html). Accessed June 18, 2018.

Weltevrede, E., and Helmond, A. (2012) 'Where do bloggers blog? Platform transitions within the historical Dutch blogosphere', *First Monday*, 17(2) (http://www.uic.edu/htbin/cgiwrap/bin/ojs/index.php/fm/article/view/3775/3142). Accessed June 18, 2018.

Williams, R. (1983) *Keywords: A Vocabulary of Culture and Society*. New York: Oxford University Press.

Winer, D. (1996) 'What is Frontier?', *Scripting News* (http://scripting.com/frontier/beginning/whatFrontierIs.html). Accessed June 18, 2018.

Yahoo! Internet Life (2002) *Top of the Net 2001*, 8: 56–8.

# The History of Online Social Media

Christina Ortner, Philip Sinner and Tanja Jadin

## INTRODUCTION

In our changing world, terms such as globalization, individualization, digitalization or information society have become popular buzzwords. All these concepts refer to a transformation process where technological innovations, changing lifestyles, new work and life patterns and emerging needs are inextricably linked (Carpentier et al., 2014). In communication and media studies, this fundamental change is primarily discussed as the '*meta process*' (Krotz, 2014: 137, emphasis in original) of mediatization (for discussion see Livingstone, 2009; Lunt and Livingstone, 2016: 462), which is shaped by both, technological and social change (see Hepp, 2012).

Within the last decades, one of the driving factors of mediatization was the rise of social media – a phenomenon that appeared in the late 1990s, passed through a period of rapid proliferation in the 2000s and has since become an important part of online culture. Today, we face a wide range of different social media platforms, new ones emerging every day. As they strongly influence the way people interact with each other, they have developed into an integral part of our societies. Against this background, the present chapter sets out to reconstruct the history of social media in the wider context of web history. Hence, it will tell how this specific form of web-based services evolved in relation to the overall progress of the web.

Subsequent to a clarification of terms, the chapter will deal with different phases in this development: 1) the first period before the rise of modern social media when online interaction was mainly realized via discussion boards, newsgroups, mailing lists, chats or instant messenger, 2) the second phase when new web-based services such as wikis, weblogs, podcasts or social bookmarking became popular, 3) the third phase which is characterized by a diversification of social media services offering new possibilities for social interaction, and 4) finally, the recent time, when apps for mobile devices allow us to interact via social media anytime and anywhere.

Like always in history, different developments may exist at the same time and new patterns do not necessarily replace older structures. Therefore, these four phases cannot be seen separately. They are overlapping and strongly interwoven. Nevertheless, we argue that they mark major changes in the evolution of social media. Moreover, a brief history like this is necessarily far from complete. Thus, the aim rather lies in drawing the big picture than in giving detailed insights into single technologies or platforms.

## THE CONCEPT OF SOCIAL MEDIA

According to Bercovici (2010), the term social media appeared in the early 1990s for the first time, yet it took until the mid 2000s for it to become established in scientific and public discourse. Since then, social media have been commonly perceived as a specific category of Internet services. 'However, what exactly is meant by social media is a matter of debate' (Hunsinger and Senft, 2014: 1).

According to Treem et al. (2016), there is some consensus that social media are services based on the web which enable social interaction between human beings. Yet what kind of social interaction this could be differs from author to author (see Fuchs, 2017). Other approaches focus on the type of content provided by social media and identify user-generated content (UGC) as their main characteristic (e.g. Kaplan and Haenlein, 2010, 2012; Kietzmann et al., 2011). As UGC has already been around since the late 1970s Kaplan and Haenlein further limit social media to applications 'that build on the ideological and technological foundations of Web 2.0' (2010: 61). However, as we will see later in this chapter, these foundations are quite ambiguous.

Given the difficulties of a single definition, many authors tend to use social media as an umbrella term for services with similar features. Yet what types of platforms it involves is also open to discussion. Blogs, microblogs, social networking sites, wikis and multimedia platforms are included by most authors even if they use slightly different names. Some add podcasts and videocasts as a new form of personal publishing similar to blogging (e.g. Schmidt, 2011). Whether messengers or even e-mails are part of social media is still debated (Sajithra and Patil, 2013: 70), as it is Kaplan and Haenlein's (2010, 2012) suggestion to include virtual worlds or multiplayer game worlds.

There are several reasons why it is so difficult to find a common understanding. First of all, social media are associated with a wide variety of diverse applications using different technologies, providing different functions, satisfying different needs. Second, these applications tend to incorporate features of already existing web-based services, which makes it hard to draw the line at related tools. Last but not least, 'social media platforms, rather than being finished products, are dynamic objects' (Van Dijck, 2013: 7), permanently adapting to new developments. Thus, the field of social media is in a constant state of flux (Lomborg, 2016: 6).

However, it is exactly their diversity and volatility that makes social media so fascinating. Therefore, we agree with Treem et al. that 'the ambiguity around social media should not be viewed (…) as a source of frustration' (2016: 770) but rather as an integral principle of the phenomenon we investigate.

In this chapter, we therefore understand social media in a broad sense, trying to meet their diverse and dynamic nature. In the following sections, we will trace the development of web-based tools that allow users to create, publish and share own content easily and that support social interaction, communication and collaboration. On the one hand, the focus is on services that do not provide such functions as additional features but are primarily designed for these purposes. On the other hand, we mainly consider applications that allow public or semi-public communication. Moreover, we take into account services with similar functions developed in the pre-web era in the 1970s, 1980s and 1990s that can be seen as precursors of modern social media.

In doing so, we choose an approach that puts concrete services with specific communicative features in the core of the definition. These services depend on the availability of respective technologies, on actors who develop and offer social media tools and on people who make use of them. Hence, we address the evolution of social media as a process that is shaped by technological change, by important actors and companies and by the communicative practices of its users.

## THE PRECURSORS OF MODERN SOCIAL MEDIA

Quite often, social media are seen as a ground-breaking novelty. Yet, although they actually change the ways we interact online, the basic idea behind social media is anything but new (see Brügger, 2015; Kaplan and Haenlein, 2010; Sajithra and Patil, 2013; Treem et al., 2016). It is rather based on the need for sociality, which 'is an integral part of human life' (Brügger, 2015) and 'existed long before the creation of digital social media platforms' (Treem et al., 2016: 773). Therefore, some authors trace the origins of social media back to the first postal services (Guru et al., 2016) or the invention of smoke signals (Adams, 2011).

Even if we do not go that far, but focus on social interaction via computer, we have to start in the pre-web era, namely in the 1960s. In these years, first tests with local e-mails took place (Clark, 2003: 175; Peter, 2004) and researchers such as Licklider and his colleagues at the Advanced Research Projects Agency (ARPA) experimented on possibilities for collaboration (Allen, 2004). The creation of the ARPANET, which from 1969 on linked universities all over the United States, increased the potential of computers as a means of social interaction, e.g. via Internet e-mail service available from 1971 on (see Clark, 2003). In the same period, early learning management systems (such as PLATO in 1960), first bulletin boards (such as Community Memory in 1973) and collaborative software (such as EIES in 1978) were developed (Allen, 2004; Jones, 2003; Senft, 2003a).

Building on some of these ideas, new network services for social interaction entered the stage in the late 1970s, most notably bulletin board systems (BBSs), Usenet and mailing lists. A bulletin board system is an early forum software where users can post or read news, exchange messages and share files. The first BBS – the Computerized Bulletin Board System (CBBS) – was developed by Suess and Christensen in 1979 (Senft, 2003a). Only one year later, Truscott and Ellis created a similar service called Usenet (Chen, 2003), which provides a discussion platform organized in the form of newsgroups. Its communicative structure is quite similar to mailing lists, another instrument for group communication that came up at the end of the 1970s.

Throughout the 1980s, innumerable BBSs emerged all over the world functioning as platforms for various communities. In parallel, Usenet developed into a worldwide discussion system with newsgroups on all sorts of topics. At the beginning, both BBSs and Usenet operated within their own networks; however, later they were connected among each other as well as with the Internet. In the same period, mailing lists became widespread, especially after the launch of an automation program called LISTSERV by Thomas in 1986 (Featherly, 2003).

Yet another important service for online interaction began to spread in the late 1980s, namely the Internet Relay Chat (IRC) developed by Oikarinen (Senft, 2003b). It established the communicative genre chat and is seen as one of the ancestors of instant messaging (Larson, 2003). IRC is a text-based chat system that allows multiple users to send messages in real-time. Communication is mainly organized through public channels, although IRC also allows one-to-one communication.

The idea of synchronous online communication was not new at that time. Oikarinen was inspired by an already existing technology used within BITNET called Bitnet Relay (Senft, 2003b). Moreover, chat software had been integrated into earlier systems since the 1970s (e.g. Talkomatic in PLATO or the CB Simulator in CompuServe). However, none of these were as widespread as IRC. Within only a few years, IRC evolved into a worldwide phenomenon. 'People in over 120 countries and territories have used IRC, and one can easily find conversations flourishing in English, German, Japanese, French, Finnish and other languages there' (Senft, 2003b: 256).

By providing means of interaction among larger groups, BBSs, Usenet and IRC – together with e-mail and mailing lists – shaped the way people shared ideas via computers for a long time. However, from the mid 1990s on they lost their significance. The reason lies in the rise of the WorldWideWeb (WWW) as a universal service, which today for many represents the Internet itself. After its launch in 1991 by Berners-Lee, the web was yet another Internet service next to various existing systems, all designed for a specific purpose: IRC for chat, Usenet for newsgroups and so on (Brügger, 2015). At that time, it merely concentrated on hypertextuality. Yet, step by step it 'began to absorb the functions that each of the other software systems possessed' (Brügger, 2015). As a result, BBSs, Usenet and IRC – like many others – were slowly replaced by web-based services. Even if they are still used by specific technical communities, today they are rather a marginal phenomenon. Nevertheless, they had an important impact on online communication and web culture.

From that time on, the web was the main driver for online sociality. In the 1990s, its dominant role was only challenged by instant messengers like ICQ or AOL Messenger (Guru et al., 2016), which operated within the Internet but outside the web. These services existed next to numerous web forums and chat groups, where people met to socialize, exchange ideas or share common interests. In addition, the web opened up new possibilities for self-expression through personal websites (Sajithra and Patil, 2013: 72). Even if people had to code their own sites and therefore needed programing skills in the beginning, a vivid culture of web publishing emerged. It shaped the early days of the web and can be seen as the roots of the blogosphere (see later in this chapter).

As a reaction to these practices, automated web publishing software was developed. GeoCities (since 1994) was the first service that provided free web hosting combined with tools for website creation (see Milligan, chapter 23). 'For the first time, users could create their own web pages without having to worry about the intimidating acronym soup of FTP, HTML, and the like' (Milligan, 2017: 137). This led to 'a popularity surge in homepages, whereby the Average Joe could share information' (Kaplan and Haenlein, 2010: 60). Another prominent example is Blogger, the first weblog publishing system, which was developed to support the blogging scene in 1999.

These automated software tools enabled users without specific skills to publish online and therefore can be seen as a significant step towards social media. In the second half of the 1990s, we can moreover observe first versions of wikis such as WikiWikiWeb (in 1995) or social networking sites such as Classmates (in 1995) or SixDegrees (in 1997). However, it took several more years – in the case of social networking sites even longer – until these types of media gained the importance they have today.

## THE RISE OF SOCIAL MEDIA IN THE WAKE OF WEB 2.0

The first social media services that became widespread among larger groups of Internet users were wikis, weblogs and social bookmarking sites. Their success story is closely linked to a bundle of trends in the development of the web which were later discussed under the heading Web 2.0 and are seen as a major point in web history. After the burst of the dotcom bubble in 2000, the Internet industry was in an economic crisis. Yet, at the same time, the Internet hit the mainstream as larger groups of the population got access. Moreover, several technological innovations led to the emergence of new tools following quite different principles than traditional web-based services before.

As a reaction, O'Reilly Media and CMP Technology planned a conference in 2004 to discuss new trends and business models in the Internet industry. When trying to find a possible title, Dougherty suggested the term Web 2.0, not knowing that this would be the buzzword of a new web era (Musser and O'Reilly, 2006). Although the wording recalls a software update, Web 2.0 does not refer to a new technical version of the web. It is rather 'a set of economic, social, and technology trends that collectively form the basis for the next generation of the Internet' (2006: 4). The concept was meant to express the feeling that the web had reached a new level and hence should help attract novel capital investments (Fuchs, 2017: 35).

In a well-known blog article, O'Reilly (2005) describes Web 2.0 by mapping typical applications (flickr, del.icio.us, BitTorrent, Napster, Wikipedia, blogs), typical features (GoogleAdSense, eBay reputation, Amazon reviews), typical practices (tagging, folksonomy) and new technologies (RSS, AJAX). Based on this map he tries to identify a set of principles that characterize the new phenomenon. These include the tendency to use the web as a platform, to apply lightweight programing models, to deliver software as a service, to optimize it for different devices, to build application around data, to enrich user experience and to harness the power of the crowd (see also Anderson, 2007).

With regard to social media, the last principle is the most important as it refers to the core role of users. In Web 2.0 applications, content is no longer published by single authors but provided by multiple end users in a collective manner. Therefore, the value of such services depends on the participation of individuals who exchange ideas, share resources, connect with each other and work together. According to Van Dijck (2009), this provoked the notion of a participation shift. However, the core idea of user participation is anything but new. Content provided by end users already built the backbone of early network services, and the web was meant to foster worldwide collaboration right from the beginning – as its founder Berners-Lee stated (Anderson, 2007).

Moreover, Van Dijck (2009) argues that the participation shift is rather an ideal than a real phenomenon. Although the barriers are lowered, only a limited number of Internet users actively makes use of this potential. Still, educational as well as socio-economic backgrounds remain the main factors for Internet usage patterns (e.g. Hargittai and Walejko, 2008; Van Deursen and Van Dijck, 2014). Finally, online activities do not merely result in benefits for the users. By creating major parts of the content, they provide unpaid creative work. Moreover, they leave personal data, on which web companies build their business models (Van Dijck, 2009: 46).

Nevertheless, there is some evidence that Web 2.0 applications actually did foster participatory web cultures in the early 2000s (e.g. Dooley et al., 2012). This applies particularly for blogs and wikis: while blogs allow people to publicly express their opinion, the strength of wikis lies in collaborative content production. A wiki is a system of interlinked web pages that can be edited by 'any user with a forms-capable web browser client' (Leuf and Cunningham, 2001: 14). The history function of wikis enables users to follow the changes of a document and easily switch to an older version of the text.

The first wiki, called WikiWikiWeb, was launched in 1995 by Cunningham and gave this genre its name (Wagner, 2004: 269). However, it was the launch of Wikipedia in 2001 that made wikis really popular. This free multilingual online encyclopaedia run by the Wikipedia Foundation is by far the most prominent representative of this genre. (see Famiglietti, chapter 21) Today, it consists of more than five million articles stored on approximately 41 million pages that are cultivated by more than 100,000 active users (Wikipedia, 2017). It is one of the main free information resources online and demonstrates the enormous potential of wikis for collaborative texting.

Another flagship of participatory web culture are blogs. (see Siles, chapter 24) In 1997 Barger (www.robotwisdom.com) coined the term weblog for a type of website that had been around for a while (see Siles, in this volume). The original idea of these sites was to collect and comment on other web sources. Therefore, Barger defined weblogs as web pages, where 'Web loggers' note all sorts of other sites they find interesting (Blood, 2004: 54). Later the meaning of the term slightly changed, focusing less on the type of content and more on the way it is presented.

Although the practice of blogging has existed since the mid 1990s, it only became widespread after automated weblog publishing systems such as Blogger or WordPress emerged around the year 2000. Since that time a wide range of more or less professional blogs on all sorts of topics have been published all over the world. While in the beginning prominent weblogs were mainly of private nature, nowadays the most known blogs are integral parts of bigger websites designed by professionals such as Mashable, Huffington Post or TechCrunch (eBizMBA Guide, 2017).

Right from the beginning, bloggers had a strong sense for community building. By commenting on or linking other blogs, they established relations between different sites. Step by step a network of blogs with some focal points and a big number of peripheral members developed – the so-called blogosphere. An important technology in this context is RSS (Really Simple Syndication or Rich Site Summary). This innovation made it possible to integrate content from other websites into their own sites. In addition, a so-called RSS feed reader allowed users to subscribe to blogs or web pages and automatically follow their updates. Another technique, which was and still is used to establish connections between different blogs is tagging. By enhancing information with specific key words – so-called tags – websites with similar content can be identified more easily.

The technique of tagging is closely linked to social bookmarking, which appeared around 2003 and took the original idea of blogging – namely sharing interesting web sources – to the next level. Social bookmarking platforms allow people to collect and organize links just like they do in their web browser. Yet, as these bookmarks are not stored locally but on web-based platforms, they can easily be shared with and commented on by others. The most prominent representative of social bookmarking is Schachter's website del.icio.us, which triggered the whole phenomenon (Anderson, 2007).

At around the same time, the idea of blogging was applied to audio and later video content. A new form of publishing – called podcasting – began to spread. Podcasts are regularly updated audio or video blogs that can be published via blogging software and subscribed to via RSS feed reader. Their appearance is an indicator for the shift from text-based publishing to multimedia services. This trend became apparent with the advent of the first photo-sharing tools like flickr (in 2004) or video-sharing sites such as vimeo (in 2004) or YouTube (in 2005). In addition, social networking sites – most notable Friendster (in 2001) and myspace (in 2003) – tried to gain ground, yet still with limited success. In these years, we can also see the first tendencies towards commercialization – a trend that directly leads us to the next period in the history of social media when this tendency intensified.

## DIVERSIFICATION, PROLIFERATION AND COMMERCIALIZATION

In the mid 2000s, the field of social media entered a new phase characterized by a diversification of services, a rapid proliferation and the trend towards commercialization. User figures rose up to hitherto undreamt heights all over the world, turning social media into a global mass phenomenon. This rapid increase in active users led to rising costs and the need to professionalize the business.

Around this time, we can observe the advent of several new types of social media. Most apparent is the rise of social networking sites (SNS), driven by the success of Facebook. Early versions of SNS such as SixDegrees (in 1997), Friendster (in 2001) or myspace (in 2003) had been around for years (boyd and Ellison, 2007: 214). Yet it was Facebook that made social networking so popular. Launched for students of Harvard University in 2004, it opened its registration to almost everyone in the world in 2006. By September 2016, Facebook had 1.79 billion monthly active users and was available in 140 languages (Facebook, 2017).

Other social networking sites went online in this period but were not able to sustain. Myspace may be the most prominent example of what happens if a service fails to live up to its users' changing demands (Gillette, 2011). A lack of technological innovations and an overloaded, old-fashioned design are named as reasons for its decline, which began in 2008. Even Google's networking site Google+ is struggling and has so far not got beyond the status of a niche product (see Denning, 2015).

Its rapid growth and the acquisition of additional platforms such as Instagram or WhatsApp are key factors for Facebook's success. Moreover, Brügger (2015) argues that the service is so attractive because it provides an empty digital space that structures user interactions but can be used for all sorts of purposes. Like many other social media organizations, Facebook started as a low-cost-oriented start-up with a promising idea but sooner or later became a highly commercialized company. It is therefore a good example of a development we can observe in the overall field of social media: step by step it turned into an internationalized market.

To sustain in this highly competitive field, it is necessary to push innovation, introduce new features or occupy new niches. As a result, we can observe the emergence of several new types of social media in the second half of the 2000s. One of these new genres is microblogging. Although it has its roots in blogging (see Siles, in this volume), microblogging was designed for other purposes and its communicative dynamics strongly differ from traditional blogging (Van Dijck, 2011: 335). The most famous representative of microblogging is Twitter. It was launched in 2006, had more than 300 million active users by June 2016 (Twitter, 2017) and is extensively used by politicians, journalists, organizations and companies.

New types of social media also emerged when specialized services for different types of content came up. This had already started in the period before but gained dynamic as time went on. Several image-sharing sites such as flickr (in 2004), Pinterest (in 2010) and Instagram (in 2010) or multimedia blogging tools like Tumblr (in 2007) entered the stage. YouTube, the dinosaur among video-sharing sites, was launched in 2005 and rapidly spread around the world. In 2006 it was bought by Google and turned into a highly commercial platform (see also Burgess and Green, 2013). It is now a prosperous venture with around one billion users in more than 88 countries (YouTube, 2017). Similar services such as the short-form video-hosting service Vine (in 2012) were less successful. In the field of radio, music and audio, SoundCloud (since 2007) – a music database owned by CBS-Interactive Inc. – has established itself as the biggest player.

In the course of time, many of these services expanded their features and turned into multimedia platforms. As a reaction to new applications even big players like Twitter, YouTube or Facebook widened their areas of interest to be able to sustain their position (see Brügger, 2015). However, diversification was not only driven by innovative features but likewise by specialization on particular groups with common identities or areas of interest. Hidden champions in different spheres are highlighting their wide range and diverse character. We see offerings for LGBTQ+ people such as the SNS PlanetRomeo (since 2002) or Grindr (launched in 2009), which have had great influence on social life and the economy (see Lemke et al., 2015: 2), and millions of people are gathering in certain networks to share their activities. Fishbrain (since 2010) for fishing, Strava (since 2009) to track and share athletic activities or Ravelry (since 2007) for fiber arts are only a few examples.

Moreover, business and employment-oriented platforms such as LinkedIn (2002) and XING (2003) or networks for special sectors such as Academia.edu and ResearchGate for scientists became popular (Thelwall and Kousha, 2014, 2015). Digital curation is now also closely linked to business-related services. Offers such as TripAdvisor (since 2000), Yelp (since 2004) or later Foursquare (since 2009) bring together companies with the aim of presenting their products and users with their desire for participation (see Jenkins, 2009: 7).

Finally, we should bear in mind that – though many of the best-known social media companies are located in the United States – social media are as diverse as the world itself. Especially in large linguistic areas, regional services became the market leader. While some of them had to face substantial decline or even shut down – such as Orkut in Brazil, India and the United States or StudiVZ, SchülerVZ and meinVZ in the German-speaking area (Hasebrink and Rohde, 2011: 104f.) – domestic platforms are still the major player in other countries.

The Russian market, for example, is dominated by VKontakte and Odnoklassniki (Classmates), both regional services, and China – the largest linguistic area – is a world unto itself. Due to restrictive legislation and censorship, most Western social media are not available there (see also King et al., 2013). Therefore, domestic offerings such as the social networking sites QZone, RenRen and Kaixin001, the microblogging services Tencent Weibo, SINA Weibo and Fanfou, the video-sharing sites YOUKU, 56.com and iQIYI, or the messenger services QQ and WeChat share the market (see Millward, 2016).

To sum up, from the mid 2000s on, social media entered into a highly dynamic phase characterized by rapid proliferation and enormous diversification. Next to economic and social factors, the main drivers were technological developments. Therefore, it is not surprising that it was the rise of yet another technological invention which brought about major changes in the field of social media by the end of the 2000s, namely the smartphone.

## THE SHIFT TOWARDS SOCIAL MEDIA APPS AND MOBILE USAGE

On 9 January 2007, Steve Jobs presented Apple's new mobile phone with the words: 'This is one device … and we are calling it iPhone' (quoted from Noriega, 2011). In the years to come, this product would change the way we use mobile Internet in general and social media in particular. Although the iPhone was neither the first smartphone nor perfect or flawless, it has influenced the way such products look like up to the present day. With regards to the handling, all-over multi-touch displays replaced both small displays and tiny QWERTY keyboards.

In 2008 Apple opened the iPhone for external developers and launched the first app store via iTunes. In such online marketplaces developers can offer their software tools – so-called apps (Jansen and Bloemendal, 2013: 195). In the same year, Google published the Google Play Store (Butler, 2011: 4) and other companies such as Microsoft, BlackBerry and Amazon followed (Hyrynsalmi et al., 2012: 64). In subsequent years, smartphones have virtually replaced older versions of mobile phones in many regions of the world.

This success story had tremendous influence on the development of social media. The whole Internet became accessible via smartphones and people could now chat, read, watch, vote or post any content at any time and any place (e.g. Humphreys et al., 2013; Vorderer et al., 2016). The more intensively people made use of these possibilities, the more social media developed into an integrated part of their daily lives and the more people found themselves in a state of permanent connection.

Soon, social media companies realized the potential of mobile usage and started publishing mobile versions of their offerings. In addition, more and more new services were released as independent 'social networking apps' (Johnson, 2015) for mobile use only. Many of them built their functionalities on the possibility to track users' whereabouts. These location-based services such as Foursquare, Traces and Recho (for hidden notes and records), Bubbly (a voice-oriented network), or Findery (a location-related database) have rapidly gained importance over recent years. In addition, mobile dating apps, such as the above-mentioned Grindr or picture-based Tinder (launched in 2012) started to make use of positioning services to optimize results.

Another recent trend is live video streaming – very often tied to certain locations, too. Google Hangouts was the first to offer this feature in 2013, followed by Facebook in 2015 in the United States and one year later in the rest of the world. In 2015, two important mobile apps specializing in live video were launched, namely Meerkat and Periscope. While Meerkat stopped all its services in 2016, Periscope is still on the market and is owned by Twitter. The app is mainly designed for broadcasting live videos to a wider public. Nevertheless, users can limit access to selected persons within their own network. The latest development in the field of mobile live streaming is Houseparty. It was launched in 2017 by the Meerkat team and specializes in sharing video streams among smaller groups.

Although all these innovative services are important for the further development of social media, until now they have not reached the mainstream. Quite contrary to this, the genre of mobile messaging rapidly developed into a mass phenomenon. The most popular representatives are WhatsApp and Snapchat. WhatsApp was launched in 2009, bought by Facebook in 2014 and is by now well established among all age groups.

Snapchat is extremely popular among young people, mainly because of its numerous functions and periodically updated (geo)filters. As its most distinguishing feature, photo- and video-snaps disappear after a few seconds. This supposed transience contrasts with the idea of the Internet as an everlasting memory. Although Snapchat has been online since 2011, the company still has a promising future: in 2017 Snap Inc. went public successfully, and at the moment competitors are busy adopting more and more of Snapchat's functions.

At this point the history of social media turns into a vivid present that points to an interesting future. The success of picture- and video-based networks and the acceptance of augmented reality give a hint as to which direction the game may be heading. However, in such a highly dynamic field, future developments are hard to predict.

## CONCLUSIONS

To conclude, online social media have a long and dynamic history, which is closely related to web history. Although their roots go back to the pre-web period when services such as bulletin board systems, Usenet or IRC introduced basic functions for online interaction, the emergence of modern social media depended on the success of the web as a universal service. In the mid and late 1990s the web became the main driver for online sociality, people met in various web forums and chat rooms, a culture of web publishing supported by automated software developed and the first versions of modern social media such as wikis, weblogs and social networking sites came up. At that time, these offers were only marginal phenomena. Nonetheless, they indicated the major opportunities of the Internet, later labeled as Web 2.0.

In the wake of this transformation, weblogs, podcasts, wikis and social bookmarking sites gained significance. They offered new ways for sharing information and represented the new participatory character of the web. From the mid 2000s on, we can observe rapid proliferation, a diversification of services, the advent of new types of social media and a trend towards commercialization. The enormous success of smartphones around 2010 triggered further changes in the field of social media. Nowadays, nearly all social media platforms offer apps for mobile devices and new tools for mobile use only are emerging. As a consequence, social media usage is continuously shifting from web-based services towards mobile social media apps. Trends like location-based services, video live streaming or augmented reality programs point to a vivid future.

Looking back, one can observe some overall strands that shaped the history of social media throughout all these periods. These are diversification, internationalization, professionalization and commercialization. Since the late 1990s, when the first blogs, wikis and SNS appeared, the number and types of social media have continuously increased. Today we face a wide range of different platforms focusing on all sorts of features, content, interests, groups, branches, regions and areas of life. As new tools are emerging every day, trying to find yet another niche to operate in, the diversification of services is still ongoing. Right from the beginning, this process went hand in hand with a trend towards internationalization. Although most innovations in this field had their starting point in the United States, they quickly spread around the world. It did not take long for special services for specific countries or regions to emerge – some of them dominating the market in large linguistic areas today.

Finally, the history of social media is shaped by professionalization and commercialization. In the beginning, the 'empty structure' (Brügger, 2015) of social media offers was mainly filled by end users. Today, social media content is produced by journalists, newspapers, TV channels, political parties, NGOs and all sorts of firms, associations and organizations. (Semi-)professional YouTubers, bloggers or Instagrammers make (part of) their living via their social media activities, and social media companies are facing the challenge of finding models for monetarization. Altogether, these developments have resulted in a growing relevance of social media for societies and economies all over the world – a trend that has not yet come to an end.

## REFERENCES

Adams, D. (2011) The History of Social Media (http://www.instantshift.com/2011/10/20/the-history-of-social-media/) Date Accessed: 17 June 2018.

Allen, C. (2004) Tracing the Evolution of Social Software (http://www.lifewithalacrity.com/2004/10/tracing_the_evo.html) Date Accessed: 17 June 2018.

Anderson, P. (2007) 'What is Web 2.0? Ideas, Technologies and Implications for Education', *JISC Technology and Standards Watch*, 1(1): 1–64.

Bercovici, J. (2010) Who Coined 'Social Media'? Web Pioneers Compete for Credit (http://blogs.forbes.com/jeffbercovici/2010/12/09/who-coined-social-media-web-pioneers-compete-for-credit) Date Accessed: 17 June 2018.

Blood, R. (2004) 'How Blogging Software Reshapes the Online Community', *Communications of the ACM*, 47(12): 53–55.

boyd, D.M. and Ellison, N.B. (2007) 'Social Network Sites: Definition, History, and Scholarship', *Journal of Computer-Mediated Communication*, 13(1): 210–230.

Brügger, N. (2015) 'A Brief History of Facebook as a Media Text: The Development of an Empty Structure', *First Monday*, 20(5) (http://firstmonday.org/ojs/index.php/fm/article/view/5423/4466) Date Accessed: 17 June 2018.

Burgess, J. and Green, J. (2013) *YouTube: Online Video and Participatory Culture*. Hoboken: John Wiley & Sons.

Butler, M. (2011) 'Android: Changing the Mobile Landscape', *IEEE Pervasive Computing,* 10(1): 4–7.

Carpentier, N., Schrøder, K.C. and Hallett, L. (2014) 'Audience – Society Transformations', in N. Carpentier, K.C. Schrøder and L. Hallett (eds.), *Audience Transformations. Shifting Audience Positions in Late Modernity*. New York: Routledge. pp. 1–12.

Chen, S.-L.S. (2003) 'USENET', in S. Jones (ed.), *Encyclopedia of New Media: An Essential Reference to Communication and Technology*. Thousand Oaks, London, New Delhi: Sage. pp. 457–459.

Clark, N. (2003) 'E-Mail', in S. Jones (ed.), *Encyclopedia of New Media: An Essential Reference to Communication and Technology*. Thousand Oaks, London, New Delhi: Sage. pp. 175–177.

Denning, S. (2015) 'Has Google+ Really Died?' *Forbes*, 23 April 2015 (http://www.forbes.com/sites/stevedenning/2015/04/23/has-google-really-died/#6374b0d916e9) Date Accessed: 17 June 2018.

Dooley, J.A., Jones, S.C. and Iverson, D. (2012) 'Web 2.0 Adoption and User Characteristics', *Web Journal of Mass Communication Research*, 42 (June) (http://ro.uow.edu.au/cgi/viewcontent.cgi?article=1027&context=sspapers) Date Accessed: 17 June 2018.

eBizMBA Guide (2017) The 15 Most Popular Blogs. The eBizMBA Guide (http://www.ebizmba.com/articles/blogs) Date Accessed: 17 June 2018.

Facebook (2017) Newsroom. Company Info (http://newsroom.fb.com/company-info) Date Accessed: 17 June 2018.

Featherly, K. (2003) 'LISTSERV', in S. Jones (ed.), *Encyclopedia of New Media: An Essential Reference to Communication and Technology*. Thousand Oaks, London, New Delhi: Sage. pp. 293–294.

Fuchs, C. (2017) *Social Media: A Critical Introduction*. 2nd edn. Thousand Oaks: Sage.

Gillette, F. (2011) 'The Rise and Inglorious Fall of Myspace', *Bloomberg Businessweek*, 23 June 2011 (https://www.bloomberg.com/news/articles/2011-06-22/the-rise-and-inglorious-fall-of-myspace) Date Accessed: 17 June 2018.

Guru, M.C., Motaghem, S., Kumar, D. and Devanoor, G. (2016) 'History of Social Media', *International Journal of English Language, Literature and Humanities*, 4(2): 294–303.

Hargittai, E. and Walejko, G. (2008) 'The Participation Divide: Content Creation and Sharing in the Digital Age', *Information, Community and Society*, 11(2): 239–256.

Hasebrink, U. and Rohde, W. (2011) 'Die Social Web-Nutzung Jugendlicher und junger Erwachsener: Nutzungsmuster, Vorlieben und Einstellungen' [Social Web Usage of Adolescents and Young Adults: Patterns, Preferences and Attitudes], in J.-H. Schmidt, I. Paus-Hasebrink and U. Hasebrink (eds.), *Heranwachsen mit dem Social Web [Growing up with the Social Web]*, together with T. Brüssel. Berlin: Vistas. pp. 83–120.

Hepp, A. (2012) *Cultures of Mediatization*. Cambridge: Polity Press.

Humphreys, L., Pape, T. von and Karnowski, V. (2013) 'Evolving Mobile Media: Uses and Conceptualizations of the Mobile Internet', *Journal of Computer-Mediated Communication*, 18(4): 491–507.

Hunsinger, J. and Senft, T.M. (2014) 'Introduction', in J. Hunsinger and T.M. Senft (eds.), *The Social Media Handbook*. New York: Routledge. pp. 1–5.

Hyrynsalmi, S., Mäkilä, T., Järvi, A., Suominen, A., Seppänen, M. and Knuutila, T. (2012) 'App Store, Marketplace, Play! An Analysis of Multi-Homing in Mobile Software

Ecosystems', in S. Jansen, J. Bosch and C. Alves (eds.), *Proceedings of the Fourth International Workshops on Software Ecosystems*, CEUR Workshop Proceedings 879. pp. 59–72 (https://ssrn.com/abstract=2281670) Date Accessed: 17 June 2018.

Jansen S. and Bloemendal E. (2013) 'Defining App Stores: The Role of Curated Marketplaces in Software Ecosystems', in G. Herzwurm and T. Margaria (eds.), *Software Business. From Physical Products to Software Services and Solutions*. ICSOB 2013. Lecture Notes in Business Information Processing 150. Berlin, Heidelberg: Springer. pp. 195–206.

Jenkins, H. (2009) *Confronting the Challenges of Participatory Culture: Media Education for the 21st Century*, together with K. Clinton, R. Purushotma, A.J. Robison and M. Weigel. Chicago: The MacArthur Foundation (https://www.macfound.org/media/article_pdfs/JENKINS_WHITE_PAPER.PDF) Date Accessed: 17 June 2018.

Johnson, M. (2015) History of Social Media Part III (http://www.booksaresocial.com/history-of-social-media-part-iii/) Date Accessed: 17 June 2018.

Jones, S. (2003) 'PLATO', in S. Jones (ed.), *Encyclopedia of New Media: An Essential Reference to Communication and Technology*. Thousand Oaks, London, New Delhi: Sage. pp. 375–377.

Kaplan, A.M. and Haenlein, M. (2010) 'Users of the World, Unite! The Challenges and Opportunities of Social Media', *Business Horizons*, 53(1): 59–68.

Kaplan, A.M. and Haenlein, M. (2012) 'Social Media: Back to the Roots and Back to the Future', *Journal of Systems and Information Technology*, 14(2): 101–104.

Kietzmann, J.H., Hermkens, K., McCarthy, I.P. and Silvestre, B.S. (2011) 'Social Media? Get Serious! Understanding the Functional Building Blocks of Social Media', *Business Horizons*, 54(3): 241–251.

King, G., Pan, J. and Roberts, M.E. (2013) 'How Censorship in China Allows Government Criticism but Silences Collective Expression', *American Political Science Review*, 107(2): 326–343.

Krotz, F. (2014) 'Mediatization as a Mover in Modernity: Social and Cultural Change in the Context of Media Change', in K. Lundby (ed.), *Mediatization of Communication*. Berlin: de Gruyter. pp. 131–162.

Larson, G.W. (2003) 'Instant Messaging', in S. Jones (ed.), *Encyclopedia of New Media: An Essential Reference to Communication and Technology*. Thousand Oaks, London, New Delhi: Sage. pp. 236–237.

Lemke, R., Tornow, T. and PlanetRomeo.com (2015) Gay Happiness Monitor – Results overview from a global survey on perceived gay-related public opinion and gay well-being. Mainz: Johannes Gutenberg University (https://www.planetromeo.com/wp-content/uploads/2015/05/GAY_HAPPINESS_MONITOR_2015.pdf) Date Accessed: 17 June 2018.

Leuf, B. and Cunningham, W. (2001) *The Wiki Way. Quick Collaboration on the Web*. Boston: Addison-Wesley.

Livingstone, S. (2009) 'On the Mediation of Everything. ICA Presidential Address' 2008, *Journal of Communication*, 59(1): 1–18.

Lomborg, S. (2016) 'A State of Flux: Histories of Social Media Research', *European Journal of Communication*, 32(1): 6–15.

Lunt, P. and Livingstone, S. (2016) 'Is "Mediatization" the New Paradigm for our Field? A Commentary on Deacon and Stanyer (2014, 2015) and Hepp, Harvard, and Lundby (2015)', *Media, Culture and Society*, 38(3): 462–470.

Milligan, I. (2017) 'Welcome to the Web: The Online Community of GeoCities During the Early Years of the World Wide Web', in N. Brügger and R. Schroeder (eds.), *The Web as History. Using Web Archives to Understand the Past and the Present*. London: UCL Press. pp. 137–158.

Millward, S. (2016) WeChat's Global Expansion Has Been a Disaster (https://www.techinasia.com/wechat-global-expansion-fail) Date Accessed: 17 June 2018.

Musser, J. and O'Reilly, T. (2006) Web 2.0. Principles and Best Practices [excerpt] (http://cursa.ihmc.us/rid=1211300618980_550838356_10465/web20_report_excerpt.pdf) Date Accessed: 17 June 2018.

Noriega, M. (2011) iPhone Keynote 2007 Complete (https://www.youtube.com/watch?v=t4OEsI0Sc_s) Date Accessed: 17 June 2018.

O'Reilly, T. (2005) What Is Web 2.0? Design Patterns and Business Models for the Next

Generation of Software (http://www.oreilly.com/lpt/a/1) Date Accessed: 17 June 2018.

Peter, I. (2004) The History of Email (http://www.nethistory.info/History%20of%20the%20Internet/email.html) Date Accessed: 17 June 2018.

Sajithra, K. and Patil, R. (2013) 'Social Media – History and Components', *IOSR Journal of Business and Management*, 7(1): 69–74.

Schmidt, J.-H. (2011) *Das neue Netz. Merkmale, Praktiken und Folgen des Web 2.0. [The New Net. Characteristics, Practices and Consequences of Web 2.0]*. Konstanz: UVK.

Senft, T.M. (2003a) 'Bulletin-Board Systems', in S. Jones (ed.), *Encyclopedia of New Media: An Essential Reference to Communication and Technology*. Thousand Oaks, London, New Delhi: Sage. pp. 45–48.

Senft, T.M. (2003b) 'Internet Relay Chat', in S. Jones (ed.), *Encyclopedia of New Media: An Essential Reference to Communication and Technology*. Thousand Oaks, London, New Delhi: Sage. pp. 256–258.

Thelwall, M.A. and Kousha, K. (2014) 'Academia.edu: Social Network or Academic Network?' *Journal of the Association for Information Science and Technology*, 65(4): 721–731.

Thelwall, M.A. and Kousha, K. (2015) 'ResearchGate: Disseminating, Communicating and Measuring Scholarship?' *Journal of the Association for Information Science and Technology*, 66(5): 876–889.

Treem, J.W., Dailey, S.L., Pierce, C.S. and Biffl, D. (2016) 'What We Are Talking About When We Talk About Social Media: A Framework for Study', *Sociology Compass*, 10(9): 768–784.

Twitter (2017) Twitter Usage – Company Facts (https://about.twitter.com/company) Date Accessed: 17 June 2018.

Van Deursen, A.J. and Van Dijck, J. (2014) 'The Digital Divide Shifts to Differences in Usage', *New Media & Society*, 16(3): 507–526.

Van Dijck, J. (2009) 'Users Like You? Theorizing Agency in User-Generated Content', *Media, Culture & Society*, 31(1): 41–58.

Van Dijck, J. (2011) 'Tracing Twitter: The Rise of a Microblogging Platform', *International Journal of Media and Cultural Politics*, 7(3): 333–348.

Van Dijck, J. (2013) *The Culture of Connectivity: A Critical History of Social Media*. New York: Oxford University Press.

Vorderer, P., Krömer, N. and Schneider, F.M. (2016) 'Permanently Online – Permanently Connected: Explorations into University Students' Use of Social Media and Mobile Smart Devices', *Computers in Human Behavior*, 63(2016): 694–703.

Wagner, C. (2004) 'Wiki: A Technology for Conversational Knowledge Management and Group Collaboration', *Communications of the Association for Information Systems*, 13(1): 264–290.

Wikipedia (2017) Wikipedia: About (https://en.wikipedia.org/wiki/Wikipedia:About) Date Accessed: 17 June 2018.

YouTube (2017) Statistics (https://www.youtube.com/yt/press/statistics.html) Date Accessed: 17 June 2018.

PART V

# Web History and Users, some Case Studies

26

# Cultural Historiography of the 'Homepage'

Madhavi Mallapragada

## INTRODUCTION

Technically speaking, the homepage refers to the designated main page or starting page of a website that is located in the site's root directory (root in the Domain Name System's hierarchical structure refers to the top-level directory and is the starting point of the file system) (W3C Technical Architecture Group, 2004). The URL (Uniform Resource Locator) or Web address for a homepage is typically just the domain name of the site (for example, www.utexas.edu). The homepage was and remains a fundamental unit of the Web's architecture, albeit the specific practices and politics shaping the design, usability, access, and experience of homepages are not the same across time (from the 1990s to the present) and space (cultural and social contexts).

As websites proliferated by the mid 1990s, a key area of scholarly attention was the Web's hypertextuality, namely the non-linear intertextual nature of a website wherein HTML links on a given page would lead to another page (within the site or possibly outside it) with its own set of hyperlinks that, in turn, were pathways to other pages and links (Chun and Keenan, 2006; Landow, 2006). Theoretically, then, the website is a decentered text, made up of nodes and linkages; this in turn helped (partly) shape the language of travel, mobility, fluidity, and dispersal that is evoked in historical and contemporary theorizations about user experience of the Web as well as the Web's discursive politics vis-à-vis ideologies of time-space, place, territory, identity, and the 'real/virtual' (see note for examples).[1] It is in this broader context of discrete but interconnected links and globally dispersed network of websites that the spatial–temporal unit of the homepage gains prominence beyond (but intertwined with) its technical significance as the root document.

I argue here and elsewhere (Mallapragada, 2014a) that the 'homepage', so central to Web culture, must be understood as a cultural metaphor. At the core of the category of 'homepage' is an idea that has enduring power as a material, affective, and political idea: the idea of *home*. The homepage, rising to prominence in the early-to-mid 1990s, must be understood in the broader context of the destabilization of cultural narratives that historically privileged rootedness, authenticity that was tied to place and tradition, and a time–space framework that was shaped by a nationalist optic (Clifford, 1994; Brah, 1996; Appadurai, 1997; Ong, 1999). Drawing on my research on websites targeting Indian immigrants in the United States since the 1990s (Mallapragada, 2000, 2006a, 2006b, 2010, 2014a, 2014b), I argue that the homepage is a metaphor that anchored ideas of belonging at the turn of the twentieth century as the world was transformed by digital capitalism, new media communicative practices, unprecedented global mobility and transnational lives and work (Castells, 1996; Cohen, 1997; Schiller, 1999; Ang, 2001; Karim, 2003; Lee and Wong, 2003; Grewal, 2005; Nakamura, 2008). While the need for belonging is arguably a universal one, imaginaries of belonging as well as how one experiences belonging or its lack thereof (being 'at home'/feeling out of place) are both historically and socially contingent (Douglas, 1991; Massey, 1994; Naficy, 1999; Morley, 2000).

My research on the online cultures of Indian immigrants revealed that the Web, and its spatial trope the homepage, were crucial to the construction and negotiation of imaginaries of belonging by a diverse set of players – including individual creators of personal homepages, commercial entities offering community-oriented websites, non-profit sites for community building and activism or predominantly e-commerce sites. It is worth pausing here and clarifying why I include different genres of sites – personal, community, commercial, organizational – within this present discussion of the 'homepage'. While there are clear differences in the institutional and ideological cultures of these types of sites, my frame for understanding them is how they all differently, but in the same socio-historical period of the mid 1990s to the mid 2000s, anchored 'the ideals and ideologies of belonging online in relation to two dominant imaginaries associated with the time-space of the home – namely, the domestic, familial household and the public, national homeland' (Mallapragada, 2014a: 1).

The historical context of the 1990s as it pertains to Indian immigration to the United States is another key factor that anchors my study of websites. While the migration of Indians to American shores dates back to the mid-to-late nineteenth century, it wasn't until the passage of the US Immigration Family Reunification Act in 1965 that Indian immigration to the United States took on a steady pattern (Takaki, 1989). That said, the 1990s were a particularly significant decade for Indian immigrant culture for a few reasons: all-time high levels of Indian immigration to the United States; a growing recognition of diversity within the Indian immigrant and Indian American community at large (generational, political, cultural differences); strategic overtures by the Indian state to embrace its diaspora within its national fold; and more visible efforts by immigrant subjects to enact and negotiate their sense of cultural citizenship through media and popular culture, especially the Web (Mallapragada, 2014a: 1–19).

Scholars writing at the intersections of Web studies and immigrant/diasporic/migrant/exile studies (sometimes categorized as studies of 'digital diaspora') have called attention to the homology between the condition of transnational migration and the condition of virtual communication via the Web (see for instance, Lee and Wong, 2003; Georgiou, 2006; Gajjala and Gajjala, 2008; Everett, 2009; Alonso and Oiarzabal, 2010). Both involve a pattern of deterritorialization and reterritorialization. Migrants leave a national territory and relocate to a new country. Websites transcend physical geography and take 'root' (as homepages, servers, country code domain names) in digital, virtual spaces (Shklovski and Struthers,

2010). Relatedly, ideas of real and virtual are also invoked in this homologous relationship because migrants on the one hand could be said to experience their symbolic real (their home country) virtually through memory, community formation, and cultural reproduction, while websites on the other hand allow one to virtually experience our sense of time, space, and place (Kyra Landzelius, 2006). Or, another way to think about it is that both the immigrant condition and the condition of Web communication fundamentally disrupt traditional place-based orientation and sense of time and open up the space for renewed imaginations about temporality, presence, and connection.

## CHAPTER OVERVIEW, THEORETICAL AND METHODOLOGICAL FRAMEWORK

This chapter offers a cultural historiography of the homepage by drawing on my research on Indian immigrants and their online cultures in the United States. I do not offer a comprehensive set of historical facts about specific websites, nor do I cover the Web from its emergence to the present. Instead, I offer details from homepages, focusing on the period from the mid 1990s to the mid 2000s, as a form of historical evidence to make a larger argument about the role and politics of the homepage in Web culture. As a researcher working in the media and cultural studies tradition, issues of epistemology (ways of knowing the subject of our research), methodology (how we study it), and theoretical agenda (what issues we seek to engage and why we consider them relevant), are inter-related aspects of my research that co-exist and shape each other. In my book *Virtual Homelands* (2014a), which I am drawing on for this chapter, I employed a combination of textual, institutional, and discursive analyses. I situated the textual and institutional details of the homepages I discussed within a broader socio-cultural context to demonstrate why and how 'the homepage' needed to be understood as a cultural form. My intellectual framework was and is shaped by the fields of diaspora studies, cultural studies of media, postcolonial studies, critical race, and feminist studies – fields that have routinely put home and homeland and their nexus at the locus of their disciplinary interrogations. Such an intellectual framing allowed me to engage the question of how power shapes the production of normative understandings of 'home' and 'homepage'.

Normative understanding of home (private household and public homeland) and homepages rely on a hierarchy of social axes of identity and difference such as national affiliation, race, gender, class, sexuality, and language (Morley, 2000). By examining the politics of homepage in an immigrant context, my research questions the a priori nature of the category of the homepage – in other words, the implicit sense of its always already 'home-ness'. By demonstrating how belonging was actively constructed and negotiated by US immigrant-centric homepages specifically by employing the tropes of immigrant household and virtual homeland, my research makes a case for interrogating how normative understandings of belonging (in domestic spaces, in community spaces, within the nation) are embedded within homepages that are not necessarily explicitly targeting any specific community or group but are more broadly imagined around a general, mainstream audience/users. Although utopian narratives about the Web, especially around issues relating to access and its ahistorical 'newness', have been vigorously dismantled and new conceptual and methodological frames have been offered (for example, see Bolter and Grusin, 2000; Norris, 2001; Brügger, 2010), there still remains, as Gerard Goggin and Mark McLelland (2008) note, a Euro-American bias in how knowledge about the Web and its trajectories is produced. Most often, such a bias reveals itself in universal accounts of aspects or features of the Web, often framed as technological histories. While the implication is that technological histories transcend cultural context, in reality they are mutually implicated. In this vein, I note that there is no universal history of the homepage, only micro histories (and that a cultural historiography of Indian immigrant homepages reveals how the technological and institutional aspects of the homepage (hyperlinking, domain name symbolism, advertising and sponsorship, discussion forums, aesthetic features, entrepreneurial capital, and corporate identity) are shaped by and, in turn, shape the latter's cultural politics). In the next sections, I will draw on some key and diverse examples to establish my larger argument about understanding homepages as a cultural metaphor for the recasting of belonging in the age of new media and migration.

## THE PERSONAL HOMEPAGE: REPRESENTING THE TRANSNATIONAL SELF

In my research, I found that many of the personal pages were maintained by Indian graduate students at US universities or those who were employed at US firms, many of the latter being IT and software companies. While many of these pages hosted by Geocities Angelfire or Tripod are no longer active, one could potentially access at least some of them through online archives such as Reocities, The Internet Archive's Geocities Special Collection 2009, Oocities, and GeoCities.ws. Writing about them in the current is an act of memory, limited archive and noticeable absence of 'evidence', and as such makes visible a research conundrum faced by Web scholars and historians who might have been witnesses but not necessarily diligent recorders of that which they witnessed. Beyond that, as a way of acknowledging my blind spots in the act of writing about homepage culture in the Indian immigrant context, I recall Michel Trouillot's insight in *Silencing the Past* (1995), that in the production of historiography may be also embedded moments of erasure – when source materials are not recorded, archives are not preserved, or narratives are not told.

Some of the personal pages I examined were in the tradition of a personal diary or biography with links to 'about me', 'my interests', 'my work', and 'my family'. In these examples, the focus of the page was on self-expression of identity and personal details. As late-1990s and early-2000s scholarship on personal homepages has discussed, the textual and aesthetic choices made by personal homepage creators sometimes included appropriating features of physical rooms (a wall poster for instance) or homes (doorways), but more crucially involved the strategic presentation of self articulated as a hypertextual map of individual interests and interpersonal connections (Wakeford, 1997; Chandler and Roberts-Young, 1998; Papacharissi, 2002; Cheung, 2004). A common feature I found in these pages was details about Indian 'origins' and current location in the US homeland. As if answering the perennial question, 'where are you (really) from?' asked of immigrants in a new locale, a question eloquently deconstructed by media and postcolonial theorist Ien Ang (2001: 10–11), the authors of the homepages in most cases posted details about their past and present residences in the quintessential immigrant frame of, 'I am originally from ___in India and now I live in __in the United States'.[2] The personal homepage also bears testimony to how 'internet surfing' emerged in the 1990s as a legitimate hobby alongside the usual suspects – reading, traveling, listening to music, etc. Graduate students, many of them from engineering and computer science backgrounds, maintained their pages with a mix of purpose, it appeared. In some cases, the pages were an attempt to speak to their dual homeland affiliations – so, for example, links to news outlets and sports teams from India were arranged alongside links to their favorite US national sports teams and media outlets. The placement of images of the Indian and American flags as a top banner on pages was a common visual strategy to represent the emergent transnational imaginary around cultural belonging and citizenship.[3] In recent years, studies of homepages maintained by transnational subjects such as international students and immigrants have highlighted how ideas of original homeland (country of citizenship, the 'there') and present home-spaces (country of residence, the 'here and now') are intertwined with ideas of self and belonging in the transnational space (see for instance, Collins, 2009). In a few instances, the personal homepage was little more than an elaborate CV with a strategic performance of the professional self for future employers. Here, in addition to personal details, the page contained links to the latest news in their area of study.

While these different examples offer a glimpse of how different subjects personalized the homepage to either narrate their selves online or reproduce a strategic version to negotiate their continued belonging in the United States (students wanting to impress future employers, get a work permit, and thereby extend their stay in the United States), there were a few other examples that show how the personal homepage had hardly anything to do with private self or personal homes and everything to do with public selves and original homeland. Examples include pages which essentially functioned as a virtual library of links to Indian newspapers and cultural magazines, pages that paid tribute to their homeland of India by creating a database of website links to cultural and religious tradition, iconic places and linguistic cultures, and pages that offered a culturally nationalist take (in most case, a Hindu-centric one) on the greatness of past and present India.[4] These types of personal homepages exemplified how some users, no doubt responding to both their cultural and nationalist identification as well as the challenge to such identification brought about by migration to a new country, were more invested in recreating an ideology of the homeland on the Web than an individually oriented sense of self. This is an important point to note because most studies of personal homepages have been focused on the latter (self) and relatedly on noting the analogous relationship between the brick and mortar spaces of real homes with the virtual spaces produced on homepages, rather than on the relationship between personal homepages and homelands (Chandler and Roberts-Young, 1998; Dominick, 1999; Döring, 2002; Cheung, 2004). The personal homepages of immigrant subjects articulating an overlapping investment in private selves and public identities thereby complicate the already blurry boundaries between private and public in online spaces (Marwick and Boyd, 2014) but do by mapping the contours of the private and public in a transnational context. Personal homepages that, for instance, functioned as a database of news, sports, entertainment, and information from India and Indian America were essentially drawing on media stories or links from the public square but repurposing them to cater to the 'private' interests and needs of themselves and others like them. Private in this context reveals that there is no universal sense of individual self, only one marked by social relations such as, in this instance, one's identity as an immigrant in the United States, an ethnic minority whose taste and interests in popular and public culture do not get catered to by mainstream American media.

## HOMELAND IDEOLOGIES AND THE INSTITUTIONAL CONTEXTS OF THE WEB

Community-oriented homepages targeting Indian immigrants in the United States in their earliest iterations (1994) recognized transnational subjectivity as the locus of the imagined user. This did not mean, however, that ethnocentrism or inward-looking nationalistic discourses did not appear on some of these sites (Lal, 2003). Relatedly, although website names like indiainfoonline.com, indolink.com, nriol.com, indiaworld.com are obvious examples of marking the URL as a nation-centric space (Shklovski and Struthers, 2010), when we examine the content and discursive politics of immigrant sites, we note, as Emily Ignacio (2005) and Kyra Landzelius (2006) among others have discussed, that the act of immigrants making themselves 'at home' in an online space fundamentally complicates the relationship between identity and place and problematizes the idea of a stable national discourse in diasporic settings.

Some of the websites targeting Indian immigrants in the United States in the late 1990s also contended with a related issue of a website's country of origin and its potential implications for audience engagement. For example, between 1996–2001, India-based sites like samachar.com (1998; news and information), khoj.com (1998; job search portal), indiaworld.com (entertainment, sports, news), shaadi.com (1997; matrimonial), and rediff.com (1996; news and popular culture) were very popular among US users. Many of these sites were hosted by formidable media and information technology players in India and the United States and were clearly targeting Indian immigrants (Rajghatta, 2001). The Indian Internet marketplace was robust on the production side but facing obstacles on the consumption/usage end due to infrastructural, bandwidth, and cost-related factors (Aguiar, 1999). During this same period, Indian immigration to the United States was at an all-time high and the diverse needs of the community along generational, class, social identity, and ethnic–racial politics were becoming more pronounced and visible. In addition to providing news about India and Indians in the United States, a key way in which these sites targeted Indian immigrants was through their advertising, notably, international calling cards, money remittance services, matrimonial ads, shopping for consumer products, and insurance (for US homes, travel to India and medical insurance for visiting relatives from India).

When US-based sites like indolink.com (1998), nriol.com (1997) (NRIOL standing for Non Resident Indians Online), Namaste.com (1998), and indianmatches.com (2003) entered the fray, the company narrative expressed through its 'About us' or 'Mission' sections and press releases and interviews with the Indian American press (popular publications included *India Currents*, *India Abroad*, *India West*) almost always called attention to the immigrant identity of the company founders as well as to the fact that the website was headquartered in a US city. In some cases, such as indolink.com, the company first started in Santa Clara, CA and then established satellite offices in New York and Mumbai. To be fair, in many cases it was hard to really see a big difference in the cultural ideologies espoused by India-based sites and US-based ones. For example, samachar.com and indolink.com both offered a fairly similar version of a Hindu-centric culturally nationalist India; the difference was more in the minor details – while samachar.com presented its role as showcasing India on the net, indolink.com, like many US sites of the time, presented its role as linking and connecting Indians worldwide. In reality, India-based sites did not necessarily lose out on their popularity because of the advent of US competitors. In fact, over the course of the late 1990s to early 2000s, we see a complicated mesh of Indian and US players shape the Web space. For instance, AT&T and Western Union frequently advertised on Indian sites and Indian players like ICICI Bank and Citibank advertised on US sites (as did American companies such as Western Union).[5]

While, in many instances, the immigrant sensibility of the company's founders and, by extension, the website was mentioned in a matter-of-fact way, in some cases it was presented more vigorously as a key factor in the appeal of the site. A case in point is webindia.com, a California-based Web portal for businesses based in India, founded in 1994, around the same time as Yahoo and Netscape Navigator made their entry on the Internet. In its marketing promos, the company framed itself as 'an opportunity for businesses in [...] motherland to compete in the global market...' and 'erase the advantages of foreign companies' (Internet Archive). No ambiguity here when it comes to identifying the site's homeland affiliation. On the other hand, sites like bayareaindian.com (1999) and indianmatches.com (2003) used their US home location to make a larger argument about their cultural appeal. While bayareaindian.com's USP was its ability to mobilize local networks and cater to the local needs of the immigrant community (for example, a list of Indian nannies in the area), indiamatches.com, which was essentially a set of twin sites, indiandating.com and indianmatrimonials.com, sought to appeal to Indian American youth by including a dating service separate from conventional matchmaking services and set itself apart from the marriage-focused services offered by the India-based leading matrimonial site shaadi.com (the Hindi word for marriage). In the manner in which the institutional identity of a site was managed or presented, there was either a flickering or, in some instances, a direct invocation of the site's institutional home as a key signifier of the politics of belonging advanced by the site at large.

A unique and temporary phenomenon is observed in the case of Rediff.com, which emerged in the late nineties as a leading Indian site and portal that had a large following of US users. The story goes that when Rediff.com launched its website, it received one million hits in the first month, but almost all of them were from Indians based in the United States (Aguiar, 1999). In 2000, the site launched a US version of the site, and over the next few years acquired three Indian American media businesses. They included an online portal (thinkindia.com), an Internet phone company (Value Communications), and the most high-profile of its acquisitions, the longest-running (since 1970) and most prominent Indian American print newspaper, *India Abroad* (Financial News, 2000; Business Wire, 2001a, 2001b). Rediff.com's business strategies over the next few years revealed its efforts to market itself as a transnational company and mobilize an expanded sense of its cultural citizenship that aimed to cater to Indian Americans as well as Indians in India. The company redefined itself as an Indian American company (both in the sense of the hyphenated cultural identity of immigrants as well as a company with businesses in India and the United States). A highlight of Rediff.com's US storyline included its successful alliance with another Indian entity, ICICI Bank, in the early 2000s, which foregrounded how crucial the construct of the 'home' was to enable these Indian players to recast themselves as part of the immigrant family (see Mallapragada, 2014a: 103–12). ICICI Bank, the business leader for Web-based banking in India and a dynamic player in global banking, was looking to create a new online campaign for its online services that targeted Non-Resident Indians (NRIs) in the United States. Among the services were transnational banking (dual currencies being valid), money remittance to India, and home loans for properties in Indian locations. ICICI frequently placed ads on Rediff.com, sponsored its finance channel, and, much like Rediff.com, articulated a transnational space – a virtual Indian American network – as its authentic space of belonging. In a one-time promotion campaign orchestrated to coincide with the Indian state's announcement of August 6 as the 'Day of the Diaspora', icicibank.com placed sponsored messages that read 'High Achieving NRIs, we have a lot in common...It's not that lonely at the top when we're right there with you' in the newspaper *India Abroad*, which since 2001 has been rebranded as a Rediff.com publication (ICICI Bank, 2003). The messaging was the most direct attempt at establishing an analogy between Indian immigrants' experience of border crossings, leaving 'old' homes and establishing 'new' ones, and the bank's journey of leaving behind Indian and physical boundaries and reemerging as a virtual bank. Although Rediff.com as of 2016 shifted its attention back to the Indian market, delisted from Nasdaq and sold *India Abroad* to another Indian American company, icicibank.com continues to capitalize on its virtualization of home services, be they personal finance, getting access to virtual tours of Indian home properties, or sending money to family back home; the only difference since the early 2000s is that it is now using social media platforms such as Facebook and Twitter to expand its reach.

## DOMESTIC AGENDAS, FAMILY TROPES, AND EXCLUDED COMMUNITIES

> He was born in Kansas and raised in Delaware County, but the place Vivek Srivastava feels most American is not on U.S. soil. It's in space. Cyberspace. Each day, Srivastava clicks onto his computer server from his house in Media, Pa., and, for at least two hours, mingles with thousands of other Indian Americans on the Internet's World Wide Web. (Sudarshan, 1999: 73)

In this section, I offer a few prominent and diverse examples to highlight this argument. As I have argued earlier, the distinction between commercial and community websites is untenable precisely because one of the key selling points of the Web was its ability to transgress boundaries. Hence my discussion here moves freely between commercial websites and commercially sponsored community websites.

A very common template that many of these sites followed was to have the homepage feature a gallery of topics that appeared as channels or links on the main page, with sub-links (in some instances) and advertising alongside them. What might seem to be a cluttering of the main page was in fact a gesture to accommodate a strategically constructed image of Indian American identity, cultural affiliations, and transnational investments. Among commercially sponsored community sites (indolink.com (1998), rediff.com (1996), sulekha.com (1998), indusladies.com (2004), for example), commonly appearing topics were news, entertainment, religion, lifestyle, parenting, immigration, stock markets, education, sports, jobs, matrimony, and discussion forums. In essence, the spatial arrangement of these topics on the main page of these sites, many of whom often described themselves as 'ethnic portals' in their press and marketing reports, was an attempt to capture the temporal as well as the socio-cultural context of the immigrant condition. By constructing memory and foregrounding core areas (community, finance, shopping, culture, religion), in essence the page was inviting the user to relate to these links and see them as emblematic of the aspects of home and homeland that need preservation, connection, and representation. For example, on a site like indolink.com, while the 'Immigration' channel would offer guidance on navigating the US visa system, the 'Parenting' channel would give advice and solicit discussion on the challenges of and resources for first-generation immigrant parents raising Indian American children.

Who is the transnational subject? How is community articulated to location and mobility? In my research, I found that the contours of community formation were mapped across diverse variables. For gopio.net (1999), the home of the Global Organization of People of Indian Origin, it was an Indian-origin story with global spin-offs that was at the heart of its community identity. Early sites like bayareaindian.com and pittsburghindian.com were more invested in functioning as a community center and bulletin board and engendering a local, intimate sense of neighborhood rather than a vast transnational space of virtual belonging.

As I have discussed elsewhere (Mallapragada 2014a), there is plenty of evidence that the homepage was crucial to the maintenance of hegemonic and conservative ideologies around nation, gender, class, and caste in the Indian immigrant community. For instance, a community site like TANA.org, which represents the Telugu-speaking linguistic sub-group of the immigrant community, also reveals a bias towards specific caste groups (Reddy and Kamma) that are politically and financially highly influential in India and its diasporic circles. While hindunet.com (1994) promised access to an 'interactive Hindu universe', its institutional backers had strong ties to conservative Hindu nationalist groups in the United States and India. Namaste.com, an online shopping site specializing in Indian consumer products, strategically advertised images of traditionally dressed 'Indian' immigrant women to drive home the point that, 'no matter where you live everything you love about India, movies, snacks, music, health and beauty products, is just a click away' (Namaste.com, 2000). The metaphorical association between Indian immigrant women (placed centrally in the ad) and the 'India' in the site's tagline, 'Bring India home!', is crucial because a site like namaste.com is digitally remastering an older imaginary of the Indian cultural nationalism (middle-class Hindu women as bearers of cultural authenticity and tradition) (Bhattacharjee, 1992) to position itself as an authentic brand in the e-commerce domain. The associative linking of women's social roles within the family (as wives and mothers) with the consumption and virtualization of Indian culture was frequently made on shopping sites or links that sold products relating to the domestic and familial space of the immigrant home. For example, images of young women (representing brides) on matrimonial sites and older women (representing mothers or ageing parents) for services around international phone cards or money remittances were very common.[6]

The homepage was, however, not limited to the consolidation of hegemonic and conservative narratives about gendered social roles or cultural nationalism. Sawnet.org (1995), home to a feminist South Asian collective of female users, often addressed the challenges to belonging within the nation as it is clothed in patriarchal and regressive cultural ideologies around gender roles, women's spaces, and cultural gatekeeping in the diaspora (see Gajjala, 2014). On a community site, indusladies.com, a US-centric discussion forum, 'H4 Indus Ladies' (2005) exemplifies how immigrant women feeling trapped and experiencing a sense of un-belonging in the United States as a result of restrictions placed on them because of their H4 visa status (most notably, being barred from being employed while on the visa) critically evaluates the patriarchal politics of imagining the domestic home space as a pleasant retreat from the busy world.[7] In their conversations, women frequently call attention to how the home can be a site of displeasure, anxiety, and boredom. Furthermore, they re-route the discussion about belonging to the virtual 'home' of the discussion forum, noting that for some marginalized voices such as theirs, home territories, to recall David Morley's (2000) term, are dynamic, transnational zones of online agency and connectivity.

## CONCLUSION

Despite recent news reports wondering if 'homepages are dead', both homepages and the idea of 'home' continue to be central to the imagination and organization of Web spaces (Kamdar, 2015). In the present media environment – where social media has emerged as a key driver of traffic to websites where Facebook's profile and personal pages can be considered the twenty-first-century version of the 1990s' 'free personal homepages' (with a whole new dynamic with regards to commodification, surveillance, privacy, and interactivity), and where mobile viewing of online content has changed the design and experience of websites – it is important to recognize that while today's homepages catering to Indian immigrants in the United States are still articulated to imaginations of home and belonging, the specific practices they employ to engender belonging and, relatedly, the visual and cultural economy of webpage design and flow are different from the 1990s–2000s iteration. Most remarkably, the main pages of websites are increasingly incorporating social media icons as a way to direct users to the site's social media presence. And, relatedly, the social media pages of commercial and community websites are using the platform to guide users back to the website. Arguably, what is unfolding in the current moment is an intensification of the idea of home and belonging as mobile, affective, interactive spaces that can be accessed by touch or voice recognition.

In different historical and cultural contexts, the homepage appears very differently to its different users. When we are forced to contend with the homepage as a historical phenomenon, then we are also led to interrogate what the 'home' in the homepage means across different historical and cultural contexts. For instance, while ideologies of nostalgia woven around India as the original homeland were central to many of the early websites targeting Indian immigrants in the mid 1990s, by the mid 2000s (with social media and participatory culture) there were more instances of websites trying to articulate belonging by interrogating how Indian immigrants were impacted by ideologies of race, gendered immigration policy, and inter-racial political alliances.[8] Two things are important to note here. One, recalling Raymond Williams' (1975) insight that technology and society exist in a symbiotic relationship, one can understand the shifts in how homepages articulated belonging as emblematic of evolving ideas about identity and politics within the Indian immigrant community. Two, the status and experience of the homepage in online culture in the late 2000s is different from that of the 1990s. For instance, when the key hyperlinks on the homepage of a website lead to social media platforms like YouTube, Facebook, or Twitter, both the 'look' of the page and the practices by which one could interact with the homepage and engender a sense of belonging are remarkably different from that of a homepage from the 1990s, where no such access existed. How belonging is invited and enacted is different in both instances; nevertheless, my larger point is that imaginaries of belonging are central to understanding the work homepages 'do' in our Web-based culture.

Metaphors are integral to Web aesthetics and app design. Icons such as the shopping cart in online stores, a pen and paper for the Pages app, a camera for Instagram, and a house for the home screen all visually index the digital and the virtual through the physical and the familiar. The ubiquity of such metaphors in online media, coupled with the fact that the Web is more than a quarter century old, makes it especially challenging to separate the elements of architecture and technical design from those of metaphors and cultural imaginaries. Yet, to assess the significance of a given medium, we need to not just know how it functions as a technology but, more importantly, examine that technology as a cultural form. In other words, it is to understand how the institutions, practices, features, and histories of a technology shape everyday life, culture, and meaning making in a social context.

Finally, I also take note of the fact that at the time of this writing (March 2018) advertising for products such as Amazon Alexa and Google Home are increasingly linking the everyday domestic, familial, and house-centric activities to the technological capacity and cultural significance of these smart home technologies (for example, creating a grocery shopping list, looking up a recipe while in the act of cooking) (O'Shea, 2018). In other words, 'home' as both a real place and imagined space of belonging has been, and continues to be, a very potent idea to produce and manage the material and discursive power and value of networking technologies, be they websites, smart home devices, or social media apps (Facebook's Home, for example, while not successful, still reveals the efforts to articulate ideas of home to digital social networking) (Turner, 2013). Granted, industry narratives are tied to investments in the consumer Web, but it is worth noting that, historically as well as in contemporary times, the constructs of the 'house' and the 'home' have shaped and continue to shape the financial, institutional, and social imaginaries of websites in particular and the Web at large.

## Notes

1 For example, Sherry Turkle (1995: 14) in her discussion of the Windows interface (and how one can have multiple applications simultaneously open on a computer screen) has argued that 'windows' are a metaphor for the fluidity and multiplicity of self and identity. Ella Shohat (1999) has thoughtfully critiqued the utopian narratives of cybertravel and electronic frontiers in 1990s popular and public discourse and in turn argued that the Web is shaped by a tension between mobility and fixity, between transcending borders and creating boundaries.

2 http://members.tripod.com/~abhayj/whoami.html, URL when active, print-out from 10/26/02.

3 http://www.public.iastate.edu/~sach/ URL when active, print-out from 11/4/99.

4 http://members.home.com/draj99/india.html, URL when active, print-out from 11/4/99.

5 See, for example, Indolink.com's list of advertisers at http://www.indolink.com/advertise.html. As of 2018, Indolink.com is an inactive site.

6 Example of sites where these images appeared include matrimonial sites such as shaadi.com and H1Bmatrimonials.com, as well as the Facebook page of ICICI Bank's NRI banking services for Indians in the United States.

7 The H4 visa, also known as the dependent visa, is given to the spouse and child(ren) of the H1B visa holder. The H1B visa is given to foreign workers in a 'specialty occupation' who perform 'specialized and complex' duties, such as those in the information technology sector. US Citizenship and Immigration Services, 'H-1B Specialty Occupations, DOD Cooperative Research and Development Project Workers, and Fashion Models'. https://www.uscis.gov/working-united-states/temporary-workers/h-1b-specialty-occupations-dod-cooperative-research-and-development-project-workers-and-fashion-models

8 See chapters 3 and 4 in Mallapragada (2014a) for a more detailed discussion of these themes.

## REFERENCES


Aguiar, A.A. (1999) 'Indian Internet Users Multiplying Fast', *News India-Times*, October 22: 36.

Alonso, A., and Oiarzabal, P.J. (Eds) (2010) *Diasporas in the New Media Age, Identity, Politics and Community*. Reno, NV: University of Nevada Press.

Ang, I. (2001) *On Not Speaking Chinese: Living Between Asia and the West*. London: Routledge.

Appadurai, A. (1997) *Modernity at Large: Cultural Dimension of Globalization*. Minneapolis, MN: University of Minnesota Press.

Bhattacharjee, A. (1992) 'The Habit of Ex-Nomination: Nation, Woman and the Indian Immigrant Bourgeoisie', *Public Culture*, 5(1): 19–44.

Bolter, D.J., and Grusin, R. (2000) *Remediation: Understanding New Media*. Cambridge: MIT Press.

Brah, A. (1996) *Cartographies of Diaspora: Contesting Identities*. London: Routledge.

Brügger, N. (2010) (Ed.) *Web History*. New York: Peter Lang.

Business Wire (2001a) 'Rediff.com Completes Acquisition of Value Communications Corporation: New Entity To Leverage Strengths and Offer Expanded Services to Indian Americans in the U.S', *Business Wire*, April 12.

Business Wire (2001b) 'Rediff.com Re-Launches India Abroad Weekly Publication', *Business Wire*, August 1.

Castells, M. (1996) *The Rise of the Network Society*. Malden: Blackwell Publishing.

Chandler, D., and Roberts-Young, D. (1998) 'The Construction of Identity in the Personal Homepages of Adolescents', Nov, 1998. visualmemory.co.uk/daniel/Documents/short/strasbourg.html

Cheung, C. (2004) 'Identity construction and self-presentation on personal homepages: Emancipatory potentials and reality constraints', in David Gauntlett and Ross Horsley (Eds), *Web.Studies*. London: Arnold. pp. 53–68.

Chun, W.H.K., and Keenan, T. (Eds) (2006) *Old Media, New Media: A History and Theory Reader*. New York: Routledge.

Clifford, J. (1994) 'Diasporas', *Cultural Anthropology*, 9(3): 302–338.

Cohen, R. (1997) *Global Diasporas: An Introduction*. Seattle: University of Seattle Press.

Collins, F.L. (2009) 'Connecting "Home" with "Here": Personal Homepages in Everyday Transnational Lives', *Journal of Ethnic and Migration Studies*, 35(6): 839–859.

Dominick, J.R. (1999) 'Who Do You Think You Are? Personal Home Pages and Self-Presentation on the World Wide Web', *Journalism & Mass Communication Quarterly*, 76(4): 646–658.

Döring, N. (2002) 'Personal Home Pages on the Web: A Review of Research', *Journal of Computer-Mediated Communication*, 7(3) http://www.ascusc.org/jcmc/vol7/issue3/doering.html

Douglas, M. (1991) 'The Idea of Home: A Kind of Space', *Social Research*, 58(1): 287–307.

Everett, A. (2009) *Digital Diaspora: A Race for Cyberspace*. Albany, NY: State University of New York Press.

Financial News (2000) 'Silicon Valley Portal to Merge with Rediff.com to Create Rediff USA: Merger will extend the reach of Rediff.com's content, services and marketplace offerings to the Indian-American community in the U.S', *Financial News*, October 27.

Gajjala, R., and Gajjala, V. (Eds) (2008) *South Asian Technoscapes*. New York: Peter Lang.

Gajjala, R. (2014) *Cyberselves: Feminist Ethnographies of South Asian Women*. Walnut Creek: AltaMira Press.

Georgiou, M. (2006) *Diaspora, Identity and the Media: Diasporic Transnationalism and Mediated Spatialities*. Cresskill, NJ: Hampton Press.

Goggin, G., and McLelland, M. (Eds) (2008) *Internationalizing Internet Studies: Beyond Anglophone Paradigms*. New York: Routledge.

Grewal, I. (2005) *Transnational America: Feminisms, Diasporas, NeoLiberalisms*. Chapel Hill, NC: Duke University Press.

ICICI Bank (2003) 'The Day of the Diaspora', *India Abroad*, January 10 sec. S: 1–4.

Ignacio, E.N. (2005) *Building Diaspora: Filipino Cultural Community Formation on the Internet*. New Brunswick, NJ: Rutgers University Press.

Internet Archive, 'About us,' www.webindia.com. https://archive.org/

Kamdar, S. (2015) 'Is the Homepage Dead?' *Forbes*, December 27. https://www.forbes.com/sites/sachinkamdar/2015/12/27/is-the-homepage-dead/#16e189872344

Karim, H. (Ed.) (2003) *The Media of Diaspora: Mapping the Globe*. New York: Routledge.

Landow, G.P. (2006) *Hypertext 3.0: Critical Theory and New Media in an Era of Globalization*. 3rd edn. Baltimore, MD: Johns Hopkins University Press.

Kyra Landzelius, K. (Ed.) (2006) *Native on the Net: Indigenous and Diasporic Peoples in the Virtual Age*. London: Routledge.

Lal, V. (2003) 'North American Hindus, the Sense of History, and the Politics of Internet Diasporism', in Rachel Lee and Sau-Ling Cynthia Wong (Eds), *Asian America.Net: Ethnicity, Nationalism and Cyberspace*. New York: Routledge. pp. 98–138.

Lee, R., and Wong, S.-l.C. (Eds) (2003) *Asian America.Net: Ethnicity, Nationalism and Cyberspace*. New York: Routledge.

Mallapragada, M. (2000) 'The Indian Diaspora in the USA and around the Web', in David Gauntlett (Ed.), *Web.Studies: Rewiring Media Studies for the Digital Age*. London: Arnold & OUP. pp. 179–185.

Mallapragada, M. (2006a) 'Home, Homeland, Homepage: Belonging and the Indian-American Web', *New Media and Society*, 8(2): 207–227.

Mallapragada, M. (2006b) 'An Interdisciplinary Approach to the Study of Cybercultures', in David Silver and Adrienne Massanari (Eds), *Critical Cyberculture Studies: Current Terrains, Future Directions*. New York: New York University Press. pp. 194–204.

Mallapragada, M. (2010) 'Desktop Deities: Hindu Temples, Online Cultures and the Politics of Remediation', *South Asian Popular Culture*, 8(2): 109–121.

Mallapragada, M. (2014a) *Virtual Homelands: Indian Immigrants and Online Cultures in the United States*. Urbana-Champaign, IL: University of Illinois Press.

Mallapragada, M. (2014b) 'Rethinking Desi: Race, Class and Online Activism of South

Asian Immigrants in the United States', *Television and New Media*, 15(7): 664–678.

Marwick, A., and Boyd, d. (2014) 'Networked Privacy: How Teenagers Negotiate Context in Social Media', *New Media and Society*, 16(7): 1051–1067.

Massey, D. (1994) *Space, Place and Gender*. Minneapolis, MN: University of Minnesota Press.

Morley, D. (2000) *Home Territories: Media, Mobility, Identity*. London: Routledge.

Naficy, H. (Ed.) (1999) *Home, Exile, Homeland: Film, Media and the Politics of Place*. New York: Routledge.

Nakamura, L. (2008) *Digitizing Race: Visual Cultures of the Internet*. Minneapolis, MN: University of Minnesota Press.

Namaste.com (2000) Advertisement in *Silicon India*, 4(7): 69.

Norris, P. (2001) *Digital Divide: Civic Engagement, Information Poverty and the Internet Worldwide*. Cambridge, UK: Cambridge University Press.

Ong, A. (1999) *Flexible Citizenship: The Cultural Logics of Transnationality*. Durham, NC: Duke University Press.

O'Shea, D. (2018) 'Amazon's Alexa Being Integrated into Smart Homes', *Retail Dive*, February 22, https://www.retaildive.com/news/amazons-alexa-being-integrated-into-smart-homes/517591/

Papacharissi, Z. (2002) 'The Self Online: The Utility of Personal Home Pages', *Journal of Broadcasting & Electronic Media*, 46(3): 346–368.

Rajghatta, C. (2001) *The Horse that Flew: How India's Silicon Gurus Spread Their Wings*. New Delhi: HarperCollins.

Schiller, D. (1999) *Digital Capitalism: Networking the Global Market System*. Cambridge, MA: MIT Press.

Shklovski, I., and Struthers, D.M. (2010) 'Of States and Borders on the Internet: The Role of Domain Name Extensions in Expressions of Nationalism Online in Kazakhstan', in *Policy & Internet*, 2(4), http://www.psocommons.org/policyandinternet/vol2/iss4/art5/

Shohat, E. (1999) 'By the Bitstream of Babylon: Cyberfrontiers and Diasporic Vistas', in Hamid Naficy (Ed.), *Home, Exile, Homeland: Film, Media and the Politics of Place*. New York: Routledge. pp. 226–227.

Sudarshan, R. (1999) 'Ethnic Roots in Cyberspace; Isolated in America, Immigrants are Uniting Online To Cherish Their Culture', *Little India*, January 31, 9(73).

Takaki, R. (1989) *Strangers from a Different Shore: A History of Asian Americans*. Boston: Little, Brown and Company.

Trouillot, M. (1995) *Silencing the Past*. Boston: Beacon Press.

Turkle, S. (1995) *Life on the Screen: Identity in the Age of the Internet*. New York: Touchstone.

Turner, A. (2013) 'A Place to Call Home: A Social Media Giant Has Reinvented the Smartphone Interface', *The Age*, April 28, http://www.theage.com.au/digital-life/mobiles/a-place-to-call-home-20130425-2ifn3.html

W3C Technical Architecture Group (2004) 'Architecture of the World Wide Web Volume One', The World Wide Web Consortium, https://www.w3.org/TR/webarch/

Wakeford, N. (1997) 'Networking Women and Grrls with Information/Communication Technology', in Jennifer Terry and Melodie Calvert (Eds), *Processed Lives: Gender and Technology in Everyday Life*. London: Routledge. pp. 35–46.

Williams, R. (1975) *Television: Technology and Cultural Form*. New York: Schocken Books.

# Consumers, News, and a History of Change

Allie Kosterich and Matthew Weber

## INTRODUCTION

As we near the third decade of the Web, attention is needed on the integral impact of the Web's historical development on a range of social, cultural, economic, and political facets of society. The influence of the history of the Web is particularly significant with regard to the ways that humans connect, share, and communicate. In this context, the impact has been deeply evident in the transformation of consumption within the news industry. In essence, a history of news media has quickly become a history of the Web. As such, this chapter provides a comprehensive review of Web history as related specifically to the news media industry. The chapter focuses on Web history and the context of news media in the United States from 1990 through 2015. Specifically, the scope covers a history of change on the Web and related impacts with regards to the ways in which consumers engage with the news media ecosystem. Emphasis is placed on production, distribution, and consumption patterns related to print news media and key legacy broadcast news media. In doing so, this chapter examines the ways that consumers access news and information by mapping out the changes in consumer behavior with regard to Web history and access to news. A key point throughout this chapter is the notion that many present-day changes in news media consumption can be traced back to historical changes in news media content on the Web, thus providing a window into best practices for future adaptation.

The means by which consumers seek and obtain information and news evolved significantly over the past several decades. In 1990, 67 percent of households in the United States reported buying a newspaper; by 2000 that number dropped to 53 percent (Editor and Publisher Yearbook, 2003). Conversely, while online news was slow to find an audience in the 1990s, today 38 percent of Americans report getting their news from online sources (Mitchell et al., 2016b).

The general importance of the news media industry, paired with the marked change resulting from engagement with Web technology, has led to significant research focused on the transformation of the news industry since the introduction of the Web. Despite this large body of relevant work, a comparatively small body of work has focused on changes on the Web from the perspective of the consumer and consumption of Web-based news media content. And yet the consumer perspective of Web history is a key driver of change in the news ecosystem (Hamilton, 2004). To that point, a 2015 Reuters Institute Digital News Report found that 25 percent of consumers across the globe use a smartphone as the main device for news consumption; in the United States alone, 44 percent use a smartphone to access the news (Newman et al., 2015). Dependence on the smartphone for news is remarkable given that the Apple iPhone, the most popular smartphone in the United States, launched in 2007. Consumer dependence on Web access via smartphone grew at an alarming rate. Yet legacy news organizations have struggled to adjust delivery systems to a Web-based digital environment, and they have also struggled to adjust to the emergence of Web-based digital-first intermediaries such as Facebook, Twitter, and Google through which many of today's consumers obtain their news. To wit, the 2015 Reuters Institute Digital News Report also found that 41 percent of the consumers sampled in their study use Facebook for news each week.

Thus, the history of the Web and associated technological change underlying the growth of the Web continues to impact and explain change in the news industry as consumers shift to a digital environment. This point is particularly salient as mobile and social technologies continue to occupy a more central role in the industry. In many ways, the transformation today mirrors historical trends from the history of the Web. In recent decades, the news industry has experienced three significant disruptions related to consumption trends: the transition from traditional printed newspaper to digital newspapers, the rise of social media, and the influence of mobile technology (Bell et al., 2017). This chapter thus focuses on Web history through the lens of the evolution of consumer interaction with news media by reviewing the core technologies and key media outlets over the past two decades from the consumer perspective. To that end, we focus specifically on the rise of early Web technology (e.g. webpages as a means of distribution), the growth of social media as a platform for news consumption, and, most recently, the dominance of mobile technology as a new means for accessing and consuming news media from the Web. In the closing sections, recent shifts to a mobile consumer environment are addressed, with a focus on the impact of the development of mobile applications on the consumer news environment.

## A RECENT HISTORY OF US NEWS CONSUMPTION

In order to better understand Web history and related changing patterns of news consumption, this chapter reviews the past 25 years in US news consumption. As noted, the focus herein is placed on the transition to digital news, the increasing prominence of social media, and the introduction of mobile technology and mobile news apps. In general, the story of US news consumption since the advent of the Web is punctuated by the advent of new technologies and the increasing ability of publishers to deliver rich and interactive content via digital technology. And yet, as de Sola Pool (1983) noted, advances in electronic technology often result in a reversal, whereby audiences are increasingly fragmented and afforded more choices for consuming news. The consumer perspective is thus particularly important to this narrative, given the central role of the consumer in driving trends with regards to the patterns of production in response to consumption of news on the Web.

## Newspapers on the Web

Few would argue against the narrative that the 1990s and early 2000s proved fiscally disastrous for the majority of the print newspaper industry. In general, the narrative of news media adapting to Web technology is one of responding to changes in consumer demand. The early period of the Web (e.g. the 1980s and 1990s) is one notable exception, as US newspapers responded to the advent of new technology in an attempt to anticipate changes in consumer demand. For instance, in the 1980s newspapers experimented with Telex technology as a way to send news digitally, although it was clear there was not a significant consumer market for the product (Khaw, 1983). Similarly, in 1992 Prodigy and America Online, two early online Internet Service Providers, experimented with bulletin board system formats for distributing digital news, despite relatively small user bases (Boczkowski, 2004). Early Web technology, as used by news media organizations, can be viewed as a means of experimentation, rather than as a means of responding to direct consumer demand.

The transition to news on the Web, however, is better understood as two periods – the movement of newspapers on to the Web, and the introduction of digital-only newspapers. Indeed, one of the most significant changes in the history of the Web and the evolution of news consumption is related to the advent of digitally native news organizations. Digitally native news refers to news content that is developed exclusively for distribution via online mediums (Nee, 2013). By definition, digitally native news media organizations emerge and develop entirely online, differentiating themselves from traditional news media organizations in a variety of ways. These digitally native news organizations run the gamut from popular national and international companies such as The Huffington Post, Buzzfeed, and Vice to smaller companies targeting niche needs and audiences such as Baristanet, New Brunswick Today, and Syria Deeply.

### Broad trends in Web news consumption

Undoubtedly, print and Web-based news are two inherently different products. There are innate differences in the products: print news articles are generally presented on one to two pages, and the reader is easily able to peruse the content. Web-based content is presented online and read via a desktop computer, laptop computer, tablet, or mobile device. The consumer reading Web-based content will often see a headline and brief abstract, and will then have to click to open the article, and to then read further. Often, Web-based news articles are spread across multiple webpages (Mitchelstein and Boczkowski, 2009). In addition, the distinctly different nature of the products, as well as the ecosystems (printed products vs. digital products), contributes directly to the distinct nature of the business models in print and online (Ahlers, 2006).

Despite the unique nature of Web-based news content, recent research suggests that, beyond the experience of consumption, there are no major differences with regards to recall of news read online versus news read in print (d'Haenens et al., 2004). Consumption of printed news has continued to decline at a remarkable rate. A Reuters Institute report on digital news noted that from 2012 to 2016, consumption of print news declined from approximately 37 percent to 25 percent based on sources of news in a given week (Cornia et al., 2016). Early shifts to online news consumption raised questions regarding the impact of online news on civic engagement. Many feared that as audiences moved online, civic participation would decline. Research on the impact of online consumption on civic participation is mixed, as some studies have found little to no connection between online news consumption and civic participation (Bimber, 2001; Margolis and Resnick, 2000), whereas others have found evidence that there is a positive relationship (Amadeo, 2007; Norris, 2003). Continued research is needed with regards to the impact on civic participation, as ongoing research continues to point to mixed findings (de Zuniga et al., 2014).

As for digitally native news organizations, exact numbers are hard to come by since there is no single tracking data source. Pew Research notes that the audience for news in this category is growing significantly, and that nearly 50 percent of the digitally native news organizations that they track reported double-digit growth in audience in 2015 (Mitchell et al., 2016b). Interestingly, the rate of growth has slowed somewhat; in 2009, growth rates for top online news websites averaged 27 percent year-over-year (Center, 2008), but by 2015 growth slowed to just above 10 percent (Mitchell et al., 2016b).

The historical impact of news on the Web as a disruption within the evolution of news consumption behaviors is connected to the development of Internet capabilities, which helps to feed consumer interest in online news. As of 2016, the percentage of US adults reportedly consuming news from print newspapers fell to 20 percent (down from 27 percent in 2013), compared with 38 percent consuming news online via websites, apps, or social media (Mitchell et al., 2016a). From the perspective of the news producer, this change is further reflected through an examination of Web traffic.

### *History of Web news consumption*

In order to contextualize technological change during this period, it is helpful to remember how nascent Web technology was in the 1990s. Early in the history of newspapers on the Web, change was slow because consumers were still adapting to the technology. In 1990, only 42 percent of the population had even tried using a computer. The first website went online in December of 1990 and it remained the only one for some time as the Web source code wasn't released until 1991 (CERN, n.d.).

Just a few years later, in 1994, the number of Americans with online access had skyrocketed to 11 million. In 1995, that number was 18 million, but only 3 percent of Americans had accessed the World Wide Web. Just three years later, in 1998, 20 percent of Americans were getting their news online at least once a week (Pew Research Center, 2014). Early experimentation shifted to a period of accelerated innovation in response to consumer demand as traditional print newspapers quickly ramped up models for online news production. In 1997, an estimated 745 newspapers had a website, and that number jumped to 1,749 in 1998 (Editor and Publisher Yearbook, 2003). As of 2000, it was clear that online news delivered via websites was likely to be a permanent component of the news industry.

As the industry evolved, this period in the history of news on the Web reflects an era of marked change and replacement. The evolution was slow as first, but in the later years, from the late 1990s onwards, the pace of change increased notably. During this time, many print newspapers found themselves losing circulation, staff, and prestige. Indeed, Gilbert (2005) notes that, in most cases, successful innovation in the transition to Web content required newspapers to create new business units or new divisions in order to foster substantial innovation.

The focus of many print newspapers during this time was a shift to multi-platform production, although the transition was slow to occur (Doyle, 2013). For print newspapers, a multi-platform model of news production recognizes the business model for print has eroded, and, in turn, focuses on repurposing print content across multiple technological platforms (e.g. print newspaper, social media, websites). During this historical evolution, the main focus was on transferring print content to the Internet with the overriding strategy of print newspapers being to horizontally translate content to the Web, rather than reinventing content for the Web (Rothmann and Koch, 2014).

Following the early rise of newspapers on the Web, increased access to Internet technologies fostered a landscape for both the production and consumption of news media anytime and anywhere. Early on, however, consumption was often driven by key events. For example, a 2002 analysis found that the majority of online news Web traffic was driven by consumption of news pertaining to key events such as the Clinton–Lewinsky scandal (Wu and Bechtel, 2002), or by immediate need-based consumption such as weather-related news. As technology proliferated, and Internet access speeds increased, usage became more ubiquitous. According to Pew, for example, 2010 marked the first time surveyed respondents said the Internet was the platform of choice for news; 65 percent of participants said they got most of their news from the Internet as opposed to television, newspapers, or radio (Rosenstiel and Mitchell, 2011). As such, there was a rapid acceleration of new news organizations on the Web.

Larger legacy organizations such as *The New York Times*, CNN, and the BBC migrated toward a stronger and more dominant online presence. The presence of organizations such as CNN and the BBC on the Web points to a continued pattern of change; consumer demand was and is not specific to a single medium – as a result, news media online is often an agglomeration of diverse media channels. Notably, this period also saw an increase in startup organizations born on the Web such as Propublica, Business Insider, and Quartz (Mitchell et al., 2014). An examination of the digitally native landscape indicates that many of these organizations are focused specifically on content that has been negatively impacted by the industry's economic struggles, including local news, investigative journalism, and international content (Jurkowitz, 2014). Today, online consumption of news is a given, but the patterns of consumption are far more nuanced. Patterns of user distribution have developed online in ways that often mirror what was once seen in print; users with mainstream political views congregate on mainstream news websites, but there is a diverse and rich population of niche websites to serve other points of view (Fletcher and Park, 2017). On the other hand, online news audiences engage and interact with news in a far more meaningful way than in the days of print-dominated news. Online news allows consumers to engage and interact with news sources, providing commentary, asking questions, and interacting with other readers (Ksiazek et al., 2016).

### Tensions between Web news consumers and producers

The advent of online news and digitally native news leaves news producers to contend with the response and management of technological and associated behavioral changes as they grapple with new ways to produce and distribute news. In some ways, digitally native news producers are at an advantage with regards to managing changes in news consumption. As digitally native news producers, these news organizations are inherently capable of benefitting from social media as a contributor to content creation, distribution, and engagement (Wu, 2016). This is crucial for the survival of news media organizations as an increasing number of users consume news through social media platforms, which is in the next section of this chapter. Similar benefits exist due to the inherent ability of digital news media organizations to integrate mobile into organizational routines. Indeed, digitally native news media organizations lead mobile news advertising revenue (Wu, 2016), which proves important as 25 percent of respondents use a smartphone as the main device for news consumption (Newman et al., 2015). In addition, digitally native news media organizations strive to innovate by creating new styles and forms of storytelling (Mitchell and Page, 2014) facilitated by the difference in distribution of costs from traditional news media companies (Thompson, 2014). As a whole, digitally native news media organizations continue to expand in terms of growth and profit (Wu, 2016).

### *Implications for the news ecosystem*

This discussion of digitally native news is inextricably linked to an understanding of the news media resource space and represents an evolution that can only be told by understanding the history of news consumption on the Web. In response to the development of digitally native news, legacy organizations must diversify and engage with these new entrants, and competition over resources such as funding and audience is unavoidable. For example, a 2014 report from the Pew Research Center noted that in the preceding year there had been 'a dramatic and conspicuous migration of high-profile journalists to digital news ventures': specifically, digitally native news ventures such as Vice employed 1,100 staff, the Huffington Post employed more than 500 staff, and Politico had more than 100 staff on payroll at the time (Jurkowitz, 2014). The shift in employment has not been one-to-one, and hand-in-hand with changes in consumption patterns there has been an accompanying change in the underlying business model that has resulted in a decrease in the overall employment level in the news media industry (Picard, 2014). In order to remain competitive, both legacy and digitally native news organizations must continue to adapt to the accelerated changes evident in news consumption behaviors.

## *Social Media Intermediaries*

Digital intermediaries such as platforms and search engines, as well as algorithms that are used to sort and display news, play an increasingly significant role in shaping and structuring digital life – especially evident via changes in news consumption, which are increasingly mediated, delivered, and curated by social media companies. Within the context of this chapter, *digital intermediaries* refers to online content platforms, news aggregators, search engines, and social media sites that serve as third-party hosts and distributors, bringing news content from creators and publishers to consumers (Braun and Gillespie, 2011; Foster, 2012). According to Bell et al. (2017), the role of these media platforms and technology companies within the news ecosystem is even greater a disruption than the movement from print to digital.

In examining the history of news on the Web and the rise of social media, it is important to understand that many of these intermediaries utilize mechanisms such as software or algorithms to achieve these processes. Broadly speaking, algorithms are 'encoded procedures for transforming input data into a desired output, based on specified calculations' (Gillespie, 2014: 167). They are designed by humans, influenced by human behavior, but still 'the result of sequential decisions made by a machine' (Usher, 2015: 1); as such, algorithms are technically complex with potentially biased and complex operating logics (Diakopoulos, 2014). As a mechanism utilized by digital intermediaries, they facilitate the discovery and dissemination of news in their responsive design as reflective of individual users (Webster, 2010). Indeed, these algorithms hold substantial independent authority to affect the flow of news (Napoli, 2014) to consumers.

### *Broad trends in social media and news consumption*

Social media and related technology represent the cusp of evolution in the news media industry. The advent of social media is a significant disruption in the transformation of news consumption on the Web. Cornia et al. (2016) found that the number of consumers surveyed who reported using social media as an outlet for news consumption each week increased from 25 percent in 2013 to 46 percent in 2015. The report also found that 41 percent of the sample use Facebook for news each week. Echoing the same trends, Pew's recent study found that half of Web-using adults in the United States get political news from Facebook (Mitchell and Page, 2015). The prior trends identified in this chapter suggest that these changing patterns of consumption are likely to accelerate moving forward.

### History of social news consumption

Social media emerged from the growth of Web 2.0 technologies in the late 1990s with social blogs such as Slashdot (founded in 1997) and Metafilter (founded in 1999) that list links to posts by users. Algorithmic distribution of social news, however, did not develop as a medium for news distribution until the late 2000s. To wit, Facebook launched in 2004 as a Harvard-only social network with the news feed component launching in 2006 – the year that also brought the launch of Twitter. Four years later came the introduction of Instagram (2010), followed by Snapchat and Apple Newsstand (2011), and Google Newsstand (in 2013). Notably, where there was a decades-long gap between the advent of the Internet and the rise of the World Wide Web, the development of social media as a news platform has occurred in a significantly shorter time period. Beginning in 2014, the frequency of social media and news-related developments began to greatly accelerate, including, but not limited to, developments such as Snapchat Discover, Facebook Instant Articles, Google AMP, and Instagram Stories (Bell et al., 2017).

The case of the Web history of Facebook, in particular, helps shed light on the role of social media and digital intermediaries in news consumption. Since its inception in 2004, Facebook evolved to play a significant role in social life and specifically in relation to the news media ecosystem, as it appears to play an important role in increasing traffic to individual news stories (Alpert, 2015; Mitchell and Page, 2014). Indeed, Facebook is responsible for about 20 percent of referrals to news publishers (Persio, 2015). Facebook's news feed algorithm always occupied some type of news editorial role in that its programing decisions select the types of news stories featured in user feeds (Bell, 2015).

More recently, in 2015 Facebook announced its *Instant Articles* partnership with several news organizations, which allows for hosting of exclusive content within Facebook's own website instead of linking out to the news organization. Ostensibly, the incentive is to minimize the slower loading speed from linking out to the news organization website and to increase revenue opportunity (Constine, 2015); however, the broader implication of such a reality is increasingly centralized news from one powerful platform where news stories are sorted and delivered via a proprietary algorithm.

### Tensions between social news consumption and production

The increasingly powerful role of social media and digital intermediaries in the consumption of news raises concerns for a number of reasons. Echoing the attitude of other technology companies, Facebook, for example, does not see itself as a publisher. Rather, as Facebook's head of news partnerships Andy Mitchell explains, Facebook is 'first and foremost, a platform where people connect with people' (Menichini, 2015). When asked if Facebook felt any responsibility for the integrity of its news feed, Mitchell evaded acceptance of the role of news publisher and responded only by saying 'that the company cared about improving user experience' (Bell, 2015). Indeed, Facebook is very involved in what content is distributed; in fact, users only see about 6 percent of their friends' posts (Timm, 2015). Perhaps more importantly, most users aren't even aware of these processes. A recent study from Eslami et al. (2015) found that 62.5 percent of sampled users were not aware that Facebook's news feed algorithm hid stories; instead, they thought every single story from their followed pages and friends appeared in the feed.

The role of social media and technology companies has become increasingly integrated into the relationship between news producers and consumers; indeed, this transition is accelerating in a short time frame. In response to such significant shifts in the ways that audiences find and consume news, news producers themselves are beginning to incorporate these digital intermediaries into their own formal business processes. Legacy news organizations and digital news organizations alike now have teams dedicated to creating content solely for social media platforms and messaging applications. According to Bell et al. (2017), this speed of transformation may lead to a reduction or even an elimination of publishing, distributing, hosting, and monetizing content from the main business processes of news organizations.

### *Implications for the news ecosystem*

The global news ecosystem is changing in fundamental ways as audiences increasingly consume news through social media platforms and digital intermediaries – and the modern state of the news media ecosystem is a significant evolution from the early history of news on the Web. Third parties such as Google, Facebook, Twitter, and Apple (along with their proprietary software and algorithms) are mediating news access and consumption and, as such, raising concerns regarding public interest and media diversity. Third-party organizations frequently use algorithms, software, platforms, and other mechanisms to bring news content to consumers, acting neither as 'neutral pipes, nor full media companies' but instead as 'gatekeepers, controlling information flows, selecting, sorting, and then distributing information' (Foster, 2012: 6). As such, the use of algorithms and other technology is directly impacting consumption patterns, and has long-term implications for the ways in which the news media ecosystem will develop over time – although the exact implications are unknown at present.

Intermediaries such as Google and Apple are commercial companies with values not necessarily aligned with media diversity and the public interest, which are traditional foundations of the Western notion of free press. The absence of public knowledge regarding what happens from the creation of news to how it is consumed raises broader issues for democracy (Bell, 2015). In fact, the means by which these digital intermediaries operate are economically sensitive, proprietary, and generally opaque. Such contradiction between the stated values of these companies and the significance of the role they play within the news ecosystem 'raises the question of if or how the normative dimensions of their governance frameworks reflect the realities of their function and significance' (Napoli, 2015: 2).

Indeed, the selective presentation of information by any intermediary is potentially detrimental to public interest ideals when the service personalizes what it presents and uses a 'proprietary recipe to draw from boundless ingredients' to deliver the news (Zittrain, 2014). The difference, however, is that while traditional news organizations are indeed built around principles of editorial oversight, such behavior is historically paired with industry-wide standards, guidelines, or codes of conduct that provide some level of transparency into the process. These kinds of self-regulatory instruments are not yet a component of digital intermediaries such as Facebook, Twitter, Apple, and Google in their involvement with the news ecosystem. In actuality, many of these companies are still publicly distancing themselves from identifying as news organizations and corresponding editorial responsibilities (Napoli, 2015).

As discussed, in response to changes in news consumption behaviors that reflect an increase in the use of social media intermediaries, news producers continue to push content to these technology companies without any guarantee of a consistent benefit to their business models. Such a scenario has created a critical dilemma for the greater news media ecosystem:

> Should they continue the costly business of maintaining their own publishing infrastructure, with smaller audiences but complete control over revenue, brand, and audience data? Or, should they cede control over user data and advertising in exchange for the significant audience growth offered by Facebook or other platforms? (Bell et al., 2017: 50)

## Mobile News Apps

One of the most significant disruptions in the evolution of consumer news behaviors is related to the introduction and growth of mobile news, a term used here to signify the multiple ways in which consumers engage with news via a mobile device. Indeed, mobile news consumption involves a variety of different access points of engagement including customized news alerts, mobile websites of news organizations, and mobile news applications (apps) (Westlund, 2013). Mobile news is also used here to represent consumer engagement with news produced specifically for third-party platforms such as Snapchat and Instagram, as well as with news stories on social feeds like Facebook and Twitter.

### Broad trends in mobile news consumption

The disruption of mobile news with regards to the evolution of news consumption on the Web is inextricably linked to the diffusion of smartphones and improved access to mobile Internet, which have helped to feed consumer interest in mobile services such as mobile news (Nel and Westlund, 2012). Over the past five years, US adult smartphone ownership has increased from 46 percent to 82 percent (Knight Foundation, 2016). Broadly speaking, news has always been an integral component of public life; indeed, more than 70 percent of current US adults closely follow the news (Mitchell et al., 2016a). Furthermore, a growing portion of news consumption now occurs via mobile intake, with 89 percent of the US mobile population (144 million users) accessing news and information on mobile devices (Knight Foundation, 2016). A recent Pew study estimates that news consumption specifically on mobile devices has increased from 54 percent in 2013 to 72 percent in 2016 (Mitchell et al., 2016a). These broad trends speak to the significance of mobile news as the most recent disruption in the historical evolution of news consumption on the Web.

### History of mobile news consumption

Mobile devices are deeply embedded into everyday life. What began as an innovation of the telecommunication industry evolved to become a media-rich platform (Wei, 2008) encompassing a variety of audio, video, graphical, and textual communication processes (Westlund, 2008). Early research found a hesitation toward mobile news consumption, behaviors restricted to breaks in a daily schedule (Dimmick et al., 2011). This evolved quickly, however, with research that found people accessed mobile news both between and during scheduled activity (Westlund et al., 2011).

This turning point of mobile news as a significant disruptor of consumption patterns can be traced back to 2011 when half of the US adult population owned a smartphone or tablet and nearly one-third of them got news on a mobile device at least once per week, and by 2012 over half (51 percent) of smartphone owners used mobile devices for news (Rosenstiel and Mitchell, 2012). This increased slightly to 54 percent in 2013, when 21 percent also reported that mobile news consumption is 'frequent' (Mitchell and Page, 2014). In 2015, Pew's State of the News Media report recognized a 'mobile majority' as mobile traffic was greater than desktop traffic for 39 of the top 50 digital news websites analyzed (Mitchell and Page,

2015: 4), and the number of news sites with greater mobile traffic than desktop traffic continued to increase in 2016 (Mitchell et al., 2016b). In a similar vein, a Reuters Institute report found that the percentage of the US population that said they used a smartphone to access the news in the last week increased from 30 percent in 2013 to 48 percent in 2016 (Cornia et al., 2016).

### *Tensions between mobile news consumers and producers*

Consumption of news on the Web evolved quite rapidly, with the disruption of mobile news and associated technological developments leaving news organizations to contend with managing changes in the creation and distribution of news. For instance, evolving consumer demand for mobile news could impact the amount of resources spent on other mediums (Nel and Westlund, 2012) or it could complement consumer choices regarding other media (Newell et al., 2008). News organizations grapple with the shift to mobile news in terms of attracting audiences, formatting and delivering content, and the influence of technological aspects such as screen size and loading speed (Dunaway, 2016). Whether an opportunity or a threat, the disruption of mobile news for consumers causes tensions for the news producers as they grapple with new production- and distribution-related activities.

Historically, legacy news organizations endeavor toward cross-media news production. In fact, news organizations first experimented with mobile news as early as the 1990s, when some organizations published news for the pager (Westlund, 2013). The turn of the millennium brought the development of pushed news alerts (Fidalgo, 2009) and customized mobile news websites, experiments implemented with the goal of meeting evolving user demands of better exposure and usability (Westlund, 2013). In 2007, Apple's iPhone launched in the United States and spurred the growth of a new mobile ecosystem, a formative turning point in the evolution of news production and consumption on the Web. The mobile-focused efforts of news producers were two-fold: first, to ensure news was accessible on mobile Web browsers and, second, to develop their own native apps (Westlund, 2013). The late 2010s saw the development of an increasing number of emerging mobile platforms, such as Snapchat and Instagram, each of which adds to the tension between news produced and consumers as they navigate the ever-evolving field.

As we reach present day, the longstanding patterns of this historical shift leads to mobile news, which continues to afford consumers with access to news at any place and any time. On the flipside, news producers continue to struggle with where best to invest resources and development efforts. While some news organizations adopted a 'mobile first' strategy, others tend to focus on a 'more platform-agnostic approach' (Westlund, 2013: 13). While some news organizations see value in developing native mobile news apps, others are focusing on building out mobile-responsive websites (Knight Foundation, 2016). No matter the strategic organizational approach, changes in news consumption on the Web continue to cause tension for news producers responding to the disruption of mobile news.

### *Implications for the news ecosystem*

Indeed, the disruption of mobile news and associated changes in consumption behaviors is having a profound impact on the greater news ecosystem. The emergence of mobile news enables consumption at any time and any place, but, furthermore, it enables new forms of personalization, curation, and aggregation of distributed news (Sheller, 2015). This affects both the production and consumption of news on the Web as we know it.

Almost all adults with mobile devices consume news on their devices, further enabling news organizations to develop and target specific audiences (Knight Foundation, 2016). Early research suggested the mobile news consumers followed the news more frequently, but with specific user patterns and preferences (Chan-Olmsted et al., 2012). Two-thirds of all online activity is expected to take place on mobile devices by 2020; as a result, more time is spent consuming the news than was historically possible (Dunaway, 2016). In the shift to a mobile news landscape, news organizations must learn from the lessons of the history of the Web and better understand the longstanding patterns of change with regards to the consumption of news.

## CONCLUSION

This chapter constructs a narrative that traces changes in news media consumption from the early rise of Web pages, to the growth of social media, to the proliferation of mobile platforms. At each stage, the trajectory of the history of the Web is central to understanding the next stage in the evolution of news media consumption and corresponding production. In sum, news consumption has indeed evolved since the advent of the Web, but changes in consumption are interwoven with the history of the Web. The introduction of the Web first brought the rise of online news; however, several decades later further significant changes have impacted the ways that humans communicate and connect. This chapter depicts such transformation in the context of the news industry by highlighting the evolution of news consumption behavior over the last two decades. In tracing the news industry's movement to digital, the rise of social, and the influence of mobile, this work sheds light on the history of news evolution with specific regard to the consumer perspective.

## REFERENCES

Ahlers, D. (2006) 'News consumption and the new electronic media', *Harvard International Journal of Press/Politics* 11(1): 29–52.

Alpert, L.I. (2015) 'Publishers warily embed with Facebook: Social network's power to steer readers could grow with "Instant Articles" initiative', May 11, *The Wall Street Journal*.

Amadeo, J.A. (2007) Patterns of Internet Use and Political Engagement Among Youth. In: Dahlgren P (ed) *Young Citizens and New Media: Learning for Democractic Participation*. New York: Routledge. pp. 125–148.

Bell, E. (2015) 'Google and Facebook are our frenemy. Beware', *Columbia Journalism Review*. Available at: https://www.cjr.org/analysis/google_facebook_frenemy.php

Bell, E., Owen, T., Brown, P., Hauka, C. and Rashidian, N. (2017) 'The platform press: How Silicon Valley reengineered journalism', *Tow Center for Digital Journalism at Columbia University*.

Bimber, B. (2001) 'Information and political engagement in America: The search for effects of information technology at the individual level', *Political Research Quarterly* 54(1): 53–67.

Boczkowski, P.J. (2004) *Digitizing the News: Innovation in Online Newspapers*, Cambridge, USA: MIT Press.

Braun, J. and Gillespie, T. (2011) 'Hosting the public discourse, hosting the public: When online news and social media converge', *Journalism Practice* 5(4): 383–398.

Center, P.R. (2008) 'Internet overtakes newspapers as news outlet', Pew Research Center.

CERN. (n.d.) The Birth of the Web. (https://home.cern/topics/birth-web)

Chan-Olmsted, S., Rim, H. and Zerba, A. (2012) 'Mobile news adoption among young adults: Examining the roles of perceptions, news consumption, and media usage', *Journalism & Mass Communication Quarterly* 90(1): 126–147.

Constine, J. (2015) 'Facebook starts hosting publishers: Instant Articles', *TechCrunch*. Available at: https://techcrunch.com/2015/05/12/facebook-instant-articles/

Cornia, A., Sehl, A. and Nielsen, R.K. (2016) 'Private sector media and digital news', *Reuters Institute for the Study of Journalism*.

d'Haenens, L., Jankowski, N. and Heuvelman, A. (2004) 'News in online and print newspapers: Differences in reader consumption and recall', *New Media & Society* 6(3): 363–382.

de Sola Pool, I. (1983) *Technologies of Freedom,* Cambridge, USA: Harvard University Press.

de Zuniga, H.G., Copeland, L. and Bimber, B. (2014) 'Political consumerism: Civic engagement and the social media connection', *New Media & Society* 16(3): 488–506.

Diakopoulos, N. (2014) *Algorithmic accountability reporting: On the investigation of black boxes,* Tow Center for Digital Journalism.

Dimmick, J., Feaster, J.C. and Hoplamazian, G.J. (2011) 'News in the interstices: The niches of mobile media in space and time', *New Media and Society* 13(1): 23–39.

Doyle, G. (2013) 'Re-invention and survival: Newspapers in the era of digital multiplatform delivery', *Journal of Media Business Studies* 10(4): 1–20.

Dunaway, J. (2016) 'Mobile vs. computer: Implications for news audiences and outlets', *Harvard Kennedy School Shorenstein Center on Media, Politics and Public Policy.*

Editor and Publisher Yearbook. (2003) *Editor and Publisher Yearbook Online Data,* 1940–2003.

Eslami, M., Rickman, A., Vaccaro, K., et al. (2015) 'I always assumed that I wasn't really that close to [her]: Reasoning about invisible algorithms in news feeds', *CHI 2015.* Seoul, Korea.

Fidalgo, A. (2009) 'Pushed news: When the news comes to the cellphone', *Brazilian Journalism Research* 5(2): 113–124.

Fletcher, R. and Park, S. (2017) 'The impact of trust in the news media on online news consumption and participation', *Digital Journalism* 5(10): 1281–1299.

Foster, R. (2012) 'News plurality in a digital world', *Reuters Institute for the Study of Journalism.*

Gilbert, C.G. (2005) 'Unbundling the structure of inertia: Resource versus routine rigidity', *Academy of Management Journal* 48(5): 741–763.

Gillespie, T. (2014) The Relevance of Algorithms. In: Gillespie T, Boczkowski P and Foot K (eds) *Media Technologies.* Cambridge: MIT Press. pp. 167–194.

Hamilton, J. (2004) *All the News that's Fit to Sell: How the Market Transforms Information into News,* Princeton, USA: Princeton University Press.

Jurkowitz, M. (2014) 'The growth in digital reporting', *Pew Research Center.*

Khaw, A. (1983) 'Changing old habits with new technology in newspapers', *Media Asia* 10(3): 168–169.

Knight Foundation. (2016) 'Mobile-first news: How people use smartphones to access information', *Knight Foundation.*

Ksiazek, T.B., Peer, L. and Lessard, K. (2016) 'User engagement with online news: Conceptualizing interactivity and exploring the relationship between online news videos and user comments', *New Media & Society* 18(3): 502–520.

Margolis, M. and Resnick, D. (2000) *Politics as Usual: The Cyberspace Revolution,* Thousand Oaks, USA: Sage.

Menichini, R. (2015) 'Facebook: More collaboration, not competition, with media', *La Repubblica.*

Mitchell, A., Gottfried, J., Barthel, M., et al. (2016a) 'The modern news consumer: News attitudes and practices in the digital era', *Pew Research Center.*

Mitchell, A., Holcomb, J. and Weisel, R. (2016b) 'State of the news media 2016', *Pew Research Center.*

Mitchell, A., Jurkowitz, M., Anderson, M., et al. (2014) 'State of the news media 2014', In: Mitchell A (ed) *State of the News Media.* Washington DC: Pew Research Center. Available at: http://assets.pewresearch.org/wp-content/uploads/sites/13/2017/05/30142556/state-of-the-news-media-report-2014-final.pdf

Mitchell, A. and Page, D. (2014) 'State of the news media 2014: Growth in digital reporting: What it means for journalism and news consumers', *Pew Research Center.* (http://www.journalism.org/files/2014/03/Shifts-in-Reporting_For-uploading.pdf)

Mitchell, A. and Page, D. (2015) 'State of the news media 2015', *Pew Research Center.*

Mitchelstein, E. and Boczkowski, P.J. (2009) 'Between tradition and change: A review of recent research on online news production', *Journalism* 10: 562–586.

Napoli, P.M. (2014) 'Automated media: An institutional theory perspective on algorithmic media production and consumption', *Communication Theory* 24(3): 340–360.

Napoli, P.M. (2015) 'Social media and the public interest: Governance of news platforms in the realm of individual and algorithmic gatekeepers', *Telecommunications Policy* 39(9): 751–760.

Nee, C.R. (2013) 'Creative destruction: An exploratory study of how digitally native news nonprofits are innovating online journalism practices', *International Journal on Media Management* 15(1): 3–22.

Nel, F. and Westlund, O. (2012) 'The 4C's of mobile news: Channels, conversation, content, and commerce', *Journalism Practice* 6: 744–753.

Newell, J., Pilotta, J.J. and Thomas, J.C. (2008) 'Mass media displacement and saturation', *International Journal on Media Management* 10(4): 131–138.

Newman, N., Levy, D.A.L. and Nielsen, R.K. (2015) 'Digital news report 2015: Tracking the future of news', *Reuters Institute for the Study of Journalism.*

Norris, P. (2003) 'Tuned out voters? Media impact on campaign learning', *Ethical Perspectives* 9(3): 200–221.

Persio, S.L. (2015) 'Facebook's plans to feed us news', *International Journalism Festival 2015 WebMagazine.*

Pew Research Center. (2014) 'World wide web timeline', *Pew Research Center.*

Picard, R.G. (2014) 'Twilight or new dawn of journalism? Evidence from the changing news ecosystem', *Digital Journalism* 2(3): 273–283.

Rosenstiel, T. and Mitchell, A. (2011) 'The state of the news media 2011', *Pew Research Center.*

Rosenstiel, T. and Mitchell, A. (2012) 'The future of mobile news: The explosion in mobile audiences and a close look at what it means for news', *Pew Research Center.*

Rothmann, W. and Koch, J. (2014) 'Creativity in strategic lock-ins: The newspaper industry and the digital revolution', *Technological Forecasting and Social Change* 83: 66–83.

Sheller, M. (2015) 'News now', *Journalism Studies* 16(1): 12–26.

Thompson, B. (2014) 'Is Buzzfeed a tech company?', *Stratechery.*

Timm, T. (2015) 'The most concerning element of Facebook's potential new power', *Columbia Journalism Review.* Available at: https://www.cjr.org/criticism/facebook_news_censorship.php

Usher, N. (2015) 'Who's afraid of the big bad algorithm?', *Columbia Journalism Review.* Available at: https://www.cjr.org/analysis/whos_afraid_of_a_big_bad_algorithm.php

Webster, J.G. (2010) 'User information regimes: How social media shape patterns of consumption', *Northwestern University Law Review* 104(2): 593–612.

Wei, R. (2008) 'Motivations for using the mobile phone for mass communications and entertainment', *Telematics and Informatics* 25(1): 36–46.

Westlund, O. (2008) 'From mobile phone to mobile device: News consumption on the go', *Canadian Journal of Communication* 33(3): 443–463.

Westlund, O. (2013) 'Mobile News', *Digital Journalism* 1(1): 6–26.

Westlund, O., Gomez-Barroso, J.-L., Compano, R., et al. (2011) 'Exploring the logic of mobile search', *Behaviour & Information Technology* 30(5): 691–703.

Wu, H.D. and Bechtel, A. (2002) 'Web site use and news topic and type', *Journalism & Mass Communication Quarterly* 79(1): 73–86.

Wu, L. (2016) 'Did you get the buzz? Are digital native media becoming mainstream?', *#ISOJ* 6(1). Available at: https://isojjournal.wordpress.com/2016/04/14/did-you-get-the-buzz-are-digital-native-media-becoming-mainstream/

Zittrain, J. (2014) 'Engineering an election', *Harvard Law Review Forum* 127: 335–341.

# Historical Studies of National Web Domains

Niels Brügger and Ditte Laursen

This chapter sets out to investigate national web domains, and it argues that research on how national web domains have developed is a cornerstone in web history studies at large. However, studying a national web domain over time is challenging in a number of ways, including how to conceptualize a national web, let alone the technical challenges of studying large amounts of web data. The chapter starts by presenting some of the arguments for why the history of web domains is a relevant field of study. Then a brief research history of studies of national webs is outlined. In the following section some of the major research themes and challenges are discussed, including which sources to use, how to delimit a nation on the web, and how to use the archived web as a source. Finally, there follows an overview of case studies of national webs, and then the chapter is concluded.

## WHY STUDY THE HISTORY OF NATIONAL WEB DOMAINS?

At first sight it may seem counterintuitive to use the term 'national web' in the same sentence as the World Wide Web. The web is undoubtedly 'world wide' in the sense that no matter where web users are located they can make content available to anyone located anywhere, and they can access content made available by others, no matter their location. However, there is evidence that web users to a large extent use a 'national web'. In a study based on an analysis of 4,000 websites, already in 2000 Halavais argues that the web is to some degree part of a national web domain (Halavais, 2000). In the 2009 survey *The media menus of Danish internet users 2009*, transnational web use was examined, and the conclusion was that the web is largely used as a national (or even local) medium: 'national horizon is strong except for "Searching" info about and "Buying goods"' (Finnemann et al., 2012: 31–5). In the monograph *Social Theory after the Internet*, it is debated whether the web is global or not when it comes to its use, and after evaluating various ways of measuring this it is concluded that 'Whatever the most important factors may turn out to be, the web is not becoming a single whole, but rather a series of clusters: linguistic plus those that develop due to the policies of states and sites promoting shared interests such as economic development strategies' (Schroeder, 2018: 121–2). Finally, if looking at content providers, a comparative study of news websites in nine different countries showed that online news is strongly nation-centred (Curran et al., 2013: 887–91). Thus, the web may potentially be global, but when it comes to users and content it is actually in many cases national. However, although the national web seems to play a role for web users, the rest of this chapter will show that from a web researcher's perspective it can be a challenge to determine exactly how 'the national web' should be approached, in particular when it comes to the history of a national web.

But still there are good arguments for considering the national web an analytical entity of relevance to web historians. First of all, it is important to study a national web and its historical development, because it constitutes the backdrop for other web historical studies of analytical entities that are smaller than the national web. For instance, when studying the history of one website or of a cluster of interrelated websites about an event such as elections, sports events, or natural disasters it is important to contextualize such a study, and one of the contexts of the websites is the entire national web in which they are embedded. Therefore, it is relevant to study a national web as an object of study in its own right, and to include it as a contextualizing element in other web studies.

However, web historical studies of national webs do not only provide relevant historical knowledge. If national web studies are based on the archived web as a source, they can also help develop and test adequate methods and analytical tools for Big Data studies of this important part of the digital cultural heritage. Since many national web archiving institutions now hold large collections of archived web historical studies, these large quantities of archived material can help develop novel methods that can be used on a smaller scale when studying other web entities. In this sense, historical studies of national webs can be understood as extreme cases that can bring web archive studies to a head, as is the case with the Danish research project 'Probing a Nation's web domain', in which both authors of this chapter have participated, and which will be used to illustrate some of the points throughout the chapter; hence the many Danish examples (cf. Brügger, 2017). In addition, historical studies of national webs are also important as drivers for the establishment of national – and even transnational – research infrastructures. On a national level this includes High Performance Computer facilities as well as procedures and technical solutions for extracting large amounts of data from national web archives, and on a transnational scale could include simple look-up facilities to help researchers find national material in other countries' web archives, and eventually the possibility of including such material in an analysis (for instance, based on a derived dataset such as a link graph). Finally, the playfulness that is a part of studying developments in such large quantities of archived web should not be neglected, since the iterative process of gaining experience with working with large amounts of archived web can help researchers develop and test research questions that would probably not have occurred with smaller amounts of data, but that can now be asked, and in many cases also answered.

## A BRIEF RESEARCH HISTORY

Studies of national web domains can be divided into three waves, each with a different focus.

National web domains have been studied since the early 2000s (cf. Brügger, 2017: 62), and include studies of a number of national web domains such as the Austrian, Brazilian, and Portuguese web domains, among others, with a focus on language, page size, page age, and hyperlinks (cf. the overview in Baeza-Yates et al., 2007: 3–5). With the exception of Halavais' study from 2000 of the relation between 4,000 websites and national borders (Halavais, 2000) these early studies mainly focused on the technical content of the web, and their aim was by and large to improve either the web (browsers, hyperlink structure, etc.) or the process of web archiving. These studies rarely adopted a historical perspective.

In contrast, the second wave sets out to study national webs as a source in their own right that can be used to inform research projects within the social sciences and the humanities. These studies emerge out of the research environment Digital Methods Initiative at the University of Amsterdam, and they are by and large based on the idea that the online web's ways of working (e.g. the use of search engines) are repurposed as research tools (Rogers, 2013). This also means that focus is on the online web and not on the archived web, as it has been archived by a web archive in the past, and these studies do not aim to study the historical development of national domains. Some of the studies emerging out of the second wave are studies of the development of the Iranian web (Rogers et al., 2013) and a study of the Arabic webspace in Israel (Ben-David, 2014).

The third wave starts to emerge almost in parallel with the second wave, although a little later, but in contrast to the latter the research projects of the third wave have a clear historical approach, and in most cases they include the archived web as a source, although not as the only source in all cases. And in some cases the insights that characterized the second wave have been supplemented with historical studies of the archived web, such as Ben-David's study of the history of the web domain of the former Yugoslavia (Ben-David, 2016, cf. also 'A disappeared nation' section later in this chapter). An early project is the Australian 'Internet History in Australia and the Asia-Pacific' (2010–13), which is investigating the development of the internet in Australasia; however, this project is focused not only on web history, but on internet history. Then follows 'Big Data: Demonstrating the Value of the UK Web Domain Dataset for Social Science Research', which makes the first digs into trends in the development of the UK web domain (UK, 2012–14; cf. Hale et al., 2014, and also section 'A nation's sub-domains – the case of the UK web' later in this chapter), 'WebART: Enabling Scholarly Research in the KB Web Archive', which investigates the Dutch web (the Netherlands, 2012–16), 'Probing a Nation's Web Sphere – the Historical Development of the Danish Web', which analyses file types, link structures, and web content on the Danish web, and how this has developed (Denmark, 2013–; cf. Brügger, 2017), 'Big UK Domain Data for the Arts and Humanities (BUDDAH)', in which the development of the UK web domain is studied in more depth through a number of case studies (UK, 2014–15; cf. Cowls, 2017 for an overview), 'A Longitudinal Analysis of the Canadian World Wide Web as a Historical Resource', which focuses on the development of the Canadian web (Canada, 2014–15), and, finally, 'Web90–Patrimoine, Mémoires et Histoire du Web dans les années 1990', which is a broader research project in which the development of the French web in the 1990s is placed in a wider cultural context and in a longer time span going back to the 1970s (France, 2014–17; cf. Schafer and Thierry, 2016; Schafer, 2018, and also section 'A national web domain' later in this chapter). Also in this period the first edited volumes about the web in different national settings were published (Brügger and Schroeder, 2017; Brügger and Laursen, 2018).

Thus, national webs have been studied since the early 2000s, in the beginning mainly with a technical aim, which from the second wave is supplemented with social science and humanities studies, and in the beginning without a historical approach, which does not emerge until the third wave, when the archived web in web archives also starts to be used as one of the primary source types. In addition, the studies tend to move from broad mappings towards more detailed studies, including reflections on how a national web domain can be delimited at all. Finally, it is worth mentioning that in parallel with these research projects more and more national web archives are established, which in many cases is a condition as well as an incentive to undertake these research projects, and more of the projects are made in close collaboration with web archives.

## RESEARCH THEMES AND CHALLENGES

Studies of national web domains are facing a number of challenges, such as determining which sources to base the study on, how to delimit a national web domain on the web, and, in particular, to what an extent the archived web can be used as a source.

### *A Broad Range of Sources*

When introducing studies of national webs above it has been taken for granted that such studies are based on the archived web. However, this need not be the case. As with any other historical study a variety of source types can – and should – be used. This could include user statistics, reports on government initiatives, on web use and similar, government policies, articles/features in the printed or audio-visual media, internal documents from web companies, and oral history interviews with relevant individuals, to mention just a few. In addition, sources such as 'How to…' books published from the early 1990s onwards, like 'How to use the web' and similar, also constitute an important source type since they are the most comprehensive presentation of what the web looked like and what a user could find on the web of the time, including the national web; in many cases these types of books are the only sources to help show the actual web content, primarily regarding the old web. In a similar vein, the archived internet or web can be used, but not as the object of study as such, but rather indirectly; for instance, the web may have been mentioned in newsgroups, just as national search engines/portals may give an overview of the categories of content that were available, including links to that content. Finally, lists of the domain names on a given Country Code Top-Level Domain name (ccTLD), such as .uk and .fr for the UK and France, respectively, constitute an invaluable source.

An example of a study of a national web that is based on a broad range of source types is the above-mentioned French research project 'Web90 – Patrimoine, Mémoires et Histoire du Web dans les années 1990'. In addition to the archived web, this project also studied press and audio-visual archives (mainstream media and specialist press dedicated to the web and the internet), reports, newsgroups, and interviews with web professionals (Schafer and Thierry, 2016: 1145; Schafer, 2018).

The challenges related to these types of sources are in general not particular to web history studies or to studies of national webs, and in brief they mainly relate to the finding of the material. The printed press and audio-visual media have usually been collected and preserved, but online media such as newsgroups and search engines/portals can be harder to find, since they may not have been archived. Regarding statistical material about web use this is often not available for entire national webs, and in particular for the early years not much statistical information of this kind exists. Lists of web domains on ccTLDs come with challenges of their own, and are discussed below.

## *Delimiting a Nation – on the Web*

Defining how a nation can be delimited is in itself a challenge, and with the web this challenge does not become smaller. In general, one can delimit the boundaries of a nation either by focusing on the concrete geo-physical space, that is, where the nation's territory starts and ends, or one can focus on the cultural space, that is, how the inhabitants within a certain territory construct a cultural national community and its boundaries. The latter approach is put forward by Benedict Anderson when he argues that 'nation-ness, as well as nationalism, are cultural artefacts' (Anderson, 1996: 4). But to Anderson nations are not only cultural artefacts, they are also imagined, since 'the members of even the smallest nation will never know most of their fellow-members [...] yet in the minds of each lives the image of their communion' (Anderson, 1996: 6).[1] Therefore, Anderson argues, one of the main conditions for the emerging nation-ness in the late eighteenth century is the spread of print-capitalism, that is, the advent of the printed book as a commodity (Anderson, 1996: 22–46). The printed book, and later newspapers, offers a shared space that enables the inhabitants of a given geo-physical area to imagine a nation populated by fellow members, and to do this across physical distance and over time.

Inspired by Anderson's idea of this close relation between print media and the establishment of an imagined nation-ness, one could argue that, in general, the territory and the cultural artefact of the nation are interwoven through media, since the imagined community of the nation does not exist ex nihilo – on the contrary, the imagination of fellow members of a nation is conveyed by and with media that are distributed within a certain geo-physical territory. Although newspapers could be posted globally, by and large their distribution network (postal system (routes, stamps, etc.), street vendors, bicycles) has stayed within the territory of the nation. As for analogue electronic media such as radio and television, global broadcasting is possible, for instance with short-wave radio and satellite television, but the majority of broadcasters have usually limited their broadcast activities to the national territory, in the main based on a national terrestrial broadcasting network. Thus, although national print media and analogue electronic media could have a global reach, their actual distribution networks tend to stay within the geo-physical boundaries of the nation, which implies that in the pre-web era there was a high degree of concordance between the national territory and the media that carry the imagined community.

With the web this close mutual interdependency between territory and media distribution network is loosened to such an extent that the limits of the territory do not constitute the natural boundaries for the web as carrier of the imagined national community. However, as mentioned at the beginning of this chapter, this does not imply that no national borders can be identified on the web, but due to the absence of a close and unequivocal material relation between territory and media distribution the boundaries of the nation are not as obvious as before the web. In contrast, these boundaries have to be established by reconstructing them in the vast material of the global web.

The most obvious way of delimiting a national web is to use the web's own institutionalized national delimitations, as expressed in the above-mentioned Domain Name System where a given Country Code Top-Level Domain name is allocated to a given nation, such as .uk for the UK, .fr for France, and .nl for the Netherlands. Delimiting a nation's web based on ccTLD is the most obvious way forward if the archived web is used as a source. The big advantage of this approach is that it is easy to automate, and it scales to large quantities of web material of which the reconstructed national web is composed. However, this way of delimiting a nation on the web also comes with a number of challenges.

The first cluster of challenges revolves around the extent to which the ccTLD mirrors the online activities related to a given nation. Although the ccTLD may cover some of these activities, in most cases it does not cover all of them on a 1:1 scale since a certain portion of a nation's web can be located on other top-level domain names such as .com, .edu, etc. (a so-called generic Top-Level Domain (gTLD)), or on transnational domains such as .eu. Also, there may be a certain degree of randomness related to the link between a given ccTLD and the content's relation to the nation in question; for instance, the ccTLD .tv for the island of Tuvalu is used by a large number of broadcasters and streaming services, and it would not tell much about that island nation, just like the domain name 'youtu.be' does not relate to Belgium. In some countries the ccTLD plays an important role on the national web (like .uk, .fr), whereas in other countries the ccTLD is not that well used by the nation's citizens (like .us, .ca; cf. Milligan and Smyth, 2018 regarding .ca). In addition, cities within a nation may have their own TLD, like .amsterdam (Teszelszky, 2018). The challenge regarding material on gTLDs and similar is that it has to be tracked manually, by researchers or web archive curators.[2] Finally, in some nations there exist more than one ccTLD on the same territory, such as in the Netherlands where the .nl exists along with the .frl domain, the ccTLD of Friesland, the region of the Frisian people (Teszelszky, 2018).

The second challenge relates to finding and accessing information about a given ccTLD. It is preferable to have the entire list of a given ccTLD from the investigated period because it constitutes the authoritative list of what was included in the nation's web domain. But a list of a given country's ccTLD is normally not accessible, either because it does not exist any longer (the national ccTLD handler may not have preserved it), or it is not freely available (because of privacy issues, or other). Therefore, if this list is not available one has to reconstruct it by searching existing web archives for the relevant ccTLD name, and then perform a hyperlink analysis of the found material to discover new domain names on the ccTLD (an iterative process that can be repeated). For instance, this is the method developed and used in a study of the Yugoslav web and the ccTLD .yu (Ben-David, 2016, cf. also section 'A disappeared nation' later in this chapter).

A third challenge relates to the ccTLDs themselves, because even if one has access to the authoritative list or has reconstructed (parts of) it, a ccTLD's domain names tend to be dynamic in the sense that they come and go, and this happens rapidly. An illustrative example of this is a historical study of the Danish ccTLD .dk where the authoritative ccTLD list was compared with the holdings of the US-based Internet Archive. The study showed that the Internet Archive had archived more web domains than the ones on the initial ccTLD list that the Danish national web archive Netarkivet used when starting a web archiving of the entire Danish web domain (Brügger et al., 2018). The reason for this is that the archiving of a national web domain takes time, often several months, and during this time the ccTLD's domain names are changing. Therefore, this temporal discrepancy between a ccTLD list and the changes during the time it takes to archive a national web domain implies that the ccTLD list itself does not mirror the national web as it may look during the archiving, and it may then be necessary to consult other web archives.

Another way of delimiting a nation on the web would be to look for language. However, this is only useful in very few cases where a given language is spoken in only one country (as for instance Danish in Denmark). In many other cases searching for a nation's main language would not be useful because the language is widely spoken (like English or Spanish).

In summary, delimiting a nation on the web is challenging. In many cases the ccTLD can be a distinctive element, but it usually has to be supplemented, whereas in other cases the ccTLD is not much help.

## *The Archived Web as a Source*

As mentioned above, the archived web may not be the only useful historical source in a study of a national web, but nevertheless it is still an important source, and it is therefore necessary to reflect on some of the challenges related to its use, because it is distinct from other source types (written, print, electronic, digitized, as well as online sources). The online web can be archived in a number of ways (Brügger, 2018a, 2018b), but for historical studies of a nation's web domain the most obvious place to look for relevant source material is national or transnational web archives.[3] In the main these web archives have collected and preserved the online web by the use of web crawling. With web crawling a list of web domains to be crawled is set up in the crawling software, then the web crawler contacts the web server where the web domain is hosted, retrieves the web pages, finds all the hyperlinks on these pages, and follows these hyperlinks and retrieves the web pages to which they point. And this process can be repeated in as many iterations as the web archiving institution specifies in the scope of the web crawler. The result of web crawling is a number of files (HTML and other) that are usually preserved in a compressed file format such as ARC or WARC. In addition, web crawling also produces supplementary material such as the seed list (the list of web domains used by the web crawler) and the crawl log, which is a log file that records everything that happened during the web crawl.[4] General knowledge about web crawling is important to have in mind to better understand the challenges related to this type of material.

In general, the main challenge when basing studies of national web domains on the archived web in web archives is how the holdings of the web archives can be used to reconstruct 'the national web domain'. As will be shown in more detail below, in some countries this is a question of having more material than is needed by the web historian to cover 'the national web domain', and therefore selections have to be made, whereas in other cases the reconstruction of the national web domain is a matter of the web historian not having enough material, and therefore the material at hand may have to be combined. In brief, the challenge is how one can reconstruct a corpus of archived web that can be maintained to cover a national web domain.

Before looking more closely at these two cases of establishing a corpus, it is important to remind oneself that when using archived web in national web archives it is not only a matter of reconstructing the national web based on archival holdings – these holdings are themselves (re)constructions of the online web (Brügger, 2018a, 2018b). For various reasons web archiving, including web crawling, cannot collect and preserve the online web on a 1:1 scale, so when reconstructing a national web in a web archive this reconstruction is taking place on top of the initial construction that took place during the archiving. In that sense what is analysed is the web as archived and not the online web as it was in the past.

When reconstructing a corpus that can be claimed to constitute 'a national web', the researcher is dependent on how the web archive in question has collected and preserved the online web, and how it is made available to researchers. There are great differences regarding this between web archives, and in each case the choices impact the research. It is worth mentioning that corpus building is not the same as crawling the web with a view to establishing a collection. Most web archives have collected more material than is needed by the web historian, and therefore they cannot be dealt with as a single unit. Thus, selections have to be made to establish a corpus.

In some countries more material has been archived than is needed by the web historian to cover 'the national web domain', in some cases deliberately, in other cases accidentally, as an effect of web crawling as an archiving method. And in both cases selections have to be made to establish a corpus that is as accurate as possible. The Danish case can illustrate these points (Brügger et al., 2018). The Danish web is archived by Netarkivet, and the entire Danish ccTLD .dk is crawled two to four times per year (including some material on gTLDs).[5] Thus, the first choice is to choose between these crawls. When one of these has been selected, then comes a more complicated round of selections. The challenge is that the web crawling process has implied that more versions of the same web page are likely to have been collected during the two to four months it takes to archive .dk. The reason for this is that hyperlinks may point to HTML pages that were already archived (or that are later being archived), and these web pages will then occur in the material more than one time. However, since this is not a systematic bias (it is based on the accidental presence of link targets), the researcher has to make selections as to which of these versions should be included in the corpus.[6] Therefore, when this type of web archive collection is used, 'the national web' has to be established in a two-step selection procedure: first, one chooses which of the annual crawls to be used; and, second, versions of the same web page should be identified and selections have to be made, and neither identification nor selection are trivial to perform.

That there is too much archived web to choose from is not necessarily only a matter of having too much material in the same web archive, as in the Danish case. It can also be a matter of having too many web archives that each collect parts of the same national web, but with different archiving strategies and aims. This is, for instance, the case in the UK, where the British Library performs a broad crawl of the entire ccTLD .uk and some other non-.uk sites as well (since 2013), but in addition to this the library holds selective archivings from before 2013, and parts of the UK web domain are also archived by the UK Government Web Archive at The National Archives as well as by the UK Parliament Web Archive (Winters, 2018). Thus, the researcher who wants to establish a corpus of the UK web domain may start with the British Library's ccTLD crawl, but the other collections may be included as well, because they can possibly supplement the broad crawl. However, combining web collections across web archives is in itself challenging because of differences as to archiving strategies and software, quality of the material, terms of searching and accessing the archive, archiving format, etc. (Brügger, 2012: 316–18).

In other countries the challenge is not having too much material, but rather the opposite: there is not enough archived web for the web historian to reconstruct a corpus that is close to the national web. This lack of material can come in different forms, ranging from that something but not all is available, to that nothing is available at all. In the Netherlands, for instance, there exists a national web archive at the National Library of the Netherlands, but it does not make crawls of the entire .nl ccTLD (only a small number of selected web domains are archived, not based on legal deposit), but as was the case in the UK there also exist a few smaller web archiving initiatives such as the Archipol web archiving project at the Documentation Centre for Dutch Political Parties (Teszelszky, 2018). Thus, in this case one cannot base the reconstruction of the Dutch web on a ccTLD crawl, supplemented with material from other web collections; one can only try to combine as many bits and pieces as possible from the national selective web archive with material in other Dutch web archives to get as close as possible to the national web. And if it has not been possible to provide an authoritative list of all existing web domain names on the Dutch ccTLD it can be difficult to know exactly how (in)complete the constructed national web is (as mentioned above, a hyperlink analysis of what is already included in the corpus may help remedy this).[7]

In yet other countries there does not even exist a national web collection, but only smaller collections. This is the case in Belgium, where a number of web archiving initiatives exist, for instance at Felix Archive in Antwerp, the AMSAB Institute of Social History in Ghent, and Ghent University Library (Chambers and Mechant, 2018), as well as in Italy where there exists only a small collection of the Italian ccTLD .it from 2006 and a collection of PhD theses from Italian universities (Nanni, 2017).[8]

Finally, some countries did not manage to establish a national web archive before they disappeared as countries, which is the case with Yugoslavia, and in such cases one has to reconstruct the national web based on material in other web archives (cf. Ben-David, 2016, and section 'A disappeared nation' below).

It is worth mentioning that a national web may also be constructed on the basis of what can be found in a transnational web archive such as the Internet Archive. But the Internet Archive's collection of material from a given ccTLD is not necessarily as complete as it would have been if the collection had been initiated on the basis of a complete list of the domain names of the ccTLD. Thus, the Internet Archive's collections are a great help either to supplement existing national collections or to be used as the core of a national corpus, but one should not expect to find a complete copy of the national web domain.[9]

In summary, when constructing a national web it is a great help to have access to an authoritative list of all web domains on the nation's ccTLD (although the list is dynamic), and to have access to broad crawls of the relevant ccTLD, which may then eventually be supplemented with material from other collections. In cases where neither a list of the ccTLD nor a broad crawl is accessible, one may have to reconstruct the list of domain names of the ccTLD as well as combine parts of the national web as it can be found in the collections at hand. And, in any case, there are challenges to having too much as well as too little material, but the challenges are different.

## HISTORICAL CASE STUDIES

As mentioned in the brief research history above, since the mid 2010s a number of case studies have been made of national web domains. This section will briefly introduce some examples of studies with a view to illustrating how national web studies can be made, and how the general challenges outlined above have been dealt with, in particular the question of delimiting the nation on the web.

### *A National Web Domain*

The French research project 'Web90', dedicated to the French heritage, memories, and history of the web in the 1990s led by Valérie Schafer (France, 2014–17) outlines the multiple challenges of defining the research field of a national web domain. In investigating how the French web of the nineties can be mapped out, the project works on several scales – macro and micro, collective and individual – and bases itself on a variety of heterogeneous sources, using multi-method approaches, i.e. qualitative and quantitative methods, close and distant readings, and science and technology studies approaches.

In delimiting their object of study, the researchers do not begin with the introduction of the .fr domain in 1987 nor with the first websites created in the 1990s. In contrast, they follow a thread which leads back to the first French contacts with the internet and the first expressions of interest among the research community in the internet and the web, in the 1970s. Another part of the study centres around the Minitel, which for most French people was their first online experience of messaging, directories, and commercial services (cf. also Schafer and Thierry, 2012). Yet another line of study revolves around the cyber cafes as spaces for learning, socialization, and communication (Schafer, 2018). These studies are good illustrations of the challenges and perspectives in the study of where a nation's web begins.

The boundaries of the nation's web are also explored in the project's investigation of the French web domain, i.e. the set of digital resources spanning multiple websites relevant or related to the French nation, not only websites with the Country Code Top-Level Domain name .fr (cf. Schneider and Foot, 2005). The project analyses a case where a request to the Internet Archive for all top-level domains generically or geographically relating to France only produced one single .fr domain featured among the largest 200 domains (Schafer, 2018). This was wanadoo.fr, while the largest domains included infospace.com and amazon.com, as well as yahoo.com and geocities.com. A further example is the story of the pioneering site in the museum field, Weblouvre, developed by a student, Nicolas Pioch, from 1994, which won a Best of the Web Award. When the Louvre found that Nicolas Pioch was using its name, it decided to recover the domain and launch its own website, and Nicolas Pioch transferred his site. Although no longer hosted in France and although entirely in English, this site has a significant place in the early history of digital culture and museum sites in France, and also, despite its subsequent migration, in the history of domain name allocation.

## *A Nation's Sub-Domains – the Case of the UK Web*

In the Domain Name System hierarchy, a second-level domain (SLD) is a domain that is directly below a top-level domain (TLD). Second-level domains often refer to the organization that registered the domain name with a domain name registrar. Some domain name registries introduce a second-level hierarchy to a TLD that indicates the type of entity intended to register an SLD under it. For example, in the .uk name space a college or other academic institution would register under the .ac.uk ccSLD, while companies would register under .co.uk. This allows for studies on the relative size of second-level domains and the role of different sectors on the web. One such study is Hale et al. (2014), which investigates the growth of the entire .uk domain between 1996 and 2010, broken down into its four largest constituent parts, .co.uk, .org.uk, .gov.uk, and .ac.uk, showing, for instance, that .co.uk is the predominant second-level domain throughout the entire period. A particular second-level domain, the academic sub-domain .ac.uk, is analysed in relation to linking practices compared with institutional affiliation, league table ranking, and geographic location, showing clear patterns in terms of higher inlinks to the highest-status academic institutions and stronger connections between geographically closer institutions.

Studying second-level domains may have some limitations, as in the above case where several British companies and organizations may operate domains in generic top-level domains (.com, .org, etc.). Another approach to studying sub-domains is taken by Musso and Merletti (2016). They propose a methodology based on the usage of historical web directories to access and map past sub-domains. Web directories were lists that could be found on web portals such as Yahoo!, where readers could get an overview with hyperlinks to websites related to different topics, such as 'Culture', 'Sport', and

'Business'. In the study, the directories preserved in the Internet Archive are used as the entry door to the archived .uk web. The directories allow the quantitative reconstruction of specific webspaces because they conserve the memory of many hyperlinks that have not been archived by any archive but that existed at the time in which the directory was on the live web. As mapped through several business directories, Musso and Merletti reconstruct the early approach of UK business to the web between 1996 and 2001.

### *Trans-National Web Domains*

While some Country Code Top-Level Domains are allocated to a given nation, such as .uk for the United Kingdom, .fr for France, and mirror some of its national online activities, a certain portion of a nation's web can be located on other top-level domain names such as .com, .edu, or .eu. The challenge regarding national material on these top-level domains is that it has to be tracked manually or semi-automatically (cf. above), and that – in their entirety – these top-level domains do not naturally fall under any national memory institution's remit since they cover multiple nations.

The .eu is a curious case as it is region specific, created to promote the European single market on the internet (Hockx-Yu et al., 2018). With 3.7 million registered domains, the .eu domain is also one of the biggest top-level domains in Europe (in comparison France has 2.5 million registered domains (DomainTyper, The .fr domain)), and it is the sixth most popular ccTLD in Europe (DomainTyper, The .eu domain). However, a comprehensive web archive for .eu does not exist, because no institution has taken formal, ongoing responsibility for whole-domain archiving of .eu. The only comprehensive effort to date that focused on archiving the entire .eu domain was conducted by the Portuguese web archive, Arquivo.pt, between 2014–17 in the context of RESAW, a European network that aims to create a research infrastructure for the study of archived web materials, and the collections in such a research infrastructure will be incomplete without content on .eu. For historical studies, however, the researcher is prone to what may or may not have been harvested in different web archives. In 2014, a study showed that while 3.7 million .eu domains were registered that year, the national web archives in Denmark, Portugal, and the UK had captured only a few thousand (Gomes et al., 2014). Hockx-Yu et al. (2018) suggest aggregating content from different archives and bringing it together to serve as a .eu web archive. Even if it is incomplete, it would still provide some insight into the development of the .eu web domain for future generations' understanding of European nations on the web. The study also proposes and discusses a number of options towards sustainable, long-term archiving arrangements for .eu, such as a group or an organization taking on the long-term responsibility of collecting, preserving, and providing access to the archived European web, possibly with direct funding or involvement from the European Commission.

### *Borderland Web Domains – the Northern Irish Web Domain*

While every national web domain includes very substantial amounts of content that resides within the various geographically non-specific domains, little is known about what factors determine the choices made by webmasters as to the domain registrations they choose. This may be examined in different ways, and one exceptional case is the cross-border study of the Northern Irish web domain by Webster (2018a). On the island of Ireland two political units (the UK and the Republic of Ireland) and two ccTLDs (.uk and .ie) share a land border. Webster's study takes the case of the Christian churches in Ireland (north and south) as a case study in the mapping of the differences between the nation and the top-level domain. The churches in Ireland are organized on an all-Ireland basis: a reflection of their origins that pre-date the partition of Ireland into north and south. Using link graph data provided by the British Library, the study recreates the networks of links between individual church congregations on both sides of the border, and the national infrastructure of the churches into which local congregations fit. In examining the regional, national, and cross-border relationships, the study argues that even though there are indeed clear geographic concentrations in these link graphs, these map only very loosely indeed to the UK Country Code Top-Level Domain. For instance, it seems that Roman Catholic congregations are likely to register domains outside the UK; however, a particular prioritization of registration within the UK in relation to the Protestant churches is not borne out. The study affirms that the Country Code Top-Level Domain may be a weak proxy for the national web, including or even more so in cross-border cases such as this.

### *A Disappeared Nation and a Nation Without a Web Domain*

Nation states are not always stable and sovereign entities, whose borders and boundaries are recognized and undisputed. The history of the web has seen several deletions and re-delegations of ccTLDs of countries in transition. Some examples are the retired ccTLD of Czechoslovakia, .cs, which became the new ccTLDs to the Czech Republic (.cz) and Slovakia (.sk), and the former domain of Zaire, .zr, re-delegated as .cd after the country changed its name to the Democratic Republic of Congo (Ben-David, 2016).

Ben-David has researched the .yu, the ccTLD of Yugoslavia. The .yu was deleted from the internet's Domain Name System in 2010, after it had lost its legitimacy, since the country to which it was delegated no longer existed. When researching the domain on the live web in 2014, Ben-David found little evidence that it ever existed. With little evidence on historical addresses on the live web, the Internet Archive's Wayback Machine was of sparse use since one has to know the specific URL in order to retrieve archived snapshots. In order to reconstruct a portion of the web that no longer exists and whose archived locations are unknown, Ben-David turned to external sources to reconstruct a seed list, and then a hyperlink discovery method was used to find more .yu pages in the Internet Archive. With the method applied, the networked history of the .yu ccTLD was partially reconstructed.

In another study, Ben-David (2018) challenges the notion of the national web even further, by examining the web history of Kosovo – a disputed country that struggles for statehood, yet does not have a ccTLD. The fact that Kosovo is a national web that is not supported by the Domain Name System reveals a variety of entangled ties between geopolitics, standards, and technologies that stand behind national webs. Finally, the role of different political and regulatory institutions in determining national web borders is discussed, where recognition by the United Nations is a preliminary condition for a country's web presence, and it is compared to the process that led to the successful delegation of the Palestinian ccTLD, .ps.

## CONCLUSION

The national web as object worthy of studying has gained growing attention among internet researchers and web historians since the early 2000s. In this chapter we have argued that the research history has developed in three waves, the first with a technical aim, the second augmented by social sciences and humanities, and the third with a clear historical and national approach, and in many cases based on the archived web.

Today, national projects are well underway in Denmark, in France, and in the UK, among others. These national web studies may constitute the backdrop for web studies of other analytical entities.

The chapter has also outlined a number of methodological challenges that studies of national webs face. One perplexing question is: where is the national web? And what does it mean to think of the web in spatial and quasi-geographic terms? A way of delimiting a national web is to use the ccTLD but national webs can also be found on generic TLDs, and ccTLDs are deleted and re-delegated over time when countries transform. Hence, national projects are put in dialogue with investigations of the boundaries between national domains, and interactions across those boundaries. For historical web studies, the archived web can be used as a source; however, some countries do not have web archives or only smaller collections or no collections at all. Researchers must then turn to other countries' archives or to transnational web archives such as the Internet Archive, which may or may not have archived relevant parts. Moreover, often web archives do not have full-text search, so secondary sources for identification of relevant web addresses are crucial to retrieve the potentially archived objects. Additionally, when reconstructing the nation's past web, this reconstruction is taking place on top of the initial construction that took place during the archiving.

National web archives delimit the borderless flow of information on the web with national barriers. In addition, there are no easy ways of accessing or processing the large amounts of data, neither on a national level, nor on an international level, as web archives are not prepared for Big Data studies. This chapter has introduced some examples of studies on how national web studies can be made and how some of the above-mentioned challenges have been dealt with. These studies shed light on the historical development of specific national webs and suggest many future possibilities for research on a national and transnational level on this increasingly important digital cultural heritage.

## Notes

1 Anderson mentions three other characteristics: nations are limited, they are sovereign, and they are a community (1996: 7).
2 It can be partly automated, cf. Zierau et al. (2015).
3 For an overview of web archiving initiatives see List of Web archiving initiatives (n.d.); IIPC Members (n.d.); Webster (2018b). Historical overviews can be found in Brügger (2011: 29–32); Webster (2017)
4 See Brügger (2018a, 2018b) for an expanded discussion of the challenges related to web crawling as well as how web archives based on web crawling are made available for researcher use.
5 For more information about Netarkivet, see Schostag and Fønss-Jørgensen (2012).
6 These issues are discussed more in detail in Brügger et al. (2018).
7 A number of other countries do not make broad crawls of the entire ccTLD (e.g. Australia), and, like the Netherlands, Canada also only archives selective parts of the national Canadian web, due to the lack of a legal deposit law (cf. Milligan and Smyth (2018)).
8 A pilot project, PROMISE, for the establishment of a national Belgian web archive was launched in 2017 (Chambers and Mechant, 2018).
9 The coverage of the Internet Archive compared with the Danish Netarkivet is discussed in Brügger et al. (2018).

## REFERENCES

Anderson, B. (1996) Imagined communities: Reflections on the origin and spread of nationalism. London: Verso.

Baeza-Yates, R., Castillo, C., and Efthimiadis, E.N. (2007) 'Characterization of national Web domains', ACM Transactions on Internet Technology (TOIT), 7(2). DOI 10.1145/1239971.1239973.

Ben-David, A. (2014) 'Mapping minority webspaces: The case of the Arabic webspace in Israel', in D. Caspi and N. Elias (Eds.), Ethnic minorities and media in the Holy Land. London: Vallentine-Mitchell Academic. pp. 137–157.

Ben-David, A. (2016) 'What does the web remember of its deleted past? An archival reconstruction of the former Yugoslav top-level domain', New Media & Society, 18(7): 1103–1119.

Ben-David, A. (2018, forthcoming) 'National web histories at the fringe of the web: Palestine, Kosovo and the quest for online self-determination', in N. Brügger and D. Laursen (Eds.), The historical web and Digital Humanities: The case of national web domains. Abingdon: Routledge.

Brügger, N. (2011) 'Web archiving – between past, present, and future', in M. Consalvo and C. Ess (Eds.), The Handbook of Internet Studies. Oxford: Wiley-Blackwell. pp. 24–42.

Brügger, N. (2012) 'Historical network analysis of the web', Social Science Computer Review, 31(3): 306–321.

Brügger, N. (2017) 'Probing a nation's web domain: A new approach to web history and a new kind of historical source', in G. Goggin and M. McLelland (Eds.), The Routledge companion to global internet histories. New York: Routledge. pp. 61–73.

Brügger, N. (2018a) The archived web: Doing web history in the digital age. Cambridge, MA: MIT Press.

Brügger, N. (2018b) 'Understanding the Archived Web as a Historical Source', in N. Brügger and I. Milligan (Eds.), The SAGE Handbook of web history. London: Sage. pp. 16–29.

Brügger, N., and Laursen, D. (Eds.) (2018, forthcoming) The historical web and Digital Humanities: The case of national web domains. Abingdon: Routledge.

Brügger, N., Laursen, D., and Nielsen, J. (2018) 'Establishing a corpus of the archived web: The case of the Danish web from 2005 to 2015', in N. Brügger and D. Laursen (Eds.), The historical web and Digital Humanities: The case of national web domains. Abingdon: Routledge.

Brügger, N., and Schroder, R. (2017) (Eds.) The web as history: Using web archives to understand the past and the present. London: UCL Press.

Chambers, S., and Mechant, P. (2018, forthcoming) 'Towards a national web in a federated country: A Belgian case study', in N. Brügger and D. Laursen (Eds.), The historical web and Digital Humanities: The case of national web domains. Abingdon: Routledge.

Cowls, J. (2017) 'Cultures of the UK web', in N. Brügger and R. Schroeder (Eds.), The web as history: Using web archives to understand the past and the present. London: UCL Press. pp. 220–237.

Curran, J., Coen, S., Aalberg, T., Hayashi, K., Jones, P.K., Splendore, S. Papathanassopoulos, S., Rowe, D., and Tiffen, R. (2013) 'Internet revolution revisited: A comparative study of online news', Media, Culture & Society, 35(7): 880–897.

DomainTyper, The .eu domain, https://domaintyper.com/domain-names/top-level-domains/ccTLD/eu-domain (accessed 16 March 2018).

DomainTyper, The .fr domain, https://domaintyper.com/domain-names/top-level-domains/ccTLD/fr-domain (accessed 16 March 2018).

Finnemann, N.O., Jauert, P., Jensen, J.L., Povlsen, K.K., and Sørensen, A.S. (2012) The media menus of Danish internet users 2009. Aarhus: The Research Project 'Changing Borderlines – Mediatization and Cultural Citizenship'. https://research.ku.dk/search/?pure=en/publications/the-media-menus-of-danish-internet-users-2009(7ac0e756-6479-41c3-a80c-f911b565f230).html (accessed 30 June 2018).

Gomes, D., Hockx-Yu, H., and Laursen, D. (2014) Archiving .eu – pilot project. RESAW Seminar, London, UK.

Halavais, A. (2000) 'National Borders on the World Wide Web', New Media Society, 2(1): 7–28.

Hale, S.A., Yasseri, T., Cowls, J., Meyer, E.T., Schroeder, R., and Margetts, H. (2014) 'Mapping the UK Webspace: Fifteen Years of British Universities on the Web', WebSci '14 Proceedings of the 2014 ACM conference on Web science, Bloomington, Indiana, June.

Hockx-Yu, H., Laursen, D., and Gomes, D. (2018, forthcoming) 'The curious case of archiving .eu', in N. Brügger and D. Laursen (Eds.), The historical web and Digital Humanities: The case of national web domains. Abingdon: Routledge. pp. xx–xx.

IIPC Members (n.d.) http://netpreserve.org/about-us/members

List of Web archiving initiatives (n.d.) https://en.wikipedia.org/wiki/List_of_Web_archiving_initiatives

Milligan, I., and Smyth, T.J. (2018, forthcoming) 'Studying the Web in the shadow of Uncle Sam: The case of the .ca domain', in N. Brügger and D. Laursen (Eds.), The historical web and Digital Humanities: The case of national web domains. Abingdon: Routledge.

Mussu, M., and Merletti, F. (2016) 'This is the future: A reconstruction of the UK business web space (1996–2001)', New Media & Society, 18(7): 1120–1142.

Nanni, F. (2017) 'Reconstructing a website's lost past methodological issues concerning the history of Unibo.it', Digital Humanities Quarterly, 11(2). http://digitalhumanities.org/dhq/vol/11/2/000292/000292.html (accessed 19 Sep 2018).

Rogers, R. (2013) Digital methods. Cambridge. MA: MIT Press.

Rogers, R., Weltevrede, E., Borra, E., and Niederer, S. (2013) 'National web studies: The case of Iran online', in J. Hartley, J. Burgess and A. Bruns (Eds.), A companion to new media dynamics. Oxford: Blackwell. pp. 142–166.

Schafer, V. (2018, forthcoming) 'Exploring the "French Web" of the 1990s', in N. Brügger and D. Laursen (Eds.), The historical web and Digital Humanities: The case of national web domains. Abingdon: Routledge.

Schafer, V., and Thierry, B. (2012) Le Minitel: L'enfance numérique de la France. Paris: Nuvis, Cigref.

Schafer, V., and Thierry, B. (2016) 'The "Web of pros" in the 1990s: The professional acclimation of the World Wide Web in France', New Media & Society, 18(7): 1143–1158.

Schneider, S.M., and Foot, K.A. (2005) 'Web sphere analysis: An approach to studying online action', in C. Hine (Ed.), Virtual methods: Issues in social research on the Internet. Oxford: Berg Publishers: pp. 157–170.

Schostag, S., and Fønss-Jørgensen, E. (2012) 'Webarchiving: Legal deposit of internet in Denmark, a curatorial perspective', Microform & Digitization Review, 41: 110–120.

Schroeder, R. (2018) Social theory after the internet. London: UCL Press.

Teszelszky, K. (2018, forthcoming) 'The historic context of web archiving and the web archive: Reconstructing and saving the Dutch national web using historical methods', in N. Brügger and D. Laursen (Eds.), The historical web and Digital Humanities: The case of national web domains. Abingdon: Routledge.

Webster, P. (2017) 'Users, technologies, organisations: Towards a cultural history of world web archiving', in N. Brügger (Ed.), Web 25: Histories from the first 25 years of the World Wide Web. New York: Peter Lang Publishing. pp. 175–190.

Webster, P. (2018a) 'Understanding the limitations of the ccTLD as a proxy for the national web: Lessons from cross-border religion in the Northern Irish web sphere', in N. Brügger and D. Laursen (Eds.), The historical web and Digital Humanities: The case of national web domains. Abingdon: Routledge.

Webster, P. (2018b) 'Existing web archives', in N. Brügger and I. Milligan (Eds.), The SAGE Handbook of web history. London: Sage. pp. 30–41.

Winters, J. (2018, forthcoming) 'Negotiating the archives of UK web space', in N. Brügger and D. Laursen (Eds.), The historical web and Digital Humanities: The case of national web domains. Abingdon: Routledge.

Zierau, E., Brügger, N., and Moesgaard, J. (2015) 'Defining a National Web Sphere over time from the Perspectives of Collection, Technology and Scholarship'. Paper presented at the RESAW conference, Aarhus, June 2015.

29

# The Origins of Electronic Literature as Net/Web Art

James O'Sullivan and Dene Grigar

Readers of this chapter might benefit from the knowledge that 'electronic literature' (or e-lit) refers to born-digital works which embrace the creative, as opposed to just the disseminative, potential of computation. As defined by Hayles: 'Electronic literature, generally considered to exclude print literature that has been digitized, is by contrast "digital born," a first-generation digital object created on a computer and (usually) meant to be read on a computer' (2008: 3). A useful primer for those looking to develop some perquisite understanding might be 'Electronic Literature: Contexts & Poetics', wherein Heckman and O'Sullivan argue that e-lit can take many forms, but 'could only exist in that space for which it was developed/written/coded' (2018). Electronic literature (or e-lit) did not start with the Web – works of art merging the literary with the digital had found their way into circulation long before the Net had permeated public consciousness and consumptive habits to the extent that we know it in contemporary contexts. It is difficult to point with any certainty to *the first* work of electronic literature, though many commentators attribute this accolade to Christopher Strachey, who, in 1952, designed an algorithm on the University of Manchester's Ferranti Mark I capable of generating love letters (Wardrip-Fruin, 2008: 163). Literary experiments like Strachey's predate what we now consider 'the Internet' by some 30 years, and indeed even conceptual precursors like Ted Nelson's Project Xanadu, introduced in 1960, and computer poetry like Alison Knowles and James Tenney's *The House of Dust*, produced on a Siemens 4004 computer with Fortran in 1967, by the better part of a decade. Judy Malloy's *Uncle Roger*, largely considered to be one of the first commercial works of electronic literature in the United States, was published between 1987 and 1988 and set the stage for stand-alone software that marks the early period of e-lit development (Grigar and Moulthrop, 2015). While the circulation of electronic literature is now largely confined to Web-based platforms, the early history of this domain is one of floppies, diskettes, and compact discs.

We can see the reality of this history in the material emphasis of resources like the Electronic Literature Lab (ELL) at Washington State University Vancouver, where scholars and practitioners can get a sense of the field's earliest incarnations through interaction with those pieces. The central mission of this initiative is to preserve pieces in their release state, so that the literary experience is not modified by migration to more current technologies or emulation on contemporary software. How does one capture the experience of first-generation e-lit works as objects, replicating the smell of the plastic, the computer's loading screen, the learning curve attached to the traversal method? The electronic literary experience is bound to the quirks of intended platforms, the peculiarities of the technology, and the variety of glitches that such configurations offer. The ELL then, resembles something of a Mac museum,[1] where vintage machines are used as reading devices for outmoded formats. It is difficult to provide any precise periodisation of the field – electronic literature is inherently *literary*, and with any literary movement, genres and modes are comprised of further genres and modes. It might be useful, however, to think of 'first-generation' e-lit as largely hypertextual, that is to say, screen-based works whose digital aesthetics were largely drawn out of the idea of links, and how narrative can be constructed and disrupted in a fragmentary manner. Second generation might be considered to be more algorithmic or computationally 'sophisticated', as is the case with generative literature. The most contemporary of electronic literary works might be seen as inherently ludo-literary, availing of the affordances of technologies made popular by the video game industry, though (usually) privileging language over play.

But while the history of electronic literature is not exclusively Web-based, the significance of the Net as a means of sharing – which is what publishing, an activity so central to literature, is all about – needs to be recognised, as does the influence of hypertextuality, which again, while arguably predating the Internet as a *literary* concept, certainly became more pronounced once authors recognised the potential syntheses between the world of writing and the World Wide Web. In treating the history of electronic literature in the context of the history of the Web, this chapter will detail the form as both a pre- and post-Web practice, drawing particular attention to the Net art movement and contemporary e-lit situation, while arguing for a more comprehensive electronic literary history.

Many of the first-generation hypertextual works that dominated the field in its earliest days were published by Eastgate Systems, Inc., founded in Watertown, Massachusetts by Mark Bernstein. With some notable exceptions, like Sarah Smith's *King of Space* (1991), written in HyperGate, Deena Larsen's *Marble Springs* (1993), created in HyperCard, and M. D. Coverley's *Califia* (2000), produced with ToolBook, works for stand-alone systems were mostly written with Storyspace, an intuitive hypertext authoring system created by Jay David Bolter, Michael Joyce, and John B. Smith (Landow, 1992: 40) that is now maintained by Bernstein under his imprint. 'The Eastgate School', or as Hayles calls it, the 'Storyspace school' (2008: 6), is synonymous with the origins of the movement, incorporating many of the electronic hypertexts to first garner significant critical attention: Michael Joyce's *afternoon, a story* (1990),[2] Stuart Moulthrop's *Victory Garden* (1992), Jane Yellowlees Douglas' 'I Have Said Nothing' (1994), and Shelley Jackson's *Patchwork Girl* (1995).

The earliest works of electronic literature were disseminated as floppy disks (Fig 29.1), and later, as CDs – as noted, e-lit had a life before the Web. But the influence of the Web is not entirely absent from the origins of the field. As mentioned, one of the earliest examples of commercially available electronic literature, Malloy's *Uncle Roger*, first emerged in 1986 as a serialised novel on The WELL, an

**Figure 29.1 Stuart Moulthrop's *Victory Garden* (1992), published by Eastgate Systems.**

online community started in 1985 by Stewart Brand and Larry Brilliant.[3] Research by the seminal *Pathfinders*[4] project shows an advert from an 1988 *Art Com* catalogue (Fig 29.2), advertising copies of *Uncle Roger* packaged as floppy disks (Grigar and Moulthrop, 2015).

**Figure 29.2 Advert for Judy Malloy's 'Uncle Roger: A Party in Woodside', from *Pathfinders*.**

There are six digital versions of *Uncle Roger*; the first began, as already noted, as a serial novel for the net published on The WELL's Art Com Electronic Network (ACEN). The second version was an interactive narrative also published by ACEN. The third version, created as a database narrative on Malloy's own authoring software, Narrabase, however, constitutes the 1987–8 commercial packaging on three 5.25-inch floppy disks. Often described as a trilogy, the segregation between discs was more of a consequence of storage constraints rather than any narrative construction. Version 4.0 was produced in 1988 for galleries and other venues that used PCs instead of Macintosh computers. These four early versions were produced almost simultaneously with Malloy starting one version and developing another alongside it. The fifth version – the one produced for the Web – came seven years later in 1995 and recompiles the work into one environment (Grigar, 2015). This version, according to Malloy, is the authorised version and reflects Malloy's awareness of the changing audience from that of the intellectually elite one of The WELL and the more mainstream one of the Web (Moulthrop and Grigar, 2017: 93–106). The final digital version is the emulation of Version 4 with edited content of Version 5, produced for the DOSBox Emulator. It creates, to a certain extent, some of the unique features of the pre-Web experience. This trend, re-releasing first-generation Web-based e-lit, as Eastgate Systems, Inc. has done with *afternoon: a story* and *Patchwork Girl*, both on flash drive, may become a trend as interest in early digital literary work continues to grow. Thus, as we have pointed out, not all e-lit started on the Web, but like most cultural artefacts influenced by the migration to cloud technology, this is where it is ending up, and that has profound repercussions for the ways in which renovated pieces are received, and indeed, how the movement is conceived.

## A CASE FOR ELECTRONIC LITERARY HISTORY

Lev Manovich traces the origins of digital art to the post-WWII era, citing co-occurring shifts in technology and artistry as the motivating factors: 'In the last few decades of the twentieth century, modern computing and network technology materialized certain key projects of modern art developed approximately at the same time' (2003: 15). For Manovich, the creative potential offered by emerging technologies 'actualized the ideas behind projects by artists, they have also extended them much further than the artists originally imagined' (2003: 15). Manovich, like many other theorists and critics operating in this domain, recognises the difficulty in isolating, with any certainty, the exact origins of the field.[5] In many respects, this is to be expected, as most artistic movements do not result from a Big Bang-like reaction, instantly materialising out of a collision between aesthetic forces. Artistic and literary movements are the product of slow, and sometimes unintentional, exchanges with the changeable affordances of form and content – the same fluctuations are usually happening in multiple places at once, situated in varying contexts, but all contributing to the emergence of something other than what has gone before.

But there is a second, more explicit reason as to why it is difficult to identify the origins of electronic literature – the lack of a deliberate historical account of the field:

> ...future theorists and historians of computer media will be left with not much more than the equivalents of the newspaper reports and film programs from cinema's first decades. They will find that analytical texts from our era recognize the significance of the computer's take-over of culture yet, by and large, contain speculations about the future rather than a record and theory of the present. (Manovich, 2001: 6–7)

The paucity of deliberate historical accounts of this field has been alleviated in recent years,[6] but considering the long history of the field, and its explosion since the introduction of the browser, more historical accounts are needed. Projects like *Pathfinders*, which provides a concerted effort to develop the methodology for a detailed documentation of works that strives to capture their multimedia and interactive features, follows in the footsteps of other digital literary histories in contributing to the future of electronic literature by documenting its past. Literature has many pasts, and the past that Grigar and Moulthrop are documenting in *Pathfinders* focuses on the digital literary experiments that emerged in the late eighties to mid nineties, and continued to grow and develop into what we now call 'e-lit'. *Pathfinders* takes an unusual approach to its research methodology in that it asks authors of early digital literature to perform their work on a computer and with software with which the work was originally intended to be read at the time of its publication. Grigar and Moulthrop videotape this performance, as well as record an interview with the author. They also bring in two additional readers to interact with and share the experiences of the work, which is also recorded. Much has been gleaned from these interactions, the materials ensuring that future generations will be able to appreciate the origins of the field, achieving a sense of the historical and cultural framework of which one must be aware if they are to critique a work within the contexts of its precursors. While *Pathfinders* has undertaken in-depth research into a select few works, the fact remains that there are countless more which are yet to be documented and written about, and as a result, preserved. Without this work, knowledge about these precursors, and the expression they sought in the digital, would be lost.

The vital work being accomplished by initiatives like *Pathfinders* should serve as a warning to the current generation, who have mistaken the ease by which the digital can be disseminated for protection against obsolescence. Even when one cannot experience a work, we should at least know that it existed – the sad reality of this field is that many of those literary experiments that contributed to its emergence have undoubtedly been lost, and it is the fault of the academy that they cannot be recovered. The contemporary situation is worsening in a marketplace where authors are distributing their work on proprietary cloud-based architectures maintained by profit-motivated organisations like Google and Apple. It may well be that the issue to which Manovich points will only amplify, to the point where we will only ever have an awareness of popular – and thus preserved – first-generation and contemporary electronic literature, with nothing in between.

This has ramifications beyond this particular community. Take issues around gender, for example. Malloy programmed and coded *Uncle Roger* by hand with UNIX Shell Scripts (Version 2), AppleSoft BASIC (Version 3), GW-BASIC (Version 4), and HTML (Version 5). As notable was the authoring software she created for e-lit, Narrabase developed at approximately the same time as Storyspace and George Landow's Intermedia. These achievements are significant from a feminist perspective in that it shows that women were among the pioneers of this creative and technological movement, a reality that is often neglected (Walker Rettberg, 2012a). The history of electronic literature is not just a history of computational art, it is a social and cultural history that has relevance far beyond the literary. Such a lack of visibility may well be one of the chief contributors to the ambiguity that surrounds our discipline. Electronic literature is increasingly piquing the interest of literary scholars, and indeed, finding its way into the third-level curriculum, but, in many respects, it remains esoteric. This may well be due to the inherent computational element, which puts its critique beyond the expertise, and perhaps interest, of many scholars, but it may also be owing to this historical blind spot.

## THE RISE OF E-LIT AS NET ART

A definite milestone in the advent of digital literature as something more than merely hypertextual was the publication of the ELO's first *Electronic Literature Collection* in October 2006 (Fig. 29.3), described as 'the first major anthology of contemporary digital writing' (Funkhouser, 2007b). Edited by Hayles, Nick Montfort, Scott Rettberg, and Stephanie Strickland, the collection marks the progression towards increasingly multimodal forms.

But the anthology was more than just a demonstration of the 'the perpetual metamorphosis of electronic literature' (Marino, 2008); it also heralded a new era for e-lit – an era in which literatures of the Web would come to prominence in an increasingly paperless world.

Manovich is acutely aware of the symbiosis that exists between computation and culture, noting that their effects are commutative in essence – the computer is being shaped by culture, as much as culture is being transformed by the computer:

> To use another concept from new media, we can say that they are being composited together. The result of this composite is a new computer culture – a blend of human and computer meanings, of traditional ways in which human culture modeled the world and the computer's own means of representing it. (2001: 46)

This bi-directional exchange between culture and computation is key to the evolution of electronic literature. The Web transformed the ways in which artists looked at composition – quite simply, authors recognised where their audiences were going, and started writing for the Web. Such a conscious decision had profound repercussions for the history of the form, as it determined the technologies

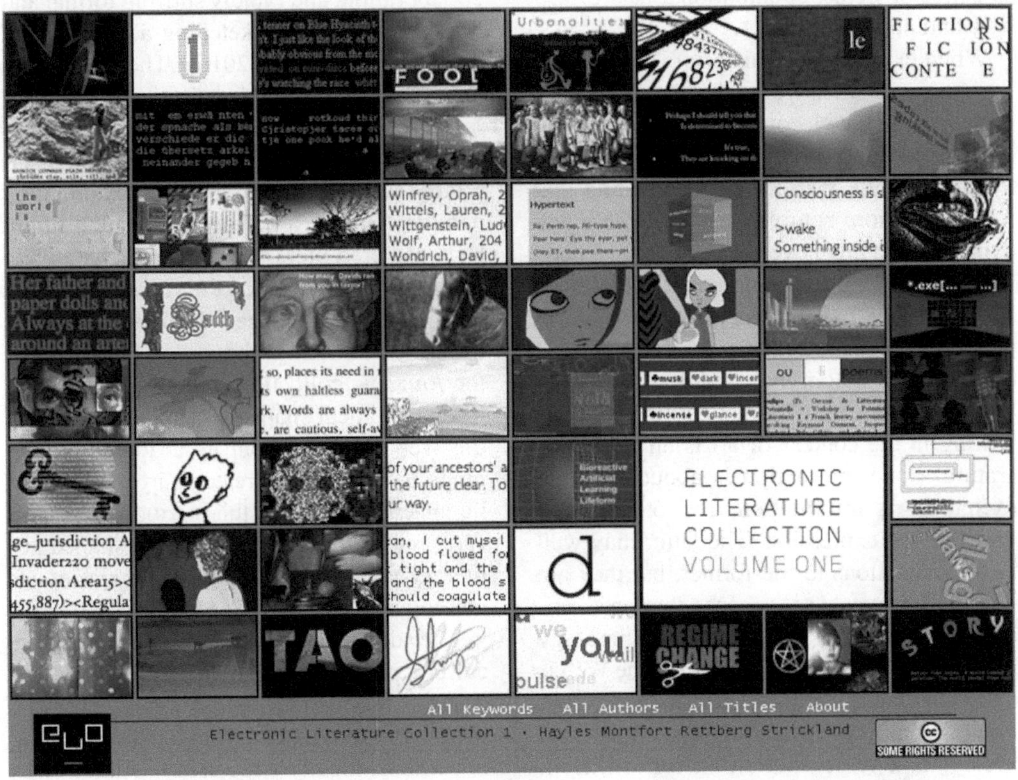


**Figure 29.3 Electronic Literature Collection: Volume 1, from collection.eliterature.org.**

and literary techniques available to e-lit practitioners. To say that the Web had a profound influence on the field might seem like an obvious statement – the Internet was a game changer, there is nothing revelatory in this – but the extent of this influence far outweighs that felt by e-lit's counterparts. The broader publishing industry, for example, recognised the disseminative potential of e-books and sought to remediate print literature in a bid to capture a share of the emerging e-reader market. But print has retained its dominance of this industry, and while the Web has undoubtedly transformed the ways in which publishers operate, the codex is thriving. The same cannot be said of electronic literature, which has undergone more complex transformations in the age of the Web, with most e-lit now, as already noted, *written for*, not just disseminated via, Web technologies – editions circulated as hardware are now seen as collector items, or intentional acts of artistry and preservation.

When exploring the history of the Web in the context of artistry, there is a danger of conflating channel with constituent. Historicising digital art, Manovich asserts that the 'greatest hypertext is the Web itself', contending that it is even 'more complex, unpredictable and dynamic than any novel that could have been written by a single human writer, even James Joyce' (2003: 15). This is an arbitrary comparison in many respects; a fresh example of the old dichotomy: the Internet as hypertext is an act of communication, whereas writing in the context of art is an act of literature – one transaction is about the clear exchange of information, the other about unrestrained expression. The latter may well have connections to the former, but they are not interchangeable in a sense that one criticism can be readily applied to any technology intended for broader social utility. The Web is undoubtedly the zenith of hypertextuality, but it is a social hypertext, socially complex and irresolute; a vessel, not an artwork in itself. Perhaps Manovich is right to treat the Web as one great work of art, as a great anthology of fact and fiction, open to uninhibited human intervention, the hallmark of creativity. But if we are to trace the emergence of electronic literature in the context of Net art in a manner that is useful to this volume's readership, we must do so in a slightly more conservative manner, primarily so that we avoid confusing technological innovation with literary developments – they are related, but not quite an amalgam.

On October 27th, 2016, *Rhizome* premiered its *Net Art Anthology*,[7] an iterative online exhibition that is seeking to retell the history of Net art from the 1980s through the present day, restaging 100 artworks across four pre-determined periods: 1984–98, 1999–2005, 2006–11, and 2012–18. The series aims to 'take on the complex task of identifying, preserving, and presenting exemplary works in a field characterized by broad participation, diverse practices, promiscuous collaboration, and rapidly shifting formal and aesthetic standards, sketching a possible net art canon' (Connor, 2016). The Anthology also includes a useful definition of Net art 'as an expansive, hybrid set of artistic practices that overlap with many media and disciplines' (Connor, 2016), but our examination revolves largely around works which might be considered literary in the sense that, while incorporating the ludic,[8] the visual, and aural, they privilege language.[9] While unfinished at the time of writing, the 1984–98 section of the *Rhizome* collection is live, and thus represents an ideal snapshot of the era in which the Web emerged from its academic beginnings to become a greater part of the public sphere. Entries in this period reveal how early interactions with the Web reshaped key literary notions around language, space, and ideology.

The advent of the Web heralded deep sociocultural progression, but, in a more pragmatic sense, it was also the realisation of HTML as the principal standard through which text was to be semantically structured – authors who wished to create text-based Net art would be writing in HTML. The relationship between form and content is such that the structural semantics imposed by HTML would have forced authors to think about their writing in different ways, adapting their creative processes to a pre-defined system of elements and sub-elements, embedding, and selective rendering. It is in this sense interesting that we use the term 'Net' art, when the Net was a largely linear underlying technical structure that would go on to facilitate the 'Web' as a more omnidirectional means of ordering information as a constellation – the net influenced the dissemination of art, true, but it was the Web, the idea of hypertextuality, that arguably brought about the greater cultural and artistic repercussions. One could quite readily argue that electronic literature's origins are not as Net art, but as Web art. Furthermore, authors had to re-think how to transact with the readers – HTML structures literary content, but its appearance to an audience is determined by Web technologies like CSS and JavaScript. All writing is subject to constraint, but authorial media selections are about the recognition of affordance; what it is that a particular medium can do in the service of an author's aesthetic vision. The Web's earliest authors traded the constraints of the page for those of the screen, and that meant writing differently, adapting their processes to allow for such constraint so as to avail of the potentialities.

Authors had already recognised the aesthetic possibilities of hypertextual narratives by the time artists began writing for the Web – there is little structural difference between the work of the Eastgate School and that of Net art's earliest writers. Nonetheless, the rise of the Net had a profound effect, drawing authors towards a public space composed of a language designed to facilitate multimodality – the transaction between creator and audience had fundamentally changed, and would continue to change as the Web advanced towards more participatory principles, collapsing, in some cases, the distinction between producer and consumer. HTML is a textual system, and so it is unsurprising that the 1990s were dominated by literary Net art that privileged the word. But the decade also witnessed considerable advances across other screen media, particularly cinema and video gaming, and so many of these works were situated within a progressively visual culture. We see the foundations of this convergence between language, the visual, and the ludic in the work of authors like Olia Lialina. Rhizome's *Net Art Anthology* describes the former's 'My Boyfriend Came from the War' (1996) as a piece which 'highlights the parallels and divergences between cinema and the web as artistic and mass mediums, and explores the then-emerging language of the net' (2016). Lialina herself remarked: 'If something is in the net, it should speak in net. language' (Lialina, 2016), accentuating the demarcation between the Web as a platform for dissemination, and the Web as an authorial instrument.

Beyond the multimodality of HTML, artists saw the Net as a space for the renewed politicisation of art, a space in which they could better immerse their audiences within ideological frameworks. Art had always been political, but now it could be truly public, and somewhat participatory. Martine Neddam used her fictional 'Mouchette' (1997) to tackle the issue of suicide, inviting participants to contribute to the topic, thus rendering her adolescent persona 'a character who doubles as a platform of exchange' (Neddam, 2016). While *The File Room* (1994) existed as an installation piece at various points throughout its existence, Antoni Muntadas undertook the project knowing that it could never be completed (Muntadas, 2016). The publication of these artworks came alongside the rise of Web 2.0, which heralded the shift towards Net platforms as dynamic systems composed through mass participation. It was an era in which the transaction between producer and consumer became an act of co-creation. Burgess and Green discuss this in the context of popular sites like YouTube, and how it transitioned 'from the idea of the website as a personal storage facility for video content to a platform for public self-expression', a transition that amounts to a 'user-led revolution' (2013: 4).

For all the rhetoric of democratisation that accompanies participatory concepts, the convergence between art and the affordances of the Web increases the potential for corporate forces to exert control over public expression. As noted by Lanier, users of the Web, however participatory it may be at present, always 'lose control of their own personal content' (2013: 207). The utopia of Web 2.0 belies something of a dystopic reality, wherein the crowd, and in this context, the authors and artists, are simply doing the creation for the producers, but sharing in few of the spoils, and having no say in the governance. But the same could be said of most institutions which support the creation and dissemination of artistic practice, and if one is to subvert a system, it is best to do so through direct engagement. It is in such a context that we can appreciate Net art as being political in itself, not merely a form open to the encapsulation of political content. Shulgin's 'Form Art' (1997) was published some 20 years after the earliest literary games, titles like Will Crowther's *Adventure* (1976), and *Zork* (1977/80), but it is nonetheless historically significant, transforming 'the most bureaucratic, functional, and unloved aspects of the web into aesthetic, ludic elements' (Shulgin, 2016). Drawing readers through a series of inane Web forms, 'Form Art' challenged its audience to traverse the maelstrom of forms as if they were playing a game that they could win or lose. In this respect, Shulgin was one of the first artists to really question the pervasiveness of emerging Web technologies and the ways in which the interface has dictated our use of such innovations. Shulgin describes the 'Form Art' as 'a declaration of the fact that a computer interface is not a "transparent" invisible layer to be taken for granted, but something that defines the way we are forced to work and even think' (2017). By creating a competition that solicited other submissions of form art – a critique of the Prix Ars Electronica – Shulgin used participatory mechanisms to reinforce the ideology of his piece.

Art which interacts with capitalist tools and processes is always in danger of advancing such instruments, a tension which Shulgin expressed in relation to his artistic movement:

> In general, now I am having mixed feelings about early net art because I see how the strategies developed by net artists are now used by corporations and in politics. But that's the destiny of avant-garde art – developing communication and aesthetic tools for the future capitalists and politicians. (2017)

His prediction proved accurate in some respects: many artists and critics recognised the power of the participatory, of the role of the receiver in the creative process, long before major commercial entities realised that survival in the Web 2.0 era was dependent on their capacity to embrace 'the power of the web to harness collective intelligence' (O'Reilly, 2010: 230). But in many respects, the converse of what Shulgin anticipated has turned out to be true, wherein artists now tend to reuse commercially driven tools for creative purposes. Artistic appropriation of capitalist media technologies is a disruptive act which serves to subvert the profit motives driving the development of such tools. Flash, Twitter, Unity – these are all examples of proprietary systems and spaces which artists have distorted and occupied for the purposes of facilitating some artistic purpose. In this respect, the history of art and literature and the Net is one of subversion.

Distinct communities have been treated in tandem here in the sense that practitioners within the Net art community do not always identify with those from the e-lit movement. Grigar explores this issue in some detail:

> For the most part, digital media theory has been dominated by scholars and critics trained in formalistic theories of cinema and visual art. Lev Manovich uses Russian formalism, for example, as his lens for formulating views of 'new' media, while Oliver Grau focuses his attention on Italian

> Futurism. What chance does an emergent form with literature in its name have when faced with such a strong art history perspective? Likewise, Stephen Wilson devotes little attention in his 900+ page book Information Arts to early hypertext work with no mention of more contemporary elit pieces. That 'net art' became the name of choice for some working in the area of web-based elit should come as no surprise under these circumstances since the term 'literature' in the name of elit may have limited its inclusion in media art festivals, exhibitions, and art scholarship. (2008)

There are, of course, figures who have transcended often arbitrary distinctions like 'community' and 'movement', such as Mez Breeze, an artist and writer whose work has appeared in both the *Net Art Anthology* (2016) and the third volume of the ELO Collection (Campbell and Breeze, 2012), but, typically, artistic groups relevant to this space have operated as considerably independent cohorts. Mark Amerika figures largely as a cross-disciplinary artist who straddles media art gallery installations and e-lit performance space.

Furthermore, this treatment is largely Anglocentric in its focus, and for every artist, artwork, or artistic group mentioned, many more have been omitted. But the purpose in drawing reference to these few examples has not been to privilege certain works over others, but rather to trace some of the key trends that are of relevance to the history of electronic literature as net art, and indeed, emphasise the one consistent element of all of these works – language. Whatever term you think most appropriate to such works, be it 'net art' or 'e-lit', the word as text is the dominant force throughout. The history of electronic literature as net art is a history of artists – be they authors or otherwise – responding to the affordances and constraints of the Web as a space for *writing*. The Web was not the first digital technology which writers adopted, but it is undoubtedly one of the most significant. This significance is represented in the reality that those artistic trends that emerged throughout the 1990s are still dominant today in the prospering modal exchange between literature, sound and visual art, video games, and an increasingly diverse range of realities.

## THE CONTEMPORARY SITUATION

While electronic literature had an existence before the Web, its beginnings and evolution

**Figure 29.4** ***All the Delicate Duplicates*, by Mez Breeze and Andy Campbell (2013).**

can be tied to the cultural diffusion of the Internet age – networking changed the way authors thought about writing, its processes, and dissemination. Hayles describes electronic literature as that which is usually meant to be read on a screen, but the field's recent history is one in which most works have been designed to be read in a browser. Perusing the Electronic Literature Organisation's collections, one encounters a high volume of works which rely on Web technologies. The influence of the Net is waning in contemporary contexts – as the fields of electronic literature and video gaming continue to converge, the Web is gradually reverting to its disseminative role. Where authors once predominantly wrote in the languages of the Web, electronic literature's localised traditions are seeing something of a resurgence with the rise of literary games. The critical discourse surrounding electronic literature and video games draws from a large pool of terms – interactive fiction, digital literary, literary games – but all of these concepts point to works with similar essential traits: they combine the 'ludic (from the Latin *ludus*: game or play) and literary (from Latin *littera*: alphabetic letter, or plural *litterae*: piece of writing) elements' (Ensslin, 2014: 1). We can think of electronic literature with ludic traits quite simply as 'creative media that has both *readerly* and *playerly* characteristics' (Ensslin, 2014: 1).

The creators of contemporary electronic literature are availing of increasingly sophisticated technologies to develop complex narrative spaces, such as those typified by the productions of The Chinese Room, or the work of Mez Breeze and Andy Campbell. The latter's recent piece, *All the Delicate Duplicates* (Fig 29.4), exemplifies a new wave of electronic literature wherein the literary is juxtaposed with the technologically immersive to forge game-like literary spaces that are shared, but not played, online.

Electronic literature is utterly reflective of the mechanics of its era, and as technology continues to progress at an exponential rate, so too will our notions of what it means to be contemporary in this domain. Where authors once wrote in HTML, they now code in Javascript; where they once animated in Flash, they now build worlds in Unity; where they once displayed their work on screens, they now immerse their audiences in augmented and virtual realities. As it stands, most of the form's emerging trends are independent of internetworking, shifting from the Web back towards localised systems, and indeed, experiences driven by physical peripherals like headsets. The reality of the practice is that most authors do not have the resources nor the desire to develop such literary spaces as participatory. Contemporary electronic literature, certainly, at the level of critical acclaim enjoyed by the likes of Breeze and Campbell (O'Sullivan, 2017), is about downloading and installing – the floppies have made a resurgence. The Net has had its moment, and the Web, while still visible in the aesthetics of electronic literature, is slowly being relegated to a means of distribution – but this should not diminish the legacy of either, which will undoubtedly rise again.

## Notes

1 Many early works of electronic literature were produced for Macintosh computers. It wasn't until the Windows operating system was available for PCs that e-lit works for that platform became common.
2 *afternoon, a story* was not published by Eastgate until 1990, though an earlier incarnation had been released three years prior, at the 1987 Association for Computing Machinery conference.
3 For more on The WELL, or Whole Earth 'Lectronic Link, see http://www.well.com/aboutwell.html.
4 Details on the *Pathfinders* project can be found at http://dtc-wsuv.org/wp/pathfinders/, while the project's open-access book, published in Scalar, is at http://scalar.usc.edu/works/pathfinders/index.
5 By 'origins', we do not refer to works that might be considered the first of many – there is little to be gained from extensive exploration of what came when, as all that this tells us is the order in which particular pieces gained publicity; rather, we see origins as being concerned with the complexities of the entire network of practice that

was operating throughout the era in which e-lit was formed. Origin stories are less about chronology than they are contribution.

6 Readers interested in further exploring the literary history of this field might consider one of many detailed accounts Funkhouser (2007a, 2007b); Kac (2007); di Rosario (2011); Walker Rettberg (2012b); Emerson (2014); Pawlicka (2014); Rettberg et al. (2015); Flores.

7 Unfinished at the time of writing, *Rhizome's* Net Art Anthology can be found at https://anthology.rhizome.org/.

8 By ludic, we mean relating to 'play'.

9 For more detailed disambiguation of the different forms of digital art, and the means by which language plays a role in this process, readers should see Ensslin's literary-ludic spectrum (2014: 43–5).

## REFERENCES


Breeze, M. (2016) 'Mezangelle', in Connor, M. (Ed.), *Net Art Anthology*. Rhizome. (https://anthology.rhizome.org/mez-breeze) Accessed May 2, 2017.

Burgess, J., and Green, J. (2013) *YouTube: Online Video and Participatory Culture*. Cambridge & Malden, Massachusetts: Polity Press.

Campbell, A., and Breeze, M. (2012) 'The Dead Tower', in Boluk, S., Flores, L., Garbe, J., and Salter, A. (Eds.), *Electronic Literature Collection: Volume 3*. Cambridge, Massachusetts: Electronic Literature Organization. (http://collection.eliterature.org/3/work.html?work=dead-tower) Accessed May 2, 2017.

Connor, M. (Ed.) (2016) *Net Art Anthology*. Rhizome. (http://anthology.rhizome.org/) Accessed April 10, 2017.

Emerson, L. (2014) *Reading Writing Interfaces: From the Digital to the Bookbound*. Minneapolis, Minnesota: University of Minnesota Press.

Ensslin, A. (2014) *Literary Gaming*. Cambridge, Massachusetts: The MIT Press.

Flores, L. I ♥ E-Poetry. *I ♥ E-Poetry*. (http://iloveepoetry.com/). Accessed May 2, 2017

Funkhouser, C. T. (2007a) *Prehistoric Digital Poetry: An Archaeology of Forms, 1959–1995*. Tuscaloosa, Alabama: The University of Alabama Press.

Funkhouser, C. (2007b) Electronic Literature circa WWW (and Before). *Electronic Book Review*. (http://www.electronicbookreview.com/thread/electropoetics/collected). Accessed March 16, 2017.

Grigar, D. (2008) Electronic Literature: Where Is It? *Electronic Book Review*. (http://www.electronicbookreview.com/thread/technocapitalism/invigorating) Accessed March 16, 2017.

Grigar, D. (2015) 'The Structure of Uncle Roger', in *Pathfinders: Documenting the Experience of Early Digital Literature*. Vancouver, Washington: Nouspace Publications. (http://scalar.usc.edu/works/pathfinders/the-structure-of-uncle-roger-by-dene-grigar?path=malloys-critical-essays) Accessed April 9, 2017.

Grigar, D., and Moulthrop, S. (2015) 'History of Judy Malloy's Uncle Roger', *Pathfinders: Documenting the Experience of Early Digital Literature*. Vancouver, Washington: Nouspace Publications. (http://scalar.usc.edu/works/pathfinders/history-of-judy-malloys-uncle-roger?path=judy-malloy) Accessed April 9, 2017.

Hayles, N. K. (2008) *Electronic Literature: New Horizons for the Literary*. Notre Dame, Indiana: University of Notre Dame Press.

Heckman, D., and O'Sullivan, J. (2018) 'Electronic Literature: Contexts and Poetics', in Price, K. M. and Siemens, R. (Eds.), *Literary Studies in a Digital Age*. New York: Modern Language Association. (https://dlsanthology.mla.hcommons.org/electronic-literature-contexts-and-poetics/) Accessed Feb 1, 2018.

Kac, E. (2007) *Media Poetry: An International Anthology*. Bristol and Chicago: Intellect Books.

Landow, G. P. (1992) *Hypertext: The Convergence of Contemporary Critical Theory and Technology*. Baltimore and London: The Johns Hopkins University Press.

Lanier, J. (2013) *Who Owns the Future?* London: Allen Lane, Penguin.

Lialina, O. (2016) 'My Boyfriend Came Back from the War', in Connor, M. (Ed.), *Net Art Anthology*. Rhizome. (https://anthology.rhizome.org/my-boyfriend-came-back-from-the-war)

Manovich, L. (2001) *The Language of New Media*. Cambridge, Massachusetts: The MIT Press.

Manovich, L. (2003) 'Mew Media from Borges to HTML', in Wardrip-Fruin, N. and Montfort, N. (Eds.), *The New Media Reader*. Cambridge, Massachusetts: The MIT Press. pp. 13–25.

Marino, M. C. (2008) The Electronic Literature Collection Volume I: A New Media Primer. *Digital Humanities Quarterly*, 2(1). (http://digitalhumanities.org/dhq/vol/2/1/000017/000017.html) Accesed March 1, 2017.

Moulthrop, S., and Grigar, D. (2017) *Traversals: The Use of Preservation for Early Electronic Writing*. Cambridge, Massachusetts: The MIT Press.

Muntadas, A. (2016) 'The File Room', in Connor, M. (Ed.), *Net Art Anthology*. Rhizome. (https://anthology.rhizome.org/the-file-room) Accessed May 3 2017.

Neddam, M. (2016) 'Mouchette', in Connor, M. (Ed.), *Net Art Anthology*. Rhizome. (https://anthology.rhizome.org/mouchette) Accessed May 4, 2017.

O'Reilly, T. (2010) 'What Is Web 2.0? Design Patterns and Business Models for the next Generation of Software', in Donelan, H. M., Kear, K., and Ramage, M. (Eds.), *Online Communication and Collaboration: A Reader*. Abingdon, Oxon: Routledge. pp. 225–235.

O'Sullivan, J. (2017) 'Electronic Literature's Contemporary Moment: Breeze and Campbell's *All the Delicate Duplicates*'. *Los Angeles Review of Books*. (https://lareviewofbooks.org/article/electronic-literature-turns-a-new-page-breeze-and-campbells-all-the-delicate-duplicates/) Accessed Nov 11, 2017.

Pawlicka, U. (2014) Towards a History of Electronic Literature. *CLCWeb: Comparative Literature and Culture*, 16(5). (http://docs.lib.purdue.edu/clcweb/vol16/iss5/2) Accessed March 10, 2017.

Rettberg, S., Tomaszek, P., and Baldwin, S. (2015) *Electronic Literature Communities*. Morgantown, West Virginia: West Virginia University Press.

di Rosario, G. (2011) Electronic Poetry: Understanding Poetry in the Digital Environment. (https://jyx.jyu.fi/dspace/bitstream/handle/123456789/27117/9789513943356.pdf) Accessed October 10, 2013.

Shulgin, A. (2016) 'Form Art', in Connor, M. (Ed.), *Net Art Anthology*. Rhizome. (https://anthology.rhizome.org/form-art) Accessed April 13, 2017.

Shulgin, A. (2017) A Net Artist Named Google. (http://rhizome.org/editorial/2017/jan/12/a-net-artist-named-google-1/) Accessed April 13, 2017.

Walker Rettberg, J. (2012a) 'Electronic Literature Seen from a Distance: The Beginnings of a Field'. *Dichtung Digital: A Journal of Art and Culture in Digital Media* (41). (http://www.dichtung-digital.de/en/journal/archiv/?postID=278) Accessed Jan 23, 2018.

Walker Rettberg, J. (2012b) The History of the Term 'Electronic Literature'. *jill/txt*. (http://jilltxt.net/?p=2665) Accessed Jan 23, 2018.

Wardrip-Fruin, N. (2008) 'Reading Digital Literature: Surface, Data, Interaction, and Expressive Processing', in Schreibman, S. and Siemens, R. (Eds.), *A Companion to Digital Literary Studies*. Oxford: Blackwell. pp. 163–182.

30

# Exploring the Memory of the First World War Using Web Archives: Web Graphs Seen from Different Angles

Valérie Beaudouin, Zeynep Pehlivan and Peter Stirling

## INTRODUCTION

Web archives are a rich source for performing hyperlink network studies within the social sciences, but their use creates methodological questions in applying network analysis to archived web material. This chapter explores these general questions about the construction and analysis of web archives: how to define and archive a collection of websites? How to extract and visualise hyperlink information from the archives? How to interpret the network of websites?

This chapter is based on a specific case: an analysis of the network of websites related to the First World War with the aim of understanding how the collective memory of the war is constructed online. The methodology presented for representing a network of websites using a web archive collection was developed as part of a project, 'The future of digitised heritage online: the example of the Great War', which aimed to study the circulation of digitised documents online. This particular part of the project was dedicated to creating a map of websites related to the war. Because websites have a purpose (here, history and memory), it is important to understand what activities they support, and how, and which communities use them in order to interpret their structure and their interrelations. Our exploratory analysis aims to understand how the memory of the war is socially organised on the web using hyperlink networks, and in particular to identify the social and publishing activity of amateurs. The approach chosen allowed us to study how this web space is organised and in particular the place of a discussion forum which was identified as having an important role for WWI history (Amar and Chevallier, 2013).

The chapter aims to provide, first, an in-depth look at different methodological challenges for network analysis of large web archives, including the importance of decisions regarding collection construction; second, an overview of the relative strengths of different strategies for reducing 'noise' within large collections and creating a network of websites that support the researcher's work; and, finally, a discussion of the importance of qualitative work in addition to quantitative network analysis.

The analysis was based on the internet legal deposit collections of the Bibliothèque nationale de France (BnF), and specifically a collection of websites selected for a BnF crawl on the centenary of WWI. This collection was defined by BnF librarians and partners independently of the research project, allowing the researchers to analyse a rationally constructed collection with a collection policy aimed at representing all aspects of the WWI web space, with each site classified by type of producer. The use of the BnF web archives therefore allowed the creation of a stable, well-documented corpus, the long-term preservation of which is assured (Stirling et al., 2012a). For researchers studying the web archives, it is necessary to understand how the collection was constituted, to ensure that the analysis takes into account the nature of this kind of source. Web archiving implies fixing content that is in constant movement and evolution, by collecting the different elements of which websites are made, in such a way as to recreate the site as it was at the time of crawling. To achieve this end, a whole set of choices and processes are involved, concerning both technical and collection aspects, and determining the content of the archives that the researcher will use. It is also necessary to consider technical limits, as web archiving technologies frequently encounter difficulties due to the rapid evolution of the technologies used on the web, and indeed technologies specifically intended to block web crawlers. Finally, the legal deposit framework also determines the form of the collection. This was the first use of data mining approaches on these collections.

This chapter is organised in three sections. First, the creation of the collection is studied, as well as the impact that the legal context, the selection policy and the technical aspects of the collection have on the corpus analysed by the researchers. The second section discusses how the metadata from the corpus was used to generate graphs, and in particular the three different strategies that can be combined to produce networks that best support the work of interpretation. Finally, the last section explores the network of WWI websites to analyse the online collective memory of WWI, shows how the interpretation of the network of websites was enriched by qualitative analysis (content analysis and interviews of contributors) and underlines the value of working on web collections prepared and archived by libraries.

## SOURCES: CREATING THE COLLECTION

Using web archives as a source for network analysis of the web brings many advantages: it was decided to base the analysis on the internet legal deposit collections of the BnF in order to benefit from a stable, well-documented corpus that will be preserved over the long term, allowing the possibility for other researchers to reproduce, complement or challenge the analysis that has been performed. However, the nature of web archives must be taken into account in developing a research methodology. The web archive is an artefact constructed from the live web, and the content and nature of the collection is therefore in large part determined by different aspects: the legal framework governing its construction, the technical characteristics used in its creation and the collection policy choices involved. This section explores how these aspects determine the content of the corpus analysed and the elements that researchers must take into account in developing their methodology.

### *Web Archiving at the BnF: The Legal and Technical Framework*

Legal deposit is used in France, as in many other countries, to ensure the preservation of web content (Stirling et al., 2012b); legal deposit of the internet is entrusted to the National Audiovisual Institute (INA) for websites of television and radio stations and websites mainly dedicated to them, and the Bibliothèque nationale de France for the rest of the French domain. The law ensures that web content is conserved in the same way as publications on other media, but it is necessary to adapt the principles of legal deposit to the nature of the web.

First of all, the idea of territoriality is central to legal deposit. Three criteria are used to determine whether web content is French, each one being sufficient for the content to be covered by legal deposit: if the content is on the top-level domain (TLD) .fr; if it is produced by a person or organisation resident in France; or if it is produced in France. This covers a large quantity of sites and web content, but, as we will see, the legal scope can mean 'breaking' links between French sites and those in other countries which could interest a researcher studying a corpus.

Second, legal deposit concerns that which is published, or 'communicated to the public by electronic means', in the expression used in the law. Information transmitted via the internet but considered as private correspondence does not come into the scope of legal deposit. This includes private emails but also any information on social networks accessible only to those that are logged in and with the authorisation of the person who has put the information online. It remains the case, however, that the border between what is public and what is private on the internet is unclear, including for internet users themselves; sensitive information, in particular that of a personal nature, could therefore be found in internet legal deposit collections. The role of the researcher and of the analysis that is performed can therefore raise ethical questions such as the anonymisation of sources.

Finally, it is important to note that legal deposit in all its forms aims in principle to be exhaustive. As regards the internet, this becomes difficult even to imagine, due not only to the volume of data but also the dynamic nature of the web, where it becomes impossible to define a stable 'publication'. Legal deposit of the internet, rather than being exhaustive, aims to be representative regarding the French web. This approach is necessary because it is impossible to judge in advance what might interest a researcher, and legal deposit in any case does not make a judgement regarding the interest or value of a given site. It is necessary therefore to allow researchers the possibility to define corpora within the collections.

The BnF uses the open-source software Heritrix for web archiving (https://webarchive.jira.com/wiki/display/Heritrix/Heritrix). This software, generally called a robot or crawler, starts from a list of seed URLs and identifies links within pages to collect all webpages and associated files (such as images and stylesheets), within the limits of the technical settings that have been defined. Some settings apply to all crawls, and specific settings are defined for each seed URL, depending both on the technical characteristics of the site and the target of the crawl defined by the collection policy (Le Follic et al., 2012).

These settings concern in particular the depth of crawl: the robot can collect a whole site (domain), a sub-site or a blog hosted on a platform (host), or a specific section of a site (path, page + 2 clicks). A budget in terms of numbers of files collected is also defined, mainly in relation to the size of the site, and a crawl frequency is set depending on the nature of the crawl. Multiple crawls allow the study of the evolution of sites over time, but imply multiple occurrences within the archives. It is necessary for a researcher to have sufficient information to be able to interpret these occurrences.

These technical settings determine the content of the archives, which can only be a representation of the site as it existed online: content may be missing and, at best, web archives cannot recreate the entire network of links in which a site is placed, or the constant flow of information and updates. Web archives are thus a new kind of object for researchers to study; while indispensable for studying the web, they are an artefact created from the web and not the web itself, their form largely determined by the technology used to create them. In this they can be compared to other sources used by researchers, which have their own characteristics in terms of what is missing, and the choices and limitations in their creation. Part of the work of a researcher is to define and explain the nature of the source and to take this nature into account in any interpretation that is made. This is why it is vital for researchers to have an understanding of the technologies used to archive the web.

### *Collection Policy and the WWI Collection*

It is equally important for researchers to have information about the choices that have been made regarding the content of the web archives, which also determine their form. The BnF has put in place a system combining broad and focussed crawls (Bonnel and Oury, 2014) to fulfil its legal deposit mission. Broad crawls take place once a year and concern a very large number of sites, based on lists of domain names registered in France, while focussed crawls collect more frequently and/or in greater depth a smaller number of sites that have been selected by BnF librarians or by partners. In these focussed crawls, the selection of seed URLs and the technical settings of the crawl are defined in relation to a collection policy.

'The Great War on the Web' is a focussed crawl, which therefore follows a collection policy intended to ensure that there are no gaps or incoherencies in the collection. The crawl was created by the Philosophy, History and Human Science Department at the BnF, in collaboration with the Maps Department, and the group of selectors was progressively broadened to include partner institutions with an interest in the subject, including regional libraries in areas particularly affected by the First World War: the Bibliothèque de documentation internationale contemporaine (BDIC), the Ministry of Defence section for Memory, Heritage and Archives (DMPA), the Bibliothèque nationale et universitaire de Strasbourg (BNUS) and Amiens Library.

The first step was to define the scope of the collection. While it was originally planned to concentrate on sites covering the centenary and the commemoration of the First World War, it was decided to broaden the scope to any content relating to WWI. This was partly due to the fact that the distinction between 'commemoration' and other approaches is difficult to define, and sometimes controversial. In addition, the use of the crawl by the project 'The future of digitised heritage online: the example of the Great War' was already being considered, and this wider scope would allow a study of the evolution of the sites over a longer period, with crawls planned two to three times a year over the period 2013 to 2019.

As this scope is potentially very wide, different criteria were applied to ensure that the collection remained coherent. Some general criteria are applied to all focussed crawls at the BnF: that sites selected should be active, and that they should provide original content, to avoid sites that merely duplicate content published elsewhere. Other guidelines were specific to this crawl: to include all official partners of the commemoration; to avoid concentrating on certain geographical areas or types of media, etc. How much of a site should be collected, in relation to the 'depth' setting described above, also depends both on the specific collection and the overall legal deposit framework. In general, a site or blog is collected as a whole (that is, using the depth settings 'domain' or 'host'), but in cases where only part of the site is relevant the specific sections can be collected using the depth settings 'path' or 'page + 2 clicks', depending on size and amount of relevant content. Even in the latter case, from a legal deposit point of view it is useful to widen this scope, as other content may interest a researcher; for example, when bloggers talk about WWI, what else do they have on their blog? Different settings are thus applied to different sites in the collection; however, each receives the same budget. The definition of 'entities' within the collection is therefore a combination of expert judgement (the selection of a seed URL) and technical factors (the settings applied) – to which can be added the interpretation made by the researcher.

One of the main ways to structure the collection was that a typology of sites was established to guide the selection and ensure its coherence. This typology was based on the producer, that is, the organisation or individuals responsible for the site. This approach has already been used for other crawls at the BnF, in particular those covering electoral campaigns, and ensures that the coverage and balance of the collection is as complete and equitable as possible, while also providing a means of dividing up the work of selection. It can also be used in analysing the collection.

During the initial sampling the most common categories of sites were identified, using both information in sections called 'About this site', 'Who are we?', etc., and additional information from authority notices in the BnF catalogue. These categories included institutions (political, scientific, heritage), educational sites (online resources, teachers' blogs), research sites (researchers, laboratories), associations (regional, genealogical, veterans), amateurs, media, and memorial tourism. These categories were used to create a typology similar to that used for previous collections:

- Official
  - National
  - Territorial
  - European
- Public
  - Heritage
  - Educational
  - Scientific
- Personal
- Association
- Media

While this kind of typology is very important, its use did create some problems. Sites and blogs can often be a mix of categories and require a closer analysis to decide where they should be placed in the typology; for example, the blog of a researcher may mention the institution without being under its responsibility. The distinction between 'Official' and 'Public' was intended to distinguish between government sites and those produced by public bodies but which do not have the same official role; this distinction was not always easy for the librarians to maintain, and also created problems for the researchers. Similarly, the 'Association' category was not limited to those organisations with the official status of an association under French law, creating potential overlap with 'Personal' sites. Finally, the 'Media' category was intended to cover news sites with sections specifically dedicated to WWI, but not all sites have such a section. In this case the sites are generally already included as part of a separate dedicated crawl of news sites by the BnF. This means that articles from sites not selected for this crawl should still be in the web archives of the BnF, but not as part of the 'Great War on the Web' collection, meaning researchers will have to decide whether to include them in their analysis. The 'Media' category was also broadened to include other sites of a commercial nature, such as video games.

The selection was created progressively and for the first capture, held in late 2013 to coincide with the start of the official events relating to the centenary, it was decided to ensure that as a minimum the official sites and other sites or sections specifically created for the occasion should be included; this corresponds largely with the 'Official' and 'Public' categories. This was then widened to include the other categories, starting with any site that could be related to or commented on the centenary events, and from the third crawl

**Table 30.1 Evolution of the collection 'Great War on the Web'**

| *Date* | *Size of collection* | *Number of URLs collected* | *Volume* |
|---|---|---|---|
| November 2013 | 41 sites | 1,198,732 | 35,75 Gb |
| March 2014 | 99 sites | 1,689,613 | 47,29 Gb |
| August 2014 | 482 sites | 7,323,201 | 402,83 Gb |
| November 2014 | 555 sites | 9,698,633 | 313,85 Gb |

onwards to cover the overall scope outlined above of sites about the First World War in general. The collection continued to grow, but more gradually than over these first few captures (see Table 30.1). As noted above, this is another aspect that researchers must be aware of in analysing the evolution of the collection over time, to distinguish between changes in the sites themselves and changes due to the addition of sites.

Other methods were also used in the process of searching for and selecting sites. A list of keywords was established both to guide searches for relevant material and to describe sites selected in the selection tool BnF Collecte du Web (BCWeb) (Le Follic et al., 2012). This list was based on existing research on the First World War (the main sources used were: Cervoni and Cervoni, 2005; Loez, 2013; Meyniel, 2010), to avoid any gaps due to a lack of knowledge of a given theme: battles, diplomacy, life at the front, etc.

However, this vocabulary proved to be of only limited use in web searching, due not only to the fact that terms frequently produced too many or hardly any sites, but also that sites were often poorly referenced in search engines. Two main ways of identifying sites were thus used:

- Using links from sites already identified; official sites frequently have lists of related sites, blogrolls indicate other sites on related subjects, etc.
- Searching by type of site: when one site has been selected, other similar sites are identified, all sites of local archives, all tourist sites for regions affected by battles, etc.

This strategy proved effective; the cartography produced by the project did not identify any obvious gaps in the selection, within the criteria and the legal framework described above.

## METADATA: GENERATING THE GRAPHS

This section explores the challenges that must be overcome in order to build a network of websites from a web archive. In particular, it studies the choices made to increase the relevance and the readability of the networks. Network analysis offers an opportunity to analyse the social organisation of a community of interest. In our case study, the aim is to explore the social structure of online memory of the First World War: who is involved? How are institutions and amateurs connected? This interpretative work, described in greater detail in the section on the results below, must rely on an interpretable and relevant hyperlink network.

The approach chosen was to generate a directed network graph based on the BnF web archives to study the relations, materialised by hyperlinks, between the websites in the WWI collection. Rather than using the archived files directly, the analysis used both metadata extracted from the collections (including hyperlinks, which are considered as metadata representing the relationship between sites) and additional descriptive metadata from the selection tool. This section describes the different methods of generating graphs from these metadata that were tested in order to produce results that allow the researchers to study the research questions.

**Figure 30.1 Framework.**

The World Wide Web is a vast network: webpages can be represented as nodes in a graph, where the links between the nodes, known as edges, are the URL hyperlinks connecting the pages. The analysis of these web graphs is important for a number of purposes in different domains such as crawler optimisation, information retrieval or community detection. It has also become common practice to analyse web archives using web graphs; however, it is not always clear how best to generate and interpret them. Brügger (2013) divides the challenges of network analysis on web archives into two categories: constitutive challenges and practical challenges. Practical challenges such as access to the archive are beyond the scope of this chapter, but we will study some of the constitutive challenges and propose some solutions.

Researchers using web archives work, most of the time, with topic-centric collections (focussed crawls) which are dedicated to specific subjects such as elections, WWI, etc. Crawling procedures have an impact on the interpretation of graphs (Achlioptas et al., 2009; Meusel et al., 2014; Serrano et al., 2007), and this impact is more remarkable for topic-centric collections, as the frequency and/or the depth of crawl of different sites can vary. Their heterogeneity should be taken into account during graph analysis. Another important issue is content, which can be considered 'off topic' for the purposes of the analysis, and is introduced into the collection due to crawler settings or by outgoing links (whether or not these are crawled).

## From Metadata to Web Graph

The web graphs are generated from metadata files in WAT format[1]; these files contain an extraction from the web archive files, with in particular the URL of each file collected as well as an extraction of all the outgoing hyperlinks and their properties.

The elements listed below are extracted from the WAT files by using adapted Apache Pig scripts from the Internet Archive:[2]

- URL
- Status: http response status code (ex: 404 page not found)
- Mime type: a two-part identifier for file formats and format contents transmitted on the internet (ex: text/html or application/pdf)
- Outgoing links: list of hyperlinks found on the page
- Types of outgoing links, such as anchor tags (A), image tags (IMG)
- Date: crawled date of the file

These links are then aggregated according to the specified aggregation level and a graph file is generated in GEXF format, as shown in Figure 30.1.

## Ensuring Quantity and Quality

While generating network graphs from web archives, there are two main issues: quantity and quality. The main problem with analysis and visualisation of graphs is their readability. Beyond a certain density, the analysis algorithms cannot be executed on an 'average' server or their results become uninterpretable (cf. Figure 30.4). Thus, the data should be filtered to decrease the quantity for reasons of readability and interpretability.

As described earlier, the crawler begins with one or more URLs that constitute a *seed list*, and crawls each URL according to the configuration criteria, such as frequency of crawl, depth of links to follow, etc. The seed list is reliable because it is created by curators and by experts in the domain, but different factors can introduce 'interference' in the collection. The crawling procedure can archive pages not relevant to the subject of the analysis because it simply follows links on the page. This is particularly the case for websites where a sub-section is dedicated to the topic. As the structure of the website is based on hypertext links, a part of these links may not be related to the topic. These links, whether archived or not, appear in the list of outgoing links on a page and thus potentially in the graph.

Let us take the example of the page *Le Monde*, which proposes a sub-section dedicated to the Great War: http://www.lemonde.fr/Centenaire14-18. This seed URL is reliable, but contains links to other sub-sections unrelated to WWI, such as Economy, Sport, etc., as well as links to external sites. The crawler that follows the links to build the corpus, or the outgoing links on pages that are archived, potentially introduce a large number of URLs which are not relevant to the subject. In order to build a correct graph, it is necessary to eliminate this interference.

We present three different strategies that can be used to solve these issues, separately or in combination: Aggregation, Filtering and Scope.

## Aggregation

To make large-scale graphs readable, the usual method is the '*aggregation* of nodes'. This consists of grouping nodes that share the same attributes and presenting them as a single node in the graph. Three aggregation methods can be distinguished (see Meusel et al., 2015):

- Page-Level Aggregation: The nodes are aggregated based on page, which is defined as a single page within the web crawl, uniquely identified by its URL. For example, a page with URL http://pages14-18.mesdiscussions.net/pages1418/forum-pages-histoire/liste_sujet-1.htm is represented as a node.
- Host Aggregation: The nodes are aggregated based on a host of a URL, which is defined in RFC 1738 (Berners-Lee et al., 1994): informally, everything after the protocol double slash and the following slash, but excluding port and authentication information. The same example is aggregated to the node 'pages14-18.mesdiscussions.net'
- Pay-Level Domain (PLD) Aggregation: The nodes are aggregated based on pay-level domain, which is a sub-level domain of a top-level domain like .com, .tr, etc. The example is aggregated to the node 'mesdiscussions.net' in this case.

We add a new method for generating graphs from web archives: *seed-URL aggregation*, where the nodes are aggregated based on the seed URL, that is the URL chosen as a seed, or starting point, to archive this source. This information is drawn from the selection tool BCWeb. For the example above, the URL is aggregated on 'pages14-18.mesdiscussions.net', which is the URL chosen by the librarians.

## Filtering

*Filtering* techniques allow the reduction or elimination of interference in the collection. This can be done by several methods, from using advanced webpage classification algorithms (Markkandeyan and Devi, 2015) to manual selection. Classification approaches can be divided into binary and multi-class. Binary classification categorises instances into two classes; in our case these can be 'relevant' and 'non-relevant'. To classify each page, there is a need to work with its content. In web archives, as we mentioned, depending on crawler configuration, each outgoing link is not archived, thus we do not have the contents of all pages to run a classifier. In addition, classification is often taken as a supervised machine learning problem where a set of annotated data is needed to train a classifier and we do not have annotated data for our corpus. On the other hand, the manual annotation at page level of the entire archive content on this scale is often infeasible.

The URLs of the archived webpages can contain the necessary information and can offer an efficient way to classify pages as relevant or not. It has been shown that URL tokens are sufficient to classify the pages (Hernández et al., 2012). A recent work (Souza et al., 2015) showed that the URLs of the archived web documents can contain semantic information and can offer an efficient way to obtain initial semantic annotations for the archived documents. We tested this solution to eliminate 'off topic' pages from our corpus. A set of keywords (war, 1418, 1914, etc.) was defined by studying the seed URLs selected by curators. Links that do not contain at least one of these keywords are eliminated. The result is very dependent on the choice of the keywords: while we can obtain a corpus without interference, much relevant content can also be excluded.

### *Scope*

The corpus can be restricted to the scope of collection, in other words by using the seed list and only keeping pages whose URLs/hosts match those of seed URLs. The alternative is that all pages are kept, including outgoing links not captured by the crawler. Restricting the corpus based on the seed URLs is reliant on the hypothesis that the curators are able to find the most important sources to archive and the quality of the archive is assured. Without this restriction, the link analysis can also be used to discover new pages to enrich the archive.

## *Qualitative Analysis*

We can thus generate graphs more adapted to visualisation by improving the quality of the information and decreasing its quantity based on three methods: aggregation, filtering and scope. In this section we will compare the combined effects of the three strategies presented in order to find the most useful combinations. To the best of our knowledge, there are no measures to compare these different strategies: thus, only a qualitative assessment is used.

Table 30.2 shows for each combination of strategies the number of nodes and links for the capture from August 2014. This collection was chosen to compare the strategies based on its medium size (7,323,201 URLs) that facilitates the experiments and the variety of seed URLs.

### *Aggregation*

In this section, we compare the visualisation of the host graph to the seed-URL graph. In both graphs, we keep only the URLs that match the seed list, in other words, we apply 'scope' strategies to better observe the effects of different aggregation levels. To be able to visualise the differences between these two graphs, the nodes have been filtered with respect to their degree, that is, the sum of the number of outgoing and incoming links: the nodes whose degrees are less than 80 have been excluded from visualisation. It should be noted that degree filtering does not have

**Table 30.2 Comparison of strategies for generating the graph**

| *Aggregation level* | *URL filtering* | *Scope* | *# Nodes* | *# Links* |
|---|---|---|---|---|
| Host | Filtered | Corpus | 456 | 3,356 |
| Host | Filtered | All | 15,148 | 27,968 |
| Host | Not filtered | Corpus | 483 | 6,603 |
| Host | Not filtered | All | 252,207 | 521,414 |
| Seed URL | Filtered | Corpus | 419 | 2,274 |
| Seed URL | Filtered | All | 15,310 | 28,910 |
| Seed URL | Not filtered | Corpus | 462 | 3,469 |
| Seed URL | Not filtered | All | 252,399 | 525,460 |

the same impact on both graphs: aggregation by host will group more nodes into one and therefore the distribution of degrees is different.

In Figure 30.2, corresponding to aggregation by host, we note that the central place is occupied by nodes like youtube.com and facebook.com, which can be considered as main poles, whereas these social network nodes disappear in the second graph (cf. Figure 30.3), with aggregation by seed URL. We take the example of facebook.com to illustrate the comparison. In the seed list, there are two URLs chosen by the experts:

> https://www.facebook.com/pages/Bicyclette-Pliante-Gérard/254241421345914
> https://www.facebook.com/pages/Centenaire-de-la-Première-guerre-mondiale-en-Haute-Saône/400310596705578

These two URLs represent two different nodes in the seed-URL graph, which is not visible in Figure 30.3 as they do not have a degree greater than our threshold (80). On the other hand, in Figure 30.2, they are aggregated in the facebook.com node with all the links that have facebook.com as host. In addition, many pages contain outgoing links to social networks (in our example Facebook) to promote the sharing of articles or the related social media accounts. Here are some examples of URLs that are located in the facebook.com node:

> http://www.facebook.com/pages/Ministère-de-la-défense/11091233228
> http://www.facebook.com/sharer.php?u=http://centenaire.org/fr/agenda?nid=2015

This increases the degree of the Facebook node. When we examine the URLs aggregated to the Facebook node, we realise that a very small part of the links concerns sites chosen by curators; indeed, only those from centenaire.org point to a Facebook page chosen in the seed list. This example illustrates how the interpretation of the network visualisation can change based on the choices made during the generation of the graphs.

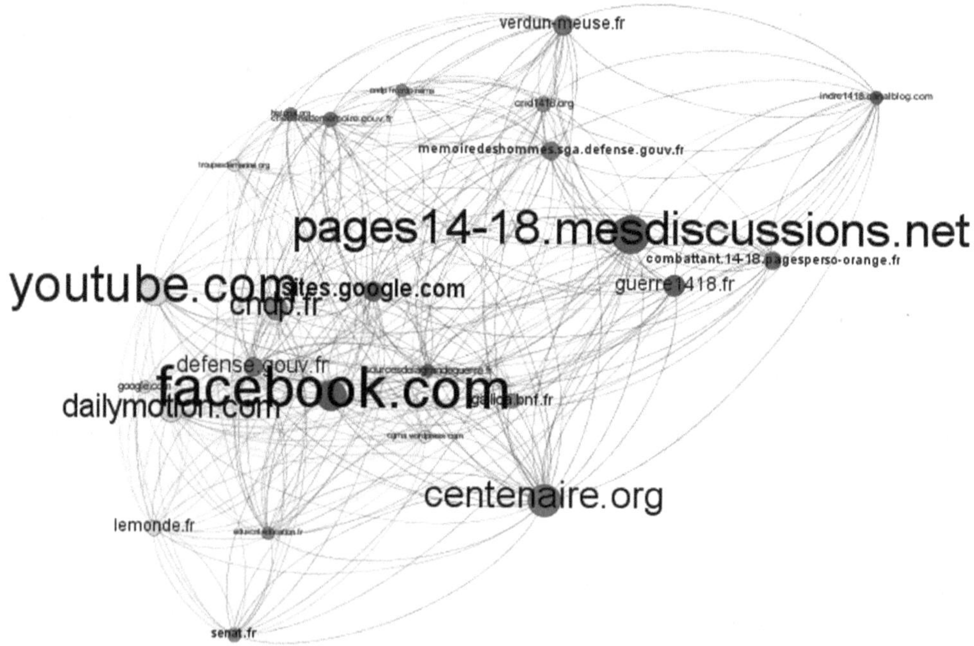


**Figure 30.2 Hyperlink network visualisation with host aggregation (scope Corpus).**

**Figure 30.3 Hyperlink network visualisation with aggregation by seed URL (scope Corpus).**

### *Filtering*

In this section, we compare the effect of filtering by keywords in URLs on the graph aggregated by host. The use of filtering increases the readability of the graph and ensures that all pages that do not concern WWI are eliminated. Figure 30.4 shows a graph without filtering, which is very difficult to open and manipulate with Gephi. After filtering the graph, we obtain Figure 30.5, which is much easier to manipulate and allows an interpretation by the researcher.

Using the example of a seed URL http://www.lemonde.fr/centenaire-14-18/8.html that has outgoing links to different URLs:

1 http://television.telerama.fr/tele/chaine-tv/france-3,80.php
2 http://www.lemonde.fr/centenaire-14-18-livres/
3 http://www.lemonde.fr/idees/article/2013/10/08/l-europe-ce-n-est-pas-la-paix-c-est-la-consequence-de-la-paix_3492063_3232.html

By using filtering, URLs 1 and 3, which are offtopic, are eliminated and only URL 2, which contains the terms 'centenary' and '14-18', is retained. This method is very dependent on the choice of the keywords: an overly selective choice of keywords can lead to the elimination of pages that are nevertheless relevant. The August 2014 capture contains approximately 240 million URLs, but after filtering only 22 million URLs remain. Thus, 90% of the corpus is considered 'off topic', a level that seems unacceptably excessive.

### *Scope*

In this section, we compare the graphs generated by staying in the scope of the corpus

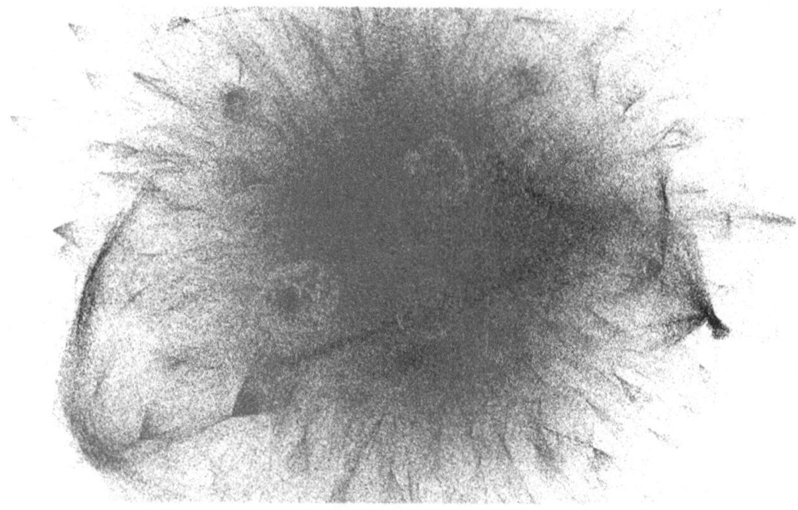

**Figure 30.4 Hyperlink network visualisation without filtering, with host aggregation (scope: all).**

as archived, that is, including only those URLs collected based on the seed list, or by including all the outgoing URLs cited whether or not they form part of the corpus. In both cases the nodes are aggregated by host. The second graph, very difficult to manipulate, corresponds to Figure 30.4. Figure 30.6 represents the graph produced by remaining in the scope of the seed list.

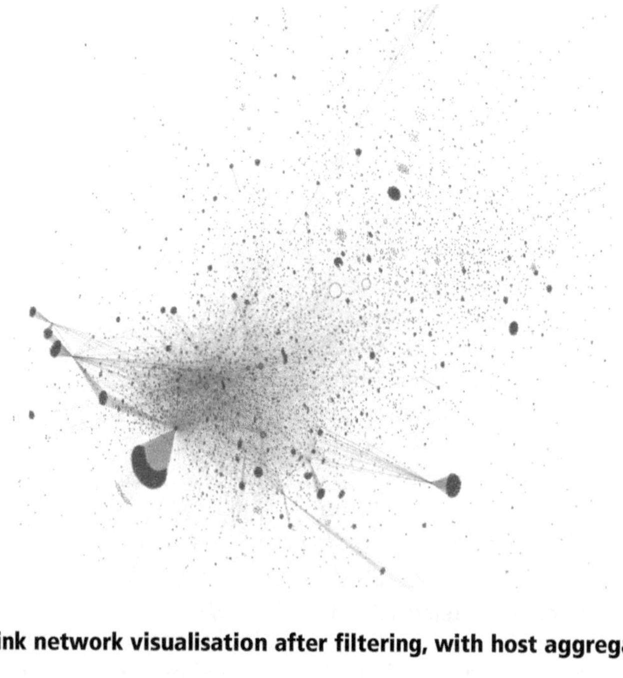

**Figure 30.5 Hyperlink network visualisation after filtering, with host aggregation (scope: all).**

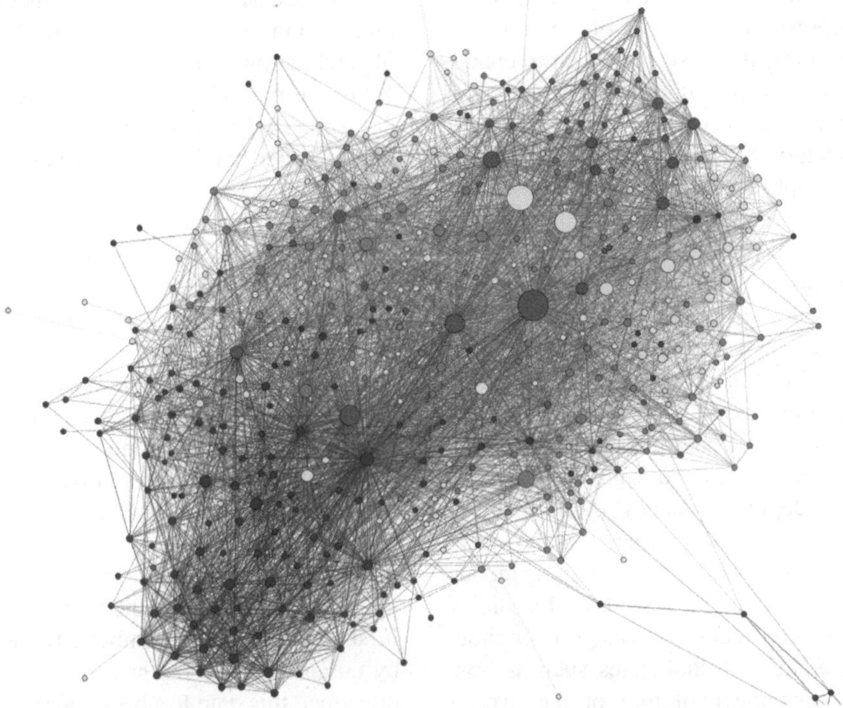

**Figure 30.6 Hyperlink network visualisation without filtering, aggregated by host, remaining in the scope of the seed list.**

By staying within the scope of the collection, the seed list plays the role of a filter, regardless of whether or not URL keyword filtering is applied. If we do not restrict the dataset to this scope, it is necessary to use filtering to have a readable and interpretable graph, eliminating the 'interference' that comes from outgoing links.

For the aggregation of the nodes, the comparison above led us to choose to aggregate by seed URL rather than by host, which gives too much importance to sites that are only partially dedicated to the Great War (examples: websites of social networks, media, etc.). The graphs presented in the following sections respect the scope of the collection with nodes aggregated by seed URL and without any keyword filtering.

## *Dealing with Dynamic Graphs*

One of the interests of working on web archives is to be able to retrace the evolution of documents and their relationships. In our case, the various captures should make it possible to evaluate how the structure of the network of sites devoted to the Great War changed over time.

Dynamic (temporal) graphs, where nodes and links appear and disappear over time, have been the subject of an increasing interest in computer science as a challenging topic due to the complexity introduced by this temporal dimension. Various techniques have been proposed to respond to the challenges related to integrating time into the visualisation of graphs (Albano et al. 2015; Heymann and le Grand, 2014). The most common way in practice consists of studying the series of graphs representing the state of the corpus at different times. It is also important to ensure stability in the layout in order to preserve the user's mental map, which is essential for readability, memorability and interpretability of dynamic graphs (Archambault and Purchase, 2013). Two kinds of analysis can be done by using dynamic graphs: studying the general evolution of the overall graph over time or focussing on a specific node (dynamic egocentric graph) and studying only its evolution over time (Shi et al., 2015).

For homogeneous web archive collections, which are constructed by following the same seed URLs and same crawler configuration (depth, frequency, etc.), all these challenges remain the same. On the other hand, while working with non-homogeneous web archives where the seed URLs and/or the crawler configuration change over time, we have additional challenges such as how to distinguish the evolution of the overall graph from the evolution of the collection. We would like to underline that these issues are independent of the aggregation, filtering and perimeter decisions. On the other hand, generating a seed-URL graph raises another issue: which version of the seed list to use. This is one reason why it is crucial for researchers to understand how the web archive collections are created.

We generated four graphs for four different captures made between November 2013 and November 2014. For each capture, the seed list is enriched with new sources and is updated (changes to URLs or crawler configuration for sources already in the collection). The appearance of a new source in the seed list does not necessarily mean that it is a new site on the web: the site could already exist but not have been spotted or have been considered to be irrelevant by curators before. Thus, we face a great deal of uncertainty: is the intensification of relationships from one capture to another due to better identification of sites in the archiving process or rather to changes in activity in terms of the number of sites online and links between them? If the metadata in WAT files could indicate the date of publication of the archived documents, it would be possible to detect if it is one phenomenon or the other, but this is not the case. On the other hand, we will never be certain because, for web documents in general, no trustworthy timestamp for publication is available. This is due to its decentralised nature and the lack of standards for time and date; only the date of crawl can be considered as truly reliable.

In the timescale of this project, we were not in a position to make a reliable temporal analysis, although the context of events relating to the centenary encourages us to think that network densification is indeed an effect of increased online activity. Thus, we have taken the option of working on a collection that reflects the state of the web related to the First World War in November 2014 as defined by curators. Since the growth of the collection since this date has been more gradual, it would be interesting to perform a temporal analysis on the subsequent captures, which represent a more stable corpus.

## RESULTS: INTERPRETING THE NETWORK OF WWI WEBSITES

This section aims to show the interpretive work that can be carried out from a network of sites built from a web archive. It shows how the analysis can be enriched by content analysis and by interviews, and the interest of working on web archives.

Websites are usually built for one or several purposes; they are designed and used by specific populations with such purposes in mind. These functional aspects deeply inform the content and structure of websites, as well as their relations with other websites and resources. That is why, in this case as in any case of data analysis, the background knowledge of the domain is essential for the analyst to see what is relevant in the statistics and maps, to be able to tell the wood from the trees.

The aim of our larger research, to study how the memory of WWI is constructed on the web, provided us some such background. WWI, of course, corresponds to an important moment for the collective memory: it concerned a whole generation and the nations involved developed a significant activity around the commemoration of the dead before the end of the conflict (Olick and Robbins, 1998). It is notable that this memory activism, still alive one century afterward, was reinforced by the fact that since the 1980s we have been facing a profusion of references to memory, 'the *boom mémoriel*' as it is called in French. Pierre Nora, by introducing the concept of '*lieu de mémoire*' (or 'place of memory'), proposes an interpretation of memory transformation, focussing on the externalisation of memory: '*Lieux de mémoire* originate with the sense that there is no spontaneous memory, that we must deliberately create archives, maintain anniversaries, organize celebrations, pronounce eulogies, and notarize bills because such activities no longer occur naturally' (Nora, 1989). WW1 websites participate in that ecology. But Nora's seven-volume book was published before the growth of internet as a media. What are the equivalent of the *lieux de mémoire* on the web? A century after the events, who are the main actors involved in constructing the history and memory of WWI through websites (amateurs, experts, associations, institutions…)? What kind of links are established between these websites? What is the role of online heritage collections in this territory? To understand this ecology, our approach combines the sociology of memory (Gensburger and Lavabre, 2005), in the Halbwachs (1994, 1997) tradition, enriched by Nora's (1989), Rousso's (2016) and Ricoeur's (2003) reflections on memory with research on new media.

As our aim is to describe the digital organisation of WWI memory on the web, we focus on a specific aspect of this collection as seen earlier in this chapter: the relations between websites through hyperlinks. The idea is to establish the network of websites, thereby giving a vision of social or intellectual distance between actors and providing information on the popularity and notoriety of different actors (Cardon et al., 2014; Severo and Venturini, 2016).

After presenting the main results that emerge thanks to the WWI website network, we focus on the role of qualitative analysis, content analysis and interviews for enhancing the interpretation. We will then examine which conditions are necessary in using a corpus initially constituted for a heritage purpose for a research one.

## Observations from the Network of WWI Websites

The archived collection of WWI (captured in November 2014) has almost 500 websites: 35% are institutional websites[3], and 11% are websites from media that propose specific sections dedicated to the world conflict. But more than half are *non-professional* websites published by individuals (37%) or by associations (17%).

To visualise the graph, generated by the treatment chain presented above, a force-directed layout is used to spatialise the network, ForceAtlas2: 'Nodes repulse each other like magnets, while edges attract their nodes, like springs. These forces create a movement that converges to a balanced state' (Jacomy et al., 2014). Figure 30.7 gives a 2D representation of the WWI web network. The absolute position of the nodes is arbitrary, while the relative positions are correlated to the interrelationships. Figure 30.8 retains the nodes with a degree greater than 30.

The first remark is that media are quite invisible in the map, certainly because they are less connected to the other sites but also because there is not always a clear identification of the section dedicated to WWI.

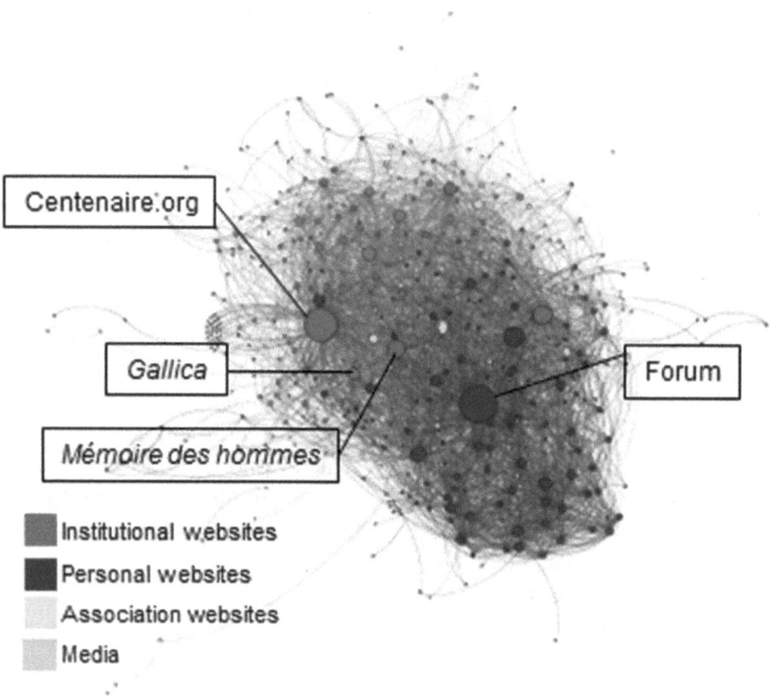


**Figure 30.7 Network visualisation of websites dedicated to WW1.**

Although there are no truly independent clusters, we can notice a clear distinction between a zone dominated by institutional websites (in red) and another one where personal websites (in blue) are the most frequent. We interpret the latter as the amateur sphere. The main actor, with the highest degree (see earlier in chapter), i.e. the most connected to other websites, in the institutional zone is centenaire.org, the official website dedicated to the centenary.

In the blue zone, the main node is an amateur forum, surrounded by a lot of blogs or personal websites. The density of the connections between the websites is highest in this part of the graph. It is important to notice that not all the non-professional websites are located in this lower part of the map. Some of them are clearly integrated in the institutional zone, such as sourcesdelagrandeguerre.fr or troupesdemarines.org, due to their specific network of connections: they are more connected to institutional websites and do not interact with the amateur sphere.

Finally, we can notice that some institutional websites, like Gallica or Mémoire des hommes, are close to the personal websites on the map because they are frequently cited through hyperlinks.

## *Improving Interpretation*

The exploration of the network map reveals some elements of the structure of the territory of WW1 memory, especially the distinction between the institutional and the amateur zone. In order to improve the understanding of the communities engaged in WWI memory, the network analysis should be combined with qualitative approaches to understand the content of nodes and the nature of interactions between stakeholders. We would like to underline the interest of 1)

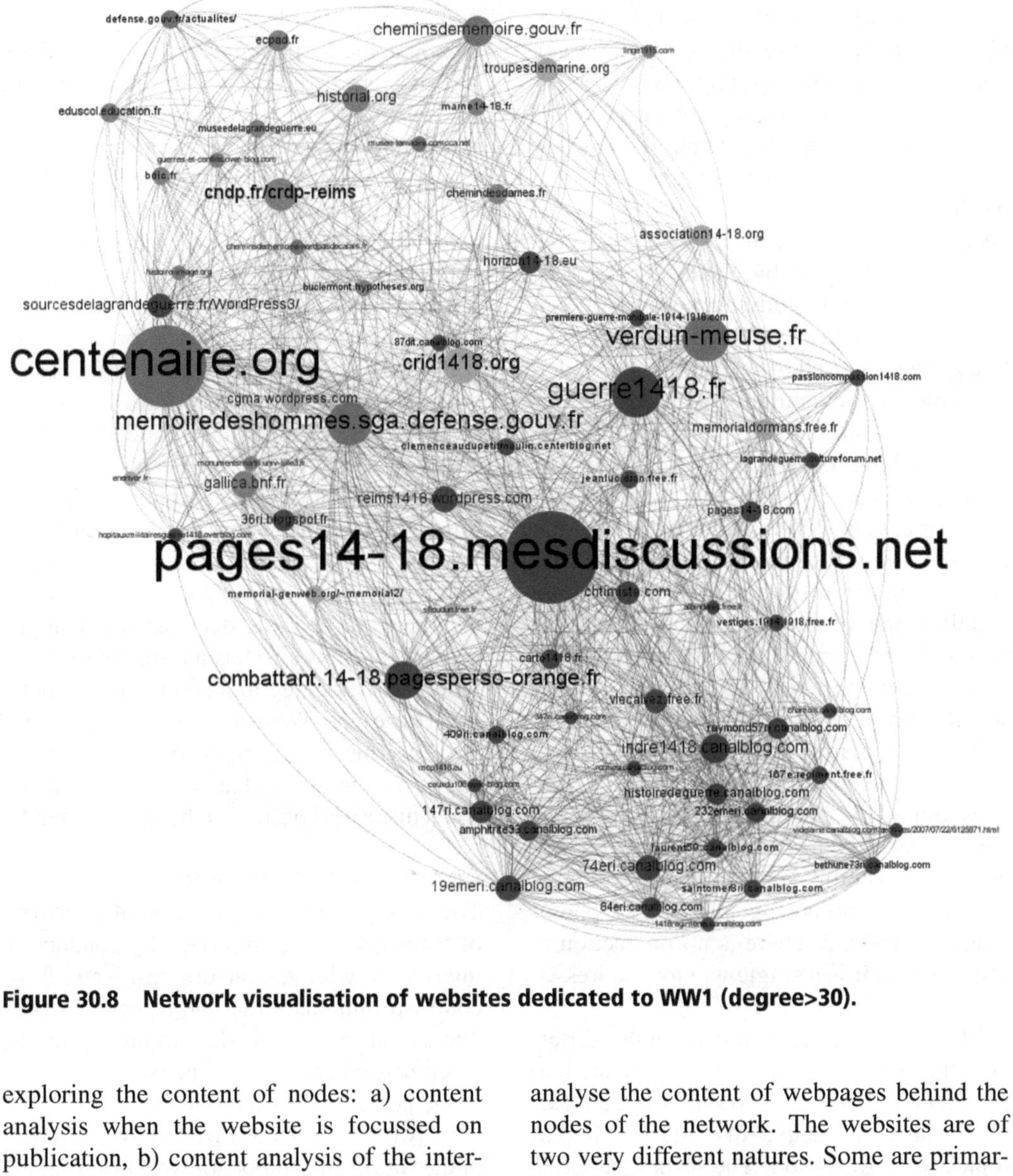


**Figure 30.8 Network visualisation of websites dedicated to WW1 (degree>30).**

exploring the content of nodes: a) content analysis when the website is focussed on publication, b) content analysis of the interactions between contributors when the website, like a forum, is dedicated to interactions and 2) conducting interviews with the actors of this interaction space to capture their own perspective.

## *Analysing the contents of websites and interactions*

To better understand the social structure behind a network of websites, it is helpful to analyse the content of webpages behind the nodes of the network. The websites are of two very different natures. Some are primarily places of publication, while others are places of interaction, such as forums, although, on the web, the activity of publication is closely intertwined with the activity of interaction. Both require specific approaches, one focussing on content analysis and the other on analysis of interactions.

This content exploration helps us to understand the social organisation of the group, the presence of a common culture, the existence of norms, statuses and roles that are reflected in the network structure. It usually implies an observation of the milieu in the tradition of virtual ethnography (Hine, 2000), which means participating for an extended period of time, reading what is said and published, observing what happens, exploring hyperlinks, collecting conversations and documents. This kind of approach was conducted, for example, by Nancy Baym in the early 1990s while studying a group of fans of soap opera (Baym, 1993) in a forum or by Beaudouin and Velkovska (2000) for understanding a peer-community of technical assistance, which implied interactions in a forum, self-publishing of websites, exchanges by mailing list, etc.

In our case of WWI memory, this exploration shows a real difference in the way sites are cited. In the institutional sphere, links are mainly based on the content; in the amateur sphere the meaning of the hyperlinks is twofold: highlighting both the *content and the social relation*. We can better understand this point by comparing the main nodes of each zone. Centenaire.org gathers all the initiatives around the centenary of WWI. It is like a portal, referencing every exhibition, conference, demonstration, publication, educational action… and proposing archives of photographs, maps, etc. There is no interaction in this website; it is a single window addressed to a large audience.

The nature of the forum is totally different: this space is principally dedicated to *interactions* between participants. The sections and threads help to distinguish different topics of conversation. The forum gathers a group of people working together to build the memory of the war: they are connected because they share information and data, because they build knowledge together but also because friendship helps in organising relations between them. In this space, where there are no professional obligations, the involvement is also sustained by the social relations between the members (Beaudouin, 2016).

Around the forum, and connected to it, we noticed the network of personal websites. The ethnographic exploration shows that these websites are dedicated to specific aspects of the war, based on the knowledge and documents (public and personal documents and photographs) that their authors have been accumulating. Many of these websites concern infantry regiments and reconstitute the memory of each soldier, battle and place occupied. Most of the authors of websites in the environment of the forum are or were also contributors to the forum. Signs of friendship are visible on the websites: most of the sections offering external links are called '*Blogs et sites amis*' ('friends' blogs and sites'), and in the presentation of each blog the interactions with other amateurs are often mentioned. We have shown on the map that the density of links was higher in the amateur zone, and the ethnographic analysis demonstrates that the network of links also has a different meaning reflecting belonging to a community of practice (Lave and Wenger, 1991) engaged in a work of collective memory (Halbwachs, 1994, 1997), in the sense that the way of talking about history is constructed by the community.

### Conducting interviews

The quality of the interpretation of a network of websites can be improved by conducting interviews with the actors involved. It of course presupposes that the research is conducted shortly after the archive process, when participants are still active.

We performed 11 interviews (nine face-to-face, two by telephone) with active members of the forum and authors of websites from the amateur sphere involved in WWI memory. Interviews lasted on average 1h 50 (between 50 minutes and three hours)[4]. We presented the web graph to the various interviewees at the end of the interaction. They were able to react to this representation of a universe that sounds familiar to them, especially in the amateur zone. Conversely, the institutional zone is for them a space that is less known, less useful, less frequented.

These interviews were very helpful for understanding the specific position of heritage websites in the map. These document warehouses, which offer digitised collections to readers, are clearly institutional websites. This is true for *Mémoire des hommes*, a huge database from the Ministry of Defence, which contains all the data concerning the soldiers killed during the war ('*Morts pour la France*') and the digitised war diaries of each regiment. It is also the case for Gallica, the digital library of Bibliothèque nationale de France. Despite their institutional character, they are located close to the amateurs' sphere. These non-professional historians or genealogists show an intensive use of the digitised documents, confirmed during the interviews, by frequently mentioning these sources in their messages, blogs and websites. In that sense these amateurs bring life to heritage websites that are institutional by definition.

Finally, the interviews had an unexpected use: the exploration of the map by the actors made it possible to identify the limits of the network of WWI websites. Some noted the absence of fundamental sites for their research, such as the site of the Red Cross which lists all prisoners of war, or dedicated sites in countries other than France... Others were surprised by the small size of the MemorialGenWeb site, which is in a sense the amateur ancestor of *Mémoire des hommes*. And more generally, the low presence of genealogy sites was often noted. This points to three different problems. The archiving of the web is part of a legal deposit mission and does not concern foreign sites, which is obviously regrettable in the study of a world conflict. Second, the limited presence of MemorialGenWeb is due to the fact that at the time the archive being studied was created the site was in the process of leaving its original hosting service provider, so that the address of the site was in transition. Finally, archiving does not currently cover commercial sites that charge fees, which is the case for most genealogy sites. Presenting the map to the actors makes possible the work of co-construction of the interpretation between actors and researchers and also allows us to identify the limits of the map. It also offers a potential loop of interactions with the constitution of the collection.

## Methodological Reflections

After explaining the strategy used in this study to interpret and control the quality of the representation, this final section discusses two aspects of the methodology chosen for this research: doing research on a corpus constituted for a heritage purpose; and working with web archives instead of working with the live web.

### Delegating the establishment of the corpus

Can a corpus constituted for a heritage purpose be useful for a research one? At the end of this experience, the answer is evidently yes, but at the starting point it was not evident at all. Usually, the researcher considers that the constitution of the corpus is part of his/her research work and will not volunteer to delegate this task. The constitution of the corpus corresponds to the moment where the researcher discovers the field and is when hypotheses emerge. For example, with Navicrawler, a tool used by many scholars to perform mapping of websites (Boullier and Lévy, 2016; Diminescu and Pasquier, 2010), at each step as a new website is proposed by the tool, the researcher takes the decision to keep it or to exclude it from the collection. Evidently, this method can also introduce some bias in the sense that the principle of choice may change over time.

What are the conditions for working on a collection that researchers have not constituted? The main condition is the quality of description of the process of selection. In our case, as the collection was constituted by librarians and experts, in a professional context where rules are clearly defined and written, we were presented with a corpus that was clearly documented with the seed URL, the categorisation of the author, the keywords, the person responsible for the selection… and also the method of crawling applied. This set of metadata is an exceptional resource because it allows the researcher to check the perimeter of the collection, to define sub-corpora, to exclude some websites if needed.

Evidently, it is not only a question of documenting the process but also a question of interaction: the essential element is the possibility of interacting with the experts in charge of the collection, for understanding certain choices, for suggesting missing websites, for signalling changes in a URL… This feedback gives researchers a role in creating the archive, at the risk of creating a bias in the collection; it is rare for researchers to create primary archive sources, even if it is more common for readers to suggest books for library collections. The loop of interactions between the team in charge of the collection and the team that will do research on a corpus extracted from the collection is a condition of quality.

### *Working on web archives*

Since the web came into existence, and since research on the internet has emerged, the necessity of working on archives was so evident that nobody really sought to explain it. Many tools, such as httrack, were available for crawling and making local copies of websites. For researchers in social sciences it was obvious that due to the ephemeral character of the web it was necessary to archive corpora. The initiative of the Internet Archive and the building of the Wayback Machine arise from the same observation: as the web is in constant transformation, it is vital to preserve the different states. Researchers have developed archives, without imagining that they would prove to be so ephemeral: the disk cannot be read any more, the copy is partially damaged, the browser cannot support old versions…. Digital documents are particularly fragile compared with other media, such as books. Archiving the web demands a high level of expertise and it is essential to delegate this task to specific institutions or organisations.

Many researchers have underlined that the archive cannot correspond exactly to the 'real' websites (Brügger, 2013), because the process of archiving cannot guarantee an identical copy of the documents, but rather a mere representation of the websites.

Nonetheless, working on web archives represents a great improvement for the research community: it allows the possibility to verify the results by returning to the raw data and it ensures that the research can be reproduced. As Halbwachs (1997) mentioned, the memory is the collective reconstruction of the past. We know that the memory of the war that we study during the centenary is specific to our time and that it differs from the memory just after the war and of what it will be for the bicentenary of the war. For historians, it is essential to keep the memory of those different periods.

## CONCLUSION

This chapter gives an account of a research methodology for analysing web uses based on the archives of the web, as preserved by the French National Library (BnF). It is based on a specific research question: the memory of the First World War on the web. This case study demonstrates how the three stakeholders involved, librarians, computer scientists and social scientists, cooperate to produce quality work with frequent interaction and feedback between the constitution of the collection, the data extraction and the analysis and interpretation, the latter being fed by the exploration of the archived documents and by the interviews with the actors. The treatment chain has been designed to be used on other topics and by other researchers.

As noted above, web archives are a new kind of source for many researchers, and can be difficult to interpret if the researchers do not understand the way they have been created. For librarians, the work with the researchers on this project was very useful in helping to define what information needs to be provided on the way sites have been selected and collected. The different publications on the project are one way of providing this kind of information for future researchers.

Working on web archives is a major opportunity for social science research: it allows the use of documented and stabilised collections to constitute corpora. This opens the possibility of a reproducibility of the research and allows the testing of new methodologies on the same corpus, which opens the possibility of both confrontation and enrichment of the analyses.

What are the challenges for developing the use of web archives in social science research? The first one relates to the availability of archives, which is limited by law: in the digital era, having to be physically on-site at the BnF to consult the archives is an obvious limitation. The second is the flexibility of the archiving process, which needs to adapt to the evolutions of the web. If it is still relevant to archive websites, it becomes essential to archive the social media platforms on which a large part of the activity is deployed. In our case study, social media were partially integrated, knowing that in parallel another researcher was involved in archiving the WWI on Twitter (Clavert, 2016). Finally, on subjects of international dimension, such as ours, interoperability between the national archives will have to be envisaged in order to allow the creation of transnational corpus. An International Internet Preservation Consortium (IIPC) initiative around the First World War is underway.

Through this experience, we have been able to show how, at the time of the first centenary, an original memory work was built on the web around the First World War, which involves institutions as well as a network of amateurs. These results constitute a reference base for further studies.

## ACKNOWLEDGEMENTS

'The future of online digitised heritage: the example of the Great War' is a research project conducted by the BnF, the BDIC and Télécom ParisTech as part of the Cluster of Excellence, Pasts in the present, Investissements d'avenir, réf. ANR-11-LABX-0026-01 (Nicolas Auray, Valérie Beaudouin, Philippe Chevallier, Lionel Maurel, Josselin Morvan, Zeynep Pehlivan, Peter Stirling).

## *Notes*

1 https://webarchive.jira.com/wiki/display/Iresearch/Web+Archive+Transformation+(WAT)+Specification,+Utilities,+and+Usage+Overview (visited 6 June 2017).

2 https://webarchive.jira.com/wiki/display/Iresearch/Web+Archive+Analysis+Workshop (visited 6 June 2017).

3 We used the librarian's categories, with only marginal changes: we merged 'official' and 'public' websites into a global category 'institutional websites' and changed the categorisation of a very small number of websites.

4 Three of them were conducted by Philippe Chevallier, eight by Valérie Beaudouin.

## BIBLIOGRAPHY

Achlioptas, D., Clauset, A., Kempe, D., and Moore, C. (2009) 'On the bias of traceroute sampling: Or; power-law degree distributions in regular graphs', *Journal of the ACM*, 56(4): 1–28.

Albano, A., Guillaume, J.-L., Heymann, S., and Grand, B. Le (2015) 'Studying Graph Dynamics Through Intrinsic Time Based Diffusion Analysis', in Kazienko, P. and Chawla, N. (Eds), *Applications of Social Media and Social Network Analysis*. Springer International Publishing (Lecture Notes in Social Networks). pp. 103–124.

Amar M., and Chevallier P. (2013) *Rapport d'étude sur les usages des corpus numérisés de Gallica sur la Grande Guerre', Technical Report*. Paris: BnF.

Archambault, D., and Purchase, H.C. (2013) 'The "Map" in the mental map: Experimental results in dynamic graph drawing', *International Journal of Human-Computer Studies*, 71(11): 1044–1055.

Baym, N.K. (1993) 'Interpreting soap operas and creating community: Inside a computer-mediated fan culture', *Journal of Folklore Research*, 30: 143–176.

Beaudouin, V., and Velkovska, J. (2000) 'Structuring a communication space on the Internet', *Réseaux. The French Journal of Communication*, 7(2): 183–222.

Beaudouin V. (2016) 'Forums en ligne: des espaces de co-production de la connaissance et du lien social', in Martin, O. and Dagiral, E. (Eds), *L'ordinaire d'internet*. Paris: Armand Colin. pp. 164–182.

Berners-Lee, T., Masinter, L., and McCahill, M. (1994) 'RFC 1738: Uniform Resource Locators (URL)', https://www.ietf.org/rfc/ rfc1738.txt.

Bonnel, S., and Oury, C. (2014) 'Selecting websites in an encyclopaedic national library: A shared collection policy for internet legal deposit at the BnF', in *IFLA WLIC 2014*.

Boullier, D., and Lévy, J. (2016) 'Topographies/topologies. Langages spatiaux, spatialités, espaces', *Réseaux*, 34(195): 9–162.

Brügger, N. (2013) 'Historical network analysis of the Web', *Social Science Computer Review*, 31(3): 306–321.

Cardon, D., Fouetillou, G., and Roth, C. (2014) 'Topographie de la renommée en ligne', *Réseaux*, 6(188): 85–120.

Cervoni, J.-R., and Cervoni, M.-F. (2005) *Petit dictionnaire de la Grande guerre*. Bastia: Anima Corsa.

Clavert, F. (2016) '#ww1. The Great War on Twitter', in *Digital Humanities 2016: Conference Abstracts.* Jagiellonian University & Pedagogical University, Kraków. pp. 461–462.

Diminescu, D., and Pasquier, D. (Eds) (2010) Les migrants connectés – TIC, mobilités et migrations. *Réseaux,* 1(159): 196.

Gensburger, S., and Lavabre, M. (2005) 'Entre "devoir de mémoire" et "abus de mémoire": la sociologie de la mémoire comme tierce position', in Müller, B. (Ed.), *Histoire, mémoire et épistémologie. A propos de Paul Ricoeur.* Paris: Payot. pp. 76–95.

Halbwachs, M. (1994) *Les cadres sociaux de la mémoire*. Paris: Albin Michel (First edition, 1925, Librairie Alcan).

Halbwachs, M. (1997) *La mémoire collective*. Paris: Albin Michel (First edition, 1950).

Hernández, I., Rivero, C.R., Ruiz, D., and Arjona, J.L. (2012) 'An Experiment to Test URL Features for Web Page Classification', in Rodríguez, J.M.C., Pérez, J.B., Golinska, P., Giroux, S., and Corchuelo, R. (Eds), *Trends in Practical Applications of Agents and Multiagent Systems*. Berlin and Heidelberg: Springer (Advances in Intelligent and Soft Computing). pp. 109–116.

Heymann, S., and Le Grand, B. (2014) 'Exploratory network analysis: Visualization and interaction', Complex Networks and their Applications, in Cherifi, H (Ed.), *Complex Networks and their Applications*. Cambridge: Cambridge Scholars Publishing. pp. 174–211.

Hine, C. (2000) *Virtual ethnography*. London: Sage.

Jacomy, M., Venturini, T., Heymann, S., and Bastian, M. (2014) 'ForceAtlas2, A continuous graph layout algorithm for handy network visualization', *PLoS ONE*, 9(6): 1–22.

Lave, J., and Wenger, E. (1991) *Situated learning: Legitimate peripheral participation*. Cambridge: Cambridge University Press.

Le Follic, A., Stirling, P., and Wendland, B. (2012) 'Putting it all together: Creating a unified web harvesting workflow at the Bibliothèque nationale de France'. International Internet Preservation Consortium (IIPC).

Loez, A. (2013) *Les 100 mots de la Grande guerre*. Paris: Presses universitaires de France.

Markkandeyan, S., and Devi, M.I. (2015) 'Efficient machine learning technique for web page classification', *Arabian Journal for Science and Engineering*, 40(12): 3555–3566.

Meusel, R., Vigna, S., Lehmberg, O., and Bizer, C. (2014) 'Graph Structure in the Web – Revisited: A Trick of the Heavy Tail', in ACM (WWW '14 Companion), pp. 427–432.

Meusel, R., Vigna, S., Lehmberg, O., and Bizer, C. (2015) 'The graph structure in the web – analyzed on different aggregation levels', *The Journal of Web Science*, 1(1): 33–47.

Meyniel, J. (2010) *Vocabulaire illustré de la Grande guerre: 1914–1918*. Fontaine: EP.

Nora, P. (1989) 'Between memory and history: Les lieux de mémoire', *Representations*, 0(26): 7–24.

Olick, J.K., and Robbins, J. (1998) 'Social memory studies: From "collective memory" to the historical sociology of mnemonic practices', *Annual Review of Sociology*, 24(1): 105–140.

Ricoeur, P. (2003) *La mémoire, l'histoire, l'oubli*. Paris: Seuil.

Rousso, H. (2016) *Face au passé. Essais sur la mémoire contemporaine*. Paris: Belin.

Serrano, M.Á., Maguitman, A., Boguñá, M., Fortunato, S., and Vespignani, A. (2007) 'Decoding the structure of the WWW: A comparative analysis of web crawls', *ACM Trans. Web*, 1(2), http://dx.doi.org/10.1145/1255438.1255442

Severo, M., and Venturini, T. (2016) 'Enjeux topologiques et topographiques de la cartographie du Web', *Réseaux*, 34(195): 84–105.

Shi, L., Wang, C., Wen, Z., Qu, H., Lin, C., and Liao, Q. (2015) '1.5D egocentric dynamic network visualization', *IEEE Transactions on Visualization and Computer Graphics*, 21(5): 624–637.

Souza, T., Demidova, E., Risse, T., Holzmann, H., Gossen, G., and Szymanski, J. (2015) 'Semantic URL Analytics to Support Efficient Annotation of Large Scale Web Archives', in Cardoso, J., Guerra, F., Houben, G.-J., Pinto, A.M., and Velegrakis, Y. (Eds), *Semantic Keyword-based Search on Structured Data Sources*. Cham: Springer International Publishing (Lecture Notes in Computer Science). pp. 153–166.

Stirling, P., Chevallier, P., and Illien, G. (2012a) 'Web archives for researchers: Representations, expectations and potential uses', *D-Lib Magazine*, 18(3–4), http://www.dlib.org/dlib/march12/stirling/03stirling.html.

Stirling, P., Illien, G., Sanz, P., and Sepetjan, S. (2012b) 'The state of e-legal deposit in France: Looking back at five years of putting new legislation into practice and envisioning the future', *IFLA Journal*, 38(1): 5–24.

31

# A History with Web Archives, Not a History of Web Archives: A History of the British Measles–Mumps–Rubella Vaccine Crisis, 1998–2004

Gareth Millward

The media storm over the measles–mumps–rubella vaccine (MMR) is often attributed to a now-retracted *Lancet* article from February 1998 (Wakefield et al., 1998). Allegations that the vaccine might be linked to rising autism diagnoses in the UK caused significant problems for public health authorities. Vaccination rates dropped as parents received conflicting information from the medical profession, the press and, increasingly, the World Wide Web. In England, 92 per cent of children under the age of two received at least one dose of MMR in 1996. In 2004 this had dropped to 80 per cent (Health and Social Care Information Centre, 2005). Although the uptake of MMR then began to recover, it was not until 2012 that rates returned to pre-crisis levels. Conveniently, the Internet Archive begins in 1996, and covers this entire period. Given that the web was often credited as an influence during the crisis, this is a critical resource in writing the history of MMR.

But accessing the archive is no simple task. There is far too much information for any one human to read in detail. Moreover, most historians – even those dealing with the more-recent past – are not trained to use, or have experience using, web archives. Many do not have the resources or the inclination to build their projects around 'the web' as their main object of study. With so much information available, how can historians use the archived web as one source among many? How can they select and read documents? And how problematic is this for our understanding of the 1990s and 2000s?

This chapter is a review of one historian's research involving the Internet Archive. Through a case study, it shows historians without experience of web archives what is possible – as well as the methodological pitfalls. In doing so, it also emphasizes to digital historians and web archivists how 'traditional' historians with little experience of web archives might approach this source base. This may help to explain what historians will want from digital repositories and what training they may need to physically and practically access them in a meaningful way.

This chapter begins with an outline of the project. Next, it explores the methodological challenges of using the Internet Archive, especially for historians who are using close textual reading of these sources as part of a wider study. After explaining the historical context of MMR and British internet usage, it then outlines three different websites. These give not just examples of the empirical data gleaned from the archive, but also the methods for identifying and using that material. As a whole, it shows that the Internet Archive can be used as one source among many in larger history projects that span a wider time frame than that in which the web has existed. However, it is still a flawed and problematic process. Historians will be confronted with these problems more regularly over the next few years, and it is important that we begin to tackle them sooner rather than later.

## A HISTORY OF POLICY

I am a historian of medicine, specializing primarily in the history of government policy. Between 2014 and 2017 I wrote a monograph on the history of British vaccination policy from the 1940s through to MMR in the twenty-first century.[1] The main source base comprised official records (such as reports, internal governmental procedural documents and parliamentary proceedings), contemporary publications and newspapers. Web archives were an important addition to this body of literature. There were websites which were in themselves official government documents. Similarly, websites created by other organizations and individuals inform analysis of how and why the British public may have supported or rejected official government policy. Not all these sites were still on the live web, or at least not in the form they would have taken during the period under discussion. I used the Internet Archive's (2017) Wayback Machine in conjunction with the SHINE interface – a faceted search tool developed on a comprehensive index of the .uk domain by the British Library (2017). These tools allow historians to inspect historical snapshots and contextualize them with other primary sources.

Yet web archives were not (and could not be) central to the overall analysis. The period they cover was limited to the final book chapter on MMR. Any large-scale analysis of hyperlink networks or corpus linguistics was impractical. I lacked the training or expertise to embark on such an endeavour, and in practical terms I lacked the time to do so. It would also have created an unbalanced project, with completely different historical techniques and research questions employed for around one-fifth of the monograph compared with the other time periods. The aim, therefore, was to integrate archived web sources; albeit with a critical eye on how born-digital sources must be inspected within a different context to other archived materials (Brügger, 2008). This was not a history *of MMR on the web*. Such a project would undoubtedly shed light on the impact of the web just as contemporary sociologists and media studies academics have been invaluable in assessing the impact of the media on public discourse (Hargreaves et al., 2003; Speers and Lewis, 2004). Ackland and Evans (2017) give us an example of how this might be done with another contentious debate of medical and social significance, abortion in Australia. Instead, this was a history of MMR *which included the web*.

While the work of digital historians has been invaluable in opening up these sources to wider historical analysis, it is important that 'traditional' historians are able to work *with* as well as *on* internet archives. Not all research questions will be designed with web archives as the central source. Wider social and political studies will also need to analyse data which are neither born-digital nor originally published on the internet. At the same time, any history of the 1990s and 2000s has to engage with the fact that increasing numbers of Britons were using the web in their day-to-day lives. In order to write such histories, researchers need to be aware of the power as well as the limits of available depositories. The Big UK Domain Data for the Arts and Humanities (BUDDAH, 2015) project with the Institute of Historical Research and British Library (Winters, 2017) revealed that web archival sources are not the same as fully catalogued 'physical' collections such as those at The National Archives or local history centres. Similarly, they are not as accessible, coherent or well-curated as digitized depositories such as the Old Bailey records or newspaper collections.[2]

As part of BUDDAH, I had done some work on the Internet Archive. I was therefore not a complete novice, though I would also lay no claims to be an accomplished digital historian. The experience from this and from my colleagues showed that naïve search methods could lead to large, unwieldy corpora that were difficult to analyse (see esp. Deswarte, 2015; Millward, 2015). With MMR, I decided to focus on websites which were cited in my other primary sources. Mostly, these were URLs mentioned in correspondence and news reports in the leading medical journals *The Lancet* and the *British Medical Journal*. This produced a concentrated group of documents for which there was evidence of impact in the historical record. Martin Gorsky (2015) employed a similar methodology in his investigation of Primary Care Trust websites from the 1990s and 2000s. Web archives were crucial in these endeavours. The Wayback Machine allowed me to examine captures of websites from the time that they were cited by other publications. The well-known problem of 'link rot' in academic journals (Zittrain et al., 2014) meant that this was also, in many cases, the only way to access any version of URLs long since removed from the live web. This form of triangulation provided richer insight from the primary sources.

## THE MMR CRISIS IN THE CONTEXT OF BRITISH WEB HISTORY FROM THE 2000s

MMR became part of the routine vaccination programme for children in 1988. Immunization rates against the three diseases had been sub-optimal for public health authorities, and this trivalent vaccine was more effective and convenient for parents (Department of Health and Social Security, 1987; Badenoch, 1988). Uptake of the vaccine was good. By 1996 over 90 per cent of children under the age of two had received MMR (Health and Social Care Information Centre, 2005). But confidence in the vaccine dropped significantly in the late 1990s. In 1998, a paper was published in *The Lancet* (Wakefield et al., 1998) which appeared to show a link between MMR and a new type of autism. The paper itself was inconclusive. However, in a press conference called to launch the paper, the lead author, Andrew Wakefield, claimed that it would be safer for parents to give their children separate measles, mumps and rubella vaccines. Despite repeated assertions that there was no evidence of a link between MMR and autism – including in the same edition of *The Lancet* as Wakefield et al.'s paper (Chen and DeStefano, 1998) – the press continued to report that the medical community was divided on the issue (Speers and Lewis, 2004).

The crisis hit its peak in late 2001 and early 2002 (Speers and Lewis, 2004). Prime Minister Tony Blair refused to confirm or deny whether his own young son Leo had received MMR, citing his right to privacy. Then, a BBC documentary series *Panorama* reported on Wakefield and John O'Leary's work on the MMR–autism link, casting new doubt on the vaccine's safety (Dobson, 2002). The government was forced into a defensive publicity campaign. The Department of Health eventually regained some control over the MMR story. The weight of scientific evidence in MMR's favour meant that the Legal Services Commission (2003) withdrew funding for a case against the Department brought by the parents of autistic children who had received MMR. Then, in the following year, the investigative journalist Brian Deer (2004) published a series of exposés on Wakefield's research practices in the *Sunday Times*. Ten of the 12 co-authors of Wakefield et al. (1998) formally withdrew their support for the 1998 paper (Murch et al., 2004), and Deer's documentary for the Channel 4 series *Dispatches* (Berger, 2004) further damaged Wakefield's reputation and reaffirmed the scientific basis for the MMR programme. The General Medical Council (2010) began proceedings against Wakefield, and he was eventually struck off the medical register for serious professional misconduct.

There are two main reasons for studying the MMR crisis. For public health professionals and researchers, the period was considered a 'crisis' because the vaccination rate among children for MMR dropped significantly, leading to several measles outbreaks, notably in 2008–09 and 2012–13 (Eaton, 2009; McCartney, 2013; Keenan et al., 2017). They study MMR in its own right or as a comparison with similar events in other countries and time periods to learn lessons and avoid such events in the future. For historians and media studies scholars, the crisis is of interest as an example of a public debate played out in the popular press, doctors' surgeries and the internet (Fitzpatrick, 2004; Horton, 2004; Speers and Lewis, 2004). The media coverage of MMR was bound up in the political and cultural context of its time, and tells us much about public attitudes towards science, medicine, infectious disease and state authority. Any research questions around these topics must involve the internet. There is a temporal overlap. Although placing exact dates on the MMR crisis is difficult, the most concentrated period of activity is from the publication of Wakefield et al. (1998) to the Deer (2004) exposés. A wider view may take in the decline in MMR uptake – 1996

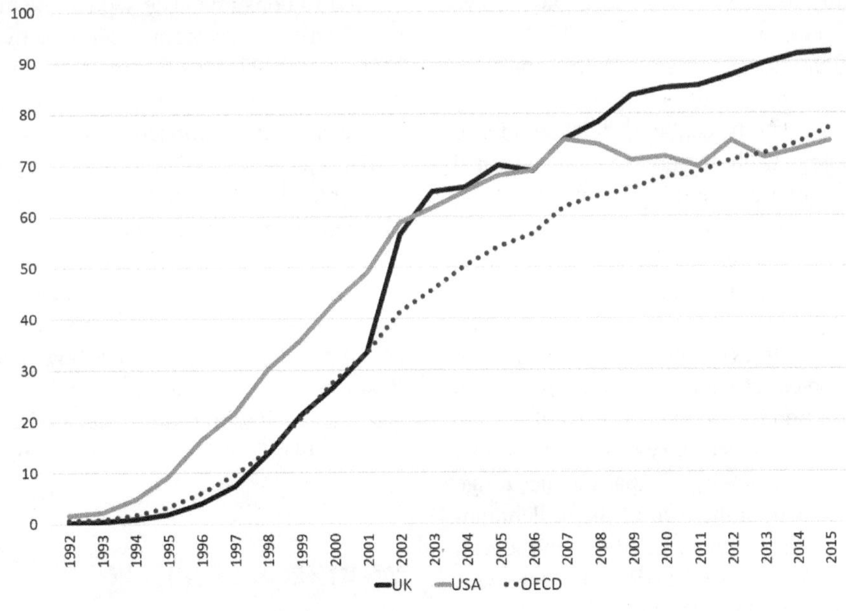


**Figure 31.1 Internet users (per 100 people).**
*Source*: UNdata (2017).

(Health and Social Care Information Centre, 2005) – and present-day measles outbreaks in Europe and North America (Larson et al., 2016). However defined, this is contemporaneous with the holdings in the Internet Archive. Moreover, the internet was continually cited as an influence on the debate.

Knowing exactly who and how many people read about MMR on the internet is difficult to know with absolute precision. These questions are currently asked as part of surveys on parents' attitudes and the trend has been towards increased usage, but they were not discussed in the peak period of the crisis (Ramsay et al., 2002; Campbell et al., 2017). In a 2003 study (Hargreaves et al., 2003), only 5 per cent of respondents said that they consumed their science news primarily from the internet. Undoubtedly, however, the general trend has been towards increased internet usage and coverage in Britain. This period of greatest growth coincided with the intensification of the MMR crisis (UNdata, 2017). It is therefore understandable that commentators at the time, at least in part, attributed the spread of rumour and negative publicity over the vaccine to 'the internet' (Selway, 1998; Horton, 2004; Speers and Lewis, 2004).

Web archives can certainly help to uncover these trends, but the definition of 'the internet' in this context has to be challenged. It can refer to the technology itself, the information contained on it or the cultures around how it was used and the meanings attributed to them (Abbate, 2017; Turner, 2017). Moreover, the meaning and use of the internet has not been static; nor should we succumb to the temptation of writing either Whiggish narratives of internet 'progression' or uncritical polemics against the 'dangers' of the democratization of knowledge (Russell, 2017). However, this is not a history *of* the web. Instead it is one that acknowledges that internet usage and web content at the turn of the millennium were part of the cultural milieu that influenced public discourse about MMR. The focus was on content – on closer reading of the information contained in select webpages – rather than a fully theorized and evidenced analysis of how the internet was used by different groups. What information was accessible to the general public? How did the government or other authors make use of this emerging technology? And if 'the internet' was to blame, what specific websites or resources on that internet were particularly worrisome or empowering to different communities involved in the crisis? This has necessarily limited the conclusion that one can draw from the material, but has also made the documents easier to integrate into my existing primary source analysis. Historians need to be conscious of their choices and the politics inherent in the definition of 'the internet' that they used (Abbate, 2017).

With these caveats, this article now presents three examples of how the Internet Archive might be used. The first concerns a government website called MMR The Facts, hosted on the nhs.uk domain. It sought to educate parents about MMR, borrowing from sociological research on risk communication. The government used the web because of the internet's growing importance (perceived or real) and because it could provide as little or as much information as parents or health professionals wished to consume. The second example is a report written by vaccine-sceptic activist Alan Phillips in 1997. This document was hosted as a text file on an American university's server. While the actual impact of the document is difficult to measure, it was quoted by a health worker in the *British Medical Journal* who claimed many parents in his/her circle had read and shared it widely. The final example concerns the website of the Society for the Autistically Handicapped. This was discovered through SHINE. It shows how potentially 'lost' documents can be traced within the archive, albeit with limitations in what historians can then do with this information.

## MMRTHEFACTS.NHS.UK

The British government attempted to combat negative publicity about MMR from the day of the infamous Wakefield press conference. In the face of increased doubt and declining vaccination rates, it renewed its campaign in 2001 (Ramsay, 2001). This failed to reverse the trend. In 2002, the Department of Health launched a new public-facing website called MMR The Facts (Figure 31.2), which it believed would educate parents and make use of an increasingly important technology (Department of Health, 2002d). It borrowed from techniques outlined in the growing field of risk communication, amid criticism from sociologists that the Department's strategy had hitherto been too proscriptive and inflexible (Ramsay, 2002; Alaszewski and Horlick-Jones, 2003). The site's URL appeared in contemporary news reports, particularly in the *British Medical Journal* (Muminovic, 2002).

The Internet Archive provided an opportunity to analyse what information the Department felt was important and to see whether and how these messages changed over time. The news section, for example, provided regular updates on stories that reaffirmed the government's MMR message (Department of Health, 2002c). A world map showed which countries used MMR and the varying rates of infectious disease between them. The Department showed that most high-income nations used the vaccine, emphasizing its safety record – especially in relation to the outbreaks of diseases such as measles in low-income countries. Statistical models showed what could happen if vaccination rates dropped too far. An interactive map allowed users to scan the globe, though unfortunately the Wayback Machine has not preserved this Flash application (Department of Health, 2002e). A 'myths and truths' section refuted the main claims made against MMR, especially the Wakefield et al. (1998) article. This 'quick reference' section was supported by a much longer page about MMR, why the government preferred it over other public health measures and the

**Figure 31.2 'MMR The Facts' – front page captured 8 September 2002.**
*Source*: Department of Health (2002d).

importance of achieving a high uptake among the entire population (Department of Health, 2002b). Other than the 'news' section, these pages appear to have remained static for the lifespan of the website. A more dynamic and interactive page came in the form of 'your questions answered' (Figure 31.3). If parents felt the website did not answer their questions sufficiently, they could complete a webform with a specific question. This was then forwarded to an 'expert' within the Department of Health who would provide an answer. The Wayback Machine has archived 40 of these questions, and they covered a range of topics from specific enquiries about allergies to requests for more empirical data (Department of Health, 2002f).

Related to this website was a specific page dedicated to health professionals. Written in a more technical format, it provided a comprehensive summary of the sort of questions parents were likely to ask and the reasons why the Department believed MMR was still the best course of action for children. While MMR The Facts could perform this role too, this concise, detailed page was held on the Department of Health's (2002a) own domain. The Department felt this necessary because it was clear that health workers were members of the public too. They had also been affected by constant media coverage and were themselves unsure about the precise reasons behind the MMR programme. The official 'Green Book' on vaccination was updated once every few years, but was only available in hard copy and could not adapt quickly to the changing discourse around MMR and vaccine technology.[3] General practitioners and nurses were known to have the greatest impact in educating and changing parents' behaviour. Therefore, it was important that information was made available through the

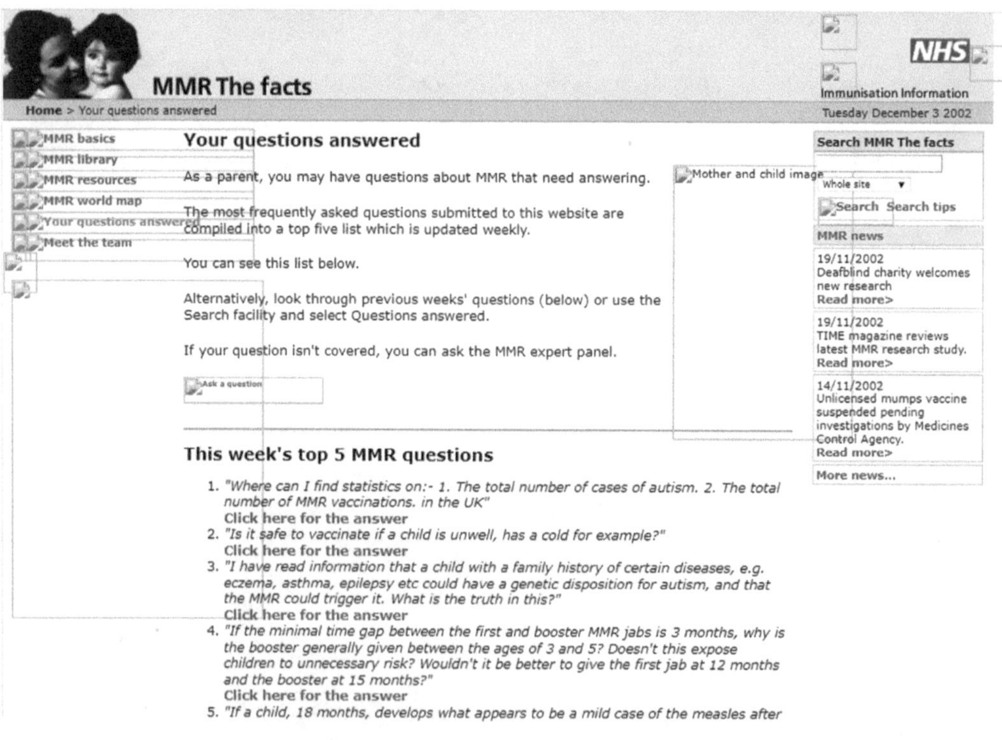


**Figure 31.3 'MMR The Facts – Your Questions Answered' – Captured 3 December 2002.**
*Source*: Department of Health (2002b).

most up-to-date and timely medium (Petrovic et al., 2001; British Medical Journal, 2002).

It is interesting that the sites appear to have been maintained for a relatively short amount of time. After 2004, the copyright information on MMR The Facts was no longer updated; and when the Department of Health's domain changed from 'doh.gov.uk' to 'dh.gov.uk', the MMR briefing page did not migrate with it. It was replaced with a generic 'immunisation' section, with a link to MMR The Facts for anyone who wanted further information (Department of Health, 2004). Triangulating this with other sources, we can begin to answer why this might be so. The core period of press activity over MMR began in 1998 and ended in 2004. By the time of the domain switch, the Department was confident that it had convinced the majority of parents to vaccinate their children. MMR The Facts had served a useful purpose and would continue to do so. However, the remarkable drop-off in articles on MMR in *The Lancet*, the *British Medical Journal* and the general press after 2004 (Speers and Lewis, 2004) shows that the government no longer felt the need to publicize MMR's benefits as forcefully to health care professionals. It is through all these sources of information that these archived websites help us to tell the story of the government's education practices during the MMR crisis.

## UNC.EDU/~APHILLIP/WWW/VACCINE/DVM.TXT

While MMR The Facts was the most directly useful website for analysing government policy and educational strategies in the 2000s, the Internet Archive also retained documents that gave a sense of the vaccine-sceptic material circulating during the crisis. A correspondent to the *British Medical Journal* (Selway, 1998) drew readers' attention to an American report on the dangers of vaccination (Phillips, 1999).[4] Hosted on a university server and written like an official medical journal article, it had been shared around Selway's non-medical friends. Its impact on the general public is unclear. We only have the author's own claims to its importance from his present-day personal website (Phillips, 2017).[5] However, as an individual document it can tell us more about anti-vaccination campaigning and its place within the wider history of the movement. Historians of the nineteenth and twentieth centuries have shown that there were multiple objections to vaccination in Britain and other countries (Durbach, 2005; Colgrove, 2006). Even today, parents have a wide range of beliefs, which are flexible depending on the vaccine in question, attitudes towards infectious disease and trust in medical and state authorities (Larson et al., 2014). By employing the techniques of contemporary scientific literature, Phillips' report shares many characteristics with the pamphleteers of the previous century. Whether or not Phillips himself was influential, this was a good example of the sort of literature that public health workers believed was circulating among parents. There are limits to how far we can generalize about all anti-vaccination literature at this time, but it certainly fits within what else we know about the longer history of the movement.

Through triangulation with other sources, Phillips' report also becomes useful as a window onto the attitudes of the general public. Contemporary newspaper reports in the UK may not have cited it, but they amplified similar concerns – such as the claim that safety testing was inadequate, the diseases being prevented were not particularly harmful or that the authorities might be hiding key evidence of harm (Speers and Lewis, 2004). Many of these were then refuted in the 'myths' section of MMR The Facts (Department of Health, 2002b) (Figure 31.4). Attitudinal surveys from the early 2000s show that these concerns were present, even if not all parents fully believed them (Evans et al., 2001; Hargreaves et al., 2003). Other

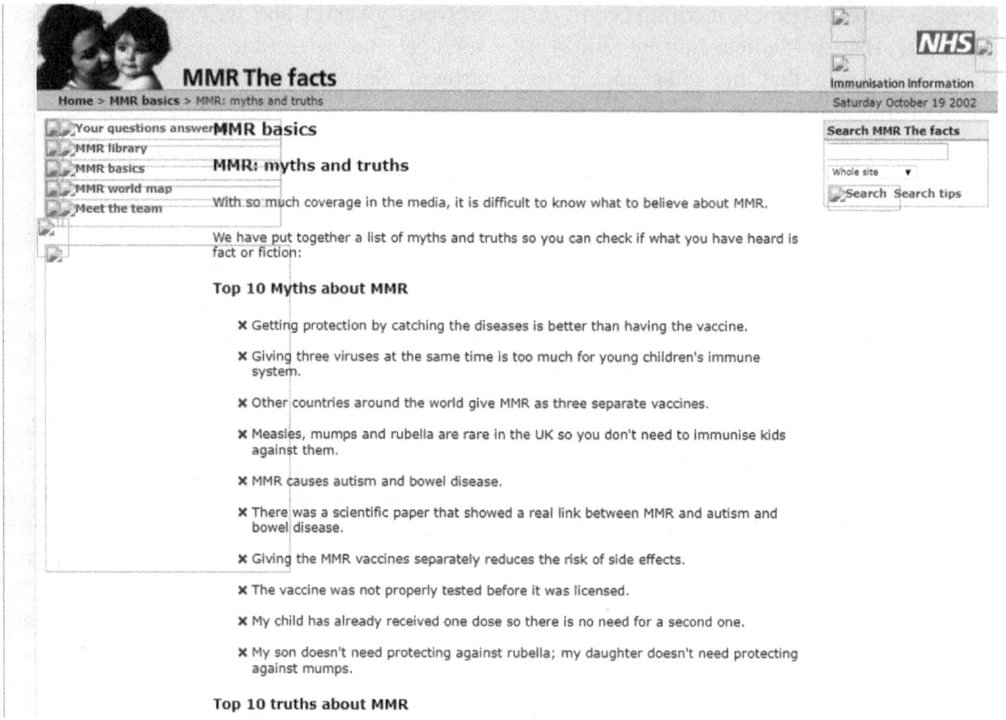


**Figure 31.4 'MMR The Facts – Myths and Truths' – Captured 19 October 2002.**
*Source*: Department of Health (2002f).

health crises from the late twentieth century had reduced faith in medical authorities, meaning that these concerns about MMR had become more believable. The most prominent of these was the bovine spongiform encephalopathy (BSE) scandal (Speers and Lewis, 2004), but there was also adverse publicity over heart surgery in Bristol (Kennedy, 2001), the removal of organs from deceased children without parental permission in Liverpool (Redfern, 2001) and the tainted blood scandal in which haemophiliacs were infected with blood-borne diseases (Dyer, 2001). When Phillips questioned whether 'public health officials always place health above other concerns' in his report (Phillips, 1999), there were reasons why this might resonate with a British audience.

We can also place the author in context because he has remained an active vaccine sceptic and has maintained his presence on the World Wide Web. The page on the University of North Carolina (UNC) server has long gone. Yet his personal site (Phillips, 2017) carries a curriculum vitae. We learn through this and the report itself that Phillips' own child had become injured after receiving vaccination. He had worked at UNC as an IT technician, before studying law and becoming an attorney specializing in securing exemptions for parents with conscientious objections to vaccination. This helps to explain why the author was motivated to write and why he had the skills to write an official-sounding report and build a convincing argument. This made him similar to other charismatic campaigners for vaccination reform in the UK, such as Rosemary Fox and Jackie Fletcher, and helps historians to put these debates into a wider narrative of continuity and change over time.[6] These transnational comparisons between Britain and the United States are fruitful for those trying to understand how lay scientific information spread across borders during the internet age. Thus, while the report is not a central part of the crisis in its own right, it becomes a jumping-off point for asking further questions about the social and cultural history of vaccination. This is possible through using the documents retrieved in the Internet Archive, subjecting them to close reading and placing them in the context of other primary and secondary sources.

## RMPLC.CO.UK

The final example is a useful reminder of how information can be lost. Web archives and search tools can be employed forensically to track down documents and information about events that might otherwise be obscured. Soon after Wakefield's press conference, a health worker named Rouse (1998) wrote to *The Lancet* to question Wakefield's interests. He noted that 'a simple internet search … quickly found the Society for the Autistically Handicapped', and that this site contained a report from lawyers building a case against the Department of Health that clearly showed Wakefield's involvement. This evidence appeared to show that funding for Wakefield's research had come partly through Legal Aid Board (later the Legal Services Commission) money which had been used to build the case on behalf of parents of autistic children. Brian Deer (2004) would later widely publicize such conflicts of interest, and they formed part of the judgment handed down by the General Medical Council (2010) that stripped Wakefield of his licence to practice. That this information seemed to be readily available in 1998 raises questions. If this was well known, why was it apparently ignored by the majority of the media criticizing government MMR policy? Similarly, while the medical press was quick to dismantle Wakefield's scientific claims (Chen and DeStefano, 1998), they had been mostly quiet about this and other potential interests (such as Wakefield's ownership of a patent on an alternative measles vaccine).

The URL that Rouse provided was not in the Wayback Machine. At the time of my study, searching was not possible – and even a subsequent search on the new interface did not produce any results. The domain – 'mplc.co.uk' – was owned by a web services company (e-crew, 2004). To see if this was an error, I searched 'The Society for the Autistically Handicapped' (in quotation marks) with the British Library's SHINE interface. The Society appeared to be British, and since the quoted URL was on the .uk top-level domain I hoped that the site would be indexed. Limiting the results to 1999 (the earliest year with any results for the search string) returned the site. It was hosted on 'rmplc.co.uk'. A simple spelling mistake had left the site invisible. Without a search engine like SHINE, it would have remained so. The report (Society for the Autistically Handicapped, 2000) could only be found on a successor website on a different domain. Nonetheless, it bore out Rouse's claims. Written by lawyers known to have been involved in the case (including Richard Barr: Barr, 2002; Deer, 2004), Wakefield appears as one of the experts to whom parents are encouraged to listen. The lawyers openly claim to be working with Wakefield, citing his research and the court case.

This page is not crucial to the MMR story in itself, nor was it essential in the proceedings against Wakefield. Rouse's claims were subsequently made elsewhere in the printed and digital press, and there was enough evidence for Wakefield to be struck off the medical register. Yet, for social historians wishing to dig deeper into the ways in which voluntary organizations fought against the government, these sorts of pages are useful sources. This page – and presumably dozens like it – would have been lost without search tools. The use of printed URLs as a method of selecting documents is not sufficient in itself. Broken links may require further, manual searching before the cited information can be discovered.

## CONCLUSIONS

This review of the MMR crisis presents a partial story. The use of printed URLs in other primary sources necessarily skewed which websites were discoverable and, in turn, which websites were included in this history of MMR. Inevitably, the views of the Department of Health received far more attention than those of other actors. As with any documentary history, evidence bases are biased towards not just those who had the power to create information, but those who have been able to maintain and archive that information for future scholars.

This survival bias is exacerbated with internet sources because of link rot and the archival practices of different organizations. Historians are acutely aware that information will be lost at the same time as so much more data are being stored than ever before (Rosenzweig, 2003). But we should not think that because documents from 'official' sources are more likely to survive, this guarantees access to them. Many of the materials from the General Medical Council, for example, are no longer available on the live web. Even for government agencies such as the Legal Services Commission, the press releases around MMR are not available through The National Archives' collection of government websites. Instead, they were found through the comprehensive online archive maintained by Brian Deer (2017).[7] It is not difficult to see why this is problematic. While Deer has taken care to declare the provenance of his documents, the material he presents is undeniably biased towards his particular investigation into Wakefield. There is plenty of other material on MMR that will not and cannot be included in such an archive, and so the research questions we can ask of it will be necessarily limited. We do not have extensive reactions from parents or other members of the public. Anti-government material (such as that written by Wakefield and his colleagues), is only included as it pertains to Deer's investigations. Without better archives with better discovery tools – both in terms of the digital technology and methodological techniques for storing and searching data – our histories will continue to skew towards those sources we find easiest to get our hands on (Hitchcock, 2013).

Out of the thousands of scholars who consider themselves historians, very few work with web archives. Historians are often conservative about how close to the present they can work and the value of 'historical distance'. In Britain, the end date for projects has usually coincided with the '30-year rule' (referencing the fact that most official procedural documents are released in The National Archives 30 years after creation). The rise in Freedom of Information, digitized official reports and accessible web archives, however, is giving us much more material to work with from the near-past. Combine this with the passage of time, and it will not be long before there will be a sizable cohort of historians of 1990s and 2000s Britain. How will they make use of internet archives? Undoubtedly, my research was aided by my experiences with BUDDAH and attendance at conferences on web archiving. Yet this is the sum total of my 'training' on the subject; a product both of muddling through by getting my hands dirty with the material and making copious mistakes. Before I started with MMR, I was aware of the limits of what I would be able to read, of what conclusions could be drawn from the way the archiving process works, and what sorts of questions would be answerable. This has resulted in a limited foray into the archive, but not an unsubstantial one. Without even this basic awareness, would other social or policy historians be able to access such material and use it in a productive way alongside their other sources? Are historians even aware that web archives are a potential trove of information? It could be that I am isolated in my particular networks, but conversations with colleagues in the field of contemporary British history suggest that there is an acute lack of awareness. As events around the turn of the millennium will become more and more relevant to historical inquiry, it is essential that those working with web archives pass on their experiences.

I am aware there are limits to what this project can say about the UK's MMR crisis. There is much more that could be done with the Internet Archive to shed light on other voices, especially in conjunction with deeper readings of other media and oral history techniques. As an adjunct to my main project, however, the archive has proved particularly fruitful. It helped me to answer my specific research questions on government policy. While I knew of the existence of MMR The Facts, it was only through reading and analysing the material contained within it that the Department of Health's educational tactics became more visible. For historians who still work with 'small' rather than 'big' data, Alan Phillips' and the Society for the Autistically Handicapped's pages give us insights into how individuals and voluntary organizations embraced the new technology of the World Wide Web to communicate their positions. It will be up to future projects and historians to get the most out of this and the other material still waiting to be analysed in the archive. One potential criticism of close reading approaches to this material is that we may place too much emphasis on the documents that we can find at the expense of the wider picture.[8] Again, this is where triangulation can help. While it is difficult to measure the precise audience or the impact that any one document had, the fact that these pages were referenced in leading medical journals gives us some indication that certain publics had begun to take notice. Further work with link analysis and linguistic analyses of larger corpora may be able to ask different questions of this material and give us wider insights into the crisis.

## Notes

1 This work was conducted at the London School of Hygiene & Tropical Medicine through the Placing the Public in Public Health Wellcome Investigator award project led by Alex Mold (grant number WT-100586-Z-12-Z). This chapter was originally prepared as a paper for the RESAW conference at the University of London, held in July 2017. The author would like to thank all those who attended and provided valuable feedback.

2 Web archives often contain duplicates of the same document, or files with such small changes they are effectively the same. Similarly, archives can only collect what crawlers are able to access and store, meaning large sections of the web have almost certainly not been catalogued. We have no way of telling what or how much. This is just the beginning. That said, even when these are well-curated they can cause significant problems that historians do not always confront. Research questions are often biased to what information is available and how easy it is to work with. As a result, Hitchcock (2013) worries that there may be an over-reliance on the criminal records of the Old Bailey in London, depriving us of important potential projects and conclusions about other parts of the United Kingdom.

3 For the latest version of this – which is now available online – see Public Health England (2013).

4 Although the document states that it was last revised in 1997, the first available copy through the Wayback Machine of the report on Phillips' archived site is from May 1999.

5 Phillips (2017) claims that the report was 'published around the world and translated into Russian, Chinese, and several European languages in the late 1990's [sic]. It has been used in medical school classrooms in three different countries, appears on websites around the world, and has appeared in publications including an Australian grassroots newsletter, Indian homeopathic journals, the Hindustan Times, and American and European magazines'.

6 Rosemary Fox (2006) led a campaign for changes in vaccination compensation law in Britain in the 1970s. Although not a professionally trained campaigner or academic, her daughter Helen had been diagnosed with brain damage following a polio vaccination in the 1960s. Jackie Fletcher led a group called Justice Awareness and Basic Support (2001) during the MMR crisis, and campaigned for a court case against the Department of Health and more informed choice for parents. Her son had developed epilepsy after receiving MMR.

7 The Legal Services Commission (LSC) withdrew legal aid funding for the case against the Depart-

ment of Health in October 2003. The first instance of the LSC's website in The National Archives is December 2003, and the press release is not accessible. Brian Deer holds a copy, which can be corroborated through the Wayback Machine (Legal Services Commission, 2003, 2004; Deer, 2017).

8 Although it would be simplistic to suggest that this is not an inherent problem with any source base. Selection is inevitable in any historical investigation, and subject to the biases of the researcher. It is only through being open about our methodologies that we can put historical claims into appropriate context.

## REFERENCES


Abbate, J. (2017) 'What and where is the Internet? (Re)defining Internet histories', *Internet Histories*, 1(1–2): 8–14.

Ackland, R., and Evans, A. (2017) 'Using the web to examine the evolution of the abortion debate in Australia, 2005–2015', in Niels Brügger and Ralph Schroeder (eds), *The Web as History*. London: UCL Press. pp. 159–89.

Alaszewski, A., and Horlick-Jones, T. (2003) 'How can doctors communicate information about risk more effectively?', *British Medical Journal*, 326(7417): 728–31.

Badenoch, J. (1988) 'Big bang for vaccination', *British Medical Journal*, 297(6651): 750–1.

Barr, R. (2002) 'Autism, bowel inflammation, and measles', *The Lancet*, 359(9323): 2112–3.

Berger, A. (2004) 'Dispatches. MMR: What they didn't tell you', *British Medical Journal*, 329: 1293.

Big UK Domain Data for the Arts and Humanities (BUDDAH) (2015) Bursaries. (https://buddah.projects.history.ac.uk/news/bursaries/). Retrieved 29 July 2017.

British Medical Journal (2002) 'Letters: Health professionals' attitudes to MMR vaccine', *British Medical Journal*, 322(7294): 1120–1.

British Library (2017) UK Web Archive, SHINE (https://www.webarchive.org.uk/shine). Retrieved 24 July 2017.

Brügger, N. (2008) 'The archived website and website philology: A new type of historical document?', *Nordicom Review*, 29(2): 155–75.

Campbell, H., Edwards, A., Letley, L., Bedford, H., Ramsay, M., and Yarwood, J. (2017) 'Changing attitudes to childhood immunisation in English parents', *Vaccine*, 35(22): 2979–85.

Chen, R.T., and DeStefano, F. (1998) 'Vaccine adverse events: Causal or coincidental?', *The Lancet*, 351(9103): 611–2.

Colgrove, J. (2006) *State of Immunity: The Politics of Vaccination in Twentieth-Century America*. Berkeley: University of California Press.

Deer, B. (2004) 'MMR: The truth behind the crisis', *Sunday Times*, 22 February: 12.

Deer, B. (2017) Taxpayer cash for MMR action is stopped after £15m that stoked fear was spent (http://briandeer.com/mmr/lancet-lsc.htm). Retrieved 28 July 2017.

Department of Health (2002a) Measles, Mumps and Rubella Vaccine (MMR) (http://web.archive.org/web/20021213092753/http:/www.doh.gov.uk/mmr/). Retrieved 28 July 2017.

Department of Health (2002b) MMR: Myths and Truths (https://web.archive.org/web/20021019073221/http:/www.mmrthefacts.nhs.uk:80/basics/truths.php). Retrieved 28 July 2017.

Department of Health (2002c) MMR News (https://web.archive.org/web/20021202234730/http://www.mmrthefacts.nhs.uk:80/news/). Retrieved 28 July 2017.

Department of Health (2002d) MMR The Facts (https://web.azchive.org/web/20020908120649/http://www.mmrthefacts.nhs.uk/). Retrieved 28 July 2017.

Department of Health (2002e) MMR World Map (https://web.archive.org/web/20021214014604/http://www.mmrthefacts.nhs.uk:80/worldmap/). Retrieved 28 July 2017.

Department of Health (2002f) Your Questions Answered (https://web.archive.org/web/20021203001027/http://www.mmrthefacts.nhs.uk:80/questions/). Retrieved 28 July 2017.

Department of Health (2004) Immunisation (http://web.archive.org/web/20040301041356/http://www.dh.gov.uk:80/PolicyAndGuidance/HealthAndSocialCareTopics/Immunisation/fs/en). Retrieved 28 July 2017.

Department of Health and Social Security (1987) *Promoting Better Health: The Government's Programme for Improving Primary Care*. London: HMSO.

Deswarte, R. (2015) 'Revealing British Euroscepticism in the UK Web Domain and Archive Case Study'. London: Institute of Historical Research (http://sas-space.sas.ac.uk/6103/#undefined).

Dobson, R. (2002) 'Parents' champion or loose cannon?' *British Medical Journal*, 324(7334): 386.

Durbach, N. (2005) *Bodily Matters: The Anti-vaccination Movement in England, 1853–1907*. Durham: Duke University Press.

Dyer, C. (2001) 'NHS told to pay £10m to patients infected with hepatitis C', *British Medical Journal*, 322(7289): 751.

Eaton, L. (2009) 'Measles cases in England and Wales rise sharply in 2008', *British Medical Journal*, 338: b533.

e-crew (2004) Holding page (http://web.archive.org/web/20040330011552/http://www.mplc.co.uk:80/). Retrieved 28 July 2017.

Evans, M., Stoddart, H., Condon, L., Freeman, E., Grizzell, M., and Mullen, R. (2001) 'Parents' perspectives on the MMR immunisation: A focus group study', *The British Journal of General Practice*, 51(472): 904–10.

Fitzpatrick, M. (2004) *MMR and Autism: What Parents Need to Know*. Abingdon: Routledge.

Fox, R. (2006) *Helen's Story*. London: John Blake.

General Medical Council (2010) *Dr Andrew Jeremy Wakefield: Determination on Serious Professional Misconduct (SPM) and Sanction*. London: General Medical Council.

Gorsky, M. (2015) 'Into the dark domain: The UK Web Archive as a source for the contemporary history of public health', *Social History of Medicine*, 28(3): 596–616.

Hargreaves, I., Lewis, J., and Speers, T. (2003) *Towards a Better Map: Science, the Public and the Media*. London: Economic and Social Research Council.

Health and Social Care Information Centre (2005) 'NHS immunisation statistics: England, 2004–05' London: National Statistics.

Hitchcock, T. (2013) 'Confronting the digital: Or how academic history writing lost the plot', *Cultural and Social History*, 10(1): 9–23.

Horton, R. (2004) *MMR: Science and Fiction – Exploring a Vaccine Crisis*. London: Granta Books.

Internet Archive (2017) The Wayback Machine (https://archive.org/web/). Retrieved 29 July 2017.

Justice Awareness and Basic Support (2001) Fair warning (http://web.archive.org/web/20011025144125/http://www.jabs.org.uk:80/jabsinformation.htm). Retrieved 28 July 2017.

Keenan, A., Ghebrehewet, S., Vivancos, R., MacPherson, P., and Hungerford, D. (2017) 'Measles outbreaks in the UK, is it when and where rather than if? A database cohort study of childhood population susceptibility in Liverpool, UK', *BMJ Open*, 7(3): e014106.

Kennedy, I. (2001) *The Report of the Public Inquiry into Children's Heart Surgery at the Bristol Royal Infirmary 1984–1995: Learning from Bristol*. London: TSO.

Larson, H., Jarrett, C., Eckersberger, E., Smith, D., and Paterson, P. (2014) 'Understanding vaccine hesitancy around vaccines and vaccination from a global perspective: A systematic review of published literature, 2007–2012', *Vaccine*, 32(19): 2150–9.

Larson, H., Figueiredo, A. de, Xiahong, Z., Schulz, W.S., Verger, P., Johnston, I.G., Crook, A.R., and Jones, N.S. (2016) 'The state of vaccine confidence 2016: Global insights through a 67-country survey', *EBioMedicine*. DOI: 10.1016/j.ebiom.2016.08.042

Legal Services Commission (2003) Decision to remove funding for MMR litigation upheld on appeal (https://web.archive.org/web/20031010112531/http://www.legalservices.gov.uk/misl/news/press/press-13-03.htm). Retrieved 28 July 2017.

Legal Services Commission (2004) Legal Services Commission (http://webarchive.nationalarchives.gov.uk/20040105011642/http://www.legalservices.gov.uk/). Retrieved 28 July 2017.

McCartney, M. (2013) 'MMR, measles and the South Wales Evening Post', *British Medical Journal*, 246: f2598.

Millward, G. (2015) 'Digital barriers and the accessible web: Disabled people, information and the internet'. London: Institute of

Historical Research (http://sas-space.sas.ac.uk/6104/#undefined).

Muminovic, M. (2002) 'MMR', *British Medical Journal*, 325(7364): 604.

Murch, S.H., Anthony, A., Casson, D.H., Malik, M., Berelowitz, M., Dhillon, A.P., Thomson, M.A., Valentine, A., Davies, S.E., and Walker-Smith, J. (2004) 'Retraction of an interpretation', *The Lancet*, 363(9411): 750.

Petrovic, M., Roberts, R., and Ramsay, M. (2001) 'Second dose of measles, mumps, and rubella vaccine: Questionnaire survey of health professionals', *British Medical Journal*, 322(7278): 82–5.

Phillips, A. (1999) Dispelling Vaccination Myths https://web.archive.org/web/19990503175555/http:/www.unc.edu:80/~aphillip/www/vaccine/dvm.txt Retrieved 28 July 2017.

Phillips, A. (2017) Allan Phillips, J.D. Attorney and Counselor at Law (http://www.vaccinerights.com/attorneyphillips.html). Retrieved 28 July 2017.

Public Health England (2013) *Immunisation against Infectious Disease*. London: Public Health England (2nd ed.) (https://www.gov.uk/government/collections/immunisation-against-infectious-disease-the-green-book). Retrieved 21 May 2015.

Ramsay, S. (2001) 'UK starts campaign to reassure parents about MMR-vaccine safety', *The Lancet*, 357(9252): 290.

Ramsay, S. (2002) 'UK government tries to control MMR panic', *The Lancet*, 259(9306): 590.

Ramsay, M.E., Yarwood, J., Lewis, D., Campbell, H., and White, J.M. (2002) 'Parental confidence in measles, mumps and rubella vaccine: Evidence from vaccine coverage and attitudinal surveys', *The British Journal of General Practice*, 52(484): 912–6.

Redfern, M. (2001) *The Royal Liverpool Children's Inquiry Report*. London: TSO.

Rosenzweig, R. (2003) 'Scarcity or abundance? Preserving the past in a digital era', *American Historical Review*, 108(3): 735–62.

Rouse, A. (1998) 'Autism, inflammatory bowel disease and MMR vaccine', *The Lancet*, 351(9112): 1356.

Russell, A.L. (2017) 'Hagiography, revisionism & blasphemy in Internet histories', *Internet Histories*, 1(1–2): 15–25.

Selway, J. (1998) 'MMR vaccination and autism 1998', *British Medical Journal*, 316(7147): 1824.

Society for the Autistically Handicapped (2000) Vaccines fact sheet (http://web.archive.org/web/20000902060843/http://www.autismuk.com:80/index1sub4.htm). Retrieved 28 July 2017.

Speers, T., and Lewis, J. (2004) 'Journalists and jabs: Media coverage of the MMR vaccine', *Communication & Medicine*, 1(2): 171–81.

Turner, F. (2017) 'Can we write a cultural history of the Internet? If so, how?', *Internet Histories*, 1(1–2): 39–46.

UNdata (2017) Internet users (per 100 people) (http://data.un.org/Data.aspx?d=WDI&f=Indicator_Code%3AIT.NET.USER.P2). Retrieved 22 June 2017.

Wakefield, A.J., Murch, S.H., Anthony, A., Linnell, J., Casson, D.M., Malik, M., Berelowitz, M., Dhillon, A.P., Thomson, M.A., Harvey, P., Valentine, A., Davies, S.E., and Walker-Smith, J.A. (1998) 'RETRACTED: Illeal-lymphoid-nodular hyperplasia, non-specific colitis, and pervasive developmental disorder in children', *The Lancet*, 351(9103): 637–41.

Winters, J. (2017) 'Breaking into the mainstream: Demonstrating the value of internet (and web) histories', *Internet Histories*, 1(1–2): 173–9.

Zittrain, J., Kendra, A., and Lessig, L. (2014) 'Perma: Coping and addressing the problem of link and reference rot in legal citations', *Legal Information Management*, 14(2): 88–99.

32

# Religion and Web History

Peter Webster

## INTRODUCTION

It was the English explorer Sir Walter Raleigh who wrote that if 'whosoever in writing a modern history, shall follow truth too near the heels, it may haply strike out his teeth' (Raleigh, 1614: preface). Raleigh's remark, written in 1614 and often quoted since, showed the danger for the historian in writing about the very recent past. For historians of contemporary religion, the difficulties are greater still, in that we follow close on the heels not only of the present, but of scholars in several other disciplines who study religions in something close to real time. The literature on the phenomenon of religion in computer-mediated contexts is now very large, having built up over two decades. That literature is also produced both in, and in the spaces between, more than one discipline: Internet Studies, which concerns itself with the nature of the medium (see the survey by Campbell, 2011); the sociology of religion (for example, Cheruvallil-Contractor and Shakkour, 2016); and from scholars of religious studies concerned in particular with the relationship between religion and the media in general (Beckerlegge, 2001; Mitchell and Marriage, 2003). The disciplinary labels vary between countries, but however it is named, little of this writing concerns itself directly with the kind of questions that most preoccupy historians, although in time it will itself become the raw material for historical study, much as the pioneering religious social science now is for historians of the 1960s.[1]

Given both the size and the methodological eclecticism of the literature to hand, this chapter can make no claim to exhaustiveness. Rather, its first half attends to some debates of particular historical and methodological note with which the emerging history of religions on the Web may fruitfully be brought into conversation. These include debates concerning both the Web itself as a technological system, and religious responses to technological change in general. It also sets out some points of contact between Web history and three key themes in contemporary religious history: secularisation; religious radicalism; and the place of religion in civic life and the law. It also argues for a fresh integration of the Web, and the archived Web in particular, with the study of offline religion, in pursuit of an ideal state in which the archived Web is merely one of many kinds of primary sources with which historians work.

The second half then takes a fourfold schema of different aspects of religions as they may be studied, setting out an agenda for future Web history research on each aspect. The references cited throughout the chapter are indicative and exemplary of particular questions and approaches, rather than specific recommendations of this or that piece of work in its substantive claims. The chapter as a whole takes its examples predominantly from the Christian tradition, but would assert that the picture it paints has a more general applicability.

## RELIGIOUS VIEWS OF THE WEB AS A SYSTEM

Both the Internet and the Web have been screens onto which all manner of cultural and social aspirations and fears, both utopian and dystopian, have been projected, both strictly relating to religion and more widely. The Internet has been feted as a great disruptor: a solvent of established privilege and the outlet for previously marginal opinions, and a liberator of suppressed creative energy, in politics, commerce and the arts. It has equally well been denounced as the harbour of criminality, the accelerator of falsehood, the destroyer of traditional industries, communities, languages and cultures (Krotoski, 2014). Whilst these twin discourses of technological utopia and dystopia have been widespread, religious thinkers have themselves also adopted versions of both (an example of the latter is Shallis, 1984). To a degree, a utopian accent was also audible in some of the early scholarship in Internet Studies in general, and on the religious Web in particular (Hoejsgaard and Warburg, 2005; Wellman, 2011:18–9). The degree to which both crazes and moral panics are a natural accompaniment to far-reaching technological change need not detain us here. But both positive and negative discourses of the Web have been expressed in both implicit and explicit theological, or at least ethical and moral, terms. If we are to understand the engagement of religious people and institutions with the Web, we must attend to the history of the paradigms in which they conceive of the Web as a system.

This task would be relatively straightforward were it not for a significant strand of secular thinking that viewed both the Internet and the Web in quasi-mystical terms *as technologies;* a trend which owed something to the Christian and post-Christian culture of the West out of which it grew (see, for instance, Davis, 1998, *passim*). This particular phenomenon is also related to what David E. Nye dubbed the 'technological sublime', in which new technologies become objects of awe and wonder (Nye, 1994; see also Mosco, 2004). The term *cyberspace* – a spatial metaphor where none was necessarily required by the intrinsic nature of the technology – has indirectly given occasion to considerable philosophical, not to say mystical, reflection on the online as an alternative plane of existence, even as reflective of the nature of God: a fifth dimension, in a sense (Burke, 2016: 158; Cobb, 1998). These understandings are ripe for historical examination (for which, see Webster, 2018b), but here one observes simply that to understand the history of the idea of the Web must involve attending to these discourses, their origins and their mutations over time.

As well as understanding religious and quasi-religious paradigms of the nature of the Web as a system, historians have also the task of attending to what might be termed the 'religious Web'. I define this as the sum of the activities of, and interactions between, religious institutions and those individuals who articulate or act out their own religious faith online. (An alternative designation might be the 'religious Web sphere'.) Historians of this religious Web need also to attend to the ethical and philosophical frameworks in which religious people have tended to view their specific activities online. To take Christians in Europe and North America as an example, some of the early dystopian visions of the computerised future were not the product of mere ignorance and fear of change but of concerns about key ethical issues. To question the economic effects of the Web on certain industries or on certain countries was to make a statement about economic justice based on much older Christian understandings of neighbourliness between citizens and between nations. To express concern about the distancing effect of computer mediation on human relationships was to make a statement about the nature of the human person and the relational nature of God himself (see, for instance, Houston, 1998; Lochhead, 1997; Webster, 2018b). Concerns about the effect of anonymity on online behaviour were intimately connected with much older concerns about the spiritually damaging effect of dissimulation on the individual: of portraying oneself as someone other than the person visible to God. The rationalisation by American evangelicals observed by Kelsy Burke – that anonymity was acceptable since God himself was witness to their conduct online – bears comparison with the thinking of Protestants under threat of persecution and death in Catholic countries in the Reformation period (Burke, 2016: 158; Dixon, 1997: 144–9; Pettegree, 1996: 85–96). These various debates about a cluster of technologies and their social and economic effects are as much a part of the history of the religious Web as individual sites and pages.

## THE RELATIONSHIP OF ONLINE AND OFFLINE

Some early studies of religion on the Web were marked by a concentration of attention on the online alone: what one scholar has referred to as 'immanent Internet analysis' (Krüger, 2005: 17). This was unsurprising as scholars came to terms with the nature of the medium and the new methods required to study it. More recently there has been greater attention paid to the interaction between online and offline. Recent studies have attended to the relationship between the two in theory, and in particular to the direction in which influence is exerted: the degree to which offline roles and organisations are reflected online, and (conversely) the degree to which the online experience changes the expectations that religious people have of their face-to-face relationships with others (for example, Becker, 2011; Lundby, 2011). At the same time, more empirical studies have employed an approach that uses the evidence of the Web in combination with other sources, such as direct observation and interview evidence with key actors (Burke, 2016; Krüger, 2005). These have been accompanied by calls for a multi-modal approach, or (to translate the matter into historical terms), the integrated study of many classes of primary source (Cheong et al., 2016). This is to be welcomed, and when viewed in terms of the history of the discipline of history, parallels the methodological work done to incorporate new or neglected kinds of sources, such as broadcast media, recorded music or material culture simply as particular kinds of primary source amongst many (see, for example, Harvey, 2009).

In this respect, the study of history using the *archived* Web is a step behind again. The history of Web archiving itself is only 20 years long, and scholarly engagement with the archives produced younger still (Webster, 2017b). Given this, historians using Web archives are themselves in the process of understanding the nature of the material with which they must deal, and consequently have been less concerned with its integration with other kinds of sources. In this sense this body of work is at the same stage of development as that of scholars of online religion, perhaps 15 years ago. The (so far) small number of studies of religious history using Web archives have begun to retrieve the element of change over time that is often missing from other disciplines, but without yet an integration with other source types, in some cases explicitly so (Hofheinz, 2010: 106; Webster, 2017a: 202). Use of the historic Web which is both diachronic and multi-modal must be the aim; only at that point will the enterprise look like historical research as is commonly understood.

## LONGER-RANGE HISTORICAL QUESTIONS

For religious historians there is another and rather larger task at hand: to relate the development of religion on the Web to larger and longer-range questions of religious history. This presents problems, since very few historians of religion have begun serious study of periods more recent than the late 1980s. As such, what follows is a projection forward in time of three particular historical debates currently underway regarding the 1960s, 1970s and 1980s which are germane to the more recent past. The examples given here are particularly pertinent in European and North American contexts, and historians of the non-Western world will have different sets of problems and preoccupations to which to refer, but certain similarities may be observed.

Perhaps pre-eminent is the continuing legacy of secularisation. Religious historians are still deeply engaged in understanding how European, North American and Australasian nations – once religiously homogenous with highly observant populations, socially powerful churches and legal systems which privileged Judeo-Christian moral principles – became religiously diverse societies, with secularised systems of law, increasingly non-religious populations and relatively insignificant churches. Secularisation theory in its classic form attributed great agency to economic, social and technological modernisation in the weakening of religious belief and adherence (for a summary in relation to the Web in particular, see Han, 2016: 1–11). In more recent years, greater stress has been placed not so much on economic and political change as on change in the terms of religious discourse, and also on the ways in which religious practice has not so much declined as mutated (see, *inter alia*, Brown, 2009, and Davie, 2000). Others have stressed the significant *growth* in religious practice outside the mainstream Christian denominations, and of the so-called New Religious Movements (Goodhew, 2012; Hunt, 2003). The present literature on online religion speaks both directly and obliquely to these concerns in particular contemporary contexts, but without beginning the work of understanding them in historical terms. Insofar as the Web as a technology may be understood as an agent of modernisation, how far can it be said to have been either inimical to or supportive of religious belief and practice as understood before the Web came about? Understanding to what degree the religious Web is a reflection of social changes occurring offline according to their own logic, as opposed to (or as well as) being an agent in fostering, shaping or hindering those changes, is perhaps the major challenge for contemporary religious historians of the next generation.

Secondly, the events of 9/11 may in time come to be seen as epoch-making and epoch-ending: the kind of marker with which historians divide the past into periods that may be examined and understood, such as 1789 or 1914. But the religious radicalisation of which the attacks on the United States and elsewhere in subsequent years were a symptom had a long pre-history, bound up in part with the wider 'clash of civilisations' identified by Samuel P. Huntington (1997). There was as well a specific history of the growth and strengthening of conservative elements in several of the world religions, intimately connected to the progress (or otherwise) of secularisation, into which it is now time to begin placing the history of the Web (Herbert and Wolffe, 2005; McLeod, 2007: 207–12). Is it the case that the affordances of the Web have sharpened religious radicalism, as people more easily encounter those things to which they object? Alternatively, the story may be one of a pre-existing radicalism, growing according both to its own logic, the communication of which is facilitated and made more visible. Only a reading of religious radicalism on the Web alongside its offline history will provide answers to these questions. (For an example of such work, see Howard, 2011.)

Thirdly, the lifetime of the Web has also coincided with a sharply renewed public debate concerning the place of religious faith, speech and practice in public life, in relation to the law in particular. In part this is a function of debates to which the growth of the Internet itself gave greater force: over censorship, freedom of speech and the idea of hate speech and its subjection to criminal or civil law penalties. But the questions are wider, taking in the right or otherwise of both religious and non-religious people to protection from religious offence; the place of religious buildings, rituals and symbolic objects in local communities; the right or otherwise to religious expression in the workplace. Each of these has its own histories in different cultures. In the Christian West these include the de-Christianisation of the secular law, which has unfolded piecemeal over several decades; the history of integration of immigrant communities and the contested urban spaces which they often inhabit; and the rise of more assertive atheist and non-religious voices, partly in reaction to the increased religious conservatism noted above (Amarasingam, 2010; Garnett and Harris, 2013; Webster, 2015a: 65–90). Just as with secularisation and the growth of conservatism, any history of religion and the Web must attend to the ways in which these debates are played out online, and the interplay of local, physically bounded events with their networked representations.

## AN HISTORICAL MODEL OF RELIGIONS

The remainder of this chapter considers the recent history of religion on the Web under four heads. The first of these is doctrine and religious knowledge: the symbols and forms of words that describe the divine, the world, the human person and their interrelations. Second are religious organisations and their representatives (clerical or lay), which are mostly responsible for the codification and interpretation of doctrine and the framing and regulation of communal ritual. Third is religious practice: those communal and solitary activities of prayer, worship and other rituals through which religious people address the divine and represent their religion to each other and to others. Finally, the section on religions and the Other deals with all the various modes in which religious people and organisations encounter those outside: as potential proselytes, as discussion partners in debate about wider social and economic issues and as antagonists.

### *Doctrine*

Most of the major world religions are textual to some significant degree. Sacred texts – some directly given by God, others created by humans acting in response to divine prompting – provide perhaps the principal way in which doctrine is fixed and transmitted. Surrounding sacred scripture is a wealth of commentary, exposition and critique, written variously by priestly figures, by those whose profession it is to think and write, and by those in the wider circle of believers. The earliest affordances of the Web were ideal for the reproduction of text; it was technically straightforward, and economic at a time when many users paid for their usage by the metering of data. Many of the earliest ventures of religious organisations onto the Web were in the reproduction of texts, both for study by the devout and in order to engage others (to adopt the distinction made by Hutchings, 2016). In the case of the Bible, this built on pre-existing ventures in software designed for study, dating back as far as the 1950s.

When compared with the interactions between individuals (examined below under 'Religious Practice') these early ventures in a new form of religious publishing have attracted relatively little scholarly attention. This may have been in part because, for scholars of the Web as a technology, this represented a use of the medium of limited technical inventiveness. But opportunities abound, particularly using the archived Web, not only for historians of religion, but also of education, publishing, media and reading. From the very beginning, to what extent did the move online represent a duplication of print publishing or a replacement of it? What opposition did it arouse, and on what grounds? More recent years have seen the advent of social media accounts, notably on Twitter, publishing single verses of a sacred text at a time. Sociologists of religion have already asked questions about the effect this may have had on reading habits (Hutchings, 2016). Historians might also ask what relation such practices bear to the evangelical Christian culture of the Bible verse on a car bumper sticker, poster or bookmark (Harvey, 2008).

There are also questions, the asking of which the scale of Web archives allows. Scholars of the nineteenth century have made inventive use of corpora of digitised books and newspapers to reconstruct the flow of texts from publication to publication across great geographical distances (Beals, 2016). The archived Web now affords rich opportunities to observe the spread of religious texts from site to site, and their different framing and interpretation in each new publication context. There is an opportunity now to examine the ways in which religious organisations have sought to control the reuse of these texts, by use of copyright law or other means, and for which reasons.

As well as examining the lives sacred texts lead online, another fruitful area of inquiry is the effect the Web has had on the shaping of religious texts themselves: not so much ancient texts as theological and other writings which are still being produced. It seems likely that the content of preaching has been changed by the ready accessibility of a vast range of texts and other resources online (not least other sermons), previously unobtainable by, and perhaps also unknown to, local ministers. The time is also ripe for an historical assessment of the effect of the Web on the disciplines of theology and religious studies, both in terms of the availability of primary texts for research, but also in the field of Open Access publishing. It is likely that the present chapter could not have been written, or at least would have been very different, without being able to locate and then access scholarship on every religious tradition in many nations. One of the oldest online theological periodicals celebrated its 20th anniversary in 2013; a span of time which invites serious historical reflection (Keown and Prebish, 2013).

## Organisations

A prominent theme in much of the scholarship so far has been that of the authority of religious institutions and their representatives. Studying the spirituality of Generation X in 1998, Tom Beaudoin identified a suspicion of institutions as one of its four key markers (Beaudoin, 1998: 56–60). Not unlike other institutions and industries being 'disrupted' by the Web, religious institutions were faced with the most fundamental of capitalist forces, a competition of ideas, and for attention and for loyalty. Intimately connected with broader narratives of the culture of the Web as 'virtual communitarian' and entrepreneurial (Castells, 2001: 36–63), part of the early utopian narrative was about a new religious freedom. This might be the freedom to experiment with new forms of organisation whilst still in good standing with an existing institution, or to extend the range of activities of that institution to meet needs hitherto unmet (Burke, 2016, *passim*; Prebish, 2004: 145). It might equally include the freedom to found new religious movements entirely outside, and indeed possibly inimical to, existing institutions (Hoejsgaard, 2005).

Each of those aspects continues to merit investigation, but the literature has also seen a more recent turn to try to understand the organisations themselves: the degree to which organisations and people with authority within them adapted the way their authority is articulated and gains assent. Based on a case study from Chinese Buddhism, Cheong et al. (2016) outlined a phenomenon of 'strategic arbitration' in which authoritative figures were able to re-define their offline authority to include a role as 'arbiters of knowledge and encounters' online as well as offline. Heidi Campbell's study of the blogs of American Christians stressed the degree to which bloggers were also already clergy or other authoritative figures in their local churches: here, authority offline is replicated online rather than overturned (Campbell, 2010).

Even this more nuanced examination of institutional adaptation has tended to be at the level of the individual. The growing availability of the archived Web at scale now opens up a new frontier: of investigating the online relationships *within* and *between* organisations and their evolution over time. To understand local and national organisations within the same denomination, historians have often examined the ways in which formal hierarchical relations between individual local congregations and the superstructure of their denomination have functioned, and how information, people and funds have circulated around the different parts of the structure (for an example of this kind of institutional history, see Chandler, 2006). The archived Web now offers the means to reconstruct the 'Web sphere' of each individual denomination: how individual congregations are connected to each other in a particular locality, within larger geographic units and with other nodes in larger national and international denominational networks that transcend locality (see Webster, 2018a; on the notion of a 'Web sphere', see Brügger, 2010).

A related theme in the religious history of the twentieth century amongst the Christian churches was the great hopes invested in co-operation, and indeed potential reunion, between the different denominations, reversing the great schisms of the Reformation period. Such questions were traditionally studied in terms of high-level diplomatic contact between denominations – the formulation of statements and the holding of conferences – but also in the face-to-face contact between Christians in particular localities (Power, 2007; Webster, 2015a: 21–48). The archived Web offers the opportunity to observe those ecumenical contacts within religious traditions – international, national and local – as they are replicated on or transferred to the Web.

## Religious Practice

Of the four aspects of religion under examination here, perhaps the most attention from scholars of the Web has been paid to *practice*: what is it that religious people *do* when being religious online? Much of this work has been implicitly and explicitly ethnographic and indeed anthropological in approach, observing, as it were, the behaviour of an isolated tribe. This approach has its counterpart in offline research, such as the method employed by James Steven to investigate worship amongst English charismatic Christians (Steven, 2002: 42–54). Using a combination of participant observation and interviews, scholars have examined several different kinds of religious activities transferred to online spaces. Obvious continuities may be observed, such as those between the television or radio broadcasting of worship (a feature of British life from the 1920s onwards) and live webcasting of the same. One of the earliest studies examined charismatic Christians 'meeting' in small groups for communal prayer in a virtual reality environment, a direct transference of a common practice into a new space (Schroeder et al., 1998). Becker (2011) examined the dynamics of Islamic rituals such as the *shahada*, or conversion ritual, in Dutch and German chatrooms. Particularly counter-intutive, it might seem, has been the migration of pilgrimage online – a form of religious observance which traditionally drew its very validity from the sacrifices involved in physically travelling to a particular place. One example of cyber-pilgrimage is that to Croagh Patrick in the Republic of Ireland (in the Roman Catholic tradition), but many others could be mentioned (MacWilliams, 2004).

From the point of view of the historian, much of the discussion of the 'success' of such transference of offline activity to online is beside the point. Whether or not such transferred rituals fulfil the criteria for a valid and effectual religious observance must remain a question for theologians and liturgists. However, specific historical attention has turned towards changing expectations of what constitutes an 'authentic' religious experience (a related but different question to that of validity), and how the Christian churches in particular have responded to this perceived demand (Garnett et al., 2006). Prayer, corporate worship, pilgrimage, particular buildings and religious 'events' such as festivals all come into focus under this rubric, with a sharpened emphasis on the aesthetic and communal aspects of shared experience in a particular place. To what extent have both worshippers and religious organisations recognised online ritual as 'authentic', if the recent historical trend has been towards greater emphasis on physical presence?

As such online ritual comes into historical focus, the questions will rather be to do with how widespread these practices were, and how many believers engaged in them, as a proportion of the faith community as a whole. Did such rituals attract those who were not already habitually engaged in worship in a physical location? How did participants understand what they were doing, and how it related to their offline worship or pilgrimage? As such, a methodological shift will be required. The archived traces of the online rituals themselves offer some evidence. Whatever textual traces of comment from participants that have been preserved will also be key, as will the contemporary investigations made by sociologists of religion and others. However, sustained oral history investigation will be essential to understand how and why people did so participate, and what they took from their participation. Direct engagement with site owners will also be required to secure access to statistics relating to usage. Offline published commentary and interview evidence from religious leaders and others will also be key to understanding the attitudes of religious professionals to these various migrations of practice online: were they a disruption, or an opportunity, or both?

## *Religions and the Other*

Perhaps the most significant area in which the Internet has not simply provided spaces for the replication of existing religious activity, but allowed new kinds of activity, is in the contact between individual religious people of different faiths and with those who profess no religion. Before the Web, when examined internationally, the study of these interactions was necessarily confined to the high-level summitry between official representatives of religions, since these were by and large the only channels available for such contact (Webster, 2015b). It was also possible to study the representation of minority faiths in print and in mainstream media, but given their broadcast nature, to recover the reception of and reactions to those representations was relatively difficult. To recreate the contact between individuals of different faiths and none was a task of very detailed local and oral history; rarely did a local encounter leave a significant documentary trace (one exception is documented by Maiden, 2015).

The Web in general, and social media in particular, have afforded the opportunity for individuals to engage directly with others, either as a means of fostering greater understanding or in a more antagonistic mode. There has been relatively little scholarly attention paid to this so far, perhaps because the contacts between individuals of opposed views are harder to identify in the mass than are communities of the like-minded. However, the work of Stephen Pihlaja on Christian-atheist antagonism on YouTube suggests a fruitful approach to the small-scale interactions of individuals, which might be replicated using archived blog comment threads and other discussion fora (Pihlaja, 2016).

We noted above the opportunity to begin to investigate the growth and change of religious organisations as reflected in the archived Web. Another particular opportunity for scholars that the archived Web affords is understanding the way in which religious organisations, large and small (as distinct from individuals) have interacted online with other organisations. The recent study by Ackland and Evans (2017) on the debate over abortion in Australia is instructive, using data from the live Web collected in 2005 and 2015 to reconstruct the network of pro-life and pro-choice sites and to analyse the terms in which the issue was discussed. Webster (2017a) also provided a case study of how the imprint of one religious leader's site in the link structures of the UK Web changed as a result of a single controversial public statement. Such studies point the way towards longitudinal analyses of evolving debates over social issues in which religious organisations play only a part.

As well as public online encounters between religious people and those who are not, religious historians studying the Web will need also to attend directly to anti-religious groups and the ways in which they have attempted to influence the shape of public discourse about religion. Although they are by no means identical, the phenomena of racism, xenophobia, anti-religious sentiment and far-right politics overlap, and the far-right was early to adopt the Internet as a means of internal communication and outward dissemination (Halavais, 2010). Controversies such as those over cartoons of the prophet Muhammad in Denmark in 2005 or the film *The Innocence of Muslims* are objects of historical study not only for the reactions from those whose sensibilities were offended, but for understanding the support amongst the anti-religious for them (al-Rawi, 2016; Khan, 2015).

## CONCLUSION

The 'Great Commission' given by Jesus Christ was to 'go and make disciples of all nations', and most (although not all) of the world religious traditions have been proselytic in their aims. In this, we see both another spur to historical investigation and a reminder of the limits of Web history. Certainly, some of the materials of such evangelism have been made available online: sacred texts and expositions of them, and live broadcasts of worship and the preaching that is often embedded within it. The online text has its counterpart in the printed tract so widely distributed by Christian evangelists in earlier periods; the online sermon is prefigured by the televangelist of the 1970s, or the street corner preacher before him. However, whilst the call to conversion may be studied online, the response is much less easily recovered, which perhaps explains the relative lack of emphasis on this in the research to date. The stories of Christian conversion that have survived tend to stress the quietness and the inwardness of the process by which people come to adopt a position of faith:

processes which tend to leave no trace whatever at the time, and are often only recorded much later. (On the exceptionally well-documented but yet still complex case of C.S. Lewis, see McGrath, 2013: 131–59.) In closing, then, this chapter suggests that to write the history of proselytisation and response in the early twenty-first century requires not only the study of the Web, but also an integration of both the live and archived Web with the full range of other primary sources that are the raw material of historical writing: personal testimonies of both evangelist and convert; the experience of the local congregations into which the converted pass; changing institutional strategies and the growth and decline of membership overall. Such an investigation is complex, and the sources often incomplete, but the achievement of such an integration would mark the point at which Web history had become part of history as a whole.

## Note

1 For instance, the work of the educationalist Harold Loukes (1961) on religious attitudes amongst British teenagers is now a key source for historians of the 1950 and 1960s.

## REFERENCES


Ackland, R., and Evans, A. (2017) 'Using the Web to examine the evolution of the abortion debate in Australia, 2005–2015', in N. Brügger and R. Schroeder (Eds), *The Web as History*. London: UCL Press. pp. 159–89.

al-Rawi, A. (2016) 'Facebook as a virtual mosque: The online protest against *Innocence of Muslims*', *Culture and Religion*, 17(1): 19–34.

Amarasingam, A. (Ed.) (2010). *Religion and the new atheism: A critical appraisal.* Leiden: Brill.

Beals, M. (2016) 'The role of the Sydney Gazette in the creation of Australia in the Scottish public sphere', in J. Hinks and C. Feely (Eds), *Historical Networks in the Book Trade*. London: Routledge. pp. 148–70.

Beaudoin, T. (1998) *Virtual faith. The irreverent spiritual quest of Generation X.* San Francisco: Jossey Bass.

Becker, C. (2011) 'Muslims on the path of the *Salaf al Salih*. Ritual dynamics in chat rooms and discussion forums', *Information, Communication and Society*, 14(8): 1181–203.

Beckerlegge, G. (Ed.) (2001) *From sacred text to internet.* Farnham: Ashgate.

Brown, C.G. (2009) *The death of Christian Britain: Understanding secularisation, 1800–2000.* 2nd edition, London: Routledge.

Brügger, N. (2010) 'Introduction', in N. Brügger (Ed.), *Web History.* New York: Peter Lang, pp. 1–25.

Burke, K. (2016) *Christians under covers: Evangelicals and sexual pleasure on the internet.* Oakland, CA: University of California Press.

Campbell, H. (2010). 'Religious authority and the blogosphere', *Journal of Computer-Mediated Communication*, 15(2): 251–76.

Campbell, H. (2011) 'Internet and religion', in M. Consalvo and C. Ess (Eds), *The Handbook of Internet Studies.* Chichester: Wiley-Blackwell. pp. 232–50.

Castells, M. (2001) *The Internet galaxy: Reflections on the internet, business and society.* Oxford: Oxford University Press.

Chandler, A. (2006) *The Church of England in the twentieth century: The Church commissioners and the politics of reform.* Woodbridge: Boydell.

Cheruvallil-Contractor, S., and Shakkour, S. (Eds) (2016) *Digital methodologies in the sociology of religion.* London: Bloomsbury.

Cheong, P.H, Brummans, B.H.J.M., and Hwang, J.M. (2016) 'Research authority in religious organizations from a communicative perspective: A connective online-offline approach', in S. Cheruvallil-Contractor and S. Shakkour (Eds), *Digital Methodologies in the Sociology of Religion*. London: Bloomsbury. pp. 137–46.

Cobb, J. (1998) *Cybergrace: The search for God in the digital world*. New York: Crown.

Davie, G. (2000) *Religion in Modern Europe: A memory mutates.* Oxford: Oxford University Press.

Davis, E. (1998) *Techgnosis: Myth, magic and mysticism in the age of information.* New York: Harmony.

Dixon, P. (1997) *Cyberchurch: Christianity and the Internet*. Eastbourne: Kingsway.

Garnett, J., Grimley, M., Harris, A., White, W., and Williams, S. (Eds) (2006) *Redefining Christian Britain. Post 1945 perspectives*. London: SCM Press.

Garnett, J., and Harris, A. (Eds) (2013) *Rescripting religion in the city: Migration and religious identity in the modern metropolis*. Farnham: Ashgate.

Goodhew, D. (Ed.) (2012) *Church growth in Britain: 1980 to the present*. Farnham: Ashgate.

Halavais, A. (2010) 'Evolution of U.S. white nationalism on the Web', in N. Brügger (Ed.), *Web History*. New York: Peter Lang. pp. 83–103.

Han, S. (2016) *Technologies of religion: Spheres of the sacred in a post-secular modernity*. Abingdon: Routledge.

Harvey, D. (2008) 'Seen to be remembered: Representation and recollection in contemporary British evangelicalism', in M. Smith (Ed.), *British Evangelical Identities Past and Present: volume 1. Aspects of the History and Sociology of Evangelicalism in Britain and Ireland*. Carlisle: Paternoster. pp. 180–200.

Harvey, K. (Ed.) (2009) *History and material culture: A student's guide to approaching alternative sources*. Abingdon: Routledge.

Herbert, D., and Wolffe, J. (2005) 'Religion and contemporary conflict in historical perspective', in J. Wolffe (Ed.), *Religion in History: Conflict, Conversion and Co-existence*. Manchester: Manchester University Press. pp. 286–320.

Hoejsgaard, M. (2005) 'Cyber-religion: On the cutting edge between the virtual and the real', in M.T. Hoejsgaard and M. Warburg (Eds), *Religion and Cyberspace*. London: Routledge. pp. 50–63.

Hoejsgaard, M.T., and Warburg, M. (2005) 'Introduction: waves of research', in M.T. Hoejsgaard and M. Warburg (Eds), *Religion and Cyberspace*. London: Routledge. pp. 1–9.

Hofheinz, A. (2010) 'A history of Allah.com', in N. Brügger (Ed.), *Web History*. New York: Peter Lang. pp. 105–35.

Houston, G. (1998) *Virtual morality: Christian ethics in the computer age*. Leicester: Apollos.

Howard, R.G. (2011) *Digital Jesus: The making of a new Christian fundamentalist community on the Internet*. New York: New York University Press.

Hunt, S.J. (2003) *Alternative religions: A sociological introduction*. Farnham: Ashgate.

Huntington, S.P. (1997) *The clash of civilizations and the remaking of world order*. London: Simon and Schuster.

Hutchings, T. (2016) 'Studying apps: Research approaches to the digital Bible', in S. Cheruvallil-Contractor and S. Shakkour (Eds), *Digital Methodologies in the Sociology of Religion*. London: Bloomsbury. pp. 97–108.

Keown, D., and Prebish, C. (2013) 'Celebrating twenty years of the *Journal of Buddhist Ethics*', *Journal of Buddhist Ethics*, 20: 37–9, accessed on 16 December 2016 at http://blogs.dickinson.edu/buddhistethics/

Khan, R.J. (2015) *Muhammad in the digital age*. Austin, TX: University of Texas Press.

Krotoski, A. (2014) 'Inventing the Internet: Scapegoat, sin eater and trickster', in M. Graham and W.H. Dutton (Eds), *Society and the Internet: How networks of information and communication are changing our lives*. Oxford: Oxford University Press. pp. 23–35.

Krüger, O. (2005) 'Discovering the invisible Internet: Methodological aspects of searching religion on the Internet', *Online: Heidelberg Journal of Religions on the Internet* 1: 1, accessed at http://heiup.uni-heidelberg.de/journals/index.php/religions/article/view/385/360

Lochhead, D. (1997) *Shifting realities: Information technology and the Church*. Geneva: World Council of Churches.

Loukes, H. (1961), Teenage religion. London: SCM Press.

Lundby, K. (2011) 'Patterns of belonging in online/offline interfaces of religion', *Information, Communication and Society*, 14(8): 129–35.

MacWilliams, M.W. (2004) 'Virtual pilgrimage to Ireland's Croagh Patrick', in L.L. Dawson and D.E. Cowan (Eds), *Religion Online: Finding Faith on the Internet*. London and New York: Routledge. pp. 223–37.

Maiden, J. (2015) '"What could be more Christian than to allow the Sikhs to use it?" Church redundancy and minority religion in Bedford, 1977–8', *Studies in Church History*, 51: 399–411.

McGrath, A. (2013) *C.S. Lewis, a life: Eccentric genius, reluctant prophet*. London: Hodder.

McLeod, H. (2007) *The religious crisis of the 1960s*. Oxford: Oxford University Press.

Mitchell, J., and Marriage, S. (Eds) (2003) *Mediating religion: Conversations in media, religion and culture*. London: T. & T. Clark.

Mosco, V. (2004) *The digital sublime: Myth, power and cyberspace*. Cambridge, MA: MIT Press.

Nye, D.E. (1994) *American technological sublime*. Cambridge, MA: MIT Press.

Pettegree, A. (1996) *Marian Protestantism: Six studies*. Aldershot: Scholar.

Pihlaja, S. (2016) 'Analysing YouTube interaction: A discourse-centred approach', in S. Cheruvallil-Contractor and S. Shakkour (Eds), *Digital Methodologies in the Sociology of Religion*. London: Bloomsbury. pp. 49–58.

Power, M. (2007) *From ecumenism to community relations: Inter-church relationships in Northern Ireland 1980–2005*. Dublin: Irish Academic Press.

Prebish, C. (2004) 'The Cybersangha: Buddhism on the Internet', in L.L. Dawson and D.E. Cowan (Eds), *Religion Online: Finding Faith on the Internet*. London and New York: Routledge. pp. 135–47.

Raleigh, W. (1614) *The history of the world*. London.

Schroeder, R., Heather, N., and Lee, R.M. (1998) 'The sacred and the virtual: Religion in multi-user virtual reality', *Journal of Computer-Mediated Communication*, 4(2). DOI: https://doi.org/10.1111/j.1083-6101.1998.tb00092.x

Shallis, M. (1984) *The silicon idol: The micro revolution and its social implications*. Oxford: Oxford University Press.

Steven, J. (2002) *Worship in the Spirit: Charismatic worship in the Church of England*. Carlisle: Paternoster.

Webster, P. (2015a) *Archbishop Ramsey: The shape of the Church*. Farnham: Ashgate.

Webster, P. (2015b) 'Race, religion and national identity in Sixties Britain: Michael Ramsey, archbishop of Canterbury and his encounter with other faiths', *Studies in Church History*, 51: 385–98.

Webster, P. (2017a) 'Religious discourse in the archived Web: Rowan Williams, archbishop of Canterbury, and the sharia law controversy of 2008', in N. Brügger and R. Schroeder (Eds), *The Web as History*. London: UCL Press. pp. 190–203.

Webster, P. (2017b) 'Users, technologies, organisations: Towards a cultural history of world Web archiving', in N. Brügger (Ed.), *Web 25: Histories from the First 25 Years of the World Wide Web*. New York: Peter Lang. pp.175–90.

Webster, P. (2018a, forthcoming) 'Lessons from cross-border religion in the Northern Irish web sphere: Understanding the limitations of the ccTLD as a proxy for the national web', in N. Brügger and D. Laursen (Eds), *The Historical Web and Digital Humanities: The Case of National Web domains*. London: Routledge.

Webster, P. (2018b) 'Technology, ethics and religious language: Early Anglophone Christian reactions to "cyberspace"', *Internet Histories*. 2(3–4).

Wellman, B. (2011) 'Studying the Internet through the ages', in M. Consalvo and C. Ess (Eds), *The Handbook of Internet Studies*. Chichester: Wiley-Blackwell. pp. 17–23.

33

# Hearing the Past: The Sonic Web from MIDI to Music Streaming

Jeremy Wade Morris

## INTRODUCTION

In a recent round of spring cleaning, I came across an old cassette tape, one of about a dozen or so recorded cassettes and personal mixtapes that I had saved from the earlier days of my music collection. I'm not sure whether it helps or hurts my academic credibility to mention the tape was entitled 'Smashing Pumpkins, Dusseldorf Germany', a bootleg of a concert the titular band played in 1996. The tape is decidedly analog…it has a handmade photocopied cover image and the physical casing of the tape is degraded. But the tape is also forever digital in my mind. It was the first piece of music (and perhaps the first commodity of any kind) that I purchased 'from the Internet', and in 1996, it was well before standard conventions of web commerce had fully developed. There was no 'click here to buy now' button linked to my Amazon account, no shopping cart icon to which I could add the purchase. The tape, instead, came from a music newsgroup I had been a part of called alt.music.smashing-pumpkins (again, do these details hurt or help my story?). Another user in the forum was selling the tape and all I had to do was send $5 in the mail to somewhere in the United States and the tape would, supposedly, be mailed back to me. Being a cost-conscious Canadian college student who had never purchased anything from the Internet before, I worried this deal would go sour. But such was my reckless fandom for the band that potentially losing $5 seemed like a risk worth taking on this other user, whose only credentials were that they frequented the same newsgroup I did.

The tape arrived as promised a few weeks later and, 20 years later, it stands as a reminder of the many ways in which analog and digital collided in the mid 1990s, and the ways new technologies like the Web reconfigured social, economic and cultural practices around cultural goods like music. Even if computers and network technologies in the early 1990s were limited in their capacities to produce, distribute, sell and play sound, a variety of communities and companies nevertheless found ways to use the Web towards sonic ends. From early websites and bulletin board sites where users traded sound-related texts like MIDI files, song lyrics, guitar tablature, to the noises of new technologies like the sound of the dial-up modem or 'You've got Mail!', to higher-bandwidth audio practices like file sharing, mp3 downloads, streaming music and podcasts, the Web's sounds have shaped the industrial, legal and cultural logics of the platform.

Despite this rich sonic past, histories of the Web generally focus on the visual; we track website snapshots over time with tools like the Wayback Machine, focus on different eras of web design styles like Web 2.0 or flat design and praise the Web's visual technical innovations. What if we amplified this knowledge of the Web's visual and technical history by listening to it as well? Accordingly, this chapter explores some of the Web's sonic past by considering technologies that made sound playable on the Web and some of the early communities that formed around new modes of music distribution. I focus particularly on developments in North America, given that a number of these technologies come from US tech companies like Winamp, Real Player, Napster, etc. Even if the reach of many of these technologies was international, sound and its meanings are always positional so the analysis provided here should be complemented with sounds and sonic experiences from other regions. I track the rise of commercial efforts to sell and stream sound online and the recent explosion in popularity of podcasts and other new sonic forms. Then I move on to address both the importance of sound/sound commodities as elements of the Web's development and the difficulties posed by web sounds as objects of history. While all web histories are marked by their absences, web sounds are doubly vulnerable. Efforts and tools geared towards preserving, archiving and displaying the historic Web, such as the Internet Archive's Wayback Machine, are visually oriented, relying on snapshots, web crawls and archived web pages as windows to the Web's past. These techniques often treat sound as secondary or present technical challenges for capturing sounds and sonic media. Further, as with other digital formats, early sound files are often unplayable through today's technologies, either because of the ever-quickening pace of obsolescence or because of technical barriers resulting from long and inconsistent battles over proprietary formats and digital rights management. Even more open and available sonic objects, like podcasts, are at risk of becoming inaccessible to researchers because of increasing commercialization and a lack of urgency around preserving something that's seen as both mundane and ubiquitous.

I begin with a section called Web of Sounds, where I provide an overview of the changing sound of the Web over the past several decades, including some key sonic technologies that have shaped the Web. Then I move into a second section, Sound Histories, which focuses on the challenges sound files, formats and soundscapes present for digital historians. The Web's rich sonic history has been muted or muffled to date, but like all web histories, the challenge is how we gather the material to tell it.

## WEB OF SOUNDS

### *Early Sounds (1960s–1980s)*

Buried in the timeline for 'A Little History of the World Wide Web', which The World Wide Web Consortium maintains on their website, is a 'snapshot of the WWW Project Page as of 3 Nov 1992' (W3C 2000b). Although a troublesome historical document as the 'first' web page (Gitelman, 2006), it nevertheless offers a representation of what early web pages looked like and contained. Built as a directory structure, the page offers a link to 'What's out there?' sorted by subject of interest (e.g. Mathematics, Literature, Computing, etc.) or by type of service (e.g. Network News, Gopher, Telnet). Halfway down the 'Subjects' page is the heading

'Music', which includes links to 'MIDI Interfacing' and 'Song Lyrics', immediately followed by a parenthetical note that reads '(apparently disabled for copyright reasons)' (W3C, 2000a). The music links no longer resolve, nor do they appear in the Internet Archive's Wayback Machine. While web historians might never know which MIDI files and song lyrics they'd find if these links still worked, the existence of these links is at least evidence that, even in the Web's earliest stages, sound and music were key areas of interest for potential web users.

These links aren't, of course, the first evidence of sound on the Internet. In fact, for many early Internet users, the very sound of connecting to the network was an iconic and instrumental part of the experience. From the acoustic couplers in the 1960s that helped send modem sounds through telephones and connect two computers (Mann, 1998) to the dial-up modem technology that emerged in the late 1970s and early 1980s from work at universities and on NSFnet (Abbate, 1999; Baym, 1994; Hauben and Hauben, 1997), sound has been a core component of network technology. In the 1970s and 1980s users would employ a modem to dial into bulletin board systems (BBSs), Usenet or similar service providers and the sounds of that connection process would play aloud. Dial-up modems made a peculiar though not entirely unfamiliar sound (for a nostalgic reminder, listen to willterminus, 2008). The dial-up sound began like a phone call, with dial tones and number tones, but turned into something more akin to a distorted fax machine: a set of high-pitched screeching tones bouncing back and forth, negotiating the terms of connection before giving way to a wash of static. Technically, the sound represented a handshake between two computers; the protocols by which further communication could take place (Madrigal, 2012). Culturally, it meant so much more:

> Of all the noises that my children will not understand, the one that is nearest to my heart is not from a song or a television show or a jingle. It's the sound of a modem connecting with another modem across the repurposed telephone infrastructure. It was the noise of being part of the beginning of the Internet. (Madrigal, 2012)

For users who sat through the process countless times, the dial-up sound meant connection; it opened up the isolated machine users were on to a network of people, places and possibilities. It was a fusion of the analog and digital; sound waves that carried data across phone lines to enable contact, communication and community.

BBSs grew in popularity in the 1980s, sparking networked discussions on everyday subjects like politics, business and music as well as other more niche subcultures and scenes (Driscoll, 2016). While primarily textual interfaces for asynchronous discussions, BBSs also had a sonic component to them. As BBS creators became proficient with the use of the ANSI text standard to create highly visual login screens, with many becoming part of the larger 'artscene' and 'demoscene' movement in computer graphics (Driscoll and Diaz 2009), some programmers learned to add basic musical tones to their BBSs, giving them a distinct sonic as well as visual character (Scott, 2005).

The sounds of dial-up modems and BBSs in the 1980s and early 1990s were, like the soundscapes of any period, limited by the sound-producing capabilities of the primary technologies of the time. Although early mainframe computers of the 1960s and 1970s were entirely capable of processing sound, and many electronic music composers had been experimenting for decades with computer music (Manning, 2004), audio was largely secondary when 'personal' computers emerged in the late 1970s. The first personal computers were extensions of office tools (Venkatesh, 1996; Venkatesh and Vitalari, 1987), calculating machines to enhance productivity at work (Friedman, 2005: 102–10, 121; Kirschenbaum, 2016). Computers at the time were not designed for, or perceived as, entertainment devices (Friedman, 2005, Venkatesh, 1996), though developments in video game sound on consoles like Atari and Intellivision in the early 1980s helped shift these conceptions. New affordances for making digital sounds and new kinds of sound communities, like the chiptune scene[1] (Driscoll and Diaz, 2009), meant that while computer audio wasn't yet mainstream, it certainly wasn't silent.

### *Multimedia Sounds (1980s–1995)*

Along with advances in gaming, the multimedia 'revolution' of the late 1980s and early 1990s brought a number of changes to the computer's audio and video capabilities (Friedman, 2005: 121; Venkatesh, 1996). Companies like Apple, which had developed specialty audio technologies in the late 1970s and early 1980s, began to include advanced audio as standard features on all kinds of personal computers, giving everyday users the ability to create, record, mix and master music. As a 1991 review for a Macintosh desktop computer noted:

> Recently, sound on the Mac has gotten even better, suitable for general users rather than just for musicians. Stereo-sound-output ports now come standard with every Mac except the LC, which has a mono-output port. The LC and IIsi come standard with sound-input ports and microphones as well, and with third-party products, you can add sound-input capabilities to other Macs. (Gruberman and McQuillin, 1991)

Additionally, the late 1980s and early 1990s saw the introduction of the sound card: an internal electronics card or chip that provided a user's computer amplified and more customizable sound than the standard internal speaker. For more adventuresome users, companies like AdLib and Creative Labs provided cards like SoundBlaster and GameBlaster that users could install on their machines for enhanced sonic capabilities. CD-ROM drives also served as Trojan horses for getting recorded music onto the computer. Designed originally to store data, play games, or offer encyclopedias, they were reconfigured through programs like Trantor's Music Box (1991) that let users play audio CDs in CD-ROM drives (Grunin, 1991).

The multimedia 'revolution', then, was more of a disparate effort on the part of manufacturers, software developers and tech journalists to expand the market for personal computers than a cohesive movement, and sound and video played key roles in this technical and cultural re-imagining of computers and computing. Hardware like CD-ROM drives, sound cards and stereo ports, as well as audio playback software, served as building blocks for the sonic web; they were part of a series of technologies that made the computer an all-purpose sonic machine that could make, rip, store, play and burn music. They were also reminders of how foreign the concept of using computers for music and sound playback was, even with the advances of the multimedia 'revolution'. Using the device for general music production or playback often required user effort and technical skill, like installing sound cards and the translation of a whole series of technologies and practices onto the computer (Petzold, 1991). Yet even if it was slow and uneven, and more hype than happening, the multimedia 'revolution' helped turn computers from office extensions to personal media devices, something more akin to the 'small-scale technologies [...] for the transformation of consciousness and community' and tools for individual self-fashioning we consider them today (Friedman, 2005; Turner, 2005: 489.

As a variety of communities used these newly capable 'personal' computers to connect in BBSs, newsgroups, FTP or Gopher Sites and other networks, users traded files that were sonic in intent, if not in practice. MIDI files, for example, were some of the earliest ways users swapped 'music' online, even if those files were more data than sound (Alderman, 2001: 28–30; Haring, 2000: 83–5). MIDI or Musical Instrument Digital Interface was a file standard that emerged in the early 1980s. It was an open standard designed to coordinate communication between musical instruments and computers by storing and transferring data about specific signals or events (e.g. pitch, volume, velocity, panning, tempo, etc.), but it was also the perfect way for artists and fans to send musical ideas and 'performances' across a relatively low-bandwidth system (Théberge, 1997: 83–90). MIDI files, after all, were merely the instructions that, when combined with the synthesizers and sound cards capable of processing and sequencing MIDI, could then create sound. There were also many lyrics sites and web spaces devoted to sharing musical notation and tablatures, like the alt.guitar.tab newsgroup that become the Online Guitar Archive (OLGA), one of the largest repositories of guitar tablature on the early Web.

In the mid 1990s, as the Web became the primary interface for navigating the Internet, these sonic communities migrated to websites that allowed for more direct distribution of sound. What had been vibrant communities of users trading MIDI files, song lyrics and other textual representations of sonic objects became thriving sites for making and sharing actual sounds and songs. Sites like the Internet Underground Music Archive (IUMA) were some of the first digital hubs and most-cited places to visit on the burgeoning network (Alderman, 2001: 12–4; Haring, 2000: 36–8). A pre-cursor to mp3.com, MySpace and other music-focused social networks, the IUMA encoded and converted music sent from artists (usually on cassettes or CDs) into compressed digital formats and provided a web space for artists to post songs and band photos and offer merchandise for sale. There and elsewhere on the Net, music enthusiasts were converting and uploading bootleg versions of concerts, b-sides and other rarities, creating websites for their favourite artists and posting MIDI files for users to download and play. Using primitive software media players like XingSound – the first commercially available real-time audio encoder launched in 1993 – or XMCD, users could rip CDs to their computers or play songs they had downloaded from the Web (Amorim, 2007; Ness, 1993).

Internet companies at this time also started thinking sonically. An online service provider in the United States and Canada called Quantum Link (Q-Link) hired a voice actor named Elwood Edwards to voice a few stock phrases and help make their Internet service stand out. When Q-Link changed its name in 1991 to AOL and began blanketing the United States with a flood of start-up CDs, millions of users heard Elwood's 'Welcome!', 'File's done', 'Goodbye' and 'You've Got Mail!' each time they started surfing the Net. Estimates from around that time suggested the sounds might have been heard more than 27 million times a day (Sittenfeld, 1998). Minor as they may have been, the sounds brought visual interfaces to life and humanized technology that had bureaucratic and militaristic historical lineage. Like the modem sound, AOL and other service provider sounds became sonic souvenirs of the early Web's soundscape in the United States (AOL used different voice actors in other countries). Together with sounds such as the Intel Chime, the various operating system start-up sounds and online game sounds, these noises helped form the soundscape of early web use.

## *Web Sounds (1995–2000s)*

By the mid 1990s, there was little doubt that the Web was a thriving environment for those interested in sound and music. A variety of formats and services emerged to cater to the millions of users who were turning to the Web for all kinds of news, information and entertainment. College radio stations like WXYC in Chapel Hill, WREK out of Atlanta, and KJHK in Lawrence raced to be the 'first' to provide an Internet broadcast in late 1994 (Bottomley, 2016), while AudioNet brought many terrestrial radio stations online when it launched in 1995. That year also saw the launch of Progressive Networks' RealAudio, which brought a range of streaming audio to the Web, from music to talk to sports radio. Designed to address the frustratingly long wait times posed by downloading large media files over slow modems, RealAudio's service worked by allowing users to listen to a file in real time. Its streaming innovations made it a pioneer in attempts to bring radio and television online (Rothenberg, 1999), even if they were ultimately disadvantaged in an online audio and digital music market that preferred the direct download for most of the 2000s (Alderman, 2001: 40).

This proliferation of new services, sites and media players brought new modes of delivery and new audio formats for creators and users alike. The mp3 format, for example, which was the result of research conducted on behalf of a broader consortium of radio and television broadcasters and the film industries (the Motion Picture Experts Group), proved itself to be a relatively convenient and efficient format for sending songs via Internet connections and to portable music players (Katz, 2004; Sterne, 2012). A host of competing formats that never gained the prominence of the mp3, such as a2b, Liquid Audio, Windows Media Audio and Ogg Vorbis, also emerged around this time and each offered different levels of proprietary control, digital rights management or openness (Morris, 2015). From the sheer number of these competing formats, it's clear the story of sound on the Web in the late 1990s and early 2000s was contradictorily about disseminating sound further, faster and more conveniently, and about controlling this dissemination in order to profit from it. The battles over the various formats were ostensibly about which format should prevail or which company(ies) might provide the infrastructure for this burgeoning market, but these format wars also very much affected the way users could and couldn't use digital audio in this new environment (Burkart and McCourt, 2006; Gillespie, 2007). Some formats limited the players on which you could play back the music; others only allowed for music to be played once the copy was authenticated as a legitimate purchase.

In addition to new formats, there were a host of new interfaces for finding and playing music and sound as well. Playback programs like Winamp, Windows Media Player, iTunes and others gave users new tools for building playlists, storing collections and visualizing music, while file-sharing networks such as Napster, Gnutella, Limewire and Kazaa provided users spaces to socialize, share and discover music through alternative outlets (Morris, 2015). Some of these programs were more industrially approved (e.g. iTunes) than others (e.g. Napster), setting off a decade-long contest between entrenched music industry interests and upstart tech companies that saw music and sound as just another form of information that was meant, like other information on the Web, to be free. Although the passing of the Digital Millennium Copyright Act in 1996 and the formation of the Secure Digital Music Initiative in 1998 were early warning signs of the court cases and lawsuits that followed in the 2000s (Burkart and McCourt, 2006), the struggle against piracy and the implementation of digital rights management technologies (Gillespie, 2007) defined much of the debate around music and sound on the Internet in ways that still shape music online to this day.

Complicating these legal battles was the rise, in the early and mid 2000s, of various sound- and music-focused social networks that offered the distribution of free sounds. Although there had been other social network sites before it, MySpace was the first mainstream music-focused social network site to connect a vast number of established and emerging musicians with their fans. It offered users general social networking features but MySpace stood out for the ways it allowed artists to market themselves and their music (Suhr, 2012). Every artist could create a profile and could add their music to it, all of which was offered freely, while users had more intimate access to their favorite artists and music. Subsequent social networks and communities like imeem, GarageBand.com, Last.Fm, Bandcamp and SoundCloud built on MySpace's legacy by turning audiences into communities based around sound, music and music creation (Suhr, 2012).

Beyond music, the Web also became a prime outlet for audio blogging and podcasting in the 2000s. Although there had been experiments in personal audio broadcasting as early as 1993, with hobbyists and technologists like Carl Malamud broadcasting online with a technology called Mbone (Bottomley, 2016) or with more mainstream programs like Winamp's SHOUTcast, the roots of podcasting more fully took hold in the audio blogging practices of the early 2000s. By the time journalist Ben Hammersley (2004) accidentally coined the term 'podcasting' in an article for *The Guardian*, personal broadcasting on the Web was already a burgeoning cultural form. Podcasting crystallized and institutionalized through the 2000s (Sterne et al., 2008), as larger players like iTunes (2005) incorporated podcasts into their software and other aggregators, like Podcast Alley, offered access to thousands of podcast episodes from amateurs, public radio stations and commercial media alike. Although critics claim we are currently experiencing a 'golden age' of podcasts (Blattberg, 2014; Roose, 2014), personal broadcasting online has been growing steadily since the advent of the Web itself.

So, while I remember my purchase of the Smashing Pumpkins bootleg tape as a pioneering act in the history of online music and e-commerce, there's plenty of evidence suggesting it was simply a tiny transaction in the much longer history of the Internet as a tool for sound and for commerce[2]. Still, it was only in 1995 that the US National Science Foundation lifted the prohibition of commercial enterprise on the Internet, so my 1996 purchase, and the many other downloads, shares and trading of sounds described above, still stand as examples of practices around digital sonic objects that were still under negotiation with users, technology companies, regulators and media producers. What were once gray and unsure markets are now flourishing areas for growth, with digital formats comprising half of all purchases and streaming eclipsing most other forms of consumption (IFPI, 2017). Downloadable mp3s are still of value, and valuable, to users and companies alike, but the future that companies like RealAudio and mp3Tunes bet on in the early 1990s resonates anew in music service providers like YouTube, Spotify, Apple Music, Google Play, Pandora, Tidal and others. These services co-exist uneasily with less industrially sanctioned file sharing and bit torrent sites, as well as private tracker communities. Fans continue to trade lyrics, mp3s, MIDI files and other sonic texts in a variety of sound-focused communities. Newer technologies to connect to the Web, like smartphones, tablets and home assistants bring new sounds, alerts and notifications that are defining the contemporary web soundscape.

Yet this partial sampling of the Web's sonic history raises a number of issues about how researchers, archivists and anyone interested in their own sonic pasts will keep track of the Web's current and future sounds. I turn now to consider some of the challenges web audio presents for sonically inclined historians by looking at some of the current repositories for historical web sounds. If the Web's early decades were hard to archive, future decades may be even harder.

## SOUND HISTORIES

While all web histories are marked by their absences – by what cannot be captured in a dynamic and often-changing environment of code, objects, pages, sites and spheres (Brügger, 2009) – web sounds are doubly vulnerable. First, web archiving tools are primarily built on visual metaphors and thus neglect the role of audio. Second, preserving audio formats often requires preserving the sounds themselves as well as the technologies on which to play those sounds. Like so many other digital media, web audio is hard to hear not just because it is hard to find and save but because it is hard to know what to save along with it to make it playable in the future. Driscoll and Diaz's claim that 'the role of music, sound, and noise in computer games remains relatively under examined' (2009:2) applies to web history more broadly and to the sonic elements of the web's past and present.

### The Sounds of the Internet Archive

The current tools for archiving and displaying older versions of the Web are highly visual. The Internet Archive's Wayback Machine, for example, can certainly help us to see what Napster's website looked like between 1998 and 2001, or what people were talking about on Winamp's early forums (Morris, 2015). There's even screengrabs of the IUMA dating back to 1996, where users can see that the IUMA was boasting that the site was 'Now Real Audio Enriched!', though the links return error pages when trying to play music from the artists or genres listed. Like so many of the other audio and media links in the Wayback Machine's archives, the source audio has either moved or is no longer playable. This snapshot-based approach to web preservation and display is crucial, allowing users to time-hop through various representations of the past, but it foregrounds the visual and ensures a site's text/layout is preserved while capturing less of the other media associated with historical sites.

This is not to say that the Internet Archive is absent of audio. The site has a robust audio archive, with millions of audio files uploaded by dedicated web users and historians. There are, for example, 45,036 results in the 'IUMA (Internet Underground Music Archive) Collection', which is made up of songs that were posted to the site over time. The broader audio collection has thousands of files, including podcasts, popular music, local terrestrial and web radio, audiobooks and a vast collection of live bootleg concerts. These collections are invaluable, but they are also stripped of much of their original context. The IUMA Collection, for example, provides access to sounds but doesn't really provide a sense of how these songs and sounds appeared within the original site. If the visual snapshots from the Wayback Machine are silent, the sound collections are hard to visualize.

### The Sounds of YouTube and User-Generated Repositories

In addition to songs and other popular audio, the Internet Archive also has some of the iconic computer and Internet sounds from early days of the Web. The 'You've Got Mail!' sound, for example, is preserved, as is the sound of a dial-up modem, though many others are absent. Some of these sounds have not changed since their earliest iterations (e.g. 'You've Got Mail!'), while others seem to be re-creations or approximations of the sounds as users remember them. The archived dial-up modem sound, for example, comes from a YouTube video that was uploaded in 2008, along with the caption:

> I was bored so I wanted to see if I could get free dial up internet so I found that NetZero still has free service so I put in the number and heard the glorious sound of the Dial-up. Remind me of years gone. Unfortunately I was not able to make a connection. (willterminus, 2008)

It's not exactly the sound of a modem from the early 1990s, but it represents the sound close enough to satisfy close to 6,000 commenters, who chime in with responses like 'Ah yes, the sound of my childhood' or memories like 'Get off the Internet, I'm on the phone'. However, responses from users from different countries (or different locations within certain countries) serve as a reminder that what's past for some is present for many. Dial-up is only a 'historical' sound for those privileged enough to live in cities and countries where the Internet infrastructure is developed, or for users with the financial means to be able to afford faster connections. Even in the United States, some 3% of the population, or close to ten million users, still regularly connect to the Internet via dial-up (PEW, 2013). The sounds of the Web, in other words, point to the sounds of the various digital divides that have structured and continue to structure the technology.

On YouTube, videos of users trying to connect 56k modems using 2017 technology, or grainy old home videos showing users starting up their computers in the 1990s, point to a second challenge of saving the sonic web: like other media, preserving the historical sounds associated with the Web also means preserving the technologies on which to play those sounds. RealAudio, for example, was a crucial audio format in the 1990s and a significant portion of early online broadcasts were made using RealAudio and RealPlayer technologies. As with the many other proprietary formats released at the time, RealAudio requires RealPlayer to decode and play the audio, making any sound saved in that format dependent on the continued maintenance and support of RealPlayer technology (which is currently supported, but only for Windows). Other sound formats and services, such as the Yahoo Music Store or the inaccurately named Windows PlaysForSure designation are evidence of how a good portion of web-related audio can be protected and privatized to the point of inaccessibility, once the technologies for maintaining the infrastructure shut down or close (Morris, 2015).

## The Sounds of Institutional Archives

There are more official and institutional sound archives online that take greater care in preserving, cataloguing and making researchable a variety of sounds and sound recordings. These archives tend to focus on history (e.g. the British Library, The Library of Congress, etc.), genre (e.g. Cornell's Natural Sound Archive, Smithsonian Folkways World Music Collection, etc.), technology (e.g. Radio Archives, Cylinder Audio Archive, etc.) or artist (e.g. The Studs Terkel Archive, Alan Lomax Sound Archive, etc.) in their collections. They don't, however, address the Web or many of the new noises Internet-related technologies have brought since the 1990s. More unofficial repositories, such as the Museum of Endangered Sounds[3], fill in some of these gaps, but hardly in a way that is systematic or comprehensive.

Unlike analog audio objects that leave physical traces and copies of sounds that historians can listen back to in the future, digital sounds are often intimately tied to the technologies that produce them. The start-up chimes or BBS home page sounds exist within a particular machine or website for a particular period of time exclusively unless they are preserved in other formats or migrated to new hardware and software. Analog media are, of course, not immune to these challenges; cassettes need cassette players, Betamax tapes need Betamax machines and analog materials decay over time, whether it's valuable film stock or my Smashing Pumpkins cassette. But the intertwining of format, software and hardware that comprise many web sounds complicate the process of accessing those sounds as time wears on. Trying to run a Flash-based video game or play a Liquid Audio file downloaded from a file-sharing site in the mid 1990s is a whole other matter, given the copy protection schemes and rapid pace of obsolescence of many Internet-dependent technologies. Depending on the severity of the digital rights management, or the networked links between the audio format, the software media player and the hardware itself, it may be next to impossible.

## The Sounds of Streams

The shift towards streaming as a dominant form of delivery for sound (and other media) on the Web is a prime example of the ways this assemblage of format–software–hardware complicates the ability to save and store audio. While streaming offers the ability to play music and sound from multiple devices and doesn't take up space on devices with limited storage space (i.e. some mobile phones, tablets or ageing computers), it also leaves no – or at least no easy way to access and copy – trace of the audio in question. Despite all the outcry around digital rights management through most of the 2000s, and how the technology prevented users from sharing files with other devices and users, making multiple copies of songs or editing files, streaming is celebrated even though it upholds these same restrictions. Although most of the songs in Spotify's library come from other sources (i.e. Spotify's version is rarely the only copy), audio on sites like SoundCloud and other music communities are increasingly born-digital and exclusively digital. As streaming becomes a dominant mode of delivery for all kinds of web-based media, these natively digital goods may be less copy-able and save-able than their predecessors. Much of what remains from the early days of the IUMA or mp3.com remains because users downloaded and saved those sounds. Today's streaming sites rely less on providing users their own copy of sounds, than on providing access to a vast catalogu of sounds in exchange for a subscription fee or for advertisements. Increasingly, our web-based technologies are prizing the mobile and the ubiquitous, the dynamic over the static, causing difficulties for those trying to write the histories of sound on the Web or anyone interested in listening to the past.

We know from the histories of other media, like television, film or radio, that the early years of a developing medium are invaluable for researching intersections of technology, industry, culture and power. We also know that these early years are some of the hardest to preserve, not just because of the logistics of preserving, but often because we seem to realize too late that the latest technology is neither mundane nor permanent. Huge percentages of early silent film, television and radio have been lost, destroyed or are otherwise inaccessible.[4] Given how ubiquitous and available digital sound files are, one might assume these web artifacts would not face the same preservation risks as, say, old radio tape reels, transcription discs or celluloid film stock. But similar preservation challenges face new and old media alike. For instance, there's no general exemption in current US copyright law for the copies that libraries and preservationists might want to make in order to keep digital formats up to date and properly preserved – updating from, say, wma files to something more current – leaving merely a complex and shifting patchwork of policies regulating digital preservation.

Ultimately, it's not just a question of what the Internet Archive or the Library of Congress has (or doesn't) or what other archives might or might not. Rather, it's about whether we should be trying to save sounds of the early Web, or saving its soundscapes. Schafer's (1977) original conception of the soundscape is primarily a sonic one, but the link to landscapes emphasizes how sound is shaped by the structures, bodies and objects that make up any given scene. On the Web, it's often not enough to save the sound of a particular song, technology or web object; the contextual material that helps create that sound must be preserved as well. Preserving the soundscape means preserving much more than just the sounds; it requires a multi-sensorial effort to document the Web in all its multimediated complexity. If 'digital sources necessitate a rethinking of the historian's toolkit' (Milligan, 2012: 23), they also require rethinking how the very practices of archiving and historiography take place.

## CONCLUSION

As I was finishing this article, there was a flurry of articles about the death of the mp3 (e.g. Beadon, 2017; Flanagan, 2017). The articles were in response to an announcement from the organization that created the mp3, the Fraunhofer Institute, noting that the licensing program for some mp3 patents and software was ending. Of course, as critics were quick to point out, this didn't mean that the worldwide stashes and stores of mp3s would suddenly vanish. Rather, it recognized the more dull and pragmatic fact that Fraunhofer could no longer collect licenses on technology like media players, audio editors, etc. since its patents were expiring. Instead, Fraunhofer was shifting its efforts to more profitable formats, like Advanced Audio Coding (AAC) or other efficient compression codecs that are used by many of the current streaming services.

Media historians are trained to recognize that the death of formats or media is rarely as final or certain as the label 'death' implies. Media and their formats persist over time and interact with the media formats that come after it (Bolter and Grusin, 1999; Gitelman, 2006). Our music libraries didn't simply shed the vinyl or cassettes or CDs once digital files came along; they likely remained in some liminal state made up of multiple formats from multiple eras, each taking up varying amounts of physical and emotional real estate in our collections. But Fraunhofer's announcement does signal that the download model that has driven much of the innovation in web music since the mid 1990s is giving way to streaming, and that the mp3, long the favored format of file sharers and legal downloaders alike, will have less institutional and industrial support moving forward. Obsolescence is rarely a moment; it's a process (Parks, 2007; Sterne, 2007). Like modem sounds and AOL start-up discs, the mp3 will persist and be put to novel uses even as it becomes less ubiquitous, common and used than it has been in the past.

All history is marked by its absences. As Sterne notes, the very endeavor of doing media historiography would not be possible without absence: 'It is the absence of the past, the impossibility of finding direct access to it, that makes possible the writing, reading, and contemplation of history. History's condition of impossibility – the irreducible distance of finitude – is thus its condition of possibility' (Sterne, 2010: 80). We can recover sounds from the Web's past but even the most complete archive (like a download of all the IUMA files) is still merely an archive of fragments and gaps. They are, as Sterne argues, 'already not the history they described' and therefore it is up to historians to 'find linkages across documents, registers, genres, and problems to give history meaning and intelligibility for ourselves and our readers' (Sterne, 2010: 86).

The sounds of the Web, from MIDI to streaming, are an integral part of its history; a part of its history that is often ignored through tools like the Internet Archive's Wayback Machine. They are often the absence in highly visual representations of the Web's past. These sounds are not only nostalgic reminders of technologies and experiences past; they contain important clues as to how machines were used, how particular websites or technologies worked, and what experiences early web users might have had. Sound researchers can always cobble together an archive through unofficial or accidental archives like YouTube or through more institutional efforts, but only by repacking our toolkit so that it also includes a focus on web sounds can we better preserve those sounds moving forward. What today's podcasters, web musicians, computer sound engineers, etc. are producing today will have value in the future, if not for its content, but for what it tells us about audio's longer history, about who has the right to communicate and by what means. If we're not making efforts to preserve these sounds now, we'll likely find ourselves in the same sonic conundrum many radio historians now find themselves in: writing, researching and thinking about a past they can't fully hear.

## Notes

1 'The strictest definition of chiptune refers to a song composed exclusively for performance by a microchip capable of synthesizing sound' but the chiptune culture that emerged from the Sound Interface Device era in the 1980s, the tracking scene, and the Gameboy musicians in the 1990s took 'the term and aesthetics far beyond that simple definition' (Driscoll and Diaz, 2009).
2 Apparently, there's evidence of the sale of marijuana between university students via ARPAnet in the early 1970s (Markoff, 2006) and, certainly, videotex services like Minitel and CompuServe in the 1980s offered a number of e-commerce options (Carey and Elton, 2009).
3 The Museum is supposedly the project of ubernerd and sound archivist Brendan Chilcutt, but in a story line built for Internet historians, Chilcutt is actually a fictional creation of three former advertising students at Virginia Commonwealth University (Pardes, 2016). The trio created Chilcutt as a spoof, but the sounds they preserved have driven serious interest and attention to the site.
4 With many thanks to Eric Hoyt for helping me formulate these ideas on preservation more clearly and effectively.

## REFERENCES


Abbate, J. (1999) *Inventing the Internet.* Cambridge, Mass: MIT Press.

Alderman, J. (2001) *Sonic Boom: Napster, MP3, and the New Pioneers of Music.* Cambridge, Mass: Perseus Pub.

Amorim, R. (2007) 'XingSound MP2 Player' [Online]. *Really Rare Wares.* Available: http://web.archive.org/web/20070214091726/http://www.rjamorim.com/rrw/xingsound.html [Accessed 8 December 2007].

Beadon, L. (2017) 'The MP3 Is Dead, Long Live the MP3' [Online]. *Hypebot.* Available: http://www.hypebot.com/hypebot/2017/05/the-mp3-as-dead-as-pepe-the-frog.html [Accessed 18 May 2017].

Blattberg, E. (2014) 'The Podcast Enters a New Golden Age'. [Webpage]. *Digiday* Nielsen. Available: http://digiday.com/publishers/nielsenes-rise-podcast/ [Accessed 12 February 2016].

Bolter, J. D. & Grusin, R. A. (1999) *Remediation: Understanding New Media.* Cambridge, Mass: MIT Press.

Bottomley, A. (2016) *Internet Radio: A History of a Medium in Transition.* PhD Dissertation, University of Wisconsin-Madison, Department of Communication Arts.

Brügger, N. (2009) 'Website History and the Website as an Object of Study'. *New Media & Society,* 11(1&2): 115–32.

Burkart, P. & McCourt, T. (2006) *Digital Music Wars: Ownership and Control of the Celestial Jukebox.* Lanham, Maryland: Rowman & Littlefield Publishers.

Carey, J. & Elton, M. C. J. (2009) 'The Other Path to the Web: The Forgotten Role of Videotex and Other Early Online Services'. *New Media & Society,* 11(1–2): 241–60.

Driscoll, K. (2016) 'Social media's dial-up roots'. *IEEE Spectrum,* 53(11): 54–60.

Driscoll, K. & Diaz, J. (2009) 'Endless Loop: A Brief History of Chip Tunes', *Transformative Works and Culture,* 2(1). Available: http://journal.transformativeworks.org/index.php/twc/article/view/96/94 [Accessed 21 June 2017].

Flanagan, A. (2017) 'The MP3 Is Officially Dead, According To Its Creators' [Online]. *NPR.* Available: http://www.npr.org/sections/therecord/2017/05/11/527829909/the-mp3-is-officially-dead-according-to-its-creators [Accessed 13 May 2017].

Friedman, T. (2005) *Electric Dreams: Computers in American Culture.* New York, NY: New York University Press.

Gillespie, T. (2007) *Wired Shut: Copyright and the Shape of Digital Culture.* Cambridge, Mass: MIT Press.

Gitelman, L. (2006) *Always Already New: Media, History And The Data Of Culture.* Cambridge, Mass: MIT Press.

Gruberman, K. & McQuillin, K. (1991) 'Multimedia and Audio'. *MacUser.* Ziff-Davis.

Grunin, L. (1991) 'Utility Coaxes Cd-Audio Out Of Your Rom Drive'. *PC Magazine.* Ziff Davis.

Hammersley, B. (2004) 'Audible Revolution'. *The Guardian*, February 12.

Haring, B. (2000) *Beyond the Charts: MP3 and the Digital Music Revolution.* Los Angeles, Calif.: JM Norther Media LLC.

Hauben, M. & Hauben, R. (1997) *Netizens: On the History and Impact of Usenet and the Internet.* Los Alamitos, Calif.: IEEE Computer Society Press.

IFPI (2017) IFPI Global Music Report 2017. London: International Federation of the Phonographic Industry.

Katz, M. (2004) *Capturing Sound: How Technology Has Changed Music.* Berkeley, Calif.: University of California Press.

Kirschenbaum, M. G. (2016) *Track Changes: A Literary History of Word Processing.* Cambridge, Mass: The Belknap Press of Harvard University Press.

Madrigal, A. C. (2012) The Mechanics and Meaning of That Ol' Dial-Up Modem Sound. *The Atlantic* [Online]. Available: https://www.theatlantic.com/technology/archive/2012/06/the-mechanics-and-meaning-of-that-ol-dial-up-modem-sound/257816/ [Accessed 22 September 2017].

Mann, Hugh. (1998) 'The Internet from Payphones' [Online]. Web Page. Available: http://www.wrybread.com/WryRoad/gadgets/coupler.htm. [Accessed 16 February 2017]

Manning, Peter. (2004) *Electronic and Computer Music.* Oxford; New York: Oxford University Press.

Markoff, J. (2006) *What the Dormouse Said: How the Sixties Counterculture Shaped the Personal Computer Industry.* New York, NY: Penguin Books.

Milligan, I. (2012) 'Mining the "Internet Graveyard": Rethinking the Historians' Toolkit'. *Journal of the Canadian Historical Association,* 23(2): 21–64.

Morris, J. W. (2015) *Selling Digital Music, Formatting Culture.* Berkeley, Calif.: University of California Press.

*Museum of Endangered Sounds* [Online]. Available: http://savethesounds.info [Accessed 20 January 2017].

Ness, L. (1993) 'Xing Technology Ships XingSound MPEG Audio Compression Software' [Online]. *Business Wire* 12 October.

Pardes, A. (2016) 'Where the Sounds of Your Childhood Go to Rest' [Online]. *Medium – Mel Magazine*. Available: https://melmagazine.com/where-the-sounds-of-your-childhood-go-to-rest-28e0812bbe52 [Accessed 15 May 2017].

Parks, L. (2007) 'Falling Apart: Electronics Salvaging and the Global Media Economy'. *In:* Acland, C. R. (ed.) *Residual Media.* Minneapolis, Minn: University of Minnesota Press: 32–47.

Petzold, C. (1991) 'Putting Sound on PCs: An Introduction to Waveform Audio'. *PC Magazine.* Ziff Davis.

PEW. (2013) '3% of Americans Use Dial-Up at Home' [Online]. *PEW Research Center*. Available: http://www.pewresearch.org/fact-tank/2013/08/21/3-of-americans-use-dial-up-at-home/ [Accessed 15 May 2017].

Roose, K. (2014) 'What's Behind the Great Podcast Renaissance?' *New York Magazine*, 30 October.

Rothenberg, R. (1999). 'Rob Glaser, Moving Target'. *Wired,* 7(8): 126–33.

Schafer, R. M. (1977) *The Tuning of the World.* New York, NY: Knopf.

Scott, J. (Director) (2005) *BBS: The Documentary.*

Sittenfeld, C. (1998) 'He's the Voice of the Net Generation' [Online]. *Fast Company.* Available: https://www.fastcompany.com/35450/hes-voice-net-generation%7D [Accessed 20 January 2017].

Sterne, J. (2007) 'Out With The Trash: On the Future of New Media'. *In:* Acland, C. R. (ed.) *Residual Media.* Minneapolis, Minn: University of Minnesota Press: 16–31.

Sterne, J. (2010) 'Rearranging the Files: On Interpretation in Media History'. *The Communication Review,* 13(1): 75–87.

Sterne, J. (2012) *MP3: The Meaning of a Format.* Durham, NC: Duke University Press.

Sterne, J., Morris, J. W., Baker, M. & Moscote Freire, A. (2008) 'The Politics of Podcasting'. *Fibreculture,* (13). Available: http://thirteen.fibreculturejournal.org/fcj-087-the-politics-of-podcasting/ [Accessed 13 December 2008].

Suhr, C. (2012) *Social Media and Music: The Digital Field of Cultural Production,* New York, NY: Peter Lang.

Théberge, P. (1997) *Any Sound You Can Imagine: Making Music/Consuming Technology.* Hanover, Conn: Wesleyan University Press.

Turner, F. (2005) 'Where the Counterculture Met the New Economy: The Well and the Origins of Virtual Community'. *Technology and Culture,* 46: 485–512.

Venkatesh, A. (1996) 'Computers and Other Interactive Technologies for the Home'. *Communications of the ACM,* 39(12): 47–54.

Venkatesh, A. & Vitalari, N. (1987) 'A Post-Adoption Analysis of Computing in the Home'. *Journal of Economic Psychology,* 8: 161–80.

W3C. (2000a) 'Information by Subject' [Online]. *World Wide Web Consortium*. Available: https://www.w3.org/History/19921103-hypertext/hypertext/DataSources/bySubject/Overview.html [Accessed 20 January 2017].

W3C. (2000b) 'A Little History of the World Wide Web' [Online]. *World Wide Web Consortium*. Available: https://www.w3.org/History.html [Accessed 20 January 2017].

willterminus. (2008, 9 November). 'The Sound of Dial-Up Internet'. *YouTube*. Available: https://www.youtube.com/watch?v=gsNaR6FRuO0 [Accessed 9 January 2018].

# 34

# Memes

Jim McGrath

## INTRODUCTION

In digital contexts, the word *meme* has been used to describe a wide range of media: text, photographs, video clips, audio files, image macros, GIFs. Broadly speaking, a digital object is often labeled an 'internet meme' once it begins to spread (often quickly, or 'virally', to embrace a popular metaphor) across various social media networks and digital publication platforms, especially when the object is seen moving far beyond the network of the individual who first circulated it. In recent years it has become more conventional to see 'internet memes' more generally referred to as 'memes' in informal discussions, media commentary, and academic scholarship. The erasure of 'internet' in these contexts suggests that the term may feel redundant or unnecessary; it seems taken for granted that discussions of memes inevitably refer to 'the internet'. Echoing scholars of web history who ask us to consider the political dimensions of where, how, and why the internet is described and defined (Abbate, 2017), this chapter is interested in where, how, and why the metaphor of the meme is used to describe particular modes of expression in digital contexts with a specific focus on the web.

Memes (as they were explicitly called by certain users) began circulating on the newsgroups of Usenet in the early 1990s. The meme metaphor continued to be invoked in the 2000s, mainly to describe popular jokes and references circulated by commenters on forums like *Something Awful* and blogs like *Metafilter*. But memes were a concept that didn't often travel far beyond these smaller communities and coteries. The first English-language Wikipedia article for the term 'internet meme' was created in March 2005; until December 2006 the page was simply a stub that redirected readers to the article for 'internet phenomena' (CesarB, 2005). The words 'meme' and 'internet meme' are absent from *Time* magazine's 2006 'Person of the Year' cover story on 'Web 2.0' and its users (Grossman, 2006). Their ubiquity on (and beyond) the web in the second decade of the twenty-first century is a fairly recent development.

The absence of memes from these texts and contexts is a useful reminder of how rapidly the web has changed over a short period of time. Whereas in the mid 1990s we saw a 'desire among users to situate themselves on the web' via creating personal web sites on GeoCities and elsewhere (Milligan, 2017: 138), many twenty-first-century users instead gravitate towards the networks and interfaces of social media networks. Ian Milligan highlights the 'geographical community metaphor' governing GeoCities and similar uses of spatial language to describe and 'map' the terrain of the web during this period (2017: 138). While online community formation remains a key interest of many web users, these particular manifestations of spatial and geographic resonances are arguably muted in the constructions of later communities through social media, communities tied to particular mobile apps, and other kinds of group and identity formations on the twenty-first-century web. Memes have been read as essential components in these more recent efforts of community formation, in that their arguments, materials, and uses have been shown to construct, critique, and reimagine ideas of normative and subversive online behavior (Gal et al., 2016).

Memes are seemingly everywhere: they have come to dominate the online discourse of social media networks, they receive extensive press coverage on news and entertainment web sites and blogs, they have been appropriated by advertising and marketing firms across the globe, they are the subjects of serious critical inquiry by scholars and archivists, and they have even warranted direct commentary (and even re-use) by politicians and heads of state. Generally speaking, memes seem to have particularly flourished during what Niels Brügger calls the 'third wave' in the development of 'the nexus between the Web, social media, and mobile media', a period 'characterized by the emergence of new social media that are born on and with mobile media, and that are app-based only, most notably Instagram, but also Snapchat and Tinder' (2016: 1064). Memes are arguably the digital objects we most frequently associate with online behavior during this particular period. How did we come to inhabit what Ryan Milner (2016) calls 'the world made meme?'.

To answer this question, this chapter will consider the long history of memes, focusing particularly on the earliest forms of memes to circulate on the web. It argues that an understanding of the aesthetics, uses, and reception of memes in the twenty-first century benefits from examining the earliest examples of memes. But it also suggests that highlighting these dimensions of earlier memes might also improve our understanding of web history, by highlighting both recurring traits in online behavior as well as changes in behavior that reflect the transformation of how we access, inhabit, and imagine the web in our contemporary moment. At our current moment in the twenty-first century, we see memes that frequently travel back and forth with relative ease between and across the web, social media, and mobile media. A closer look at what memes are being created and circulated and where they travel can teach us much about the ways the web is utilized, populated, and imagined by particular individuals at specific historical and cultural moments in time.

In other words, while memes might often be described as freely or 'virally' circulating rapidly across and beyond the web, we might also see in them traces of constraints, conventions, and communities from the web's past. Some of these traces materialize in the form of particular points of reference from these earlier moments: images and texts popular among smaller online communities that are now familiar to much larger audiences. For example, 'Godwin's Law', a meme created in 1991 by Usenet user Mike Godwin, continues to circulate on news web sites, tweets, and Facebook comments in the twenty-first century. Why does 'Godwin's Law' continue to resonate on the web for particular users? Does the meme have value for particular demographics of users, and do these demographics change over time? When considering why particular memes hold the attention of various web users at various points in time, we would do well to remember who does and does not have access to particular technologies, cultural references, and other dimensions and conventions of online discourse. How do the earlier communities of Usenet compare to the communities of users sharing ideas across the web, social media, and mobile apps in later contexts?

Looking at earlier memes can also highlight the ways that the material dimensions of knowledge production have changed over the history of the web. 'Godwin's Law', which we will discuss in greater detail later, is a meme created in static text and then distributed through the particular network of Usenet. The material and networked dimensions of Godwin's Law are visible in its successful reception beyond Usenet on the web at large and in other contexts like print: this particular meme can be physically replicated and remediated with relative ease. Other meme formats, like GIFs, image macros, or short videos circulated on the social media app Vine, become popular among certain users in part because of limitations in technology: these formats came to be preferred by users because they were easy to create and circulate on the parts of the web and social media that they inhabited at various points in time. And we also see memes shaping the material affordances of particular online spaces when they travel across networks: for example, in recent years Twitter, Facebook, and other social media networks have made it easier for users to share, upload, and display memes in GIF and video formats to meet demands among users related to memes.

This chapter brings recent examples of internet memes on Twitter and Facebook into conversation with earlier investments in the meme metaphor in digital contexts like Usenet and internet message boards. It draws parallels and identifies points of comparison between early ideas and uses of memes and more recent iterations, but it also calls attention to the differences in the particular material and historical conditions, rhetorical strategies, and social uses of these particular networks and the different kinds of memes created and circulated there. The history of memes is a history of technology, in the sense that the creation and dissemination of memes over the last three decades is greatly informed by the digital tools, sites of publication, and devices enabling users to read, create, share, and remix these materials. The speed at which devices, editing software, and publication platforms have become more readily available and less expensive has resulted in a significant increase in producers and consumers of internet memes. A decelerated, deliberately detail-oriented approach to the reading and curation of memes might help present and future web historians attend to what is getting lost in these rapid exchanges of cultural information.

## WHAT IS A MEME?

In *The Selfish Gene*, Richard Dawkins searched for a more precise way to meet 'the formidable challenge of explaining culture, cultural evolution, and the immense differences between human cultures around the world' (1989: 191). Analogies 'between cultural and genetic evolution' favored by other scientists and sociologists seemed, to Dawkins, to rely too much on an interpretation of Darwin that went 'looking for "biological advantages"' in their justifications of the longevity of certain cultural practices (1976: 191). Dawkins believed that replication and imitation in cultural behavior (like the frequency of the belief in the existence of God) was not necessarily due to 'genetic advantages' in the brains capable of creating and subscribing to those ideas (1976: 191). He searched for 'a name for the new replicator, a new noun that conveys the idea of a unit of cultural transmission, or a unit of imitation', a term that might rhyme with 'gene' to playfully acknowledge the influence of Darwinian thinking but might also afford a kind of critical inquiry that is not dominated by its reasoning (1976: 192). He settled on 'meme'.

With the idea of the 'meme' as a framing device, Dawkins invites us to use it to think about the shared traits in disparate things like 'tunes, ideas, catch-phrases, clothes fashions, ways of making pots or of building arches' (1976: 192). Dawkins unites these texts, objects, and referents under the rhetorical framework of the meme by noting the ways they are all continuously 'leaping from brain to brain via a process which, in the broad sense, can be called imitation' (1976: 192). He classifies memes as possessing three qualities: 'longevity, fecundity, and copying-fidelity' (1976: 194). While he provides this list of traits to his readers, Dawkins sees them more as a 'speculative' framework than a set of descriptive mandates (1976: 199). He is reluctant to explicitly designate 'what a single unit-meme' is (or is not): an entire song, a lyric, a brief section of music, a particular performance. He is more interested in the circumstances that lead a particular meme to 'dominate the attention of a human brain' (1976: 197). Milner argues that 'it may be better to diminish the connections between Dawkins' argument and participatory media', given the differences between the idea of the meme outlined in *The Selfish Gene* and the connotations this descriptive lens has generated in digital contexts (2016: Loc. 3968). On the other hand, Dawkins himself has noted that the meaning of the word 'meme' in the particular context of the internet 'is not that far away from the original' (Solon, 2013). In fact, Dawkins seems to have embraced these connotations: for example, he performed in a 'theatrical piece' about memes organized by the ad agency Saatchi and Saatchi at the 2013 Cannes Advertising Festival (Solon, 2013).

Most book-length projects with 'meme' in the title have focused on memetics in a general sense and are primarily intended for STEM audiences, though this research has at times considered and intersected with the more particular topic of internet memes as well as academic investments in humanistic research. For example, Susan Blackmore's *The Meme Machine* has a chapter titled 'Into the Internet', in which she considers the impact of new forms of 'replication machinery' within the larger narrative of 'the evolution of meme replication' (1999: 205). In the same way that 'memes took a great step forward when they got into books' with the advent of the printing press, the internet and its comparatively inexpensive publishing mechanisms are situated as key factors in enabling more forms and modes of reception, duplication, and distribution of memes (1999: 209–10). On the other hand, Blackmore seems more interested in 'traditional' forms of replication that aspire to exact or precise copies in digital publication and communication platforms. For example, she describes the benefits of 'bots' designed with artificial intelligence as 'small and simple units that together do clever things' (1999: 217). These programs might be designed to resemble 'insects laying chemical trails' and put to work on 'error-correction tasks or censorship duties' (1999: 217). Replicating mechanisms are becoming more prevalent in online discourse. For example, we have seen YouTube, Facebook, and other sites automate processes to regulate the circulation of content in ways that address concerns about copyright protection, and we find traces of bots dedicated to mundane formatting tasks in Wikipedia's edit histories. But generally speaking, bots are frequently viewed as distinct from 'memes' in terms of their perception and social uses.

## GODWIN'S LAW

Despite the productivity of researchers in the emerging field of memetics, one of the most memorable experiments in 'memetic engineering' did not take place in a university lab or require research funding (Godwin, 1994). In the early 1990s, lawyer Mike Godwin was a frequent contributor to Usenet, an online hub of various 'newsgroups' dedicated to text-centric discussions about a host of topics. Godwin had grown tired of the prevalence of what he called the 'Nazi-comparison meme', a rhetorical move that Godwin believed 'trivialized the horror of the Holocaust and the social pathology of the Nazis' in its frequent invocation on various newsgroups (1994). He channels these frustrations into the creation of 'Godwin's Law', a 'counter-meme' situated as a call to arms, a critique that its author hopes will compel 'net.dwellers [sic] to make a conscious effort to control the kinds of memes they create or circulate' (1994).

In an earlier version of the law posted to the rec.arts.sf-lovers newsgroup on August 18, 1991, 'Godwin's Rule of Nazi Analogies' states that 'As a Usenet discussion grows longer, the probability of a comparison involving Hitler or Nazis approaches one' (Godwin, 1991). The rule became a 'law' due to the frequency with which the Usenet community seemed to inevitably replicate this behavior, whether it was in a discussion of the allegedly homophobic views of science fiction author Orson Scott Card (as it was in this instance) or in a 1999 thread about the benefits of bicycling in pdx.general, a Portland (Oregon) newsgroup, to take one example at random from the Usenet archives. Beyond his sense that these comparisons to Hitler or the Nazis do a disservice to the historical specificity of these atrocities when they are invoked to discuss comparatively mundane subjects, Godwin desires a level of intellectual and rhetorical rigor that meets his image of a 'Net' that is 'filled with diverse critical thinkers' (1994).

Godwin explicitly situates his law within the context of memetics in a 1994 essay published in *Wired* magazine. He embraces the 'viral' resonances of the metaphor: while he commends a meme's ability to 'crystallize whole schools of thought' and create a shared vocabulary and shorthand for conversation, Godwin is more immediately concerned with the limits of consensus-oriented online discourse. '[V]iral memes are capable of doing lasting damage', he warns, and he wonders if there is a 'moral imperative' or 'obligation to improve our information environment' that might drive the creation and circulation of additional 'counter-memes' on the web (1994). Godwin suggests that memes might also be sites of critique and resistance, spaces where both familiar topics and the conventions of discourse might be subverted or productively critiqued.

Originality often has less to do with a meme's successful replication than its authors or inventors would like us to believe. In fact, several factors likely contributed to the popularity of Godwin's Law on Usenet and beyond this original site of publication. The frequency of the Nazi comparison had been flagged by other users before Godwin: a list of 'FAQs' (Frequently Asked Questions) about Godwin's Law highlights a comment by Richard Sexton on October 16th, 1989, noting that 'You can tell when a USENET discussion is getting old when one of the partcipents [sic] drags out Hitler and the Nazis' (Skirwin, 1999). Godwin's framing calls attention to itself, is part playful and part challenge, inviting readers to test its veracity, whereas Sexton's (misspelled) remark is delivered in an offhand manner and quickly forgotten. Many successful memes adopt rhetorical strategies that have proven successful in other digital and non-digital contexts: for example, the framing of Godwin's Law might be productively compared to philosophical or legal language as well as the branding strategies of advertisers. And, like a successful advertising campaign, 'Godwin's Law' likely spreads in part because its author is both committed to circulating its message across various Usenet newsgroups and in possession of the time, technology, and additional resources needed to maintain a presence on this digital communication network.

In Godwin's recollection of the rise of 'Godwin's Law', he notes that he 'seeded' his observation 'in any newsgroup or topic where I saw a gratuitous Nazi reference' and then quickly found that other people picked up on it, even occasionally forming 'corollaries' about Nazi-related discussions or trends (1994). In his version of the story, Godwin invents the meme, introduces it to particular discussion threads, it is accepted and embraced by other users, and it is quickly adopted and redistributed. Godwin narrates a story about control and invention: he is the conductor of an experiment, the originator of an idea, the designer and orchestrator of a rhetorical campaign. His history is one that places his own authority and agency at the center, a retelling of events that renders the success of his meme predictable, a logical outcome that confirms his perceptive interpretation of the ways information circulates on Usenet. While he seemed to accept that its spread was 'far beyond my control', Godwin does seem to enjoy the ability to dictate the terms of the meme's narrative in the pages of *Wired* and elsewhere (2008).

Based on the attention it received beyond Usenet in North American news media, Godwin's Law is a useful context for understanding how the language of memetics became prevalent in descriptions of modes of digital behavior. That being said, there are other ways to begin a 'pre-history' of memes. For example, Patrick Davison suggests that the introduction of the emoticon marker ':-)' to Carnegie Mellon's bulletin boards in 1982 might be a generative point of origin for the history of memes, given their popularity on social media networks and in text messaging (2012: 124). 'Emoticons are a meme', Davison argues, and they are a particularly popular and malleable kind of meme (2012: 124). Read through the lens of memetics, and the early emoticon certainly seems like a meme, given the frequency with which it can be (and still is) quickly composed and replicated on various devices. Davison notes how this particular method of 'contextualizing one's written messages with an emoticon to indicate emotional intent' has become a staple of online communication, most visibly in the ubiquity of emojis and emoji keyboards on mobile devices (2012: 124). The uses and forms of emoticons have changed with the introduction of newer digital publication platforms and networks, and other digital material has served to accentuate the emotional or rhetorical weight of digital content.

Since 'Godwin's Law', we have seen similar claims that attempt to combat and critique conventions of online behavior by calling them out as clichéd, illogical, or otherwise unwanted. The idea of 'jumping the shark' – the moment when a once-popular serialized work (generally fiction) takes a turn that vocal parts of its audience find absurd or illogical – originated in a University of Michigan dorm room conversation about of Arthur Fonzarelli's waterskiing mishaps in an episode of *Happy Days* (Fox Jr., 2010); it spread beyond these walls in 1997 when Jon Hein, one of the undergrads participating in this conversation, created *jumptheshark.com*, a popular web site dedicated to documenting these moments in the history of television (Fox Jr., 2010). Similarly, 'The Bechdel Test', a checklist of film tropes designed to expose how frequently their stories of women in films were dominated by the male figures in their lives, began as a conversation between two characters in a 1985 installment of Allison Bechdel's *Dykes To Watch Out For* comic serial; it eventually found a wider audience when 'lefty blogs' began referencing it, leading to its reappearance and redistribution in digital form via a scan posted to the artist's blog (Bechdel and Cathy, 2005). Bechdel and Hein do not call their observations 'memes', but they resonate in many ways with Godwin's sense of the 'counter-meme' (and have been classified as memes by the popular *Know Your Meme* web site). These phrases and their contexts quickly spread and reappear across blogs and message boards, in print publications, on television programs dedicated to popular culture, in offline conversation.

Early internet memes like Godwin's Law, the Bechdel Test, and 'jumping the shark' are all text-based, enabling them to easily and quickly circulate across various discussion boards and web sites. Text-centric memes circulate on social media networks and are sometimes transformed by the technical affordances available there: Instagram and Twitter users may turn static memes into hyperlinked hashtags, for instance.

Some scholars have noted the ways in which memes seem to function as 'signatures of topics and events [that] propagate and diffuse over the web' (Leskovec et al., 2009). Memes like 'jumping the shark' quickly became 'networked' in digital contexts, in that they could be hyperlinked in certain sites of publication to sites providing additional context, or users could often run searches to find additional use-cases. But the ubiquity of hashtags on platforms like Twitter makes the networked dimensions and the potential for replication more visible and explicit, and the aesthetic dimensions of digital interfaces inviting users to create, recirculate, or click on these networked memes has certainly shaped their reception and popularity.

## DANCING BABIES

In 1996, LucasArts employee Ron Lussier was able to 'fix up' a 3D animation of a dancing baby found on Character Studio, a digital animation tool (Lussier, n.d.). After showing his results to some co-workers, Lussier got some requests to email the 'Dancing Baby' file, and he soon found that 'people…had received it back again from people outside the company, across the country' (Lussier, n.d.). The animation originally circulated without a soundtrack, though a version in which the baby appears to be dancing to the song 'Hooked on a Feeling' as performed by the band Blue Suede in 1974 was arguably the most popular dancing baby of them all, serving as the inspiration for the 'Dancing Baby' that appeared as a hallucination in several episodes of the FOX sitcom *Ally McBeal* in 1998. Dancing babies would go on to appear in advertisements, as GIFs, and in other digital and commercial contexts, though Lussier was only directly involved in and compensated for a small number of these appearances.

The 'Dancing Baby' meme primarily circulated via email, and while it could be consumed, it was difficult to revise: alterations required a technical skill level and a familiarity with both digital animation and distribution that limited who could participate in the creation of meme variations. Lussier created a GIF from his 'original' dancing baby in 1996 to enable the smaller file to more widely and freely circulate via email and on web sites, but it would have been difficult for many internet users to remix even this file. Lussier clearly had conflicted feelings about the forms of distribution and uses of his 'Dancing Baby' files. A page concerning 'Copyright Info' on his company's web site notes that 'the original net-baby…has become a "loose property" (not a legal definition!!), by way of being many peoples [sic] work, and because it was a great promotional phenomenon' (Lussier, n.d.). Despite his own admitted unfamiliarity with legal terms and protections concerning copyright in digital contexts, Lussier warns against 'reformatting, cropping, using, or otherwise modifying someone else's work without written permission' and claims that his files can only be distributed 'for private use' (Lussier, n.d.). 'Only stills of the dancing baby may be displayed on a private, non-commercial web page', he cautions, and these snapshots must be republished alongside the web address of Lussier's company, Burning Pixel Productions (Lussier, n.d.). Newer incarnations and variations of the 'Dancing Baby' created by Lussier also feature large reproductions of his URL in their JPEG and GIF versions.

The solutions Lussier comes up with to address perceived failures to properly, ethically, or even legally compensate him for his work on the 'Dancing Baby' meme may seem inelegant or even incorrect to some contemporary readers, but they do suggest the ways in which claims for copyright or ownership of materials can impact the creation, distribution, and study of internet memes. For example, while Twitter's Terms of Service note that the social media network 'will respond to notices of alleged copyright infringement', it also notes, on a page concerning its interpretation of 'Fair Use' and similar global concepts governing 'uses of copyrighted material [that] may not require the copyright owner's permission', that 'there is no clear formula' to determining strict guidelines informed by this concept (2016). Other social media networks are more proactive in policing users who may willingly or unwittingly engage in copyright violation: for example, many users of Facebook's 'Facebook Live' video streaming tool have discovered that the network will disrupt or refuse to publicly archive material checked 'against files in [its] Rights Manager Reference library' (Brogan, 2016). While it is easy for many users to download, screenshot, edit, and re-upload memes to social media on mobile and desktop devices, networks that choose to enforce copyright through automated modes of surveillance or compliance checks in the name of intellectual property may limit the abilities of users to create memes or content that may one day be re-used or appropriated itself for the purposes of meme creation.

## ALL YOUR BASE ARE BELONG TO US

As it became comparatively easier to create, edit, and redistribute a wider range of media on web sites, beyond text, message boards, and forums, internet memes began to take on increasingly multimodal dimensions in the late 1990s. Message boards began to be areas online where contributors could embed or link to media files found elsewhere on the web, sometimes even images of their own invention. While Usenet survived as a communications platform into the early years of the twenty-first century, other digital hubs for conversation were emerging, creating their own communities, modes of online discourse, and, of course, memes. In the late 1990s and early 2000s, forums hosted on sites like *Fark* and *Something Awful* became hotbeds of activity where global networks of users would distribute and dissect various forms of popular culture, solicit and provide advice on personal matters, tell jokes, and seek out kindred spirits. While these digital spaces often looked 'unprofessional' and lo-fi compared with the sleeker output of commercial organizations, marketers, news media outlets, and scholars of popular culture paid attention to what was happening in spaces like *Something Awful* when they noticed the popularity of content created and made. It is for this reason that institutions like the US Library of Congress have taken an interest in archiving and curating the records of these conversations, which they view as forms of 'digital folklore' essential to collections that 'reflect contemporary traditional culture on the web and beyond' (Saylor, 2014). In many respects, the beginnings of the aesthetic and stylistic conventions and formalist dimensions of internet memes as they came to be known in the twenty-first century began in these discussion boards.

When the phrase 'All Your Base Are Belong To Us' began circulating in various online and offline contexts at the start of the twenty-first century, journalists quickly discovered that the origins of the phrase could be found within these newer iterations of internet message boards. As recounted by *Wired* reporter Jeffrey Benner, 'All Your Base Are Belong To Us' is a phrase from a 1992 English translation of a 'cut scene' describing the world of a mostly forgotten 1989 Toaplan video game named *Zero Wing* (2001). These cut scenes were extracted and compiled in an Adobe Flash animation file, which then began circulating on forums like *Metafilter, Something Awful*, and memepool, among many others (Benner, 2001). One popular video compilation anticipated the spread of 'All Your Base Are Belong To Us' beyond digital contexts, mixing the robotic voice from *Zero Wing* into club-ready techno mixes, photoshopping the text onto street signs, fortune cookies, comic strips, even the mugshot file photo of O.J. Simpson (Bad-CRC, 2008). Benner meets the popularity of the phrase's 'mutations and gossip' across internet chat rooms with some skepticism, but he also acknowledges that the meme has outperformed '[a]rmies of marketers toiling for years' and finds its success ultimately indicative of 'a medium that refuses to be tamed into predictability' (Benner, 2001).

## THE GROWING FIELD OF MEME STUDIES

In the years following the initial spread and popularity of 'All Your Base Are Belong To Us', memes appear to have become a familiar and recognizable medium to marketers and many other content creators on the web. Scholars interested in new media, sociology, internet culture, and other fields and research interests have begun to describe their now-predictable conventions, their common revisions, their reception histories, and their various capacities for redistribution. For example, MIT Press has published two book-length surveys of internet memes in recent years: Limor Shifman's *Memes in Digital Culture* (2012) and David Milner's *The World Made Meme: Public Conversations and Participatory Media* (2016). Bradley Wiggins and Bret Bowers also attempt a 'tenable genre development of Internet memes' (2015: 1903). These projects are perceptive surveys of patterns in meme creation, consumption, and distribution. In these studies, memes are frequently evaluated and even venerated for their role in forming communities and social bonds in digital spaces, and for their status as important artifacts in identity formation. For example, Shifman argues that memes are 'rooted in economic, social, and cultural logics of participation', forces that draw our attention 'not only on the texts' that comprise individual units of memes but also 'the cultural practices surrounding them' (2012: 33–4). Social networks may invite performances of 'accelerated individualism', but these performances '[demonstrate] an enduring human longing for communality' that pre-dates the web' (2012: 33). Shifman further argues that memes play a vital role in fostering more varied forms of community formation; to her, the most interesting memes reveal 'a new arena of bottom-up expression' on the web, a world wide web whose occupants 'can blend pop culture, politics, and participation in interesting ways' (2012: 4).

Milner similarly highlights the variety of ways memes are created and deployed to meet a wide range of 'communicative ends'; they can circulate in networks and contexts that can be 'vastly public, communally social, or intimately interpersonal' (2016: Loc. 510). For Milner, memes are the coin of the realm in popular spaces of 'participatory media' like social networks: these are digital environments where 'it's relatively cheap and easy to make a statement, remix a text, or spread an idea' (2016: Loc. 429). Milner argues that all memes are 'made by collective practices more substantial than any individual text', and his book applies a particular grammar and inventorying mechanism to memes in an attempt to draw connections between the range of motives, identities, and communities of 'cultural participants' involved in making memes, as well as the varied multimodal dimensions, methods of appropriation (and, as Milner puts it, 'reappropriation'), and distribution networks involved in their spread and reception (2016: Loc. 970).

Shifman and Milner invent terms and methods of classification that may prove useful to scholars interested in these forms of digital media. They are more critical lenses than comprehensive surveys of the field, invitations to apply observations about general methods of creation, reception, and distribution to specific memes and their attendant communities of reception and socio-historical contexts. Both surveys are geographically and temporally limited: Milner notes, for instance, his book 'is almost entirely situated in Western contexts, most specifically English-language contexts within the United States' (2016: Loc. 366). General surveys of internet memes also tend to be preoccupied with the material conditions and forms of memes that are popular in their historical moment of composition. Wiggins and Bowers remind us that 'memes are a *developing* genre of communication' (2015: 1892), but in doing so they also suggest that case studies of internet memes in their particular historical, cultural, and digital contexts might yield more compelling insights than attempts to unify and classify memes in such a generalized fashion.

The particular memes selected as examples or case studies by authors in scholarly editions or monographs are inevitably dated. Shifman's book begins with memes related to 'Gangnam Style', a 2012 song by Korean pop artist Psy with an accompanying music video that, at the time of Shifman's writing, 'was the first [YouTube video] to surpass the one-billion-view mark' (2012: 1). Milner starts his discussion with memes related to American hip-hop artist Kanye West's interruption of fellow celebrity musician Taylor Swift at MTV's 2009 Video Music Awards, a televised moment that led to 'a flurry of "Kanye Interrupts" remixes' across social media and entertainment news sites once it was re-broadcast and discussed by news, entertainment, and social media outlets (2016: Loc. 486). These memes both rely on content distributed by corporate-driven media channels (MTV and YouTube) and feature individuals familiar to consumers of traditional outlets of global news media. They are both memes that arguably oversaturated the press and social media outlets they circulated in: their impact was transformed by the speed with which they were championed and then discarded. Encyclopedic indexes and aggregators of memes (like *Know Your Meme* or *BuzzFeed*) that are primarily circulated as web sites can avoid being fixed in amber by publication deadlines and the material limitations of print media. On the other hand, these digital publications can still quickly become outdated themselves if they fail to secure audiences, contributors, web designers, and revenue streams, among other factors.

Some scholars have tended to disassociate internet memes from their particular temporal and material dimensions in favor of highlighting the 'spread' of the meme across time and space. Jenkins et al. eschew periodization in favor of a 'top down to bottom up' or 'grassroots to commercial' narrative of viral media like internet memes (2015: 1). 'If it doesn't spread, it's dead' is the shorthand Jenkins uses for determining 'value and meaning' in twenty-first-century digital contexts. Nooney and Portwood-Stacer argue that 'In meme culture, flow takes primacy over origin, as the creator of an object and even the conditions in which it was made often remain unknown to the legions of users who remix it and pass it on' (2014: 2). There are certainly instances where the 'flow' or 'spread' of an internet meme remediates it in surprising or troubling ways beyond its original context, and creators of memes (or the material appropriated for the creation of a meme) often lack a degree of agency or control over where and how their content is re-used. The materiality of memes varies greatly: memes can be snippets of text, multimodal works, photos, screenshots, digitally edited images, cartoons, found footage. And it is true that what we know about their authors and audiences can also vary greatly: some internet memes have citational information, while others circulate anonymously or travel across networks populated by pseudonyms, and some are even rendered unrecognizable by their original authors.

But origins and conditions in which internet memes are first created are not always so hidden or obscured, thanks to archivists and scholars invested in highlighting, collecting, and preserving these materials.

What are the ethical dimensions worth considering when individuals who are not public figures find themselves starring in memes? Moya Bailey has discussed the benefits and challenges of a methodology of 'collaborative consent' in surveys of digital culture, a perspective that allows subjects of analysis the right to refuse to be discussed or named in scholarship (2015). While these refusals may create gaps or silences in a scholar's discussion of social media activity, Bailey argues that 'citation itself may be the thing that creates the harm to the community' (2015). Debates surrounding the presence, absence, redaction, and remediation of citational data in memes are indicative of the particular challenges facing scholars interested in contemporary digital media. Milner claims that in his own survey of memes, 'finding their creator and site of origin is largely impossible, and arguably inconsequential when considering how they resonate' (2016: Loc. 531). While it is true that it is at times difficult to identify points of origin and creators of memes, knowledge of the original sites of publication and distribution of memes, even if some of that information is incomplete, can yield important insights about online discourse, its various communities and coteries, and where these groups overlap and intersect.

Additionally, the visibility and presence of a diverse and varied set of perspectives within the global web can be muted by generalized discussions of memes and their uses. For example, Laur M. Jackson observes that 'in the tenuous trade of meme profiteering, the actual authors remain largely absent from the monetary benefits of their own creations' (2016). She calls for a more careful and precise consideration of the ways 'memes in their emergence, development, transformation, and resurgence are imbued with a semantically Black mode of improvisation and revitalization' (2016). Contextual details about the political, racial, economic, and social dimensions of digital communication platforms offer important information about why and how particular memes are generated and distributed. Lisa Nakamura argues that 'media scholarship needs to explore the genealogy, distribution, aesthetics, and visual history of memetic culture, so much of which is racist, sexist, and comes to us from circuitous and pseudonymous paths' (2014: 260). Gabriella Coleman notes, for instance, that the aesthetic and performative dimensions of what she calls 'the lulz' are 'lighthearted jokes...enjoyed by many internet nerds around the world', but she also wants us to remember the 'cruel' and troll-like dimensions of this form of comedy in its point of origin on 4chan and other message boards (Coleman, 2015). These earlier contexts continue to haunt this mode of online expression as memes travel beyond these initial sites of publication.

Jackson, Nakamura, Coleman, and other scholars are arguing for more site-specific, user- and context-oriented approaches to the reading and making of memes. Recent developments suggest that the futures of memes and their analysis will frequently highlight the creators and users who star in and circulate them. For example, in July 2017, media attention focused on President Donald Trump's redistribution of a meme on his personal Twitter page that imagined him in a wrestling match with a CNN logo (Kaczynski, 2017). The attention paid to Trump's retweet, to the meme's initial popularity on Reddit, and to the Reddit user who first posted the meme (and the critiques of CNN's decision not to reveal the identity of the user to its reader) suggest that claims for the 'subtle poetic ambiguity' of memes (Goldsmith, 2011) can be productively challenged at times when additional context about particular meme creators, distributors, and networks reveals more explicit political and social dimensions informing their creation and reception.

## THE FUTURES OF MEMES

Scholars interested in the present state of memes can learn a lot from excavating the digital objects and networks of the recent past, as well as their attendant contextual and material dimensions. More recent developments impacting the creation and spread of memes include the rise of meme aggregators like Giphy, which make memes searchable and more easily transferable to social media networks (as well as professional spaces like Slack) but which also rely upon user-generated metadata and third-party support to index, preserve, and keep this content in circulation. The increasing reliance on mobile platforms and networks has resulted in new variations on memes that reflect the ease of smart phone screencapping: instead of image macros, many users have taken to remediating content from other platforms like text message conversations, Twitter exchanges, and Facebook comment threads. These new iterations of memes create new challenges for archivists, given that screenshots are frequently lower-quality versions of media that had already been compressed in the first place. Users distributing these memes beyond spaces that encourage the use of tags to improve visibility and accessibility frequently care little about citation or best practices for linking content to contextual information, and 'content farms' devoted to the economics of memes will frequently (and often willfully) obscure contextual details in their campaigns for attention.

This lack of context becomes more concerning if (or when) you wake up one morning and find that you or something you've created has become a meme. Some subjects of memes have leveraged their visibility into endorsement deals and other employment opportunities: for example, in 2015 Delta Airlines employed several 'stars' and visuals affiliated with then-popular internet memes in a safety video that aired as part of the boarding procedures used on its planes (Grayson, 2015). Others have taken steps to have images removed or digital distributors of memes legally punished: a 2015 *Washington Post* article called 'How Copyright is killing your favorite memes' directs readers to a page where the encyclopedic *Know Your Meme* site has recorded the various Digital Millennium Copyright Act notices it has received over the years (Dewey, 2015).

Jon Ronson's *So You've Been Publicly Shamed* profiles individuals who have lost jobs and relationships due to the negative attention they received from 'starring' in internet memes critical of their actions or language (2015). More recently, we have seen the 'Pepe The Frog' meme – centered on a cartoon frog who originally appeared in a series of print and digital comics in 2006 by Matt Furie – move from the alternative comics community to 4chan message boards to Tumblr to aggregated content on *BuzzFeed* to Donald Trump propaganda and anti-propaganda. An image once used in parodies of 'slacker' millennial behavior is now tied to images classified as hate speech by the Anti-Defamation League. While initially pleased with the spread of the image before its embrace by members of the 'alt-right' political spectrum in the United States, Furie has since responded to the controversy surrounding the lifespan of these memes in comics (featuring Pepe having nightmares about his transformation), in a #SavePepe hashtag campaign designed to reject these recent affiliations (Furie, 2016), and ultimately in the act of 'killing' his creation in a 2017 comic book (Fortin, 2017). 'I understand that it's out of my control', Furie notes in an editorial for *Time* magazine published after the Anti-Defamation League controversy, 'but in the end, Pepe is whatever you say he is, and he and I, the creator, say that he is *love*' (Furie, 2016). Despite this acknowledgment of a content creator's inevitable loss of control in digital spaces populated by millions of users with little regard for copyright law's dictates regarding re-use and redistribution, Furie's frustrations are clear in his repeated attempts to contextualize Pepe and regain some semblance of control.

Furie's stated wishes (and the national press attention they received) may influence some users of social media and internet meme creators to avoid uploading and remixing images of Pepe, but the announcement of a meme's 'death' is little more than ceremonial in this particular instance.

On Twitter, Facebook, Instagram, and other social media networks, we see meme producers and 'stars' enjoying the benefits of celebrity or the negative consequences of public shaming, we watch marketing firms mimic, purchase, or outright steal viral content and aesthetic conventions, and we see journalistic outlets and content farm publishers discover new ways to cover, curate, and monetize the attention paid to popular memes. But the economics of attention are complicated, and these networks are making decisions that may improve their bottom line while simultaneously alienating or disrupting creators of internet memes. For example, Brian Feldman has noted how Tumblr's status as a hub of 'internet culture' and the site of origin for numerous internet memes has not translated into a successful business model, and that Twitter 'still has trouble turning a profit' in 2017 (2017). These observations raise questions about the future of internet memes and whether that future will be encouraging or restrictive; for example, Feldman argues that recent innovations like Facebook and Instagram's 'algorithmic timelines' are 'terrible for internet culture' (2017). The instability of these networks suggests that archivists may need to act sooner rather than later to document and preserve internet memes and important contextual materials that might help future generations understand their popularity and perceived value to earlier generations of the web.

## REFERENCES


Abbate, J. (2017) 'What and Where is the Internet? (Re)defining Internet Histories', *Internet Histories*, 1(1–2): 8–14.

Bad-CRC. (2008) 'All Your Base Are Belong To Us (Original Version)', *YouTube* (https://youtu.be/8fvTxv46ano) Accessed August 1, 2018.

Bailey, M. (2015) '#transform(ing)DH Writing and Research: An Autoethnography of Digital Humanities and Feminist Ethics', *Digital Humanities Quarterly*, 9(2), (http://www.digitalhumanities.org/dhq/vol/9/2/000209/000209.html) Accessed August 1, 2017.

Bechdel, A. and Cathy. (2005) 'The Rule', *Alison Bechdel* (http://dykestowatchoutfor.com/the-rule) Accessed August 1, 2017.

Benner, J. (2001) 'When Gamer Humor Attacks', *WIRED* (https://www.wired.com/2001/02/when-gamer-humor-attacks/) Accessed August 1, 2017.

Blackmore, S. (1999) *The Meme Machine*. New York: Oxford University Press.

Brogan, J. (2016) 'Facebook Live's Biggest Problem Isn't Porn. It's Copyright', *Future Tense (Slate)* (http://www.slate.com/blogs/future_tense/2016/04/12/facebook_live_video_has_a_problem_with_copyright_not_porn_despite_rights.html) Accessed August 1, 2017.

Brügger, N. (2016) 'Introduction: The Web's First 25 Years', *New Media and Society*, 18(7): 1059–65.

Cesar B. (2005) 'Internet Meme', *Wikipedia* (https://en.wikipedia.org/w/index.php?title=Internet_meme&oldid=17287330) Accessed August 1, 2017.

Coleman, G. (2015) *Hacker, Hoaxer, Whistleblower, Spy: The Many Faces of Anonymous*. New York: Verso Books.

Davison, P. (2012) 'The Language of Internet Memes', in Michael Mandiberg (ed.), *The Social Media Reader*. New York: NYU Press. pp. 120–34.

Dawkins, R. (1989) *The Selfish Gene (new edition)*. New York: Oxford University Press.

Dewey, C. (2015) 'How Copyright Is Killing Your Favorite Memes', *The Washington Post* (https://www.washingtonpost.com/news/the-intersect/wp/2015/09/08/how-copyright-is-killing-your-favorite-memes/?utm_term=.684b32e941f3) Accessed August 1, 2017.

Feldman, B. (2017) 'Tumblr's Unclear Future Shows That There's No Money In Internet Culture', *Select All (New York Magazine)* (http://nymag.com/selectall/2017/06/theres-no-money-in-internet-culture.html) Accessed August 1, 2017.

Fortin, J. (2017) 'Pepe The Frog is Dead, Or So His Creator Hopes', *New York Times* (https://www.nytimes.com/2017/05/08/us/pepe-the-frog-comic.html) Accessed August 15, 2017.

Fox Jr., F. (2010) 'First Person: In Defense of *Happy Days'* "Jump the Shark" Episode', *Los Angeles Times* (http://articles.latimes.com/2010/sep/03/entertainment/la-et-jump-the-shark-20100903) Accessed August 1, 2017.

Furie, M. (2016) 'Pepe The Frog's Creator: I'm Reclaiming Him. He Was Never About Hate', *Time* (http://time.com/4530128/pepe-the-frog-creator-hate-symbol/) Accessed August 15, 2017.

Gal, N., Shifman, L., and Kampf, Z. (2016) '"It Gets Better": Internet Memes and the Construction of Collective Identity', *New Media and Society*, 18(8): 1698–714.

Godwin, M. (1991) 'Untitled', *Rec.arts.sf-lovers* (http://groups.google.com/groups?selm=1991Aug18.215029.19421%40eff.org) Accessed August 1, 2017.

Godwin, M. (1994) 'Meme, Counter-Meme', *WIRED* (https://www.wired.com/1994/10/godwin-if-2/) Accessed August 1, 2017.

Godwin, M. (2008) 'I Seem To Be A Verb: 18 Years of Godwin's Law', *Jewcy* (http://jewcy.com/jewish-arts-and-culture/i_seem_be_verb_18_years_godwins_law) Accessed August 1, 2017.

Goldsmith, K. (2011) 'The Meme Museum', *Harriet (The Poetry Foundation)* (https://www.poetryfoundation.org/harriet/2011/04/the-meme-museum) Accessed August 1, 2017.

Grayson, N. (2015) 'Delta Airlines' Meme Safety Video Is Garbage', *Kotaku* (https://kotaku.com/delta-airlines-meme-safety-video-is-garbage-1705916797) Accessed August 1, 2017.

Grossman, L. (2006) 'You – Yes, You – Are *Time's* Person Of The Year', *Time* (http://content.time.com/time/magazine/article/0,9171,1570810,00.html) Accessed August 1, 2017.

Jackson, L.M. (2016) 'The Blackness of Meme Movement', *Model View Culture* (https://modelviewculture.com/pieces/the-blackness-of-meme-movement) Accessed August 1, 2017.

Jenkins, H., Ford, S., and Green, J. (2016) *Spreadable Media: Creating Value and Meaning in a Networked Culture.* New York: NYU Books.

Kaczynski, A. (2017) 'How CNN found the Reddit user behind the Trump wrestling GIF', *CNN* (https://www.cnn.com/2017/07/04/politics/kfile-reddit-user-trump-tweet/index.html) Accessed August 1, 2017.

Leskovec, J., Backstrom, L., and Kleinberg, J. (2009) 'Meme-tracking and the Dynamics of the News Cycle', *ACM SIGKDD International Conference on Knowledge Discovery and Data Mining (ACM KDD).*

Lussier, R. (n.d.) 'Dancing Baby FAQ', *Burning Pixel Productions* (http://www.burningpixel.com/Baby/BabyFAQ.htm) Accessed August 1, 2017.

Milligan, I. (2017) 'Welcome To The Web: The Online Community of GeoCities during the Early Years of the World Wide Web', in Niels Brügger and Ralph Schroeder (eds), *The Web As History*. London: University College London Press. pp. 137–58.

Milner, R. (2016) *The World Made Meme: Public Conversations and Participatory Media.* Cambridge (MA): MIT Press. Kindle Edition.

Nakamura, L. (2014) '"I WILL DO EVERYthing That Am Asked": Scam-Baiting, Digital Show-Space, and the Racial Violence of Social Media', *Journal of Visual Culture*, 13(3): 257–74.

Nooney, L. and Portwood-Stacer, L. (2014) 'One Does Not Simply: An Introduction to the Special Issue on Internet Memes', *Journal of Visual Culture*, 13(3): 248–52.

Ronson, J. (2015) *So You've Been Publicly Shamed.* New York: Riverhead Books.

Saylor, N. (2014) 'Getting Serious About Collecting And Preserving Digital Culture', *Folklife Today (Library of Congress)* (https://blogs.loc.gov/folklife/2014/06/getting-serious-about-collecting-and-preserving-digital-culture/) Accessed August 1, 2017.

Shifman, L. (2012) *Memes in Digital Culture.* Cambridge (MA): MIT Press.

Skirwin, T. (1999) 'How to post about Nazis and get away with it – the Godwin's Law FAQ', *alt.usenet.kooks,alt.usenet.legends,alt.*

*answers,news.answers.* (http://wiki.killfile.org/projects/usenet/faqs/godwin/) Accessed August 1, 2017.

Solon, O. (2013) 'Richard Dawkins on the internet's hijacking of the word "meme"', *WIRED (UK)* (http://www.wired.co.uk/article/richard-dawkins-memes) Accessed August 1, 2017.

Twitter. (2016) 'Terms of Service', *Twitter* (https://twitter.com/en/tos) Accessed December 15, 2016.

Wiggins, B. and Bowers, G.B. (2015) 'Memes as Genre: A Structurational Analysis of the Memescape', *New Media and Society*, 17(1): 1886–906.

# 35 Years of the Internet: Vernacular Creativity before, on and after the Chinese Web

Gabriele de Seta

## INTRODUCTION: YEAR OF THE INTERNET

> In the hype-ridden People's Republic of China, 1996 was the 'Year of the Internet.' No matter that, by the highest estimates, only 150,000 Chinese people – barely 1 in 10,000 – are actually wired. (Barmé and Sang, 1997)

Technically speaking, the Internet arrived in Mainland China[1] on August 26th, 1986, through an X.25 connection established between Karlsruhe University and the Chinese Institute of Computer Applications (ICA) in Beijing (Hauben, 2005). Its early years in the country were characterized by academic frustration, technical pessimism, bureaucratic impediments and international mistrust (Zheng, 1994: 236). Offered to the country's general public in 1996, ten years after its first infrastructural link, the Internet has become, in the span of little more than two decades, a fundamental part of the everyday life of the majority of Chinese citizens. In the words of a local literature professor, going online in the late 1990s through the precarious configuration of a 386 personal computer, a telephone set, a CNY 500 modem and CNY 200 worth of phone connection fees offered the experience of a 'speed never seen in history before' (Yan, 1997: 3). Similarly, in macro-economic and infrastructural terms, the development of networked communications in China is commonly described as 'break-neck', 'momentous', 'accelerated' and 'compressed', adjectives that give a sense of how Chinese authorities and local IT industries have managed to leapfrog technological advancements and catch up with an imagination of the Internet largely shaped by the Silicon Valley model.

This chapter offers an episodic chronology of Internet use in China by singling out six landmark years and highlighting how creative practices have been shaping the adoption of the technology before, during and after the popularization of the World Wide Web as the primary information space for hundreds of millions of users. One peculiar consequence of the accelerated and compressed development of ICTs in China has been the conflation of the Internet (as a network of networks) and the Web (as an information-sharing protocol) in the experience of a large majority of users. The first web server in China was installed in 1994 (Zhou, 2006: 136), when only a minimal fraction of the population had access to the Internet, so that the users coming online during and after the 'Year of the Internet' of 1996, along exponential growth rates propelling the Chinese user population to 2.1 million by the end of 1998 (Du, 1999: 405), could already experience the Internet not only through e-mail and bulletin boards, but also through web browsers and link directories. As of today, the Mandarin Chinese terms *hulianwang* [literally 'interconnection net'] and *wangluo* [literally 'network'] are routinely used to refer to both the Internet and the Web, while more technical translations of World Wide Web such as *wanweiwang* and *huanqiuwang* remain outside of popular parlance. The *wang* character, present in all these terms to translate both 'web' and 'net', exemplifies this blurring of technology and protocol: checking if something is *wang shang* ['on the network'] could mean either verifying a device's wireless access to the Internet, the online presence of a friend on a messaging application, the existence of information on a webpage, or the successful upload of data to a cloud server. As in other local contexts, the vernacular conflation of Internet and Web testifies to the centrality of the protocol to the experience of the underlying technology.

Recent calls for histories of both the Internet and the Web (Brügger, 2011; Wellman, 2011) have urged scholars to move beyond the amply chronicled pasts of networked communications in the United States and Europe (Abbate, 1999; Roy, 1998). Sensitive to these concerns, a growing body of academic literature on Chinese media history has been charting the three decades of the country's Internet development from different angles and perspectives (Qiu, 2004; Tai, 2006; Zhou, 2006). Yet, as is increasingly often recognized, these inquiries have disproportionately focused on the political implications and democratizing potential of ICTs (Herold and de Seta, 2015), leading many to ignore 'the myriad ways in which the Internet might potentially affect Chinese life' (Kluver and Yang, 2005: 306). As more recently noted, the study of usage, users and user experiences is fundamental to understanding the relationship between the Internet, the Web and society (Schroeder and Brügger, 2017: 2). Perhaps as a result of the terminological conflation highlighted above, much of the scholarship on the Chinese *wangluo* has focused on the Internet rather than the Web, tending to privilege infrastructural concerns over user practices. Yet the existence of a Chinese Web cluster is hardly disputed, and recent studies attribute its accretion more to language and content preferences of local users than to the much-discussed censorship mechanisms developed by the authorities (Taneja and Wu, 2014).

In this chapter, I historicize the modest advent, massive popularity and creeping enclosure of the Web in China by linking it to the continuities in the *vernacular creativity* of Internet users. After introducing the early years of local Internet development, explaining the situated experience of both the Internet and World Wide Web, and arguing for a historical perspective that highlights how the creative practices of users have accompanied networked communications in the country throughout three decades, I chronicle six historical turning points exemplified by different forms of vernacular creativity, each connected to the rise and fall of communication protocols, coding standards, content-management systems, messaging software and social media platforms. Starting from the pre-Web examples of e-mail and BBSs, I follow everyday creative usage through the boom of amateur homepages, community portals and blogs, towards the looming enclosure of the Web hidden behind contemporary social media platforms. In the conclusion, I argue that vernacular creativity provides a productive thread through which the advent, popularity and disappearance of the Web can be followed from the point of view of local populations of Internet users.

## A HISTORY OF VERNACULAR CREATIVITY

The idea of the 'vernacular' was introduced as early as 1960 by anthropologist Margaret Lantis to describe forms of everyday culture and speech that are different 'from the literary language or from the language of straight news reporting' (1960: 202–3). This attention to everyday forms of speech has been extended, most famously by the work of Michel de Certeau, to the larger 'lexicon of users' practices' (1984: 31) resulting from the consumers' tactical engagement with popular culture and media. The category has been more recently discussed by various authors in linguistics, media and cultural studies, including Henry Jenkins' use of 'vernacular culture' to define the experimental productions created by amateurs (2006: 132), David Barton's idea of 'vernacular writing on the Web' (Barton, 2010: 109) to discuss literacy practices rooted in locality and everyday life, and Jean Burgess' definition of 'vernacular creativity' as:

> a productive articulation of consumer practices and knowledges (of, say, television genre codes) with older popular traditions and communicative practices (storytelling, family photography, scrapbooking, collecting). (Burgess, 2007: 207)

With the popularization of Internet access and digital media platforms, these communicative practices become increasingly central in everyday life, and the rift between active producers and passive consumers shrinks into a permeable boundary. The emergence of ASCII compositions out of the limited affordances of e-mail writing (Danet, 2001) and of ANSI artworks on Bulletin Boards (Scott Sadofsky, 2005) are widely documented as early examples of vernacular creativity on the Internet[2], but it is with the popularization of the World Wide Web in the mid 1990s that vernacular creativity is embraced by larger populations of amateur users (Lialina, 2009a, 2009b). In this chapter, I adopt Burgess' definition of vernacular creativity as 'both an ideal and a heuristic device' (2007: 206) in order to distill a chronology of the Web in China from the point of view of the creative practices of its users. Grounded on ethnographic research on Internet use in the country, my periodization playfully appropriates the media hype rhetorics that recurrently describe China as going through 'the Year of' whatever emerging media technologies happen to achieve widespread adoption at any specific point in time. From e-mail greeting cards to amateur web design, from personal blogs to smartphone video clips, my chronology singles out significant years for the uptake of specific media forms, protocols and platforms, and connects them to the corresponding practices of vernacular creativity through which users experiment with the communicative possibilities of each medium.

## 1987: YEAR OF THE E-MAIL

> Ueber die Grosse Mauer erreichen wie alle Ecken der Welt
>
> Across the Great Wall we can reach every corner in the world

So read the first e-mail sent on September 20th, 1987 from the Institute of Computer Applications (ICA) in Beijing, China to research partners at the University of Karlsruhe, Germany, one year after the Chinese Academic Network (CANet) was established in cooperation between the two institutions (Hauben, 2005). For five years, after these first steps achieved through the painstaking efforts of joint teams of Chinese and foreign computer scientists, expensive and precarious e-mail links were 'the only network connectivity that could reach the rest of the world [from China]' (Hauben, 2005). During this period of time, academic researchers and an increasing number of university students were the first Chinese users to register e-mail addresses and experience the possibilities of corresponding at a distance with other users inside the country and abroad. Given the lack of international encoding standards for *hanzi* ['Chinese characters'], most of these exchanges happened in foreign languages and through alphabetic scripts. A second well-documented e-mail message symbolizes the adoption of the Internet in China by its early users. It was sent on April 10, 1995 from Peking University, and it read:

> Hi,
>
> This is Peking University in China, a place of those dreams of freedom and democracy. However, a young, 21-year old student has become very sick and is dying. The illness is very rare. Though they have tried, doctors at the best hospitals in Beijing cannot cure her; many do not even know what illness it is. So now we are asking the world – can somebody help us?
>
> [...]
>
> This is the first time that Chinese try to find help from Internet, please send back E-mail to us. (Fung, 1995)

Classmates of Zhu Ling, a Tsinghua University sophomore who fell mysteriously ill, posted this message on various mailing lists seeking medical help from abroad, and received a flood of helpful responses. Geremie Barmé and Ye Sang recount how 84 of these responses were in fact correct diagnoses of thallium poisoning: 'Zhu Ling was treated and eventually began a slow recovery; the Chinese public was enthralled. A television miniseries is reportedly in the works' (Barmé and Sang, 1997). Another account of what was arguably the first large-scale example of user-led crowdsourcing information in China correlates it with the country's booming informatization: 'she [Zhu Ling] was really lucky that this happened right during the year in which the Internet began to penetrate massively in China' (Yan, 1997: 109).

For roughly a decade, before being partly substituted by discussion boards, Web-based services and messaging applications, e-mail was the central medium through which Chinese Internet users could experiment with the creative possibilities of computerized textual communication. The ASCII graphic compositions collected by folklorist Seana Kozar throughout the early 1990s, circulated by Chinese students as 'electronic greeting cards' during Christmas or Spring Festival holidays (Figure 35.1), are a striking example of the practices of vernacular creativity through which early Internet users figured out ways of reproducing traditional symbols and playful motifs in spite of the limitations of character encoding and textual formatting of the time (Kozar, 1995). For the few hundred thousand Chinese users who experienced a pre-Web Internet, vernacular creativity offered ways of rendering the visuality of the Chinese script and the lack of consistent encoding standards (McLelland, 537–550), foreshadowing a desire for localization that kept driving many of the practices described in the following sections.

## 1995: YEAR OF THE BBS

According to the detailed chronology provided by Zhou Yongming, the first BBS was set up in China in 1991. It was only in 1994, though, that the first local Internet-based BBS (the *Dawn BBS*) was opened to the public, beginning a two-decade-long history of bulletin board use in the country.

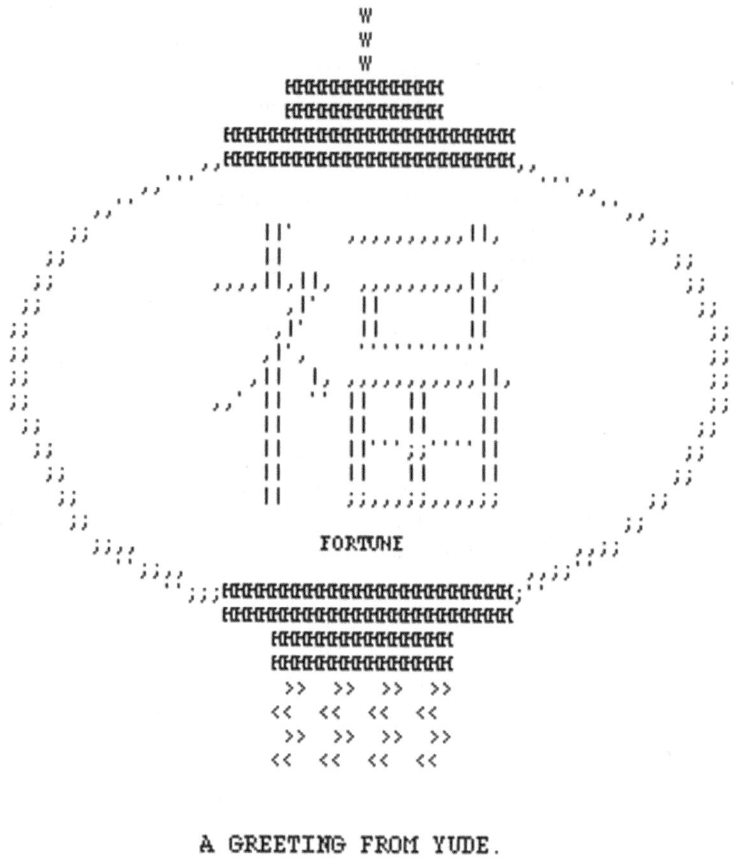


**Figure 35.1 A 'good fortune lantern' ASCII graphic sent via e-mail by a Chinese student during the 1992 New Year celebrations (Kozar, 1995).**

Local BBSs quickly overtook the use of e-mail newsgroups such as *alt.chinese.text.big5*, which required additional shareware software in order to input, encode and display Chinese characters on the user's terminal in the various standards available at the time, including zw-DOS, GB (*guobiao* 'national standard') for simplified characters, and Big5 for traditional ones (Kozar, 1995). The example of the Tsinghua University *Shuimu Tsinghua* BBS (Figure 35.2), which implemented Web-based access in 1995 after a few months of TCP/IP-only service (Xinlang Keji, 2008), highlights how the arrival of the Web was rapidly embraced by users and admins alike. As a result of this rapid shift to Web-based bulletin board access – and in contrast with the specific meaning of the acronym in English-language usage – the term 'BBS' was adopted in Chinese parlance to indicate all sorts of online forums, from older bulletin board systems to newer, Web-based forums and image boards. This local usage of the 'BBS' acronym persists until today for the description of both massive online community platforms with multimedia content affordances such as Baidu Tieba as well as government-backed forums like the People's Daily Online *Qiangguo Luntan* ['Strong Nation Forum'].

Besides supporting the formation of new collective identities and facilitating

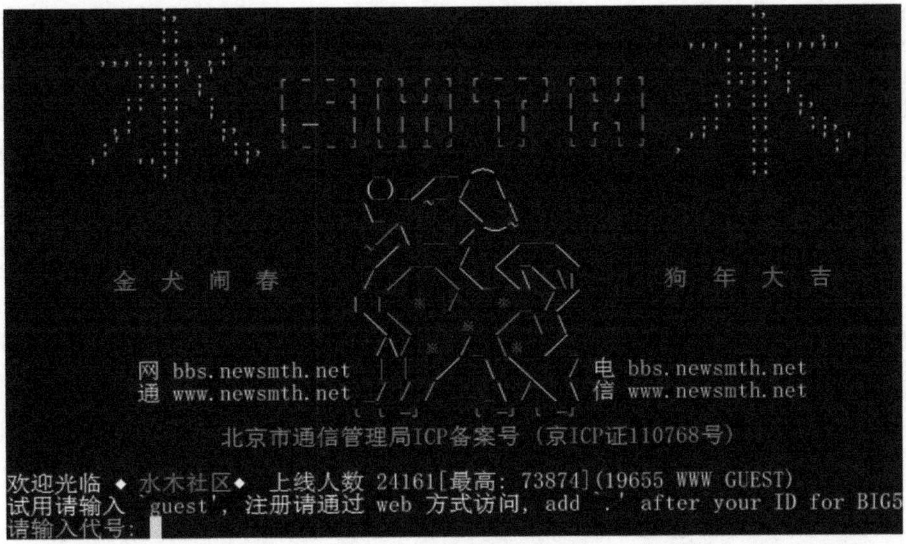


**Figure 35.2 Log-in page screenshot of the Tsinghua University *Shuimu Tsinghua* BBS, originally set up on a 386 computer running Linux, using the same PalmBBS behind the National Taiwan University *Coconut Trees* BBS (Xinlang Keji, 2008).**

large-scale community interaction on a national geographical scale (Damm, 2007: 288), the expanded textual affordances, the possibilities of account personalization and the increasingly varied multimedia affordances of BBS platforms have rapidly sustained their users' experimentation with various forms of vernacular creativity. Early user creativity was largely linguistic, pushing lexical and rhetorical choices into the contentious realms of flaming and personal attacks (Huang, 1999). The development of neologisms, in-jokes and slang terms understood only by community members was seen as a form of resistance against the official language of public discourse (Clark, 2012: 162), and contributed to the emergence of a first wave of online political satire during the late 1990s and early 2000s (Luqiu, 2017: 124).

As communities diversified beyond university campuses, and as enthusiastic early Internet adopters were overtaken by new users flocking towards commercial and government-sponsored platforms – 2006 was widely acclaimed as 'the year of online communities', as Pang (2008: 60) notes – the creative uses of BBSs flourished around political extremization, particularly in the realms of both right-wing nationalism and leftist revival (Hu, 2007). Community-based vernaculars moved beyond the textual, including personalized emoticons, satirical images and even amateur video productions, as the repertoires of *egao* [bad taste humor, literally 'evil making'] content became increasingly deployed in the practices of confrontation accurately described in Han (2015). The rapid shift from TCP/IP bulletin boards to Web accessibility, and the following popularization of Web-native discussion forums and large-scale online communities proves how the history of the various platforms that in China are all called BBS is tightly linked to the World Wide Web and its protocols.

## 1998: YEAR OF THE HOMEPAGE

In May 1994, the CAS Institute of High Energy Physics marked another milestone for Internet development in China by setting up the first www server in the country and developing the first homepage hosted within its national borders (Zhou, 2006: 136). As noted by McLelland (537–550), the popularization of Internet connectivity in China coincided with a historical moment in which the World Wide Web was becoming the predominant way through which users around the world created and navigated online content. It is thus not surprising that, along with e-mail interactions and BBS-based communities, creating websites, following hyperlinks and exploring web directories were some of the chief forms of Internet usage in late-1990s China (Yan, 1997: 100). It is also not surprising that the majority of early Chinese webmasters were academics and college students: according to a 2002 survey, one in eight students had started using the Internet before 1998 (Clark, 2012: 161), acquiring the literacy in HTML language and web design necessary to create simple yet highly personal homepages hosted on university servers or free hosting service providers like GeoCities, Tripod or Angelfire. The diffusion of encoding standards with increasingly comprehensive character sets contributed to lowering the linguistic barriers for users to navigate and design an increasingly rich Chinese Web.

Emerging in parallel to the local commercial and governmental developments of the World Wide Web, the 'vernacular web' (Lialina, 2009a: 22) of Chinese homepage-making amateur culture wasn't that different from its American or European counterparts, and remains a precious testimony of how early users latched onto the creative possibilities offered by the HTML protocol and created their own online homes as bricolages of starry backgrounds and navigation icons, personal beliefs and biographical details, low-resolution photographs and animated GIFs, hyperlinks and guestbooks (Chandler, 1998). While structurally similar to their global counterparts, Chinese amateur websites also had their defining features. National pride and cultural heritage contributed to a clearly local look of many Chinese amateur websites (Gevorgyan and Manucharova, 2009: 396); as evidenced by an analysis of Chinese GeoCities webpages created between 1996 and 1998, a substantial part of them was dedicated to introductions to the country, tea-savoring instructions, coin divination guides, classical literature and other explicitly 'cultural' topics (Figure 35.3). Language was also a defining feature of the Chinese vernacular Web: even if *hanzi* characters were introduced in UNICODE in 1992, most web designers kept encoding their pages in either the national standard GB2312 for simplified characters, or the Big5 standard for traditional characters, a choice mostly guided by personal tastes and regional preferences[3]. Many websites provided multiple versions of their pages in different encodings to avoid visualization problems, and some webmasters offered bilingual contents to cater to both local and international visitors.

Zhai Zhenming, who is today a Professor of Philosophy at Sun Yat-sen University, Guangzhou, was one of the first Chinese users of GeoCities, where he set up his personal homepage in 1997 with the intent to promote his academic output and share his poetry compositions. He remembers his experience as an amateur web designer:

> I did very little coding with HTML, I basically just used the templates provided by GeoCities, plus some additional marking adjustment with simple HTML tags. I remember I also linked to my musical clips on the webpage, it's me playing the Chinese instrument *erhu*… I don't know if you can still find those recordings online. (Interview with the author, July 2015)

Another amateur web designer, Song Gang, whose website is a colorful potpourri of borrowed graphic elements and painstakingly nested HTML tables (Song, 1998), successively went on to establish one of China's earliest grassroots environmental protection organizations. He believes his successful career was helped by his early tinkering with web design, and he takes pride in his dedication to the craft:

> My personal website was made in 1998 using HTML – design and coding are all done by me. I taught myself how to do it because I was interested

**Figure 35.3 Bilingual coin divination page from one of the earliest Chinese websites hosted on GeoCities. Screenshot by the author, courtesy of the GeoCities Research Institute archive.**

> in it, I bought some books in Zhongguancun [a technology hub in Haidian district, Beijing] to study, and I had many exchanges with colleagues who were specializing in computing. (Interview with the author, October 2014)

Before GeoCities and similar free hosting providers were either blocked in China or fell out of fashion, and before hosting websites inside the country was subjected to increasingly strict regulations and controls, amateur web designers explored the potentialities of the Web by cobbling together personal homepages to introduce themselves and their country to the world.

## 2001: YEAR OF QQ

In February 1999, a few months after being founded, Chinese Internet company Tencent Inc. released a proprietary messaging application called OICQ, an acronym standing for 'Open ICQ'. Following a lawsuit filed by AOL, which at the time owned the increasingly popular instant messenger software ICQ, Tencent had to rename its application QQ. Struggling during its first two years of operation, Tencent QQ eventually managed to achieve a breakthrough in popularity in 2001, quickly moving from one million to 50 million users, and started experimenting with sustainable business models (CIW Team, 2014). In the early 2000s, the stylized penguin with a red scarf that QQ used as an icon and mascot became instantly recognizable among Chinese Internet users. For many, registering a QQ number (a unique identifier used for both login and for contact exchange across Tencent services, both Web-based and proprietary) is the earliest memory of accessing the Internet, even before setting up an e-mail account or a BBS profile (Wallis, 2011: 414).

Besides the instant messaging capabilities of the software, having a personal QQ number introduced Internet users to a growing number of Web-based Tencent services such as QZone (a social networking and content-sharing platform) and QQ Mail (an e-mail inbox), as well as to other software-based services such as QQ Music (a music streaming and download application) or QQ Pinyin (an input method for Chinese characters alternative to the Microsoft Pinyin offered by Windows operating systems). As QQ moved away from its beginnings as an ICQ clone through the addition of features such as virtual currency (QCoin), in-software videogames (QQ Games) and paid memberships (QQ Vip), it quickly became an essential application for the lives of Chinese Internet users, younger ones in particular. A large majority of my interviewees, who were children or teens in the early 2000s, still used their first QQ number and QQ Mail address after more than a decade, and connect the Tencent media ecology to affective moments and intimate memories: some opened their account in elementary school and used QZone to keep in touch with classmates and family members, experiencing first-hand the plights of context collapse when posting something too racy or vulgar; others registered their QQ numbers in high school, and sometimes got two or more accounts to divide personal and work connections (de Seta, 2015: 124).

I registered my own QQ number in the mid 2000s, as it was evidently a necessary medium to keep contact and interact with Chinese friends and acquaintances. Over the years, my contact list has grown to include hundreds of names and dozens of chat groups discussing the most varied topics (Figure 35.4), and my QQ account has played a central role

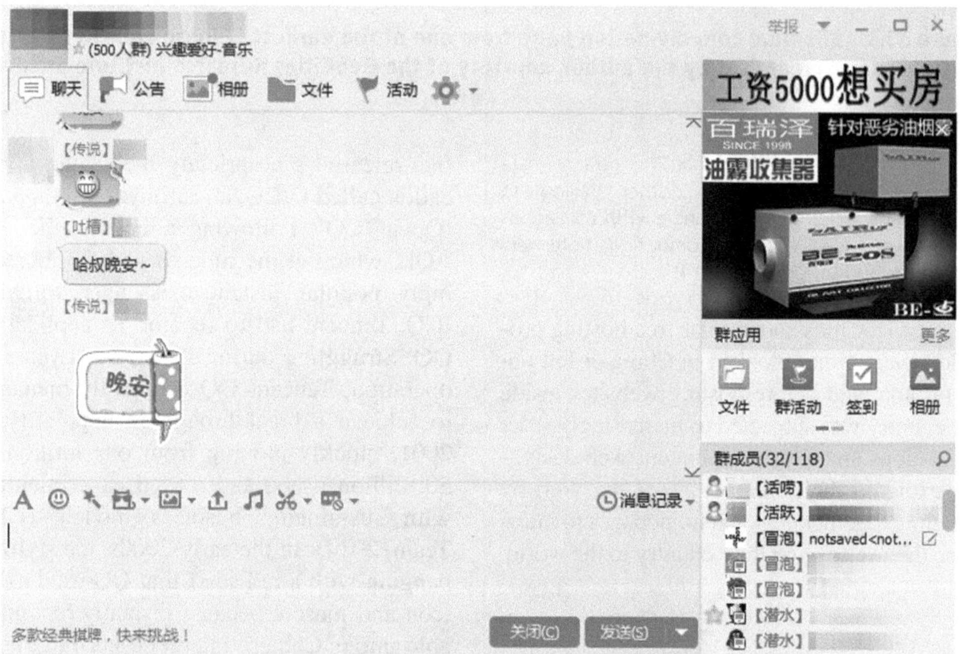


**Figure 35.4 A QQ group chat window, including a common message feed, a textbox with multimedia uploading options, different toolbars to access additional services and a list of the 118 group members. Screenshot by the author.**

in both my private life and my professional research projects, offering the convenience of logging into numerous local web services and mobile apps through its verified user credentials. Similarly, for more than 15 years, QQ has provided an indispensable communicational space and an array of interactional tools to hundreds of millions of Chinese users, expanding the social possibilities offered by mailing lists and BBSs into a more immediate and personalizable experience that moves (sometimes clumsily[4]) between Web-based services and proprietary software. It is through QQ chat windows that slang terms circulate beyond the boundaries of online communities, coalescing in an ever-growing, nation-wide repertoire of *wangluo yuyan* ['Internet language']; similarly, it is because of the possibility of importing and editing images of multiple formats as emoticons ready to be exchanged among users that genres of visual content like *egao* achieve wide popularity online; finally, it is thanks to the convenience of managing groups, organizing activities, exchanging files and sharing screenshots that communities of practice (such as subtitling and translation groups) as well as entire companies have adopted QQ as a fundamental software tool for professional productivity.

While the QQ messenger itself is not a Web-based service but rather an instant messaging software operating through a proprietary Tencent protocol (originally released as a computer application and today also widely used in its mobile app version), it is undeniable that its usage has from the beginning been closely tied to the experience of Web content: on launch, its starting screen offers a crammed collage of news headlines, images and video previews linking to the QQ News section of the Tencent portal; hyperlinks and screengrabs of Web content are routinely shared and commented upon across private conversations and group discussions; a simple click on the small icons in the main window of the application opens the QQ Mail or Qzone Web interfaces in the system browser. Moreover, in late 2009 Tencent launched a Web-based version of the QQ messenger, which offers a comprehensive, desktop-like user experience accessible on any computer through a simple scanning of an in-browser QR code. From its ungainly beginnings as a knockoff messaging application in the early 2000s, Tencent QQ has developed into a sprawling media ecology of software and platforms that are as self-enclosing as they are intricately woven with the Chinese Web.

## 2005: YEAR OF THE BLOG

In the mid 2000s, the World Wide Web of static homepages was shifting towards the dynamic content and interoperable protocols promised under the banner of Web 2.0 (O'Reilly, 2005). Along with social networking websites and media streaming services, blogs emerged as one of the most popular kinds of platform, and China was no exception. For many of the Internet users who encountered the Web without any coding experience, blogging was the first opportunity to construct a personal online space (Sima and Pugsley, 2010: 292). Blogging websites existed in China since 2002, but the turning point for this media form happened in 2005 – widely recognized as the 'Year of the Blog' (Yu, 2007: 425) – when the posts of 4.3 million active bloggers proved to have a resounding social and cultural impact. In late 2006, search engine provider Baidu launched its own blog platform alongside other companies like Sina, NetEase and Sohu, and by 2008 the country had a population of 105 million active bloggers (Wang and Hong, 2010: 67). Due to their low participation threshold, their social networking features and their strong authorial identity, blogs supported the expansion of online interactions beyond BBSs and QQ group chats, providing a space to growing networked audiences engaging in celebrity fandom and large-scale debates following

**Figure 35.5 The Sina Blog of Zhou Xiaoping, a 1981-born blogger popular for his nationalist and anti-American views, as of September 2010. Screenshot by the author.**

popular or controversial blog posts (Wallis, 2011: 414).

As Wu (2012) notes, it was precisely the booming of blogging practices in China that catapulted online debate culture – with its vernacular slang and rhetorical positions – into the realm of public opinion and everyday life at large. What was once limited to mailing lists and university discussion boards became discussed throughout comment sections and blog posts, while popular bloggers such as race car driver Han Han or nationalist writer Zhou Xiaoping rose to the status of widely followed celebrities and opinion leaders (Figure 35.5). The blogging boom of the late 2000s led many journalists and academics to identify a 'Chinese blogosphere' that could function as an incubator for a local civil society mediating between individuals and the state (Tang, 2009). Blog posts displaying a skillful use of ambiguous language and clever *egao* humor were widely regarded as a forceful pushback against authoritarian control and censorship: 'Chinese are speaking truth to each other, and by doing so in a widely accessible manner, are speaking truth to power' (Esarey and Xiao, 2008: 753).

In the wake of the July 2009 Ürümqi riots and the subsequent shutdown of the first Chinese micro-blogging service Fanfou (along with the blockage of foreign websites like Facebook, Twitter and YouTube), the Sina Corporation launched Sina Weibo, a micro-blogging website through which users could publish 140-chararacter multimedia posts, follow accounts and comment or re-blog each other's content. In the span of a few months, competing blogging providers such as NetEase, Sohu and Tencent all released their own Weibo platforms, trying to attract users to their own micro-blogging service. The intensification of censorship practices commonly summarized through the 'Great Firewall' metaphor (Tsui, 2007), combined with the opportunistic proliferation of local blogging and micro-blogging platforms, contributed to enclose the activities of hundreds of millions of users in increasingly walled social media gardens amenable to state control and delegated censorship.

Yet, despite the number of analyses that frame blogs and micro-blogs as either safety valves for dissent or pressure cookers for activism (Hassid, 2012), most users of these platforms didn't engage with politics or social issues, but largely blogged to keep a public record of their daily lives, to share and discuss their hobbies and passions, or to participate in larger communities of interest or fandom (Clark, 2012: 129). Even when channeled towards the discussion of political topics, the vernacular creativity of Chinese bloggers did not necessarily fit the bill of an emerging public sphere: on the one hand, nationalist, conservative and even reactionary blogs sprang up along their more liberal and pro-democracy counterparts (Leibold, 2011: 1034); on the other, the activities of amateur bloggers and online celebrities were accompanied by 'Red Blogs' set up by party organs and official accounts managed by Chinese authorities with the goal of promoting political stability (Esarey, 2015).

## 2011: YEAR OF WECHAT

A decade after launching QQ – by then an extremely successful application used across personal computers, smartphones and tablets – Tencent released a mobile-oriented messaging app called Weixin [literally meaning 'micro-message'], better known in English as WeChat. Profiting from an already existing population of hundreds of million QQ accounts, and helped by a societal shift towards mobile devices and wireless connectivity, WeChat quickly accrued a massive userbase. Tencent learned from its previous experience with messaging applications, and included social networking functions in WeChat through a *pengyouquan* ['friend circle'] content feed, the possibility of following official accounts managed by brands, organizations, news outlets and celebrities, as well as a Web-based version of the app, accessible in any browser through the simple scanning of a QR code. Other functions added to the platform over the years include WeChat Pay, a digital wallet enabling users to perform mobile payments and send money to each other; City Services, a booking system for different kinds of public and private services in urban areas; and even WeChat Search, a proprietary search engine. WeChat epitomizes a major shift that characterized Chinese Internet development in the early 2010s: the drastic growth of mobile Internet access and the broad uptake of smartphones and tablets throughout the country. As the Internet is predominantly accessed through app interfaces and proprietary protocols, the Web seems to disappear behind fluttering messaging windows and endlessly scrolling social media feeds.

The affordances offered by smartphones and tablets – wireless Internet access, front and rear camera imaging, audiovisual playback and recording – played a central role in the kinds of vernacular creativity practiced on WeChat and shaped the larger ecology of mobile apps and online platforms coalescing around it. Besides exchanging textual messages and voice snippets, users of WeChat could communicate through emoticons, in-app stickers, funny images, short video 'sights' shot through the app itself, longer videos imported from other platforms, locational data, and even *hongbao* ['red envelopes'] used to transfer small amounts of money between accounts (Figure 35.6). The multimedia messaging possibilities provided by WeChat also directly contributed to the emergence of new genres of digital content. Alongside the emoticons and stickers offered by the platform, users imported and exchanged vibrant repertoires of personalized *biaoqing* [literally 'expressions'], giving a new lease of life to the *egao* humor popularized by BBSs and micro-blogging platforms. Dividing their time between chat conversations and *pengyouquan* feeds, users chronicled their daily activities through edited *zipai* ['selfies'] and short videos ready to be liked and commented on. Exposed to the activities

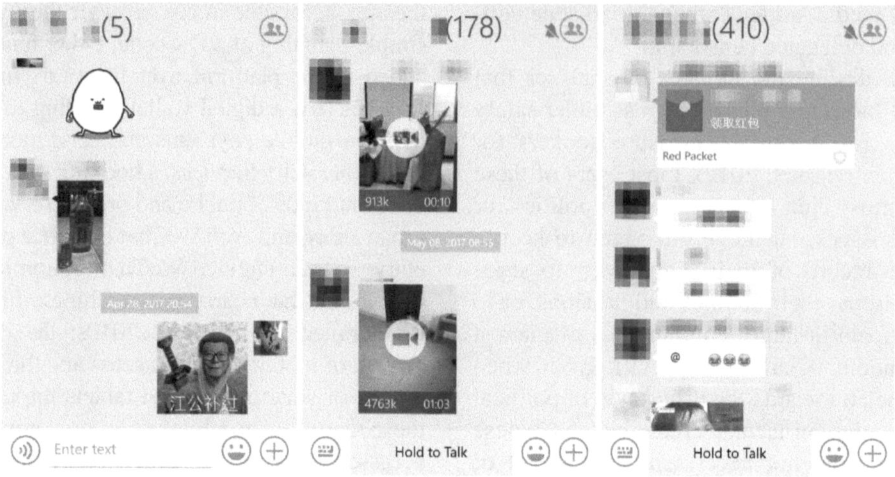


**Figure 35.6 In-app stickers, photos, personalized *biaoqing* images, short videos, *hongbao* red envelopes and emoticons used in interactions across three WeChat group chats. Screenshots by the author, 2017.**

of official accounts and the discussions taking place in massive chat groups, they took advantage of their devices' affordances to engage first-hand in activities like coordinating nationalist campaigns (Han, 2015), marketing and reselling branded products (Zhang, 2015) or participating in everyday practices of citizen activism (Pan, 2017).

WeChat's success story, grounded on Tencent's experience with the development of QQ and its ecology of services, and culminating in its overtaking of sister software QQ with almost 900 million users and ten million official accounts by Q4 2016 (Penguin Intelligence, 2017), also marks an important year for the Chinese Web, which users increasingly experience through the selective curation of social media feeds, and which seems to slowly disappear as browsers become just one of the many ways of interfacing with the Internet among the many app icons pinned to mobile device screens. Yet proclaiming the death of the Chinese Web might be exaggerated: while it is true that social media platforms push for app-based experiences and for the enclosure of both proprietary and user-generated content, it is also true that much of the users' creative activity on WeChat still passes through the Web, or draws the Web back into the app, in different shapes and forms. WeChat's proprietary browser is the default way of opening hyperlinks shared in WeChat conversations, but two extra taps in the menu allow users to launch their own default browser; WeChat posts shared by public accounts are actually HTML webpages designed through a Web-based editor and hosted on the WeChat Official Account website; WeChat stickers, stories and screenshots are also collected by individual users and uploaded in Web-based repositories to facilitate circulation and preservation. As social media platforms seek to enclose user activity and content, vernacular creativity pulls the Web back into their app-based ecologies from unexpected sociotechnical backdoors.

## 2020: YEAR OF THE FUTURE

A few years from now, perhaps 2015 will be remembered as China's 'Year of e-payments', 2016 as the 'Year of the gig economy', 2017 as the 'Year of livestreaming', and 2018 as the 'Year of mobile gaming', while predictions for the tech hype of 2019 are still open. What is less disputable is that the development of digital media in the country will not grind to a halt anytime soon: both the National Informatization Plan (2006–20) and the 13th Five-Year Plan (2016–20) identify the year 2020 as a symbolic yet pressing deadline for completing the transformation of the country into a 'world-class information society' (Austin, 2014: 3). Along with the rather general goals outlined by policy documents, it is expected that the near future of the Internet in China will see the emergence of new networked devices and online platforms, new kinds of services and modes of participation, as well as new forms of vernacular creativity introduced by users through their everyday interaction with different media. Alongside these innovations, it is likely that some of the existing media forms, protocols and practices will subside, while others will remain current, or even see unexpected resurgences.

The history sketched in this chapter has no pretense of completeness, and relies on necessary elisions: the six significant years I chose (1987, 1995, 1998, 2001, 2005, 2011) to describe the various kinds of protocols and platforms (e-mail, BBSs, websites, QQ, blogs, WeChat), their relationship to the modest advent, massive popularity and creeping enclosure of the Chinese Web, and the forms of vernacular creativity practiced by their users are simply one of the many possible ways of chronicling the history of the Internet in China. My choices prioritize radical shifts in protocol adoption, platform design and device usage, and in doing so they necessarily conceal the variety of media under analysis. Similar discussions could be dedicated to the rise of social networking websites like Kaixin001, Renren or Douban, the fortune of online marketplaces like JD or Taobao, the adoption of foreign platforms like MySpace, Facebook or Twitter, or the recent uptake of livestreaming apps. Similarly, the decision to structure this history as a year-based chronology doesn't imply that usage of the media described in each section remained limited to its breakout year – conversely, each of those protocols and platforms has a peculiar history that is best investigated ethnographically: some have become widely used throughout the world at large, some have remained popular only locally, and others have slowly shrunk or quickly disappeared.

Twenty years after China's 'Year of the Internet' described by Geremie Barmé and Ye Sang (1997), the online interactions of hundreds of millions of users have surely come a long way from the struggles with composing Spring Festival greeting cards through a limited set of ASCII characters to be carefully copy-pasted across e-mails and BBSs. After experiencing a *wangluo* environment already Web-centric since its early years of popular adoption, most of the Chinese Internet users of today spend a large part of their online time in the enclosed playgrounds of platforms like WeChat, Baidu, Taobao, Bilibili or Zhihu, and rarely need to tinker with HTML tags, character encoding or FTP uploads in order to create, share and circulate a large amount of multimedia content. Yet the practices of vernacular creativity through which users make themselves at home in the media ecologies shifting around them remain a constant presence, pulling back the Web into the walled gardens of social media platforms. Vernacular creativity emerges as a shaping force of political economy through which users open up unpredicted spaces of maneuver in the media at their disposal (Li, 2016), and offers a productive category through which to rethink where the boundaries of the Web lie today. Regardless of what the next 'Year of the Internet' will turn out to be about, users will rewrite its history and contribute to shaping the future of the Chinese Web.

## Notes

1 Mainland China, or Chinese mainland, are terms commonly used to define the geographical area

under the jurisdiction of the People's Republic of China (PRC), excluding the Special Administrative Regions (SAR) of Hong Kong and Macau. Given that the development of the Internet and the Web in the Chinese mainland have been intimately shaped by the peculiar geopolitical and legal configuration of the PRC, the terms 'China' and 'Chinese' are used throughout this chapter as shorthands to refer to this area.

2 ASCII (American Standard Code for Information Interchange) is a character encoding standard published in 1963 used to represent text by encoding 128 characters into seven-bit integers. The ANSI (American National Standards Institute) is a private non-profit organization that facilitates the development of national consensus standards. ASCII characters have been arranged in visual compositions to create emoticons and pictures since the introduction of the standard, and its expansion through extended character tables and ANSI color encoding have resulted in the creative practice termed ANSI art.

3 The Big5 encoding was prevalently used in Hong Kong, Taiwan, Singapore and other Chinese-speaking regions, including diasporic communities around the world. Yet some Mainland Chinese webmasters preferred encoding their pages in the traditional characters mapped by Big5 over the simplified ones offered by the GB national standards – some for their geographic or biographic closeness to Hong Kong or Taiwan, others for aesthetic or literary preference.

4 Attributing virtually any problem encountered during the use of a computer to the bloated interfaces of Tencent software was a common diagnosis I repeatedly heard throughout my fieldwork: many informants saw QQ-branded applications as unreplaceable but aggressive software that took unwanted liberties with their machine. The 2010 'Qihoo 360 vs. Tencent' dispute over unfair competition and software bundling practices highlights how the QQ messenger had become much more than a single piece of proprietary software.

## REFERENCES


Abbate, J. (1999) *Inventing the Internet*. Inside Technology. Cambridge, MA: MIT Press.

Austin, G. (2014) *Cyber policy in China*. China Today. Cambridge, United Kingdom: Polity Press.

Barmé, G.R., and Sang, Y. (1997) 'The Great Firewall of China'. *Wired*, June. Available at: http://archive.wired.com/wired/archive/5.06/china_pr.html (accessed 12 January 2015).

Barton, D. (2010) 'Vernacular writing on the Web', in: Barton D and Papen U (Eds) *The anthropology of writing: Understanding textually-mediated worlds*. London, United Kingdom: Continuum. pp. 109–125.

Brügger, N. (2011) 'Web archiving – Between past, present, and future', in: Consalvo M and Ess C (Eds) *The handbook of Internet studies*. Handbooks in Communication and Media. Malden, MA: Wiley-Blackwell. pp. 24–42.

Burgess, J. (2007) *Vernacular creativity and new media*. PhD Thesis. Queensland University of Technology, Brisbane, Australia. Available at: eprints.qut.edu.au/16378/1/Jean_Burgess_Thesis.pdf (accessed 18 February 2015).

Chandler, D. (1998) Personal home pages and the construction of identities on the Web. Available at: http://visual-memory.co.uk/daniel/Documents/short/webident.html (accessed 19 September 2014).

CIW Team (2014) The story of the rise of Tencent Empire. Available at: https://www.chinainternetwatch.com/6031/tencent-rising-of-penguin-empire/ (accessed 20 May 2017).

Clark, P. (2012) *Youth culture in China: From Red Guards to netizens*. New York, NY: Cambridge University Press.

Damm, J. (2007) 'The Internet and fragmentation of Chinese society', *Critical Asian Studies*, 39(2): 273–294. DOI: 10.1080/14672710701339485.

Danet, B. (2001) *Cyberpl@y: Communicating online*. Oxford, United Kingdom: Berg.

de Certeau, M. (1984) *The practice of everyday life*. Berkeley, CA: University of California Press.

de Seta, G. (2015) *Dajiangyou: Media practices of vernacular creativity in postdigital China*. PhD Thesis. The Hong Kong Polytechnic University, Hong Kong, China.

Du, X. (1999) 'Internet diffusion and usage in China', *Prometheus*, 17(4): 405–420. DOI: 10.1080/08109029908632119.

Esarey, A. (2015) 'Winning hearts and minds? Cadres as microbloggers in China', *Journal of Current Chinese Affairs*, 44(2): 69–103.

Esarey, A., and Xiao, Q. (2008) 'Political expression in the Chinese blogosphere: Below the radar', *Asian Survey*, 48(5): 752–772. DOI: AS.2008.48.5.752.

Fung, M. (1995) Help needed in Beijing. Available at: http://www.bio.net/bionet/mm/bioforum/1995-April/014054.html?utm_ (accessed 26 March 2015).

Gevorgyan, G., and Manucharova, N. (2009) 'Does culturally adapted online communication work? A study of American and Chinese Internet users' attitudes and preferences toward culturally customized Web design elements', *Journal of Computer-Mediated Communication*, 14(2): 393–413. DOI: 10.1111/j.1083-6101.2009.01446.x.

Han, R. (2015) 'Defending the authoritarian regime online: China's "voluntary fifty-cent army"', *The China Quarterly*, 224: 1006–1025. DOI: 10.1017/S0305741015001216.

Hassid, J. (2012) 'Safety valve or pressure cooker? Blogs in Chinese political life', *Journal of Communication*, 62(2): 212–230. DOI: 10.1111/j.1460-2466.2012.01634.x.

Hauben, J. (2005) Across the Great Wall – The China-Germany email connection 1987–1994. Available at: http://www.columbia.edu/~hauben/china-email.doc (accessed 12 November 2013).

Herold, D.K., and de Seta, G. (2015) 'Through the looking glass: Twenty years of Chinese Internet research', *The Information Society*, 31(1): 68–82. DOI: 10.1080/01972243.2014.976688.

Hu, A.Y. (2007) 'The revival of Chinese leftism online', *Global Media and Communication*, 3(2): 233–238. DOI: 10.1177/1742766507078420.

Huang, E. (1999) 'Flying freely but in the cage – An empirical study of using Internet for the democratic development in China', *Information Technology for Development*, 8(3): 145–162. DOI: 10.1080/02681102.1999.9525303.

Jenkins, H. (2006) *Convergence culture: Where old and new media collide*. New York, NY: New York University Press.

Kluver, R., and Yang, C. (2005) 'The Internet in China: A meta-review of research', *The Information Society*, 21(4): 301–308. DOI: 10.1080/01972240591007616.

Kozar, S. (1995) 'Enduring traditions, ethereal transmissions: Recreating Chinese New Year celebrations on the Internet', *Journal of Computer-Mediated Communication*, 1(2). DOI: 10.1111/j.1083-6101.1995.tb00329.x.

Lantis, M. (1960) 'Vernacular culture', *American Anthropologist*, 62(2): 202–216.

Leibold, J. (2011) 'Blogging alone: China, the Internet, and the democratic illusion?', *The Journal of Asian Studies*, 70(4): 1023–1041. DOI: 10.1017/S0021911811001550.

Li, L.N. (2016) 'Rethinking the Chinese Internet: Social history, cultural forms, and industrial formation', *Television & New Media*, 18(5): 393–409. DOI: 10.1177/1527476416667548.

Lialina, O. (2009a) 'A vernacular web', in: Lialina O and Espenschied D (Eds) *Digital folklore*. Stuttgart, Germany: Merz & Solitude. pp. 19–33.

Lialina, O. (2009b) 'A vernacular web 2', in: Lialina O and Espenschied D (Eds) *Digital folklore*. Stuttgart, Germany: Merz & Solitude. pp. 58–69.

Luqiu, L.R. (2017) 'The cost of humour: Political satire on social media and censorship in China', *Global Media and Communication*, 13(2): 123–138. DOI: 10.1177/1742766517704471.

O'Reilly, T. (2005) What is Web 2.0: Design patterns and business models for the next generation of software. Available at: http://www.oreilly.com/pub/a/web2/archive/what-is-web-20.html (accessed 21 May 2017).

Pan, W. (2017) 'Under the Dome: Un-engineering digital capture in China's smog', *Asiascape: Digital Asia*, 4(1–2): 13–32. DOI: 10.1163/22142312-12340066.

Pang, C. (2008) 'Self-censorship and the rise of cyber collectives: An anthropological study of a Chinese online community', *Intercultural Communication Studies*, 17(3): 57–76.

Penguin Intelligence (2017) 2017 Weixin yonghu & shengtai yanjiu baogao [2017 research report on WeChat users & ecology]. Available at: http://tech.qq.com/a/20170424/004233.htm#p=1 (accessed 28 August 2017).

Qiu, J.L. (2004) 'The Internet in China: Technologies of freedom in a statist society', in: Castells M (Ed.) *The network society: A cross-cultural perspective*. Cheltenham, United Kingdom: Edward Elgar Publishing Limited. pp. 99–124.

Roy, R. (1998) 'Wizards, bureaucrats, warriors, and hackers: Writing the history of the Internet', *The American Historical Review*, 103(5): 1530–1552. DOI: 10.1086/ahr/103.5.1530.

Schroeder, R., and Brügger, N. (2017) 'Introduction: The web as history', in: Brügger N and Schroeder R (Eds) *The web as history: Using web archives to understand the past and the present*. London, United Kingdom: UCL Press. pp. 1–19. DOI: 10.14324/111.9781911307563.

Scott Sadofsky, J. (2005) *BBS: The documentary*. Documentary. Bovine Ignition Systems.

Sima, Y., and Pugsley, P.C. (2010) 'The rise of a "me culture" in postsocialist China: Youth, individualism and identity creation in the blogosphere', *International Communication Gazette*, 72(3): 287–306. DOI: 10.1177/1748048509356952.

Song, G. (1998) Song Gang's Cyberspace Villa. Available at: http://www.grchina.com/qiang/cybervilla.htm (accessed 22 May 2017).

Tai, Z. (2006) *The Internet in China: Cyberspace and civil society*. Abingdon, United Kingdom: Routledge.

Taneja, H., and Wu, A.X. (2014) 'Does the Great Firewall really isolate the Chinese? Integrating access blockage with cultural factors to explain Web user behavior', *The Information Society*, 30(5): 297–309. DOI: 10.1080/01972243.2014.944728.

Tang, H. (2009) 'Blogging in China: Freedom of expression vs political censorship in sexual and satirical blogs', *Networking Knowledge*, 2(1): 1–17.

Tsui, L (2007) 'An inadequate metaphor: The Great Firewall and Chinese Internet censorship', *Global Dialogue*, 9(1–2): 60–68.

Wallis, C. (2011) 'New media practices in China: Youth patterns, processes, and politics', *International Journal of Communication*, 5: 406–436.

Wang, S.S., and Hong, J. (2010) 'Discourse behind the Forbidden Realm: Internet surveillance and its implications on China's blogosphere', *Telematics and Informatics*, 27(1): 67–78. DOI: 10.1016/j.tele.2009.03.004.

Wellman, B. (2011) 'Studying the Internet through the ages', in: Consalvo M and Ess C (Eds) *The handbook of Internet studies*. Handbooks in Communication and Media. Malden, MA: Wiley-Blackwell. pp. 17–23.

Wu, A.X. (2012) 'Hail the independent thinker: The emergence of public debate culture on the Chinese Internet', *International Journal of Communication*, 6: 2220–2244.

Xinlang Keji (2008) 1995 nian Qinghua Shuimu Qinghua BBS chengli [In 1995, Qinghua University sets up the Shuimu Qinghua BBS]. Available at: http://tech.sina.com.cn/i/2008-11-12/18262575131.shtml (accessed 19 May 2017).

Yan, F. (1997) 'Shenghuo zai wangluo zhong – Shangpian [Living in the Internet – First part]', in: *Shenghuo zai wangluo zhong [Living in the Internet]*. Wangluo wenhua congshu. Beijing, China: Zhongguo Renmin Daxue Chubanshe. pp. 3–114.

Yu, H. (2007) 'Blogging everyday life in Chinese Internet culture', *Asian Studies Review*, 31(4): 423–433.

Zhang, L. (2015) 'Fashioning the feminine self in "prosumer capitalism": Women's work and the transnational reselling of Western luxury online', *Journal of Consumer Culture*. DOI: 10.1177/1469540515572239.

Zheng, C. (1994) 'Opening the digital door: Computer networking in China', *Telecommunications Policy*, 18(3): 236–242.

Zhou, Y. (2006) *Historicizing online politics: Telegraphy, the Internet, and political participation in China*. Stanford, CA: Stanford University Press.

36

# Cultural, Political and Technical Factors Influencing Early Web Uptake in North America and East Asia

Mark McLelland

## INTRODUCTION

Today internet histories is a developing field with more attention being paid to regional histories (Goggin and McLelland, 2017) as well as pre-internet developments in computer mediated communication (CMC). As Carey and Elton (2010) argue, there is a growing acknowledgement of the many alternate developments in online services that prefigured and prepared the ground for the internet applications that became ubiquitous with the roll-out of the World Wide Web in the mid-to-late 1990s. For instance, they refer to teletext in the United Kingdom and videotext in the United States in the 1970s, which provided news and other information in a text format that could be displayed on a television screen and navigated with the remote control (2010: 221–3). Although uptake of the services was low, they did get people 'used to the idea of information retrieval and display' (2010: 226). Numerous database and computer conferencing systems also prefigured aspects of the Web that we take for granted today. However, there were technical limitations that made the use of these services outside of North America and Europe problematic due to the lack of international protocols surrounding language and script input and retrieval. As Nishigaki (1998) has noted, the complexity of some of the world's writing systems has 'often hinder[ed] the rapid development of text processing technology'. In this chapter I look at early developments in CMC across four of the currently most densely networked societies in East Asia: Taiwan, mainland China, South Korea and Japan, to assess how both common and specific challenges faced by these societies influenced their uptake of Web-based applications in the mid 1990s.

It is important to recall that in Euro-American societies the roll-out of public internet access, which was accelerated by the introduction of the Web and the first Web browsers in 1994, took place in a context where large segments of the population already had some prior experience of personal computing (Fouser, 2001: 274). The fact that most high-school graduates already had a familiarity with the QWERTY keyboard, originally popularised by the Remington typewriter in 1873, meant that prior to the development of the mouse and the graphic interface, the use of the keyboard to interface with a computer screen was easily intelligible. Despite the fact that the QWERTY layout, originally devised to prevent the jamming of commonly occurring letters in English words, is not the most efficient for computer input, the familiarity established by the typewriter has made the keyboard difficult to change (Castillo, 2011: 613). The centrality of the QWERTY keyboard to early computer input and navigation systems meant that speakers of East Asian languages needed to develop familiarity with this counter-intuitive system in order to process their own languages.

Given the complex input and display issues associated with non-Roman scripts such as Chinese, Japanese and Korean, which made interoperability between different encoding systems challenging, the introduction of Web-based platforms was less straightforward in East Asia than in North America and Europe. Although the ascendancy of Web-based applications may seem inevitable if we look at the development of the internet from a Euro-American perspective, a review of the history of Web uptake in East Asia reveals a number of culturally embedded issues with the technology that first had to be resolved before the Web could be embraced by a majority of internet users.

This chapter reviews aspects of pre-Web internet communications systems in East Asia, focusing specifically on the BBS cultures where the majority of early adopters were first introduced to native script processing. It then considers how the affordances of these early systems and the cultures that developed around them paved the way for the different pace and scope of Web uptake in the mid-to-late 1990s and explains the persistence of non-Web-based applications in some contexts in East Asia today.

## THE ROLE OF ENGLISH IN THE DEVELOPMENT OF COMPUTER NETWORKS

The dominance of English-speaking countries in the development of computing in the middle of the last century led to a situation where the Roman alphabet and the English language were the default script and language used both for the construction of computer code and commands and for discussion concerning research and development (Breen and Tokita, 2004: 1; UNESCO, 2005). The 7-bit code that was established by the US standards agency in the early 1970s, generally known as the American Standard Code for Information Interchange (ASCII), allowed for 128 basic characters including lower- and uppercase letters from a–z, numerals 0–9 and punctuation marks. With the extension to 8-bits, a further 128 characters were made available that included accented letters and additional punctuation marks (Breen and Tokita, 2004: 1; UNESCO, 2005: 71–3). Most countries using European languages were thus able to deploy the standard ASCII set while using the extra character capacity to configure diacritic, punctuation and other marks to suit the local writing system. Non-Roman alphabets such as Greek or Cyrillic were able to use the extended code space to configure their own alphabets. However, languages such as Chinese and Japanese, which use several thousand distinct Chinese characters, could not be written by such a restricted number of options.

In North America publicly available networked computing emerged on a small scale in 1978 with the founding of the Computerized Bulletin Board System (CBBS), a dial-up technology that enabled a limited number of users to access message boards housed on central computers. The establishment of ASCII at this time as the standard input and display code across applications in North America enabled a range of text-based networks such as FidoNet,

CompuServe and later AOL to begin to offer services nationally and later overseas. One of the key features that allowed networked communication was the development in 1978 (and release onto ARPANET in 1983) of the TCP/IP set of protocols that allowed computers with different operating systems to communicate with each other via telephone lines (Carey and Elton, 2010: 217). However, an important caveat is needed here – these protocols were also based on the alphabet as well as numerals and punctuation marks used in English, thus assuming familiarity with a specific script (not to mention keyboard layout), making it difficult to use the TCP/IP protocols to send and receive data in scripts other than Roman.

Subsequent to the implementation of TCP/IP, the next development that increased the capacity for information to be sent and received via the internet was the World Wide Web, made available to the public in 1993. The Web had numerous advantages when compared with earlier applications, especially its capacity for handling formatted text, embedded graphics and sound and visual media. However, Web programming and mark-up languages carried over existing biases in terms of their reliance on Roman script. Initially languages using scripts other than Roman needed to upload their Web pages as image files, resulting in slow download speeds and lack of searchability. Hence, as Pargman and Palme, in their analysis of 'ASCII imperialism', concluded, 'there does exist a bias among the organisations, institutions, and individuals' involved in setting the standards for computer communication 'that works in favour of English-speaking Internet users' (2009: 197).

By 1994, the development of Web browsers able to launch applications that displayed content using earlier internet protocols meant that much information embedded in previous systems was still available. This fact, added to the ability to search for content across different platforms, enabled the Web to become the most popular internet application across many jurisdictions within a few years of its development. In North America the transition from early internet applications such as Usenet and various Bulletin Board Systems (BBS) was largely seamless since the Web included many features already made familiar in these contexts and it simply enhanced the user experience, making the retrieval and upload of information more straightforward for those with less computer literacy. These factors resulted in a large imbalance in the amount of material available in English vis-a-vis other (especially non-European) languages in the late 1990s. For instance, one of the earliest surveys of language presence on the internet conducted by the Babel Project discovered that as of June 1997, 84 percent of Web content was in English, followed by 4.5 percent in German. At this time only 3.1 percent was in Japanese and Chinese usage had yet to register (cited in Gerrand, 2007). This massive imbalance in the amount of information available in English led some Korean and Japanese commentators to complain at the time of an American 'hegemony over Internet culture' (Auh, 1998; see also Nishigaki, 1998).

## CHALLENGES TO COMPUTING WITH CHARACTER-BASED SCRIPTS

As mentioned earlier, many non-European-language users, particularly those in East Asia whose written languages were not alphabet based but depended to some extent upon the reproduction of complex characters originating in China (such as Chinese, Japanese and, to an extent, Korean), were not familiar with the typewriter. Although typewriters for Asian scripts did exist, they were cumbersome and could only be used by highly trained operatives, making it impossible to reproduce the typing pools that had developed across Western businesses and government departments (Choi, 2013: 42; Gottlieb, 2000: 136–7).

The possibilities for easier text input, display and retrieval afforded by computers were therefore of great interest to East Asian businesses and governments and from the 1970s onward various schemes and protocols were explored across the region. However, unlike the close cooperation between North American and European researchers and manufacturers at the time, there was little attempt at achieving standardisation between countries in the region (Contreras, 2014). One major problem was the restricted memory available in early computers, making it difficult to develop code to deal with characters beyond the 26 letters of the Roman alphabet, Arabic numerals and a small number of key punctuation symbols associated with written English. The fact that the internet and CMC more generally were pioneered in the United States, a largely English-speaking jurisdiction, meant that there had been little inclination to invest in technology to expand this character range. Hence, as Breen (2007: 1) points out, at the time of these early developments in computing, it made little sense to speak of 'computing in English' – since the use of the English language was embedded in the very architecture of computer programs and English was the default language for international communication on the early internet (Breen and Tokita, 2004: 1; Pargman and Palme, 2009: 184; Weber, 1997: 16). However, 'computing in Japanese' (or Chinese or Korean) raised a whole set of issues particular to these languages and there have been a number of studies dedicated to the specific computing problems raised by the use of East Asian scripts (see, for example, Gottlieb, 2000; Lunde, 1999; Unger, 1987).

During the 1970s separate attempts were made in countries of the East Asian region by computer manufacturing companies and other bodies to develop 'double byte character sets' that could cope with a non-phonetic ideograph-style writing system, but unlike in North America and Europe where the American system had become standard, there was no unifying system in place for the input and conversion of Chinese characters (used across all three languages) nor for the local *hiragana* and *katakana* syllabaries used in Japan or for the *hangul* alphabet in Korea. Only during the 1980s did the need for texts to move across national boundaries as well as for the use of multiple scripts in the same document become apparent (Breen and Tokita, 2004: 2).

It was not until 1993 that Unicode, a system that integrated aspects of the ISO 10646 code that the International Organization for Standardization, an independent NGO based in Geneva, had developed, was publicly released. Unicode was a 16-bit system allowing a potential 65,536 characters that finally allowed for the inputting and displaying of 'unified CJK [Chinese, Japanese and Korean] ideographs' across platforms and applications. However, this code could not itself address some fundamental biases concerning script built into the architecture of the internet. For instance, Japanese and Chinese text is traditionally written from right to left in a vertical manner from top to bottom of the page. Also, unlike European languages, which separate words on the page and screen, other than paragraph spaces, Chinese and Japanese are written without word breaks (Unger, 1987: 29–31). This distinctive writing style requires conversion software to recognise not just individual words but also lexemes.

Another fundamental bias concerning script is the reliance on the Roman alphabet plus numerals and common punctuation devices in the coding of internet protocols and Web domain addresses. In 1998 the Multilingual Internet Names Consortium, an NGO that had emerged from a research project based in Singapore, began to address this issue and in 2003 a standard conversion algorithm was developed and approved by the Internet Engineering Task Force. This allowed for a domain name to be written in a local script familiar to end users (deploying Unicode) and then converted into the international format familiar to Web browsers that utilised the limited ASCII character set (Breen and Tokita, 2004: 3). It thus took a decade after the introduction of the Web before users in Japan and China were able to use their character-based scripts in the designation of Web addresses.

## EARLY ONLINE NETWORKING: BULLETIN BOARD SYSTEMS

For the majority of early adopters across East Asia it was in the context of various Bulletin Board Systems (BBS) that they became accustomed to CMC, especially in regard to the input and display of native scripts. BBS are among the earliest forms of social networking and information-sharing systems that introduced users to many of the online activities that we take for granted today. These included message boards used for news sharing and the posting of ads and personal requests, file sharing, online gaming, self-advertisement, chat and debate. However, despite the fact that these systems pioneered some of these familiar applications, technical limitations meant that they offered a communications environment that lacked the immediacy of the modern internet. Lack of memory and slow data speeds have already been discussed regarding script input and display, but these issues also affected the kind of material that could be exchanged online, limiting it mostly to text. In addition, the number of phone lines that were able to link to a mainframe at any one time was limited, leading to connectivity issues. It was also not unusual for phone companies to charge for connectivity by the minute, encouraging users to avoid peak times and take advantage of lower off-peak rates late at night.

BBS have generally been supplanted by newer, Web-based applications such as online forums and commercial sites like Facebook. From 1995 onward, news sharing, an important early function, was replaced by portal sites such as yahoo.com, and chat functions were replaced by instant messaging tools such as those supported by MSN. Yet for over a decade prior to the launch of the Web, BBS played an important role in the development of internet culture globally. BBS were supported by a set of internet protocols known as Telnet that in the days of limited bandwidth and computer memory enabled a no-frills display of textual information. The display was in plain text and without the use of images, or sound and video files. There was no mouse to navigate the screen and commands needed to be issued by hotkey combinations such as Ctrl + R for replying to a message. Thus, a familiarity with the QWERTY keyboard was necessary for these early users, but once the commands had been memorised the navigation of services was fairly straightforward. It was also not too difficult to set up a BBS of one's own and many individuals and small groups dedicated to niche interests and pastimes took advantage of the technology to network.

The introduction of the Web in the mid 1990s did not immediately supplant the use of BBS. Instead BBS sites were reconfigured to allow access from a Web browser in addition to a Telnet connection and support site navigation via a mouse, not key commands. Increased bandwidth also granted enhanced functionality, particularly support for multimedia formats. However, as more sophisticated Web-based services were developed many users simply migrated to these new and more powerful applications, preferring to search for information via Google or chat and exchange opinions on MSN. As in North America and Europe, BBS played an important role in the initial development of computer literacy and communication across East Asia, where Web-based BBS have remained influential in Japan and mainland China, and earlier Telnet versions are still in use in Taiwan, as outlined below.

## THE PERSISTENCE OF BBS IN TAIWAN

As a small and relatively resource-poor island that supports a large population of over 23 million, keeping a competitive edge in exports has been vital for Taiwan's development. Hence, in the early 1980s there was growing awareness among government agencies that Taiwan needed to do more to keep up with developed nations in terms of computerisation and office automation. Yet, as Wang points out, given language and other differences, 'computerization and automation [could not] be accomplished by just purchasing the hardware' (1984: 15) since a number of changes needed to take place, including the abolition of martial law in 1987 and the subsequent deregulation of the telecommunications industry.

Internationally networked communication began in Taiwan in 1988 when an existing network of local Taiwanese computer hobbyists established a connection to FidoNet, which allowed previously independent and isolated BBS to be linked together in a network spanning international borders (Li et al., 2017: 183). However, at this time the bandwidth restrictions of dial up and problems with handling of Chinese script limited the uptake of the technology. In 1990 the Taiwanese government took the lead in internet development, funding internet centres across three national universities, providing subsidised access to all staff and students. This initial network soon spread to other universities where it became common to provide internet access portals to students living in campus dormitories. At this time students were introduced to a number of CMC features including BBS; however, unlike the previous costly and limited dial-up system deployed by the original BBS innovators, the Taiwanese system used a TCP/IP model providing enhanced bandwidth that also supported the use of Chinese script (Li et al., 2017: 184–5).

Universities generally embraced student use of BBS, viewing the technology as a means to communicate efficiently with the student body. However, the systems were often set up and run by student volunteers, causing tension between the institutional owners of the system and the everyday administrators. The need to negotiate with institutions about technical innovations frustrated many students, who looked for ways to develop their own private networks using the infrastructure provided by their universities. Student innovators developed a number of plug-in packages that enabled individuals to easily set up their own BBS on existing university networks, leading to a boom where up to 400 large Telnet BBS were in operation between 1996 and 2000, a significant number for the island's population of only 21 million at the time (Li et al., 2017: 188).

During the late 1990s, even though other Web-based networking forums were now available, there was a strong preference among Taiwanese students for continued interaction via BBS. This was partly to do with language – there was simply much more content in Chinese on existing BBS forums than on the Web at this time, but there was also the perception that Web pages were somewhat 'static', difficult to update in real time and separated from the needs and interests of their users. Campus-based BBS on the other hand seemed to speak much more directly to their student audiences in a language all could use and deploying technology developed by the students themselves. It is for these reasons that Li et al. (2017) point to the continued salience of BBS technology in Taiwan at a time when Web-based systems were proving much more popular in Euro-American contexts. As one of their informants pointed out, 'Back in the old days, when other countries were crazy for Web sites, for several years college students in the whole [of] Taiwan were mad about developing and improving BBS systems' (2017: 188). Indeed, BBS have maintained their popularity among Taiwanese students today, especially the PTT network originally founded by a National Taiwan University student in 1995, which still uses a Telnet protocol offering a primarily text-based environment.

The continuing popularity of BBS use among students in particular can be put down to the strong sense of community and ownership as requisite technical skills and administrative duties have been handed down from generation to generation of student users. BBS in Taiwan maintained their critical edge and autonomy at a time when Web-based networks were becoming increasingly commercialised and dominated by advertising. PTT is now the most popular BBS in Taiwan, with more than 20,000 discussion boards. Indeed, it has been such an important part of the life of generations of students that in 2012 it was the topic of a major movie supposedly based on 'true events' taking place on the discussion boards (*Taiwan Today,* 2010). Like Japan's 2-channel, which also utilises a BBS format (albeit Web based), PTT has developed its own online lingo and art and become a major part of the country's media landscape, accessed by both current and former students. The continuing interest in and access to BBS networks across the population in Taiwan is distinct from the situation in mainland China (discussed below) where, due to legislation introduced in 2005 that required all college BBS to 'transform into exclusive, on-campus communication platforms based on real name registration', off-campus users and alumni are barred from participating (Jin, 2008: 22–3).

## MAINLAND CHINA: FROM BBS TO THE WEB

Early computer networking in mainland China between 1986 and 1992 was limited to email applications shared between university computer research labs. China, spurred on by the Clinton administration's strong support for internet infrastructure, was first linked to the internet via a dedicated line connecting to the United States in 1994 (Jin, 2008), at a time when the Web was already becoming the most popular means of creating and navigating internet content. However, the costs of computer purchase plus connecting to the network as well as a lack of computer literacy were initial barriers to widespread adoption.

China's first TCP/IP-based BBS, known as the Dawn BBS, was established soon after China's connection with the World Wide Web in April 1994, and hosted by the National Research Centre for Intelligent Computing Systems. It was the first public internet-based BBS in China, offering services such as news updates, online forums and chat rooms. Universities, among the first institutions to be given internet access, allowed students easy access to the new communications technology, initially via BBS. Telnet-based commercial BBS such as the 'sports salon' affiliated with Sitong Lifang Information Technology Company also gained mass audiences at this time. These early BBS communities were established on CFidoNet, a branch of the international FidoNet system, with a user-base of around 10,000 at its peak in 1997. These early adopters were well-educated and tech-savvy individuals from the economically developed south-east of the country and tended to be liberal in political outlook, supporting a wide variety of discussion topics (Li, 2010: 67). Yet, unlike in Taiwan where private student-run BBS were able to grow outside of government and university control, on the mainland government interference, including the closing of popular sites, soon tempered the liberal outlook of these first forums (Li, 2010: 69).

1997 saw the roll-out of popular commercial portal websites such as Sina.com. In 1998 Sitong was incorporated into Sina, which became the largest Web portal in the Chinese-speaking world (Yang, 2017: 372), inaugurating the era of Web-based BBS. Other commercial developments encouraged Web uptake at this time, with major news outlets setting up their Web presence and internet startups such as Netease.com offering free space for users to build their own Web pages (Yang, 2017: 372). Web-based BBS still remain popular, focusing as they do on topics and issues of social concern, as opposed to other more people-centric social networks (*Inside China,* 2012).

## EARLY KOREAN APPLICATIONS ANTICIPATE THE WEB

In Korea the development of internet cultures can be traced back to 1982, when the government introduced a research-oriented computer communication network using TCP/IP protocols. As Jo comments, although there had been some use of computers in Korea dating from the late 1970s, 'the effective implementation of a Korean character code and the search for an optimal standard were key factors necessary before new information and communication technologies could become part of popular and mass culture' (2017: 199). Although Korean script has also traditionally employed *hanja* (the Korean equivalent of Chinese characters), these have mostly fallen out of use, albeit they are still studied at school and widely comprehended. Hence, the development of code for the processing of the native *hangul* alphabet does not pose the same challenges as character-based scripts such as Chinese and Japanese, given that *hangul* consists of a finite set of 19 consonants and 21 vowels. The main problem was one of consistency, since before 1987 there were numerous competing and incompatible software programs for the processing of the *hangul* script before the KS C 5601 character set was adapted as the national standard.

The Data Communication Company of Korea (DACOM) was established by the government in 1982 and was intended to be the main artery for data flow. It was established on a top-down broadcast model with limited interaction from users. Developments included a video text service known as Chollian, inaugurated in 1987, with terminals set up in airports, major hotels and event venues. This limited access meant that the service was not widely used, and it was relaunched in 1988 with an expanded number of services, including home shopping, but still failed to catch on with a broad public.

Jo (2017) argues that the first internet cultures in Korea did not develop around users of the Chollian terminals but instead emerged from early adopters of email communication. In 1984 DACOM established an email service that was connected to the United States and made available to research institutions and major corporations, but the system was only formatted to handle text in English and did not prove popular with individual users. At the time an alternative system that could receive and display messages in the *hangul* script, known as H-mail, was already being used among DACOM employees and was gradually rolled out to its corporate clients and, from 1987, it was made available to the general public. Uptake was not rapid, however, for a number of reasons, mainly due to low PC penetration rates and the need for expensive hardware such as modems.

Despite the relatively few users, H-mail saw some important developments that prefigured in many ways the kinds of collaborative cultures that were to come into their own with the roll-out of Web-based social media platforms in the early 2000s. For instance, affordances of the system such as BBS news groups and chat-like electronic conferencing spaces proved extremely popular. Unlike the Chollian system, where users accessed predetermined information, the information on H-mail was mostly provided by and shared among the users themselves. Like on early internet networks in North America, and paralleling the experience in Taiwan at this time, H-mail boards provided the perfect environment for networking among computer nerds and hackers who were interested in providing an enhanced user experience, often against the directives of the network owners. These networks led to the establishment of the first BBS systems in 1988, which, like in Taiwan at the time, became extremely popular among university students. However unlike in Taiwan where one board, PTT, developed rapidly on the back of government support for university networks, the early BBS systems in Korea were 'skunkworks'-style developments set up by individuals or small teams since, as Jo points out, at the time private usage of a modem and unauthorised communications systems like the BBS were regarded as potential threats to national security (2017: 204–5). It was on these early BBS that *donghohoe* or popular 'friendship associations' developed, challenging the information retrieval model of internet communication anticipated by the authorities (Jo, 2017: 205). Hence, when major internet portals began to offer Web-based internet café and communication-style services in the late 1990s, they were tapping into cultures of use and expectation that had already been established in the BBS era, albeit extending these services to users beyond their original tech-savvy and student-based cohorts.

## JAPAN AND THE EARLY ADOPTION OF THE MOBILE INTERNET

The difficulty of inputting Japanese text and the lack of familiarity with computing technology among the general public meant that computer literacy was very low in Japan in the early 1980s (McLelland, 2017). There were also industry and policy factors that slowed the development even of a hobbyist cohort of computer pioneers (Contreras, 2014: 919). Due to restrictions on the use of Japanese telephone lines, prior to industry reform in 1985 those hobbyists who wanted to access computer networks had to do so via overseas systems such as CompuServe in the United States, requiring expensive international dial-up fees and some fluency in English (Shapard, 1993: 260). Even after the establishment of a growing number of local networks, Japan's overpriced leased lines and expensive metered call charges made it difficult for individuals to engage with these new opportunities.

Hence, by the early 1990s, unlike the situation in North America, there was 'no strong tradition of grassroots approaches in info-communications and no extensive experience in the use of electronic community networks via CATV or computer networks' in Japan (Latzer, 1995: 524). The computing environment was largely defined by mainframes and proprietary systems complete with bundled software, and the price of personal computers remained high (Parker Smith, 1997: 26). Established business practices prioritising face-to-face meetings and the exchange of hand-written documents via tele-fax also delayed the take-up of email exchange. The exchange of email, which encourages lateral connections between employees, was also a cause for concern in many of Japan's major businesses used to top-down communication structures (Parker Smith, 1997: 29). The uptake of personal computers was also low compared with other developed nations. Research in 1994, for instance, showed a PC penetration rate of 15.8 percent for the United States and only 5.7 percent for Japan. Significantly, of these American computers, 52 percent were linked to local area networks compared with only 8.6 percent of Japanese computers that were similarly linked (Latzer, 1995: 524). Japanese people's relative lack of familiarity with computers is also seen in a 1997 survey comparing Japanese with American and Korean computer literacy. It was found that the Japanese had least familiarity with a keyboard, only 23.7 percent of Japanese indicating that they could 'type fast' compared with 31.6 percent of Koreans and 54.4 percent of Americans. In Japan 50.8 percent of respondents indicated they had never used a computer, in comparison to only 21.8 percent of American respondents (Fouser, 2001: 274). This situation meant that the discourse about Japan and the internet in journalistic venues such as *Wired* was framed in terms of bureaucratic incompetence and cultural entrenchment, stressing a need for 'catch-up' based on American models (see, for example, Abate, 1996; Johnstone, 1994).

As in Taiwan, mainland China and Korea, issues of interoperability raised by different encoding systems needed to be overcome before the widespread adoption of CMC was possible. The situation in Japan was even more complex than in these other nations since in addition to 2,000 or so basic *kanji* (Chinese characters), Japanese also uses two native syllabaries, *hiragana* and *katakana*, which function like alphabets. Prior to 1995 there had been little attempt to develop a unified approach to language input and display problems, leading to Japan's major computer manufacturers developing their own proprietary systems (Seo, 2013: 186). This meant that although there were several BBS-style computer networks, including NEC's PC-Van and Fujitsu's Nifty-Serve, each with about half a million subscribers by 1994, the networks could not link with each other (McLelland, 2017).

These companies pioneered what is known in Japanese as *pasokon tsūshin* or 'personal computer communication' – initially based on a BBS that enabled users to seek out information from various news feeds as well as participate in online discussions and send emails to other users – albeit, in the early years at least, only with those on the same system (McLelland, 2017). The interoperability problem was finally overcome, not by Japanese computer companies, but by an outside intervention from IBM, which licensed its DOS/V software in 1995, allowing computer manufacturers to market open systems that allowed anyone to install Japanese fonts onto their PCs (Parker Smith, 1997: 28). The launch of a Japanese version of Windows 95 at the end of 1995 made available a host of new applications and was a major boost to PC sales among the general public, with smaller and lighter laptops proving the most popular. This early familiarity with BBS-style communication in Japan helps to explain the phenomenal rise of the 2-channel Web-based BBS site established in 1999, which at its peak in the mid 2000s was receiving 2.5 million posts a day. Like the PTT BBS system in Taiwan discussed earlier, 2-channel has played a major role in Japan's internet culture, becoming an alternative news outlet and developing its own distinct language and art forms (Katayama, 2007).

However, the major boom in internet connectivity in Japan did not eventuate as a result of gradually increasing PC penetration, but as a result of the early adoption of the mobile internet accessed via the *keitai denwa* (handheld phone). In the late 1990s in Japan internet access was expensive, requiring investment in a computer, modem and line rental and, as telecoms were still charging for dial-up calls by the minute, Web browsing could rack up large bills. In 1999 NTT's 'i-mode' system allowed access to specially configured sites using a cell phone and charged only for downloads, not time spent browsing. I-mode did not deploy WAP (Wireless Application Protocol), which was developed by an industry-wide consortium in Europe and North America and failed to connect with consumers at the time, largely due to the impoverished Web environment that could be provided on a screen capable of displaying only a few lines of text (Vincent, 2001: 16). Instead, the Japanese system used a simplified form of HTML that required sites to be specifically designed or converted for the system, meaning that i-mode was only available in Japan and able to be accessed via the specially configured *keitai* handsets. As a result, early advertising for the medium avoided discussion of specifications and even avoided mention of the internet or the Web, stressing instead the convenience of the various applications offered (such as ticket reservations, email and music downloads) (Natsuno, 2003: 77).

The sudden boom of interest in i-mode can be understood in the context of earlier developments that had introduced consumers to the convenience of handheld communication devices. The popularity of pagers among Japanese teens, for example, has been noted, especially the manner in which schoolgirls used the pagers' numerical display capacity to send coded messages (Kohiyama, 2005: 64). Matsuda argues that early adopters among the nation's youth simply carried over this message-exchange function when they moved to mobile phones, pointing out that 'the *keitai* Internet is substantially different from that accessed by personal computers' (2005: 124). The relative absence of a widespread PC-based internet culture in Japan, alongside the functionality of the specially designed i-mode sites and handsets containing several short-cut buttons, made mobile internet access seem efficient and attractive. The *keitai* also saw an innovation in input method for the Japanese language, using a limited numerical keypad where each number on the pad is associated with a sequence of *kana* syllables – such as ka, ki, ku, ke, ko – with the desired syllable being selected according to the number of button presses. Once the phonetic spelling of the desired term is visible on screen, conversion to the required *kanji* can be achieved by the use of an arrow button, allowing the entire process to be navigated just by using one thumb – giving rise to the moniker *yubi-zoku* or 'thumb tribe' to describe young people who soon became proficient in this input style.

It is subsequent to the advent of mobile internet access via the *keitai* that the history of the internet in Japan can no longer be framed as a matter of 'catch up'. Indeed, by the end of May 2001, 40 million Japanese were able to access a version of the internet on their mobiles, while in August 2000 only four million North Americans had such access (Miyata et al., 2005: 145). Yet the i-mode system allowed access to a limited internet environment, isolated from the World Wide Web, where sponsored commercial sites allowed users to purchase information, items and services and have the cost added to their monthly phone bill, thus obviating the need for credit card transactions. One particular success of this model has been the licensed download of music, ring tones and e-books. For over a decade i-mode was a distinct ecology within the wider internet world, complete with its own navigation and custom-designed streamline services that were both inexpensive and light on battery use. It is only in recent years that i-mode's appeal has begun to be challenged by smart phones offering a much richer Web experience and the full range of apps expected by modern consumers (Akimoto, 2011).

## CONCLUSION

This chapter has looked at language, cultural and political issues on the early internet, investigating how they affected the take-up of internet applications in North America and East Asia prior to the advent of the Web. I have argued that in the case of North America and Europe, the move from early text-based systems to the multimedia graphics interface offered by the Web was largely seamless due to the internet and the Web already sharing basic protocols, most notably reliance on ASCII, TCP/IP and the QWERTY keyboard as the main human/computer interface. Bulletin Board Systems were shown to be important precursors to Web applications in that they already anticipated many of the affordances that the Web made more widely available. While the move from BBS to Web-based applications was fairly seamless in a Euro-American context, I noted how specific cultural, language and political issues complicated the uptake of the Web to an extent in an East Asian context.

For the first few years after the roll-out of the Web, English was undoubtedly still the global language of the internet, leading students in Taiwan to remain embedded in their local Chinese-speaking BBS systems, while Japanese users developed a separate internet ecology based on i-mode mobile applications. Mainland China, due to its government's longstanding desire for information sovereignty (Qiu, 1999: 2), developed its own proprietary Web-based platforms.

However, in no sense has this chapter been arguing for cultural essentialism. It did not take long for users across East Asia to become enthusiastic adopters of Web-based platforms once issues of script input, display and interoperability had been overcome. Indeed, by 2002, 6 percent of Web content was estimated to be in Japanese (ahead of Spanish and French), and by 2005 Chinese speakers had emerged as the second-largest bloc of internet users after speakers of English (cited in Gerrand, 2007). Instead, I have argued for the need for an enhanced scrutiny of hidden biases in internet infrastructure, including the manner in which the Web extended and amplified these biases, in order to understand the complex and distinct regional negotiations that needed to take place across the globe before Web use could become the seemingly natural and default mode of internet access that it has become today.

## REFERENCES


Abate, T. (1996) 'The Midnight Hour: Japan Ventures onto the Net in the Dark of Night', *Scientific American*, January, 37.

Akimoto, A. (2011) 'In the Battle with Smart Phones is I-Mode Dead?' *Japan Times*, April 20 (http://www.japantimes.co.jp/life/2011/04/20/digital/in-the-battle-with-smart-phones-is-i-mode-dead/#.V_2l7DVH5W0), accessed 18 June 2018.

Auh, T.-S. (1998) 'Promoting Multiculturalism on the Internet: Korean Experience', paper, Graduate School of Journalism and Mass Communication, Korea University, Republic of Korea (http://www.unesco.org/Webworld/infoethics_2/eng/papers/paper_8.htm), accessed 17 March 2017.

Breen, J., and Tokita, A. (2004) 'The WWW in Japan: A Threat to Cultural Identity or a Domesticated System?' First International Conference on Cultures and Technologies in Asia, Mumbai, India, Feb 2004 (http://www.edrdg.org/~jwb/paperdir/jwww.html), accessed 18 June 2018.

Breen, J. (2007) 'Computing in Japanese: What Are the Frontiers Now?' Workshop on Computational Japanese Studies, University of Tokyo (http://www.csse.monash.edu.au/~jwb/cj_abstract.html), accessed 17 March 2017.

Carey, J., and Elton, M. (2010) *When Media Are New: Understanding the Dynamics of New Media Adoption and Use*. Ann Arbor: MIT Press.

Castillo, M. (2011) 'QWERTY, @, &, #', *American Journal of Neuroradiology*, 32: 613–14.

Choi, Y.B. (2013) 'Path Dependence on the Korean Keyboard', *Journal of Economic Behaviour and Organization*, 88: 37–46.

Contreras, J. (2014) 'Divergent Patterns of Engagement in Internet Standardization: Japan, Korea and China', *Telecommunications Policy*, 38: 914–32.

Fouser, R. (2001) '"Culture", Computer Literacy and the Media in Creating Public Attitudes to CMC in Japan and Korea', in Charles Ess (ed.), *Culture, Technology, Communication: Towards an Intercultural Global Village*, Albany: SUNY Press, pp. 261–78.

Gerrand, P. (2007) 'Estimating Linguistic Diversity on the Internet: A Taxonomy to Avoid Pitfalls and Paradoxes', *Journal of Computer Mediated Communication*, 12(4): 1298–321.

Goggin, G., and McLelland, M. (2017) 'Global Coordinates of Internet Histories', in Gerard Goggin and Mark McLelland (eds), *The Routledge Companion to Global Internet Histories*, New York: Routledge, pp. 1–20.

Gottlieb, N. (2000) *Word Processing Technology in Japan: Kanji and the Keyboard*. Richmond: Curzon.

*Inside China*. (2012) 'Chinese BBS – The Social Activity that Never Grows Old' (http://thinkingchinese.com/chinese-bbs-the-social-activity-that-never-grows-old)

Jin, L. (2008) 'Chinese Online BBS Sphere: What BBS Has Brought to China', Master's thesis, Massachusetts Institute of Technology (http://pdf.textfiles.com/academics/liwen-jin2008.pdf), accessed 18 June 2018.

Jo, D. (2017) 'H-mail and the Early Configuration of Online User Culture in Korea', in Gerard Goggin and Mark McLelland (eds), *The Routledge Companion to Global Internet Histories*, New York: Routledge, pp. 197–208.

Johnstone, B. (1994) 'Wiring Japan: A Bitter Cultural Clash Has Reduced Japan to a Third-Rate Power in Networking', *Wired*, 1 February (http://archive.wired.com/wired/archive/2.02/wiring.japan_pr.html)

Katayama, L. (2007) '2-Channel Gives Japan's Famously Quiet People a Mighty Voice', *Wired*, 19 April (http://archive.wired.com/culture/lifestyle/news/2007/04/2channel), accessed 18 June 2018.

Kohiyama, K. (2005) 'A Decade in the Development of Mobile Communications in Japan (1993–2002)', in Mizuko Ito, Daisuke Okabe, and Misa Matsuda (eds), *Personal, Portable, Pedestrian: Mobile Phones in Japanese Life*, Cambridge: MIT Press, pp. 61–70.

Latzer, M. (1995) 'Japanese Information Infrastructure Initiatives', *Telecommunications Policy*, 19(7): 515–29.

Li, S. (2010) 'The Online Public Space and Popular Ethos in China', *Media, Culture and Society*, 32(1): 63–83.

Li, S.L., Lin, Y.-R., and Huang, A.H.-M. (2017) 'Brief History of Taiwanese Internet: The BBS Culture', in Gerard Goggin and Mark McLelland (eds), *The Routledge Companion to Global Internet Histories*, New York: Routledge, pp. 182–96.

Lunde, K. (1999) *CJKV Information Processing*. Sebastopol, CA: O'Reilly & Associates.

Matsuda, M. (2005) 'Mobile Communication and Selective Sociality', in Mizuko Ito, Daisuke Okabe, and Misa Matsuda (eds), *Personal, Portable, Pedestrian: Mobile Phones in Japanese Life*, Cambridge: MIT Press, pp. 123–42.

McLelland, M. (2017) 'Early Computer Networks in Japan 1984–1994', in Gerard Goggin and Mark McLelland (eds), *The Routledge Companion to Global Internet Histories*, New York: Routledge, pp. 171–80.

Miyata, K., Boase, J., Wellman, B., and Ikeda, K. (2005) 'The Mobile-izing Japanese: Connecting to the Internet by PC and Webphone in Yamanashi', in Mizuko Ito, Daisuke Okabe, and Misa Matsuda (eds), *Personal, Portable, Pedestrian: Mobile Phones in Japanese Life*, Cambridge: MIT Press, pp. 143–63.

Natsuno, T. (2003) *The i-mode Wireless Ecosystem*. Chichester: John Wiley & Sons.

Nishigaki, T. (1998) 'Multilingualism on the Net', Paper presented at UNESCO INFOethics '98 (http://www.unesco.org/Webworld/infoethics_2/eng/papers/paper_5.htm), accessed 17 March 2017.

Pargman, D., and Palme, J. (2009) 'ASCII Imperialism', in Martha Lampland and Susan Leigh Star (eds), *Standards and their Stories: How Quantifying, Classifying and Formalizing Practices Shape Everyday Life*, Ithaca: Cornell University Press, pp. 177–99.

Parker Smith, N. (1997) 'Computing in Japan: From Cocoon to Competition', *Computing*, March, 26–33.

Qiu, J.L. (1999) 'Virtual Censorship in China: Keeping the Gate between Cyberspaces', *International Journal of Law and Communications Policy*, 4: 1–25.

Seo, D. (2013) *Evolution and Standardization of Mobile Communications Technology*. Hershey, PA: Information Science Reference.

Shapard, J. (1993) 'Islands in the (Data)Stream: Language, Character Codes, and Electronic Isolation in Japan', in Linda M. Harasim (ed.), *Global Networks: Computers and International Communication*, Cambridge, MA: MIT Press, pp. 255–70.

*Taiwan Today*. (2010) 'BBS-themed Movie Stirs Up Campuses', June 8 (http://taiwantoday.tw/ct.asp?xitem=106214&ctnode=1730&mp=9), accessed 18 June 2018.

UNESCO. (2005) 'Measuring Linguistic Diversity on the Internet', UNESCO, Paris (http://www.unesco.org/new/en/communication-and-information/resources/publications-and-communication-materials/publications/full-list/measuring-linguistic-diversity-on-the-internet/), accessed 18 June 2018.

Unger, J.M. (1987) *The Fifth Generation Fallacy: Why Japan Is Betting its Future on Artificial Intelligence*. New York: Oxford University Press.

Vincent, G. (2001) 'Learning from I-Mode [Packet-Based Mobile Network]', *IEE Review*, 47(6): 13–18.

Wang, G. (1984) 'Information Revolution in Taiwan: Economic Concerns and Beyond', in AMIC-ISEAS-EWC Workshop on Information Revolution in Asia-Pacific, Singapore, Dec 10–12, 1984, Singapore: Asian Mass Communication Research & Information Centre (https://dr.ntu.edu.sg/bitstream/handle/10220/311/AMIC_DEC10-12_1984_10.pdf?sequence=1), accessed 18 June 2018.

Weber, G. (1997) 'Top Languages: The World's Top 10 Languages', *Language Today*, 2: 22–8.

Yang, L. (2017) 'Platforms, Practices, and Politics: A Snapshot of Networked Fan Communities in China', in Gerard Goggin and Mark McLelland (eds), *Routledge Companion to Global Internet Histories*, New York: Routledge, pp. 370–84.

# 37

# Online Pornography

Susanna Paasonen

Pornography has played a crucial, albeit often neglected role in the development of Web solutions and Web economy since their very earliest days. The enterprises of online gaming and shopping began to pick up towards the end of the 1990s, whereas pornography remained, virtually from the launch of the first graphic Web browsers, one of the few forms of content that users were consistently willing to pay for (Lane, 2001: xiii; Perdue, 2002). Safe credit card processing systems, streaming video technologies, hosting services, promotional design practices such as banner advertisements, mousetrapping, and pop-ups were first developed for and applied on porn sites (Bennett, 2001; Lane, 2001: 70; Johnson, 2010; McNair, 2013: 27–9). Pornography has often been heralded as a 'killer app' as a form of content that quickly migrates to new media platforms with commercial success: this was certainly the case with the Web in the 1990s.

Despite both online pornography's remarkable perennial popularity among consumers and the vocal public concerns that it tends to evoke, academic studies concerning it – and particularly ones focusing on commercial platforms – remained few up until the 2010s. The rare in-depth studies that did exist focused almost exclusively on US contexts (Lane, 2001), on alternative and independent pornographies (Jacobs, 2007), or both (Magnet, 2007). It is fair to state that Web porn long remained one of the most understudied areas in Internet research. Significant knowledge gaps continue to exist when it comes to the production, distribution, and consumption of Web pornography in a historical perspective.

More porn is available on the Web than ever to date and massively popular video aggregator sites modelled after YouTube (est. 2005) sport multiple billion annual visits. This development seems to resonate with the broad diagnoses on the pornification of media culture, according to which pornographic aesthetics have grown ubiquitous enough to infiltrate diverse visual media practices from advertising to the circulation of nude selfies. At the same time, pornography's role and position is currently crucially different than in the Web cultures of the 1990s. Despite its perennial popularity, the role of porn as a driving force of dot.com enterprise and technical innovation has clearly passed, as has the period when one could create quick profits by simply setting up an adult site. Pornographic content is actively weeded out from the targeted advertising and linked content on social media sites such as Facebook, Instagram, and Pinterest. As tech journalist Cade Metz notes,

> with the rising power of companies like Apple and Google and Facebook, the adult industry doesn't drive new technology. In many respects, it doesn't even have access to new technology. The big tech companies behind the big platforms control not only the gateway services (the iPhone app store, Google Search, the Facebook social network) but the gateway devices (the iPhone, Android phones, Google Chromecast, the Amazon Fire TV, the Oculus Rift virtual reality headset). And for the most part, they've shut porn out. (Metz, 2015)

All this results in a complex nexus where the abundant accessibility and diversity of Web porn meets its limited visibility on social media and app markets, insufficient knowledge of the working practices and economies of pornography, and public discourses of concern on the pornification of culture. Exploring these connections and disconnections, this chapter first maps out the development of Web pornography from the home-grown enterprises of the early 1990s to the increasing visibility of sexual subcultures and the presence of established companies on online platforms. It then examines the shifts that have occurred in porn production with the ubiquity of proam (a.k.a. professional amateur), reality, and amateur productions, as well as the centralization of porn distribution on video aggregator sites. The chapter explains how Web technologies and the centrality of search functions and metadata in particular have affected the development and uses of pornographic content, what kinds of sexual taste cultures have emerged, how the public visibility of pornography has been altered in the course of its online distribution, and how this connects to the policing of online content in national-level media regulation and policy, as well as in terms of the moderation carried out by online platforms. All this necessitates understanding the production of Web pornography, as well as the notion of the porn industry that it connects to, as characterized by inner distinctions and constant fragmentation on the one hand, and by the increasing centralization of ownership and distribution, on the other.

## PORN AND THE WEB: A PERFECT MATCH?

Graphic Web browsers such as Mosaic (1993), Netscape Navigator (1994), and Microsoft Explorer (1995) made it possible to embed image files and, gradually, animated GIFs and video clips into the interface. Multimodal interface design possibilities were understandably lucrative for the distribution of pornography, which relies heavily on visual and audiovisual material, despite the continuing popularity of literary porn, especially in its user-generated forms (Lane, 2001: 69–70; Paasonen, 2010a). At the time, the market of porn was dominated by VHS, DVD, and magazine releases sold in special shops and newsagents, as well as through mail order.

Pornography was readily and plentifully available on Usenet and bulletin board systems (BBSs) alike as binary files, and it soon migrated to Web platforms. Initially, the most visible and successful Web porn enterprises were small-scale ventures that occasionally had the same people performing in front of the camera as writing the HTML. Some – such as the amateur star 'Wifey' of Wife's World – had established their reputation on Usenet, while others – such as Danni Ashe, the owner and star of Danni.com – also had modelling and stripping experience before starting to run their own sites (Perdue, 2002: 27, 156–8; Mash, 2004; Paasonen, 2011: 35, 93–5). Large, established video production studios and print publishers, from Playboy to Penthouse, Hustler, Vivid, and Private, did not similarly pioneer in establishing their Web presence, coin innovative online services, or by any means invest extensively in them (Perdue, 2002: 63). These companies advertised their productions online but were relatively slow in extending their business models to Web distribution. The dwindling markets of DVD and magazine retail later considerably hurt such established brands. Playboy temporarily dropped sexually explicit images in 2016 in response to feedback from its younger readers, while both Hustler and Penthouse have struggled to keep up their print production.

Code remained simple and easily manageable during the first years of the Web. Before the development of Web professions and design solutions such as cascading stylesheets (CSS) and JavaScript, it took relatively little skill to set up and run a site. Since the professional standards of Web design were yet to be established (Kotamraju, 1999), the playground was notably level for both aspiring independent pornographers and multimillion-dollar companies trading in porn superstars. Consequently, 1990s Web porn was heterogeneous in terms of its agents, economies, aesthetics, and agendas. Porn was made available in limited 'free tour' sections of pay sites, as pirated content, as thumbnail teasers on link sites, as free content, and as materials protected by pay walls. US products dominated the markets of Web porn, yet low distribution costs, coupled with the increasing affordability of digital cameras and the gradual demographic diversification of Internet users in terms of nationality, age, and ethnicity, broadened the base of porn production. Combined with the increased circulation and accumulation of pre-digital pornographies on online platforms and the rise in the distribution of amateur content, this resulted in the clear expansion of available pornographies, from sites specializing in erotica writing to queer experimental porn and glossy commercial pornography targeted at straight male audiences.

While Web hosting was never exactly free, especially when involving larger user bases and audiovisual content necessitating more bandwidth, online distribution was particularly tempting for independent entrepreneurs that had little or no resources to engage in DVD or print production. Online distribution was an attractive option for porn producers on a number of levels. First of all, it afforded a potentially global audience unlimited by restrictions in local regulation, store hours, and access to retail opportunities. Content not allowed for distribution in one country could easily be placed on a server outside its borders, which eroded the viability of established systems of media regulation based on pre-screening and classification developed for the distribution of film, video, and print materials. Furthermore, by doing away with theatres, mail-order companies, and stores that have traditionally gained considerably from selling porn, Web platforms gradually redefined the ways in which porn producers reach consumers. Meanwhile, other middlemen profiting from the traffic, such as credit card companies, continued to thrive.

For consumers, online platforms drastically changed the accessibility and uses of pornography. Since porn use no longer necessitated the acquisition of material commodities, it was unnecessary to visit a specialty shop or indeed to move anywhere from one's computer. Despite the factual tracking capacities inbuilt in IP addresses and cookies, online porn consumption allowed for an unprecedented impression of anonymity. The range of available Web pornographies very soon grew, allowing for a degree of option unavailable even in the largest of porn retail stores. Given the volume of freely accessible teasers and pirated files, it was not even necessary to pay for the content downloaded beyond the connectivity charges themselves. The costs of dial-up connections were generally calculated either by second or by the bytes downloaded, and access to free pornography was therefore not all free.

## AMATEURS, PROAMS, AND INDIE PRODUCERS

The spread of digital cameras, camcorders, and smart phones provided both amateurs and semi-professional producers with inexpensive tools for making their own pornography. While amateurs have produced their own explicit content in virtually all media known to man, it was not easy to circulate on VHS tapes or as printed matter beyond one's immediate social circles (Esch and Mayer, 2007: 101). People shared their own digital content in newsgroups and through IRC (Internet Relay Chat), which allowed for exchanges between people with similar sexual palates (Slater, 1998; Dery, 2007). Amateur Web porn was successful throughout the 1990s (e.g. Lane, 2001: 209–12), yet its visibility and popularity peaked in the mid 2000s as porn distribution began to shift to platforms emulating the operating principles of social media sites. The rise in amateur porn therefore runs parallel to the overall rise in user-generated content crucial to the operating principles and business models of Web 2.0 and social media (Dijck, 2013; Marwick, 2013: 21–66; Jarrett, 2015: 7–10).

The central promise and attraction of amateur porn involves its unpolished look of realness and authenticity, which is seen to contrast with the stylized scenarios and trimmed bodies of commercial productions (e.g. Hardy, 2009; Hilderbrand, 2009: 66–7; Paasonen, 2010b). Uploaded on both general-interest video aggregator sites and platforms specialized in amateur content, user-generated clips have been shared for free, in return for gift vouchers and fixed fees. The performers of the most popular – and hence also the most visible – amateur videos have generally conformed to the body norms of (female) youth, whiteness, and thinness. The acts, gestures, and positions performed have similarly followed the choreographies of commercial porn, which are used as templates in making amateur clips look like pornography (Doorn, 2010). At the same time, videos need to have a domestic feel in order to come across as amateur productions. Amateur porn production therefore involves particular forms of gendered domestic labour even as it is presented as no work at all (Hofer, 2014: 335, 343–4). Their aesthetic of homey intimacy is connected to the assumed ethics of production, according to which amateur content is voluntarily produced for the sake of pleasure rather than for profit, and it therefore remains detached from the oppressive work conditions of the porn industry (Paasonen, 2010b: 1302–4). Images and videos leaked, stolen, and otherwise distributed without permission on revenge porn sites have a different sort of appeal, one geared towards slut shaming (Stroud, 2014). For their part, celebrity sex tapes have been both leaked and knowingly produced as the means of building one's star image (e.g. Esch and Mayer, 2007; Hilderbrand, 2009: 68–71; Cruz, 2011).

The rise in amateur pornography has been a key trend of Web porn for over a decade. The appeal of immediacy and realness is crucial to the genre of pornography, which has promised to convey sexual acts through the lens of the camera as they unfold ever since the advent of film (Williams, 1989). Gonzo porn rose to popularity in the 1990s with its seemingly improvised scenes, nonprofessional performers, and subjective camera shots (Maina and Zecca, 2016; Stella, 2016). On Web platforms, the concept of gonzo gave way to reality porn, such as the sites run by the Miami-based Reality Kings. Shot on streets and in cars, motels, and private residencies, reality porn makes use of proam performers and the constant, renewable stream of new young talent. Inexpensive to produce, reality porn balances amateur codes of authenticity with repetitive thematic and narrative patterns: the standard plot of Backroom Casting Couch, for example, involves ingénue actresses performing sexual favours in the hope of landing a part, whereas, in Bait Bus, young women are assumedly lured to have sex with the promise of money they are never to receive.

Parallel to the staged and rehearsed authenticity of reality sites and the avalanche of amateur porn, Web porn has afforded a broader public visibility to a range of sexual niches and subcultures while also commodifying them in different degrees. Be it a question of preferences concerning body size, age, ethnicity, hirsuteness or the lack thereof; tastes in role-play, bondage or discipline; fetishes involving uniforms, hiking boots, balloons, or fake fur; interest in the sexual frolicking of cartoon characters or Hollywood stars, Web platforms cater to virtually any fantasy scenarios and participatory possibilities. This has contributed to the ever clearer articulation of sexual taste cultures in the realm of pornography.

Established in 2001, Suicide Girls became the best-known soft-core alt porn site, with its emphasis on female sexual agency and subcultural body styles. The models featured tattoos, piercings, and punk and Goth coiffures, and users were invited as members to read their blogs and engage with them: in this sense, Suicide Girls framed membership as a lifestyle choice (Attwood, 2007; Magnet, 2007). The adult performer and producer Joanna Angel established Burning Angel in 2002 as the more sexually explicit alt porn site. In their applications of subcultural capital and sexual titillation, alt porn became, in Feona Attwood's (2007: 449–50) phrasing, representative of 'new sex taste cultures', which defined 'themselves through a variety of oppositions to mainstream culture – and especially mainstream porn – as creative, vibrant, classy, intelligent, glamorous, erotic, radical, varied, original, unique, exceptional and sincere'.

While alt and indie porn have been argued to challenge the porn industry in terms of their ethics of production and their community feel, they have, seemingly paradoxically, equally been identified as 'the research and development arm of the porn industry' (Cramer and Home, 2007: 165). In order to evoke the interest of users with novelties and specialities, so-called mainstream porn companies have long drawn on sexual subcultures and niche pornographies for inspiration, hence also familiarizing them in the process (McNair, 2002: 206; Dery, 2007).

All kinds of porn sites have turned towards alt porn when seeking out new audiences, diverse content, and novel principles of operation (Attwood, 2007: 452). Tattooed and pierced female models have long ceased to be exceptional in so-called mainstream productions – quite the contrary – while community features have grown increasingly central to how users are invited to engage with sites, comment on content, grade it, and upload material themselves.

Some scholars have identified the transformations fuelled by digital production and online distribution as entailing a rupture in the history of pornography. In the mid 2000s, these perspectives were united under the rubric of netporn, defined as pornographies particular to online platforms and networks (Jacobs, 2007; Jacobs et al., 2007). Netporn referred to the blurred boundaries of porn producers and consumers, and the rise in alternative body aesthetics and amateur, sex activist, and art projects, as well as the slipperiness of the very notion of porn caused by the proliferation of queer, independent, and alternative content. It was contrasted with 'porn on the Net', namely the recycling of the same old pornographic images and videos online (Shah, 2007). The notion of netporn, as outlined in the two Netporn conferences held in Amsterdam in 2005 and 2007, a listserv, and an edited reader (2007), was premised on technological, aesthetic, ethical, political, and economic particularity. It helped to mark out the increasing visibility of non-normative sexual palates and minoritarian sexual cultures, yet its binary premises and dynamics were of less assistance in mapping out the transformations that the production, distribution, consumption, and range of pornography were undergoing (Paasonen, 2010b). Furthermore, it was the Web, and not the Net more generally, that had become the norm in porn distribution on a global scale. While scholarly interest towards alternative and independent pornographies remains, the vocabulary of netporn is currently in scarce use.

## METADATA, SEARCHABILITY, AND PORN TAXONOMIES

Pornographic images distributed in newsgroups, BBSs, IRC, or Gopher were indexed through file names and categories. In contrast, the searchability of visual and audiovisual Web content necessitated a much more clear and complex textual marking out of subcategories, terms, names, titles, acts, and preferences (Chun, 2006: 106). Such contextual metadata was necessary for the functionality of search engines but equally for the search functions of porn sites themselves, as they grew in size to host hundreds of thousands of files. Porn images and videos are indexed on the basis of factors such as date, file size and length, subgenre, popularity of content, number of views, body types, national origins, performers, production studios, and the acts performed. Metadata remains crucial to the diverse categorizations and tagging functions of aggregator sites appropriating the participatory models of social media. Dictated by the necessities of information architecture, metadata has helped to render the inner distinctions within the genre of pornography more manifest than ever.

Print, VHS, and DVD porn were all broadly categorized through parameters such as straight or gay, as being focused on specific acts or scenarios (e.g. anal sex, BDSM), through their stars, and production styles such as amateur and gonzo pornography. Such distinctions provided users with broad options to navigate in between. The range and plethora of tagging practices marks the latest stage in the development that has, throughout the history of Web porn, rendered the variety of body styles, roles and positions, niches, and fetishes increasingly articulate and therefore also more recognizable. This has also involved the familiarization – if not precisely the domestication – of fringe pornographies that were previously deemed too marginal for mainstream consumption.

This has perhaps most obviously been the case with Japanese pornographic anime, hentai, which routinely depicts penetrative sex between humans, demons, and monsters, notably often in scenarios of non-consensual domination and submission. Hentai remained a specialty niche too bizarre for DVD appeal distribution in the 1990s, only to enter the menus of all kinds of porn Web sites during the following decade (Dahlqvist and Vigilant, 2004). The popularity of hentai has since only increased in connection with both the rise of cartoon porn and Japanese game porn fandom. Another equally visible example involves transgender porn targeted at heterosexual male consumers. While so-called 'shemale' and 'chicks with dicks' pornography – a field distinct from transgender porn produced and consumed within queer communities – had long been produced in Brazil in particular, the subgenre was more thoroughly commodified and modified on Web platforms as it grew into a staple element of the palette of online porn in the early 2000s (Paasonen, 2011: 147–50). The relatively early entry of both transgender porn and hentai into the interfaces of so-called mainstream porn speaks of the fragmentation and diversification of online pornography in ways that call into question the veracity of the very notion of the mainstream.

The promise of the Web was, since the mid 1990s, one of abundant and diverse pornography that only waited to be found. In practice, finding it was not, however, always easy. Content remained fragmented across the

Web, occasionally brought together as Web rings pointing users from one affiliated site to another, and as listed on directory sites that were the default means of finding content before search engines were in common use. Persian Kitty's Adult Links was one of the best-known link sites facilitating access to free porn images. Established by Beth Mansfield, 'a Tacoma, Washington homemaker and mother of two' (Lane, 2001: 89) in 1995, Persian Kitty was a simple directory page with links to featured sites that paid for advertising space and an alphabetical listing of sites with information on the number of images that each of them contained. By 1998, Persian Kitty attracted over half a million visitors per day and made tens of thousands in monthly profit. During a period when finding pornography, and free porn in particular, was cumbersome, Persian Kitty grew into one of the prime portals for accessing it (Lane, 2001: 190–2).

The earliest version of Persian Kitty available through the Internet Archive (archive.org) is from November 26, 1996. Its featured content includes the site's sponsor, Danni's Hard Drive, as well as Amateur Hardcore with 'A quarter-million fast downloading *hardcore* amateur pix and totally raw movie clips, in AVI, Quicktime & Mpeg. *Unlimited* downloads! *Instant* Access! And it's all Keyword-searchable! Thumbnails and descriptions, too! Raunchy! Nasty! Extreme Hardcore!' The description of the alphabetically listed link sites remained much more straightforward, as this excerpt illustrates:

HENTAI MANGA ANIME PAGE – 50 hentai pix
HERMITAGE – 20 Asian pix
HEUY'S PAGE – 12 pix
HOLLYWOOD HILLS HOOCHIES – 25 babe pix, no preview
HONNEAMISE ASIANS – 20 pix, no preview
HORNY TOADS – 9 babe pix, 1 avi
HOT CHICKS – 30 babe pix, no preview
HOT PEPPERS – 15 pix, no preview
HOTTEST BABE ON THE WEB – 20 pix a week, vote for your favorite
THE HOTZONE – 18 pix, no preview

Some of the sites listed offered as few as five or six images, while only two promised more than 1,000 images. The contextual metadata describing the style, genre, and content of the images remained thin or even absent. Since thumbnail preview was by no means always in use, it was necessary to first download the images in order to see what they were. Given the speed of dial-up connections, this would have been a slow enterprise. Dial-up modems had the maximum download speed of 56 kilobytes per second, which severely constrained the use of images and video clips. Larger files easily took minutes to download and small thumbnails were in broad use for giving the user some idea of the awaiting visual content. Rough black-and-white bitmap (BMP) raster images were also used for similar purposes, gradually fading away from the background as the desired JPG or GIF file of the same width and height grew visible. Indeed, according to an early Web design rule-of-thumb, individual pages should not exceed 100K in size, were they to download smoothly.

Web directories were not necessarily maintained frequently enough to keep their links fully up to date. Meanwhile, porn sites tried to knowingly derail users to click on lucrative links, independent of what the users may have been specifically looking for. The optimization of clicks emerged early as a strategy of profit generation, while other solutions, including mouse-trapping and pop-ups, were designed to force users to stay on the site, or to become acquainted with content against their will (Perdue, 2002). For porn users, the landscape of Web porn was therefore one of endless, optimistic yet frustrating waiting, searching and clicking, getting stuck, and regularly ending up with different content than that advertised (Patterson, 2004).

Altavista, the leading search engine preceding the reign of Google, was launched in 1995, the year that Yahoo! started out as a Web directory and a year after the equally popular search tools Lycos, Infoseek, and WebCrawler were introduced. The increasing use of search engines marked a gradual shift from link sites to keyword searches in porn use. Pornography was remarkably popular with early searches: in 1997, almost 17 per cent of search queries were connected to pornography and sexuality. In contrast, in 2005, porn comprised less than 4 per cent of all searches (Spink et al., 2006). This proportional drop does not speak of a decrease in the popularity of pornography – quite the contrary, both the volume and use of Web porn continued to grow, and they continue to do so to this date. It rather speaks of expansive increase in all Web content and in the diversification of its user base: to mention only a few examples, during this period, public broadcasting companies started making their content available through online archives and streaming video services; banks shifted their services online; online learning platforms emerged; online shopping had grown steeply with giants such as Amazon and eBay leading the way; and social media platforms were about to make a breakthrough. In 1995, there were an estimated 23,500 websites (that is, unique hostnames): the number grew to over three million by 1999. Out of these, an estimated 30,000 were focused on pornography (Lane, 2001: 135). By 2005, the total number of sites was close to 65 million and by 2015, over 860 million (Internet Live Stats, 2017). As the volume of Web content rapidly grew in number and variety, the proportional volume of porn sites decreased. The same applied to search queries.

Directories, link and click sites continue to live on in a range of forms, from personally curated fan selections to metasites that routinely guide users to different directions than those of their own choosing – and even Persian Kitty is still up and running. The rhythms and temporalities of porn browsing have nevertheless undergone clear transformations since the 1990s when one needed to constantly wait for servers to respond and for materials to download. The gradual spread of broadband connections around the new millennium allowed for image resolutions to increase to the point that high-definition became a profitable novelty while streaming video, and the format of the video clip in particular, began to dominate as the default format of porn consumption.

## VIDEO AGGREGATOR SITES AND THE IMPLICATIONS OF CENTRALIZATION

Porn sites adopted streaming video technologies early on since many users found applications requiring plug-ins, such as Real Player and Microsoft Media Player, too cumbersome (Perdue, 2002: 140–3). In 2002, pornographic content was estimated to take 30 to 70 per cent of all bandwidth, largely for the reason that other forms of video content remained much less popular (Perdue, 2002: 179–84). The success of porn video aggregator sites such as YouPorn (est. 2006), RedTube (2006), Xtube (2006), XVideos (2007), xHamster (2007), and Pornhub (2007) means that pornography continues to occupy server space and user attention, yet with platforms such as YouTube, Netflix, and Hulu in the mix, the landscape of streaming video looks clearly different than it did in the early 2000s. In 2016, an impressive 92 billion videos were watched on Pornhub, the world's second most popular porn site, yet YouTube's number was 20 times higher, with almost five billion daily views.

Aggregator sites marked a departure from the free and centralized accessibility of video clips. As more and more video became available online as torrents shared in P2P networks and as tube content shared by studios for marketing purposes, uploaded by users with little regard for copyright, and produced by the users themselves, DVD sales began to steeply and permanently drop (Moye, 2013; Rosen, 2013). This drop equalled the transformations that had occurred in the music industry since the launch of peer-to-peer sharing app Napster in 1999 (Leyshon et al., 2005), yet it took place significantly later, around the financial crisis of 2008.

Pornography was long considered 'recession-proof' in the sense that its profits tended to steadily increase despite any oscillations in national or international economy. More pornography is being produced than ever to date, there is factually more pornography available, and the number of visits to porn sites continues to increase, yet the profits of the porn industry have, as a whole, decreased. Users have grown unwilling to pay subscription fees even for specialized and premium content. Kink.com (est. 1997), one of the success stories of Web porn, specializing in rough scenarios of domination and control, announced in 2016 that its revenues had recently been cut in half due to drastic drop in membership subscriptions. Webcams, with their live nature and interaction possibilities with porn stars, amateurs, and proams alike, remain virtually the only form of adult content that users are willing to broadly pay for. Pornographic webcams have been popular for as long as the technology has been available (Lane, 2001: 249–58; Senft, 2008; Hillis, 2010), yet webcamming has also increasingly centralized around hubs. At the time of writing, the largest of these were the Hungarian-born site LiveJasmin (est. 2001), the California-based Chaturbate (est. 2011), and the Cyprus-based BongaCams (est. 2012).

The money flows of Web porn have not suddenly dried up, but they are following different routes than during the previous decades. As studios focused on DVD production and pay content have suffered, many of them have been bought up. The originally Montreal-based MindGeek (formerly known as Manwin) alone has bought major brand names such as Men.com, Brazzers, Reality Kings, and Digital Playground. This has resulted in an unprecedented centralization of ownership in both porn production and distribution, given that MindGeek also runs the most popular video aggregator sites (with the exception of XVideos and xHamster). Analysing MindGeek's dominant role in porn, technology writer David Auerbach (2014) notes that its 'producers make porn films mostly for the sake of being uploaded on to MindGeek's free tube sites, with lower returns for the producers but higher returns for MindGeek, which makes money off of the tube ads that does not go to anyone involved in the production side'. In other words, the profits of online pornography revolve around distribution, while the income streams have grown considerably thinner in its production.

Production studios have moved from establishing long exclusive contracts with models to a system where producers hire the necessary crew and cast for each title. As Heather Berg (2016: 161) points out, this 'gig economy' builds on a reserve army of labour that is 'willing to perform in porn even when pay and conditions are poor' and the workers of which are placed 'in shifting positions as entrepreneurs, independent contractors, employees, contracted and freelance managers, and producers'. On the one hand, the economy of Web porn has grown increasingly corporate and centralized, especially in North America. On the other hand, the labour of porn has grown increasingly precarious as a source of income for its makers.

Just as the traffic of views, links, and clicks connected to news items, memes, and video clips is driven through globally leading social media hubs, the traffic of online porn is increasingly centralized and organized through aggregator sites. If, throughout the 1990s and beyond, porn consumption was characterized by endless searching, in the 2010s, tube sites promise to host all possible content within one interface: users need merely to browse through the available categories and conduct key term searches within the site. This centralization follows similar patterns to those followed by developments connected to corporations like Google, Microsoft, and Facebook, which buy up smaller enterprises, aggressively expand their operations within the online economy, and collect massive volumes of data on user activities, preferences, and trends while doing so. This means that select companies have considerable power to modulate the accessibility of content and forms of usage while not needing to be transparent as to the parameters of operation. Most Web porn companies are not listed, and the financial specificities are therefore not subject to public knowledge. It then follows that there is much opaqueness to their flows of money and labour.

The work of video aggregator sites largely involves tasks such as running servers, the management of data, and the tweaking of algorithms. As is the case with any social media platforms or online services, the successful operation of porn tubes necessitates large-scale investments into software engineering and programming. The careers available at MindGeek – including PHP and Web development, project management, customer service, sales, support, video editing, website optimization, mobile design, legal counsel, financial, data, security, Web analysis, marketing, sales, and PR – differ notably little from those in other tech companies. Alongside this partial redefinition of porn labour as tech work runs the mainstreaming of companies such as MindGeek as brands with more general cultural visibility. Adult entertainment companies have abroad social media presence, yet, with the exceptions of Twitter and Tumblr, social media terms of service generally ban gratuitous displays of nudity and sex with the explicit aim of blocking pornographic content from platforms such as Facebook, Pinterest, and Instagram. Since this sets automated limits to the circulation of sexually explicit content, porn companies have resorted to a range of publicity stunts.

In the case of Pornhub, such efforts have ranged from their globally circulated annual infographics detailing search trends, lengths, and the volume of visits within the calendar year (since 2013) to campaigns against breast cancer (since 2012) and for the protection of sperm whales (in 2016) and media stunts such as the Pornhub theme song (2014) and advert contests (2014). These campaigns afford broad social media publicity for virtually no expense (see Paasonen et al., forthcoming). In an *Adweek* interview, Pornhub's vice president, Corey Price, explained how the company wants to let 'people know that watching porn shouldn't be an underground activity that's to be seen as shameful. Everyone does it, why not just bring that out in the open?' (Monnlos, 2014). The overall aim of the campaigns is to build an entertainment brand with mainstream recognizability of the kind previously gained by Playboy or Hustler.

## PORNIFICATION AND FILTERING

The increased public visibility of Web pornography and its key brands, together with the more general flirtation with sexual representation across the fields of media, have given rise to a myriad of diagnoses on the pornification culture (McNair, 2002; Paasonen et al., 2007; Attwood, 2009; Smith, 2010; Mulholland, 2013; Paasonen, 2016). While these diagnoses remain notably diverse in their examples and premises, they share a focus on how pornography has grown mundane in its abundant availability and how its codes and conventions travel across media platforms. The mainstreaming of pornography is mapped in terms of its sheer popularity, as well as the cultural presence of pornography in the guise of porn stars turned mainstream media celebrities, and in its aesthetics circulated in films, television shows, journalistic overviews, and art projects (Attwood, 2009: xiv). It is nevertheless online pornography that has become the key symptom of and symbol for such developments.

In public discourse, online porn is frequently posed as a problem in its exaggerated displays of gendered and racialized relations of control and in its arguably addictive qualities. The access of minors to online porn has similarly been a key concern since the mid 1990s. A range of filtering software has been developed for blocking adolescents' access to porn and Google introduced SafeSearch, namely the automatic filtering of pornographic content, in 2009 (Paasonen, 2011: 32, 43–5). Concerns over the exposure of minors to sexually explicit content remain vocal, especially given the increasing ubiquity of smart phones, which also allow minors to generate and share their own content. Incidents concerning sexting have given rise to bullying as well as legal action: in the United States, adolescents taking naked selfies have been identified as sex offenders for producing and distributing child pornography (Zhang, 2010). Child pornography remains a topic of great public concern, especially in connection with the distribution facilities allowed by networked communications. Since child pornography is illegal and heavily policed internationally, it is primarily distributed in the so-called deep Web rather than on openly accessible platforms. It is also a form of content actively filtered out from virtually any website.

Parallel to the concern about the public accessibility of all kinds of online smut runs a range of filtering and censorship practices ranging from governmental firewalls in countries such as China and Saudi Arabia to the filtering of hentai in Australia and the application of obscenity laws to niche pornographies in the UK. Few politicians or tech-sector professionals are willing to defend pornography with other arguments than possibly those concerning the freedom of speech: the work or content of porn would not be included in most considerations of creative labour or innovation. On the contrary, the well-acknowledged presence and ubiquity of smut online and the harmful resonances it is seen to involve have been rationale for a broad range of content policing practices from traffic filtering to nation-specific acts of blocking, tracking, and banning. Such governance practices are by no means limited to porn, yet they gain political and public support through attempts to fight it. Pornography is, in sum, despite its public visibility and perennial popularity among consumers, considered to be the quintessentially 'bad' form of online content that would be best weeded out.

The history of Web pornography is one of simultaneous and possibly paradoxical fragmentation, diversification, and centralization. Despite the recent increase in academic interest and in examinations of the webcam sector in particular, many white areas remain in studies of Web porn, its economies, and labour practices in perspectives both historical and contemporary. Porn may sit awkwardly in the overall palette of Web content, not least in terms of the content allowed on most social media platforms, yet there is no doubt as to the central role that it has played in technological and economic developments throughout the history of the Web. Rather than continuing to routinely fence off pornography as a special concern, a social problem, or a marginal field of activity, it is crucial to acknowledge the role it has played in online content production and distribution, and to account for it in analyses thereof. The tenacious exclusion of pornography from studies of e-commerce, site design, Web technology, user cultures, and their affective entanglements can ultimately only obscure the overall understanding of how the Web has developed, and how it continues to do so. This would mean both reproducing existing knowledge bias and ignoring the insights brought forth in scholarship on online pornography.

## REFERENCES

Attwood, F. (2007) 'No money shot? Commerce, pornography and new sex taste cultures', *Sexualities,* 10(4): 441–56.

Attwood, F. (2009) 'Introduction: The sexualization of culture', in F. Attwood (ed.), *Mainstreaming Sex: The Sexualization of Western Culture*. London: I.B.Tauris. pp. xiii–xxiv.

Auerbach, D. (2014) 'Vampire porn', *Slate*, 23 October. (http://www.slate.com/articles/technology/technology/2014/10/mindgeek_porn_monopoly_its_dominance_is_a_cautionary_tale_for_other_industries.html)

Bennett, D. (2001) 'Pornography-dot-com: Eroticising privacy on the Internet', *The Review of Education/Pedagogy/Cultural Studies,* 23(4): 381–91.

Berg, H. (2016) '"A scene is just a marketing tool": Alternative income streams in porn's gig economy', *Porn Studies,* 3(2): 160–74.

Chun, W.H.K. (2006) *Control and Freedom: Power and Paranoia in the Age of Fiber Optics.* Cambridge: MIT Press.

Cramer, F. and Home, S. (2007) 'Pornographic coding', in K. Jacobs, M. Janssen and M. Pasquinelli (eds), *C'Lick Me: A Netporn Studies Reader.* Amsterdam: Institute of Network Cultures. pp. 159–71.

Cruz, A. (2011) 'The black visual experience: Hendrix, porn, and authenticity', *Camera Obscura,* 26(1): 65–93.

Dahlqvist, J.P. and Vigilant, L.G. (2004) 'Way better than real: Manga sex to tentacle hentai', in D. D. Waskul (ed.), *Net.seXXX: Readings of Sex, Pornography, and the Internet.* New York: Peter Lang. pp. 91–103.

Dery, M. (2007) 'Paradise lust: Pornotopia meets the culture wars', in K. Jacobs, M. Janssen and M. Pasquinelli (eds), *C'lick Me: A Netporn Studies Reader.* Amsterdam: Institute of Network Cultures. pp. 125–48.

Dijck, J. van (2013) *The Culture of Connectivity: A Critical History of Social Media.* Oxford: Oxford University Press.

Doorn, N. van (2010) 'Keeping it real: User-generated pornography, gender reification, and visual pleasure', *Convergence,* 16(4): 411–30.

Esch, K. and Mayer, V. (2007) 'How unprofessional: The profitable partnership of amateur porn and celebrity culture', in S. Paasonen, K. Nikunen and L. Saarenmaa (eds), *Pornification: Sex and Sexuality in Media Culture.* Oxford: Berg. pp. 99–111.

Hardy, S. (2009) 'The new pornographies: Representation or reality?', in F. Attwood (ed.), *Mainstreaming Sex: The Sexualization of Western Culture.* London: I.B.Tauris. pp. 3–18.

Hilderbrand, L. (2009) *Inherent Vice: Bootleg Histories of Videotape and Copyright.* Durham: Duke University Press.

Hillis, K. (2010) 'Historicizing webcam culture: The telefetish as virtual object', in N. Brügger (ed.), *Web History.* New York: Peter Lang. pp. 137–54.

Hofer, K.P. (2014) 'Pornographic domesticity: Amateur couple porn, straight subjectivities, and sexual labour', *Porn Studies,* 1(4): 334–45.

Internet Live Stats (2017) 'Total number of websites'. (http://www.internetlivestats.com/total-number-of-websites)

Jacobs, K. (2007) *Netporn: DIY Web Culture and Sexual Politics.* Lanham: Rowman & Littlefield.

Jacobs, K., Janssen, M. and Pasquinelli, M. (eds) (2007) *C'Lick Me: A Netporn Studies Reader.* Amsterdam: Institute of Network Cultures.

Jarrett, K. (2015) *Feminism, Labour and Digital Media: The Digital Housewife.* London: Routledge.

Johnson, J.A. (2010) 'To catch a curious clicker: A social network analysis of the online pornography industry', in K. Boyle (ed.), *Everyday Pornography.* London: Routledge. pp. 147–63.

Kotamraju, N.P. (1999) 'The birth of Web site design skills: Making the present history', *American Behavioral Scientist,* 43(3): 464–74.

Lane, F.S. III (2001) *Obscene Profits: The Entrepreneurs of Pornography in the Cyber Age.* New York: Routledge.

Leyshon, A., Webb, P., French, S., Thrift, N. and Crewe, L. (2005) 'On the reproduction of the musical economy after the Internet', *Media, Culture & Society,* 27(2): 177–209.

Magnet, S. (2007) 'Feminist sexualities, race and the Internet: An investigation of suicidegirls.com', *New Media & Society,* 9(4): 577–602.

Maina, G. and Zecca, F. (2016) 'Harder than fiction: The stylistic model of gonzo pornography', *Porn Studies,* 3(4): 337–50.

Marwick, A. (2013) *Status Update: Celebrity, Publicity, and Branding in the Social Media Age.* New Haven: Yale University Press.

Mash, T. (2004) 'My year in smut: Inside Danni's Hard Drive', in D.D. Waskul (ed.), *Net.Sexxx: Readings on Sex, Pornography, and the Internet.* New York: Peter Lang. pp. 237–58.

McNair, B. (2002) *Striptease Culture: Sex, Media and the Democratization of Desire.* New York: Routledge.

McNair, B. (2013) *Porno? Chic! How Pornography Changed the World and Made it a Better Place.* London: Routledge.

Metz, C. (2015) 'The porn business isn't anything like you think it is', *Wired,* 15 October. (https://www.wired.com/2015/10/the-porn-business-isnt-anything-like-you-think-it-is/)

Monnlos, K. (2014) 'Inside Pornhub's crusade to tear down the taboos of watching sex online?', *Adweek,* 18 December. (http://www.adweek.com/brand-marketing/inside-pornhubs-crusade-tear-down-taboos-watching-sex-online-161910/)

Moye, D. (2013) 'Porn industry in decline', *The Huffington Post*, 19 January. (http://www.huffingtonpost.com/2013/01/19/porn-industry-in-decline_n_2460799.html)

Mulholland, M. (2013) *Young People and Pornography: Negotiating Pornification.* New York: Palgrave.

Paasonen, S. (2010a) 'Good amateurs: Erotica writing and notions of quality', in F. Attwood (ed.), *Porn.com: Making Sense of Online Pornography.* New York: Peter Lang. pp. 138–54.

Paasonen, S. (2010b) 'Labors of love: Netporn, Web 2.0, and the meanings of amateurism', *New Media and Society,* 12(8): 1297–312.

Paasonen, S. (2011) *Carnal Resonance: Affect and Online Pornography*. Cambridge: MIT Press.

Paasonen, S. (2016) 'Pornification and the mainstreaming of sex', in N. Rafter (ed.), *Oxford Encyclopedia of Criminology*. Oxford: Oxford University Press. (http://criminology.oxfordre.com/view/10.1093/acrefore/9780190264079.001.0001/acrefore-9780190264079-e-159.)

Paasonen, S., Nikunen, K. and Saarenmaa, L. (2007) 'Pornification and the education of desire', in S. Paasonen, K. Nikunen and L. Saarenmaa (eds), *Pornification: Sex and Sexuality in Media Culture*. Berg, Oxford. pp. 1–20.

Paasonen, S., Jarrett, K. and Light, B. (forthcoming) *Not Safe for Work: Sex, Humor and Risk in Social Media*. Cambridge: MIT Press.

Patterson, Z. (2004) 'Going on-line: Consuming pornography in the digital era', in L. Williams (ed.), *Porn Studies*. Durham: Duke University Press. pp. 104–23.

Perdue, L. (2002) *Erotica Biz: How Sex Shaped the Internet*. New York: Writers Club Press.

Rosen, D. (2013) 'Is the Internet killing the porn industry?', *Salon*, 30 May. (http://www.salon.com/2013/05/30/is_success_killing_the_porn_industry_partner/)

Senft, T.M. (2008) *CamGirls: Celebrity & Community in the Age of Social Networks*. New York: Peter Lang.

Shah, N. (2007) 'PlayBlog: Pornography, performance and cyberspace', in K. Jacobs, M. Janssen and M. Pasquinelli (eds), *C'Lick Me: A Netporn Studies Reader*. Amsterdam: Institute of Network Cultures. pp. 31–44.

Slater, D. (1998) 'Trading sexpics on IRC: Embodiment and authenticity on the Internet', *Body & Society,* 4(4): 91–117.

Smith, C. (2010) 'Pornographication: A discourse for all seasons', *International Journal of Media and Cultural Politics,* 6(1): 103–8.

Spink, A., Partridge, H. and Jansen, B.J. (2006) 'Sexual and pornographic Web searching: Trend analysis', *First Monday,* 11(9). (http://www.firstmonday.org/ojs/index.php/fm/article/view/1391/1309)

Stella, R. (2016) 'The amateur roots of gonzo pornography', *Porn Studies,* 3(4): 351–61.

Stroud, S.R. (2014) 'The dark side of the online self: A pragmatist critique of the growing plague of revenge porn', *Journal of Mass Media Ethics,* 29(3): 168–83.

Williams, L. (1989) *Hard Core: Power, Pleasure, and the 'Frenzy of the Visible'*. Berkeley: University of California Press.

Zhang, X. (2010) 'Charging children with child pornography: Using the legal system to handle the problem of "sexting"', *Computer Law & Security Review,* 26(3): 251–9.

# Spam

Finn Brunton

## THE COUNTERHISTORY OF THE WEB

This chapter builds on a larger argument about the history of the Internet, and makes the case that this argument has something useful to say about the Web; and, likewise, that the Web has something useful to say about the argument, expressing an aspect of what is distinctive about the Web as a technology. The larger argument is this: spam provides another history of the Internet, a shadow history. In fact, following the history of 'spam', in all its different meanings and across different networks and platforms (ARPANET and Usenet, the Internet, email, the Web, user-generated content, comments, search engines, texting, and so on), lets us tell the history of the Internet itself entirely through what its architects and inhabitants sought to *exclude*. Identifying and describing spam, from the terminals of time-shared mainframes in the 1970s to the elaborate automated filtering systems of Gmail, meant having to talk about what the network is for, what the rules are, and who's in charge. And the first conversation, over and over again: what exactly is 'spam?'. Briefly looking at how this question got answered will bring us to the Web and what made it different.

Before the Web, before the formalization of the Internet, before Minitel and Prestel and America Online, there were graduate students in basements, typing on terminals that connected to remote machines somewhere out in the night (the night because computers, of course, were for big, expensive, labor-intensive projects during the day – if you, a student, could get an account for access at all it was probably for the 3 a.m. slot). Students wrote programs, created games, traded messages, and played pranks and tricks on each other. Being nerds of the sort that would stay up overnight to get a few hours of computer access, they shared a love of things like science fiction and the absurd comedy of *Monty Python's Flying Circus.* Alone at the terminals, together on the network, they would volley lines from *Python* sketches back and forth

– the dead parrot sketch, the dirty fork sketch, the spam sketch. This last was particularly popular because most of the dialogue was just the repetition of 'spam', whether sung by Vikings or shouted by the waitress, and it was therefore trivial to generate. You could write a simple program that, at the right spot in the dialogue, would post 'SPAM! SPAM! SPAM! SPAM! SPAM! SPAM! SPAM! SPAM!' over and over, relentlessly and without pause, filling the screen, killing the discussion, and often overloading the chat platform completely, kicking people offline. Jussi Parikka and Tony Sampson (2009), in the context of their larger analysis of spam, have shown that the sketch itself is built around a communications breakdown: the point where noise on the line overwhelms any particular signal. It was annoying, but playful and mischievous rather than malign, like unexpectedly blowing a vuvuzela in the middle of a conversation. This kind of noisy, frustrating behavior was dubbed 'spamming'.

The term came in useful in the ensuing decade-plus – though not with reference to advertising or commercial messages, which were their own category of etiquette violation. 'Spamming' remained the domain of noise and the indiscriminate, wasting time, attention, and bandwidth on redundant copies of messages, on overly verbose and off-topic postings, on tedious rants and cut-and-pasted slabs of text. Dave Hayes, prominent on the discussion system Usenet, wrote a manifesto in 1997 itemizing the forms of social misbehavior online – with 'commercial self-promotion' as a separate entry from 'SPAM', which meant precisely being a high-noise low-signal attention hog over a precious and expensive medium (Hayes, 1996). This definition shifted irrevocably in the spring of 1994, when two lawyers from Arizona posted a message across Usenet – that is, to computers around the world, to many thousands of users, indiscriminately – offering their services with the process of entering the US Green Card lottery. (We know this event best through the responses that quote it at the time – for instance (Larson, 1994).) The lottery was an initiative to simplify and speed up the process of getting papers to live and work in the United States as a foreign national: a subject of obviously narrow interest, which they had broadcast to computers from Singapore to Australia to the Netherlands – and, of course, throughout the United States, where the vast majority of recipients were citizens already. To enter the lottery, furthermore, only required sending in a postcard, but the message suggested that paid legal help would be needed – a sleazy commercial misrepresentation. Abuse of the network's many-to-many tools and global reach had been combined with a moneymaking scheme.

In the process of trying to describe this event, the global community on Usenet settled on *spam* as the term of art for their message and their action: the American lawyers had spammed the network. The word had jumped into the domain in which we identify today … or rather, it had come closer to our current understanding, in a way that is intimately intertwined with the development of the Web.

After assembling the whole history of spam, from an anti-Vietnam War message distributed on MIT's early time-sharing system in 1971, to a Digital Equipment Corporation ad on ARPANET in 1977, to present-day phishing, comment spam, 'spammy' posts and social network activity, clickbait and 419 ('Nigerian price') emails, I arrived at a working definition. What is 'spam'? *Spam is the manipulation of information technology infrastructure to exploit existing aggregations of human attention.* That is the meaning of 'spam' once all the technological particulars of search engine spamming or phishing campaigns have been worn away: following the term's broad application across the decades – both in English and as a loanword in other languages on the Internet – includes commercial and noncommercial activities, criminal and legitimate, with many different technologies and platforms, from email to

Twitter to content production. What remains consistent, I argue, is the model: spammers identify already existing collections of human attention, and imitate and manipulate their particular properties to extract value. I want to say a few more words explaining this before focusing on the Web in particular.

Spam is an information technology phenomenon. Across their many modes and domains, spammers push the properties of information technology to their extremes: the capacity for automation, algorithmic manipulation, and scripting; the leveraging of network effects and vast economies of scale; distributed connectivity and free or very low-cost participation. So many neglected blogs and wikis and other social spaces are out there on the Web: automatic bot-posted spam comments, one after another, will fill the limits of their server space. What this means – beyond characterizing spam as an activity – is that spammers take advantage of existing infrastructure in ways that make it difficult to extirpate them without making changes for which we would pay a high price. Indeed, in Geert Lovink's argument (2005), spam is akin to other network failures like identity theft in being inherent in the design – constitutional elements of yesterday's network architecture. Spammers partially survive by finding places where the potential value lost and effort expended in locking-down could exceed the harm they do – which reveals those places, and their value, to us.

More exactly, spammers find places where the open and exploratory infrastructure of the network hosts gatherings of humans, however indirectly, and where their attention is pooled. The use they make of this attention is exploitative not because they extract some value from it but because in doing so they devalue it for everyone else – that is, in plain language, they waste our time for their benefit. Recall the objections against the Green Card spam campaign on Usenet: it wasn't simply that the lawyers were acting commercially but that they didn't respect salience, barraging everyone indiscriminately with their lame message, treating the whole network as a passive audience whose time was theirs to spend. (Some of the complex distinctions inherent in spam, 'trash', 'junk', and 'waste' are considered in the analysis collected in Parikka and Sampson (2009), especially Galloway and Thacker's 'On Narcolepsy' (2008), and Gansing (2011).) Two consequences follow from studying spam in this light. First, we can see the history of networked computing as a thread in the history of the management and distribution of attention – Alessandro Ludovico (2005) has argued that spam is best seen as one instance in a long history, from traveling salesmen to personalized bulk postal mail to eye-catching billboards, of trying to interfere with our thoughts and provoke us into some form of consumer desire. Second, we can see in concrete terms how the nebulous shape of community online used spam to define itself. The intersection of these two topics brings us back to the distinctive history of the Web, the ways it gathered attention and formed communities, shown to us anew through spam's crass, hustling, inventive counterhistory. I will break this counterhistory up into four sections, which describe from spam's side how the Web became searchable, central, and social.

## JUNK RESULTS

How, though, could spam have come to play a role in the Web? My brief sketch of spam's origins, above, is all social spaces: conversation threads on Usenet, chat on time-sharing computer networks, and of course email, where 'spam' as a concept and a business scaled up. The Web, though, was a kind of document navigation system at first – a markup language and set of protocols for authoring and exploring knowledge through hypertext. It was a project suited to a polyglot scientific community: developed by an English computer scientist, revised by a

Belgian, with the first site built in French, hosted on a Californian machine in the walls of a Swiss research institute, a knowledge presentation and navigation tool for one of the twentieth century's biggest capital-S Scientific communities. It's a context, and a technology, in which you can no more imagine spam thriving than you can imagine mold growing on a space station.

But mold does in fact grow in outer space, behind panels, on gaskets and insulation, on walls, under clothes. As human attention condensed, collected, and pooled on the Web, from Erwise to ViolaWWW to NCSA Mosaic, techniques began appearing to absorb and exploit it. Take a year, from the middle of 1994 to 1995, when we can see many different factors picking up speed: the global growth of users away from computer science professionals to the general population; the end of the noncommercial restrictions on the network in the United States; the shift in power from sysadmins to lawyers and entrepreneurs as social arbiters; and events like the Green Card lottery spam on Usenet (with subsequent publicity in newspapers – the first appearance of 'spam' in print – and major advertisers scenting blood in the water); Mosaic's booming download numbers; and the publication of *How to Make a Fortune on the Information Superhighway* – a cash-in book by those same Arizona lawyers, promising to teach readers how to market across the global network and get rich quick by exploiting the technology.

There were 20-odd websites in the fall of 1992, 10,000 by the end of summer in 1995, and millions by mid 1998. There were so many sites by then that finding what you were looking for – even knowing what was available to be found – was an enormous challenge, eloquently described in a paper published on April Fool's Day of 1998: 'The Anatomy of a Large-Scale Hypertextual Web Search Engine', by Sergey Brin and Larry Page. Others had already tried to solve the problem of abundance on the Web by developing search engines. The issue was, as Brin and Page put it, that 'some advertisers attempt to gain people's attention by taking measures meant to mislead automated search engines. ... "Junk results" often wash out any results that a user is interested in' (2). Or, as a paper published on the very same day more bluntly put it: 'Some authors have an interest in their page rating well for a great many types of query indeed – spamming has come to the web' (Pringle et al., 1998: 1).

The form that spamming took reflects the unique particulars of the Web and search technology: it was designed not simply to dominate a conversation, as in chat, or flood a channel with messages, as with email and Usenet, but to make assertions of *relevance* and *salience.* We can see, through spam's development, how generations of search engines tried to model information on the Web in terms of what it meant for a user's query. The spiders that the first search engines sent out would go through the HTML source of a page, using the structure of the markup to assess the significance of words with greater or lesser degrees of importance and relevance to a search. A word in a URL (for uniform resource locator, the 'address' of the page) or in the first header tag – which is the markup for what the human reader would see as the 'title' of the page, as in <h1>My Homepage</h1> – was probably more important than one in the body text of a page and would be rated accordingly in the index. A set of elements called 'meta tags' were used in HTML specifically for the benefit of search engine spiders, with keywords listed for the page such that they would be invisible to the human reader but helpful to search indexing. Helpful in theory, anyway: though meta tag elements were popularized by early search engines such as AltaVista and Infoseek, they were so aggressively adopted by spammers that metadata was largely ignored by the turn of the century, with AltaVista abandoning the influence of meta tags on search results in 2002: 'the high incidence of keyword repetition and spam made it an unreliable indication of site content and quality' (Sullivan, 2002).

What precisely was the business plan of these early search spammers, and what were they putting in their web pages? Keywords were repeated in the meta tags and gathered in the page itself, hidden from the casual human reader's eye. One of the details that HTML can specify is the color of text, so the page's author could set the page's background to gray and make text the same shade of gray, invisible on the human reader's display while appearing to be normal text on the page as far as the spider was concerned. Innocuous pages with some form of spammy intent would have a mysterious gap at the bottom of the page. (Such techniques could also be used playfully or prankishly, part of the toolkit of the 'vernacular web' of bespoke HTML (Lialina, 2009).) The text on the page ended and there were no images, just a few inches of the gray background before the bottom. In that gap, in background-matching color and often minuscule font size, lay a magma flow of obscenity and pornography, product names, pop stars, distinctive phrases, cities and countries, odd terms seemingly plucked from Tristan Tzara's hat, selected because they happened to get good returns at that time. The text reads as though a Céline character worked for *Entertainment Tonight:* toyota ireland ladyboy microsoft windows hentai pulp fiction slut nirvana.

Such blocks of text illustrate a recurring theme in the development of spam on the Web and elsewhere: a matter-of-fact distinction between humans and machines, with different strategies for dealing with each. Almost every piece of spam, whether over email or in the context of spam blogs or comment spam, became *biface*, capable of being read in two ways with very different messages for the algorithm and for the human. (We will return to this distinction and its consequences for the Web at the end.) Spamming the early Web exacerbated this process, with techniques like 'cloaking'. Search engine spiders identify themselves by the way in which they request a page. This identification is part of the set of protocols that help to distinguish a normal Web browser from other platforms, like a phone, or a Braille display, making it possible to serve a compact page to the phone and text instead of images to the Braille device. This means you can serve one page to a spider, to be indexed and delivered as a search result, and an entirely different page to the user who clicks on the link. The signatures of spider requests, which trigger the cloak page, proved very difficult to disguise from spammers – which brings us back to Google's embryonic form in 1998: 'a prototype of a large-scale search engine which makes heavy use of the structure present in hypertext', created precisely to solve the problem posed by 'junk results', spammy web pages – and creating in turn a new way for spam to reshape the Web (Brin and Page, 1998: 1).

## MUTUAL ADMIRATION SOCIETY

'The citation (link) graph of the web is an important resource that has largely gone unused in existing web search engines', wrote Brin and Page. 'These maps allow rapid calculation of a web page's "PageRank," an objective measure of its citation importance that corresponds well with people's subjective idea of importance' (3). Inspired by academic citation structure, they argued for reputation, essentially treating links as a measurable expression of social value. They were not the first to do this – earlier search engine projects, trying to beat the keyword-stuffing of the Web's first spammers, had tried to use numbers of links to roughly evaluate the meaningfulness of results. In response, spammers had started *link farms,* pages of nothing but links between spam sites, providing a cheap-and-easy boost to that metric. Part of Google's brilliance lay in the flaw in this strategy: spam pages are lonely. They may link to thousands of other sites, but the only *inbound* links, as a rule, come from other spam pages.

Links, in theory, carry an implicit endorsement, a vote of relevance made by a person. The spam-fighting question is: who is the person, and how much does their endorsement count for? Google's PageRank equation answered those questions with the behavior of the 'random surfer', an abstracted user of the late-1990s Web. This rather depressing model of a person starts on 'a web page at random and keeps clicking on links, never hitting "back," but eventually gets bored and starts on another random page' (4). The likelihood that this idle character, clicking ever forward along the link graph, will land on a given page defines PageRank. This means that other sites linking to your site matters – as does which sites link to those that link to you. It's a reputational model that works transitively, with links weighted differently by their significance: 'pages that have perhaps only one citation from something like the Yahoo! homepage are also generally worth looking at' (Yahoo! being, at the time, a directory of human-curated significant links.) What were spammers to do? Building on the algorithmic inference of social data, Google could make it 'nearly impossible to deliberately mislead the system'. The only workaround for spammers would be to build their own artificial societies.

A variety of strategies developed as Google's market share grew and other search engines around the world developed similar models. Websites with a high PageRank were transformed into kingmakers. A link from them could move a site onto the first page or top three returns of the different search sites, boosting attention and revenue. Sites took advantage of preexisting ideas for the human-curated Web, like 'Best of the Web' awards, 'Top 100 Sites' awards, and so forth; these awards included a badge, a little image, and a snippet of code to be copied into the winning site – a snippet that included a link to the award-giving site. The human user saw a little badge image, but the search engine spider saw an outgoing link: a digital endorsement. New habits of use and etiquette appeared among ordinary users of the Web: a comment in a blog post included the commenters' websites along with their names, to rack up another link. Posting something without including a 'via' link to the person you got it from – the 'via' being an additional outbound link as a kind of thanks for using their discovery – became increasingly rude, the sign of an uncouth person. 'Mutual admiration societies' arose, huge link-heavy sets of sites, each page linking to many of the others – all sites kept carefully unspammy, maintaining the pretense of legitimate use of the Web. Their business was not to produce spam sites themselves, but to charge for outbound links from the society. They were renting out their accumulated 'votes'. But even those had a characteristic shape: heavy cross-linking within a group of sites, all with only a few inbound links (because spam pages are lonesome), creating little islands of intense self-endorsement with no outside involvement. To analytic tools, it's a pattern as obvious as the newspaper ads taken out by vanity publishing houses for their new releases with the blurbs from friends and family – and easy for Google to discount accordingly.

In 1999, a company called Pyra Labs launched a service called Blogger. (Google would buy it in 2003.) Blogger's goal, as of so many related systems, from Flickr to Wikipedia, was to provide people with an intuitive means for publishing their content on the Web. It was remotely hosted, so you did not have to own a website domain name or pay for hosting; many of its processes were automated, so you did not have to design it or do any coding behind the scenes; and it had a useful and increasingly sophisticated Application Programming Interface (API) for connecting with other Web applications and automating processes. With the boom in weblog popularity and the peculiar chronological publishing model of blogs, came another three-letter acronym, RSS, 'Really Simple Syndication', which makes new posts or other changes on a site available in forms that are easy to use. (For the sake of Web history completeness: RSS originally stood for 'RDF Site Summary', which highlights its relationship with the history of Web document formatting – but was retroactively changed to the more straightforward meaning.) Feed readers can gather the latest entries from RSS-enabled sites (which blogs soon were by default), material can be forwarded to mobile devices, and a page can feature the headlines or recent posts from other sites.

What does this have to do with Web spam? Consider the toolkit laid out by these developments: a content publishing system that can be easily automated (new accounts, posts on a prearranged schedule, modified settings), without the detailed work and paper trail of registering domain names and paying for Web hosting, and – with RSS – a faucet of other people's words, content that looked real and human because it actually was, unlike a lot of spam production. Hooked together with the right software tools, you can generate a new kind of mutual admiration and endorsement society with a network of spam blogs – or 'splogs'.

A splog production system will pull in RSS feeds from other blogs and news sources, chop them up and remix them, insert relevant links, and post the resulting material, hour after hour and day after day, with minimal human supervision. You can turn the machine on and leave the room while it makes money for you. With contextual advertising (including ads as a launching point for browser malware) you can make money through pageviews and the occasional click by running 'excerpt model' splogs, with fragments taken from other people's posts that are polling particularly well in Google's keyword metrics. A more ambitious system is 'full content' splogs, cross-linking in their hundreds and thousands to distort the shape of the Web. Each splog is assigned a set of keywords and feeds from which to pull related text, and in turn links to other splogs, which link to still more, forming an insular community on a huge range of sites – a kind of PageRank greenhouse that is not in itself meant to be read by people, but solely by search engine spiders. The splogs only work from a distance, appearing to be groups of people, the language and links functioning in aggregate. Taken in statistical total and algorithmic analysis, splogs resemble the patterns of a thriving community. Their posts are pitched at precisely the level of complexity the spider requires to accept their input as human, and they adapt human text for other machines to read and act on; affecting humans happens only indirectly – boosting the search ranking of a spammy appliance review site, for instance, that makes money through ads and affiliate links, or leading a human searcher into a fraudulent destination, whether a simple rip-off with ads and no meaningful content, or a site that might middleman a transaction, tacking on an additional fee or trying to force-download some adware.

This section opened with 'Google', a new-minted concept for a ranking algorithm, and ends with Google, a massively successful advertising company that runs a search engine. One question raised by this chronicle of spam's relationship to the Web and Web search is how complicit, or symbiotic, Google is with its own antagonist. Consider splogs: built and hosted on a platform Google owns, using text for content drawn from other sites hosted by Google, optimized to best fit Google's search engine algorithms, to boost the results for Google searches for sites that make money by hosting ads served through Google's affiliate advertising program (which, of course, also makes money for Google). Search engine spammers running their vast stables of spam blogs and sites are not anomalous, quantitatively or qualitatively; splogs now account for more than half of the total number of all blogs (Fetterly et al., 2004). They are the optimal users, from Google's perspective, constructing a system in which all the extraneous matter of people and conversation has been pruned away in favor of the automation of content production, search results, clicks, and ads served. This system in turn puts Google in the contradictory position of having to analyze and expel many of their most dedicated customers: those who overexploit, and accidentally overexpose, the financial and attention economies and technologies that underlie the contemporary Web. Google is hardly alone in this problem, as we will see.

## THE LANDING PAGE

Another shift in the dynamics of spam was developing, meanwhile, which reflects the Web's role as what Christian Sandvig (2013) calls an 'emerging essential'. It had been something that ran *on* infrastructure – running on top of the Internet, which ran in turn on top of the infrastructure of telephony – which became infrastructure itself, in the negative sense defined by Paul Edwards (2003: 187), 'those systems without which contemporary societies cannot function'. The Web became a key component for banking, health care, work and administration, and content creation and consumption, with browser standards and shared protocols becoming matters of urgent negotiation, monopolistic strategy, and even public safety (as in the push to standards like HTTPS) – with international implications from the top-level domains issued within the United States to legal decisions on hate speech in the EU (Goldsmith and Wu, 2008). In other words, it was not simply an aggregation of human attention around documents and content, navigated through search and hyperlinks, but a portal into many vulnerable and intimate parts of our working and personal lives. To understand how spam shifted accordingly, it helps to briefly look back for the last time to that Green Card lottery message in 1994.

What the lawyer-spammers were offering was, technically, an actual service (a misleading, borderline fraudulent one, but let that pass), whereas much of the spam we receive now has a very different agenda. You could call the real, working telephone number and schedule an appointment with the lawyers, just as, with much of the spam in the years following 1994, you could actually purchase the quack weight-loss pills, the deadstock toys, the counterfeit watches. Spam – spam of this era and this meaning – was loathed and despised, but it was also still somewhat legitimate, if only by accident. It thrived in the regulatory shadow of direct mail marketing, a powerful and moneyed interest that didn't want a legal precedent set that could close off a future advertising venue, and in the novelty of the increasingly popular and commercial Web, growing faster than legislation and defensive software could keep up. International guides to legal redress for spamming sprang up, their constantly updated confusion of potential laws – from CAN-SPAM in the United States to economic crime units in Norway to Canada's Department of Justice task force on pyramid schemes – highlighting the problem of figuring out where criminal lines were crossed (for example, Hollis, 2005). Many spammers were able to present themselves as brashly inventive promoters, with postal addresses and registered trademarks, seeking recognition in the classic tradition of entrepreneurial hustlers. What they produced is still what many people think of when they think of spam: the enthusiastic pitches full of mangled grammar and implausible stock photography, in the service of a recognizable, even traditional, class of dubious pleasures from timeshares and self-help books to diets and pornography.

But as the Web became an infrastructural system – and spam, for reasons too complex to go into here, became a progressively more embattled industry with less easy money – a new predatory spam technique took shape, to trick humans rather than machines. As far back as the mid 1990s, hackers and spammers alike had been finding ways to fool people into giving up their login information. Initially, the goal was to send spam from trustworthy-looking accounts, or within closed networks (whose members were often more naïve and easier to exploit).

In early 1996, in the Usenet newsgroup for the hacker magazine *2600*, the term for this technique makes its first appearance: 'phishing' ('mk590', 1996).

A representative spam business in the mid 1990s – who spelled it 'fishing' – used a simple ASCII picture, '<><', to note AOL accounts they'd captured to deluge people within the AOL network with spam ads (Brunton, 2013: 76). That was small change, though, compared with the uses to which phishing would be put. Targeted phishing messages used the same biface aspect of HTML – one side of the markup visible to people, the other for machines – to send email purporting to be from a bank, a credit card company, an email provider, or an employer, with a link whose innocuous text ('To resolve this block on your credit card, click here') disguises a suspicious URL (mastercard.l337haxx0r.ru, or whatever). Following the link reveals a careful – or sometimes not-so-careful – counterfeit of the original 'landing page' for the legitimate site. Careful study of spammer landing pages reveals how much HTML and CSS – the markup and styling vocabulary of early Web design – could convey the 'realness' of a particular online destination. Some crudely copy-and-pasted the HTML available through 'view source' commands for the sites they were pirating; others, faced with better-protected sites, reverse-engineered the design of their counterfeit, replicating color schemes, trying to duplicate the placement of images, and lifting or in some cases amusingly improvising the text.

Phishing sites are now often hosted on the compromised computers or servers that make up 'botnets', networks of many thousands of machines under the remote control of the spammer. These botnets generate the great bulk of the spam that we encounter (and much that we don't – spam can be upwards of 85% of *all* email on the Internet at peak times, most of it stopped by filters well before a person receives it (Messaging Anti-Abuse Working Group, 2011)). That verb, 'generate', is carefully chosen here: the botnet machines can run semi-autonomously, receiving command-and-control instructions for new spam campaigns and then spewing out messages in the millions, adjusting each one individually ('per-message polymorphism') and shifting strategy if they receive an unusually high number of rejections (Kreibich et al., 2008). In fact, a unique, targeted 'spear-phishing' attack, like the one that got John Podesta's Gmail login and disrupted the 2016 American election, is a flashback to a more artisanal, personal time in the Web. It had a carefully designed trick URL ('myaccount.google.com-securitysettingpage.tk') and a beautiful HTML email and login landing page, both mimicking Google's style to the pixel. (Similar care was taken with attempts to get internal email from the campaign of Emmanuel Macron in France – a tactic now so common that his staff prepared for it in advance.) That kind of attack is now the exception rather than the rule, the human touch for high-value targets. When we encounter a spam comment, a spam blog, a spam email, a message on Twitter @'d to you by a bikini avatar with a high-entropy name, we are very likely the first people to have ever seen it. It is the product of layers of wholly computational work, for which the humans merely set the parameters, assembled and passed around the world on a chain of mechanical writers and readers. This brings us to the last chapter of the Web's counterhistory, the closing act of those linkfarms and mutual admiration societies: the rise of the post-human social Web.

## WE STILL BELIEVE THERE IS HUMAN INVOLVEMENT

The Web had always been social, of course, alight with cultures of linking, authoring, sharing, and citing, with forums, boards, comments, and 'virtual communities'. But as a matter of terminology, the Web became 'social' after it became searchable and increasingly central, when Friendster, MySpace, Facebook, Orkut, LinkedIn, Bebo, Sina Weibo, Twitter, the *Marie Celeste* ghost ship that is Google+, and a million other social networks came to dominate much of the experience and use of the Web. This was an aggregation, a pooling, of human attention on a scale beyond a spammer's wildest dreams.

Furthermore, it was a model for aggregating human attention to which spamming came quite naturally. It was – and is – a terrain dominated by clickbait and linkbait, by eyeball-grabbing fake news (a technique pioneered by spam emails with links that launched malware downloads) and you'll-never-guess headlines bannered over the thinnest content, by the endlessly refilled candy bowl of meme culture, and advertisements indistinguishable from old-school spam come-ons (weight loss, penile enlargement, predatory home-loan scams, and other dragnets for dim fish). Even the legitimate human users developed spam-like approaches to their activity. Merlin Mann, a bemused witness to the dot-com scene, dubbed this activity on Twitter *personality spamming*, the work of arrogating attention for oneself, using social media to build an audience – often a very carefully quantified audience of 'followers' and 'rebloggers' – rather than a network of friends. It is the socially acceptable but aggressively eyeball-hungry work of those who would be, or act like, celebrities, 'influencers', or 'thought leaders'. From the Web 2.0 status culture analyzed by Alice Marwick (2013) to Whitney Phillips's media-savvy trolls (2015), to Limor Shifman's circulating memes (2013) and Sarah Jeong's 'Internet of Garbage' (2015), studies of the social Web capture how difficult it can be to distinguish from what its own users call spam.

Spam was a natural fit for this set of platforms and practices – so much so that it produced a similar paradox to that faced by Google, for which its most optimal customers were spammers. Spammers jumped into creating fake Twitter accounts and Facebook pages and YouTube accounts, serving up porn links and browser exploits and selling armies of Twitter followers, blocks of tens of thousands of Facebook 'likes' and YouTube views and upvotes. A huge portion of human time on the Web became devoted to interacting with and producing content that sought the illusion of salience through popularity – and if there was one thing spammers were good at, it was producing exactly that illusion. In a sweatshop model that recalls the early days of email spamming, employees of 'likefarming' firms will 'like' a particular brand or product for a fee. The going rate is a few US dollars for 1,000 likes (Schneider, 2004). Performed in narrowly focused bursts of activity devoted to liking one thing or one family of things, from accounts that do little else, this tactic is easy to spot, so they have to generate the appearance of casual use. They do this by liking pages recently added to the feed of Page Suggestions, which Facebook promotes according to its model of the user's interests – they behave, in other words, as ideal Facebook citizens, heavy users constantly clicking the thumbs-up and endorsing whatever Facebook's recommendation algorithm thinks they will endorse.

Twitter, likewise, has an enormous bot problem. It must regularly conduct sweeps to purge the bot accounts from its ranks, but the bots follow paying users in packs of thousands to make them look important and popular, as well as random humans to create the illusion of normalcy for their other activities. A too-successful purge is rewarded with outrage as users see their follower numbers plummet (and Twitter as a company sees its value drop, likewise, as the pool of active users shrinks). The same is true of buying views for your YouTube video, listens for your song on Soundcloud, or clicks on your ads. In a Web 2.0 version of Goodhart's Law ('When a measure becomes a target, it ceases to be a good measure', or, 'What gets evaluated, gets gamed'), any metric meant to describe human interest, esteem, or attention more generally will spur the development of customized code to take it over for pay (Goodhart, 1981: 116). All of these vast social Web platforms have created models in which the spammers boost the metrics in exactly the way they're supposed to be boosted – just not as legitimate human users. (What these models say about the expectations for the humans, those hoof-clicking attention cattle, is left to the reader.)

I would like to close with a final problem, a ubiquitous mark on the structure of the Web left by spam, one that points towards the future: the humble CAPTCHA. The CAPTCHA system – the deformed letters on weird backgrounds that only humans can read, in theory, to verify their non-bot status – is meant to block automated posting, commenting, and account-creation tools, key components in the contemporary spammer arsenal. CAPTCHAs make it harder to start new Blogger blogs or open more free email accounts, and spammers have been working assiduously on different fronts to overcome them. In May 2008, the security company Websense documented a series of attacks on the account-creation process of email services. Many requests for accounts kept hitting the CAPTCHA stage, and most, but not all, failed (Whoriskey, 2008). The pace (replies in six seconds) and the failure rate (nine to one) suggested that computers were doing the solving. 'We still believe there is human involvement', said the company's statement. Botnet attacks on text recognition have improved enough since then that new forms of CAPTCHAs rely on identifying somewhat ambiguous visual information, like picking storefronts out of a set of pictures of buildings. To solve this, spammers have turned to automating humans with services like Captcha King, which retrieves the CAPTCHA images from things like the Twitter account-creation process for manual entry. An outsourced staff sits there all day banging out CAPTCHAs, with a guaranteed 'success rate of 95% with a response time of less than 90 seconds' (Krebs, 2012; Motoyama et al., 2010). Those poor souls, whose work makes regular data entry look exceedingly pleasant by comparison, are essentially being paid to be human – to exhibit a theoretically solely human characteristic.

In that labor, and in the statement 'We still believe there is human involvement', we can see a Web increasingly and finally dominated by the activity and content not of humans but of software, and humans directly responding to and directed by software. As Ben Light (2016) points out, human agency was always the centerpiece of Web 2.0 – but, observed more closely, it's clear we miss the real story of the contemporary Web if we fail to account for all the *nonhuman* agency and activity on it. This is an appropriately grim and paradoxical note for the close of this counterhistory of the Web: with Twitter accounts made by humans solving problems for machines, to provide other humans with the illusion of social activity, of 'Web presence'.

We have followed the work of drawing the line defining spam and non-spam through the history of the Web, from links and sites to blogs and search to the exquisite fakes that mislead users of the Web's infrastructure. Throughout, I have argued that the act of calling something 'spam' tells as much about what is being excluded as what is being identified: junk results and salient searches, personality spamming and meaningful social content, fake-out landing pages and the real thing, abusive advertising and legitimate applications. I hope I have also conveyed how blurry those categories can be. As we follow the movement of the word and the systems to which it is applied, spam exposes how vague and tricky the distinctions can be, and will continue to be. Spam exposes the failures and holes in models: how relevance is calculated, what a valuable collection of interlinked Web pages looks like, how people understand the pages they see and how their machines construe them, what constitutes approval, interaction, relationships, society, even humanness. In some of the cases I've described here, spam indicts the very systems it exploits; it produces optimal users, pushing business models to their logical extreme. Following all these developments provides a different history of the Web – searchable, central, and social – through the ways each development created communities, attention, and the possibility of their own failure.

Which brings us back to the present and future of the Web, seen from spam's point of view: in which the humans involved have never been less important, mere fodder for content production and analytic stats, under the watchful eye of the platforms. The end of the line.

## REFERENCES


Brin, S., and Page, L. (1998) 'The Anatomy of a Large-Scale Hypertextual Web Search Engine', *Computer Networks & ISDN Systems* 30(1–7): 107–117.

Brunton, F. (2013) *Spam: A Shadow History of the Internet*. Cambridge, MA: MIT Press.

Edwards, P. (2003) 'Infrastructure and Modernity: Force, Time, and Social Organization in the History of Sociotechnical Systems', in Thomas Misa, Philip Bray, and Andrew Feenberg (Eds.), *Modernity and Technology* (pp. 185–225). Cambridge: MIT Press.

Fetterly, D., Manasse, M., and Najork, M. (2004) 'Spam, Damn Spam, and Statistics: Using Statistical Analysis to Locate Spam Web Pages', *Proceedings of the 7th International Workshop on the Web and Databases* 67 (2004): 1–6.

Galloway, A.R., and Thacker, E. (2008) 'On Narcolepsy', in Jussi Parikka and Tony D. Sampson (Eds.), *The Spam Book: On Viruses, Porn, and Other Anomalies from the Dark Side of Digital Culture* (pp. 251–263). Cresskill, NJ: Hampton Press.

Gansing, K. (2011) 'Spamculture: The Informational Politics of Functional Trash', in Miyase Christensen, André Jansson, and Christian Christensen (Eds.), *Online Territories: Globalization, Mediated Practice and Social Space* (pp. 89–109). New York: Peter Lang.

Goldsmith, J., and Wu, T. (2008) *Who Controls the Internet?: Illusions of a Borderless World*. Oxford: Oxford University Press.

Goodhart, C. (1981) 'Problems of Monetary Management: The U.K. Experience', in Anthony S. Courakis (Ed.), *Inflation, Depression, and Economic Policy in the West* (pp. 111–146). Lanham, MD: Rowman & Littlefield.

Hayes, D. (1996) 'An Alternative Primer on Net Abuse, Free Speech, and Usenet' (http://www.jetcafe.org/dave/usenet/freedom.html).

Hollis, K. (2005) 'alt.spam FAQ or "Figuring out Fake E-Mail & Posts"' (Rev. 20050130, 30 January 2005) (http://digital.net/~gandalf/spamfaq.html).

Jeong, S. (2015) *The Internet of Garbage*. New York: Forbes Media.

Krebs, B. (2012) 'Virtual Sweatshops Defeat Bot-or-Not Tests' (Krebs on Security, 9 January 2012) (http://krebsonsecurity.com/2012/01/virtual-sweatshops-defeat-bot-or-not-tests/).

Kreibich, C., Kanich, C., Levchenko, K., Enright, B., Voelker, G., Paxson, V., and Savage, S. (2008) 'On the Spam Campaign Trail', *Proceedings of the 1st Usenix Workshop on Large-Scale Exploits and Emergent Threats* (http://cseweb.ucsd.edu/~savage/papers/LEETStormspam08.pdf).

Larson, W.L. (1994) 'Re: Green Card Lottery – Final One?' in news.admin.policy, 12 April 1994.

Lialina, O. (2009) 'A Vernacular Web 2', in Olia Lialina and Dragan Espenschied (Eds.), *Digital Folklore Reader* (pp. 58–69). Stuttgart: Merz Akademie.

Light, B. (2016) 'The Rise of Speculative Devices: Hooking Up with the Bots of Ashley Madison', *First Monday*, 21(6) (http://firstmonday.org/ojs/index.php/fm/article/view/6426/5525).

Lovink, G. (2005) 'The Principle of Notworking (Concepts in Critical Internet Culture)' (lecture, Hogeschool van Amsterdam), 24 February 2005.

Ludovico, A. (2005) 'Spam, the Economy of Desire' (Neural.it, 1 December 2005) (http://www.neural.it/art/2005/12/spam_the_economy_of_desire.phtml).

Marwick, A. (2013) *Status Update: Celebrity, Publicity, and Branding in the Social Media Age*. New Haven: Yale University Press.

Messaging Anti-Abuse Working Group (2011) 'Email Metrics Program: The Network

Operators' Perspective. Report #15 – First, Second and Third Quarter 2011' (http://www.maawg.org/sites/maawg/files/news/MAAWG_2011_Q1Q2Q3_Metrics_Report_15.pdf).

'mk590' (1996) 'AOL for Free?' in alt.2600, 28 January 1996.

Motoyama, M., Levchenko, K., Kanich, C., McCoy, D., Voelker, G., and Savage, S. (2010) 'Re:CAPTCHAs – Understanding CAPTCHA-Solving Services in an Economic Context', *Proceedings of the USENIX Security Symposium* (August 2010): 435–452.

Parikka, J., and Sampson, T.D. (2009) 'On Anomalous Objects of Digital Culture: An Introduction', in Jussi Parikka and Tony D. Sampson (Eds.), *The Spam Book: On Viruses, Porn, and Other Anomalies from the Dark Side of Digital Culture* (pp. 1–18). Cresskill, NJ: Hampton Press.

Phillips, W. (2015) *This Is Why We Can't Have Nice Things: Mapping the Relationship between Online Trolling and Mainstream Culture*. Cambridge, MA: MIT Press.

Pringle, G., Allison, L., and Dowe, D. (1998) 'What Is a Tall Poppy among Web Pages?', *Computer Networks & ISDN Systems* 30(1–7): 369–377.

Sandvig, C. (2013) 'The Internet as Infrastructure', in William Dutton (Ed.), *The Oxford Handbook of Internet Studies*. Oxford: Oxford University Press.

Schneider, J. (2004) 'Likes or Lies? How Perfectly Honest Business can be Overrun by Facebook Spammers' (TheNextWeb, 23 January 2004) (http://thenextweb.com/facebook/2014/01/23/likes-lies-perfectly-honest-businesses-can-overrun-facebook-spammers/).

Shifman, L. (2013) *Memes in Digital Culture*. Cambridge, MA: MIT Press.

Sullivan, D. (2002) 'Death of a Meta Tag' (*Search Engine Watch,* 30 September 2002) (http://searchenginewatch.com/article/2066825/Death-Of-A-Meta-Tag).

Whoriskey, P. (2008) 'Digital Deception', *Washington Post*, 1 May 2008.

39

# Trolls and Trolling History: From Subculture to Mainstream Practices

Michael Nycyk

## INTRODUCTION

The internet and its component the World Wide Web (web) brings many benefits to humankind, such as communication and information exchanges, yet humans have struggled with the freedoms it offers. Trolling, cyberbullying, hacking and other practices have confronted internet users, governments and lawmakers with the challenges of how to manage them and what measures should be introduced to punish trolls. This chapter documents the history of trolls and trolling, informed by the idea that technological developments and increased access to the internet have supported trolling, and that, once a relatively contained activity, trolling has spread to become a widely practised one. While other reasons account for it, such as changes in the civility and conduct of humans in societies, the chapter's thesis is driven by this underlying concept. This historical account documents this view.

This account's time period addresses trolling from pre-web (before 1989), Web 1.0 (1989–2005) and Web 2.0 (2004 to present). It begins by defining trolls, trolling and the technologies where it takes place. Stories of trolling discussed demonstrate its spread, development and sophistication, seen especially in the organized trolling groups that have caused harm to internet users. The concentration of pre-web Usenet groups in this account is important because it demonstrated the first accounts of the severity of trolling and its consequences. The discussion then moves to the way in which trolling is supported by the extended reach and ease of use of internet and web platforms, such as social media, and its prevalence as a mainstream practice is identified. The chapter then concludes with suggestions of how the future of trolling may look.

## TROLLS, TROLLING AND TECHNOLOGY: DEFINITIONS AND CONTEXTS

Trolls and trolling, as they are used in internet contexts, are associated with stories of ugly, supernatural creatures in Scandinavian and Norse (Middle Age Icelandic and Norwegian languages) folklore. Lindow (2014: 5–6) claims the origin of the word 'troll' is still unknown, but in Norse language they were so called because they were troublesome, shifting, changing and hard to pin down. This analogy seems appropriate when applying it to trolls on the internet. Over time the troll figure from this period of history has been associated with those who use the internet for trolling; hence the original meaning of troll has morphed into being used to describe humans who do mischief using electronic communication.

Bishop's (2013: 28) definition of trolls encompasses qualities we have come to expect from trolling behaviours: they post messages and image content via electronic networks intended to be provocative, offensive, menacing and disruptive. Bergstrom (2011) vividly compares an internet troll to a mythical Norse troll that has malicious intent to do harm. Many trolls consider themselves comedians doing it for the Lulz (laughs) and think their work is harmless, but scholars often report them as being antagonistic for the sake of amusement (Hardaker, 2013: 58). Another common term for trolls is keyboard warriors.

Bishop (2014a: 8-9) describes the historical origins of trolls and trolling as originating from the US military in the 1960s, where fighter pilots' strategies were fishing and 'reeling in' one's opposition in a form of dog-fighting. He argues that trolling has been understood since 2001 as a form of abuse (Bishop, 2014b: 9). Further, it is argued that it is also a form of humour and a type of transgressive disruptive behaviour that became associated with the hacker group Anonymous and the bulletin board group 4chan, where members made trolling a source of enjoyment (Bishop 2014b: 9).

Trolling is practised across many types of electronic communication and software, mainly through text, image and video. The strategy is to bait people into being hurt or shocked by the content, but it is the disruption to the internet user's experience and offline life, when using any online space, that is of concern. Trolling that causes hurt or disruption is done by (but not limited to): posting sexist, racist and homophobic comments, human body shaming, physical and mental disability, publication of private details called doxxing, sexting and revenge porn publication, fake news reports, false accusations of paedophilia, attacking people's political and religious beliefs and desecrating human and animal online memorial sites.

Trolls can act alone but are also highly organized into co-operative groups. Trolling behaviours have been attributed to what Suler (2004: 321) states is a form of disinhibition where people do not feel any consequences for posting harmful content about others. Suler's work has been frequently cited as offering causes for such behaviours. Other terms that scholars have applied to trolls include sadism, Machiavellianism (named after an Italian Renaissance politician), self-interested, psychopathic, sociopathic and deceitful. From these it is evident that trolls are usually portrayed in books and the mass media as causing harm and as criminals.

Trolling is practised in electronic communication environments requiring mostly password access and software skill mastery to operate. The increased ease of access and use of software, as exemplified in social media like Facebook and Twitter, has played a part in trolling, which became more common as the software became easier to use. A clear divide can be delineated, with technology becoming more accessible and easy to use. Pre-web and Web 1.0 applications were limited to those with expertise or willingness to learn them, whereas Web 2.0 represented new and easier ways to take up trolling. However, Ankerson (2015: 1) cautions against forming neat categories of technology development, especially the distinction between Web 1.0 and Web 2.0. Though there are differences, trolls used many pre-web and Web 1.0 software such as newsreaders or Internet Relay

Chat well past 2004 when Web 2.0 was said to have begun.

Therefore, a brief description of the context of internet and web technologies is given to show where trolls practise trolling. The development of the web, attributed to Tim Berners-Lee and launched in 1989, is described as a document collection in an information space identified by Uniform Resource Locators (URLs) (The World Wide Web Consortium (W3C), 2004). Characterizing this was the term 'read-only web', where information could be found but limited opportunities to post content existed.

Web 1.0 and 2.0 had an overlap in terms of functionality; however, the advantage of increased web and internet development was a more interactive, useful and interconnecting user experience with easier posting of content (Naik and Shivalingaiah, 2008). Cormode and Krishnamurthy (2008) describe the impact of this change as a shift from passive consumer use in Web 1.0 to a participatory model where users became content creators.

For this chapter, the technological timeline for describing trolling is informed by the periods of pre-web, Web 1.0 and 2.0. However, to fully cover the changes in trolling, references are also made to other software where trolling is now abundant, such as phone applications (apps), gaming and virtual environments.

## PRE-WEB AND WEB 1.0 TROLLING: A BOUNDED SUBCULTURE

Calling the pre-web and Web 1.0 a bounded subculture means that trolling took place in limited areas on the internet and was less known by the public. It occurred on the web, but also on non-web applications such as Telnet bulletin boards, Usenet, chat rooms, email, Multi-User Domains (MUDS) and virtual communities, the last one being an example of a subculture bounded by rules and moderation to protect members' privacy. As virtual communities are online spaces where human relationships are built through support and information exchange, they can act as a form of psychotherapy (Rheingold, 1993: 4–7). Protected spaces can be infiltrated by trolls, hence the energy expended by owners of websites and internet spaces, who struggle to protect users from the negative experiences trolls provide.

Throughout internet and web studies the word 'culture' is used to describe activities done in cyberspace; hence the use of the word cyberculture. Scholars speak of trolling culture but settling on a precise definition is difficult. For this trolling history, the definition of culture is based on Kroeber and Kluckhohn's (1952: 53) claim that peoples' beliefs and values inform action. A subculture has beliefs at odds with a dominant culture, often challenging the main culture's values. Therefore, trolls are a subculture because their beliefs and attitudes inform negative actions such as disruption and hurt, the antithesis of co-operative, respectful communities. If pre-web and Web 1.0 are more bounded, with trolling occurring only in limited parts, in Web 2.0 and beyond, trolling is considered mainstream. This means it is common and occurs across the internet and web, fostered by better technologies and changing societal attitudes to civility.

To demonstrate this core argument of trolling history – its move from bounded subculture to mainstream practice – the evidence is in the reporting of significant incidents. These are discussed in the next two sections, but again the pre-web, Web 1.0 and Web 2.0 are merely markers of time where improved technology and access to the internet meant trolling became more widespread.

### *The LambdaMOO Troll Incident*

The publication of Julian Dibble's (1993) 'A Rape in Cyberspace: Or how an Evil Clown, a Haitian Trickster Spirit, Two Wizards and a Cast of Thousands Turned a Database into a Society' was significant for two reasons.

First, it challenged people to question trolling, especially the concept that sexual assault took place online. Was virtual rape the same as physical rape? Second, it highlighted the dilemmas faced by those who ran any internet space. Freedom to post was at odds with the censure and moderation of troll activity. Some people called for punishments such as banning, but others saw no legitimate harm in the troll's action.

To illustrate, a short description of the incident is needed to appreciate its significance in trolling history. Dibble was involved in a Multi-User Domain Object Orientated space called LambdaMOO, a text-based program where people chatted and interacted with each other in public and private spaces. He stated it was a harmonious environment where trust was given freely and people supported each other. Into this came a troll named Mr Bungle, described by Dibble (1993) as an evil-looking clown in a harlequin suit with a belt buckle displaying a swear word. The troll, or perhaps trolls, as Dibble suggests it may have been more than one person, maliciously disrupted the MOO by forcing female participants to perform sexual acts on him and each other.

Despite the troll eventually being banned, the success of the disruption was an early account of how troll acts cause problems and how managing trolling is difficult. It was not just the act that disrupted the room but the troll's attempt to return under a new name and the division between members who did not see the trolling as a serious issue. Dibble's story is important for scholars, albeit critically, as debates exist over the use of the term 'virtual rape' as a valid act. However, as an early account of the problematic nature of troll behaviour, it is an invaluable resource for reflecting on the commonplace dilemma of controlling it.

## *The Usenet and Flame Wars*

The bounded system of Usenet brought trolling, and its mischievous nature, to scholars and the public. Created in 1979 at the University of North Carolina, the computer-based distributed discussion system was a significant communication channel for information exchange, emotional support and sharing of interests. Newsgroups in Usenet consisted of topics and message threads within them. Messages were cross-posted, meaning they appeared in many newsgroups, which became a factor in widespread unconstrained trolling activity. Moderation and censorship of messages, including banning of trolls, were attempted, but trolls did not adhere to such rules.

Usenet users were unhappy with the constraints on language and topic use in the groups, and pressured Usenet's owners to create a subculture called alternative (alt). Smith (1999: 201) observed that many Usenet groups seemed to be dedicated to non-co-operative interactions, with people challenging, insulting and threatening each other. Trolling became a standard part of Usenet use, with a number of documented events that came to public attention. Trolls succeeded in derailing conversations and eroding trust between people, but also involved other Usenet groups as unwilling participants drawn into trolling behaviours (Sindorf, 2013: 201).

The historical significance of Usenet trolling was around the group alt.folklore.urban (Bartlett, 2014). Krappitz (2012: 40) claimed alt.flame, a Usenet group devoted to insulting and flaming other members, contained one of the first appearances of the word 'troll', as reported in this post:

> Just some credentials: I am called Troll. I didn't get the name because I'm a fun guy. I am the champion of channel +insult on irc and I have thrice defended the title before the channel went down, so I can flame with the best. Flame away if you like, but 'I'm gonna deal it back to you in spades. 'Cause when I'm havin' fun ya know I can't conceal it. Because I know you'd never cut it in my game.' -Guns N' Roses' 99

This example of the word troll was applied increasingly to people who were disrupting others' internet experiences through name-calling and making fun of people. Note in the quote the threat that retaliation will earn the person more vitriol from the troll.

Trolls also flame people as a form of baiting others to respond to their comments. Bartlett's (2014) account in *The Dark Net: Inside the Digital Underworld* comprehensively covers the Usenet troll battles that became infamous but also stimulated research enquiry into trolling practices. He wrote of the story of a Usenet member Moby who wanted to invite a female to his apartment. However, his cats were on heat, messing up his apartment. Though only posted in the Usenet group alt.tasteless, his dilemma was cross-posted to many groups, including pet groups.

The alt.tasteless members would troll other Usenet groups, posting Moby's message to groups where explicit language was banned, such as pet discussion groups. Trolls from other Usenet groups in turn began trolling alt.tasteless in return with messages involving sexual acts with cats, torture and execution. This caused outrage in many groups because cross-postings would disrupt the flow of exchanges between members posting about their hobbies and interests, as well as flooding the groups with irrelevant and offensive messages. Trolls were relentless in posting content about Moby's predicament with messages about cats that were sexual and violent, causing problems with moderating the groups, which were overwhelmed by the volume of messages.

In 1996 another well-known Usenet incident highlighted the organized nature of trolling. A group of Harvard University students found an abandoned Usenet group called alt.fan.karlmalden.nose, named after the American actor Karl Malden, who had a bulbous nose after it was broken. It was meant to be a group that only discussed campus events. Lee (2016) on the website 'The One True History of Meow' stated that the Harvard Usenet members decided to target another Usenet group with disruptive messages. They chose a group named alt.tv.beavis-n-butthead after two Music Television (MTV) cartoon characters.

Displaying the nature of co-operation that existed across Usenet, the beavis-n-butthead group were warned of the Harvard group's intention of trolling. A Harvard student, Matt Bruce, urged trolls to compose messages using big words and immaculate grammar. Bruce had meant this for amusement, but it was seen as arrogant by the other group. In retaliation against the Harvard students, the beavis-n-butthead group Usenet members banded together and posted multiple offensive messages in the Karl Malden Harvard group.

This trolling achieved the aim of driving many Harvard members to stop using Usenet because of the excessive and relentless number of troll messages. One Harvard member who was targeted was called C.A.T., the name inspiring the beavis-n-butthead trolls to use cat phrases in messages as jokes (Lee, 2016):

> Suddenly, afk-mn, alt.college.college-bowl, and scores of other groups were flooded to the gills and beyond with hundreds upon hundreds of huge meow articles from all corners of Usenet. Cascades, ASCII cats, hundred-line 'meow' hello-world-type flood posts, and more were posted, reposted, munged, pureed, and regurgitated all over the servers of the world. The Harvard kids' protests were quickly lost in the feline tidal wave. Every post by a Harvard snot would result in fifty cascade follow-ups. alt.college.college-bowl, a known regular haunt of Matt Bruce, was reduced to a smoldering crater, so inundated with meows that its regulars could no longer use it.

Bruce tried to appeal to all to stop the trolling but was further ridiculed for his attempt to do so. This trolling incident is significant as it demonstrates how a subculture's beliefs and attitudes impacted on all users of an internet space. The Harvard students were seen as elitist, deserving the flame war waged on them. This suggested that trolls, although seen as pranksters and disruptors, had genuine beliefs about another group in society that made that group the object of derision and hate.

These incidents captured scholars' interest in theorizing about trolls, particularly the motivations of trolls in disrupting the internet and websites using vitriol against groups in society. Mitra's (1996) study of the Usenet group soc.cult.indian concluded that, despite the group having rules on behaviours, those identified as coming from Pakistan openly racially attacked those living in India. This replicated the historical conflict between the countries as trolls disrupted the civil conversations between group members. Spender's (1995) study of women's forums illustrated what has become common trolling behaviour: using sexist and misogynistic terms to disparage women's achievements. Jane (2012) researched trolling and flaming of women online, terming the treatment they received 'e-bile'. Although unpleasant, Jane (2015: 66) argues that over 30 years of trolling research has assisted well for understanding the hostile discourse trolls take.

The selected historical troll incidents that took place in bounded spaces online within subcultures were increasing as more people began using the internet and web. Moderators, also known as administrators and on some sites wizards, began to struggle to control trolls. As Usenet studies showed, trolls could organize themselves into highly efficient groups capable of attacking many others they had disdain for. This period laid the basis for understanding trolling behaviours, which were breaking out of the subcultures and corners of the internet and web, finding their way into the mainstream culture of the internet.

## WEB 2.0 TROLLING: BECOMING MAINSTREAM

While Ankerson (2015: 1) stated the temporal move from Web 1.0 to Web 2.0 was not seamless, increased functionality of online software and growing access to the internet encouraged a growth in trolling activity. Researchers recognized trolling's growing perverseness in moving from Usenet and virtual forums to social networks, online magazines and newspapers, blogs and web-based virtual worlds and computer games (Coles and West, 2016: 233). They sought answers for why trolling was occurring, drawing upon Suler's (2004) disinhibition work. Research began recognizing new motivations for trolling, with Buckels et al. (2014: 97) arguing that research on trolling was needed to diversify and explore motivations for it, incorporating sadism, narcissism, Machiavellianism and psychopathic factors. These explanations marked a shift in which trolling began to increasingly concern the public, with demands for severe actions to punish trolls.

Whitney Phillips, a scholar who studied trolling using ethnographic methods, described Web 2.0 as the period when internet trolling became mainstream. She argues that it reflects both the societal and technological changes that have caused trolling to become a mainstream activity (Phillips, 2015: 137):

> As agents of cultural digestion, trolls are subject to and directly reflect shifting political, historical, and economic sands. It would stand to reasons, then, that changes in mainstream culture would result in corresponding changes in trolling subculture, a critical point when considering the differences between the emerging troll space of the mid-2000s, the established troll space of 2008–2011, and the scattershot troll space of 2012–2015.

Usenet required specific software and use of passwords, but new sites such as 4chan did not ask for such requirements. The web-based bulletin board of 4chan has been widely researched and attracts criticism from scholars as being a centre of organized trolling, with behaviours described as divorced from a moral hinge and joining a 'hivemind' where trolls could attack individuals (Manivannan, 2013: 122). However, it is only one of many online spaces where trolls now practise their pranking and disruption skills.

To illustrate the spread of trolling into the mainstream daily life of the internet, a number of important internet spaces are discussed. With these are examples of trolling that demonstrate this shift, and how trolling has become a practice that is almost taken-for-granted, only punctuated by occasional outrage that brings it back to public focus.

## Internet Memes and Online Memorial Vandalism

Internet memes have become a widely used artefact to troll and prank online, but have also been used to convey messages about serious issues, beginning with the Occupy Wall Street movement of 2011. By contrast, trolls are seen by the public as villains, for example the trolling of online memorials for people and pets, referred to as vandalism. Memes are multimodal artefacts often created in response to events in popular culture for public comment (Milner, 2013: 2359) but over time may become ghoulish and attention seeking (Rintel, 2013: 266).

A popular image of trolls was created by Carlos Ramirez in 2008, called troll face. Shown as a bald head with large teeth and a grinning mouth, it was often placed over people's faces to display humour or contempt.

Burgess (2008: 9) states that video and image memes are deeply situated in the everyday use of the internet and are simply users performing mundane and creative traditions. In her study of the meme website LOLCats, Miltner (2014) argues that feline memes became a harmless participatory practice. Yet the meme can also cause hurt and offence if used with the intent to harm.

Trolls vandalizing online memorial sites invokes greater outrage among internet users and the public. The term 'memorial vandalism' officially emerged in 2010 to describe the provocative, insensitive and inflammatory text and photos posted on human and animal memorial websites and social media. Leaver (2013: 221) questions whether such practices are trolling, suggesting that the term trolling is being diluted and as such memorial vandalism is not a form of harm. Yet Marwick and Ellison (2012: 390–1) claim such practices are a serious form of trolling with an impact not seen before in trolling history.

Phillips (2011) argues that early memorial vandalism trolling came from 4chan, in a post making light of an attack by a killer whale on a Sea World trainer in 2010:

> The date was 25 February 2010. That afternoon, Sea World trainer Dawn Brancheau was thrashed to death by Tillikum, a 12,000 pound killer whale, as the two performed in front of a live stadium audience (Martinez, 2010). Within minutes of Brancheau's death, trolls began uploading macros onto /b/ featuring a homicidal whale ('Killed the bitch cos she didn't bring fishs') as well as variations on Rule 34 (an unofficial rule of the internet declaring that whatever 'it' is, there is porn of it; if on the off-chance there isn't, one is expected to promptly create or PhotoShop some).

Public outrage of such vandalism is often met with more posts from trolls making further fun of the tragedy. There have been arrests and incarceration in many countries for such behaviours, though court action is often prohibitive by cost and is not a deterrent to trolls. Memes and online memorial vandalism trolling have become notorious as weapons trolls use to hurt and disrupt others on a large scale.

## Social Media Trolling

Social media web-based platforms allow text, image and video posts to be shared with an unlimited audience. Although they require membership through the provision of an email address, fake accounts are abundant, and flaming, baiting and name-calling exist across all of them. Although privacy settings are offered, these are often not in bounded systems, so message content can be seen by anyone. Curran (2012: 56) argues that trolling has been caused by the fact that the internet has over time fostered a cumulative shift from values and beliefs that prioritize the collective good of the community, and of groups within it, to ones that give priority to the satisfaction of the needs, desires and aspirations of the individual.

What is significant is the move away from Donath's (1999: 45) description of trolling being a 'game' about identity deception, to people exposing themselves by stating their real names. This disclosure has changed our understanding of trolls, for they are no longer invisible, anonymous, under-the-bridge internet users. People seem willing on some social media sites to use their accounts for public trolling that can, and has, resulted in bans and defamation court cases. Their behaviours are like the Usenet trolls but now they have a face and a name.

## *Facebook and Twitter Trolling*

Facebook and Twitter are frequently criticized as platforms for trolls. Facebook has widespread trolling on it, prevalent on pages for media news sites, celebrities, politicians and controversial human figures. Users will argue and fight with each other, leaving posts public. Pressure has been placed on Facebook to enact stricter punishments for trolling. This has proven to be difficult to consistently apply and often people who are not trolling are banned for publishing comments and photographs that were not intended to bait and disrupt others. Clearly, the decision as to what is trolling on Facebook, undertaken by several content-watching offices around the world, is subjective. Page owners have the ability to ban trolls from their sites, but it is the decision of Facebook to ban someone permanently.

Twitter was created in 2006 as a micro-blogging service where messages are called tweets, but its unique branding is that each tweet is limited to only 140 characters (boyd et al., 2010: 2). It has become controversial because of the prevalence of trolls and the failure of Twitter to manage them. The platform is also notorious for the number of anonymous accounts and fake profiles of personalities, as well as trolls posting about fake deaths of celebrities.

Trolling on Twitter can be sophisticated and organized, like Usenet groups. In 2016 mass trolling occurred that was even more efficiently organized and inflamed mob mentality behaviours. This behaviour is reinforced by the use of hash tags (#) and re-tweeting, where messages can be posted across accounts and, although it is a bounded system, public tweets can be seen by anyone. Examples of mass trolling during 2016 included: England's vote to leave the European Union (Brexit), the 2016 Clinton–Trump US presidential campaign, continued opposition to marriage equality in the United States, and harassment of African American actor Leslie Jones, who acted in a remake of *Ghostbusters*, by conservative blogger Milo Yiannopoulos.

Another example was reported by Simon Hattenstone (2013) of *The Guardian* online newspaper site, who interviewed Caroline Criado-Perez, a feminist campaigner. She became a victim of Twitter trolls for her success in having a woman placed back on English banknotes. As she states:

> Then there were the death threats. 'One was from a really bright guy who said: "I've just got released from prison."' She shows me her phone: "I'd do a lot worse than rape you. I've just got out of prison and would happily do more time to see you berried [sic]. #10feetunder." The tweet is signed Ayekayesa. There is another one, equally chilling. "I will find you, and you don't want to know what I will do when I do. You're pathetic. Kill yourself. Before I do. #Godie."

She was successful in having some of the trolls jailed. Another reported Twitter trolling case was New Zealand model and television presenter Charlotte Dawson. It was reported that she was targeted because she posted on Twitter back at the trolls when they posted tweets such as 'It's a very good thing that you cannot breed', and 'please go hang yourself' (The New Zealand Herald: 2012). Dawson's case was unique because the trolling was considered a factor in her suicide, bringing greater awareness to the public about the consequences of trolling. The mainstream commercial media began extensively reporting and analysing trolling, often in a sensational manner.

Over time, trolling on social media has not only become more organized but is an industry in some countries, for example China and Russia. One example from Russia involved hackers who, it was suggested, had been interfering in the country's political system by spreading fake news on Twitter. They were investigated by Finnish journalist Jessikka Aro during 2014, resulting in her being trolled on her Twitter account. Interviewing Aro, Miller (2016: 4) describes the systematic, relentless and personal trolling Aro experienced:

> Last spring someone sent her a text message pretending to be from her father – who died 20 years ago – telling her he was 'watching her'. Another wrote a song, mocking her as a bimbo 'James Bond' NATO agent with a drug habit. There is even a music video online, with Aro portrayed by an actress in a leotard and wig. It would be funny if it wasn't dripping with venom'.

Social media trolling has become mainstream because of the reporting of incidents such as Aro and Dawson. Trolls usually do prefer fake accounts but, unlike Usenet, Twitter and Facebook became significant for open trolling where full disclosure of people's names occurred. The term trolling became generic rather than just being a dark part of the web only experienced by some users.

## *Video Sharing, Gaming and Mobile Computing Trolling*

Trolling also occurs on video and knowledge-sharing platforms such as YouTube and Wikipedia and increasingly on smart phone apps such as dating sites. Web gaming sites and the virtual reality world *Second Life*, a sophisticated graphical version of Dibbell's LambdaMOO, also experience trolling. These mainstream websites are used daily so trolling, while tolerated, does place pressure on the owners of these websites to regulate them against trolls.

YouTube, founded in 2005, shares videos posted by users and invites users to comment on them. Videos are posted by trolls showing their online exploits across the web and internet. However, YouTube's user comments section is often unmoderated despite community guidelines that users who join agree to adhere to. What is concerning is that trolling can appear on any video unless users disable comments. Trolling comments are often used to cause arguments, although controversial issues, political figures, criminals, religion, celebrities and people's sexuality are also frequently targeted by trolls. Trolls turn debates on YouTube into arguments that become hateful with often discriminatory remarks used to further inflame users who willingly participate in such debates.

A significant study of trolling was conducted by Shachaf and Hara (2010: 357) using Wikipedia, a collaborative encyclopedia, which illustrated the reasons why trolls practise disruptive trolling activities. The authors found that the Wikipedia trolls they interviewed were motivated by boredom and the need to find challenges, viewing the harm they did as entertainment. This study is frequently cited because the authors were able to interview a small but significant sample of trolls, giving insights into why people will troll a site, suggesting that pleasure in harming is part of the reason for trolling behaviours.

Web-based role-playing sites like *Second Life*, founded in 2003, have trolls that interrupt the residents' activities. This is through sexual harassment of residents and posting text and images not allowed by the world's owner. Krappitz (2012: 112) documented the activities of *Second Life* troll Ralph Pootawn, who gained fame by making videos of his trolling. Owners constantly banned him for watching residents having intimate encounters. Trolls who did this in virtual worlds came to be known as professional griefers. *Second Life* trolling is a more sophisticated version of Dibbell's (1993) depiction of text-only trolling, but it is a more accepted and mainstream activity compared with the outrage that virtual world trolling previously caused.

Significant trolling now also occurs on smart phone apps. Dating sites such as Tinder, Grindr and OkCupid are especially targeted. Because of the immediacy of contact between members, people will often play with the trolls through humorous conversations. In an Australian study of 357 Tinder users, March et al. (2017: 139) found that trolling on this app resulted from traits of psychopathy, sadism and dysfunctional impulsivity. In terms of troll history, such studies found a shift in society that needs further validation but is a reflection of changing societal values. Much trolling is associated with younger males. However, this study suggests an equalling of male and female trolling, with females' growing access and skill in trolling activities being more frequently reported.

This section has presented the argument that trolling history has shifted from a bounded system activity to a public mainstream one. Griffiths (2014: 85) reflects that little has changed, as it appears trolling is an act of intentionally provoking and/or antagonizing users in an online environment that creates an often desirable, sometimes predictable, outcome for the troll. The difference is simply in the increase in types of, and numbers of, trolls that exist. However, added to this is how we define trolls and trolling, as these terms are applied to many forms of abuse web users experience in many areas of the web. Yet it is clear from the examination of the sample of web and internet trolling presented in this chapter that it has become a widespread issue that is still manifest, despite safeguards and policies that exist to protect web users.

## CONCLUSIONS AND FUTURE SPECULATIONS ON TROLLING ACTIVITY

In this historical account of trolling I have given a chronological order of events through the pre-web, Web 1.0 and 2.0 eras: how trolling operates, what it looks like and how it has developed. Although such an account risks a biased view and leaves out many other events, as is the nature of historical accounts, it has demonstrated that trolling has developed into a sophisticated, organized and accessible phenomenon that grew out of bounded subcultures into a mainstream, taken-for-granted part of using the internet. Web 1.0 and 2.0 are representations of the shift the technology has allowed in supporting greater content creation and ease of use that has in some way encouraged trolling. However, the use of the word troll has developed a new meaning as it has morphed into those who simply like to argue and fight with each other online.

A rapid increase in research has contributed to our understanding of why trolls act as they do, using perspectives. There are still calls for more research, as well as the need to develop theories of trolling. Trolling behaviours may stay consistent in intent – to inflame, upset and disrupt – yet the incidence and shape of them have changed. It is a mainstream phenomenon because the web technologies and platforms we use are integrated into our daily lives. Therefore, it is not just the technology that has changed opportunities to troll, but also the generic use of the term troll to describe mere arguments between web users has become convoluted.

Speculation on the future history of web trolling lies in two possible areas: technology development and changing definitions of what trolling is. First, technology will continue to evolve. Will virtual reality be a space for trolling on a larger scale than the current virtual worlds? What if artificial intelligence develops a trolling side to it? Second, our perceptions of trolling and civility towards others will evolve over time. Will the insults of trolls have less importance as we become a more tolerant society no longer willing to accept racism, sexism, homophobia and other issues to cloud our interactions towards others in our global community? Importantly, will trolls have further influence on our lives as opinion shapers when world events occur?

Calls to minimize and eliminate trolling will continue as governments consider harsher penalties for its practice. As we continue to refine our theoretical conceptions of trolling we must also use that knowledge to assist us in making decisions as to how we can accomplish the elimination of it. This imperative is supported by the concerning ability for trolls to influence government and societal affairs. Trolling was once bounded within spaces, yet its flow into the mainstream has been to the web and internet user's detriment. The internet will grow further; trolling will take on new characteristics, with users who are finding themselves the victim of trolling struggling to contain their influence. This is the price we pay for trolls coming into our mainstream culture, but with research and willingness to take action against them, it is not a battle that will necessarily be lost.

## REFERENCES


Ankerson, M.S. (2015) 'Social media and the "read-only" web: reconfiguring social logics and historical boundaries', *Social Media + Society*, 1(2): 1–12.

Bartlett, J. (2014) *The Dark Net: Inside the Digital Underworld*. London: William Heinemann.

Bergstrom, K. (2011) '"Don't feed the troll": shutting down debate about community expectations on Reddit.com', *First Monday*, 16(8) (http://firstmonday.org/article/view/3498/3029).

Bishop, J. (2013) 'The effect of de-individuation of the internet troller on criminal procedure implementation:an interview with a hater', *International Journal of Cyber Criminology*, 7(1): 28–48 (http://www.cybercrimejournal.com/Bishop2013janijcc.pdf).

Bishop, J. (2014a) 'Dealing with internet trolling in political online communities: towards the this is why we can't have nice things scale', *International Journal of E-Politics*, 5(4): 1–20.

Bishop, J. (2014b) 'Representations of "trolls" in mass media communication: a review of media-texts and moral panics relating to "internet trolling"', *International Journal of Web Based Communities*, 10(1): 7–24.

boyd, D.M., Golder, S., and Lotan, G. (2010) 'Tweet, tweet, retweet: conversational aspects of retweeting on Twitter', *HICSS-43, IEEE*, Kauai, Hawaii (https://www.danah.org/papers/TweetTweetRetweet.pdf).

Buckels, E.E., Trapnell, P.D., and Paulhus, D.L. (2014) 'Trolls just want to have fun', *Personality and Individual Differences*, 67: 97–102.

Burgess, J.E. (2008) "'All your chocolate rain are belong to us?" viral video, YouTube and the dynamics of participatory culture', in G. Lovink and S. Niederer (Eds.), *Video Vortex Reader: Responses to YouTube*. Amsterdam: Institute of Network Cultures. pp.101–109.

Coles, B.A., and West, M. (2016) 'Trolling the trolls: online forum users constructions of the nature and properties of trolling', *Computers in Human Behavior*, 60: 233–244.

Cormode, G., and Krishnamurthy, B. (2008) 'Key differences between Web 1.0 and Web 2.0', *First Monday*, 13(6) (http://firstmonday.org/article/view/2125/1972).

Curran, J. (2012) 'Rethinking internet history', in J. Curran, N. Fenton, and D. Freedman (Eds.), *Misunderstanding the Internet*. London: Routledge. pp. 34–65.

Dibbell, J. (1993) 'A rape in cyberspace: or how an evil clown, a Haitian trickster spirit, two wizards and a cast of thousands turned a database into a society', *The Village Voice*, 38(51): 26–42 (http://www.villagevoice.com/news/a-rape-in-cyberspace-6401665).

Donath, J.S. (1999) 'Identity and deception in the virtual community', in P. Kollock and M. Smith (Eds.), *Communities in Cyberspace*. London: Routledge. pp. 29–59.

Griffiths, M.D. (2014) 'Adolescent trolling in online environments: a brief overview', *Education and Health*, 32(3): 85–87.

Hardaker, C. (2013) '"Uh.....not to be nitpicky,,,,,but...the past tense of drag is dragged, not drug": an overview of trolling strategies', *Journal of Language Aggression and Conflict*, 1(1): 57–85.

Hattenstone, S. (2013) 'Caroline Criado-Perez: "Twitter has enabled people to behave in a way they wouldn't face to face"'. *The Guardian* (http://www.theguardian.com/lifeandstyle/2013/aug/04/caroline-criado-perez-twitterrape-threats).

Jane, E.A. (2012) "'Your a ugly, whorish, slut" – understanding e-bile', *Feminist Media Studies*, 14(4): 531–546.

Jane, E.A. (2015) 'Flaming? what flaming? the pitfalls and potentials of researching online hostility', *Ethics and Information Technology*, 17(1): 65–87.

Krappitz, S. (2012) 'Troll Culture', Honours Thesis, Gestaltung, Kunst und Medien, Stuttgart (http://wwwwwwwww.at/downloads/troll-culture.pdf).

Kroeber, A.L., and Kluckhohn, C. (1952) *Culture: A Critical Review of Concepts and Definitions*. Cambridge, MA: Peabody Museum of American Archaeology and Ethnology, Harvard University.

Leaver, T. (2013) 'Olympic trolls: mainstream memes and digital discord?', *Trolls and the Negative Space of the Internet: The Fibreculture Journal*, 22: 216–233 (http://twentytwo.fibreculturejournal.org/fcj-163-olympic-trolls-mainstream-memes-and-digital-discord/).

Lee, X. (2016) 'The one true history of meow', *Netiquette Anthropology* (http://xahlee.info/Netiquette_dir/_/meow_wars.html).

Lindow, J. (2014) *Trolls: An Unnatural History*. London: Reaction Books.

Manivannan, V. (2013) 'Tits or GTFO: the logics of misogyny on 4chan's random – /b/', *Trolls and the Negative Space of the Internet: The Fibreculture Journal*, 22: 108–131 (http://twentytwo.fibreculturejournal.org/fcj-158-tits-or-gtfo-the-logics-of-misogyny-on-4chans-random-b/).

March, E., Grieve, R., Marrington, J., and Jonason, P.K. (2017) 'Trolling on Tinder® and other dating apps: examining the role of the dark tetrad and impulsivity', *Personality and Individual Differences*, 110: 139–143.

Marwick, A., and Ellison, N.B. (2012) '"There isn't wifi in heaven!" negotiating visibility on Facebook memorial pages', *Journal of Broadcasting and Electronic Media*, 56(3): 378–400.

Miller, N. (2016) 'Trolling the messenger in the name of propaganda', *The Sun Herald* (http://www.smh.com.au/world/finnish-journalists-jessikka-aros-inquiry-into-russian-trolls-stirs-up-a-hornets-nest-20160310-gng8rk.html).

Milner, R.M. (2013) 'Pop polyvocality: internet memes, public participation, and the Occupy Wall Street movement', *International Journal of Communication*, 7: 2357–2390.

Miltner, K.M. (2014) '"There's no place for lulz on LOLCats": the role of genre, gender, and group identity in the interpretation and enjoyment of an internet meme', *First Monday*, 19(8) (http://firstmonday.org/ojs/index.php/fm/article/view/5391/4103).

Mitra, A. (1996) 'Nations and the internet: the case of a national newsgroup, "soc.cult.indian"', *Convergence: The International Journal of Research into New Media Technologies*, 2(1): 44–75.

Naik, U., and Shivalingaiah, D. (2008) *Comparative Study of Web 1.0, Web 2.0 and Web 3.0*. Paper presented to the International CALIBER-2008 meeting University of Allahabad, Allahabad, India (http://ir.inflibnet.ac.in/handle/1944/1285).

Phillips, W. (2011) 'LOLing at tragedy: Facebook trolls memorial pages and resistance to grief online', *First Monday*, 16(12) (http://firstmonday.org/article/view/3168/3115).

Phillips, W. (2015) *This Is Why We Can't Have Nice Things: Mapping the Relationship between Online Trolling and Mainstream Culture*. Cambridge, MA: The MIT Press.

Rheingold, H. (1993) *The Virtual Community: Homesteading on the Electronic Frontier*. New York: Harper Perennial.

Rintel, S. (2013) 'Crisis memes: the importance of templatability to internet culture and freedom of expression', *Australasian Journal of Popular Culture*, 2(2): 253–271.

Shachaf, P., and Hara, N. (2010) 'Beyond vandalism: Wikipedia trolls', *Journal of Information Science*, 36(3): 357–370.

Sindorf, S. (2013) 'Symbolic violence in the online field: calls for "civility" in online discussion', *Trolls and the Negative Space of the Internet: The Fibreculture Journal*, 22: 193–215 (http://twentytwo.fibreculturejournal.org/fcj-162-symbolic-violence-in-the-online-field-calls-for-civility-in-online-discussion/).

Smith, M.A. (1999) 'Invisible crowds in cyberspace: mapping the social structure of the Usenet', in P. Kollock and M. Smith (Eds.), *Communities in Cyberspace*. London: Routledge. pp.195–219.

Spender, D. (1995) *Nattering on the Net: Women, Power and Cyberspace*. North Melbourne: Spinifex.

Suler, J. (2004) 'The online disinhibition effect', *CyberPsychology and Behavior*, 7(3): 321–326.

The New Zealand Herald. (2012) 'Charlotte Dawson Hospitalised after Troll War' (http://www.nzherald.co.nz/lifestyle/news/article.cfm?c_id=6&objectid=10830456).

The World Wide Web Consortium (W3C). (2004) *Architecture of the World Wide Web, Volume One W3C recommendation 15 December 2004* (https://www.w3.org/TR/webarch/#acks).

PART VI

# The Roads Ahead

40

# Web Archives and (Digital) History: A Troubled Past and a Promising Future?

Jane Winters

## INTRODUCTION

'For more than four decades, the Internet has grown and spread to an extent where today it is an indispensable element in the communication and media environment of many countries, and indeed of everyday life, culture and society' (Brügger et al., 2017: 1). So begins the introduction to the journal *Internet Histories: Digital Technology, Culture and Society*, launched in 2017. The World Wide Web, which unlocked the full potential of the Internet, has been with us for nearly 30 years; and in October 2016 the Internet Archive celebrated 20 years of capturing, preserving and republishing the Web (Hanamura, 2016). These are pleasingly round figures, indicating the passage of substantial time and the relative maturity both of the Web itself and the processes that have evolved to ensure that it is archived for the benefit of researchers. But those same researchers, and historians in particular, remain largely oblivious to the richness of the archived Web as a primary source for the study of the recent past, if not oblivious to the very existence of Web archives.[1] This chapter will examine the reasons for historians' relative failure to engage with the archived Web, and suggest why it is critical for contemporary, political and digital historians at least to do so. It will go on to explore the changing relationship between archivists, librarians and historians, which is beginning to break down researchers' reluctance to work with born-digital materials and big data. Finally, it will propose an exciting future for (digital) historical research, which employs a combination of quantitative and qualitative approaches to recover the lives and voices of ordinary people.

## HISTORIANS AND WEB ARCHIVES

The Web, like the newspapers that it now incorporates, contains material of interest for every sub-discipline of history – politics, sport, finance, culture, food, fashion, conflict are all present in infinite varieties. Web archives, imperfect though they may be,[2] reflect this range and diversity; there is something for everyone. But there are three (overlapping) groups for whom Web archives might be expected to hold immediate and particular interest: contemporary, political and digital historians. Why is there so little evidence that they are engaging with this new primary source, or indeed with a whole range of born-digital archives?

## Contemporary History

According to Kandiah (2008), 'the aim of contemporary history is to conceptualise, contextualise and historicise – to explain – some aspect of the recent past or to provide a historical understanding of current trends or developments'. Web archives are an invaluable lens through which to study life in the developed West in the late twentieth and early twenty-first centuries, but perhaps that past is still too recent, the digital apparently still too new. Weber (2017: 26) reports that 'When I told people I was researching the history of the Web in early 1995, about half of them were amused: "But it's too young to have a history!"' The strong connection between the Web and journalism may also be a problem here. As Kandiah (2008) notes, 'Critics of the discipline feared that contemporary history could … at best be nothing more than a form of journalism because its concerns were so closely rooted to the present'. In relation to Web archives, and the history of the Web, it is the desire to historicise that seems to be most dominant. A conference on 'History and the Internet' organised by History and Policy[3] in December 2016, for example, included presentations on the Domesday Book as big data and parliament and print culture in the seventeenth century, but only limited treatment of the Internet itself. For historians who approach the Web in this way it is not necessary to engage with its archives, although arguably to do so would enrich their understandings of our most recent twentieth-century media revolution. It is to be hoped that this engagement will come with greater chronological distance, as the early technologies of the Internet become as unfamiliar as those of the printing press or the scriptorium.

## Political History

The question of how to work with born-digital data is more pressing for political historians, some of whom, of course, would also think of themselves as working in the field of contemporary history. Governments have taken to the Web with marked enthusiasm and no little skill, as they seek to engage with, provide support for and learn more about their citizens. A 2016 United Nations report (Department of Economic and Social Affairs, 2016: 82), for example, identified the UK as world-leading in e-government, noting 'a Whole-of-Government approach in online service delivery'. Data portals like data.gov.uk, open.canada.ca and data.gouv.fr are increasingly making the workings of government transparent, but they serve as an early warning to political historians that they will have to change how they work. In the sphere of government, the adoption of digital means of communication, both internally and externally, has been definitive and startlingly quick. Political historians will soon have little choice but to seek information from Web archives because government plays out on the Web. They 'will need to transpose their long-established disciplinary skills and instincts into a digital register: asking the usual critical questions about their source material – how it was produced and why it has survived – and establishing a deep and rich set of contexts through which to interpret it' (McCarthy, 2016).

For historians in both these and other fields, however, the key reason for failing to use Web archives is the requirement to develop new skills, or to refresh old ones.[4] This was an important, if not unexpected, finding of the Big UK Domain Data for the Arts and Humanities (BUDDAH) research project.[5] The project case studies are revealing of the problems faced by researchers: 'we do not have enough case studies or methodological literature to help us design this research' (Millward, 2015: 10); 'Keyword full-text searching as the standard methodology needs to be critically reconsidered' (Deswarte, 2015: 9); archived Web pages bring 'the challenge of defining the analytical object itself' (Huc-Hepher, 2015a: 8). Some of the missing skills are technical ones – manipulating and cleaning large quantities of data is much easier if you have an understanding of Regular Expressions,[6] for example – but others relate to historians' (in)ability to work with statistics, to undertake even the most basic quantitative analysis. A lack of statistical understanding impedes both analysis at scale and the sampling that might facilitate closer reading and micro-analysis. The turn away from quantitative methods and approaches that has characterised much recent historical research and training has left historians singularly ill-equipped to deal with increasingly vast Web and other born-digital archives.[7]

## Digital History

If a dearth of appropriate skills, and skills training, is hindering many historians from studying Web history, or from adding Web archives to their basket of primary sources, one might assume that this would not be the case for our third group: digital historians. But until very recently, the focus of even digital history has lain elsewhere. This lack of attention is both striking and, in my view, surprising. Digital humanities 'has its origins in the research carried out … in textually focused computing'; it has diversified admirably in the second decade of the twenty-first century, but as recently as 2004 there could be no argument that 'it remains deeply interested in text' (Schreibman et al., 2004). Web archives contain vast quantities of text, but they are far removed from a digital scholarly edition or a corpus prepared for linguistic analysis.[8] Digital history, by contrast, has no such unifying thread. It encompasses Geographic Information Systems (GIS) and approaches drawn from historical geography; significant elements of public history, as exemplified by the work of the Roy Rosenzweig Center for History and New Media; scholarly editing and textual scholarship; economic and social research, influenced by social science methodologies; prosopographical, biographical and genealogical investigation; and so on. Its proponents are interested in digital pedagogy, in scholarly communication, in big and small data, micro- and macro-analysis. All of these approaches and interests may be brought to bear on the historical Web, yet digital historians have generally displayed the same 'tepid interest' in Web archives and Internet histories as other humanities researchers (Weber, 2017: 27).

One explanation is that while digital history has embraced a range of historical sub-disciplines, and borrowed readily from cognate subjects like archaeology and historical geography, it has largely failed to take account of developments in two crucial areas: library, archive and information studies; and digital preservation. Libraries and archives have necessarily been at the forefront of Web archives research and practice: it is they who have been responsible for developing the tools and protocols to harvest the Web, for running Web crawls, for devising preservations tools and standards, for exploring how to document and search Web archives of varying size and scale. This is work that is discussed among the members of the International Internet Preservation Consortium (IIPC), but not among historians, digital or otherwise. Webster (2017) rightly notes that much of the debate about the impact of 'the transition from paper to digital in records management and archiving … is to be found in the journals of the archival profession, into which historians rarely look'. The boundaries between digital history and digital preservation are even more clearly delineated; as with the conservation of books and manuscripts, digital preservation may only be noticed when it has failed in some way.[9] The first reaction of a historian on seeing an archived Web page is more likely to be 'Why are those images missing?' than 'How has so much of this page been successfully preserved?' The narrative of the 'digital dark age', which sometimes seems ubiquitous in the mainstream media, only persists because of a general lack of awareness of, and appreciation for, the scope of existing digital preservation work and expertise (Winters, 2017a: 45).

## CHANGING TIMES?

But there are signs that this is beginning to change. In the UK, for example, the Arts and Humanities Research Council (AHRC) has funded two separate research networks which bring together historians, archivists, librarians and digital preservation specialists, among others, to discuss the challenges posed by collecting, preserving, publishing and using born-digital data of all kinds.[10] The much larger European network RESAW (A Research Infrastructure for the Study of Archived Web Materials)[11] similarly includes both humanities researchers, including several historians, and representatives of memory institutions with a responsibility for archiving the Web. More events are being organised which offer something to multiple sectors. There has generally been very little exchange of ideas and personnel between the 'Digital history' and 'Archives and society' seminars hosted by the Institute of Historical Research in London, for example, but in January 2017 a joint seminar was organised on 'Sensitivity review and digital records' (Seles, 2017). In June 2017, RESAW and the IIPC collaborated to run a conference which considered 'Researchers, practitioners and their use of the archived Web', highlighting the value and importance of cross-sectoral conversations. The strict separation of spheres that has obtained for so long is beginning to break down in the face of the challenges posed by born-digital data, and nowhere is this more apparent than in relation to Web archives.

## MEDIATING ACCESS: HISTORIANS, LIBRARIANS, ARCHIVISTS AND THE ARCHIVED WEB

If some historians are still prone to confuse Web archives with archives of historical data which happen to have been published on the Web – 'archive' is not a particularly helpful term here, as Brügger (2016) has discussed – it does seem as though a turning-point has been reached. It no longer seems entirely fanciful to argue that we are moving towards the promising future of this chapter's title; a future in which many different types of historian, not just those with an interest in contemporary politics or digital methods, can integrate Web archives into their research. For most of those historians, early encounters with Web archives are likely to be mediated by archivists and librarians (another reason to ensure that disciplinary silos are breached). Given the scale of most Web archives,[12] and the consequent limitations of keyword searching, curated special collections provide an easy and obvious route in to the data. They are also more likely to be openly available than the broad national crawls undertaken by libraries and archives on a statutory basis.

To date, the British Library has published 45 special collections around themes which have been deemed 'useful and interesting' by curators.[13] They immediately showcase both the chronological span of the archive and the range of human activity represented within it. One of the earliest special collections is concerned with the terrorist attacks that took place in London on 7 July 2005, which killed 52 people and injured more than 700; the most recent deals with the UK general election of 2015. A special collection capturing the 2016 EU referendum debate is in preparation, and will soon be made available to researchers (Kunze, 2016). There is plenty of material here for political historians: a series of UK general elections from 2005 to 2015; the Scottish parliamentary election of 2007 and the Scottish Independence referendum of 2014; the London mayoral election of 2008 (although not those of 2012 or 2016); the European Parliament election of 2009; the Credit Crunch, 2008–10. Other areas of strength include sport (the Commonwealth Games held in Glasgow in 2014, the London Olympic and Paralympic Games of 2012), anniversaries of national significance (the 200th anniversary of the birth of Charles Darwin, Queen Elizabeth II's Diamond Jubilee in 2012, the centenary of the Easter Rising in 2016), health (collections dedicated to mental health, personal experiences of illness, the 2012 Health and Social Care Act and even pandemic influenza outbreaks since 2005) and religion (a general collection on religion, politics and law since 2005 and more specific ones concerned with the Quakers and the Free Churches).

These special collections are enormously rich and diverse, but that very eclecticism poses something of a problem for Web history and historians. Why, for example, are there collections relating to Cornwall and Hampshire but to no other counties in the UK? What was it about the Cambridge Network, 'a membership organisation based in the vibrant high technology cluster of Cambridge', which led to its being singled out in this way? Why have 26 websites concerned with e-publishing trends been given special status alongside those dealing with national politics? Clearly, certain types of predictable event generate special collections in the Web archive – elections, anniversaries, major sporting occasions; other clusters are responses to the unexpected, to natural disasters like the Indian Ocean tsunami in December 2004 or to terrorism. This latter trend is also apparent in the collections developed through Archive-It, which is described as 'The leading web archiving service for collecting and accessing cultural heritage on the web'.[14] Archive-It involves more than 400 institutions in 16 countries who between them have curated more than 4,000 special collections. Of these, 178 (4.25 per cent) are categorised as arising from 'Spontaneous events', and while the first collection on the list is an archive of the 100,000 Poets for Change website,[15] many concern shocking and more or less unpredictable events, from the 2013 Boston Marathon bombing to Hurricane Katrina.[16] Politics looms large too: for example, 412 collections (9.83 per cent) are categorised as relating to 'Government', and there are numerous smaller and perhaps overlapping clusters concerned with particular elections or states in the United States.[17]

In both of these instances, the special collections serve an important role in illuminating the wider Web archives from which they are derived, respectively those of the British Library and the Internet Archive. They act as a shop window for archives that are challenging to encounter at scale, encouraging initial browsing which might then lead on to more in-depth analysis and research. This necessarily imbues them with an importance that may not always have been considered by those responsible for their creation. A particular collection almost certainly has enormous value for the curator(s), and for the many others who will explore it in years to come, but what does it say about the shape and significance of the wider Web archive? The British Library's remit to preserve and make available the UK's intellectual and cultural heritage is apparent in the Web archive collections that deal with significant and/or traumatic events, but others are suggestive of personal interest and enthusiasm or a serendipitous partnership.[18] This is even more the case for Archive-It, where some collections have been curated in specific teaching contexts, for example.[19] This is still an evolving landscape, and experimentation is entirely appropriate, but there is a risk that these early experiments may begin to 'fix' a particular view of Web archives and the kinds of historical research for which they are most suitable. This is particularly true if access to the larger archives remains restricted, for legal, technical or other reasons. The choices that are made now could resonate for decades to come, and some of the consequences might be unintended: as Schwartz and Cook (2002: 2) note, 'Archives – as records – wield power over the shape and direction of historical scholarship, collective memory, and national identity, over how we know ourselves as individuals, groups and societies', and archivists have the power to shape how we access those records.

## THE HISTORIAN AS ARCHIVIST

If librarians and archivists will play an important role in determining not just what is included in Web archives but how that archived material is used by historians, even the kinds of questions that they will ask, there is also considerable scope for historians to take personal responsibility. Web archiving at scale is a highly technical process, requiring investment in expertise and equipment, but researchers can build their own collections. This tendency towards personal archiving has been present from the very earliest days of Web history. Brügger, for example, noted in 2010 that his personal Web archive 'contains a substantial part of the Danish web activity in relation to the Olympic Games in 2000' (2010: 351). There are a number of options available to researchers who would like to assume some control over the archiving process. They might, for example, choose to collaborate with archivists and programmers, as described in Milligan et al. (2016); or they might investigate the various open-source Web archiving tools that have been developed, like Warcbase and Wget.[20] Milligan in particular has shown what can be achieved when historians embrace these approaches and participate in the creation as well as the analysis of Web archives (2012; 2017a). Both of these approaches to Web archiving, however, require a degree of technical expertise with which many historians are, and are likely to remain, uncomfortable. Fortunately, there are alternatives that do not involve such a steep technical learning curve, notably Webrecorder.[21]

Webrecorder allows anyone 'to create high fidelity, context rich and interactive archives of the dynamic web' (Espenschied, 2016). The resulting collections of WARC files are not just personal but personalised: the pages are captured as the researcher moves through a website, keeping a record of her chosen pathway. This personalisation even extends to the faithful recording of the 'logged-in' experience on online social media. A shallow hierarchical structure is present in these archives, with 'sessions' organised into collections, and simple descriptions can be added to aid future navigation and discoverability. All of this functionality is available in the browser, but the archived files can also be downloaded and replayed offline using a desktop app, the Webrecorder Player.[22] This is a very different approach to Web archiving from the comprehensive full domain crawl undertaken by large memory institutions, one which supports a micro-level approach both to the harvesting and study of the Web. Archiving a website of any size, for example that of a major public broadcaster, would be difficult and time-consuming using this method, with all links having to be followed to ensure their successful capture. The collections that can be created in this way will remain relatively small, and focused narrowly on a researcher's interests and experiences. In some instances they will record and reflect her personal social and research networks online, providing some of the ethnographic context that is missing from the larger automated Web crawls. There are layers of interest and value in such archives, which can only be fully realised if they are shared, with other researchers and perhaps ultimately with libraries and archives.

## CAPTURING THE VOICE OF THE INDIVIDUAL

This focus on the small, on the personal, is one possible future for Web history; and one which reflects growing interest in the value of digital storytelling (see, for example, Burgess, 2006; Coleborne and Bliss, 2011). Web archives, which record so many different voices, hold out the promise of a new golden age of history from below.[23] It is not true to say that anyone can create online content which might find its way into a Web archive – certain groups are still privileged, depending on education, age, social class, geographical location, and so on[24] – but there are unprecedented opportunities to self-publish, to comment on the publications of others. The sheer diversity of authors who may be represented in Web archives is highlighted by a Blogs special collection in the UK Web Archive: among the 763 blogs included, alongside those of politicians and protest groups, are 'Alan in Belfast', who writes about 'cinema, books, technology, and the occasional rant about life'; 'Nelly's Garden', which presents the thoughts of Nelly Culleybackey from County Antrim; and 'Lizzy's Literary Life', 'celebrating the pleasures of a 21st century bookworm'.[25] Ian Milligan's work on the GeoCities archive has begun to recover the voices of the children who were active participants in the early Web, and specifically in the Enchanted Forest 'neighbourhood' (Milligan, 2017a and 2017b); Megan Dougherty has shone a spotlight on the brief flourishing of the subcultural Islamic punk movement in North America from the early 2000s (Dougherty, 2017); and Saskia Huc-Hepher has explored the histories of French communities in London through their archived blogs (Huc-Hepher, 2015b). But this volume and variety poses challenges for historians. How do we make sure that we find individual voices among all the noise? How can we judge the significance of what they are saying when any and all points of view will have been captured, but we have little or no data indicative of circulation or popularity?

## BIG HISTORY AND THE MACROSCOPE

Alongside this renewed emphasis on close reading, the current abundance of digital data has led to calls for a return to 'big' history and the *longue durée* (Guldi and Armitage, 2014), for the adoption of the distant reading approach first proposed by Franco Moretti for the study of digitised literary corpora (Moretti, 2013). Graham et al. (2015) argue for historians to embrace big data – one chapter is even titled 'The joys of big data for historians'. The authors are among an increasing number of historians to apply the concept of the macroscope (see, for example, Jockers, 2013; Hitchcock, 2014), which 'instead of allowing you to see things that are small or far away … makes it easier to grasp the incredibly large. It does so through a process of compression, by selectively reducing complexity until once-obscure patterns and relationships become clear' (Graham et al., 2015: 15). This is a far more nuanced approach than Culturomics, which more or less completely failed to take account of humanities research practices and concerns (Michel et al., 2011). The proponents of the macro-historical are not suggesting that the micro-historical should be abandoned in the face of the data deluge, rather that there is value in considering both; and, indeed, the interactions between the two can produce new insights and interpretations.

## THE SMALL AND THE LARGE: A QUESTION OF SCALE

As is so often the case, the most promising approaches for historical research in this field bring together the small and the large, 'the general and the particular' (Manovich, 2016). The challenge is for historians to find new ways of working without losing the emphasis on the individual that has long distinguished humanities research. Using the framework of cultural analytics, Lev Manovich proposes that 'we may combine the concern of social science, and sciences in general, with the *general* and the *regular*, and the concern of humanities with *individual* and *particular* … analysing massive datasets to zoom in on the unique items' (Manovich, 2016). Tim Hitchcock argues that, in contrast with 'the categories of knowing that dominated the nineteenth and twentieth centuries', born-digital data, and Web archives in particular, provide 'an opportunity to re-think what is possible, and to re-think what it is we are asking; how we might ask it, and to what purpose'; but while historians must 'be able to wield the tools of large-scale visualization … we need to do so at the same time as we preserve the values and practices that underpin traditional academic history, while going beyond the standards of scholarship we have inherited' (Hitchcock, 2015; 2013: 20).

## A PROMISING FUTURE?

These are provocative calls to action, which speak to an exciting future for historical research – one which is predicated on the ever-increasing availability of digital sources and the development, and widespread adoption, of innovative digital methods that build on the best traditions of humanistic exploration. It is, however, an exciting future that has been invoked before in the current life-cycle of digital history. A report on the impact of digital resources published in 2011, for example, considered whether 'they simply make research easier, cheaper (to the researcher), more convenient, and less time consuming, or whether there is evidence that they open up *new avenues for* research'. The story here is one of enormous potential: researchers are perceived to be developing new methods and even theories, but 'How these perceived changes result in new research questions across the humanities in the long run is still emerging' (Meyer, 2011: 39). Perhaps it is unfair to consider 16 years as 'the long run', but this description of humanities research, and digital history, would not seem out of place today. The promise of transformation is still tantalisingly there, but how close is it to being realised?

Web archives, and other kinds of born-digital data, do bring the possibility of, and perhaps even necessitate, a radical reframing of digital history – through their scale, their heterogeneity, their complexity, their fragility. Some historians will undoubtedly continue to focus solely on the textual elements of the archived web, abstracting words from their rich digital context. But others will work with text, sound, and still and moving images in the round. In doing so they might engage with the history of art and design, media and communication studies, the history of technology, linguistics, film studies – and with other researchers in those fields. They might move across the boundaries of the (social) sciences, arts and humanities, learning new skills themselves or building partnerships. They might, as Marc Weber urges, turn their attention to the materiality of the Web, learning from the work of museums.[26] They might do some or all of these things in combination. And they might, by combining big data approaches with humanistic understandings, at last begin to develop genuinely new research questions and generate new knowledge.

It is vitally important that historians, digital or otherwise, should carve out a space for themselves in the study of both the live and the historical Web, especially where these are conceived first and foremost as big data. The individual, the human, risks becoming lost in the face of arguments that 'Causality ... is being knocked off its pedestal as the primary foundation of meaning. Big data turbocharges non-causal analyses, often replacing causal investigations' (Mayer-Schönberger and Cukier, 2017: 66); or claims that 'Culturomic results are a new type of evidence in the humanities' (Michel et al., 2011: 181). Large-scale trends are, of course, enormously important to understand, as Mayer-Schönberger and Cukier demonstrate, but historians are very well placed to combine an appreciation of broader patterns and movements with a forensic understanding of the small-scale and the human – of ordinary lives not just data points. And the archives of the Web are a unique record of many millions of ordinary lives, alongside histories of celebrities, institutions and nations. As yet those archives remain largely unexplored, but there are many Web histories to be uncovered, many pathways to be explored and many new questions to be asked.

## Notes

1 A 2010 study into the 'state of the art' noted the gap 'between the *potential* community of researchers who have good reason to engage with creating, using, analysing and sharing web archives, and the *actual* (generally still small) community of researchers currently doing so' (Dougherty et al., 2010: 5).

2 The problems of working with Web archives have been well rehearsed by, among others, Brügger (2012a and 2012b), Brügger and Finnemann (2013), Milligan (2016) and Winters (2017b).

3 History and Policy is a UK network of historians which 'promotes better public policy through a greater understanding of history' (http://www.historyandpolicy.org/).

4 I am unconvinced by the argument that historians are reluctant to use Web archives because they are concerned 'that they will not be able to replicate their historical research process when using web archives, and may not find essential and authoritative records' (Belovari, 2017: 60). This seems to me simultaneously to underestimate the variety of humanities research methodologies, the fuzziness of concepts like 'essential' and 'authoritative', and the ability of historians to navigate uncertainty and devise new approaches.

5 BUDDAH was funded by the Arts and Humanities Research Council (AHRC) as part of its Digital Transformations in the Arts and Humanities theme (https://buddah.projects.history.ac.uk/; grant reference AH/L009854/1). Cowls (2016) usefully summarises the progress made and challenges faced by the ten researchers who were awarded bursaries to use Web archives in their research.

6 'Regular expressions ... are a way of defining patterns that can apply to sequences of things ... and they are incorporated into most general programming languages' (Knox, 2013).

7 There are many reasons for the current lack of interest in, even distrust of, quantitative methods among historians, but at least some of it may be traced back to the overblown claims made for the 'Cliometrics Revolution' of the 1960s and 1970s. The fall from grace experienced by Cliometrics was dramatic, and echoes of it may be seen in the heated debates that followed the publication of Michel et al. (2011), and reactions to 'Culturomics'. For a fuller discussion of these issues, see Winters (2018).

8 Compare, for example, the order and structure of the Corpus of Global Web-Based English (Davies, 2014) with the disorder and relative chaos of the UK Web Archive.

9 In the UK, the most resonant example is still that of the BBC Domesday project. This ambitious initiative to create a comprehensive digital record of life in Britain, 900 years after the compilation of the original Domesday Book, was an early and very high-profile digital preservation failure. It cost £2.5 million, but the special BBC Micro computers required to read the 12-inch video disks rapidly became obsolete and the data was inaccessible just 15 years after it was collected (McKie and Thorpe, 2002). The contrast with its medieval – analogue – predecessor could not have been greater. What is much less remarked is that there were a number of efforts to recover the data, and indeed in 2011 the contents of the 'Community' disk were published online as part of Domesday Reloaded. In another failure of digital preservation, this recovered data was until recently accessible on the live web at http://www.bbc.co.uk/history/domesday, but at the time of writing it is only partially available via the Internet Archive.

10 The two interdisciplinary networks are: Born-digital Big Data and Approaches for History and the Humanities (https://borndigitaldata.blogs.

sas.ac.uk/; grant reference AH/N006178/1) and Record DNA (https://recorddna.wordpress.com/; grant reference AH/P006868/1).

11 RESAW (http://resaw.eu/).

12 There are some exceptions to this. At the time of writing, the UK Parliament Web Archive (http://webarchive.parliament.uk/) only includes around 37 websites. Individually, some of these might be very large (the Hansard Archive from 1803 is one example), but the collection as a whole remains manageable and susceptible to qualitative analysis. By contrast, the full domain crawl of the .uk country code Top Level Domain (ccTLD) undertaken by the British Library in 2014 captured 2.5 billion web pages and other assets (Hartmann, 2015).

13 UK Web Archive: Browse by Special Collection (https://www.webarchive.org.uk/ukwa/collection/).

14 Archive-It (https://archive-it.org/).

15 100,000 Poets (https://archive-it.org/collections/2845).

16 There are, in fact, three special collections dealing with the Boston Marathon bombing: Blasts in Boston Marathon (https://archive-it.org/collections/3752); 2013 Boston Marathon Bombing (https://archive-it.org/collections/3649); and Boston Marathon Bombing: Twitter and RSS Feeds (https://archive-it.org/collections/3645). Hurricane Katrina warrants two: Hurricane Katrina (https://archive-it.org/collections/174); and Hurricane Katrina Blogs Web Collection (https://archive-it.org/collections/7625). This multiplicity of collections relating to single events is an additional problem for the historian, as the relationship between them is unclear. In the Boston example, two have been curated by the Virginia Tech: Crisis, Tragedy, and Recovery Network, so there is presumably no overlap, but what of the collection curated by Internet Archive Global Events? Detailed comparison is required to establish the ways in which these three collections differ from or are similar to each other.

17 Government special collection (https://archive-it.org/explore?show=Collections&fc=meta_Subject%3AGovernment). Examples of smaller collections on a similar theme are Government – US Federal (https://archive-it.org/explore?show=Collections&fc=meta_Subject%3AGovernment-usfederal) and SF [San Francisco] Government (https://archive-it.org/explore?show=Collections&fc=meta_Subject%3ASF+Government).

18 This is explicitly the case with the Live Art collection, which has been produced in partnership with the Live Art Development Agency in London (https://www.webarchive.org.uk/ukwa/collection/26312782/page/1).

19 See, for example, the K-12 Web Archiving Program in the United States, which at the time of writing has generated more than 300 student collections (https://archive-it.org/k12/). I owe this reference to Ian Milligan.

20 Warcbase (https://github.com/lintool/warcbase) has been developed by Jimmy Lin at the University of Waterloo; Wget (https://www.gnu.org/software/wget/) is part of the GNU Operating System.

21 Webrecorder (https://webrecorder.io/). Webrecorder has been developed by Ilya Kramer at Rhizome, with funding from the Andrew W. Mellon Foundation.

22 Webrecorder Player 1.0.5 (https://github.com/webrecorder/webrecorderplayer-electron/releases/tag/v1.0.5).

23 See Taylor (1997), for a discussion of history from below and modern British social history.

24 Just in the UK, a 2017 survey of digital skills published by the Tech Partnership, in association with Lloyds Banking Group, found that '21% (11.5m) of the UK are classified as not having Basic Digital Skills'. A heatmap of digital exclusion derived from the survey data reveals significant geographical variation (http://heatmap.thetechpartnership.com/). Even where relatively advanced digital skills are present, there are a range of other factors influencing whether or not people choose to participate in the creation of online content (see, e.g., Hargittai and Walejko (2008); Blank (2013).

25 Alan in Belfast (https://www.webarchive.org.uk/ukwa/target/18710548/collection/100698/source/collection); Nelly's Garden (https://www.webarchive.org.uk/ukwa/target/7176221/collection/100698/source/collection); Lizzy's Literary Life (https://www.webarchive.org.uk/ukwa/target/65208425/collection/100698/source/collection).

26 Weber sees 'the history of the online world as not just about the Web itself, or networks like the Internet, or computers, but as all of these within the long tradition of tools we have created for sharing and refining information: books and clay tablets and talking drums and more' (Weber, 2017: 34). Web90 – Patrimoine, mémoires et histoire du Web dans les années 1990, at L'Institut des sciences de la communication du CNRS, is an exemplary project in this respect (http://web90.hypotheses.org/).

## REFERENCES

Belovari, S. (2017) 'Historians and Web archives', *Archivaria*, 83: 59–79.

Blank, G. (2013) 'Who creates content? Stratification and content creation on the Internet', *Information, Communication and Society*, 16(4): 590–612. DOI: 10.1080/1369118X.2013.777758.

Brügger, N. (2016) 'Webraries and Web archives – the Web between public and private', in D. Baker and W. Evans (eds), *The End of Wisdom? The Future of Libraries in a Digital Age*. Oxford: Chandos Publishing. pp. 185–90.

Brügger, N. (2012a) 'Web history and the Web as a historical source', *Zeithistorische Forschungen*, 9(2): 316–25.

Brügger, N. (2012b) 'When the present Web is the later past: Web historiography, digital history, and Internet studies', *Historical Social Research/Historische Sozialforschung*, 37(4): 102–17.

Brügger, N. (ed) (2010) *Web History*. Bern, Switzerland: Peter Lang US.

Brügger, N. and Finnemann, N. O. (2013) 'The Web and digital humanities: theoretical and methodological concerns', *Journal of Broadcasting and Electronic Media*, 57(1): 66–80. DOI: 10.1080/08838151.2012.761699.

Brügger, N., Goggin, G., Milligan, I. and Schafer, V. (2017) 'Introduction: Internet histories', *Internet Histories: Digital Technology, Culture and Society*, 1(1–2): 1–7. DOI: 10.1080/24701475.2017.1317128.

Burgess, J. (2006) 'Hearing ordinary voices: cultural studies, vernacular creativity and digital storytelling', *Continuum: Journal of Media and Cultural Studies*, 20(2): 201–14. DOI: 10.1080/10304310600641737.

Coleborne, C. and Bliss, E. (2011) 'Emotions, digital tools and public histories: digital storytelling using Windows Movie Maker in the history tertiary classroom', *History Compass*, 9(9): 674–85. DOI: 10.1111/j.1478-0542.2011.00797.x.

Cowls, J. (2016) 'Cultures of the UK Web', in N. Brügger and R. Schroeder (eds), *The Web as History: Using Web Archives to Understand the Past and the Present*. London: UCL Press. pp. 220–37.

Davies, M. (2014) Corpus of Global Web-Based English (GloWbE) (https://corpus.byu.edu/glowbe/).

Department of Economic and Social Affairs (2016) *United Nations E-Government Survey 2016: E-Government in Support of Sustainable Development*. New York: United Nations (http://workspace.unpan.org/sites/Internet/Documents/UNPAN97453.pdf).

Deswarte, R. (2015) Revealing British Euroscepticism in the UK Web domain and archive. London: School of Advanced Study. pp. 1–10 (http://sas-space.sas.ac.uk/6103/1/Deswarte%20case%20study.pdf).

Dougherty, M. (2017) '"Taqwacore is dead. Long live Taqwacore" or punk's not dead? Studying the online evolution of the Islamic punk scene', in N. Brügger and R. Schroeder (eds), *The Web as History: Using Web Archives to Understand the Past and the Present*. London: UCL Press. pp. 204–19.

Dougherty, M., Meyer, E. T., Madsen, C. M., van den Heuvel, C., Thomas, A. and Wyatt, S. (2010) *Researcher Engagement with Web Archives: State of the Art*. Jisc Report (https://papers.ssrn.com/sol3/papers.cfm?abstract_id=1714997).

Espenschied, D. (2016) Introduction to Webrecorder (https://www.youtube.com/watch?v=n3SqusABXEk&feature=youtu.be).

Graham, S., Milligan, I. and Weingart, S. (2015) *Exploring Big Historical Data: The Historian's Macroscope*. London: Imperial College Press (http://www.themacroscope.org/2.0/).

Guldi, J. and Armitage, D. (2014) *The History Manifesto*. Cambridge: Cambridge University Press (https://www.cambridge.org/core/books/the-history-manifesto/AC1A1EC711AE91A4F9004E7582D79AFD#).

Hanamura, W. (2016) The Internet Archive turns 20! Internet Archive Blogs (https://blog.archive.org/2016/09/19/the-internet-archive-turns-20/).

Hargittai, E. and Walejko, G. (2008) 'The participation divide: content creation and sharing in the digital age', *Information, Communication and Society*, 11(2): 239–56. DOI: 10.1080/13691180801946150.

Hartmann, S. (2015) 2015 UK domain crawl has started. UK Web Archive blog (http://blogs.bl.uk/webarchive/2015/09/2015-uk-domain-crawl-has-started.html).

Hitchcock, T. (2015) The UK Web Archive, born-digital sources, and rethinking the future of research. Web Archives for Historians (https://webarchivehistorians.org/tag/tim-hitchcock/).

Hitchcock, T. (2014) Big data, small data and meaning. Historyonics blog (http://historyonics.blogspot.co.uk/2014/11/big-data-small-data-and-meaning_9.html).

Hitchcock, T. (2013) 'Confronting the digital: or how academic history writing lost the plot', *Cultural and Social History*, 10(1): 9–23. DOI: 10.2752/147800413X13515292098070.

Huc-Hepher, S. (2015a) Searching for home in the historic Web: an ethnosemiotic study of the London-French habitus as displayed in blogs. London: School of Advanced Study. pp. 1–27. (http://sas-space.sas.ac.uk/6252/1/Huc-Hepher%20case%20study.pdf).

Huc-Hepher, S. (2015b) 'Big Web data, small focus: an ethnosemiotic approach to culturally themed selective Web archiving', *Big Data & Society*, 2(2) (http://journals.sagepub.com/doi/abs/10.1177/2053951715595823).

Jockers, M. L. (2013) *Macroanalysis: Digital Methods and Literary History*. Urbana-Champaign: University of Illinois Press.

Kandiah, M. D. (2008) Contemporary history. Making History (http://www.history.ac.uk/makinghistory/resources/articles/contemporary_history.html).

Knox, D. (2013) Understanding Regular Expressions. *The Programming Historian* (https://programminghistorian.org/lessons/understanding-regular-expressions).

Kunze, S. (2016) Capturing and preserving the EU Referendum debate (Brexit). UK Web Archive blog (http://blogs.bl.uk/webarchive/2016/06/capturing-and-preserving-the-eu-referendum-debate-brexit.html).

McCarthy, H. (2016) Political history in the digital age: the challenges of archiving and analysing born digital sources. Impact of Social Sciences – LSE Blogs (http://eprints.lse.ac.uk/66690/).

McKie, R. and Thorpe, V. (2002) Digital Domesday Book lasts 15 years not 1000. *The Guardian* (https://www.theguardian.com/uk/2002/mar/03/research.elearning).

Manovich, L. (2016) 'The science of culture? Social computing, digital humanities and cultural analytics', *Journal of Cultural Analytics*. DOI: 10.22148/16.004 (http://culturalanalytics.org/2016/05/the-science-of-culture-social-computing-digital-humanities-and-cultural-analytics/).

Mayer-Schönberger, V. and Cukier, K. (2017) *Big Data: The Essential Guide to Work, Life and Learning in the Age of Insight*. London: John Murray (Publishers).

Meyer, E. T. (2011) Splashes and Ripples: Synthesizing the Evidence on the Impacts of Digital Resources. Jisc Report (https://ssrn.com/abstract=1846535).

Michel, J.-B., Shen, Y. K., Aiden, A. P., Veres, A., Gray, M. K., The Google Books Team, Pickett, J. P., Hoiberg, D., Clancy, D., Norvig, P., Orwant, J., Pinker, S., Nowak, M. A. and Aiden, E. L. (2011) 'Quantitative analysis of culture using millions of digitized books', *Science*, 331(6014): 176–82. DOI: 10.1126/science.1199644.

Milligan, I. (2017a) 'Welcome to the Web: the online community of GeoCities during the early years of the World Wide Web', in N. Brügger and R. Schroeder (eds), *The Web as History: Using Web Archives to Understand the Past and the Present*. London: UCL Press. pp. 137–58.

Milligan, I. (2017b) 'Pages by kids, for kids': unlocking childhood and youth history through the GeoCities Web archive. Researchers, practitioners and their use of the archived Web, International Internet Preservation Consortium/RESAW Conference, London.

Milligan, I. (2016) 'Lost in the infinite archive: the promise and pitfalls of web archives', *International Journal of Humanities and Arts Computing*, 10(1): 78–94. DOI: 10.3366/ijhac.2016.0161.

Milligan, I. (2012) 'Mining the "Internet graveyard": rethinking the historians' toolkit', *Journal of the Canadian Historical Association/Revue de la Société historique du Canada*, 23(2): 21–64. DOI: 10.7202/1015788ar.

Milligan, I., Ruest, N. and St. Onge, A. (2016) 'The great WARC adventure: using SIPS, AIPS, and DIPS to document SLAPPS', *Digital Studies/Le champ numérique*, 2015–16 open issue (http://www.digitalstudies.org/ojs/index.php/digital_studies/article/view/325/412).

Millward, G. (2015) Digital barriers and the accessible web: disabled people, information and the internet. London: School of Advanced Study. pp. 1–12 (http://sas-space.sas.ac.uk/6104/1/Millward%20case%20study.pdf).

Moretti, F. (2013) *Distant Reading*. London: Verso.

Schreibman, S., Siemens, R. and Unsworth, J. (2004) 'The digital humanities and humanities computing: an introduction', in S. Schreibman, R. Siemens and J. Unsworth (eds), *A Companion to Digital Humanities*. Oxford: Blackwell (http://www.digitalhumanities.org/companion/).

Schwartz, J. M. and Cook, T. (2002) 'Archives, records, and power: the making of modern memory', *Archival Science*, 2(1–2): 1–19. DOI: 10.1007/BF02435628.

Seles, M. (2017) 'It always seems impossible until it is done': sensitivity review and digital records. Archives & Society and Digital History seminars (https://www.youtube.com/watch?v=ncdbLdshhel).

Taylor, M. (1997) 'The beginnings of modern social British history?', *History Workshop Journal*, 43: 155–76.

Tech Partnership (2017) Basic digital skills UK 2017: summary of findings (https://www.thetechpartnership.com/globalassets/pdfs/basic-digital-skills-standards/basicdigital-skills2016_findingssummary.pdf).

Weber, M. (2017) 'A common language', *Internet Histories: Digital Technology, Culture and Society*, 1(1–2): 26–38. DOI: 10.1080/24701475.2017.1317118.

Webster, P. (2017) Book review: The Silence of the Archive by David Thomas, Simon Fowler and Valerie Johnson. Review of Books – LSE Blogs (http://blogs.lse.ac.uk/lsereviewofbooks/2017/08/11/book-review-the-silence-of-the-archive-by-david-thomas-simon-fowler-and-valerie-johnson/).

Winters, J. (2018) 'Digital history', in P. Burke and M. Tamm (eds), *Debating New Approaches in History*. London: Bloomsbury Publishing. pp. 277-300.

Winters, J. (2017a) 'Will history survive the digital age?', *BBC History Magazine*, 3: 41–5.

Winters, J. (2017b) 'Coda: Web archives for humanities research – some reflections', in N. Brügger and R. Schroeder (eds), *The Web as History: Using Web Archives to Understand the Past and the Present*. London: UCL Press. pp. 238–48.

# Index

Note: Page numbers in *italics* indicate tables and figures. Page numbers followed by n indicate end-of-chapter notes.

FSC
www.fsc.org
MIX
Papier | Fördert gute Waldnutzung
FSC® C083411

Kolibri 360 GmbH
Ferdinand-Jühlke-Straße 7
99095 Erfurt, Deutschland
produktsicherheit@kolibri360.de